KU-794-035

The Practice of Econometrics: Classic and Contemporary

University of Nottingham
Hallward Library

ERNST R. BERNDT

Massachusetts Institute of Technology and the National Bureau of Economic Research

ADDISON-WESLEY PUBLISHING COMPANY

Reading, Massachusetts · Menlo Park, California · New York
Don Mills, Ontario · Wokingham, England · Amsterdam · Bonn
Sydney · Singapore · Tokyo · Madrid · San Juan

ADDITIONAL CREDITS:

Arrow: Reprinted with permission of the Econometrica Society. Nordhaus: Reprinted with permission of The Brookings Institution. Klein: Reprinted with permission of the author. Schultz: Reprinted with permission. Musgrave: Reprinted with permission. Ohta, Griliches, Terleckyj: Reprinted with permission. Ashenfelter: Reprinted with permission. Stigler: Reprinted with permission. Schultz: Reprinted with permission. Watson: From Morgan and Langford, *Facts and Fallacies,* Exeter, England: Webb & Bower, 1981, p. 44. Reprinted with permission. From Cerf and Navasky, *The Experts Speak: The Definitive Compendium of Authoritative Misinformation,* NY: Pantheon Books, 1984, p. 209. Morley: Reprinted with permission. Einstein: NY: Crown Publishers, 1954, p. 274. Malkiel. NY: W.W. Norton and Co., Inc., 1985, p. 152. Reprinted with permission. Spence: Copyright 1981. Reprinted from *The Bell Journal of Economics,* with permission of The RAND Corporation. *The Price Statistics of the Federal Government,*
(Credits continue on p. 680, which constitutes a continuation of the copyright page.)

1005357234

IBM and IBM PC are registered trademarks of International Business Machines Corporation. Lotus, 1-2-3, and Symphony are registered trademarks of Lotus Development Corporation. MicroTSP is a trademark of Quantitative Micro Software. Time Series Processor and TSP are trademarks of TSP International. MINITAB is a registered trademark of Minitab, Inc. Other products mentioned as examples may also be trademarked by their manufacturers.

Addison-Wesley makes no warranties, either expressed or implied, regarding the enclosed computer software, its merchantability or fitness for any particular purpose. The exclusion of implied warranties is not permitted by some states. The above exclusion may not apply to you. This warranty provides you with specific legal rights. There may be other rights that you may have which vary from state to state.

It is a violation of copyright law to make a copy of this software except for backup purposes to guard against accidental loss or damage.

Library of Congress Cataloging-in-Publication Data

Berndt, Ernst R.

The practice of econometrics : classic and contemporary / Ernst R. Berndt.

p. cm.

Includes bibliographical references and index.

ISBN 0-201-17628-9

1. Econometrics. I. Title.

HB139.B47 1990

330'.01'5195--dc20

90-46332

CIP

Copyright © 1991 by Addison-Wesley Publishing Company, Inc.

All rights reserved. No part of this publication may be reproduced, stored in a retrieval system, or transmitted, in any form or by any means, electronic, mechanical, photocopying, recording, or otherwise, without the prior written permission of the publisher. Printed in the United States of America.

Reprinted with corrections February, 1996

Package ISBN 0-201-49900-2

Book ISBN 0-201-17628-9

Disk ISBN 0-201-54598-5

12131415161718-MA03020100

printing 11

Preface

The term "econometrics" was apparently first used by Pawel Ciompa in 1910 in a somewhat obscure book published in Germany. To Ciompa, the goals of "oekonometrie" were to describe economic data series mathematically and to display them geometrically and graphically. According to the Nobel Laureate Ragnar Frisch, however, Ciompa's view of econometrics was too narrow, since it emphasized only the descriptive side of econometrics.[1] Writing as founding editor in the inaugural issue of *Econometrica* in 1933, Frisch defined econometrics in more general terms:

> Econometrics is by no means the same as economic statistics. Nor is it identical with what we call general economic theory, although a considerable portion of this theory has a definitely quantitative character. Nor should econometrics be taken as synonomous (sic) with the application of mathematics to economics. Experience has shown that each of these three view-points, that of statistics, economic theory, and mathematics, is a necessary, but not by itself a sufficient, condition for a real understanding of the quantitative relations in modern economic life. It is the *unification* of all three that is powerful. And it is this unification that constitutes econometrics.[2]

To Frisch, econometrics embodies a creative tension between theory and observation:

> Theory, in formulating its abstract quantitative notions, must be inspired to a large extent by the technique of observation. And fresh statistical and other factual studies must be the healthy element of disturbance that constantly threatens and disquiets the theorist and prevents him from coming to rest on some inherited, obsolete set of assumptions.[3]

The field of econometrics has developed and matured enormously since Frisch wrote in 1933. It is my belief, however, that the way in which we typically teach econometrics today often loses sight of the underlying goals identified by Frisch. In particular, in the customary classroom teaching environ-

[1] For a brief discussion, see Ragnar Frisch, "Note on the Term 'Econometrics,'" *Econometrica*, 4:1, 1936, p. 95.
[2] Ragnar Frisch, "Editorial," *Econometrica*, 1:1, January 1933, p. 2.
[3] Ibid.

ment it is tempting to focus primarily on econometric theory and to lose sight of the driving forces behind econometrics, namely, to increase our "real understanding of the quantitative relations in modern economic life."

This book focuses exclusively on such quantitative relations—important applications and empirical implementations of econometrics. It is not a textbook in econometric theory but is complementary to such a text.

I have structured and written this text for primary use in four types of learning environments:

1. As a supplementary textbook in a first-year graduate econometrics and forecasting course for students in economics or business or for a similar course at the advanced undergraduate level.
2. As the primary textbook in an applied econometrics course that focuses on important classic and contemporary applications and empirical implementations of econometric techniques.
3. As a "hands-on" textbook for students who wish to learn, on their own or in training seminars, how to implement and interpret econometric techniques.
4. As a reference material for students doing term paper exercises or theses in a variety of applied areas, for example, labor economics.

Computation and Econometrics

The usefulness of this text is due in large part to recent developments in computation. The continued steady drop in costs of mainframe computing, the greater accessibility to students of mainframe computers, as well as the diffusion of increasingly affordable personal computers and workstations, have removed most previous obstacles and now make it feasible for students early in their training to become seriously involved in implementing empirically the theory taught in econometrics and forecasting courses.

In this textbook I exploit these and other recent computational developments. I do this in three ways:

1. For a number of important topical applications this text provides students with readable surveys on the underlying economic theory, major issues in measurement and econometric implementation, and the principal empirical findings obtained to date.
2. This text makes accessible to students a variety of classic and contemporary data bases, thereby encouraging replication and extension of the existing empirical literature. These data bases are provided on a floppy disk accompanying this textbook. Since the data are in files written using ASCII conventions, the data should be readable by virtually all computers.
3. For individuals who have access to IBM or compatible personal computers or to Apple Macintoshes, this text provides information on avail-

able software sources, including free software and inexpensive student editions. This information enables students and instructors to choose software and then to implement and experiment with, at minimal cost, a good portion of the econometric techniques used by empirical researchers today.

Organization of the Book

The book consists of an introductory chapter followed by ten applied topics of interest to economics and business students, emphasizing one set of tools per chapter. The order of the chapters corresponds with the sequence of topics that is typically taught in econometrics and forecasting courses, beginning with the bivariate regression model (Chapter 2), moving on to multiple regression and effects of omitted variables (Chapters 3 and 4), dummy variables and specification issues (Chapters 4 and 5), then to generalized least squares and distributed lags (Chapters 6 and 7), forecasting with generalized least squares and time series analysis (Chapter 7), causality and simultaneity (Chapter 8), systems of equations (Chapter 9), simultaneous equations (Chapter 10), and discrete dependent variable models (Chapter 11).

The amount of material in this text is substantial, and instructors may well choose to work with only a subset of the chapters in a one-semester or even a year-long course. Two chapters, "Explaining and Forecasting Aggregate Investment Expenditures" (Chapter 6), and "Causality and Simultaneity between Advertising and Sales" (Chapter 8) are considerably longer than the other chapters; these two chapters have been designed for instructors in economics or business who wish to have their students focus on one particular topic for a substantial time period, such as a quarter or a semester. Alternative ways of using these and other chapters in this text are discussed further in the Instructor's Resource Guide.

Each chapter begins with a discussion of the economic theory underlying the application, outlines issues in econometric implementation (including measurement issues), summarizes important empirical findings to date, and then engages the student in a carefully designed set of eight to ten empirical exercises involving replication and extension of classic and contemporary empirical findings.

Applications and "Hands-on" Exercises

Several aspects of these exercises are worth noting. First, this applications textbook will be most helpful to users if its exercises are coordinated with their econometric theory textbook. To facilitate such coordination, a cross-reference of exercises in this book with relevant chapters in the leading econometric theory textbooks is provided in the Instructor's Resource Guide. Second, in most chapters the initial exercises involve students in examining the data before using them in further econometric analyses. I believe that exploratory data analysis is an important component of good econometric research. Third, the exercises have been tested and have served students well in a number of courses at MIT and elsewhere. But the practice of econometrics is diverse, and instructors might wish to augment or revise the exercises to meet their particular needs and preferences. The text allows for such flexibility, and I expect considerable diversity in how this text is used.

Fourth, data for each of the exercises are provided on a floppy disk accompanying this text. Classic data sets can be updated by consulting the cited data sources. Ideas and sources for additional data are discussed in the Instructor's Resource Guide. Fifth, rather than presenting students with only one data base and one set of exercises per topic, in most chapters a number of data series are provided; students (and instructors) are invited to choose among them and experiment. This selection permits a greater degree of individualization and self-learning. Sixth, while the empirical exercises encourage experimentation and are designed particularly with the personal computer in mind, they can of course be carried out on mainframe computers.

Finally, each application chapter contains exercises that correspond to two levels of difficulty. Most of the exercises initially focus on the use of econometric procedures, but the final few exercises often introduce procedures that might not yet have been covered in class. Students are therefore encouraged to return to a particular topic later in a typical course, perhaps several times, after more sophisticated econometric techniques have been presented and learned.

The emphasis in this text on empirical implementation and self-learning contains at least one significant potential liability. Since all the data required to perform the exercises are provided on a floppy disk students are not really required to "dig" for data or gain understanding of how data are actually gathered and compiled. That is unfortunate. Nonetheless, I believe that the strategy of giving students complete access to data is justifiable, since it is important for students to begin to understand quickly and at minimum cost that the process of replication is extremely important in empirical research.

Supplements

Three manuals are available to help readers implement the "hands-on" exercises in each chapter of the text using well-known econometrics software packages for microcomputers (as well as mainframes with PC-TSP and SHAZAM):

Greenberg, *A Computer Handbook Using MicroTSP*
White/Bui, *A Computer Handbook Using SHAZAM*
White/Hall, *A Computer Handbook Using PC-TSP*

The data disk bundled with the textbook is written in ASCII code and can be used with these software packages or with other common statistical software.

A detailed Instructor's Resource Guide is also available and includes the following:

Solutions to many "hands-on" exercises
Suggested course outlines
Guide for using the textbook with major econometric theory books
Sources for additional data sets

Acknowledgments

This textbook has benefited from the comments and insights of a large number of people, particularly my students at MIT. Numerous colleagues and friends have also provided constructive and challenging suggestions. I owe special thanks to G. Campbell Watkins, Ken White, and Paul Greenberg, who read each chapter with great care and offered many constructive suggestions. Also, Steve Lerman of Project Athena at MIT provided seed money for this project as part of the process of introducing personal computers and workstations into the MIT curriculum. In addition, is a pleasure to thank the following people who in various ways contributed to one or more of the chapters:

Susanne Ackum, Dennis Aigner, William Alberts, Richard Anderson, G. Chris Archibald, David Atlas, Richard Blundell, Linda Bui, Charles A. Capone, Jr., Ron Cartwright, Judy Wang Chiang, Robert Chirinko, Barry Chiswick, Klaus Conrad, Clint Cummins, Linda Datcher-Loury, George Day, Erwin Diewert, Ellen Dulberger, Robert Engle, Ray Fair, Hank Farber, Frank Fisher, M. Therese Flaherty, Peter Fortune, Don Fullerton, Mel Fuss, David Garman, Robert J. Gordon, William Greene, Zvi Griliches, Gudmundur Gunnarson, Morley Gunderson, Robert Halvorsen, Robert Hall, John Ham, Dan Hamermesh, Ray Hartman, Arnoldo Hax, Bertil Holmlund, George Houlihan, Hendrik Houthakker, Dennis W. Jansen, Dale Jorgenson, Chris Kemerer, Mark Killingsworth, Lawrence R. Klein, Jan Kmenta, Richard Kopcke, Nalin Kulatilaka, Julia Lane, Edward Lazear, Pierre Lasserre, Robert E. Lucas, Jacques Mairesse, Terry Marsh, Ben McCallum, Dan McFadden, Claudio Migliore, Jacob Mincer, Mathew J. Morey, Catherine Morrison, Thomas Mroz, Stewart Myers, Alice Nakamura, Masao Nakamura, Charles Nelson, J. Randolph Norsworthy, Ronald Oaxaca, Tae Oum, Kristian Palda, Leslie Papke, Stephen Peck, John Pencavel, Richard Pollay, James Poterba, Harvey Rosen, Shelley Rosenstein, Julio Rotemberg, Thomas Sargent, Richard Schmalensee, Fiona Scott-Morton, Mark Showalter, Alvin Silk, V. Kerry Smith, John Solow, Robert Solow, Bruce Stangle, Leslie Sundt, Paul Taubman, John Taylor, Lester Telser, Jack Triplett, Luc Valle, Joachim Wagner, G. C. Watkins, David Wood, Eric Wruck, C. K. Woo, Bengt-Christer Ysander, and Arnold Zellner.

Although each of these individuals has made direct contributions to the chapters of this text, it is of course the case that the contents and style of the book reflect in many ways the lasting impacts of those who have taught me most about the practice of econometric theory: Lau Christensen, Erwin Diewert, Art Goldberger, Zvi Griliches, Dale Jorgenson, and Larry Lau. I am deeply indebted to each of them.

The experience of transforming an overdue manuscript into final book form has been surprisingly enjoyable. This process is due in large part to the dedication, thoroughness, and highest professional standards of the publishing team at Addison-Wesley. In particular, it is a pleasure for me to thank my editor, Barbara Rifkind, as well as Christine O'Brien, Kari Heen, Kazia Navas, Ann Kilbride, Jason Jordan, Mary Dyer, and Marshall Henrichs. Special thanks also to Lynn Steele, my assistant at MIT.

This effort would not have been possible without the patient support of my friend and wife, Cathy Morrison. The essential ideas for this text germinated while we were both on leave at Stanford University in 1985, and Cathy's support encouraged me to risk limiting attention on traditional research, and instead devoting energies and efforts to this textbook.

While this effort has been hard and at times frustrating, you have stood with me. To you, Cathy, I dedicate this book. Thank you.

Cambridge, MA E.R.B.

Cover:
Astronomers analyze and predict the movements of planets, stars and galaxies, combining theory with observation. Just so, the practicing econometrician endeavors to predict changes in economic variables over time and space, using economic theory and empirical observations typically based on non-experimental data. Surprises, measurement errors, and the lack of a completely satisfactory theory often result in prediction errors for both astronomers and econometricians. This inability to predict with sufficient precision induces revisions to the underlying theory. In this way, theory and observation work together in helping us better understand our world.

Contents

"If you think . . . that anything like a romance is preparing you, reader, you were never more mistaken. Do you anticipate sentiment, and poetry, and reverie? Do you expect passion, and stimulus, and melodrama? Calm your expectations, reduce them to a lowly standard. Something real, cool and solid lies before you; something unromantic as Monday morning, when all who work wake with the consciousness that they must rise and betake themselves thereto."

CHARLOTTE BRONTË

Prelude to *Shirley*

Chapter 1

Computers and the Practice of Econometrics

"I think there is a world market for about five computers."

THOMAS J. WATSON,[1] Chairman of the Board—IBM, 1943

"There is no reason for any individual to have a computer in their home."

KENNETH OLSON,[2] President, Digital Equipment Corporation, 1977

"One machine can do the work of fifty ordinary men. No machine can do the work of one extraordinary man."

ELBERT (GREEN) HUBBARD[3]

The purpose of this book is to engage you in direct "hands-on" empirical applications of econometric tools, using classic and contemporary data sets. To become involved in such experiences, you will need to work with a computer. Although this text is designed primarily with personal microcomputers in mind (especially the IBM-PC and its compatibles or the Macintosh), all the exercises in this book can be performed using mainframe computers.

The goal of this chapter is to help you get going with the implementation of econometrics. In Section 1.1 we begin with a brief historical overview of computers in econometrics, and then in Section 1.2 we introduce you to some basics of computer equipment (hardware) and computer programs (software), focusing in particular on the most important software accompanying any computer, called its operating system.

With this as background, in Section 1.3 we acquaint you with procedures necessary for accessing the classic and contemporary data sets from the floppy diskette accompanying this text. Although particular procedures for doing this vary among computers, certain steps are almost universal, and we focus attention on them. In Section 1.4, we briefly overview the structure of the exercises found at the end of each chapter. Finally, in Section 1.5 we involve you in a very simple hands-on application, to make sure you are ready and able to take on the applications and exercises of subsequent chapters. Two appendices accompany this chapter. In Appendix A we overview a variety of statistics and econometric software packages for the IBM-PC and the Apple Macintosh. In Appendix B we provide you with references for obtaining further information and product reviews.

1.1 HISTORICAL PERSPECTIVES ON COMPUTERS AND ECONOMETRICS

The empirical implementation of econometric procedures is much simpler and easier today than it was even a decade ago, owing in large part to the development and diffusion of increasingly inexpensive and powerful computer hardware and software. Although recent developments appear particularly dramatic, remarkable improvements in computational capabilities for econometrics have been occurring for quite some time.

For example, one might characterize the first generation of empirical econometrics as one in which computations were done entirely by hand. The advent of hand-crank and electronic calculators improved matters considerably, but such second-generation developments still implied enormous computational times for typical problems in empirical econometrics. For example, at meetings in 1946 of members of the Cowles Commission staff (an institution associated with numerous pioneering developments in econometrics), the following exchange took place concerning the estimated time required to undertake econometric computations:

> In answer to a question by Girshick, Koopmans mentioned that one supervisor and one to two computers had worked two to three months on an eight equation system, by hand calculating. Rubin estimated that a ten equation system with fifty unknown parameters by hand computing with an ordinary calculator requires seventy 24-hour computer days.[4]

Today, with personal computers and modern statistical software, such computations take less than 20 seconds.

The history of computation in econometrics is not yet well chronicled.[5] A few interesting facts are known, however. One is that in 1944, when Guy H. Orcutt became an assistant professor of economics at the Massachusetts Institute of Technology, he also began working for Professor George Wadsworth of the MIT Mathematics Department to build and then operate a "regression analyser," the design of which was based on Orcutt's Ph.D. thesis in economics at the University of Michigan, a thesis complete with electronic circuit diagrams.[6] Although Orcutt's prototype analog machine had only two-digit accuracy and stored data for only 33 item time series on punched cards, which were continuously read many times per second, one might charitably think of it as being the first portable computer. In particular, according to Orcutt,

> As events unfolded, the planned prototype machine was built and used successfully for a few months as World War II was beginning to wind down. I took my regression analyser with me to Cleveland and demonstrated it at the annual Christmas meetings. Since I was grossly overloaded, I was unable to take along the cathode ray tube which served as a graphical display device for showing time series and scatter diagrams derived from the three time series segments being read into the regression analyser. But I was able to borrow one from Case University in Cleveland.[7]

The regression analyser traveled even farther. During the 1945–1946 academic year, Orcutt was invited by Richard Stone to come to the newly established Department of Applied Economics at Cambridge University, with the expressed hope that "I would bring the machine and put it to use in developing tests of significance of apparent relationships between autocorrelated economic time series."[8] It was there that Orcutt used his regression analyser in working with autocorrelated time series generated by stochastic time series models that were estimated by using data from Jan Tinbergen's pioneering macroeconometric model. The regression analyser played an essential role in making it feasible to carry out Monte Carlo computations for testing the significance of apparent relationships between economic time series having autocorrelated characteristics.[9]

Apparently, the first article published by an econometrician based on results from a digital electronic calculator having a stored memory program is that by Hendrik S. Houthakker.[10] Houthakker's research involved working

GUY ORCUTT

A Pioneer in Econometric Computation

Born in a Detroit suburb in 1917, Guy Orcutt spent much of his spare time as a high school student experimenting with electricity and chemistry, even accidentally creating an explosion that redecorated part of his bedroom ceiling. After graduating from the University of Michigan with majors in physics and mathematics, Orcutt spent the summer of 1939 at a Quaker work camp in a severely depressed coal mining region of West Virginia. This experience kindled an interest in economics and led him to enroll as a graduate student in economics at Michigan, even though he had not taken a single undergraduate economics course.

Mentored by Arthur Smithies, as a graduate student Orcutt was encouraged to expand on his interests in using electronic devices for undertaking complex mathematical computations. This led to Orcutt's design of a "regression analyser," the theory and circuit diagrams of which are prominently displayed in his Ph.D. dissertation.

Since the actual construction of such a machine required considerable time, funds for materials, and help from machinists (support that was not available to Orcutt as a graduate student), it was not until late 1945 that a prototype of Orcutt's regression analyser was successfully constructed. This took place at the Massachusetts Institute of Technology, where Orcutt was hired in 1944 to teach beginning economics courses to engineering undergraduates but was simultaneously involved with Professor George Wadsworth of the MIT Mathematics Department in an effort to improve weather forecasting by relating the weather at a given location to the weather somewhat earlier at other locations.

Orcutt's regression analyser was successfully demonstrated at the annual meetings of the American Economic Association in Cleveland in 1945, and his interest in autocorrelated time series attracted the attention of Richard Stone, who invited Orcutt to Cambridge University beginning in the fall of 1946.

There, in the newly created Department of Applied Economics under the direction of Stone, Orcutt refurbished his regression analyser, availing himself of facilities at the Cavendish Laboratory. He then used the regression analyser in Monte Carlo studies that focused on developing tests of significance of apparent relationships between time series having autocorrelated characteristics similar to actual time series being used in econometric modeling of national economies. These efforts resulted in two papers, one in the 1948 volume of the *Journal of the Royal Statistical Society*, Series A, and the other with S.F. James in the December 1948 issue of *Biometrika.*

Together with a Cambridge graduate student named Donald Cochrane, Orcutt also developed the now widely used Cochrane-Orcutt estimator for models with first-order autocorrelated disturbances, which was described in the March and September 1949 issues of the *Journal of the American Statistical Association.*

In addition to his pioneering work on electronic computations and the estimation of autocorrelated time series models, Orcutt is widely known for research on the measurement of price elasticities in international trade and for the development of microanalytic models of socioeconomic behavior.

Guy Orcutt retired from Yale University in 1988 and now lives with his wife Geil (and his personal computer) in Grantham, New Hampshire.

with the EDSAC—the Electronic Delay Storage Automatic Calculator of the University Mathematical Laboratory at Cambridge University.[11] (In Chapter 7 of this book you will have an opportunity to work with Houthakker's classic data set, and to reproduce his EDSAC results.) The EDSAC provided numerous advantages over electric hand-calculators:

> It takes about 7 minutes on the EDSAC to compute all the 55 weighted sums of squares and cross-products of 10 variables with 40 observations in addition to about 4 hours for punching and checking the number tape

Photo of EDSAC—the Electronic Delay Storage Automatic Calculator.

> and verifying the results by a sum-check. A human computer with an electric desk machine would probably need about 75 hours for this job, so that 71 hours of labor are replaced by 7 minutes of machine time.[12]

Since the EDSAC, numerous other very important developments have occurred that have lowered enormously the computational costs of implementing empirical econometrics. For example, major product innovations include the installation of the first UNIVAC machine at the U.S. Census Bureau in 1951; the delivery of IBM's first electronic computer, the 701, to Los Alamos in 1953; the IBM debut of FORTRAN, the first high-level computer language, in 1957; the Digital Equipment Corporation introduction of the minicomputer in 1963; the unveiling of the IBM System/360 in 1964, the first family of computers; the introduction of mass-produced pocket calculators into the United States in 1971; the initial offering of the Apple II personal computer in 1977; and the entry of IBM into the personal computer market in 1981.

Although the history of these developments makes for fascinating reading, for our purposes it is more useful here to focus on the last of these developments, namely, the personal computer and its usefulness for econometric research.[13] To this we now turn our attention.

1.2 BACKGROUND: COMPUTER HARDWARE AND COMPUTER SOFTWARE

At the heart of the personal or microcomputer is the *microprocessor*, a chip that performs most of the computer's work. Quite frequently, microprocessors are characterized in terms of the number of *bits* they are able to process at one time. The word "bit," incidentally, is a contraction of the words "binary digit," each bit being either a zero or a one. A 32-bit microprocessor can process 32 zeros and ones simultaneously. Although earlier microcomputer models often had 8- or 16-bit microprocessors, today models in the IBM PS/2 series contain a 32-bit Intel 80386 microprocessor, while the Macintosh II utilizes a 32-bit Motorola 68020 unit.[14]

Most personal computer software and statistical data come in the form of a *floppy disk*, made from a thin film of mylar plastic coated with ferrous oxide and placed inside a lubricated plastic protective jacket; common sizes for these diskettes are 5.25″ and 3.5″. When blank floppy disks are purchased from a store, they are typically usable in any personal computer, since the millions of tiny magnets in the ferrous oxide coating are arranged randomly on the disk, that is, the disk is unformatted.

The first operation users typically perform with a floppy disk is to *format* it, which means magnetically inscribing pie-shaped sectors and concentric tracks onto the disk. Precisely how these sectors and tracks are laid out on the disk varies depending on the specifications adopted by the various hardware and software manufacturers. When a disk is formatted, each of the tiny magnets in the ferrous oxide coating is "lined up" so that each points in the direction that indicates "zero."

Once the disk is formatted, data can be stored on it. Each magnetic dipole in the ferrous oxide coating has a north and a south pole; when the dipole is pointing left, a "zero" or "off" is indicated, and when the dipole is pointing right, a "one" or "on" is implied. Each bit is either "on" or "off." A series of eight bits is called a *byte*; a byte is also often called a character and can be a letter, a number, or some other symbol.

The standard code used to convert letters, numbers, and symbols into bits and bytes is called the ASCII (*A*merican *S*tandard *C*ode for *I*nformation *I*nterchange) code. Examples of ASCII code include the following:

Character	*ASCII Code*
A	0100 0001
B	0100 0010
C	0100 0011
D	0100 0100
0	0011 0000
1	0011 0001
2	0011 0010
3	0011 0011
*	0010 1010
!	0010 0001

The standard ASCII code contains 256 distinct characters (2 raised to the eighth power), including numbers, symbols, uppercase and lowercase alphabetical elements, and some foreign language characters. The data series provided on the floppy disk accompanying this text have been coded following ASCII conventions and therefore should be readable by almost any micro, mini, or mainframe computer.

Floppy disks can store a great deal of information. The precise amount of storage capacity of a disk depends on the number of sectors and tracks inscribed on it by the operating system when the disk was most recently formatted. One of the earliest common formatting procedures for an IBM or IBM-compatible machine was the 360K format, in which 512 bytes per sector were generated, there were nine sectors per track, and 40 tracks per disk for each of the two sides of the floppy disk. This yielded a total of 368,640 bytes (or 2,949,120 bits); such disks are commonly referred to as having 360K (kilobyte) capacity. Disks with 720K, 1.2 MB (for megabyte), and 1.4 MB capacity are now commonly used for both IBM and Macintosh machines.

Personal computers usually have at least one floppy disk drive; many have an additional floppy drive and/or a hard disk drive, the latter essentially being equivalent to several floppy drives but permitting more convenient storage of data and programs on the computer. Data, programs, and files contained in the floppy disk drives can usually be accessed by addressing the appropriate drive; typically, A: and B: refer to the floppy drives, while C: (or D:) refers to the hard disk drive.

The *operating system* is the lowest level of software on the personal computer. It interacts directly with the computer's microprocessor to perform the most basic and important housekeeping functions, such as formatting disks, copying disks, saving and loading files, checking the status of a disk, and keeping a directory of the files on the disk. For the IBM-PC the operating system is typically stored partly on a ROM (*R*ead *O*nly *M*emory) chip inside the microcomputer and partly on the DOS (*D*isk *O*perating *S*ystem) master diskette or on the hard disk. This means that certain commands—those stored in ROM—can be performed by the IBM-PC computer without even loading the DOS diskette. We now overview some of the most important functions performed by DOS on the IBM-PC and its compatibles.

With data stored in files on disks it is often convenient to organize the files into separate groups. One function of DOS is to create distinct directories or groups of files, where the files within each directory are kept separate from the files in other directories. With DOS, each disk has a main, or root, directory. To this root directory, one can add new subdirectories where files can be kept in distinct groups.

Consider, for example, the data files that must be accessed to perform the empirical exercises at the end of each chapter in this text. The various data series for each chapter are stored as distinct files in chapter-specific subdirectories. For example, in the data diskette provided with this text, the root directory contains the names of one documentation file, README.DOC, one data file, COLORTV, and ten subdirectories: CHAP2.DAT, CHAP3.DAT, CHAP4.DAT, . . . , CHAP11.DAT. Within each of the ten subdirectories, you will find a number of data files containing data for hands-on exercises from the appropriate chapter.

As an example, take the CHAP2.DAT subdirectory. It contains over 20 data files, each containing data on rates of return on securities for some particular company, such as MOBIL, GERBER, DELTA, and TANDY. Similarly, the CHAP3.DAT subdirectory contains data files on production costs for the manufacture of polyethylene (POLY) and titanium dioxide (TIO2), as well as a rather strange data set named WEIRD.

One particularly important function of DOS is to make backup copies of important floppy disks. Right now is a very good time to make a backup copy of your data disk. To do this, use the XCOPY /S command, as noted in your DOS manual. (*Important:* Do *not* use the COPY command, since the data diskette contains a number of subdirectories; the COPY command will usually not copy subdirectories. If your computer uses a version of DOS earlier than 3.2, however, the XCOPY command is not available; instead you can employ the DISKCOPY command, even though it is somewhat cumbersome.)

Since subdirectories branch off of directories, they are said to form a "tree" structure. *Paths* or *pathnames* are used to climb through the branches of the trees. More specifically, the pathname is a routing device that indicates, through a sequence of addresses, just where a file can be accessed. For example, the data file GOLD in the subdirectory CHAP2.DAT on a floppy in disk drive B can be called from any current working subdirectory by typing the pathname

```
B:\CHAP2.DAT\GOLD
```

Note that the backslashes (\) are used to separate the names of directories and files in the pathname. Also, when operating the computer, you will notice that one directory is always the default; it is called your *current working directory.*

To move between directories, type "CD\" (Change Directory) followed by the pathname of the directory to which you want to move. To create a directory, type the "MD" (Make Directory) command, followed by the name of the directory. For example, if you want to create a directory called BACKUP on the disk drive B, type

```
B:\MD BACKUP
```

To change disk drives, type the letter name of the drive you want to access, followed by a colon. For example, if you are currently in the A drive and want to change to the B drive, type "B:".

Files can be named by using a combination of up to eight letter and/or number characters. (Some statistical programs, however, restrict the number of characters to six or fewer. Check your econometric software program documentation for further details.) File names often have an extension, which is a period just after the filename, followed by a maximum of three characters. Extensions such as .EXE and .COM indicate to the computer that the file has been rearranged (compiled) by software so that it can be executed immediately. Often, however, users employ an extension to aid in quickly identifying a file's contents.

Files can be copied by using the COPY command. For example, if you wished to copy a file named GOLD in the directory CHAP2.DAT, which is currently on a floppy disk in the A drive, onto a file named GOLD in a directory named BACKUP on a floppy disk in the B drive (assuming that the BACKUP directory has been created), you would type

```
COPY A:\CHAP2.DAT\GOLD B:\BACKUP\GOLD
```

At times you might change your mind and decide to rename a file. This can be done very simply. For example, the GOLD data file mentioned in the previous paragraph could be that for the gold market in London; to remind yourself of that, you might want to change its name from GOLD to GOLD.LON by typing

```
RENAME B:\BACKUP\GOLD B:\BACKUP\GOLD.LON
```

A very common operation involves examining the contents of a file visually on the monitor screen. For example, you might have performed an operation using an econometric software program and might then want to examine the output file to determine whether you made any programming mistakes. Any file stored in ASCII characters can be displayed on the monitor screen by using the command

```
TYPE FILENAME.EXT
```

where the location of the filename is identified by a pathname. If you want to have the file contents shown one screen at a time, add "/P" to the TYPE FILENAME.EXT command. If you decide to have the material currently displayed on the monitor screen printed, simultaneously hit the keyboard keys ⟨Shift⟩ and ⟨PrtSc⟩. Finally, if you want to have the entire contents of an ASCII file printed out (not just the portion displayed on your monitor screen), type out the DOS command

```
TYPE FILENAME.EXT > PRN
```

Finally, it should be noted that to work with data files, to create sets of commands for statistical software programs, or to modify any ASCII files, it is often most convenient to employ computer software that is specifically designed to allow you to edit files. For the IBM PC and its compatibles the most common *text editor* software is EDLIN (a component of DOS) and the BASIC Program Editor. More sophisticated and powerful text editor software programs are typically called *word processors.* A wide variety of word processor programs are available commercially, and some are even in the public domain at virtually no cost. Reviews and comments on various word processor software packages can be found in numerous magazines available at newsstands. You will find that having access to and being familiar with a word processor software package will help you enormously in doing the exercises in this textbook.

While this review of the IBM-PC and the DOS operating system is admittedly *very* brief, it should be sufficient to get you started. Whenever you are in doubt about the appropriate choice of commands, refer to your DOS manual; if you are working on a computer other than the IBM-PC or its compatibles or on a mainframe computer, examine its documentation, check with the mainframe computer operators, or see your instructor.[15]

1.3 ACCESSING DATA FROM DISKETTES FOR USE IN COMPUTER SOFTWARE PROGRAMS

As was noted in the previous section, the data necessary to do the empirical exercises at the end of each chapter have been written onto a data diskette. These data are written using the almost universal ASCII free format procedures and thus can be read and edited or modified by virtually any word processor program. The data have been organized according to the structure presented in Table 1.1.

Regression and statistical/forecasting software programs vary consider-

Table 1.1 Structure of Data Diskette Accompanying the Practice of Econometrics

Root Directory	Subdirectory	Number of Files in Subdirectory	Number of Characters in Subdirectory
Contains names of subdirectories, a documentation file called README.DOC, and a data file called COLORTV.	CHAP2.DAT	23	38,781
	CHAP3.DAT	6	14,774
	CHAP4.DAT	4	29,840
	CHAP5.DAT	3	59,798
	CHAP6.DAT	2	16,392
	CHAP7.DAT	3	5,558
	CHAP8.DAT	8	52,385
	CHAP9.DAT	2	6,717
	CHAP10.DAT	4	10,397
	CHAP11.DAT	2	61,624

ably in the way in which they input or read data from diskettes. In most statistical software programs the data are first described in terms of the number of observations and the names of the variables. This part of the data input is typically called the *header.* The header provides information enabling the software program to read the data correctly. For example, are the data organized by variable or by observation? The second portion of data input in most statistical software programs consists of the *data* itself—rows and columns of numbers, delimited by spaces or commas. Some software programs require that the data be organized (formatted) in a particular manner, while a good number of programs are now more flexible and permit "free format" entry of data. The third and final component of a typical data input is a word, symbol, or set of characters immediately following the last data entry, indicating that the data series has terminated. This is often called a *data terminator.*

You should check your statistical software manual for complete information on how the header, data, and data terminator or their equivalents must be specified in order that your input data can be read correctly. Note that it will most likely be necessary for you to use a word processor program to modify (edit) the data files on the data diskette accompanying this text.

The number of powerful statistics, econometrics, and forecasting software programs that can be executed on the personal computer is growing very rapidly, as are the features that these programs incorporate. Although this text cannot possibly provide readers with up-to-date lists of all available software and features—the computer environment is changing too rapidly—two types of important information can be given here.

First, in Appendix A to this chapter we provide some general comments concerning several "extended families" of software programs. Software that is currently either free or relatively inexpensive in the form of special student or instructional editions is highlighted.

Second, since the available menu of statistical software is changing rapidly, in Appendix B to this chapter we furnish the addresses and phone numbers of vendors of the most common statistics, econometrics, and forecasting software for the IBM-PC and compatibles and for the Macintosh. While this list is not exhaustive, it is representative.

You are strongly encouraged to contact vendors listed in Appendix B to obtain current information on prices, hardware requirements, and features. When examining prices, you might examine not only the list price, but also the availability of quantity discounts, special educational prices, and site license fees. In addition to standard statistical features, you might also compare the programs in terms of their ability to display data graphically and their amenability to importing or exporting data consistent with protocols of other widely used data base programs, such as Lotus® 1-2-3® or Symphony®.

Statistical software programs are frequently reviewed in computer magazines such as *PC Magazine*, *PC Week*, and *Info World* (for the IBM-PC and compatibles) and *MacWorld*, *MacUser*, and *MacWeek* (for Apple Macintosh machines). These magazines are typically available at most newsstands.[16] Further, *The American Statistician*, a quarterly publication of the American Statistical Association, regularly contains a special section devoted to summarizing and reviewing recent statistical software for the personal computer.[17] Also, Springer-Verlag Press publishes a readable journal devoted to statistics and computing, called *CHANCE*.[18] Finally, for a periodic survey and update of available statistical software, see the *Directory of Statistical Microcomputer Software*.[19]

1.4 A NOTE ON THE END-OF-CHAPTER EXERCISES

The exercises at the end of each remaining chapter in this book have been carefully designed to enable you to obtain hands-on experience in implementing empirical research. One important feature of this text is that its chapters are ordered to correspond with ever increasingly advanced econometric procedures—techniques typically learned in a sequential manner in most econometrics and forecasting courses. Therefore it is expected that you will work through Chapter 2 before considering, say, Chapter 8.

However, the empirical topics are of considerable inherent interest, and much insight and understanding would be lost if the specific topics were addressed only once during a course. For that reason, while most of the exercises at the end of each chapter deal with a particular set of econometric tools, in almost all chapters the final two or so exercises use more advanced procedures. This means that you can undertake the vast majority of exercises at the end of each chapter as you initially proceed through a typical econometrics/forecasting course. However, the last few exercises usually involve techniques and procedures that are customarily learned later in such courses; you might not be able to do them until your instructor introduces the appropriate procedures.

You are most likely to gain a deeper appreciation of the empirical aspects of each specific topic if, as your course of studies proceeds, you return to the final, more difficult exercises of earlier chapters. In this way you can examine issues of robustness, observing by yourself how results might be affected by changes in assumptions and estimation methods. More generally, returning to the same topic several times during a course enables you to experience the special satisfaction of observing your own maturation as you employ increasingly sophisticated research tools and methods.

1.5 HANDS ON WITH AN EXPLORATORY DATA SET

The purpose of this section is to involve you in practicing some basic computer skills to ensure that you are ready and able to perform the empirical exercises found at the end of each remaining chapter in this book. The following exercise involves entering data directly from the keyboard and then, alternatively, accessing the same data from a data file on the data diskette provided. It is assumed that you have access to a personal, mini, or mainframe computer, that you have available and understand how to use a text editor/word processor software program, and that you also have statistical software at your disposal.

Table 1.2 displays time series data for the unit price and cumulative production of color television sets in the United States over the 1964–1979 time period. This type of data is often used to analyze the effects of learning on production costs and prices, where it is assumed that, as cumulative production increases, learning occurs, resulting in lower unit costs and prices. The subject of learning curves, incidentally, is discussed in considerable detail in Chapter 3 of this text. As is seen in Table 1.2, the average price of color TVs has tended to decline as cumulative production has increased.

EXERCISES

EXERCISE 1: Ensuring That Data Are Properly Entered and Transformed

The purpose of this exercise is to have you practice some basic computer skills to ensure that you are able to enter data into your statistical software program, both from the keyboard directly and from a data file provided on your data diskette.

(a) Boot (start) up your computer, make sure that DOS or its equivalent is loaded, and then load into memory your statistical software program.
(b) Using direct keyboard entry, note the appropriate sample size (16 observations) and then enter into your program historical values of the vari-

Table 1.2 Prices and Cumulative Production of Color Television Sets in the United States, 1964–1979

Year	Price Index (TVPRICE)	Cumulative Production (in Millions) (TVCUMPR)
1964	777	3.104
1965	779	5.798
1966	787	10.910
1967	746	16.373
1968	662	22.588
1969	615	28.779
1970	624	34.099
1971	549	41.373
1972	520	50.218
1973	474	60.289
1974	448	68.700
1975	442	74.919
1976	430	83.113
1977	407	92.454
1978	380	103.674
1979	360	113.170

Notes: The Price Index variable is computed as the average price of color televisions deflated by the GNP deflator, where the deflator is indexed to 1979 = 1.00. The data were kindly provided by Strategic Planning Associates, Washington, D.C., which obtained it from the 1981 TV Factbook No. 49.

ables TVPRICE and TVCUMPR (for color television price index and cumulative production, respectively) as given in Table 1.2, following the directions provided by your statistical software program documentation. Print the data on these variables to the monitor screen and then to a hard copy on a printer. Verify that the data series on the printed paper are identical to those in Table 1.2. (It's easy to make keypunch errors!)

(c) Compute and print the means and standard deviations of these two variables, as well as their sample correlations and their variance-covariance matrices. Do you expect the sample correlation between TVPRICE and TVCUMPR to be negative or positive? Why? Is this what you in fact find?

(d) Generate two new variables, one the natural logarithm of the TVPRICE and the other the natural logarithm of TVCUMPR; choose names for these variables, and then plot the logarithm of TVPRICE against the logarithm of TVCUMPR. Is this plot consistent with your expectations? Why?

(e) Now check whether you obtain the same results when you use data from the diskette rather than typing it directly in from the keyboard. Read your statistical software program manual and discover how data on disk files must be formatted in order to be read in properly by your statistical software. (You might also want to reread Section 1.3 of this chapter.) Next, to ensure that you are able to enter data indirectly from your data diskette, read in the data file COLORTV found in the root directory on your data diskette, containing the variables YEAR, PRICETV, and CUMPRTV.

(f) In parts (a) through (d), you used data that you entered directly via the keyboard. Now, having entered data indirectly via data files on diskettes, repeat parts (c) and (d), noting that in the COLORTV data file the TVPRICE variable is called PRICETV and that TVCUMPR is named CUMPRTV. Verify that the results obtained here are identical to those you obtained originally with parts (c) and (d).

(g) Next, perform a simple linear regression of the logarithm of PRICETV on a constant term and the logarithm of TVCUMPR. Do the regression results seem plausible? Why or why not?

(h) Compute and plot the residuals from your regression, and comment on the time series pattern of the residuals.

(i) Having completed this practice exercise, you should now be able to proceed with exercises from subsequent chapters of this book. Good luck!

APPENDIX A

An Overview of Statistics and Econometrics Software for the PC

Although software vendors typically expend considerable efforts in differentiating their products from others, certain commonalities exist within groups of software. One of the first major statistical programs written for use by econometricians on mainframe computers was TSP (*T*ime *S*eries *P*rocessor). It is a widely used program, and various incarnations and modifications of it with differing characteristics are available for the PC. These include PC-TSP, MicroTSP®, ESP, and Soritec. MicroTSP® offers a special student edition at a relatively inexpensive price. A somewhat smaller version of Soritec, called Soritec Sampler, is available free of charge from the Sorites Group.

Another software program originally written for econometricians working on mainframe computers, but now designed for personal computers, is SHAZAM. Like the various incarnations of TSP, SHAZAM incorporates a wide range of features that are typically employed by practicing econometricians. Personal computer versions of SHAZAM are available both for the IBM-PC and compatibles and for the Apple Macintosh.

A widely used microcomputer software program is RATS (*R*egression *A*nalysis of *T*ime *S*eries). It is a very powerful package with particular strengths in time series applications, although it incorporates a wide variety of other features as well. Researchers who enjoy and are somewhat skilled at programming have tended to prefer the RATS software over that in the TSP family; the latter tends to be more user-friendly and well-documented but is not as efficient, although differences between them are diminishing with time. RATS is available for the IBM-PC and compatibles and for the Macintosh. A relatively inexpensive student version of RATS is also available. PDQ, SCA SYSTEM, PC-GIVE, and DATA-FIT are examples of other software programs with particular strengths in time series analysis, model specification analysis, and forecasting. The vendor of PDQ has special financial arrangements for classroom use of the program.

A large family of statistical software has principal roots in disciplines other than economics, such as in statistics, or other social or physical sciences. While this software might not have all the features currently used by state-of-the-art practitioners of econometrics, the power and range of the features offered are often considerable. In many cases this type of software is particularly designed to deal with very large data bases and produces excellent graphic display summaries of data. This family of software includes BMDP/PC, MINITAB, P-STAT, SAS/STAT, SPSS/PC+, STATVIEW 512+, STATA, STATGRAPHICS, STATPRO, and SYSTAT. SYSTAT offers a downsized version, called MYSTAT, free of charge for instructional use. BASSSTAT is somewhat similar to SAS but is smaller and considerably less expensive.

Another family of software was originally designed for estimation of models in which the dependent variable is discrete, rather than continuous. This software group includes LIMDEP and SST; both of these programs, as well as a recent entrant from the LIMDEP family called ET, have expanded the set of offered features considerably beyond the original discrete dependent variable orientation and now include many common econometric procedures.

A different set of software was originally designed to perform matrix algebra calculations in a computationally efficient manner and then was expanded to include a number of the more common econometric procedures as simple sets of commands. Currently, the best-known such program is GAUSS. Another example is MATLAB, which is available for the IBM-PC, the Macintosh, and a number of other microcomputers, minicomputers, and workstations.

Finally, several large data base service companies have developed and marketed software enabling users to download data from mainframe computers and then to perform statistical operations on decentralized personal computers. Users are also typically given the option of performing more sophisticated or exotic econometric procedures by using the large library of programs available on the mainframe computers. Two examples are the ECONOMIST WORKSTATION from Data Resources/McGraw-Hill, and AREMOS/PC from Wharton Econometric Forecasting Associates, Inc.

This concludes our brief overview of the rapidly growing set of statistics, econometrics, and forecasting software programs that are available for the personal computer. It is worth repeating that prices, features, and hardware requirements for these programs change rapidly and that before making a major purchase decision you should contact vendors and read magazine reviews to obtain current information. The information contained in Appendix B should be of considerable help in this process. Finally, if you are using a mainframe computer, contact your instructor or computer operator for information concerning available statistical software. Many of the PC programs mentioned above are also available for selected mainframe computers.

APPENDIX B

Statistics and Econometrics Software for the IBM-PC and Compatibles and for the Apple Macintosh: A Partial List of Products and Vendors

IBM-PC and Compatibles

AREMOS/PC. Wharton Econometric Forecasting Associates, 3624 Science Center, Philadelphia, PA 19104. (215)-386-9000.

BASSSTAT. BASS Institute Inc., P.O. Box 349, Chapel Hill, NC 27514. (919)-933-7096.

BMDP/PC. BMDP Statistical Software Inc., 1440 Sepulveda Blvd., Suite 316, Los Angeles, CA 90025. (213)-479-7799

DATA-FIT. Oxford Electronic Publishing, Oxford University Press, Walton Street, Oxford OX2 6DP, U.K.

ECONOMIST WORKSTATION. Data Resources/McGraw-Hill, 24 Hartwell Avenue, Lexington, MA 02173. (617)-863-5100.

ESP. Economic Software Package. 76 Bedford St., Suite 33, Lexington, MA 02173. (617)-861-8852.

ET. William H. Greene, Stern Graduate School of Business, New York University, 100 Trinity Place, New York, NY 10006.

GAUSS. Aptech Systems Inc., 26250 196th Place SE, Kent, WA 98042. (206)-631-6679.

LIMDEP. William H. Greene, Stern Graduate School of Business, New York University, 100 Trinity Place, New York, NY 10006.

MATLAB. MathWorks, Inc., 20 N. Main St., Sherborn, MA 01770. (617)-653-1415.

MICRO TSP. Quantitative Micro Software, 4521 Campus Drive, Suite 336, Irvine, CA 92715. (714)-856-3368.

MINITAB. Minitab, 3081 Enterprise Dr., State College, PA 16801. (814)-238-3280.

PC-GIVE. University of Oxford, Institute of Economics and Statistics, St. Cross Building, Manor Rd., Oxford OX1 3UL U.K. (0865)-249631.

PC-TSP. TSP International, P.O. Box 61015, Palo Alto, CA 94306. (415)-326-1927.

PDQ. Charles R. Nelson, 4921 NE 39th St., Seattle, WA 98105.

P-STAT. P-STAT Inc., P.O. Box AH, Princeton, NJ 08542. (609)-924-9100.

RATS. VAR Econometrics, P.O. Box 1818, Evanston, IL 60204-1818. (312)-864-8772.

SAS/STAT. SAS Institute Inc., P.O. Box 8000, SAS Circle, Cary, NC 27511-8000. (919)-467-8000.

SCA SYSTEM. Scientific Computing Associates, Lincoln Center, 4513 Lincoln Ave., Suite 106, Lisle, IL 60532. (312)-960-1698.

SHAZAM. Kenneth J. White, Department of Economics, University of British Columbia, Vancouver, BC V6T 1Y2 Canada. (604)-228-5062.

SORITEC. The Sorites Group Inc., P.O. Box 2939, 8136 Old Keene Mill Road, Springfield, VA 22152. (703)-569-1400.

SPSS/PC+. SPSS Inc., 444 N. Michigan Ave., Chicago, IL 60611. (312)-329-3600.

SST. Dubin/Rivers Research, 1510 Ontario Ave., Pasadena, CA 91103. (818)-577-8361.

STATA. Computing Resource Center, 10801 National Blvd., 3rd Floor, Los Angeles, CA 90064. (800)-STATAPC; in California, (213)-470-4341.

STATGRAPHICS. STSC Inc., 2115 E. Jefferson St., Rockville, MD 20852. (800)-592-0050; in Maryland, (301)-984-5123.

STATPRO. Penton Software Inc., 420 Lexington Avenue, Suite 2846, New York, NY 10017. (800)-221-3414; in New York, (212)-878-9600.

SYSTAT. Systat Inc., 1800 Sherman Ave., Evanston, IL 60201. (312)-864-5670.

Apple Macintosh

MATLAB. MathWorks, Inc., 20 N. Main St., Sherborn, MA 01770. (617)-653-1415.

PC-TSP. TSP International. P.O. Box 61015, Palo Alto, CA 94306. (415)-326-1927.

RATS. VAR Econometrics, P.O. Box 1818, Evanston, IL 60204-1818. (312)-864-8772.

SHAZAM. Kenneth J. White, Department of Economics, University of British Columbia, Vancouver, BC V6T 1Y2 Canada. (604)-228-5062.

STATVIEW 512+. Brain Power, Inc., Suite 250, 24009 Ventura Blvd., Calabasas, CA 91302.

CHAPTER NOTES

1. From remarks attributed to Thomas J. Watson, quoted from Chris Morgan and David Langford, *Facts and Fallacies*, Exeter, England: Webb & Bower, 1981, p. 44.
2. From David H. Ahl in an interview with Kenneth Olson. Quote from Christopher Cerf and Victor Navasky, *The Experts Speak: The Definitive Compendium of Authoritative Misinformation*, New York: Pantheon Books, 1984, p. 209.
3. American businessman, writer, and printer; lived from 1856 to 1915. Quote taken from Martin H. Manser, *The Chambers Book of Business Quotations*, Edinburgh: W & R Chambers, Ltd., 1987, p. 42.
4. Quote taken from Minutes of Discussion of Papers on "Multivariate Analysis for Non-Experimental Data and Related Problems of Matrix Computation," The Cowles Commission, August 23–24, 1946, Ithaca, New York, authored by Theodore W. Anderson and Tjalling Koopmans, p. 8.
5. For a brief overview, see Lawrence R. Klein, "The History of Computation in Econometrics," remarks prepared at the Institute for Advanced Study at Princeton University honoring John von Neumann, undated and unpublished.
6. For a description of this machine, see Guy H. Orcutt, "A New Regression Analyser," *Journal of the Royal Statistical Society*, Vol. 111, Series A, Part I, 1948, pp. 54–70.

7. Guy H. Orcutt, "From Engineering to Microsimulation," an autobiographical reflection, to be published in 1990 in the *Journal of Economic Behavior and Organization*, along with a collection of papers presented in connection with a conference in honor of Orcutt sponsored by the Social Systems Research Institute and the Department of Economics at the University of Wisconsin, May 1988.
8. Ibid.
9. Results from these computations were published in Guy Orcutt, "A Study of the Autoregressive Nature of the Time Series Used for Tinbergen's Model of the Economic System of the United States, 1919–1932," *Journal of the Royal Statistical Society*, Vol. 10, No. 1, Series B (Methodological), 1948, pp. 1–45; and Orcutt and S.F. James, "Testing the Significance of Correlation between Time Series, *Biometrika*, Vol. 25, Parts III & IV, December 1948.
10. See Hendrik S. Houthakker, "Some Calculations on Electricity Consumption in Great Britain," *Journal of the Royal Statistical Society*, Series A, No. 114, Part III, 1951, pp. 351–371.
11. For a discussion of the EDSAC computer and its development, see Maurice V. Wilkes, *Memoirs of a Computer Pioneer*, Cambridge, MA: The MIT Press, 1985, especially Chapter 13, pp. 127–142.
12. From J.A.C. Brown, H.S. Houthakker, and S.J. Prais, "Electronic Computation in Economic Statistics," *Journal of the American Statistical Association*, 48:263, September 1953, p. 423.
13. For a well-written historical overview of computers large and small, see Stan Augarten, *Bit by Bit: An Illustrated History of Computers*, New York: Ticknor & Fields, 1984; historical issues in econometrics are addressed by Roy J. Epstein, *A History of Econometrics*, Amsterdam: North-Holland, 1987.
14. Incidentally, mathematical operations on the IBM-PC, the IBM-PC AT, or the IBM PS/2 can be speeded up considerably by installing an Intel 8087, 80287, or 80387 mathematical coprocessor, respectively. Some statistical regression programs require such a mathematical coprocessor. Check your econometrics software documentation to determine whether your machine is properly configured.
15. Numerous books are available to help you learn DOS. One of the best is that by Peter Norton, *MS-DOS and PC-DOS User's Guide*, Bowie, MD: Robert J. Brady Company for Prentice-Hall, 1984. Also see Peter Norton, *Programmer's Guide to the IBM PC*, Bellevue, WA: MicroSoft Press, 1985.
16. For further information, contact *PC Magazine*, One Park Avenue, New York, NY 10016; *PC Week*, P.O. Box 5970, Cherry Hill, NJ 08034 (609-428-5000); *Info World*, 1060 Marsh Road, Suite C-200, Menlo Park, CA 94025 (415-328-4602); *MacWorld*, PCW Communications, Inc., 501 Second St., San Francisco, CA 94107; *MacUser*, P.O. Box 56986, Boulder, CO 80321-2461 (800-627-2247); and *MacWeek*, 525 Brannan St., San Francisco, CA 94107 (415-882-7370).
17. The American Statistical Association, 1429 Duke St., Alexandria, VA 22314.
18. For further information, write to CHANCE, Springer-Verlag New York, Inc., Journal Fulfillment Services, 44 Hartz Way, Secaucus, NJ 07096-2491.
19. Published by Marcel Dekker, Inc., 270 Madison Avenue, New York, NY 10016 (212-696-9000).

Chapter 2

The Capital Asset Pricing Model: An Application of Bivariate Regression Analysis

"In investing money, the amount of interest you want should depend on whether you want to eat well or sleep well."

J. KENFIELD MORLEY, "Some Things I Believe," *The Rotarian*, February 1937

"October. This is one of the peculiarly dangerous months to speculate in stocks in. The others are July, January, September, April, November, May, March, June, December, August and February."

MARK TWAIN, *Pudd'nhead Wilson's Calendar* (1899), p. 108

"Nature is the realization of the simplest conceivable mathematical ideas."

ALBERT EINSTEIN, *Ideas and Opinions* (1954), p. 274

"Financial forecasting appears to be a science that makes astrology look respectable."

BURTON MALKIEL, *A Random Walk Down Wall Street* (1985), p. 152

One of the most sought-after possessions for a typical private investor or securities market analyst is a reliable equation predicting the return on alternative securities. A first step in developing and empirically implementing such an equation involves gaining an understanding of why a particular stock has a low or high rate of return. In this chapter we focus attention on the capital asset pricing model (CAPM), a model that helps considerably in developing such understanding. As we shall see, a remarkable feature of CAPM is that its most important parameters can be estimated by using the very simplest of econometric techniques, namely, a bivariate linear model in which a dependent variable is regressed on a constant and a single independent variable. The simple CAPM framework therefore provides a useful introduction to empirical econometrics.

The empirical analysis of stock markets has had a very important role in the development of econometrics. In 1932, Alfred Cowles III, a quantitatively oriented investment analyst, provided leadership to found the Econometric Society.[1] Cowles also initiated funding support to establish the Cowles Commission for Research in Economics. Some of the most important developments in econometric theory, including the theory underlying simultaneous equations estimation and identification, were conceived by researchers at the Cowles Commission, first at the University of Chicago and now at Yale University. In this context it is interesting to note that in the first volume of *Econometrica*, the official publication of the Econometric Society, Cowles published an article purporting to show that the most successful records of stock market forecasters "are little, if any, better than what might be expected from pure chance. There is some evidence, on the other hand, to indicate that the least successful records are worse than what could reasonably be attributed to chance."[2]

It is therefore appropriate that our first application in this hands-on econometrics text involves an empirical examination of stock markets. We begin this chapter with a summary discussion of the financial theory underlying the CAPM, consider the role of diversification, derive the principal estimating equations, interpret them, and then consider issues in empirical implementation.[3] Finally, in the hands-on applications we examine ten years of monthly returns data for a variety of companies and for the market as a whole, estimate company-specific betas using bivariate regression procedures, assess why gold is a special asset, interpret the R^2 measure in terms of the proportion of total risk that is nondiversifiable, evaluate properties of certain portfolios, conduct event studies, estimate a generalized version of CAPM, and then test assumptions concerning stochastic specification.

2.1 DEFINITIONS AND BASIC FINANCE CONCEPTS

Assume that when investors act in the securities markets, their behavior is perfectly rational in the sense that their only concern is the myopic one of assessing returns from their own investments. Define the rate of return on an investment as

$$r \equiv \frac{p_1 + d - p_0}{p_0} \tag{2.1}$$

where

$p_1 \equiv$ price of security at the end of the time period,
$d \equiv$ dividends (if any) paid during the time period,
$p_0 \equiv$ price of security at the beginning of the time period.

Although the return r can be easily calculated ex post (once the investment has been made), r is of course uncertain ex ante (before the investment decision has been made). Hereafter, we interpret r as the expected or ex ante rate of return.

Typically, investors (other than those who enjoy gambling for its own sake) are not only interested in the most likely or *expected return* on an investment; they are also concerned with the possible *distribution* of r, where r is taken as a random variable. The *risk* accompanying a possible investment is typically characterized by the distribution of such possible returns. Returns are often assumed to be distributed normally, and in such cases the distribution can be completely described by two measures, the expected value and the variance σ^2 (or the square root of the variance, σ, called the standard deviation). Under the normality assumption, in the empirical finance literature risk is typically measured by the standard deviation σ.[4]

While investors are virtually unanimous in preferring higher returns to lower ones, other things equal, it is also the case that most investors are risk-averse, that is, investors prefer a lower standard deviation to a higher one, given the same expected return. This implies that if the risk on an investment or portfolio of investments appears to be large, investors are likely to accept such high risk only if it is accompanied by a high expected return; similarly, an investment with a low expected return will be acceptable only if it has a small risk.[5] But how much of a premium will investors require in order to assume greater risk?

If investors were to purchase an asset having zero risk, they would still demand a return as an inducement to postpone current consumption. Such a return is called the *risk-free rate of return*, and we denote it here by r_f; empirical analysts of the U.S. securities market often employ as a measure of r_f the 30-day U.S. Treasury bill rate held until maturity, apparently because investors believe that the probability of default on such a security is virtually zero.[6] We can use these concepts to define compensation for risk, or the risk premium on the jth asset, as the excess return over the risk-free rate r_f, that is,

$$\text{Risk premium}_j \equiv r_j - r_f \tag{2.2}$$

With these definitions in mind we now turn to a consideration of diversification and risk management.

2.2 DIVERSIFICATION AND PORTFOLIO OPTIMALITY

How do intelligent investors manage risk on their investments? To examine the risk management process, it is useful to introduce the notion of *diversification*. Although mathematical discussions of the diversification process can easily become very involved, here we summarize the principal results, using a combination of relatively simple analysis and intuition, based in large part on the pioneering work of Harry M. Markowitz.[7]

If an investor holds two securities, the expected return on the total portfolio r_p is simply the weighted average of the expected returns on each of the assets, the weights being the relative shares invested in each of the two securities,

$$r_p = w_1 r_1 + w_2 r_2 \tag{2.3}$$

where w_j is the proportion of total funds invested in asset j, $j = 1, 2$, and $w_1 + w_2 = 1.0$. Further, the total variance of the portfolio, σ_p^2, is

$$\sigma_p^2 = w_1^2\sigma_1^2 + w_2^2\sigma_2^2 + 2 \cdot w_1 w_2 \sigma_{12} = w_1^2\sigma_1^2 + w_2^2\sigma_2^2 + 2 \cdot w_1 w_2 \rho_{12}\sigma_1\sigma_2 \tag{2.4}$$

where

$\sigma_j^2 \equiv$ variance of return on security j, $j = 1, 2$,
$\sigma_j \equiv$ standard deviation of return on security j, $j = 1, 2$,
$\sigma_{12} \equiv$ covariance of returns on securities 1 and 2, and
$\rho_{12} \equiv$ simple correlation between returns on securities 1 and 2.

The second equality in Eq. (2.4) holds, since by definition, $\sigma_{12} = \rho_{12}\sigma_1\sigma_2$.

We now want to show that for a given amount of funds to be invested, diversification generally reduces risk. To see this, assume first the unlikely situation in which returns on securities 1 and 2 are perfectly correlated, that is, assume that ρ_{12}, the simple correlation coefficient between returns on assets 1 and 2, equals 1.0. In this case, $\sigma_{12} = \sigma_1\sigma_2$, which is the largest possible value that σ_{12} can take. But as can be seen by inspecting Eq. (2.4), whenever σ_{12} is at a maximum, given σ_1 and σ_2, so too is the variance on the total portfolio σ_p^2. As the covariance and therefore the correlation between returns on assets 1 and 2 decreases and becomes less than perfect, the final term in Eq. (2.4) becomes smaller, and so too does the total portfolio variance σ_p^2. This is intuitively appealing: By holding two assets whose returns do not move together in perfect harmony, the lower return on one asset can be partially offset by a relatively higher return on the other asset, resulting in a reasonable overall portfolio return yet a reduced total portfolio risk.

It is instructive to demonstrate this with several examples of portfolio risk and return under alternative diversification behavior. Consider the simple case in which the expected returns on securities 1 and 2 both equal 10%, where the standard deviation of returns σ for each is equal to 2.0 and where it is initially assumed that returns on the two securities are perfectly correlated, that is, $\rho_{12} = 1.0$, which implies that $\sigma_{12} = 4.0$.

HARRY M. MARKOWITZ

Father of Modern Portfolio Theory

The basic finance theory underlying modern portfolio analysis is due in large part to the pioneering work of Harry M. Markowitz. Markowitz is a product of Chicago. He was born there in 1927, attended its elementary and secondary schools, and received three degrees from the University of Chicago—a bachelor's, master's, and doctorate in economics. In his Ph.D. dissertation, Markowitz developed the basic portfolio model summarized in this chapter. His seminal analysis appeared in a 1952 issue of the *Journal of Finance*, and a more complete treatment was published in 1959 as a Cowles Foundation report by John Wiley and Sons.

Markowitz's professional career has been in and out of academia and in and out of finance. Leaving Chicago in 1952 with all but his dissertation completed, Markowitz joined the Rand Corporation in Santa Monica, California. In 1960 he took a position at the General Electric Corporation, and then in 1961 he returned to Rand. At Rand and at GE, Markowitz wrote computer code for programs that simulated logistic and/or manufacturing processes. His interests in simulation programming grew, and in 1963 he became Chairman of the Board and Technical Director of Consolidated Analysis Centers, Inc., a computer software firm. One year after assuming an academic position at UCLA in 1968, Markowitz became portfolio manager and later president of an investment firm called Arbitrage Management Company. From 1974 to 1983 he served as a Research Staff Member at IBM's Thomas J. Watson Research Center, focusing on the design of data base computer languages.

Markowitz is a Fellow of the Econometric Society and of the American Academy of Arts and Sciences and has served as President of the American Finance Association. In 1989 he was awarded the John von Neumann Theory Prize by the Operations Research Society of America and The Institute of Management Science, in part for his research on portfolio theory and the SIMSCRIPT programming language. Although he is still very actively involved in real-world financial matters, Harry M. Markowitz currently holds the Marvin Speiser Distinguished Professor of Finance and Economics chair at Baruch College at the City University of New York.

One possible investment strategy is to place funds entirely into security 1, implying that $w_1 = 1.0$ and $w_2 = 0.0$; we name this Case A, and its consequences are presented in the first row of Table 2.1. In Case A the expected portfolio return, based on Eq. (2.3), is calculated as $r_p = 1.0\ (10\%) + 0.0\ (10\%) = 10\%$. Substituting the Case A values into Eq. (2.4) yields a portfolio variance of 4.0, or a standard deviation of 2.0.

A second investment strategy, called Case B, involves putting all funds into security 2 and none into security 1, implying that $w_1 = 0.0$ and $w_2 = 1.0$; this case is presented in the second row of entries in Table 2.1. Use of Eqs. (2.3) and (2.4) again implies that $r_p = 10\%$, while $\sigma_p^2 = 4.0$ and risk σ equals 2.0. Since the risk and return consequences of following Case A or Case B are identical, investors will be indifferent between these two cases.

A third alternative investment strategy, Case C, is to diversify the portfolio by purchasing equal amounts of securities 1 and 2, implying that $w_1 = w_2 = 0.5$. If one substitutes Case C entries in Table 2.1 into Eqs. (2.3) and (2.4), one again obtains the same portfolio return of 10% and standard deviation of 2.0. Notice that in each of these three Cases A, B, and C, because of the perfect correlation assumption, the portfolio risk and return are the same whether the investor holds only security 1, only security 2, or a combination of these assets. If returns on these two securities had not been perfectly correlated, however, the portfolio variance would have been smaller.

To see this, first consider Case D in Table 2.1. Here the correlation between returns on assets 1 and 2 is positive but less than perfect, that is, $\rho_{12} = 0.5$. All other features of this case are the same as in Case C. Notice that owing to diversification (equal amounts of securities 1 and 2 are purchased), the investor is able to exploit the less than perfect correlation between asset returns and obtain the same portfolio return of 10%, yet at a reduced variance of 3.0 and standard deviation of about 1.7. On the basis of Eqs. (2.3) and (2.4) it is simple to show that, in the presence of less than perfect correlation between asset returns, had the investor not diversified and purchased only security 1 (Case E) or only security 2 (Case F), the same 10% return would have been attained but at a higher variance of 4.0 and standard deviation of

Table 2.1 Examples of Risk and Return Under Alternative Portfolio Diversifications

	$r_1 = r_2$	w_1	w_2	σ_1	σ_2	ρ_{12}	σ_{12}	r_p	σ_p^2	σ_p Risk
Case A	10%	1.0	0.0	2.0	2.0	1.0	4.0	10%	4.0	2.0
Case B	10%	0.0	1.0	2.0	2.0	1.0	4.0	10%	4.0	2.0
Case C	10%	0.5	0.5	2.0	2.0	1.0	4.0	10%	4.0	2.0
Case D	10%	0.5	0.5	2.0	2.0	0.5	2.0	10%	3.0	1.7
Case E	10%	1.0	0.0	2.0	2.0	0.5	2.0	10%	4.0	2.0
Case F	10%	0.0	1.0	2.0	2.0	0.5	2.0	10%	4.0	2.0
Case G	10%	0.5	0.5	2.0	2.0	−1.0	−4.0	10%	0.0	0.0

2.0, as in Cases A, B, and C. Cases D, E, and F therefore clearly demonstrate the benefits of diversification in reducing risk.

Finally, in the most unlikely case that returns on assets 1 and 2 were perfectly negatively correlated, diversification could eliminate risk entirely. For example, in Case G, $\rho_{12} = -1.0$, but if $w_1 = w_2 = 0.5$, $\sigma_p^2 = \sigma_p = 0$.

Now consider the case of an investor diversifying by holding n securities, where n can be larger than 2. As before, the expected return on the total portfolio is a weighted average of security-specific expected returns r_j, where the w_j weights are shares of total funds invested in each asset, that is,

$$r_p = \sum_{j=1}^{n} w_j r_j \tag{2.5}$$

Once again, with n securities the total variance of the portfolio depends not only on the variances of the n individual securities, but also on their covariances. Specifically, the portfolio variance is calculated as

$$\sigma_p^2 = \sum_{i=1}^{n} \sum_{j=1}^{n} w_i w_j \sigma_{ij} = \sum_{i=1}^{n} w_i^2 \sigma_i^2 + 2 \cdot \sum_{i=1}^{n} \sum_{j=i+1}^{n} w_i w_j \sigma_{ij} \tag{2.6}$$

where σ_{ij} is the covariance between returns on securities i and j and σ_i^2 is the variance. Note that the total portfolio variance in Eq. (2.6) has n variance terms and $n(n - 1)$ covariances, with $n(n - 1)/2$ of them being different. Therefore the larger is n, other things equal, the greater is the relative importance of asset covariances to total portfolio variance. For example, when n is 5, there are five variances and 20 covariances; when n is doubled to 10, the number of variances doubles to 10, but the number of covariance terms in Eq. (2.6) increases to 90! As n becomes very large, the portfolio variance approaches a (weighted) average of the covariances. Hence covariances are extremely important in the diversification process.

The above discussion focused on the average return and variance of a diversified portfolio. For portfolio decision-making purposes, marginal returns and variances are also important. Suppose that in the initial portfolio of n assets held by an investor, there were zero holdings of security k, implying that initially $w_k = 0$. Next, assume that the investor decided to acquire a very small positive amount of security k, but that other holdings remained unchanged. Define the *marginal return* of the kth asset on r_p as the change in r_p, given a small change in w_k. From Eq. (2.5) this marginal return is simply equal to r_k:

$$\text{Marginal return}_k \equiv \partial r_p / \partial w_k = r_k \tag{2.7}$$

This small change in asset holdings also affects the portfolio variance. Define the *marginal variance* of the kth asset as the change in σ_p^2 given a small change in w_k. From Eq. (2.6) and using the fact that a weighted sum of individual covariances with security k equals the covariance of security k with the portfolio—itself a weighted sum of other securities—it follows that the marginal variance is simply

$$\text{Marginal variance}_k \equiv \frac{\partial \sigma_p^2}{\partial w_k} = 2 \cdot \sum_{i=1}^{n} w_i \sigma_{ik} = 2\sigma_{kp} \tag{2.8}$$

where σ_{kp} is the covariance between security k and the portfolio p.[8] Hence the marginal variance—the change in total portfolio variance as a result of a small change in the holdings of asset k—depends simply on the covariance between returns on asset k and the portfolio.

Given these definitions, we can now present an important principle of portfolio optimality derived in finance theory. If two securities in a portfolio have the same marginal variance but different expected returns, then that portfolio cannot be optimal in the sense of providing a maximum return for given risk. The reason such a portfolio could not be optimal is that it would be possible to obtain a higher return without increasing risk by holding more of the asset with the higher return (the marginal variances of the two assets are assumed to be identical). Therefore if a portfolio is *optimal*, all securities with the same marginal variance must have identical expected returns.

The marginal variance and the variances and covariances in Eqs. (2.6) and (2.8) all depend on units of measurement. Like the economists' notion of elasticity, financial economists have found it convenient to adopt relative measures that are independent of units of measurement. Perhaps the best-known relative measure is the *beta value* for security k, computed simply as

$$\text{Beta}_k \equiv \sigma_{kp}/\sigma_p^2 \tag{2.9}$$

Since a security's beta value depends on its covariance, which in turn is closely related to its marginal variance, one can combine Eqs. (2.8) and (2.9) to derive a factor of proportionality between beta and marginal variance:

$$\text{Marginal variance}_k = 2\sigma_{kp} = 2\sigma_p^2 \cdot \text{beta}_k$$

Given this relationship, the previous discussion on portfolio optimality can be expressed equivalently in terms of beta values rather than marginal variances. Specifically, if a portfolio is optimal, then all securities with the same beta value relative to the portfolio must have identical expected returns.

2.3 DERIVATION OF A LINEAR RELATIONSHIP BETWEEN RISK AND RETURN

To this point we have related variances, covariances, marginal variances, and beta values, and we have presented an important principle of portfolio optimality. But how might one move from these insights to portfolio choice and an empirically implementable relationship between risk and return? In the next few pages we summarize the very important contribution of the CAPM to facilitating relatively simple empirical analysis, and we show that the relationship between risk and return is a linear one.[9]

Suppose an investor has a portfolio, called a, consisting of a mix of two assets. The blend of these two assets generates an expected portfolio return r_a and has a variance of σ_a^2. Now let there be a risk-free asset whose return is r_f, and let the investor be able to borrow or lend indefinitely at the risk-free rate of return r_f. One possibility facing this investor is to combine portfolio a with the risk-free asset into a new portfolio. In such a case the expected return on the new portfolio would equal

$$r_p = (1 - w_a)r_f + w_a r_a \tag{2.10}$$

where w_a is the proportion of total funds invested in portfolio a. The variance of this new portfolio would be

$$\sigma_p^2 = w_a^2\sigma_a^2 + (1 - w_a)^2\sigma_f^2 + 2w_a(1 - w_a)\sigma_{af} \tag{2.11}$$

where σ_{af} is the covariance between the expected return of portfolio a and that on the risk-free asset. However, since by definition the risk-free asset has a zero variance return, this risk-free return is also uncorrelated with that on any other security, implying that $\sigma_f^2 = \sigma_{af} = 0$. Thus Eq. (2.11) reduces to

$$\sigma_p^2 = w_a^2\sigma_a^2 \qquad \text{or} \qquad \sigma_p = w_a\sigma_a \tag{2.12}$$

Rearranging the second expression in Eq. (2.12) yields $w_a = \sigma_p/\sigma_a$ and $(1 - w_a) = 1 - \sigma_p/\sigma_a$, which, after substituting back into Eq. (2.10) and collecting terms, gives us

$$r_p = r_f + \left[\frac{r_a - r_f}{\sigma_a}\right]\sigma_p \tag{2.13}$$

In Eq. (2.13) we have a simple linear relationship between portfolio return r_p and portfolio risk σ_p, one that even Albert Einstein would admire (recall the Einstein quote at the beginning of this chapter). Specifically, the total portfolio return r_p is the sum of two terms: the risk-free rate of return r_f and $(r_a - r_f)/\sigma_a$ times the portfolio risk σ_p. This linearity is shown in Fig. 2.1 in which the expected return is measured on the vertical axis, risk is on the horizontal axis, the intercept term is r_f, and the slope term is $(r_a - r_f)/\sigma_a$.

Several features of Fig. 2.1 are worth noting. First, if the investor chose to invest only in the risk-free asset such that $w_a = 0$, then by Eq. (2.10), r_p would equal r_f, and by (2.11), σ_p would equal zero. Second, if the investor instead chose to invest only in the a portfolio and entirely avoided the risk-free asset (say, at point a in Fig. 2.1), then $w_a = 1$, $r_p = r_a$, and $\sigma_p = \sigma_a$. Third, the slope of the line in Fig. 2.1 represents the reward to the investor of accepting increased risk, that is, of increasing the proportion of funds invested in the risky portfolio a.

Portfolio a is, of course, but one of many possible risky portfolios constructed by our investor; assets 1 and 2 could have been combined in numerous alternative combinations. This raises the interesting issue of what the risk-

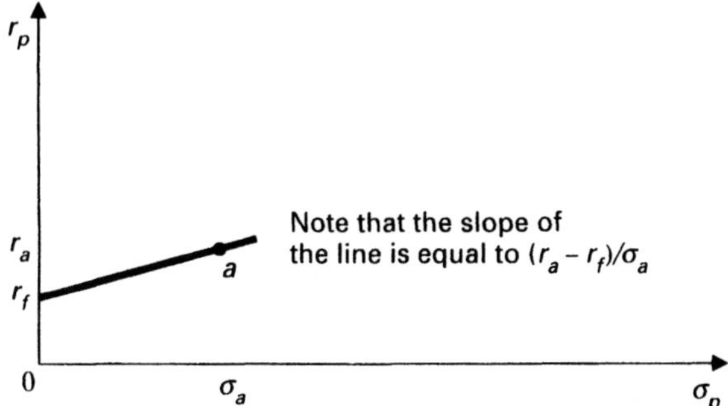

FIGURE 2.1 The linear relationship between risk and return

return frontier would look like for an investor who is considering other alternative possibilities of a portfolio blended from these two risky assets.

Suppose we place two securities on a risk-return diagram, as in Fig. 2.2. Let asset 1 be low risk–low return, while asset 2 is high risk–high return. Further, let the correlation between returns on assets 1 and 2 be less than perfect. As was pointed out in Eq. (2.3), a combination of the two stocks will yield an expected return of $r_p = w_1 r_1 + w_2 r_2$, a weighted average of returns on the two assets. However, because of diversification, the total portfolio risk σ_p will be smaller than the weighted average of the standard deviations, since $(w_1\sigma_1 + w_2\sigma_2)^2$ is less than the right-hand side of Eq. (2.4) whenever $\rho_{12} < 1$. As a result, provided that $\rho_{12} < 1$, the risk-return frontier for various combinations of assets 1 and 2 will look like the concave curve depicted in Fig. 2.3. Incidentally, it is worth noting that as $\rho_{12} \rightarrow 1$, the concave curve converges to a straight line.

Our investor is now faced with the following problem: Among all the possible risky asset portfolio combinations in Fig. 2.3, which blend of a portfolio of risky assets with the risk-free asset will yield the maximum return for

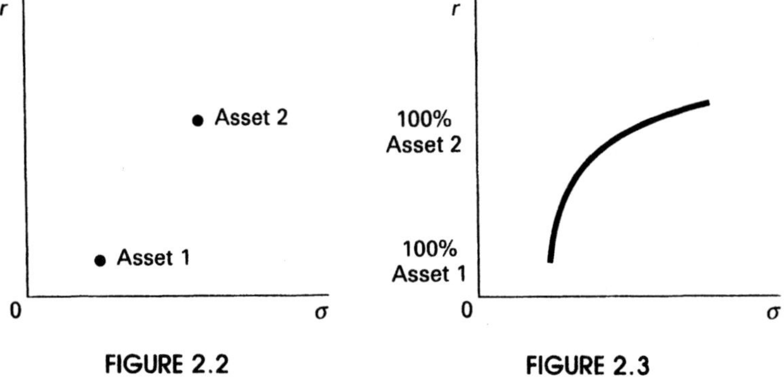

FIGURE 2.2

FIGURE 2.3

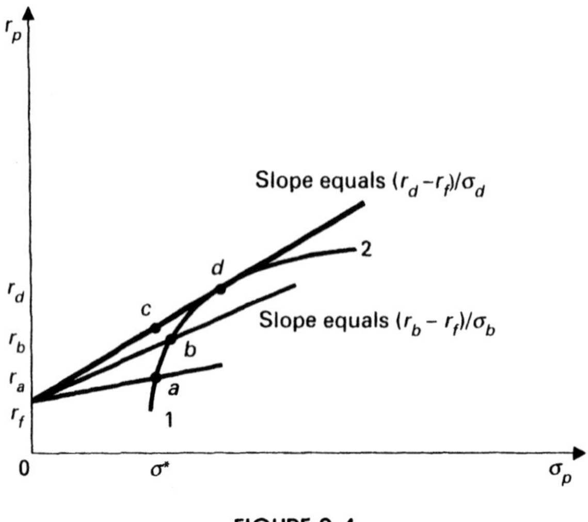

FIGURE 2.4

any given portfolio risk? The CAPM solution to this optimality problem is in fact quite simple.

One possible strategy is one that we considered earlier when we constructed portfolio *a*: holding assets 1 and 2 in the proportions corresponding to, say, point *a* in Fig. 2.4. Note that at point *a* on the $(r_f - a)$ bottom line in Fig. 2.4, the total portfolio risk is σ^* and the return is r_a. We now show that while such a strategy would be feasible, it would not be optimal in the sense that the investor could attain an even higher return given total risk σ^* by lending a portion of funds, say, $1 - w_p$, at the risk-free rate r_f and then investing the remaining portion of funds, w_p, according to the portfolio proportions represented by some other point on the concave risk-return frontier in Fig. 2.4 (as we shall soon see, portfolio *d*). An investor who followed this mixed strategy would be able to reach point *c*, where the return is larger than at point *a*, yet the σ^* risk is the same as at point *a*.

To see this, consider another portfolio (called *b*) and the risk-return possibilities available when this risky portfolio is combined with the risk-free asset. Specifically, if we repeated our analysis that began just above Eq. (2.10) and derived a linear relationship between risk and return for various mixes of portfolio *b* with the risk-free asset, we would obtain a linear equation analogous to Eq. (2.13), having intercept r_f and slope equal to $(r_b - r_f)/\sigma_b$. Such a line is the middle one drawn in Fig. 2.4; its slope is larger than that obtained with various mixes of the earlier portfolio *a* and the risk-free asset, implying that the rewards to risk are higher when portfolio *b* is mixed with the risk-free asset instead of portfolio *a*. An important result here is that with this *b* portfolio, as is shown in Fig. 2.4, one could hold a mixture of it and the risk-free asset to attain any desired return on the straight line through points r_f and b; except at the intercept point where $\sigma_p = 0$, for any given risk the portfolio return r_p is larger on the portfolio b line than on the portfolio a line. In this sense, portfolio b dominates portfolio a.

But why stop with portfolio b? Using the very same reasoning as with portfolios a and b, consider yet another portfolio combination of assets 1 and 2, say, that at point d on the concave risk-return frontier in Fig. 2.4. Analogous to Eq. (2.13), one could now blend portfolio d with a risk-free asset in numerous ways to obtain a risk-return linear equation relating r_p to σ_p, having intercept r_f and slope now equal to $(r_d - r_f)/\sigma_d$. Such a straight line is the top one in Fig. 2.4; note that its slope is larger than that based on portfolio b. Points on this $r_f - d$ line indicate the expected return r_p corresponding with alternative levels of risk σ_p.

Note that with a strategy based on a mix of portfolio d with the risk-free asset, the investor could always attain a higher return for the same risk than with the b mixture, since the straight line connecting r_f through point d is always above the $r_f - b$ line except at the point where $\sigma_p = 0$. Furthermore, since this $r_f - d$ line is tangent to the concave risk-return frontier, there is no other portfolio superior to d, for any other line emanating from r_f and having a larger slope would not touch the concave risk-return frontier and therefore would not be feasible. Portfolio d is said to be *efficient*.

The implication of this analysis is startling: Each investor should hold portfolio d, regardless of his or her risk-return preferences, and then achieve the desired amount of risk by borrowing or lending at the risk-free rate r_f. In particular, if σ^* is the desired maximum amount of risk given the investor's preferences, the optimal procedure for the investor is to mix assets 1 and 2 according to portfolio d and then blend by borrowing or (in this case) lending funds at the risk-free rate until point c is attained. Note that each investor is therefore involved in only two investments—a risky portfolio d and borrowing or lending on a risk-free loan.[10]

This same line of reasoning can easily be generalized to more realistic situations in which the number of risky securities available to investors is greater than two. In the case of n securities the CAPM best strategy for each investor is to hold the n assets in optimal proportions on the concave risk-return frontier and then adjust for the person-specific desired risk level by borrowing or lending at the risk-free rate.[11]

The thoughtful reader might now ask, "But just where is this optimal portfolio d really located?" Although in general it might in fact be very hard to plot out the entire concave frontier of attainable risk-return combinations and its tangency with the risk-free lending line, under CAPM assumptions this calculation is simple, perhaps even unnecessary. Specifically, if one makes the assumption that all investors have the same information and opportunities and that there are no taxes or transactions costs, then, even if people's attitudes toward risk differ, everyone will process information in the same way and will view their investment prospects identically. In such a case, everyone will hold exactly the same portfolio *d* mix of securities 1 and 2, but each person will then blend portfolio *d* and the risk-free asset to suit his or her own risk-return tastes. In this case the total market portfolio for all investors will simply be a blowup of portfolio *d*. Alternatively, each investor's portfolio will be a microscopic clone of the market as a whole. Therefore, according to the CAPM, the optimal strategy is to invest in securities in the same proportion as they are in the overall market, since these are the same as those of the best attainable portfolio, and then adjust for person-specific risk preferences by borrowing or lending at the risk-free rate.

2.4 FURTHER INTERPRETATION OF THE CAPM RISK-RETURN LINEAR RELATIONSHIP

We have shown that diversification is effective in reducing risk because prices of different stocks are imperfectly correlated. We now examine risk in greater detail. In a classic experimental study by Wayne Wagner and Sheila Lau [1971] it was shown that diversification reduces risk very rapidly at first, but that after some point, additional diversification has little effect on risk or variability. Specifically, using portfolios of different size drawn from an historical sample of stocks, Wagner and Lau demonstrated that diversification can almost halve the variability of returns but that most of this benefit can be obtained by holding relatively few stocks; the improvement becomes rather small when the number of securities is increased beyond, say, ten.[12]

Diversification cannot, of course, eliminate risk entirely. The risk that can be potentially eliminated by diversification is called *specific*, unique, or unsystematic risk. Specific risk derives from the fact that many of the dangers or opportunities that surround an individual company are peculiar to that company and, perhaps, its immediate competitors; specific risk can therefore be eliminated by holding a well-diversified portfolio. But there is also some risk that cannot be avoided no matter how much one diversifies. This risk is generally known as *market* or systematic risk. Market risk derives from the fact that there are other economywide and global dangers and opportunities that are faced by all businesses. The fact that stocks have a tendency to "move together" reflects the presence of market risk, risk that cannot be eliminated through diversification. Note that this risk will remain even when an optimal portfolio is attained.

To explore further this dependence of stock returns on market risk, note that one implication of the CAPM is that the risk of a well-diversified portfolio depends only on the market risk of the securities included in the portfolio. Suppose, therefore, that you had a well-diversified portfolio (say, a microscopic clone of the entire stock market portfolio) and that you wanted to measure the dependence of stock returns on risk further by computing the sensitivity of a particular company's stocks in your portfolio, say, those of company *j*, to variations in the overall market return. Obviously, you would not want to compute this by looking at company j's returns in isolation. Rather, you would want to use the covariance information from Eqs. (2.8) and (2.9) relative to the market as a whole.

Specifically, recall that we noted earlier that one measure of the relative marginal variance of a security, say, the kth asset, is called its beta value relative to the portfolio; in Eq. (2.9) this was defined as $\text{beta}_k = \sigma_{kp}/\sigma_p^2$. One interpretation of this relative variance notion is that if the return on the portfolio is expected to increase by, say, 1%, then the return on the kth asset is expected to increase by beta_k times 1%. The investment beta is therefore a measure of the sensitivity of the return on the kth asset to variation in returns on the portfolio; beta_k summarizes the dependence on portfolio risk.

It will be useful to think of the portfolio as the entire market's portfolio. Let us therefore define an investment beta for, say, company j relative to the entire market portfolio as

$$\text{Beta}_j \equiv \sigma_{jm}/\sigma_m^2 \tag{2.14}$$

where σ_{jm} is the covariance between company j's return and that of the market as a whole and σ_m^2 is the variance of the market's returns.

There is one problem, however, in relating beta_j to the CAPM framework. The covariance and variance terms for beta_j in Eq. (2.14) refer to the *total* returns on assets, whereas by contrast in the CAPM development to this point we have dealt with variations in risk *premiums*, that is, the excess return over the risk-free rate, such as $r_m - r_f$, where r_m is the return on the entire market's assets. Can one rewrite Eq. (2.14) in terms of risk premiums rather than total returns? As we now show, we can, since beta_j is unaffected by this change.

To see this, note that since the ratio of the covariance term σ_{jm} to the variance term σ_m^2 is unaffected by subtracting the risk-free return from the total return, the investment beta ratio Eq. (2.14) holds even when it is defined in terms of risk premiums rather than in terms of total returns. This has an important implication in the CAPM context, where we deal with risk premiums rather than with total returns. Specifically, since Eq. (2.14) is invariant to rescaling in terms of risk premiums rather than total returns, the value of beta for a particular company equals the covariance of its risk premium with the market portfolio risk premium, divided by the variance of the market's risk premium. This suggests that the beta_j summary measure of dependence on market risk has wide applicability.

Securities vary considerably in the value of their investment betas; some, for example, have values as large as 2, indicating that a 1% rise or fall in the market results in a 2% rise or fall in the value of that security. Such securities are relatively risky. Other truly "blue chip" stocks, on the other hand, are not as sensitive to market movements and have much smaller betas of, say, 0.5, implying that a 1% rise or fall in the market results in a ½% rise or fall in their value. Traditionally, holding stocks with betas greater than 1 is called an "aggressive" stance, while holding stocks with betas less than unity is called "defensive." As we shall see in Exercise 3 of this chapter, for some assets, beta can even be negative—these are "superdefensive" assets!

Investment betas can also be defined for portfolios of assets (rather than individual assets) relative to the market as a whole. For example, consider a portfolio q consisting of n assets, and define its beta value relative to the market as a whole as $\text{beta}_{qm} \equiv \sigma_{qm}/\sigma_m^2$. Given the definition of covariances, one can rewrite beta_{qm} as

$$\text{Beta}_{qm} = \sum_{i=1}^{n} w_{iq} \cdot \text{beta}_{im} \tag{2.15}$$

where w_{iq} is the proportion of portfolio q invested in asset i and beta_{im} is asset i's beta value relative to the market's portfolio. Hence the beta value of a portfolio is simply a weighted average of the beta values of the component securities, the weights being the portfolio investment shares.

Obviously, for the stock market as a whole the covariation with itself is the same as its variance, implying that the beta ratio for the stock market as a whole is 1.0. Moreover, since by Eq. (2.15) the beta of a well-diversified entire market portfolio depends on the weighted average betas of the securities included in the portfolio, it follows that, on average, individual stocks have a beta of 1.0. Finally, it is worth noting that since the covariance of a riskless asset with the market portfolio is zero, beta_{im} equals zero whenever asset i is risk-free.

2.5 ECONOMETRIC ISSUES INVOLVED IN IMPLEMENTING THE CAPM

We now want to move toward econometric implementation of the CAPM framework. Our first objective is to derive an estimable equation. Consider a small portfolio p whose sole security is j and a large, well-diversified portfolio m, which is the entire market's portfolio. Substituting j for p and m for a into Eq. (2.13), we can rewrite the CAPM linear relationship (2.13) as

$$r_j - r_f = (\sigma_j/\sigma_m) \cdot (r_m - r_f) \tag{2.16}$$

where r_j and r_f are returns to security j and to a risk-free asset, respectively; r_m is the return on the overall securities market portfolio; and σ_j/σ_m is the ratio of the standard deviations of returns on asset j and the market portfolio m. The term $r_j - r_f$ is the risk premium for security j, while $r_m - r_f$ represents the overall market's risk premium. By the way, over the last 60 or so years in the United States the average market risk premium has been about 8.4% per year.[13]

According to Eq. (2.16), the risk premium on the jth asset is simply a factor of proportionality σ_j/σ_m times the market risk premium; this factor of proportionality expresses the dependence of security j's return on the market return, a dependence highlighted by the CAPM. Such reasoning suggests that the proportionality factor σ_j/σ_m must be related in some way to the investment beta$_j$ discussed in the previous section.

To explore this relationship further, let us generalize Eq. (2.16) by adding to it an intercept term α_j and a stochastic disturbance term ϵ_j, and then define a new parameter β_j as being equal to the proportionality factor, that is, $\beta_j \equiv \sigma_j/\sigma_m$. This gives us an estimable equation relating the total risk premium of security j to the market risk premium and to the stochastic disturbance term:

$$r_j - r_f = \alpha_j + \beta_j(r_m - r_f) + \epsilon_j \qquad \textbf{(2.17)}$$

In Eq. (2.17) the stochastic disturbance term ϵ_j reflects the effects of specific (unsystematic) and diversifiable risk. We will assume that ϵ_j has an expected value of zero and a variance of σ_ϵ^2 and that it is also independently and identically normally distributed.

Now comes the clincher: The least squares estimate of β_j in Eq. (2.17) is in fact identical to the investment beta defined in Eq. (2.14)! To see this, consider the bivariate regression model $y = \alpha + \beta x + \epsilon$. The least squares estimate of β is COV(x, y)/VAR(x). Now let $y \equiv r_j - r_f$ from Eq. (2.17), and let $x \equiv r_m - r_f$. Then the least squares estimate of β_j is simply $\hat{\beta}_j$ = COV$(r_j - r_f, r_m - r_f)$/VAR$(r_m - r_f)$. But this is precisely equal to σ_{jm}/σ_m^2, the investment beta defined in Eq. (2.14). Intuitively, the least squares estimate of the factor of proportionality β_j is simply the ratio of the standard deviations of the risk premiums for asset j and for the market m.

These results imply that, for any security j, one can estimate β_j using bivariate least squares procedures on Eq. (2.17). Graphically, the covariance-variance ratio is the least squares estimate of the slope of a regression line relating the risk premium of a particular security j on the vertical axis to the market risk premium on the horizontal axis; the linearity of this relationship derives from Eq. (2.13). Although one can use least squares procedures, in the bivariate regression framework, estimating β_j is in fact trivial: Once one has values of the appropriate covariances and variances, all one need do is simply compute β_j as their ratio.

To estimate the β_j parameter based on time series data of individual companies, it must of course be assumed that, for a particular company, β_j is relatively stable over time. Quite frequently, monthly data are employed that are based on returns from the New York Stock Exchange. Econometric studies based on such data have found that in many studies (but with some notable exceptions), β_j has tended to be relatively stable over a five-year (60-month) time span.[14] There are cases, however, in which the conditions in an industry or a firm abruptly change, implying that the relevant β_j might also vary. Oil company stocks, for example, had a beta below unity before the 1973 OPEC oil embargo, but this soon changed after 1973, and since then oil company betas have typically increased. Similarly, when the airline industry in the United States was deregulated in 1978, the betas of most major U.S.

airline companies rose; analogous changes in betas occurred for electric utilities, particularly for those with substantial nuclear-generating capacity, after the Chernobyl nuclear power accident in 1986. This stability of beta remains a problematic issue, however, and therefore in Exercises 6 and 7 of this chapter we will encourage you to examine the variability of estimated betas over time, using statistical techniques known as Chow tests and event study methodologies.

While the parameter β_j is of obvious interest and importance, in our estimable Eq. (2.17) another parameter appears that was added in an ad hoc manner, namely, α_j. Specifically, recall that α_j does not appear in Eq. (2.16), the linear equation analogous to Eq. (2.13). On the basis of the finance theory underlying the CAPM and summarized in Eq. (2.16), one should therefore expect estimates of α_j to be close to zero on average (more on this later, however). In fact, a typical empirical result obtained when one estimates parameters of Eq. (2.17) is that the least squares estimate of α_j is insignificantly different from zero. The null hypothesis that $\alpha_j = 0$ can be tested of course simply by determining whether the t-statistic corresponding to the estimate of α_j is greater than the critical value at some predetermined significance level. Moreover, if one wants to impose the restriction that $\alpha_j = 0$ in (2.17), most computer regression programs provide options that allow the user to omit an intercept term.

It is worth noting that in some investment houses, portfolio managers' performances have occasionally been evaluated by computing the predicted returns the manager would have earned given the betas of the companies in his or her portfolio and subtracting this predicted return from realized returns, thereby obtaining an implicit estimate of the manager's α; if the realized return were larger than that predicted by the overall portfolio β, then the portfolio manager was said to have produced a positive α, and he or she was compensated accordingly. Such simple compensation schemes are seldom used today, but they suggest an interesting interpretation of α for portfolio managers.[15]

Suppose that a securities market analyst employed monthly time series data on returns of a particular company over the preceding five years and estimated the parameters α and β using conventional linear regression techniques. Perhaps the analyst obtained the empirical finding that for a particular company the estimate of α was positive and significantly different from zero. This would imply that even if the market as a whole were expected to earn nothing (that is, if $r_m - r_f$ in Eq. (2.17) equalled zero), investors in this company expected a positive rate of price appreciation. (Note that, for example, an estimate of 0.67 for α based on monthly data is interpreted as an annual rate of price appreciation of approximately 12 times 0.67, or about 8% per year.) For some other company the analyst might find that the estimated α was negative and significantly different from zero. True adherents to the CAPM would therefore argue that, on average, one should expect estimates of α to be zero.

This raises the important issue of whether one can test the CAPM. Five remarks are worth making in this context. First, the finance theory underlying the CAPM explicitly employs *expected* or ex ante returns, whereas all we can observe is *realized* or ex post returns. This makes rigorous testing of the CAPM more difficult, although not impossible if more sophisticated econometric techniques are employed.[16]

Second, according to the CAPM, the market portfolio should include *all* risky investments, whereas most market indexes and estimates of r_m contain only a sample of stocks, say, those traded on the New York Stock Exchange (thereby excluding, for example, all risky assets traded in the rest of the world—even human capital, private businesses, and private real estate). Collecting sufficient data on risky assets to estimate r_m reliably could be a formidable and prohibitively expensive task. In this context it is worth noting that early empirical studies based on the CAPM discovered that estimates of β depended critically on the choice of r_m; specifically, r_m measures based on the Dow Jones 30 Industrials Index provided different results from those based on the Standard & Poor 500 Index or the Wilshire 5000.[17] Today, funded in large part by Merrill, Lynch, Pierce, Fenner & Smith, Inc., the Center for Research on Securities Prices (CRSP) at the University of Chicago makes available to researchers estimates of r_m based on the value-weighted transactions of all stocks listed on the New York and American Stock Exchanges. Fortunately, such data series on r_m have been made available to us, and in the hands-on applications of this chapter we will employ the CRSP measures of r_m.

Third, the typical measure of a risk-free asset is something like the 30-day U.S. Treasury bill rate, which really is risk-free only if it is held to maturity. Further, it is risk-free only in a nominal sense, for even if it is held to maturity, the uncertainty of inflation makes the real rate of return uncertain. Therefore it is difficult, if not impossible, to obtain a good measure of the risk-free return. This makes testing of the CAPM model even more troublesome.

Fourth, there is a strong tradition within statistics that argues that it is not possible to test a specific model unless there is an alternative viable model against which it can be compared. In the case of the CAPM, one alternative that might be used is the ingenious arbitrage pricing model (APM) developed by Stephen Ross, which in its simplest interpretation essentially involves adding right-hand variables to Eq. (2.17), such as the rate of unexpected price inflation.[18] Provided that the above issues were properly taken into account, one could in principle test the CAPM against the APM merely by testing the null hypothesis that the parameters on the additional right-hand variables were simultaneously equal to zero against the alternative hypothesis that these parameters were simultaneously not equal to zero.

Fifth and finally, a more informal method of testing the CAPM involves checking whether its predictions are consistent with what is observed. In this context, two aspects of the CAPM model appear to be inconsistent with observation.

STEPHEN A. ROSS

Generalizing the CAPM

Although the capital asset pricing model of modern finance theory is widely taught and implemented today, the validity of the CAPM hinges on a number of restrictive assumptions. One very useful generalization of the CAPM is called the arbitrage pricing model (APM). The APM allows for factors other than the market risk premium to affect returns on securities. The APM was developed in 1976 by Stephen A. Ross, a financial economist then at the University of Pennsylvania.

Ross's research on the APM has attracted a great deal of interest and controversy and has raised important methodological issues of whether it is possible to test the CAPM as a special case of the APM (see the text for further details and references).

Born in Boston in 1944, Stephen Ross developed a strong interest in applied mathematics. He received his B.S. degree with honors from the California Institute of Technology, majoring in physics. His attention shifted to economics and finance, however, and in 1969 he earned a doctorate in economics from Harvard.

Although Ross is widely recognized as a rigorous theoretical financial researcher, he is also respected as an unusually clear expositor. At the University of Pennsylvania, for example, he was nominated for distinguished teaching awards three years in succession. In 1977, Ross moved to Yale University, and today he holds its Sterling Professor of Economics and Finance chair, a chair previously held by Nobel Laureate James Tobin.

In addition to undertaking academic research in finance theory, Ross regularly travels from Yale to Wall Street and New York City, where he engages in financial consulting and serves as a principal with Richard Roll in Roll and Ross Asset Management Corporation. Ross is on the editorial board of numerous professional journals, is a Fellow of the Econometric Society, and in 1988 was elected President of the American Finance Association.

1. One important implication of the CAPM framework is that the relationship between risk and return is not only linear but is also positive. As has been noted by Fischer Black, Michael Jensen, and Myron Scholes [1972], however, there have been a number of instances in which this relationship has appeared to be negative rather than positive. Specifically, Black, Jensen, and

Scholes found that over the entire nine-year period from April 1957 through December 1965, securities with higher βs produced lower returns than less risky (lower-β) securities. Why this happened is not yet entirely clear and constitutes a puzzling contradiction of the CAPM framework.

2. Another implication of the CAPM framework is that a security with a zero β should give a return exactly equal to the risk-free rate. Black, Jensen, and Scholes exhaustively studied security returns on the New York Stock Exchange over a 35-year period and found instead that the measured zero-β rate of return exceeded the risk-free rate, implying that some unsystematic (or non-β) risk makes the return higher for the zero-β portfolio than is predicted by the CAPM. Moreover, the actual risk-return relationship examined by Black, Jensen, and Scholes appeared to be flatter than that predicted by the CAPM. It is therefore not clear what factors other than the market risk premium are being valued in the marketplace. According to the CAPM, it is only market risk that matters, since unsystematic risk can be diversified away. Much research is currently underway that attempts to examine whether factors other than r_m affect market risk.

In this context it is worth noting that some securities firms such as Merrill, Lynch, Pierce, Fenner and Smith regularly publish a "beta book" in which they report estimates of α and β based on standard OLS regression methods, as well as "adjusted β" estimates that attempt to deal with the zero-β portfolio problem mentioned above, using more complex Bayesian statistical procedures. Although these Bayesian procedures are of considerable interest, they are beyond the scope of this chapter.

Several other econometric issues should be briefly noted. The printed output of computer regression programs typically includes measures of R^2, the standard error of the regression, and t-statistics. These and other standard statistical measures have a particularly interesting interpretation and application within the CAPM. Consider, for example, the simple correlation between the risk premium on the security j $(r_j - r_f)$ and the market risk premium $(r_m - r_f)$—variables that are on the left- and right-hand sides, respectively, of the CAPM regression equation (2.17). The sample correlation coefficient between them can be rewritten as follows:

$$\rho_{jm} = \frac{\hat{\sigma}_{jm}}{\hat{\sigma}_j \hat{\sigma}_m} = \frac{\hat{\sigma}_{jm}}{\hat{\sigma}_m^2} \cdot \frac{\hat{\sigma}_m}{\hat{\sigma}_j} = \hat{\beta}_j \cdot \frac{\hat{\sigma}_m}{\hat{\sigma}_j} \tag{2.18}$$

where $\hat{\sigma}_{jm}$, $\hat{\sigma}_m^2$, $\hat{\sigma}_j^2$ are sample covariances and variances for $r_m - r_f$ and $r_j - r_f$, and $\hat{\beta}_j$ is the least squares estimate of β_j. Hence the sample correlation between the portfolio and market risk premiums is simply the product of the least squares estimate of β_j and the relative sample standard deviations of the market and j-portfolio risk premiums.

The standard error of the residual in the regression equation (2.17) also has a useful interpretation. Specifically, while the left-hand side of Eq. (2.17) reflects the effects of both specific (unsystematic) and market (systematic) risk on the portfolio in company j, the $\beta_j(r_m - r_f)$ term on the right-hand side reflects only the impact of market risk. It therefore follows that the estimated residual in Eq. (2.17) incorporates only the effects of specific (unsystematic) risk. The standard error of the residual (also often called the standard error of the regression), computed as the square root of s^2, defined as

$$s^2 = \sum_{t=1}^{T} e_t^2/(n - 2) \tag{2.19}$$

where e_t is the least squares residual for the tth observation, therefore measures the standard deviation of the specific (unsystematic) risk—portfolio risk that is not responsive to market fluctuations. A large standard error of the residual, say, $s = 15\%$ per month, would indicate that a substantial amount of change in the portfolio j risk premium could not be explained by changes in the market risk premium.

Further, since the R^2 value from regression computer output indicates what proportion of the variation in the dependent variable is explained by variation in the right-hand or independent variables, in the CAPM context of Eq. (2.17), R^2 measures the market (systematic) portion of total risk. On the other hand, $1 - R^2$ is the proportion of total risk that is specific (unsystematic). William F. Sharpe [1985, p. 167] notes that for an individual company a typical R^2 measure from a CAPM equation is about .30 but that as one diversifies across companies' assets into a larger portfolio, the R^2 measure increases, owing to the reduction of specific risk through diversification.

It is important to note that, since in the bivariate regression model $R^2 = \rho_{jm}^2$, high R^2 values do not necessarily correspond with large estimates of β_j. To see this, note that from Eq. (2.15),

$$R^2 = \rho_{jm}^2 = \hat{\beta}_j^2 \cdot \frac{\hat{\sigma}_m^2}{\hat{\sigma}_j^2} \tag{2.20}$$

It follows that for some stocks with very large variance $\hat{\sigma}_j^2$, R^2 can be low even while the estimate of β_j is high; in such cases the reaction of the particular stock (or portfolio) to market variations is very sharp, yet market variation explains only a small portion of the stock's large variability. The regression equation for other stocks might have a high R^2 but a low β_j estimate; this can occur when variation in the stock's (or portfolio's) risk premium is small in relation to variation in the market risk premium, that is, the ratio of sample variances in Eq. (2.20) is large. Moreover, note that a very low R^2 does not invalidate the CAPM framework; rather, it simply indicates that the total risk of a particular company's assets is almost entirely company-specific, unrelated to the market as a whole.

The final typical regression output of particular interest to us here is the t-statistic. Earlier, it was noted that the t-statistic on the estimate of α can be used to test directly the null hypothesis that $\alpha = 0$ against the alternative hypothesis that $\alpha \neq 0$. Failure to reject this null hypothesis might be viewed as evidence in support of the CAPM.

The t-statistic on the estimate of β corresponds to an analogous null hypothesis, namely, that $\beta = 0$, against the alternative hypothesis that $\beta \neq 0$. Quite frequently, it is of interest to test a different hypothesis, namely, that the movement of asset prices of a particular company is the same as that of the market as a whole; this corresponds to a test of the null hypothesis that $\beta = 1$ against the alternative hypothesis that $\beta \neq 1$. To conduct such an hypothesis test, simply take the estimated standard error of the β estimate (usually provided on computer regression outputs), construct a confidence interval given some reasonable level of confidence (e.g., 95% or 99%), and then determine whether $\beta = 1$ falls within this confidence interval. If it does, the null hypothesis is not rejected; if $\beta = 1$ does not fall within this confidence interval, the null hypothesis is rejected.

One other remark is worth making before we go on to hands-on empirical implementations. Since within the CAPM framework, β enables one to calculate what the required return on a particular stock might be, it also indirectly allows one to compute the all-equity firm's cost of capital. For a well-managed firm that is considering a particular investment project, the combination of expected return and its β should, of course, place the project above its cost of capital if the project is to be accepted. However, if the company is considering a new project that is more risky than the company's average projects, a larger expected return should be required by the firm before investing, since such a project would increase the average risk of the company and, according to the CAPM model, would result in investors' requiring a higher return. This implies that, analogous to Eq. (2.15), projects also have their own betas, and if the β of a particular project is higher than the company's average β, so too should be the required expected rate of return.[19]

This completes our discussion of the theory underlying the CAPM and our brief review of econometric issues involved in estimating its parameters. We are now ready to become directly involved in implementing the CAPM empirically.

2.6 HANDS ON WITH THE CAPM

The purpose of the exercises in this chapter is to help you gain an empirical hands-on experience and understanding of the CAPM using bivariate least squares regression techniques. Exercise 1 is particularly useful, since in it you become acquainted with data used in subsequent exercises. In Exercise 2 you obtain and interpret least squares estimates of β, while in Exercise 3 you encounter the β of a very interesting asset—gold. In Exercise 4 you are given the opportunity to learn how you can recover from mistakes—running a regression of X on Y rather than of Y on X for Delta Airlines. In Exercise 5 you gain a better understanding of the benefits of diversification by employing the CAPM to construct a portfolio.

The last five exercises of this chapter employ slightly more sophisticated econometric techniques; therefore you might want to return to these exercises later after becoming more familiar with the requisite econometric tools. In particular, in Exercise 6 you test for the stability of β using the Chow test procedure. In Exercise 7 you employ dummy variables in "event studies" for the Three Mile Island nuclear power accident and for the bidding war between DuPont and Dow Chemical in their takeover attempt of Conoco. In Exercise 8 you employ Chow tests and dummy variables to assess whether January returns are different from those of other months, as has apparently been observed. Then in Exercise 9 you assess an alternative to the CAPM framework, the arbitrage pricing model, by comparing results from multivariate and bivariate regressions. In the final application, Exercise 10, you conduct a number of tests to determine the empirical validity of the stochastic specification.

●●●●●●●●●●

On the data diskette provided, you will find a subdirectory called CHAP2.DAT with numerous data files. In these data files a number of data series are provided, including data on ten years of monthly returns for 17 companies over the time period January 1978 to December 1987 (values for r_p). In another data file named MARKET, you will find a data series taken from the Center for Research on Securities Prices (often called CRSP) that measures r_m; specifically, MARKET is a value-weighted composite monthly market return based on transactions from the New York Stock Exchange and the American Exchange over the same ten-year time span. Note that the CRSP measure of r_m includes data on all stocks listed at the New York and American Stock Exchanges, not just the 30 used for the Dow Jones index or the Standard & Poor 500. Another data file is called RKFREE, and it provides you with a measure of r_f, namely, the return on 30-day U.S. Treasury bills. The 17 companies whose returns are in the master file of CHAP2.DAT operate primarily in eight industries:

Industry	*Company*	*File Name*
Oil	Mobil	MOBIL
	Texaco	TEXACO
Computers	International Business Machines	IBM
	Digital Equipment Company	DEC
	Data General	DATGEN
Electric utilities	Consolidated Edison	CONED
	Public Service of New Hampshire	PSNH
Forest products	Weyerhauser	WEYER
	Boise	BOISE
Electronic components	Motorola	MOTOR
	Tandy	TANDY
Airlines	Pan American Airways	PANAM
	Delta	DELTA

Banks	Continental Illinois	CONTIL
	Citicorp	CITCRP
Foods	Gerber	GERBER
	General Mills	GENMIL

These firms and industries display considerable variation in risk and returns. Several other data files are in the CHAP2.DAT subdirectory, such as GOLD, EVENTS, and APM. The contents of those data files are discussed in the exercises below.

At numerous times in the following exercises we will ask you to test an hypothesis using a "reasonable level of significance." Since what is "reasonable" is to some extent discretionary, you are asked to follow the convention of stating precisely what percent significance level is being used to test hypotheses; in that way, others with different preferences can still draw their own inferences.

Note: Remember that before the data diskette can be used, the data files must be properly formatted. For further information, refer back to Chapter 1, Section 1.3. MAKE SURE THAT ALL DATA FILES TO BE USED BELOW ARE FORMATTED.

EXERCISES

EXERCISE 1: Getting Started with the Data

The purpose of this exercise is to help you become more familiar with the data series in your subdirectory CHAP2.DAT and to have you speculate on what values company-specific betas might take.

(a) Using data in the file named MARKET, print and plot returns for the last 36 months in the data series, from January 1985 through December 1987. (The output of most computer regression programs looks rather messy if the full time period of 120 months is plotted.)

(b) Next, using data from the MARKET and RKFREE files covering the entire 120-month time span, construct the risk premium measure ($r_p - r_f$) for any company of your choice and the overall market risk premium ($r_m - r_f$). (*Note:* It is possible that for some months the risk premium of a particular company's assets, or that for the market as a whole, is negative. Does this occur in your sample? In particular, check for October 1987. What happened in that month?) Compute and print out sample means for r_p, r_m, r_f, $r_p - r_f$, and $r_m - r_f$. Note that these returns are monthly, not annual. One way of converting the mean monthly returns to annual equivalents is based on the formula

$$r_{\text{annual}} = (1 + \bar{r})^{12} - 1$$

where r_{annual} is the annual return and $\bar{r}$ is the mean monthly return. A resulting value of .060, for example, corresponds to a 6.0% annual return. Compute annual returns for r_p, r_m, r_f, $r_p - r_f$, and $r_m - r_f$. Do these values appear plausible? Why or why not?

(c) Next plot both the company's and the market's risk premium for the last 36 months in the data series, from January 1985 through December 1987 (make sure months coincide for the two series). Are there any noteworthy aspects of these plots? Do you think that this company's β for this time period will be greater than or less than unity? Why? Does this make intuitive sense?

(d) Finally, calculate the variance and the standard deviation of the company's and market's risk premiums over the same 36-month time period as in part (c), as well as the simple correlation coefficient between them. Using Eq. (2.18) and the above values, calculate the implied β for this company. Is this β roughly equal to what you expected?

EXERCISE 2: Least Squares Estimates of β

From the list of industries on pages 42–43, choose one industry that you think is highly risky and another industry that you think is relatively "safe." Divide your sample into the first half (January 1978–December 1982) and the second half (January 1983–December 1987) and choose the half with which you will work.

(a) Using your computer regression software, the 60 observations you have chosen, and Eq. (2.17), estimate by ordinary least squares the parameters α and β for one firm in each of these two industries. Do the estimates of β correspond well with your prior intuition or beliefs? Why or why not?

(b) For one of these companies, make a time plot of the historical company risk premium, the company risk premium predicted by the regression model, and the associated residuals. Are there any episodes or dates that appear to correspond with unusually large residuals? If so, attempt to interpret them.

(c) For each of the companies, test the null hypothesis that $\alpha = 0$ against the alternative hypothesis that $\alpha \neq 0$, using a significance level of 95%. Would rejection of this null hypothesis imply that the CAPM has been invalidated? Why or why not?

(d) For each company, construct a 95% confidence interval for β. Then test the null hypothesis that the company's risk is the same as the average risk over the entire market, that is, test that $\beta = 1$ against the alternative hypothesis that $\beta \neq 1$. Did you find any surprises?

(e) For each of the two companies, compute the proportion of total risk that is market risk, also called systematic and nondiversifiable. William F.

Sharpe [1985, p. 167] states that "Uncertainty about the overall market . . . accounts for only 30% of the uncertainty about the prospects for a typical stock." Does evidence from the two companies you have chosen correspond to Sharpe's typical stock? Why or why not? What is the proportion of total risk that is specific and diversifiable? Do these proportions surprise you? Why?

(f) In your sample, do large estimates of β correspond with higher R^2 values? Would you expect this always to be the case? Why or why not?

EXERCISE 3: Why Gold Is Special

The purpose of this exercise is to acquaint you with features of a rather remarkable asset whose peculiar covariance of returns with the market as a whole often makes it attractive to investors.

(a) There is one asset in the data directory whose data file is named GOLD. The GOLD data file contains series on monthly returns for GOLD, as well as data series for the market (MARK76) and risk-free (RKFR76) variables, all for the January 1976–December 1985 time period. Using the January 1976–December 1979 four-year time period and the CAPM, generate variables measuring the GOLD-specific and market risk premiums, and then estimate the β for GOLD. Compute a 95% confidence interval for β. Do your estimates make sense? Why might such an asset be particularly desirable to an investor who is attempting to reduce risk through diversification? What does this imply concerning the expected return on such an asset?

(b) Now estimate the β for GOLD using data from January 1980–December 1985. Construct a 95% confidence interval for β. Has anything changed? Comment on supply and demand shift factors possibly altering the β of GOLD.

EXERCISE 4: Consequences of Running the Regression Backward

The purpose of this exercise is to explore the consequences of running a regression backwards, that is, of regressing X on Y rather than Y on X, and to discover how one can recover the "correct" estimates from the computer output of the "incorrect" regression.

(a) Using data from January 1983 through December 1987 for Delta Airlines in the data file DELTA, as well as data on r_m in MARKET and on r_f in RKFREE, construct the risk premium for Delta Airlines and for the market as a whole. To simplify notation, now define $Y_t \equiv r_{pt} - r_{ft}$ (the risk premium for Delta Airlines) and $X_t \equiv r_{mt} - r_{ft}$ (the market risk premium), $t = 1, \ldots, 120$.

Suppose that instead of specifying the "correct" CAPM regression equation

$$Y_t = \alpha + \beta X_t + \epsilon_t \tag{2.21}$$

you inadvertently specified the "incorrect" reciprocal regression equation

$$X_t = \delta + \gamma Y_t + v_t \tag{2.22}$$

Show that in the incorrect equation, one can still find the original CAPM parameters and disturbances, that is, solve Eq. (2.21) for X_t in terms of Y_t and ϵ_t and show that $\delta = -\alpha/\beta$, $\gamma = 1/\beta$, and $v_t = (-1/\beta)\epsilon_t$.

(b) Now estimate by OLS the parameters in the incorrect equation (2.22), and denote these estimates of δ and γ by d and g, respectively. What is the R^2 from this incorrect regression? At a reasonable level of significance, test the null hypothesis that $\gamma = 0$ against the alternative hypothesis that $\gamma \neq 0$. Next, construct implicit estimates of the CAPM β and α parameters from this incorrect regression as $b_x = 1/g$ and $a_x = -d/g$ (the subscript x indicates that the estimate is obtained from a regression of X on Y).

(c) Having suddenly discovered your mistake, now run the correct regression and estimate by OLS the α and β parameters in Eq. (2.21), and denote these parameter estimates as a_y and b_y (the subscript y indicates that the estimate is obtained from a regression of Y on X). What is the R^2 from this regression? At a reasonable level of significance, test the null hypothesis that $\beta = 0$ against the alternative hypothesis that $\beta \neq 0$.

(d) Notice that the R^2 from the correct equation (2.21) in part (c) is identical to the R^2 from the incorrect equation (2.22) in part (b) and that so too are the t-statistics computed in parts (b) and (c). Why does this occur? Using the formula for R^2 from your econometric theory textbook and for the OLS estimates of β in Eq. (2.21) and γ in Eq. (2.22), show that

$$R^2 = b_y \cdot g = b_y/b_x \tag{2.23}$$

Notice that what Eq. (2.23) implies is that if you run the wrong regression (Eq. 2.22) and obtain g rather than b_y, you can simply use your R^2 from this incorrect regression, your value of g and Eq. (2.23) to solve for b_x—the estimated value of β you would have obtained had you run the correct regression! Verify numerically that this relationship among R^2, b_y, g, and b_x occurs with your data for Delta Airlines.

(e) Finally, notice that since R^2 is always less than unity, Eq. (2.23) implies that $b_y < b_x$. Which estimate of β do you prefer—the smaller b_y or the larger b_x? Why?

EXERCISE 5: Using the CAPM to Construct Portfolios

The purpose of this exercise is to provide you with a greater appreciation of the benefits of diversification. Imagine that in December 1982 your rich uncle died and bequeathed to you one million dollars, which he specified that you must invest immediately in risky assets. Further, according to the terms of the estate, you could not draw on any funds until you graduated. Therefore in late 1982 you needed to decide how to invest the proceeds of this estate so that upon graduation you would have ample funds for the future. You will now examine the effects of diversification upon risk and return, given three alternative portfolios that you might have chosen in January 1983.

Choose one industry that you think is relatively risky and another industry that is relatively safe, from the list on pages 42–43. Choose two companies in the safe industry and two in the relatively riskier industry.

(a) Calculate the means and standard deviations of the returns for each of the four companies over the January 1983–December 1987 time period. Do the risk-return patterns for these companies correspond with your prior expectations? Why or why not? In which might your uncle have invested? Why?

(b) Construct three alternative (one million dollar total) portfolios as follows. Portfolio I: 50% in a company in the safe industry and 50% in a company from the risky industry. Portfolio II: 50% in each of the two companies in the safe industry. Portfolio III: 50% in each of the two companies in the risky industry. Calculate the sample correlation coefficient between the two company returns in each of the three portfolios. Comment on the size and interpretation of these correlations. For each of the three portfolios, calculate the means and standard deviations of returns over the January 1983–December 1987 time period. Are there any surprises?

(c) Which of the three alternative portfolio diversifications would have been most justifiable in terms of reducing the unsystematic risk of investment? Why? (Choose your words carefully.)

(d) Next estimate the CAPM equation (2.17) for each of these three portfolios over the same January 1983–December 1987 time period. For each portfolio, using a reasonable level of significance, test the null hypothesis that $\beta = 1$ against the alternative hypothesis that $\beta \neq 1$. Which portfolio had the smallest proportion of unsystematic risk?

(e) For Portfolio I, compare the R^2 from the portfolio regression in part (d) with the R^2 from the separate regressions for the two companies. Would you expect the R^2 from the portfolio equation to be higher than that from the individual equations? Why or why not? Interpret your findings.

EXERCISE 6: Assessing the Stability of β over Time and Among Companies

An important maintained assumption of much empirical work in the CAPM framework is that the β parameter is stable over time. To the extent that companies within the same industry are relatively similar, one might also expect that the βs are equal across companies in the same industry. In this exercise, such assumptions are tested, using the Chow test for parameter stability.[20]

(a) From your data file, choose two industries. To allow for possible structural change, for each company in the sample, divide the historical data series into two halves, one for January 1978–December 1982 and the other for January 1983–December 1987. Using Eq. (2.17) and a reasonable level of significance, test the null hypothesis that for each company the parameters α and β are equal over the two half-samples, that is, that for each company these parameters are constant over time.

(b) Now, for each industry, using a reasonable level of significance, test the null hypothesis that the parameters α and β are identical for all firms in the industry over the entire January 1978–December 1987 time period. (Be particularly careful in how you compute degrees of freedom.)

(c) Finally, for each industry, using a reasonable level of significance, test the null hypothesis that the parameters α and β are identical for all companies in the industry *and* are equal over *both* the January 1978–December 1982 and January 1983–December 1987 time intervals. (Be particularly careful in calculating degrees of freedom.) What do you conclude concerning the stability of parameters over companies and time?

EXERCISE 7: Three Mile Island and the Conoco Takeover: Event Studies

An important behavioral assumption underlying the CAPM is that all investors efficiently use whatever information is available to them. It is also typically assumed that all investors have equal access to information. One implication of this is that if an unexpected event occurs that generates information to all investors concerning changes in the expected future profitability of a particular company, such a release of information should immediately raise or lower the price of that company's securities. This sharp change in the value of a company's assets will often, but not always, tend to be a "once and for all" shift, and thereafter movements in the company's securities are often again determined by its β and the overall market risk premium.

In this exercise we examine and quantify the effects of certain events that generated information relevant to investors. We consider two cases:

(1) the effect of the Three Mile Island nuclear power plant accident on March 28, 1979, on the returns earned by General Public Utilities, the parent holding company of the Three Mile Island generating plant[21]; and (2) the effect of the bidding war between, among others, DuPont and Dow Chemical in their attempt to take over Conoco in June–August 1981.[22] Incidentally, in both cases it will be implicitly assumed that the companies' subsequent betas were unaffected by the new information.

In your subdirectory CHAP2.DAT is a data file named EVENTS, containing 120 months' data on monthly returns for GPU, DUPONT, and DOW as well as the RKFREE return and the overall MARKET return; these data cover the time period from January 1976 through December 1985. This file also includes data for CONOCO, but the data cover only the time period of January 1978 through September 1981, since Conoco was taken over at that time.

(a) First, generate values of the company-specific and overall market risk premiums for GPU, DUPONT, and DOW over the January 1976–December 1985 time period and for CONOCO covering the January 1976–September 1981 time interval. Compute sample means and print them out.

(b) Then, using the CAPM equation (2.17), estimate the α and β of General Public Utilities over the January 1976–December 1985 time period, but exclude from your sample the month of April 1979. On the basis of your regression model, compute the fitted value for April 1979 and then the residual for April 1979, the period just after the Three Mile Island nuclear power accident occurred. (*Note:* The monthly data are daily averages, and since the accident occurred in the last days of March 1979, it does not substantially affect the monthly March 1979 data.) How do you interpret this residual?

(c) Now form a dummy variable (denoted TMIDUM) whose value in April 1979 is unity and whose value is zero in all other months. Using least squares regression methods, estimate an expanded CAPM model in which Eq. (2.17) is extended to include the dummy variable TMIDUM. Compare the value of the estimated coefficient on the TMIDUM variable with the value of the residual in part (b) for April 1979. Also compare the estimated slope coefficients in the two regressions. Why are these equal? Finally, using a reasonable level of significance, test the null hypothesis that the coefficient on the TMIDUM variable is equal to zero against the alternative hypothesis that it is not equal to zero. Was the Three Mile Island accident a significant event?

(d) Using the CAPM equation (2.17) and as lengthy a time period sample as possible, estimate the α and β of the three companies involved in the Conoco takeover event: DuPont (the eventually successful takeover bidder), Dow (an unsuccessful bidder), and Conoco (the takeover target); note that for Conoco, the data series terminates in September 1981, since at that time the takeover was completed. For each company, construct the average of the regression residuals for the months of June, July, August, and September 1981.

(e) Next, construct for DuPont, Dow, and Conoco a dummy variable whose value is 1 during the four months of June, July, August, and September 1981 and whose value is 0 in all other months. Using least squares regression methods, estimate an expanded CAPM model over the January 1976–December 1985 time period for DuPont and Dow (and for January 1976–September 1981 for Conoco), in which Eq. (2.17) is extended to include the June–September 1981 dummy variable. Compare the value of the estimated coefficient on this dummy variable for each company with the arithmetic average value of its residuals over the June–September 1981 time period from part (d). Then compare the estimated betas. Why does the equality relationship of part (d) no longer hold here? How do you interpret the signs of these estimated coefficients; in particular, which shareholders were the winners and which were the losers during the Conoco takeover efforts? Is this plausible? Finally, using a reasonable level of significance, for each of the three companies test the null hypothesis that the coefficient on the June–September 1981 dummy variable is equal to zero against the alternative hypothesis that it is not equal to zero.

EXERCISE 8: Is January Different?

There is some tentative evidence supporting the notion that stock returns in the month of January are, other things being equal, higher than in other months, especially for smaller companies.[23] Why this might be the case is not clear, since even if investors sold losing stocks during December for tax reasons, the expectation that January returns would be higher would shift supply and demand curves and thereby would tend to equilibrate returns over the year via the possibility of intertemporal arbitrage.[24] However, the "January is different" hypothesis does seem worth checking out empirically. In this exercise you investigate how this hypothesis might be tested.

(a) First, if the "January premium" affected the overall market return r_m and the risk-free return r_f by the same amount, say, j_m, show that the market risk premium would be unaffected. In this case, could the "January is different" hypothesis be tested within the CAPM framework of Eq. (2.17)? Would it not make more sense, however, to assume that the "January is different" hypothesis referred only to risky assets? Why or why not?

(b) Suppose instead, therefore, that the "January premium" did not affect risk-free assets. In this case, one might hypothesize that in January the overall market return would change from r_m to r'_m, where $r'_m \equiv r_m + j_m$

and j_m is the January premium. Would the market risk premium be affected? Why or why not? Further, if the CAPM model were true and the α and β parameters were constant, show that in January the expected portfolio return should increase to r_p', where $r_p' \equiv r_p + \beta \cdot j_m$. Rewrite Eq. (2.17) using the right-hand sides of the above r_m' and r_p' expressions in place of r_m and r_p, respectively; then, noting that $\beta \cdot j_m$ is unobservable, subtract $\beta \cdot j_m$ from both sides. With what are you left compared to Eq. (2.17)? What does this indicate concerning the possibility of testing the "January is different" hypothesis within the CAPM framework?

(c) Given the conclusions that emerged from parts (a) and (b), it would seem to make sense to abandon the CAPM framework and instead to examine alternative ways of testing the "January is different" hypothesis. To do that, choose any three industries in your January 1978–December 1987 sample. Form a dummy variable called DUMJ that takes the value of unity if the month is January and is zero for all other months; also ensure that for each company the variable r_p is accessible from your data files (*not* the $r_p - r_f$ risk premium variable used in the CAPM regression). Now for each company run the regression of r_p on an intercept term and on the dummy variable DUMJ. Using a reasonable level of significance, test the null hypothesis that the coefficient on the DUMJ variable is zero against the alternative hypothesis that it is not equal to zero. Is January different?

(d) Now suppose that in spite of the reservations developed in parts (a) and (b) concerning the possibility of testing the "January is different" hypothesis within the CAPM framework, sheer perseverance compels you still to estimate Eq. (2.17). More specifically, for each company in the same sample as in part (c), form a subsample that consists only of the ten January observations (one from each year). Then form the complementary subsample consisting of the remaining 11 months of each year for each company. Next, using the Chow test procedure,[25] test the null hypothesis that the parameters of the CAPM in January are equal to those of the remaining months of the year. Interpret your results carefully. What is the alternative hypothesis in this case?

(e) Yet one other way of examining this "January is different" hypothesis within the CAPM framework is to assume that the β parameter is constant over all months but that the January intercept term might differ from that for the remaining 11 months of the year. Set up and estimate a CAPM model, using the same companies as in parts (c) and (d), in which the slope coefficient β is the same for all months, while the intercept term for January and the common intercept term for all other months of the year are permitted to differ. Using a reasonable level of significance, test the null hypothesis that "January is different." Then test the null hypothesis that "January is better."

(f) Comment on the various tests and test results in parts (a) through (e). What do you conclude? Is January different?

EXERCISE 9: Comparing the Capital Asset and Arbitrage Pricing Models

As was noted in the text, an alternative model of asset pricing has been developed by Stephen A. Ross and has been called the arbitrage pricing model (APM).[26] In our context the APM is of interest in that the CAPM might be viewed as a testable special case of a more general model. More specifically, in the APM, securities are allowed to respond differentially to economywide "surprises," such as unexpected oil price shocks, or unexpected changes in the overall rate of inflation. In this exercise, the CAPM is treated as a special case of the APM using the multivariate linear regression model. It is worth noting here that while typical applications of the APM use quite sophisticated empirical methods, such as factor analysis, for pedagogical purposes here we will simply treat the CAPM and the bivariate regression model as a special case of the APM in the multiple regression context.

A data file named APM in the subdirectory CHAP2.DAT contains monthly time series for three data series: the consumer price index (CPI), the price of domestic crude oil (POIL), and the Federal Reserve Board index of industrial production (FRBIND). Make sure that all these data series are properly formatted (see Chapter 1, Section 1.3 for further details).

(a) Choose two industries whose companies, in your judgment, might be particularly sensitive to aggregate economic conditions. For each firm in this sample, using the entire January 1978–December 1987 time span, first construct a data series called RINF reflecting the rate of inflation (CPI in month t minus CPI in month $t - 1$ divided by CPI in month $t - 1$); another data series called ROIL—the growth rate in the real price of oil—computed as $(\text{POIL/CPI})_t - (\text{POIL/CPI})_{t-1}$, all divided by $(\text{POIL/CPI})_{t-1}$; and finally, a data series GIND reflecting growth in industrial production, computed as FRBIND in month t minus FRBIND in month $t - 1$, divided by FRBIND in month $t - 1$. (*Note:* The data series for CPI, POIL, and FRBIND begin in December 1977, not January 1978; this permits you to compute changes in these variables for the full January 1978–December 1987 time period.) Compute the sample means of RINF, ROIL, and GIND and then generate simple "surprise" variables SURINF, SUROIL, and SURIND as RINF minus its sample mean, ROIL minus its sample mean, and GIND minus its sample mean, respectively. Print out the data series for SURINF, SUROIL, and SURIND.

(b) Next, estimate the standard CAPM model for your chosen company and then estimate a multiple regression model in which the right-hand variables include a constant, the market risk premium of the CAPM model, and the "surprise" variables SURINF, SUROIL, and SURIND.

Using a reasonable level of significance, test the joint null hypothesis that the coefficients of these three additional variables are simultaneously equal to zero. Interpret the results.

(c) On the basis of your results in part (b), develop and defend a model specification for each company that best reflects the factors affecting company returns. Do you conclude that the CAPM model is supported, or do you reject it? Is market risk entirely captured by the market risk premium, or do other variables affect market risk? Are any of these results surprising? Why?

EXERCISE 10: What about Our Assumptions Concerning Disturbances? Did We Mess Up?

In order for the ordinary least squares estimator to have the optimal properties, it has been assumed that the ϵ_j disturbances are independently and identically normally distributed with mean zero and variance σ^2. In this exercise we test these assumptions. Note that parts (a), (b), (c), and (d) are independent questions and, in particular, are not sequential; hence any subset of them can be performed once the requisite econometric procedures have been learned.

(a) Testing for homoskedasticity: A number of tests have been proposed to test the null hypothesis of homoskedasticity against an alternative hypothesis consisting of either a specific or some unspecified form of heteroskedasticity. Here we employ a very simple test, due to Halbert J. White [1980].

From your master data file in CHAP2.DAT, choose any two firms. For the first firm in the sample, on the basis of the entire January 1978–December 1987 data series, estimate parameters in the CAPM equation (2.17) using ordinary least squares. Retrieve the residuals from this OLS regression and then generate a new variable defined as the square of the residual at each observation. (*Note:* Take a look at the residual for October 1987. Is it unusual? Why might this be the case?) Next, run an auxiliary OLS regression equation in which the dependent variable is the squared residual series from the first regression and the right-hand variables include a constant term, the market risk premium r_{mt}, and the square of the market risk premium, that is, r_{mt}^2. If one assumes that the original disturbances are homokurtic (that is, the expected value of ϵ_t^4 is a constant), then under the null hypothesis, T (the sample size, here, 120) times the R^2 from this auxiliary regression is distributed asymptotically as a chi-square random variable with two degrees of freedom. Compute this chi-square test statistic for homoskedasticity and compare it to the 95% critical value. Are your data from the first firm consistent with the homoskedasticity assumption? Perform the same White test for the second firm. If the null hypothesis of homoskedasticity is rejected for any firm, make the appropriate adjustments and reestimate the CAPM equation using an appropriate weighted least squares procedure. In such cases, does adjusting for heteroskedasticity affect the parameter estimates significantly? The estimated standard errors? The *t*-statistics of significance? Is this what you expected? Why or why not?

(b) Testing for first-order autoregressive disturbances: From your master data file in CHAP2.DAT, choose two industries. For each firm in the January 1978–December 1987 sample of these two industries, use the Durbin-Watson statistic and test for the absence of a first-order autoregressive stochastic process employing an appropriate level of significance. If the Durbin-Watson statistic for any firm reveals that the null hypothesis of no autocorrelation either is rejected or is in the range of "inconclusive" inference, reestimate the CAPM equation for those firms using either the Hildreth-Lu or Cochrane-Orcutt estimation procedure.[27] Are the estimated parameters, standard errors, and/or *t*-statistics affected in any important way? Are any of the above results surprising? Why?

(c) Testing for first-order moving average disturbances: From your master data file in CHAP2.DAT, choose two industries. For each firm in the January 1978–December 1987 sample of these two industries, estimate the CAPM model allowing for a first-order moving average disturbance process. Using either an asymptotic *t*-test or a likelihood ratio test statistic and a reasonable level of significance, test the null hypothesis that the moving average parameter is equal to zero against the alternative hypothesis that it is not equal to zero.[28]

(d) Testing for normality: From your data file, choose two industries. For each firm in the January 1978–December 1987 sample of these industries, use residuals from CAPM regression equations and the chi-square goodness-of-fit test (or the Kolmogorov-Smirnov test procedure) to test for normality of the residuals.[29]

CHAPTER NOTES

1. For an historical account of the founding of the Econometric Society, see Carl F. Christ [1983].
2. Alfred Cowles III [1933], p. 324.
3. For a more complete discussion of the CAPM, see any textbook in modern corporate finance, e.g., Richard Brealey and Stewart Myers [1988], Chapters 7–9, or William Sharpe [1985], Chapters 6–8, as well as the references cited therein.
4. It might be argued that risk should be measured only by downside surprises. However, if the distribution of returns is symmetric, as is the case with the normal distribution, then use of either the variance or the standard deviation as a measure of risk is appropriate. Incidentally, although the issue remains somewhat controversial, there is a substantial amount of evidence suggesting that returns are dis-

tributed reasonably symmetrically and approximately normally; see, for example, Franco Modigliani and Gerald A. Pogue [1974a, b].

5. There is a substantial body of literature demonstrating that, on average, investors in the United States have in fact received higher rates of return for bearing greater risk. See, for example, the empirical study by Roger Ibbotson and Rex Sinquefield [1986] covering the 60-year time span from 1926 to 1985.
6. Note, however, that the price of this asset is guaranteed only if it is held to maturity. Further, although the *nominal* return is known with certainty if the asset is held to maturity, the extent of inflation is uncertain, and thus its *real* rate of return is not risk-free.
7. For a more complete treatment of diversification, see the seminal article by Harry M. Markowitz [1952].
8. This exposition is admittedly very simple and ignores complications of shares adding to unity, as well as the source of funding for the additional purchases of security k. For a more detailed and rigorous discussion, see Harry M. Markowitz [1952, 1959]. An intuitive exposition using discrete changes is found in William F. Sharpe [1985], pp. 154–156.
9. Two seminal articles on the CAPM are those by William F. Sharpe [1964] and John Lintner [1965]. A third pioneering article on CAPM by Jack L. Treynor [1961] has never been published.
10. This two-step procedure has been called the separation theorem and was first derived by James Tobin [1958].
11. Obviously, the concave risk-return frontier in this case represents alternative optimal portfolios composed of n assets. To ensure that the portfolio is on the frontier rather than under it, each portfolio mix must fulfill the portfolio optimality conditions discussed near the end of Section 2.2.
12. Other useful studies demonstrating the rapid benefits of diversification are by Franco Modigliani and Gerald Pogue [1974a, b] and, in an international context, Bruno Solnik [1974].
13. Richard A. Brealey and Stewart C. Myers [1988], p. 136, taken from Roger Ibbotson and Rex Sinquefield [1986].
14. Studies examining the historical stability of β include Marshall E. Blume [1971]; Robert A. Levy [1971]; William F. Sharpe and Guy M. Cooper [1972]; and Fischer Black, Michael C. Jensen, and Myron Scholes [1972].
15. For further discussion, see Burton Malkiel [1985], Chapter 9.
16. For one attempt to circumvent the ex ante, ex post problem, see Eugene F. Fama and James D. MacBeth [1973].
17. See, for example, Richard Roll [1983].
18. For further discussion of the arbitrage pricing model, see modern finance textbooks such as Richard A. Brealey and Stewart C. Myers [1988], pp. 163–164, or William F. Sharpe [1985], Chapter 8, pp. 182–201. The classic article on the arbitrage pricing theory is that by Stephen A. Ross [1976]. Empirical implementations of the APM typically involve rather sophisticated econometric techniques, including various types of factor models. Some examples of APM empirical implementations include Richard Roll and Stephen A. Ross [1980]; Edwin Burmeister and Kent D. Wall [1986]; Nai-Fu Chen, Richard Roll, and Stephen A. Ross [1986]; and Marjorie B. McElroy and Edwin Burmeister [1988a, b].
19. Most modern finance texts have discussions on procedures for estimating project-specific betas and incorporating them properly into cost of capital calculations.

See, for example, Richard A. Brealey and Stewart C. Myers [1988], Chapter 9, pp. 173–203. An analytical framework for envisaging such project-specific betas has been developed by William F. Sharpe [1977].

20. The Chow test is described in most standard econometrics textbooks. The original reference is Gregory C. Chow [1960]; an expository treatment is provided in Franklin M. Fisher [1970], and a further discussion is found in Damodar N. Gujarati [1970].
21. For further discussion on the effects of the Three Mile Island accident on securities prices of GPU and other electric utility companies, see Carl R. Chen [1984] and Thomas J. Laslavic [1981]; for an analysis of the effects of the Chernobyl nuclear power accident on U.S. electric utility security prices, see Juanita M. Haydel [1988].
22. For a description and analysis of the Conoco takeover, see Richard S. Ruback [1982].
23. See, for example, Richard H. Thaler [1987a]; Philip Brown, Allan W. Kleidon, and Terry A. Marsh [1983]; Donald B. Keim [1983]; Josef Lakonishok and Seymour Smidt [1984]; and Richard Roll [1983]. Incidentally, empirical evidence has also been reported supporting the notion of Monday, end of weekend, holiday, and even intraday effects; see, for example, Kenneth R. French [1980] and, for additional discussion and references, Richard Thaler [1987b]. Finally, the May/June 1978 (Vol. 6, No. 2/3) issue of the *Journal of Financial Economics* is devoted entirely to articles discussing a variety of anomalous returns.
24. However, see Burton G. Malkiel [1985], pp. 179–180, for a discussion of the role of relatively large transactions costs for securities of small companies in reducing possible intertemporal arbitrage.
25. For references on the Chow test, see footnote 20.
26. For references, see footnote 18.
27. The Durbin-Watson test statistic and the Hildreth-Lu and Cochrane-Orcutt estimation procedures are described in considerable detail in most standard econometrics textbooks. Your instructor can provide you with further details.
28. Most graduate econometrics textbooks now include discussions of estimation and inference in models with moving average disturbances. A useful and readable specialized reference text on time series estimation and inference is Charles Nelson [1973].
29. Chi-square goodness-of-fit tests are described in most statistics textbooks, as is the Kolmogorov-Smirnov test; in the context of econometrics textbooks a brief review of tests for normality is found in Judge et al. [1985], pp. 826–827. An alternative test procedure is the studentized range test procedure. For an application in the CAPM context and for tables, see Eugene F. Fama [1976], especially pp. 8–11 and Table 1.9, p. 40.

CHAPTER REFERENCES

Black, Fisher, Michael C. Jensen, and Myron Scholes [1972], "The Capital Asset Pricing Model: Some Empirical Tests," in Michael C. Jensen, ed., *Studies in the Theory of Capital Markets*, New York: Praeger, pp. 79–121.

Blume, Marshall E. [1971], "On the Assessment of Risk," *Journal of Finance*, 26:1, March, 1–10.

Brealey, Richard A. and Stewart C. Myers [1988], *Principles of Corporate Finance*, Third Edition, New York: McGraw-Hill.

Brown, Philip, Allan W. Kleidon, and Terry A. Marsh [1983], "Stock Return Seasonalities and the Tax-Loss Selling Hypothesis: Analysis of the Arguments and Australian Evidence," *Journal of Financial Economics*, 12:1, June, 105–127.

Burmeister, Edwin and Kent D. Wall [1986], "The Arbitrage Pricing Theory and Macroeconomic Factor Measures," *The Financial Review*, 21:1, February, 1–20.

Chen, Carl R. [1984], "The Structural Stability of the Market Model After the Three Mile Island Accident," *Journal of Economics and Business*, 36:1, February, 133–140.

Chen, Nai-Fu, Richard Roll, and Stephen A. Ross [1986], "Economic Forces and the Stock Market," *Journal of Business*, 59:3, July, 383–403.

Chow, Gregory C. [1960], "Tests of Equality between Sets of Coefficients in Two Linear Regressions," *Econometrica*, 28:3, July, 591–605.

Christ, Carl F. [1983], "The Founding of the Econometric Society and Econometrics," *Econometrica*, 51:1, January, 3–6.

Cowles, Alfred III [1933], "Can Stock Market Forecasters Forecast?" *Econometrica*, 1:3, July, 309–324.

Einstein, Albert [1954], *Ideas and Opinions*, New York: Crown Publishers.

Fama, Eugene F. [1970], "Efficient Capital Markets: A Review of Theory and Empirical Work," *Journal of Finance*, 25:2, May, 383–417.

Fama, Eugene F. [1976], *Foundations of Finance*, New York: Basic Books.

Fama, Eugene F. and James D. MacBeth [1973], "Risk, Return and Equilibrium: Empirical Tests," *Journal of Political Economy*, 81:3, May, 607–636.

Fisher, Franklin M. [1970], "Tests of Equality between Sets of Coefficients in Two Linear Regressions: An Expository Note," *Econometrica*, 38:2, March, 361–366.

French, Kenneth R. [1980], "Stock Returns and the Weekend Effect," *Journal of Financial Economics*, 8:1, March, 55–70.

Gujarati, Damodar N. [1970], "Use of Dummy Variables in Testing for Equality between Sets of Coefficients in Two Linear Regressions—A Note," *American Statistician*, 24:1, February, 50–52.

Haydel, Juanita M. [1988], "The Effect of the Chernobyl Nuclear Accident on Electric Utility Security Prices," unpublished M.S. thesis, Massachusetts Institute of Technology, A.P. Sloan School of Management, June.

Heck, Jean Louis [1988], *Finance Literature Index*, New York: McGraw-Hill.

Ibbotson, Roger G. and Rex A. Sinquefield [1986], *Stocks, Bonds, Bills, and Inflation: 1986 Yearbook*, Chicago: Ibbotson Associates.

Judge, George G., William E. Griffiths, R. Carter Hall, Helmut Lutkepohl, and Tsoung-Chao Lee [1985], *The Theory and Practice of Econometrics*, Second Edition, New York: John Wiley and Sons.

Keim, Donald B. [1983], "Size Related Anomalies and Stock Return Seasonability: Further Empirical Evidence," *Journal of Financial Economics*, 12:1, June, 13–32.

Lakonishok, Josef and Seymour Smidt [1984], "Volume and Turn of the Year Behavior," *Journal of Financial Economics*, 13:3, September, 435–455.

Laslavic, Thomas J. [1981], "A Market Shock: The Effect of the Nuclear Accident at Three Mile Island upon the Prices of Electric Utility Securities," unpublished M.S. in Management thesis, Massachusetts Institute of Technology, A.P. Sloan School of Management, June.

Levy, Robert A. [1971], "On the Short-Term Stationarity of Beta Coefficients," *Financial Analysts Journal*, 27:6, November/December, 55–62.

Lintner, John [1965], "The Valuation of Risk Assets and the Selection of Risky Investments in Stock Portfolios and Capital Budgets," *Review of Economics and Statistics*, 47:1, February, 13–37.

Malkiel, Burton G. [1985], *A Random Walk down Wall Street*, New York: W.W. Norton.

Markowitz, Harry M. [1952], "Portfolio Selection," *Journal of Finance*, 7:1, March, 77–91.

Markowitz, Harry M. [1959], *Portfolio Selection: Efficient Diversification of Investments*, New York: John Wiley & Sons.

McElroy, Marjorie B. and Edwin Burmeister [1988a], "Arbitrage Pricing Theory as a Restricted Nonlinear Multivariate Regression Model," *Journal of Business and Economic Statistics*, 6:1, January, 29–42.

McElroy, Marjorie B. and Edwin Burmeister [1988b], "Joint Estimation of Factor Sensitivities and Risk Premia for the Arbitrage Pricing Theory," *Journal of Finance*, 43:3, July, 721–735.

Modigliani, Franco and Gerald A. Pogue [1974a], "An Introduction to Risk and Return: I," *Financial Analysts Journal*, 30:2, March/April, 68–80.

Modigliani, Franco and Gerald A. Pogue [1974b], "An Introduction to Risk and Return: II," *Financial Analysts Journal*, 30:3, May/June, 69–86.

Nelson, Charles R. [1973], *Applied Time Series Analysis for Managerial Forecasting*, San Francisco: Holden-Day.

Reinganum, Marc R. [1983], "The Anomalous Stock Market Behavior of Small Firms in January: Empirical Tests for Tax-Loss Selling Effects," *Journal of Financial Economics*, 12:1, June, 89–104.

Roll, Richard [1983], "Vas Ist Das?" *Journal of Portfolio Management*, 9:2, Winter, 18–28.

Roll, Richard and Stephen A. Ross [1980], "An Empirical Investigation of the Arbitrage Pricing Theory," *Journal of Finance*, 35:5, December, 1073–1103.

Ross, Stephen A. [1976], "The Arbitrage Theory of Capital Asset Pricing," *Journal of Economic Theory*, 13:4, December, 341–360.

Ruback, Richard S. [1982], "The Conoco Takeover and Stockholder Returns," *Sloan Management Review*, Cambridge, Mass.: MIT Sloan School of Management, 23:2, Winter, 13–32.

Sharpe, William F. [1964], "Capital Asset Prices: A Theory of Market Equilibrium under Conditions of Risk," *Journal of Finance*, 19:3, September, 425–442.

Sharpe, William F. [1977], "The Capital Asset Pricing Model: A 'Multi-Beta' Interpretation," in Haim Levy and Marshall Sarnat, eds., *Financial Decision Making Under Uncertainty*, New York: Academic Press.

Sharpe, William F. [1985], *Investments*, Third Edition, Englewood Cliffs, N.J.: Prentice-Hall.

Sharpe, William F. and Guy M. Cooper [1972], "Risk-Return Classes of New York Stock Exchange Common Stocks, 1931–1967," *Financial Analysts Journal*, 28:2, March/April, 46–54.

Solnik, Bruno [1974], "Why Not Diversify Internationally Rather Than Domestically?" *Financial Analysts Journal*, 30:4, July/August, 48–54.

Thaler, Richard H. [1987a], "Anomalies: The January Effect," *Journal of Economic Perspectives*, 1:1, Summer, 197–201.

Thaler, Richard H. [1987b], "Anomalies—Seasonal Movements in Security Prices: II. Weekend, Holiday, Turn of the Month, and Intraday Effects," *Journal of Economic Perspectives*, 1:2, Fall, 169–177.

Tobin, James M. [1958], "Liquidity Preference as Behavior toward Risk," *Review of Economics and Statistics*, 25:1, February, 65–86.

Treynor, Jack L. [1961], "Toward a Theory of Market Value of Risky Assets," unpublished manuscript.

Twain, Mark (Samuel Clemens) [1899], *Pudd'nhead Wilson*, New York: Harper and Row.

Wagner, Wayne H. and Sheila C. Lau [1971], "The Effect of Diversification on Risk," *Financial Analysts Journal*, 27:6, November/December, 48–53.

White, Halbert J. [1980], "A Heteroskedasticity-Consistent Covariance Matrix Estimator and a Direct Test for Heteroskedasticity," *Econometrica*, 48:4, May, 817–838.

FURTHER READINGS

Cragg, John G. and Burton G. Malkiel [1982], *Expectations and the Structure of Share Prices*, Chicago: University of Chicago Press. A rigorous empirical analysis of stock market returns.

Fama, Eugene F. [1976], *Foundations of Finance*, New York: Basic Books. Especially Chapters 1–4. A readable and useful classic text.

Huang, Chi-fu and Robert H. Litzenberger [1988], *Foundations for Financial Economics*, Amsterdam: North-Holland. Especially Chapter 10, "Econometric Issues in Testing the Capital Asset Pricing Model." Contains a useful summary of recent research issues.

Malkiel, Burton G. [1985], *A Random Walk down Wall Street*, New York: W.W. Norton. Especially Chapters 8 and 9. Enjoyable and stimulating reading.

Markowitz, Harry M. [1959], *Portfolio Selection: Efficient Diversification of Investments*, New York: John Wiley & Sons. A classic treatment of portfolio theory.

Chapter 3

Costs, Learning Curves, and Scale Economies: From Simple to Multiple Regression

> *"Understanding of the underlying causes of the experience curve is still imperfect. The effect itself is beyond question. It is so universal that its absence is almost a warning of mismanagement or misunderstanding. Yet the basic mechanism that produces the experience curve effect is still to be adequately explained. . . . Our entire concept of competition, anti-trust, and non-monopolistic free enterprise is based on a fallacy if the experience curve effect is true."*
>
> BOSTON CONSULTING GROUP (1973, p. 2)

> *"The learning curve creates entry barriers and protection from competition by conferring cost advantages on early entrants and those who achieve large market shares."*
>
> A. MICHAEL SPENCE (1981, p. 68)

In this chapter we focus on econometric issues that are encountered in estimating the cost effects of scale economies and learning curves. This focus will help us to understand differences between simple and multiple regression, to assess the effects of incorrectly omitting variables from a regression equation, and to implement alternative ways of testing hypotheses.

The existence of scale economies, as well as the cost reductions due to learning curve effects, have important implications for market structure and economic welfare, since such phenomena can create barriers to entry, thereby protecting early entrants from effective market competition. On the other hand, acting in the interests of their shareholders, effective managers must focus a great deal of attention on these and other factors that might reduce their production costs.

According to one line of thinking, potential *economies of scale* can be exploited, resulting in average or unit cost decreases as the level of output increases per time period. If such economies of scale are available, then it may be rational for profit-maximizing or cost-minimizing managers to accelerate investment plans, reduce prices, and thereby achieve higher levels of production at lower unit cost than if scale economies were absent. Scale economies also have important implications for the competitive structure of an industry. But from what do economies of scale derive?

Economies of scale might arise because of the large fixed capital expenditures often required before any production can take place. Such reasoning has been used in explaining, for example, increasing returns to scale in the generation of electricity. Other sources of scale economies include physical-technical relationships and laws of nature. For example, in the case of boilers or pipelines, costs are typically closely related to the surface area of the boiler or pipeline, yet output (throughput) depends primarily on the potential volume. From basic geometry it is known that the area of a sphere or cylinder of constant proportions increases by the two-thirds power of its volume; this implies that the surface area increases less rapidly than the potential volume, suggesting that for both boilers and pipelines, one might expect economies of scale to be available. In the engineering literature this is known as the "two-thirds" or "six-tenths" rule, and it implies a rule of thumb that costs should increase by only about 60–67% as output or potential volume doubles.[1]

While these particular engineering examples are striking, one would not expect the two-thirds rule to apply to all types of production activities. Therefore obtaining estimates of scale economies is a very important issue; as we shall see, such a task can be carried out by using econometric methods.

Another important determinant of production costs is called the *learning curve* effect, a concept that is closely related to progress functions and experience curves. It is not clear precisely when the learning curve was first discovered.[2] A particularly well-known historical example occurred when it was noticed that, for certain emergency shipbuilding yards that were involved in the construction of the Liberty vessel during World War II, unit costs tended to fall over time as production experience accumulated, even when the annual level of operations remained unchanged; similar cost-reduction trends were noted for aircraft.[3] More generally, in numerous assembly line operations in which tasks are performed in a repetitive manner, it has frequently been found that workers tend to learn from their experiences, thereby reducing the time and labor costs required to perform prescribed tasks.[4] Even in operations that are less repetitive, such as the construction of coal-burning or nuclear power plants, learning curve effects have been found to occur.[5]

Today the notion that unit costs and unit prices tend to decline systematically in real terms as cumulative output increases is widespread and important in both the private and public sectors. In strategic management, for example, the existence of such experience or learning curve effects can provide a rationale for a pricing and marketing strategy in which producers initially price low (perhaps even below current marginal cost) in order to expand sales and gain market penetration rapidly, thereby quickly accumulating experience and exploiting the cost-reducing effects of such learning.[6] In modern industrial economics and marketing, the effects of learning curves on optimal pricing policies, make-or-buy decisions, market structure, and consumers' welfare are currently being modeled and analyzed, using increasingly sophisticated dynamic optimization techniques.[7] Finally, in the public policy sphere it has been argued by some that because of the existence of learning curves, it may make sense for governments to provide limited temporary protection to domestic manufacturers from foreign competitors.[8]

The above examples clearly demonstrate that learning or experience curves are very important in the formulation of strategy and policy. But how are they estimated, how might they be used in forecasting costs, and how are they related to scale economies?[9]

Chapter 3 is organized as follows. We begin by summarizing the economic theory of cost and production, define returns to scale, and characterize the effects of learning as shifts in production or cost functions. Next we derive estimating equations based on the Cobb-Douglas production function, discuss several measurement and econometric issues, and then present an overview of empirical research findings on scale economies and learning curves. Finally, we present a number of exercises based on classic data sets that involve you in the estimation of scale economies in the generation of electricity, as well as in the estimation and interpretation of learning curve effects in the manufacture of polyethylene and titanium dioxide. These exercises involve simple and multiple regressions, single and joint hypothesis tests, and the interpretation of R^2 in simple and multiple regressions.

3.1 THE UNDERLYING ECONOMIC THEORY OF COST AND PRODUCTION

The relationship among inputs and output is summarized by a production function. More specifically, denote flows of n input services as x_i, $i = 1, \ldots, n$, and the flow of output as y; the production function f indicates the maximum possible output y given any combination of inputs x_i, $i = 1, \ldots, n$,

$$y = f(x_1, x_2, \ldots, x_n) \tag{3.1}$$

Essentially, therefore, the production function is an engineering relationship reflecting technology and the laws of nature.

While laws of nature do not change over time, our understanding of technology and nature has improved over the years, as has our ability to exploit technological possibilities. At any point in time, therefore, the various possible ways in which output y can be produced with differing combinations of inputs x_i can be thought of as a book containing alternative "blueprints." Since the number of pages in the book of such blueprints has grown with advances in knowledge, empirical analysts of production and cost relationships often add a variable into Eq. (3.1) to reflect such improvements in the state of technical knowledge. In this spirit, therefore, we insert a state of technical knowledge variable, called A, into Eq. (3.1) as follows:

$$y = f(x_1, x_2, \ldots, x_n; A) \tag{3.2}$$

One important characteristic of Eq. (3.2) is the notion of *returns to scale*. Suppose that all inputs are increased proportionately, say, by the factor μ, while A is held constant. If output y then increases by a factor greater than, equal to, or less than μ, returns to scale are said to be increasing, constant, or decreasing, respectively. As an example, if all inputs are increased by 100% and output increases by 115%, 100%, or 85%, then returns to scale are increasing (equal to about 1.15), constant (1.00), or decreasing (about 0.85), respectively. Further, *economies of scale* are typically computed as returns to scale minus 1; in the above example, economies of scale are positive (0.15), zero, or negative (−0.15), respectively.

While the production function (3.2) is essentially an engineering notion, economic content can be obtained by making assumptions concerning the economic behavior of firms. The two most common assumptions are those of profit maximization and cost minimization. Since the latter hypothesis is less stringent, we now adopt it.

The usual set of assumptions surrounding cost minimization behavior by firms includes the presumption that the level of output y produced by the firm is predetermined (it is not a contemporaneous endogenous variable chosen by the firm), that the prices of the n inputs, $p_1, \ldots, p_n$, are fixed and exogenous, and that the firm chooses its bundle of input quantities so as to minimize the total costs of producing y. This implies that, dual to the production function (3.2), there exists a *cost function* relating the minimum possible total cost $C \equiv \Sigma_i p_i x_i$ of producing a given level of output to the prices of the n inputs, the level of output y, and the state of technical knowledge A. The dual cost function can therefore be written as

$$C = g(p_1, p_2, \ldots, p_n, y; A) \tag{3.3}$$

Now define average or unit cost c as $c \equiv C/y$. If returns to scale are increasing, then doubling all inputs more than doubles output, and average cost falls; similarly, if returns to scale are decreasing, then doubling all inputs results in less than a doubling of output, and average cost increases; finally, if returns to scale are constant, then doubling all inputs results in an equiproportional doubling of output, and average cost is unaffected.

The relationship between returns to scale, output level, and average costs can be seen graphically by observing the long-run average cost curves in Fig. 3.1. For both average cost curves drawn in Fig. 3.1, at levels of output to the left of y_0, average cost is falling as output increases; therefore in this range of outputs, returns to scale are increasing. To the right of y_0, average cost is increasing with output; therefore in this range of outputs, returns to scale are decreasing. Finally, at the point y_0, average cost is at a minimum, and returns to scale are constant.

The above discussion on returns to scale focused on relationships among inputs and output, given that the state of technical knowledge A was unchanged. But how might improvements in the state of technical knowledge—increases in A—affect production and costs? It is convenient to think of such improvements as shifting the production function (or production possibility frontier) outward, since given the same combination of inputs, the maximum possible output increases with improvements in technical knowledge. This implies that the total and average costs of producing output decline with improvements in technical knowledge, that is, that the average cost curve shifts downward with increases in A.

One example of special interest here is the case of learning. To the extent that cumulative experience with the production of output results in improvements in technical knowledge, one might think of A as being affected by cumulative experience, or learning. In such cases the effects of learning are to change A in Eq. (3.3) from, say, A_0 to A_1 and thus to shift the cost curve in

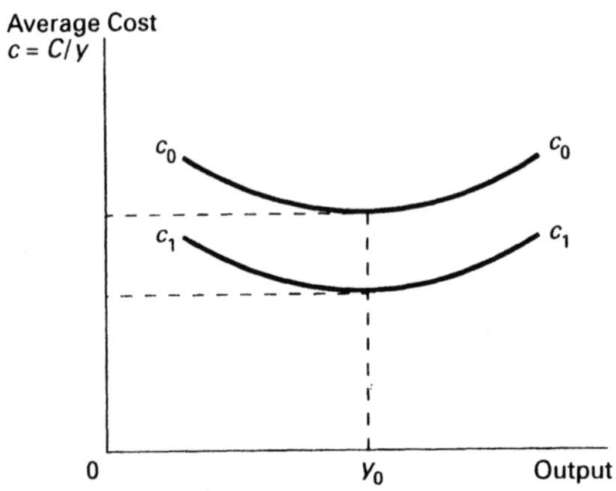

FIGURE 3.1

Fig. 3.1 downward from the curve $c_0 - c_0$ to the lower curve $c_1 - c_1$. Incidentally, it is worth noting that changes in returns to scale correspond with movements *along* the average cost curves in Fig. 3.1, whereas changes in the state of technical knowledge induce *shifts* in these curves.

In terms of the calculus, one can write the cost minimization problem facing the firm as a constrained optimization problem:

$$\min_{x_i} \mathcal{L} = \sum_{i=1}^{n} p_i x_i + \lambda[y - f(x_1, \ldots, x_n; A)] \tag{3.4}$$

where λ is the Lagrange multiplier.[10] The first-order conditions for minimization of costs are

$$\begin{aligned} \frac{\partial \mathcal{L}}{\partial x_1} &= p_1 - \lambda f_1(x_1, x_2, \ldots x_n; A) = 0 \\ &\vdots \\ \frac{\partial \mathcal{L}}{\partial x_n} &= p_n - \lambda f_n(x_1, x_2, \ldots, x_n; A) = 0 \end{aligned} \tag{3.5}$$

and

$$\frac{\partial \mathcal{L}}{\partial \lambda} = y - f(x_1, x_2, \ldots, x_n; A) = 0 \tag{3.6}$$

where f_i is the first partial derivative (here, marginal product) of the production function (3.2) with respect to the ith input quantity, $i = 1, \ldots, n$.

Assuming that the second-order conditions for minimization are satisfied, we can solve for the cost function g in Eq. (3.3) dual to the production function f in Eq. (3.2) in a sequential manner, first by taking ratios of first-order conditions (3.5) to eliminate λ (reflecting cost minimization):

$$\begin{aligned} \frac{p_1}{p_n} &= \frac{f_1(x_1, x_2, \ldots, x_n; A)}{f_n(x_1, x_2, \ldots, x_n; A)} \\ &\vdots \\ \frac{p_{n-1}}{p_n} &= \frac{f_{n-1}(x_1, x_2, \ldots, x_n; A)}{f_n(x_1, x_2, \ldots, x_n; A)} \end{aligned}$$

then solving for each x_i by repeated substitution into Eq. (3.6)—call these $\hat{x}_i$—and finally by substituting these optimal $\hat{x}_i$ into the expression for total costs, $C \equiv \Sigma_i p_i \hat{x}_i$.

It might also be noted here that in many cases it is impossible to solve analytically for the cost function g dual to a particular production function f, particularly when the production function becomes mathematically complex. In the last two decades, however, there have been important advances in the economic theory of duality that now facilitate theoretical and empirical implementations of cost functions dual to rather general production functions. While such duality theory issues are very important for empirical research on costs and production (and are discussed in further detail in Chapter 9), they are beyond the scope of this chapter.[11]

3.2 BRIEF OVERVIEW OF LEARNING CURVE LITERATURE

The essential features underlying learning curves—curves relating unit real cost or real price to cumulative production—were briefly summarized in the introduction to this chapter. There it was emphasized that, given exposure to repetitive tasks, workers are likely to learn from cumulative experience how such tasks can be performed more quickly and efficiently. Not only are assembly line workers able to exploit their experiences, but so too are plant managers and other company officials. For example, plant engineers and managers can call upon their experience to improve the operations management of the plant, rearranging its layout, modifying job assignments, and reducing material wastes. Further, machines that are involved in the productive process are also affected by experience, not in the sense that they learn, but rather that they may undergo a number of technical improvements and in some cases can be replaced altogether by machines embodying newer technologies.[12]

The literature on the cost effects of learning has occasionally differentiated learning curve effects from experience curve effects: the former was confined to the learning and increased effectiveness of workers, while the latter incorporated the complete effects of experience, from workers' training to technical improvements to better management. Be they learning or experience curve effects, however, their impacts on costs are typically computed by developing a measure of cumulative previous production. For the moment we interpret cumulative previous production as a measure incorporating the effects of learning or experience.[13]

Consider, for example, the historical record of the Ford Motor Company in producing its Model T Ford over the 1909–1923 time period. Ford decided to make relatively standard models with few customized options.[14] Because of the experiences gained by management and labor, dramatic cost reductions occurred as cumulative production increased; these cost declines were then passed on to consumers in the form of price reductions.[15]

To see what happened at Ford, observe Fig. 3.2, which indicates the average list price in 1958 dollars of the Model T as cumulative production increased.[16] The vertical axis displays the natural logarithm of prices in thousands of 1958 dollars, while the horizontal axis displays the natural logarithm of cumulative production. A simple regression line with a negative slope of about -0.25 "fits" these data very nicely and suggests that price fell substantially with increases in cumulative production. As has been noted by a number of analysts, slopes of -0.20 to -0.30 on diagrams analogous to Fig. 3.2 are very common for a number of manufactured products.[17]

The learning curve has been formulated in a variety of ways. The simplest and most common form of the learning curve is as follows:[18]

$$c_t = c_1 n_t^{\alpha_c} e^{u_t} \tag{3.7}$$

where

$c_t \equiv$ average or unit real costs of production in time period t (nominal average costs adjusted for inflation using a GNP-type deflator)

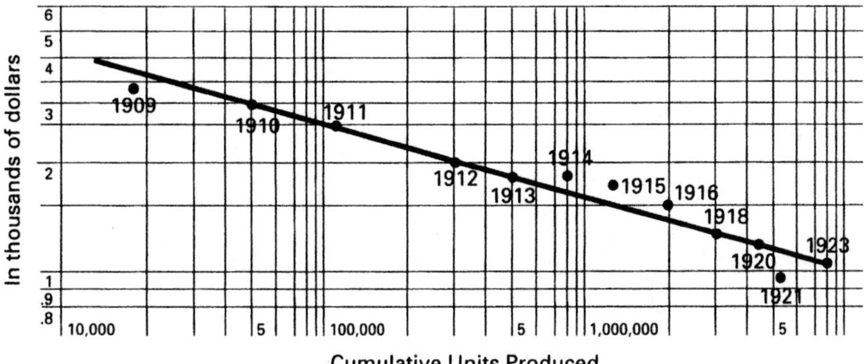

FIGURE 3.2
(*Source:* W.J. Abernathy and K. Wayne, "Limits of the Learning Curve," *Harvard Business Review*, September/October, 1974.) Reprinted by permission of *Harvard Business Review*.

c_1 ≡ real unit or average costs in the initial production time period
n_t ≡ cumulative number of units of output produced up to (but not including) time period t
α_c ≡ elasticity of unit costs with respect to cumulative volume (typically negative)
u_t ≡ a stochastic disturbance term reflecting the effects of inherent randomness in cost-production processes

Typically, it is assumed that the u_t disturbance term is independently and identically normally distributed with mean zero and constant covariance matrix (more on this later).

Equation (3.7) can be written in logarithmic form as

$$\ln c_t = \ln c_1 + \alpha_c \cdot \ln n_t + u_t \tag{3.8}$$

The learning curve elasticity parameter α_c can then be estimated by least squares, provided that appropriate data on unit costs and production are available.[19]

The mathematics of logarithmic transformations implies that each time cumulative experience doubles, costs (prices) will decline to d% of its previous level, where

$$d = 2^{\alpha_c} \tag{3.9}$$

Therefore if cost (price) declines to 80% of its previous level as cumulative production doubles, then the experience or learning curve is said to have an 80% slope. Simple calculations imply that the numerical relationship between d and α_c is approximately as follows:

α_c:	−0.50	−0.33	−0.25	−0.16
d:	0.71	0.80	0.84	0.89

An example is found in Fig. 3.2, where the slope of the simple regression line on Model T Fords is about −0.25; on the left-hand side of this figure it is noted that the experience curve has an 85% slope. From the above example an α_c estimate of about −0.25 implies a d estimate of about 0.84.

While other formulations of the learning curve relationship have been employed, it is the double logarithmic relationship (3.8) that has been most widely estimated in the empirical learning curve literature. In the next section of this chapter we examine what economic theory and what mathematical relationships could be called upon to justify employing an equation such as the popular learning curve (3.8).

3.3 DERIVATION OF COST FUNCTION BASED ON COBB-DOUGLAS PRODUCTION FUNCTION

In Section 3.1 we overviewed the economic theory underlying cost and production functions and focused on the notions of returns to scale and advances in technical knowledge. Then in the Section 3.2 we briefly outlined the learning curve literature. In this and the following section we synthesize these two literatures and move toward empirical implementation. First we employ economic theory and derive a Cobb-Douglas cost function equation, apparently related to the learning curve equation (3.8), whose parameters can be estimated by using linear multiple regression techniques. Then in Section 3.4 we explicitly integrate the learning curve equation (3.8) with the Cobb-Douglas cost function.

It is worth emphasizing that our focus here is the rather simple one of obtaining and interpreting an estimable learning curve equation that is consistent with the theory of cost and production. Students who are interested in pursuing more complex mathematical issues further may wish to consult a microeconomic theory textbook, such as those referenced in footnote 11.

To obtain a cost function whose parameters have clear interpretations, it is useful to specify a particular functional form for the production function f in Eq. (3.2). A very convenient, albeit somewhat restrictive, functional form is known as the Cobb-Douglas production function. Similar mathematical representations were used by the economist Knut Wicksell as early as 1896, but this form became particularly well known following an important published study by Charles Cobb and Paul Douglas [1928].[20]

In several of the empirical exercises in this chapter you will deal with the estimation of returns to scale in the generation of electricity based on the three inputs of capital, labor, and fuel. We therefore begin by writing a slightly more general version of the constant returns to scale, two-input functional form than that originally presented by Cobb and Douglas in their 1928 paper. In particular, we write the three-input Cobb-Douglas production function as

$$y = A \cdot x_1^{\alpha_1} \cdot x_2^{\alpha_2} \cdot x_3^{\alpha_3} \tag{3.10}$$

where α_1, α_2, and α_3 are unknown parameters to be estimated. If each of the x's is multiplied by the proportionality factor μ, then substitution into Eq. (3.10) implies that the resulting output equals $y \cdot \mu^r$, where $r \equiv \alpha_1 + \alpha_2 + \alpha_3$. This means that returns to scale for the Cobb-Douglas function, hereafter denoted as r, equal the sum of the exponents in Eq. (3.10), that is,

$$\text{Returns to scale} \equiv r = \alpha_1 + \alpha_2 + \alpha_3 \tag{3.11}$$

Further, economies of scale are computed as $r - 1$. If, for example, r equalled 1.15, 1.00, or 0.85, then returns to scale would be increasing, constant, or decreasing, respectively, and economies of scale would be positive (0.15), zero, or negative (−0.15), respectively.

To derive the cost function dual to the Cobb-Douglas production function, substitute Eq. (3.10) for $f(x_1, x_2, \ldots, x_n)$ into Eq. (3.4) and rewrite the corresponding first-order conditions in Eqs. (3.5) and (3.6). After rearranging, the first-order conditions in Eqs. (3.5) turn out to be, for this Cobb-Douglas case,

$$x_i = \lambda \cdot y \cdot \alpha_i / p_i \qquad i = 1, 2, 3 \tag{3.12}$$

Now take ratios of these first-order conditions in Eq. (3.12) to eliminate λ and y; for example, take ratios x_2/x_1 and x_3/x_1. Given these ratios, solve for x_2 and x_3, substitute into Eq. (3.6), and rearrange to solve for, say, x_1 as a function of y, A, α_i, and p_i, $i = 1, 2, 3$. This yields the derived demand for x_1 as a function of the level of output y, the parameters of the Cobb-Douglas production function, and the prices of the three inputs. Follow analogous procedures to obtain derived demands for x_2 and x_3. Then, using these analytical expressions for x_1, x_2, and x_3, obtain the functional form for the cost function g dual to the Cobb-Douglas production function (3.10) as

$$C = p_1 x_1 + p_2 x_2 + p_3 x_3 \tag{3.13}$$

which, after simple but tedious algebraic computations, turns out to be

$$C = k \cdot y^{1/r} \cdot p_1^{\alpha_1/r} \cdot p_2^{\alpha_2/r} \cdot p_3^{\alpha_3/r} \tag{3.14}$$

where

$$k = r \cdot [A \cdot \alpha_1^{\alpha_1} \cdot \alpha_2^{\alpha_2} \cdot \alpha_3^{\alpha_3}]^{-1/r} \tag{3.15}$$

and r is the returns-to-scale parameter defined in Eq. (3.11).

While the Cobb-Douglas cost function (3.14) and (3.15) appears formidably nonlinear, a linear specification that is amenable to conventional linear multiple regression techniques can be obtained by taking natural logarithms. This logarithmic transformation yields the much simpler equation

$$\begin{aligned} \ln C = {} & \ln k + (1/r) \cdot \ln y + (\alpha_1/r) \cdot \ln p_1 \\ & + (\alpha_2/r) \cdot \ln p_2 + (\alpha_3/r) \cdot \ln p_3 \end{aligned} \tag{3.16}$$

where ln denotes the natural logarithm. Notice in particular that if one estimated Eq. (3.16) using conventional linear multiple regression techniques (ignoring for the moment the absence of a stochastic disturbance term), the reciprocal of the estimated coefficient on the ln y variable would provide a direct estimate of returns to scale. However, and this will turn out to be very important, since r is a constant parameter, returns to scale with this Cobb-Douglas cost function cannot vary with the level of output; this implies that the average cost curve in Fig. 3.1 corresponding to the Cobb-Douglas cost function would always slope downward if $r > 1$, would be a horizontal straight line if $r = 1$, and would always slope upward if $r < 1$.

One other additional constraint can be imposed before estimating Eq. (3.16). Specifically, according to economic theory, in order that cost functions are well behaved, it is necessary that they be homogeneous of degree 1 in input prices, no matter the extent of scale economies.

The underlying intuition for homogeneity of degree 1 in input prices is as follows: For a given level of output, if all input prices double, one would expect that total costs should also double. (Note that this constraint involving prices and costs, holding output fixed, is different from the returns-to-scale relationship whereby $r \equiv \alpha_1 + \alpha_2 + \alpha_3$. See any microeconomic theory text for further details.) This homogeneity of degree 1 in input prices (also called linear homogeneity) implies the constraint that the coefficients on the input price variables in Eq. (3.16) sum to unity, that is, that

$$\alpha_1/r + \alpha_2/r + \alpha_3/r = (\alpha_1 + \alpha_2 + \alpha_3)/r = 1 \qquad \textbf{(3.17)}$$

This restriction can be imposed by solving Eq. (3.17) for, say, α_3/r:

$$\alpha_3/r = 1 - \alpha_1/r - \alpha_2/r \qquad \textbf{(3.18)}$$

substituting Eq. (3.18) into Eq. (3.16), collecting terms, and then rearranging. This results in

$$\begin{aligned}\ln C - \ln p_3 &= \ln k + (1/r)\cdot \ln y \\ &\quad + (\alpha_1/r)\cdot(\ln p_1 - \ln p_3) + (\alpha_2/r)\cdot(\ln p_2 - \ln p_3)\end{aligned} \qquad \textbf{(3.19)}$$

A convenient way of rewriting Eq. (3.19) is as follows:

$$\ln C^* = \beta_0 + \beta_y \cdot \ln y + \beta_1 \cdot \ln p_1^* + \beta_2 \cdot \ln p_2^* \qquad \textbf{(3.20)}$$

where

$$\begin{aligned}\ln C^* &\equiv \ln C - \ln p_3 \\ \ln p_1^* &\equiv \ln p_1 - \ln p_3 \\ \ln p_2^* &\equiv \ln p_2 - \ln p_3 \\ \beta_0 &\equiv \ln k \\ \beta_y &\equiv (1/r) \\ \beta_1 &\equiv \alpha_1/r \\ \beta_2 &\equiv \alpha_2/r\end{aligned} \qquad \textbf{(3.21)}$$

Equation (3.20) highlights the linearity and empirical simplicity of the Cobb-Douglas cost function equation.

An important issue now emerges: If one estimated the parameters in Eq. (3.20) using linear multiple regression techniques, how could one employ them to recover estimates of the underlying Cobb-Douglas production function parameters and returns to scale? As was noted earlier and implied in the fifth line of Eqs. (3.21), $r \equiv 1/\beta_y$; similarly, by using the last two lines of Eqs. (3.21),

$$\alpha_1 = \beta_1 \cdot r = \beta_1/\beta_y \quad \text{and} \quad \alpha_2 = \beta_2 \cdot r = \beta_2/\beta_y \tag{3.22}$$

Finally, employing Eq. (3.18) and the bottom two lines of Eqs. (3.21) the implicit parameter α_3 can be recovered from the parameters directly estimated in Eq. (3.20) as

$$\alpha_3 = (1 - \beta_1 - \beta_2)/\beta_y \tag{3.23}$$

Hence by estimating parameters of the dual cost function equation (3.20), one can recover estimates of all other Cobb-Douglas production function parameters.

In the exercises at the end of this chapter, you will become involved with estimation of parameters in Eq. (3.20) and will obtain estimates of returns to scale in the generation of electricity for various electric utility companies in the United States.

3.4 INTEGRATING THE LEARNING CURVE WITH THE COBB-DOUGLAS COST FUNCTION

We have now discussed two apparently rather different strands of literature, one dealing with learning and experience curves and the other with Cobb-Douglas production and dual cost functions. In this section we integrate these discussions.

It is useful to recall that the most common equation used to estimate parameters of the learning curve is that of Eq. (3.8), namely,

$$\ln c_t = \ln c_1 + \alpha_c \cdot \ln n_t + u_t \tag{3.8}$$

while the Cobb-Douglas cost function equation (with a stochastic disturbance term now included) was derived in Eq. (3.16) as

$$\begin{aligned} \ln C = \ln k &+ (1/r) \cdot \ln y + (\alpha_1/r) \cdot \ln p_1 \\ &+ (\alpha_2/r) \cdot \ln p_2 + (\alpha_3/r) \cdot \ln p_3 + u_t \end{aligned} \tag{3.16}$$

To integrate the learning curve and Cobb-Douglas discussions, in essence we ask what restrictions or changes must be made to Eq. (3.16) so that it reduces to the simple learning curve equation (3.8).

The first important difference to note between Eqs. (3.16) and (3.8) is that the variable reflecting the effects of learning and experience, measured in Eq. (3.8) by cumulative previous production and denoted n_t, is entirely absent from the Cobb-Douglas cost function equation (3.16). However, recall that the constant term in Eq. (3.16) is simply ln k, where k was defined in Eq. (3.15) to depend on A and where in turn A reflected advances in the state of knowledge. Surely advances in knowledge are closely related to learning curve effects, and therefore it should be relatively straightforward to integrate A with n_t.

In this spirit, define the state of knowledge in time period t as cumulative production up to time period t, all raised to the power α_c, where α_c is the experience curve elasticity parameter to be estimated, that is,

$$A_t \equiv n_t^{-\alpha_c} \tag{3.24}$$

Substituting Eq. (3.24) into Eq. (3.14), adding time subscripts to the cost, output, and price variables, and then taking logarithms yield a modified version of the Cobb-Douglas cost function equation (3.16) with experience effects included:

$$\begin{aligned}\ln C_t = \ln k' + (\alpha_c/r) \cdot \ln n_t + (1/r) \cdot \ln y_t + (\alpha_1/r) \cdot \ln p_{1t} \\ + (\alpha_2/r) \cdot \ln p_{2t} + (\alpha_3/r) \cdot \ln p_{3t}\end{aligned} \tag{3.25}$$

where k' is the same as k in Eq. (3.15) except that the effects of A are removed, that is,

$$k' = r \cdot [\alpha_1^{\alpha_1} \cdot \alpha_2^{\alpha_2} \cdot \alpha_3^{\alpha_3}]^{-1/r} \tag{3.26}$$

While the Cobb-Douglas cost function equation (3.25) now has learning or experience curve effects included, it also contains a number of variables that are not found in the learning curve equation (3.8), such as the three input prices and the output variables.

With respect to the three input prices, one could simply make the grandiose assumption that over whatever time period the data spanned, the relative input prices were constant. In such a case, prices could simply be ignored, and their effect would be included in a composite intercept term. However, while such an assumption is convenient, it is heroic indeed.

One could instead make a different assumption that effectively removes the price variables as regressors from the Cobb-Douglas cost function equation. In particular, one could assume that the effects of the three input prices in Eq. (3.25) could be captured by using an appropriate deflator from the national income and product accounts, such as the deflator for gross national product (GNP). Denote such a GNP deflator as GNPD, set GNPD equal to the Cobb-Douglas function of prices in Eq. (3.25),

$$\ln \text{GNPD}_t \equiv (\alpha_1/r) \cdot \ln p_1 + (\alpha_2/r) \cdot \ln p_2 + (\alpha_3/r) \cdot \ln p_3 \tag{3.27}$$

and then define total costs in constant dollars (denoted C_t') as total costs in current dollars (C_t) divided by GNPD_t, that is,

$$C_t' \equiv C_t/\text{GNPD}_t \quad \text{or} \quad \ln C_t' = \ln C_t - \ln \text{GNPD}_t \tag{3.28}$$

If we solve Eq. (3.28) for ln C_t and then substitute Eq. (3.27) into Eq. (3.25), the Cobb-Douglas cost function equation becomes

$$\begin{aligned}\ln C_t &= \ln C_t' + \ln \text{GNPD}_t \\ &= \ln C_t' + (\alpha_1/r) \cdot \ln p_{1t} + (\alpha_2/r) \cdot \ln p_{2t} + (\alpha_3/r) \cdot \ln p_{3t} \\ &= \ln k' + (\alpha_c/r) \cdot \ln n_t + (1/r) \cdot \ln y_t + (\alpha_1/r) \cdot \ln p_{1t} \\ &\quad + (\alpha_2/r) \cdot \ln p_{2t} + (\alpha_3/r) \cdot \ln p_{3t} + u_t \end{aligned} \tag{3.29}$$

Notice that since the terms involving price variables appear on both sides of the second equal sign in Eq. (3.29), the price terms can be subtracted from both sides, thereby generating a modified Cobb-Douglas cost equation that looks very much like the learning curve equation (3.8), specifically,

$$\ln C_t' = \ln k' + (\alpha_c/r) \cdot \ln n_t + (1/r) \cdot \ln y_t + u_t \tag{3.30}$$

It is important to note that this similarity in the Cobb-Douglas and learning curve equations depends critically on the assumption that the effects of input prices on costs of production can be measured by using the GNP deflator, that is, that Eq. (3.27) is valid. Of course, that involves a rather strong assumption and is unlikely to be appropriate whenever the shares of the inputs in total costs of production for a particular company or firm differ significantly from the weights used by national income accountants in constructing the national GNP deflator. This aspect of the learning curve equation should therefore be viewed with considerable skepticism. With this strong caveat firmly in mind, however, let us now proceed with the final integration of the learning curve and the Cobb-Douglas cost function equations.

The major remaining differences between Eqs. (3.8) and (3.30) appear to be the fact that the dependent variable in the learning curve equation (3.8) is unit or average real cost, while in the modified Cobb-Douglas equation (3.30) the dependent variable is total real cost; further, an output variable appears as a right-hand side variable in the Cobb-Douglas equation (reflecting the effects of returns to scale), while such an output variable is omitted in the learning curve equation.

Since total and average costs are related by the identity $c_t \equiv C_t'/y_t$ (average real costs equal total real costs divided by the level of output in time period t), it follows that $\ln c_t = \ln C_t' - \ln y_t$. Subtracting $\ln y_t$ from both sides of Eq. (3.30) gives

$$\begin{aligned}\ln C_t' - \ln y_t &= \ln c_t \\ &= \ln k' + (\alpha_c/r) \cdot \ln n_t + ((1 - r)/r) \cdot \ln y_t + u_t\end{aligned} \tag{3.31}$$

Notice that the dependent variables in Eqs. (3.8) and (3.31) are now identical and that the only remaining difference in these two equations is that $\ln y_t$ appears as a right-hand variable in the Cobb-Douglas cost function equation (3.31) but is not present in the learning curve equation (3.8).

How should one interpret this current output variable in the modified Cobb-Douglas cost equation (3.31)? If returns to scale were increasing (if $r > 1$), then the value of the parameter on the $\ln y_t$ variable (equal to $(1 - r)/r$) should be negative, indicating that, given the effects of experience, unit costs would fall with increases in current output. Similarly, if returns to scale were decreasing ($r < 1$), then the value of this parameter would be positive, implying that, given the effects of experience, unit costs would rise with increases in current output. Finally, if returns to scale were constant ($r = 1$), then the value of the $(1 - r)/r$ parameter would be zero, and the $\ln y_t$ term would drop out of the estimating equation (3.31).

This suggests the following. To obtain an estimating equation based on the Cobb-Douglas cost function but identical to that commonly used in the experience curve literature, one must also make an assumption concerning returns to scale. Specifically, if one makes the additional assumption that returns to scale are constant, that is, that $r = 1$, then $\ln y_t$ disappears completely from Eq. (3.31), leaving

$$\ln c_t = \ln k' + \alpha_c \cdot \ln n_t + u_t \tag{3.32}$$

an equation that is identical to the learning curve equation (3.8).[21]

The above discussion can be summarized as follows. To synthesize the estimating equations based on Cobb-Douglas cost functions with those on the effects of learning curves, one must make two assumptions: First, it must be assumed that the effects of input price changes on costs of production can be accurately measured by using a GNP deflator; this assumption is stated explicitly in Eq. (3.27). Second, one must also assume that returns to scale are constant, that is, that $r = 1$.

While each of these assumptions is subject to serious question, the second assumption involving returns to scale is of particular interest to us here. In particular, note that if returns to scale are not constant, then instead of estimating Eq. (3.32), one should estimate Eq. (3.31):

$$\ln c_t = \ln k' + (\alpha_c/r) \cdot \ln n_t + (1 - r)/r \cdot \ln y_t + u_t$$

which can be conveniently rewritten as

$$\ln c_t = \beta_0 + \beta_1 \cdot \ln n_t + \beta_2 \cdot \ln y_t + u_t \tag{3.33}$$

where

$$\beta_0 \equiv \ln k', \qquad \beta_1 \equiv \alpha_c/r, \qquad \text{and} \qquad \beta_2 \equiv (1 - r)/r \tag{3.34}$$

Because the learning curve equation (3.32) is based on the assumption of constant returns to scale, in empirical work it may be of interest to test whether such a restriction is in fact supported by the data. Such a test is relatively straightforward, since by Eq. (3.34), $\beta_2 \equiv (1 - r)/r$. Specifically, one could simply estimate Eq. (3.33) by least squares regression methods and then test the null hypothesis of constant returns to scale ($r = 1$) against the alternative hypothesis of nonconstant returns to scale ($r \neq 1$) by employing a t-test and assessing whether, at a predetermined reasonable level of significance, the estimate of β_2 is statistically different from zero. If this hypothesis is rejected, then a key assumption underlying the most commonly used learning curve equation is invalid, and an equation such as Eq. (3.33) should be employed rather than Eq. (3.32). On the other hand, if the null hypothesis that $\beta_2 = 0$ is not rejected, then the constant returns to scale assumption underlying the learning curve equation is empirically validated.

Note also that if one estimates Eq. (3.33) by linear multiple regression techniques, one can employ Eq. (3.34) to recover indirectly an estimate of the learning curve elasticity parameter α_c and the returns-to-scale parameter r based on the direct estimates of β_1 and β_2. Specifically,

$$r = 1/(1 + \beta_2) \qquad \text{and} \qquad \alpha_c = \beta_1 \cdot r = \beta_1/(1 + \beta_2) \tag{3.35}$$

Unfortunately, since the estimates of the indirectly estimated parameters r and α_c involve nonlinear transformations of the directly estimated β_1 and β_2 parameters, one cannot in general directly employ the estimated standard errors of β_1 and β_2 to compute confidence intervals for r and α_c.[22]

3.5 ECONOMETRIC ISSUES

Having derived and synthesized estimating equations based on the learning curve and the Cobb-Douglas function, we now turn attention to important econometric issues, beginning with measurement issues and an examination of the bias effects of incorrectly omitting an explanatory variable.

3.5.1 Measurement Issues

A number of important measurement issues arise in implementing empirically the learning curve model. Here we briefly mention two important issues.[23] First, according to the learning curve framework, deflated unit costs should be the dependent variable. Since unit costs are typically calculated in current year dollars, to compute real (inflation adjusted) costs, one must deflate the cost data using some type of deflator. In many studies a GNP or CPI deflator is employed. Montgomery and Day [1985, p. 215] argue that an overall deflator such as the GNP deflator is preferable to an industry-specific output deflator, since if the latter is used, the learning curve effect may be "washed out" owing to the price deflator already capturing a substantial portion of the learning-induced productivity gains in that particular industry. Note also that the unit cost series should include all costs—labor, capital, energy, materials, and so on. Some learning curve studies focus only on labor costs and therefore are not comparable with studies using more comprehensive input cost measures unless labor and other input costs change at the same rate over time.

Second, since cost data are often difficult to obtain and, even if available, may be proprietary, a substantial number of empirical learning curve studies have substituted the deflated unit cost variable with a real price variable and then regressed the logarithm of real price on a constant term and the logarithm of cumulative production. This procedure introduces a major complication and makes separate identification of the learning curve effect very difficult if not impossible.

To see this, consider two firms with identical learning curve experiences. Assume one firm adopted a penetration pricing strategy in which the initial price was very low, thereby increasing demand, market share, and production, while the other firm adopted a "cream-skimming" pricing strategy in which the initial price was very high and was lowered only gradually. If one regressed price on cumulative production for these two firms, one would obtain very different estimates of the learning curve elasticity, even though the potential learning curve effects were identical. Had unit cost data been employed instead, however, this discrepancy would not have occurred. This demonstrates that it is preferable to employ unit cost rather than price data to estimate learning curve relationships, since unlike the case with unit cost, use of price data confounds the effects of pricing strategy with learning curves.

3.5.2 Omitted Variable Bias

Recall from Eq. (3.33) that in the Cobb-Douglas cost function equation with nonconstant returns to scale, the equation to be estimated has as right-hand variables a constant term, the logarithm of cumulative previous production $\ln n_t$, the logarithm of current output $\ln y_t$, and a disturbance term u_t:[24]

$$\ln c_t = \beta_0 + \beta_1 \cdot \ln n_t + \beta_2 \cdot \ln y_t + u_t \tag{3.33}$$

On the other hand, the equation most commonly estimated in the learning curve literature is Eq. (3.8), which can be rewritten as

$$\ln c_t = \alpha_0 + \alpha_1 \cdot \ln n_t + \omega_t \tag{3.36}$$

where $\alpha_0 \equiv \ln c_1$, $\alpha_1 \equiv \alpha_c$, and ω_t is a random disturbance term.

Suppose that one incorrectly estimated Eq. (3.36) when the parameters of Eq. (3.33) should have been estimated instead. Will the least squares estimate of α_1 be larger, equal to, or smaller than the least squares estimate of β_1? What bias results from incorrectly omitting $\ln y_t$ from the learning curve equation (3.36), and on what will the magnitude of the bias depend? These issues all concern the *omitted variable bias* and are very important. In our context, omitted variable bias issues involve (1) examining whether the learning curve elasticity is underestimated or overestimated when returns to scale are nonconstant, that is, when $\ln y_t$ is incorrectly omitted from Eq. (3.36), and (2) determining on what the magnitude of the underestimation or overestimation depends.

To analyze these omitted variable bias issues, it will be convenient to introduce a new equation, often called an auxiliary regression equation, in which the omitted right-hand variable is related to the included right-hand variable and a stochastic disturbance term ϵ_t,

$$\ln y_t = \delta_0 + \delta_1 \cdot \ln n_t + \epsilon_t \tag{3.37}$$

Now label the least-squares estimates of the α's, β's, and δ's in Eqs. (3.33), (3.36), and (3.37) as a's, b's, and d's, respectively. The omitted variable bias questions can then be stated simply as follows: What is the relationship between a_1 (the least squares estimate of α_1 in Eq. (3.36)) and b_1 (the least squares estimate of β_1 in Eq. (3.33))? On what does the difference between a_1 and b_1 depend?

Since the mathematics underlying this question are presented in a number of econometric theory textbooks,[25] here we simply note that the relationship between a_1 and b_1 can be shown to be as follows:

$$a_1 = b_1 + d_1 b_2 \quad \text{or} \quad a_1 - b_1 = d_1 b_2 \tag{3.38}$$

The *bias* from omitting ln y_t from Eq. (3.36) is simply equal to $a_1 - b_1$, which from Eq. (3.38) can be seen to equal $d_1 b_2$. This omitted variable bias will therefore be zero only if at least one of the following two conditions is satisfied:

1. $d_1 = 0$, that is, the logarithms of current output and cumulative previous production in Eq. (3.37) are uncorrelated;
2. $b_2 = 0$, that is, current average cost in Eq. (3.33) does not depend on current production. Alternatively, by Eq. (3.35), returns to scale are constant.

If neither of these two conditions is satisfied, then an omitted variable bias will result, implying that if one estimated the learning curve elasticity parameter using Eq. (3.36) and incorrectly omitting ln y_t, one would obtain a biased estimate of the true learning curve parameter. But will the bias be positive or negative, that is, will the learning curve elasticity be underestimated or overestimated?

To calculate the sign of the bias, recall from Eq. (3.38) that

$$a_1 - b_1 = d_1 \cdot b_2$$

Therefore the sign of the bias depends on the sign of the product of d_1 and b_2. Since cumulative production is the sum over time of current production, n_t and y_t are positively correlated, and d_1 will be positive. On the other hand, whether b_2 is positive, zero, or negative depends on whether returns to scale are decreasing, constant, or increasing, that is, whether $r < 1$, $r = 1$, or $r > 1$.[26] With d_1 positive this therefore implies that

- $a_1 - b_1 > 0$ if $r < 1$ (there are decreasing returns to scale),
- $a_1 - b_1 = 0$ if $r = 1$ (there are constant returns to scale), and
- $a_1 - b_1 < 0$ if $r > 1$ (there are increasing returns to scale).

As was noted in the introduction, in many cases, one might expect returns to scale to be increasing, so it is plausible to expect that in many cases the last of the above three cases will occur. Further, since a_1 and b_1 are typically negative, $a_1 - b_1 < 0$ corresponds with b_1 being smaller in absolute value than a_1. In such a case, estimation of the simple learning curve equation (3.36) yields a larger estimate of the learning curve elasticity (in absolute value) than if one includes the current output variable as in Eq. (3.33); hence in this case the learning curve elasticity is overestimated in absolute value.

The interpretation of this result is as follows: By incorrectly omitting the current output variable, one attributes to the learning curve elasticity what in fact is due in part to the effects of returns to scale. In the learning curve context, omitted variable bias could be very important.

Fortunately, in the exercises at the end of this chapter you will have an opportunity to verify these numerical relationships among least squares estimates and to assess the magnitude of the omitted variable bias.

3.5.3 Individual and Joint Hypothesis Tests

A second set of econometric issues that merits attention here involves hypothesis testing. The computer output of typical regression program software includes *t*-statistics on each of the estimated coefficients, as well as an equation *F*-statistic. We now examine hypothesis testing in the context of the integrated Cobb-Douglas production–learning curve model, where it is assumed that the disturbance term appended to Eq. (3.33) is independently and identically normally distributed with mean zero and constant variance.

As noted earlier, to test the null hypothesis of constant returns to scale against the alternative hypothesis of nonconstant returns, all one need do is estimate Eq. (3.33) by least squares and then perform a *t*-test on β_2; the null hypothesis is $\beta_2 = 0$, and the alternative hypothesis is $\beta_2 \neq 0$.

Similarly, one could test the null hypothesis that the learning curve effect is zero. Having estimated Eq. (3.33) by least squares, this hypothesis test could also be performed by using a *t*-test; the null hypothesis is $\beta_1 = 0$, while the alternative hypothesis is $\beta_1 \neq 0$.

Suppose, however, that one wanted to test the above two hypotheses simultaneously. In this case the joint null hypothesis that both the learning curve elasticity is zero and returns to scale are constant would correspond with the joint null hypothesis that $\beta_1 = \beta_2 = 0$; the alternative hypothesis would of course be that $\beta_1 \neq 0, \beta_2 \neq 0$. Note that under the joint null hypothesis, Eq. (3.33) reduces to an equation in which real unit cost is simply regressed on a constant term; no other regressors remain.

To perform such a joint hypothesis test, however, one should employ an *F*-statistic rather than individual *t*-statistics. The reason is that the individual *t*-tests are not, in general, independent; by contrast, the calculation underlying the *F*-statistic properly accounts for the dependence among the individual hypothesis tests. In this particular case the dependence between the individual *t*-tests depends primarily on the covariance between the least squares estimates b_1 and b_2.

Because the *F*-test statistic properly accounts for dependence between the two individual t-tests, an inference based on the F-statistic might not necessarily agree with that based on the two t-tests. Specifically, any of the following six cases is possible:

1. reject the joint null on the basis of the F-statistic, but do not reject each separate null on the basis of the individual t-tests;
2. reject the joint null on the basis of the F-statistic, reject one individual hypothesis on the basis of a t-test, and do not reject other individual hypothesis on the basis of a t-test;
3. reject the joint null on the basis of the F-statistic, and reject each separate null on the basis of individual t-tests;
4. do not reject the joint null on the basis of the F-statistic, and do not reject each separate null on the basis of individual t-tests;
5. do not reject the joint null on the basis of the F-statistic, reject one individual hypothesis on the basis of a t-test, and do not reject other individual hypothesis on the basis of a t-test;
6. do not reject the joint null on the basis of the F-statistic, but reject each separate null on the basis of individual t-tests.

Although they are possible, in practice, cases 1 and 6 occur only very rarely. As we shall see with the learning curve exercises in which, on the basis of individual t-tests, the estimated learning curve elasticity is statistically significant but returns to scale are only marginally different from unity, cases 2 and 3 are relatively common, particularly with time series data.

3.5.4 Brief Overview of Empirical Findings on Returns to Scale and Learning Curves

We now briefly summarize the principal empirical findings on returns to scale and on learning curve elasticities. We begin with learning curves.

Over the years, hundreds of studies, many of them involving the Boston Consulting Group, have focused on estimating parameters of the learning or experience curves. Obviously, such a large number of studies cannot be summarized here. Rather, what we do is to comment on a recent survey by Pankaj Ghemawat [1985], published in the *Harvard Business Review*, in which 97 academic studies from the learning and experience curve literature are reviewed. The results of this summary are presented in Table 3.1.

In Ghemawat's survey, the 97 studies are classified according to the size of the learning or experience curve slope. Recall from our earlier discussion that the relationship between the slope of the learning curve d and the size of the learning curve elasticity α_c is, from Eq. (3.9),

$$d = 2^{\alpha_c}$$

Hence for each experience curve slope range presented in Ghemawat's study, we first employ the above relationship and calculate the corresponding range for the learning curve elasticity.

Table 3.1 Summary of Variation in Learning Curve Elasticity Estimates by Product

Learning Curve Elasticity (in Absolute Value)	Learning Curve Slope	Number of Products
0.63–0.74	0.60–0.64	3
0.52–0.62	0.65–0.69	3
0.42–0.51	0.70–0.74	10
0.33–0.41	0.75–0.79	23
0.25–0.32	0.80–0.84	30
0.16–0.24	0.85–0.89	26
0.08–0.15	0.90–0.94	6
0.01–0.07	0.95–0.99	1

Average learning curve slope: 0.85
Total number of products surveyed: 97

Source: Data from Pankaj Ghemawat, "Building Strategy on the Experience Curve," *Harvard Business Review*, March/April 1985, Exhibit II, p. 146.

As can be seen in Table 3.1, the largest number of products have learning curve elasticities in the range −0.25 to −0.32, with corresponding learning curve slopes of 0.80 to 0.84; this range covers approximately 30% of the products and studies examined. The vast majority of products (79 of the 97 examined) fall in the learning curve elasticity range of about −0.16 to −0.41, which corresponds with learning curve slopes ranging from 0.75 to 0.89. Hence while there is considerable variation among products in the size of the learning curve elasticities and slopes, it is quite unusual to obtain learning curve elasticity estimates smaller than 0.15 or larger than 0.41 (in absolute value).

Ghemawat notes in his survey that, in general, manufacturing activities are associated with larger learning curve elasticities than those from the raw materials purchasing, marketing, sales, or distribution companies. Moreover, Ghemawat finds a pattern to the learning curve elasticities, stating (p. 144) that "manufacturing costs decline particularly steeply in industries with standardized product ranges and complex, labor-intensive production processes such as the airframe assembly or machine tool businesses."

It might also be noted here that, like other experience and learning curve analysts, Ghemawat is rather cautious about interpreting these experience curves; in particular, he does not rule out the possibility that their magnitude may also reflect the presence of nonconstant returns to scale.[27] Recall that the advantage of the regression equation such as Eq. (3.33) is precisely that it permits separate estimation and identification of learning curve and returns-to-scale effects.

We now move on to a brief discussion of empirical findings on returns to scale. The first important point is that measures of returns to scale can be expected to vary as one moves from the plant level to the company and then to the industry as a whole. In particular, even if there are increasing returns to scale at the plant level, companies can build additional plants such that doubling the number of plants doubles the output at any given level of cost. This may therefore show up at the company level as constant returns to scale. Similar arguments suggest that returns to scale may be constant at the industry level but could be increasing at the company level.

Since the number of industries is very large and the number of firms or companies is even larger, there is no compact way in which the voluminous empirical literature on returns to scale can be summarized. Given this, we focus here on but one particular industry in which the presence of alleged increasing returns to scale has brought about considerable government regulation, namely, the electric utility industry.

A number of studies have attempted to measure returns to scale in the generation of electricity over the last three decades; these studies have been summarized and critiqued by Thomas G. Cowing and V. Kerry Smith [1978]. The classic econometric study of returns to scale in the electric utility industry is by Marc Nerlove [1963] and is based on the Cobb-Douglas cost function examined earlier in this chapter. An attractive feature of Nerlove's study is that it includes a data appendix with all data listed. In the hands-on exercises at the end of this chapter you will have the opportunity to work with Nerlove's original data, as well as data of more recent vintage, to estimate returns to scale and attempt to replicate classic findings.

Cowing and Smith summarize a number of econometric studies, including those based on production functions, input demand models, cost functions, and profit functions. Evidence of increasing returns to scale is widespread, particularly in the era preceding the 1970s in the United States. Nerlove, for example, used 1955 data and obtained returns to scale estimates of 0.97 to a rather large 1.91; not surprisingly, he also found that returns to scale tended to fall as the size of the electric utility company increased. For the very largest utilities, returns to scale were approximately constant. Returns to scale estimates ranging from 1.1 to 1.2 are common and typical in the econometric studies surveyed by Cowing and Smith.

A particularly interesting study is that by Laurits R. Christensen and William H. Greene [1976], who used Nerlove's original 1955 data base and then updated it to 1970. Further, Christensen and Greene employed a translog cost function, a mathematical formulation that is considerably more general than the Cobb-Douglas form considered in this chapter. One attractive feature of the translog form is that it allows returns to scale to vary, depending on input prices and on the level of output.[28] Christensen and Greene [1976, p. 655] summarized their principal findings based on the translog function as follows:

> We find that in 1955 there were significant scale economies available to nearly all firms. By 1970, however, the bulk of U.S. electricity generation was by firms operating in the essentially flat area of the average cost curve. We conclude that a small number of extremely large firms are not required

MARC NERLOVE

Estimating Returns to Scale

Marc Nerlove's classic article on estimating returns to scale in the supply of electricity was not written in the traditional research ambience of academia or the private sector. Rather, it was begun while Nerlove was serving in the U.S. Army from 1957 to 1959. Nerlove undertook research on economic factors affecting the supply of electricity, since the adequacy of national energy supplies was clearly an issue of strategic importance. Although most of the research work was done while he was in the Army, Nerlove completed his article at the University of Minnesota in 1960. A major innovation in Nerlove's model of electricity supply was that it was firmly based on the theory of production; in fact, it is the first empirical application using the dual cost function approach. As is discussed in this chapter, a principal econometric finding in Nerlove's study was that while scale economies were substantial, they tended to decline with firm size.

Marc Nerlove was born in Chicago in 1933. At the age of 15 he enrolled as an undergraduate at the University of Chicago, majoring in mathematics. Graduating with honors at age 18, he became interested in economics and decided to pursue graduate studies at the Johns Hopkins University. His 1954 M.A. thesis focused on the demand for meat in the United States, and his 1956 Ph.D. dissertation dealt with estimating supply elasticities for corn, cotton, and wheat. With his Ph.D. degree in hand, Nerlove took a position in 1956 as an analytical statistician for the Agricultural Marketing Service of the U.S. Department of Agriculture. In 1959, after spending two years in the U.S. Army, he initiated an academic career at the University of Minnesota. Since then, Nerlove has held academic appointments at Stanford, Yale, Chicago, Northwestern, and, since 1982, the University of Pennsylvania, where he is now University Professor of Economics and Research Fellow at the International Food Policy Research Institute.

Nerlove's research has ranged widely, from the analysis of nonstatic expectations, distributed lags, the pooling of cross-sectional and time series data, time series approaches, and univariate and multivariate logit models to applications in agriculture, macroeconometric modeling, population economics, advertising, income distribution, and inventory behavior. He has been elected a Fellow of the Econometric Society, served as its President in 1981, is a Fellow of the American Statistical Association and the American Academy of Arts and Sciences, and is an elected Member of the National Academy of Sciences. Nerlove's thesis and articles have won publication awards from the American Farm Economics Association, and his 1958 Agricultural Handbook No. 141 from the U.S. Department of Agriculture, *Distributed Lags and Demand Analysis*, has been cited for an enduring publication commendation.

for efficient production and that policies designed to promote competition in electric power generation cannot be faulted in terms of sacrificing economies of scale.

In summary, the econometric literature on estimated returns to scale in the electric utility industry in the United States appears to suggest that substantial economies of scale have been available, that such scale economies may have been largely exploited by the early 1970s, and that today the bulk of electricity generation comes from firms generating electricity at the bottom of their average cost curves.

This completes our discussion of costs, scale economies, and learning curves. It is now time to move on and engage you in hands-on applications.

3.6 HANDS ON WITH COSTS, LEARNING CURVES, AND SCALE ECONOMIES

The purpose of the following exercises is to enable you to gain an empirical understanding of cost curves, scale economies, and learning curves, using a variety of simple and multiple regression techniques. Exercises 1, 2, and 3 are particularly useful. In Exercise 1 you examine typical learning curve data on costs and cumulative output and use the simple regression procedure to estimate a learning curve elasticity. Then in Exercise 2 you assess the possible omitted variable bias on learning curve elasticity estimates resulting from incorrectly assuming that returns to scale are constant. In this exercise you employ both simple and multiple regression procedures, and you perform a number of single and joint hypothesis tests. To help you better understand relationships among simple and multiple regressions, in Exercise 3 you compare the R^2 goodness-of-fit measure from various regressions and find that in one very strange data set (appropriately called WEIRD) you obtain a striking and memorable result.

In Exercise 4 you examine and attempt to replicate the returns-to-scale estimates in the classic study of the U.S. electric utility industry by Marc Nerlove. You also construct confidence intervals and diagnose the least squares residuals. Then in Exercise 5 you employ information from the residual diagnostics and, following Nerlove, estimate returns to scale using a number of alternative equation specifications. You also test for the empirical validity of the constant returns to scale assumption. In Exercise 6 you compare returns-to-scale estimates from Nerlove's 1955 data with the Christensen-Greene data for 1970, and you evaluate the Christensen-Greene finding that by 1970 the bulk of U.S. electricity generation was being produced by firms operating on relatively flat portions of their average cost curves.

In the next two exercises you focus on stochastic specification and information gained from examining least squares residuals. Specifically, in Exercise 7 you examine the effects of first-order autocorrelation on estimates of the learning curve elasticity and its statistical significance. In Exercise 8 you employ the Durbin-Watson test statistic (usually applied in a time series context) with Nerlove's cross-sectional data to help you in uncovering model misspecification.

The issue of whether returns to scale are identical for firms of varying size can also be examined by estimating subsets of the entire data set separately and then testing whether parameters are equal across subsets. In Exercise 9 you perform such a procedure, called the Chow test, using both the Nerlove 1955 data and the Christensen-Greene 1970 data sets for electric utilities.

Finally, in Exercise 10 you employ an estimated learning curve model to forecast unit costs in the future, after further learning will have occurred. You will also estimate the forecast error variance and will uncover some disconcerting implications of using small data sets to make such forecasts.

••••••••••

In the data diskette provided, you will find a subdirectory called CHAP3.DAT, having five data files. In these data files a number of data series are provided, including data from the Nerlove returns-to-scale study in the electricity industry on 145 electric utility companies in 1955 (named NERLOV), as well as updated data from Laurits R. Christensen and William H. Greene for 1970 on 99 electric utility companies (called UPDATE). Data files on unit costs and production in the manufacture of polyethylene (POLY) and titanium dioxide (TIO2) are also found in the CHAP3.DAT subdirectory. Finally, there is a rather strange data set in this file called WEIRD.

Note: Remember that before you can use the data diskette in this exercise, you must properly format the data files. For further information, refer back to Chapter 1, Section 1.3. MAKE SURE THAT ALL DATA FILES TO BE USED BELOW ARE PROPERLY FORMATTED.

At numerous times in the following exercises you will be asked to test an hypothesis using a "reasonable level of significance." Since what is "reasonable" is to some extent discretionary, you are asked to follow the convention of stating precisely what percent significance level you use to test hypotheses; in that way, others with different preferences can still draw their own inferences. Alternatively, you may wish to state the level of significance at which the parameter estimate is significantly different from zero or at which the null hypothesis is rejected.

EXERCISES

EXERCISE 1: Estimating Parameters of a Learning Curve

The purpose of this exercise is to have you estimate and interpret parameters of a learning curve. In this exercise you have a choice of using one of two data files, both of which are in your data diskette subdirectory CHAP3.DAT. One file, called POLY, contains annual data on deflated unit costs (UCOSTP), current production (PRODP), and cumulative production to year $t - 1$ (CUMP) for a typical manufacturer of polyethylene over the 13-year period from 1960 to 1972. The second file, called TIO2, contains annual data for the DuPont Corporation in its production of titanium dioxide from 1955 to 1970. The variables in this data file include *undeflated* unit costs (UCOSTT), current production (PRODT), cumulative production to year $t - 1$ (CUMT), and a GNP-type deflator (DEFL).[29] The YEAR variable is called YEARP in the POLY file and YEART in the TIO2 file. Notice that both files contain data on *costs* and production, which are typically more difficult to obtain than data on *prices* and production.

Choose one of these two data files, and then perform steps (a) and (b). *Important note:* If you are using the TIO2 data file, you will first need to deflate the UCOSTT data by dividing UCOSTT by DEFL.

(a) Take the logarithm of cumulative production up to time period $t - 1$, and name this variable LNCP. Do the same for unit cost (LNUC) and current output (LNY). Plot unit cost against cumulative production, and then plot LNUC against LNCP. Comment on the two plots and what they might imply for the mathematical form of the learning curve relationship.

(b) Using least squares, estimate the parameters of the simple learning curve model (3.8) in which LNUC is regressed on a constant and on LNCP. Interpret your estimate of the learning curve elasticity. Is this estimate reasonable? What is the corresponding slope of the learning curve? Using a reasonable level of significance, construct a confidence interval for your estimated learning curve elasticity, and then test the null hypothesis that the learning curve elasticity is zero against the alternative hypothesis that it is not equal to zero.

EXERCISE 2: Testing the Simple Learning Curve Specification

In this exercise you test the simple learning curve specification as a special case of the more general Cobb-Douglas cost function. You also consider the effects of incorrectly omitting a right-hand variable.

As in Exercise 1, in this exercise you have a choice of using one of two data files, both of which are in your data diskette subdirectory CHAP3.DAT. One file, called POLY, contains annual data on deflated unit costs (UCOSTP), current production (PRODP), and cumulative production to year $t - 1$ (CUMP) for a typical manufacturer of polyethylene over the 13-year period from 1960 to 1972. The second file, called TIO2, contains annual data for the DuPont Corporation in its production of titanium dioxide from 1955 to 1970 on undeflated unit costs (UCOSTT), current production (PRODT), cumulative production to year $t - 1$ (CUMT), and a GNP-type deflator (DEFL). The YEAR variable is called YEARP in the POLY file and YEART in the TIO2 file.

Choose one of these two data files, and then perform steps (a) through (d). *Important note:* If you are using the TIO2 data file, you will first need to deflate the UCOSTT data by dividing UCOSTT by DEFL.

(a) Just as in Exercise 1, take logarithms of cumulative production up to time period $t - 1$ (call it LNCP), unit cost (LNUC), and current output (LNY). Using ordinary least squares, now estimate the parameters of a *multiple* regression model based on Eq. (3.33) in which LNUC is regressed on an intercept, LNCP, and LNY. Using a reasonable level of significance, test the null hypothesis that because technology is characterized by constant returns to scale, the coefficient on LNY in this multiple regression equals zero. What is the point estimate of returns to scale with this model and data?

(b) Suppose that you instead estimated the simple learning curve specification (3.36) with LNY omitted as a right-hand variable. To evaluate the bias consequences on the learning curve elasticity estimate of incorrectly omitting LNY, run the simple regression (3.36) as well as the auxiliary regression (3.37). Verify numerically that the analytical relationship between the two estimates of the learning curve elasticity is in fact expressed by Eq. (3.38). In this particular case, why is the bias large or small?

(c) On the basis of your results from part (b), compare the R^2 from the simple regression equation (3.36) with that from the multiple regression equation (3.33). Why is the latter R^2 larger? Is this always true? Why?

(d) Using a reasonable level of significance, test the joint null hypothesis that both slope coefficients in the regression equation (3.33) of part (a) are simultaneously equal to zero. Perform this test using the analysis-of-variance approach based on changes in the sum of squared residuals and on the basis of the R^2 approach. Compare the inference based on the two individual t-tests with that based on the joint F-test. Are these results mutually consistent? Why or why not?

EXERCISE 3: R^2 in Simple and Multiple Regressions: A Surprise

The purpose of this exercise is to provide you with a dramatic example of possible relationships among R^2 measures in simple and multiple regressions. The common experience of practitioners is that the R^2 from a multiple regression of Y on X1 and X2 is less than the sum of the R^2 from the two simple regressions, Y on X1 and Y on X2. As you will see in this exercise, however, this need not always be the case.

In your data subdirectory CHAP3.DAT is a data file called WEIRD. It contains 15 observations on three variables: Y, X1, and X2.[30]

(a) Print the data series on Y, X1, and X2, and compute the simple correlations among these three variables. Does anything look particularly strange? Why or why not?

(b) Comment on why, especially with time series data, R^2 from a multiple regression of Y on a constant and K regressors is typically less than the sum of the R^2 from K simple regressions of Y on a constant and X_k, $k = 1, \ldots, K$.

(c) Now do an ordinary least squares regression of Y on a constant and X1. Then do an ordinary least squares regression of Y on a constant and X2. Are there any striking results on t-statistics in these two regressions? Compute the sum of the R^2 measures from these two regressions.

(d) Next do a multiple regression, using ordinary least squares, of Y on a constant, X1 and X2. Are there any striking results on t-statistics in this regression? What is the R^2 from this multiple regression? Compare this R^2 to the sum of the R^2 from the two regressions from part (c). Why is this result rather surprising? To what do you attribute it?

EXERCISE 4: Replicating Nerlove's Classic Results on Scale Economies

The purpose of this exercise is to engage you in attempting to replicate some of the principal returns-to-scale results reported by Nerlove in his classic 1955 article. The equation estimated by Nerlove is Eq. (3.20). In the data file NERLOV, data are provided on total costs (COSTS) in millions of dollars, output (KWH) in billions of kilowatt hours, and prices of labor (PL), fuels (PF), and capital (PK) for 145 electric utility companies in 1955. There are 145 observations, and the observations are ordered in size, observation 1 being the smallest company and observation 145 the largest.

(a) Using the data transformation facilities of your computer software, generate the variables required to estimate parameters of Eq. (3.20) by least squares. In particular, for each of the 145 companies, form the variables LNCP3 (≡ ln (COSTS/PF)), LNP13 (≡ ln (PL/PF)), LNP23 (≡ ln (PK/PF)), and LNKWH (≡ ln (KWH)). Print the entire data series for LNKWH, and verify that the observations are ordered by size of output, that is, that the first observation is the smallest output company, whereas the last observation has the largest output.[31]

(b) Given the data for all 145 firms from (a), estimate Eq. (3.20) by least squares, where your constructed variable LNCP3 ≡ ln C^*, LNKWH ≡ ln y, LNP13 ≡ ln p_1^*, and LNP23 ≡ ln p_2^*. Nerlove [1963, p. 176] reports parameter estimates for β_y, β_1, and β_2 as 0.721, 0.562, and −0.003, respectively, with standard errors of 0.175, 0.198, and 0.192, respectively, and an R^2 of 0.931. Can you replicate Nerlove's results? (*Note:* You will not be able to replicate Nerlove's results precisely. One reason for this is that he used common rather than natural logarithms; however, this should affect only the estimated intercept term. According to Nerlove, the data set published with his article is apparently an earlier one that includes errors, while a revised data set was used in the estimation. This final data set has never been found.)

(c) Using the estimates you obtained in part (b) and a reasonable level of significance, construct a confidence interval for β_y. Is the null hypothesis that $\beta_y = 1$ rejected? What does this imply concerning a test of the null hypothesis that returns to scale are constant? Using line 5 of Eqs. (3.21), compute the point estimate of returns to scale based on your estimate of β_y. Are estimated returns to scale increasing, constant, or decreasing? Are economies of scale positive, zero, or negative?

(d) According to Eq. (3.12), demands for each factor of production will be positive only if α_i is positive, $i = 1, 2, 3$. What is the implied estimate of α_2 from part (c)? Is it significantly different from zero? Why do you think Nerlove was unsatisfied with this estimate of α_2?

(e) Compute and plot the residuals from estimated regression equation (3.20). Nerlove noticed that if the residuals were plotted against the log of output, the pattern was U-shaped, residuals at small levels of output being positive, those at medium levels of output being negative, and those at larger levels of output again becoming positive. Do you find the same U-shaped pattern? How might this pattern of residuals be interpreted? Finally, what is the sample correlation of residuals with LNKWH across the entire sample? Why is this the case?

EXERCISE 5: Assessing Alternative Returns-to-Scale Specifications

Because of the pattern of residuals noted by Nerlove (see Exercise 4, particularly part (e)), Nerlove hypothesized that estimated returns to scale varied with the level of output. In this exercise you evaluate Nerlove's conjecture and assess alternative specifications that relax the assumptions implicit in Eq. (3.20). To facilitate grouping the data in this exercise, in the data file NERLOV in the CHAP3 subdirectory is a variable named ORDER; the first 29 values of this variable are numbered 101 to 129, the second set of 29 values are 201 to 229, and so forth, the final 29 values of the variable ORDER taking on the values 501 to 529.

(a) Following Nerlove, divide the sample of 145 firms into five subsamples, each having 29 firms. Recall that since the data are ordered by level of output, the first 29 observations will have the smallest output levels, whereas the last 29 observations will have the largest output levels. Then using least squares regression techniques, estimate parameters of Eq. (3.20) for each of these subsamples. Nerlove [1963, p. 176] reports the following results (estimated standard errors are in parentheses):

	Parameter Estimated			
	β_y	β_1	β_2	R^2
Subsample I	0.398	0.641	−0.093	0.512
	(0.079)	(0.691)	(0.669)	
Subsample II	0.668	0.105	0.364	0.635
	(0.116)	(0.275)	(0.277)	
Subsample III	0.931	0.408	0.249	0.571
	(0.198)	(0.199)	(0.189)	
Subsample IV	0.915	0.472	0.133	0.871
	(0.108)	(0.174)	(0.157)	
Subsample V	1.045	0.604	−0.295	0.920
	(0.065)	(0.197)	(0.175)	

How well can you replicate Nerlove's reported results? To what might you attribute any discrepancies? (*Note:* See the brief discussion at the end of part (b) of Exercise 4.)

(b) On the basis of your parameter estimates of β_y in part (a), compute the point estimates of returns to scale in each of the five subsamples. What is the general pattern of estimated scale economies as the level of output increases? How might this pattern be interpreted? Does this suggest an alternative specification?

(c) Now construct data variables such that a regression equation (3.20) will be estimated, except that while each of the five subsamples has common estimated "slope" coefficients for β_1 and β_2, each of the five subsamples has a different intercept term and a different estimate of β_y. Given the results in part (b), why might such a specification be plausible? Estimate this expanded model, and assess your success in replicating Nerlove, who reported the five subsample estimates of β_y as being 0.394 (0.055),

0.651 (0.189), 0.877 (0.376), 0.908 (0.354), and 1.062 (0.169), respectively, where numbers in parentheses are standard errors. The common estimates of β_1 and β_2 reported by Nerlove are 0.435 (0.207) and 0.100 (0.196), respectively. Nerlove's reported R^2 was 0.950.

(d) For each of the five subsample estimates of β_y in part (c), compute the implied estimate of returns to scale. What is the general pattern of estimated scale economies as the level of output increases?

(e) How would you compare estimates in part (c) versus those in part (a)? In particular, since part (a) estimates constitute a special case of part (c), using an F-test and a reasonable level of significance, formulate and test the restrictions implicit in part (a) against the alternative hypothesis in part (c). Is the null hypothesis rejected or not rejected? Comment on your results.

(f) To exploit the fact that estimated returns to scale seemed to decline with the level of output in a nonlinear fashion, Nerlove formulated and estimated a slight generalization of Eq. (3.20) in which the variable $(\ln y)^2$ was added as a regressor; call the corresponding coefficient β_{yy}. Using the full sample of 145 observations, estimate the equation

$$\ln C^* = \beta_0 + \beta_y \cdot \ln y + \beta_{yy} \cdot (\ln y)^2 + \beta_1 \cdot \ln p_1^* + \beta_2 \cdot \ln p_2^*$$

by least squares. How well can you replicate Nerlove's reported results, which he reported as 0.151 (0.062), 0.117 (0.012), 0.498 (0.161), and 0.062 (0.151) for β_y, β_{yy}, β_1, and β_2, respectively, and an R^2 of 0.952? Now, using a reasonable level of significance, test the joint null hypothesis that returns to scale are constant, that is, that $\beta_y = 1$, $\beta_{yy} = 0$, against the null hypothesis that returns to scale are nonconstant, that is, that $\beta_y \neq 1$, $\beta_{yy} \neq 0$. How does inference based on the joint F-test compare with that based on the individual t-tests? Finally, since returns to scale in the above expanded model vary with the level of output and can be shown to equal $r = 1/(\beta_y + 2 \cdot \beta_{yy} \cdot \ln y)$, compute the implied range of returns-to-scale estimates using the median value of LNY in each of the five subsamples.

EXERCISE 6: Comparing Returns-to-Scale Estimates from 1955 with Updated 1970 Data

Nerlove's returns to scale results were based on 1955 data for 145 electric utility companies in the United States. These data have been updated to 1970 and have been used for estimation by Christensen and Greene [1976]. In this exercise you compare returns-to-scale estimates based on the 1955 and the 1970 data and then evaluate the Christensen-Greene finding that by 1970 the bulk of electricity generation in the United States came from firms operating very near the bottom of their average cost curves.

The 1970 data are presented in the CHAP3.DAT subdirectory data file called UPDATE. The 1970 data sample is smaller, consisting of 99 observations, and like the data in NERLOV, the observations are ordered by size of firm, as measured by kilowatt hour output. The variables in the UPDATE data file include the original Christensen-Greene observation number (OBSNO), total costs in millions of 1970 dollars (COST70), millions of kilowatt hours of output (KWH70), the price of labor (PL70), the rental price index for capital (PK70), and the price index for fuels (PF70). (Notice that the numbers "70" have been added to the COST, KWH, PL, PK, and PF variables to distinguish these 1970 updated data from the Nerlove 1955 data.)[32]

(a) Using the 1970 updated data for 99 firms, construct the appropriate variables needed to estimate Eq. (3.20) by least squares. In particular, for each of the 99 observations, generate the following variables: LNC70 ≡ ln (COST70/PF70), LNY70 ≡ ln (KWH70), LNP170 ≡ ln (PL70/PF70), and LNP270 ≡ ln (PK70/PF70), where your just-constructed LNC70 is the same as $\ln C^*$ in Eqs. (3.20) and (3.21), LNY70 is $\ln y$, LNP170 is $\ln p_1^*$, and LNP270 is $\ln p_2^*$. Compute the sample mean for KWH70, and compare it to the sample mean for KWH in Nerlove's 1955 data set, found in the data file NERLOV. On average, are firms generating larger amounts of electricity in 1970 than in 1955? What might you therefore expect in terms of returns-to-scale estimates for 1970 as compared to those for 1955? Why?

(b) Now estimate by least squares the parameters of the equation

$$\text{LNC70} = \beta_0 + \beta_y \cdot \text{LNY70} + \beta_1 \cdot \text{LNP170} + \beta_2 \cdot \text{LNP270} + \epsilon$$

and then construct a confidence interval for β_y, using a reasonable level of significance. Is the null hypothesis of constant returns to scale ($\beta_y = 1$) rejected? Using line 5 of Eqs. (3.21), calculate the implied estimate of returns to scale. Compare this result, based on the 1970 data, with that reported by Nerlove for his 1955 data (see Exercise 4, part (b), for a list of Nerlove's results). Are you surprised by these results? Why or why not?

(c) A slightly generalized version of Eq. (3.20) involves adding $(\text{LNY70})^2$ as a regressor. Such an equation,

$$\text{LNC70} = \beta_0 + \beta_y \cdot \text{LNY70} + \beta_{yy} \cdot (\text{LNY70})^2 + \beta_1 \cdot \text{LNP170} + \beta_2 \cdot \text{LNP270} + \epsilon$$

cannot be derived from the Cobb-Douglas production function (3.10) but has the advantage of permitting returns to scale to vary with the level of output. In particular, in the above equation, returns to scale can be shown to equal $r = 1/(\beta_y + 2 \cdot \beta_{yy} \cdot \ln y)$. Note also that the equation in part (b) of this exercise (analogous to Eq. (3.20) in the text) is a special case of the expanded equation here, being valid if and only if $\beta_{yy} = 0$. Using the 1970 data, estimate by least squares the parameters of the above expanded equation. Then, based on a reasonable level of significance, test the null hypothesis that returns to scale do not vary with the level of output, that is, test the null hypothesis that $\beta_{yy} = 0$ against the alternative hypothesis that $\beta_{yy} \neq 0$. Next test the joint null hypothesis that returns to scale are constant, that is, that $\beta_{yy} = 0$ and $\beta_y = 1$, against the alternative hypothesis that $\beta_{yy} \neq 0$, $\beta_y \neq 1$. Interpret these two different test results. Are they mutually consistent?

(d) Next, calculate the implied range of returns to scale by splitting the 1970 sample into five groups, ordered by size, where the first four groups consist of 20 firms each and the last group has only 19 firms. Estimate by least squares the parameters of the equation in part (b) separately for each of the five groups. For each group, compare the returns-to-scale estimates based on 1970 data with those reported by Nerlove and based on 1955 data, namely, 2.92, 2.24, 1.97, 1.84, and 1.69.

(e) Finally, how might one best evaluate the Christensen-Greene finding that by 1970 the bulk of U.S. electricity generation was being produced by firms operating "very close" to the bottom of their average cost curves? Do you agree or disagree with Christensen and Greene? Why?

EXERCISE 7: Autocorrelation in the Learning Curve Model

The purpose of this exercise is to assess whether disturbances in the simple and expanded learning curve models are independently distributed or appear to follow a first-order autoregressive pattern.

(a) Using the data described in Exercises 1 and 2 and least squares regression methods, choose either the polyethylene or the titanium dioxide data and estimate the parameters of the simple learning curve model (3.36) as well as the generalized learning curve model (3.33). On the basis of the Durbin-Watson test statistic and using a reasonable level of significance, test the null hypothesis of no autocorrelation against the alternative hypothesis of a first-order autoregressive disturbance structure.

(b) Using either the Hildreth-Lu or the Cochrane-Orcutt estimation procedures, estimate both the simple and generalized learning curve models under the assumption that disturbances follow a first-order autoregressive scheme. Compare the estimated learning curve elasticities, as well as their statistical significance, with and without allowing for first-order autocorrelation. Are there any surprises? Why or why not?

EXERCISE 8: Misspecification in the Nerlove Returns-to-Scale Model

The purpose of this exercise is to acquaint you with one somewhat unorthodox procedure for examining misspecification in the cross-sectional data set on electric utility companies in 1955. Even though the data are cross-sectional, the Durbin-Watson test statistic will be seen to provide some useful (although not particularly powerful) evidence concerning model misspecification.

(a) Using the 1955 data for 145 electric utility firms described in Exercise 4 (see especially part (a) of that exercise), estimate by least squares the parameters of the regression equation (3.20).
(b) A particular feature of this data set is that it is ordered by size of output, that is, the first observation is that from the firm with the smallest output in 1955, while the last observation is that from the firm with the largest output. If average cost curves are U-shaped, then returns to scale will vary with the level of output. The specification of Eq. (3.20), however, assumes that the degree of returns to scale is the same regardless of the level of output. If in fact returns to scale varied with the level of output but a regression equation like Eq. (3.20) were estimated by least squares where the data were ordered by size of output, what might the pattern of residuals look like? In what sense is this lack of independence among residuals in this cross-sectional context similar to first-order autocorrelation in the time series context?
(c) Given this different interpretation of first-order autocorrelation, use a reasonable level of significance and the Durbin-Watson test statistic from part (a) to test the null hypothesis that disturbances are independent. Interpret the alternative hypothesis. Would it make sense to reestimate this model by using the Hildreth-Lu or Cochrane-Orcutt procedures, or does the above analysis suggest instead that the apparent presence of autocorrelation here indicates a fundamental problem with specification that cannot simply be "fixed" by using generalized least squares? Defend your position carefully. (The results in the first parts of Exercise 5 might be of help.)

EXERCISE 9: Testing for the Equality of Coefficients in the 1955 and 1970 Returns-to-Scale Models

The purpose of this exercise is to give you experience in performing a number of tests on the equality of the returns-to-scale estimates based on various subsamples of the 1955 and 1970 electric utility companies. The data necessary for this study are described at the beginning of Exercises 4 and 6. The hypothesis tests involve use of the Chow test procedure.[33]

(a) The 145 companies in the 1955 data base are ordered by size of output. Disaggregate this sample into five groups with 29 observations each and estimate Eq. (3.20) for each group and for the entire 145-company sample. Using the Chow test procedure, test the null hypothesis that parameters in each of these five subgroups are equal. (*Note:* Take special care in computing degrees of freedom.)

(b) The 99 companies in the 1970 data base are also ordered by size of output. Disaggregate this 1970 sample into five groups with 20 observations in each of the first four groups and 19 observations in the last group. Then estimate Eq. (3.20) for each group and for the entire 99-company sample. Using the Chow test procedure, test the null hypothesis that parameters in each of these five subgroups in 1970 are equal.

(c) Now pool the 1955 and 1970 data, estimate Eq. (3.20) for the pooled sample, and then test the null hypothesis that parameters in each of the ten subgroups (five in 1955 and five in 1970) are equal; also test the null hypothesis that parameters in 1970 (assumed to be the same for all companies in that year) equal those from 1955 (assumed to be the same for all companies in that year).

(d) Finally, using least squares procedures and a reasonable level of significance, estimate the generalized Cobb-Douglas model with $(\ln y)^2$ added as a regressor, that is, estimate the parameters of

$$\begin{aligned} \text{LNC70} = {} & \beta_0 + \beta_y \cdot \text{LNY70} + \beta_{yy} \cdot (\text{LNY70})^2 \\ & + \beta_1 \cdot \text{LNP170} + \beta_2 \cdot \text{LNP270} + \epsilon \end{aligned}$$

first for the entire 145-company sample in 1955, then for the entire 99-company sample in 1970, and finally for the pooled 1955–1970 sample. Using the Chow test procedure, test the null hypothesis of parameter equality in 1955 and 1970 for this generalized Cobb-Douglas model.

(e) Comment on how one might interpret the entire set of test results in parts (a) through (d), in particular, on how they might be of help in choosing a preferred specification.

EXERCISE 10: Forecasting Unit Cost after Further Learning Occurs

One of the principal reasons why analysts are interested in the effects of learning curves is that, if estimated reliably, the parameters can be used to forecast unit costs after further learning occurs. In fact, as was noted earlier in this chapter, if unit costs can reliably be forecasted to fall at a certain rate as cumulative production increases, in some cases it may be optimal to reduce current prices in order to increase current demand and production and thereby accelerate learning. The purpose of this exercise is to forecast unit costs after cumulative production doubles and to obtain an estimate of the forecast error variance.

Recall from Eq. (3.36) that the bivariate regression model underlying the simple form of the learning curve is $\ln c_t = \alpha_0 + \alpha_1 \cdot \ln n_t$; for notational simplicity, rewrite this equation as $z_t = \alpha_0 + \alpha_1 \cdot x_t$, where $z_t \equiv \ln c_t$ and $x_t \equiv \ln n_t$. When an identically and independently normally distributed random disturbance term is appended to this equation, and given a known future value of x_t denoted x_τ, as is shown in numerous econometric theory textbooks,[34] the estimated forecast error variance s_f^2 equals

$$s^2_{f,\tau} = \text{VAR}(a_0) + 2 \cdot x_\tau \cdot \text{COV}(a_0, a_1) + x_\tau^2 \cdot \text{VAR}(a_1) + s^2$$
$$= s^2 \cdot \left[1 + \frac{1}{T} + \frac{(x_\tau - \bar{x})^2}{\sum_{t=1}^{T} (x_t - \bar{x})^2} \right]$$

where a_0 and a_1 are least squares estimates of α_0 and α_1, T is the number of observations used in the sample to estimate the parameters, $\bar{x}$ is the sample mean of x_t (here, ln n_t) over the estimation sample, x_τ is the known value of x (ln n) at time τ in the future, and s^2 is the sum of squared residuals in the estimation divided by $T - 2$.

(a) Using the data on unit costs and cumulative production of either the polyethylene or the titanium dioxide data discussed in Exercise 1, obtain least squares estimates of α_0 and α_1, their variances and covariances, and s^2.
(b) Given the above formula and the estimates in part (a), calculate the forecasted value of unit costs, as well as the estimated forecast error variance at a level of cumulative production equal to twice that at the last historical observation. *Note:* To do this, double the value of n_t at the last historical observation, and then form x_τ as the natural logarithm of this doubled n_τ.
(c) Given the forecasted value of unit costs in part (b) brought about by additional learning, as well as the estimated forecast error variance, use a reasonable level of significance and construct a confidence interval for forecasted unit costs at $x = x_\tau$.
(d) After examining the above equation for the estimated forecast error variance, comment on the effects of increasing the sample size on the magnitude of the estimated forecast error variance. Since the number of observations in data sets underlying typical learning curve studies is rather small (often fewer than 20 observations), how reliable would you expect forecasts of unit costs to be? How would reliability be affected by the difference between x_τ and the sample mean of x? With these points in mind, comment on the range of the confidence interval estimated in part (c).

CHAPTER NOTES

1. More extended discussions on the six-tenths rule, scale economies at the product-specific and plant level, and a list of important references are found in F. Michael Scherer [1980], Chapter 4.
2. In the industrial psychology literature, learning functions go back at least as far as 1930; see L. L. Thurstone [1930] and, for an attempt to provide a statistical framework in an experimental setting, William K. Estes [1950]. For historical overviews and references in the management context, see Louis E. Yelle [1979] and John M. Dutton, Annie Thomas, and John E. Butler [1983].

3. For shipbuilding, see Allan D. Searle [1945], and for aircraft, see Kenneth A. Middleton [1945]; also see Leonard Rapping [1965].
4. Classic discussions of the learning curve in production economics include Frank J. Andress [1954], Armen Alchian [1963], Werner Hirsch [1952], and Wilfred B. Hirschmann [1964].
5. For nuclear power, see Martin L. Zimmerman [1982], and for coal-burning plants, see Paul L. Joskow and Nancy L. Rose [1985].
6. This pricing strategy is often identified with the Boston Consulting Group, which made it a central focus of its corporate consulting practice. See Boston Consulting Group [1973, 1974, 1982], A. Michael Spence [1981], and Arnoldo Hax and Nicolas J. Majluf [1982] for further discussion.
7. For an overview, see Jean Tirole [1989], Chapters 6–10. Also see Robert J. Dolan and Abel P. Jeuland [1981], Drew Fudenberg and Jean Tirole [1983], and Saman Majd and Robert S. Pindyck [1989]. On make-or-buy decisions, see James J. Anton and Dennis A. Yao [1987].
8. See, for example, Partha Dasgupta and Joseph Stiglitz [1985] and Elhanan Helpman and Paul R. Krugman [1985].
9. The relationship between scale economies and learning curve effects has often been unclear in the strategic management literature; see William Alberts [1989] for a critical review. For an empirical study that carefully distinguishes these notions and relates them to pricing behavior and market structure in the chemical processing industries, see Marvin B. Lieberman [1984].
10. Notice that in this case, λ also equals the marginal cost of producing output, that is, $\partial \mathcal{L}/\partial y = \lambda$.
11. Discussions of duality theory can be found in numerous advanced microeconomic theory textbooks. See, for example, Walter Nicholson [1985], Chapter 2, or R. Robert Russell and Maurice Wilkinson [1979], especially Chapters 5 and 9. A more complete discussion is found in Hal R. Varian [1984], especially Chapters 1 and 4.
12. The interpretation of learning and experience curves is not without controversy. For a recent critique that includes questions of the direction of causality, see William W. Alberts [1989].
13. For further discussions of strategic implications of learning and experience curves, see Arnoldo Hax and Nicolas Majluf [1982; 1984, Chapter 6], George S. Day and David B. Montgomery [1983], Boston Consulting Group [1982], Michael E. Porter [1980], and William W. Alberts [1989].
14. Ford did this in part to take advantage of the cost-reducing effects of learning by experience. However, learning was not the only reason; volume buying of input parts also reduced input prices and therefore costs of production.
15. The measurement of learning curve effects is complicated when one uses price rather than unit cost data; see Section 3.5.1 for further discussion.
16. Figure 3.2 is taken from William J. Abernathy and Kenneth Wayne [1974].
17. See William Abernathy and Kenneth Wayne [1974], as well as David B. Montgomery and George S. Day [1985]; also see Thomas H. Naylor, John M. Vernon, and Kenneth L. Wertz [1983], especially Chapter 12.
18. More complex formulations are considered in, among others, A. Ronald Gallant [1968], N. Keith Womer and J. Wayne Patterson [1983], N. Keith Womer [1984], and John McDonald [1987].
19. Learning curve effects are typically assumed to affect costs. The extent to which such cost reductions are passed on to consumers in the form of price decreases

depends, of course, on market structure and other strategic pricing decisions. See Section 3.5.1 for further discussion.

20. For an historical overview of the Cobb-Douglas form and its estimation, see Paul A. Samuelson [1979].
21. Note, however, that the interpretation of the intercept term in the two equations still differs. In Eq. (3.32), ln k' reflects the effects of the α parameters as shown in Eq. (3.26), while in Eq. (3.8) the intercept represents c_1—unit costs in the initial production time period.
22. Estimation and statistical inference issues arising in models that are nonlinear in the parameters are beyond the scope of this chapter but are discussed in many graduate econometric theory textbooks. See, for example, Thomas B. Fomby, R. Carter Hill, and Stanley R. Johnson [1984], Appendix, pp. 603–616, and George G. Judge et al. [1985], Chapter 6.
23. These and other measurement issues are discussed in further detail in George S. Day and David B. Montgomery [1983] and in Montgomery and Day [1985].
24. The additive disturbance term in the Cobb-Douglas cost function equation (3.33) can be derived from a multiplicative random disturbance term appended to the original Cobb-Douglas production function (3.10). Specifically, if the multiplicative disturbance term on Eq. (3.10) is denoted as u and the additive disturbance term on the Cobb-Douglas cost function equation (3.36) is v, then it can be shown that $v = (-1/r) \cdot \ln u$.
25. See, for example, Arthur S. Goldberger [1968], Chapter 3, in which the omitted variable bias algebra is worked out for both the 2- and the k-regressor case, for $k > 2$. Other early derivations are found in Zvi Griliches [1957] and Henri Theil [1957].
26. See the discussion in the paragraph underneath Eq. (3.31).
27. For additional discussion on the interpretation of learning or experience curves, see William W. Alberts [1989]. The effect of possible first-order autocorrelation of disturbances on the estimation of learning curve elasticities is considered by David Montgomery and George Day [1985].
28. The translog form is discussed and implemented empirically in Chapter 9.
29. The polyethylene data have been in the public domain for some time and are usually attributed to some early studies by the Boston Consulting Group, a consulting firm that has specialized in analyzing the effects of learning on optimal pricing and production strategies. The DuPont titanium dioxide data are taken from the Federal Trade Commision Docket No. 9108, U.S. Government Printing Office, Washington, D.C. They are described in further detail by Pankaj Ghemawat [1986].
30. These data are taken from David Hamilton [1987].
31. The careful student will note that it is not clear on what basis company size ranking is determined. Although Nerlove suggests that it is on the basis of company output (KWH), in fact there are several minor discrepancies in this ranking; see, for example, observations whose ORDER numbers are 119–120, 324–325, and 408–409.
32. Further, although not used in this exercise, the UPDATE data file also contains 1970 cost share data for labor, capital, and fuel, denoted SL, SK, and SF, respectively.
33. The Chow test procedure is described in most standard econometrics textbooks, often under the name "tests for parameter equality." The original article is by Gregory C. Chow [1960].

34. See, for example, Robert S. Pindyck and Daniel L. Rubinfeld [1981], Chapter 8, especially Section 8.1., pp. 206–211.

CHAPTER REFERENCES

Abernathy, William J. and Kenneth Wayne [1974], "Limits of the Learning Curve," *Harvard Business Review*, 52:5, September/October, 109–119.

Alberts, William W. [1989], "The Experience Curve Doctrine Reconsidered," *Journal of Marketing*, 53:3, July, 36–49.

Alchian, Armen [1963], "Reliability of Progress Curves in Airframe Production," *Econometrica*, 31:4, October, 679–693.

Andress, Frank J. [1954], "The Learning Curve as a Production Tool," *Harvard Business Review*, 32:1, January/February, 87–97.

Anton, James J. and Dennis A. Yao [1987], "Second Sourcing and the Experience Curve: Price Competition in Defense Procurement," *Rand Journal of Economics*, 18:1, 57–76.

Boston Consulting Group [1973], "The Experience Curve—Reviewed, II: History," *Perspectives*, No. 125.

Boston Consulting Group [1974], "The Experience Curve—Reviewed, III: Why Does It Work?" *Perspectives*, No. 128.

Boston Consulting Group [1982], *Perspectives on Experience*, Boston: Boston Consulting Group, Inc.

Chow, Gregory C. [1960], "Tests of Equality between Sets of Coefficients in Two Linear Regressions," *Econometrica*, 28:3, July, 591–605.

Christensen, Laurits R. and William H. Greene [1976], "Economies of Scale in U.S. Electric Power Generation," *Journal of Political Economy*, 84:4, Part 1, August, 655–676.

Cobb, Charles and Paul H. Douglas [1928], "A Theory of Production," *American Economic Review*, 18:1, Supplement, March, 139–165.

Cowing, Thomas G. and V. Kerry Smith [1978], "The Estimation of a Production Technology: A Survey of Econometric Analyses of Steam-Electric Generation," *Land Economics*, 54:2, May, 157–170.

Dasgupta, Partha and Joseph Stiglitz [1985], "Learning-by-Doing, Market Structure and Industrial and Trade Policies," London: Centre for Economic Policy Research, Discussion Paper No. 80, October.

Day, George S. and David B. Montgomery [1983], "Diagnosing the Experience Curve," *Journal of Marketing*, 47:2, Spring, 44–58.

Dolan, Robert J. and Abel P. Jeuland [1981], "Experience Curves and Dynamic Demand Models: Implications for Optimal Pricing Strategies," *Journal of Marketing*, 45:1, Winter, 52–73.

Dutton, John M., Annie Thomas, and John E. Butler [1983], "The History of Progress Functions as a Managerial Technology," *Business History Review*, 58:2, Summer, 204–233.

Estes, William K. [1950], "Towards a Statistical Theory of Learning," *Psychological Review*, 57:2, March, 94–107.

Fomby, Thomas B., R. Carter Hill, and Stanley R. Johnson [1984], *Advanced Econometric Methods*, New York: Springer-Verlag.

Fudenberg, Drew and Jean Tirole [1983], "Learning-by-Doing and Market Performance," *Bell Journal of Economics*, 14:2, Autumn, 522–530.

Gallant, A. Ronald [1968], "A Note on the Measurement of Cost/Quantity Relationships in the Aircraft Industry," *Journal of the American Statistical Association*, 63:324, December, 1247–1252.

Ghemawat, Pankaj [1985], "Building Strategy on the Experience Curve," *Harvard Business Review*, 63:2, March/April, 143–149.

Ghemawat, Pankaj [1986], "DuPont in Titanium Dioxide," Cambridge, Mass: Harvard Graduate School of Business, Case Study 9-385-140, 1984; revised June 1986.

Goldberger, Arthur S. [1968], *Topics in Regression Analysis*, New York: Macmillan.

Griliches, Zvi [1957], "Specification Bias in Estimates of Production Functions," *Journal of Farm Economics*, 39:1, March, 8–20.

Hamilton, David [1987], "Sometimes $R^2 > r^2_{yx1} + r^2_{yx2}$: Correlated Variables Are Not Always Redundant," *The American Statistician*, 41:2, May, 129–132.

Hax, Arnoldo and Nicolas J. Majluf [1982], "Competitive Cost Dynamics: The Experience Curve," *Interfaces*, 12:5, October, 50–61.

Hax, Arnoldo and Nicolas Majluf [1984], *Strategic Management: An Integrative Perspective*, Englewood Cliffs, N.J.: Prentice-Hall.

Helpman, Elhanan and Paul R. Krugman [1985], *Market Structure and Foreign Trade*, Cambridge, Mass.: MIT Press.

Hirsch, Werner [1952], "Manufacturing Progress Functions," *Review of Economics and Statistics*, 34:2, May, 143–155.

Hirschmann, Wilfred B. [1964], "Profit from the Learning Curve," *Harvard Business Review*, 42:1, January/February, 125–139.

Joskow, Paul L., and Nancy L. Rose [1985], "The Effects of Technological Change, Experience, and Environmental Regulation on the Construction Cost of Coal-Burning Generating Units," *Rand Journal of Economics*, 16:1, Spring, 1–27.

Judge, George G., William E. Griffiths, R. Carter Hill, Helmut Lutkepohl, and Tsoung-Chao Lee [1985], *The Theory and Practice of Econometrics*, Second Edition, New York: John Wiley and Sons.

Lieberman, Marvin B. [1984], "The Learning Curve and Pricing in the Chemical Processing Industries," *Rand Journal of Economics*, 15:2, Summer, 213–228.

Majd, Saman and Robert S. Pindyck [1989], "The Learning Curve and Optimal Production under Uncertainty," *Rand Journal of Economics*, 20:3, Autumn, 331–343.

McDonald, John [1987], "A New Model for Learning Curves, DARM," *Journal of Business and Economic Statistics*, 5:3, July, 329–335.

Middleton, Kenneth A. [1945], "Wartime Productivity Changes in the Airframe Industry," *Monthly Labor Review*, 62:2, August, 215–225.

Montgomery, David B. and George S. Day [1985], "Experience Curves: Evidence, Empirical Issues, and Applications," Chapter 3.6 in Howard Thomas and David Gardner, eds., *Strategic Marketing and Management*, New York: John Wiley and Sons, pp. 213–238.

Naylor, Thomas H., John M. Vernon, and Kenneth L. Wertz [1983], *Managerial Economics: Corporate Economics and Strategy*, New York: McGraw-Hill.

Nerlove, Marc [1963], "Returns to Scale in Electricity Supply," Chapter 7 in Carl F. Christ, ed., *Measurement in Economics: Studies in Honor of Yehuda Grunfeld*, Stanford, Calif.: Stanford University Press, pp. 167–198.

Nicholson, Walter [1985], *Microeconomic Theory*, Third Edition, Chicago: The Dryden Press.

Pindyck, Robert S. and Daniel L. Rubinfeld [1981], *Econometric Models and Economic Forecasts*, Second Edition, New York: McGraw-Hill.

Porter, Michael E. [1980], *Competitive Strategy*, New York: The Free Press, Macmillan.

Rapping, Leonard [1965], "Learning and World War II Production Functions," *Review of Economics and Statistics*, 47:1, February, 81–86.

Russell, R. Robert and Maurice Wilkinson [1979], *Microeconomics: A Synthesis of Modern and Neoclassical Theory*, New York: John Wiley and Sons.

Samuelson, Paul A. [1979], "Paul Douglas' Measurement of Production Functions and Marginal Productivities," *Journal of Political Economy*, 87:5, Part 1, October, 923–939.

Scherer, F. Michael [1980], *Industrial Market Structure and Economic Performance*, Second Edition, Chicago: Rand McNally.

Searle, Allan D. [1945], "Productivity Changes in Selected Wartime Shipbuilding Programs," *Monthly Labor Review*, 61:6, December, 1132–1147.

Spence, A. Michael [1981], "The Learning Curve and Competition," *Bell Journal of Economics*, 12:1, Spring, 49–70.

Theil, Henri [1957], "Specification Errors and the Estimation of Economic Relationships," *Review of the International Statistical Institute*, 25:1, 41–51.

Thurstone, L. L. [1930], "The Learning Function," *Journal of General Psychology*, 3, 469–493.

Tirole, Jean [1989], *The Theory of Industrial Organization*, Cambridge, Mass.: MIT Press.

Varian, Hal R. [1984], *Microeconomic Analysis*, Second Edition, New York: W.W. Norton.

Womer, N. Keith [1984], "Estimating Learning Curves from Aggregated Monthly Data," *Management Science*, 30:8, August, 982–992.

Womer, N. Keith and J. Wayne Patterson [1983], "Estimation and Testing of Learning Curves," *Journal of Business and Economic Statistics*, 1:4, October, 265–272.

Yelle, Louis E. [1979], "The Learning Curve: Historical Review and Comprehensive Survey," *Decision Sciences*, 10:2, April, 302–328.

Zimmerman, Martin L. [1982], "Learning Effects and the Commercialization of New Energy Technologies: The Case of Nuclear Power," *Bell Journal of Economics*, 13:2, Autumn, 297–310.

FURTHER READINGS

Diewert, W. Erwin [1974], "Applications of Duality Theory," in Michael Intriligator and David Kendrick, eds., *Frontiers of Quantitative Economics*, Vol. 2, Amsterdam: North-Holland. A classic development of duality theory and its applications.

Johnston, J. [1960], *Statistical Cost Analysis*, New York: McGraw-Hill. An early study of cost and production economics.

Nerlove, Marc [1965], *Estimation and Identification of Cobb-Douglas Production Functions*, Chicago: Rand McNally. A classic and detailed econometric study using the Cobb-Douglas function.

Rosenberg, Nathan [1982], *Inside the Black Box*, Cambridge, England: Cambridge University Press. See especially Chapter 6, "Learning by Using."

Walters, Alan A. [1963], "Production and Cost Functions: An Econometric Survey," *Econometrica*, Vol. 31, January/April, pp. 1–66. A survey of econometric findings through 1962 based on the Cobb-Douglas production function.

Chapter 4

The Measurement of Quality Change: Constructing an Hedonic Price Index for Computers Using Multiple Regression Methods

"If a poll were taken of professional economists and statisticians, in all probability they would designate (and by a wide margin) the failure of the price indexes to take full account of quality changes as the most important defect in these indexes."

NATIONAL BUREAU OF ECONOMIC RESEARCH (1961, p. 35)

"My own point of view is that what the hedonic approach tries to do is estimate aspects of the budget constraint facing consumers, allowing thereby the estimation of 'missing' prices when quality changes."

ZVI GRILICHES (1988, p. 120)

". . . if the automobile and airplane businesses had developed like the computer business, a Rolls Royce would cost $2.75 and run for 3 million miles on one gallon of gas. And a Boeing 767 would cost just $500 and circle the globe in 20 minutes on five gallons of gas."

TOM FORESTER (1985, p. i)[1]

In this chapter we develop an understanding of how price indexes are constructed and interpreted, how quality and price are related, and how multiple regression analysis can be used to account for the effects of quality change. We focus attention on the interpretation of estimated coefficients in a multiple regression, including the dummy variable parameters.

Price indexes play a very important role in today's economies. For example, contracts between employers and employees often contain specific cost-of-living provisions for the automatic adjustment of wages or salaries due to changes in the Consumer Price Index (CPI). Similarly, government payments to senior citizens and other recipients of Social Security depend explicitly on changes over time in the CPI. Many long-term contracts between sellers and buyers include detailed provisions specifying how future transactions are to be affected by inflation, depending on changes in some particular price index. Policymakers, businesspeople, and analysts often want to know how measures such as sales, output, and costs should be deflated by a price index in order to obtain "real" quantity measures that adjust for the effects of inflation.

Because price indexes are so pervasive in today's economies, it is important that they be constructed with as much reliability and accuracy as is practically possible. Much has been written concerning the large number of important conceptual and statistical sampling issues encountered in constructing and interpreting both individual and aggregate price indexes.[2]

One very important issue concerns how price indexes should be adjusted to account properly for quality change. For products such as stylized raw materials, the physical specifications and characteristics typically remain unchanged over long periods of time; and for such products, quality change usually does not present a problem. However, for some products whose specifications and characteristics evolve rapidly over time, accounting properly for quality change becomes a very significant issue. In this chapter we will focus on one aspect of this problem and examine how regression methods can be used to construct quality-adjusted price indexes for individual products. In particular, we will construct an hedonic price index for computer-related products using multiple regression procedures.

The chapter proceeds as follows. In Section 4.1 we briefly summarize traditional procedures used in constructing price indexes that attempt to account for quality change. In Section 4.2 we examine the relationship between price and quality for a product at a given point in time. We show how this price-quality relationship can be analyzed by using regression analysis in which transaction prices are regressed on a number of explanatory variables, each measuring an important quality characteristic of the product. Then in Section 4.3 we extend the price-quality analysis into the intertemporal domain by showing how multivariate regression analysis can be used to measure the extent to which prices have changed over time, adjusting for quality by holding its level fixed. This procedure involves considerable use of dichotomous independent variables, more often simply called dummy variables.

In Section 4.4 we apply this general framework of hedonic price analysis to the specific problem of constructing a price index for computers. Computers are a particularly interesting application, since quality change in this industry has been very rapid and pervasive. Here we survey and review the empirical literature to date, including the recent innovations adopted by the U.S. Bureau of Economic Analysis. In Section 4.5 we discuss a number of econometric issues: the use of weighted least squares to adjust for heteroskedasticity, the choice of functional form, and the conditions under which parameters can be directly interpreted as estimates of the marginal costs or marginal consumer valuations of changes in the quality characteristics.

Finally, the exercises presented in this chapter involve you in the replication and extension of classic results reported in the empirical literature to date and are based on three very interesting data sets. The first is that gathered and employed by Frederick V. Waugh [1928] in his pioneering study of the effects of quality on vegetable prices. The second data set was constructed by Gregory C. Chow [1967] in his seminal study of demand for computers over the 1955–1965 era, and the third is a portion of one involving computers and computer peripheral products constructed by IBM in its recent study in conjunction with the U.S. Bureau of Economic Analysis.[3] The econometric procedures that you employ in these exercises include multiple regression analysis, the interpretation of R^2 and multiple correlation, dummy variables, hypothesis testing, tests for parameter stability, weighted least squares and tests for homoskedasticity, and Box-Cox estimation.

4.1 TRADITIONAL PROCEDURES FOR INCORPORATING QUALITY CHANGES INTO PRICE INDEXES

The traditional procedure for controlling for the effects of quality change on price is commonly called the "matched model" method. In this procedure the only prices used in constructing the index are those for models or varieties that are unchanged in specification between two adjacent time periods. The idea underlying this method is that matching the models ensures that any differences between the prices collected for the two time periods solely reflect price change, rather than a change in what in fact was purchased. In the United States the Producer Price Indexes (PPI), used for deflating many components of producers' durable equipment, are constructed by using the matched model method.

Two problems can arise with the matched model method that may prevent it from properly accounting for quality change.[4] One error can arise when the price changes observed for matched models do not accurately represent the price movements taking place for all models. For example, if new models of some product are introduced that embody an improved technology, and if the price index is based only on information gained from following prices of the incumbent models until they disappear from the market, it is possible that a substantial portion of the overall price change would not be uncovered by using matched model methods.

A second error can occur when models that are in fact not identical are nevertheless matched. This can arise when information on some of the specifications and characteristics of the models is unavailable or is not taken into account, so that some models that appear to be matches are in fact different. Alternatively, in some cases the statistical agency may know that the two models are not truly identical but may conclude that if the differences are small, it is preferable to make the match rather than drop the price information from the index entirely.

Dealing with each of these two possible errors involves facing a tradeoff. The stricter the criteria for accepting two models as a match, the greater the number of models that will be excluded from the price index. This implies that, with the matched model method, the more one guards against the second possible error (matching not completely identical models), the more likely it is that the index will contain the first error (inferring incorrect information for unmatched models based on that observed for matched models).

Regression analysis can help considerably in reducing the severity of this tradeoff. After years of encouragement from a number of distinguished economists, in 1986 the U.S. Bureau of Economic Analysis published and incorporated into its official statistics the results of a study on computer prices in which the matched model method was augmented by a particular type of regression analysis known as *hedonic price analysis*.[5] In one type of hedonic price analysis the matched model method is employed whenever the appropriate data are available, and then hedonic regression methods are used to impute missing prices for newly introduced or just discontinued models, thereby accounting more fully for the price changes associated with turnover of models available in the market. In another type of hedonic price analysis the price index is estimated directly from a regression equation.[6] In either case, hedonic price analysis forms the basis of the measurement of quality change.

4.2 ANALYZING THE PRICE-QUALITY RELATIONSHIP AT A GIVEN POINT IN TIME

In this section we discuss the relationship between price and quality at a given point in time by reviewing some of the early empirical literature. In terms of today's standards for econometric practice, this pioneering literature leaves much to be desired. Interestingly, while much recent hedonic price research has focused on quality-adjusted prices for computers, the first hedonic price equations were estimated without the benefit of any computers whatsoever. Therefore in assessing this early literature, it is worth bearing in mind that today's computational hardware and software tools were simply not available in the 1920s. As we shall see, however, an important contribution of the early studies consisted of establishing the notion that price variations reflect quality differentials.

The early empirical research on measuring the effects of quality on price was for the most part not concerned with implications for price indexes, but had other purposes in mind. Apparently, the first empirical study relating price and quality was that of Frederick Waugh, an agricultural economist who in 1927 wrote a paper entitled "Quality Factors Influencing Vegetable Prices."[7] The goal of Waugh's research was, using statistical analysis, "to discover the important quality factors which cause high or low prices" [1928, p. 186]. In his paper, Waugh reported results, based on multiple correlation analysis, in which he considered the effects of physical characteristics—size, shape, color, maturity, uniformity, and other factors—on the prices of asparagus, tomatoes, and hothouse cucumbers as recorded in daily sales transactions at the Faneuil Hall wholesale market in downtown Boston, Massachusetts.

Waugh had rather practical motivations for his research. Noting that profit-maximizing farmers can to some extent adjust both the quantity and quality of commodities produced to meet market demand conditions, Waugh emphasized the usefulness of his research by stating that [1928, p. 187]

> If it can be demonstrated that there is a premium for certain qualities and types of products, and if that premium is more than large enough to pay the increased cost of growing a superior product, the individual can and will adapt his production and marketing policies to market demand.

To eliminate the effects of seasonal and day-to-day changes in prices, Waugh used as a left-hand or dependent variable in his regression equations the ratio of the actual price recorded for a wholesale market lot transaction of a particular commodity (denoted P_{in}) to the average market quotation for that commodity that day (PM_i). Call this relative price of the nth lot transaction for the ith commodity p_{in}, and note that it is defined as

$$p_{in} \equiv P_{in}/PM_i \tag{4.1}$$

Waugh regressed p_{in} on the physical characteristics of vegetables that he believed were related to their actual or perceived quality variations. Although he reported separate results for asparagus, tomatoes, and hothouse cucumbers, here we confine our attention to his analysis of asparagus.

Waugh inspected 200 individual lots of asparagus in Boston over the time period of May 6 to July 2, 1927. Apparently, a great deal of quality variation existed among lots of asparagus, since even on the single day of July 2, prices per bushel box varied from a low of \$4.50 to a high of \$12.00. Waugh characterized qualitative differences among lots as follows:

> One lot was extra fancy. It was green from tips to butts. The stalks were large, straight and of uniform size. The bunches were compact. The other

lot was classified as "junk." It was white. The stalks were small, crooked, and uneven in size. The bunches were loose. The butts were jagged and uneven.[8]

To quantify the effects of quality variables on relative prices, Waugh chose three measures that he believed were related to perceived quality. The first was the number of inches of green color on the asparagus; name this variable GREEN. The second variable was designed to capture the average size of stalks and was measured by the number of stalks in the bunches; call this variable NOSTALKS. Since the standard size of bunches was about 18 ounces, the number of stalks in a bunch increased as their size or diameter became smaller. Finally, to capture the effect of uniformity, a record was kept of the actual diameter of each stalk, and then the variation in size was measured by using the quartile coefficient of dispersion; denote this variable DISPERSE.

Waugh is not completely clear on precisely how he performed his regression analysis, but it appears to have had some problems, at least by today's standards. Waugh's aim was to estimate parameters in the multiple regression equation

$$p_n = \beta_0 + \beta_1 \cdot \text{GREEN}_n + \beta_2 \cdot \text{NOSTALKS}_n + \beta_3 \cdot \text{DISPERSE}_n + u_n \tag{4.2}$$

for $n = 1, \ldots, 200$, where the least squares estimates of β_1, β_2, or β_3 could be interpreted as representing the partial effect of a change in one quality characteristic on price, all other quality characteristics being held fixed. Although Waugh assumed that u_n was a random disturbance term with mean zero, he did not give it a specific interpretation.

Using what he called the method of multiple correlation analysis, Waugh [1929, p. 144] reports the following estimates of the regression equation parameters in Eq. (4.2), where e_n is the equation residual:

$$p_n = \beta_0 + 0.13826 \cdot \text{GREEN}_n - 1.53394 \cdot \text{NOSTALKS}_n - 0.27553 \cdot \text{DISPERSE}_n + e_n \tag{4.3}$$

No estimate is provided for the intercept term β_0, nor are values given for the estimated standard errors and t-statistics.[9]

Waugh commented on his empirical findings as follows. First, he reported that green color is by far the most important quality factor influencing asparagus prices in Boston: "Boston wants green asparagus" [1928, p. 188]. Waugh noted that the predicted price per dozen bunches of asparagus that were green throughout a length of six inches from the tip was 38.5 cents more than asparagus having only five inches of green color. The coefficient of determination for the GREEN variable was 0.40837, which led Waugh to state that [1928, p. 188] "the influence of this one factor explained 41 percent of the variation in prices found in the 200 inspections."

With respect to size of the asparagus, Waugh [1929, p. 144] commented that on the basis of his estimated regression coefficient, for each additional stalk in the bunch the price was predicted to decrease by about 4.6 cents per dozen bunches. In terms of explanatory power, Waugh reported that the coefficient of determination for the NOSTALKS variable was 0.14554. Finally, concerning uniformity, Waugh's analysis revealed that the premium paid for uniformity in size was small; further, the coefficient of determination for the DISPERSE variable was also rather small, equaling only 0.02133.

The size of the relative coefficients of determination for these three separate regressors led Waugh to conclude that the uniformity variable

> was about one-seventh as important as size of stalk and one-twentieth as important as green color in its effect on prices. The three together explained 58 percent of the price variation. The coefficient of multiple correlation between these three quality factors and prices received was 0.76.[10]

To interpret Waugh's regression results, we focus on two questions. First, were his estimates of the multiple regression coefficients correctly computed? Apparently not. This issue will be dealt with in Exercises 1 and 2 at the end of this chapter. Second, did he measure goodness of fit properly? Here the answer is clearly no, at least by today's standards. Waugh relied heavily on the notion of the coefficient of determination in interpreting which variables were most important and how they contributed to explaining variation in prices.

In the multiple regression context it may be tempting to decompose the R^2 from an estimated equation into additive components, indicating what proportion of the variance in the dependent variable is distinctly attributable to variations in each of the right-hand variables.

This temptation should be resisted. The problem with such a decomposition is that in general it is impossible to compute unambiguously the individual contribution of each right-hand variable to the explanation of variations in the dependent variable. The only exception to this is when each of the right-hand variables is orthogonal to each of the other regressors.

Coefficients of determination attempt to measure contributions of variables, but since there is some ambiguity about the definition of coefficient of determination, it will be useful for us first to distinguish partial from separate coefficients of determination.

Consider first the *partial* coefficient of determination, which attempts to measure the marginal proportional contribution of a regressor to the explanation of variance in the dependent variable, *given all the other regressors.* The partial coefficient of determination for variable X_j is computed as the R^2 from a regression equation in which two sets of residuals are regressed against each other, one from a regression of Y on all X's except X_j and the other from a regression of X_j on all other X's.[11] The major problem with this measure is that the sum of the marginal contributions over the various right-hand variables does not in general equal the R^2 from the original multiple regression equation, in part because each of the partial coefficients of determinations is computed given a different set of other regressors.

An alternative measure used by some to attempt to measure the contribution of an individual regressor is called the *separate* coefficient of determination. Suppose we had a multiple regression equation of the form

$$Y_i = \beta_0 + \beta_1 X_{1i} + \beta_2 X_{2i} + \beta_3 X_{3i} + \cdots + \beta_K X_{Ki} + u_i \qquad i = 1, \ldots, n \tag{4.4}$$

and denote least squares estimates of the β's with b's. The separate coefficient of determination for the *j*th regressor is computed as

$$d^2_{Y,X_j} = b_j \frac{\sum_{i=1}^{n} (X_{ij} - \overline{X}_j) \cdot (Y_i - \overline{Y})}{\sum_{i=1}^{n} (Y_i - \overline{Y})^2} \tag{4.5}$$

It may be tempting to sum the separate coefficients of determination over all the regressors and interpret the result as the total proportion of variation "explained" by the regressors, that is, to interpret this sum as equaling the conventional R^2 goodness-of-fit measure. Unfortunately, however, there is no clear relationship between the conventional R^2 measure from multiple regression equation analysis and the $\Sigma_{j=1}^{K} d^2_{Y, X_j}$.

Which notion of the coefficient of determination did Waugh have in mind? We do know that the 58% total coefficient of determination figure reported by him equals the sum of the coefficient of determination values from the three separate regressors—0.58 = 0.41 + 0.15 + 0.02. Moreover, as we shall see in Exercise 2, Waugh apparently computed coefficients of determination using Eq. (4.5), that is, he computed separate coefficients of determination.

It is important to note that unless the regressors GREEN, NOSTALKS, and DISPERSE are pairwise uncorrelated (and this in fact was not the case), the 0.58 figure calculated as this sum is not equal to the traditional R^2 figure computed in today's typical regression programs.[12] Hence not only was it incorrect for Waugh to attribute the relative importance of contributions from the regressors GREEN, NOSTALKS, and DISPERSE as equaling 0.41, 0.15, and 0.02, respectively, but it was also incorrect for him to state, as was quoted above, "The three [regressors] together explained 58 percent of the price variation." An implication of this is that without being able to examine further the original data, it is not clear what statistical significance can be attributed to Waugh's empirical results. Fortunately, Waugh published his original data in appendices at the end of his 1929 book, and this will enable us to analyze them further in Exercises 1 and 2 at the end of this chapter.

By today's computational and statistical standards, therefore, Waugh's analysis was somewhat flawed. However, for our purposes it should be borne in mind that Waugh's particularly valuable and enduring insight was to see the possibility of using statistical methods for assessing the relationship between price and quality at a given point in time, having eliminated the effects of seasonal and day-to-day price variations by using relative prices. In the next section we extend Waugh's reasoning by examining how quality variations among varieties and over time can be dealt with simultaneously by using multiple regression analysis.

4.3 MEASURING PRICE-QUALITY RELATIONSHIPS OVER TIME

Although one often observes quality differentials among goods at a given point in time, quality changes also occur over time, owing in part to the forces of technological change. As we shall now see, regression analysis, particularly involving dummy variables, can help considerably in dealing with quality adjustment of price indexes over time. This type of regression analysis has become known as hedonic price analysis. A brief historical background on hedonic prices may be of particular interest here.

In the late 1930s in the United States, owing in part to the relatively large size of General Motors (GM) and the existence of substantial cyclical unemployment, public policy debates arose in Congress and elsewhere over whether GM should be required to vary prices of its automobile models in order to stabilize production volumes and employment levels. Some critics argued that GM had been using its monopoly power ruthlessly and that it could be employed more constructively. As evidence, they noted that over the 1925–1935 time period, the U.S. Bureau of Labor Statistics (BLS) official new car price index for the GM brands had increased 45%; moreover, the index of GM new car sales demonstrated considerable variability from year to year.

Stung by this criticism and alarmed at the prospect of such government intervention, in 1938 GM funded a study by Andrew T. Court of the Automobile Manufacturers' Association to assess the effects of auto price changes on the total volume of auto sales.[13]

One of the first issues that Court faced was the choice of the price variable to be used as an explanatory variable in the demand for automobile equation. Should it be average list price? If it were, it would not properly account for the quality improvements over the 1925–1935 time period in the increased horsepower, comfort, speed, and reliability of the GM models. Court could have used the BLS official new car price index, but at that time this price index was based simply on average list prices by brands, and no account was taken of changing specifications and quality improvements.[14] In particular, within a brand, no distinction was made between standard, fully equipped cars and special, stripped economy models that were offered without starter, battery, generator, and spare tire. This sole reliance on brand contrasted with the BLS procedures that were operative at that time for farm tractors and trucks, the official price indexes of which were computed by using matched model methods involving certain physical specifications. Apparently, the BLS believed that use of matched model methods for automobiles would have been inadequate because of the complexity of the problem.

Court devised an alternative procedure, which he called the hedonic pricing method. Invoking utilitarian philosophies that promoted hedonistic thinking—seeking the greatest happiness of the community as a whole—Court [1939, p. 107] defined hedonic price comparisons as "those which recognize the potential contribution of any commodity, a motor car in this instance, to the welfare and happiness of its purchasers and the community." Automobiles, he noted, produce a number of services that consumers enjoy. It would be desirable to measure directly the amount of happiness and increased welfare provided by automobile services, but such quantification would, of course, be impossible. However, it might be reasonable to relate the enjoyment consumers receive from automobiles to physical design and operating characteristics, such as power, speed, internal room, safety, and the like. Court then argued as follows:

> In the case of passenger cars, if the relative importance to the customer of horsepower, braking capacity, window area, seat width, tire size, etc., could be established, the data reflecting these characteristics could be combined into an index of usefulness and desirability. Prices per vehicle divided by this index of Hedonic content would yield valid comparisons in the face of changing specifications.[15]

Following a suggestion made to him by Sidney W. Wilcox, then the Chief Statistician of the U.S. Bureau of Labor Statistics, Court proceeded to measure the relative importance of automobile characteristics to customers by estimating parameters in a multiple regression equation, based on historical data, by model and by year, on list prices and measures of relevant automobile characteristic specifications.

As an example of Court's thinking, consider the case of various new automobile models introduced in three model years, say, 1925, 1926, and 1927. Suppose, as did Court, that three characteristics relate to automobile quality: the dry weight of the car in pounds (WT), the length of the wheelbase in inches (LH), and the advertised horsepower (HP). Denote the price of model i as P_i, and in addition to the intercept term, define two dummy variables, $D_{1926,i}$, a variable that takes on the value of 1 if model i is from the model year 1926 and zero otherwise, and $D_{1927,i}$, a variable that takes on the value of 1 if model i is from model year 1927 and zero otherwise.

Within this context, Court proposed estimating the following hedonic regression equation:

$$\ln P_i = \alpha_0 + \alpha_1 \cdot D_{1926,i} + \alpha_2 \cdot D_{1927,i} + \beta_1 \cdot \text{WT}_i + \beta_2 \cdot \text{LH}_i + \beta_3 \cdot \text{HP}_i + u_i \tag{4.6}$$

where the α's and β's are unknown parameters to be estimated and u_i is assumed to be an identically and independently normally distributed disturbance term with mean zero and variance σ^2. Incidentally, the intercept term α_0 refers to the 1925 year, and so it is necessary to have only two dummy variables, $D_{1926,i}$ and $D_{1927,i}$, even though data from three years are being employed. Data necessary to estimate parameters in Eq. (4.6) consisted of a number of observations on different new car models sold in model years 1925, 1926, and 1927.

The importance of this hedonic regression equation to the construction of price indexes that account for quality change emerges from the interpretation of the regression coefficients, particularly α_1 and α_2. Suppose that two automobile models were introduced, alike in all quality respects except that one was introduced in model year 1925 and the other in model year 1926; denote their common weight, length, and horsepower as WT*, LH*, and HP*, respectively, and their distinct prices as P_{1925} and P_{1926}. Since quality-related characteristics are identical, any price change between the two years is a pure price change, unrelated to quality variations. The least squares predicted price for the model introduced in 1925 is

$$\ln \hat{P}_{1925} = \hat{\alpha}_0 + \hat{\beta}_1 \cdot \text{WT*} + \hat{\beta}_2 \cdot \text{LH*} + \hat{\beta}_3 \cdot \text{HP*} \tag{4.7}$$

while the predicted price for the model introduced in 1926 is

$$\ln \hat{P}_{1926} = \hat{\alpha}_0 + \hat{\alpha}_1 + \hat{\beta}_1 \cdot \text{WT*} + \hat{\beta}_2 \cdot \text{LH*} + \hat{\beta}_3 \cdot \text{HP*} \tag{4.8}$$

where the $\hat{\alpha}$'s and $\hat{\beta}$'s refer to least squares estimates of α and β (obtained, say, from a larger sample), and the $\hat{P}$ implies the predicted or fitted log-price.

Since in this example any price change between years 1925 and 1926 is a pure price change unrelated to quality variations, we can compute the pure price change simply by taking differences in the predicted prices of 1926 and 1925. Subtracting Eq. (4.7) from Eq. (4.8) yields

$$\ln \hat{P}_{1926} - \ln \hat{P}_{1925} = \hat{\alpha}_1 \tag{4.9}$$

Hence the estimate of α_1 represents the estimated change in the natural logarithm of the price index for new car models from 1925 to 1926, quality being held fixed.

If an identical model were also sold in 1927, similar reasoning would yield an interpretation of the estimate of α_2 as representing the estimated total change in the natural logarithm of the quality-adjusted price index for new car models over the two years from 1925 to 1927. The change in the natural logarithm of the estimated quality-adjusted price index for new cars over the single year from 1926 to 1927 would therefore be equal to the difference between the estimates of α_2 and α_1.

While the above interpretation of α_1 and α_2 is based on an example in which quality levels have been constrained to be identical in 1925 and 1926, this interpretation holds much more generally. Recall that in a multiple regression equation the least squares estimate of a parameter refers to a change in one right-hand variable, all others being held fixed. In this particular case we can therefore interpret the estimate of α_1 as reflecting the estimated change in $\ln P_i$ due to the passage of time, holding all other variables—in this case, including all quality variables—constant. Thus in a very natural way the estimated coefficients on the time dummy variables represent changes in the natural logarithm of the price index for new cars, quality being held fixed.

Let us now arbitrarily normalize the level of the quality-adjusted new car price index to 1.00 in 1925. To create estimates of this price index for 1926 and 1927, we take appropriate antilogarithms, that is, we exponentiate as follows:[16]

$$\begin{aligned}&\text{Quality-adjusted price index for 1926:}\quad e^{\hat{\alpha}_1}\\ &\text{Quality-adjusted price index for 1927:}\quad e^{\hat{\alpha}_2}\end{aligned} \tag{4.10}$$

Incidentally, had Court specified a regression equation in which the dependent variable was P rather than $\ln P$, then the quality-adjusted price indexes would have been computed as 1.00, $1 + \hat{\alpha}_1$, and $1 + \hat{\alpha}_2$ for 1925, 1926, and 1927, respectively. The reason Court chose the semilogarithmic equation specification over the linear one was grounded in goodness-of-fit criteria; on the basis of a preliminary analysis, Court reported that the semilogarithmic form was found to give "higher simple correlations."[17]

Within the context of Court's hedonic price equation it is possible to test statistically a number of interesting hypotheses. One hypothesis is of the form that "quality does not matter," that is, that price variations in no way reflect quality differences. Notice that if in Eq. (4.6) $\beta_1 = \beta_2 = \beta_3 = 0$, then variations in WT, LH, and HP would not be associated with changes in $\ln P$. Hence the "quality does not matter" hypothesis could be implemented empirically by testing the joint null hypothesis that $\beta_1 = \beta_2 = \beta_3 = 0$ against the alternative hypothesis that $\beta_1 \neq 0$, $\beta_2 \neq 0$, or $\beta_3 \neq 0$.

In addition to this joint test involving three coefficients, one could of course also test that one particular quality characteristic is not significant. In the case of Eq. (4.6), for example, one could test the hypothesis that wheelbase length (LH) does not matter, simply by testing the null hypothesis that $\beta_2 = 0$ against the alternative hypothesis that $\beta_2 \neq 0$.

A different hypothesis is that all price variations from 1925 to 1927 correspond with quality variations and therefore that during this time span there has been no change in the quality-adjusted price index, that is, once adjusted for quality change, there has been no inflation. In the context of Eq. (4.6), such a null hypothesis is $\alpha_1 = \alpha_2 = 0$, while the alternative hypothesis is that $\alpha_1 \neq 0$ and $\alpha_2 \neq 0$. The null hypothesis that there has been no quality-adjusted price change between only two years, say, 1926 and 1927, could be implemented by testing $\alpha_2 - \alpha_1 = 0$ against the alternative $\alpha_2 - \alpha_1 \neq 0$.

Finally, suppose one wanted to measure how much quality change per automobile had in fact taken place over the 1925–1927 time interval. Recall that while prices per automobile had risen considerably over the 1925–1927 time period, according to Court, at least some of this price increase should be attributed to quality improvements. The quality levels embodied in 1927 models as compared to 1925 models could be computed in two different, but numerically equivalent, ways. This can be seen by subtracting estimates of $(\alpha_1 \cdot D_{1926,i} + \alpha_2 \cdot D_{1927,i})$ from both sides of the estimated version of Eq. (4.6) as follows:

$$\ln \hat{P}_i - \hat{\alpha}_1 \cdot D_{1926,i} - \hat{\alpha}_2 \cdot D_{1927,i} = \hat{\alpha}_0 + \hat{\beta}_1 \cdot \mathrm{WT}_i + \hat{\beta}_2 \cdot \mathrm{LH}_i + \hat{\beta}_3 \cdot \mathrm{HP}_i \quad \textbf{(4.11)}$$

To interpret this equation, let us suppose that two models were being compared, model $i = A$ from 1925 and model $i = B$ from 1927. Given the values of the characteristics of these two models and the estimated parameters, one could focus on and compute either side of Eq. (4.11). If one calculated the left-hand side, in essence the logarithm of the quality-adjusted price index (the logarithm of Eq. (4.10)) would be subtracted from the least squares fitted quality-unadjusted price in logarithms. This is equivalent to taking the logarithm of the *ratio* of the fitted quality-unadjusted price to the estimated quality-adjusted price. The difference between these two is the logarithm of the estimated quality difference between models A and B.

Alternatively, one could focus on the right-hand side of Eq. (4.11) and simply substitute into it the values of the WT, LH, and HP characteristics for models A and B along with the corresponding parameter estimates. The difference between the two model values would then be directly interpreted as the logarithm of their quality ratio.

Note that in either case the hedonic technique converts the "quality problem" into a quantity measure. Court's methodological contribution to the construction of quality-adjusted price indexes was therefore a most important and significant one. As we shall see in the next section, much recent work—including that on computers—has been based on the framework established by Court in 1939.

The curious reader might wonder what ultimately became of Court's hedonic price research. In terms of contributing to the public policy debate involving more cyclical pricing behavior by GM, Court's findings were dramatic and significant. While the BLS official new car price index rose 45% over the 1925–1935 time period, Court's proposed quality-adjusted new car price index *decreased* approximately 55%.[18] GM officials used these empirical findings along with other data in developing their argument that automobile manufacturers had already been reducing quality-adjusted prices and that any further price decreases designed to stabilize employment would likely lead the auto manufacturers to the "brink of insolvency," since the required break-even volume would be much larger than the price-induced increase in demand for new cars.[19]

In terms of generating new empirical research, however, it is somewhat surprising that Court's methodological contributions were not immediately influential. Indeed, for more than two decades the only subsequent research

ZVI GRILICHES

Father of Modern Hedonic Price Analysis

The ongoing professional interest in the use of regression analysis to adjust price indexes for quality change is due in large part to the work of Zvi Griliches, who in 1961 presented before hearings in the U.S. Congress a seminal analysis entitled "Hedonic Price Indexes for Automobiles: An Econometric Analysis of Quality Change." Griliches' research is widely recognized as having formed the basis of modern hedonic price analysis.

Zvi Griliches was born in Lithuania of Jewish parents in 1930. At age 11, Griliches was moved, along with his parents, into the German-occupied Kaunas Ghetto, where he remained until 1944, when he and his father were separated from his mother and were shipped to a working camp of the Dachau concentration system. Orphaned at the age of 14, Griliches was liberated by Patton's 3rd Army in May 1945 and arrived in Palestine via the "underground railroad" (actually a boat) in September 1947 after a seven-month internment in a British camp on Cyprus. He then spent several years in various kibbutzim, focusing much of his spare time on learning English and mathematics, teaching himself enough to pass an external high school equivalence examination in 1950.

After studying history for a year at the Hebrew University, Griliches applied to and was accepted by the University of California at Berkeley. Griliches chose agricultural economics as his major field of study because to leave Israel at that time, one had to be going to study something "essential." Griliches completed Berkeley's undergraduate degree requirements in two years, receiving a B.S. degree with highest honors in 1953 and an M.S. in 1954, and learned his first econometrics from George Kuznets (Simon's brother). He then transferred to the University of Chicago, where he studied additional econometrics with Roy Radner, Henri Theil, Trygve Haavelmo, and Carl Christ. His 1957 Ph.D. dissertation, "Hybrid Corn: An Exploration of the Economics of Technological Change" (published in *Econometrica*) earned him the best published research award from the American Farm Economic Association.

Although Griliches is widely recognized for his work on hedonic price analysis, his research has ranged widely, and today he is equally well known for major contributions to the analysis of productivity growth and technical change (see Chapter 9 of this book), estimating rates of return to education (Chapter 5), analyzing patent statistics, and the econometric specification and interpretation of distributed lags (Chapters 6, 7, and 8).

Zvi Griliches' initial academic appointment was at the University of Chicago. In 1969 he moved to Harvard University, where he now is the Paul M. Warburg Professor of Economics. He teaches graduate courses in applied econometrics and econometric methods and conducts two seminars, one in econometrics and the other in labor. He is a Fellow of the Econometric Society, served as its President in 1975, was coeditor of *Econometrica* for a decade, and is a recipient of the distinguished John Bates Clark Medal from the American Economic Association. He is also an elected Member of the National Academy of Sciences.

To Zvi Griliches, doing empirical econometrics involves one in a wonderful research venture that can involve numerous frustrations and surprisingly circuitous paths. In a 1977 *Econometrica* article he described this process, quoting from A. A. Milne's *The House at Pooh Corner* as follows:

> "How would it be," said Pooh slowly, "if, as soon as we're out of sight of this Pit, we try to find it again?"
>
> "What's the good of that?" said Rabbit.
>
> "Well," said Pooh, "we keep looking for Home and not finding it, so I thought that if we looked for this Pit, we'd be sure not to find it, which would be a Good Thing, because then we might find something that we weren't looking for, which might be just what we were looking for, really."
>
> "I don't see much sense in that," said Rabbit.
>
> "No," said Pooh humbly, "there isn't. But there was going to be when I began it. It's just that something happened to it on the way."

published on hedonic pricing was relatively obscure, consisting of several theoretical notes and empirical illustrations, including one by Richard Stone on computing a "price per unit of inebriation" for alcoholic beverages.[20]

Court's hedonic multiple regression approach to the construction of price indexes was finally revived in 1961 by Zvi Griliches.[21] Unlike Court's, Griliches' work immediately stimulated a substantial and very influential body of new research, both theoretical and empirical, that continues to this day.[22] Although Court's notion of hedonic prices focused on the demand side, the post-Griliches research typically envisages hedonic prices as the outcome of shifting supply and demand curves for characteristics. Further, as was noted in the introduction to this chapter, Griliches' revival of the hedonic method has now attained an official status; in 1986 the U.S. Bureau of Economic Analysis released official price indexes for computers based in part on the results of hedonic multiple regressions.[23]

4.4 APPLICATIONS OF THE HEDONIC METHOD TO PRICE INDEXES FOR COMPUTERS

Although Court's hedonic price framework has been applied in a host of empirical studies analyzing quality change in various goods and commodities, it is computers and automobiles that have received the greatest share of attention from applied econometricians. In this section we survey and review various applications of the hedonic price procedure to the estimation of quality-adjusted price indexes for computers. Computers provide a particularly interesting application, since quality improvement in the computer industry has been rapid and pervasive. Before we begin this survey, however, we first make some more general comments on the hedonic pricing procedure.

Implicit in the hedonic price framework is the assumption that the numerous models and varieties of a particular commodity can be viewed as consisting of various combinations, bundles, or composites of a smaller number of characteristics or basic attributes. In brief, the hedonic hypothesis is that heterogeneous goods are aggregations of characteristics. Moreover, implicit marginal prices for the characteristics can be calculated as derivatives of the hedonic price equation with respect to levels of the characteristics.

Once one views heterogeneous goods as aggregates of individual characteristics, it becomes clear that the relationship between the overall bundle price and the level or quantity of the various characteristics need not be constant over time, that is, implicit prices may change over time. Firms can be viewed as supplying various combinations of characteristics, and consumers can be envisaged as demanding them. When supply or demand curves for characteristics shift, the implicit price relationships between the overall price of the bundle and the individual characteristics might also change.

For example, recall the motivation of Waugh's research on quantifying the effects of consumers' valuations of vegetable quality on price. Suppose producers responded to a particularly perceived premium and increased the supply of, say, green asparagus. Would this change the size of the market premium for green asparagus? More generally,

> Will the premium paid for products of high quality tend to remain constant, or will it change with variations in the proportion of the different grades of qualities on the market?[24]

The answer to this question depends, of course, on the underlying supply and demand relationships for the characteristics. As we shall see later on, while in general it is difficult to recover consumers' utility functions and/or producers' cost functions from the hedonic regression equation, viewing observations of price-characteristic combinations as representing the outcomes of an underlying and potentially changing supply-demand framework suggests that in empirical implementations, particular care should be given to checking whether the parameters of hedonic price equations are stable over time.

In this context it is useful to note very briefly the major changes that have occurred since the 1950s in the computer industry.[25] It is traditional to characterize the commercial history of mainframe computers as consisting of three generations. By most accounts the first generation of computer history began with the earliest models sold commercially in the United States, beginning in 1953 and 1954, and ended in about 1959–1960, when models were introduced in which solid-state transistors replaced vacuum tubes. This second generation of computers reigned until about 1964 or 1965, when integrated circuit technology was introduced. The third-generation computers embodying the integrated circuit technology, exemplified by the IBM 360 series, displayed a considerably improved price-performance ratio relative to its predecessors.

In addition to these changes in computer hardware, the marketing of software, previously bundled with hardware, was altered considerably beginning in the mid- to late 1960s. In particular, by the late 1960s, computer hardware began to become unbundled from software and associated maintenance. Moreover, whereas in the past, bundled computers were primarily rented on a monthly basis, by around 1968 or so the outright purchase of unbundled computers became the norm.

One implication of these computer hardware and marketing changes for the construction of price indexes is the following: If price indexes are to adjust properly for quality change, then it would seem to be important that the construction of indexes over the 1965–1972 time period should incorporate the effects of quality reductions associated with unbundling and that rental prices should be properly distinguished from purchase prices.

With this as background, let us now examine the pioneering study of demand for computers by Gregory Chow [1967]. The purpose of Chow's study was to explain the growth in demand for computer services in the United States over the 1955–1965 time period, in particular to separate out the effects on demand that would have occurred had technological change (quality improvements) not occurred from demand changes induced by technological change. To do this, it was necessary for Chow to construct a quality-adjusted price index for computer services, using hedonic price analysis and multiple regression techniques. Incidentally, since Chow's data spanned the time in which computers were rented, his measure of price is the rental price per month in thousands of dollars. Moreover, all his data come from an era in which computer software and hardware were bundled.

Recognizing that it would be impossible to obtain measures of all relevant quality variables, Chow chose but three characteristics and hoped that any omitted variables would be very highly correlated with the variables that he included.

The first variable chosen was multiplication time, computed as the average time required to obtain and complete the multiplication instruction, in microseconds. Chow expected this multiplication time variable, named MULT, to have a negative effect on computer rental price. Presumably, the MULT variable measures one aspect of the speed of the computer.

GREGORY C. CHOW
A Pioneer in Econometrics

Although Gregory C. Chow is undoubtedly best-known to econometrics students as developer of the widely used "Chow test" for parameter equality in differing data samples, his contributions have spanned a wide range of other topics as well. Chow's 1967 *American Economic Review* article on the demand for computers, discussed in detail in this chapter, is recognized as the first hedonic price analysis of quality changes embodied in computers; his work on using optimal control theory in dynamic economic models and his research on computational algorithms for econometric estimators are also regarded as seminal.

Born in Macau, South China, in 1929, Chow emigrated to the United States in the late 1940s. He received a B.A. degree from Cornell University in 1951 and M.A. (1952) and Ph.D. (1955) degrees from the University of Chicago, all in economics. After initiating an academic career at the Massachusetts Institute of Technology (1955–1959) and Cornell University (1959–1962), Chow moved in 1962 to the IBM Thomas J. Watson Research Center in Yorktown Heights, New York, where he served as Staff Member and Manager of Economic Models. In 1970, Chow returned to academia, becoming Professor of Economics and Director of the Econometric Research Program at Princeton University.

In the last decade, much of Chow's attention has focused on economic issues in the People's Republic of China (PRC). He has served as Chairman of the American Economic Association Committee on Exchanges in Economics with the PRC, has taught in the PRC on numerous occasions, holds honorary professorships and an honorary degree from Chinese universities, and has written econometric theory and economics textbooks that have been widely read by university students in China. Chow is a Fellow of the Econometric Society and has served on the editorial boards of numerous professional economics journals.

However, since computers are able to execute a wide variety of instructions, multiplication time might not necessarily be representative of the typical tasks executed on the computer. Other single-instruction speed measures could include addition time, but a more preferable measure might be a weighted composite of all of the instruction execution rates for a typical job mix (such as MIPS—millions of instructions per second). As is noted in the survey by Triplett [1989], there is some controversy among computer industry experts concerning the choice of speed measure, in part because it is thought that some measures favor one computer architecture (and therefore the manufacturer adopting it) over another.[26]

The second characteristic chosen by Chow as a measure of quality was memory size, called MEM, which was computed as the product of the number of words in the main memory (in thousands) and the number of binary digits per word, with allowances made for different types of digits.[27] Chow expected MEM to be positively related to quality and so expected the estimated coefficient of MEM in the hedonic price equation to be positive.

The third characteristic used by Chow was also related to speed and involved the average time required by the computer to retrieve information from the memory. This access time variable is named ACCESS. Chow predicted that the effect of ACCESS on rental price would be negative.

Chow obtained data for his study from a number of sources, including a published U.S. government survey of computer rentals and characteristics and issues of the monthly magazine *Computers and Automation*. For each year from 1955 to 1959, Chow obtained data on nine to eleven models rented (but not necessarily newly introduced) that year, while from 1960 to 1965 his data included only newly introduced models, which varied from a sample of 10 new models in 1960 to 18 in 1964.

In terms of empirical results, Chow reported that addition time was considered as a measure of speed instead of MULT but that results with it were slightly inferior. The estimated coefficients obtained by Chow based on separate, year-by-year regressions are reproduced in Table 4.1.[28]

Chow comments on his results as follows:

> Judging from the 11 cross section regressions for the individual years, memory size has a larger coefficient (in absolute value) than either access time or multiplication time. Three of the coefficients of multiplication time, and one coefficient of access time, have wrong signs, though they are small fractions of their standard errors. While the standard errors are large for many coefficients, as a result of the high correlations among the three explanatory variables and of the small sample sizes, the orders of magnitude of the three coefficients do not appear to have changed drastically through time. Note also that the intercept tends to be smaller for later years, but its decline is far from being uniform.[29]

Because his pre-1960 data was scarce, and to avoid mixing first- and second-generation computer models, Chow pooled his data for the years 1960 to 1965, constraining the slope coefficients on the three quality variables to be equal across all years but specifying dummy variable intercept terms for each year 1961 to 1965. The test statistic corresponding to the null hypothesis that these slope coefficients were equal across the six years suggests nonrejection of the null hypothesis; Chow reports a test-statistic of 0.74, which is considerably less than the critical value of the F-statistic at any reasonable level

Table 4.1 Chow's Estimated Hedonic Price Equations for Computer Services, 1955–1965; Estimated Standard Errors in Parentheses (All variables in natural logarithms)

Year	Intercept Term	Multiplication Time	Memory Size	Access Time	R^2	s^2	Number of Observations
1955	2.027	0.0108	0.4297	−0.2895	0.947	0.0461	9
		(0.1021)	(0.1530)	(0.0618)			
1956	1.675	−0.0505	0.4495	−0.1991	0.890	0.2081	11
		(0.1911)	(0.1624)	(0.1076)			
1957	0.140	0.0549	0.5651	−0.2187	0.941	0.1476	10
		(0.1596)	(0.1481)	(0.0807)			
1958	0.542	−0.0171	0.5311	−0.1617	0.976	0.0972	10
		(0.0891)	(0.0697)	(0.0565)			
1959	2.489	−0.2116	0.3562	−0.1270	0.993	0.0360	10
		(0.0366)	(0.0395)	(0.0337)			
1960	1.205	−0.1523	0.4234	−0.1208	0.943	0.1924	10
		(0.1009)	(0.1797)	(0.0783)			
1961	0.005	−0.0615	0.5507	−0.1755	0.944	0.1159	12
		(0.0729)	(0.1078)	(0.0519)			
1962	−2.404	0.0786	0.8264	−0.2571	0.916	0.2414	11
		(0.1411)	(0.1525)	(0.1167)			
1963	−0.801	−0.0675	0.5750	−0.0412	0.951	0.0794	15
		(0.0690)	(0.0732)	(0.1228)			
1964	−1.590	−0.1486	0.6867	0.0412	0.895	0.0978	18
		(0.0525)	(0.0754)	(0.1048)			
1965	−1.354	−0.0411	0.5778	−0.1465	0.877	0.2518	16
		(0.0779)	(0.0821)	(0.0999)			
Pooled Run: 1960–1965	−0.1045	−0.0654	0.5793	−0.1406	0.908	0.1476	82
		(0.0284)	(0.0354)	(0.0293)			
	$-0.1398 \cdot D_{61}$	$-.4891 \cdot D_{62}$	$-0.5938 \cdot D_{63}$	$-0.9248 \cdot D_{64}$		$-1.163 \cdot D_{65}$	
	(0.1665)	(.1738)	(0.1661)	(0.1663)		(0.166)	

Note: D_{61}, D_{62}, D_{63}, D_{64}, and D_{65} are dummy variables for the years 1961–1965.

Source: Data from Gregory C. Chow, "Technological Change and the Demand for Computers," *American Economic Review*, Vol. 57, No. 5, December 1967, pp. 1117–1130.

of significance. Results from this pooled regression are presented in the bottom rows of Table 4.1.

A number of points are worth noting. First, in spite of strong correlations among the explanatory variables, each of the coefficients on the three quality variables, MULT, MEM, and ACCESS, is statistically significant, the MEM variable having a particularly large implied t-statistic (0.5793/0.0354 = 16.36). Second, since the regression involves logarithms of both the dependent and explanatory variables, the estimated coefficients can be interpreted directly as elasticities. The three elasticities are estimated to be 0.58 for MEM, −0.14 for ACCESS, and −0.07 for MULT. Third, coefficients on the dummy variables decrease uniformly as time increases, reflecting sustained price declines for computers, adjusted for quality change. An examination of these coefficients reveals that the price decline is particularly large from 1961 to 1962 (corresponding with the substantial market penetration of second-generation solid-state computers); another considerable decline in quality-adjusted price occurred in 1964, coinciding with price reductions on existing models following the announced introduction of the new IBM Series 360 models.

Quality-adjusted price indexes for computers could be computed in a number of ways. Chow suggests choosing a base year, say, 1960, and computing the base period quantity of computer services as the fitted value of the regression equation (with the −0.1045 intercept for 1960), using the arithmetic mean of the model characteristics for that year as measures of MULT, MEM, and ACCESS. Following the procedure completely analogous to that described for automobiles in the previous section of this chapter beneath Eq. (4.11), the average quantities of (quality-adjusted) computer services for other years are then computed, using the same 1960 intercept but replacing 1960 values of the characteristics with values for each of the models introduced in each year, 1961 to 1965. The quality-adjusted price index for each model could then be computed simply as the rental price divided by the above model-specific quantity-quality index. To calculate an aggregate price index for the year over all models, Chow simply employed an arithmetic average over each of the models introduced that year.[30]

An alternative procedure is much more direct and simply involves taking antilogarithms of the estimated coefficients of the dummy variables in the bottom row of Table 4.1. Normalizing the base year value to unity in 1960, one obtains a time series of quality-adjusted price indexes over the 1960–1965 time period, presented in the middle column of Table 4.2. This hedonic price index computed directly from the regression coefficients can be compared with that obtained using Chow's first suggested procedure, which is presented in the final column of Table 4.2. A comparison of these two columns indicates that in this case the two alternative methods outlined above for computing quality-adjusted price indexes give very similar results.

The above quality-adjusted price indexes can be used to compute their average annual growth rate (AAGR). When this is done for the directly com-

Table 4.2 Quality-Adjusted Price Indexes for Computers, 1960–1965. Based on Chow's Dummy Variable Coefficient Estimates and on Chow's Arithmetic-Weighted Procedure

Year	Estimated Coefficient	Price Index (Antilogarithm)	Price Index* (Arithmetic-Weighted)
1960		1.0000	1.0000
1961	−0.1398	0.8695	0.8438
1962	−0.4891	0.6132	0.6414
1963	−0.5938	0.5522	0.5330
1964	−0.9248	0.3966	0.3906
1965	−1.163	0.3125	0.3188

*Entries in the final column are taken from Chow [1967, Table 2, p. 1124], normalized to unity in 1960.

puted hedonic price index, one finds that the AAGR is approximately −20.8% per year, which implies that the quality-adjusted price index for computers declined approximately 21% per year over the 1960–1965 time period. Such a result is, of course, dramatically different from that implicitly assumed by the U.S. Bureau of Economic Analysis (BEA) until 1986, namely, that the price index for computers was constant at 1.000 over the entire 1953–1985 time period.[31]

Chow's research on the demand for computers marked the beginning of a substantial number of studies estimating quality-adjusted price indexes for computers. These studies have recently been surveyed by Triplett [1989].[32]

Triplett divides the various hedonic price studies on computers into those using data before 1972 and those using post-1972 data. With respect to the pre-1972 studies, Triplett notes that none reports any attempt to deal with the consequences of unbundling, which began to occur in the late 1960s. As a result, Triplett argues that the price indexes for the late 1960s and early 1970s estimated by the hedonic method quite likely overstated quality improvements, although the size of the bias is unknown. Triplett conjectures that it is conceivable that computer prices, quality-adjusted, actually rose slightly in the late 1960s or early 1970s.

After critically surveying a number of empirical studies, Triplett combines their hedonic price index estimates judgmentally, using weights that reflect what he calls "best practice" research criteria, such as quality of the underlying data sources, choice of index computation method used, and investigator effects. This yields a most interesting set of results, reproduced here in Table 4.3.

A number of comments are worth noting. First, a striking result in Table 4.3 is that the quality-adjusted price of computers declined every year from 1953 to 1972. Second, and even more striking, by 1972 a computer's quality-adjusted price was approximately only 1% of what it cost when computers first came on the market in 1953. Third, the advent of second-generation computers in 1958–1959 set off an accelerated rate of price decreases of about

Table 4.3 Triplett's "Best Practice" Research Price Index for Computers, 1953–1972

Year	Price Index (1965 = 100)	Annual % Change	Year	Price Index (1965 = 100)	Annual % Change
1953	1320		1963	183.0	−23.6
1954	1139	−13.7	1964	139.0	−24.2
1955	1010	−11.3	1965	100.0	−27.8
1956	862	−14.7	1966	38.0	−61.5
1957	761	−11.8	1967	26.9	−30.1
1958	689	−9.4	1968	24.3	−9.7
1959	591	−14.2	1969	24.2	−0.4
1960	435	−26.4	1970	23.3	−3.7
1961	332	−23.7	1971	18.1	−22.3
1962	239	−27.9	1972	14.8	−18.2

Source: Data from Jack E. Triplett, "Price and Technological Change in a Capital Good: A Survey of Research on Computers," Chapter 4 in Dale W. Jorgenson and Ralph Landau (eds.), *Technology and Capital Formation,* Cambridge, Mass.: MIT Press, 1989, Table 4.6A, p. 176.

25% per year, which increased dramatically to over 60% when third-generation computers were delivered in 1966. Over the 1967–1970 time period these price decreases slowed considerably; they then picked up again in 1971–1972 with the introduction of the IBM Model 360 series. Note, however, that failure to account for the unbundling of computers implies that the post-1968 price indexes may be biased downward. Fourth and finally, the AAGR of the quality-adjusted price index for computers over the entire 1953–1972 time period is about −27%, implying that quality-adjusted price decreases in computers over this time period have occurred at a prodigious rate.

Turning now to the post-1972 time period, we begin by noting that a substantial number of empirical studies examining computer price movements have been published over this time period. Although Triplett surveys these in considerable detail, here we confine our attention to just one hedonic price study, the IBM analysis published by Cole et al. [1986], which in turn formed part of the basis of the official computer price index later published by the U.S. Department of Commerce, Bureau of Economic Analysis.

One aspect of the Cole et al. study that is worthy of special note was its focus on the individual components or "boxes" of a computer system, rather than on the system as a whole. In particular, Cole et al. separately examined computer processors, intermediate and large (hard) disk drives, printers, and general-purpose displays (keyboards and monitors).

Although they experimented with a number of alternative functional forms (e.g., log-log, semilog, and linear), Cole et al. obtained preferred results with the log-log specification. For the computer processors the quality characteristics chosen were speed (MIPS, or millions of IBM 370-equivalent instructions per second) and memory (in megabytes); for disk drives the characteristics used were speed and capacity. While capacity was relatively straightforward to measure (the number of megabytes that could be stored on the disk drive), speed (in units of kilobytes per second) was computed as 1 over the sum of three elements: average seek time (the average time for the read/write head to locate and arrive at the correct track on the disk) plus average rotation delay (the time required by the disk to rotate so that the read/write head is lined up at the correct point on the track) plus the transfer rate (the time required to transfer the data between the drive and the main memory once the correct position on the disk has been located).[33] Data were taken from a number of sources, including IBM sales manuals and trade and general press sources such as *Datamation* and *Computerworld.* Prices for the various models are list prices for a quantity of one and so do not necessarily correspond with transactions prices, particularly in the case of large-volume discounting.

Since they employed a log-log specification, Cole et al. were able to interpret the coefficient estimates on the characteristic variables as elasticities of price with respect to quality characteristics. One hypothesis that they examined in detail was what they called homogeneity, by which they meant the hypothesis that the sum of the elasticities (coefficient estimates) on the quality characteristic variables equaled 1. Under this type of homogeneity, a doubling in the values of each of the characteristic variables would double the price. Significantly, for each of the four types of computer equipment that Cole et al. examined, the null hypothesis that the characteristics coefficients summed to 1 could not be rejected.

On the basis of their hedonic regression results, Cole et al. constructed a number of alternative price indexes. Here we confine our discussion to their estimates for processors and intermediate-large disk drives, estimates that are reproduced in columns 1–4 of Table 4.4.

The most striking result that is observed in Table 4.4 is that the traditional matched model procedure for accounting for quality change appears to be woefully inadequate. For example, while the matched model procedure generates an AAGR of −8.5% for computer processors, the hedonic regression procedure yields a much larger (in absolute value) AAGR of −19.2%; for disk drives, the matched model and hedonic regression procedures yield price indexes that grow at an AAGR of −6.9% and −16.8%, respectively.

Finally, in column 5 of Table 4.4 we reproduce from Cartwright [1986] the new official U.S. Department of Commerce, Bureau of Economic Analysis, price index for the commodity aggregate of computers and computer-peripheral equipment types, based largely on hedonic regression procedures.[34] Note that this price index continues the steady decline over time first revealed earlier for the 1953–1972 time period in Table 4.3. Over the 1972–1984 era, the AAGR of this quality-adjusted price index is −13.8%.

If one combines the results from Table 4.3 for the 1953–1972 time interval with those of Table 4.4 for the 1972–1984 epoch, one finds that, quality adjusted, computers that cost $531.88 in 1953 cost only $1.00 in 1982; in

Table 4.4 Price Indexes for Processors and Disk Drives Based on the Cole et al. Study* and New Official Hedonic-Based BEA Price Indexes for Computers** (1982 = 100)

	Processors		Disk Drives		Computers
Year	(1) Matched Model	(2) Hedonic Regression	(3) Matched Model	(4) Hedonic Regression	(5) New Official BEA Price Index
1972	214.1	990.1	201.7	427.4	408.1
1973	214.6	1047.5	200.9	429.5	369.3
1974	219.9	814.8	154.5	345.3	291.1
1975	228.9	792.1	143.4	313.2	265.1
1976	223.6	778.2	134.0	291.5	231.1
1977	183.5	499.0	133.5	150.0	199.7
1978	147.3	262.4	131.1	147.0	169.3
1979	136.4	242.6	107.7	111.0	146.2
1980	115.4	177.2	91.0	96.2	117.5
1981	111.1	112.9	92.9	96.6	107.4
1982	100.0	100.0	100.0	100.0	100.0
1983	89.7	90.1	86.5	54.3	77.1
1984	73.7	77.2	85.1	46.9	68.5
AAGR 1972–1984	−8.5	−19.2	−6.9	−16.8	−13.8

**Source:* Cole et al. [1986, Table 7, p. 49].
***Source:* Cartwright [1986, Table 1, p. 8].

other words, what would have cost more than half a million dollars in 1953 cost only $1000 in 1984. Moreover, since the calculations in Cole et al. and Cartwright involve only mainframe and minicomputers and exclude personal (micro) computers, it is possible that this price index understates the amount of quality improvement.

This concludes our survey of empirical hedonic research on price indexes for computers. We now change our focus and consider several econometric issues that arise in the estimation of hedonic regression equations.

4.5 ECONOMETRIC ISSUES IN THE ESTIMATION OF HEDONIC PRICE EQUATIONS

Our survey of empirical hedonic research on price indexes for computers has already raised a number of econometric issues. In this section we briefly consider some other important topics.

4.5.A Heteroskedasticity

One econometric issue that has received some attention in the hedonic price literature concerns heteroskedasticity of the disturbance terms. Suppose, for example, that data consist of average prices of each computer model and that the various models have rather different sales volumes. Let the disturbance term u_i in the regression equation

$$Y_i = \beta_0 + \beta_1 \cdot X_{1i} + \beta_2 \cdot X_{2i} + \cdots + \beta_K \cdot X_{Ki} + u_i \qquad i = 1, \ldots, N$$

originally involving N individual computer observations be distributed normally with mean zero and variance σ^2, but let the M observations consist of average prices for each of the M models, where $M < N$. Denote the volume of sales for the mth model as S_m. When M model-specific averaged data observations are used rather than the original data for each of the N computers, the variance of the disturbance term u_i^* is no longer σ^2 but instead equals σ^2/S_m. This implies a heteroskedastic disturbance term, large-volume models having smaller disturbance variances than models with low-volume sales.

In order that estimates of the parameters be efficient and that estimated standard errors be consistent, it is necessary to use generalized or weighted least squares rather than ordinary least squares. Intuitively, in this case, generalized least squares weights the large-volume, low-disturbance-variance models more and the low-volume, high-disturbance-variance models less than does ordinary least squares. Note, however, that in this particular example, if one first transforms each of the variables (including the vector of ones for the intercept term) by multiplying them by $\sqrt{S_m}$ and then performs ordinary least squares on the transformed data, the results obtained will be numerically equivalent to employing generalized or weighted least squares on the untransformed data. For further details on generalized least squares, see your econometric theory textbook.

4.5.B Choice of Functional Form

Several times in the previous sections we noted that, on the basis of economic or other theory, few if any restrictions were placed on the functional form of the hedonic price equation. While Waugh considered only the linear form, Court compared the semilog form with the linear one and noted that on the basis of goodness-of-fit criteria, with his automobile data the semilog form was preferable. Similarly, Cole et al. compared results based on the linear, semilog, and log-log specifications and, on the basis of their data for four different types of computer equipment, found that in general the log-log specification was preferred. It should be noted here that a comparison of goodness of fit from the various functional forms is not necessarily straightforward, since explaining variations in the natural logarithm of price is not the same as explaining variations in price.

Although a full discussion is beyond the scope of this chapter, it is worth mentioning here briefly that there is a statistical basis that can be used to compare alternative functional forms, and not just the log-log, semilog, and linear specifications. This procedure is known as the Box-Cox or Box-Tidwell transformation.[35] The Box-Cox procedure involves transforming a variable from X_i to X_i^* as follows:

$$X_i^* = \frac{X_i^\lambda - 1}{\lambda} \tag{4.12}$$

where λ is a parameter to be estimated. When $\lambda = 1$ for all variables (Y and the X's), the functional form is linear, and in the limit as $\lambda \rightarrow 0$ for each variable, $Y_i^* \rightarrow \ln Y_i$ and the $X_i^* \rightarrow \ln X_i$, implying a log-log specification. One can also specify a different λ for Y_i than for all of the X_i right-hand variables, in which case one would have a mixed specification; if the λ for Y were restricted to 0 and that for all the X's to 1, a semilogarithmic functional form would result. In the Box-Tidwell procedure the individual X's are permitted to have differing λ's as well.

An important point here is that λ need not be restricted to values of 0 or 1 but can take on a wide variety of other values, including those outside the 0–1 interval.[36] In fact, in his survey, Triplett [1989] notes that the log-log specification used in many econometric studies is inconsistent with certain a priori knowledge of the computer industry. He suggests that values of λ other than 0 or 1 should also be investigated, including negative values.[37]

4.5.C Choice of Variables, Make Effects, and Effects of Omitted Variables

The hedonic hypothesis essentially involves treating varieties of products as alternative bundles of a smaller number of characteristics. These characteristics should of course reflect measures of quality. But how should measures of quality be chosen? In the case of computers, Cole et al. report that the IBM study group spent considerable effort in understanding the views of computer industry engineering design and marketing personnel and that on the basis of such discussions they settled on a number of quality variables. This approach is attractive, since knowledge of the particular industry is most useful in choosing measures of quality.

As Chow, Cole, and others have freely acknowledged, however, it is impossible to specify all the relevant quality variables entering an hedonic price equation for computers. In general, unless the omitted variables are either perfectly correlated or perfectly uncorrelated with each of the included variables, the omission of significant quality variables can result in biased estimates of the parameters.

Some have argued that one particularly important quality variable that is typically omitted from computer hedonic price equations concerns the reliability of the model, or the service and maintenance it may require. Presumably, this variable is omitted because of difficulty in obtaining an accurate measure of it. However, if such a quality were associated with the manufacturer of the model, and if it were assumed that this quality effect is constant over time, then one could incorporate it into the hedonic equation by specifying dummy variables for various manufacturers. When this is done, estimates of the resulting parameters are often called "make effects."[38]

More generally, it is often the case that the quality variables employed in hedonic regression equations are not in themselves measures of quality but are presumed to be highly correlated with consumers' perceptions of qualities. In the automobile study by Court, for example, the weight of the auto model in pounds was used as a measure of quality. Consumers surely do not judge the quality of an auto by its weight, yet in fact weight has often been highly correlated with other quality attributes, such as safety and power.

This raises the issue of how one can properly estimate parameters of the hedonic price equation when the quality attributes are unobserved or are measured with error. There is a great deal of literature elsewhere in econometrics on coping with measurement error or unobserved variables, but that literature is only now finally beginning to be applied to the estimation of hedonic price equations.[39] We can expect much more research on this topic in the future.

4.5.D Identification of Underlying Supply and Demand Functions

Earlier in this chapter it was noted that since price-quality observations can be viewed as the market outcome of underlying supply-demand relations for characteristics, shifts in either function could result in volatile parameter estimates in the estimated hedonic price equation. To be specific, recall that implicit prices of the characteristics can be computed as partial derivatives of the price of the product with respect to the level of the characteristic. With a linear functional form, these derivatives are simply the parameters, and in that case the parameters provide direct estimates of the implicit prices. With other functional forms, such as the semilog or log-log specifications, these derivatives can depend on levels of the characteristics and the product price as well as the parameter estimates. This therefore suggests that tests for parameter stability in the hedonic price equation are closely related to tests for shifts in the underlying supply-demand relationships for characteristics.[40]

This type of reasoning has led a number of researchers to extend the hedonic price framework and to attempt to estimate, in addition to the hedonic price equation, the underlying supply and demand equations for characteristics. However, this more ambitious analysis of hedonic markets raises a number of important econometric issues.

Note first that the estimated hedonic price equation contains three pieces of information: the price of the product, the quantities of the characteristics, and the implicit prices of the characteristics. This information makes it possible to define the budget constraint facing consumers; for example, how much of characteristic *i* must be given up in order to obtain more of characteristic *j*, product price being held constant. Second, since with many functional forms the implicit prices depend on the levels of the characteristics, the slope of the budget constraint is not necessarily constant, and so the budget constraint is nonlinear. This contrasts with the usual case dealt with in economics texts, in which the budget constraint for products is linear.

Owing in large part to nonlinearity of the budget constraint, it turns out that in general it is very difficult, and at times even impossible, to obtain consistent estimates of the supply and demand functions underlying the hedonic price equation. This has been shown in important papers by Sherwin Rosen [1974] and Dennis Epple [1987]; also see Timothy J. Bartik [1987].

There are, however, some special cases in which one can interpret these implicit prices as reflecting directly the marginal costs of production or the valuations of consumers. Suppose first that the supply of characteristics is fixed, that is, supply is perfectly price inelastic. In such a case, demand curves for the various characteristics will intersect with vertical supply curves at the implicit prices estimated by the hedonic price equation. Hence in such cases, implicit prices will reflect the market's valuations of the characteristics. If in addition it is assumed that all consumers are alike, then the implicit prices reflect valuations of the representative consumer. In practice, empirical hedonic studies based on perfectly inelastic supply assumptions have often dealt with secondhand markets such as those for automobiles, trucks, or housing.[41]

Alternatively, suppose that supply curves for characteristics are perfectly flat and elastic, firms are identical, and markets are competitive. In such cases the demand curves for the various characteristics will always intersect with the supply curves at an implicit price that is equal to the average (and marginal) costs of production, since with competitive markets, price equals average and marginal costs.[42] Incidentally, the perfect competition assumption can be relaxed to that of a constant markup situation; for an empirical implementation, see Makoto Ohta [1975].

In general, however, the strong results reported by Rosen, and especially by Epple, indicate that while hedonic prices reflect the shape of budget constraints, identification of the underlying supply and demand functions for characteristics is very difficult and that a great deal of care is required in both the specification and the estimation of equations in order to obtain a valid inference. The subtleties involved become even more complex if one specifies that markets for new products can be in temporary disequilibrium in the sense that supply prices are not necessarily instantaneously adjusted to equality with consumers' valuations.[43]

4.5.E Final Comments

In this section we have briefly raised a number of important econometric issues that are involved in the estimation and interpretation of parameters in hedonic price equations. Exciting features of the hedonic price framework are that its practical importance is obvious, it can be implemented relatively easily, and yet it raises a host of very significant and difficult econometric issues. Therefore the analysis of hedonic prices provides both beginning and advanced econometricians with opportunities for challenging research. With that as background we now take a hands-on approach and involve you in the estimation and interpretation of hedonic price equations.

4.6 HANDS ON WITH HEDONIC REGRESSIONS, PRICE INDEXES, AND COMPUTERS

The purpose of the following exercises is to help you gain an empirical understanding of hedonic regression equations, of price indexes constructed from estimated hedonic regression equations, and of the importance of selected characteristics on prices of computers. Although you might not experience hedonistic pleasures from these exercises involving hedonic regressions, in fact they are very useful, and you might even enjoy them!

Exercise 1 is particularly enlightening; in it you attempt to replicate Waugh's pioneering study and find that replication is not possible. This is a useful (and, unfortunately, not uncommon) experience in applied econometrics. This leads you to examine his data more carefully. In Exercise 2 you perform a number of simple and multiple regression estimations using Waugh's data, and then you examine relationships among their R^2 measures, as well as coefficients of determination and correlations.

In Exercise 3 you compute a number of alternative price indexes for computers, using Chow's data set, multiple regression techniques, and dummy variables. You also test an hypothesis involving the specification of the MEM variable. Again, you will experience some problems in attaining complete replication of Chow's original findings. Then in Exercise 4 you replicate (with success!) the findings reported by Cole et al. in their analysis of hard disk drives of computers, findings that were later adopted in part by the U.S. Department of Commerce for its official computer price index. You will test for homogeneity of the characteristics and will also examine alternative ways of modeling price changes over time.

Whether the hedonic coefficients are stable over time is an important issue; therefore in Exercise 5 you have the opportunity to test this hypothesis, using a variety of parameter equality tests, including the well-known Chow test. The application here involves examining parameter stability over the first and second generations of computer models and employs Chow's data. Then in Exercise 6 you investigate a different way of constructing price indexes based on hedonic equations, namely, using adjacent year regression procedures and Chow's data.

Finally, for students with more advanced backgrounds, in Exercise 7 you engage in an examination of choice of functional form, using the Box-Cox estimation method and your choice of either the Waugh asparagus data or the Chow computer data.

••••••••••

In the data diskette provided (have you made a backup?), you will find a subdirectory called CHAP4.DAT with data files. In these data files, three data series are provided, including the asparagus data from the original Waugh study (in a file named WAUGH), the data series collected and used by Chow in his 1967 study of demand for computer services (CHOW), and a portion of the large data set used by Cole et al. in the IBM study for the U.S. Department of Commerce. The Cole et al. data here are those for intermediate and large (hard) disk drives and are found in the file named COLE.

Note that before the data diskette can be used, the data files must be properly edited and formatted, depending on the requirements of your particular computer software. For further information, refer back to Chapter 1, Section 1.3. MAKE SURE THAT ALL DATA FILES TO BE USED IN THE EXERCISES BELOW ARE PROPERLY FORMATTED.

EXERCISES

EXERCISE 1: Examining Waugh's 1927 Asparagus Data

In a number of exercises in this book you will be asked to replicate a researcher's reported empirical findings. The appropriate data will be provided to you, and unless your software is flawed, you should be able to replicate successfully previously reported results. In some cases, however, it will not be possible to achieve a complete replication or reconciliation of findings, and this will require you to dig further and examine the underlying data more closely. That is what we ask you to do in this exercise. The purpose of this exercise, therefore, is to involve you in an important part of the scientific method, namely, to attempt to replicate others' empirical findings.

In your data diskette subdirectory CHAP4.DAT is a file called WAUGH, which contains 200 data points on four variables: (1) the relative price per bunch of asparagus, named PRICE; (2) the number of inches of green color on the asparagus (in hundredths of inches), called GREEN; (3) the number of stalks of asparagus per bunch, denoted NOSTALKS; and (4) the variation in size (the interquartile coefficient) of the stalks, denoted DISPERSE.[44]

(a) Using these data, estimate the parameters of the multiple regression equation in which PRICE is regressed on a constant term, GREEN, NOSTALKS, and DISPERSE. Compare the parameter estimates that you obtain with those reported by Waugh, reproduced in Eq. (4.3) of this chapter. Which parameter estimates differ the most from those of Waugh?

(b) Since the results differ, further investigation appears to be warranted. In his Appendix, Waugh [1929, Table 4, p. 144] reports summary statistics of his underlying data. In particular, he reports the arithmetic means of the variables PRICE, GREEN, NOSTALKS, and DISPERSE to be 90.095, 5.8875, 19.555, and 14.875, respectively. Compute means of these variables. Are his statistics consistent with those based on the data in your file WAUGH? Do you have any hunches yet on the source of the inability to replicate Waugh's findings?

(c) Waugh's Appendix also provides statistics on the product moments (variances and covariances) of the four variables, as follows:

	PRICE	GREEN	NOSTALKS	DISPERSE
PRICE	1063.64	3430.89	−100.92	−82.35
GREEN		24317.19	−17.01	−154.54
NOSTALKS			61.33	25.51
DISPERSE				83.07

Using your computer software and the data provided in the file WAUGH, compute the moment matrix and compare it to Waugh's, as reproduced above. Notice that the sample variances for the variables GREEN and DISPERSE are very similar to those reported by Waugh,[45] they are not quite as close for NOSTALKS, and are very different for PRICE. Are all your covariances larger than those reported by Waugh, or does the relative size vary? Does there appear to be any pattern to the differences that might help to reconcile the findings?

(d) Even though it does not appear to be possible to reconcile Waugh's data with his reported estimates of regression coefficients, are any of his principal *qualitative* findings concerning the effects of variations in GREEN, NOSTALKS, and DISPERSE affected? How different are your findings from his concerning the *quantitative* effects of one-unit changes in each of the regressors on the *absolute* price per bunch of asparagus? (To do these calculations, you will need to refer back to Section 4.2 and will also need to know that the average market quotation PM_i was \$2.782.) Comment also on the statistical significance of the parameter estimates.

(e) Do you have any final thoughts on why results differ? (Hint: Compute least squares estimates using his estimated variances and covariances, reproduced above.)

EXERCISE 2: Exploring Relationships among R^2, Coefficients of Determination, and Correlation Coefficients

Earlier in this chapter we noted the extensive use Waugh made of his estimated coefficients of determination and how he apparently erred in interpreting his results. The purpose of this exercise is to gain an understanding of relationships among the various coefficients of determination, R^2, and correlation coefficients, as well as to comprehend better the implications of the extent of correlation among regressors.

(a) In the data file WAUGH of subdirectory CHAP4.DAT you have observations on the variables PRICE, GREEN, NOSTALKS, and DISPERSE. Using your computer software, compute simple correlations between each of these variables. The correlation matrix that you obtain should be the following:

	PRICE	GREEN	NOSTALKS	DISPERSE
PRICE	1.00000	0.74834	−0.40656	−0.32464
GREEN		1.00000	−0.01403	−0.12605
NOSTALKS			1.00000	0.35003
DISPERSE				1.00000

Which variables are most highly correlated? Which variables are almost orthogonal?

(b) Run three simple regressions, PRICE on GREEN, PRICE on NOSTALKS, and PRICE on DISPERSE, where each regression also includes a constant term. Take the R^2 from each of these three simple regressions, and compute its square root. Then compare its value with the appropriate correlation coefficient reported in the first row of the above table. Why are they equal (except for sign)? Now suppose you had messed up and had inadvertently run the "reverse" regressions, GREEN on PRICE, NOSTALKS on PRICE, and DISPERSE on PRICE. What R^2 measures would you have obtained? Why do they equal those from the "correct" regressions?

(c) Notice the value of the R^2 measure from the simple regression of PRICE on GREEN, computed in part (b). What do you expect to happen to this value of R^2 if you now add the regressor NOSTALKS, that is, run a multiple regression equation with PRICE on a constant, GREEN, and NOSTALKS? Why? Given the correlation between the GREEN and NOSTALKS variables shown in the above table, do you expect the change in R^2 to be large or small? Why? Run this regression equation, and check to see whether your intuition is validated. Then comment on the change in the R^2 value from the simple regression of PRICE on GREEN or PRICE on DISPERSE when PRICE is regressed on both GREEN and DISPERSE; is this change consistent with the sample correlation between GREEN and DISPERSE? Similarly, what is the change in the R^2 value from the simple regression of PRICE on NOSTALKS or PRICE on DISPERSE when PRICE is regressed on both NOSTALKS and DISPERSE? Is this change consistent with the sample correlation coefficient between NOSTALKS and DISPERSE? Why?

(d) In all three cases considered in part (c), the R^2 from the multiple regression (with two regressors in addition to the constant) is less than the sum of the R^2's from the corresponding two simple regressions. Is the R^2 from the multiple regression equation with all three regressors (GREEN, NOSTALKS, and DISPERSE) greater than or less than the sum of the R^2 from the three simple regressions? *Note:* It might be tempting to conclude from this that the R^2 from a multiple regression with a constant term and K regressors is *always* less than or equal to the sum of the R^2 values from the K simple regressions. However, this is not always the case, as has been shown in an interesting theoretical counter example by Harold Watts [1965] and validated empirically by David Hamilton [1987]. (See Exercise 3 in Chapter 3 in this book for further details.)

(e) Using Eq. (4.5) in this chapter to compute separate coefficients of determination, based on the regression coefficient estimates reported by Waugh and reproduced in Eq. (4.3), see whether you can replicate Waugh's reported coefficient of determination values for the GREEN, NOSTALKS, and DISPERSE variables as 0.40837, 0.14554, and 0.02133, respectively. You should be able to replicate Waugh for NOSTALKS and DISPERSE but not for GREEN. Waugh [1929, p. 113] states: "The sum of the coefficients of determination is .57524, indicating that 57.524 per cent of the squared variability in the percentage prices is accounted for by the three factors studied." Is this correct? What should Waugh have stated instead? Why?

(f) As in part (a) of Exercise 1, estimate parameters in the multiple regression equation of PRICE on a constant, GREEN, NOSTALKS, and DISPERSE. Note the value of the R^2 from this regression, and then compute and retrieve the fitted or predicted values. Now run a simple regression equation in which the dependent variable is PRICE and the regressors include a constant and the fitted value from the previous regression equation. Compare the R^2 from this regression to that from the first regression. Why does this result occur? Why is the value of the estimated intercept term zero and the estimated slope coefficient unity in this regression?

EXERCISE 3: Constructing Alternative Price Indexes for Computers Based on Chow's Data

The purpose of this exercise is to construct a price index for computers using hedonic regression techniques and then to assess the sensitivity of the price index to changes in the specification of the underlying hedonic regression equation.

In the data file CHOW in the subdirectory CHAP4.DAT you will find data series consisting of 137 observations on 11 variables. These variables (not necessarily in the same order as they appear in the data file) include the number of new installations of that computer model in that year (VOLUME), the monthly rental of computers (RENT), the number of words in main memory, in thousands (WORDS), the number of binary digits per word (BINARY), the number of equivalent binary digits (DIGITS), the average time required to obtain and complete multiplication or addition instructions (denoted as MULT and ADD, respectively), the average time required to access information from memory (ACCESS), the year in which the model was introduced (YEAR), a dummy variable taking on the value of 1 if the model was manufactured by the IBM corporation (IBMDUM), and the number of the observation (ORDER). These data were provided by Gregory Chow.

(a) Construct the appropriate variables. In particular, take natural logarithms of the variables RENT, MULT, ACCESS, and ADD, and rename them using the prefix LN (e.g., LNRENT). Form the variable for memory space, MEM, as the product WORDS*BINARY*DIGITS, and then take the natural logarithm of this new MEM variable and call it LNMEM. Finally, construct the dummy variables D_{61}, D_{62}, D_{63}, D_{64}, and D_{65} that take on the value of unity if the model was introduced in the year 1961, 1962, 1963, 1964, or 1965, respectively, and otherwise are zero. Note that if a model was introduced in, for example, 1962, the value of the variable YEAR for that observation would be 62. Using the data from 1960 through 1965, and then from 1954 to 1959, compute and examine the correlation matrices measuring simple correlations among the above variables. Are the correlations among variables roughly the same over the two time intervals? Was Chow's concern over collinearity among regressors justified?

(b) Having constructed these data, replicate Chow by estimating parameters of the multiple regression equation of LNRENT on a constant term, D_{61}, D_{62}, D_{63}, D_{64}, D_{65}, LNMULT, LNMEM, and LNACCESS, using observations from 1960 through 1965 (observations 56 to 137 in the variable ORDER). Unless your software (or data construction procedures) is flawed, you should be able to obtain the same results as Chow reported, reproduced in the bottom rows of Table 4.1 in this chapter. Finally, normalize the price index for computers to 1.000 in 1960, take antilogarithms of the estimated coefficients on the dummy variables, and then form a price index covering the 1961–1965 time period. Compare this price index series to that reported in Table 4.2.

(c) Arguments can be made that for purposes of computational accuracy the number of equivalent binary digits per word (the product BINARY*DIGITS) might be more important than the number of words in memory (WORDS). Show that in Chow's logarithmic specification of the variable MEM in the hedonic price equation, the logarithms of these two variables (BINARY*DIGITS and WORDS) are implicitly assumed to have equal slope coefficient estimates. Now construct a new separate variable measuring word length, LENGTH = BINARY*DIGITS; then form the two separate logarithmic variables LNLENGTH and LNWORDS. Next, estimate parameters in the multiple regression equation of LNRENT on a constant term, D_{61}, D_{62}, D_{63}, D_{64}, D_{65}, LNMULT, LNLENGTH, LNWORDS, and LNACCESS, using observations from 1960 through 1965 (observations 56 to 137 in the variable ORDER). Test the null hypothesis that coefficient on LNLENGTH equals that on LNWORDS, using a reasonable level of significance. Is this null hypothesis rejected or not rejected? Which specification do you prefer, and why?

(d) Next construct dummy variables D_{55}, D_{56}, D_{57}, D_{58}, D_{59}, and D_{60} that take on the value 1 if the appropriate year is 1955, 1956, 1957, 1958, 1959, or 1960, respectively. Using the entire sample of 137 observations, estimate parameters in the multiple regression equation of LNRENT on the dummy variables D_{55} through D_{65}, LNMULT, LNMEM, and LNACCESS. On the basis of values of the estimated dummy variable coefficients, construct a price index for computers covering the 1954–1965 time period, normalized to unity in 1954. Compare this price index with the "best practice" index computed by Triplett, reproduced in Table 4.3. (You might want to renormalize one of the two series so that the base years are common.)

(e) In Section 4.5.A of this chapter it was noted that if the differing computer models range considerably in their volumes of sales, and if the pure data reflected arithmetic means over varying amounts of sales by model, then the disturbance terms may be heteroskedastic. Chow collected data on the number of computers installed by year for each model; in the data file CHOW this variable is named VOLUME. Using the pooled data over the 1960–1965 time period, follow the procedures outlined in Section 4.5.A, transform the variables appropriately (including the intercept and dummy variables), and then estimate parameters of the transformed model data by ordinary least squares. Are any of the parameter estimates affected significantly? What is the effect on the estimated standard errors of adjusting for this type of heteroskedasticity? Is the rationale for this type of heteroskedasticity correct, since LNRENT rather than RENT is the dependent variable? Why or why not?

EXERCISE 4: Price Indexes for Disk Drives: A Closer Look at the IBM Study

The purpose of this exercise is to replicate, interpret, and extend selected results reported by Cole et al. in the IBM study of price indexes for hard disk drives. Using data consisting of 91 observations on 30 devices marketed by 10 vendors over the 1972–1984 time period in the United States, Cole et al. obtained the following results, in which LN refers to the natural logarithm, PRICE is the list price, SPEED is 1 over the sum of average seek time plus average rotation delay plus transfer rate, CAP is the capacity of the disk drive in megabytes, the numbers in parentheses are t-statistics, and s is the estimated standard error of the residuals:

$$\text{LNPRICE}_i = \text{Dummies} + \underset{(3.3)}{0.41}\ \text{LNSPEED}_i + \underset{(5.8)}{0.46}\text{LNCAP}_i + e_i$$

$$i = 1, \ldots, 91 \qquad R^2 = 0.844 \qquad s = 0.051$$

The data used by Cole et al. are found in the data file COLE within the subdirectory CHAP4.DAT. This file also contains a number of other variables, discussed in the README.DOC file of the CHAP4.DAT subdirectory. Further information can also be obtained by reading the article by Cole et al. in the January 1986 *Survey of Current Business.*

Very important note: After publishing their article, Cole et al. discovered several data errors. Three data corrections have been made since the original research was published. These data revisions affect parameter estimates. The data now appearing at the beginning of the COLE file reflect these corrections, while original values for these data are found in the last part of the COLE data file. Further information is available in the README.DOC data file of the CHAP4.DAT subdirectory.

(a) Using the original data, construct the variables LNPRICE, LNSPEED, and LNCAP, as well as dummy variables by year for each year from 1973 to 1984. Estimate parameters of the multiple regression model of LNPRICE on a constant, the 12 yearly dummies, LNSPEED, and LNCAP. You should be able to replicate successfully the Cole et al. results reproduced above.

(b) Now construct the same variables using the corrected data, and estimate parameters of the same regression equation. Compare the results. Are any of the parameter estimates affected in a substantial manner?

(c) Cole et al. report that in many cases they were unable to reject the null hypothesis of homogeneity, which they interpreted to imply that the sum of the estimated regression coefficients on LNSPEED and LNCAP equals unity. Since most computer regression software programs permit you to print out or retrieve the estimated variance-covariance matrix of the estimated coefficients, you should be able to obtain estimates of the variances and covariances of these two regression coefficients. Given your parameter and variance-covariance estimates from part (b), construct a 95% confidence interval for the sum of the regression coefficients on the LNSPEED and LNCAP variables. (You will need to use the variance of a sum rule—see any statistics text to refresh your memory.) Is the null hypothesis of homogeneity rejected? Why or why not? Comment on your test results.

(d) The model specification employed in parts (a) and (b) allows the annual rate of price decrease, quality adjusted, to vary over time. A more restrictive assumption is that this annual rate of price decrease is constant. Show that if one replaces the 12 dummy variables in part (a) or (b) with the single variable TIME, where TIME takes on the value 1 in 1972, 2 in 1973, . . . , and 12 in 1984, then such a model specification imposes the restriction that the annual rate of price decrease is constant. Generate the TIME variable, and then, using the corrected data and the variable TIME in place of the annual dummy variables, estimate such a model. Test the null hypothesis of constant rate of price decreases against the alternative hypothesis of differing rates of price decrease for each year. Do the data support the constant rate of price decrease assumption? Why or why not?

EXERCISE 5: Assessing the Stability of the Hedonic Price Equation for First- and Second-Generation Computers

In this exercise we assess the stability of the hedonic price equation for computers over time. One implicit hypothesis underlying the hedonic method is that goods such as computers can be viewed as the aggregate of a number of characteristics. Since firms supply various computer models embodying alternative combinations of characteristics and consumers demand them, the relationship between price and characteristics reflects the outcome of a market process. When dramatic technological changes occur, factor prices vary, or if consumer preferences change, the relationship between the overall price of the bundle and the individual characteristics might also change. The data to be used are in the file CHOW within the subdirectory CHAP4.DAT; names of variables are described at the beginning of Exercise 3 above.

(a) Conventional wisdom in the computer industry dates the first generation of computers as occurring from 1954 to about 1959 and the second generation as taking place between 1960 and about 1965. Chow [1967, p. 1123] reports that he tested the null hypothesis that the three "slope" coefficients were equal over the 1960–1965 time period and could not reject the null hypothesis; his F-test statistic was 0.74, much less than the critical value at any reasonable level of significance. Construct the appropriate variables as in part (a) of Exercise 3, and then estimate parameters in two models, one in which the slope coefficients are constrained to be the same in all years 1960–1965 (a pooled regression) and the other in which these coefficients are allowed to differ (separate, year-by-year regressions). You should be able to replicate Chow's results, reproduced in Table 4.1 of this chapter. Based on the sums of squared residuals from these regressions, test the null hypothesis that the slope coefficients are equal over the 1960–1965 time period. Be particularly careful in calculating the appropriate degrees of freedom for the F-test.

(b) Form appropriate dummy variables for each of the years from 1955 to 1959, and then repeat part (a) and test the null hypothesis that the slope coefficients are equal over the 1954–1959 era, first by running a pooled regression over the 1954–1959 data and then by doing year-by-year regressions, 1954 to 1959. Incidentally, the year-by-year results that you will obtain for 1955–1958 will differ somewhat from those reported by Chow and reproduced in Table 4.1; the reason for these discrepancies is unclear, although for years 1957 and 1958 the CHOW data set has only nine observations, whereas in Chow's [1967] original article he indicates the use of ten observations for both years.

(c) In essence, parts (a) and (b) tested for slope parameter stability *within* the first and the second generations of computers, respectively. To test whether the hedonic relationship changed *between* the first and second generations, it will be useful to run one additional regression covering the entire 1954–1965 time period, namely, a specification in which LNRENT is regressed on a constant, year-specific dummy variables for 1955 through 1965, LNMEM, LNMULT, and LNACCESS. Having run this regression, and initially assuming equality of the slope parameters within the first (1954–1959) and the second (1960–1965) generations, test the null hypothesis that the slope coefficients of the first generation equal those of the second generation. Does this result surprise you? Why or why not? Next, relax the assumption of slope parameter equality within each generation, and test the null hypothesis that slope parameters are equal over the entire 1954–1965 time span against the alternative hypothesis that these slope coefficients varied from year to year. Note that calculation of the appropriate F-statistic requires comparing the sums of squared residuals from the 12 separate year-by-year regressions with that from the pooled 1954–1965 regression and then adjusting by the appropriate degrees of freedom. Interpret your results. Are the two test results of part (c) mutually consistent? Why or why not?

(d) The above tests for parameter stability are in essence a variant of the well-known Chow test (yes, the same Gregory Chow who wrote the computer article), described in most econometrics textbooks. In order that this test statistic be valid, it is necessary to assume that disturbances are distributed independently among models and over time and, perhaps more important, that their variance is constant over time. Chow's estimates of the disturbance variance, denoted s^2, are reproduced in Table

4.1. Using any one of the tests for homoskedasticity described in your econometrics textbook, test whether the homoskedasticity assumption is valid within the two generations and between the two generations. What do your results imply concerning the validity of the tests performed in parts (a) through (c)?

EXERCISE 6: Using Time-Varying Hedonic Price Equations to Construct Chained Price Indexes for Computers

The procedures for constructing quality-adjusted price indexes for computers based on estimated hedonic price equations discussed in this chapter assumed that the slope coefficients were constant over time. In this exercise we relax the assumption of constant parameters over the entire data sample and instead employ adjacent year regression procedures to construct chained price indexes. The data used in this exercise are in the file named CHOW, within the subdirectory CHAP4.DAT, and are described at the beginning of Exercise 3.

(a) Consider the following regression equation, based on data from two adjacent years, for example, 1954 and 1955:

$$\begin{aligned}\mathrm{LNRENT}_i = \beta_0 + \beta_t\,\mathrm{DUM}_{it} + \beta_1\,\mathrm{LNMEM}_i \\ + \beta_2\,\mathrm{LNMULT}_i + \beta_3\,\mathrm{LNACCESS}_i\end{aligned}$$

where DUM_{it} is a dummy variable taking on the value of 1 if model i was introduced in the current year (say, 1955) and 0 if it was introduced in the adjacent previous year (1954). The estimate of β_t indicates the change in the natural logarithm of the price from 1954 to 1955, holding quality fixed. Such a regression equation could be specified for each pair of adjacent years, such as 1954–1955, 1955–1956, 1956–1957, . . . , 1964–1965. An attractive feature of the adjacent year regression approach is that the slope coefficients are allowed to vary over time. Using the data in the file CHOW, construct the appropriate variables, estimate the 11 adjacent year regression equations by ordinary least squares, and then retrieve the 11 estimates of β_t, denoted as β_{1955}, β_{1956}, β_{1957}, . . . , β_{1965}. Next, using data covering the entire 1954–1965 time period, estimate the more traditional hedonic regression equation in which LNRENT is regressed on a constant, 11 dummy variables D_{1955} to D_{1965}, LNMEM, LNMULT, and LNACCESS. Compare year-to-year *changes* in the estimated coefficients of these 11 dummy variables with the *levels* of the 11 β_t estimates. Why is it appropriate to compare year-to-year changes in the estimated dummy variable coefficients with levels of the estimated β_t? Comment on and interpret any differences that appear to be substantial.

(b) Calculate a traditional hedonic price index for computers over the 1954–1965 time period, normalized to unity in 1954, by simply exponentiating values of the estimated coefficients on the 11 dummy variables, D_{1955} to D_{1965}. Then construct a chained price index, using the following sequential procedure: For 1955, exponentiate β_{1955}; for 1956, exponentiate the sum $(\beta_{1955} + \beta_{1956})$; for 1957, exponentiate the sum $(\beta_{1955} + \beta_{1956} + \beta_{1957})$. Continue this for each year, until for 1965 the quality-adjusted price index is computed as the antilogarithm of the sum $(\beta_{1955} + \beta_{1956} + \beta_{1957} + \cdots + \beta_{1965})$. Why is such an index called a chained price index? Empirically compare this chained price index with the traditional hedonic price index. Do they differ in any substantial or systematic manner? Which index do you prefer, and why?

EXERCISE 7: Exploring Alternative Functional Forms for the Hedonic Price Equation Using Box-Cox Procedures

In Section 4.5 it was noted that the choice of a functional form for the hedonic price equation is often one made with a priori information having only limited influence, and goodness-of-fit criteria instead play a major role. The purpose of this exercise is to use the Box-Cox procedure to choose among alternative functional forms for the hedonic price equation. To do this exercise, you will need to have access to software programs that are capable of doing Box-Cox transformations.[46] The following nomenclature will be adopted: A Box-Cox transformation of the dependent variable involving a λ variable as in Eq. (4.12) will be called a λ_y transformation, while a Box-Cox transformation of the independent variables will be called a λ_x transformation. There are four common special cases of the Box-Cox transformation:

1. $\lambda_y = \lambda_x = 1$: a linear equation ($y$ on x),
2. $\lambda_y = \lambda_x = 0$: a log-log equation ($\ln y$ on $\ln x$),
3. $\lambda_y = 0, \lambda_x = 1$: a semilog equation ($\ln y$ on x), and
4. $\lambda_y = 1, \lambda_x = 0$: another semilog equation (y on $\ln x$).

It is important to note, however, that λ_y and λ_x can take on values other than 0 or 1. This implies that the Box-Cox procedure is not limited to the set of linear, log-log, and semilogarithmic functional forms.

For this exercise, choose and work through either part (a), dealing with the Waugh asparagus data, or part (b), based on the IBM study of disk drives. (Note: If you choose to work with the Waugh data, you will need to delete the 10 observations for which DISPERSE = 0.)

(a) Using the data on asparagus PRICE, GREEN, NOSTALKS, and DISPERSE in the data file WAUGH of the subdirectory CHAP4.DAT, estimate the four above special cases of the Box-Cox transformation, where in each case the same λ_x transformation is applied to each of the regressors GREEN, NOSTALKS, and DISPERSE. On the basis of the sample value of the log-likelihood function, which of these four functional forms is preferred? Now estimate the parameters λ_y and λ_x, where λ_x is still constrained to be the same for all three regressors but differs from λ_y. Are the estimated values of λ_y and λ_x close to any of the four special cases outlined above? Comment on the signs of the estimated coefficients and the implied shape of the hedonic price function. Using the likelihood ratio testing procedure, test each of these four special cases as a null hypothesis, where in each case the alternative hypothesis leaves λ_y and λ_x unconstrained. Finally, test the null hypothesis that $\lambda_y = \lambda_x$ against the alternative hypothesis that $\lambda_y \neq \lambda_x$.

(b) Data on PRICE, SPEED, and capacity (CAP) for hard disk drives in the United States over the 1972–1984 time period are found in the file COLE within the subdirectory CHAP4.DAT. Form a set of 11 dummy variables, $D_{73}, D_{74}, \ldots, D_{84}$, that take on the value of unity if the disk drive model was introduced in that particular year and is zero otherwise. In this exercise, Box-Cox transformations are performed on PRICE, SPEED, and CAP, but not on the intercept term or the dummy variables. Estimate the four above common special cases of the Box-Cox transformation, where in each case the same λ_x transformation is applied to each of the regressors SPEED and CAP. On the basis of the sample value of the log-likelihood function, which of these four functional forms is preferred? Does this result concur with that reported by Cole et al., discussed in Section 4.4? Now estimate separately the parameters λ_y and λ_x, where λ_x is still constrained to be the same for both slope regressors. Are the estimated values of λ_y and λ_x close to any of the four special cases outlined above? Comment on the signs of the estimated coefficients and the implied shape of the hedonic price function. Do values of the transformation parameters all lie in the 0–1 domain, or are some, as Triplett [1989] conjectured, in the negative domain? Using the likelihood ratio testing procedure, test each of these four special cases as a null hypothesis, where in each case the alternative hypothesis leaves λ_y and λ_x unconstrained. Then test the null hypothesis that $\lambda_y = \lambda_x$ against the alternative hypothesis that $\lambda_y \neq \lambda_x$. Finally, briefly outline how you would construct a price index series for disk drives based on your preferred functional form.

CHAPTER NOTES

1. A similar quote is attributed by Robert J. Gordon [1989, fn. 2] to the December 22, 1980 issue of *Forbes* magazine, which in turn attributes it to an unspecified issue of *Computerworld*.
2. For a discussion of such issues and appropriate references, see U.S. Department of Labor, Bureau of Labor Statistics [1982, Vol. II], Franklin M. Fisher and Karl Shell [1983], and Robert A. Pollak [1989].

3. See Rosanne Cole et al. [1986].
4. For a more detailed discussion of these issues, see Jack E. Triplett [1986] and the references cited therein.
5. See Rosanne Cole et al. [1986] and David W. Cartwright [1986].
6. Yet another approach also involves regression analysis but focuses on changes in the prices of characteristics.
7. This paper was part of Waugh's Ph.D. dissertation at Columbia University. It built on earlier work dating back to 1923 and was subsequently published as Frederick V. Waugh [1928].
8. Waugh [1928, p. 188].
9. Since Waugh [1929, p. 144] provides means for the dependent and independent variables, it is possible to work backwards and, using his parameter estimates for the slope coefficients and the fact that the least squares line always passes through the point of means, calculate the estimate of β_0. In this case this calculation turns out to be: $90.095 - 0.13826 \cdot 588.75 + 1.53394 \cdot 19.555 + 0.27553 \cdot 14.875 = 42.789$.
10. Waugh [1928, p. 189].
11. A discussion of partial and separate coefficients of determination is found in, among others, Arthur S. Goldberger [1964, pp. 197–200].
12. For a discussion of R^2 relationships in multivariate and multiple simple regression equations, see Arthur S. Goldberger [1968], especially Chapter 4.
13. This study was published in Andrew T. Court [1939].
14. It appears that the BLS price index was based primarily on data about the Ford Model T, a model that was relatively unchanged from year to year, and for which the matched model method worked quite well until the acceleration of technical change in the early 1930s.
15. Court [1939, p. 107].
16. If one exponentiates Eq. (4.6) and then takes expected values, the expected value of the exponentiated disturbance term is no longer zero but instead equals $0.5\sigma^2$; for discussion, see John Aitchison and James A. C. Brown [1966] or Dale M. Heien [1968]. An implication of the Aitchison-Brown result is that the estimate of $0.5\sigma^2$ should be added to each predicted price index before exponentiating Eq. (4.6). This adjustment is seldom done by empirical researchers, however, perhaps because it is typically quantitatively insignificant. Furthermore, if one is interested only in examining differences in predicted price indexes between years, for practical purposes this term will drop out.
17. Court [1939, p. 110].
18. Although a reduction in the growth rate of price indexes is common when one attempts to adjust for quality change, it is not always the case that price indexes based on hedonic regressions yield lower growth rates in times of technical progress than those obtained using traditional matched model techniques. For interesting counterexamples, see Meyer L. Burstein [1961] and Jack E. Triplett [1971].
19. See, for example, the interpretation of Court's findings by a GM official in Stephen M. Dubrul [1939].
20. See, for example, Hendrik S. Houthakker [1952], Richard Stone [1956], Jan Tinbergen [1956], and an obscure paper by William M. Gorman [1957].
21. See Zvi Griliches [1971] and Irma Adelman and Zvi Griliches [1961].
22. Some of this research in the 1961–1970 decade is summarized and referenced in

Zvi Griliches [1971]. This volume also contains a number of other important papers commissioned by the Price Statistics Committee of the Federal Reserve Board. A more recent review is given in Griliches [1988, Part I].

23. It might be noted, however, that for about 20 years previously the BLS had used hedonic procedures to construct a new housing price index. In private correspondence, Jack Triplett has indicated that "the new house price index is a price index for characteristics—it is the ratio of current characteristics prices to those prevailing in 1982, weighted by the total quantities of characteristics sold."
24. Waugh [1929, p. 95].
25. For more detailed historical accounts, see, among others, Stan Augarten [1984]. Historical economic issues, particularly those involving mainframe computers and the International Business Machines Corporation, are discussed in Franklin M. Fisher, John J. McGowan, and Joen E. Greenwood [1983]. Also see Jack E. Triplett [1989] and Robert J. Gordon [1989].
26. On this, also see Cole et al. [1986].
27. A decimal digit counted as four binary digits, while an octal digit counted as three binary digits.
28. Table 4.1 corrects two typographical errors in Chow [1967, Table 1], namely, the signs on the estimated coefficients of the MEM and ACCESS variables in Chow [1967] are incorrect for the year 1961.
29. Chow [1967, pp. 1121–1122].
30. Chow reports that results were virtually identical when geometric means replaced the arithmetic means.
31. As of 1990, the official BEA price index for computers over the 1953–1969 is still constant; it is only from 1970 onward that it declines.
32. Also see Robert J. Gordon [1989].
33. Calculations were done under the assumption that the average amount of data transferred at one time is 2 kilobytes. Further, if multiple read/write heads appeared on a device, the speed of the device was measured as the speed per set times the number of sets.
34. The Cartwright deflator is in effect a Paasche price index with a moving reference year. For a deflator with fixed 1972 weights based on Laspeyres procedures, see Triplett [1989, Table 4.14, p. 196].
35. For further discussion, see your econometric theory textbook. A compact textbook treatment is given in George G. Judge et al. [1985, Chapter 20]. The original articles are George E. P. Box and David R. Cox [1964] and George E. P. Box and Paul W. Tidwell [1962]. Issues concerning estimation, inference, and computational algorithms are discussed by, among others, John J. Spitzer [1982, 1984].
36. In private correspondence, Ellen R. Dulberger has indicated that in her own research in Dulberger [1986] she employed Box-Cox transformations varying λ from 0 to 1 in increments of 0.1.
37. A related issue concerns the set of quality variables that should be included in the hedonic regression equation. Since alternative variables are often highly correlated with one another, parameter estimates frequently vary considerably with the choice of included variables. One possible procedure, used by Phoebus Dhrymes [1971] but little since then, employs factor analysis or principal components. Discussion of factor analytic methods, however, is also beyond the scope of this chapter; on this, see Harry H. Harman [1976].

38. For further discussion, see Fisher, McGowan, and Greenwood [1983]. It is worth noting that make effects might also capture manufacturer-specific pricing policies, such as failing to keep up with competitive price reductions.
39. See Dean F. Amel and Ernst R. Berndt [1986] and the references cited therein.
40. For an interesting application involving the effects of changes in gasoline prices on the valuations of fuel-efficiency characteristics of used automobiles, see Makoto Ohta and Zvi Griliches [1986].
41. See, for example, Robert E. Hall [1971] as well as the bibliographies at the end of Griliches [1971, 1988].
42. For a related application, see Franklin M. Fisher, Zvi Griliches, and Carl Kaysen [1962].
43. On this, see, for example, Fisher, McGowan, and Greenwood [1983] and Ellen R. Dulberger [1986].
44. The data are taken from Waugh [1929, Appendix, Table 1, pp. 127–131].
45. Your computed sample variances may be identical to those of Waugh, depending on whether your computer software computes sample variances by dividing the squared deviations around the mean by $n = 200$ or by $n - 1 = 199$.
46. Information on modifying conventional nonlinear least squares programs to perform Box-Cox estimation, as well as other computational issues, are discussed in John J. Spitzer [1982, 1984].

CHAPTER REFERENCES

Adelman, Irma and Zvi Griliches [1961], "On an Index of Quality Change," *Journal of the American Statistical Association*, 56:295, September, 535–548.

Aitchison, John and James A. C. Brown [1966], *The Lognormal Distribution*, Cambridge, England: Cambridge University Press.

Amel, Dean F. and Ernst R. Berndt [1986], "Depreciation in the Swedish Automobile Market: An Integration of Hedonic and Latent Variable Approaches," Cambridge, Mass.: Massachusetts Institute of Technology, Center for Energy Policy Research, Working Paper MIT EL 86-007WP, March.

Augarten, Stan [1984], *Bit by Bit: An Illustrated History of Computers*, New York: Ticknor & Fields.

Bartik, Timothy J. [1987], "The Estimation of Demand Parameters in Hedonic Price Models," *Journal of Political Economy*, 95:1, January, 81–88.

Box, George E. P. and David R. Cox [1964], "An Analysis of Transformations," *Journal of the Royal Statistical Society*, Series B, 26:2, April, 211–243.

Box, George E. P. and Paul W. Tidwell [1962], "Transformation of the Independent Variables," *Technometrics*, 4:4, November, 531–550.

Burstein, Meyer L. [1961], "Measurement of Quality Change in Consumer Durables," *The Manchester School of Economics and Social Studies*, 29:3, September, 267–279.

Cartwright, David W. [1986], "Improved Deflation of Purchases of Computers," *Survey of Current Business*, 66:3, March, 7–9.

Chow, Gregory C. [1967], "Technological Change and the Demand for Computers," *American Economic Review*, 57:5, December, 1117–1130.

Cole, Rosanne, Y.C. Chen, Joan A. Barquin-Stolleman, Ellen Dulberger, Nurhan Helvacian, and James H. Hodge [1986], "Quality-Adjusted Price Indexes for Computer Processors and Selected Peripheral Equipment," *Survey of Current Business*, 66:1, January, 41–50.

Court, Andrew T. [1939], "Hedonic Price Indexes with Automotive Examples," in *The Dynamics of Automobile Demand*, New York: The General Motors Corporation, 99–117.

Dhrymes, Phoebus J. [1971], "Price and Quality Changes in Consumer Capital Goods: An Empirical Study," Chapter 4 in Zvi Griliches, ed., *Price Indexes and Quality Change: Studies in New Methods of Measurement*, Cambridge, Mass.: Harvard University Press, 88–149.

Dubrul, Stephen M. [1939], "Significance of the Findings," *The Dynamics of Automobile Demand*, New York: The General Motors Corporation, 123–139.

Dulberger, Ellen R. [1986], *The Application of an Hedonic Model to a Quality Adjusted Price Index for Computer Processors*, unpublished Ph.D. dissertation, City University of New York, Department of Economics. Portions of this dissertation were published as "The Application of a Hedonic Model to a Quality-Adjusted Price Index for Computer Processors," Chapter 2 in Dale W. Jorgenson and Ralph Landau, eds., *Technology and Capital Formation*, Cambridge, Mass.: MIT Press, 1989, pp. 37–75.

Epple, Dennis [1987], "Hedonic Prices and Implicit Markets: Estimating Demand and Supply Functions for Differentiated Products," *Journal of Political Economy*, 95:1, January, 59–80.

Fisher, Franklin M. and Karl Shell [1983], *The Economic Theory of Price Indexes: Two Essays on the Effects of Taste, Quality and Technological Change*, Cambridge, Mass.: MIT Press.

Fisher, Franklin M., Zvi Griliches, and Carl Kaysen [1962], "The Costs of Automobile Model Changes since 1949," *Journal of Political Economy*, 70:5, October, 433–451.

Fisher, Franklin M., John J. McGowan, and Joen E. Greenwood [1983], *Folded, Spindled and Mutilated: Economic Analysis and U.S. vs. IBM*, Cambridge, Mass.: MIT Press.

Forester, Tom, ed. [1985], *The Information Technology Revolution*, Cambridge, Mass.: MIT Press.

Goldberger, Arthur S. [1964], *Econometric Theory*, New York: John Wiley and Sons.

Goldberger, Arthur S. [1968], *Topics in Regression Analysis*, New York: Macmillan.

Gordon, Robert J. [1989], "The Postwar Evolution of Computer Prices," Chapter 3 in Dale W. Jorgenson and Ralph Landau, eds., *Technology and Capital Formation*, Cambridge, Mass.: MIT Press, pp. 77–125.

Gorman, William M. [1957], "A Possible Procedure for Analyzing Quality Differentials in the Egg Market," Iowa Agricultural Experiment Station, Working Paper, revised, February. Reissued in January 1976 as Discussion Paper No. B4, London: London School of Economics.

Griliches, Zvi [1961], "Hedonic Price Indexes for Automobiles: An Econometric Analysis of Quality Change," in *The Price Statistics of the Federal Government*, General Series No. 73, New York: Columbia University Press for the National Bureau of Economic Research, pp. 137–196. Reprinted in Zvi Griliches, ed., *Price Indexes and Quality Change: Studies in New Methods of Measurement*, Cambridge, Mass.: Harvard University Press, 1971, pp. 55–87.

Griliches, Zvi [1971], "Introduction: Hedonic Price Indexes Revisited," in Zvi Griliches, ed., *Price Indexes and Quality Change: Studies in New Methods of Measurement*, Cambridge, Mass.: Harvard University Press, pp. 3–15.

Griliches, Zvi [1988], *Technology, Education, and Productivity*, New York: Basil Blackwell.

Hall, Robert E. [1971], "The Measurement of Quality Change from Vintage Price Data," Chapter 8 in Zvi Griliches, ed., *Price Indexes and Quality Change: Studies in New Methods of Measurement*, Cambridge, Mass.: Harvard University Press, pp. 240–271.

Hamilton, David [1987], "Sometimes $R^2 > r^2_{yx1} + r^2_{yx2}$: Correlated Variables Are Not Always Redundant," *American Statistician*, 41:2, May, 129–132.

Harman, Harry H. [1976], *Modern Factor Analysis*, Third Edition, Chicago: University of Chicago Press.

Heien, Dale M. [1968], "A Note on Log-Linear Regression," *Journal of the American Statistical Association*, 63:323, September, 1034–1038.

Houthakker, Hendrik S. [1952], "Compensated Changes in Quantities and Qualities Consumed," *Review of Economic Studies*, 19(3), 155–164.

Judge, George G., William E. Griffiths, R. Carter Hill, Helmut Lutkepohl, and Tsoung-Chao Lee [1985], *The Theory and Practice of Econometrics*, Second Edition, New York: John Wiley and Sons.

National Bureau of Economic Research [1961], *The Price Statistics of the Federal Government*, General Series No. 73, New York: Columbia University Press for the National Bureau of Economic Research.

Ohta, Makoto [1975], "Product Technologies of the U.S. Boiler and Turbo Generator Industries and Hedonic Price Indexes for Their Products: A Cost Function Approach," *Journal of Political Economy*, 83:1, February, 1–26.

Ohta, Makoto and Zvi Griliches [1986], "Automobile Prices and Quality: Did the Gasoline Price Increases Change Consumer Tastes in the U.S.?" *Journal of Business and Economic Statistics*, 4:2, April, 187–198.

Pollak, Robert A. [1989], *The Theory of the Cost-of-Living Index*, New York: Oxford University Press.

Rosen, Sherwin M. [1974], "Hedonic Prices and Implicit Markets: Product Differentiation in Pure Competition," *Journal of Political Economy*, 82:1, January/February, 34–55.

Spitzer, John J. [1982], "A Primer on Box-Cox Estimation," *Review of Economics and Statistics*, 64:2, May, 307–313.

Spitzer, John J. [1984], "Variance Estimates in Models with the Box-Cox Transformation: Implications for Estimation and Hypothesis Testing," *Review of Economics and Statistics*, 66:4, November, 645–652.

Stone, Richard [1956], *Quality and Price Indexes in National Accounts*, Paris: Organization for European Economic Cooperation.

Tinbergen, Jan [1956], "On the Theory of Income Distribution," *Weltwirtschaftliches Archiv*, 77, 155–175. Reprinted in L.H. Klaassen, L.M. Koyck, and H.J. Witteveen, eds., *Selected Papers of Jan Tinbergen*, Amsterdam: North-Holland, 1959, pp. 243–263.

Triplett, Jack E. [1971], "Quality Bias in Price Indexes and New Methods of Quality Measurement," Chapter 6 in Zvi Griliches, ed., *Price Indexes and Quality Change*, Cambridge, Mass.: Harvard University Press, pp. 180–214.

Triplett, Jack E. [1986], "The Economic Interpretation of Hedonic Methods," *Survey of Current Business*, 66:1, January, 36–40.

Triplett, Jack E. [1989], "Price and Technological Change in a Capital Good: A Survey of Research on Computers," Chapter 4 in Dale W. Jorgenson and Ralph Landau, eds., *Technology and Capital Formation*, Cambridge, Mass.: MIT Press, pp. 127–213.

U.S. Department of Labor, Bureau of Labor Statistics [1982], *BLS Handbook of Methods*, Vols. I and II, Washington, D.C.: U.S. Government Printing Office.

Watts, Harold W. [1965], "The Test-o-Gram: A Pedagogical and Presentational Device," *American Statistician*, 19:4, October, 25–28.

Waugh, Frederick V. [1928], "Quality Factors Influencing Vegetable Prices," *Journal of Farm Economics*, 10:2, April, 185–196.

Waugh, Frederick V. [1929], *Quality as a Determinant of Vegetable Prices: A Statistical Study of Quality Factors Influencing Vegetable Prices in the Boston Wholesale Market*, New York: Columbia University Press. Reprinted by the AMS Press, Inc., New York, 1968.

FURTHER READINGS

Gordon, Robert J. [1990], *The Measurement of Durable Goods Prices*, Chicago: University of Chicago Press. See especially Chapter 6, "Electronic Computers."

Griliches, Zvi, ed. [1971], *Price Indexes and Quality Change: Studies in New Methods of Measurement*, Cambridge, Mass.: Harvard University Press. A collection of classic articles.

Griliches, Zvi [1988], *Technology, Education, and Productivity*, New York: Basil Blackwell. See especially Part I, which updates the material in Griliches [1971].

Lancaster, Kelvin [1971], *Consumer Demand: A New Approach*, New York: Columbia University Press. A theoretical framework emphasizing the role of characteristics and attributes in demand analysis.

Stigler, Stephen M. [1986], *The History of Statistics: The Measurement of Uncertainty before 1900*, Cambridge, Mass.: Harvard University Press. An enjoyable historical account of statistical measurement issues.

Chapter 5

Analyzing Determinants of Wages and Measuring Wage Discrimination: Dummy Variables in Regression Models

"The Lord said to Moses, 'Say to the people of Israel, . . . your valuation of male from twenty years old up to sixty years old shall be fifty shekels of silver, according to the shekel of the sanctuary. If the person is a female, your valuation shall be thirty shekels. . . . And if the person is sixty years old and upward, then your valuation for a male shall be fifteen shekels, and for a female ten shekels.'"

The Bible, Revised Standard Version, Leviticus 27:3–7

"An investment in knowledge pays the best interest."

BENJAMIN FRANKLIN, *Poor Richard's Almanack*

"The improved dexterity of a workman may be considered in the same light as a machine or instrument of trade which facilitates and abridges labour, and which, though it costs a certain expence, repays that expence with a profit."

ADAM SMITH, *The Wealth of Nations*, Book II, Chapter 1

"Let us remember the unfortunate econometrician who, in one of the major functions of his system, had to use a proxy for risk and a dummy for sex."

FRITZ MACHLUP (1974)

The differences in earnings capacities among people have long been noted and debated. Craftsmen with greater experience typically have larger annual earnings than apprentices. On average the lifetime earnings of college graduates are greater than those of people who hold but a high school diploma. College graduates generally expect rather different lifetime earnings depending on the subsequent training and career paths they choose. For example, the expected lifetime earnings of clergymen, musicians, history professors, elementary school teachers, and public interest lawyers are typically less than those of corporate financial officers, computer scientists, plastic surgeons, and investment bankers. Further, substantial differences in earnings streams are also known to exist in the United States between males and females, between nonwhites and whites, and between union and nonunion employees.

The causes of variations in wages and earnings among people are complex and controversial. One purpose of this chapter is to acquaint you with a widely accepted economic framework for thinking about wage differentials, to provide you with a selective survey of principal empirical findings on determinants of wages, and to help you interpret measures of wage discrimination by race and gender. A second major purpose of this chapter is to give you hands-on experience in implementing econometric methods using recent U.S. data and to encourage you to pursue on your own further research on the determinants of wages.

One econometric tool that will be of particular importance in analyzing wage determinants is the categorical variable, more commonly called a "dummy variable." Dummy variables are useful when certain categories are not easily quantified. For example, wage rates may depend on whether an individual is categorized as male or female. Although the quantification of gender is problematic, the effects of gender on wages can still be incorporated into a regression equation through the use of a male-female dummy variable. Dummy variables can also be employed to capture nonlinear aspects of categorical variables through the use of interaction terms. In this chapter, both linear and interaction forms of dummy variables will be used extensively.

The chapter is organized as follows. We begin in Section 5.1 with a review of the currently dominant theoretical framework for analyzing wage differentials, the human capital model. We also briefly discuss an alternative model, called the signaling or screening hypothesis. With this theoretical discussion as background, in Section 5.2 we discuss a number of econometric issues that arise in implementing empirically the human capital framework. Among these implementation issues are measurement problems, choice of functional form and stochastic specification, use of dummy variables, and bias due to omitted variables—the most prominent being abilities. Then in Section 5.3 we provide a selective but representative survey of empirical studies on determinants of wages. Estimates from a number of studies on returns to education, returns to on-the-job training, and wage differentials between union and nonunion employees will be presented. In Section

5.4 we discuss how econometricians have estimated and interpreted the wage effects of discrimination by race and gender. In Section 5.5 we summarize other econometric issues in modeling determinants of wages.

Finally, in the hands-on exercises we provide opportunities for you to engage in econometric estimation on your own. Two data sets are furnished, one a random sample from the May 1978 U.S. Census Current Population Survey and the other from the May 1985 survey. Each data set contains observations on 20 variables for about 550 individuals. The exercises involve examining the distribution of wages, demonstrating the equivalence of alternative dummy variable specifications, using and interpreting interaction terms, calculating rates of return to education and experience, examining age-earnings profiles, estimating union-nonunion wage differentials, measuring and interpreting wage discrimination by race and gender, performing tests for parameter equality, and assessing the effects of heteroskedasticity.

5.1 CONSIDERATIONS FROM ECONOMIC THEORY: THE HUMAN CAPITAL MODEL

The dominant economic theory of wage determination is human capital theory. Its development is due to important contributions by Jacob Mincer [1957, 1958, 1962], Theodore Schultz [1960, 1961], and Gary Becker [1962, 1964]. In turn, modern human capital theory clearly has its roots in the classic eighteenth-century writings by Adam Smith on equalizing differentials; there is even some evidence that the notion of human capital was developed as early as 1691 by Sir William Petty.[1] We begin this section with a review of Smith's notion of equalizing differences.

5.1.A Adam Smith and Equalizing Differences

Work activities vary considerably in their nonmonetary advantages and disadvantages. Some jobs and occupations provide very desirable amenities, while others offer obvious disamenities and are held in low esteem. Furthermore, in many cases, people differ in how they evaluate the nonmonetary aspects of particular jobs and occupations.

On numerous occasions in Book I of *The Wealth of Nations*, Adam Smith argued that the wages paid to workers should compensate for or equalize the differences in workplace amenities and disamenities. For example, if two jobs requiring identical skills varied in the nonmonetary amenities provided, the employer providing greater nonmonetary disamenities would be forced to pay higher wages; otherwise, no one could be hired. In Smith's words,

> The whole of the advantages and disadvantages of the different employments of labor and stock must, in the same neighborhood, be either perfectly equal or continually tending to equality. If in the same neighbor-

> hood there was any employment evidently either more or less advantageous than the rest, so many people would crowd into it in one case, and so many would desert it in the other, that its advantages would soon return to the level of other employments.[2]

Smith's line of reasoning implies that observed wage differentials reflect in part workers' tastes for various amenities and disamenities. Further, this theory of equalizing differences is a theory of long-run equilibrium. In the short run, workers may not be sufficiently mobile to change employment, but in the long run, supply is more elastic. Hence short-run wage premiums eventually tend to be reduced as supply curves shift.

For equalizing differentials to reflect market efficiency, however, employees and employers must have symmetric and perfect information. For example, if, unknown to employees, the working environment contained potentially fatal toxic substances, it might not be necessary for employers to pay higher wages to attract workers. Yet if workers knew of this disamenity, any efficient outcome would most likely involve some form of additional cost to the employer.[3]

Further, since the equilibrium wage depends on both supply and demand, in some cases workplace disamenities need not be rewarded by higher wage rates. For example, since people's tastes differ, it is possible that while 95% of the populace viewed a particular workplace attribute with absolute disdain, a 3% minority might view it with no opinion, and 2% might even value it highly. In this case, if the market demand by employers for workers at workplaces with such an attribute amounted to, say, less than 1% of the population, then employers could attract sufficient workers without offering a compensating wage premium; in this case the 2% would actively search and compete for such employment. The important point here is that since people's tastes differ, market supply curves for jobs with particular combinations of amenities and disamenities are likely to contain both flat and upward sloping portions; the equilibrium wage rate will occur where supply and demand curves intersect.

Smith's theory of equalizing differentials has been used to explain in part a substantial number of observed occupational wage differentials.[4] For example, workers holding jobs that have substantial risks to health and longevity, such as test pilots and offshore oil-rig workers, command sizable wage premiums, as do workers in positions with extreme severity of working conditions, such as Alaskan pipeline welding.[5] Other jobs offer amenities that are valued highly only by some people and thus might entail lower wages. For example, there is some empirical evidence suggesting that even after controlling for differences in age, school quality, and academic performance, public interest lawyers earn some 20% less than other lawyers in more traditional practices.[6] Building on a notion discussed centuries earlier by Adam Smith, Robert Hall [1970] has suggested that some workers are willing to accept a higher probability of temporary layoff and unemployment, provided that they are compensated with a higher wage while employed. Moreover, firms are willing to pay a wage premium for the privilege of drawing on an inventory of potential workers in the market.[7] In brief, each of these examples demonstrates that the principle of equalizing differences has important empirical implications. As we shall also see, Smith's concept of equalizing differentials has formed the basis of the modern theory of human capital.

5.1.B Schooling as Investment

A rather straightforward extension of Smith's notion of equalizing differences involves the wage implications of investment in human capital, such as schooling, on-the-job training, job search, and migration. We begin by briefly outlining the human capital implications of education.

Although there is undoubtedly a certain amount of sheer enjoyment and consumption value to life as a student, schooling also represents an investment. In particular, additional schooling entails opportunity costs in the form of forgone earnings, as well as direct expenses such as tuition.

The schooling implications of modern human capital theory can be stated in a nutshell as three propositions.[8] First, on the labor supply side: In order to induce a person to forgo earnings, pay tuition, and undergo additional schooling, that worker must be compensated by sufficiently higher lifetime earnings. Second, on the labor demand side: In order to be able to command higher earnings, the more schooled workers must be sufficiently more productive in employment than their less schooled fellow workers, that is, marginal products of workers must increase with the level of schooling; otherwise, employers would not pay premium wages for more highly educated workers. Third, on market equilibrium: In long-run competitive equilibrium the relationship between schooling and lifetime earnings must be such that the supply of and demand for workers of each schooling level are equated, and no worker wishes to alter his or her level of schooling.

On the basis of these three propositions and other observations, a number of theoretical results have been derived by human capital theorists.[9] One important result is that a worker's incentives for human capital accumulation are largest at younger ages, implying that it is primarily the young who will undertake schooling. There are several reasons for this. First, from the marginal benefit point of view, since additional schooling results in higher earnings, the earlier one accumulates human capital, the longer the remaining working life over which benefits can be recouped (provided that one begins work immediately after completing schooling and continues working full time until retirement). Second, from the marginal cost vantage, since earnings tend to increase with experience (more on that shortly), the forgone earnings of the younger ages are typically less than those of older age. Third, the ability and hence the time cost to accumulating human capital varies over the life cycle. Some evidence suggests that the most productive time to learn is relatively early in the life cycle.[10] Therefore human capital theory can help explain why it is primarily the young who attend school.

Another implication of human capital theory concerns the dispersion of earning power among individuals. In choosing education levels so as to maximize the present value of their wealth, individuals will consider the costs and benefits of schooling. Individuals with high aptitude and abilities will find it relatively easy to accumulate human capital, since learning comes easily to them. Therefore the human capital benefits of one hour of studying for the more able may be larger than for the less able. Suppose that the more able individuals also have relatively easy access to investable funds owing to, say, scholarships given on the basis of ability. If true, these conditions would imply that high-ability individuals would have greater incentives to accumulate human capital in the form of education than would individuals with fewer abilities.[11] Therefore it is reasonable to expect that abilities and years of schooling would be correlated. The resulting positive correlation between abilities and human capital accumulation implies a greater dispersion of earnings capacity than would occur if everyone had equal abilities and equal access to investable funds, in which case abilities and schooling would be uncorrelated. In this latter case the only reason for observed wage inequality would be nonwage differences in job characteristics.

5.1.C On-the-Job Training as Investment

Although formal schooling is one way in which human capital can be accumulated, it is not the only route. Many labor market skills are acquired through on-the-job training, ranging from formal training sessions and structured apprenticeships to the much more informal "learning by doing." The wage and labor supply implications of on-the-job training human capital accumulation have been considered by, among others, Gary Becker [1962, 1964] and Jacob Mincer [1962, 1974].

In order to analyze the wage implications of on-the-job training, it is useful to distinguish two polar forms of training. *General training* refers to activities that generate extremely versatile skills or characteristics, equally usable or salable in any firm or industry. Hence general training increases the productivity of a worker at any task.

One important feature of general training is that if labor markets are competitive, firms will be unwilling to assume any of the training costs. The reason is that since general training is completely transferable, any worker who receives general training paid for by the firm could quit upon completion of training, and the firm would be unable to recoup any of its general training investment in the worker. Hence workers bear the cost of general training, often in the form of reduced wages during the training period.

A polar contrast to general training is called *specific training*. It refers to on-the-job training that can be used only in the particular firm providing the training. Specific training therefore raises the productivity of a worker only at that firm and is completely nontransferable.

Specific training raises some interesting issues in terms of who bears the costs of training and who recoups the gains from investment. If firms could prevent trained workers from moving elsewhere, firms might be willing to bear the entire costs of specific training, provided that they could also appropriate all the returns. However, if trained workers were mobile, firms would find it in their interest to share some of the returns from specific training with their trained workers by paying them a wage that was slightly larger than they could earn elsewhere. In this way, costly turnover could be mitigated.[12] Note that in such a case the wage rates paid to workers with specific training would reflect the combined effects of the workers' innate productivity and a portion of the return to the firm's specific investments in workers.

It is worth noting that firms can design wage-experience compensation schemes for workers with specific training in ways that provide incentives that are compatible with the firms' interests; for an elaboration of this notion, see Edward Lazear [1979b, 1981]. For example, the use of nonvested pension funds can reduce the labor turnover of highly trained workers.

General and specific on-the-job training are polar extremes, and in many cases, investments in workers represent a mix of these two types of training. Regardless of the mix, human capital theory assumes that additional human capital can be accumulated by incremental job experience. However, human capital can also depreciate. Such depreciation can occur through work interruption or unemployment, obsolescence (facility with the slide rule is no longer a very valuable skill), and also the passage of time. As workers age, for example, their human capital can depreciate in the form of "forgetting," not remembering as quickly, or simply taking a longer period of time to perform tasks.

An important issue addressed by human capital theory concerns the optimal timing of work and training during the life cycle. Recall our earlier discussion in which we argued that it is generally optimal for workers to invest in schooling at an early age. To the extent that work experience is an investment in on-the-job training, incentives for this form of human capital accumulation also decline with age. The principal reason is that the present value of any returns-to-training investment decline as the remaining worklife of the worker decreases.

Gilbert Ghez and Gary Becker [1974] and Alan Blinder and Yoram Weiss [1976] have derived life cycle profiles for wages, hours worked, and earnings that reflect discount rates, working horizons, returns to investment, tastes for leisure, and either wealth or present value utility-optimizing behavior by individuals. Following their example, let us ignore schooling, assume that all training is general, and assume that workers' discount rates are less than the sum of the rate of return to capital plus the depreciation rate on human capital.

In this case the principal results are that, owing to the decreased present value of returns to investment as one ages, it is generally optimal to increase *hours worked* with age early in one's life and rapidly accumulate human capital through on-the-job training, to work peak hours per year somewhere during midlife, and then gradually to reduce hours worked as incentives to invest decline owing to the onset of retirement. The corresponding optimal *wage* profile by age is one of rapidly increasing wage rates early in one's life as human capital is accumulated, a peak in wage rates near the point in midlife when human capital is at its largest, and then a decline in wage rates as the effects of human capital depreciation dominate reduced accumulation. Finally, the optimal *earnings* profile (the product of wage rate and hours worked per year) by age has a similar shape, but the peak in hours worked generally occurs before that for wages and earnings. However, as has been emphasized by, among others, James Heckman [1976], Mark Killingsworth [1982], and Yoram Weiss [1986], the shapes and peaks of these life cycle optimum profiles can change considerably when training is specific or when the discount rate becomes very large.

Finally, it is worth noting that on average, those individuals who receive the largest amount of formal education also tend to receive more on-the-job training.[13] This may reflect in part employers' beliefs that individuals with greater formal education can be trained at less cost, since they have already demonstrated an ability to learn. Note that if the more educated also become the more trained, then their human capital will accumulate very rapidly, resulting in a steeper experience-earnings profile than that of less educated workers.

This brief summary of on-the-job training appears to suggest that human capital theory is testable, since it is capable of generating testable predictions concerning the shape of the age-hours worked, age-wage, and age-earnings profiles for individuals with differing levels of schooling. But is this really so? As we shall now see, that is not necessarily the case.

5.1.D Screening as an Alternative to Human Capital Theory

Although the human capital theory of wage determination is widely accepted, it has its detractors. One prominent alternative is called the screening hypothesis. Its formal development is due to Kenneth Arrow [1973] and Michael Spence [1973, 1974].

Suppose that education does very little if anything in terms of improving the productivity of workers. However, suppose that firms nonetheless view degrees and diplomas as signals indicating that degree holders have superior abilities and productivity. In such a case, educational degrees provide a signal and serve as a convenient screen but do not directly affect workers' productivities. This notion is called the screening hypothesis of education.

Why might employers use education as a screen? There are at least two reasons. First, it may be very costly for firms to determine the abilities and productivities of individuals. Using educational degrees as a screening device may be a cost-effective way to identify high-quality workers. Second, it may in fact be the case that on average, holders of educational degrees have greater abilities and skills. Why would this be the case? Arrow and Spence argue that even if individuals with varying abilities all recognized that employers use educational degrees as screens, it is the most able who could obtain the degrees at lowest personal cost in terms of the effort and time input required to satisfy degree requirements. Moreover, the private costs of schooling to the more able would be reduced even further if the more able were recipients of scholarships awarded on the basis of ability.

According to the screening hypothesis, therefore, an educational degree is an admission ticket to higher-paying jobs in which there are attractive opportunities for further training and promotion. Less educated workers are screened from such positions, not necessarily because they are less able, but simply because they do not have the "sheepskin" to grant them access to the position.

It is worth noting that from the point of view of an individual evaluating potential private returns to schooling as an investment, it makes little if any difference whether the human capital or the screening hypothesis is valid; in either case the same private return to education can be expected. But from the point of view of society as a whole, if the screening hypothesis is valid, then the social return to schooling is overstated. In such a case, instead of subsidizing education, society might better invest scarce funds by finding and utilizing less costly ways to screen high-quality workers. Which theory is correct therefore has important normative implications for society as a whole.

It would of course be very useful if one could employ historical data and econometric methods to discriminate between the human capital and screening theories of education; indeed, there have been some attempts to do so.[14] The essential problem, however, is that since the more able will self-select themselves into educational degree programs regardless of which theory is correct, in some sense the two theories are observationally equivalent, and so it is difficult if not impossible to distinguish between them using historical data. If conventions and protocol regarding use of humans as experimental research objects permitted, it might in theory be possible to devise an experiment that could discriminate between the screening and human capital theories; but even in such a case, one would also need to overcome notoriously difficult problems in measuring abilities.[15]

5.2 ISSUES IN ECONOMETRIC IMPLEMENTATION OF THE HUMAN CAPITAL MODEL

The human capital framework for analyzing determinants of wages has generated a very substantial empirical literature. Before reviewing representative empirical findings, however, we first address a number of important issues concerning econometric implementation. We begin with measurement issues and common data sources.

5.2.A Measurement Issues and Common Data Sources

The notions of wage rates, hours worked, and earnings are pervasive in human capital theory, but how one obtains empirical measures of these theoretical constructs is not always entirely clear. In practice, the data sets that are most commonly used by empirical labor economists are based on answers to questions asked of two types of respondents, either households or business firms and establishments. In either case a great deal of effort is expended to ensure that the confidentiality of respondents is maintained.

In the United States the Census Bureau conducts an entire census of the population decennially and also carries out a much smaller survey on a monthly basis (the Current Population Survey).[16] Nongovernmental agencies producing household data that are of interest to labor economists include the Center for Human Resource Research at Ohio State University (National Longitudinal Surveys, often called the Parnes data) and the Survey Research Center at the University of Michigan (Survey of Working Conditions or the Quality of Employment Survey and the Panel Study of Income Dynamics). Data provided by business firms and establishments for all manufacturing firms are collected by the Census Bureau once every five or six years (Census of Manufactures), while a smaller sample of manufacturing firms is surveyed each year (Annual Survey of Manufactures). In addition, data from a sample of all firms and establishments are gathered on a monthly basis and are then published in summary form by the Bureau of Labor Statistics (Employment and Earnings Surveys).[17]

According to economic theory, an individual's wage rate is the value of market goods that can be purchased for, say, an hour of work. The wage rate data collected from household sources typically measure this theoretical notion with considerable error. For example, a substantial proportion of jobs not only involve an hourly rate of pay, but also include payments into private pension funds, health plans, social security, unemployment insurance, and other programs. In some cases, executives receive compensation and bonuses in the form of stock options. In 1987 in the United States, fringe benefits alone accounted for more than 25% of the total compensation of an average employee.[18] It has also been found that the amount and, in some cases, the proportion of nonwage benefits in total compensation rise with wages[19] and that the proportion of fringe benefits in total compensation is larger for males than for females.[20] Further, Walter Oi [1983] has presented evidence suggesting that the percentage of employees who receive important nonwage benefits rises steeply with firm size, whereas wages paid rise less dramatically. He interprets this in the context of firm-specific investment, arguing that "[w]orkers in large firms are paid higher wages as well as compensation in the form of pensions and fringes that are designed in part to reduce the turnover of specifically trained employees."[21] These remarks imply that use of wage rate data in empirical studies of wage determination may reveal only a portion of the total compensation differentials among workers.

Another problem with wage rate data is that at times, wage is computed as weekly earnings divided by weekly hours worked. In some cases, individuals may have difficulty accurately remembering these figures. Errors can also emerge when individuals are salaried rather than paid by the hour, since it is often difficult to obtain accurate data on hours worked by salaried people.

A final important issue on wage rate data concerns periodicity. Alternative possibilities here include hourly, weekly, or annual data; while human capital theory often refers to lifetime earnings concepts, such data are virtually nonexistent. In practice, the choice between hourly, weekly, or annual earnings data is important because, as human capital theory suggests, optimal hours worked vary over the life cycle and with the level of educational attainment. Hence in using annual data, care must be taken to distinguish the effects on earnings of hours worked from those due to variations in wages.

The wage rate variable is not the only variable whose empirical measurement is problematical. The measure of educational attainment that is typically used in empirical studies of wage determination (or of the dollar amount invested in education) is simply the highest grade attended. Hence the schooling variable is 12 for high school graduates and 16 for college degree holders. Note that for some people it may take more or less than 16 years to complete a college degree. Moreover, given a wide variation in schooling quality, number of years schooling completed is a very crude measure of educational attainment. Some attempts have been made, however, to incorporate measures of school quality into empirical analyses. These include measures such as expenditures per pupil, days of school attended per year, and an external quality rating of colleges.[22]

Another variable whose accurate measurement presents serious difficulties is the stock of on-the-job training human capital. Following Mincer's pioneering studies, researchers have typically attempted to measure this stock by years of labor force experience. But since that variable is hardly ever directly measured in survey questionnaires, in practice researchers usually compute this stock as the individual's age minus years of schooling minus 6, thereby implicitly assuming that all workers begin elementary school at age six and that no time is spent outside the labor force or school.[23] Note in particular that for females raising children at home, such a computation is inappropriate; it is also invalid for people who are in the Armed Forces, on extended vacation, or doing full-time volunteer work.[24]

In summary, therefore, the practicing econometrician in labor economics is typically forced to make use of data that are considerably less than ideal. As we shall see, however, in spite of these serious measurement problems, much has been learned concerning the determinants of wages.

5.2.B Functional Forms for Statistical Earnings Functions

The brief summary of human capital theory presented in Section 5.1 was a verbal one, with no discussion of mathematical derivations or exact functional forms. To implement this theory empirically, however, one must use specific functional forms. From where do they arise, and what form should they take? These are important issues to which we now turn our attention.

A number of researchers have examined data on the distribution of earnings or wages and have noticed that typically the data are skewed, with median earnings usually being less than the mean. Some researchers have attempted to fit various types of statistical distributions directly to earnings data, using distributions such as the normal or log-normal. The log-normal distribution is a skewed distribution that fits actual earnings distributions quite well, perhaps better than any other rather simple distribution, but it is generally unable to predict the relatively numerous occurrences of very high earnings.

One interesting strand of literature has attempted to relate earnings distributions to the distributions of underlying abilities. Beginning with the observation that there are many different and valuable types of abilities—intelligence, physical strength, calmness under pressure, manual dexterity, grittiness, and so on, researchers have made specific assumptions concerning their statistical distributions. A. D. Roy [1950], for example, showed that if each of the relevant abilities is normally distributed but earnings vary with the product of two or more uncorrelated kinds of ability, then the logarithm of earnings, rather than earnings themselves, will be normally distributed. It is worth noting here that there is very little evidence suggesting that specific forms of ability are normally distributed; with intelligence tests, for example, it is the I.Q. test scores that are normally distributed by construction and not necessarily the underlying intelligence.

The econometric literature on wage determination has for the most part been based on regression equations of the form

$$\ln y_i = f(s_i, x_i, z_i) + u_i \qquad i = 1, \ldots, n \tag{5.1}$$

where $\ln y_i$ is the natural log of earnings or wages for the ith individual, s_i is a measure of schooling or educational attainment, x_i indexes the human capital stock of experience, z_i are other factors affecting earnings such as the race, gender, and/or geographical region of the individual, and u_i is a random disturbance term reflecting unobserved ability characteristics and the inherent randomness of earnings statistics. It is usually assumed that u_i is normally distributed with mean zero and constant variance.[25] Equation (5.1) is often called a *statistical earnings function*.

Attempts have been made to derive an equation similar to Eq. (5.1) on the basis of wealth-maximizing individuals choosing career paths and forms of human capital formation, subject to their utility functions and intertemporal budget constraints. As Robert Willis [1986] has emphasized, however, these attempts have generally been unsuccessful in that so far it has proven impossible to obtain analytic or closed form solutions to such intertemporal choice problems. Statistical earnings functions such as Eq. (5.1) must therefore be viewed as approximations to the solutions of intertemporal choice problems.

It is possible, however, to obtain some guidance on functional form using the human capital framework, provided that one makes certain assumptions.[26] For example, suppose that the only costs of schooling are those of forgone earnings. The rate of return on the first year of education, r_1, is then computed as incremental benefits divided by incremental costs, that is,

$$r_1 \equiv (Y_1 - Y_0)/Y_0 \tag{5.2}$$

where Y_1 is earnings after one year's education and Y_0 is earnings without education, where both are assumed to be constant over the remaining life cycle.[27] Equation (5.2) can be rewritten as

$$Y_1 \equiv Y_0(1 + r_1) \tag{5.3}$$

Similarly for year 2 of schooling, the rate of return r_2 is defined as

$$r_2 \equiv (Y_2 - Y_1)/Y_1 \tag{5.4}$$

where Y_2 is earnings after two years' education. This implies that

$$Y_2 \equiv Y_1(1 + r_2) \equiv Y_0(1 + r_1)(1 + r_2) \tag{5.5}$$

After s years of schooling, it follows that

$$Y_s \equiv Y_0(1 + r_1)(1 + r_2) \cdots (1 + r_s) \tag{5.6}$$

If one assumes that the rate of return to education is the same for all levels of schooling, that is, $r_1 = r_2 = \cdots = r_s = r$, and if one approximates $(1 + r)$ by e^r, as one can provided that r is small, then Eq. (5.6) becomes

$$Y_s = Y_0 e^{rs} \tag{5.7}$$

which, with a multiplicative disturbance term e^u appended, can be rewritten in logarithmic form as

$$\ln Y_s = \ln Y_0 + rs + u \tag{5.8}$$

Equation (5.8) is the most basic form of the earnings function. Notice that if this equation is fitted by least squares to data on schooling and the logarithm of earnings, the estimated slope coefficient provides an estimate of r, the private rate of return to schooling, and the estimated intercept indicates the predicted level of log earnings in the absence of schooling.[28] It is worth noting that this estimated rate of return ignores tuition and other direct costs of schooling. It also overlooks earnings while attending school, but it does take into account forgone earnings. To the extent that direct schooling costs exactly offset earnings while at school, these estimated schooling costs are appropriate. Further, the estimated return is private in that this specification ignores any public subsidization of schooling, and it omits any positive or negative externalities to schooling, such as the possible benefits to society of having a more informed and educated electorate.

This simple specification of the earnings function has been generalized by Jacob Mincer [1974] to take into account the effects of on-the-job general training.[29] One possibility is to amend Eq. (5.8) to have the form

$$\ln Y_i = \ln Y_0 + \beta_1 s_i + \beta_2 k_i X_i + u_i \tag{5.9}$$

where β_1 is the rate of return to schooling, β_2 is the rate of return to on-the-job training, k_i is the proportion of the ith worker's time devoted to training investment, and X_i is the ith worker's years of labor market experience, usually measured as age minus s_i minus six years. Unfortunately, data on k_i are generally unavailable. Further, for reasons discussed in Section 5.1, human capital theory suggests that earnings should generally not be constant after leaving school but should follow a parabolic shape, peaking somewhere in midlife. This has led Mincer and others to amend Eq. (5.9) to have a form that is linear in schooling but quadratic in experience:[30]

$$\ln Y_i = \ln Y_0 + \beta_1 s_i + \beta_2 X_i + \beta_3 X_i^2 + u_i \tag{5.10}$$

If the earnings function is concave in experience, as is suggested by human capital theory, then estimates of β_2 should be positive, while those of β_3 should be negative. Further, to calculate the years of experience for which $\ln Y_i$ is greatest, one can differentiate Eq. (5.10) with respect to X_i, set the result equal to zero, and then solve for X^*. This yields that level of experience for which $\ln Y_i$ is maximized,

$$X^* = -\beta_2/2\beta_3 \tag{5.11}$$

which is independent of the level of schooling s_i. Note, however, that the age at which earnings peak will vary with schooling, since the age variable is the sum of six years plus years at school plus years of experience.

One implication of human capital theory, discussed in Section 5.1, is that if abilities are correlated with years of schooling and if individuals with more schooling receive more on-the-job training, then the posteducation age-earnings profile of the more educated should be steeper than that of the less educated. One way of incorporating such effects is to specify interaction terms between schooling and experience. For example, in a generalization to Eq. (5.10),

$$\ln Y_i = \ln Y_0 + \beta_1 s_i + \beta_2 X_i + \beta_3 X_i^2 + \beta_4 s_i X_i + u_i \tag{5.12}$$

the effect of experience on log earnings, $\partial \ln Y_i/\partial X_i = \beta_2 + 2\beta_3 X_i + \beta_4 s_i$, depends on the level of experience X_i *and* on the level of schooling s_i. A sufficient condition for experience-earnings profiles of the more educated to be steeper is that $\beta_4 > 0$.

5.2.C Dummy Variables in Earnings Functions

Empirical research in wage determination often makes use of dummy variables. To see how dummy variables are used, recall that in an equation such as Eq. (5.11), the intercept term $\ln Y_0$ represents the log of earnings of an individual with no schooling and no experience. Suppose that an identifiable population subgroup existed for which, for a variety of reasons, earnings levels were always a constant percentage less than those for the remaining population, regardless of the level of schooling or experience. Equivalently, assume that the logarithm of earnings for these people always differed by a constant absolute amount. Call members of this population subgroup Category 1 individuals; Category 1 individuals might consist of, say, physically handicapped people, while the remaining population consisted of all nonhandicapped individuals. Note that if it is assumed that differences between Category 1 individuals and the remaining population are constant and independent of schooling and experience, it is thereby implicitly assumed that rates of return on schooling or experience are identical for Category 1 individuals and the remaining population, that is, all population members have the same slope parameters β_1, β_2, β_3, and β_4 in Eq. (5.12). However, intercept terms will differ.

The earnings function (5.12) can be modified to incorporate these effects for Category 1 individuals by first defining a dummy variable called C_{1i} that takes on the value 1 if the individual is a member of Category 1 and otherwise is zero. This dummy variable C_{1i} is then added to Eq. (5.12), yielding

$$\ln Y_i = \ln Y_0 + \alpha_1 C_{1i} + \beta_1 s_i + \beta_2 X_i + \beta_3 X_i^2 + \beta_4 s_i X_i + u_i \quad \textbf{(5.13)}$$

where α_1 now represents the constant difference in log earnings for being a member of Category 1 rather than being from the remaining population, regardless of the level of schooling or experience. Notice that in terms of percentage changes, $\alpha_1 = \ln(1 + d_1)$, where d_1 is the percentage change in earnings attributable to membership in Category 1; for small values near zero, $\alpha_1 \approx d_1$, but if α_1 is larger than, say, 0.15 or 0.20, the antilog of α_1 is usually taken to obtain an estimate of d_1.

An alternative procedure for incorporating the differential earnings of Category 1 individuals involves specifying two distinct dummy variables, each representing a different intercept term. Specifically, define a dummy variable C_{0i} that is 1 if the individual i is a member of the non–Category 1 population (call this Category 0) and that is zero otherwise. Then define the dummy variable C_{1i} as above, and specify the earnings function as

$$\ln Y_i = \alpha_0 C_{0i} + \alpha_1' C_{1i} + \beta_1 s_i + \beta_2 X_i + \beta_3 X_i^2 + \beta_4 s_i X_i + u_i \quad \textbf{(5.14)}$$

where α_0 is the log earnings for Category 0 individuals with no schooling or experience and α_1' is the log earnings for Category 1 individuals with no schooling or experience. On the basis of the discussion in your econometric theory textbook you should be able to show that least squares estimates of the β's are identical in Eqs. (5.13) and (5.14) but that the estimate of α_1' in Eq.

(5.14) equals that of ln $Y_0 + \alpha_1$ in Eq. (5.13). To test the null hypothesis that Category 0 and Category 1 individuals have identical earnings, given schooling and experience, in Eq. (5.13) one would test whether the estimate of $\alpha_1 = 0$, whereas in Eq. (5.14) one would test whether the estimated $\alpha_0 = \alpha_1'$. In either case, one would obtain the same value of the appropriate t-test statistic.

This simple dummy variable specification can be expanded. Suppose, for example, that all individuals were either male or female and that it was hypothesized that the earnings effects of being male were different from those of being female but that rates of return to schooling and experience were identical for all individuals. Define a dummy variable for gender, D_{Gi}, that takes on the value 1 if the individual is a female and 0 otherwise. An equation specification having both Category 1 and gender dummy variables is

$$\begin{aligned} \ln Y_i = \ln Y_0 &+ \alpha_1 C_{1i} + \alpha_G D_{Gi} + \beta_1 s_i \\ &+ \beta_2 X_i + \beta_3 X_i^2 + \beta_4 s_i X_i + u_i \end{aligned} \tag{5.15}$$

where α_G is interpreted as the difference in log earnings for females rather than males, regardless of whether the individual is in Category 0 or 1, given his or her level of education and experience. In Eq. (5.15) a test corresponding to the null hypothesis that gender does not matter is simply a test of $\alpha_G = 0$.

A further elaboration of the dummy variable specification (5.15) permits interaction effects. Suppose, for example, that it was hypothesized that the earnings effects of being male were different from those of being female for Category 1 individuals; equivalently, let the effect of being in Category 1 on log earnings depend on gender. A simple procedure for incorporating this interaction between categories and gender is to define a new dummy variable $D_{G1,i}$ as the product of C_{1i} and D_{Gi}, that is, let $D_{G1,i} \equiv C_{1i} \cdot D_{Gi}$, $i = 1, \ldots, n$, and then add this interaction dummy variable to Eq. (5.15). This results in

$$\begin{aligned} \ln Y_i = \ln Y_0 &+ \alpha_1 C_{1i} + \alpha_G D_{Gi} + \alpha_{G1} D_{G1,i} \\ &+ \beta_1 s_i + \beta_2 X_i + \beta_3 X_i^2 + \beta_4 s_i X_i + u_i \end{aligned} \tag{5.16}$$

Care must be taken in interpreting parameters of this specification. For simplicity, let the schooling and experience variables all equal zero. According to Eq. (5.16), the expected log earnings for a male in Category 0 is ln Y_0, that for a female in Category 0 is ln $Y_0 + \alpha_G$, that for a male in Category 1 is ln $Y_0 + \alpha_1$, and that for a female in Category 1 is ln $Y_0 + \alpha_1 + \alpha_G + \alpha_{G1}$. Hence in this interaction specification the effect of gender on expected log earnings depends on whether the individual is in Category 0 or 1, and the effect of being in Category 1 depends on gender. The null hypothesis that these interaction effects equal zero corresponds to a test of whether $\alpha_{G1} = 0$.

These remarks demonstrate that dummy variable procedures can be very useful in incorporating the effects of categorical or qualitative variables into regression equations. It is worth noting that over the years, important controversies have emerged in the literature, based in part on the appropriate interpretation of dummy variables in statistical earnings functions. For example, in addition to schooling, gender, and race variables, some analysts have included dummy variables for occupation or industry; this complicates the interpretation of the schooling and occupational coefficients.[31] Further, although the discussion here has limited parameter differences among population subgroups to differences in intercept terms, one might also want to allow slope coefficients to vary among subgroups. Such possibilities will be examined further in Section 5.4, where we measure the wage effects of discrimination by race and by gender.

5.2.D Omitted Variable Bias: Abilities

One issue of great concern to empirical researchers assessing determinants of wages is the possible parameter bias due to omitting from the regression equation variables measuring individuals' abilities. It is widely believed that since abilities are likely to be positively correlated with schooling, omitting the ability measures from the regression equation biases upward the estimated returns to schooling. In practice, three procedures have been used to address this omitted variables bias. These include use of data on intelligence ability, use of data from identical twins, and use of panel data with fixed effects assumed.

In a pioneering study, Zvi Griliches and William Mason [1972] analyzed data on intelligence test scores of males drafted into the U.S. armed forces. These intelligence data were augmented by a reinterview undertaken a number of years after the individuals were discharged from service in the armed forces. The reinterview included questions on earnings. In examining these data, Griliches and Mason found that, surprisingly, abilities measures were virtually uncorrelated with schooling. As a result, the omitted variables bias on returns to education was negligible. This result also held when an instrumental variable technique was employed to account for possible error in measuring mental ability.[32]

A rather different approach to accounting for abilities has been pioneered by Paul Taubman [1976a, b]. Arguing that it is reasonable to assume that the abilities and family backgrounds of identical male twins are equivalent, Taubman sought to control for abilities and family background by examining the educational attainment and earnings of 1000 identical male twins aged 45 to 55 in 1973. Taubman found that when differences in the log of earnings between pairs of twins were related to differences in schooling, the estimated rate of return to schooling was only about 3%, much less than the typical findings of about 8% found elsewhere in the literature. Taubman's findings implied that for males, contrary to the findings of Griliches and Mason, abilities and schooling may be very highly correlated. However, Griliches [1977, 1979] has questioned the reliability of Taubman's results, arguing that random errors in the measurement of schooling in Taubman's model result in substantially downward biased estimates of returns to education.[33]

Yet another approach to dealing with difficulties in obtaining measures of individuals' abilities and family backgrounds involves making the assumption that however one might measure these characteristics, for each individual they are constant or fixed over time. This implies that if one can obtain repeated observations on the same individuals over time, one can first difference the data and thereby remove the fixed effects, that is, one can control for differences in individuals' unmeasured abilities and family backgrounds. This type of data, in which a cross section of individuals is repeatedly sampled over time, is called panel data. A discussion of econometric procedures for efficiently using the information contained in panel data sets is beyond the scope of this chapter; for further details on panel data techniques, see Griliches [1977] and Gary Chamberlain [1978]. Suffice it to say that at this time there does not yet appear to be convincing evidence that differences in abilities account for a sizable proportion of the earnings differentials among individuals who have differing amounts of schooling.

5.3 SELECTED EMPIRICAL RESULTS ON DETERMINANTS OF WAGES

The empirical literature on returns to education and to on-the-job training is extremely large, and it is impossible within the confines of this chapter to provide an exhaustive survey of that literature.[34] Our goal in this section is therefore the more modest one of providing a flavor of typical results obtained by empirical researchers. We begin in Section 5.3.A with an overview of results on returns to education, then examine returns to training in Section 5.3.B, comment on some findings concerning the productivity of the more highly paid workers in Section 5.3.C, and conclude in Section 5.3.D with a brief summary of union-nonunion relative wages.

Mincer's basic statistical earnings function framework, discussed in Section 5.2, has formed the basis of a very substantial empirical literature. According to Robert Willis [1986],

> the Mincer earnings function has been one of the great success stories of modern labor economics. It has been used in hundreds of studies using data from virtually every historical period and country for which suitable data exist.

Willis goes on to say, however, "To me, perhaps the most fascinating question concerning the human capital earnings function is why it should work so well."[35] Recall that there are numerous reasons why one might expect the human capital model not to work particularly well in practice, given the potentially serious measurement issues involving wages, schooling, experience, and ability and the relatively modest theory underlying the functional form specification of the statistical earnings function.

JACOB MINCER

Distinguished Labor Economist

Jacob Mincer is widely known for pathbreaking analyses in empirical labor economics. His contributions include pioneering studies on factors that affect the distribution of personal income, the labor force participation decisions of married women, the extent of hidden unemployment, variations in labor mobility, and the effects of work or career interruptions on wage rates and lifetime incomes.

A distinctive feature of Mincer's applied econometric research, as exemplified by his statistical earnings functions examined in this chapter, is that both the underlying economic theory and the econometric tools employed are kept as simple as possible. Yet the results from this empirical research are widely cited and often serve as benchmarks in assessing other studies.

After receiving his B.A. degree from Emory University in Atlanta, Georgia, Mincer attended graduate school at Columbia University, where in 1957 he received his Ph.D. degree in economics. His dissertation, a study of the effects of human capital investments on the distribution of personal income, built on the earlier theoretical foundations of Milton Friedman and Simon Kuznets. At the invitation of Theodore Schultz, Mincer spent the following year as a postdoctoral fellow at the University of Chicago. His subsequent work in labor economics interacted closely with contemporaneous theoretical human capital research by Gary Becker. Except for occasional visiting appointments, Mincer has spent his academic career since 1960 at Columbia, where he is now the Buttenweiser Professor of Economics and Human Relations. At Columbia, Mincer has helped make the Labor Workshop one of the most prestigious in the profession.

Jacob Mincer is a Fellow of the Econometric Society and of the American Statistical Association and is a Member of the American Academy of Arts and Sciences and of the National Academy of Education. In 1989 the American Economic Association named him a Distinguished Fellow, citing his "rare combination of imaginative empirical analysis guided by a command of theory."

5.3.A Rates of Return to Education

The early empirical research on returns to education was for the most part noneconometric. Researchers such as Jacob Mincer [1957, 1958, 1962], W. Lee Hansen [1963], and Gary Becker [1964] typically cross-classified the annual earnings from a cross-sectional sample of the U.S. population census by age and years of schooling, used this average earnings data to estimate average forgone earnings for individuals while they attended school, assumed that differentials by educational attainment remained constant over the remaining worklives of individuals, and then used standard formulae to compute internal rates of return.[36] In some cases, estimates of direct tuition costs for education were included, as were estimates of earnings while in school. In most cases, however, both direct education costs and earnings while in school were omitted, which is appropriate if the two offset each other.

To obtain an idea of how simple calculations are performed under such assumptions, in Table 5.1 we list mean annual earnings of year-round full-time workers by gender, age, and years of schooling for the United States in 1983. In the first row of Table 5.1 it is shown that mean earnings of male college graduates ages 18–24 in 1983 were $17,534, while mean earnings for high school graduates of the same age were $12,902. For females the comparable figures are $14,469 and $10,337. One very simple way to calculate the internal rate of return to college education is to use the formula, based on Eq. (5.3),

$$(1 + r)^n = Y_1/Y_0 \tag{5.17}$$

where Y_1 is the mean earnings of college graduates, Y_0 is the mean earnings of high school graduates, n is the number of years required from high school

Table 5.1 Mean Earnings of Year-Round Full-Time Workers by Age and Schooling, 1983; Annual Earnings in Dollars, by Schooling Completed

Age	Male High School Graduates	Male College Graduates	Female High School Graduates	Female College Graduates
18–24	12,902	17,534	10,337	14,469
25–29	18,082	23,244	13,018	17,094
30–34	20,668	27,472	13,832	19,788
35–39	22,465	31,057	14,630	20,430
40–44	24,098	36,553	14,114	20,373
45–49	24,992	38,834	14,700	18,496
50–54	24,548	38,791	14,233	18,149
55–59	24,158	38,829	13,926	19,917
60–64	23,618	36,483	14,602	18,866
65+	20,472	30,460	na	na
Total	20,869	30,990	13,413	18,584

Source: U.S. Census Bureau, *Current Population Reports*, Series P-60, #146, April 1985, Table 48.

to obtain a college degree (usually four years), and r is the real before-tax internal rate of return. If the entries from the first row of Table 5.1 are substituted into Eq. (5.17) and Eq. (5.17) is solved for r, one obtains a real private rate of return for males of 7.97% and for females of 8.77%. Computational formulae that are more complex than Eq. (5.17) can be employed to take account of the finite remaining worklife of individuals (this becomes increasingly important at higher ages) and to account for income taxes.[37]

Based on data for the 1950s and 1960s and these types of calculations, the private before-tax rate of return to college education was generally estimated to be between 10% and 15%. Becker [1964, Table 14, p. 128], for example, computed rates of return to college graduates based on data from the 1940 and 1950 census and subsequent surveys. His rate of return estimates were 14.5% in 1939, 13+% in 1949, 12.4% in 1956, and 14.8% in 1958; analogous estimates for high school graduates were 16%, 20%, 25%, and 28%, respectively.

These rates of return are averages, but the distribution of earnings by educational level around the average is often very wide. While the average return to a college degree may be 12%, for some people the return will be negative, while for others it may be as large as 50%. Lester Thurow [1975], for example, has noted that on the basis of 1972 data, about 28% of people with college degrees had income *below* the median high school income (implying negative rates of return to college), and approximately 21% of people with only high school degrees had incomes above the median *college* income level.[38]

Although these noneconometric analyses of returns to education are informative, they do not enjoy the advantages of a regression approach, since with the latter one can "hold constant" the effects of other variables, and one can also undertake more detailed statistical inference. The most thorough early econometric study of returns to education is a 1965 University of Chicago Ph.D. dissertation by Giora Hanoch, eventually published as Hanoch [1967]. Using data from the 1 in 1000 sample of the 1960 census, Hanoch examined earnings, schooling, age, and demographic relationships for more than 57,000 males over age 14. The sample not at school in 1959 was divided into 24 groups defined by race (white, nonwhite), region (South, non-South), and six age groups (14–24, 25–34, 35–44, 45–54, 55–64, 65 and over). Within each of these 24 groups, Hanoch regresssed earnings (not log earnings) on 23 variables, most of them being dummy variables.

One of the most interesting findings reported by Hanoch is that there appeared to be a pattern of decreasing marginal rates of return to schooling. This is shown in Table 5.2, which reproduces a portion of Hanoch's Table 3. Note in particular that marginal rates of return to college (16 years) are smaller than those to a high school diploma (12 years), which in turn are smaller than those from completion of elementary school (8 years).[39]

A rather different issue concerns whether returns to schooling are stable

Table 5.2 Hanoch's Estimates of Private Internal Rates of Return to Successive Levels of Schooling, United States, 1959

	Schooling Level					
Race/Region	5–7	8	9–11	12	13–15	16
Whites/North	21.8	16.3	16.0	7.1	12.2	7.0
Whites/South	14.4	18.2	18.8	9.3	11.0	7.3

Source: Adapted from Giora Hanoch, "An Economic Analysis of Earning and Schooling," *Journal of Human Resources*, Vol. 3, No. 2, Summer 1967, Table 3.

over time. Since wage rates by schooling depend on supply and demand, stability of wage rates will occur only if demand and supply curves shift equiproportionally. Richard Freeman [1975, 1976] has argued that rates of return to college degrees fell sharply in the 1970s, owing in part to the relative increase in the supply of graduates induced by more heavily publicly subsidized college training. Freeman [1975] estimates that private rates of return to college training for men were 11.0% in 1959, 11.5% in 1969, and 10.5% in 1972, but only 8.5% in 1974; his corresponding estimates of social rates of return are 10.5%, 11.1%, 9.5%, and 7.5%.

Findings similar to those of Freeman have been reported by George Psacharopoulos [1981]; these are reproduced in Columns A and B of Table 5.3. There it is seen that while rates of return to secondary education varied modestly around a mean of about 12% from 1939 to 1976, rates of return to college education remained relatively constant at about 11% from 1939 to 1969 but then began falling sharply, reaching lows of about 5% in 1976.

Whether the lower rates of return to a college education have been con-

Table 5.3 Gross Private Rates of Return to Education in the United States by Educational Attainment, Selected Years, 1939–1982

Year	A Secondary	B Higher	C Higher	Year	A Secondary	B Higher	C Higher
1939	18.2	10.7	na	1974	14.8	4.8	8.5
1949	14.2	10.6	na	1975	12.8	5.3	8.9
1959	10.1	11.3	na	1976	11.0	5.3	8.3
1967	na	na	8.2	1977	na	na	8.5
1968	na	na	8.7	1978	na	na	8.5
1969	10.7	10.9	9.0	1979	na	na	7.9
1970	11.3	8.8	9.0	1980	na	na	8.3
1971	12.5	8.0	9.2	1981	na	na	8.7
1972	11.3	7.8	8.5	1982	na	na	10.2
1973	12.0	5.5	8.9				

Sources: Columns A and B, Psacharopoulos [1981], Table V; Column C, based on unpublished cross-sectional regressions using Current Population Survey tapes, provided to Willis [1986] by Finis Welch. This table reproduced from Willis [1986], Table 10.2.

stant since the 1970s, or have rebounded in the United States in the 1980s is not yet completely clear, although the accumulating evidence suggesting a rebound is strong. In his survey article on human capital, Willis [1986] presents evidence gathered by Finis R. Welch suggesting instead that rates of return to college education have been relatively constant, even into the 1980s. In Column C of Table 5.3 we reproduce rates-of-return calculations based on Welch's regression results, as reported by Willis. There it is seen that returns to a college degree varied only modestly between 1967 and 1981, from 7.9% to 9.2%, and then increased to 10.2% in 1982. Precisely why the Welch-Willis results differ from those reported by Freeman and by Psacharopoulos is not clear.[40] Other studies, such as that by Kevin Murphy and Finis Welch [1988], present persuasive evidence that rates of return have risen greatly in the 1980s from their low levels in the 1970s. This type of evidence has led labor economics textbook writers, such as Daniel Hamermesh and Albert Rees [1988, Chapter 3], to conclude that the evidence suggests that in the United States and elsewhere in the 1980s, the rates of return to college degrees have in fact rebounded to their 1960s levels, if not to higher ones.[41]

5.3.B Returns to On-the-Job Training and Experience

An important implication of the human capital framework, discussed in Section 5.2, is that age-earnings profiles for the more educated should be steeper than for those with less schooling, owing in part to the fact that people with more schooling tend to receive more on-the-job training. We now briefly review empirical and econometric findings concerning interactions between returns to schooling and returns to on-the-job training.

As with the literature on returns to education, the early empirical research on returns to on-the-job training was for the most part noneconometric and was based on calculations involving cross-sectional variations in earnings data. In Mincer [1962], for example, rates of return were calculated on apprenticeship training in three trades in 1949: metal, printing, and building. Preferred estimates were 9.5% for metal, 9.0% for printing, and 9.7% for building trades. For medical specialization, incomes of residents and specialists (after residency) were compared with incomes of general practitioners, again using 1949 data. This yielded best estimates of before-tax returns of 12.7% and, after a rough adjustment for taxes, after-tax returns of 11.3%.[42] Such returns were approximately equal to those estimated by Becker and by Mincer on returns to schooling.

A classic econometric study of returns to on-the-job training is that by Mincer [1974]. Mincer reports results from a number of regressions, each implicitly based on the assumption that all training is general. Several regressions are of particular interest to us. For example, using 1959 data on 31,093 white, nonfarm, nonstudent males up to age 65 from the 1960 1 in 1000 census sample, Mincer began by running a simple least squares regression of log earnings on schooling, as in Eq. (5.8). This yielded

$$\ln Y = 7.58 + \underset{(43.8)}{0.070s} \qquad R^2 = 0.067 \tag{5.18}$$

where the number in parentheses is the t-statistic. Notice that the estimated schooling coefficient implies a 7% annual return to schooling and is highly significant. However, the proportion of variation in log earnings "explained" by variation in schooling is small, since the R^2 is but 0.067.

When experience (X) and its square (X^2) are added as regressors as in Eq. (5.10), where X equals age minus years schooling minus 6, the goodness of fit improves enormously from 0.067 to 0.285.[43] This is seen in Eq. (5.19):

$$\ln Y = 6.20 + \underset{(72.3)}{0.107s} + \underset{(75.5)}{0.081X} - \underset{(-55.8)}{0.0012X^2} \qquad R^2 = 0.285 \tag{5.19}$$

Here the estimate of the returns to schooling increases to 10.7%, and, as predicted by human capital theory, returns to experience are positive and decline with increases in experience. Using Eq. (5.11), estimates in Eq. (5.19) imply that peak earnings occur at $X^* = 33.75$ years, just under age 52 for a person with a high school education and just under 56 for a person with a college degree.

Mincer also reports estimates of a model allowing for interactions between schooling and experience, as in Eq. (5.12). Further, he allows for diminishing returns to schooling by adding as a regressor years of schooling squared (s^2). He reports an estimated equation having the form

$$\ln Y = 4.87 + \underset{(2.34)}{0.255s} - \underset{(-7.1)}{0.0029s^2} - \underset{(-31.8)}{0.0043sX} + \underset{(63.7)}{0.148X} - \underset{(-66.2)}{0.0018X^2}$$
$$R^2 = 0.309 \tag{5.20}$$

Note that the effect of schooling on log-earnings in Eq. (5.20),

$$\partial \ln Y/\partial s = 0.255 - 0.0058s - 0.0043X \tag{5.21}$$

now depends on schooling and experience and exhibits diminishing returns to schooling. Specifically, if Eq. (5.21) is evaluated at $X = 8$, then marginal rates of return to schooling are 17.4% at 8 years of schooling, 15.1% at 12 years, and 12.8% at 16 years.

To assess the effects of experience on earnings at various levels of schooling, one can differentiate Eq. (5.20) with respect to X, obtaining

$$\partial \ln Y/\partial X = 0.148 - 0.0043s - 0.0036X \tag{5.22}$$

indicating that returns to experience decrease with increases in educational attainment and in years of experience. Of particular interest in Eq. (5.22) is the implication that peaks in the age-earnings profiles among people with differing levels of schooling occur more closely together than is implied by an equation such as Eq. (5.19) that does not allow for interactions between schooling and experience. In particular, if one sets Eq. (5.22) equal to zero and solves for the X^* that maximizes ln Y, one obtains

$$X^* = (0.148 - 0.0043s)/0.0036 \tag{5.23}$$

For $s = 8$, 12, and 16 the peak log earnings occur at $X^* = 31.6$, 26.8, and 22.0 years of experience; if one adds to X^* the years of schooling plus 6, then the age at which log earnings is maximized is virtually the same: age 45.6 for elementary school graduates, 44.8 for high school graduates, and 44.0 for college graduates. Significantly, since the ages at which log earnings are maximized are virtually the same, and since postschool earnings for the more educated begin at a later age, it follows that the age-earnings profile is steeper for the more educated, as was hypothesized by the human capital framework discussed near the end of Section 5.1.C.

Mincer's econometric research refers only to males. It has long been observed that the age-earnings profiles of females are much flatter than those for males, regardless of the level of schooling. (To see this, compare male-female earnings in the United States in 1983, displayed in Table 5.1.) Further, Mincer [1962, p. 67] estimated that the amount of training investment in females in 1949 was perhaps only 10% as much as that in males.

Although discrimination by gender will be discussed more fully in Section 5.4.C, it is worth noting here that if employers and female employees both expect female employees to leave the work force for prolonged periods to rear children, then the incentives to invest in training and schooling are smaller for females, since the remaining work period over which benefits from such investments can be recouped is likely to be smaller. Further, as has been emphasized by Mincer and Solomon Polachek [1974] and Mincer and Haim Ofek [1982], incentives for undertaking training investment are further reduced if investment in human capital depreciates quickly when the individual is not in the work force. Citing these reasons, Mincer [1962] argues that one should expect differentials among age-earnings profiles at various levels of schooling to be smaller for females than for males. Note, however, that such reasoning also implies that differences should be smaller if not zero for single, "career-oriented" females who are not expected to leave the work force to rear children. Further, similar differential age-earnings profiles should be observed for males who are expected to spend substantial portions of their adult life out of the work force.

An econometric implication of this discussion is that one might expect parameters of the statistical earnings function to differ between males and females. If true, it would not be sufficient to attempt to accommodate such differences merely by specifying a male-female dummy variable for the intercept term, as in Eq. (5.14), since the above arguments suggest that the slope coefficients on schooling, and especially on experience, might also be expected to differ between males and females.

5.3.C The Productivity of Highly Paid Workers

The empirical literature on returns to training discussed up to this point is based on the assumption that workers are paid the value of their marginal product. This equality between wages and values of marginal products breaks down if training is specific rather than general.[44] Further, if training is in part specific, then in a statistical earnings function it should be the case that the cumulative time working for the present employer (often called the seniority), and not just overall work experience, affects current wages.

A number of econometric studies have included as regressors in a statistical earnings function not only schooling and overall work experience since leaving school, but also the length of time worked for the present employer. In most such studies it is found that both overall experience and seniority with the current employer affect current wages. For example, based on the Michigan Panel Study of Income Dynamics data, Richard Kamalich and Solomon Polachek [1982] estimated the following wage equation by OLS:

$$\ln w = \underset{(163.0)}{4.92} + \underset{(34.6)}{0.075s} + \underset{(10.3)}{0.0070X_1} + \underset{(16.2)}{0.0014X_2} \qquad R^2 = 0.28 \qquad \textbf{(5.24)}$$

where numbers in parentheses are t-statistics, X_1 is the number of years worked since age 18, and X_2 is the number of months worked for the present employer. According to Eq. (5.24), wages depend not only on general training (the coefficient on X_1 is positive and statistically significant), but also on specific training obtained from the current employer (the coefficient on X_2 is also positive and significant). Note that while the coefficient on X_1 is five times larger than that on X_2, X_1 is measured in years, while X_2 is measured in months. Hence an "annualized" coefficient on X_2 would approximately equal 0.0168 (0.0014 times 12), which is twice as large as that on X_1. Therefore it appears that at least a substantial portion of training is specific.

But if training is specific, wages may differ from marginal products. Specifically, with specific training it is typically optimal for employers to share some of the returns to specific training investment with workers in order to avoid costly labor turnover. This may result in an implicit contract between employers and employees in which wages paid to employees are initially smaller than alternative wages (in other firms) but are greater in later years. In such an implicit contract a portion of compensation may be deferred to later years of employment.

As was discussed at the end of Section 5.1.C, this type of compensation policy may create incentives for shirking on the part of specifically trained workers and may also induce them to want to work to a greater age than is optimal from the employers' vantage point. Optimal compensation schemes in such contexts are one focus of the rapidly growing principal-agent and efficiency-wage literatures.[45] In our context, such issues have been discussed by, among others, Edward Lazear [1979b, 1981] and Jacob Mincer and Boyan Jovanovic [1981].

A critical empirical issue is therefore the extent to which the more highly paid are more productive. If it can be established that the more highly paid are in fact more productive, then there is support for the Mincer general training hypothesis as explaining age-earnings profiles. On the other hand, if the higher wage–higher productivity link is not a strong one, then there may instead be support for an implicit contract notion with specific training.

Empirical research on this issue is still in its formative stages. Early research by James Medoff and Katherine Abraham [1980, 1981] examining the relationship between a worker's wages and the evaluation of his or her performance by supervisors suggests that productivity and pay are not as closely linked as is suggested by human capital theory and general training theory.

A related hypothesis on why earnings tend to increase with experience is not directly related to the Mincer-Becker distinction between general and specific training. This alternative theory rationalizes the positive relationship between experience and earnings by hypothesizing that individuals with more experience have had more time to find a good job and/or a good match.[46]

The search/match and general and specific training hypotheses have been examined and compared empirically by Katherine Abraham and Henry Farber [1987]. Their findings conflict somewhat from those of Medoff and Abraham. Specifically, Abraham and Farber find that returns to seniority are rather modest in comparison to those from overall work experience and that earnings deferral under implicit contracts does not seem to be an important overall factor in labor markets. However, for nonunion blue collar workers, Abraham and Farber find evidence supporting the notion that experience facilitates sorting into either a better job or a better job match.

These various theories relating seniority, overall experience, and job search to wages are the focus of much current research. In some cases the econometric techniques involved have become very sophisticated, such as those involving duration analysis.[47] Other literature has attempted to discern how these alternative theories might be discriminated empirically. Already it is clear that this line of research will produce important empirical findings on determinants of wages and earnings.

5.3.D Union-Nonunion Relative Wages

Another empirical issue that has attracted a great deal of attention from applied econometricians is the extent to which wage differentials exist between union and nonunion employees. This empirical issue is somewhat subtle and is not identical to the issue of the effects of unions on wage rates. Such a distinction must be made, since unions may have an impact on the wages of nonunion workers. In particular, as has been stressed by H. Gregg Lewis [1963] and others, nonunion employers may set higher wages in an attempt to prevent their firms from becoming unionized or simply to compete with union employers in recruiting qualified labor. Moreover, union-nonunion differentials may take on the forms of nonwage compensation (such as health insurance). Hence observed union-nonunion wage differentials are rather imperfect estimates of the effects unions have had on total compensation.

A further market response that may affect observed union-nonunion wage differentials in the other direction involves the fact that high union wages and the resulting possibly higher product prices would tend to reduce employment in the union sectors (and in nonunion establishments where threats of union organization are significant) and increase the supply of labor to the nonunion sector. Thus nonunion wages would fall, and union-nonunion wage differentials would increase.

A common finding of empirical research in this area is that there tends to be a positive correlation between unionization (or, more precisely, whether workers are covered by union contracts) and wage rates. Although one interpretation of such a finding is that the existence of union contracts has an impact on wages, an alternative interpretation stresses causality in the other direction. In particular, it may be the case that preexisting high wage rates, perhaps in industries with price-inelastic product demand, attract union membership drives.

One of the simplest procedures for assessing union-nonunion wage differentials is to gather data on wages, educational attainment, work experience, and perhaps some other variables and then estimate a statistical earnings function such as Eq. (5.12) by least squares including also a dummy variable for whether the individual is or is not covered by a union contract. The coefficient on the union dummy variable could then be interpreted as the effect of union contracts on wages, holding all other variables fixed.

The major problem with such a simple procedure is that it implicitly assumes that the effects of variables such as education and experience on log wages are the same in the union and nonunion sectors, that is, it implicitly constrains the slope coefficients to be equal for union and non-union workers.

Although one might expect the coefficients on education and experience to have the same sign in union and nonunion wage equations, there are a number of reasons why one would expect their magnitudes to differ. It is commonly believed, for example, that owing to the prevalence of seniority systems in unions, the effects of education on wages are smaller in union than in nonunion establishments; this differential effect is likely to be particularly important if older union workers have relatively low formal educational attainment.[48] In general, it is also believed that unions appear to have a flattening impact on the age-earnings profile, with peak effects of experience on log wages occurring earlier than in nonunion establishments.[49]

In practice, union-nonunion wage differentials have been computed in at least three different ways. The simplest procedure is that just discussed, namely, use of a dummy intercept term in a statistical earnings function. A second procedure involves separating the sample into union and nonunion workers and estimating separate wage equations with both intercept and slope coefficients differing. Mean differences in the explanatory variables in the union and nonunion sectors are then weighted by the union wage structure to estimate wage differentials.

More specifically, let $\ln W^u$ and $\ln W^n$ represent logs of individual wage rates in the union and nonunion sectors, let β^u and β^n be the vectors of estimated parameters in the union and nonunion equations, and let Z^u and Z^n be the corresponding vectors of explanatory variables. If the union wage structure applies to workers in both union and nonunion establishments, then the mean wage differentials between them, controlling for differences in mean union-nonunion characteristics of workers, can be estimated as

$$\overline{\ln W^u} - \overline{\ln W^n} = \beta^u(\overline{Z}^u - \overline{Z}^n) \tag{5.25}$$

where the overbars indicate sample means.[50] Note that according to Eq. (5.25), mean wage differentials between union and nonunion workers reflect differences in mean characteristics of variables explaining wages (the Z's), where these differences are evaluated by using union parameters β^u.

A third procedure for estimating union-nonunion wage differentials is similar to Eq. (5.25) but instead evaluates differences in mean characteristics of explanatory variables by using the estimated nonunion parameters, β^n:

$$\overline{\ln W^u} - \overline{\ln W^n} = \beta^n(\overline{Z}^u - \overline{Z}^n) \tag{5.26}$$

Farrell Bloch and Mark Kuskin [1978] have used these three procedures in estimating union-nonunion wage differentials on the basis of data from the May 1973 U.S. Current Population Survey, limited to 12,573 white, non-Spanish males between ages 25 and 64 who were employed in the private sector. Using a Chow test, Bloch and Kuskin decisively reject the null hypothesis that slope coefficients are equal in the union and nonunion sectors; this result implies that use of a simple dummy variable procedure is inappropriate. Nonetheless, using such a procedure, they obtain an estimated coefficient on the union-nonunion dummy variable of 0.14734 with a standard error of 0.00855; the antilog of this coefficient yields a union-nonunion wage differential estimate of 15.87%. When separate equations are estimated for union and nonunion workers, use of Eq. (5.25) results in a mean logarithmic differential of 0.0888, while that based on Eq. (5.26) is 0.1461. The corresponding percentage union-nonunion wage differentials (the antilogs) are 9.29% and 15.73%. Block and Kuskin therefore find that despite strong evidence of differing wage structures in the union and nonunion sectors, the estimate of wage differentials based on the simple dummy variable technique is larger, but not dramatically different from those based on models with differing wage equation coefficients.

The literature on union-nonunion wage differentials is a large one; it has recently been surveyed by Lewis [1986]. Lewis concludes that evidence to date for the United States suggests that union-nonunion wage differentials are roughly similar for males and females, are slightly larger for blacks than for whites, are larger in the construction industry than in other nonmanufacturing sectors, are smaller in manufacturing than in nonmanufacturing industries, are larger in the South than in other regions, are positive but decline with level of schooling and with age up to 25–30 years of experience, and are larger in the private sector than in the public sector.

One interesting strand of the literature surveyed by Lewis attempts to take into account the possibility that instead of union membership causing higher wages, the probability of an establishment being unionized depends positively on preexisting wage rates. Orley Ashenfelter and George Johnson [1972] and Peter Schmidt and Robert Strauss [1976], for example, have estimated models in which a union membership equation is estimated simultaneously with a wage equation. Significantly, in both cases the authors find a much smaller positive effect of unions on wages than was obtained by using a single-equation framework.[51] On the basis of these and other considerations, Lewis concludes by stating that in the United States from 1967 to 1979 the mean union-nonunion wage gap was often estimated as high as 14%, "but I suspect that the average was lower. By how much? I wish that I knew."[52]

Finally, it is worth noting that a substantial related empirical literature focuses on the more general issue of modeling individuals' and unions' joint behavior, particular attention being devoted to how workers and unions deal with potential tradeoffs involving employment and wages. Students who are interested in this topic might read recent surveys and contributions by Henry S. Farber [1983, 1986], Andrew J. Oswald [1985], John Pencavel [1984], and Thomas MaCurdy and John Pencavel [1986].

5.4 ESTIMATING THE WAGE EFFECTS OF DISCRIMINATION

It is widely known that in the United States there is substantial inequality in earnings by gender and by race. In Table 5.4 the median weekly earnings of full-time workers in the United States are given for selected years from 1967 to 1984, by sex and by race. The table shows that weekly earnings of females have been about 62% those of males, only slightly larger than the 60% ratio announced thousands of years ago in the quotation from the Old Testament at the beginning of this chapter. This ratio has increased slightly in the 1980s. The median black/white earnings ratio averages about 0.78 and is higher than the female/male average of about 0.62. Hence differences in median earnings by gender are larger than those by race. An important issue concerns the extent to which earnings differentials represent variations in individual endowments of productive attributes such as schooling and experience or instead reflect the effects of discrimination. We now consider how one might employ econometric techniques to measure the effects of discrimination on wages.

Table 5.4 Median Weekly Earnings of Full-Time Workers by Race and Sex for Selected Years, 1967–1984, in Current Dollars

Year	By Sex		Female/Male Ratio	By Race		Black/White Ratio
	Males	Females		Whites	Blacks*	
1967	$125	$ 78	0.62	$113	$ 79	0.70
1969	142	86	0.61	125	90	0.72
1971	162	100	0.62	142	107	0.75
1973	188	116	0.62	162	129	0.80
1975	221	137	0.62	190	156	0.82
1977	253	156	0.62	217	171	0.79
1978	272	166	0.61	232	186	0.80
1981	345	217	0.63	292	236	0.81
1984	400	259	0.65	339	256	0.76

*Includes other nonwhites.
Sources: Data from U.S. Department of Labor, *Handbook of Labor Statistics*, 1980, p. 118; and *Employment and Earnings*, January 1985, p. 210. This table is taken from Campbell R. McConnell and Stanley L. Brue, *Contemporary Labor Economics*, New York: McGraw-Hill, 1986, Table 11-1, p. 291.

5.4.A Issues in Defining and Estimating the Wage Effects of Discrimination

Labor market discrimination in the United States has been defined as occurring when female or minority group workers with abilities, education, training, and experience equal to those of white male workers are provided inferior treatment in hiring, occupational access, promotion, or wage rates. In our context it is useful to distinguish several possible sources of discrimination. First, members of a particular group might have less access than others to productivity-augmenting opportunities, such as schooling. Second, given equal qualifications such as schooling, members of a particular group might occupy less favorable jobs than do advantaged group members. Third, given employment in a particular job, members of a disadvantaged group might receive lower pay than members of the advantaged group. When truly similar jobs are being compared, this third source of differences is called wage discrimination. Furthermore, while the first two sources may reflect previous conditions of discrimination, wage discrimination as defined here is current.

The classic treatment of wage discrimination is by Gary Becker [1971]. Becker demonstrates that a wage difference can arise in competitive circumstances between, say, blacks and whites in a given job if whites have a distaste for working or associating with blacks. In many cases the preferred distance between workers may be more "social" than physical, that is, males may protest working with female superiors but be comfortable with female subordinates. Customers might also exercise tastes for discrimination, particularly in service jobs in which clients might prefer that providers of services be members of the clients' group. Depending on the positions of the resulting supply and demand curves, such tastes for discrimination can result in higher wages for members of advantaged groups and higher prices for services rendered by advantaged group members. In the absence of tastes for discrimination the forces of competition would eventually eliminate any such wage and price differentials. It follows that tastes for discrimination result in an opportunity cost in terms of forgone productive efficiency. One 1980 U.S. study concludes that if racial discrimination were eliminated, the level of GNP would have been 4.4% higher in the 1970s.[53] In Becker's model, majority group individuals are willing to bear such efficiency costs.[54]

A somewhat different notion of discrimination involves the exercise of economic power, not just tastes for discrimination. It occurs when one group colludes in discriminating against others and thereby raises the incomes of its own membership. Examples here include a majority group restricting minority group access to education (for example, by providing less public funding to schools with a substantial proportion of minority group students) or by restricting apprenticeships (as has occurred in certain crafts unions).[55] In such cases the job opportunities and incomes of advantaged group members are enhanced at the expense of the disadvantaged.

A related source of discrimination involving economic power occurs when employers are able to exploit monopsony power (the ability of the employer to affect the wage rate of its employees) in a labor market. For example, even when males and females are equally productive (have equal marginal products), if the supply curve for females is less wage elastic than that for males, the profit-maximizing monopsonistic employer will pay females lower average wages than males, although the gender-specific marginal costs of labor will be equal. This occurs because the employer facing upward sloping supply curves for both male and female workers will employ each type of labor at a level at which the gender-specific marginal cost of labor equals the common marginal product. Note that in contrast to Becker's taste for discrimination case, if monopsony is present, profit maximization and competition among firms will not reduce discrimination over time but will in fact maintain it.

Two issues should be considered, however, when evaluating the monopsony argument. First, monopsony power is generally dissipated when the number of employers in a region increases. One would therefore expect monopsony to be most prevalent in remote areas and "one-company towns" and be less likely in areas with multiple employers, since if multiple employers coexisted, competition among them would eliminate wage differentials. With multiple employers, monopsony power could be maintained only by collusive behavior. Second, the monopsony argument as applied to female workers is of doubtful empirical validity, since there is considerable empirical evidence suggesting that the labor supply of females, particularly married females, is more wage elastic, not less elastic, than that of males. Hence the empirical conditions that are necessary for such monopsony discrimination to occur are unlikely to hold.[56]

Yet another source of discrimination is called statistical discrimination. Lester Thurow has defined this as occuring

> whenever an individual is judged on the basis of the average characteristics of the group, or groups, to which he or she belongs rather than upon his or her own personal characteristics. The judgments are correct, factual, and objective in the sense that the group actually has the characteristics that are subscribed to it, but the judgments are incorrect with respect to many individuals within the group.[57]

The rationale underlying statistical discrimination is similar to the market signaling and screening literature discussed in Section 5.1.D. This form of discrimination occurs because it is costly or simply infeasible for employers to obtain detailed information on each potential employee. Further, the limited information that is available is insufficient to enable the employer to predict accurately which applicants will be the most productive employees. As a result, the employer uses simple considerations such as race, gender, or age in choosing among applicants, criteria that on average may be appropriate indicators of productivity but that are often inaccurate for given individuals.

A hiring policy that assumes that group or average differences apply in each individual case may minimize employers' hiring costs. This form of discrimination is therefore rather different from the taste for discrimination notion in which employers clearly suffer adverse cost consequences from discriminating. The employer who statistically discriminates may well be profitable on the average, even though many workers who differ from the group average will suffer adverse consequences. It is also worth noting that unless the average differences among groups change, there is no compelling reason why competition among firms would diminish discrimination over time.

The above discussion on definitions and sources of discrimination is, unfortunately, very brief. For further details on this fascinating topic, readers are referred to well-known textbooks in labor economics (such as those referenced at the end of this chapter) and the survey by Glen Cain [1986].

With this brief background we now examine how measures of discrimination are constructed and interpreted.

A very substantial literature exists that addresses how one might decompose variations in workers' earnings into differences in productive endowments and effects of discrimination. Important references in this literature include Dennis Aigner and Glen Cain [1977], David Bloom and Mark Killingsworth [1982], Glen Cain [1986], and Thomas Johnson [1978].

The most common econometric framework for measuring the effects of wage discrimination was developed by Alan Blinder [1973] and Ronald Oaxaca [1973b]. Essentially, it assumes that in the absence of discrimination the estimated effects of workers' endowments on earnings are identical for each group. Discrimination is revealed by differences in the estimated coefficients. Differences are not confined to intercept terms through simple dummy variable specifications, but also include variations in estimated slope coefficients.

More specifically, suppose that data on log wages and workers' characteristics were collected from two groups, an advantaged group, denoted with a superscript asterisk, and a disadvantaged group, denoted with a subscript asterisk. Using these data on workers' wages and their endowments of productivity-enhancing characteristics (years of schooling, experience, etc.), first estimate by least squares the separate statistical earnings functions equations for these two groups, that is, estimate parameters in $\ln y^* = X^*\beta^* + u^*$ for the advantaged group and $\ln y_* = X_*\beta_* + u_*$ for the disadvantaged group, where y and u are vectors of wages and random disturbance terms and X is a matrix of observations on explanatory variables (schooling, experience, etc., with observations on the same explanatory variables in each of the two groups). Define the least squares estimates of β^* and β_* as b^* and b_*, respectively, and note that the sample variance of $(b^* - b_*)$ equals $\text{Var}(b^*) + V(b_*)$, for $\text{Cov}(b^*, b_*) = 0$.

A fundamental property of the least squares estimator is that the fitted regression line passes through the point of sample means. This implies that

$$\overline{\ln y^*} = \bar{X}^* b^* \qquad \text{and} \qquad \overline{\ln y_*} = \bar{X}_* b_* \tag{5.27}$$

and that the mean difference in the predicted log wages for the two groups is

$$\overline{\ln y^*} - \overline{\ln y_*} = \bar{X}^* b^* - \bar{X}_* b_* \tag{5.28}$$

The difference between the advantaged and disadvantaged coefficient vectors is

$$\Delta b \equiv b^* - b_* \qquad \text{implying that} \qquad b_* = b^* - \Delta b \tag{5.29}$$

Substituting the second equation in Eq. (5.29) into Eq. (5.28) and rearranging yields

$$\overline{\ln y^*} - \overline{\ln y_*} = b^*(\bar{X}^* - \bar{X}_*) + \bar{X}_* \Delta b \tag{5.30}$$

Equation (5.30) is very important, since as stressed by Blinder and Oaxaca, it states that the mean difference in log earnings between the advantaged and disadvantaged groups can be decomposed into the effects of differences in their average endowments (the first term on the right-hand side of Eq. (5.30)), and the effects of discrimination, as revealed by differences in estimated coefficients (the second term).[58] Note that average endowment differences in Eq. (5.30) are weighted by advantaged workers' estimated coefficients, while differences in the estimated coefficients are weighted by average characteristics of the disadvantaged workers.

An equally plausible alternative procedure involves solving the first term in Eq. (5.29) for b^* rather than b_*, substituting for b^* into Eq. (5.28), and then rearranging. This yields a variant of Eq. (5.30),

$$\overline{\ln y^*} - \overline{\ln y_*} = b_*(\bar{X}^* - \bar{X}_*) + \bar{X}^*\Delta b \qquad \textbf{(5.31)}$$

where average endowment differences are now weighted by disadvantaged workers' estimated coefficients and coefficient differences are weighted by mean characteristics of the advantaged workers.

The choice between use of Eq. (5.30) or Eq. (5.31) to measure discrimination is essentially a classic index number problem involving a decision on which weights to employ.[59] In practice, empirical researchers have typically employed both equations, arguing that together they bracket the estimated effects of discrimination on wages. Note also that the above framework can easily be extended to apply to comparisons of numerous disadvantaged groups with a common advantaged group and with each other.

Two important caveats are worth mentioning. First, regardless of which procedure is employed, to provide an accurate measure of discrimination, the list of regressors in Eq. (5.27) must include all relevant variables measuring individuals' productive endowments. Second, if there were any reason why one might expect coefficients to differ among groups in the absence of discrimination, then the Blinder-Oaxaca procedure would be inappropriate.

With this as background we now turn to a brief discussion of estimates of discrimination by race and by gender, based on Eqs. (5.30) and (5.31).

5.4.B Discrimination by Race

An interesting feature of the econometric literature on discrimination between blacks and whites is that most of it has focused on males, since racial differences in female wages have become very small. Further, since there is now greater income inequality among blacks than among whites, it is not surprising that very substantial black/white wage differentials exist for males.[60] Using a variety of equations, including ones similar to Eqs. (5.27) and (5.30) and 1967 data from the Michigan Panel Study of Income Dynamics, Blinder [1973] measured the mean wage differential for white over black males as 50.5%. Approximately 60% of this mean wage differential was attributed to differences in endowments, and about 40% reflected discrimination by race.[61] Using more recent data, Mary Corcoran and Greg Duncan [1979] estimate that productivity differences account for about 53% of earnings differentials between black and white men and discrimination accounts for about 47%.

Other studies have focused attention on whether federal legislation in the United States, especially the 1964 Civil Rights Act, has reduced black/white wage differentials, either by improving blacks' endowments or through reducing discrimination. Richard Freeman [1981] has argued that black Americans have made substantial labor market progress in recent years, most of the gains coming since the middle 1960s and coinciding with the passage and enforcement of the Civil Rights Act. Weighting mean differences in black/white characteristics by whites' regression coefficients, Freeman finds

ALAN BLINDER

Measuring the Wage Effects of Discrimination

As a second-year graduate student at MIT who was very much concerned with factors affecting the distribution of personal income, Alan Blinder developed a statistical multiple regression procedure for measuring the effects of race or gender discrimination on wages. This research involved using a large cross-sectional data base consisting of thousands of observations. Such an effort severely strained the econometric software capabilities that existed at MIT in 1971, particularly since some of the research involved using two-stage least squares. Blinder was greatly assisted in this research by Robert Hall, then an Assistant Professor at MIT. According to Blinder, Hall helped him learn how to use a statistical program called CSP (Cross-Sectional Processor) that involved first using other software to form the $X'X$ and $X'Y$ matrices and then punching out these matrices onto 80-column cards and reading them into CSP; Hall also helped Blinder interpret the error messages, written as hexadecimal dumps. A procedure similar to Blinder's was coincidentally and independently developed by Ronald Oaxaca. The Blinder-Oaxaca procedure, which is described in detail in this chapter, has formed the basis of numerous attempts to measure the wage effects of discrimination.

Alan S. Blinder was born in 1945 in Brooklyn, New York, attended suburban Long Island elementary and secondary public schools, and then enrolled at Princeton University, where in 1967 he graduated summa cum laude in economics. After spending one year at the London School of Economics, Blinder came back to the United States for further graduate study; within two years he earned a Ph.D. degree from MIT, having written his dissertation for a committee consisting of Robert Solow, Robert Hall, and Peter Diamond. He then returned to his alma mater, Princeton, and aside from several visiting appointments, he has been there since 1971. Blinder now holds the Gordon S. Rentschler Professorship of Economics chair at Princeton.

Blinder's research typically focuses on policy-related issues. Although issues of income inequality have always been important to him, Blinder is also widely known for his research in macroeconomics, particularly on the effectiveness of government stabilization policies. Blinder has frequently been asked to testify before the U.S. Congress on economic policy matters, and he has often written in the popular press, not only as the author of *Hard Heads, Soft Hearts: Tough-Minded Economics for a Just Society*, but also as an economics columnist for *Business Week*, *The Boston Globe*, *The Washington Post*, and *Newsday*.

One theme that Blinder often develops with his graduate students is that the most harmful thing he was taught in econometrics at MIT was "You don't get the hypothesis from the data." While he clearly recognizes the dangers of data mining, he also asks, "From where else do you get the hypothesis?" Blinder's advice: "Look at the data. Look at plots. Look at means and moments. Print out the data, look for outliers, and for observations with decimal points off by several places. Learn to know your data."

that only about 3% of the average earnings differences between black and white young workers (17 to 27 years of age) is due to discrimination, while 32% of the difference for black and white older men (48 to 62 years of age) represents discrimination. When blacks' regression coefficients are used to weight differences in mean characteristics, the results obtained are very similar, indicating that only 3% of wage differences for black/white young workers is due to discrimination and 22% for older workers. Freeman suggests that the estimated effects of discrimination are larger for the older group of workers, since older blacks probably received schooling that was significantly below the quality of that received by older whites. This implies that for older blacks, measurement error in endowments appears incorrectly as current wage discrimination.

Freeman's results are somewhat controversial.[62] Edward Lazear [1979a] has argued that employers have responded to federal government antidiscrimination activities by equalizing the starting salaries of blacks and whites but simultaneously have reduced training opportunities for young blacks. If true, this implies that owing to less training investment, years from now blacks will find themselves with relatively lower wages. Interestingly, a recent study by James P. Smith and Finis R. Welch [1989] concludes that while black/white wage differentials continued to improve in the 1980s for older blacks (age 45 and above), the differentials remained constant for those in the 35–44 year age group, but for younger cohorts ages 20–24 and 25–34, black/white wage differentials actually increased in the 1980s.[63] This evidence can be viewed as being consistent with Lazear's hypothesis.

In another study, Richard Butler and James Heckman [1977] disputed Freeman's findings, arguing that the improvement in blacks' earnings after the mid-1960s was only coincidentally related to governmental antidiscrimination activities and instead simply reflected the fact that low-income blacks withdrew from the labor force and instead participated in various income maintenance programs initiated as part of the War on Poverty in the 1960s.

More recently, in their summary of black economic progress in the

United States from the 1940s to the 1980s, Smith and Welch [1989] discuss the apparent widening of wage gaps between blacks and whites in the 1980s. One factor of particular importance is the apparent rebound in the rate of return to schooling; among men 25–34 years old, college graduates earned 24% more than high school graduates in 1980, but 42% more in 1986. To the extent that education endowments are larger for whites than blacks, this increase in returns to schooling increases wage inequality, *ceteris paribus*. Citing research by Kevin Murphy and Finis Welch [1988], Smith and Welch suggest that the increased premiums on skills in the 1980s are due in part to the changing structure of international trade. In particular, the rising levels of foreign imports, intensive in unskilled labor, reduced the demand for domestic low-skill U.S. labor in the 1980s. According to Murphy and Welch, the post-1980 slowdown in racial economic progress reflects the enhanced value of skills in the U.S. labor market. Smith and Welch summarize this argument as follows:

> Just as blacks gained (relative to whites) from the falling value of schooling during the 1970s (as the highly educated baby boom cohorts hit the labor market), they suffered more from these demand shifts that raised the income benefits from schooling.[64]

Econometric analyses of discrimination by race have not been confined to black-white studies. Geoffrey Carliner [1976] has found that substantial variations exist in the United States among Hispanics, those from Cuba encountering less wage discrimination than those from Puerto Rico. Cordelia Reimers [1983] reports that on the basis of 1975 data, endowment differences, including the ability to communicate effectively in English, account for 83% of the wage gap between Mexican-Americans and white Anglos, 55% for Puerto Ricans, and 39% for blacks. Gilles Grenier [1984] also concludes that if one accounts for language facility in English, measures of discrimination against various Hispanic groups are virtually zero. Barry Chiswick [1983a] finds that American-born workers of Chinese and Japanese descent encounter no wage discrimination (it might even be negative), while Filipinos do considerably less well and, in particular, appear to earn lower rates of return to schooling. Chiswick [1983b] reports that, other factors being held fixed, male American Jews have 16% higher earnings than non-Jewish white males and have a 20% higher rate of return to schooling. He hypothesizes that this reflects the greater productivity of Jews in creating and using human capital.

These various studies demonstrate that measures of discrimination by race vary considerably among racial and ethnic groups in the United States. They also appear to suggest that if one includes an expanded set of explanatory variables in regression equations, such as facility in the English language, the effects of discrimination are estimated to be smaller. Ultimately, this raises issues of what are the appropriate human capital, productivity-enhancing variables that one should include in regression equations such as Eq. (5.27). This issue will arise again when we examine discrimination by gender.

5.4.C Discrimination by Gender

As was noted at the beginning of Section 5.4 and summarized in Table 5.4, it is now well known that earnings inequalities by gender tend to be larger than those by race. Blinder's [1973] decomposition of mean differences in log earnings of males and females attributes 34% of this gap to productivity endowment differences and 66% to discrimination; the more recent estimates of Corcoran and Duncan [1979] suggest that productivity differences account for 44% of the male-female gap, while discrimination is reckoned at 56%. Other empirical studies arrive at similar results, although there is some evidence suggesting that the discrimination proportion has recently been declining slightly.[65] Therefore two facts account for greater market discrimination against women than against blacks: (1) the overall earnings differential is larger by gender than by race, and (2) a smaller proportion of the gender differential can be explained by productivity differences.

In contrast to race, for which the principal productivity difference has been found to be less schooling for blacks, the primary differences for women appear to be less on-the-job training and seniority with the present employer. Recent research on discrimination by gender has in part been inspired by the empirical finding that, other things being held equal, average hourly earnings of never-married females appear to be much closer to average hourly earnings of males than are average hourly earnings of married females. This finding suggests that marriage and time devoted to child-raising may have a significant impact on male-female wage differentials. Further, some researchers now argue that gender differences in payoffs to productive traits (what Blinder and Oaxaca called discrimination) may really be due to factors other than discrimination, such as differences in type of schooling (college major or professional degree) or type of job (career path chosen).

More specifically, for a substantial proportion of married women a large amount of time is spent out of the labor force in order to bear and raise children. In 1967, for example, a sample of women in the United States aged 30–44 indicated that white married women with children spent 6.4 years in the labor force after leaving school and 10.4 years out of it; for never-married women, comparable numbers are 14.5 years in the labor force and 1.5 years out.[66]

Recent research has attempted to measure the loss of earnings power by married women with intermittent labor force participation due to atrophy of skills and forgone job-oriented human capital investments. One study by Jacob Mincer and Simon Polachek [1974] segmented postschooling training investment into three components: the first ending with the birth of the first child, the second encompassing a broad labor force nonparticipation interval in which children are reared, and the third comprising the period of reentry to continuous work. Mincer and Polachek conjectured that little training would be undertaken during the first segment, and disinvestment might occur during the second segment. Within the third segment they expected new investment, perhaps in the form of refresher courses and on-the-job training.

In their empirical analysis, Mincer and Polachek found that for white married women, the coefficient on the length of current job tenure is positive, statistically significant, and higher than the coefficient on the time length of the first segment; moreover, the coefficient on the second segment (the time at home raising children) is negative and statistically significant. The negative coefficient on home time implies a net depreciation of earning power of about 1.2% per year and is higher for women with greater levels of schooling. For never-married women the home time coefficient is negative but statistically insignificant, reflecting perhaps job search activities during this time interval. These results suggest that for women, investment and earnings depend strongly on family commitments.[67]

More recent research by Mincer and Haim Ofek [1982] is based in part on retrospective and panel data and finds that the long-run effect of temporary withdrawal from the labor force is to reduce wages by approximately 1.5–2.0% per year of nonparticipation, about two thirds of the loss being due to atrophy and one third to forgone experience. The age-earnings profile for women permanently reentering the labor force is also found to be very steep, as predicted by human capital theory. Further, Mincer and Ofek use procedures similar to Eqs. (5.27), (5.30), and (5.31) to decompose the 40% male/female wage differential, taking account of endowment differences and the intermittent labor force participation of married women. Their results suggest that if one makes such adjustments, the male/female earnings gap shrinks to something like 20–32% rather than 40%.

A related line of research argues that women who expect to be absent from the labor force for either long or frequent intervals, along with their employers, may rationally elect to invest less than males in on-the-job training. Hence given identical schooling, women may rationally present themselves for employment in those occupations in which the penalty for intermittent employment is lowest. Moreover, this expectation may affect women's choice of college major and professional degree, or as Jere R. Behrman, Robert A. Pollak, and Paul Taubman [1986] have argued, it may affect parents' willingness to invest in their daughters. For example, Thomas Daymont and Paul Andrisani [1984] argue that between one third and two thirds of the gender gap can be accounted for by male/female differences in college majors and occupational preferences. Similar findings on the empirical significance of male/female differences in tastes and personalities have been reported by Randall K. Filer [1983].

A troubling aspect of this research is that it is not at all clear what is exogenous and what is endogenous. For example, one might argue that the reason women tend to choose certain careers and develop distinctive personality traits is not because of male/female differences in inherent endowments or preferences, but rather because females expect to encounter future labor market discrimination, perhaps in the form of occupational discrimination. In other words, women's current choices may well reflect adaptation to expected future discrimination by gender. According to this line of reasoning, discrimination by gender not only manifests itself in differences in regression coefficients, measured by procedures such as Eqs. (5.27)–(5.31), but is also evident in distinctive career choices and in other variables that should be treated as endogenous, not exogenous, in regression equations. Precisely what measurable variables can appropriately be viewed as ultimately exogenous in such equations is not at all clear. Note that this reasoning is not confined to gender discrimination, but is also relevant for measuring and assessing discrimination by race.

As the above brief discussion indicates, the measurement and interpretation of discrimination by race and gender remain very important but controversial issues. Some of the research on this topic calls into question the usefulness of the human capital approach to explaining variations in earnings.[68] Much has been written on this topic, including analyses of comparable worth initiatives,[69] as well as on implications for other policies to reduce discrimination. The chapter references and suggested further readings contain a great deal of useful discussion, sophisticated econometric analyses, and important information on these topics.

5.5 OTHER ECONOMETRIC ISSUES IN MODELING DETERMINANTS OF WAGES

An implicit theme in this chapter has been that the econometric procedures that are typically employed in examining determinants of wages and earnings are attractive in that their implementation is rather straightforward, involving alternative dummy variable specifications, with separate regressions for members of differing race and gender. In spite of this it is worth repeating that empirical implementation of the human capital framework is not mechanical and involves important assumptions and judgments. For example, issues of endogeneity versus exogeneity, and more generally, questions of equation specification are very critical in implementing and evaluating empirical findings.

One important assumption that is made in virtually all the studies cited in this chapter is that, for the equation to be estimated, the expected value of the random disturbance term in the sample is zero. Suppose, however, that for certain individuals the wages earned were they to participate in the labor market would not be sufficient and that these individuals therefore choose not to be in the labor force. Notice that wages of such individuals are not observed in the sample, since these people do not work. Under plausible assumptions it can be shown that when such individuals are selectively excluded from the sample, although the expected value of the disturbance term for the population as a whole may be zero, for the observed sample it is likely to be nonzero.

Further, in such cases, estimation by ordinary least squares yields biased estimates of the intercept and slope parameters.[70]

James Heckman [1979] has shown that this sample selection problem can be viewed as a specification error in which a variable is incorrectly omitted from the regression equation. Further, Heckman develops a procedure for statistically accounting for the omitted variable bias. Although detailed discussion of Heckman's paper is beyond the scope of this chapter (see Chapter 11), in essence, Heckman's procedure involves first estimating a probit equation relating the probability of an individual being in the labor force to a number of determinants, and then, on the basis of this estimated probit equation, computing the inverse Mills ratio. This last variable is then added as a regressor to the statistical earnings function equation, whose parameters can then be consistently estimated by ordinary least squares.[71]

Another theme of this chapter has been that the measurement of wage discrimination by race and by gender is controversial and raises not only the common but important issue of measurement error, but also profound issues of exogeneity and endogeneity. These issues have recently generated intense practical problems, since econometricians are now increasingly involved as expert witnesses in legal cases dealing with damages sought by individuals alleging discrimination by race or by gender.

An intriguing line of empirical research on estimating the wage and earnings effects of discrimination is called reverse regression. It has attracted attention not only because some of its advocates are distinguished statisticians and empirical researchers, but also because in virtually every case it has generated much lower estimates of discrimination than the "forward regression" procedures of Blinder and Oaxaca.

More specifically, advocates of reverse regression such as Richard Kamalich and Solomon Polachek [1982] and Delores Conway and Harry Roberts [1983] argue that, for example, instead of viewing discrimination against women in terms of lower wages given schooling, one should measure it as the increased schooling required of women in order to earn the same wages as men. Advocates of reverse regression also frequently contend that explanatory variables in forward regressions such as schooling and experience are difficult to measure accurately. For these reasons and others it is asserted that regression equations should be estimated with productivity endowment measures such as years of schooling and experience as dependent variables and wages as a right-hand variable. Since such a specification reverses the role of dependent and independent variables, it is known as reverse regression.

Whether forward or reverse regression is appropriate depends of course on what one assumes concerning endogeneity, exogeneity, measurement error, and stochastic specification. Arthur Goldberger [1984] has formalized a number of measurement error and simultaneous equations models known as multiple indicator models with multiple latent variables and has derived conditions under which the reverse regression procedure is appropriate. Goldberger also demonstrates why reverse regression typically results in lower estimates of discrimination. Significantly, he concludes with a strong preference for the forward regression technique, noting that only under a rather implausible set of circumstances will the reverse regression procedure yield estimates with desirable statistical properties. He also emphasizes that with the reverse regression procedure, one will obtain different estimates of the effects of discrimination depending on which productivity attribute (e.g., years of schooling or years of experience) is the dependent variable. While the evaluation of reverse regression procedures is still controversial, empirical research by Carole Green and Marianne Ferber [1984] lends strong empirical support to Goldberger's conjectures and conclusions.[72]

Although a substantial amount of literature has been cited in this chapter on determinants of wages, it is worth noting that the topics considered here come nowhere near to exhausting the domain of related recent labor economics research. For example, one issue that is not considered here deals with the effects of cyclical variations in the macroeconomy on wage differentials. An important finding here is that when labor markets are tight, employers are more willing to "experiment" and hire workers they might otherwise not employ. As a result, the absolute and relative earnings of the disadvantaged tend to improve in periods of tight labor markets.[73] Another body of literature—that on efficiency wages—has been referred to on several occasions[74] but has not been discussed in detail, since this chapter is already quite long.

It is clear that the opportunities for aspiring econometricians to do significant empirical research in labor economics are virtually unlimited. This is due in part to the fact that much microdata on the labor market behavior of individuals is publicly available, and so it is feasible to examine in detail numerous issues of labor force supply and the determinants of wages.[75] Along with such data the underlying body of economic theory in labor economics is now well developed, and the set of available econometric tools and techniques is impressive. Good luck!

5.6 HANDS ON WITH ESTIMATING DETERMINANTS OF WAGES AND EARNINGS

We now come to the hands-on portion of this chapter. The goals of the following exercises are to help you gain firsthand experience in constructing and interpreting coefficients on dummy variables and on interaction terms, to enable you to discover by yourself what factors affect individuals' wages and earnings, to estimate rates of return to schooling, to calculate union-nonunion wage differentials, and to compute measures of discrimination by race and by gender.

The exercises of this chapter have been carefully designed to introduce you to important current issues in measuring determinants of wages, but they only begin to scratch the surface of potential empirical research in this area. Your instructor may therefore use the data sets of this chapter for other innovative exercises (for example, occupational data and employment by industry data are not used in the exercises here, even though they are available in the data sets) or may provide you with different data sets.

Typically, it is very useful to examine data sets before implementing econometric estimation. You have a good opportunity to do this in Exercise 1, "A Review of Essential Facts: Inspecting the Data." In Exercises 2 and 3 you can confirm and build on your knowledge of econometric theory by comparing empirically alternative dummy variable specifications, including those involving dummy interaction terms. In Exercise 4 you have the opportunity to assess whether your own estimates of experience-earnings profiles are in general agreement with those reported in the literature. Whether union members earn premium wages, and whether this premium is declining with time, is the focus of Exercise 5. Then in Exercises 6 and 7 you are invited to employ econometric methods in measuring and interpreting wage discrimination by race and by gender. You can also examine whether such discrimination appears to have changed between 1978 and 1985. Finally, in Exercise 8 you test whether disturbances in the statistical earnings function are homoskedastic.

●●●●●●●●●●●

In other chapters of this book, classic data sets are provided on diskette, in part so that readers can engage in replicating and extending well-known empirical results. However, the data sets used by researchers in the studies cited in this chapter are typically very large, often involving over 10,000 observations, and it is simply not feasible to provide such a large data base on your data diskette.

Instead, two smaller data sets have been provided in the subdirectory called CHAP5.DAT of your data diskette. The first data file is called CPS78; the second is CPS85. Each is a random sample taken from the May Current Population Survey by the U.S. Census Bureau, the first from May 1978 and the second from May 1985. The data file CPS78 contains observations on 20 variables for 550 individuals, while there are 534 observations on 19 variables in CPS85.

The first variable is years of schooling (ED), and the next seven entries are 0–1 dummy variables taking on the value 1 if the individual resides in the South (SOUTH), is nonwhite and non-Hispanic (NONWH), is Hispanic (HISP), is female (FE), is married with spouse present or in the military (MARR), and is female and married with spouse present or in the military (MARRFE). The next two variables measure potential years of experience (named EX), computed as age minus years schooling minus 6, and this potential experience measure squared (EXSQ). The dummy variable UNION equals 1 if the individual works on a union job. The natural logarithm of the average hourly earnings in dollars is denoted as LNWAGE, and the age of the individual in years is AGE. The number of dependent children under age 18 in the household is denoted as NDEP; this variable is available only for the 1978 random sample (CPS78), not for 1985 (CPS85).

Several other variables are available on the data diskette but are not used in the exercises of this chapter. Specifically, the next two variables in both data files are industry dummies that take on the value 1 if the individual works in manufacturing or mining (MANUF) or in construction (CONSTR); if the individual works in some other industry, such as services, that individual's values for the MANUF and CONSTR variables are both zero. The last five variables are occupational dummies that are equal to 1 if the individual's occupation is managerial or administrative (MANAG), sales worker (SALES), clerical worker (CLER), service worker (SERV), or professional or technical worker (PROF); if an individual works in some other occupation, such as tradesperson or assembly line worker, the values of all these dummy variables are zero.

EXERCISES

EXERCISE 1: A Review of Essential Facts: Inspecting the Data

The purpose of this exercise is to help you become familiar with features of the data in CPS78 and CPS85. In examining the data you will compute and compare arithmetic means, geometric means, and standard deviations for the entire sample and for the data sorted into various subgroups. An optional section offers you the opportunity to compare simply the normal and log-normal statistical distributions to the distribution of wage rates.

(a) Using the data in CPS78, compute the arithmetic mean and standard deviation of LNWAGE. The geometric mean is calculated by first computing the arithmetic mean of LNWAGE, and then exponentiating it. Compute this geometric mean wage rate, in dollars. Assuming that a work year consists of 2000 hours, what is the implied geometric mean of annual wages? Exponentiate LNWAGE, and then compute its mean. Compare this arithmetic with the geometric mean wage rate. What are the arithmetic means and standard deviations of years of schooling (ED) and years potential experience (EX)?

(b) The dummy variable NONWH in CPS78 equals 1 if the individual is nonwhite and non-Hispanic (the vast proportion of NONWH individuals are black). What is the sample mean of NONWH? Since there are 550 observations in CPS78, how many individuals in your sample are nonwhite and non-Hispanic? Another dummy variable is HISP, and it equals 1 if the individual is nonwhite and is of Hispanic origin. What is its sample mean, and how many individuals in your sample are Hispanic? Finally, the dummy variable FE equals 1 if the individual is female. What proportion of the sample is female? How many individuals are female?

(c) A common procedure used to inspect a data set is to sort it into subgroups by certain variables and then compute and compare means and standard deviations for the various subgroups. Sort your data in CPS78 by gender. What are the mean and standard deviation of years of schooling (ED) for males and for females? The geometric mean wage rates? Next sort your data by race into whites, nonwhites and non-Hispanics (NONWH), and Hispanics (HISP). For each of these groups, compare the arithmetic mean and standard deviation of ED and the geometric mean and standard deviations of the wage rate. Whose LNWAGE has the largest dispersion, as measured by the standard deviation?

(d) Now repeat parts (a) through (c), using the 1985 data in CPS85. (*Note:* There are 534 observations in CPS85 and 550 in CPS78.) Are there substantial changes in the sample proportions of individuals by gender or race in 1985 as compared to 1978? Using a consumer price index deflator that equals 1.000 in 1978 and 1.649 in 1985, compute and compare the geometric mean of real wage rates in 1978 and 1985, for (i) the entire sample, (ii) by gender, and (iii) by race. Which subgroups appear to have attained higher real wages? Have any subgroups suffered real wage losses? Finally, compare years of schooling by gender and by race for 1978 and 1985. Are changes in years of schooling and mean geometric wages broadly consistent with the human capital model for the various subgroups? Why or why not?

(e) *(Optional)* It has often been observed that wages tend to be more log normally than normally distributed. You now conduct a simple, preliminary empirical comparison of these two distributions. Choose either the 1978 or 1985 data set, and compute the arithmetic mean and standard deviation of LNWAGE; call these w and σ, respectively, and denote the LNWAGE of the ith individual as w_i. Assuming that LNWAGE is normally distributed, assign each individual to one of six groups, consisting of (i) $w_i < w - 2\sigma$; (ii) $w - 2\sigma \leqslant w_i < w - \sigma$; (iii) $w - \sigma \leqslant w_i < w$; (iv) $w \leqslant w_i \leqslant w + \sigma$; (v) $w + \sigma < w_i \leqslant w + 2\sigma$; and (vi) $w_i > w + 2\sigma$. What is the number of observations in each of the six groups? What is the proportion of individuals in each group? How well do these proportions compare to predictions based on the normal distribution? Employ a chi-square goodness-of-fit test procedure (or the Kolmogorov-Smirnov test statistic) to test for normality.[76]

Now exponentiate LNWAGE for each observation, call this WAGE, and compute the *arithmetic* mean and standard deviation of WAGE. Using procedures analogous to those above, but assuming that WAGE rather than LNWAGE is normally distributed, partition your sample into six corresponding groups. What are the number and proportion of individuals in each group? How well does this correspond to predictions based on the normal distribution? Again, employ a chi-square goodness-of-fit test procedure (or the Kolmogorov-Smirnov test statistic) to test for normality.

Which do you think more closely follows the normal distribution, LNWAGE or WAGE? Why?

EXERCISE 2: Confirming Relationships among Alternative Dummy Variable Specifications: Earnings and Returns to Schooling

The purpose of this exercise is to have you confirm empirically the relationships that theoretically should occur among alternative simple dummy variable specifications in the linear regression model. This exercise involves examining least squares coefficients in a stylized human capital model where LNWAGE is affected by years of schooling (ED) with a slope coefficient that is identical for everyone but where the intercept terms differ by union status (UNION = 1 if the individual works on a union job).

Choose either the 1978 (CPS78) or the 1985 (CPS85) data set. Employ this data set for each section of this exercise.

(a) Using least squares, estimate parameters in a simple model where LNWAGE is regressed on a constant term and years of schooling (ED). What is the value of the estimated slope coefficient? When can this coefficient be interpreted as the rate of return to schooling? Construct and interpret a 95% confidence interval for this coefficient. What is the R^2 in this model? Interpret this R^2, and compare it (as well as the estimated rate of return to schooling) to that reported by Mincer in Eq. (5.18), based on 1959 data.

(b) The specification in part (a) assumes that the intercept and slope coefficients are identical for all individuals. Now assume instead that the effect of schooling on wages differs between union and nonunion members by a constant factor of proportionality; that is, for nonunion members WAGE $= \alpha_N \, e^{\beta \text{ED}} \, e^{\epsilon}$, whereas for union members, WAGE $= \alpha_U \, e^{\beta \text{ED}} \, e^{\epsilon}$, where WAGE is the wage rate, α_N and α_U are differing factors of proportionality, β is the common rate of return to schooling, and ϵ is a random disturbance term. Show that this implies that when LNWAGE rather than WAGE is the dependent variable, union and nonunion workers have different intercept terms α_N and α_U but a common slope coefficient β. Now estimate by least squates parameters in a regression model

$$\text{LNWAGE} = \alpha + \alpha' \cdot \text{UNION} + \beta \cdot \text{ED} + \epsilon$$

where UNION is the dummy variable equal to 1 if the individual works at a union job and ϵ is a random disturbance term. Interpret your estimates of α and α', relating α and α' to α_N and α_U above. Formulate and test the null hypothesis that intercept terms for union and nonunion individuals are identical, using a 5% level of significance. What happens to the estimated rate of return to schooling when union and nonunion individuals have different intercepts? Can you interpret this?

(c) An alternative procedure for formulating the regression relationship in part (b) is as follows. First, create a new nonunion dummy variable called NONU, where NONU ≡ 1.0 − UNION. (Note that for each individual, NONU + UNION = 1.0. Why is this important?) Then estimate parameters in an equation without a constant term:

$$\text{LNWAGE} = \alpha_0 \cdot \text{NONU} + \alpha_1 \cdot \text{UNION} + \beta \cdot \text{ED} + \epsilon$$

Interpret α_0 and α_1, and relate them to α_N and α_U in part (b). According to econometric theory, what should the relationship be among estimates of α_0 and α_1 and of α and α' (see part (b))? Why? Are your estimates numerically consistent with this relationship? Why or why not? Formulate and test the null hypothesis that intercept terms for union and nonunion workers are identical. Your test result should be precisely equivalent to that in part (b). Is this the case? Compare the estimated rate of return to schooling and R^2 here with that obtained in part (b). Why does this occur?

(d) A seemingly plausible specification is the equation

$$\text{LNWAGE} = \alpha^* + \alpha_0^* \cdot \text{NONU} + \alpha_1^* \cdot \text{UNION} + \beta \cdot \text{ED} + \epsilon$$

in which LNWAGE is related to a common intercept term α^*, to separate terms α_0^* and α_1^* for nonunion and union members, and to ED by a common coefficient β. What is wrong with this specification? Why is least squares unable to estimate parameters of this model uniquely? What happens when you try to estimate this model using your software? Interpret this phenomenon.

(e) One other logical possibility is to estimate parameters in an equation in which the NONU dummy variable in part (b) replaces the UNION dummy variable. Such an equation would be of the form

$$\text{LNWAGE} = \alpha^0 + \alpha^1 \cdot \text{NONU} + \beta \cdot \text{ED} + \epsilon$$

Interpret the regression estimates of α^0, α^1, and β in this equation. What do you expect to be the relationship among estimates of α^0, α^1, and β here with those of α, α', and β in part (b)? Why? Verify your conjectures empirically by estimating the above equation.

EXERCISE 3: Dummy Interaction Variables: The Earnings of Single and Married Males and Females

The purpose of this exercise is to help you construct and interpret dummy variables involving interaction terms. The empirical implementation focuses on the earnings of single and married males and females. Recall from the chapter text (Section 5.4.C) that, according to the human capital framework, to the extent that married females differ from single females and from married or single males in their frequency of leaving the labor force temporarily to rear children, other things being equal, the statistical earnings functions of married females might differ from those of married or single males or from single females. In this exercise you take a preliminary look at this empirical issue, using dummy interaction variables.

Choose either the 1978 (CPS78) or the 1985 (CPS85) data set. Employ this data set for each section of this exercise.

(a) Begin by estimating a model allowing for no differences by gender or marital status. In particular, using least squares procedures, estimate parameters in the simple, stylized human capital model (5.10):

$$\text{LNWAGE} = \alpha + \beta_1 \cdot \text{ED} + \beta_2 \cdot \text{EX} + \beta_3 \cdot \text{EXSQ} + \epsilon$$

where EX and EXSQ are potential experience (age minus years schooling minus 6) and potential experience squared. Are your estimates plausible? Why?

(b) Now allow for intercepts to vary by gender. The dummy variable FE is 1 if the individual is female and 0 if the individual is male. Using least squares, estimate parameters in the expanded equation

$$\text{LNWAGE} = \alpha + \alpha_F \cdot \text{FE} + \beta_1 \cdot \text{ED} + \beta_2 \cdot \text{EX} + \beta_3 \cdot \text{EXSQ} + \epsilon$$

Interpret these parameter estimates. Using a reasonable level of significance, formulate and test the null hypothesis that there are no differences in intercept terms for males and females.

(c) Next examine whether marital status affects the statistical earnings function in a linear manner. The dummy variable MARR equals 1 if the individual is married with spouse present or in the military and otherwise is 0. Using least squares, estimate parameters in the equation

$$\begin{aligned}\text{LNWAGE} = {} & \alpha + \alpha_F \cdot \text{FE} + \alpha_M \cdot \text{MARR} \\ & + \beta_1 \cdot \text{ED} + \beta_2 \cdot \text{EX} + \beta_3 \cdot \text{EXSQ} + \epsilon\end{aligned}$$

Interpret estimates of α, α_F, and α_M. Show that the effect of marital status on LNWAGE in this specification, given ED, EX, and EXSQ, is the same for males and females. Within this specification, formulate and then test the null hypothesis that marital status has no effect on LNWAGE.

(d) As was noted above, human capital theorists have argued that the effect of marital status on earnings might be expected to depend on gender; in particular, being married may have a larger negative effect on earnings for females than for males, *ceteris paribus*. The restrictive specification in part (c) does not allow you to test this hypothesis. Why? Construct an interaction dummy variable for each of the i individuals in your sample that takes on the value of unity if the individual is married with spouse present or in the military *and* is female. For each of the i individuals this variable is constructed as $\text{INFMAR}_i \equiv \text{FE}_i^* \text{MARR}_i$. Generate the dummy interaction variable INFMAR_i. INFMAR should be identical to the dummy variable in your data set entitled MARRFE. To verify this, construct a temporary variable called CHECK, defined as $\text{CHECK}_i \equiv \text{INFMAR}_i - \text{MARRFE}_i$, for $i = 1, \ldots, n$. If you have properly constructed INFMAR_i, CHECK should equal 0 for all observations. Print out CHECK for the entire sample, and verify that you have properly constructed this dummy interaction variable. Comment on why INFMAR_i is an interaction variable rather than a simple additive dummy variable.

(e) Finally, using least squares procedures, estimate parameters in the equation with both additive and interaction dummy variables:

$$\text{LNWAGE} = \alpha + \alpha_F \cdot \text{FE} + \alpha_M \cdot \text{MARR} + \alpha_{F,M} \cdot \text{INFMAR} + \beta_1 \cdot \text{ED} + \beta_2 \cdot \text{EX} + \beta_3 \cdot \text{EXSQ} + \epsilon$$

Interpret the parameter estimates of α, α_F, α_M, and $\alpha_{F,M}$. Are they consistent with the human capital argument noted above? Why or why not? Formulate and test the null hypothesis that the effect of marital status does not depend on gender. How do you interpret this finding?

EXERCISE 4: Examining Experience-Earnings Profiles

The purpose of this exercise is to engage you in employing econometric tools to estimate and interpret the shape of the experience-earnings profile and to assess whether the evidence is consistent with implications of human capital theory.

Choose either the 1978 (CPS78) or the 1985 (CPS85) data set. Employ this data set for each section of this exercise.

(a) Begin by estimating the "base model" of the experience-earnings function, Eq. (5.10) with several dummy variables added:

$$\text{LNWAGE} = \alpha + \alpha_F \cdot \text{FE} + \alpha_U \cdot \text{UNION} + \alpha_N \cdot \text{NONWH} + \alpha_H \cdot \text{HISP} + \beta_1 \cdot \text{ED} + \beta_2 \cdot \text{EX} + \beta_3 \cdot \text{EXSQ} + \epsilon$$

where the variables are defined in the paragraph just before Exercise 1. Note that EX is potential experience, defined as AGE minus ED minus 6. What are the sign predictions for estimates of β_2 and β_3 based on the human capital framework? Are your parameter estimates consistent with this prediction? Why or why not? At what level of EX is LNWAGE maximized? (*Hint:* Refer back to Eq. (5.11) and the associated discussion.) Compute the years experience (and the implied ages) at which LNWAGE is maximized for individuals with 8, 12, and 16 years of schooling.

(b) With exp (LNWAGE) on the vertical axis and AGE on the horizontal axis, use the parameter estimates from part (a) and graph the estimated age-earnings profile, evaluated at the sample means of FE, UNION, NONWH, HISP, and ED (these were computed in Exercise 1). It may be tempting to interpret this age-earnings profile as suggesting that as an individual ages, his or her earnings decline. Why is this interpretion incorrect? (*One hint:* Is the profile that you are graphing one of age-earnings or of age-wage rate? What is the difference, and why might the difference become larger as one ages?)

(c) As was noted in Section 5.2.B, if individuals with more schooling receive more on-the-job training, then the posteducation age-earnings profiles of the more educated should be steeper than those of the less educated. To allow for this, following Eq. (5.12), generate a new variable EDEX, which for the ith individual is defined as $\text{EDEX}_i \equiv \text{ED}_i \cdot \text{EX}_i$. Then estimate by least squares the parameters of an equation with EDEX added as a regressor,

$$\begin{aligned}\text{LNWAGE} = \alpha &+ \alpha_F \cdot \text{FE} + \alpha_U \cdot \text{UNION} + \alpha_N \cdot \text{NONWH} \\ &+ \alpha_H \cdot \text{HISP} + \beta_1 \cdot \text{ED} + \beta_2 \cdot \text{EX} + \beta_3 \cdot \text{EXSQ} \\ &+ \beta_4 \cdot \text{EDEX} + \epsilon\end{aligned}$$

What sign do you expect for β_4? Why? How precise is your estimate of β_4? Is it consistent with the text discussion by Eq. (5.11)? Might your ability to obtain a precise estimate of β_4 be affected by the relatively small sample size available here? Note that in this equation the effect of experience on LNWAGE depends on education, for $\partial\text{LNWAGE}_i/\partial\text{EX}_i = \beta_2 + 2 \cdot \beta_3 \cdot \text{EX}_i + \beta_4 \cdot \text{ED}_i$, since $\text{EDEX}_i \equiv \text{ED}_i \cdot \text{EX}_i$. Verify that the value of EX for which LNWAGE is maximized, denoted EX_i^*, can be computed analytically as $\text{EX}_i^* = -(\beta_2 + \beta_4 \cdot \text{ED}_i)/(2*\beta_3)$. Using your parameter estimates, calculate EX_i^* for individuals with 8, 12, and 16 years of schooling; then calculate the ages at which LNWAGE is maximized for individuals with 8, 12, and 16 years of schooling. Compare these peaks in the age-earnings profiles with those obtained in part (a).

(d) Using the parameter estimates obtained in part (c) and with exp (LNWAGE) on the vertical axis and AGE on the horizontal axis, graph three age-earnings profiles, one each for individuals with 8, 12, and 16 years of schooling, where each is evaluated at the overall sample means of FE, UNION, NONWH, and HISP. Is the posteducation age-earnings profile steeper for the more highly educated? Interpret these results.

(e) Finally, restrict your sample to females, and repeat parts (c) and (d) separately for single and married females (but delete the FE dummy variable of part (c)). What do you expect concerning the shapes of the age-earnings profiles for single versus married females? Why? Is your empirical evidence consistent with this expectation? Why or why not?

EXERCISE 5: Do Union Workers Earn Premium Wages?

The purpose of this exercise is to involve you in comparing dummy variable and separate regression procedures in measuring the extent to which union workers earn premium wages, other workers' characteristics being held fixed. In addition, you also implement a Chow test for parameter equality. Finally, you examine the interesting issue of whether union-nonunion wage differentials have fallen from 1978 to 1985.

(a) Using data from the CPS78 data file for all 550 observations, calculate and retrieve for later use the sample means of LNWAGE, FE, UNION, NONWH, HISP, ED, EX, and EXSQ. Then estimate by OLS parameters in the equation

$$\text{LNWAGE} = \alpha + \alpha_F \cdot \text{FE} + \alpha_U \cdot \text{UNION} + \alpha_N \cdot \text{NONWH} + \alpha_H \cdot \text{HISP} + \beta_1 \cdot \text{ED} + \beta_2 \cdot \text{EX} + \beta_3 \cdot \text{EXSQ} + \epsilon$$

What are the estimated value and statistical significance of the UNION dummy variable coefficient? Interpret the antilog of this estimated coefficient. Is this consistent with evidence reported in Section 5.3.D? Critique the use of this equation for assessing whether union workers earn premium wages.

(b) Next sort your CPS78 data set according to whether the individual works in a union job (UNION = 1). Calculate sample means for LNWAGE, FE, NONWH, HISP, ED, EX, and EXSQ separately for union and nonunion workers. Then for each of these variables, calculate differences in the sample means between the union and nonunion individuals. What is the mean difference in LNWAGE between union and nonunion workers? On average, do union workers have less or more schooling than nonunion workers? What are the potential experience differences between union and nonunion individuals? Are there substantial differences by race or by gender between union and nonunion workers?

(c) Using the sorted union-nonunion data from part (b), estimate parameters in separate union and nonunion equations, each of the form

$$\text{LNWAGE} = \alpha + \alpha_F \cdot \text{FE} + \alpha_N \cdot \text{NONWH} + \alpha_H \cdot \text{HISP} + \beta_1 \cdot \text{ED} + \beta_2 \cdot \text{EX} + \beta_3 \cdot \text{EXSQ} + \epsilon$$

Compare magnitudes of the estimated coefficients in the union and nonunion equations. In particular, are union-nonunion wage differentials larger for females than males, other characteristics being held fixed? Does the union-nonunion wage differential vary by race?

As was noted in Section 5.3.D, it has been hypothesized that the effects of education on log earnings are smaller in the union sector, owing in part to effects of the seniority system. Are your results consistent with this hypothesis? Why or why not? Finally, compare your estimated age-earnings profile for union and nonunion workers, evaluating FE, NONWH, HISP, and ED at their overall sample means from part (a). Is the profile flatter for union workers, consistent with evidence reported by Lewis [1986]?

(d) Now, using a reasonable level of significance, do a Chow test of the null hypothesis that all intercept and slope coefficients are simultaneously equal in the union and nonunion estimated equations. To do this, first reestimate the equation in part (a) with the UNION variable omitted (why is this the "constrained" regression?). Compute the sum of squared residuals from this constrained regression. Then compute the sum of squared residuals from the two separate regressions in part (c) (the "unconstrained" regressions). Using the Chow test procedure, test the null hypothesis of complete parameter equality in the union and nonunion equations. (Be particularly careful in calculating degrees of freedom for this test.) Interpret your results.

(e) In addition to the dummy variable procedure used in part (a), in Section 5.3.D, two additional procedures for estimating union-nonunion wage differentials were outlined. Following Bloch and Kuskin [1978], you now implement the procedure summarized in Eq. (5.25). In particular, first subtract the sample mean of LNWAGE for nonunion workers from the sample mean of LNWAGE for union workers. Then for each of the independent variables employed in part (c), subtract the sample mean for nonunion from that for union workers. Next, weight each of these sample mean differences in the regressors by the estimated union parameters, as in Eq. (5.25), and subtract the sum of these weighted differences in regressors from the LNWAGE difference. Exponentiate this value. Why can this exponentiated difference be interpreted as an estimate of the union-nonunion wage differential, workers' characteristics being held fixed? How large is it? What proportion of the observed mean difference in LNWAGE between union and nonunion workers is "explained" by differences in mean values of worker characteristics FE, HISP, NONWH, ED, EX, and EXSQ? Which of these worker characteristics mean differences are particularly important in explaining union-nonunion wage differentials? Are your results similar to those of Bloch and Kuskin, discussed in Section 5.3.D? Why or why not?

(f) Now do the same calculations as in part (e), but instead of weighting union-nonunion sample mean differences in the regressors by the estimated union parameters, employ Eq. (5.26) and weight using the estimated nonunion parameters. What is the value of the estimated union-nonunion wage differential now? Compare and interpret the three alternative estimates of the union-nonunion wage differential, from part (a), part (e), and here. Which, if any, do you prefer, and why?

(g) Much ink has been spilt concerning the willingness of U.S. unions to accept wage reductions during the 1980s. A priori, it is not clear whether such actions resulted in reduced union-nonunion wage differentials. To examine this issue empirically, redo parts (a)–(f), using the May 1985 data from the data file CPS85. (*Note:* CPS85 contains 534 observations, while CPS78 has 550.) Have the wage premiums earned by union workers fallen over the 1978–1985 time period? Interpret your findings. (*Optional:* Is this difference in wage premiums statistically significant? *Hint:* See the discussion in the paragraph before Eq. (5.27)).

EXERCISE 6: Measuring and Interpreting Wage Discrimination by Race

The purpose of this exercise is to have you implement empirically and then interpret three alternative procedures for measuring wage discrimination by race. The econometric methodology employed is based on that developed by Blinder [1973] and Oaxaca [1973b], as discussed in Sections 5.4.A and 5.4.B. You also conduct a Chow test for parameter equality.

Choose either the 1978 or the 1985 data set in CPS78 and CPS85, respectively, and use this data set for all portions of this exercise.

(a) Begin by estimating the effects of wage discrimination by race using simple dummy variable procedures. Specifically, using OLS, estimate parameters in the equation

$$\begin{aligned} \text{LNWAGE} = {} & \alpha + \alpha_F \cdot \text{FE} + \alpha_U \cdot \text{UNION} + \alpha_N \cdot \text{NONWH} \\ & + \alpha_H \cdot \text{HISP} + \beta_1 \cdot \text{ED} + \beta_2 \cdot \text{EX} + \beta_3 \cdot \text{EXSQ} + \epsilon \end{aligned}$$

Interpret the estimated coefficients α_N and α_H. Test the null hypothesis that, gender, union status, education, and experience being held fixed, racial status has no effect on log wages. Then test and interpret the null hypothesis that the coefficients on NONWH and HISP are equal to each other but are not necessarily equal to zero.

(b) Next sort your data set into three subsamples, according to whether the individual is nonwhite and not Hispanic (NONWH = 1), Hispanic (HISP = 1), or other (primarily whites, hereafter denoted OTHER). How many observations are there in each of the three subsamples? Calculate sample means for the variables LNWAGE, FE, UNION, ED, EX, and EXSQ separately for each of the three subsamples. Then for each of these variables, calculate differences in the sample means between the OTHER and NONWH samples and between OTHER and HISP. What is the mean difference in LNWAGE in the OTHER and NONWH samples? What is the mean difference in LNWAGE between OTHER and HISP? On average, do NONWH and HISP workers have less or more schooling than OTHER workers? What are the potential experience differences among these three subsamples? Are there substantial gender (FE) differences by race?

(c) Using the sorted data by race from part (b), estimate parameters in separate NONWH, HISP, and OTHER equations, each of the form

$$\begin{aligned} \text{LNWAGE} = {} & \alpha + \alpha_F \cdot \text{FE} + \alpha_U \cdot \text{UNION} \\ & + \beta_1 \cdot \text{ED} + \beta_2 \cdot \text{EX} + \beta_3 \cdot \text{EXSQ} + \epsilon \end{aligned}$$

Now compare magnitudes of the estimated coefficients in the three equations, calculating the standard errors of differences in estimated coefficients between subsamples using the formula discussed just before Eq. (5.27). In particular, is the effect of schooling (ED) on LNWAGE different between OTHER and NONWH? Between OTHER and HISP? Interpret these results. Does the gender-related (FE) wage differential vary significantly by race? In what ways does the age-earnings profile differ by race? How do you interpret this?

(d) Using a reasonable level of significance, perform a Chow test of the null hypothesis that all intercept and slope coefficients are simultaneously equal in the NONWH, HISP, and OTHER equations. To do this, first reestimate the equation in part (a), omitting the NONWH and HISP variables, and retrieve the sum of squared residuals from this equation. Using the Chow test procedure (be careful in computing degrees of freedom), compare this sum of squared residuals with the sum from the three separate regressions in part (c). Interpret your results. Outline what additional information would be required in order to test the null hypothesis that parameters from the HISP sample are equal to those from the OTHER sample. Calculate and interpret results from such a test.

(e) Now implement the Blinder-Oaxaca procedures to measure wage discrimination by race. In particular, using sample mean data from part (b) and Eq. (5.30), where OTHER is the advantaged group and NONWH is the disadvantaged group, decompose the difference in mean LNWAGE between the OTHER and NONWH groups into that portion due to differences in endowments (weight the differences in sample means of the regressors by the estimated coefficients from the OTHER equation) and the residual part due to discrimination by race. (Note that according to Eq. (5.30), the discrimination portion can be calculated indirectly as the above residual or directly as the difference in the estimated coefficients Δb weighted by mean values of the NONWH regressors.) What proportion of mean differences in LNWAGE between OTHER and NONWH is due to differences in endowments? Which endowment differences appear to be particularly important? What proportion of the mean differences in LNWAGE can be attributed to effects of discrimination by race? How do these proportions compare with empirical results reported in Section 5.4.B? With the dummy variable procedure in part (a) of this exercise?

(f) Now measure wage discrimination for Hispanics. Specifically, repeat procedures in part (e), but replace NONWH with HISP, thereby contrasting the HISP and OTHER groups. Compare your results with those obtained in part (e) in terms of relative endowments and the proportions of differences in LNWAGE attributable to differences in endowments and to discrimination. What can you say concerning the relative wage discrimination experienced by members of NONWH as compared to HISP? How do these proportions compare with empirical results reported in Section 5.4.B? With the dummy variable procedure in part (a) of this exercise?

(g) The measures of discrimination by race computed in parts (e) and (f) of this exercise involve weighting differences in endowments by the estimated parameters of the advantaged (OTHER) group, as in Eq. (5.30). An alternative procedure, discussed in Section 5.4.A and summarized in Eq. (5.31), involves weighting differences in mean endowments by estimated parameters of the disadvantaged group. Using the estimated parameters from the NONWH equation from part (c) and OTHER-NONWH mean differences in endowments, substitute into Eq. (5.31) and compute this alternative measure of wage discrimination. What proportion of the mean difference in LNWAGE between OTHER and NONWH is now estimated as being due to differences in mean endowments? What portion represents wage discrimination by race? Compare these estimates to results obtained in part (e). Finally, use parameters from the estimated HISP equation, mean differences between OTHER and HISP in LNWAGE and endowments, and Eq. (5.31) to compute an alternative estimate of the effects of wage discrimination by race experienced by HISP individuals. Compare these new results to those obtained in part (f).

(h) On the basis of these alternative measures of wage discrimination by race, what do you conclude concerning the relative importance of racial discrimination in the United States? Defend your conclusions.

EXERCISE 7: Measuring and Interpreting Wage Discrimination by Gender

The purpose of this exercise is to have you compute and interpret the effects of wage discrimination by gender, using three alternative procedures: a traditional dummy variable approach and the two weighted differences in mean endowments procedures introduced by Blinder and by Oaxaca, discussed in Section 5.4.A. You will also do a Chow test and then examine whether wage discrimination by gender has declined in the United States over the 1978–1985 time period.

(a) Using data in the data file CPS78, begin by estimating the effects of wage discrimination by race using simple dummy variable procedures. Specifically, using OLS, estimate parameters in the equation

$$\text{LNWAGE} = \alpha + \alpha_F \cdot \text{FE} + \alpha_U \cdot \text{UNION} + \alpha_N \cdot \text{NONWH} + \alpha_H \cdot \text{HISP} + \beta_1 \cdot \text{ED} + \beta_2 \cdot \text{EX} + \beta_3 \cdot \text{EXSQ} + \epsilon$$

Interpret the estimated coefficient α_F and its value exponentiated. Test the null hypothesis that, holding race, union status, education, and experience fixed, gender has no effect on log wages.

(b) Next sort your CPS78 data set into two subsamples, according to whether the individual is female (FE = 1) or male (FE = 0). How many observations are there in each of the two subsamples? Calculate sample means for the variables LNWAGE, NONWH, HISP, UNION, ED, EX, and EXSQ separately for males and for females. Then for each of these variables, calculate differences in the sample means between the FE = 1 and FE = 0 samples. What is the mean difference in LNWAGE in the male and female samples? On average, do male workers have less or more schooling than females? What are the potential experience differences between males and females? For which gender is the potential experience variable EX more likely to measure on-the-job training? Why? Are there substantial differences in the proportions of HISP, NONWH, and all other individuals by gender? Does the proportion of unionized workers vary considerably between males and females?

(c) Using the data sorted by gender from part (b), estimate parameters in separate male and female equations, each of the form

$$\text{LNWAGE} = \alpha + \alpha_N \cdot \text{NONWH} + \alpha_H \cdot \text{HISP} + \alpha_U \cdot \text{UNION} + \beta_1 \cdot \text{ED} + \beta_2 \cdot \text{EX} + \beta_3 \cdot \text{EXSQ} + \epsilon$$

Now compare magnitudes of the estimated coefficients in the male and female equations, calculating the standard errors of differences in estimated coefficients between subsamples using the formula discussed just before Eq. (5.27). In particular, does the effect of schooling (ED) on LNWAGE differ by gender? What about the effect of race on LNWAGE—does it differ by gender? Interpret these results. In what ways does the age-earnings profile differ between males and females? How do you interpret this?

(d) Using a reasonable level of significance, do a Chow test of the null hypothesis that all intercept and slope coefficients are simultaneously equal in the male and female equations. To do this, first reestimate the equation in part (a), omitting the FE dummy variable. Retrieve the sum of squared residuals from this regression. Then sum the sum of squared residuals in the two gender-specific regressions of part (c). Using the Chow test procedure based on the comparison of sum of squared residuals (be careful in computing degrees of freedom), calculate the Chow test statistic and compare it to the critical value. Interpret your results.

(e) Next implement the Blinder-Oaxaca procedures to obtain the first of two alternative measures that bracket the estimated effects of wage discrimination by gender. Specifically, using sample mean data from part (b) and Eq. (5.30), where males are the advantaged group and females are the disadvantaged group, decompose the difference in mean LNWAGE by gender into that portion due to differences in endowments (weight the differences in sample means of the regressors by the estimated coefficients from the male equation) and the residual part due to discrimination by gender. (Note that according to Eq. (5.30), the discrimination portion can be calculated indirectly as the above residual or directly as the difference in the estimated coefficients Δb weighted by mean values of the regressors in the female equation.) What proportion of mean differences in LNWAGE by gender is due to differences in endowments? Which endowment differences appear to be particularly important? What proportion of the mean differences in LNWAGE can be attributed to effects of discrimination by gender? How do these proportions compare with empirical results reported in Section 5.4.C? With the dummy variable procedure in part (a) of this exercise?

(f) The alternative Blinder-Oaxaca measure of wage discrimination by gender weights mean differences in endowments by the estimated female (rather than male) coefficients. Using the estimated parameters from the female equation from part (c) and male/female mean differences in regressors, substitute into Eq. (5.31) and compute this alternative measure of wage discrimination. What proportion of the mean difference in LNWAGE by gender is now estimated as being due to differences in mean endowments? What portion represents wage discrimination by gender? Compare these estimates to results obtained in part (e). What range brackets the estimated proportion of differences in LNWAGE by gender due to discrimination?

(g) Now examine empirically whether discrimination by gender has been declining in the United States over the 1978–1985 time period. In particular, repeat steps (a)–(f) using data from the CPS85 data file, rather than from CPS78. What has happened to the size of the LNWAGE differential from 1978 to 1985? Have differences in mean endowments by gender declined from 1978 to 1985? Interpret your results. Has the proportion of gender differences in LNWAGE due to discrimination changed from 1978 to 1985? Interpret these results, and comment on the reliability of your estimates. Are there any surprises here? Why or why not?

(h) (*Optional*) In Section 5.4.C it was noted that the statistical earnings functions of single and married women might differ, since married women with commitments to child-rearing might be expected to have extended periods of intermittent labor force participation. With data from CPS78 and CPS85, use the Blinder-Oaxaca procedures to estimate the wage discrimination experienced by married and single females, each relative to males. Interpret your findings. What additional data would help you obtain a more definitive set of findings on this empirical issue?

EXERCISE 8: Heteroskedasticity in the Statistical Earnings Function

The purpose of this exercise is to have you assess whether disturbances in an estimated statistical earnings function are homoskedastic, to compare traditional and robust estimates of standard errors of coefficients when heteroskedasticity may be present, and to examine the sensitivity of estimated coefficients to alternative stochastic specifications involving heteroskedasticity.

Choose either the 1978 or the 1985 data set in CPS78 and CPS85, respectively, and use that data set for all portions of this exercise.

(a) Begin by estimating a traditional statistical earnings function. More specifically, employing OLS, estimate parameters in the equation

$$\begin{aligned} \text{LNWAGE} = \alpha + \alpha_F \cdot \text{FE} + \alpha_U \cdot \text{UNION} + \alpha_N \cdot \text{NONWH} \\ + \alpha_H \cdot \text{HISP} + \beta_1 \cdot \text{ED} + \beta_2 \cdot \text{EX} + \beta_3 \cdot \text{EXSQ} + \epsilon \end{aligned}$$

If your computer software permits, compute both the traditional and the heteroskedasticity-consistent standard errors. (*Note:* Computational formulae for calculating consistent standard errors in the context of heteroskedasticity have been developed by Halbert J. White [1980]. Many regression software programs now permit use of this robust standard error procedure as an option. If your program does not, try using the simple and equivalent three-step instrumental variable procedure using traditional regression software, as discussed by Karen Messer and Halbert White [1984].) Are the heteroskedasticity-consistent standard error estimates always larger than the (inconsistent) OLS estimates? Is this what you expected? Why or why not?

(b) Even though OLS estimated parameters in part (a) are consistent if heteroskedasticity is present, they are not efficient. To obtain efficient estimates, a generalized least squares (GLS) procedure is required. To do GLS, first retrieve the residuals from the estimated equation in part (a) and square each of these residuals. Mincer [1974], Willis [1986], and others have argued that the variance of disturbances in a statistical earnings function might be positively related to variables such as ED and/or EX. To examine this possibility, use OLS and run a regression of the squared residual from part (a) as the dependent variable, and employ as regressors a constant, ED, EX, EXSQ, FE, UNION, NONWH, and HISP. Experiment with alternative combinations of these regressors, and then choose a preferred residual regression equation in which each of the regressors has a statistically significant coefficient. Then use square roots of the fitted values from your preferred residual regression to transform all your data, and do OLS on the transformed data, which is numerically equivalent to doing GLS on the untransformed data. *Note 1:* You might run into a problem doing such a transformation if any of the fitted values from your residual regression are nonpositive. Check to make sure that this does not occur with your estimated model. Compare your GLS and OLS estimated parameters and standard errors. Any surprises? Why or why not? *Note 2:* Some computer programs allow you to do GLS or weighted least squares without actually requiring you to transform the data. If your software permits this, simply use as a weight in weighted least squares the fitted value from your preferred residual regression equation.

(c) In typical econometric theory textbooks a number of tests are presented for testing the null hypothesis of homoskedasticity against an alternative hypothesis consisting of either a specific or some unspecified form of heteroskedasticity. One very simple test is that proposed by Halbert J. White [1980]; as you will now see, it is a variant of the somewhat ad hoc procedure used in part (b). As in part (b), retrieve the residuals from the part (a) regression, and square them. White's procedure consists of running an auxiliary regression in which the squared OLS residual is the dependent variable and the regressors consist of the original set of regressors, plus the cross-products and squares of all the regressors in the original OLS equation. In our context this implies running a regression of the residuals squared on a constant, ED, EX, EXSQ, FE, UNION, NONWH, HISP, and 17 cross-products regressors, constructed as FE · UNION, FE · NONWH, FE · HISP, FE · ED, FE · EX, FE · EXSQ, UNION · NONWH, UNION · HISP, UNION · ED, UNION · EX, UNION · EXSQ, NONWH · ED, NONWH · EX, NONWH · EXSQ, HISP · ED, HISP · EX, HISP · EXSQ, and the two squared terms ED · ED, and EXSQ · EXSQ (note that squares of the dummy variables such as FE are identical to FE, and so they are not included as additional regressors). Run this auxiliary regression, and retrieve the R^2 measure. White has shown that if the original disturbances are homokurtic (that is, if the expected value of ϵ_i^4 is a constant), then under the null hypothesis, N (the sample size) times the R^2 from this auxiliary regression is distributed asymptotically as a chi-square random variable with 27 degrees of freedom (the total number of zero slope coefficients in the auxiliary regression under the null hypothesis). Compute this chi-square test statistic for homoskedasticity, and compare it to the 5% critical value. Are your results consistent with the null hypothesis of homoskedasticity? If not, make the appropriate adjustments and reestimate the equation in part (a) by GLS using a weighted least squares procedure. Does adjusting for heteroskedasticity affect the parameter estimates significantly? The estimated standard errors? The t-statistics of significance? Is this what you expected? Why?

CHAPTER NOTES

1. A more recent precursor to modern human capital theory is John R. Walsh [1935]. For an historical discussion on the roots of human capital theory, see Billy F. Kiker [1966].
2. Adam Smith [1937], Book 1, Chapter 10.
3. This discussion abstracts from legal issues. The nature of an efficient outcome would clearly be affected, for example, if employers were subject to a liability rule that made them responsible for any damages.
4. The seminal empirical study of wages and earnings as a function of disamenities is that by Milton Friedman and Simon Kuznets [1954]. Surveys of empirical findings are found in Robert S. Smith [1979], Charles Brown [1980], and Gregory J. Duncan and Bertil Holmlund [1983]. See Sherwin Rosen [1986] for additional discussion and examples.
5. For a survey of studies relating wage rates to the risk of fatal accidents, see Robert S. Smith [1979]; for wage rates as a function of nonfatal accidents and health impairment, see W. Kip Viscusi and Charles J. O'Connor [1984].
6. Burton Weisbrod [1983]. This conclusion is controversial, however. For evidence that public interest lawyers earn no less than traditional lawyers, given their abilities, see John H. Goddeeris [1988].
7. For further discussion, see John M. Abowd and Orley Ashenfelter [1981].
8. The discussion here is based in large part on Robert J. Willis [1986].
9. In this context a classic article is that by Yoram Ben-Porath [1967].
10. On this issue, see Harold Lydall [1968].
11. Such greater incentives would be mitigated somewhat if the forgone earnings of the more able were higher.
12. Owing in part to such reasons, Walter Oi [1962] envisages labor as a quasi-fixed factor of production and works out implications for optimal responses of firms to short-run shifts in demand curves.
13. The words "on average" are important here. For example, one prominent exception involves professional athletes, such as baseball players, few of whom complete college.
14. Such studies include Paul Taubman and Terence Wales [1973], David A. Wise [1975], and Kenneth Wolpin [1977].
15. For further discussion of problems in discriminating empirically between the screening and human capital hypotheses, see John G. Riley [1976, 1979] and Joseph E. Stiglitz [1975].
16. Another less commonly used data set that focuses greater attention on sources of income than does the Current Population Survey is the U.S. Bureau of Census Survey of Income and Program Participation, undertaken as a joint project with the U.S. Department of Health and Human Services. For discussion of this data set, see U.S. Department of Commerce, Bureau of the Census [1987].
17. Detailed information on U.S. government household and business establishment surveys are found in two Bureau of Labor Statistics publications; one is an occasional one called *Handbook of Labor Statistics*, Technical Notes, while the other is the monthly publication called *Employment and Earnings*. Descriptions of the data gathered at Ohio State are found in Herbert S. Parnes et al. [1970], while those of data collected at the University of Michigan are found in James N. Morgan et al. [1966] and James N. Morgan [1974].

18. Felicia Nathan [1987].
19. B. K. Atrostic [1982].
20. Timothy Smeeding [1983]. This male-female differential is almost completely eliminated when part-time workers are excluded.
21. Walter Oi [1983], p. 105. Tax considerations might also play a role here, however.
22. Expenditures per pupil data have been used by George E. Johnson and Frank P. Stafford [1973], while college ratings measures were employed by Terence Wales [1973]. Also see studies on school quality by Anita A. Summers and Barbara L. Wolfe [1977] and Ronald Rizzuto and Paul Wachtel [1980]. For a survey discussion on school quality issues, see Eric A. Hanushek [1986].
23. For an exception to this pattern, see Eric A. Hanushek and John M. Quigley [1978], who distinguish empirically between actual cumulative and potential cumulative labor market experience.
24. However, if it is assumed that all potential experience is general and is not related just to employment for pay, then by definition, experience is gained in any activity—volunteer work, vacation, home production, etc. In such a case an experience measure computed as age minus years schooling minus 6 years is quite appropriate.
25. It is worth noting that this traditional stochastic specification has been tested by, among others, Joachim Wagner and Wilhelm Lorenz [1988], who find little empirical support for it. On the other hand, the semilogarithmic functional form in Eq. (5.1) has been tested by James J. Heckman and Solomon Polachek [1974] as a special case of the more general Box-Cox formulation; they find that the semilogarithmic form is consistent with their data.
26. The discussion that follows is based in large part on John T. Addison and W. Stanley Siebert [1979], pp. 130–132. One of the earliest derivations is found in Gary S. Becker and Barry R. Chiswick [1966].
27. Equation (5.2) can be generalized by assuming that the fraction of schooling costs represented by forgone earnings is k_s, where k_s is not necessarily equal to 1. When this is done, the left-hand side of Eq. (5.2) should be replaced by $k_s r_1$, implying that the coefficient on s in Eq. (5.8) equals $k_s r$. For further elaboration, see Gary S. Becker and Barry R. Chiswick [1966].
28. For the OLS estimator to provide consistent estimates of the parameters, it must be assumed that the schooling variable is uncorrelated with the disturbance term. This assumption would be violated if schooling were correlated with an omitted variable such as abilities (see Section 5.2.D) or if schooling were in fact an endogenous, jointly dependent variable.
29. For a critique of Mincer's derivations, see Alan S. Blinder [1976].
30. This quadratic expression can be derived rigorously when the fraction of earnings capacity invested declines linearly with age. For discussion, see Jacob Mincer [1974, pp. 11–23] and Addison and Siebert [1979, pp. 159–163].
31. Such dummy variables have reemerged in the relatively recent efficiency wage literature. See, among others, George A. Akerlof and Janet L. Yellen [1986], Joseph E. Stiglitz [1987], and Alan B. Krueger and Lawrence Summers [1988].
32. Similar findings have been reported by Arleen Leibowitz [1974].
33. These and other econometric issues involving use of twins or siblings to control for abilities and background variables are discussed in a volume edited by Taubman [1977].
34. For surveys of some of this literature, see Sherwin Rosen [1977], Gordon K.

Douglass [1977], and Mark Blaug [1976]. International comparisons are made by George Psacharopoulos [1973, 1981, 1985].

35. Willis [1986], p. 526.
36. Although net present value formulae are theoretically preferable, in practice, empirical results on returns to education based on the net present value and internal rate of return procedures are virtually identical. For a theoretical discussion distinguishing the two, see Jack Hirschleifer [1958].
37. For discussion and derivation, see Mincer [1962, 1974] and Becker [1964].
38. Thurow [1975], pp. 68–69.
39. In an earlier study in which present values of lifetime earnings were calculated for individuals at various schooling levels, Hendrik S. Houthakker [1959] found that those who began but did not complete college and those who began but did not complete high school actually had lower present value lifetime earnings than those who never even began such schooling. For these, according to Houthakker, it was not the case that "it was better to have loved and lost than never to have loved at all."
40. In footnote 2, p. 538, Willis [1986] provides an outline of procedures used by him and by Welch. In essence, the log of earnings was regressed on years of schooling and years of experience (age minus years schooling minus 5), with the schooling variable interacted with experience. Instead of using a linear and squared measure of experience as in Eq. (5.12), Welch employed what is called a spline function. This fitted regression equation was then used to simulate earnings over the remaining worklife to age 65 for high school and college graduates, and on the basis of these simulations, internal rates of return were calculated that equalized present values.
41. The international evidence on this issue has been surveyed by Psacharopoulos [1985].
42. For more recent evidence, see William D. Marden and Douglas E. Hough [1983].
43. Mincer placed great emphasis on the magnitude of the R^2, perhaps in part to counter the claims of some that noneconomic factors were primarily responsible for variations in earnings. In Mincer [1974, pp. 91–92], for example, he states, "The coefficient of determination R^2 is of special interest as an estimate of the fraction of earnings inequality that is associated with the distribution of human capital investments. The regression coefficients are not the primary concern in this study. They do, however, represent an important check on the consistency of the interpretation of the regression equations as human capital earnings functions." This raises an interesting issue: Can one put confidence in the R^2 measure but not in the individual estimated coefficients? Why or why not?
44. This equality also breaks down in a wide variety of what are called "efficiency wage" models. While this efficiency wage literature is important and fascinating, space considerations preclude further discussion of it in this chapter. For classic treatments and references, see, among others, Carl Shapiro and Joseph E. Stiglitz [1984], George A. Akerlof and Janet L. Yellen, [1986], Joseph E. Stiglitz [1987], and Alan B. Krueger and Lawrence Summers [1988].
45. See references in the previous footnote.
46. This line of reasoning was initiated formally by Kenneth Burdett [1978] and Boyan Jovanovic [1979].
47. These econometric procedures are discussed in, among others, James J. Heckman and Burton Singer [1984], Tony Lancaster [1979], and Nicholas M. Kiefer [1985].
48. For a discussion, see Sherwin Rosen [1969] and the references cited therein.

49. A useful discussion on the age-wage differential in union and nonunion establishments is found in George E. Johnson and Kenwood C. Youmans [1971]; also see H. Gregg Lewis [1986].
50. This procedure is discussed in further detail in Section 5.4.A.
51. Additional discussion of and qualifications to the original Schmidt-Strauss findings are given in Peter Schmidt [1978].
52. Lewis [1986], p. 1176.
53. U.S. Joint Economic Committee [1980], pp. 2–5.
54. It is generally believed that if tastes for discrimination result in differing wages for the same job, they are more likely to be observed between than within establishments. Specifically, disadvantaged group members will tend to be confined to lower-paying firms.
55. For discussion and examples, see Orley Ashenfelter [1973].
56. A useful survey on the supply responsiveness of female labor to wage rate changes is found in Mark Killingsworth [1983]. This topic is controversial, however, and is discussed in considerable detail in Chapter 11 of this book.
57. Thurow [1975], p. 172.
58. Blinder attempted to decompose the discrimination portion further into differences in intercepts and slope coefficients. However, F. L. Jones [1983] has demonstrated that the intercept decomposition is entirely arbitrary and is therefore uninterpretable.
59. However, David Neumark [1988] has derived Eq. (5.30) as the outcome of an optimizing process involving individuals and an employer with a specific form of tastes for discrimination. Neumark notes that other tastes for discrimation would generate alternative decompositions and that empirical results can vary substantially with the choice of decomposition; unfortunately, there appears to be little to choose among these alternative measures on an a priori basis.
60. A detailed discussion is given by David Swinton [1983].
61. Blinder also attempted to examine effects of previous discrimination on current wages. This "structural estimation" employed a simultaneous equations procedure and indicated that the 60% endowment differential could be divided equally between blacks' smaller measured endowments and discrimination in achieving education and experience levels.
62. In addition to the studies cited in the text, see Harry Holzer [1987], Smith and Welch [1977], and Welch [1973a].
63. See Table 30, p. 558, in Smith and Welch [1989].
64. Smith and Welch [1989], p. 559.
65. See, for example, the survey by Cynthia B. Lloyd and Beth T. Niemi [1979] and the more recent one by Morley Gunderson [1989].
66. Mincer and Polachek [1974].
67. Intermittent labor force participation also occurs for immigrants. The segmented labor force participation and earnings histories of immigrants have been examined empirically by, among others, Chiswick [1978]. Like reentering female labor force participants, immigrants have an age-earnings profile that is very steep.
68. See, for example, Paula England [1982] and, for a Marxian critique, Sam Bowles and Herbert Gintis [1975].
69. On comparable worth, see, for example, Ronald G. Ehrenberg [1989].
70. In the context of models of wage determination this point appears to have been first noted by Reuben Gronau [1973].
71. The OLS estimates of standard errors from this last step, however, are not consis-

tent, since disturbances are heteroskedastic. For a critique of Heckman's procedure in a related context, see Henry S. Farber [1983, Concluding Remarks].

72. For a discussion of issues on interpretation and empirical significance, see the special set of papers edited by Arnold Zellner [1984].
73. The literature on this topic is very large. See, for example, Melvin W. Reder [1955], Lester Thurow [1975], Thomas J. Kniesner, Arthur H. Padilla, and Solomon W. Polachek [1978], and the references cited therein.
74. See the references in footnote 44.
75. Frank Stafford [1986] has argued that the simple availability of such data has invigorated an area of empirical economics that would otherwise have remained dormant. For a related discussion, see Hamermesh [1990].
76. These test statistics are discussed in most statistics textbooks. For a discussion in an econometrics textbook, see Judge et al. [1985], pp. 826–827.

CHAPTER REFERENCES

Abowd, John M. and Orley Ashenfelter [1981], "Anticipated Unemployment, Temporary Layoffs, and Compensating Wage Differentials," in Sherwin Rosen, ed., *Studies in Labor Economics*, Chicago: University of Chicago Press, pp. 141–170.

Abraham, Katherine G. and Henry S. Farber [1987], "Job Duration, Seniority and Earnings," *American Economic Review*, 77:3, June, 278–297.

Addison, John T. and W. Stanley Siebert [1979], *The Market for Labor: An Analytical Treatment*, Santa Monica, Calif.: Goodyear.

Aigner, Dennis J. and Glen G. Cain [1977], "Statistical Theories of Discrimination in Labor Markets," *Industrial and Labor Relations Review*, 30:2, January, 175–187.

Akerlof, George A. and Janet L. Yellen [1986], eds., *Efficiency Wage Models of the Labor Market*, Cambridge, England: Cambridge University Press.

Arrow, Kenneth J. [1973], "Higher Education as a Filter," *Journal of Public Economics*, 2:3, August, 193–216.

Ashenfelter, Orley [1973], "Discrimination and Trade Unions," in Orley Ashenfelter and Albert Rees, eds., *Discrimination in Labor Markets*, Princeton, N.J.: Princeton University Press, pp. 88–112.

Ashenfelter, Orley [1978], "Estimating the Effect of Training Programs on Earnings," *Review of Economics and Statistics*, 60:1, February, 47–57.

Ashenfelter, Orley and George E. Johnson [1972], "Unionism, Relative Wages and Labor Quality in U.S. Manufacturing Industries," *International Economic Review*, 13:3, October, 488–508.

Atrostic, B. K. [1982], "The Demand for Leisure and Nonpecuniary Job Characteristics," *American Economic Review*, 72:3, June, 428–440.

Becker, Gary S. [1962], "Investment in Human Capital: A Theoretical Analysis," *Journal of Political Economy*, Supplement, 70:5, Part 2, S9–S49.

Becker, Gary S. [1964], *Human Capital: A Theoretical and Empirical Analysis, with Special Reference to Education*, New York: National Bureau of Economic Research.

Becker, Gary S. [1971], *The Economics of Discrimination*, Second Edition, Chicago: University of Chicago Press.

Becker, Gary S. and Barry R. Chiswick [1966], "Education and the Distribution of Earnings," *American Economic Review*, 56:3, May, 358–369.

Behrman, Jere R., Robert A. Pollak, and Paul Taubman [1986], "Do Parents Favor Boys?" *International Economic Review*, 27:1, February, 33–54.

Ben-Porath, Yoram [1967], "The Production of Human Capital and the Life Cycle of Earnings," *Journal of Political Economy*, 75:4, August, 352–365.

Blaug, Mark [1976], "The Empirical Status of Human Capital Theory: A Slightly Jaundiced Survey," *Journal of Economic Literature*, 14:3, September, 827–855.

Blinder, Alan S. [1973], "Wage Discrimination: Reduced Form and Structural Estimates," *Journal of Human Resources*, 18:4, Fall, 436–455.

Blinder, Alan S. [1976], "On Dogmatism in Human Capital Theory," *Journal of Human Resources*, 11:1, Winter 1976, 8–22.

Blinder, Alan S. and Yoram Weiss [1976], "Human Capital and Labor Supply: A Synthesis," *Journal of Political Economy*, 84:3, June, 466–472.

Bloch, Farrell E. and Mark S. Kuskin [1978], "Wage Determination in the Union and Nonunion Sectors," *Industrial and Labor Relations Review*, 31:2, January, 183–192.

Bloom, David E. and Mark R. Killingsworth [1982], "Pay Discrimination Research and Litigation: The Use of Regression Analysis," *Industrial Relations*, 21:3, Fall, 318–339.

Bowles, Samuel and Herbert Gintis [1975], "The Problem with Human Capital Theory—A Marxian Critique," *American Economic Review*, 65:2, May, 74–82.

Brown, Charles [1980], "Equalizing Differences in the Labor Market," *Quarterly Journal of Economics*, 94:1, February, 113–134.

Burdett, Kenneth [1978], "A Theory of Employee Job Search and Quit Rates," *American Economic Review*, 68:1, March, 212–220.

Butler, Richard and James J. Heckman [1977], "The Government's Impact on the Labor Market Status of Black Americans: A Critical Review," in Leonard J. Hausman et al., eds., *Equal Rights and Industrial Relations*, Madison, Wis.: Industrial Relations Research Association, pp. 235–281.

Cain, Glen G. [1986], "The Economic Analysis of Labor Market Discrimination: A Survey," in Orley Ashenfelter and Richard Layard, eds., *The Handbook of Labor Economics*, Vol. 1, Amsterdam: North Holland–Elsevier Science Publishers, pp. 693–785.

Carliner, Geoffrey [1976], "Returns to Education for Blacks, Anglos and Five Spanish Groups," *Journal of Human Resources*, 11:2, Spring, 172–184.

Chamberlain, Gary [1978], "Omitted Variable Bias in Panel Data: Estimating the Returns to Schooling, in *The Econometrics of Panel Data*, Paris: Annals of the Institut National de la Statistique et des Etudes Economiques, pp. 49–82.

Chiswick, Barry R. [1978], "The Effect of Americanization on the Earnings of Foreign-Born Men," *Journal of Political Economy*, 86:5, October, 897–921.

Chiswick, Barry R. [1983a], "Analysis of the Earnings and Employment of Asian-American Men," *Journal of Labor Economics*, 1:2, April, 197–214.

Chiswick, Barry R. [1983b], "The Earnings and Human Capital of American Jews," *Journal of Human Resources*, 18:3, Summer, 315–336.

Conway, Delores A. and Harry V. Roberts [1983], "Reverse Regression, Fairness, and Employment Discrimination," *Journal of Business and Economic Statistics*, 1:1, January, 75–85.

Corcoran, Mary and Greg J. Duncan [1979], "Work History, Labor Force Attachment, and Earnings: Differences between the Races and Sexes," *Journal of Human Resources*, 14:1, Winter, 3–20.

Daymont, Thomas N. and Paul J. Andrisani [1984], "Job Preferences, College Major, and the Gender Gap in Earnings," *Journal of Human Resources*, 19:3, Summer, 408–428.

Douglass, Gordon K. [1977], "Economic Returns on Investments in Higher Education," in Howard R. Bowen, ed., *Investment in Learning*, San Francisco: Jossey-Bass, pp. 359–387.

Duncan, Gregory J. and Bertil Holmlund [1983], "Was Adam Smith Right after All? Another Test of the Theory of Compensating Wage Differentials," *Journal of Labor Economics*, 1:4, October, 366–379.

Ehrenberg, Ronald G. [1989], "Empirical Consequences of Comparable Worth: What Have We Learned?" in M. N. Hill and Mark R. Killingsworth, eds., *Comparable Worth: Analyses and Evidence*, Ithaca, N.Y.: ILR Press, 90–107.

England, Paula [1982], "The Failure of Human Capital to Explain Occupational Sex Segregation," *Journal of Human Resources*, 17:3, Summer, 358–370.

Farber, Henry S. [1983], "The Determination of the Union Status of Workers," *Econometrica*, 51:5, September, 1417–1437.

Farber, Henry S. [1986], "The Analysis of Union Behavior," in Orley Ashenfelter and Richard Layard, eds., *The Handbook of Labor Economics*, Vol. 2, Amsterdam: North Holland–Elsevier Science Publishers, pp. 1039–1089.

Filer, Randall K. [1983], "Sexual Differences in Earnings: The Role of Personalities and Individual Tastes," *Journal of Human Resources*, 18:1, Winter, 82–99.

Freeman, Richard B. [1975], "Overinvestment in College Training," *Journal of Human Resources*, 10:3, Summer, 287–311.

Freeman, Richard B. [1976], *The Overeducated American*, New York: Academic Press.

Freeman, Richard B. [1981], "Black Economic Progress after 1964: Who Has Gained and Why?" in Sherwin Rosen, ed., *Studies in Labor Economics*, Chicago: University of Chicago Press, pp. 247–294.

Friedman, Milton and Simon Kuznets [1954], *Income from Independent Professional Practice*, New York: National Bureau of Economic Research.

Ghez, Gilbert R. and Gary S. Becker [1974], *The Allocation of Time and Goods over the Life Cycle*, New York: Columbia University Press for the National Bureau of Economic Research.

Goddeeris, John H. [1988], "Compensating Differentials and Self-Selection: An Application to Lawyers," *Journal of Political Economy*, 96:2, April, 411–428.

Goldberger, Arthur S. [1984], "Reverse Regression and Salary Discrimination," *Journal of Human Resources*, 19:3, Summer, 293–318.

Green, Carole A. and Marianne A. Ferber [1984], "Employment Discrimination: An Empirical Test of Forward vs. Reverse Regression," *Journal of Human Resources*, 19:4, Fall, 557–569.

Grenier, Gilles [1984], "The Effect of Language Characteristics on the Wages of Hispanic-American Males," *Journal of Human Resources*, 19:1, Winter, 35–52.

Griliches, Zvi [1977], "Estimating the Returns to Schooling: Some Econometric Problems," *Econometrica*, 45:1, January, 1–22.

Griliches, Zvi [1979], "Sibling Models and Data in Economics: Beginnings of a Survey," *Journal of Political Economy*, 87:5, Part 2, October, S37–S64.

Griliches, Zvi and William M. Mason [1972], "Education, Income and Ability," *Journal of Political Economy*, 80:3, Part 2, May/June, S74–S103.

Gronau, Reuben [1973], "The Effect of Children on the Housewife's Value of Time," *Journal of Political Economy*, 81:2, Part II, March/April, S168–S199.

Gunderson, Morley [1989], "Male-Female Wage Differentials and Policy Responses," *Journal of Economic Literature*, 27:1, March, 46–72.

Hall, Robert E. [1970], "Why Is the Unemployment Rate So High at Full Employment?" *Brookings Papers on Economic Activity*, 3:1970, 369–402.

Hamermesh, Daniel S. [1990], "Data Difficulties in Labor Economics," in Ernst R. Berndt and Jack E. Triplett, eds., *Fifty Years of Economic Measurement*, Chicago: University of Chicago Press.

Hamermesh, Daniel and Albert Rees [1988], *The Economics of Work and Pay*, Fourth Edition, New York: Harper & Row.

Hanoch, Giora [1967], "An Economic Analysis of Earning and Schooling," *Journal of Human Resources*, 2:3, Summer, 310–329.

Hansen, W. Lee [1963], "Total and Private Rates of Return to Investment in Schooling," *Journal of Political Economy*, 71:2, April, 128–140.

Hanushek, Eric A. [1986], "The Economics of Schooling," *Journal of Economic Literature*, 24:3, September, 1141–1177.

Hanushek, Eric A. and John M. Quigley [1978], "Implicit Investment Profiles and Intertemporal Adjustments of Relative Wages," *American Economic Review*, 68:1, March, 67–79.

Heckman, James J. [1976], "A Life Cycle Model of Earnings, Learning and Consumption," *Journal of Political Economy*, 84:4, Part 2, August, S11–S44.

Heckman, James J. [1979], "Sample Selection Bias as a Specification Error," *Econometrica*, 47:1, January, 153–162.

Heckman, James J. and Solomon Polachek [1974], "Empirical Evidence on the Functional Form of the Earnings-Schooling Relationship," *Journal of the American Statistical Association*, 69:2, June, 350–354.

Heckman, James J. and Burton Singer [1984], "A Method for Minimizing the Impact of Distributional Assumptions in Econometric Models for Duration Data," *Econometrica*, 52:2, March, 271–320.

Hirshleifer, Jack [1958], "On the Theory of Optimal Investment Decisions," *Journal of Political Economy*, 66:4, 329–352.

Holzer, Harry [1987], "Informal Job Search and Black Youth Unemployment," *American Economic Review*, 77:3, June, 446–452.

Houthakker, Hendrik S. [1959], "Education and Income," *Review of Economics and Statistics*, 61:1, February, 24–28.

Johnson, George E. and Frank P. Stafford [1973], "Social Returns to Quantity and Quality of Schooling," *Journal of Human Resources*, 8:2, Spring, 139–155.

Johnson, George E. and Kenwood C. Youmans [1971], "Union Relative Wage Effects by Age and Education," *Industrial and Labor Relations Review*, 24:2, January, 171–180.

Johnson, Thomas [1978], "Selection without (Unfair) Discrimination," *Communications in Statistics—Theory and Methods*, A7:11, November, 1079–1098.

Jones, F. L. [1983], "On Decomposing the Wage Gap: A Critical Comment on Blinder's Method," *Journal of Human Resources*, 18:1, Winter, 126–129.

Jovanovic, Boyan [1979], "Job Matching and the Theory of Turnover," *Journal of Political Economy*, 87:5, Part 1, October, 972–990.

Judge, George G., William E. Griffiths, R. Carter Hill, Helmut Lutkepohl, and Tsoung-Chao Lee [1985], *The Theory and Practice of Econometrics*, Second Edition, New York: John Wiley and Sons.

Kamalich, Richard F. and Solomon W. Polachek [1982], "Discrimination: Fact or Fiction? An Examination Using an Alternative Approach," *Southern Economic Journal*, 49:2, October, 450–461.

Kiefer, Nicholas M. [1985], ed., "Econometric Analysis of Duration Data," *Journal of Econometrics*, 28:1, April, 1–169.

Kiker, Billy F. [1966], "The Historical Roots of the Concept of Human Capital," *Journal of Political Economy*, 74:5, October, 481–499.

Killingsworth, Mark [1982], "'Learning by Doing' and 'Investment in Training': A Synthesis of Two Rival Models of the Life Cycle," *Review of Economic Studies*, 49, 263–271.

Killingsworth, Mark [1983], *Labor Supply*, Cambridge, England: Cambridge University Press.

Kniesner, Thomas J., Arthur H. Padilla and Solomon W. Polachek [1978], "The Rate of Return to Schooling and the Business Cycle," *Journal of Human Resources*, 13:2, Spring, 264–277.

Krueger, Alan B. and Lawrence Summers [1988], "Efficiency Wages and the Inter-Industry Wage Structure," *Econometrica*, 56:2, March, 259–294.

Lancaster, Tony [1979], "Econometric Methods for the Duration of Unemployment," *Econometrica*, 47:4, July, 939–956.

Lazear, Edward P. [1979a], "The Narrowing of Black-White Wage Differentials Is Illusory," *American Economic Review*, 69:4, September, 553–564.

Lazear, Edward P. [1979b], "Why Is there Mandatory Retirement?" *Journal of Political Economy*, 87:6, December, 1261–1284.

Lazear, Edward P. [1981], "Agency, Earnings Profiles, Productivity, and Hours Restrictions," *American Economic Review*, 71:4, September, 606–620.

Leibowitz, Arleen [1974], "Home Investments in Children," *Journal of Political Economy*, 82:2, Part 2, March/April, S115–S131.

Lewis, H. Gregg [1963], *Unions and Relative Wages in the United States*, Chicago: University of Chicago Press.

Lewis, H. Gregg [1986], "Union Relative Wage Effects," in Orley Ashenfelter and Richard Layard, eds., *The Handbook of Labor Economics*, Vol. 2, Amsterdam: North Holland–Elsevier Science Publishers, pp. 1139–1181.

Lloyd, Cynthia B. and Beth T. Niemi [1979], *The Economics of Sex Differentials*, New York: Columbia University Press.

Lydall, Harold [1968], *The Structure of Earnings*, Oxford, England: Clarendon Press.

Machlup, Fritz [1974], "Proxies and Dummies," *Journal of Political Economy*, 82:4, July/August, 892.

MaCurdy, Thomas and John Pencavel [1986], "Testing between Competing Models of Wage and Employment Determination in Unionized Markets," *Journal of Political Economy*, 94:3, Part 2, June, S3–S39.

Marden, William D. and Douglas E. Hough [1983], "Medical Residency as Investment in Human Capital," *Journal of Human Resources*, 18:1, Winter, 49–64.

McConnell, Campbell R. and Stanley L. Brue [1986], *Contemporary Labor Economics*, New York: McGraw-Hill.

Medoff, James L. and Katherine G. Abraham [1980], "Experience, Performance, and Earnings," *Quarterly Journal of Economics*, 95:4, December, 703–736.

Medoff, James L. and Katherine G. Abraham [1981], "Are Those Paid More Really More Productive? The Case of Experience," *Journal of Human Resources*, 16:2, Spring, 186–216.

Messer, Karen and Halbert White [1984], "A Note on Computing a Heteroskedasticity-Consistent Covariance Matrix Using Instrumental Variable Techniques," *Oxford Bulletin of Economics and Statistics*, 46:2, May, 181–184.

Mincer, Jacob [1957], "A Study of Personal Income Distribution," unpublished Ph.D. dissertation, New York: Columbia University, Department of Economics.

Mincer, Jacob [1958], "Investment in Human Capital and Personal Income Distribution," *Journal of Political Economy*, 66:4, August, 281–302.

Mincer, Jacob [1962], "On-the-Job Training: Costs, Returns, and Some Implications," *Journal of Political Economy*, 70:5, Part 2, October, S50–S79.

Mincer, Jacob [1974], *Schooling, Experience and Earnings*, New York: Columbia University Press for the National Bureau of Economic Research.

Mincer, Jacob and Boyan Jovanovic [1981], "Labor Mobility and Wages," in Sherwin Rosen, ed., *Studies in Labor Markets*, Chicago: University of Chicago Press for the National Bureau of Economic Research, pp. 21–64.

Mincer, Jacob and Haim Ofek [1982], "Interrupted Work Careers: Depreciation and Restoration of Human Capital," *Journal of Human Resources*, 27:1, Winter, 3–24.

Mincer, Jacob and Solomon Polachek [1974], "Family Investments in Human Capital: Earnings of Women," *Journal of Political Economy*, 82:2, Part 2, March, S76–S108.

Morgan, James N., ed. [1974], *Five Thousand American Families—Patterns of Economic Progress*, Ann Arbor, Mich.: Survey Research Center, University of Michigan.

Morgan, James N. et al. [1966], *Productive Americans: A Study of How Individuals Contribute to Economic Progress*, Ann Arbor, Mich.: Survey Research Center, University of Michigan.

Murphy, Kevin and Finis R. Welch [1988], "Wage Differences in the 1980s: The Role of International Trade," unpublished manuscript, University of California–Los Angeles, Department of Economics.

Nathan, Felicia [1987], "Analyzing Employers' Costs for Wages, Salaries, and Benefits," *Monthly Labor Review*, 110:10, October, 3–11.

Neumark, David [1988], "Employer Discriminatory Behavior and the Estimation of Wage Discrimination," *Journal of Human Resources*, 23:3, Summer, 279–295.

Oaxaca, Ronald [1973a], "Sex Discrimination in Wages," in Orley Ashenfelter and Albert Rees, eds., *Discrimination in Labor Markets*, Princeton, N.J.: Princeton University Press, pp. 124–151.

Oaxaca, Ronald [1973b], "Male Female Wage Differentials in Urban Labor Markets," *International Economic Review*, 14:3, October, 693–709.

Oi, Walter [1962], "Labor as a Quasi-Fixed Factor," *Journal of Political Economy*, 70:6, December, 538–555.

Oi, Walter [1983], "The Fixed Employment Costs of Specialized Labor," in Jack E. Triplett, ed., *The Measurement of Labor Cost*, Chicago: University of Chicago Press for the National Bureau of Economic Research, pp. 63–122.

Oswald, Andrew J. [1985], "The Economic Theory of Trade Unions: An Introductory Survey," *Scandinavian Journal of Economics*, 87:2, 160–193.

Parnes, Herbert S. et al. [1970], *The Pre-Retirement Years: A Longitudinal Study of the Labor Market Experience of Men*, Vol. 1, Washington, D.C.: U.S. Department of Labor, Manpower Administration.

Pencavel, John [1984], "The Tradeoff between Wages and Employment in Trade Union Objectives," *Quarterly Journal of Economics*, 99:2, May, 215–231.

Psacharopoulos, George [1973], *Returns to Education: An International Comparison*, San Francisco: Jossey-Bass.

Psacharopoulos, George [1981], "Returns to Education: An Updated International Comparison," *Comparative Education*, 17:3, 321–341.

Psacharopoulos, George [1985], "Returns to Education: A Further International Update and Implications," *Journal of Human Resources*, 20:6, Fall, 583–604.

Reder, Melvin W. [1955], "The Theory of Occupational Wage Differentials," *American Economic Review*, 45:5, December, 833–852.

Reimers, Cordelia [1983], "Labor Market Discrimination against Hispanics and Black Men," *Review of Economics and Statistics*, 65:4, November, 570–579.

Riley, John G. [1976], "Information, Screening and Human Capital," *American Economic Review*, 66:2, May, 254–260.

Riley, John G. [1979], "Testing the Educational Screening Hypothesis," *Journal of Political Economy*, 87:5, Part 2, October, S227–S252.

Rizzuto, Ronald and Paul Wachtel [1980], "Further Evidence on the Returns to School Quality," *Journal of Human Resources*, 15:2, Spring, 240–254.

Rosen, Sherwin [1969], "Trade Union Power, Threat Effects, and the Extent of Organization," *Review of Economic Studies*, 36(2):106, April, 185–194.

Rosen, Sherwin [1977], "Human Capital: A Survey of Empirical Research," in Ronald Ehrenberg, ed., *Research in Labor Economics*, Vol. 1, Greenwich, Conn.: JAI Press, pp. 3–40.

Rosen, Sherwin [1986], "The Theory of Equalizing Differences," in Orley Ashenfelter and Richard Layard, eds., *The Handbook of Labor Economics*, Vol. 1, Amsterdam: North Holland–Elsevier Science Publishers, pp. 641–692.

Roy, A. D. [1950], "The Distribution of Earnings and of Individual Output," *Economic Journal*, 60:3, September, 489–505.

Schmidt, Peter [1978], "Estimation of a Simultaneous Equations Model with Jointly Dependent Continuous and Qualitative Variables: The Union-Earnings Question Revisited," *International Economic Review*, 19:2, June, 453–465.

Schmidt, Peter and Robert P. Strauss [1976], "The Effect of Unions on Earnings and Earnings on Unions: A Mixed Logit Approach," *International Economic Review*, 17:1, February, 204–212.

Schultz, Theodore W. [1960], "Capital Formation by Education," *Journal of Political Economy*, 68:6, December, 571–583.

Schultz, Theodore W. [1961], "Investment in Human Capital," *American Economic Review*, 51:1, March, 1–17.

Shapiro, Carl and Joseph E. Stiglitz [1984], "Involuntary Unemployment as a Worker Discipline Device," *American Economic Review*, 74:3, June, 433–444.

Smeeding, Timothy M. [1983], "The Size Distribution of Wage and Non-Wage Compensation: Employer Cost versus Employee Value," in Jack E. Triplett, ed., *The Measurement of Labor Cost*, Chicago: University of Chicago Press for the National Bureau of Economic Research, pp. 237–277.

Smith, Adam [1937], *The Wealth of Nations*, Reprinted Edition, New York: Random House.

Smith, James P. and Finis R. Welch [1977], "Black-White Male Wage Ratios: 1960–70," *American Economic Review*, 67:3, June, 323–338.

Smith, James P. and Finis R. Welch [1989], "Black Economic Progress after Myrdal," *Journal of Economic Literature*, 27:2, June, 519–564.

Smith, Robert S. [1979], "Compensating Wage Differentials and Public Policy: A Review," *Industrial and Labor Relations Review*, 32:3, April, 339–352.

Spence, Michael A. [1973], "Job Market Signalling," *Quarterly Journal of Economics*, 87:3, August, 355–374.

Spence, Michael A. [1974], *Market Signalling: Informational Transfer in Hiring and Related Screening Processes*, Cambridge, Mass.: Harvard University Press.

Stafford, Frank [1986], "Forestalling the Demise of Empirical Economics: The Role of Microdata in Labor Economics Research," in Orley Ashenfelter and Richard Layard, eds., *The Handbook of Labor Economics*, Vol. 1, Amsterdam: North Holland–Elsevier Science Publishers, pp. 387–423.

Stiglitz, Joseph E. [1975], "The Theory of Screening, Education, and the Distribution of Income," *American Economic Review*, 65:3, June, 283–300.

Stiglitz, Joseph E. [1987], "The Causes and Consequences of the Dependence of Quality on Price," *Journal of Economic Literature*, 25:1, March, 1–48.

Summers, Anita A. and Barbara L. Wolfe [1977], "Do Schools Make a Difference?" *American Economic Review*, 67:4, 634–652.

Swinton, David [1983], "The Economic Status of the Black Population," in *The State of Black America*, Washington, D.C.: National Urban League.

Taubman, Paul [1976a], "Earnings, Education, Genetics and Environment," *Journal of Human Resources*, 11:4, Fall, 447–461.

Taubman, Paul [1976b], "The Determinants of Earnings: Genetics, Family and Other Environment—A Study of Male Twins," *American Economic Review*, 66:5, December, 858–870.

Taubman, Paul, ed., [1977], *Kinometrics: Determinants of Socioeconomic Success within and between Families*, Amsterdam: North-Holland.

Taubman, Paul and Terence Wales [1973], "Higher Education, Mental Ability and Screening," *Journal of Political Economy*, 81:1, January/February, 28–55.

Thurow, Lester C. [1975], *Generating Inequality*, New York: Basic Books.

U.S. Department of Commerce, Bureau of the Census [1987], *Survey of Income and Program Participation: Users' Guide*, Washington, D.C.: Customer Services, Data User Services Division.

U.S. Joint Economic Committee [1980], *The Cost of Racial Discrimination*, Washington, D.C.: U.S. Government Printing Office.

Viscusi, W. Kip and Charles J. O'Connor [1984], "Adaptive Responses to Chemical Labeling: Are Workers Bayesian Decision Makers?" *American Economic Review*, 74:5, December, 942–956.

Wagner, Joachim and Wilhelm Lorenz [1988], "The Earnings Function under Test," *Economics Letters*, 27:1, 95–99.

Wales, Terence J. [1973], "The Effect of College Quality on Earnings: Results from the NBER-Thorndike Data," *Journal of Human Resources*, 8:3, Summer, 306–315.

Walsh, John R. [1935], "Capital Concept Applied to Man," *Quarterly Journal of Economics*, 49:2, February, 255–285.

Weisbrod, Burton [1983], "Nonprofit and Proprietary Sector Behavior: Wage Differentials and Lawyers," *Journal of Labor Economics*, 1:3, July, 246–263.

Weiss, Yoram [1986], "The Determinants of Life Cycle Earnings: A Survey," in Orley Ashenfelter and Richard Layard, eds., *The Handbook of Labor Economics*, Vol. 1, Amsterdam: North Holland–Elsevier Science Publishers, pp. 603–639.

Welch, Finis R. [1973a], "Education and Racial Discrimination," in Orley Ashenfelter and Albert Rees, eds., *Discrimination in Labor Markets*, Princeton, N.J.: Princeton University Press, pp. 43–81.

Welch, Finis R. [1973b], "Black-White Differences in Returns to Schooling," *American Economic Review*, 63:6, December, 893–907.

White, Halbert J. [1980], "A Heteroskedasticity-Consistent Covariance Matrix Estimator and a Direct Test for Heteroskedasticity," *Econometrica*, 48:4, May, 817–838.

Willis, Robert J. [1986], "Wage Determinants: A Survey and Reinterpretation of Human Capital Earnings Functions," in Orley Ashenfelter and Richard Layard, eds., *The Handbook of Labor Economics*, Vol. 1, Amsterdam: North Holland–Elsevier Science Publishers, pp. 525–602.

Wise, David A. [1975], "Academic Achievement and Job Performance," *American Economic Review*, 65:3, June, 350–366.

Wolpin, Kenneth [1977], "Education and Screening," *American Economic Review*, 67:5, December, 949–958.

Yellen, Janet [1984], "Efficiency Wage Models of Unemployment," *American Economic Review*, 74:3, May, 200–208.

Zellner, Arnold, ed. [1984], "Discussion of the Statistical Analysis of Fairness and Employment Discrimination," *Journal of Business and Economic Statistics*, 2:2, April, 110–139.

FURTHER READINGS

Leading textbooks in labor economics containing one or more chapters on human capital theory and determinants of wages:

Addison, John T. and W. Stanley Siebert [1979], *The Market for Labor: An Analytical Treatment*, Santa Monica, Calif.: Goodyear.

Ehrenberg, Ronald G. and Robert S. Smith [1985], *Modern Labor Economics: Theory and Public Policy*, Second Edition, Glenview, Ill.: Scott, Foresman and Company.

Fleisher, Belton M. and Thomas J. Kniesner [1984], *Labor Economics: Theory, Evidence, and Policy*, Third Edition, Englewood Cliffs, N.J.: Prentice-Hall.

Gunderson, Morley and W. Craig Riddell [1988], *Labour Market Economics: Theory, Evidence and Policy in Canada*, Second Edition, Toronto: McGraw-Hill Ryerson, Ltd.

Hamermesh, Daniel and Albert Rees [1988], *The Economics of Work and Pay*, Fourth Edition, New York: Harper & Row.

McConnell, Campbell R. and Stanley L. Brue [1986], *Contemporary Labor Economics*, New York: McGraw-Hill.

Reynolds, Lloyd G., Stanley H. Masters, and Colletta H. Moser [1987], *Economics of Labor*, Englewood Cliffs, N.J.: Prentice-Hall.

Useful discussions on measuring and interpreting wage discrimination, and alternative policies to reduce discrimination:

Bergman, Barbara R. [1986], *The Economic Emergence of Women*, New York: Basic Books.

Hill, M. N. and Mark R. Killingsworth [1989], *Comparable Worth: Analyses and Evidence*, Ithaca, N.Y.: ILR Press.

Lloyd, Cynthia B. and Beth T. Niemi [1979], *The Economics of Sex Differentials*, New York: Columbia University Press.

Chapter 6

Explaining and Forecasting Aggregate Investment Expenditures: Distributed Lags and Autocorrelation

". . . much of the investment occurring this year is the result of decisions made last year, the year before, and even the year before that. The decisions were governed by the expectations prevailing in those years about economic conditions this year. New information about this year's conditions that became available after the launching of the projects cannot affect this year's investment in those projects. Much of this year's investment was predetermined by earlier decisions."

ROBERT HALL and JOHN TAYLOR (1988), p. 237

"The important point is that lags in the determination of the level of business investment are long."

RUDIGER DORNBUSCH and STANLEY FISCHER (1987), p. 315

". . . any time series regression containing more than four independent variables results in garbage."

ZVI GRILICHES (1974), p. 335

In this chapter we focus attention on aggregate business investment. The econometric tools that we emphasize include multiple regression estimation and forecasting with distributed lags and various forms of autocorrelation.

Over the last 40 years in the United States, business expenditures on plant and equipment gross investment have averaged approximately 10% of GNP. While such investment spending is typically small in comparison to consumption and government expenditures, for a number of reasons many economists believe that investment is the most important component of GNP.

First, plant and equipment are long-lived, durable goods. Investment outlays that renew and expand the stock of plant and equipment therefore increase potential capacity output supply, not only in the current time period but also into the future. Further, to the extent that new investment goods embody the most recent technical advances, the potential benefits of such technical progress can be realized only as investment occurs. Hence variations in investment expenditures have long-term consequences on a country's productive capacity.

Second, investment expenditures affect demands for the products of the construction and producers' durable good industries. These industries typically alter employment levels in response to variations in the demands for their products; such changes tend to spill over into other industries. This implies that changes in investment expenditures induce shifts in the aggregate levels of employment and personal income through both direct and indirect effects.

Third, the sensitivity of aggregate supply and demand to changes in investment is very important empirically, since investment is the most volatile major component of GNP, varying from about 8.5% of GNP in 1952 and 1958 to above 12.5% in 1984. This volatility of investment expenditures has important "whiplash" consequences. For example, it has been estimated that variations in business expenditures for plant and equipment investment accounted for approximately 25% of the first-year increase in GNP in the United States during the recoveries that began in the third quarter of 1980 and in the fourth quarter of 1982.[1]

Since investment expenditure is so volatile and its movements have important consequences for productive capacity, employment demand, personal income, and the balance of payments, it is critical that the fundamental causes of variations in aggregate investment be understood. If these underlying determinants of changes in investment spending were properly perceived, for example, it might be possible to predict better and accommodate such expected variations. Also, if the volatility in investment expenditures were viewed as being excessive or undesirable, it might be possible to implement government fiscal or monetary policy to control their movements in a more desirable manner.

Unfortunately, however, as we shall see in this chapter, econometricians are still not able to explain and forecast changes in aggregate investment expenditures to the desired degree of precision. Investment models and equations that work exceedingly well in explaining historical variations over one time period often turn out to be less than satisfactory in their forecasting performance into another time period. Moreover, the choice of a preferred model based on historical data often varies considerably with the time period chosen. This state of affairs is humbling, yet it also provides great challenges and opportunities for empirical econometricians.

There are several types of investment. In most industrialized countries, national income and product accountants distinguish among at least three components of investment. *Residential construction* is investment ultimately for use by homeowners and is known to be very sensitive to even minor changes in market interest rates, often written into mortgage contracts. The second major portion of aggregate investment is *changes in business inventories*, which is by far the most volatile component. Firms tend to use inventory changes as buffers against variations in the sales of goods and services, and for this reason, inventory investment is known to be very sensitive to the overall level of economic activity and especially to short-term fluctuations in sales. Inventories may also be held for speculative purposes. The third and largest component of aggregate investment is *fixed business investment*; it incorporates expenditures on nonresidential structures (plant) and producers' durable equipment.

In this chapter we focus on explaining and forecasting variations in the largest component of aggregate investment, namely, fixed business investment.[2] The econometric tools employed in our analysis of fixed business investment include the estimation of distributed lag specifications with autoregressive and moving average error structures, as well as the analysis of static and dynamic forecasting properties of alternative models having autocorrelated errors.[3] We will compare both theoretically and empirically the historical and forecasting performance of five alternative models of aggregate investment, using quarterly data from the U.S. private business sector beginning in 1954. The five alternative theoretical and empirical frameworks considered here are the accelerator, cash flow, neoclassical, Tobin's q, and time series/autoregressive models.

The outline of this chapter is as follows. In Section 6.1 a number of important definitions are presented, a general framework for representing the various models is developed, and issues of stochastic specification are briefly discussed. Then in Sections 6.2 through 6.6 a theoretical and empirical discussion of issues involved in the implementation of each of the five alternative models is presented. Additional econometric specifications and issues are discussed in Section 6.7. The five models are assessed and then compared empirically using a common data base in Section 6.8, and in Section 6.9 other important current research issues are noted. A set of interesting and engaging empirical exercises follows, grounded in a data base of quarterly investment in the U.S. private business sector, from 1952:1 to 1986:4. This data base was constructed by Richard W. Kopcke with assistance from George Houlihan and includes updates from Kopcke's [1985] study.

6.1 INVESTMENT AND CAPITAL STOCK: DEFINITIONS AND GENERAL FRAMEWORK

6.1.A Definitions

In order to understand and implement empirically the various econometric models of investment behavior, it is useful to develop definitions and to establish a general framework for assessing the alternative models. We begin with definitions of the capital stock, whose empirical measurement, as Nobel Laureate Sir John Hicks has noted, "is one of the nastiest jobs that economists have set to statisticians."[4]

Suppose that in time period $t-\tau$ the firm expends $I_{t-\tau}$ dollars for new plant or equipment. Let this $I_{t-\tau}$ value be in constant dollars, that is, define $I_{t-\tau}$ as current dollar investment divided by an asset price index, where the deflator (price index) is normalized to unity in some base year, such as 1977. It is worth noting that in most countries, separate deflators are published for distinct capital assets, such as various types of producers' durable equipment and nonresidential structures.[5]

Because investment goods are durable, they provide services over a multiperiod lifetime. The amount of real investment put in place at time $t-\tau$ and surviving to time t is denoted as $K_{t,t-\tau}$:

$$K_{t,t-\tau} \equiv s_{t,\tau} I_{t-\tau} \tag{6.1}$$

where $s_{t,\tau}$ is the survival rate for age τ investment to time period t. The aggregate of the vintages surviving to the end of time period t—the aggregate capital stock at the end of time period t, denoted K_t—is typically calculated as the sum over vintages

$$K_t \equiv \sum_{\tau=0}^{T} K_{t,t-\tau} = \sum_{\tau=0}^{T} s_{t,\tau} I_{t-\tau} \tag{6.2}$$

where T is the life of the durable good. Computations using Eq. (6.2) can be done separately for various types of capital goods. Further, for each type of capital good it is commonly assumed that the flow of available capital services is a constant proportion of the (constant dollar) capital stock.

One very important empirical issue concerns the life pattern of the survival rates $s_{t,\tau}$. A number of alternative physical deterioration age profiles have been developed. One common alternative, called "one-hoss shay" deterioration, is based on the assumption that once an asset is put into place, it provides the same amount of services during each time period until it "expires" or is scrapped.[6] Recognizing that the time at which durable goods expire is stochastic, analysts have estimated the mean and shape of mortality distributions governing the service lives of various durable assets.

One of the most famous studies of mortality distributions is that by Robert Winfrey, who in 1935 postulated and estimated various bell-shaped mortality distributions centered on the average service lives of a variety of durable goods.[7] Remarkably, until very recently, these Winfrey distributions

Table 6.1 Modified Winfrey S-3 Retirement Patterns, U.S. Department of Commerce

Percent of Mean Service Life	Cumulative Percent of Original Expenditures Discarded	Percent of Mean Service Life	Cumulative Percent of Original Expenditures Discarded
<45	0.0	105	61.6
45	1.2	110	68.8
50	2.4	115	75.4
55	4.1	120	81.3
60	6.5	125	86.3
65	9.7	130	90.3
70	13.7	135	93.5
75	18.7	140	95.9
80	24.6	145	97.6
85	31.2	150	98.8
90	38.4	155	100.0
95	46.1	>155	100.0
100	53.9		

Source: John A. Gorman, John C. Musgrave, Gerald Silverstein, and Kathy A. Comins, "Fixed Private Capital in the United States," *Survey of Current Business*, Vol. 67, No. 7, 1985, Table D, p. 43.

based on pre-1935 data remained essentially unchanged and formed the basis of U.S. Department of Commerce gross capital stock calculations.

To see how these Winfrey mortality distributions have been employed in calculating gross capital stocks based on Eqs. (6.1) and (6.2), let us take a slightly modified Winfrey S-3 retirement pattern published by the U.S. Department of Commerce, reproduced in Table 6.1.[8] For a number of different types of nonresidential capital (except autos), the mean service life is first estimated.[9] The distribution of mortality or retirement patterns $s_{t,\tau}$ is then assumed to be time-invariant, that is, $s_{t,\tau} = s_\tau$, according to the distribution given in Table 6.1.

Given a sufficiently lengthy historical series on real investment expenditures by type of asset, mean service lives, and the above Winfrey mortality distribution, national income accountants calculate the *gross capital stock* using Eqs. (6.1) and (6.2). Note that such gross capital stock series depend on the assumption of one-hoss shay deterioration, fixed expected service lives, and the modified Winfrey mortality distribution.

Although the one-hoss shay decay assumption has some plausibility, other decay patterns are also attractive. A very convenient alternative time path of physical deterioration is the constant exponential decay specification, which is based on the assumption that the rate of physical deterioration as an asset ages is constant and equal to, say, δ% per time period. With constant exponential deterioration the physical survival rate s_τ for an asset of age τ is simply $s_\tau = (1 - \delta)^\tau$. When this survival rate expression is substituted into

Eq. (6.2), the aggregate capital stock at the end of time period t, based on constant exponential deterioration, is computed simply as

$$K_t = \sum_{\tau=0}^{T} K_{t,t-\tau} = \sum_{\tau=0}^{T} (1 - \delta)^{\tau} I_{t-\tau} \tag{6.3}$$

National income accountants refer to the capital stock based on the assumption of constant exponential deterioration and calculated by using Eq. (6.3) as the *net capital stock.* Note that the net capital stock is based on the assumption of constant exponential deterioration, while the gross capital stock presumes one-hoss shay decay.[10]

A convenient way of rewriting the (end of time period) net capital stock calculation implicit in Eq. (6.3) is called the *perpetual inventory method.* It is specified as

$$K_t = (1 - \delta)K_{t-1} + I_t \tag{6.4}$$

Evidently, the word perpetual is employed because with constant exponential deterioration the quantity of services yielded by an asset as it ages approaches but never actually attains zero, and so an asset is perpetually part of the inventory of capital goods.

One could of course also use an equation like the above perpetual inventory relationship for the case of one-hoss shay decay, but since in that case the rate of scrapping over all vintages would depend on the vintage composition of the surviving capital stock, the overall rate of deterioration δ would vary over time. In such a case, Eq. (6.4) would be rewritten as

$$K_t = (1 - \delta_t)K_{t-1} + I_t \tag{6.5}$$

Another important distinction made by analysts of investment behavior is that between replacement and net investment. In each time period a certain amount of investment is designed merely to replace the amount of capital that has deteriorated or been scrapped. With exponential decay and using Eq. (6.4), *replacement investment* equals δK_{t-1}, while for one-hoss shay decay and using Eq. (6.5), replacement investment equals $\delta_t K_{t-1}$.[11] The net increment to the capital stock since the last time period, $K_t - K_{t-1}$, equals total investment minus replacement investment and is called *net investment.* With constant exponential decay, net investment therefore equals $I_t - \delta K_{t-1}$, while for one-hoss shay decay, net investment equals $I_t - \delta_t K_{t-1}$. Finally, regardless of the form of decay, gross investment, replacement investment, and net investment are related by the identity

$$\text{Gross investment} \equiv \text{replacement investment} + \text{net investment.}$$

Incidentally, in the United States, on average, replacement and net investment are roughly equal in magnitude.

The one-hoss shay and constant exponential decay assumptions generally result in different replacement investment, net investment, and therefore net or gross capital stock calculations. Moreover, other forms of decay could also be employed, such as straight-line decay, yielding yet another set of capital stock and investment calculations.[12] This raises the important issue of how one might choose among alternative physical decay assumptions. Fortunately, it is here that economic theory provides very important insights for discriminating among assumptions.

Specifically, the one-hoss shay, straight-line, and constant exponential physical *deterioration* patterns for durable goods imply explicit patterns of price *depreciation* over time as the assets age, that is, each specification of quantity deterioration implies a unique pattern of price depreciation. This relationship is based on the economic reasoning underlying the decision of how much a firm is willing to pay to purchase a used asset.

Suppose that firms seek to minimize the present value of production costs. In equilibrium the price of a used asset must just equal the discounted present value of its expected services over its remaining expected life. If the used price were higher than the present value of future services, the firm would be overinvesting in such assets, receiving services of less value than the amount paid, and would not be minimizing present value costs. On the other hand, if the used price were lower than the present value of services, the firm would be underinvesting in the asset and would be receiving services valued more highly than the price it paid. In equilibrium the present value of future services must just equal the purchase price of the used asset. This implies a relationship between expected physical deterioration and economic depreciation over the lifetime of the asset.

To understand this relationship better, assume initially that the service life of a particular asset were known with certainty and that its physical decay followed a one-hoss shay pattern. With a positive discount rate the price that firms would be willing to pay for such an asset initially would decline gradually in the early years of its service life, and then the price decline would accelerate rapidly as the date of retirement approached.

In Fig. 6.1 the price of a used asset is graphed on the vertical axis, while its age appears on the horizontal axis. The age-price profile for an asset characterized by one-hoss shay decay can be shown to be concave to the origin, as illustrated by the outward-bowed top curve in Fig. 6.1. By contrast, it can be shown that if the quantity decay of a durable good follows a constant exponential decay pattern at rate δ, then the age-price profile also follows the same pattern, that is, the rate of price depreciation is also δ% per time period. Thus with exponential decay, the age-price profile is convex to the origin, as is shown in the bottom curve of Fig. 6.1.[13]

This relationship between quantity decay assumptions and age-price depreciation profiles has stimulated a number of researchers to choose among alternative decay patterns by estimating econometrically the age-price depreciation profiles for used assets and thereby inferring the shape of the underlying s_τ distribution. Although some of the early evidence indicated little sup-

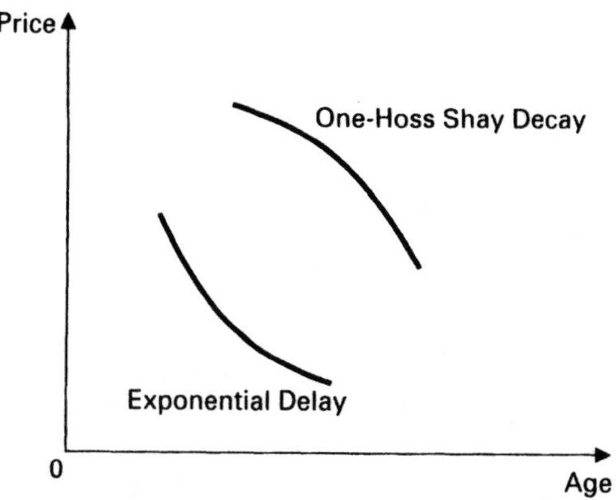

FIGURE 6.1 Age-price profiles under one-hoss shay and constant geometric decay.

port for the exponential decay assumption,[14] more recent studies have examined a larger number of alternative physical deterioration patterns using highly general Box-Cox transformations and have provided greater support for the exponential decay assumption. For example, in their examination of structures, Charles Hulten and Frank Wykoff concluded that

> depreciation patterns are accelerated vis-a-vis straight line, and perhaps also vis-a-vis the geometric [exponential] form. Certainly, the pattern of depreciation does not appear to be linear or decelerated, and obviously, our results, if correct, rule out one-horse shay depreciation as well.[15]

Hulten and Wykoff have conducted similar econometric analyses for a wide variety of differing types of equipment and structures. On the basis of these studies they conclude that while the assumption of exponential or geometric decay tends to be rejected for most assets using conventional statistical criteria, the empirical significance of these rejections is modest, since the age-price profile corresponding with the exponential decay hypothesis very closely approximates that of the more general specifications, such as the hyperbolic.[16] Other simple decay assumptions, such as straight-line or one-hoss shay, are rejected more decisively and do not approximate the more general representations as well.

Today the exponential decay assumption is by far the most widely used deterioration specification in current studies of investment expenditures, most likely owing to its convenient simplicity and its ability to track very closely the age-price profiles of a variety of used assets. It follows also that since there is more empirical support for exponential than one-hoss shay decay, most analysts currently employ as their measure of the capital stock the net rather than the gross construct. A word of caution is in order, however:

Although we will also employ the exponential decay assumption and net capital stocks in the remainder of this chapter, in fact the exponential decay assumption is very restrictive, and results from future empirical research might bring about changes in this common procedure.

6.1.B A General Framework for Representing Various Models

Most theories of investment behavior relate the demand for new plant and equipment to the gap between the desired or optimal amount of capital stock of plant and equipment, denoted K^*, and the actual amount of capital, K. In comparing alternative theories of investment, it will be useful to focus on two aspects concerning K and K^*: (1) What are the factors affecting K^*, and how can such factors be modeled and measured? (2) Why doesn't $K = K^*$, how does K adjust to K^*, and what factors affect the speed of adjustment?

These two aspects of investment behavior can be combined as follows. Let the net capital stock at the end of time period $t - 1$ be K_{t-1}, let K_t^* be the desired capital stock at the end of the current time period, and let the speed of adjustment between K_t^* and K_{t-1} be λ_t. If λ_t were zero, K would be perfectly fixed, and there would be no net investment reducing the gap between K^* and K, while if λ_t were 1, this gap would be closed entirely within one time period, that is, adjustment would be instantaneous. By definition, net investment during time period t equals $\lambda_t(K_t^* - K_{t-1})$, while under the geometric decay assumption, replacement investment equals δK_{t-1}. Since gross investment I_t is the sum of net and replacement investment, gross investment can be written as

$$I_t = \lambda_t(K_t^* - K_{t-1}) + \delta K_{t-1} = \lambda_t K_t^* + (\delta - \lambda_t)K_{t-1} \tag{6.6}$$

Note that, whenever $\delta < \lambda_t$, the $(\delta - \lambda_t)$ term on the lagged capital stock variable in Eq. (6.6) will be negative.[17]

6.1.C Stochastic Specification

To estimate parameters of an equation like Eq. (6.6), a random disturbance term must be appended, and its distribution properties need to be specified. Unfortunately, relatively little attention has been focused on the sources of these disturbances. One could of course simply assert that investment is inherently stochastic, owing to the fact that it depends on individuals' expectations, which in turn can be heterogeneous and random.

Some analysts also cite measurement error as a source of the disturbance term. Note that if the dependent variable in Eq. (6.6), gross investment, is measured with random error, then so too is the lagged capital stock, a right-hand variable, which by Eq. (6.3) is a weighted sum of previous gross investment expenditures. Hence if one specifies this type of random measurement error as the source of the disturbance term, it is necessary to employ estimation procedures other than ordinary least squares—methods that account for measurement error of a regressor—in order to obtain consistent parameter estimates.[18]

Alternatively, one could specify that at the firm level there are additional parameters affecting firms' investment, parameters that are known to the firm but unknown to the econometrician examining aggregate data. Such parameters could be randomly distributed over the population of firms and could be specified in the aggregate to be identically and normally distributed with mean α (thereby resulting in a constant term being added to Eq. (6.6)) and variance σ^2.

Moreover, since the investment spending decision is a complex one, it is likely that important variables are omitted from simple equations such as Eq. (6.6). If such omitted variables are uncorrelated with the included regressors but have a systematic pattern over time, then their impact could be incorporated in part by specifying a random disturbance term with autoregressive features.

A common procedure in empirical aggregate investment analysis is to append to Eq. (6.6) a first-order autoregressive disturbance,

$$u_t = \rho u_{t-1} + \epsilon_t \qquad t = 2, \ldots, T$$

where $|\rho| < 1$ and ϵ_t is assumed to be independently and identically normally distributed with mean zero and variance σ^2. In some cases, depending in part on the periodicity of the data (annual, quarterly, monthly, etc.), higher-order autoregressive processes may be specified instead.

Equation (6.6), with an autoregressive disturbance term appended, will form the basis of comparison among the five alternative models of investment behavior, beginning with the accelerator model, to which we now turn our attention.

6.2 THE ACCELERATOR MODEL

One of the earliest empirical models of aggregate investment behavior is the accelerator model, which was put forward by J. M. Clark in 1917 as a possible reason to rationalize the volatility of investment expenditures.[19] The distinguishing feature of the accelerator model is that it is based on the assumption of a fixed capital/output ratio. This implies that prices, wages, taxes, and interest rates have no direct impact on capital spending but may have indirect impacts. We now examine several well-known versions of the accelerator model.

6.2.A Theory

Denote real output during time period t as Y_t, and let the fixed capital/output ratio equal μ. According to the *naive accelerator model*, not only does the optimal capital stock K_t^* bear a fixed factor of proportionality to output,

$$K_t^* = \mu \cdot Y_t \tag{6.7}$$

but the capital stock is always optimally adjusted in each time period, implying that $K_t^* = K_t$ and therefore that net investment I_{nt} equals

$$I_{nt} = K_t - K_{t-1} = \mu(Y_t - Y_{t-1}) \tag{6.8}$$

This naive accelerator model has not fared well in empirical analyses, due in part to the restrictive instantaneous adjustment assumption; one common econometric finding based on estimation of Eq. (6.8) is that the least squares estimate of μ is much smaller than the observed average capital/output ratio.

6.2.B Dealing with Alternative Distributed Lag Forms

A slightly generalized version of the original accelerator model is called the *flexible accelerator* and was put forward by Leendert M. Koyck [1954]. In this specification the adjustment of capital stock to its optimal level is no longer instantaneous, but instead is assumed to be a constant proportion λ of the gap between K^* and K. Denote the partial adjustment coefficient as λ_t, set $\lambda_t = \lambda$ for all t, specify that

$$I_{nt} = \lambda(K_t^* - K_{t-1}) \tag{6.9}$$

and then substitute Eq. (6.7) into Eq. (6.9), which yields

$$I_{nt} = K_t - K_{t-1} = \lambda\mu Y_t - \lambda K_{t-1} \tag{6.10}$$

or

$$K_t = \mu\lambda Y_t + (1 - \lambda)K_{t-1} \tag{6.11}$$

An interesting aspect of Eq. (6.11) is that one can write it for different time periods such as $t - 1$, $t - 2$, $t - 3$, etc. and then repeatedly substitute each such equation back into Eq. (6.11), which then yields a distributed lag formulation with geometrically declining weights

$$K_t = \mu[\lambda Y_t + \lambda(1 - \lambda)Y_{t-1} + \lambda(1 - \lambda)^2 Y_{t-2} + \cdots]$$

or

$$K_t - K_{t-1} = \mu[\lambda(Y_t - Y_{t-1}) + \lambda(1 - \lambda)(Y_{t-1} - Y_{t-2}) + \lambda(1 - \lambda)^2(Y_{t-2} - Y_{t-3}) + \cdots] \tag{6.12}$$

Two aspects of Eqs. (6.12) merit special comment. First, in the top equation of (6.12) the level of capital depends on the levels of current and lagged output, while in the second equation the change in capital, that is, net investment, depends on current and lagged changes in output. Because *levels* of investment depend on *changes* in output, this model of investment is called the accelerator model.

Second, a change in output in period t affects investment not only in period t, but also in future time periods, that is, the effect of output changes on investment is distributed over an infinite number of future time periods.

Conversely, investment in time period t is therefore the result of current and previous output changes. However, the more distant changes are not as important, since in Eq. (6.12) each successive lagged time period is weighted by a geometrically declining factor. For these reasons the partial adjustment specification (6.9) is often called a *geometric distributed lag* formulation.

The investment equation (6.10) is in terms of net investment. Assuming constant geometric decay at rate δ, one can add replacement investment δK_{t-1} to both sides of Eq. (6.10) and obtain the gross investment formulation

$$I_t = K_t - (1 - \delta)K_{t-1} = \lambda\mu Y_t + (\delta - \lambda)K_{t-1} \tag{6.13}$$

Notice that Eq. (6.13) does not have an intercept term (although in practice this equation is typically estimated with a constant term included) and that, provided that one knew the value of δ (needed to construct the K_t series), estimation by least squares would yield implicit estimates of μ and λ.

Because of the difficulties in obtaining reliable capital stock measures, some analysts prefer to estimate an alternative form of the accelerator model. Specifically, lag Eq. (6.13) by one time period, multiply both sides by $(1 - \delta)$, and then subtract the product from Eq. (6.13). This Koyck transformation yields

$$\begin{aligned} I_t - (1 - \delta)I_{t-1} &= \mu\lambda Y_t - (1 - \delta)\mu\lambda Y_{t-1} \\ &\quad + (\delta - \lambda)K_{t-1} - (1 - \delta)(\delta - \lambda)K_{t-2} \end{aligned}$$

which can be rewritten as

$$I_t - (1 - \delta)I_{t-1} = \mu\lambda Y_t - (1 - \delta)\mu\lambda Y_{t-1} + (\delta - \lambda)I_{t-1}$$

since $I_{t-1} = K_{t-1} - (1 - \delta)K_{t-2}$. Collecting terms, we finally obtain

$$I_t = \mu\lambda Y_t - (1 - \delta)\mu\lambda Y_{t-1} + (1 - \lambda)I_{t-1} \tag{6.14}$$

Equation (6.14) can be estimated without employing any data on capital stock. Moreover, an interesting feature of Eq. (6.14) is that one can also estimate rather than assume the rate of deterioration. Specifically, the least squares estimated parameter on the lagged dependent variable identifies λ, this estimate of λ can be used along with the coefficient estimate on Y_t to identify μ, and these estimates of μ and λ can then be employed along with the estimated coefficient on Y_{t-1} to identify δ.

Note, however, that since Eq. (6.14) contains a lagged dependent variable as a regressor, if the disturbance term appended to Eq. (6.14) follows a first-order autoregressive process, then estimation by ordinary least squares yields inconsistent and biased estimates of the true parameters. Further, because the lagged dependent variable appears as a regressor, one cannot use the traditional Durbin-Watson test statistic to test for autocorrelation. Instead, one can use something like Durbin's *m*- or *h*-test statistic procedure.[20]

An attractive feature of the accelerator model (6.13) is its simplicity: Investment is a function only of current and lagged output and the lagged capital stock. The underlying rationale is also intuitively simple. Since investment intentions must pass through the various stages of planning, contracting, and ordering before becoming expenditures and then might still be subject to delivery and gestation lags, the lagged output terms represent the gradual response of investment to changes in final demand. This sequence of lagged output terms can also be interpreted as encompassing output projections, since such projections are often based in part on extrapolated past sales patterns.

The lagged capital stock term in the accelerator model (6.13) can be interpreted as serving two purposes. First, since by assumption the capital/output ratio is fixed, the recent course of output is compared to the lagged capital stock, thereby providing a calibration on whether new investment expenditures are warranted. Second, the amount of replacement investment is typically assumed to be proportional to the capital stock, and so the amount of gross investment should be affected by the level of the lagged capital stock.

While the above accelerator model involves partial adjustment with a geometric distributed lag, there is of course no reason why coefficients on the successive lagged output terms must be constrained to follow a declining geometric pattern. Some empirical researchers have therefore simply inserted a number of lagged output terms as regressors into an equation such as Eq. (6.12) without imposing any restrictions on the coefficients.

Specifically, a maximum length of the lag period is chosen, say, m periods (where $m + 2 < T$, T being the number of observations), and then an equation like

$$I_t = a_0 + \sum_{i=0}^{m-1} b_i Y_{t-i} + b_K K_{t-1} + u_t \tag{6.15}$$

is estimated with no further coefficient restrictions imposed on the m output variables. In practice, m is typically chosen on the basis of a combination of experimentation, hypothesis testing, and judgment.

One problem with unrestricted distributed lag formulations such as Eq. (6.15) is that the lagged output terms typically tend to be highly correlated, and the resulting multicollinearity often generates large standard errors for the imprecisely estimated distributed lag coefficients, leading to the "garbage" results noted by Zvi Griliches in the quote at the beginning of this chapter.

The effects of such multicollinearity can be reduced by imposing restrictions on the time pattern of distributed lag coefficients (but not as many as are found in the highly restrictive declining geometric weight specifications, Eqs. (6.12) and (6.13)). Such restricted specifications include (1) the inverted-V lag distribution introduced by Frank de Leeuw [1962] (in which the coefficients increase linearly from $b_0 = 0$ to a peak lag at $m/2$ periods, m being an even number, and then decrease symmetrically to zero where $b_m = 0$), (2) the double-lag specification of Michael K. Evans [1967], resulting in an inverted-W distribution lag pattern, and (3) forcing the coefficients to lie along a finite polynomial, the analyst specifying the degree of the polynomial and the maximal lag m. This is often called the Almon lag and is due to Shirley

Almon [1965, 1968]. The choice of the degree of the polynomial and the length of the maximal lag of course leave considerable room for experimentation and judgment.

With each of these distributed lag representations, the choice of preferred specification is to some extent arbitrary and ad hoc. To reduce such arbitrariness and to highlight the important role of hypothesis testing in choosing a preferred specification, Dale W. Jorgenson [1966] introduced the *rational lag* function. Its essential feature is that it approximates a general infinite distributed lag formulation by a ratio of two finite polynomials. An attractive feature of the rational lag distribution is that it takes on as testable special cases the Almon, geometric, and other distributed lag specifications.

Notice that with the generalization of the geometric lag specification (6.15), no restrictions are placed on the m distributed lag parameters. This implies that the rational, Almon, inverted-V, geometric lag and other distributed lag formulations can be tested as special cases of Eq. (6.15), using traditional hypothesis-testing techniques, typically in the context of autoregressive disturbances. Hypothesis testing and the estimation of alternative distributed lag formulations have been discussed extensively in the literature; useful surveys include those by Zvi Griliches [1967] and by Marc Nerlove [1972].[21]

Regardless of the distributed lag formulation chosen, most economists today criticize the accelerator model for being too simplistic.[22] On the other hand, proponents argue that while other models may be preferable on theoretical criteria, the more complicated models (such as those permitting interest rates and taxes to affect optimal capital/output ratios) tend to generate unstable parameter estimates and cannot be estimated with acceptable precision.

6.2.C Empirical Implementations

We now come to an examination of empirical results based on the accelerator model of aggregate investment, a model that has been implemented by a very large number of researchers.[23] For our purposes it will be useful to examine a series of three empirical studies by Richard W. Kopcke [1977, 1982, 1985], who estimated this and other models using quarterly U.S. data, separately for nonresidential structures and producers' durable equipment, drawn from three time periods: (i) 1954:1–1977:4, (ii) 1958:1–1973:3, and (iii) 1956:1–1979:4. In each study, Kopcke allowed for autocorrelation and reported results based on a preferred specification. For studies (ii) and (iii), Kopcke employed the Almon lag and constrained parameters to lie along a third-degree polynomial, whereas in study (i) he left the lagged coefficients unconstrained. Kopcke's results, based on the notation in Eq. (6.15), are reproduced in Table 6.2 (standard error estimates were not reported).

A number of results in Table 6.2 merit special comment. First, regarding the distributed lag coefficients, the length of the preferred lag specification

Table 6.2 Parameter Estimates of Accelerator Investment Equation (6.15) Reported by Kopcke in Three Quarterly U.S. Studies

	Nonresidential Structures			Producers' Durable Equipment		
Parameter	Study (i)	Study (ii)	Study (iii)	Study (i)	Study (ii)	Study (iii)
a_0	3.11	6.74	33.04	−38.03	−60.00	−161.11
b_0	0.025	0.023	0.028	0.095	0.083	0.090
b_1	0.014	0.022	0.021	0.022	0.048	0.067
b_2	0.004	0.015	0.015	0.054	0.036	0.049
b_3	0.028	0.007	0.011	0.028	0.035	0.036
b_4	0.018	0.002	0.007		0.032	0.027
b_5		0.006	0.005		0.015	0.021
b_6			0.003			0.017
b_7			0.003			0.014
b_8			0.002			0.012
b_9			0.002			0.008
b_{10}			0.002			
b_{11}			0.002			
b_K	−0.094	−0.092	−0.177	−0.207	−0.227	−0.272
ρ	0.91	0.995	0.966	0.91	0.997	0.966

Notes: Study (i) covers 1958:1–1973:3; study (ii) covers 1954:1–1977:4; study (iii) covers 1956:1–1979:4. Lagged variables employ earlier observations.

changes depending on the time period estimated, the shortest lags being in the first study and the longest lags being in the last study, for both plant and equipment. In the first study, for structures, $m = 5$, while in the last study, $m = 12$. Also, for equal $t-i$ time displacements the b_i distributed lag coefficients tend to be larger for equipment than for plant. This is plausible, since the time lag for equipment investment is likely to be shorter than that involved in designing and constructing nonresidential structures. In the last two studies the b_i distributed lag coefficients tend to decrease as the time lag increases, but in the first study, for both plant and equipment the distributed lag coefficients follow a reclining-S pattern, initially falling, then increasing and again falling.

Second, in all three studies and for both types of investment goods, the estimated coefficient on the lagged capital stock term is negative, which from Eq. (6.13) suggests that the one-period partial adjustment parameter is larger than the rate of depreciation; incidentally, Kopcke reports that in his net capital stock calculations he employed an annual depreciation rate of about 5% for structures and about 15% for equipment.

Third, although specific test results are not reported, in all cases, first-order autocorrelation appears to be substantial; estimates of ρ range from a low of 0.91 to a high of 0.997. As we shall see, first-order autocorrelation appears to be pervasive in studies of investment demand, no matter what model is used.

This concludes our discussion of the accelerator model. Additional remarks concerning the performance of the accelerator model in estimation and forecasting will be given in Section 6.8, where the accelerator formulation is compared with other aggregate investment models. We now turn to a second model, the cash flow model of investment.

6.3 THE CASH FLOW MODEL

It has long been postulated that the availability of funds has a significant impact on investment behavior. In turn, it has also been argued that internal cash flow is the preeminent source of funds and, in particular, is more important than the availability of external debt or equity financing. The cash flow model posits investment spending as a variable proportion of internal cash flow. Since the supply of internal funds is obviously affected by the current level of profits, it has been suggested that the optimal capital stock K^* should be made to depend not on the level of output, as in the accelerator framework, but instead on variables capturing the level of profits or expected profits.[24]

Consider the specification by Yehuda Grunfeld [1960], who assumed that the optimal capital stock is a linear function of expected profits, as proxied by the market value of the firm, V_t:

$$K_t^* = \alpha + \beta V_t \tag{6.16}$$

With Eq. (6.16) substituted into Eq. (6.6), Grunfeld obtained an investment equation with an intercept term and with V_t replacing Y_t in Eq. (6.13):

$$I_t = \lambda\alpha + \lambda\beta V_t + (\delta - \lambda)K_{t-1} \tag{6.17}$$

Equation (6.17) therefore suggests that investment is very much affected by the external market value of the firm.

Among others, John R. Meyer and Edwin E. Kuh [1957] and James Duesenberry [1958][25] have argued that there are important imperfections in capital markets. If the risks associated with firms' increasing the ratio of their debt to earnings lead them to have strong preferences for the internal cash flow financing of investment, then one might want instead to replace V_t in Eq. (6.16) with a liquidity-type variable such as profits or retained earnings after taxes.

A common variable used to measure available funds is cash flow, defined as profits after taxes plus depreciation allowances less dividend payments to shareholders. Cash flows have historically accounted for a substantial proportion of firms' sources of funding for investments in plant and equipment.

Cash flow is not, however, the sole source of available funds. After cash flow the principal source of funds for investors is debt financing. Although debt financing may allow a firm to expand its capital budget, such financing often becomes considerably more expensive than its yield would suggest. For example, debt obligations may place constraints on capital budgeting options, they may increase the risk that is inherent in owning shares of the firm, and they might even eventually increase the risk of managers and owners losing control of their investments. Most empirical analysts also believe that the cost of debt financing exceeds its yield by an increasing margin as the firm's reliance on borrowed funds increases.[26]

A third source of funds for firms is the sale of equity. This type of financing is particularly important for firms whose current or prospective investment opportunities far exceed their cash flow. New equity financing can be very expensive for firms, however, since new equityholders are entitled to their share of any dividends paid by the corporation and because under U.S. tax law these dividend payments are not tax-deductible to the firm (unlike the interest payments on debt). This cost premium can be substantial. For example, Kopcke [1985, p. 25] notes that in 1984 the real cost of investment-grade bonds was about 3%, while the real cost of equity financing exceeded 6.5%.

In summary, according to the cash flow model a firm first commits its retained earnings to financing its capital budget. Only after internal cash flow is exhausted does the firm seek external debt or equity financing. Since internal cash flow serves as a measure of profitability and as an index of the firm's capacity to attract external financing, the amount of the firm's investment is postulated to depend on its available cash flow.

One ambiguity that emerges from the above interpretation on the importance of cash flow is whether cash flow affects the desired capital stock K^* or whether it instead operates by affecting the speed of adjustment λ from K to K^*. The literature is somewhat vague on this, but it is plausible to argue that both channels are potentially significant.[27] Note, however, that if cash flow affects the speed of adjustment, then λ is time-varying and endogenous, rather than fixed and exogenous as in Eqs. (6.13), (6.14), and (6.17). Specifications in which the firm chooses the time path of λ_t as part of its optimal investment process will be considered further in Section 6.7.

The cash flow model has been implemented in a variety of ways by a large number of researchers. In most applications a distributed lag of cash flow is specified, with cash flow in nominal dollars being deflated by the price index for new investment goods. To capture replacement investment and lagged adjustment, the lagged capital stock is also added as a regressor. Note that since the cash flow model (6.18) is very similar to the accelerator model (6.15) with cash flow variables merely replacing output variables, issues of estimation and hypothesis testing tend to be very similar in the two frameworks. For that reason a discussion of these issues is not repeated here.

For our purposes it is useful again to examine the empirical studies based on quarterly U.S. data by Richard Kopcke [1977, 1982, 1985], who estimated separate equations for nonresidential structures and producers' durable equipment. In the 1977 and 1985 studies, Kopcke estimated a cash flow model having the general form

$$I_t = a + \sum_{i=0}^{m-1} b_i(F/J)_{t-1} + cK_{t-1} + u_t \tag{6.18}$$

where the b_i, a, and c are unknown parameters to be estimated, F is internal cash flow in current dollars, and J is a price index for new capital. In his 1982 study, however, Kopcke estimated a somewhat different equation in which I_t/K_{t-1} was the dependent variable and a market value variable was added as a regressor. We defer further discussion on the use of market value and Tobin's q as regressors to Section 6.5, where the Tobin's q model is treated in greater detail. For studies (ii) and (iii), Kopcke employed the Almon lag and constrained parameters to lie along a third-degree polynomial, whereas in study (i) a fourth-degree polynomial was employed.

In Table 6.3, parameter estimates of preferred models from Kopcke's first (1958:1–1977:3) and third (1956:1–1979:4) studies are presented; he did not report standard errors. A number of points merit discussion.

First, regarding the distributed lag specification, the length and shape of the estimated lag distribution vary considerably among studies and assets. In the first study, for both equipment and structures the current period cash flow does not affect current investment at all, whereas in the third study the b_0 coefficient is the largest of the estimated distributed lag parameters. The estimated b_0 through b_4 distributed lag coefficients are always larger for equipment than for plant, implying that cash flow has a more substantial effect on equipment investment than on that for longer-lived plant. In study (i), some-

Table 6.3 Parameter Estimates of Cash Flow Investment Equation (6.18) Reported by Kopcke in Two Quarterly U.S. Studies

	Nonresidential Structures		Producers' Durable Equipment	
Parameter	Study (i)	Study (iii)	Study (i)	Study (iii)
a	0.59	12.71	−19.90	12.71
b_0	—	0.0836	—	0.3702
b_1	0.0681	0.0755	0.2069	0.1677
b_2	0.0222	0.0619	0.0968	0.0963
b_3	0.0421	0.0465	0.1288	0.0898
b_4	0.0546	0.0328	0.1576	0.0818
b_5	0.0381	0.0245	0.1211	0.0062
b_6	0.0224	—	0.0406	—
b_7	—	—	0.0203	—
b_K	0.051	—	0.104	—
ρ	0.83	0.956	0.81	0.936

Notes: Study (i) covers 1958:1–1973:3, while study (iii) covers 1956:1–1979:4. For study (i), Kopcke's [1977] estimated slope coefficients have been divided by 100 to make them comparable to Kopcke's [1985] study (iii). Lagged variables employ earlier observations.

what surprisingly, the length of the lag is 6 for structures and 7 for equipment, while in study (iii) the length is 5 for both assets. Note also that while the distributed lag coefficients in the last study decline as the length of time displacement increases, in the first study for both equipment and structures the estimated distributed lag pattern is saw-toothed, falling from $t-1$ to $t-2$, then gradually increasing to $t-4$, and finally falling again. Together, these estimates indicate a lack of stability over time in the estimated distributed lag coefficients for the cash flow model.

Second, in terms of the effect of the lagged capital stock on current gross investment, only in the first study is this variable included as a right-hand variable, and here its estimated value is positive in both the plant and equipment investment equations. In the last study this variable is omitted from the preferred equation, perhaps because its estimated value was statistically insignificantly different from zero. Note that such insignificance is not entirely unexpected; our previous discussion of the accelerator model implied that the expected coefficient on lagged capital stock cannot be signed a priori, since by Eq. (6.13) it represents $(\delta - \lambda)$. Hence if $b_K \approx (\delta - \lambda)$ is insignificantly different from zero, this may simply reflect a finding that with the cash flow model, the estimate of λ is approximately equal to that of δ.

Finally, although statistical tests of significance are not reported, for both equipment and structures and in both time periods, considerable first-order autocorrelation of residuals is present. In the first study the estimated ρ are 0.83 and 0.81, while in the last study, estimates of ρ are 0.956 and 0.936.

This concludes our discussion of the cash flow model, although market value as a determinant of investment will be addressed further in the Tobin's q model of Section 6.5. Moreover, the performance of the cash flow model in estimation and forecasting will be considered again in Section 6.8, where the cash flow formulation will be compared with other aggregate investment models.

6.4 THE NEOCLASSICAL MODEL

Earlier, it was noted that one highly restrictive assumption embodied in the accelerator model of investment is that the capital/output ratio is fixed, an assumption that implies that substitution possibilities among capital, labor, and other inputs are constrained to be zero. Similarly, in the cash flow model, only internal cash flow affects the optimal capital stock, and again there is no role for input substitution. By contrast, economic theory textbooks have long emphasized the role of input substitution as a critical element in the economic theory of cost and production. This inconsistency has been highlighted by Dale Jorgenson [1963, p. 247]: "There is no greater gap between economic theory and econometric practice than that which characterizes the literature on business investment in fixed capital." In the decade that followed, Jorgenson and his associates worked at closing this gap, and their pioneering studies resulted in a model that is widely used to this day, namely, the neoclassical model of investment. Since the neoclassical model currently receives the greatest attention from econometricians, we consider it in some detail in this section.

The distinguishing feature of the neoclassical model is that it is based on an explicit model of optimization behavior that relates the desired capital stock to interest rates, output, capital prices, and tax policies. As we shall see, however, the major pitfall of the neoclassical model is that while it provides a clear framework for understanding factors affecting the firm's optimal demand for capital, it does not rationalize investment or movements toward the optimal capital stock. More specifically, as Nobel Laureate Trygve Haavelmo had explained already in 1960, "Demand for a finite addition to the stock of capital can lead to any rate of investment, from almost zero to infinity, depending on the additional hypotheses we introduce regarding the speed of reaction of capital users."[28] As a result, although econometric models of investment based on the neoclassical paradigm have explicit theoretical foundations concerning the optimal capital stock, their empirical implementation has until very recently required appending to this demand model an ad hoc specification of the adjustment process of K to K^*. Later in this chapter, however, we will discuss recent developments that allow λ_t, the speed of adjustment, to be a choice variable in the firm's overall optimization process.

6.4.A Theory

Define profits π at time t as revenue minus costs. In the case of a firm using two inputs, capital and labor, profits can be written as

$$\pi_t \equiv P_t Y_t - w_t L_t - c_t K_t \tag{6.19}$$

where P is the price of output, Y is value-added output quantity, w is the wage rate, L is the hours of labor services, c is the cost of capital services, and K is the quantity of capital services. (Recall that an assumption made in virtually all investment models is that the quantity of capital services is a constant proportion of the capital stock.) The measurement of c, often called the *user cost of capital*, will be discussed in further detail later in this section.

Jorgenson specified that the firm chooses time paths of inputs and output so as to maximize the present value of profits, subject to a neoclassical production function constraint

$$Y_t = f(K_t, L_t) \tag{6.20}$$

Since capital goods are durable, however, by purchasing long-lived plant and equipment, firms could potentially lock themselves into a situation in which they might not be able to dispose of unwanted capital goods. This implies that the present value optimization problem facing a firm is a very complex one involving uncertainties concerning lifetimes of capital goods, future input prices, and future output demands. How can such a complex problem be made more manageable and amenable to empirical implementation? To attain empirical tractability, Jorgenson and his associates made a number of important simplifying assumptions.

First, Jorgenson assumed the existence of a perfect market for used or secondhand capital goods, as well as perfect markets for all inputs and output. The existence of a perfect used market for capital goods implied that firms did not need to worry about locking themselves in by purchasing long-lived investment goods, since such goods could always be sold on the secondhand market at prices just equal to the present value of their expected services over their expected remaining lifetimes. Further, the existence of a perfect market for secondhand capital goods allowed Jorgenson to view firms as renting capital goods to themselves during each time period, charging themselves an implicit rental price for capital, a price that is called the *user cost of capital.*

Second, in his theoretical framework, Jorgenson assumed that the adjustment of K to K^* was costless. Like others before him, he assumed that the physical decay of capital goods followed an exponential pattern. Finally, Jorgenson calculated the capital stock using the perpetual inventory relation (6.4).

The above assumptions brought about a major simplification of the optimization problem facing firms. Specifically, Jorgenson showed that under these conditions the very complex present value optimization problem reduced to a sequence of one-period profit maximization problems for which the firm chooses optimal values of K_t, L_t, and Y_t so as to maximize one-period profits (6.19) subject to the production function constraint (6.20).

We now examine this one-period optimization problem in further detail. Under the above profit maximization conditions, use of the traditional Lagrangian multiplier procedure yields the familiar necessary conditions for optimality, namely, for capital,

$$P_t \cdot \frac{\partial Y_t}{\partial K_t} = c_t \rightarrow \frac{\partial Y_t}{\partial K_t} \equiv MPP_{K,t} = \frac{c_t}{P_t} \tag{6.21}$$

and for labor,

$$P_t \cdot \frac{\partial Y_t}{\partial L_t} = w_t \rightarrow \frac{\partial Y_t}{\partial L_t} \equiv MPP_{L,t} = \frac{w_t}{P_t} \tag{6.22}$$

where $MPP_{K,t}$ and $MPP_{L,t}$ denote the marginal physical products of K and L, respectively. These equations simply restate the familiar result that profit-maximizing firms will choose that set of inputs such that for each input, the marginal benefit of employing another unit of the input (the additional real output) just equals the marginal cost of employing another unit of the input (the additional real wage or real user cost of capital).

To implement an equation like Eq. (6.21) empirically, one needs to specify an explicit form of the production function f in Eq. (6.20), derive the corresponding expression for the marginal product of capital, and then solve for that level of K^* such that the marginal physical product of capital just equals the real user cost of capital, as in Eq. (6.21). In turn, this requires a measure of the user cost of capital c_t and a mathematical form for the production function f in Eq. (6.20).

6.4.B On Measuring the User Cost of Capital

Let us first examine the user cost of capital. Unlike labor input, for which wage rate data are typically readily available, the one-period user cost of capital is seldom directly observed. Although some types of capital have active rental markets (e.g., airplanes), in most cases, firms purchase capital inputs and consume them entirely by themselves. An implication of this is that because of the lack of available data, one must typically infer indirectly the user cost of capital that firms implicitly charge themselves to use their own capital inputs. If the secondhand market is assumed to be perfect and firms are indifferent between renting and owning capital, the implicit user cost of capital that firms charge themselves must just equal the price that firms could fetch were they to rent their capital to others.

In their pioneering study on the effects of tax policy on investment, Robert E. Hall and Dale W. Jorgenson [1967] emphasized that the rental price of capital must incorporate at least four effects. First, there is the opportunity cost of having funds tied up in plant and equipment. As before, let the asset price for new capital goods be J_t, and let the current one-period interest rate yield be r_t. In such a case the opportunity cost of capital equals $r_t \cdot J_t$. Second, assuming that capital decays at a constant one-period rate of δ%, the renter would need to compensate the owner for depreciation, and this depreciation would equal $\delta \cdot J_t$. Third, in addition to effects due to depreciation, durable capital goods experience price changes over time that result in capital gains or losses to their owners. Let the expected percentage change in the asset price be $\Delta J_t/J_t$. In the Hall-Jorgenson formulation the user cost of capital is the sum of the above three effects, that is,

$$c_t = J_t(r_t + \delta - \Delta J_t/J_t) \qquad \textbf{(6.23)}$$

Finally, Hall and Jorgenson noted that Eq. (6.23) should be adjusted to take into account the effects of various taxes. The introduction of taxes into the user cost formula involves an implicit assumption that firms are unable to shift taxes forward to consumers and that firms' user costs are therefore affected by taxes.[29] Through their effects on the user cost of capital, various tax policies can then be related to investment spending.

As Hall and Jorgenson emphasized, since various types of taxes affect after-tax returns, the incorporation of tax effects into the user cost of capital formula depends on the particular statutory provisions of the relevant tax laws. In the United States, such relevant taxes include the federal and state corporate income taxes, accelerated depreciation provisions, investment tax

ROBERT E. HALL

Computing the Effects of Tax Policy on Investment

As his undergraduate thesis in economics at the University of California–Berkeley in Spring 1964, Robert E. Hall elaborated on the neoclassical model of investment developed by his thesis supervisor, Dale W. Jorgenson. The following September, Hall enrolled as a graduate student at MIT, and during his first year he took a public finance course from E. Cary Brown. Public finance interested Hall, and the following summer, Hall and Jorgenson resumed working together in Berkeley, jointly deriving the famous rental price formula that incorporated the effects of tax policy. Their resulting article in the *American Economic Review*, "Tax Policy and Investment Behavior," was the first extensive examination of tax policy in a neoclassical model of investment behavior.

Hall's contributions to computation in econometrics go far beyond his work in investment modeling. When Dale Jorgenson asked him to organize software to implement empirically the computation of the effects of tax policy on investment, Hall found the available software woefully inadequate. Working originally on an IBM 1620 machine that IBM had nick-named CADET (*C*ouldn't *A*dd, *D*idn't *E*ven *T*ry—it used a table look-up to add rather than doing addition internally), Hall set about to writing the computer code for a user-friendly regression program. MIT graduate students began using the program in 1966, and after naming the program TSP (*T*ime *S*eries *P*rocessor), Hall revamped it completely in 1967, making it more modular and adding nonlinear estimation features. Hall credits Mark Eisner with helping him enormously, particularly in learning how to program analytic differentiation.

When Hall assumed an academic position at Berkeley in 1967, he took TSP with him; and with funding support to Jorgenson and Hall from David Wood of the U.S. Executive Office of the President, Office of Emergency Preparedness, TSP was essentially completed by 1968. Interestingly, much of the TSP programming took place on a remote terminal to a UNIVAC 1108 (complete with a printer, a card reader, and a 2400-baud modem that hardly ever worked), on the ground floor of a Baptist seminary, within easy walking distance of the famous 1960s People's Park student antiwar demonstrations at Berkeley.

Robert E. Hall was born in Palo Alto in 1943, received his B.A. degree from Berkeley in 1964, and received his Ph.D. from MIT in 1967. After three years at Berkeley, Hall returned to MIT, where he stayed until 1978, when he accepted an offer from Stanford University. Currently, Hall is Professor of Economics at Stanford, is a Senior Fellow at the Hoover Institution, and is Director of the Research Program on Economic Fluctuations of the National Bureau of Economic Research. Hall's research is primarily in macroeconomics, focusing on issues of inflation, unemployment, taxation, and monetary policy. With John Taylor he is coauthor of *Macroeconomics: Theory, Performance and Policy*. He has been elected a Fellow of the Econometric Society and of the American Academy of Arts and Sciences.

credits, capital gains taxes, and federal, state, and local property taxes. One user cost formula that accounts for the presence of such taxes and is commonly used in investment studies is a slightly revised version of the Hall-Jorgenson equation, derived by Laurits R. Christensen and Dale W. Jorgenson [1969]. This modified user cost formula is written as

$$c_t = TX_t \cdot [J_t r_{t-1} + \delta \cdot J_t - \Delta J_t] + b_t J_t \tag{6.24}$$

where b_t is the effective rate of property taxes and TX_t is the effective rate of taxation on capital income given by

$$TX_t \equiv \frac{1 - \Upsilon_t \cdot z_t - k_t}{1 - \Upsilon_t} \tag{6.25}$$

where Υ_t is the effective corporate income tax rate, z_t is the present value of depreciation deductions for tax purposes on a dollar's investment over the lifetime of the good, and k_t is the effective rate of the investment tax credit.

A rather serious practical problem with empirically implementing the neoclassical model of investment is that there are a number of difficult and unsettled issues in how one obtains measures of the various components in the tax-adjusted user cost of capital formulae (6.24) and (6.25). Several of these problems merit special attention.

First, to be consistent with the underlying theory, researchers usually seek data on marginal effective tax rates, not average rates. However, since tax law interpretation is complex, it is often very difficult to obtain reliable data on effective marginal tax rates. Note also that in the United States, corporate taxes (and, for that matter, subsidies) are levied at the federal, state, and local levels of government. Effective tax rate calculations should take into account these various levels and interactions of taxes and subsidies. Because of the complexity in undertaking such calculations, however, some analysts use as their measure of tax impacts the average effective tax rate or, in certain cases, marginal statutory tax rates.[30] Further, a number of U.S. and international studies have concluded that these effective and statutory tax rates vary considerably among differing types of assets, although the 1986 Tax Reform Act in the United States was designed in part to reduce such variations.[31] This suggests that in studying the effects of taxes on investment it is important to distinguish among the various types of investment goods.

A second set of issues in implementing the tax-adjusted user cost of capital empirically involves choosing "the" interest rate yield r_t. Since firms have available various possible sources of funding, including internal cash flow and external debt or equity, and since each of these sources can have distinct costs, it is not entirely clear how one should compress these various costs into a single r_t measure. In practice, researchers have used a variety of variables as their measure of r_t, including a government risk-free bond yield, a Moody's corporate bond yield such as the Baa yield, weighted averages of debt and equity costs, and ex post average internal rates of return. Econometric estimates of the neoclassical investment model parameters will depend, of course, on what measure of r_t is incorporated into the user cost formula (6.24).[32]

A third issue involved in implementing empirically the user cost of capital formula (6.24) concerns measurement of the capital gains term $\Delta J_t \equiv J_t - J_{t-1}$. This capital gains term is typically envisaged as incorporating *expected* capital gains, and so the empirical researcher must deal with the issue of measuring unobserved expectations. In practice, Christensen and Jorgenson assume perfect foresight and replace expected with realized new investment goods prices, while others have assumed static expectations, either in levels or in growth rates. Numerous alternative approaches have also been examined empirically, and it is clear that estimates of investment equations are somewhat sensitive to how one incorporates nonstatic expectations.[33] We shall return to a discussion of expectations later in this chapter (as well as in Chapter 10).

Each of these measurement issues is in principle important. One clear implication is that with the neoclassical investment model, considerable care must be taken in empirically assessing the sensitivity of one's results to alternative measures of the tax rate variables, the interest rate, and the capital gains term in user cost formulae such as Eqs. (6.24) and (6.25).

6.4.C Toward Empirical Implementation

Let us now return to the estimating equation (6.21), which serves as the basis of the neoclassical investment model. In this equation the optimal capital stock K^* is obtained by finding that level of capital at which its marginal physical product equals the real user cost. To implement this equation econometrically, one must therefore assume a specific form of the production function and obtain the marginal physical product by taking the partial derivative with respect to capital.

In the investment studies by Hall and Jorgenson and by Jorgenson a simple Cobb-Douglas form of the production function was assumed (with the implied capital-labor substitution elasticity equaling unity):

$$Y_t = A \cdot K_t^\alpha \cdot L_t^\beta \tag{6.26}$$

where, under the assumption of constant returns to scale, $\alpha + \beta = 1$. Differentiating Eq. (6.26) with respect to K_t, rearranging, and substituting into Eq. (6.21) yields

$$\alpha(Y_t/K_t) = c_t/P_t$$

This equation is then solved for the optimal capital stock K^*:

$$K_t^* = \alpha \cdot (P_t/c_t) \cdot Y_t \tag{6.27}$$

Notice that if the firm is assumed to maximize profits, then Y_t in Eq. (6.27) is an endogenous choice variable for the firm, while if it is instead assumed only that the firm minimizes costs, then Y_t is exogenous.

In his empirical research, Jorgenson assumed that Y_t was exogenous. Moreover, while his theoretical model was based on instantaneous adjustment (zero adjustment costs were assumed), in his empirical implementation, Jorgenson specified partial adjustment in the form of a distributed lag specification. This apparent inconsistency between theory and practice was rationalized by arguing that while the firm always attempted instantaneous adjustment, such attempts were perpetually frustrated by unanticipated delivery delays.

More specifically, in each period the firm was assumed to place orders for new net investment so that, had these orders been filled, it would have been the case that $K_t^* = K_t$, $K_{t-1}^* = K_{t-1}$, and so on. It therefore follows that

$$IO_t = K_t^* - K_{t-1}^* \equiv \Delta K_t^* \tag{6.28}$$

where IO_t is investment orders in time period t. Letting ϕ_j represent the proportion of all orders that take j periods to be delivered, and assuming that these ϕ_j are constant over time, Jorgenson related current net investment spending I_{nt} to a distributed lag function of current and previous investment orders $IO_{t-\tau}$, then, via Eq. (6.28), to current and previous changes in the desired or optimal capital stock $K_{t-\tau}^*$, and finally, using Eq. (6.27), to current and lagged output and real user cost, thereby ultimately obtaining

$$I_{nt} = \sum_{j=0}^{\infty} \phi_j IO_{t-j} = \sum_{j=0}^{\infty} \phi_j \, \Delta K_{t-j}^* = \sum_{j=0}^{\infty} \alpha\phi_j(P \cdot Y/c)_{t-j} \tag{6.29}$$

Provided that no orders were cancelled, the distributed lag parameters ϕ_j should sum to unity.

Equation (6.29) is in terms of net investment. Since replacement investment is proportional to the capital stock, Jorgenson added $\delta \cdot K_{t-1}$ to both sides of Eq. (6.29), thereby obtaining the estimating equation

$$I_t = \sum_{j=0}^{\infty} \alpha\phi_j(P \cdot Y/c)_{t-j} + \delta \cdot K_{t-1} \tag{6.30}$$

Jorgenson [1963] appended an additive "white noise" disturbance term to Eq. (6.30) and then approximated the infinite lag by using the rational lag specification discussed in Section 6.3.

Working with a number of associates over an extended time period, Jorgenson has reported estimates of the gross investment equation (6.30) using several differing measures of the r_t, tax variables, and expected capital gains components in the user cost formula (6.24). Some of this work is with data at an aggregated sectoral level (e.g., total manufacturing), while other studies are based on data from individual firms.[34]

One important empirical implication of virtually all of Jorgenson's empirical research on investment is that investment spending is very much influenced by tax policy that affects the user cost of capital. Notice that in the Hall-Jorgenson neoclassical framework, tax policy directly affects investment via changing the user cost of capital, whereas with the accelerator model, tax policy has only an indirect effect through induced changes in output. With the cash flow model, tax policy can have an impact, depending on whether cash flow is calculated by using before- or after-tax net revenues.

A rather common and troubling result based on Jorgenson's research, however, is that the estimate of α is very small, often less than 0.05, whereas on the basis of the Cobb-Douglas production function (6.26), one would expect a larger estimate of around 0.25.[35] While some analysts attribute this small estimate to measurement error, the source is still a matter of some controversy.

Jorgenson's neoclassical model has been generalized in a number of ways. First, if one takes a logarithmic transformation of Eq. (6.27), then differentiates with respect to the ln c_t and compares this with the partial derivative with respect to ln Y_t, it is clear that the elasticity of optimal capital with respect to output is $+1$, while that with respect to the user cost of capital is -1, that is, the elasticities are equal in magnitude but differ in sign. When one adds the distributed lag specification (6.29) to the optimal capital stock relation (6.27), the short-run, period-by-period responses of investment to changes in output and to changes in the user cost are still equal to each other (differing in sign), but now of course they are not necessarily equal to $+1$ or -1; rather, provided that the ϕ_i sum to unity, the short-run user cost responses sum to -1, while those for output sum to $+1$.

This equality of lagged investment responses to output and user costs has been questioned by Charles W. Bischoff [1971a], who argues that the response of investment to output changes should be more rapid than that to changes in user cost. More specifically, assume that capital is substitutable with labor before capital is put into place (ex ante substitutability, often called "putty") but cannot be substituted for labor once it is put into place (ex post zero substitutability, often called "clay"). Now suppose that the user cost of capital unexpectedly fell and that it was expected to remain at this lower level. This would bring about an increase in the optimal capital/labor ratio, but because of the putty-clay nature of the capital stock, the existing capital stock cannot be remolded to adapt to the new capital/labor ratio. Rather, the effects of the capital user cost change can be realized only as the older capital stock is retired or as total capacity is increased. By contrast, when output increases unexpectedly, new capital equipment is required immediately, having the same capital/labor operating attributes as the existing capital stock, and its installation is not impeded by the need to retire existing equipment first.

An important implication of this putty-clay framework is therefore that the response of investment to an increase in output should be shorter and more rapid than the response to a decrease in the user cost of capital. On the basis of this reasoning, Bischoff generalized the change in optimal capital relation (6.29), allowing for the effect of the real user cost to differ from that of output. This resulted in an investment order equation of the general form

$$IO_t = \Delta K_t^* = \alpha(P/c)_t(Y_t - Y_{t-1}) = \alpha(P/c)_t Y_t - \alpha(P/c)_t Y_{t-1} \quad \textbf{(6.31)}$$

Current net investment was then specified again to be the sum of current and lagged investment orders, where, however, the lag coefficients on output differed from those on user cost as follows:

$$I_{nt} = \sum_{j=0}^{\infty} IO_{t-j} = \alpha \sum_{j=0}^{\infty} \phi_j(P/c)_{t-j} Y_{t-j} - \alpha \sum_{j=0}^{\infty} \omega_j(P/c)_{t-j} Y_{t-j-1} \quad \textbf{(6.32)}$$

To capture the effects of replacement investment, δK_{t-1} is added to both sides of Eq. (6.32). Further, in most empirical implementations the infinite lag is approximated by using a finite lag, resulting in an equation of the form

$$I_t = a_0 + \sum_{j=0}^{m-1} b_j(P/c)_{t-j} Y_{t-j} - \sum_{j=0}^{m-1} c_j(P/c)_{t-j} Y_{t-j-1} + \delta K_{t-1} \quad \textbf{(6.33)}$$

where the b_j and c_j parameters are functions of the underlying α, ϕ_j, and ω_j parameters in Eq. (6.32). Notice that if one takes and subtracts the derivative $\partial I_t / \partial \ln (c/P)_{t-j}$ from $\partial I_t / \partial \ln Y_{t-j}$, this difference equals $c_j(P/c)_{t-j} Y_{t-j-1}$, which is positive if c_j is positive. Thus a 1% increase in output at time $t - j$ has a larger effect on I_t than a 1% decrease in the user cost of capital at time $t - j$, provided that $c_j > 0$.

In his empirical research, Bischoff found that the c_j were primarily positive and statistically significant. The null hypothesis that the price and output variables act with the same lag distribution was decisively rejected; that is, the joint null hypothesis that $c_j = 0, j = 0, \ldots, m - 1$ was rejected.[36]

A different generalization of the Jorgenson specification involved the use of a less restrictive production function underlying the marginal productivity relation (6.21). As was noted earlier, with the Cobb-Douglas specification (6.26) the elasticity of the optimal capital stock with respect to the real user cost of capital is -1; this result is obtained by taking a logarithmic transformation of Eq. (6.27) and then differentiating with respect to $\ln c_t$. A more general production function is called the CES (constant elasticity of substitution) function, and while it constrains the elasticity of substitution to be constant, it does not constrain it to equal unity.

Although a detailed discussion of properties of the CES function is outside our current focus (see Chapter 9 for further analysis), for our purposes it is sufficient to note that with the CES function, the marginal productivity relation (6.21) yields an expression for the optimal capital stock,

$$K_t^* = \alpha' \cdot (P_t/c_t)^{\sigma} \cdot Y_t \tag{6.34}$$

where σ is the elasticity of substitution between capital and labor. Note that when $\sigma = 1$, Eq. (6.34) collapses to the Cobb-Douglas optimal capital stock relation (6.27). Equation (6.34) provides the basis of an investment equation in which the long-run price response of investment to the user cost of capital is not constrained a priori to equal unity, but instead is estimated.

Earlier, it was noted that with the optimal capital stock relation (6.27) based on the Cobb-Douglas production function with constant returns to scale, the elasticity of capital with respect to output was also constrained to equal unity. Following Robert Eisner and M. Ishaq Nadiri [1968], one can allow returns to scale to differ from unity. With the CES function this implies an optimal capital relation based on the marginal productivity expression (6.21) of the form

$$K_t^* = \alpha' \cdot (P_t/c_t)^{\sigma} \cdot Y_t^{[\sigma+(1-\sigma)/\upsilon]} = \alpha' \cdot (P_t/c_t)^{\sigma} \cdot Y_t^{\eta} \tag{6.35}$$

where υ is the returns to scale parameter and $\eta \equiv \sigma + (1 - \sigma)/\upsilon$ is the elasticity of optimal capital stock with respect to output.

Instead of employing linear specifications, Eisner and Nadiri used a logarithmic regression equation based on Eq. (6.35). Specifically, taking first differences, they began with an equation of the form

$$\Delta \ln K^* = \sigma \, \Delta \ln (P/c) + \eta \, \Delta \ln Y$$

and then permitted different lagged responses to (P/c) and Y, thereby obtaining the equation

$$\Delta \ln K_t = \sum_{j=0}^{m-1} [\phi_{cj} \Delta \ln (P/c)_{t-j} + \phi_{Yj} \Delta \ln Y_{t-j}] - \sum_{i=1}^{s} \omega_i \Sigma \, \Delta \ln K_{t-i} \tag{6.36}$$

Estimates of the long-run price and output responses were shown to equal

$$\sigma = \sum_{j=0}^{m-1} \phi_{cj} \Bigg/ \left(1 + \sum_{i=1}^{s} \omega_i\right), \qquad \eta = \sum_{j=0}^{m-1} \phi_{Yj} \Bigg/ \left(1 + \sum_{i=1}^{s} \omega_i\right) \tag{6.37}$$

In implementing estimation of Eq. (6.36) empirically, Eisner and Nadiri experimented with different lag lengths for m and s and found that, regardless of the lag specification, the estimate of σ was very small (certainly less than unity and occasionally insignificantly different from zero).

Note that if one constrains the price responses to be zero ($\sigma = 0$) and the output elasticity $\eta = 1$, then the generalized neoclassical model in Eq. (6.36) reduces to the accelerator model considered earlier. The Eisner-Nadiri results imply some support for this simple accelerator specification and suggest that even when tax policy affects the user cost of capital, its direct effect on investment is nil, since investment is not sensitive to price changes (although it appears to be affected considerably by output changes).

An important empirical controversy on the effectiveness of tax policy in stimulating investment has focused in large part on the estimated value of σ, which Jorgenson and his co-workers assumed to equal unity and which others estimated, obtaining results implying that σ was close to zero.

Neither Jorgenson nor Eisner and Nadiri worried much at all about stochastic specification, simply adding disturbance terms to their equations and then estimating parameters using ordinary least squares. Recall that in Section 6.1 a number of reasons were given suggesting why the stochastic specification might follow an autoregressive process. Such considerations led Bischoff [1969] to specify a levels form of Eq. (6.36):

$$\ln K_t = a + \sum_{j=0}^{m-1} [\phi_{cj} \ln (P/c)_{t-j} + \phi_{Yj} \ln Y_{t-j}] - \sum_{i=1}^{s} \omega_i \ln K_{t-i} + u_t \tag{6.38}$$

where u_t followed a first-order autoregressive process, $u_t = \rho u_{t-1} + \epsilon_t$.

If $\rho = 0$, then OLS estimates of Eq. (6.38) would be consistent, but if $\rho \neq 0$, then because the lagged dependent variable is a regressor, estimation by OLS will yield inconsistent estimates of the parameters. On the other hand, if $\rho = 1$, then the usual procedure for dealing with first-order autocorrelation by taking generalized first differences would yield the first difference equation (6.36) estimated by Eisner and Nadiri, whose parameters in such a case could be estimated consistently by OLS. However, if ρ is between 0 and 1, regardless of whether one estimates Eq. (6.36) or Eq. (6.38), since each specification contains a lagged dependent variable as a regressor, consistent and efficient estimates of the parameters can be obtained only by using a generalized least squares estimator that allows for first-order autocorrelation.

Using the same data as that of Eisner and Nadiri (also used earlier by Jorgenson) and the Hildreth-Lu estimator, Bischoff obtained results that differed dramatically from those of Eisner and Nadiri. Bischoff's conditional maximum likelihood estimate of ρ was 0.20 (although he discovered an inferior local maximum at $\rho = 0.92$). However, the estimated likelihood function was quite flat, with a 95% confidence interval for ρ ranging from -0.02 to 0.97 for one set of data and from -0.2 to 1.0 for another set. Therefore Bischoff could not reject the null hypothesis that $\rho = 0$, and whether $\rho = 1$ was rejected was marginal.

Bischoff then proceeded to estimate σ and η, assuming a number of values for ρ. The only situation in which Bischoff was able to reject the null hypothesis that $\sigma = 1$ was when $\rho = 1$ (the Eisner-Nadiri specification), whereas in all other cases for $0 < \rho < 1$, the Jorgenson-maintained assumption that $\sigma = 1$ could not be rejected. Hence, although Bischoff's point estimates of σ were less than unity, the Eisner-Nadiri result that σ was significantly different from (less than) unity appeared to be a direct consequence of their implicit assumption that $\rho = 1$. In essence, therefore, Bischoff established the empirical significance of the autoregressive stochastic specification; unfortunately, the data were not rich enough to enable him to discriminate effectively among competing hypotheses concerning the value of σ. Note, however, that Bischoff did not examine higher-order autoregressive or other moving average processes that might have been suggested by the underlying theory.

The controversy over how large the response of investment is to changes in the user cost of capital has filled many pages of professional economic journals, and for reasons of brevity we will not consider this literature further here.[37] For our purposes, however, it is useful to examine briefly a series of three recent empirical estimates of the neoclassical investment model reported by Kopcke. Recall that Kopcke's studies cover differing time periods, study (i) encompassing the pre-OPEC oil embargo period 1958:1–1973:3, study (ii) including earlier as well as post-OPEC responses during 1954:1–1977:4, and study (iii) ranging from 1956:1 to 1979:4.

The investment equation specified and estimated by Kopcke is Eq. (6.33) and is based on the constant-returns-to-scale Cobb-Douglas production function, which assumes $\sigma = \eta = 1$. It permits distinct distributed lag responses of investment to changes in the user cost of capital and to changes in output, and it allows for first-order autocorrelation. In studies (ii) and (iii), Kopcke employs the Almon technique and constrains the distributed lag parameters to lie along a third-degree polynomial, while in study (i) a fourth-degree polynomial is specified. Although Kopcke does not report standard errors for his estimated parameters, he states [1982, p. 30] that the length of the lag was determined "by considering the sensibility of the estimated coefficients and their standard errors." Kopcke's parameter estimates for equipment are reproduced in Table 6.4, while those for structures appear in Table 6.5.

As is seen in Table 6.4, for equipment the preferred estimated neoclassical model has a very large number of estimated parameters: in studies (ii) and (iii) a total of 26 distributed lag parameters are estimated, 13 each for the output (the b's) and the user cost (the c's) lagged variables. In all three studies, for equipment, both the estimated b_j and the estimated c_j parameters follow an inverted-V pattern, first increasing to $j = 2$ (study (i)) or $j = 4$ or 5 (studies (ii) and (iii)) and then falling. Also, the estimated c_j are often as large as the b_j

able 6.4 Parameter Estimates of Neoclassical Investment Equation (6.33) for Producers' Durable Equipment Reported by Kopcke in Three Quarterly U.S. Studies

'arameter	Study (i)	Study (ii)	Study (iii)	Parameter	Study (i)	Study (ii)	Study (iii)
a_0	−18.24	−11.60	8.41	c_0	0.0060	0.019	0.0190
b_0	0.0063	0.020	0.0202	c_1	0.0080	0.029	0.0277
b_1	0.0079	0.030	0.0281	c_2	0.0086	0.037	0.0337
b_2	0.0087	0.037	0.0337	c_3	0.0081	0.042	0.0373
b_3	0.0085	0.042	0.0371	c_4	0.0068	0.044	0.0389
b_4	0.0074	0.044	0.0387	c_5	0.0050	0.045	0.0386
b_5	0.0056	0.044	0.0386	c_6	0.0030	0.043	0.0369
b_6	0.0035	0.043	0.0371	c_7	0.0013	0.040	0.0339
b_7	0.0015	0.040	0.0344	c_8	0.0001	0.036	0.0301
b_8	0.0003	0.036	0.0308	c_9		0.031	0.0257
b_9		0.031	0.0265	c_{10}		0.025	0.0210
b_{10}		0.026	0.0217	c_{11}		0.018	0.0162
b_{11}		0.020	0.0166	c_{12}		0.011	0.0118
b_{12}		0.013	0.0116	ρ	0.60	0.839	0.785
b_K	0.141	0.141	0.135				

Notes: Study (i) covers 1958:1–1973:3; study (ii) covers 1954:1–1977:4; study (iii) covers 1956:1–1979:4. In studies (ii) and (iii) the trailing term on the Almon lag is constrained to equal zero. Lagged variables employ earlier observations.

for equal time displacements j. Test results on the joint null hypothesis that the $c_j = 0, j = 1, \ldots, m - 1$, are not reported; however, the fact that Kopcke retains them suggests that they are statistically significant.

A second feature of the neoclassical investment model for equipment is that the estimated coefficient on the lagged capital stock is rather stable over the three studies, ranging only from 0.135 to 0.141. Further, in terms of sta-

ble 6.5 Parameter Estimates of Neoclassical Investment Equation (6.33) for Nonresidential Structures Reported by Kopcke in Three Quarterly U.S. Studies

'ameter	Study (i)	Study (ii)	Study (iii)	Parameter	Study (i)	Study (ii)	Study (iii)
a_0	16.84	−1.78	−50.71	b_6	0.00005	0.00045	0.0006
b_0	—	0.00074	0.0014	b_7	0.00009	0.00035	0.0005
b_1	0.00029	0.00076	0.0011	b_8	0.00015	0.00026	0.0004
b_2	0.00029	0.00074	0.0010	b_9	0.00016	0.00017	0.0004
b_3	0.00021	0.00069	0.0008	b_{10}	0.00003	0.00009	0.0003
b_4	0.00012	0.00063	0.0007	b_{11}	−0.00035	0.00003	0.0002
b_5	0.00006	0.00054	0.0006	b_K	0.048	0.025	0.096
				ρ	0.92	0.925	0.976

es: Study (i) covers 1958:1–1973:3; study (ii) covers 1954:1–1977:4; study (iii) covers 1956:1–1979:4. Lagged variables employ earlier rvations.

bility, parameter estimates on each of the distributed lag variables appear to be very similar in studies (ii) and (iii) but are generally three or more times larger than those in study (i). Whether this difference is due to different scalings of the data in the first study is not clear. One substantial difference between the three studies, however, is the extent of first-order autocorrelation. In studies (ii) and (iii) the estimate of ρ is 0.839 and 0.785, respectively, but for study (i) the estimate of ρ is but 0.60.

For nonresidential structures, point estimates of the parameters appear to suggest less stability than those for equipment. As is seen in Table 6.5, while the length of the lag is 12 quarters in each of the three studies, for equal time displacements the estimated b_j and c_j from study (iii) are larger than those from study (ii), which in turn are larger than those from the earliest study. Moreover, unlike the distributed lag pattern for equipment, which displayed an inverted-V shape, with structures the pattern in studies (i) and (iii) is one of estimated coefficients continuously falling as the time displacement increases; in study (ii) the coefficients fall after $j = 1$.

Estimates of the effect of the lagged capital stock on current gross investment in structures also vary considerably among the three studies. In the first study, $b_K = 0.048$, and with the second study this estimate falls to about half of its value, $b_K = 0.025$. Then in the last study the b_K estimate jumps dramatically to 0.096. Finally, autocorrelation appears to be important in all three studies; estimates of ρ range from 0.92 to 0.976.

In summary, the neoclassical model is attractive on theoretical criteria because it provides a rigorous framework for specifying the optimal capital stock, which depends on prices, tax policy, and output. Like the accelerator and cash flow models, however, the neoclassical model is one of optimal capital, not optimal investment, and so the choice of distributed lag specification for investment tends to be ad hoc rather than based on optimization theory. Finally, while the neoclassical model is attractive on theoretical grounds, numerous practical problems emerge in implementing it empirically, including in particular the measurement of tax, interest rate, and capital gains variables.

This concludes our discussion of the neoclassical model. Further remarks concerning the empirical performance of the neoclassical model in estimation and forecasting will be given in Section 6.8, where its properties will be compared with those of other models. We now turn to a fourth model of aggregate investment, namely, the Tobin's q specification.

6.5 TOBIN'S q MODEL

Earlier, in discussing the cash flow model of investment we noted that the optimal capital stock was postulated to be a function of expected profits, which in turn might be measured by the market value of the firm. James Tobin [1969] has generalized the cash flow model and has provided a rigorous framework for an investment model in which net investment depends on the ratio of the market value of business capital assets to their replacement value, a ratio known as "q." The theory underlying Tobin's q model is relatively straightforward and in fact is closely related to the neoclassical investment model considered in Section 6.4.

6.5.A Theory

On the basis of the expected profitability of an investment project, managers reckon the price they are willing to pay for it; call this the demand price for an asset. The demand price for an entire firm is the market value of all its securities, that is, the market value of all its debt and equity in securities markets. The cost of producing all new capital goods is the supply price and is typically measured by assessing the replacement cost of a firm's assets. In equilibrium, the demand and supply prices for plant and equipment must be equal. If the ratio of the market value of the firm to the replacement value of its assets were unity, then there would be no incentives for the firm to invest.

Suppose, however, that a firm was operating in a relatively profitable environment and that if it added \$1 to its capital stock of plant and equipment, its expected profitability would increase sufficiently that its market value would increase by more than \$1. In this case the value of the marginal q ratio would be greater than unity, and the firm should invest in the plant and equipment in order to maximize the return to its shareholders. According to Tobin, such investment should continue until the incremental market value just equaled the incremental cost of the plant and equipment, that is, investment should continue until marginal q equals unity.

A similar argument could be made for a firm operating in a relatively unprofitable environment. Suppose that the firm were already overly capital-intensive and that if it added \$1 to its capital plant and equipment stock, its expected profitability would increase negligibly, so that its market value would increase by less than \$1. In this case the value of the marginal q ratio would be less than unity, and the firm should not invest in the plant and equipment; its shareholders could earn a higher return elsewhere. Indeed, the firm might work better on behalf of its shareholders if it sold off part of its capital plant and equipment.

The above considerations suggest that in its naive form the Tobin's q model of investment implies that whenever marginal q is greater (less) than unity, there are incentives for net investment (disinvestment) in capital plant and equipment. Such reasoning has led to the specification of investment equations of the form

$$I_t = a + \sum_{j=0}^{m-1} b_j \cdot (q - 1)_{t-j} K_{t-j-1} + b_K \cdot K_{t-1} + u_t \qquad \textbf{(6.39)}$$

where the b_j are expected to be positive.

JAMES TOBIN

Expectations and the q Theory of Investment

Econometricians have long recognized that a major problem in modeling investment behavior involves dealing satisfactorily with the unobserved expectations of firms and investors. In a series of papers, some written with colleague William Brainard, James Tobin suggested using the securities market evaluation of a firm as a summary statistic of the market's expectations concerning the firm's future profitability as discounted for interest and risk. Tobin defined q as the ratio of the market value of the firm divided by the replacement value of its capital assets. He then showed that whenever the marginal value of q was greater (less) than unity, the firm should undertake investment (disinvestment); in long-run equilibrium the q of a competitive firm should equal unity. Tobin and Brainard also applied the q theory to macroeconomic models.

Tobin's q theory has had an enormous impact on the econometric modeling of investment decisions. Although the theory is simple and persuasive, econometric implementation has not been quite as straightforward. In particular, as is discussed in detail in this chapter, measurement problems occur for both the numerator and the denominator of q, and it is difficult to distinguish marginal from average q empirically.

James Tobin was born in Champaign, Illinois in 1918. His father was Athletic Publicity Director at the University of Illinois, and his mother was Executive Secretary of the local Family Service agency. After attending public high school in Urbana, Tobin won a Harvard National Scholarship and graduated from Harvard summa cum laude in economics in 1939. World War II interrupted his graduate studies at Harvard. After a brief stint in Washington as an economist in 1941–1942, he enlisted for Naval Reserve officer training and served as a line officer on a destroyer from 1942 to 1945. Tobin returned to Harvard in 1946, finished his Ph.D. in 1947, spent several years at Harvard as a Junior Fellow, and then studied in the Department of Applied Economics at Cambridge University. Tobin took an academic position at Yale University in 1950 and, aside from occasional visits, has been there ever since. He retired from teaching duties in 1988 and is now Sterling Professor Emeritus of Economics.

Tobin's contributions to economics are enormous. Tobin is the author or editor of 13 books and more than 300 articles; his main professional interests have been in macroeconomics, monetary theory and policy, fiscal policy and public finance, consumption and saving, unemployment and inflation, portfolio theory and asset markets, and econometrics (in Chapter 11 of this text, readers will implement his Tobit estimator). Also active in the public policy arena, Tobin was a member of President John F. Kennedy's Council of Economic Advisers and has frequently testified before Congress. In 1981, Tobin was awarded the Prize in Economic Science in Memory of Alfred Nobel, in part for his work on the q theory of investment.

An attractive feature of the q investment model is that because the market's expectations concerning future profitability are summarized completely by the securities market evaluation of the firm, with q as a regressor the lag distribution excludes delays due to expectational lags. Rather, lagged values of q represent only order, delivery, and gestation delays. Note also that in Eq. (6.39), $q_t \cdot K_t$ represents the market value of the firm; in this sense, Eq. (6.39) is very similar to Grunfeld's cash flow equation (6.17).

As we shall see, although the theory underlying q is seemingly persuasive, in fact, aggregate investment does not always respond to changes in market value consistent with the simple q theory.

6.5.B Issues in Empirical Implementation

In practice, there are some serious problems in empirically implementing the q model. Recall that the denominator of q is the replacement value of the firm's assets, typically measured as the sum of the replacement values of its plant, equipment, land, working capital, and inventories. A denominator computed in this way omits other assets of the firm, including intangibles such as brand recognition and goodwill. This underestimation of the denominator can lead to a situation in which measured q is greater than the firm's true q.

The measurement of the numerator of q also presents problems in empirical implementation, particularly with respect to valuing untraded outstanding and unretired debt obligations, as well as accounting properly for tax factors that drive wedges between before- and after-tax bond yields and dividends.[38]

More generally, a major problem with empirical implementation of the Tobin's q model is that a measure of q based on the market value of the firm divided by the replacement value of its assets represents an *average*, not a *marginal* value of q. For example, suppose that an unexpected energy price increase rendered obsolete a considerable portion of a firm's existing plant and equipment, yet simultaneously created substantial opportunities for profitable new investment in more energy-efficient equipment. In such a case, average q might be less than unity, while marginal q could exceed unity.

For reasons such as these, empirical researchers have tended to be rather cautious in arguing that whenever average q is greater than 1, incentives for positive net investment exist. Rather, most now simply postulate that at best, net investment should be an increasing function of measured average q. Further, since the underlying theory is vague on functional form, the q investment equation is often estimated in variants of Eq. (6.39) including, for example, having I_t/K_{t-1} as the left-hand variable. Note also that if one sets $a = 0$ in Eq. (6.39) and then divides both sides by K_{t-1}, the new intercept term is δ, and so this intercept can be interpreted as an estimate of the rate of depreciation.

The Tobin's q model of investment can be related to the neoclassical framework, as has been emphasized by Andrew Abel, Hiroshi Yoshikawa, and Fumio Hayashi.[39] More specifically, define the one-period shadow price of capital π_t as the additional profits expected in time period t if one more unit of capital were in place, and then set the one-period tax-adjusted price of uninstalled capital goods equal to the user cost of capital c_t—see Eq. (6.24). Now define an amended q as the ratio of these one-period prices, that is,

$$q_t \equiv \pi_t / c_t \qquad \textbf{(6.40)}$$

Equation (6.40) differs from the earlier definition of q in that here q is the ratio of one-period prices (often called flow prices), whereas the earlier definition of q was in terms of asset prices—the ratio of the market value of the firm to the replacement value of its assets. An advantage of the formulation in Eq. (6.40), however, is that it highlights the expectational and marginal (rather than average) nature of q. One further result explored by Hayashi in this context is that if the firm operates in an imperfectly competitive output market, in equilibrium the firm's marginal q can be greater than unity.[40]

Although the q model is attractive because of its theoretical foundations and its ability to distinguish order, delivery, and gestation from expectational lags, its empirical performance has been less than impressive to date. A number of studies have regressed investment on q, and a common finding is that variations in q are unable to explain a large part of the variation in investment; further, as with other empirical investment models, the residuals or unexplained movements in investment tend to be highly serially correlated, suggesting that important explanatory variables are omitted.[41]

The relatively poor performance of q is troubling and could be due to a number of reasons. One obvious possibility is the use of average in place of marginal q. Abel and Blanchard [1986] have reported results in which they first compute a measure of marginal q based on the expectation of a present value of a stream of marginal profits. Such a calculation involves expectations of both future profitability and the discount rate (cost of capital).

Using a number of alternative measures of marginal q, Abel and Blanchard find that, as in previous studies, q is generally a statistically significant regressor, but it leaves unexplained a large and serially correlated fraction of investment. They conclude that "Since our findings are so similar to the results obtained relating investment to average q, we find little support for the view that the low explanatory power of average q is due to the fact that average q is simply a poor proxy for the theoretically more appealing marginal q."

The incompleteness of the q model in explaining investment is also evident in that output and profit variables still enter significantly when added to the q investment equations. Finally, Abel and Blanchard examine specifications in which the two components of marginal q—the marginal profit component and the cost of capital—are specified as separate regressors. They find that the marginal profit component has a larger and more significant effect on investment than does the cost of capital component, thus lending further support to the common empirical finding in neoclassical investment studies that investment responds more to output changes than to variations in the user cost of capital.

Let us now briefly examine results from a series of three empirical studies of investment in the United States by Kopcke in which estimates of the q model are reported. Recall that Kopcke's three studies cover differing time periods, study (i) encompassing the pre-OPEC oil embargo period 1958:1–1973:3, study (ii) including earlier as well as post-OPEC responses during 1954:1–1977:4, and study (iii) ranging from 1956:1 to 1979:4.

The investment equation specified and estimated by Kopcke is Eq. (6.39) with several modifications. In study (i) and reflecting roots from the internal cash flow literature, the q_{t-j} variable is multiplied by real cash flow $(F/P)_{t-j}$ rather than by the capital stock variable K_{t-j} as in Eq. (6.39). In study (ii), Kopcke divides both sides of Eq. (6.39) by K_{t-1}, whereas in study (iii) the dependent variable is respecified as I_t/U_t, where U_t is the rate of capacity utilization.[42] The estimation of these equations allows for first-order autocorrelation and employs the Almon polynomial distributed lag technique; in studies (ii) and (iii) the coefficients are constrained to lie along a third-degree polynomial, while in study (i) a fourth-degree polynomial is specified. Kopcke specifies separate investment equations for equipment and structures. While this facilitates comparison with other models estimated by Kopcke, it is worth noting that the measure of q employed as a regressor is not specific to equipment or structures, but rather reflects their combined market value.[43]

Kopcke's results are reproduced in Table 6.6. Since the dependent variables differ in the three studies, it is not meaningful directly to compare magnitudes of the estimated coefficients across studies. Some patterns among the coefficients are, however, evident in Table 6.6.

First, the length of the estimated distributed lag estimated based on the q model varies from five to nine quarters, which is about the same length as that for the accelerator and cash flow models but is shorter than for the neoclassical model estimated by Kopcke. Second, the shape of the lag distribution varies considerably among the three studies. For structures the effect of the lag on investment peaks at zero, two, and five quarters for studies (i), (ii), and (iii), respectively, while for equipment the associated peaks are at zero, one, and four quarters. For both equipment and structures, in study (iii) the lag coefficients gradually increase with time and then taper off, while in study (i) the pattern of the lag distribution coefficients is much more complex. A curious feature of the lag coefficients from the most recent study is that simulta-

Table 6.6 Parameter Estimates in Three Versions of Tobin's q Investment Equation (6.39) Reported by Kopcke in Three Quarterly U.S. Studies

	Nonresidential Structures			Producers' Durable Equipment		
Parameter	Study (i)	Study (ii)	Study (iii)	Study (i)	Study (ii)	Study (iii)
a	2.86	0.044	12.92	−19.21	0.056	−18.52
b_0	3.338	0.004	−0.0059	11.439	0.036	−0.0260
b_1	2.278	0.012	−0.0016	4.472	0.037	−0.0020
b_2	2.333	0.015	0.0019	5.618	0.034	0.0123
b_3	2.018	0.014	0.0044	9.523	0.028	0.0188
b_4	1.015	0.011	0.0060	4.248	0.021	0.0193
b_5	0.179	0.007	0.0067		0.014	0.0159
b_6	1.532	0.003	0.0064		0.008	0.0102
b_7		0.00001	0.0053		0.002	0.0043
b_8			0.0031			
b_K	0.063	—	0.082	0.177	—	0.293
ρ	0.82	1.000	0.872	0.82	0.994	0.866

Notes: Study (i) covers 1958:1–1973:3; study (ii) covers 1954:1–1977:4; study (iii) covers 1956:1–1979:4. In studies (ii) and (iii) for both equipment and structures the trailing term in the Almon lag is constrained to equal zero. Lagged variables employ earlier observations.

neous and one-period lagged increases in q tend to decrease investment, that is, for both equipment and structures, estimates of b_0 and b_1 are negative.

Since both sides of Eq. (6.39) are divided by K_{t-1} in study (ii), the lagged capital stock is no longer included as a regressor. The intercepts therefore represent estimates of δ, which are 0.044 (structures) and 0.056 (equipment). For equipment this estimate appears to be somewhat low.

Finally, as in all of the investment equation estimates reported by Kopcke, the unexplained residuals display a marked serial correlation. For structures, estimates of ρ range from 0.82 to 1.00, while for equipment they vary between 0.82 and 0.994.

In summary, the q model is attractive on theoretical criteria because it provides a rigorous framework for specifying the effect of market value on investment. It therefore provides a theoretical foundation to an investment equation that is similar in form to some of the earlier, more ad hoc cash flow models. Although use of market value incorporates the effects of expectational lags, like the accelerator, cash flow, and neoclassical models, the underlying theory of the q model does not provide guidance on factors governing the shape and length of the distributed lag specification. Therefore in practice its form tends to be chosen on an ad hoc basis, rather than being based on optimization theory.

Further, while the q model is attractive on theoretical grounds, numerous problems emerge in implementing it empirically, including in particular measuring marginal rather than average q, accounting for intangibles that affect market value, and properly incorporating tax factors that interact among market value and the tax treatment of dividends and yields. Estimates of the q model tend to vary considerably, depending on the data time period chosen, and unexplained residuals display a substantial amount of serial correlation. Moreover, since forecasting stock market trends is known to be difficult, the q model would not seem to be very useful in the forecasting context. Finally, there is a serious question as to the imperical validity of q. If q were correct, then following a dramatic decline in stock market prices, one would expect investment plans to decline as well. As the investment banking firm Deloitte, Haskins, and Sells [1988, p. 3] has noted, this was not the case following the 1987 stock market crash: "Preliminary results from a Dun & Bradstreet (D&B) survey conducted in the wake of the [1987] stock market crash support the findings that the outlook for 1988 remains healthy. In the D&B 5,000 Survey, roughly 75% of the companies said their capital spending plans for 1988 would not be negatively affected by the stock market slump."

This concludes our discussion of the Tobin's q model, although additional remarks concerning its empirical performance in estimation and forecasting will be given in Section 6.8, where its properties will be compared with those of other models. We now turn to a fifth model of aggregate investment, namely, the time series/autoregressive formulation.

6.6 TIME SERIES/AUTOREGRESSIVE MODELS OF AGGREGATE INVESTMENT

In contrast to the four competing theories of investment discussed in the previous sections, the time series/autoregressive approach does not directly use output, cash flow, market value, prices, or taxes as determinants of investment expenditures. Rather, in its simplest form, investment is merely regressed on a series of previous investment expenditures. Such a model with m lagged investment terms could of course be interpreted as resulting from a specification in which $I_t = a + u_t$, where u_t followed an autoregressive process of degree m.

6.6.A Measurement without Theory?

Viewed in such a manner, the autoregressive model of investment would seem to be a classic example of measurement without theory, and indeed practitioners of time series modeling have encountered many such criticisms. Proponents of the time series approach have argued, however, that despite the superficial elegance of some of the economic theory-based competing models of investment, their empirical implementation requires making a number of arbitrary statistical assumptions. Rather than employing such ad hoc stochastic specification assumptions, time series practitioners argue that for a class of macroeconomic models linear in the variables, the reduced form for the investment equation can be shown to have the form

$$I_t = a + \sum_{j=1}^{m} b_j I_{t-j} + u_t \tag{6.41}$$

provided that the exogenous variables are covariance stationary. For macro models that are "nearly linear" the time series model may still approximate rather closely the unconstrained reduced form equation for investment. Hence the simple representation (6.41) can be viewed as being the "final form" derived from a more structural macro model of the economy.[44]

Critics of the time series approach contend that equations such as Eq. (6.41) are not very useful in that they do not permit forecasters or policymakers to assess directly the effects of changes in business conditions or economic policy on investment. Such criticisms merely highlight the fact that unless Eq. (6.41) is specified within a more explicit structural model, and unless appropriate cross-equation restrictions are imposed, the interpretation of parameter estimates in Eq. (6.41) is essentially unclear. Considerations such as these once led Zvi Griliches [1974, p. 335] to venture a "law" stating that "any time series regression containing more than four independent variables results in garbage."

Defenders of the more structural models of investment, however, are also somewhat vulnerable to specification issues. For example, in the accelerator and neoclassical models, output affects investment. But causality can plausibly be argued to run in the other direction from investment to output. Similarly, interest rates and market value might be influenced by investment and so might be endogenous rather than exogenous. These are issues to which we will turn our attention in the next section. However, time series practitioners take the view that the potential for misspecification is very real in the more structural models and that difficult pitfalls in model building might best be mitigated by analyzing the underlying dynamics embedded in investment outlays alone.

6.6.B Empirical Implementation

Empirical implementations of time series investment models have not been confined to purely autoregressive specifications, such as those in Eq. (6.41). Rather, as in Zellner and Palm [1974], it is common to estimate investment equations that allow both for autoregressive (AR) and moving average (MA) error structures. MA specifications are attractive in that they can be shown to emerge from expectations formations processes that are adaptive or rational, as will be discussed further in Section 6.7.

Let us now briefly examine results from a series of three empirical studies of investment in the United States by Kopcke in which estimates of the time series model are given. In studies (i) and (iii), Kopcke estimates parameters of Eq. (6.41), while in study (ii), I_t/K_{t-1} is the dependent variable, rather than I_t. Kopcke uses OLS estimation procedures in all three studies; results are reproduced in Table 6.7.

Table 6.7 Parameter Estimates of Time Series/Autoregressive Investment Equation (6.41) Reported by Kopcke in Three Quarterly U.S. Studies

	Nonresidential Structures			Producers' Durable Equipment		
Parameter	Study (i)	Study (ii)	Study (iii)	Study (i)	Study (ii)	Study (iii)
a	0.29	0.0021	0.565	0.48	0.012	0.215
b_1	1.00	1.21	1.24	1.41	1.40	1.35
b_2	—	−0.043	−0.085	—	−0.464	−0.061
b_3	—	−0.191	0.079	—	—	−0.306
b_4	—	—	−0.311	—	—	−0.143
b_5	—	—	−0.017	—	—	0.245
b_6	—	—	−0.015	—	—	−0.078
b_7	—	—	0.071	—	—	—
b_8	—	—	0.029	—	—	—

Notes: Study (i) covers 1958:1–1973:3; study (ii) covers 1954:1–1977:4; study (iii) covers 1956:1–1979:4. In Study (ii), I_t/K_{t-1} is the dependent variable, not I_t. Lagged variables employ earlier observations.

A striking result from Table 6.7 is that the preferred specification is highly unstable in the series of three studies, both for structures and for equipment. In particular, for structures the preferred number of lags is one in study (i), three in study (ii), and eight in study (iii); for equipment the number of lagged terms in the three studies is one, two, and six, respectively. Critics of the time series approach would likely interpret such instability as being due to the fact that during the 1970s a number of major economic disruptions occurred and that by failing to account properly for the effects of such disruptions the unconstrained distributed lag time series approach represents a serious misspecification. It should be noted, however, that the time series model is not alone in manifesting instability; each of the other four investment models has also displayed substantial unstable tendencies.

In Section 6.8 of this chapter we will consider in greater detail the comparative performance of each of the five models in estimation and forecasting. Before doing that, however, we digress briefly to discuss several other important econometric specifications and issues.

6.7 ADDITIONAL ECONOMETRIC SPECIFICATIONS AND ISSUES

In this section we briefly discuss a number of econometric issues that emerge from our overview of the five alternative models of investment behavior. These issues include allowing for possible simultaneity of certain regressors, incorporating moving average error structures, dealing with nonstatic expectations (including the rational expectations hypothesis), and introducing adjustment costs so that speeds of adjustment are endogenous and time-varying.

6.7.A Simultaneity Issues

In the original derivation of the neoclassical investment model, profit-maximizing firms were assumed to choose levels of K_t, L_t, and Y_t so as to maximize one-period profits (6.19). Even though Y_t is therefore an endogenous variable, Jorgenson and his co-workers typically ignored possible simultaneity issues and simply assumed that there was no correlation between Y_t and the disturbance term u_t.[45] If simultaneity (nonzero correlation between Y_t and u_t) is present, however, estimation by OLS yields biased and inconsistent parameter estimates.

The simultaneity of output and investment could be handled by assuming cost minimization rather than profit maximization, in which case, by assumption, output would be exogenous. However, under cost minimization the basic optimal capital stock equation changes from Eq. (6.27) (assuming a Cobb-Douglas production function with constant returns to scale) to

$$K_t^* = \{[\alpha/(1-\alpha)] \cdot (w_t/c_t)\}^{1-\alpha} \cdot (Y_t/A) \tag{6.42}$$

Hence if one wants to assume cost minimization rather than profit maximization, an equation that is different from Eq. (6.27) must be estimated.

Potential simultaneous equations problems are not necessarily confined to the output variable, however. Suppose, for example, that government tax policies changed, creating investment incentives. The increased demand for new investment could increase interest rates and/or the supply price of new investment goods, thereby affecting the r_t and ΔJ_t components of the user cost of capital (6.24). The market value might also be affected, implying that both the numerator and the denominator of Tobin's q could be simultaneously determined. Finally, depending on the structure of the tax rate schedule, marginal tax rates might be jointly determined with investment in response to the government investment incentives. Note that in some of these cases, simultaneity occurs at the level of the firm, while in other cases it is only at a more macro level.

Simultaneous equations problems can be addressed in a number of ways. One possibility is to solve explicitly for the reduced form and then estimate it by OLS. Alternatively, one might employ an instrumental variable estimator such as two-stage least squares and estimate the investment structural equation directly, the choice of instruments being guided by observing what exogenous variables would appear in a reduced form equation. Care must be taken, however, in choosing instruments if one has lagged dependent variables and allows for an autoregressive error structure in the structural equation. In particular, Ray C. Fair [1970] has shown that if the disturbance term follows an mth-order autoregressive process, then to purge the disturbance term of correlations with all m components, the instrument list for any $X_{t-\tau}$ regressor must include not only those from time period $t-\tau$, but also all those back to time period $t-\tau-m$, as well as the Y_{t-m}. In particular, if one includes only the $t-\tau$ current-valued instruments and excludes Y_{t-m}, estimation by instrumental variable techniques will yield biased and inconsistent estimates of the parameters.[46]

6.7.B Moving Average Errors

One very important aspect of the investment equation that has not yet been discussed concerns error structures that could be generated by alternative expectations formations. This can be illustrated by modifying slightly Tobin's q model (6.39), which we now write as

$$I_{nt} = a + b \cdot Q^*_{t+1} + \epsilon_t \tag{6.43}$$

where $Q^*_{t+1} \equiv q^*_{t+1} \cdot K_t$ is the *expected* market value of the firm at the beginning of the next time period and ϵ_t is an independently and identically normally distributed random disturbance term. Since expected market value is not observed, let us specify an *adaptive expectations* mechanism in which

$$Q^*_{t+1} - Q^*_t = (1 - \ell) \cdot (Q_t - Q^*_t) \Rightarrow Q^*_{t+1} = (1 - \ell)Q_t + \ell Q^*_t \tag{6.44}$$

where the adaptive expectations coefficient ℓ is in the range $0 \leqslant \ell < 1$. Note that ℓ is interpreted as representing the speed with which expectations adapt and not the proportion of the gap between K^* and K adjusted within one time period. In particular, according to Eq. (6.44), expected market value at time $t + 1$ is a weighted average of current market value and the market value expected in the current time period. Hence current expectations are derived by modifying previous expectations in light of current experience.

To implement the adaptive expectations empirically, repeatedly substitute $Q^*_{t-\tau}$ in $Q^*_{t-\tau+1}$ in Eq. (6.44), and then substitute the result into Eq. (6.43). This yields

$$I_{nt} = a + b \cdot (1 - \ell) \cdot (Q_t + \ell Q_{t-1} + \ell^2 Q_{t-2} + \cdots) + \epsilon_t \tag{6.45}$$

Since Eq. (6.45) contains an infinite number of regressors, it is not practical for estimation. This problem is solved by employing the Koyck transformation in which Eq. (6.45) is lagged once and multiplied by ℓ, the product then being subtracted from Eq. (6.45), yielding

$$I_{nt} = a \cdot (1 - \ell) + b \cdot (1 - \ell) \cdot Q_t + \ell \cdot I_{n,t-1} + \xi_t \tag{6.46}$$

where ξ_t is a first-order moving average process

$$\xi_t \equiv \epsilon_t - \ell \epsilon_{t-1} \tag{6.47}$$

It can also be shown that if one has additional explanatory variables in the net investment equation (6.43), each involving an adaptive expectations process, then the Koyck transformation can be applied successively, yielding a composite disturbance term involving a higher-order moving average process. In a neoclassical model, for example, one might have both expected output and expected user cost variables following adaptive expectations. More generally, considerations such as these suggest that moving average errors could be very important in the stochastic specifications of investment models.

An important econometric implication of the moving average error process in Eq. (6.47) is that since ξ_t is correlated with the lagged dependent variable $I_{n,t-1}$ (owing to the presence of ϵ_{t-1} in ξ_t), estimation by OLS yields biased and inconsistent estimates of the parameters. However, consistent estimates can be obtained by use of instrumental variables procedures or by the maximum likelihood method. Many econometric theory textbooks provide further details regarding estimation and inference of Box-Jenkins models with moving average or integrated autoregressive–moving average error (ARIMA) specifications.[47]

6.7.C Nonstatic and Rational Expectations

Expectations of future events play a very important role in economic behavior. Since anticipations are important, it is often necessary to separate out the effects of changed expectations from other explanatory variables in analyzing investment behavior. Failure to do so can result in, for example, erroneous predictions concerning the effects of changes in tax policy.[48]

In the last few decades, economists have made substantial advances in incorporating the effects of nonstatic expectations into econometric models. According to the rational expectations hypothesis (REH), economic agents efficiently use all the information at their disposal to form expectations. Indeed, omniscient economic agents are assumed to construct optimal predictors based on sophisticated economic theory and available information and data.[49] One important implication of the REH is that expectational errors should be uncorrelated with any of the variables entering into the information set used by economic agents, since if errors were correlated with these variables, the information contained in the variables could not have been employed rationally.

Optimal predictors of variables are predictors that are uncorrelated with expectational errors. Optimal predictors can be constructed in a number of ways. Suppose that in a regression equation the practicing econometrician seeks to employ as a regressor the optimal or rational predictor of X_{t+1}. John F. Muth [1960] has derived the optimal predictor in one special case. Specifically, if one assumes that X is stochastic and that its realizations are governed by a first-order moving average process of the form

$$X_t = X_{t-1} + u_t - \ell u_{t-1} \tag{6.48}$$

where u_t is an independently and identically distributed disturbance term with mean zero, then the optimal or rational predictor of X_{t+1}, denoted X^*_{t+1}, equals

$$X^*_{t+1} = (1 - \ell) \cdot (X_t + \ell X_{t-1} + \ell^2 X_{t-2} + \cdots) \tag{6.49}$$

But Eq. (6.49) is simply the adaptive expectations specification considered in the previous section, where $Q^*_{t+1} = X^*_{t+1}$. This implies that if values of X are generated as specified in Eq. (6.48)—admittedly a special case—then adaptive expectations are rational, that is, under these conditions, estimation of Eq. (6.46) incorporates the REH. Other stochastic processes can be specified that lead to different optimal predictors; such predictors often involve rather complex distributed lag representations.[50] Moreover, with many nonstatic expectations formulations, K^* is no longer a fixed target, but instead becomes a moving one.

Empirical studies of investment have incorporated nonstatic expectations in a number of ways. Eisner [1967], for example, replaced expectations variables directly with estimates based on survey data. A more common procedure, however, is to replace an expectations variable with the fitted value of a separately estimated equation. Examples of this include a Canadian study by Helliwell and Glorieux [1970] in which separate extrapolative, regressive, and trend growth elements of the expectations formation process are specified and estimated, and a British study by Feldstein and Flemming [1971]. Both studies find that this predicted variable performs well in the investment equation. Another example is provided by Ando, Modigliani, Rasche, and Turnovsky [1974], who compare empirically the importance of alternative forecasts of price changes in investment equations.

It is worth remarking that replacing an expectations variable with the fitted value from an auxiliary regression equation and then doing OLS on the new equation is of course an instrumental variables technique that in certain cases provides parameter estimates that are numerically equivalent to the two-stage least squares (2SLS) procedure.[51] Moreover, since by construction the fitted value in the 2SLS estimation procedure is orthogonal to the residual, use of 2SLS in this context ensures that elements of the information set (the variables employed in the first stage of 2SLS) are uncorrelated with the sample residuals, implying that this 2SLS procedure is consistent with the REH.[52]

6.7.D Adjustment Costs

Several times in this chapter it has been stressed that the economic theory underlying the investment models is in fact a theory of optimal capital stock, not of investment. In the last two decades, however, developments have occurred that now make it possible to implement empirically models of optimal investment, not just optimal capital. Such models are typically called adjustment cost models; we now briefly outline their salient features.

Recall that the investment process entails a number of time-consuming stages, including changing expectations, making decisions and appropriating orders, experiencing delivery delays, installing the new plant and equipment, and getting it to function. As originally presented by Robert Eisner and Robert H. Strotz [1963], the distinctive feature of the adjustment cost approach is that it is based on the assumption that when a firm expends effort to install new plant and equipment, it forgoes current output production. Internal costs of adjustment are therefore measured by the cost of the gestation lag, that is, by the value of current output forgone by devoting resources to the installation of new plant and equipment. If marginal adjustment costs are an increasing function of net or gross investment, then the firm might not wish to close the gap between K^* and K entirely within one time period and instead might find it optimal in a present value sense to reduce current adjustment costs at the expense of having a less efficient capital stock, thereby optimally spreading the adjustment process out over several time periods.[53]

While early adjustment cost specifications resulted in constant speeds of adjustment, in a series of papers Lucas and Treadway introduced important innovations that enormously facilitated empirical implementations of models with endogenous, time-varying adjustment paths.[54] On the basis of expected output demands, expected input prices, and increasing marginal costs of adjustment for capital, Lucas and Treadway employed dynamic optimization techniques and solved for the time path of investment that maximized present value. This resulted in a flexible accelerator model in which the optimal speed of adjustment λ_t is a function of substitution possibilities involving capital inputs, parameters of the adjustment cost function, and the discount rate. An interesting implication of this flexible accelerator model is that increases in interest rates have two separate but reinforcing effects on current investment. First, increases in r raise the user cost of capital and thereby reduce the optimal capital stock. Second, increases in r enhance the relative importance of current adjustment costs and thereby reduce the optimal speed of adjustment λ_t. Hence investment is a decreasing function of r.

Empirical implementation of the dynamic flexible accelerator model requires specification of cost or production functions, assumptions concerning the shape of the adjustment cost function, and expectations formation specifications. Since such models are reasonably complex and have typically been estimated in the context of many inputs—not just investment in capital plant and equipment—we omit further discussion here. For further details, see Chapter 9, "Modeling the Interrelated Demands for Factors of Production," especially Section 9.7.

6.8 EMPIRICAL COMPARISONS OF FIVE INVESTMENT MODELS

The theoretical investment literature is voluminous, and so it is not surprising that researchers have frequently compared the empirical estimation and forecasting properties of alternative investment models.[55] Rather than surveying that literature, however, we now compare results of a series of three "horse races" reported by Richard Kopcke [1977, 1982, 1985]. It would be comforting if this series of comparisons produced a consistent set of winners or losers, but as we shall see, this is unfortunately not the case, since the relative rankings of the models change dramatically from one study to the next.

Kopcke compares the five models on the basis of three aspects of performance: estimation, static forecast properties, and dynamic forecast properties. We have already discussed Kopcke's estimation of each of the models, but several other points should now be made. First, the length of the estimated lag distribution varies considerably among models, as is indicated in the second and sixth columns of Table 6.8. The time series model typically has the shortest lag (sometimes as small as 1), the neoclassical model usually has the longest (up to 13 lags), and the accelerator, cash flow, and Tobin's q models have lags of intermediate length. While increasing the length of the lag improves fit during estimation, it does not necessarily enhance forecasting properties.

Second, in each of the five models estimated by Kopcke, residuals were found to be highly autoregressive. Since allowing for first-order autoregressive errors essentially amounts to adding the lagged residual as a regressor, in esti-

Table 6.8 Selected Statistics of Five Investment Models during Estimation Period Reported by Kopcke in Three Quarterly U.S. Studies

	Nonresidential Structures				Producers' Durable Equipment			
Model	Length of Lag	Percent RMSE	% |Errors| >$1B	% |Errors| >$2B	Length of Lag	Percent RMSE	% |Errors| >$1B	% |Errors| >$2B
			Study (i) 1958:1–1973:3					
Accelerator	4	0.78	17.5	3.2	3	0.97	28.6	4.8
Cash flow	6	0.80	17.5	3.2	6	1.21	38.1	7.9
Neoclassical	11	0.78	12.7	1.6	9	0.94	28.6	1.6
Tobin's q	7	0.76	15.9	0.0	4	1.17	39.7	6.3
Time series	1	0.91	22.2	3.2	2	1.53	42.9	14.3
			Study (ii) 1954:1–1977:4					
Accelerator	6	0.82	19.8	2.1	6	1.22	42.7	10.4
Cash flow	10	0.74	15.6	1.0	9	1.58	51.0	15.6
Neoclassical	12	0.78	16.7	3.1	13	1.11	37.5	8.3
Tobin's q	8	0.78	16.7	1.0	8	1.58	42.7	17.7
Time series	3	0.89	28.1	2.1	2	1.73	41.7	18.8
			Study (iii) 1956:1–1979:4					
Accelerator	11	0.9	20	2	9	1.2	34	13
Cash flow	5	0.9	20	0	5	1.4	45	13
Neoclassical	11	0.9	25	4	12	1.2	42	9
Tobin's q	8	1.0	28	7	7	1.3	46	11
Time series	8	0.9	25	3	6	1.8	46	22

Notes: % |Errors| >$1B and >$2B refer to the percentage of absolute errors exceeding one and two billion dollars, respectively. Percent RMSE is the percent root mean squared error.

mation the goodness of fit benefits from such autocorrelation. As we shall soon see, however, this benefit for estimation does not always carry over to forecasting.

Third, goodness of fit can be measured by R^2 or by a number of other measures. In columns three and seven of Table 6.8, Kopcke reports the percent root mean squared error (RMSE) measure of fit, computed as

$$\% \text{ RMSE} \equiv \sqrt{\sum_{t=1}^{T} e_t^2/T} \qquad e_t \equiv \frac{I_t - \hat{I}_t}{I_t} \tag{6.50}$$

where $\hat{I}_t$ is the fitted value of investment in time t based on the regression estimates and T is the sample size from estimation. Note that the residual here is in percent form. The RMSE for structures never exceeds 1.0%; and although that for equipment is typically larger, it is always 1.8% or less. Differences among the models are very small, indicating that all equations can be made to track the data equally well.

In the other four columns of Table 6.8, Kopcke reports a different measure of fit, namely, the percentage of the (absolute value of) residuals that exceed one and two billion (constant 1972) U.S. dollars. Since equipment investment is on average at least twice as large as that for plant (roughly, \$120 versus \$50 billion), we expect this percentage to be larger for equipment than for plant, and indeed this is the case. The neoclassical model displays the smallest percentage of very large (>\$2 billion) residuals for equipment, while Tobin's q generally performs very well for structures; in most cases, for both equipment and structures the time series model has the largest proportion of very large residuals. This relative ranking of the neoclassical and time series models in estimation is not unexpected, since the neoclassical model generally has the longest lag structure, while the time series specification has the shortest.

Kopcke assesses forecasting properties of the five investment models using ex post static and dynamic forecasts. In ex post static forecasts, each quarterly forecast of investment spending is computed with full knowledge of the previous quarter's actual investment outlays, the actual lagged capital stock, and the corresponding lagged forecast error.[56] While such a static forecast yields little understanding of how well a forecaster would actually have fared, the error performance of the static forecast can be compared to the model's error performance during estimation. If, for example, the model is unable to track the data as well during the forecast interval as it does during the estimation period, then there is evidence indicating instability of the model.

It is therefore instructive to compare % RMSE values from estimation in Table 6.8 to the static forecast % RMSE entries in Table 6.9. On average, for both equipment and structures the % RMSE measures from the static forecast are about twice as large as those from estimation, regardless of the model estimated. Further, in most cases the percentage of large (>\$1 billion) and

Table 6.9 Selected Statistics of Five Investment Models for Static Forecasts Reported by Kopcke in Three Quarterly U.S. Studies

	Nonresidential Structures				Producers' Durable Equipment			
Model	% Mean Error	Percent RMSE	% |Errors| >$1B	% |Errors| >$2B Length	% Mean Error	Percent RMSE	% |Errors| >$1B	% |Errors| >$2B
Study (i):	*Estimation 1958:1–1973:3*				*Forecasting 1973:4–1976:4*			
Accelerator	−0.9	1.4	61.5	7.7	−0.3	1.8	53.8	15.4
Cash flow	−1.3	1.6	61.5	38.5	−1.6	2.8	84.6	69.2
Neoclassical	−0.6	1.1	30.8	7.7	−1.6	2.9	92.3	61.5
Tobin's q	−1.3	1.5	61.5	23.1	−0.7	2.1	76.9	23.1
Time series	−0.9	1.5	38.5	15.4	−0.8	2.0	61.5	23.1
Study (ii):	*Estimation 1954:1–1977:4*				*Forecasting 1978:1–1981:4*			
Accelerator	0.57	1.1	50	0	0.97	2.3	81	44
Cash flow	0.78	1.5	50	19	0.33	2.9	81	56
Neoclassical	1.00	1.6	56	25	0.82	2.1	75	44
Tobin's q	0.53	1.5	44	19	−0.16	3.2	69	56
Time series	0.52	1.3	56	19	4.70	6.3	94	88
Study (iii):	*Estimation 1956:1–1979:4*				*Forecasting 1980:1–1984:4*			
Accelerator	0.4	1.3	60	10	1.3	2.8	75	55
Cash flow	0.5	1.6	55	20	0.2	2.3	95	35
Neoclassical	−0.4	1.7	60	20	1.3	2.5	75	45
Tobin's q	1.1	2.1	70	50	0.9	2.7	75	50
Time series	0.2	1.7	70	20	0.3	3.4	85	70

Notes: % |Errors| >$1B and >$2B refer to the percentage of absolute errors exceeding one and two billion dollars, respectively. Percent RMSE is the percent root mean squared error.

very large (>$2 billion) absolute residuals also increases severalfold in the static forecast. While some deterioration in precision might be expected, this universal, substantial increase in the dispersion of errors is disconcerting and suggests that none of the equations is stable.

Additional evidence on the forecasting properties of the various models can be obtained by examining signs of the residuals. In columns two and six of Table 6.9, mean values of the percent residuals in the static forecasts are presented. In the first study, for both equipment and structures the means are all negative, indicating that each of the models systematically overpredicted investment during the 1973:4–1976:4 interval. By contrast, in both the second and third studies the % mean error values are positive in nine of ten cases, implying that over the 1978:1–1981:4 and 1980:1–1984:4 forecast intervals, the models generally underpredicted investment. Together these results suggest that the explanation of investment spending is much more complicated than any of the five models suggests or that the link between investment spending and its determinants changed from the estimation to the forecast time period.

The final set of forecast performance measures reported by Kopcke is based on ex post dynamic forecasts. With dynamic forecasts, quarterly investment forecasts do not benefit by knowing investment in the previous time period or by knowing previous forecast errors. Unlike the static forecasts, the dynamic forecast is not prevented from straying far from the trend of actual investment, since in the dynamic forecast the previous error is not checked, nor are corrections for errors incorporated into subsequent forecasts. Possibilities for substantial forecast error are therefore more likely with dynamic forecasts.

In one important sense, however, these dynamic forecasts do not reflect the actual experiences of forecasters: Values of the exogenous variable (such as output, market value, user cost of capital, internal cash flow) are based on historical data, not on forecasted values. For this reason, such forecasts are called ex post dynamic forecasts; they differ from ex ante forecasts in which all exogenous variables must be forecasted.

To obtain best linear unbiased forecasts, Kopcke computes predicted values based on the estimated regression equation for each model, and then adds to this prediction the effect of the autocorrelated residual. With first-order autocorrelation the additive effect of the last residual from the estimation period, denoted e_T, on the forecast in period $T + \tau$ equals $\rho^{T+\tau} \cdot e_T$, where ρ is the estimated first-order autocorrelation coefficient.[57] Notice that since $0 < \rho < 1$, this effect declines as τ increases, that is, the effect of the residual on the forecast diminishes as the distance between the forecast period and the estimation period increases.

While differences among the models are small in the estimation and only modest in the static forecasts, with the dynamic forecasts, Kopcke finds substantial variations among models. This highlights the fact that models that work well in estimation do not necessarily perform similarly well in forecasting. Performance measures of the ex post dynamic forecasts employed by Kopcke include % mean error, % RMSE, and % absolute errors exceeding \$4 billion and \$8 billion; these are reproduced in Table 6.10.[58] The results are very revealing.

In the first study, in nine of ten cases the % mean errors are negative, implying that almost all models failed to gauge sufficiently the weakness of investment during the immediate post-OPEC oil embargo time period. While such errors are relatively small for the accelerator model, with the time series model, average errors are huge: −8.9% for structures and −11.9% for equipment. The accelerator and Tobin's q models do not have any very large errors (% absolute errors > \$8 billion), but for equipment investment this measure varies between 30% and 70% for the neoclassical, cash flow, and time series models. The % RMSE measures range from 5.2 (accelerator) to 9.7 (time series) for structures, but for equipment investment (which is more than twice

Table 6.10 Selected Statistics of Five Investment Models for Dynamic Forecasts Reported by Kopcke in Three Quarterly U.S. Studies

	Nonresidential Structures				Producers' Durable Equipment			
	% Mean	Percent	% |Errors|		% Mean	Percent	% |Errors|	
Model	Error	RMSE	>$4B	>$8B	Error	RMSE	>$4B	>$8B
Study (i):	*Estimation 1958:1–1973:3*				*Forecasting 1973:4–1976:4*			
Accelerator	−5.1	5.2	76.9	0.0	1.8	4.2	46.2	0.0
Cash flow	−4.7	6.2	69.2	23.1	−4.1	9.2	76.9	46.1
Neoclassical	−4.6	4.9	76.9	0.0	−3.3	6.2	46.2	30.8
Tobin's q	−5.5	5.9	76.9	0.0	−1.9	4.9	53.8	0.0
Time series	−8.9	9.7	76.9	61.5	−11.9	14.3	69.2	69.2
Study (ii):	*Estimation 1954:1–1977:4*				*Forecasting 1978:1–1981:4*			
Accelerator	3.7	4.4	44	6	6.8	8.3	63	31
Cash flow	7.6	8.2	88	50	8.4	9.0	94	50
Neoclassical	9.1	10.0	88	63	6.8	8.1	75	38
Tobin's q	7.0	7.4	88	38	7.8	9.6	63	50
Time series	2.0	2.7	19	0	2.5	4.4	38	13
Study (iii):	*Estimation 1956:1–1979:4*				*Forecasting 1980:1–1984:4*			
Accelerator	2.8	3.9	30	0	8.6	10.1	85	45
Cash flow	4.8	5.9	50	30	2.0	3.9	35	0
Neoclassical	−3.0	5.3	40	15	6.9	7.6	75	40
Tobin's q	6.6	7.5	70	35	3.5	5.7	35	15
Time series	0.5	3.6	30	0	−4.8	10.7	70	45

Notes: % |Errors| >$4B and >$8B refer to the percentage of absolute errors exceeding four and eight billion dollars, respectively. Percent RMSE is the percent root mean squared error.

as large as structures) the difference is even larger, from 4.2 (accelerator) to 14.3 (time series).

There are of course many ways in which one could rank these models. If one uses the % RMSE criterion and then weights the equipment % RMSE twice that for structures (reflecting relative investment magnitudes), then in the first study the ranking is as follows: accelerator, Tobin's q, neoclassical, cash flow, and time series.

The performance of the five models changes dramatically, however, in the second of Kopcke's studies. Here the % mean error values are all positive, indicating that actual investment 1978:1–1981:4 was larger than that predicted by all the models; the underprediction is particularly large for equipment. In a sharp reversal from Kopcke's first study, in which the time series model fared worst, in this study the time series model easily outperforms the other models in all criteria. The accelerator model still does well, but its performance is clearly inferior to that of the time series model. For all models except the accelerator, the percentage of very large errors in study (ii) is larger than those of study (i). If one uses the same % RMSE criteria as noted above, then in the second study the ranking is time series, accelerator, Tobin's q, neoclassical, and cash flow.

In the final of Kopcke's three studies, a sharp change again occurs in the performance of the five models. While % mean error values are again primarily positive, indicating systematic underprediction of investment over the 1980:I–1984:IV time span, the cash flow model, which ranked last in study (ii), now dominates, particularly for equipment investment. Further, the time series model, which dominated all models for both equipment and structures in study (ii), is still dominant in study (iii) in terms of the % RMSE criterion for structures, but for equipment its % RMSE is a substantial 10.7%, and it comes in last, faring only marginally worse than the accelerator model (10.1%). If one uses the same % RMSE criteria as noted above, then in this final study the ranking is cash flow, Tobin's q, neoclassical, accelerator, and time series.

Kopcke's tables merit close attention. But one point is already abundantly clear: No investment model consistently dominates its competitors. In particular, the relative rankings of the models, summarized in Table 6.11, change dramatically from one study to the next. Further, although the accelerator, cash flow, and time series model each put in one very good effort, they also each put forth at least one very bad performance. It is also the case that Tobin's q model is reasonably consistent at second or third place and outperforms the neoclassical model in each of these ex post forecasts. However, the usefulness of Tobin's q for ex ante forecasting is rather limited, since the ability to forecast overall stock market movements accurately is still severely circumscribed.

In summary, this series of empirical comparisons of five investment models indicates that econometricians are still a long way from reaching a

Table 6.11 Rankings of Five Investment Models Based on the % RMSE Dynamic Forecast Criterion* for Kopcke's Series of Three Quarterly U.S. Investment Studies

Study Forecast Period	Model				
	Accelerator	Cash Flow	Neoclassical	Tobin's q	Time Series
Study (i) 1973:4–1976	1	4	3	2	5
Study (ii) 1978:1–1981:4	2	5	4	3	1
Study (iii) 1980:1–1984:4	4	1	3	2	5

*% RMSE for equipment is weighted twice that for structures.

consensus on what form of investment equation is most preferable. There is much—very much—that still needs to be learned.

6.9 CONCLUDING REMARKS

There is an old saying, "We are so close, and yet so far." As we have seen in this chapter, theoretical developments in dynamic demand analysis over the last 50 years have been substantial, a large amount of data has been collected, and sophisticated computational techniques are now widely available for use on increasingly inexpensive computers. But what have we learned? While theoretical and computational developments in expectations formation and in the understanding of gestation lags (adjustment costs) have provided us with necessary tools, successful measurement and forecasting still elude us. As we observed in the previous section, we are still not able to predict investment to a reasonably precise level, nor can we even conclude on the basis of empirical performance what form of the investment equation is preferable and stable. Particularly frustrating is the fact that it has proved to be very difficult to separately identify and estimate reliably the expectational, order, delivery, and gestation lags. Progress has occurred, but it has been slow. It is difficult to reduce with success the very complex investment process to a limited number of variables and parameters.

Fortunately, the analysis of investment continues to attract great attention. Researchers today are attacking investment issues from a variety of vantage points, as has been indicated in the numerous references in this chapter. Some researchers believe that we may be asking too much from our data, whose construction deserves considerably more attention, particularly with respect to timing issues (expenditures versus installation), quality adjustment, tax impacts (marginal and average, effective and statutory), and the measurement of other components of the cost of capital. Others are working on the theory of risk and focusing more attention on the stochastic nature of the investment process. Still others are investigating aggregation problems over firms, the homogeneity of capital, the implications of irreversible investments, and the effects of imperfect competition.

There is still very much to be learned. The challenge is great, the opportunities are enormous, and the pace of ongoing research is furious. For young econometricians it is the greatest of times. So let us now get on with the hands-on exercises.

6.10 HANDS-ON ESTIMATION AND FORECASTING OF INVESTMENT EQUATIONS

The purpose of these exercises is to gain experience in actual estimation of distributed lag models with autoregressive disturbances, and to better understand how one chooses among alternative investment model specifications in estimation. A particularly enlightening experience afforded by these exercises is the encounter with models that perform admirably in estimation, yet achieve only modest success in dynamic forecasting.

Exercise 1 is especially important and useful; it acquaints you with the underlying data and encourages you to think through possible hypotheses to help explain broad trends in the historical investment data. Exercises 2 through 6 then deal successively with the accelerator, time series, cash flow, neoclassical, and Tobin's q investment models. Econometric techniques that are considered in these exercises include testing for autocorrelation with lagged dependent variables, traditional regression analysis of models with autoregressive errors, and estimation of Almon polynomial distributed lags as special cases of more general specifications, with and without endpoint restrictions.

Then in the more difficult set of Exercises 7 through 9, Box-Jenkins ARIMA identification, estimation, and forecasting techniques are implemented empirically, the estimation of simultaneous equations models with autoregressive errors is introduced, and the issue of just how price-responsive is the demand for capital is addressed in the context of a putty-clay neoclassical model of investment based on the CES production function. Finally, although it is not necessarily the most difficult exercise, in Exercise 10 a "horse race" project is outlined, similar to those conducted by Kopcke. This horse race project involves considerable effort and therefore might be most suitable for a team project or term paper, rather than just a normal exercise.[59]

●●●●●●●●●●

In the directory of the data diskette provided, you will find a subdirectory called CHAP6.DAT with a data file called KOPCKE. This data file contains quarterly U.S. data, 1952:1–1986:4 on 14 variables, each having 140 observations. There are two panels of data in KOPCKE. In the first panel there are nine variables: a date variable (DATE) indicating the year and quarter (in the form YYYYQ, where YYYY is year and Q is the quarter); implicit price deflators for structures (JS) and equipment (JE), indexed to 1.000 in 1982; cash flow of nonfinancial corporate business (F) in millions of current dollars; gross private domestic investment in nonresidential structures (IS) and producers' durable equipment (IE) in millions of 1982 dollars; once-lagged capital stocks of equipment (KELAG) and structures (KSLAG); and gross domestic business product (Y), all in millions of 1982 dollars.

The five variables in the second panel of data are another date variable (TIME), indicating the year and quarter (in the YYYYQ form); the Federal Reserve Board capacity utilization rate for manufacturing (U); Tobin's q, the ratio of the market value of nonfinancial corporations to the replacement value of their net assets (Q); and the real user cost of capital for nonresidential structures (CS) and producers' durable equipment (CE). Note that the last two variables are in real, not nominal terms, that is, $C \equiv c/P$, where c is defined as in Eq. (6.24). The annual rates of depreciation employed by Kopcke in the user cost formulae (6.24) are 0.15 for equipment and .05 for structures.

Comment: These data have been provided by Richard Kopcke, with assistance from George Houlihan. There are several differences in this data set from those used in the earlier Kopcke studies, and so you will be unable to replicate exactly Kopcke's previously reported results. In particular, the current data set incorporates data revisions that were published after Kopcke's 1977, 1982, and 1985 studies. Further, units of measurement differ, since in the three Kopcke studies, investment was in millions of 1972 dollars, while in the current data set, investment is in millions of 1982 dollars. Additional details concerning these data are found in the appendices of Kopcke [1977, 1982, 1985].

Important note: Although there are 140 observations in the data set, some of these observations will essentially be lost in estimation owing to the presence of distributed lags and autoregressive or moving average error structures. Following Kopcke's last [1985] study, it is recommended that direct estimation begin with the 1956:1 observation and that the previous 16 observations be reserved for use as appropriately lagged variables.

EXERCISES

EXERCISE 1: Examining the Data

The purpose of this exercise is to help you become familiar with important features of the investment data. You examine levels and relative growth rates of investment in equipment and plant, as well as capital/output ratios, and growth rates of price deflators and user costs. You interpret high and low values of Tobin's q and capacity utilization, and you assess the internal consistency of the net capital stock and investment data with the assumed rates of depreciation.

In the data diskette directory CHAP6.DAT there is a data file called KOPCKE that contains quarterly data series 1952:1–1986:4 on real investment in equipment and structures (IE and IS), real output (Y), once-lagged capital stocks of equipment (KELAG) and structures (KSLAG), implicit price deflators for equipment and structures (JE and JS), cash flow (F), Tobin's q (Q), the rate of capacity utilization (U), and real user costs of capital for equipment and structures (CE and CS).

(a) Print out the entire data series for IE, IS, KELAG, KSLAG, JE, JS, F, Q, U, CE, and CS. Make sure that you have 140 observations on each of these variables and that printed values for the first and last observations are the same as those in the KOPCKE data file when file contents are viewed on a monitor screen. Why is this a useful procedure to follow before embarking on further data analysis?

(b) The quarterly investment data in producers' durable equipment and nonresidential structures are in millions of 1982 dollars, seasonally adjusted and at annual rates. Compare the ratio of investment in equipment to investment in structures at the beginning of the sample and at the end of the sample. Which type of investment has been growing more rapidly, equipment or structures? Do these relative growth rates also hold for capital stocks of equipment and structures? Compare relative growth rates of the asset price deflators for new equipment (JE) and structures (JS) over the entire 1952:1–1986:4 sample and then for the real user costs of capital CE and CS. What hypotheses could help explain why IE grew more rapidly than IS over this sample time period?

(c) Many students of economic development believe that countries with high investment rates and capital stocks relative to output eventually experience greater growth in output and in labor productivity. Compute capital/output ratios separately for equipment and structures in 1952:1 and 1986:4, and then construct an aggregate capital/output ratio as the sum of capital stocks of equipment and structures, divided by output. Is production in the United States becoming more capital-intensive? Comment and interpret the major trends in these capital/output data series.

(d) Tobin's q, the ratio of the market value of nonfinancial corporations to the replacement value of their net assets, has a very interesting time series. What is the lowest sample value of q, and what is the highest? What historical events might help explain these dramatically different levels of q? Do they appear to be related to relative levels of capacity utilization? When do the peaks and troughs occur for capacity utilization? For user costs of capital CE and CS? Notice that average q is less than unity for all but four observations, yet much net investment has occurred. Is it more reasonable to state that net investment is an increasing function of q or that q must be greater than 1 in order for net investment to occur? Why?

(e) The once-lagged capital stock data KELAG and KSLAG are fourth-quarter to fourth-quarter linear interpolations of annual net capital stock data published by the U.S. Department of Commerce, Bureau of Economic Analysis. Earlier, it was noted that the quarterly investment data IE and IS are seasonally adjusted and at annual rates and that in the user cost formula, Kopcke assumed rates of depreciation for equipment and structures to be $\delta_E = 0.15$ and $\delta_S = 0.05$. It is useful to compare rates of depreciation assumed by Kopcke with those embodied in the U.S. Department of Commerce net capital stock calculations. To do this, solve Eq. (6.5) for δ_t; this yields

$$\delta_t = 1 - ((K_t - I_t)/K_{t-1}) \tag{6.51}$$

For equipment, sum the four quarters of investment in 1953 and in 1986, and then divide by 4 (since the quarterly data are at annual rates); this yields annual investment for 1953 and for 1986. Then substitute this 1953 value of I_t into Eq. (6.51), let K_t, K_{t-1} be the 1953:4 and 1952:4 values, respectively, and compute δ_{1953}. Similarly, substitute the 1986 value of I_t into Eq. (6.51), let K_t, K_{t-1} be the 1986:4 and 1985:4 values, respectively, and compute δ_{1986}. How well do these values of δ_t compare with the $\delta_E = 0.15$ assumed by Kopcke? (*Note:* The Department of Commerce capital stock calculations represent sums of capital stocks for various types of equipment. While each type of equipment could have a constant exponential decay rate, the aggregate capital stock could have a time-varying decay rate, owing to the changing composition within the equipment capital stock.) Perform the same calculations for structures, and compare with Kopcke's assumed $\delta_S = 0.05$. Comment on the internal consistency of the capital stock, investment, and user cost data. Finally, for the entire 1952:1–1986:4 data sample, compute replacement investment as a proportion of total investment for equipment and for structures, using Kopcke's values for δ_E and δ_S. How important is replacement investment? Is net investment ever negative? Interpret these results.

(f) With time series data, severe multicollinearity can often occur; this can result in imprecise parameter estimates and large standard errors. Using data from 1954:1 to 1986:4, construct a simple correlation matrix for IE_t, IS_t, Y_t, Y_{t-1}, Y_{t-2}, . . . , Y_{t-8}. Construct another correlation matrix involving investment and current and lagged values for some other variable that might be used as a regressor. Are the explanatory variables highly correlated with each other? Do you think this might cause problems in estimation? How might the adverse effects of this collinearity be mitigated?

EXERCISE 2: Testing for Autocorrelation with Lagged Dependent Variables

The purpose of this exercise is to enable you to gain experience with procedures designed to test for the presence of first-order autocorrelation in models with lagged dependent variables. You will use Durbin's m and h test statistic procedures in the context of the accelerator model and will undertake estimation using the OLS, Hildreth-Lu, and iterative Cochrane-Orcutt procedures.

In the data diskette directory CHAP6.DAT there is a data file called KOPCKE that contains quarterly data series 1952:1–1986:4 on real investment in equipment and structures (IE and IS) and real output (Y).

(a) Using OLS and data corresponding to 1956:1–1986:4, estimate parameters of Eq. (6.14) for either equipment or structures investment, with an intercept term added. On the basis of these parameter estimates, construct the implicit estimates of the capital/output coefficient μ, the partial adjustment coefficient λ, and the rate of depreciation δ, as discussed in the text under Eq. (6.14). Does the implied estimate of δ correspond well with the $\delta_E = 0.15$ or $\delta_S = 0.05$ rate assumed by Kopcke? How do you interpret this? Using the reported Durbin-Watson (DW) test statistic and a 0.05 level of significance, test the null hypothesis of no autocorrelation. Since DW is approximately equal to $2(1 - \rho)$, calculate the implied estimate of ρ, the first-order autocorrelation coefficient. Why might this estimate of ρ be biased toward zero?

(b) James Durbin [1970] has developed two test statistics that are strictly valid in large samples of data but that are often employed in small samples as well. In our context, Durbin's h-statistic is calculated as

$$\text{Durbin's } h \equiv \hat{\rho} \sqrt{\frac{T}{1 - T(\text{Var } b)}} \tag{6.52}$$

where $\hat{\rho}$ is the estimated first-order autocorrelation coefficient from part (a), T is the sample size (here, $T = 124$), and Var b is estimated as the square of the standard error of the coefficient of the lagged dependent variable from part (a). In large samples, h is approximately normally distributed with unit variance. Notice that, provided $T(\text{Var } b) < 1$, the ratio in the square root term will be greater than 1, and so $h > \rho$. Using results from part (a), if possible, compute h, and then using the standard normal distribution table and a 0.05 level of significance, test the null hypothesis that $h = 0$.

In some cases, however, $T(\text{Var } b) > 1$, and in such situations one obviously cannot use Durbin's h-statistic, since square roots of negative numbers cause well-known problems! Instead, one can employ Durbin's m-test procedure. Specifically, from part (a), retrieve the 124 residuals, and denote these as e_t. Then, with the first observation now deleted, estimate by OLS an equation with e_t as the dependent variable and with regressors the same variables as in the original equation estimated in part (a) plus the lagged residual e_{t-1}; that is, estimate the equation

$$e_t = a + b_1 Y_t + b_2 Y_{t-1} + b_3 I_{t-1} + \rho^* e_{t-1}$$

over observations 1956:2–1986:4. Compare the magnitude of this estimate of ρ^* with that implied in the OLS equation estimated in part (a) and with Durbin's h-statistic (if you were able to compute it). Now test whether ρ^* here is significantly different from zero by comparing the calculated t-statistic on ρ^* with the 0.05 critical value from the normal distribution table. Does the statistical inference on whether first-order autocorrelation is present vary depending on the procedure employed? Which procedure is preferable, and why?[60]

(c) Now estimate Eq. (6.14), allowing for first-order autocorrelation, using data over the 1956:1–1986:4 time period and the Hildreth-Lu estimation technique, with the grid of values for ρ originally ranging from $\rho = 0.00$ to $\rho = 1.00$ in steps of 0.05. Does any conflict appear between local and global maxima? On the basis of the initial results, refine the grid search to steps of 0.01. Test the null hypothesis that $\rho = 0$. Compare the implicit estimates of μ, λ, and δ to those obtained in part (a). Which estimates are preferable, and why?

(d) With lagged dependent variables, one must be particularly cautious in using the iterative Cochrane-Orcutt estimator, since the first-round estimate of ρ is biased.[61] However, for numerical reasons this estimator often (but not always) coincides with the Hildreth-Lu estimator. Estimate Eq. (6.14), allowing for first-order autocorrelation using the iterative Cochrane-Orcutt estimator, and then compare parameter estimates and statistical inference with those from part (c). In this particular case, do estimates of ρ and the parameters coincide? Interpret your results.

EXERCISE 3: Regression Estimation of the Time Series/Autoregressive Model

The purpose of this exercise is to have you estimate parameters of a time series/autoregressive model and choose a preferred specification based on hypothesis testing and properties of the estimated parameters. Procedures used here involve the classical hypothesis-testing approaches of traditional regression analysis. An alternative time series approach, based on Box-Jenkins procedures, is employed in Exercise 7 of this chapter.

In the data diskette directory CHAP6.DAT there is a data file called KOPCKE that contains quarterly data series 1952:1–1986:4 on real investment in equipment and structures (IE and IS).

(a) In the three time series/autoregressive studies of Kopcke discussed in Section 6.6, the number of lagged dependent variables is one, three, and eight for structures in studies (i), (ii), and (iii), respectively, and one, two, and six for equipment. Using the quarterly U.S. investment data 1956:1–1979:4, estimate Eq. (6.41) for equipment investment by OLS, where m, the number of lagged terms, equals 8. Compare these estimates to those reported by Kopcke in his study (iii), reproduced in Table 6.7. How well are you able to replicate Kopcke's results? (*Note:* See the comment just preceding Exercise 1.) Then estimate the same equation using more recent data, that is, estimate Eq. (6.41) with $m = 8$ over the 1956:1–1986:4 time period. Do estimates of the parameters change substantially? What can you infer concerning parameter stability?

(b) Using the estimated residuals from your 1956:1–1979:4 regression equation of part (a), convert these residuals into percent form, and then compute the % root mean squared error, as in Eq. (6.50), with T now equal to 96. Compare your % RMSE to that reported by Kopcke (see Table 6.7). Then compute % RMSE for the estimated residuals from your 1956:1–1986:4 regression equation of part (a). Does the size of the % RMSE change substantially when the more recent investment data are included? Interpret these results.

(c) Repeat parts (a) and (b) but for investment in structures rather than in equipment, with $m = 6$, as in Kopcke [1985], reproduced in Table 6.7. Does the % RMSE for equipment continue to exceed that for structures, as Kopcke reported?

(d) Kopcke states that his choice of preferred specification is based on a combination of statistical significance, the sensibility of the parameter estimates, and judgment. Begin with a rather general specification, say, $m = 12$, use the full sample 1956:1–1986:4, and then conduct a series of hypothesis tests that leads you to settle on a preferred specification, both for structures and for equipment investment. Comment on the role and interpretation of the Durbin-Watson test statistic in this specification choice process. Note also that if the b_j parameters on the lagged dependent variables sum to a value greater than +1, the estimated model is nonstationary (predicted investment will increase indefinitely with time). Does this occur with any of your estimated models? Is it reasonable? Finally, for both equipment and structures, compare your preferred specifications to those reported by Kopcke in his studies (i) and (iii), reproduced in Table 6.7. Does the number of lagged variables in your preferred specification differ from those reported by Kopcke? If possible, test the number of lags reported by Kopcke as special cases of your preferred specification or vice versa. What do you conclude on the basis of these hypothesis tests?

EXERCISE 4: Almon Lag Estimation of the Cash Flow Model

The purpose of this exercise is to give you experience in using the Almon polynomial distributed lag (PDL) procedure in the estimation of a cash flow model of investment spending. You will test coefficient restrictions that are implicit in the PDL procedure and allow for first-order autocorrelation of residuals.

In the data diskette directory CHAP6.DAT there is a data file called KOPCKE that contains quarterly data series 1952:1–1986:4 on real investment in equipment and structures (IE and IS), cash flow in millions of current dollars (F), price deflators for new equipment (JE) and new structures (JS) capital goods, and the once-lagged capital stocks for equipment and structures (KELAG and KSLAG) in millions of 1982 dollars.

Note: For all parts of this exercise, choose *either* equipment investment *or* structures investment.

(a) Using the same time period (1956:1–1979:4) and specification as in Kopcke's last study (see Table 6.3), construct the real cash flow variable as the ratio of nominal cash flow (F) to the price deflator for new structures (JS) or new equipment (JE). Estimate the cash flow investment equation (6.18) using the Almon PDL procedure: As in Kopcke [1985], for both the equipment and structures equation, set m, the number of distributed lags of cash flow, equal to 6 (including the current time period), and constrain the parameters to lie along a third-degree polynomial, but impose no other constraints on the near or far PDL coefficients. Note that in Kopcke's estimated equations the lagged capital stock is omitted as a regressor, that is, the parameter c in Eq. (6.18) is constrained to zero. Test for first-order autocorrelation using the Durbin-Watson test statistic, and then estimate this PDL model allowing for first-order autocorrelation. How well can you replicate Kopcke's results, reproduced in Table 6.3? Comment on the pattern of the estimated PDL coefficients. How do you interpret the sum of the estimated PDL coefficients?

(b) Now test for restrictions implied by the above PDL estimation. Using the same time period as in part (a), that is, 1956:1–1979:4, estimate parameters of a model in which the PDL constraints are not imposed on the parameters. Specifically, estimate Eq. (6.18) with $m = 6$ and with $c = 0$, first by OLS and then by any of the procedures that allow for first-order autocorrelation (i.e., Hildreth-Lu or iterative Cochrane-Orcutt). Are any adverse effects of multicollinearity now apparent? Does the Almon PDL procedure of part (a) reduce these adverse effects? What is the difference in the number of "free" or independent parameters estimated here, relative to those estimated in the third-degree PDL of part (a)? On the basis of the OLS results here and in part (a), test for the validity of the constraints implied by the third-degree PDL using a reasonable level of significance and an F-test. Then, on the basis of the generalized least squares results (allowing for first-order autocorrelation) here and in part (a), again test for the validity of these third-degree PDL restrictions using a reasonable level of significance and the likelihood ratio test procedure. Comment on the appropriateness of your estimated PDL model.

(c) Next, check on other empirical support underlying the third-degree PDL specification. Specifically, using the PDL procedure and allowing for first-order autocorrelation over the 1956:1–1979:4 time period, estimate a model in which the number of distributed lag terms m is six as in part (a) but the degree of the PDL is 4 rather than 3. Compare results with those obtained in part (a). Are there any major changes in the parameter estimates or standard errors? Then, using a large sample test and a reasonable level of significance, test for a PDL of degree 3 (estimated in part (a)) as a special case of the PDL of degree 4 estimated here.

(d) Finally, choose a preferred cash flow investment specification for a data set including more recent data. Specifically, using the 1956:1–1986:4 data (you will need to construct the real cash flow variable as in part (a)), experiment with alternative degrees of the PDL procedure, allow for differing numbers of distributed lag terms, permit the coefficient on the lagged capital stock to be nonzero, and then estimate a number of alternative PDL equations that allow for first-order autocorrelation. From these various estimated equations, choose a preferred specification. Comment on and defend your choice.

EXERCISE 5: Putty-Clay in the Neoclassical Model of Investment

The purpose of this exercise is to engage you in estimating and interpreting parameters of a neoclassical investment equation, based on the Cobb-Douglas production function, incorporating putty-clay effects by allowing for differential impacts on investment of price and output changes. This specification was originally employed by Bischoff [1971a] and was discussed in Section 6.4.C.

In the data diskette subdirectory CHAP6.DAT there is a data file called KOPCKE that contains quarterly data series 1952:1–1986:4 on real investment in equipment (IE), the real user cost of capital for equipment (CE), a price deflator for new equipment (JE) capital goods, and the once-lagged equipment capital stock (KELAG).

(a) First you will need to construct the price-output variables that appear in the basic investment equation (6.33). Specifically, since CE is the real user cost of capital equipment defined as $CE \equiv cE/P$, where the lowercase cE is in nominal terms, on the basis of Eq. (6.33) construct new variables X_{1t} and X_{2t} defined as

$$X_{1t} \equiv (P/cE)_t Y_t = Y_t/CE_t \qquad X_{2t} \equiv (P/cE)_t Y_{t-1} = Y_{t-1}/CE_t$$

Note: Make sure that X_{1t} and X_{2t} are constructed for the data period 1952:2 to 1986:4.

(b) Having constructed the price/output variables X_{1t} and X_{2t}, you are now ready for estimation of Bischoff's putty-clay specification. As in Kopcke [1985], on the basis of the 1956:1–1979:4 time period, employ the Almon PDL procedure allowing for first-order autocorrelation, and estimate parameters of the now modified equipment investment equation (6.33):

$$IE_t = a_0 + \sum_{j=0}^{m-1} b_j X_{1,t-j} - \sum_{j=0}^{m-1} c_j X_{2,t-j} + d_K K_{t-1} + u_t \qquad \textbf{(6.33')}$$

with $m = 13$ and with the PDL coefficients constrained to lie on a third-degree polynomial. Impose no further restrictions on the PDL parameters. Compare your results to those of Kopcke, reproduced in Table 6.4, noting the negative sign in front of the c_j in (6.33′). How well are you able to replicate Kopcke's results? For small j, are your estimated c_j positive and significantly different from zero? How do you interpret these c_j?

(c) Next test whether the output responses differ from the price responses, that is, test whether Bischoff's putty-clay insight significantly improves the fit of the model. Recall from the discussion following Eq. (6.33) that for any given time displacement j, the effect on current investment I_t will be larger for an increase in Y_{t-j} than for an equal decrease in the user cost of capital $(c/P)_{t-j}$, provided that $c_j > 0$ (again note the negative sign in front of Eq. (6.33′)). This implies that the equal lag response hypothesis for prices and output corresponds to a special case of Bischoff's modified equation (6.33′) in which the c_j are simultaneously constrained to equal zero, $j = 0, \ldots, m - 1$. Using the same data sample as in part (a), $m = 13$, and a third-degree PDL specification allowing for first-order autocorrelation, estimate parameters of Eq. (6.33′) with the $X_{2,t-j}$ variables excluded from the regression equation. Impose no further restrictions on the PDL parameters. What is the number of constraints imposed in this restricted model? Using a reasonable level of significance and the likelihood ratio test procedure, test the joint null hypothesis that $c_j = 0, j = 0, \ldots, 12$, against the alternative hypothesis that these $c_j \neq 0$. Is the putty-clay hypothesis significant empirically?

(d) Finally, generate a preferred neoclassical equipment investment specification for a data set that includes more recent data. Specifically, using the 1956:1–1986:4 data (with the X_{1t} and X_{2t} variables constructed as in part (a)), experiment with alternative degrees of the PDL procedure, allow for Bischoff's putty-clay specification, and then estimate a number of alternative PDL equations that allow for first-order autocorrelation. To keep the number of regressions manageable, limit the number of distributed lag terms to $m = 13$ (including the current time period), as in Kopcke [1985]. From these various estimated equations, choose a preferred specification. Comment on and defend your choice, also comparing your results with those previously reported by Kopcke, reproduced in Table 6.4.

EXERCISE 6: Almon PDL Endpoint Restrictions in Tobin's q Model

The purpose of this exercise is to involve you in estimating a Tobin's q investment equation using Almon's polynomial distributed lag (PDL) procedure with endpoint restrictions imposed, as was done by Kopcke [1982, 1985]. Recall that PDL is a method for including a large number of lagged variables in a model but reducing the number of free coefficients to be estimated by requiring the coefficients to lie on a smooth polynomial in the lag. The purpose of endpoint constraints is to force the lag coefficients at either end of the lags over which one is estimating to go to zero. The LEADING constraint forces the coefficient of the hypothetical first lead to zero, while the TRAILING constraint forces the coefficient of the lag that is one past the last included lag to equal zero. See your econometrics theory textbook or the classic Almon [1965, 1968] references for further details.

In the data diskette directory CHAP6.DAT there is a data file called KOPCKE that contains quarterly data series 1952:1–1986:4 on real investment in equipment and structures (IE and IS), values of the Tobin's q ratio (q), and the once-lagged capital stocks for equipment and structures (KELAG and KSLAG).

Notes: For all parts of this exercise, choose *either* equipment investment *or* structures investment. The same Tobin's q variable is used in the equipment and structures investment equation, since separate measures are not available.

(a) To attempt replication of Kopcke's estimated equation (6.39), in which $(q - 1)_{t-j} \cdot K_{t-j-1}$ appear as regressors, construct a new variable called X_t and defined as $X_t \equiv (q - 1)_t \cdot K_{t-1}$. *Note:* Generate this variable for the entire 1952:1–1986:4 time period.

(b) Having constructed the X_t variable, you are now ready to proceed with estimation. Using the PDL estimation procedure and allowing for first-order autocorrelation, estimate parameters of the equation

$$I_t = a + \sum_{j=0}^{m-1} b_j \cdot X_{t-j} + b_K K_{t-1} + u_t \qquad \textbf{(6.53)}$$

over the 1956:1–1979:4 time period. Following Kopcke [1985], set $m = 9$ for the structures equation or $m = 8$ for the equipment equation, and constrain the PDL coefficients to lie on a third-degree polynomial. Impose no further restrictions on the PDL coefficients. Compare your results with those of Kopcke [1985], reproduced in Table 6.6. *Note:* You will not be able to replicate Kopcke's results, since his left-hand variable is I_t/U_t (where U is the rate of capacity utilization) rather than I_t as in Eq. (6.53). Further, he imposes the restriction that the TRAILING lag term be zero.

(c) To impose and test the restriction that the TRAILING lag term is zero, estimate Eq. (6.53) just as in part (b), but now impose the restriction that the implied coefficient on the b_m lagged variable is zero. (*Note:* Following J. Phillip Cooper [1972], most computer programs impose this endpoint restriction by subtracting the last scrambled variable from each of the other scrambled variables and then dropping the last scrambled variable from the regression.) Test for the empirical validity of this single TRAILING lag restriction by using either a t-test, F-test, or likelihood ratio test statistic and a reasonable significance level.

(d) Kopcke apparently experienced some difficulties in obtaining a desirable q investment equation in his third study, since his preferred specification involved introducing a new capacity utilization variable that did not appear in his previous studies (i) and (ii). An alternative direction on which Kopcke might have focused attention is his regressor X_t, defined in part (a). Recall that for a number of reasons discussed in Section 6.5, researchers currently tend to argue only that net investment is an increasing function of q, rather than stating the stronger hypothesis that if $q > 1$, then net investment will be positive. This suggests that one might want to define a new variable $X'_t \equiv q_t \cdot K_{t-1}$ and then substitute this into Eq. (6.53) in place of X_t. Notice that X'_t is the market value of the firm and that with this specification we are very close to the cash flow–market value specification (6.17) originally used by Grunfeld. Why will parameter estimates change when X'_t is used instead of X_t? Construct this new variable X'_t for the 1952:1–1986:4 time period. Using the same data, PDL degree, and value of m as in part (b), estimate Eq. (6.53) with the Almon PDL estimator, allowing for first-order autocorrelation. Which specification do you prefer, the one here or that from (b)? Why?

(e) Finally, generate a preferred Tobin's q investment specification for a data set that includes more recent data. Specifically, using the 1956:1–1986:4 data and staying with the third-degree PDL, experiment with the X_t or X'_t variables constructed in (a) and (d), allow for alternative TRAILING endpoint restrictions, and estimate a number of different PDL equations with first-order autocorrelation. To keep the number of regressions manageable, limit the number of distributed lag terms to at most 9, as in Kopcke [1985]. From these various estimated equations, choose a preferred specification. Comment on and defend your choice, also comparing results with those previously reported by Kopcke, reproduced in Table 6.6.

EXERCISE 7: Box-Jenkins Identification, Estimation, and Forecasting of an Investment Equation

In Exercise 3 a time series/autoregressive model was estimated using traditional regression techniques. The purpose of this exercise is to give you hands-on experience in modeling the investment time series using an alternative procedure called the Box-Jenkins time series approach. Many econometric theory textbooks now devote discussion to time series analysis. If your econometric theory text does not, see the classic reference, a book by George P. Box and Gwilym M. Jenkins [1976], or the very readable texts by Charles R. Nelson [1973], Andrew C. Harvey [1981, 1990], and Clive W. J. Granger [1989].

In the data diskette directory CHAP6.DAT there is a data file called KOPCKE that contains quarterly data series 1952:1–1986:4 on real investment in equipment and structures (IE and IS). *Note:* Since these investment series are seasonally adjusted, the series should not contain a seasonal component.

(a) The first task is to generate a transformation of the investment time series that is stationary. Using 1956:1–1979:4 data, plot the raw data series for IE and IS. Do the data appear to follow a trend? What does this imply concerning stationarity? Next construct the sample autocorrelations (and their standard errors) for IE and IS where the maximal lag m is 16. Determine whether each series is stationary. If a series is nonstationary, then difference the data one, two, or more times until the sample autocorrelation function indicates that the differenced data are stationary, that is, until the sample autocorrelations go to zero as the length of the lag increases. Denote this degree of differencing by d. In choosing d, make use of the Box-Pierce portmanteau test, typically called the Box-Pierce Q-statistic:

$$\text{Box-Pierce } Q \equiv T \sum_{k=j+1}^{m} \hat{\rho}_k^2 \tag{6.54}$$

which tests the null hypothesis that all further (longer lagged) autocorrelations are simultaneously equal to zero. At the jth lag the Box-Pierce Q-statistic is distributed independently as a chi-square random variable with degrees of freedom equal to $m - j - 1$.

(b) Having generated a stationary time series for IE and IS, now identify the order of the moving average (MA) process, denoted q, and the order of the autoregressive (AR) process, denoted p. Recall that spikes in the sample autocorrelation function often indicate MA components, while observations that are highly correlated with surrounding ones, resulting in discernible up-and-down patterns, suggest that an AR process may be generating the data. Plot the sample autocorrelation function from your stationary series, and examine its properties. Is there any evidence of an MA component? An AR component? Why or why not? The partial autocorrelation function can be also used for guidance in determining the order of the AR portion of the ARIMA process. Using the stationary data series on IE and IS, calculate partial autocorrelation functions for time displacements up to 12 quarters, and on the basis of these autocorrelation functions and the Box-Pierce Q-statistic, choose reasonable values for p and q; in particular, choose two sets of p, q for IE and two for IS. Defend your choices.

(c) Having identified several possible ARIMA(p, d, q) processes underlying the IE and IS data series, now estimate their parameters. Specifically, for each of your ARIMA(p, d, q) specifications chosen in part (b) for IE and IS, use the Box-Jenkins estimation technique and estimate the ARIMA parameters employing quarterly investment data, 1956:1–1979:4. From your four alternative ARIMA(p, d, q) specifications from part (b), choose one preferred model among these for IE and one for IS. Base your choice on the statistical significance of the estimated parameters, the sample autocorrelations, partial autocorrelations, and the Box-Pierce Q-statistics. Compare your final choices to the ARIMA specifications of Kopcke [1985], whose final (p, d, q) models, reproduced in Table 6.7, are (8, 0, 0) for IS and (6, 0, 0) for IE.

(d) Now employ eight more recent observations, redo the identification and estimation of ARIMA models, and then perform an ex post dynamic forecast. First, using the quarterly IE and IS data, 1956:1–1981:4, redo part (a) and generate a stationary data series. Next, as in part (b), identify several plausible ARIMA(p, d, q) specifications. Estimate parameters of these specifications using Box-Jenkins procedures, and choose a preferred specification for IE and IS. Compare these final specifications to those of part (c). Are the specifications robust? How do you interpret these results? Finally, on the basis of your preferred specifications for IE and IS, use the Box-Jenkins forecasting procedure and forecast for the 20 quarters following the estimation period, that is, construct a dynamic forecast over 1982:1–1986:4, using forecasted rather than actual lagged values of investment as appropriate. Compare the forecasted with the actual investment data series over this time period, compute % RMSE using Eq. (6.50), examine whether any residuals are particularly large, and comment on properties of the forecasts. How well do your ARIMA models perform?

EXERCISE 8: Estimation with Simultaneity and Autocorrelation

One important specification issue in the investment literature concerns whether certain right-hand variables are exogenous or are instead endogenous. Although a variety of variables could be viewed as being jointly determined with investment, as was noted in Section 6.7.A, most attention has been focused on the output variable. The purpose of this exercise is to help you gain firsthand experience with instrumental variable estimation of several models in the presence of simultaneity and first-order autocorrelation.

In the data diskette directory CHAP6.DAT there is a data file called KOPCKE that contains quarterly data series 1952:1–1986:4 on real investment in equipment and structures (IE and IS) and real output (Y).

Notes: (1) For all parts of this exercise, choose *either* equipment investment *or* structures investment. (2) Although this exercise suggests using the OLS estimation method, following Kopcke [1985], you might instead wish to use the Almon polynomial distributed lag (PDL) estimator. If you employ PDL, set $m = 12$ (structures) or $m = 10$ (equipment), and constrain the PDL parameters to lie on a third-degree polynomial, as in Kopcke.

(a) Using OLS and data covering the 1956:1–1986:4 time span, estimate parameters of the accelerator equation (6.15), where $m = 7$. Then estimate this same equation allowing for first-order autocorrelation. Do the AR(1) estimates differ substantially from OLS estimates? If first-order autocorrelation is present, will the OLS parameter estimates be consistent? Why or why not? (*Hint:* Note that K_{t-1} appears as a regressor and that with the perpetual inventory procedure of Eq. (6.4) the capital stock data construction methods ensure that K_{t-1} depends on lagged investment I_{t-1}.)

(b) Next, allow for simultaneity but not for autocorrelation. Assume that output Y_t is jointly determined with investment I_t but that $Y_{t-\tau}$ are predetermined, $\tau = 1, \ldots, m - 1$. From among the various variables in the KOPCKE data file, choose two variables that could serve as legitimate instruments for I_t; denote these instrumental variables as Z_{1t} and Z_{2t}. Defend your choice of Z_{1t} and Z_{2t}. Then employ the two-stage least squares (2SLS) or instrumental variable (INST) procedure and estimate parameters of Eq. (6.15), where $m = 7$. Compare results with those obtained in part (a). Do the estimates vary substantially?

(c) Now estimate allowing both for simultaneity and for autocorrelation. As discussed in Section 6.7.A, you must take care in specifying the set of instruments in this context. Specifically, Fair [1970] has shown that if the disturbances follow a kth-order autoregressive process, then in addition to Z_{1t} and Z_{2t}, the set of instruments here must include $I_{t-\tau}$, $Z_{1,t-\tau}$, and $Z_{2,t-\tau}$, for $\tau = 1, \ldots, k$. In the current context, if you specify an AR(1) process, then the set of instruments should be Z_{1t}, Z_{2t}, I_{t-1}, $Z_{1,t-1}$, and $Z_{2,t-1}$. Outline the intuition that helps explain why this expanded set of instruments must be employed in order to obtain consistent estimates of the parameters. Then, with $m = 7$ and this enlarged set of instruments, estimate parameters of Eq. (6.15) by 2SLS or INST, allowing for first-order autocorrelation. Is autocorrelation statistically significant? Do the 2SLS or INST estimates of the distributed lag parameters vary significantly when account is taken of autocorrelation? Does allowing for simultaneity matter empirically? Why or why not?

EXERCISE 9: Levels and First Differences of the CES Capital Demand Equation with Autocorrelation

The controversy over how large is the response of investment to changes in the user cost of capital has filled many pages of professional economic journals. Recall that in the investment equations employed by Jorgenson, and more recently by Kopcke, the estimating equation is derived from the Cobb-Douglas production function, and so the magnitude of the long-run price response is constrained a priori. The purpose of this exercise is to have you relax the Cobb-Douglas specification, and instead estimate capital demand equations based on the less restrictive constant elasticity of substitution (CES) production function.

In the data diskette directory CHAP6.DAT there is a data file called KOPCKE that contains quarterly data series 1952:1–1986:4 on real investment in equipment and structures (IE and IS), the real user cost of capital for equipment (CE $\equiv cE/P$) and for structures (CS $\equiv cS/P$), real output (Y), and once-lagged capital stocks for equipment and structures (KELAG and KSLAG).

Note: For all parts of this exercise, choose *either* equipment investment *or* structures investment.

(a) Following Bischoff [1969], estimate a levels form of an investment equation based on the CES function in which the distributed lag response differs for user cost and for output, as in Eq. (6.38). To do this, for all 140 observations, first form logarithmic transformations and generate $\ln K$, $\ln Y$, and $\ln P/c$ (note that this last variable is the logarithm of the inverse of the user cost of capital c/P, or the negative of log (CS) or log (CE)). Next, using data from 1956:1 to 1986:4, employ the Almon PDL estimator, constrain the ϕ parameters in Eq. (6.38) to lie along a third-degree polynomial, assume no autocorrelation, and experiment with several alternative values of m varying from 9 to 12 ($m - 1$ from 8 to 11) and of s varying from 1 to 3. Compute long-run price (σ) and output (η) responses using Eq. (6.37). Construct 95% confidence regions for σ and η.

(b) In Section 6.4 it was noted that Bischoff found that estimates of σ and η were very sensitive to the specification of autocorrelation. To assess whether Bischoff's finding holds for the quarterly U.S. data 1956:1–1986:4, assume that $\rho = 1$ and estimate parameters of Eq. (6.36), which is in first differences of $\ln K$ rather than in levels (and therefore has no constant term). Employ the PDL estimator with procedures similar to those in part (a). Compute price and income responses using Eq. (6.37). Construct 95% confidence regions for σ and η. Compare your results to those from part (a). How robust are they? Which results do you prefer, and why?

(c) As Bischoff observed, there is no reason to constrain ρ to have only two possible values, 0 and 1. Using the same data as in parts (a) and (b) and the same specifications for the PDL estimator, now estimate Eq. (6.38), allowing ρ to range between 0 and 1. On the basis of Eq. (6.37), compute long-run price and output responses, as well as 95% confidence regions for σ and η. Compare your results to those from parts (a) and (b). Like Bischoff, do you conclude that estimates of σ and η are sensitive to the specification of autocorrelation? Which joint estimates of σ, η, and ρ do you prefer, and why?

(d) Bischoff's procedure, which you have replicated in parts (a) through (c), can be criticized in that it limits the time dependence of the disturbance to a first-order autoregressive process. Note that since a lagged dependent variable appears as a regressor in Eq. (6.37), examination of the residuals from your preferred specification in part (c) is not likely to reveal accurately the presence of other autocorrelated or moving average error processes. Therefore, using your preferred specification from part (c), reestimate, allowing for higher-order AR processes and/or an MA process. Using Eq. (6.37), compute long-run price and output responses, as well as 95% confidence regions for σ and η. To the extent that tax policy affects the user cost of capital, based on your preferred model, by how much does tax policy affect investment? Test for AR(1) as a special case of your more general models. Do your new results support or undermine the Bischoff procedure? Why?

EXERCISE 10: A "Horse Race" Project Based on More Recent Data

This exercise involves a substantial amount of work, and your instructor may implement it in a number of alternative ways, some of which are suggested in the Instructor's Resource Guide accompanying this text. The purpose of this exercise is to engage you in estimating three alternative investment models from among the five discussed in the text, using more recent data than those in Kopcke [1985], and then conducting a "horse race," comparing the models in terms of performance in estimation, static forecasts, and dynamic forecasts.

In the data diskette directory CHAP6.DAT there is a data file called KOPCKE that contains quarterly data series 1952:1–1986:4 on a number of variables, defined and briefly described at the beginning of Section 6.10.

Of the five investment models, choose three that you will enter into a "horse race." On the basis of 1956:1–1981:4 data you will estimate a number of equations for each model and then choose a preferred specification from among them for equipment and for structures investment. You will also conduct ex post static forecasts for 1982:1–1986:4, and finally, you will compare the models in terms of their dynamic forecasting properties over the 1982:1–1986:4 time period.

The time periods underlying your horse races are of considerable interest because while structures investment first declined, then rose, and finally declined again during the 1982:1–1986:4 time span, equipment investment rose quite sharply, ending up in 1986:4 about 35% higher than in 1981:4. It will therefore be particularly interesting to assess the ex post forecasting properties of your alternative investment models during this volatile time period.

(a) For each of the three chosen investment models, using 1956:1–1986:4 data, estimate a variety of promising equations, varying the form of the PDL process (especially the number of lags and the degree of the polynomial) and the stochastic specification (allowing for autoregressive and/or moving average errors). As in Kopcke's three studies, use Eq. (6.50) and compute % RMSE, as well as the percent of "very large" errors. From among the various equations estimated, choose a preferred specification for structures and for equipment investment. Defend your choices, and compare them to previous equations estimated by Kopcke.

Comment on the stability of the estimated parameters over time. Does any one of the three models produce a clear winner in terms of estimation performance? Why or why not?

(b) On the basis of your preferred specifications for the IE and IS equations, use actual values for all the right-hand variables over the 1982:1–1986:4 time period, and then compute ex post static forecasts for IE and IS for all three models. Compare the % RMSE in forecast time to those from the estimation time period. Is the deterioration substantial? How does the deterioration compare to that reported by Kopcke in his three studies? Does the percent of "very large" errors also increase substantially? How do you compare your three models in terms of their static forecasting properties?

(c) Finally, again on the basis of your preferred specifications for the IE and IS equations from part (a), use actual values of all exogenous variables and simulated values for all endogenous variables that appear as regressors in the estimating equation, and compute ex post dynamic forecasts for IE and IS over the 1982:1–1986:4 time period for all three models. Incorporate the effects of the last residual in estimation (1981:4) into the forecast appropriately, depending on your AR or MA specification. How well do the dynamic forecasts capture the turning points that occurred for IE and IS over this forecast time period? Using Eq. (6.50), compute % RMSE and the percentage of "very large" errors for each model. Alternatively, you might wish to employ Theil's inequality coefficient.[62] Do the models differ substantially in their forecasting performance? Does their performance depend considerably on whether one is looking at IE or IS? Construct a criterion for an overall ranking of the three models in terms of dynamic forecasting properties, and then rank them. How does this ranking compare with those obtained by Kopcke? Who wins the horse race, and who loses?

(d) Comment on the usefulness of these types of "horse races." What have you learned, and what conclusions most surprised you?

CHAPTER NOTES

1. These numbers are taken from Richard W. Kopcke [1985].
2. For a survey on factors affecting residential investment, see Craig Swan [1970]; for inventory investment, see John C. R. Rowley and Pravin K. Trivedi [1975].
3. For other discussions of econometric issues involved in modeling aggregate investment expenditures, see Meghnad Desai [1976], especially Chapter 6, pp. 168–204; R. L. Thomas [1985], especially Chapter 9, pp. 251–291; and Kenneth F. Wallis [1973], especially Chapter 3, pp. 63–97.
4. Hicks [1981], p. 204.
5. Precisely how such price indexes should be constructed by national income accountants and statisticians is an important issue. For an example and discussion of related quality adjustment issues, see Chapter 4 in this text.

6. The expression "one-hoss shay" deterioration derives from Robert Frost's famous poem featuring a one-horse carriage. In our context, such a carriage can be envisaged as providing the same amount of services and no maintenance during each time period until it breaks, at which time its services become zero. (Note that the horse has a different life profile of services, generating virtually none during infancy and typically requiring considerably more maintenance expenditures as it approaches the end of its life expectancy.)
7. Robert Winfrey [1935].
8. Taken from John A. Gorman et al. [1985].
9. Previous and revised estimates of service lives for various assets are given in Gorman, Musgrave, Silverstein, and Comins [1985], Table C, p. 42. Steam engines and turbines, for example, are assumed to have mean service lifetimes of 32 years, ships and boats 27 years, scientific and engineering instruments 12 years, and farm tractors 9 years. These service life estimates include the expected effects of obsolescence but do not incorporate effects of unexpected obsolescence due to, for example, energy price shocks.
10. While gross capital stock calculations are almost always based on the one-hoss shay assumption, net capital stocks can be constructed by using a variety of deterioration assumptions; exponential decay is the most common assumption.
11. For a more thorough discussion of replacement investment and depreciation, see Chapter 7 in Stephen J. Nickell [1978].
12. Partly for reasons of convenience, straight line is the pattern of depreciation most often assumed by accountants.
13. For details, see Robert E. Hall [1968] and the references cited therein; also see Dale W. Jorgenson [1974].
14. See Robert E. Hall [1971], Martin S. Feldstein and David K. Foot [1971], Robert Eisner [1972], Feldstein and Michael Rothschild [1974], George C. Bitros and Harry H. Kelejian [1974], and Robert M. Coen [1975].
15. Charles R. Hulten and Frank C. Wykoff [1981a], p. 393.
16. Hulten and Wykoff [1980, 1981b].
17. Typically, U.S. researchers assume that nonresidential structures decay at between 3% and 8% per year, while producers' durable equipment decays at annual rates between 10% and 20%. In Europe, assumed rates are often smaller.
18. One possible procedure here involves instrumental variables. See your econometric theory textbook for estimation procedures in the context of measurement error.
19. J. Maurice Clark [1917]; also see Hollis B. Chenery [1952].
20. These test statistic procedures are described in most econometrics theory textbooks and are discussed further in Exercise 2 of this chapter. Alternatively, see James Durbin [1970].
21. For a detailed treatment, also see Phoebus Dhrymes [1971].
22. For an early critique, see A. D. Knox [1952].
23. In addition to studies cited earlier, see Robert Eisner [1967], Bert G. Hickman [1965], and Andrew B. Abel and Olivier Jean Blanchard [1988].
24. One of the earliest empirical applications of the cash flow model is Model I in Lawrence R. Klein [1950]. As Klein noted, however, his model could also be rationalized by using principles from Marxist economics.
25. In Duesenberry [1958], see especially Chapters 3–5.
26. This empirical observation is not necessarily consistent with the theoretical literature from financial economics. In particular, a classic theoretical result due to

Franco Modigliani and Merton H. Miller [1958] is that, in the absence of taxes, the cost of capital to a firm is independent of whether the financing is from debt or equity.

27. See Robert M. Coen [1971].
28. Trygve Haavelmo [1960], p. 216.
29. This tax incidence assumption is of course closely related to the earlier assumption of perfect competition in the output markets.
30. Note also that many firms operate across multiple tax jurisdictions. A useful discussion of many of these tax issues is found in Don Fullerton [1984].
31. See, for example, David F. Bradford and Don Fullerton [1981] and Mervyn A. King et al. [1984]. For a summary review of such tax issues, see Alan J. Auerbach [1983].
32. A discussion and empirical illustration of these issues is found in Michael J. Harper, Ernst R. Berndt, and David O. Wood [1989]. Also see Berndt [1976].
33. For a useful empirical comparison of alternative expectations formulations, see Albert K. Ando et al. [1974].
34. See, for example, Robert E. Hall and Dale W. Jorgenson [1967] and the various studies surveyed in Dale W. Jorgenson [1971]. For extensive critiques of Jorgenson's econometric studies, see the references in footnote 3.
35. Further discussion on properties of the Cobb-Douglas production and cost functions is provided in Chapter 3, especially Section 3.3.
36. There is some ambiguity in interpreting these results, however; Andrew Abel [1979] has shown that under certain conditions, putty-putty and putty-clay models can be observationally equivalent. In such cases it is not clear what hypothesis would be rejected.
37. In addition to the references cited earlier, see Robert M. Coen [1968], Robert Eisner [1969], Dale W. Jorgenson and Calvin D. Siebert [1968], and Dale W. Jorgenson, Jerald Hunter, and M. Ishaq Nadiri [1970a].
38. These and other measurement issues are discussed by, among others, John H. Ciccolo, Jr. [1978], Ciccolo and Gary Fromm [1979], Daniel M. Holland and Stewart C. Myers [1979], Lawrence H. Summers [1981], and Alan J. Auerbach [1979].
39. Andrew B. Abel [1979, especially Chapter 4], Abel [1980], Hiroshi Yoshikawa [1980], and Fumio Hayashi [1982].
40. This observation has led some analysts to employ measures of q as estimates of market power. See, for example, Michael A. Salinger [1984].
41. In addition to the references cited in footnote 38, see George M. von Furstenberg [1977], James M. Poterba and Lawrence H. Summers [1983], and Olivier J. Blanchard and Charles Wyplosz [1981].
42. Kopcke [1985, p. 32] justifies inclusion of this U_t variable into the q model by arguing that, especially for the equipment equation, when q rises, investment might not increase if the capital stock is not fully utilized. Further, Kopcke comments that the U_t variable is not included in the other investment equations, since capacity utilization effects are already captured by the output, internal cash flow, or profit variables.
43. In general, there appear to be serious problems in implementing Tobin's q empirically when there is more than one type of capital good. See David Wildasin [1984] and Berndt and Melvyn A. Fuss [1989].
44. Two important papers in this context are those by Arnold Zellner and Franz Palm [1974] and by Christopher A. Sims [1980].

45. Note that if production is characterized by constant or increasing returns to scale and if output markets are perfect, the optimal level of output is indeterminate.
46. This issue is considered further in Exercise 8 of this chapter.
47. These issues are also considered in further detail in Chapters 7, 8, and 10.
48. This is the famous "Lucas critique" (see Robert E. Lucas, Jr. [1976]); it is discussed in further detail in Chapter 10. Earlier statements of the Lucas critique are found in, for example, James Duesenberry [1948, Section I].
49. For an early clear statement of the REH, see John F. Muth [1961].
50. For a useful discussion, see Kenneth F. Wallis [1980] and the papers collected in Robert E. Lucas, Jr., and Thomas J. Sargent [1981].
51. In particular, the equation must be linear in the expectations variables. The estimated standard errors based on this direct procedure will, however, be incorrect. See Exercise 2 in Chapter 10 for further details.
52. See Lars P. Hansen and Kenneth J. Singleton [1982].
53. Internal adjustment costs are often distinguished from external adjustment costs, in which supply prices of capital goods depend on the amount of new investment goods ordered. These definitions and the shapes of the corresponding adjustment cost functions are discussed in John P. Gould [1968], Michael Mussa [1977], and Michael Rothschild [1971].
54. Robert E. Lucas, Jr. [1967a, b] and Arthur B. Treadway [1971, 1974].
55. Such comparisons studies include an early one by Jan Tinbergen [1951], as well as more recent ones by, among others, Charles W. Bischoff [1971b], Dale W. Jorgenson, Jerald Hunter, and M. Ishaq Nadiri [1970b], Peter K. Clark [1979], and Robert S. Chirinko [1986].
56. Note that the computation of each static forecast employs the previous quarter's forecast error and the estimated autocorrelation coefficient.
57. See your econometric theory text for further details. A classic treatment is by Arthur S. Goldberger [1962].
58. Other criteria that could be employed to assess forecasting performance include an analysis of missed turning points in investment and the Theil inequality measures, which decompose the forecast error into bias, variance, and covariance sources. Most econometric theory textbooks discuss Theil's measure in detail. The classic references are Henri Theil [1961, pp. 30–37] and Theil [1966, pp. 26–35].
59. A number of alternative ways of implementing Exercise 10 are discussed in the Instructor's Resource Guide accompanying this text.
60. For a discussion comparing these two procedures, including the results of Monte Carlo studies, see Andrew C. Harvey [1981, pp. 276ff.].
61. On this, see Roger Betancourt and Harry Kelejian [1981].
62. See footnote 58 for references.

CHAPTER REFERENCES

Abel, Andrew B. [1979], *Investment and the Value of Capital*, New York: Garland Publishing Company.

Abel, Andrew B. [1980], "Empirical Investment Equations: An Integrative Framework," *Carnegie-Rochester Conference Series on Public Policy*, 12, Spring, 39–91.

Abel, Andrew B. and Oliver Jean Blanchard [1986], "The Present Value of Profits and Cyclical Movements in Investment," *Econometrica*, 54:2, March, 249–273.

Abel, Andrew B. and Olivier Jean Blanchard [1988], "Investment and Sales: Some Empirical Evidence," in William A. Barnett, Ernst R. Berndt, and Halbert L. White, eds., *Dynamic Econometric Modeling*, Cambridge, England: Cambridge University Press, pp. 269–296.

Almon, Shirley [1965], "The Distributed Lag between Capital Appropriations and Capital Expenditures," *Econometrica*, 33:1, January, 178–196.

Almon, Shirley [1968], "Lags between Investment Decisions and Their Causes," *Review of Economics and Statistics*, 50:2, May, 178–196.

Ando, Albert K., Franco Modigliani, Robert Rasche, and Steven J. Turnovsky [1974], "On the Role of Expectations of Price and Technological Change in an Investment Function," *International Economic Review*, 15:2, June, 384–414.

Auerbach, Alan J. [1979], "Inflation and the Choice of Asset Life," *Journal of Political Economy*, June, 621–638.

Auerbach, Alan J. [1983], "Taxation, Corporate Financial Policy and the Cost of Capital," *Journal of Economic Literature*, 21:3, September, 905–940.

Berndt, Ernst R. [1976], "Reconciling Alternative Estimates of the Elasticity of Substitution," *Review of Economics and Statistics*, 58:1, February, 59–68.

Berndt, Ernst R. and Melvyn A. Fuss [1989], "Economic Capacity Utilization and Productivity Measurement for Multiproduct Firms with Multiple Quasi-Fixed Inputs," Cambridge, Mass.: National Bureau of Economic Research, Working Paper No. 2932, April.

Betancourt, Roger and Harry Kelejian [1981], "Lagged Endogenous Variables and the Cochrane-Orcutt Procedure," *Econometrica*, 49:4, July, 1073–1078.

Bischoff, Charles W. [1969], "Hypothesis Testing and the Demand for Capital Goods," *Review of Economics and Statistics*, 51:3, August, 354–368.

Bischoff, Charles W. [1971a], "The Effect of Alternative Lag Distributions," in Gary Fromm, ed., *Tax Incentives and Capital Spending*, Washington, D.C.: The Brookings Institution, pp. 61–125.

Bischoff, Charles W. [1971b], "Business Investment in the 1970s: A Comparison of Models," *Brookings Papers on Economic Activity*, 1:1971, 13–58.

Bitros, George C. and Harry H. Kelejian [1974], "On the Variability of the Replacement Capital Stock: Some Evidence from Capital Scrappage," *Review of Economics and Statistics*, 56:3, August, 270–278.

Blanchard, Olivier J. and Charles Wyplosz [1981], "An Empirical Structural Model of Aggregate Demand," *Journal of Monetary Economics*, 7:1, January, 1–28.

Box, George P. and Gwilym M. Jenkins [1976], *Time Series Analysis: Forecasting and Control*, San Francisco: Holden-Day.

Bradford, David F. and Don Fullerton [1981], "Pitfalls in the Construction and Use of Effective Tax Rates," in Charles R. Hulten, ed., *Depreciation, Inflation, and the Taxation of Income from Capital*, Washington, D.C.: The Urban Institute Press, pp. 251–278.

Chenery, Hollis B. [1952], "Overcapacity and the Acceleration Principle," *Econometrica*, 20:1, January, 1–28.

Chirinko, Robert S. [1986], "Business Investment and Tax Policy: A Perspective on Existing Models and Empirical Results," *National Tax Journal*, 39:2, June, 137–155.

Christensen, Laurits R. and Dale W. Jorgenson [1969], "The Measurement of U.S. Real Capital Input, 1929–1967," *Review of Income and Wealth*, 15:4, December, 293–320.

Ciccolo, John H., Jr. [1978], "Money, Equity Values and Income," *Journal of Money, Credit and Banking*, 10:1, February, 54–57.

Ciccolo, John H., Jr., and Gary Fromm [1979], "'*q*' and the Theory of Investment," *Journal of Finance*, 34:2, May, 535–547.

Clark, J. Maurice [1917], "Business Acceleration and the Law of Demand: A Technical Factor in Economic Cycles," *Journal of Political Economy*, 25:1, March, 217–235.

Clark, Peter K. [1979], "Investment in the 1970s: Theory, Performance and Prediction," *Brookings Papers on Economic Activity*, 1:1979, 73–113.

Coen, Robert M. [1968], "The Effects of Tax Policy on Investment in Manufacturing," *American Economic Review*, 58:2, May, 200–211.

Coen, Robert M. [1971], "The Effects of Cash Flow on the Speed of Adjustment," in Gary Fromm, ed., *Tax Incentives and Capital Spending*, Washington, D.C.: The Brookings Institution, pp. 131–196.

Coen, Robert M. [1975], "Investment Behavior, the Measurement of Depreciation, and Tax Policy," *American Economic Review*, 65:1, March, 59–74.

Cooper, J. Phillip [1972], "Two Approaches to Polynomial Distributed Lags Estimation: An Expository Note and Comment," *The American Statistician*, 26:2, June, 32–35.

de Leeuw, Frank [1962], "The Demand for Capital Goods by Manufacturers: A Study of Quarterly Time Series," *Econometrica*, 30:3, July, 407–423.

Deloitte, Haskins, and Sells [1988], "Expectations for 1988 Remain Favorable," *Review*, 88:3, February 1.

Desai, Meghnad [1976], *Applied Econometrics*, New York: McGraw-Hill.

Dhrymes, Phoebus [1971], *Distributed Lags: Problems of Estimation and Formulation*, San Francisco: Holden-Day.

Dornbusch, Rudiger and Stanley Fischer [1987], *Macroeconomics*, Fourth Edition, New York: McGraw-Hill.

Duesenberry, James S. [1948], "Income-Consumption Relations and Their Implications," in *Income, Employment and Public Policy: Essays in Honor of Alvin H. Hansen*, New York: W. W. Norton & Co., pp. 54–81. Reprinted in Chapter 6 in M. G. Mueller, ed. [1966], *Readings in Macroeconomics*, New York: Holt, Rinehart and Winston, pp. 61–76.

Duesenberry, James S. [1958], *Business Cycles and Economic Growth*, New York: McGraw-Hill.

Durbin, James [1970], "Testing for Serial Correlation in Least Squares Regression When Some of the Regressors Are Lagged Dependent Variables," *Econometrica*, 38:3, May, 410–421.

Eisner, Robert [1967], "A Permanent Income Theory for Investment: Some Empirical Explorations," *American Economic Review*, 57:3, June, 363–390.

Eisner, Robert [1969], "Tax Policy and Investment Behavior: Comment," *American Economic Review*, 59:3, June, 379–388.

Eisner, Robert [1972], "Components of Capital Expenditures: Replacement and Modernization," *Review of Economics and Statistics*, 54:5, August, 297–305.

Eisner, Robert and M. Ishaq Nadiri [1968], "Investment Behavior and Neo-Classical Theory," *Review of Economics and Statistics*, 50:3, August, 369–382.

Eisner, Robert and Robert H. Strotz [1963], "Determinants of Business Investment," in *Impacts of Monetary Policy*, Research Studies Prepared for the Commission on Money and Credit, Englewood Cliffs, N.J.: Prentice-Hall, pp. 59–236.

Evans, Michael K. [1967], "A Study of Industry Investment Decisions," *Review of Economics and Statistics*, 49:2, May, 151–164.

Fair, Ray C. [1970], "The Estimation of Simultaneous Equation Models with Lagged Endogenous Variables and First Order Serially Correlated Errors," *Econometrica*, 38:3, May, 507–516.

Feldstein, Martin S. and John S. Flemming [1971], "Tax Policy, Corporate Saving and Investment Behaviour in Britain," *Review of Economic Studies*, 38, October, 415–434.

Feldstein, Martin S. and David K. Foot [1971], "The Other Half of Gross Investment: Replacement and Modernization Expenditure," *Review of Economics and Statistics*, 53:1, February, 49–58.

Feldstein, Martin S. and Michael Rothschild [1974], "Towards an Economic Theory of Replacement Investment," *Econometrica*, 42:3, May, 393–423.

Fullerton, Don [1984], "Which Effective Tax Rate?" *National Tax Journal*, 37:1, March, 23–42.

Goldberger, Arthur S. [1962], "Best Linear Unbiased Prediction in the Linear Regression Model," *Journal of the American Statistical Association*, 57:298, June, 369–372.

Gorman, John A., John C. Musgrave, Gerald Silverstein, and Kathy A. Comins [1985], "Fixed Private Capital in the United States," *Survey of Current Business*, 67:7, July, 36–59.

Gould, John P. [1968], "Adjustment Costs in the Theory of Investment of the Firm," *Review of Economic Studies*, 35:1, Series No. 101, January, 47–55.

Granger, Clive W. J. [1989], *Forecasting in Business and Economics*, Second Edition, Boston: Academic Press.

Griliches, Zvi [1967], "Distributed Lags: A Survey," *Econometrica*, 35:1, January, 16–49.

Griliches, Zvi [1974], "Comments on Sims," in Michael D. Intriligator and David A. Kendrick, eds., *Frontiers of Quantitative Economics*, Vol. 2, Amsterdam: North-Holland, 1974, pp. 334–336.

Grunfeld, Yehuda [1960], "The Determinants of Corporate Investment," in Arnold C. Harberger, ed., *The Demand for Durable Goods*, Chicago: University of Chicago Press, pp. 211–266.

Haavelmo, Trygve [1960], *A Study in the Theory of Investment*, Chicago: University of Chicago Press.

Hall, Robert E. [1968], "Technical Change and Capital from the Point of View of the Dual," *Review of Economic Studies*, 35:1, 35–46.

Hall, Robert E. [1971], "The Measurement of Quality Change from Vintage Price Data," in Zvi Griliches, ed., *Price Indexes and Quality Change*, Cambridge, Mass.: Harvard University Press, pp. 240–271.

Hall, Robert E. and Dale W. Jorgenson [1967], "Tax Policy and Investment Behavior," *American Economic Review*, 57:3, June, 391–414.

Hall, Robert E. and John B. Taylor [1988], *Macroeconomics: Theory, Performance, and Policy*, Second Edition, New York: W. W. Norton.

Hansen, Lars P. and Kenneth J. Singleton [1982], "Generalized Instrumental Variables Estimation of Nonlinear Rational Expectations Models," *Econometrica*, 50:5, September, 1269–1286.

Harper, Michael J., Ernst R. Berndt, and David O. Wood [1989], "Rates of Return and Capital Aggregation Using Alternative Rental Prices," in Dale W. Jorgenson and Ralph Landau, eds., *Technology and Capital Formation*, Cambridge, Mass.: MIT Press, pp. 331–372.

Harvey, Andrew C. [1981], *The Econometric Analysis of Time Series*, Oxford, England: Phillip Allan Publishers Ltd. (Second Edition published by MIT Press, Cambridge, Mass., 1990.)

Hayashi, Fumio [1982], "Tobin's Marginal *q* and Average *q*: A Neoclassical Interpretation," *Econometrica*, 50:1, January, 213–224.

Helliwell, John F. and G. Glorieux [1970], "Forward-Looking Investment Behaviour," *Review of Economic Studies*, 37, October, 499–516.

Hickman, Bert G. [1965], *Investment Demand and U.S. Economic Growth*, Washington, D.C.: The Brookings Institution.

Hicks, John R. [1981], *Wealth and Welfare: Collected Essays on Economic Theory*, Cambridge, Mass.: Harvard University Press.

Holland, Daniel M. and Stewart C. Myers [1979], "Trends in Corporate Profitability and Capital Costs," in Robert Lindsay, ed., *The Nation's Capital Needs: Three Studies*, Washington, D.C.: Committee for Economic Development, pp. 103–188.

Hulten, Charles R. and Frank C. Wykoff [1980], "Economic Depreciation and the Taxation of Structures in U.S. Manufacturing Industries: An Empirical Analysis," Chapter 2 in Dan Usher, ed., *The Measurement of Capital*, Chicago: University of Chicago Press for the National Bureau of Economic Research, pp. 83–109.

Hulten, Charles R. and Frank C. Wykoff [1981a], "The Estimation of Economic Depreciation Using Vintage Asset Prices: An Application of the Box-Cox Power Transformation," *Journal of Econometrics*, 15:3, August, 367–396.

Hulten, Charles R. and Frank C. Wykoff [1981b], "The Measurement of Economic Depreciation," in Charles R. Hulten, ed., *Depreciation, Inflation, and the Taxation of Income from Capital*, Washington, D.C.: The Urban Institute Press, pp. 81–125.

Jorgenson, Dale W. [1963], "Capital Theory and Investment Behavior," *American Economic Review*, 53:2, May, 247–259.

Jorgenson, Dale W. [1966], "Rational Distributed Lag Functions," *Econometrica*, 34:1, January, 135–149.

Jorgenson, Dale W. [1971], "Econometric Studies of Investment Behavior: A Survey," *Journal of Economic Literature*, 9:4, December, 1111–1147.

Jorgenson, Dale W. [1974], "The Economic Theory of Replacement and Depreciation," in Willy Sellekaerts, ed., *Econometrics and Economic Theory: Essays in Honor of Jan Tinbergen*, White Plains, N.Y.: International Arts and Science Press, pp. 189–221.

Jorgenson, Dale W. and Calvin D. Siebert [1968], "A Comparison of Alternative Theories of Corporate Investment Behavior," *American Economic Review*, 58:4, September, 681–712.

Jorgenson, Dale W., Jerald Hunter, and M. Ishaq Nadiri [1970a], "A Comparison of Alternative Econometric Models of Quarterly Investment Behavior," *Econometrica*, 38:1, March, 187–212.

Jorgenson, Dale W., Jerald Hunter, and M. Ishaq Nadiri [1970b], "The Predictive Performance of Econometric Models of Quarterly Investment Behavior," *Econometrica*, 38:1, March, pp. 213–224

King, Mervyn A., Don Fullerton, and Julian Alworth, eds. [1984], *The Taxation of Income from Capital: A Comparative Study of the U.S., U.K., Sweden and West Germany*, Chicago: University of Chicago Press.

Klein, Lawrence R. [1950], *Economic Fluctuations in the United States, 1921–1941*, New York: John Wiley and Sons.

Knox, A. D. [1952], "The Acceleration Principle and the Theory of Investment: A Survey," *Economica*, 19:75, August, 269–297.

Kopcke, Richard W. [1977], "The Behavior of Investment Spending during the Recession and Recovery, 1973–76," *New England Economic Review*, Boston, Mass.: Federal Reserve Bank of Boston, November/December, 5–41.

Kopcke, Richard W. [1982], "Forecasting Investment Spending: The Performance of Statistical Models," *New England Economic Review*, Boston, Mass: Federal Reserve Bank of Boston, November/December, 13–32.

Kopcke, Richard W. [1985], "The Determinants of Investment Spending," *New England Economic Review*, Boston, Mass.: Federal Reserve Bank of Boston, July/August, 19–35.

Koyck, Leendert M. [1954], *Distributed Lags and Investment Analysis*, Amsterdam: North-Holland.

Lucas, Robert E., Jr. [1967a], "Optimal Investment Policy and the Flexible Accelerator," *International Economic Review*, 8:1, February, 78–85.

Lucas, Robert E., Jr. [1967b], "Adjustment Costs and the Theory of Supply," *Journal of Political Economy*, 75:4, August, 321–344.

Lucas, Robert E., Jr. [1976], "Econometric Policy Evaluation: A Critique," in Karl Brunner and Alan N. Meltzer, eds., *The Phillips Curve and Labor Markets*, Amsterdam: North-Holland, pp. 19–46.

Lucas, Robert E., Jr., and Thomas J. Sargent, eds. [1981], *Rational Expectations and Econometric Practice*, Minneapolis: University of Minnesota Press.

Meyer, John R. and Edwin E. Kuh [1957], *The Investment Decision: An Empirical Study*, Cambridge, Mass.: Harvard University Press.

Modigliani, Franco and Merton H. Miller [1958], "The Cost of Capital, Corporation Finance, and the Theory of Investment," *American Economic Review*, 48:3, June, 261–297.

Mussa, Michael [1977], "External and Internal Adjustment Costs and the Theory of Aggregate and Firm Investment," *Economica*, 44:174, May, 163–178.

Muth, John F. [1960], "Optimal Properties of Exponentially Weighted Forecasts," *Journal of the American Statistical Association*, 55:290, June, 299–306.

Muth, John F. [1961], "Rational Expectations and the Theory of Price Movements," *Econometrica*, 29:2, July, 315–335.

Nelson, Charles R. [1973], *Applied Time Series Analysis for Managerial Forecasting*, San Francisco: Holden-Day.

Nerlove, Marc [1972], "Lags in Economic Behavior," *Econometrica*, 40:2, March, 221–251.

Nickell, Stephen J. [1978], *The Investment Decisions of Firms*, Cambridge, England: Cambridge University Press.

Poterba, James M. and Lawrence H. Summers [1983], "Dividend Taxes, Corporate Investment, and '*q*'," *Journal of Public Economics*, 22:2, November, 135–167.

Rothschild, Michael [1971], "On the Cost of Adjustment," *Quarterly Journal of Economics*, 85:4, November, 605–622.

Rowley, John C. R. and Pravin K. Trivedi [1975], *The Econometrics of Investment*, New York: John Wiley and Sons.

Salinger, Michael A. [1984], "Tobin's *q*, Unionization, and the Concentration-Profits Relationship," *Rand Journal of Economics*, 15:2, Summer, 159–170.

Sims, Christopher A. [1980], "Macroeconomics and Reality," *Econometrica*, 48:1, January, 1–48.

Summers, Lawrence H. [1981], "Taxation and Corporate Investment: A q-Theory Approach," *Brookings Papers on Economic Activity*, 1:1981, 67–140.

Swan, Craig [1970], "Homebuilding: A Review of Experience," *Brookings Papers on Economic Activity*, 1970:1, 48–76.

Theil, Henri [1961], *Economic Forecasts and Policy*, Amsterdam: North-Holland.

Theil, Henri [1966], *Applied Economic Forecasting*, Amsterdam: North-Holland.

Thomas, R. L. [1985], *Introductory Econometrics: Theory and Applications*, London: Longman Group Limited.

Tinbergen, Jan [1951], *Business Cycles in the United Kingdom*, Amsterdam: North-Holland.

Tobin, James [1969], "A General Equilibrium Approach to Monetary Theory," *Journal of Money, Credit and Banking*, 1:1, February, 15–29.

Treadway, Arthur B. [1971], "The Rational Multivariate Flexible Accelerator," *Econometrica*, 39:5, September, 845–855.

Treadway, Arthur B. [1974], "The Globally Optimal Flexible Accelerator," *Journal of Economic Theory*, 7:1, January, 17–39.

von Furstenberg, George M. [1977], "Corporate Investment: Does Market Valuation Matter in the Aggregate?" *Brookings Papers on Economic Activity*, 2:1977, 347–397.

Wallis, Kenneth F. [1973], *Topics in Applied Econometrics*, London: Gray-Mills Publishing, Ltd.

Wallis, Kenneth F. [1980], "Econometric Implications of the Rational Expectations Hypothesis," *Econometrica*, 48:3, April, 49–73.

Wildasin, David [1984], "The q Theory of Investment with Many Capital Goods," *American Economic Review*, 74:1, March, 203–210.

Winfrey, Robert [1935], *Statistical Analyses of Industrial Property Retirement*, Ames, Iowa: Iowa Engineering Experiment Station, Bulletin 125, December 11.

Yoshikawa, Hiroshi [1980], "On the 'q' Theory of Investment," *American Economic Review*, 70:4, September, 739–744.

Zellner, Arnold and Franz Palm [1974], "Time Series Analysis and Simultaneous Equation Econometric Models," *Journal of Econometrics*, 2:1, May, 17–54.

FURTHER READINGS

Diewert, W. Erwin [1980], "Aggregation Problems in the Measurement of Capital," Chapter 8 in Dan Usher, ed., *The Measurement of Capital*, Chicago: University of Chicago Press for the National Bureau of Economic Research, pp. 433–528. An important article on aggregation issues in constructing measures of capital and investment.

Fair, Ray C. [1986], "Evaluating the Predictive Accuracy of Models," Chapter 33 in Zvi Griliches and Michael D. Intriligator, eds., *Handbook of Econometrics*, Vol. 3, Amsterdam: Elsevier Science Publishers, 1979–1995. A survey of procedures for evaluating the predictive accuracy of models.

Harvey, Andrew C. [1981], *The Econometric Analysis of Time Series*, Oxford, England: Philip Allan Publishers Ltd. A useful text on time series estimation and inference. (Second Edition published by MIT Press, Cambridge, Mass., 1990.)

Helliwell, John F., ed. [1976], *Aggregate Investment: Selected Readings*, Middlesex, England: Penguin Books, Ltd. A book of readings on classic investment studies to the mid-1970s.

Hendry, David F., Adrian R. Pagan, and J. Denis Sargan [1984], "Dynamic Specification," Chapter 18 in Zvi Griliches and Michael D. Intriligator, eds., *Handbook of Econometrics*, Vol. 2, Amsterdam: Elsevier Science Publishers, pp. 1023–1100. A survey article on procedures for evaluating the dynamic specifications of econometric models.

Keynes, John Maynard [1936], *The General Theory of Employment, Interest and Money*, London: Macmillan and Co., Ltd., especially Books II and IV. A classic treatment.

Chapter 7

The Demand for Electricity: Structural and Time Series Approaches

"Only when the country is electrified, when industry, agriculture and transport are placed on a technical basis of modern large-scale production—only then will our victory be complete."

VLADIMIR ILYICH LENIN, Address to All Russian Central Executive Committee of the Soviets, 22 December 1920.

"It is not too much to expect that our children will enjoy in their homes electric energy too cheap to meter."

LEWIS STRAUSS, U.S. Atomic Energy Commissioner (1954, p. 9)

"Forecasting is like trying to drive a car blindfolded and following directions given by a person who is looking out of the back window."

Anonymous

"The arrest in the historical decline of electricity prices, coupled with the price sensitivity of electricity demand, should contribute to slower growth rates of electricity demand than have previously occurred, unless new technologies of electricity use have a decisive impact."

TJALLING C. KOOPMANS, Committee Chair, National Research Council

After World War II and until the 1970s, the forecasting of electricity demand in the United States was rather simple: Electricity demand could be counted on to grow about 7% each year and therefore to double approximately every ten years.[1] The sharp change in energy prices in the 1970s, along with slower economic growth, brought an end to the reliability of this felicitous "double-in-ten" formula. What was not immediately clear, however, was what type of forecasting procedure should replace it. In this chapter we consider a number of alternative approaches to modeling and forecasting the demand for electricity—specifically, structural, extrapolative, and time series approaches.

There are several reasons why understanding and forecasting the demand for electricity are in practice very important. The most significant motivation is that the time required to plan, construct, and bring on-line new electricity-generating plants is often considerable, typically ranging between four and ten years.[2] This implies that to have timely capacity available to meet future electricity demand, significant lead times are necessary for planning, licensing and construction. Since the costs of underbuilding and overbuilding electricity-generating capacity are significant, use of dependable forecasting procedures is critical to rational, cost-effective planning.[3]

A second stimulus for understanding the demand for electricity is that the construction of new power plants is often accompanied by intense political controversy associated with citizens' concerns regarding plant safety, environmental impacts, and economic consequences. Although such controversies are often heated, econometricians can usefully contribute to enlightened public discussion by pointing out the factors that affect the demand for electricity, by quantifying the responsiveness of demand to electricity price changes, and by constructing forecasts that are empirically based and believable.

One purpose of this chapter, therefore, is to develop an understanding of how the earliest and more recent econometricians have modeled, estimated, and forecasted the demand for electricity. Given this background, a second purpose is to gain hands-on estimation and forecasting experience by working through a series of exercises involving the cross-sectional and time series data that were originally employed in several well-known empirical studies of electricity demand. These exercises involve the use of a number of econometric tools, including estimation by ordinary least squares, generalized least squares with first-order autocorrelation, generalized least squares with heteroskedasticity, and forecasting using structural, extrapolative, and time series approaches with autoregressive and moving average specifications.

The outline of this chapter is as follows. In Section 7.1 we begin with a background discussion of facts that are essential to understanding the demand for electricity. Of particular significance is the fact that most electricity demand is derived from the demand for the services of long-lived appliances or machines tied to the use of electricity. This implies that electricity demand changes only when the utilization of these equipment stocks varies or when the stocks are altered through new purchases, retirements, and retrofits. Hence short-run responses of electricity demand to, say, price shocks, can differ considerably from long-run reactions, since in the latter case the equipment stocks can be altered dramatically. The task facing the econometrician is therefore one of developing models incorporating these dynamic stock effects.

In Section 7.2 we consider econometric models that directly incorporate into the estimating equations measures of equipment stocks, while in Section 7.3 we elaborate on models that include these effects indirectly. This is followed in Section 7.4 by a discussion of a number of related econometric issues. Then in Section 7.5 we present a brief survey of selected econometric findings on factors that affect the demand for electricity.

Finally, the hands-on exercises presented in this chapter involve replication and extension of classic and recent results reported in the empirical literature. The first data set is that gathered and employed by Hendrik S. Houthakker [1951a] in a pioneering cross-sectional study of electricity demand in the United Kingdom, and the second is a time series data set used by Charles R. Nelson and Stephen C. Peck [1985] in their more recent study of how forecasters in the U.S. electric utility industry might have constructed their projections in the 1970s and early 1980s.

7.1 ESSENTIAL BACKGROUND FACTS CONCERNING ELECTRICITY DEMAND

When consumers purchase goods such as apples or oranges, they consume the goods directly. Electricity is somewhat different, since other than through electrocutions, it is virtually impossible for humans to consume electricity directly. Rather, most people purchase electricity because it is used in conjunction with equipment to produce services that are the true objects of consumers' demands. For example, electricity is used with air conditioners to cool air, with baseboard heaters to generate warm air, with lamps to produce light, with machines to move and lift objects, and with numerous other types of equipment to perform a wide variety of tasks. The first important fact about electricity demand is therefore that electricity demand is derived from the demand for services that involve electricity-using equipment.

A second important feature of electricity demand is that the equipment with which electricity use is combined is usually long-lived and durable. Refrigerators, for example, typically have about a ten-year life, room air conditioners have a somewhat shorter life, and machines in industry can last 20 years or longer. Furthermore, over the life of such durable equipment the amount of electricity used per hour of utilization is essentially fixed and dictated by the engineering design and operating procedures embodied in the equipment.

The fact that equipment stocks are durable and that their design characteristics are immutable means that electricity consumption for most services can be altered only by changing the utilization patterns of the equipment (varying the demand for its services) or by acquiring different equipment with altered electricity-using characteristics.[4] If real electricity prices increased, for example, consumers might reduce their air conditioning needs by tolerating a higher temperature or by scrapping their old model air conditioner and replacing it with one having a higher energy efficiency rating. Alternatively, in response to electricity price decreases, consumers might set the freezer compartment of their refrigerator to a lower temperature, and they might also put the old refrigerator into the basement or garage for purposes of cooling the household beer supply instead of scrapping the old unit. In both these examples, changing the temperature requirements affects the utilization of the cooling process, while deciding whether to scrap the model affects the electricity-using characteristics of the surviving stock of equipment.

Together, these two important facts imply that movements along or shifts in the demand curve for electricity can differ considerably in the short-run, when demand is tied to the stocks of existing equipment, from that in the long-run, when equipment stocks can be changed. It is therefore reasonable to expect that short-run own-price elasticities of demand for electricity will be smaller (in absolute value) than long-run price elasticities.

This raises a third important fact of importance in modeling electricity demand. The price schedules offered to consumers by electric utilities often contain block tariffs and increasingly include seasonal variations. For example, utilities might charge a residential customer an initial fixed fee of $5 per month for hookup and for up to 25 kilowatt hours (kwh) of consumption, 15¢ per kilowatt hour for the next 200 kwh consumed per month, 10¢ per kilowatt hour for the next 300 kwh consumed, and 8¢ per kilowatt hour for any additional consumption. This is an example of a multipart or multiblock rate schedule.[5] An important feature of such rate schedules is that they introduce wedges between the average and marginal price.

From the viewpoint of economic theory the appropriate price to employ in empirical demand analysis is the marginal price. But with a multipart tariff, several different marginal prices could exist, depending on the customer's level of consumption.[6] In practice, some econometricians have addressed this issue by using as a measure of the marginal price the price corresponding with the average number of kilowatt hours consumed per customer. Others have ignored the issue and have simply divided the total electricity bill by the number of kilowatt hours consumed and thereby obtained the average price. Note that if a multipart tariff is present, the average price clearly depends on the quantity consumed, and so bias due to simultaneity may be serious when average price is used as a regressor in ordinary least squares estimation.

Two other comments regarding electricity prices should be made. First, owing in part to the higher costs of meeting peak demands, utilities are increasingly charging residential customers premium rates during peak demand months or, in some cases, times of day. Studies of electricity demand based on annual data have for the most part ignored such seasonal price variations or else have weighted the peak and off-peak marginal prices by the corresponding consumption to obtain an "average" annual marginal price.[7] However, in recent years a number of researchers have obtained data that are disaggregated by time of day. This has enabled them to employ as a measure of marginal price the rate that is appropriate to the particular time period being analyzed.[8]

Second, it is often cost effective for utilities to meter the consumption of large industrial customers continuously and to bill these customers not only on the basis of their amount of kilowatt hours consumed (what utilities call the energy charges), but also on their peak kilowatt demand over a short time interval, often a 15-minute or one-hour time span (utilities call this the demand charge), particularly if the customer's peak coincides with the utility's systemwide peak demand. This pricing policy introduces further complications in obtaining a measure of the marginal price.

With the exception of exploratory analyses by Dennis J. Aigner and Joseph G. Hirschberg [1983, 1985], very few econometric studies of electricity demand in the industrial or commercial sector have dealt well with this peak demand issue. Instead, most have used as a marginal price that price corresponding with the off-peak demand of the average industrial customer or the average price computed as revenue from industrial customers divided by total industrial kilowatt hours consumed.[9] Again, use of the latter price measure as a regressor in ordinary least squares estimation can result in biased parameter estimates due to simultaneity.

The final fact concerning electricity demand that is of interest here is that electricity demand has been modeled and forecasted for quite some time. Until relatively recently, however, the procedures that were employed by academic researchers differed considerably from those used by industry practitioners.

The earliest econometric studies of demand for electricity, such as that by Houthakker [1951a], recognized the importance of distinguishing between short- and long-run dynamic responses, particularly those involving prices. Industry practitioners, however, typically believed that the price responsiveness of electricity demand was minimal, even in the long run, and instead often constructed forecasts using simple trend extrapolation techniques or else related electricity demand growth to projected growth in gross national product. In fact, according to one survey, in 1972 about 80% of electric utility forecasts were made by using trend extrapolation techniques.[10] This worked very well until the 1970s. Today, incidentally, only a negligible number of utilities claim that they rely on trend extrapolation.[11]

The practices of electric utility forecasters since the 1970s have been examined by Charles Nelson and Stephen Peck [1985], who have probed annual forecasts made by the North American Electric Reliability Council

(NERC). NERC was established in response to a massive power failure on November 9, 1965, that interrupted service to the entire northeast region of the North American continent, cutting off the supply of electricity to places like New York City for up to 13 hours. Since 1974, as part of its efforts to improve service reliability, NERC has summarized ten-year demand forecasts made by individual electric utilities. The utilities initially make forecasts for their own service areas, and these forecasts are submitted to NERC, which then combines, summarizes, and publishes them. It is useful to examine these NERC summary forecasts and to see how they have changed over time.

In Table 7.1 we reproduce the NERC summary ten-year forecasts (NSF) published annually since 1974.[12] Using data through the year 1973, the NSF for 1974–1983 implied an average annual growth rate (AAGR) of 7.5%, which, it turns out, was only slightly lower than the 7.8% growth rate that had been experienced by utilities over the previous 1951–1973 time period. However, the actual electricity AAGR over the 1974–1983 time period was only 2.3%, far smaller than the forecasted 7.5%. Each of the subsequent NSF, computed in light of new current industry experience, was smaller, and by 1984 the AAGR forecasted for 1985–1994 had fallen to 2.4%.

As Nelson and Peck note, the shortfall of actual electricity sales relative to sales forecasted by the industry and the persistent downward revision of projected growth rates raise a number of interesting and important issues. For example, should electricity forecasts have been more accurate, given the infor-

Table 7.1 North American Electric Reliability Council Ten-Year Forecasts and Actual Experience, 1973–1984

NERC Summary 10-Year Forecast			
Using Data Through Year	For Ten-Year Time Period	Ten-Year Average% Growth Forecasted	Ten-Year Average% Growth Realized
1973	1974–1983	7.5	2.3
1974	1975–1984	6.7	3.0
1975	1976–1985	6.3	2.9
1976	1977–1986	5.8	2.4
1977	1978–1987	5.3	2.3
1978	1979–1988	4.8	2.4
1979	1980–1989	4.1	
1980	1981–1990	3.7	
1981	1982–1991	3.3	
1982	1983–1992	3.2	
1983	1984–1993	2.8	
1984	1985–1994	2.4	

Sources: Charles R. Nelson and Stephen C. Peck [1985] and Charles R. Nelson, Stephen C. Peck, and Robert G. Uhler [1989]. Updates by E. R. Berndt.

mation and techniques that were available to forecasters at the time? Were the manner and rate in which forecasts were revised downward appropriate? Or were forecasters too slow in responding to the sharply changing environment of the 1970s? How can one assess these forecasts?

We will consider a number of these questions as we work through the exercises at the end of this chapter. Before doing that, however, we must first examine how structural econometric models can be constructed to take into account the dynamic effects of long-lived equipment stocks on the demand for electricity. We consider two distinct approaches. In Section 7.2 we present a direct procedure, while in Section 7.3 we explore indirect methods.

7.2 ECONOMETRIC MODELS OF ELECTRICITY DEMAND WITH EQUIPMENT STOCKS INCLUDED EXPLICITLY

In the previous section we emphasized that in the short run, variations in the demand for electricity are constrained to changes in utilization rates, given the fixed stock of electricity-using appliances. In the longer run, when the amount and characteristics of the equipment stock can be altered, more substantial possibilities exist for varying electricity consumption. This suggests a two-part model, and thus a two-equation framework, in which one stage is a short-run utilization model with electricity demand conditional on the equipment stock and the second is a long-run model of factors affecting the equipment stock. We begin with the first stage, a short-run utilization model.

One of the first explicit models of the short-run demand for electricity is due to Franklin M. Fisher and Carl Kaysen [1962]. Focusing primarily on the residential sector, Fisher and Kaysen called the set of electricity-using appliances and fixtures "white goods," and noted that household demand for electricity use is derived from the demand for the services of the households' various stocks of white goods.[13] In the short run these stocks are fixed. Since white goods vary in their capacity to consume kilowatts of electricity per hour of normal usage, Fisher and Kaysen proposed to measure the effects of the aggregate equipment stock on electricity consumption in terms of the total kilowatt hours that could be consumed if all appliances were employed at their normal use. This was done by obtaining engineering information on kilowatts used per hour of normal use for each type of appliance and then summing over the various household appliances.

Denote the aggregate equipment stock for the ith household at time t, measured in units of kilowatts per hour, as W_{it}. Actual electricity consumption q_{it} depends on the rates of utilization of the various stocks, called u_{it}, which in turn are hypothesized to depend on real per capita income Y_{it} and the real price of electricity, P_{it}:

$$q_{it} = u_{it} \cdot W_{it} = u_{it}(Y_{it}, P_{it}) \cdot W_{it} \tag{7.1}$$

Fisher and Kaysen specified the functional form for this relationship as

$$q_{it} = P_{it}^{\alpha} Y_{it}^{\beta} W_{it} \tag{7.2}$$

which, after a logarithmic transformation, became

$$\ln q_{it} = \alpha \ln P_{it} + \beta \ln Y_{it} + \ln W_{it} \tag{7.3}$$

In implementing this model empirically, Fisher and Kaysen expended considerable efforts in gathering data on stocks of seven major white goods, by state, over the 1944–1957 time period. Stating that the quality of this data ranged "from somewhat below the sublime to a bit above the ridiculous," Fisher and Kaysen discovered that these seven white goods did not account for enough of total residential electricity consumption and that it would be impossible to estimate stocks for other white goods. They concluded that "to estimate W_{it} by states and years with any kind of reliability is simply out of the question."[14]

Instead, they postulated that the stock of white goods in the *i*th state grew at a constant rate of γ percent per year, that is,

$$W_{i,t}/W_{i,t-1} = \exp(\gamma_i) \qquad \text{or} \qquad \ln W_{i,t} - \ln W_{i,t-1} = \gamma_i \tag{7.4}$$

Equation (7.3) was then lagged one time period, this was subtracted from Eq. (7.3), and then Eq. (7.4) was substituted in, thereby yielding the first-difference equation

$$\ln q_{it} - \ln q_{i,t-1} = \gamma_i + \alpha_i(\ln P_{it} - \ln P_{i,t-1}) + \beta_i(\ln Y_{it} - \ln Y_{i,t-1}) \tag{7.5}$$

A random disturbance term was added to Eq. (7.5), reflecting the effects of inherent stochastic elements and omitted variables (assumed to be uncorrelated with the included regressors); this random disturbance term was assumed to be independently and identically normally distributed. Fisher and Kaysen then estimated the parameters α_i, β_i, and γ_i in Eq. (7.5) for each of the states in the United States, using 1946–1957 annual data and ordinary least squares estimation.

Notice that in this model, estimates of α_i and β_i correspond to estimates of the short-run price and income elasticities of demand for electricity, conditional on the stock of white goods, while the estimate of γ_i is the constant rate of growth of the stock of white goods in state *i*. Fisher and Kaysen found that price elasticity estimates for most states were near zero, while states whose economies were younger and less developed had much larger short-run price elasticity estimates (in absolute value), although these were still less than 1.

For their long-run model, in which they attempted to explain changes in the stocks of seven white goods, Fisher and Kaysen specified what is now often called a saturation model. The dependent variable was $\ln W_{i,t} - \ln W_{i,t-1}$, and the regressors included percent changes (actually, first differences in logarithms) of population, number of wired households, real appliance purchase prices, and expected permanent income, as well as levels of current income per capita, the expected prices of electricity and gas, and the number of marriages. In effect, therefore, in their long-run model, Fisher and Kaysen regressed growth rates of appliance stocks on growth rates of noneconomic variables and on levels of economic variables (except marriages). Incidentally, the number of marriages in year *t* was included as a regressor since "the first six months or so of married life are a time of very high susceptibility to . . . appliance [purchases]."[15]

To conserve on degrees of freedom, Fisher and Kaysen pooled states into eight groups and estimated parameters for each of these eight groups by ordinary least squares. In this framework the total effect of, say, a price change on electricity demand was envisaged as the sum of the long-run effect on equipment stocks plus the short-run utilization impact.

One very important feature of the Fisher-Kaysen long-run model was its treatment of price and income variables. Since white goods are durable and since it seemed clear that the purchase of a major appliance depended not only on current income but also on a more long-run or permanent income notion, Fisher and Kaysen specified that the appropriate income measure was expected permanent income. This was calculated as a 17-year moving average of real personal income per capita, using the exponentially declining weights of Milton Friedman [1957] from his well-known analysis of the consumption function. This contrasted with the short-run utilization equation, in which the income variable was simply current per capita income. Similarly, for the expected electricity and gas price variables in the long-run model, Fisher and Kaysen employed three-year moving averages, whereas in the short-run utilization model the electricity price employed was the current one.

Fisher and Kaysen expressed considerable reservations about much of the data underlying their long-run model and introduced their empirical results by stating that "it is worth reiterating how poor our data really are" and that "No results can be better than the data on which they are based."[16] Although they obtained some evidence supporting a negative elasticity of demand with respect to real appliance price (hardly ever statistically significantly different from zero, however), the expected electricity price variable typically performed poorly, often having a positive (i.e., wrong) sign and resulting in a worsening of results for other parameter estimates. They interpreted this as implying that operating costs did not seem to affect appliance purchases in a meaningful manner. While for some appliances the income variables were significant, in most cases the economic variables (prices and income) did not appear to be as important as the demographic ones (especially the number of wired households). This last set of results might be due in part to the somewhat unorthodox specification of the Fisher-Kaysen long-run model in which growth rates of appliance stocks depended on levels of economic variables.

One important lesson to be learned from the Fisher-Kaysen study, however, is that while in principle it may be desirable to include measures of equipment stocks directly into short-run electricity demand equations and thereby to distinguish short-run utilization effects from long-run equipment stock impacts, data problems can be severe. This can result in very imprecise and unsatisfactory parameter estimates, particularly for the long-run model.[17]

This principal weakness of the approach that directly includes equipment stock measures into electricity demand equations has also been emphasized by Taylor, Blattenberger, and Rennhack [1984b], who have summarized a number of studies based on more recent data. Taylor et al. conclude by stating that "The results . . . are better than might realistically have been expected, but they are clearly much poorer than might have been hoped for. In general, the utilization equations are very good, whereas the capital stock equations leave much to be desired."[18] Concerning future work, however, they caution that additional research within this framework should be done only if "improved data on appliance stocks can be forthcoming."[19]

7.3 ECONOMETRIC MODELS OF ELECTRICITY DEMAND WITH EQUIPMENT STOCKS INCLUDED INDIRECTLY

We now consider an alternative approach that does not suffer from the disadvantage of requiring data on equipment stocks. As we shall see, however, this benefit is not gained without cost, since in the indirect approach it is no longer possible to distinguish as sharply the utilization and equipment change components of electricity demand.

Let actual electricity consumption in time period t be denoted as y_t, and let the long-run desired or equilibrium consumption be y_t^*. The long-run desired consumption is in turn affected by the level of income, prices, and other factors, denoted $x_{1t}, x_{2t}, \ldots, x_{Kt}$. A common specification is that the long-run equilibrium equation is of the logarithmic form

$$\ln y_t^* = \alpha + \beta_1 \ln x_{1t} + \beta_2 \ln x_{2t} + \cdots + \beta_K \ln x_{Kt} + \epsilon_t \tag{7.6}$$

where ϵ_t is an independently and identically normally distributed disturbance term with mean zero and variance σ^2.

The long-run, desired electricity consumption level corresponds with an equipment stock that is fully adjusted to its equilibrium level. At any point in time, however, actual electricity consumption will almost certainly differ from the long-run equilibrium consumption, since actual equipment stocks are seldom completely consistent with those in long-run equilibrium. To accommodate this fact, a partial adjustment hypothesis is often put forward.

More specifically, consumers are envisaged as attempting to bring actual electricity consumption levels y_t into line with the desired levels y_t^*, but within any time period they are only partially successful in doing so. The relationship between actual and desired electricity consumption levels is then conveniently specified to be

$$\ln y_t - \ln y_{t-1} = \phi \cdot (\ln y_t^* - \ln y_{t-1}) + \eta_t \tag{7.7}$$

where η_t is a random disturbance term. Note that when $\phi = 1$, adjustment of actual to desired electricity consumption is instantaneous, but when $\phi = 0$, the adjustment process is nonexistent and inert. For this reason it is usually specified that $0 < \phi \leqslant 1$.

If one solves Eq. (7.7) for $\ln y_t^*$, one obtains

$$\ln y_t^* = (1/\phi) \cdot \ln y_t + ((\phi - 1)/\phi) \cdot \ln y_{t-1} - (1/\phi)\eta_t \qquad \textbf{(7.8)}$$

Equation (7.8) therefore reformulates the unobserved $\ln y_t^*$ in terms of observed $\ln y_t$ and $\ln y_{t-1}$, as well as the unobserved parameter ϕ and the random disturbance term η_t.

To implement this model empirically, the right-hand side of equation Eq. (7.6) is substituted into the left-hand side of Eq. (7.8), and the resulting equation is rearranged, yielding

$$\begin{aligned} \ln y_t = {} & \alpha\phi + (1 - \phi) \ln y_{t-1} + \beta_1\phi \ln x_{1t} + \beta_2\phi \ln x_{2t} + \cdots \\ & + \beta_K\phi \ln x_{Kt} + \nu_t \end{aligned} \qquad \textbf{(7.9)}$$

where the composite disturbance term $\nu_t \equiv \phi\epsilon_t + \eta_t$. Note that the parameters of Eq. (7.9) can be estimated by using conventional econometric techniques. Moreover, if the composite disturbance ν_t is independently and identically normally distributed (which will occur if its components are identically normally distributed), then estimation by ordinary least squares yields consistent estimates of the parameters. However, if any component of ν_t is serially correlated, then because a lagged dependent variable appears as a regressor in Eq. (7.9), estimation by ordinary least squares generates biased and inconsistent estimates of the parameters. In such a case, other methods such as instrumental variable or maximum likelihood techniques can be employed to obtain consistent estimates of the parameters.

The parameter estimates corresponding to variables x_1 through x_K in Eq. (7.9) have a clear and useful interpretation, for each represents the product of the underlying structural parameters $\beta_i\phi$. Since the one-period effect of a change in $\ln x_{it}$ on $\ln y_{it}$ is $\partial \ln y_{it}/\partial \ln x_{it} = \beta_i\phi$, the $\beta_i\phi$ are short-run elasticities of demand for electricity with respect to x_i. In the long run (as $\phi \rightarrow 1$), the total or cumulative effect of a change in $\ln x_i$ on $\ln y$ is measured as β_i. Hence the β_i represent long-run elasticities.

This suggests that to construct estimates of these long-run elasticities based on estimation of parameters in Eq. (7.9), one should first obtain the estimate of ϕ by examining the coefficient estimate on the lagged dependent variable in Eq. (7.9) and then divide the coefficient estimates corresponding to the product $\beta_i\phi$ by the estimate of ϕ. Note, however, that unlike the specification when equipment stocks were directly incorporated into the estimating equation, in this indirect, partial adjustment approach, one cannot explicitly decompose the short- and long-run effects into utilization and equipment stock components.

Earlier, we emphasized that electricity is typically consumed in conjunction with the services of long-lived durable goods. In turn, it is reasonable to postulate that when consumers purchase these long-lived durable goods, they take into account the likely path of future operating and capital costs over the entire life of the asset. This suggests that if electricity demand models are to be credible, the quantity of electricity demanded in long-run equilibrium should depend on expectational variables, such as prices and income.

Suppose that several of the x's in the equilibrium electricity consumption equation (7.6) represent expectations of future movements of the x's, rather than simply being current realizations. For example, electricity consumption might depend on expected real electricity prices and expected real income. Since expectations of these variables are generally unobserved, the task facing the practicing econometrician is to specify a framework in which one can incorporate unobserved nonstatic expectations but do so in terms of observed variables. Let us denote those x's that are unobserved with asterisk superscripts, that is, denote the expectation of x_{it} as x^*_{it}, for $i = 1, 2, \ldots, I$ and $I \leq K$.

One of the most common procedures for dealing with nonstatic expectations is called the *adaptive expectations* approach; it is discussed in most econometrics textbooks in chapters dealing with distributed lags. We now briefly consider this adaptive expectations approach, focusing particularly on its applicability in modeling the demand for electricity. Other, more detailed discussions of nonstatic expectations are found in Chapters 6 and 10.

In the adaptive expectations approach, changes in the expectation of x_i from period t to period $t+1$ are proportional to the gap between actual and expected x_i in period t:

$$x^*_{i,t+1} - x^*_{it} = (1 - \lambda_i) \cdot (x_{it} - x^*_{it}) \qquad \textbf{(7.10)}$$

which can be rearranged and rewritten as

$$x^*_{i,t+1} = (1 - \lambda_i)x_{it} + \lambda_i x^*_{it} \qquad \textbf{(7.11)}$$

where $0 \leq \lambda_i < 1$. Note that in Eq. (7.11) the expectation of x_i in period $t + 1$ is a weighted average of the realized x_i in period t and the expectation of x_i in period t. Since Eq. (7.11) reflects the notion that expectations are formed by adapting previous expectations in light of current experience, this specification is called the adaptive expectations model.

An alternative interpretation of the adaptive expectations specification can be obtained by noticing that the variable x^*_{it} appears on the right-hand side of Eq. (7.11). If Eq. (7.11) is lagged one time period and then solved for x^*_{it} in terms of $x^*_{i,t-1}$, the result is substituted back into the original Eq. (7.11), and this is done repeatedly and indefinitely for $x^*_{i,t-1}$, $x^*_{i,t-2}$, $x^*_{i,t-3}$, etc., then one obtains the geometric lag representation for $x^*_{i,t+1}$ as

$$x^*_{i,t+1} = (1 - \lambda_i) \cdot (x_{it} + \lambda x_{i,t-1} + \lambda^2 x_{i,t-2} + \lambda^3 x_{i,t-3} + \cdots) \qquad \textbf{(7.12)}$$

Thus the expectation of x_i in time period $t + 1$ is the sum of a geometrically declining infinite distributed lag of realized, observed x_i, beginning in time t and proceeding backward into time.

Now suppose that our initial deterministic electricity demand equation (7.6) is rewritten so that actual electricity consumption in time period t depends on expected real electricity prices and expected real income in time period $t+1$ (denoted $x^*_{1,t+1}$ and $x^*_{2,t+1}$, respectively), on other observed exogenous variables x_{3t} through x_{Kt}, and on a random disturbance term ϵ_t:

$$y_t = \alpha + \beta_1 x^*_{1,t+1} + \beta_2 x^*_{2,t+1} + \beta_3 x_{3t} + \cdots + \beta_K x_{Kt} + \epsilon_t \qquad \textbf{(7.13)}$$

One could substitute Eq. (7.12) directly into Eq. (7.13) for both $x^*_{1,t+1}$ and $x^*_{2,t+1}$, but the resulting expression would have an infinite number of lagged values of x_1 and x_2, and so it could not feasibly be estimated econometrically given a finite number of observations.

This problem can be solved by employing the Koyck transformation repeatedly for each expectational variable.[20] Specifically, substitute $x^*_{1,t+1}$ and $x^*_{2,t+1}$ from Eq. (7.12) into Eq. (7.13), then lag this equation by one time period, multiply through by λ_1, and subtract the resulting equation from Eq. (7.13). This yields the messy-looking equation

$$\begin{aligned} y_t = {} & \alpha(1-\lambda_1) + \lambda_1 y_{t-1} + \beta_1(1-\lambda_1)x_{1t} + \beta_2(1-\lambda_2) \\ & \cdot [x_{2t} + (\lambda_2 - \lambda_1)x_{2,t-1} + \lambda_2(\lambda_2-\lambda_1)x_{2,t-2} + \cdots] \\ & + \beta_3(x_{3t} - \lambda_1 x_{3,t-1}) + \cdots + \beta_K(x_{Kt} - \lambda_1 x_{K,t-1}) \\ & + \epsilon_t - \lambda_1\epsilon_{t-1} \end{aligned} \qquad \textbf{(7.14)}$$

which still has an infinite number of lagged values of x_2 and so cannot feasibly be estimated econometrically.

However, if one again applies the Koyck transformation, this time lagging Eq. (7.14) by one time period, multiplying through by λ_2, and then subtracting the resulting product from Eq. (7.14), one obtains the estimable but still rather complicated equation

$$\begin{aligned} y_t = {} & \alpha(1-\lambda_1)(1-\lambda_2) + (\lambda_1+\lambda_2)y_{t-1} - \lambda_1\lambda_2 y_{t-2} \\ & + \beta_1(1-\lambda_1)(x_{1t} - \lambda_2 x_{1,t-1}) + \beta_2(1-\lambda_2)(x_{2t} - \lambda_1 x_{2,t-1}) \\ & + \beta_3[x_{3t} - (\lambda_1+\lambda_2)x_{3,t-1} + \lambda_1\lambda_2 x_{3,t-2}] + \cdots \\ & + \beta_K[x_{Kt} - (\lambda_1+\lambda_2)x_{K,t-1} + \lambda_1\lambda_2 x_{K,t-2}] \\ & + \epsilon_t - (\lambda_1+\lambda_2)\epsilon_{t-1} + \lambda_1\lambda_2\epsilon_{t-2} \end{aligned} \qquad \textbf{(7.15)}$$

According to Eq. (7.15), current electricity demand is a function of electricity demand lagged one and two time periods, current and once-lagged values of each of the expectational variables (here, real electricity price and real income), and current, once- and twice-lagged values of each of the other exogenous variables. This raises a number of estimation issues.

First, note that the partial adjustment equation (7.9) includes $K + 2$ regressors: an intercept term, current values of each of the K x's, and a once-lagged value of the dependent variable. By contrast, in the adaptive expectations model (7.15) the number of regressors is $[7 + 3(K - 2) = 3K + 1]$, a much larger number than $K + 2$. However, a careful examination of both these equations reveals that the adaptive expectations model (7.15) has only one more free parameter to estimate than does the partial adjustment model (7.9). This implies that estimates of the adaptive expectations model require imposing a substantial number of (nonlinear) parameter restrictions. Note that such restrictions might reduce the possible adverse effects of multicollinearity among current and lagged regressors.

Second, in the last line of Eq. (7.15) it is seen that y_t is a function of ϵ_t, ϵ_{t-1}, and ϵ_{t-2}. Since y_{t-1} and y_{t-2} also appear as regressors in this equation, the regressors are correlated with disturbances, and estimation by ordinary least squares will yield biased and inconsistent estimates.

To obtain consistent estimates of the parameters, other estimation methods, such as instrumental variable or maximum likelihood, could instead be employed. In the context of instrumental variable estimation, care must be taken in choosing instruments, given the temporal dependence in the composite error term in Eq. (7.15); legitimate instruments could include any x's not in Eq. (7.15), as well as y_{t-3} and further lagged dependent variables. Maximum likelihood estimation may also be complex, since the λ_1 and λ_2 parameters are constrained in a nonlinear manner, both as coefficients on the regressors and in the composite disturbance term (the last line of Eq. (7.15)).[21]

Fortunately, it is possible to incorporate non-static expectations in a less cumbersome manner. Suppose that in the electricity demand equation, one wishes to include as regressors the optimal or rational predictor of $x_{i,t+1}$ for, say, real electricity price ($i = 1$) and real income or output ($i = 2$). In this context a rational predictor is a prediction formed by economic agents who are efficiently using all the information at their disposal; included in their information set are the list of all relevant variables, past values of all these variables, and the form of the structural equations. With rational predictors, any expectational errors are uncorrelated with the variables in the information set. It turns out that under certain assumptions that are closely related to those made above in the adaptive expectations case, optimal or rational predictors can be constructed in a relatively straightforward manner.

Specifically, assume that x_i is stochastic and that its realizations are governed by a first-order moving average process, an MA(1), of the form

$$x_{i,t} = x_{i,t-1} + u_{it} - \lambda_i u_{i,t-1} \tag{7.16}$$

where u_{it} is an independently and identically normally distributed disturbance term with mean zero and λ_i is now a parameter in the MA(1) process. The u_{it} and $u_{i,t-1}$ must be distributed independently of the ϵ_{it} in Eq. (7.13), or else the predictor would not be employing all available information in the information set. In an important paper, John F. Muth [1960] showed that in this case the optimal or rational predictor of $x_{i,t+1}$, denoted $x^*_{i,t+1}$, is equal to

$$x^*_{i,t+1} = (1 - \lambda_i) \cdot (x_{it} + \lambda x_{i,t-1} + \lambda^2 x_{i,t-2} + \lambda^3 x_{i,t-3} + \cdots) \tag{7.17}$$

Note that Eq. (7.17) is exactly the same as Eq. (7.12), which is derived from the adaptive expectations framework.

This alternative motivation suggests a less cumbersome estimation procedure. Specifically, let us specify that in the electricity demand equation there are two expectational variables, real electricity prices and real income. For each of these variables, first estimate a univariate time series model of the form in Eq. (7.16), using the Box-Jenkins [1976] estimation technique with an MA(1) process. Then take the "fitted" or "predicted" values from this MA(1) model for both expectational variables, and use them as regressors in Eq. (7.13). In other words, estimate an equation of the form

$$y_t = \alpha + \beta_1 \hat{x}^*_{1,t+1} + \beta_2 \hat{x}^*_{2,t+1} + \beta_3 x_{3t} + \cdots + \beta_K x_{Kt} + \epsilon_t \quad \textbf{(7.18)}$$

by ordinary least squares, where the $\hat{x}^*_{i,t+1}$ for $i = 1, 2$ are fitted values from the estimated MA(1) equations in Eq. (7.16). Note that since by assumption the ϵ and u_i are independently distributed, estimation of Eq. (7.18) by ordinary least squares yields consistent estimates of the parameters.

More generally, as will be discussed further in Chapter 10 (especially Exercise 3), estimation that is consistent with rational predictors can be accomplished in a closely related manner, simply by using as instruments for the expectational variables in Eq. (7.18) values of appropriately lagged variables from the set of information available to consumers. One advantage of such an instrumental variables (IV) approach is that its validity does not depend on the assumption that expectations are adaptive, as in Eq. (7.11), or that they follow an MA(1) process, as in Eq. (7.16); rather, in the IV approach, precisely how expectations are formed is not specified.

There is one further issue. According to Eq. (7.18), the adjustment of electricity demand to its equilibrium level (given adaptive expectations) is implicitly assumed to be instantaneous. Therefore one might want to append to Eq. (7.18) a partial adjustment process, which would yield an equation of the form in Eq. (7.9), where, however, $x_{1,t}$ and $x_{2,t}$ would now be replaced by the fitted expectational variables $\hat{x}^*_{1,t+1}$ and $\hat{x}^*_{2,t+1}$ from the MA(1) estimation. In logarithmic form, such an equation would be

$$\begin{aligned} \ln y_t = {} & \alpha\phi + (1 - \phi) \ln y_{t-1} + \beta_1\phi \ln \hat{x}_{1,t+1} + \beta_2\phi \ln \hat{x}_{2,t+1} \\ & + \beta_3\phi \ln x_{3t} + \cdots + \beta_K\phi \ln x_{Kt} + \nu_t \end{aligned} \quad \textbf{(7.19)}$$

Notice that in Eq. (7.19) a lagged dependent variable appears as a regressor. As long as the ν_t in Eq. (7.19) and u_{it}, $u_{i,t-1}$ of Eq. (7.16) are independently distributed, estimation by OLS will still yield consistent estimates. If, however, ν_t follows a first-order autoregressive scheme, estimation by OLS would yield biased and inconsistent estimates of the parameters. In such a case an IV estimator, using appropriately lagged instruments, might be more appropriate.

7.4 ADDITIONAL ECONOMETRIC ISSUES

Three other econometric issues, in addition to serial correlation of disturbances, merit attention. We now consider (a) the effects of omitting the intramarginal price as a regressor, (b) the simultaneity of electricity price and quantity, and (c) the choice of functional form.

7.4.A Effects of Omitting the Intramarginal Price as a Regressor

Electric utilities typically offer customers a rate schedule with several blocks, in which prices per kilowatt hour consumed differ in each block. Under the assumption that consumers maximize utility or that firms minimize costs, given these types of rate schedules, it would seem to follow that the appropriate price to include in an electricity demand equation is the marginal price, since at that price, marginal benefits to the household or firm equal marginal costs.

In an extensive survey of empirical studies of electricity demand, Lester Taylor [1975] has argued that this view is not entirely correct, since it neglects the income effect of intramarginal electricity prices. According to Taylor, both marginal price and some measure of intramarginal price should be included as regressors in the demand equation, since if the estimated electricity demand equation is to be consistent with economic theory, then the entire rate structure has implications for the equilibrium of the consumer, not just the marginal price. Failure to include an intramarginal price variable as a regressor biases the parameter estimates.

Taylor's argument is of special interest to us because it nicely illustrates factors affecting the bias due to omitted variables. Let us look at this issue more carefully. Define intramarginal expenditures on electricity as that amount of expenditure for electricity by the consumer up to but not including the final block in which the consumer purchases electricity. Then define the average intramarginal price as this intramarginal expenditure divided by the total kilowatt hours of electricity consumed up to, but not including, the final block.

Now suppose that the utility increased the initial fixed charge for each customer but did not change any of the other portions of the multi-block rate schedule. In such a case the intramarginal expenditure and average intramarginal price would increase, although the marginal price would not. For a typical customer who still remained connected and did not change consumption sufficiently to end up in a different rate block, this rate schedule change would involve only an income effect and not a substitution effect. By contrast, a change in the rate schedule that altered marginal prices would result in both income and substitution effects.

On the basis of this reasoning, Taylor concluded that it is necessary to include as regressors in the residential electricity demand equation the marginal price of electricity faced by the typical customer and either the average intramarginal price or the intramarginal expenditure. According to Taylor, the qualitative effect of incorrectly omitting the average price or intramarginal expenditure variable is as follows:

> If average and marginal prices are positively correlated (as is likely to be the case), then use of one of the prices in absence of the other will lead, in general, to an upward bias in the estimate of the price elasticity. That this is so follows from the theorem on the impact of an omitted variable."[22]

What is not clear, however, is how important this bias is quantitatively. This turns out to be a rather interesting issue.[23]

To consider this, for simplicity let the correct demand equation be of the form

$$y_i = \alpha + \beta_1 x_{1i} + \beta_2 x_{2i} + \beta_3 x_{3i} + \cdots + \beta_K x_{Ki} + \epsilon_i \quad \textbf{(7.20)}$$

where for the ith observation, y_i is the consumption of electricity in kilowatt hours, x_{1i} is the marginal price of electricity, x_{2i} is the intramarginal average price of electricity, x_{3i} through x_{Ki} are other explanatory variables, and ϵ_i is a random disturbance term.

Now let the *estimated* least squares regression equation with all K regressors included be

$$\hat{y}_i = a + b_{y1.K}x_{1i} + b_{y2.K}x_{2i} + b_{y3.K}x_{3i} + \cdots + b_{yK.K}x_{Ki} \quad \textbf{(7.21)}$$

where $\hat{y}_i$ is the least squares fitted or predicted value of y for the ith observation, a, $b_{y1.K}$, $b_{y2.K}$, . . . , $b_{yK.K}$ are the least squares coefficients on the intercept term and x_1, x_2, . . . , x_K. Hereafter, call Eq. (7.21) the "correct" regression equation.

The misspecification emphasized by Taylor occurs when x_2 is incorrectly omitted from the regression equation (7.20). Let the misspecified least squares regression equation with x_2 omitted be

$$\hat{y}_i = a' + b_{y1}x_{1i} + b_{y3}x_{3i} + \cdots + b_{yK}x_{Ki} \quad \textbf{(7.22)}$$

where b_{y1}, b_{y3}, . . . , b_{yK} are the least squares estimated slope coefficients on x_1, x_3, . . . , x_K in the misspecified regression equation. (Under this notation, parameter estimates in Eq. (7.22) with x_{2i} deleted do not have the ".K" included in the subscript.)

The econometric consequences of this misspecification on estimates of the marginal price elasticity can be assessed by determining the difference between $b_{y1.K}$ and b_{y1}. The analytical relationship between the least squares estimates $b_{y1.K}$ and b_{y1} can be shown to be[24]

$$b_{y1.K} = b_{y1} - b_{21}b_{y2.K} \quad \textbf{(7.23)}$$

where b_{21} is the least squares coefficient in the "auxiliary" regression equation

$$\hat{x}_{2i} = a'' + b_{21}x_{1i} + b_{23}x_{3i} + \cdots + b_{2K}x_{Ki} \quad \textbf{(7.24)}$$

Here, b_{21} is the least-squares slope coefficient on marginal price when intramarginal average price is regressed on x_1, x_3, . . . , x_K.

An inspection of Eq. (7.23) permits easy determination of the qualitative consequences of incorrectly omitting x_2. Since x_1 is the marginal electricity price and x_2 represents the negative income effect of increased intramarginal expenditures, increases in x_1 or x_2 should reduce electricity consumption, *ceteris paribus*; this implies that b_{y1}, $b_{y1.K}$, and $b_{y2.K}$ should be negative. The sign of b_{21} is not clear from economic theory, but from inspection of actual rate structures it has been found that b_{21} is typically positive; utilities with high intramarginal electricity prices also tend to have high marginal prices. If these negative and positive signs are appropriately substituted into Eq. (7.23), it follows that b_{y1} is larger in absolute value than $b_{y1.K}$, and thus that b_{y1} provides an absolute upward-biased estimate of the effect of changes in the marginal price on electricity consumption. Notice, however, that from Eq. (7.23) the sign of this bias depends not only on the sign of b_{21} but also on the sign of $b_{y2.K}$.

It is useful to pursue this bias issue further, to assess whether a more precise quantitative assessment of this bias can be made. Since most of the electricity demand equations surveyed by Taylor involve double logarithmic regressions, let y and each of the x's in Eqs. (7.20), (7.21), and (7.22) be logarithmic transforms of the original variables. In this case, $b_{y1.K}$ is an estimate of the marginal price elasticity of demand for electricity, and $b_{y2.K}$ is the least squares estimate of the intramarginal average price elasticity of demand.

It turns out that microeconomic theory provides a clear interpretation of $b_{y2.K}$. Since a change in x_2 represents only an income effect and no substitution effect, $b_{y2.K}$ is the negative of the income elasticity of demand for electricity times the budget share of intramarginal electricity expenditure in the total income of the typical residential customer. Taylor's 1975 survey suggests that a reasonable estimate of the income elasticity is unity, while in another study by Taylor et al. [1977] it is reported that the mean intramarginal budget share by state over the 1961–1972 time period in the United States is about 0.01.[25] Hence if the theory and the specification are correct, a reasonable value for $b_{y2.K}$ is $-(1.0) \cdot (0.01) = -0.01$. This value can be substituted into Eq. (7.23). To complete a quantitative assessment of the misspecification, all one need do is obtain an estimate of b_{21} and insert it into Eq. (7.23).

Athough estimates of b_{21} are likely to vary among utilities, Berndt [1984] reports that reasonable values for b_{21} range from 0.25 to 1.0; the mean value of b_{21} based on examination of a number of rate schedules is about 0.5. If the values of $b_{y2.K} = -0.01$ and $b_{21} = 0.5$ are inserted into Eq. (7.23), one finds that the bias due to misspecification is

$$b_{y1.K} - b_{y1} = 0.005$$

This is a rather strong and significant result, since it suggests that if one incorrectly omits the intramarginal average price variable, then for practical purposes, the correct and the misspecified least squares estimates of the marginal price elasticity are virtually identical. For example, Taylor et al. [1977] report a correct estimate of $b_{y1.K}$ as being equal to about -0.8; this implies that the misspecified estimate would be virtually identical at -0.805.

The above discussion has focused on the effect of omitted variable bias on the estimate of the marginal price elasticity. Clearly, omitting x_2 also affects other estimated slope coefficients. Fortunately, the bias on other coefficients (such as income elasticities) will also be small. To see this, note that the difference between the correct estimate of the coefficient on x_j (denoted by $b_{yj.K}$) and the misspecified estimate on x_j due to incorrectly omitting x_2 (denoted by b_{yj}) equals

$$b_{yj.K} - b_{yj} = -b_{2j}b_{y2.K} \qquad j = 1, 3, 4, \ldots, K \tag{7.25}$$

where b_{2j} is the least-squares coefficient on x_j in the auxiliary regression equation (7.24). The parameter $b_{y2.K}$ always appears in Eq. (7.25) regardless of which regression coefficient is being checked for bias. Since we have argued that it is reasonable to expect $b_{y2.K}$ to be small (around -0.01 if income elasticities are 1.0 and mean intramarginal budget shares are 0.01), it follows that unless the b_{2j} elasticity is very large, in general the difference between any $b_{yj.K}$ and b_{yj} will be rather small.

In conclusion, the above analysis suggests that the empirical consequences of incorrectly omitting the average intramarginal price (or intramarginal expenditure) variable from the residential electricity demand equation appear to be very small and negligible. For example, if the regression analyst had insufficient data and therefore omitted x_2, he or she could still obtain estimates that were very close to the correct values by estimating the misspecified equation and then inserting reasonable estimates of b_{2j} into Eq. (7.25).[26]

7.4.B Simultaneity Between Electricity Price and Quantity

A number of econometric studies of demand for electricity have used as a measure of price the ex post average price, computed as total expenditure on electricity divided by total kilowatt hours consumed. When rate structures have multiple blocks, the average price computed in this way depends on the quantity of kilowatt hours consumed—quantity affects price. Further, since many rate structures have declining rates in the larger volume blocks, a negative relationship typically emerges between the ex post average price and the quantity of kilowatt hours consumed, due solely to the arithmetic of the rate structure. This negative relationship between price and quantity is in addition to that expected on the basis of economic theory, namely, that as the electricity price increases, the quantity demanded falls (price affects quantity).

Since quantity affects price (the rate structure) and price affects quantity (the downward-sloping demand curve), a simultaneous equations problem is present. In such a case, estimation by ordinary least squares will yield an upward-biased (in absolute value) estimate of the demand response, since the least squares estimate is not able to separate the effects of the declining block rate structure from those of the downward-sloping demand curve.

This simultaneity problem has been addressed in a number of ways. One apparent possibility, considered by Robert Halvorsen [1978], is to specify the following simple approximation to the multiblock rate structure:

$$TE = cy^d \quad \text{or} \quad \ln TE = \ln c + d \ln y \tag{7.26}$$

where TE is total expenditure, y is the quantity of kilowatt hours consumed, and c and d are parameters to be estimated. With this approximation the ex post average price, AP, is

$$AP = TE/y = cy^{d-1} \quad \text{or} \quad \ln AP = \ln c + (d-1) \ln y \tag{7.27}$$

while the marginal price, MP, is

$$MP = \partial TE/\partial y = cdy^{d-1} \quad \text{or} \quad \ln MP = \ln c + \ln d + (d-1) \ln y \tag{7.28}$$

Note that, given this simple approximation, the ratio of the marginal to the average price is constant, that is,

$$MP/AP = cdy^{d-1}/cy^{d-1} = d \quad \text{or} \quad \ln MP - \ln AP = \ln d \tag{7.29}$$

Halvorsen adds a disturbance term with traditional properties to the log-linear average price specification in Eq. (7.27), employs data from a U.S. Federal Power Commission publication, *Typical Electric Bills*,[27] and then considers estimating c and d by ordinary least squares. Note that since the rate structures of utilities are predetermined in regulatory hearings, they are not subject to simultaneity problems, and so the c and d can be estimated consistently by least squares. Halvorsen examines the effects of inserting least squares parameter estimates of c and d into the marginal price function (7.28) and then using the fitted values from this equation as instruments in estimating log-linear electricity demand equations such as Eq. (7.9).

However, as Halvorsen notes, since fitted values from the logarithmic ex post marginal price equation (7.28) are a constant proportion d of the fitted average prices based on Eq. (7.27), when estimating a log-linear electricity demand equation such as Eq. (7.9), one will always obtain numerically identical estimates of all the slope parameters using either average or marginal prices; owing to the logarithmic specifications, the constant factor of proportionality will generate only a difference in the estimated intercept term.

The basic problem with this approach is therefore that there is no difference between using average and marginal price. This reflects the fact that the simple approximation (7.26) is most likely too naive and that the multiblock feature of typical rate structures cannot adequately be approximated by continuous log-linear functions.

The most common procedure today for dealing with this simultaneity problem is to attempt to avoid average prices altogether and instead to employ an estimate of the marginal price. If the rate schedule facing customers is in fact only a two-part tariff with a fixed charge per month and a constant price per kilowatt hour consumed, then the simultaneity problem is adequately solved by utilizing the constant marginal price. For multiblock rate schedules, however, a problem arises as to which marginal price to employ.

Further, regardless of which marginal price is employed, the use of a single marginal price measure in an electricity demand equation implicitly assumes that any change in the marginal price will not be sufficiently large to induce the customer to switch to a different consumption block having yet another marginal price.

When the empirical analysis is at the state level of aggregation, recent econometric studies have increasingly used the *Typical Electric Bills* publications to compute expenditures at different levels of consumption, thereby yielding estimates of the change in average prices in moving from one consumption block to another. This information is then utilized in computing a "typical" marginal price for residential consumption in each state based on the marginal block corresponding to average consumption in each utility district. For states with several utilities a statewide measure is often computed by using a weighted average of each utility district, the weights being the proportion of state customers or total state consumption in each district.[28]

When the empirical analysis is more disaggregated, as at the household level of detail, analysts have attempted to obtain a marginal price measure by examining the associated utility's rate structure and the applicable marginal block rate.[29]

In conclusion, since the ex post average price is endogenous in multi-block rate schedules, most econometric studies of electricity demand today attempt to employ a measure of marginal price. Some ambiguity still remains in employing the marginal price of the typical customer at the average level of consumption or that relevant to an individual customer given household consumption and the applicable rate structure, since any marginal price change could induce customers to switch to other blocks having different marginal prices. Hence an important problem that remains is how best to model the simultaneous choice of which rate block the household ends up in when it also makes its electricity consumption decisions.[30]

7.4.C On the Choice of Functional Form

A substantial portion of the existing econometric research on demand for electricity has employed a log-linear functional form, such as that in Eq. (7.9). As was noted in Section 7.3, this functional specification is attractive because its estimated coefficients can directly be interpreted as short-run elasticities, and long-run elasticities can be computed in a straightforward manner.

There are several important problems with such a log-linear specification, however. First, by assumption the estimated elasticities are constant. This can create complications, particularly if in the forecast period, prices and income are quite different from those observed historically. For example, if the estimated long-run income elasticitity is greater than 1, then from basic arithmetic it is known that the budget share will increase with income. Since budget shares can never exceed unity, however, it is not possible for the income elasticity to be perpetually above unity; eventually, it must fall. Similarly, if the estimated long-run price elasticity is less than 1 in absolute value (implying a price-inelastic demand), then the budget share must rise with price increases, but again, this cannot occur indefinitely; eventually, as prices continue to increase, demand must become price elastic. The constant elasticity specifications embodied in the log-linear functional forms cannot therefore be globally valid.

One way of handling this problem is to generalize the log-linear specification by adding as explanatory variables the inverses of the original variables; for example, one could add (1/price) and (1/income) as regressors to (Eq. 7.9).[31] This yields price and income elasticity estimates that vary with the level of prices and income.[32]

However, a second and related problem is that care must be taken to ensure that the estimated model is consistent with plausible behavioral assumptions and basic economic theory. In some cases, adding regressors in a mechanical manner can introduce inconsistencies with the underlying economic theory. For example, if one assumes that the estimated demand equation is based on data representing the outcomes of consumers maximizing their utility, then one would want the log-linear demand equation (7.6) to be consistent with a well-defined utility function. To be well-defined and consistent with economic theory, the underlying utility function must at least have positive but diminishing marginal utility, and the resulting demand equations must be homogeneous of degree zero in prices and income. Further, the share-weighted sum of the income elasticities must be unity.

It turns out that Eq. (7.6) is consistent with utility maximization only if the utility function is linear logarithmic.[33] By contrast, a demand equation with (l/price) and (1/income) added as regressors to Eq. (7.6) (as was suggested above to permit varying elasticities) cannot be derived from a well-defined utility function.[34]

These two considerations—the undesirable restrictiveness of the constant elasticity assumption and the need to ensure consistency of demand equations with well-defined utility functions—have generated increasing interest in highly general utility functional form specifications that place no a priori restrictions on substitution elasticities. Such specifications are often called flexible functional forms. Two of the most common flexible forms are the translog and the generalized Leontief.

The additional generality of the flexible functional forms introduces a host of new econometric issues that are beyond the scope of this chapter. It is worth noting, however, that issues of estimation and inference involving such flexible utility functions are very similar to those encountered in estimating flexible cost or production functions; the latter are considered in Chapter 9, where the translog and generalized Leontief cost and production function specifications are discussed in great detail.

In summary, although the log-linear functional form has been employed in numerous econometric studies, it is highly restrictive and can yield constant elasticity estimates that cannot possibly be correct. For these reasons, in recent years, econometricians have increasingly employed more flexible functional form specifications. Nonetheless, precisely because it is relatively simple, the log-linear functional form is still used by a substantial number of electricity demand analysts.

7.5 A BRIEF SURVEY OF EMPIRICAL FINDINGS

We now turn to a brief survey of empirical findings, both classic and recent, concerning factors that affect the demand for electricity. The survey given here is not intended to be exhaustive, but instead is designed to present the flavor of representative results. Readers who are interested in a more complete review are referred to the Taylor [1975] survey noted earlier, as well as those by Raymond S. Hartman [1978, 1979], Douglas R. Bohi [1981], and Bridger M. Mitchell et al. [1986].

The pioneering econometric study of electricity demand is by Hendrik S. Houthakker [1951a]. This study was based on data for 42 provincial towns in Great Britain in 1937–1938 and was pathbreaking in a number of aspects. First, it appears to be the earliest published econometric article anywhere that reports least squares regression results obtained by using an electronic computer.[35]

Second, Houthakker clearly recognized the implications of a two-part tariff for modeling electricity demand and reported elasticity estimates using the marginal price rather than an ex post average price. Further, he initially ran regressions with marginal price *and* average fixed charge per customer included as regressors; he chose not to report final results with the latter variable included, since its influence was not statistically significant. Hence Houthakker's analysis implemented empirically in 1951 the theoretical framework discussed by Taylor in his 1975 survey.

Third, Houthakker employed generalized (GLS) rather than ordinary least squares (OLS) procedures. In particular, on the basis of the hypothesis that for each individual consumer the random disturbance term in the electricity demand equation was independently and identically distributed, Houthakker realized that since his data on electricity consumption were in terms of consumption per customer, the variance of the disturbance term was inversely proportional to the number of consumers in each town. To account for this heteroskedasticity, Houthakker weighted each variable in each town by the number of consumers, that is, he transformed the data and used OLS on the transformed data, which is equivalent to doing GLS on the untransformed data.[36]

Houthakker reported the following GLS estimated regression equation (standard errors are in parentheses):

$$\begin{aligned} \ln x = \text{constant} + \underset{(0.088)}{1.166} \ln M - \underset{(0.1905)}{0.8928} \ln P_{-2} \\ + \underset{(0.1165)}{0.2107} \ln G_{-2} + \underset{(0.0328)}{0.1767} \ln H \end{aligned}$$

$$R^2 = 0.934 \qquad \text{Sample size} = 42$$

HENDRIK HOUTHAKKER

Computing Demand Elasticities

As a 15-year-old student in the Netherlands, Hendrik Houthakker once came upon a book called *Mathematics for the Million*, written by Lancelot Hogben. This book contained a section outlining regression analysis, and it inspired Houthakker to calculate by hand the parameter estimates of simple demand relationships, such as the income elasticities of Engel curves. The analysis of consumer demand has been of great interest to Houthakker ever since.

Born in Amsterdam in 1924, Houthakker wrote his undergraduate thesis on the economics of electricity supply and demand in Amsterdam. He then completed his graduate work at the University of Amsterdam in 1949 and undertook postdoctoral work with Richard Stone in the Department of Applied Economics at Cambridge University. At Cambridge, Houthakker suddenly found himself engaged in what might be called "investigative econometrics."

In particular, the U.K. electricity supply industry had just recently been nationalized, and personnel at the British Electricity Authority (BEA) were vigorously lobbying government officials to commit substantial funds for the construction of new power plants, arguing that such additional supply was necessary to meet rapidly growing demand. The elder statesman Austin Robinson, then a professor at Cambridge and an occasional consultant to the Economic Section of the U.K. Cabinet Office, asked Stone whether he knew of an economist who could provide the cabinet with guidance concerning how much electricity price increases might reduce the growth in demand and thereby put less pressure on the government's scarce funds. Stone encouraged Robinson to contact Hendrik Houthakker.

Houthakker expressed great interest, but officials at the British Electricity Authority (BEA) were uncooperative and refused to provide him with data. In spite of the fact that the BEA did not want to see this research undertaken, a tenacious young Houthakker was able to gain access to the basement offices of the BEA on Great Portland Street in London, and there he uncovered old worksheets of electricity consumption data from prenationalized times. Houthakker then obtained additional necessary data, such as those on per capita incomes and appliance stocks, from other published sources.

With these data in hand, Houthakker was determined to estimate demand equations having up to ten regressors. This presented a problem because at that time it was totally impractical to do a regression with more than four variables using state-of-the-art electromechanical calculators (a regression with but four variables took an expert operator of such a machine about three days to compute). No one had ever performed a multiple regression with ten variables before, but undaunted, Houthakker set about to do just that. Using the EDSAC computer at Cambridge (see the text of this chapter and Chapter 1 for further details on the EDSAC) and benefiting from taking probably the very first computer programming course ever offered, Houthakker built up a library of subroutines. After coping with an EDSAC machine that was up and running only 5% of the time, he finally obtained the elusive least squares parameter estimates. Houthakker's results, published in 1951 and discussed in this chapter, indicated that the demand for electricity was responsive to changes in prices and in income. The British Electricity Authority was *not* happy with this study.

After doing some joint research with James Tobin on the demand for rationed foodstuffs in the United Kingdom, on January 1, 1952, Houthakker came to the United States and the Cowles Commission for Economic Research at the University of Chicago. In 1954 he moved to Stanford University, and there his research involved running regressions on an IBM 650 machine, "the first computer that worked most of the time." A 1957 visit to MIT enabled him to build on his computational interests; while there, he was able to do both regression analysis and quadratic programming on an "amazing" IBM 704 computer.

Houthakker joined the faculty of Harvard in 1960, and today he is Harvard's Henry Lee Professor of Economics. In addition to his classic research on various aspects of consumer demand, Houthakker has published extensively in economic theory, econometrics, economic policy, international economics, and commodity markets. Since 1971 he has edited *The Review of Economics and Statistics*. Houthakker is a Member of the National Academy of Sciences and the American Academy of Arts and Sciences, is a Fellow of the Econometric Society, and is a recipient of the distinguished John Bates Clark medal from the American Economic Association. He has received honorary doctorates from a number of universities and serves as a public director of the New York Futures Exchange. Houthakker still does all of his own computer programming, much of it on the three "nonstandard" personal computers at his home.

where $\ln x$ is the natural logarithm of average electricity consumption per domestic customer, M is average money income, P_{-2} is the marginal ("running") price of electricity lagged two years, G_{-2} is the two-year lagged marginal price of natural gas, and H is the average potential electricity consumption of appliances in kilowatts operated by domestic customers in 1937–1938.

These parameter estimates imply electricity income, own-price, and cross-price (with natural gas) elasticity estimates of 1.166, −0.8928, and 0.2107, respectively; except for the cross-price elasticity, each estimated coefficient is significantly different from zero at the 95% confidence level. There is some ambiguity in interpreting whether these elasticities are short- or long-run. The presence of appliance stocks H as a regressor suggests a short-run interpretation, yet the fact that the marginal price of electricity regressor is lagged two years apparently prompted Houthakker to interpret these elasticities as long-run estimates.[37] As we shall see, the size of these elasticity estimates corresponds most closely to long-run elasticity estimates.

Since 1951, a large number of studies have been published focusing on the residential, commercial, industrial, and occasionally national aggregate demand for electricity. Among these the residential sector has received the greatest attention from econometricians. We now briefly summarize findings for the residential sector based on a number of different data sets and models.

Bohi [1981, Table 3–1] reports that short-run price elasticity estimates for the residential sector based on models with explicit inclusion of appliance stocks range from −0.16 to −0.25, while corresponding short-run income elasticity estimates tend to be around 0.2. There is considerably less agreement on long-run elasticities, however. When average price is used as a regressor, the long-run price elasticity estimates tend to be in the −1.1 to −1.3 range; but when marginal price is employed instead, these long-run own-price elasticity estimates become inelastic, ranging from −0.4 to −0.7. The long-run income elasticity estimate is particularly elusive, varying from 0.4 to 1.0 in studies that employ marginal price as a regressor and from 0.7 to 1.1 in those using the average price.

One alternative to including a measure of the appliance stock as a regressor in the electricity demand equation is to incorporate dynamic effects indirectly, using some form of the partial adjustment framework discussed in Section 7.3. On the basis of these indirect approaches and using marginal price data, Bohi concludes that short-run own-price elasticity estimates tend to be smaller in absolute value than those using average price series; the mean estimate based on marginal prices is about −0.1, while that based on average prices is about −0.2. For long-run own-price elasticities a similar inequality emerges: The mean estimated elasticity using marginal price data is about −0.8, whereas that based on average prices is about −1.0. Regardless of which price series is employed, however, the long-run own-price elasticity estimates are imprecise and quite volatile, spanning from −0.45 to −1.9.

Within the class of models incorporating dynamic effects indirectly, although there tends to be relatively little variation in the short-run income elasticity estimates based on marginal or average price data (they tend to go from about 0.08 to 0.15), the long-run income elasticity estimates based on marginal price data range from 1.1 to 2.2. These estimates are generally larger than those obtained from equations in which average price appears as a regressor; for the most part the latter estimates vary from 0.1 to 0.9.

The important conclusions that emerge from this brief survey are that (1) price elasticity estimates based on marginal price data tend to be less elastic than those based on average prices; (2) however, income elasticity estimates that are taken from equations in which marginal price appears as a regressor tend on average to be larger than those employing average price; (3) long-run price elasticity estimates are smaller in studies that explicitly include appliance stock measures as regressors; (4) while there is considerable agreement on short-run price and income elasticities, long-run elasticity estimates are much more volatile, particularly for the income elasticities.

The econometric studies surveyed by Bohi provide useful information on the impact on elasticity estimates of employing a variety of different modeling procedures and measures of price. Our brief survey here would not be complete, however, if we ignored the strikingly different models recently constructed by Daniel McFadden and his research associates. As we shall see, these engineering-econometric model are very ambitious, and in many ways they set a new standard for future electricity demand research.[38]

Recall that earlier we noted that models in which appliance stocks are explicitly included as regressors are intuitively appealing, yet their data needs often make empirical implementation difficult. McFadden and a number of his research associates obtained data from the 1977–1979 U.S. Department of Housing and Urban Development Housing Surveys, an annual survey based on over 70,000 households. Data available from these surveys included information on households' appliance stocks, as well as sufficient geographic information to permit McFadden et al. to construct normal weather condition variables and the marginal price schedules facing these households. These data, along with additional microdata drawn from the U.S. Department of Labor Consumer Expenditure Survey and a variety of engineering and construction sources, were used in the formation of a set of models, collectively called the Residential End-Use Energy Planning System (REEPS).

The first module in REEPS models the appliance choice decision, given data on household socioeconomic characteristics, appliance holdings and attributes, the type and size of residence, and a variety of geographic and economic characteristics of the area in which the household resided. This appliance choice framework was modeled separately for each of a number of energy-related functions, such as space heating, water heating, room or central air conditioning, cooking, dishwashing, freezing, and refrigerating. For each appliance choice decision, explanatory variables included the household's income and demographic characteristics, normal weather conditions, and the installed capital and operating costs of various appliance choice alternatives. Households were permitted to vary in how they weighted capital versus operating costs in making their appliance decisions, and new dwellings were considered separately from old. The principal econometric technique employed in this step by McFadden et al. involved use of a discrete choice framework known as the multinomial logit model and its generalization, the nested logit model. Econometric issues involving the logit framework are beyond the scope of this chapter; they are discussed in considerable detail in Chapter 11.

One important advantage of working with these microdata is that McFadden and his associates were not restricted to using average income or other averaged data, but instead were able to work directly with individual household income and other household-specific measures. This is important because if there are non-linearities in the effects of, say, income on appliance choice, then these effects can easily be confounded if at the aggregate level, one employs only average measures. Use of the microdata therefore permitted McFadden et al. to consider effects of the entire distribution of income, rather than just its average.

The second major modeling effort in REEPS involved households' choice of utilization rates. Here, McFadden et al. specified short-run demand equations based on a specific indirect utility function that implied constant elasticities and included as explanatory variables the actual operating efficiencies of the household's appliances, marginal energy prices, and other demographic and geographic variables. Most of these utilization models were nonlinear in the parameters and were therefore estimated by using nonlinear least squares procedures.

The resulting set of appliance choice and utilization models was next "blown up" to reflect the aggregate U.S. distribution of households and was then simulated under a variety of alternative assumptions concerning energy prices, mandated energy conservation standards, income growth rates, and other demographic characteristics. In each case the REEPS set of models kept track of individual and aggregate household formation, appliance choice decisions, and the resulting vintage structure of the appliance stock.

With such a large set of models it was of course impossible for McFadden et al. to obtain analytical expressions for the various elasticities. Instead, they simulated the REEPS models under a wide variety of alternative assumptions and then used these results to summarize the sensitivity of electricity demand growth in the short and long run to changes in economic, regulatory, and demographic variables. Hence elasticity estimates are calculated from simulations and are not directly deduced from parameter estimates.

This brief discussion makes clear that the REEPS set of engineering-econometric models employ sophisticated econometric and statistical procedures, rich sets of data bases on individual households in the United States, and appliance-specific engineering information, to model factors affecting the residential demand for electricity. It is useful to note, however, that the basic conceptual framework underlying the REEPS models is the same as that considered by Houthakker in 1951 and Fisher-Kaysen in 1962. In particular, fac-

DANIEL McFADDEN
Social Scientist par Excellence

Daniel McFadden is not just an ordinary economist applying econometric tools to the demand for electricity. McFadden actually knows a great deal about electricity. Born in Raleigh, North Carolina in 1937, McFadden received a B.S. degree with High Distinction from the University of Minnesota at age 19, with physics as his major. Although physics has always fascinated him (his instructorship at Minnesota in 1957–1958 involved teaching a graduate course in electric circuitry and laboratory electronics, and from 1968 to 1970 he served as editor of the *Journal of Statistical Physics*), McFadden had a special interest in employing the rigorous tools of mathematics and statistics to the social sciences.

In 1958, McFadden switched from physics to an interdisciplinary Ph.D. program at Minnesota involving psychology, sociology, political science, anthropology, and economics. He then began to specialize in economics, and in 1962, under the tutelage of Leonid Hurwicz, he earned his Ph.D. degree in behavioral science. A research assistantship at Stanford University in the summer of 1961 proved to be very important to his career, since it was then that, working with Hirofumi Uzawa and Marc Nerlove, he became acquainted with duality concepts in the theory of cost, production, and consumer demand. McFadden's approach to modeling the demand for electricity, discussed in this chapter, relies heavily on duality theory. (See Chapters 3, 9, and 11 of this text for other applications of duality theory.) His 1984 *Econometrica* article, joint with Jeff Dubin, "An Econometric Analysis of Residential Electric Appliance Holdings and Consumption," built on duality concepts and was awarded the Ragnar Frisch medal as the best empirical article published in that journal.

McFadden began his postgraduate academic career at the University of Pittsburgh and then took a position at the University of California–Berkeley, where at the young age of 31 he was promoted to Professor of Economics. After spending 15 years at Berkeley, in 1978 McFadden accepted an offer from MIT, where he has served as Director of the Statistics Center, won the Outstanding Teacher Award, and is now the James R. Killian Professor of Economics.

McFadden's research has ranged widely, but like his teaching, it is always characterized by concise and rigorous analysis. He has made major contributions in economic theory (production theory, consumer theory, mathematical economics), econometric theory (models of consumer choice, qualitative response models, specification tests), and applied areas such as energy demand, the economics of transportation demand, economic growth and development, and health economics. McFadden is an elected Fellow of the Econometric Society, served as its President in 1985, is a recipient of the distinguished John Bates Clark Medal from the American Economics Association, and has been elected to the American Academy of Arts and Sciences, as well as the National Academy of Sciences.

tors affecting appliance choice are modeled separately from factors affecting utilization rates of existing appliance stocks. In this way the dynamic nature of electricity demand is best understood and analyzed.

7.6 HANDS ON WITH MODELING AND FORECASTING ELECTRICITY DEMAND

We have now come to the hands-on portion of this chapter. The purpose of the following exercises is to help you gain firsthand experience in constructing models of electricity demand, in replicating and interpreting classic results, and in using these and other models to construct forecasts using structural, extrapolative, and time-series approaches.

Exercises 1 and 2 are particularly useful and informative. The first exercise introduces you to features of the U.K. data employed by Houthakker in his classic 1951 study, while the second exercise involves you in examining U.S. annual data underlying the 1985 Nelson-Peck study of electric utility forecasting. In Exercise 3 you attempt to replicate Houthakker's results; he obtained these by programming the first known regressions on an electronic computer. Houthakker not only performed OLS estimation, but also did GLS. Your replications involve both OLS and GLS and the more recently developed robust standard error procedures in the context of heteroskedasticity. You also calculate demand elasticities; with the linear functional form these are observation-dependent.

In Exercise 4 you have the opportunity to examine empirically Taylor's argument concerning the effects on elasticity estimates of incorrectly omitting average intramarginal expenditures. This exercise demonstrates factors that affect the magnitude of the omitted variable bias. In Exercise 5 you become involved in implementing the Fisher-Kaysen specification of short-run electricity demand using aggregate U.S. data, 1951–1984. You consider the plausibility of the resulting short- and long-run elasticity estimates and implement tests for first-order autocorrelation of the residuals, as well as estimation by GLS.

In Exercise 6 you gain experience in implementing empirically the partial adjustment specification of demand for electricity, using the Nelson-Peck annual U.S. time series data, 1951–1984. This specification includes the lagged dependent variable as a regressor and therefore introduces complications in testing and adjusting for autocorrelation. Durbin's *m*- and *h*-statistics are employed. It turns out that with this body of data the common Cochrane-Orcutt computational algorithm that adjusts for first-order autocorrelation yields interesting problems of multiple local optima; this problem would not necessarily become apparent unless one employed the Hildreth-Lu procedure. This exercise is therefore useful in demonstrating computational problems of local versus global optima.

The last two exercises, Exercises 7 and 8, are not particularly difficult, but their execution relies on computer software that is not always available in typical regression programs. In Exercise 7 you become familiar with a variety of ad hoc extrapolative techniques when you attempt to discover what forecasting techniques yield predictions that are closest to those made by U.S. electric utility forecasters in the 1970s and 1980s. Here you will compare the forecasts made by constant exponential growth rate extrapolation, single and double exponential smoothing, and Holt's two-parameter smoothing procedure with the NERC Summary Forecasts, reproduced in Table 7.1.

Finally, in Exercise 8 you become engaged in constructing a combined time series, structural model of electricity demand, very much like that of Nelson and Peck [1985]. You then compare the forecasts from this model with the NERC Summary Forecasts.

●●●●●●●●●●

In your data diskette directory you will find a subdirectory called CHAP7.DAT with two data files. The first data file, called UKELEC, contains data employed by Hendrik Houthakker in his 1951 study of electricity demand in 42 towns of Great Britain during 1937–1938. The second data file consists of time series of several variables used by Charles R. Nelson and Stephen C. Peck in their study of how forecasters in the U.S. electric utility industry constructed electricity demand growth projections in the 1970s and 1980s. Since most of these data were initially compiled by the National Electricity Reliability Council, this data file is called NERC.

The data file UKELEC contains 42 observations (one for each town) on the following variables: The average number of consumers with domestic two-part tariffs in 1937–1938, in thousands (CUST); average income of consumers, in pounds per year (INC); the running charge (marginal cost) of electricity on domestic two-part tariffs in 1933–1934 (MC4), in 1935–1936 (MC6), and in 1937–1938 (MC8), all in pence per kilowatt hour; the marginal price of gas in 1935–1936 (GAS6) and in 1937–1938 (GAS8), both in pence per therm; consumption of electricity on domestic two-part tariffs per consumer in 1937–1938, in kilowatt hours (KWH); average holdings of heavy electric equipment leased by domestic two-part consumers in 1937–1938—a measure of appliance consumption capacity, in kilowatts (CAP); and average total expenditure on electricity by two-part consumers in 1937–1938, in pounds (EXPEN). While INC and EXPEN are in pounds, the electricity and gas marginal prices are in pence. To convert from pence to pounds, note that in

1937–1938 there were 12 pence per shilling and 20 shillings per pound; hence one pound equals 240 pence.

The other data file, NERC, contains 34 annual observations, 1951–1984, on the following variables: the year of the observation (YEAR); the total kilowatt hours consumed by all U.S. customers, in millions (KWH); the average price of electricity per kilowatt hour, in constant 1972 cents (PELEC); U.S. gross national product, in billions of 1972 dollars (GNP); and the NERC Summary Forecast average annual electricity demand growth rate forecast, in percentage points, using data up through and including the current year (NSF). The NSF variable has nonzero values only for 1973 to 1984. Further, the PELEC variable should be interpreted as an ex post average price; it is computed as total revenue from sales of utilities to all sectors (residential, commercial, industrial, etc.) in 1972 dollars, divided by the total kilowatt hours sold. Data sources for the variables in the file NERC are listed in Nelson and Peck [1985], p. 187.

EXERCISES

EXERCISE 1: Examining Houthakker's U.K. Data on 42 Towns

The purpose of this exercise is to have you become familiar with important features of the data underlying Houthakker's 1951 pioneering study on factors affecting the demand for electricity in 42 towns of Great Britain in 1937–1938. Variation in prices among towns, the importance of the intramarginal electricity budget share, the relationship between marginal and ex post average price, and the size of the fixed charge are all examined. You will find that this data analysis will be of considerable help in understanding and interpreting the regression results that you obtain in subsequent exercises.

In the data diskette directory CHAP7.DAT there is a data file UKELEC containing 42 observations on CUST, INC, MC4, MC6, MC8, GAS6, GAS8, KWH, CAP, and EXPEN; definitions of these variables were given at the beginning of this section.

(a) Print the marginal price series MC4, MC6, MC8, GAS6, and GAS8. Note that the variation in marginal electricity prices charged in the 42 towns is considerable. What are the largest and highest prices in 1933–1934? In 1935–1936? In 1937–1938? Do marginal prices of gas vary more or less than those for electricity? What do you expect to be the effect on electricity demand of changes in the price of gas when residential consumers can choose either gas or electricity energy sources for their stoves (called "cookers" at that time in the United Kingdom)? Why?

(b) Next print the data series on income (INC), electricity consumption (KWH), average total expenditure on electricity (EXPEN), appliance capacity consumption (CAP), and number of customers in each town (CUST). Is there much variation in average income per customer among towns? From "eyeballing" the data, does it appear that income and consumption are positively correlated? How important is electricity as a budget share (compute and print the ratio of EXPEN to INC)?

(c) Now compute ex post average price and intramarginal expenditure as follows. Generate a new variable, the ex post average price of electricity, as AVGPE ≡ 240 · (EXPEN/KWH). Since EXPEN is in pounds while all the price variables in part (a) are in pence, the 240 factor converts pounds into pence (in 1937–1938 there were 12 pence per shilling and 20 shillings per pound sterling). Then construct intramarginal expenditure in pounds, denoted F, as total expenditure minus marginal expenditures, that is, F ≡ EXPEN − MC8 · KWH/240. Print both AVGPE and F. Which is larger in 1937–1938, the average price AVGPE or the marginal price MC8? Why does this make sense? Roughly, how large is the intramarginal expenditure F relative to total expenditure EXPEN? What does this tell you concerning the shape of the two-part tariff in these 42 towns? What simultaneity problems might arise in estimation if one employs average rather than marginal price? Why?

(d) Houthakker employed five variables in his preferred specifications: KWH, INC, MC6, GAS6, and CAP. Construct and print a simple correlation matrix for these five variables. Did you find any surprises? Why or why not? Now construct natural logarithms of each of these five variables, and following Houthakker, denote them as LNX, LNM, LNPE2, LNPG2, and LNH, respectively (see the discussion at the beginning of Section 7.5, in which Houthakker's preferred specification is reproduced). Again, compute and print a simple correlation matrix for these five variables. Do correlations between logarithmically transformed variables look similar to those between variables in natural units?

EXERCISE 2: Examining the Nelson-Peck NERC U.S. Time-Series Data

The purpose of this exercise is to help you become familiar with important features of the data underlying the Nelson-Peck study of factors affecting total electricity demand in the United States over the 1951–1984 time period and investigate the extent to which forecasters adjusted their predictions in the light of changing experiences. You assess the variability over time in real electricity prices and real GNP, and multicollinearity among real GNP, electricity consumption, and the real price of electricity. You will find that this data analysis will be of considerable help in understanding and interpreting the regression results of subsequent exercises.

In the data diskette directory CHAP7.DAT there is a data file called NERC containing annual observations over the 1951–1984 time period on YEAR, KWH, PELEC, GNP, and NSF; definitions of these variables were given at the beginning of this section.

(a) Print the data series YEAR and PELEC. Beginning in 1951, what is the pattern of changes over time in the real price of electricity? When does this time pattern begin to change? What is the value of PELEC at the end of the sample compared to that in the beginning? What factors might have contributed to this time trend in PELEC?

(b) Now print (and if possible, plot) the time series for electricity consumption (KWH) and real U.S. gross national product (GNP). Compute and print simple correlations between KWH and GNP over the entire 1951–1984 time period, for the pre-OPEC 1951–1973 time span, and finally for the more recent 1974–1984 interval. These simple correlations are very high. How do you interpret them? Does this high correlation lend support to forecasting procedures that predict electricity consumption solely as a function of predicted GNP? Why or why not? What problems might this high correlation cause in least squares estimation? Using the above correlations, compute what the R^2 would be if you ran a simple regression of KWH on a constant term and GNP separately for the three time intervals (1951–1973, 1973–1984, and 1951–1984).

(c) A common procedure for reducing collinearity with time series data is to first-difference the data and then to work with the first-differenced data. Logarithmic first-differencing is particularly attractive, since $\ln y_t - \ln y_{t-1}$ equals $\ln (y_t/y_{t-1})$, which for small changes can be interpreted as the percentage change in y from period $t-1$ to period t. This way of computing percentage change is also attractive in that $\ln (y_t/y_{t-1})$ always yields a value between $(y_t - y_{t-1})/y_{t-1}$ and $(y_t - y_{t-1})/y_t$. Using the annual data from 1952 to 1984, compute logarithmic first differences for PELEC, GNP, and KWH, and call these new variables LNP1, LNG1, and LNK1, respectively. What are the sample means of LNP1, LNG1, and LNK1 over the 1952–1973 time interval? Is the sample mean for LNK1 consistent with the "double-ten" rule mentioned in the introduction to this chapter? Did the "double-ten" rule also hold for the 1974–1984 post-OPEC decade? Now compute and print simple correlations between LNP1, LNG1, and LNK1 over the entire 1951–1984 time period, for the pre-OPEC 1951–1973 era, and finally for the 1974–1984 decade. Are there any sign changes in simple correlations over the sub-periods? Does logarthmic first-differencing result in lower simple correlations between electricity demand and GNP growth than those from the levels data? What about the logarithmic first-differenced and levels simple correlations between electricity demand and price? Are they also smaller in absolute value?

EXERCISE 3: Replicating Houthakker's U.K. Study

The purpose of this exercise is to have you replicate Houthakker's pioneering 1951 study of factors affecting residential electricity demand in 42 U.K. towns in 1937–1938. The estimation procedures employed involve OLS and GLS.

An intriguing aspect of this replication exercise is that Houthakker's EDSAC computer at Cambridge University, to a large extent made from discarded parts of the U.K. post and telegram offices, imposed major working space constraints that caused Houthakker to worry considerably about computational accuracy. Houthakker expended great effort in ingeniously writing up the compact computer code for least squares estimation on the EDSAC. The EDSAC computer had only 480 locations, each location comprised 35 bytes, and the inversion subroutine for a 10 × 10 matrix already occupied 200 locations. It should therefore be of considerable interest to assess how well you, using today's relatively massive personal computers, can replicate the classic results that Houthakker obtained from the primitive but ingeniously programmed computer at Cambridge University.

The data file UKELEC is in the data diskette subdirectory CHAP7.DAT and contains 42 observations on variables named CUST, INC, MC4, MC6, MC8, GAS6, GAS8, KWH, CAP, and EXPEN; definitions of these variables were given at the beginning of this section.

(a) Houthakker estimated a number of regression equations, including both logarithmic and nonlogarithmic functional forms. Using a GLS technique and nonlogarithmic data, Houthakker reported the following results (note that the electricity price variable was formed as (1/MC6), not as MC6):

$$\begin{aligned} \text{KWH} = {} & -1700.0 + \underset{(0.199)}{2.378*\text{INC}} + \underset{(123.7)}{609.2/\text{MC6}} \\ & + \underset{(20.61)}{41.58*\text{GAS6}} + \underset{(60.6)}{270.1*\text{CAP}} \\ & R_2 = 0.920 \end{aligned}$$

where estimated standard errors are in parentheses. Form a new variable PRECIP defined as the reciprocal of MC6, that is, PRECIP = 1/MC6, and using OLS, run a regression of KWH on a constant term, INC, PRECIP, GAS6, and CAP. Your OLS results should differ somewhat from the GLS results reported by Houthakker and should instead look something like the following:

$$\begin{aligned} \text{KWH} = {} & \underset{(498.0)}{-1507.6} + \underset{(0.182)}{1.917*\text{INC}} + \underset{(164.9)}{752.7*\text{PRECIP}} \\ & + \underset{(34.29)}{1.751*\text{GAS6}} + \underset{(9898.69)}{286.5*\text{CAP}} \end{aligned}$$

$$R^2 = 0.776 \qquad \text{Equation } F\text{-statistic: } 31.956$$

How close are your OLS estimates to these? How do these OLS estimates compare with the GLS estimates reported by Houthakker?

(b) The dependent variable in the regression equation of part (a) is KWH and is interpreted as the average of electricity consumption per customer in each town. If electricity consumption for each customer has a constant variance σ^2, then the variance for *average* electricity consumption is σ^2/CUST, where CUST is the number of customers in each town. Therefore when considering his stochastic specification, Houthakker assumed that the independent and normally distributed disturbance term was heteroskedastic, having variance equal to σ^2/CUST. In this heteroskedastic context, OLS provides unbiased estimates of parameters, but estimates of standard errors are biased and inconsistent. To accommodate this heteroskedasticity, Houthakker multiplied each observation of each of his variables (including the vector of 1's for the constant term) by the square root of CUST and then did OLS on the transformed data. (Your econometric theory textbook will show you why doing OLS on these transformed data is numerically equivalent to doing GLS on the untransformed data.) Following Houthakker, transform the data (transform PRECIP, not MC6) appropriately and do OLS on the transformed data. It is unlikely that you will be able to replicate Houthakker's results exactly. Instead, your GLS results should look something like the following:

$$\begin{aligned} \text{KWH} = & -1666.6 + 2.341*\text{INC} + 604.0*\text{PRECIP} \\ & \quad (310.4) \quad (0.201) \qquad\quad (124.9) \\ & + 40.89*\text{GAS6} + 267.7*\text{CAP} \\ & \quad (21.2) \qquad\quad (61.9) \end{aligned}$$

R^2 = 0.684 (untransformed data)   Equation F-statistic: 48.687

How well do your GLS results match these? How well do they match the GLS results reported by Houthakker (reproduced in part (a))? Do GLS and OLS results differ substantially? What conclusions can you draw concerning your ability to replicate Houthakker's results satisfactorily? Incidentally, are estimated standard errors using GLS here uniformly larger than those based on OLS estimation? Is this what you expect? Why or why not? Which standard error estimates differ substantially?

Some computer programs enable you to use OLS estimation in the context of heteroskedasticity but provide you with standard error estimates that are robust under heteroskedasticity.[39] If your computer program provides this option, compare the robust standard error estimates with those obtained under OLS estimation, reported above. Did you find any surprises? Finally, some computer programs will do GLS directly without requiring you to do the data transformation; all that is required is that you specify the appropriate weight. If your computer program provides this option, compare the GLS estimates that it provides with those you obtained using the "brute force" data transformation approach. Are they numerically equivalent, as they should be?

(c) In the linear functional form specification in parts (a) and (b), one can employ estimated parameters and actual values of the data to compute the implied elasticities. These elasticity estimates will vary by observation. As an example, for the ith town the income elasticity can be computed as

$$\epsilon_{KWH,INC,i} \equiv \partial \ln KWH_i/\partial \ln INC_i = (\partial KWH_i/\partial INC_i) \cdot (INC_i/KWH_i)$$

Note that with the linear specification the derivative $\partial KWH_i/\partial INC_i$ equals the (constant) estimated coefficient on the income variable. Using your GLS estimates and this equation, compute an estimated income elasticity, evaluated at the point where INC = 500, MC6 = 0.5, GAS6 = 8.0, CAP = 0.5, and KWH = 1171. Houthakker reports that at this point the estimated income elasticity is 1.01. How well does your estimate compare with his? Derive the equation for the estimated own-price elasticity for electricity and compute it, evaluated at the same point. Houthakker's estimate of this price elasticity is −1.04. What is yours? Are you satisfied with your ability to replicate Houthakker's important findings? (*Optional:* These elasticity estimates vary across observations. How different are these elasticity estimates when they are evaluated at the sample means of the UKDATA, rather than at these particular values?)

(d) Houthakker also reported results based on log-log specifications, in which the coefficients are directly interpreted as constant elasticity estimates. Take natural logarithms of the variables KWH, INC, MC6, GAS6, and CAP. As in Exercise 1 and following Houthakker, denote these logarithmically transformed variables as LNX, LNM, LNPE2, LNPG2, and LNH, respectively. Then, using OLS, estimate parameters of the regression equation of LNX on a constant, LNM, LNPE2, LNPG2, and LNH. Note that Houthakker used a GLS estimation procedure, not OLS. Therefore your OLS results will differ from those reported by him. The OLS results that you obtain should be close to the following (estimated standard errors are in parentheses):

$$\begin{aligned} \text{LNX} = &\underset{(0.614)}{-0.204} + \underset{(0.082)}{1.065}*\text{LNM} - \underset{(0.212)}{0.902}*\text{LNPE2} \\ &+ \underset{(0.165)}{0.051}*\text{LNPG2} + \underset{(0.035)}{0.184}*\text{LNH} \end{aligned}$$

$R^2 = 0.839$ Equation F-statistic: 48.124 Sample size: 42

How do your OLS results compare with those above? How do they compare with the GLS results of Houthakker, reproduced near the beginning of Section 7.5? Apparently, Houthakker transformed the logarithmic data by the square root of CUST and then did GLS by doing OLS on the transformed logarithmic data. Does Houthakker's justification for this type of heteroskedasticity, summarized in part (b), carry over to the logarithmic specification? Why or why not? Transform the logarithmic data by the square root of CUST, and then do OLS on these transformed data. Your GLS coefficient and standard error results should be very close to those reported by Houthakker, reproduced at the beginning of Section 7.5. Are they? What about the R^2 values? Compare the OLS and GLS estimated standard errors. Did you find any surprises? Why or why not?

EXERCISE 4: Omitted Variable Bias: Intramarginal Electricity Price

On the basis of the economic theory of consumer demand, Lester Taylor [1975] argued that virtually all previous electricity demand studies incorrectly omitted as a regressor the average intramarginal price of electricity (or, equivalently, intramarginal electricity expenditure); instead, these studies used either only the ex post average price or the marginal price. The effect of incorrectly omitting intramarginal electricity price or expenditure as a regressor was considered in Section 7.4.A, where it was argued that the omitted variable bias could be expected to be very small quantitatively. The purpose of this exercise is to have you assess this omitted variable bias empirically, using Houthakker's data. This exercise should help provide understanding of how in some cases one might assess omitted variable biases a priori.

Note: It will be helpful if you have worked through Exercise 1 in this chapter before proceeding with this exercise.

The data file UKELEC is in the data diskette subdirectory CHAP7.DAT and contains 42 observations on variables named CUST, INC, MC4, MC6, MC8, GAS6, GAS8, KWH, CAP and EXPEN; definitions of these variables were given at the beginning of this section.

(a) The first task to accomplish is to compute the intramarginal electricity expenditure, denoted F, and the ex post average price of electricity, denoted AVGPE. Generate these variables, using the procedures presented in part (c) of Exercise 1. Then take logarithmic transformations of these variables and call them LNF and LNAVPE, respectively.

(b) The second task is to compute the budget share of intramarginal electricity expenditure in total income, denoted as SH. Compute and print SH ≡ F/INC. Compute the sample mean of SH. Is SH small in the towns of the United Kingdom in 1937–1938? (In Section 7.4.A, values of SH for the United States were reported to be less than 1%.) Recall from Section 7.4.A that the value of the coefficient on LNF in an electricity demand equation, denoted $b_{y2.K}$, should equal the product of SH and the income elasticity of demand. If this income elasticity of demand were about unity (as Houthakker reported), how large would you expect $b_{y2.K}$ to be?

(c) According to Eq. (7.23), the bias due to incorrectly omitting the intramarginal average electricity price (denoted there as x_2) can be computed algebraically and depends on the product of two terms. The first term is $b_{y2.K}$, which you computed in part (b). The second term is one of the estimated parameters, that on the logarithm of marginal electricity price (there, x_1), in an auxiliary regression equation. Your next task is to estimate this parameter, denoted b_{21}. Using OLS, run an auxiliary regression of LNF on a constant term, LNM, LNPE2, LNPG2, and LNH (the latter variables were defined in part (d) of Exercise 1). Does your estimate of b_{21} correspond at all to the 0.5 value reported in Section 7.4.A, based on U.S. and Canadian rate schedules?

(d) To evaluate the bias due to incorrectly omitting ln F, use Eq. (7.23) and your conjecture of the value of $b_{y2.K}$ (from part (b)), as well as your estimate of b_{21}. What is the value of this product? Do you expect the omitted variable bias in this case to be relatively large or small? Why?

(e) To confirm this expectation, estimate by OLS Houthakker's basic equation (reproduced near the beginning of Section 7.5) with and without LNF included as a regressor. Note that when LNF is included as a regressor, its coefficient, $b_{y2.K}$, is not constrained to equal the product of the income elasticity and SH. Your OLS estimates of b_{y1} and $b_{y1.K}$ should be about -0.902 and -0.892, respectively. Is this reasonably consistent with your expectations formed in part (d)? Why or why not?

(f) Now redo parts (c), (d), and (e), where the natural logarithm of the ex post average price, LNAVPE, replaces LNPE2 in both the regular and auxiliary regressions. Do you expect this specification to be similarly robust to the omission of LNF? Why or why not? Are your results consistent with expectations? As shown in the summary of Bohi's [1981] survey in Section 7.5, price elasticity estimates based on average prices are often larger in absolute value than those based on marginal prices. Are your results consistent with that empirical regularity?

(g) One way of imposing the restriction that the intramarginal expenditure variable reflects only an income effect is to modify the income variable to equal income minus intramarginal expenditure, that is, let INCMOD $\equiv$ EXPEN $-$ F. Generate INCMOD, take its natural logarithm and denote it as LNINCM, and then run an OLS regression of LNX on a constant, LNINCM, LNPE2, LNPG2, and LNH. Compare these estimated elasticities with those obtained from the regression in part (e). Are the differences relatively large or small? Why?

(h) On the basis of the findings of this exercise, briefly evaluate the importance of this omitted variable bias in the electricity demand context.

EXERCISE 5: The Fisher-Kaysen Specification with U.S. Time Series Data

The purpose of this exercise is to have you assess the Fisher-Kaysen specification using aggregate U.S. time series data from the Nelson-Peck study both in estimation and in forecasting.

Note: It will be useful for you to have completed Exercise 2 before proceeding with this exercise.

In Section 7.2, electricity demand specifications were considered with equipment stocks included explicitly. Owing to difficulties in obtaining data on appliance stocks, Fisher and Kaysen made the assumption that appliance stocks grew at a constant annual rate γ. This resulted in Eq. (7.5), in which first differences in the logarithms of electricity consumption were related to a constant term γ, as well as to first differences in the logarithms of real electricity price and real income. (These first differences were interpreted as percentage changes in Exercise 2.)

The data file NERC is in the data diskette subdirectory CHAP7.DAT and contains 34 observations on variables named YEAR, KWH, PELEC, GNP, and NSF; definitions of these variables were given at the beginning of this section.

(a) The first task is to generate the variables that are required to estimate parameters in Eq. (7.5). At the aggregate national level, GNP is often used as a proxy measure of real income; hence let real GNP replace the income measure in Eq. (7.5). Following procedures outlined in part (c) of Exercise 2, generate the logarithmic first-differenced series LNP1, LNG1, and LNK1 for the 1952–1984 time period (the 1951 observation is lost owing to first-differencing).

(b) Using OLS and the 1952–1984 annual observations, estimate and interpret parameters in Eq. (7.5). In particular, do these estimates represent short- or long-run elasticity measures? Are they plausible and consistent with those reported in the literature? Are they statistically significant? Why can the standard error of the regression here be interpreted as the average absolute percent residual? How large is this average error?

(c) Suppose that the real price of electricity were forecasted to fall at an annual rate of 2% but that that real GNP growth were forecasted to grow at 4% rate annually. Based on your estimated equation in part (b), what would be the growth rates forecasted for electricity demand? Would such forecasts be consistent with the "double-ten" formula mentioned at the beginning of this chapter? Why or why not?

(d) From part (b), test for the absence of first-order autocorrelation by employing the Durbin-Watson test statistic. If the null hypothesis of no autocorrelation is rejected, proceed by estimating the same equation but allowing for first-order autocorrelation (choose from among the various possible estimation procedures discussed in your econometric theory textbook—iterative Cochrane-Orcutt, Hildreth-Lu, or the maximum likelihood method in which the first observation is retained). With first-order autocorrelation permitted, are your elasticity estimates substantially changed? Which results are more plausible and credible, those in part (b) or here? Why?

(e) Now repeat parts (b), (c), and (d), employing instead data only through 1973. Peck and Nelson report that estimates based on data through 1973 are very similar to those based on data through 1984. Do you agree or disagree? Why? Over the 1951–1973 time period, average annual growth rates for GNP and PELEC were 3.5% and −2.4%, respectively. If in 1973 electric utility forecasters predicted these same growth rates to continue into the future, and if they had estimated Eq. (7.5) as you have just done using data through 1973, what would their electricity demand growth forecasts have been on the basis of these assumptions and the OLS (or GLS) estimated equation? How would their 1974–1983 forecast compare to that published by the NERC, reproduced in Table 7.1? How would their forecasts have changed had they known that GNP would grow only at an annual rate of 2.5% from 1973 to 1984 and that the real price of electricity would increase at 4.2% per annum? If they had known this, might they have adjusted their estimate of γ downward? Why?

(f) Briefly assess the empirical performance of the Fisher-Kaysen specification in terms of implied estimated elasticities and growth rates of appliance stocks, and in terms of its forecasting properties.

EXERCISE 6: Partial Adjustment Specifications with U.S. Time Series Data

The partial adjustment hypothesis provides an alternative approach to modeling and estimating factors that affect the demand for electricity. In this exercise you implement empirically the partial adjustment hypothesis, discussed in Section 7.3, using the Nelson-Peck aggregate U.S. electricity demand data, 1951–1984. You will focus particular attention on testing for autocorrelation in the presence of a lagged dependent variable and on the sensitivity of your estimates to alternative computational techniques, including problems of local and global optima.

The data file NERC is in the data diskette subdirectory CHAP7.DAT and contains 34 observations on variables named YEAR, KWH, PELEC, GNP, and NSF; definitions of these variables were given at the beginning of this section.

(a) Form logarithmic transformations of KWH, PELEC, and GNP over the 1951–1984 time period, and call these new variables LNKWH, LNPE, and LNGNP, respectively. Given these data, estimate by OLS the parameters of the partial adjustment specification (7.9), where the ln x's are LNPE and LNGNP. What is the estimate of the implied partial adjustment coefficient ϕ? Is it significantly different from zero? What are the estimated short-run price and income elasticities? Is each of these statistically significant? Using your estimate of ϕ, compute the implied long-run price and income elasticities. How do these short- and long-run elasticities compare with those found in the literature, as summarized in Section 7.5? (Note that the price variable here is an ex post average price, not a marginal price.) Compute and examine the residuals from this regression. Are any of them particularly large? How might you interpret them?

(b) Although the partial adjustment specification estimated in part (a) appears at first glance to be quite attractive, it is worth examining it in further detail. In particular, since a lagged dependent variable is a regressor, one cannot employ the Durbin-Watson (DW) test statistic to test for the absence of first-order autocorrelation. Nonetheless, using this DW test statistic and a 0.05 level of significance, test the null hypothesis of no autocorrelation. Since DW is approximately equal to $2\ (1 - \hat{\rho})$, calculate the implied estimate of ρ, the first-order autocorrelation coefficient. Why should you expect this estimate of ρ to be biased toward zero?

(c) James M. Durbin [1970] has developed two test statistics that are strictly valid in large samples of data but are often employed for small samples as well. Many econometric theory textbooks describe these tests in further detail. Why is it that Durbin's h-statistic, defined in part (b) of Exercise 2 in Chapter 6, cannot be used here? It turns out, however, that Durbin's m-statistic, also discussed in part (b) of Exercise 2 in Chapter 6, can be utilized.

Retrieve the residuals from part (a), and naming these residuals e_t, over the 1953–1984 sample period, estimate by OLS parameters in the equation

$$e_t = a + b_1\text{LNPE}_t + b_2\text{LNGNP}_t + b_3\text{LNKWH}_{t-1} + \rho^* e_{t-1} + u_t$$

where u_t is assumed to be an independently and identically normally distributed disturbance term. Compare the magnitude of this estimate of ρ^* with that implied in the OLS equation estimated in part (b). Now test whether ρ^* is significantly different from zero by comparing the calculated t-statistic on ρ^* with the 0.05 critical value from the normal distribution table. On the basis of this Durbin m-statistic, does first-order autocorrelation appear to be absent?

(d) Although Durbin's m-statistic has desirable large sample properties, as we shall now see, at times it might suffer from a problem of low power, particularly in small samples. Using the 1953–1985 sample period (one additional observation is lost because of autocorrelation), estimate parameters of the partial adjustment equation (7.9), allowing for first-order autocorrelation using the Hildreth-Lu estimation technique, with the grid of values for ρ ranging from $\rho = 0.00$ to $\rho = 1.00$ in steps of 0.05. Notice that two local minima occur, one by $\rho = 0.70$ and the other by $\rho = 0.95$. Compare the inference obtained in part (c) with the statistical significance of the estimated ρ in these two cases. What does this tell you regarding the possible power of Durbin's m-test? Now use the Hildreth-Lu technique and estimate Eq. (7.9) with a finer grid step of 0.01 in the ranges of 0.65–0.75 and 0.90–1.00. What are the estimates of ρ at the two local minima now? Of these two estimates, which corresponds to the lowest sum of squared residuals (or highest log-likelihood)? Compare the implicit estimate of the partial adjustment parameter ϕ, as well as the short- and long-run price and income elasticities for the estimated model with the global (not local) optima to that obtained in part (a) under the assumption of no first-order autocorrelation. Which estimates do you prefer on statistical criteria? Which make the most sense in terms of empirical plausibility? Why? How do estimates of standard errors compare?

(e) The presence of several local optima occasionally wreaks havoc with iterative computational procedures. This problem is complicated in the case of the iterative Cochrane-Orcutt estimator because when a lagged dependent variable is a regressor and first-order autocorrelation is present, the first-round estimate of ρ is a biased one.[40] First, use the one-step Cochrane-Orcutt estimator, and estimate parameters over the 1953–1984 time period. What is the implied estimate of ρ? Is this about what you expected? Why or why not? Then, using the iterative Cochrane-Orcutt estimator and the 1953–1984 data, estimate parameters of Eq. (7.9). Although computer programs vary, several programs used in preparing this exercise (e.g., TSP on a Micro-VAX 2000 and PC-TSP on an IBM-AT) converged to the local minima of $\rho = 0.67$ (not at $\rho = 0.94$) and stopped iterating at that point. As was noted in part (d), there is reason to believe that this is a local but not a global optimum. Does this occur with the computer program you use? What does this tell you in terms of using care when estimating models with first-order autocorrelation?

(f) Some computer programs offer users the option of employing a maximum likelihood technique that constrains the estimated ρ to lie within the unit interval and also retains the first observation. The extent to which these ML techniques generate results that are different from those of the iterative Cochrane-Orcutt or Hildreth-Lu estimators often depends on the size of the OLS residual for the first observation, which is retained by the ML estimators but usually is not in the Cochrane-Orcutt or Hildreth-Lu procedures.[41] Was the residual at the first observation from part (a) relatively large or small? What might you therefore expect of the ML estimator? If your computer program permits, estimate parameters in Eq. (7.9) over the 1952–1984 sample, using the ML estimator (retaining the 1952 observation). If possible, to mitigate potential local-global problems, begin with several alternative starting values for ρ (e.g., 0.5, 0.7, 0.90, 0.95). How do your preferred ML estimates compare with those in parts (d) and (e)? (In preparing this exercise we found an apparently global optima estimate at $\rho = 0.67$. Is this what you also obtain?)

(g) Among all these estimated equations, which do you prefer, and why? How do the elasticity estimates compare with those reported in the literature, briefly surveyed in Section 7.5?

EXERCISE 7: Forecasting Using Extrapolation and Smoothing

The National Electricity Reliability Council (NERC) annually publishes a summary of ten-year electricity demand forecasts made by electric utilities in the United States. NERC Summary Forecasts (NSF) since 1974, which were reproduced in Table 7.1, indicated that electric utility forecasters in the United States revised downward their forecasts at a very slow rate in the 1970s. According to a survey discussed by Huss [1985], in the early 1970s, more than 80% of electric utility forecasters used extrapolation techniques in constructing their forecasts.

The purpose of this exercise is to engage you in considering the forecasts that would have been made in the 1970s and 1980s, based on the data available at that time, had forecasters used a variety of extrapolation and smoothing techniques. If any of these techniques yields forecasts that are close to the NSF published by NERC, then there might be some reason to believe that such particular procedures were employed by industry practitioners at that time. Note that these NSF turned out to overstate considerably the actual growth rate of electricity demand. In this exercise you will employ a variety of extrapolative techniques, including a constant growth extrapolation based on a simple regression equation, single exponential smoothing, double exponential smoothing, and the Holt two-parameter smoothing method.[42]

The data file NERC is in the data diskette subdirectory CHAP7.DAT and contains 34 observations on variables named YEAR, KWH, PELEC, GNP, and NSF; definitions of these variables were given at the beginning of this section.

(a) One of the simplest extrapolation techniques available employs regression methods and the simple constant exponential growth functional form. Let $y_t = Ae^{rt}$, where y is the variable to be forecasted, A is a constant, r is the constant growth rate, and t is time. A forecast for τ periods ahead is given by $y^{t+\tau} = Ae^{r(t+\tau)}$. In logarithmic form, this form can be written as

$$\ln y_t = \ln A + rt$$

Its parameters $\ln A$ and r can be estimated by least squares.

One possibility is that forecasters in the 1970s used this equation and data for T previous time periods to estimate r and then forecasted future growth to occur at the constant rate r. In particular, suppose that in each year since 1974, forecasters used the previous ten years' data on LNKWH to estimate r. Construct 12 corresponding constant growth forecasts for data ending in 1973, in 1974, . . . , in 1984. (As a measure of t, use YEAR.) How well do these estimates of r compare with those in the NSF, reproduced in Table 7.1? Might electricity demand forecasters actually have used such a procedure? (*Note:* The 12 estimates of

r obtained in this way, beginning with 1964–1973, should be 7.3, 6.8, 6.2, 5.7, 5.1, 4.6, 4.3, 3.8, 3.4, 2.8, 2.6, and 2.4.)

(b) An alternative possibility is that forecasters employed smoothing techniques, such as the single exponential smoothing procedure. This procedure does not work well when there is a clear trend in the data, and so in the electricity demand context it might be useful to employ first-differenced data, such as $\text{LNK1}_t \equiv \text{LNKWH}_t - \text{LNKWH}_{t-1}$. The recursive formula for the smoothed series is of the form $\hat{y}_t = \alpha y_t + (1 - \alpha)\hat{y}_{t-1}$, where $y_t \equiv \text{LNK1}_t$. Note that the closer is α to 1, the more heavily the current value of y_t is weighted in generating $\hat{y}_t$. Hence smaller values of α imply a more heavily smoothed series. The parameter α is often estimated in computer programs by finding that value of α that minimizes the sum of squared forecast errors within the prescribed sample. Forecasts based on this method are averages and are the same for all future time periods.

Construct the logarithmic first-differenced variable LNK1 for the 1952–1984 time period, and then, using annual data from 1952–1973, 1952–1974, 1952–1975, . . . , 1952–1984, estimate α in the single exponential smoothing expression. Are the estimates of α small or large, and what is their time trend? On the basis of these 12 estimates of α, construct the forecast for the first year after the end of the sample (recall that this one-period forecast is the same as the ten-year forecast). Compare these forecasts with the NSF of electric utility forecasters, reproduced in Table 7.1, and with those obtained in part (a) under the constant exponential growth extrapolation procedure. (*Note:* The 12 forecasted growth rates obtained by exponential smoothing, beginning with 1952–1973, should turn out to be 7.8, 7.7, 5.7, 5.8, 5.6, 5.1, 4.4, 3.5, 3.2, 1.1, 1.8, and 2.9). Nelson and Peck [1985, p. 182] conclude that "a forecaster using exponential smoothing . . . to forecast future aggregate electricity sales would have produced forecasts very much like the NSF." Do you agree? Why or why not?

(c) Yet another forecasting procedure that was possibly used by electric utility forecasters is called the double exponential smoothing method. It is useful in instances in which one might want to smooth a series heavily, yet not give very much weight to the more distant data points, that is, not want a small α. In double exponential smoothing, the singly smoothed series $\hat{y}_t$ defined in part (b) is smoothed again, thereby permitting a larger value of α, yet still yielding a heavily smoothed series. In particular, denoting the doubly smoothed series $\hat{y}_t^*$, let $\hat{y}_t^* = \alpha\hat{y}_t + (1 - \alpha)\hat{y}_{t-1}^*$. Most computer programs estimate α by finding that value of α for which the sum of squared forecast errors is minimized over the prescribed sample.

On the basis of the data series for LNK1 constructed in part (b), and then using annual data from 1952–1973, 1952–1974, 1952–1975, . . . ,1952–1984, obtain 12 estimates of α based on the double exponential smoothing procedure. Are these estimates of α uniformly larger than those from the single exponential smoothing method? How do you interpret this? On the basis of these estimates of α obtained by using data through year t, construct growth rate forecasts for each year up to year $t + 10$. Compute the sample average of these ten annual growth rate forecasts. (*Note:* These average growth rate forecasts should turn out to be, beginning with 1952–1973, 5.7, 2.9, 2.2, 2.4, 2.3, 2.0, 1.6, 1.2, 1.8, 1.6, 1.4, and 1.2.) Compare the double and single exponential smoothing forecasts, and in particular assess which is closer to the NSF values, reproduced in Table 7.1. Why do the double exponential smoothing forecasts adapt more quickly to recent experiences than the single exponential forecasts? Do you think electric utility forecasters used double exponential smoothing methods in the 1970s and 1980s? Why or why not?

(d) Finally, prescient electric utility forecasters in the 1970s might have begun to notice a downward trend in electricity growth. In cases in which there appears to be a trend in the data, the exponential smoothing techniques can be modified to incorporate average changes in the long-run secular trend of a time series. One well-known procedure for doing this is Holt's two-parameter exponential smoothing method, in which the smoothed series $\hat{y}_t$ is calculated from two recursive equations, depending on two smoothing parameters, α and β (the latter a trend parameter), both of which must lie between 0 and 1. As before, the smaller are α and β, the heavier is the smoothing. These two equations are

$$\hat{y}_t = \alpha y_t + (1 - \alpha)\hat{y}_{t-1} + r_{t-1}$$
$$r_t = \beta(\hat{y}_t - \hat{y}_{t-1}) + (1 - \beta)r_{t-1}$$

where r_t is a smoothed series depicting the average rate of increase in the smoothed series $\hat{y}_t$. Note that in the first equation this trend increase is added in when computing the smoothed series $\hat{y}_t$. Once α and β are estimated, a τ-period ahead forecast can be constructed as $\hat{y}_{t+\tau} = \hat{y}_t + \tau r_t$, representing the sum of smoothed and trend effects.

To assess the potential usefulness of Holt's two parameter exponential smoothing method in the context of electricity demand, let y_t be the percentage change (logarithmic first difference) $\text{LNK1}_t \equiv \text{LNKWH}_t - \text{LNKWH}_{t-1}$, and employing annual data series 1952–1973, 1952–1974, . . . , 1952–1984, obtain 12 different estimates of α and β. You should find that in most estimations using data up to 1980 the estimate of α is usually zero, while the estimated trend parameter β is nonzero. After 1980, however, both parameters are nonzero. How do you interpret this? Then construct 12 distinct ten-year forecasts of growth rates in electricity demand beginning in year $t + 1$, where t is the last year of the sample used to estimate α and β. Since each forecast will vary over its ten-year span, compute the sample mean of the ten forecast growth rates for each of the 12 forecasts. (*Note:* These should turn out to be, beginning with the 1974–1983 forecast based on 1952–1973 data, 6.9, 5.7, 5.6, 5.6, 5.9, 4.4, 4.3, 4.2, 1.6, −1.5, −1.7, and 2.5.) How do these forecasts compare with those obtained in parts (a), (b), and (c)? Comment on why the Holt two-parameter method yields negative growth rate forecasts when using data up to 1982 and up to 1983, whereas the other methods did not. On the basis of the NSF data in Table 7.1, do you think that electricity demand forecasters actually used this Holt two-parameter in the 1970s and 1980s? Why or why not?

(e) Finally, each of the forecasting procedures you have implemented in this exercise has been criticized for being too mechanical and ad hoc and for not being sufficiently structured in economic theory. Do you agree or disagree? Why?

EXERCISE 8: Combined Structural, Time-Series Forecasting of Electricity Demand

The purpose of this exercise is to involve you in implementing empirically a combined structural, time-series (Box-Jenkins) model of demand for electricity along the lines of that published by Nelson and Peck [1985]. An issue of particular interest is whether one can plausibly interpret the overestimated electricity growth demand in the 1970s and 1980s as being due to overly optimistic forecasts of growth in real GNP and continued declines in real electricity prices.[43]

The data file NERC is in the data diskette subdirectory CHAP7.DAT and contains 34 observations on variables named YEAR, KWH, PELEC, GNP, and NSF; definitions of these variables were given at the beginning of this section.

(a) The first step in the Box-Jenkins model construction procedure is to examine the data for stationarity. Using the Nelson-Peck time series data, construct the logarithmic first-differenced data series LNK1, LNP1, and LNG1 for 1952–1984, as in part (c) of Exercise 2. Then construct and print simple and partial autocorrelations for the 1952–1973 time period, up to a lag of five periods. Nelson and Peck [1985] conclude that stationarity is achieved with no or at most one further differencing of the data series. Do you agree? Why or why not?

(b) Using annual logarithmically first-differenced data over the 1954–1973 time period (the use of differenced and lagged observations involves the loss of three observations), estimate parameters of the equation

$$\text{LNK1}_t = \alpha + \beta_1 \text{LNP1}_t + \beta_2 \text{LNG1}_t + \beta_3 \text{LNP1}_{t-1} + u_t$$

where u_t follows the first-order autoregressive scheme $u_t = \rho u_{t-1} + \epsilon_t$ and where ϵ_t is independently and identically normally distributed with mean zero and variance σ^2. With this specification, what are the implied short- and long-run elasticity estimates? Do your estimates of the income and price elasticities correspond well with the estimates discussed in Section 7.5?

(c) To use the equation in part (b) for purposes of forecasting, it is necessary to construct forecasts for LNP1 and LNG1. On the basis of their analysis of the time series properties of these variables, Nelson and Peck concluded that LNP1 and LNG1 each followed an ARIMA(0, 1, 1) process. Employing 1953–1973 data and the Box-Jenkins estimation technique, estimate the parameters of these processes for LNP1 and for LNG1. Then use these parameter estimates to construct ten-year dynamic forecasts for LNP1 and LNG1 for the 1974–1983 time period. Under what conditions are these forecasts consistent with rational expectations?

(d) Substitute into the equation estimated in part (b) the forecasts constructed in part (c) and compute forecasted growth rates in electricity demand over the 1974–1983 time period. Compute the arithmetic average of these forecasts, and compare it to the 1974–83 NERC Summary Forecast reproduced in Table 7.1. Are the results very different or quite similar?

(e) Forecasts can err because of incorrect predictions of growth rates in explanatory variables. Compute average realized annual growth rates for LNG1 and LNP1, as, for example, $AAGR_t = \{\exp[(LNP1_{t+10} - LNP1_t)/10] - 1\}$, where $t = 1973$. By how much do forecasted (from part (c)) and realized growth rates differ for LNP1 and LNG1? Insert the actual 1974–1983 AAGR into the estimated equation in part (b), and construct implied forecasts of electricity growth demand. By how much would the forecast of electricity growth over the 1974–1983 time period have changed had forecasters known what actual growth in LNG1 and LNP1 would be? Might you plausibly interpret the NSF in 1974 as being characterized by excessive optimism concerning growth in GNP and declines in real PELEC? Why or why not?

(f) Repeat steps (b), (c), and (d) for your choice of one other terminal year in the 1974–1983 time span, as well as for the final year in the sample, 1984. In each case, compare the resulting ten-year forecast with the corresponding NSF presented in Table 7.1.

(g) Finally, select several terminal historical sample years during the 1973–1984 time span, and for each terminal year, estimate the equation in part (b) assuming that the price elasticity β_1 equals zero. Substitute into your estimated equation the appropriate ten-year LNG1 forecast constructed as in part (c), and then compute the implied forecasted growth rate LNK1 for the subsequent ten-year period. Compare this zero price elasticity forecast with that from part (d). Nelson, Peck, and Uhler [1989] conclude that their analysis of these data suggests that during the 1973–1984 time span, electricity forecasters gradually learned that price effects were more powerful than they had previously thought. Would you agree? Why or why not? What additional evidence would you like to have to make this argument more plausible?

CHAPTER NOTES

1. A useful rule of thumb is that if something grows at an annual rate of $x\%$, then it takes approximately $72/x$ years for it to double. In the case of electricity demand, $72/7 \approx 10$ years. If the growth rate is compounded continuously rather than annually, then the calculation changes to $69/x$.
2. Construction times vary depending on the capacity of the generating facility, as well as on its type. For example, natural gas or coal generating facilities typically take a shorter time to construct than do hydroelectric dams or nuclear power plants of equal capacity. Compliance with regulatory proceedings to gain construction authorization and licensing can also consume a great deal of time.
3. Whether utility forecasters in fact provided sufficiently accurate predictions of electricity demand in the 1970s and 1980s has also become an issue for litigation. In the state of Washington, for example, where the Washington Public Power Systems utility defaulted on bond obligations, bondholders filed suit against the utility, claiming in part that its forecasts were not sufficiently objective and professional.
4. This is not completely true, since in some cases one can remodel or retrofit existing equipment. The cost of retrofitting is often quite considerable in relation to the cost of a new equipment model, and so retrofitting typically does not play an important role in affecting electricity demand.
5. Among electric utility analysts the marginal price in the final block is often called the running cost or the trailing block.
6. One important result from economic theory is that a multipart tariff can always be transformed into a two-part tariff without any change in revenue or consumption, where the first part (the fixed charge) consists of all intramarginal expenditures and the second part is the relevant marginal price. Hence in empirical work, many econometricians summarize a multipart tariff by using only two parts. For discussion, see Andre Gabor [1955].
7. A useful discussion of such data issues is found in Lester D. Taylor, Gail R. Blattenberger, and Robert K. Rennhack [1984a], especially Section V, pp. 96–101.
8. Such studies can become very complex, particularly if possibilities are permitted for substituting electricity consumption between hours of the day. See the various articles in Dennis J. Aigner [1984], as well as Douglas W. Caves, Laurits R. Christensen, and Joseph A. Herriges [1987].
9. For additional attempts to deal with this problem, see Michael P. Murray et al. [1978], Roger R. Betancourt [1981], J. Stephen Henderson [1983], and Chi-Keung Woo et al. [1986].
10. See William R. Huss [1985].
11. Charles R. Nelson, Stephen R. Peck, and Robert G. Uhler [1989], pp. 93–94.
12. The data are taken from Nelson and Peck [1985] and Nelson, Peck, and Uhler [1989]. Realization data through 1988 are taken from the Energy Information Administration, 1988 Annual Energy Review, Table 89, p. 207.
13. Your grandparents can attest to the fact that in earlier decades, most household appliances such as refrigerators, stoves, washing machines, and water heaters were manufactured only in the color white.
14. Fisher and Kaysen [1962], p. 27.
15. Fisher and Kaysen [1962], p. 83. Words in brackets are implicit in Fisher and Kaysen.

16. Fisher and Kaysen [1962], p. 92.
17. Yet another interpretation of these rather poor results is that they reflect insufficient attention to aggregation issues, since estimation is based on state-level data. For an approach that explores aggregation issues more thoroughly and obtains somewhat satisfactory results using aggregate data, particularly for short-run equations, see Raymond S. Hartman [1982, 1983].
18. Taylor, Blattenberger, and Rennhack [1984b], p. 123.
19. Taylor, Blattenberger, and Rennhack [1984b], p. 125.
20. See Leendert M. Koyck [1954].
21. For a discussion of instrumental variable and maximum likelihood estimation, see the chapters on moving average disturbances and distributed lags in your econometric theory textbook. These textbook discussions are often based on Phoebus J. Dhrymes [1969] and on Arnold Zellner and Martin S. Geisel [1970].
22. Taylor [1975], p. 80.
23. The discussion that follows is largely taken from Ernst R. Berndt [1984].
24. For proofs, see Zvi Griliches [1957] or Henri S. Theil [1957]. A very clear textbook treatment is given by Arthur S. Goldberger [1968], Chapter 3.
25. Lester D. Taylor, Gail R. Blattenberger, and Philip K. Verleger, Jr. [1977], p. 7.
26. Alternatively, if data are available, one can impose the theoretical restriction that $b_{y2.K}$ equals the budget share times the estimated income elasticity by redefining the income variable as income minus the intramarginal expenditure and then regressing electricity consumption on this redefined income variable and the other regressors (but excluding x_2). This procedure is considered further in Exercise 4.
27. *Typical Electric Bills* is an annual publication that provides information by state on the average amount paid for various kilowatt hours of electricity consumed, given monthly residential consumption levels of 100, 250, 500, 750, and 1000 kwh. Some data for other sectors are also published. It is available from the U.S. Department of Energy, Energy Information Administration, or the U.S. Government Printing Office in Washington, D.C.
28. Issues involved in aggregating over differing tariff schedules are considered in detail by Marie Corio [1982].
29. See, for example, the household study by Daniel McFadden, Carlos Puig, and Daniel Kirshner [1977]. This study also includes as a regressor a variable designed to reflect the rate of decline of the marginal price, computed as the difference between *Typical Electric Bills* at 750 and 1000 kwh of consumption divided by the difference between bills at 500 and 750 kwh consumption.
30. This problem is not confined to the analysis of electricity demand. For example, as will be discussed further in Chapter 11 of this text, in the analysis of labor supply, marginal income tax rates often vary over various income brackets, implying that the marginal after-tax wage rate depends on the amount of labor supplied. Again, price and quantity are simultaneously determined in a discrete, nonlinear manner. One way of handling this simultaneity problem without using the restrictive continuous log-linear functions is to employ integer or other mathematical programming techniques. For a discussion of these and other approaches, see Chapter 11 (especially Section 11.3.B), as well as Terence J. Wales and Alan D. Woodland [1979] and Gary Burtless and Jerry A. Hausman [1978].
31. This procedure was suggested by Timothy D. Mount, L. Duane Chapman, and Timothy J. Tyrrell [1973].

32. Incidentally, regardless of whether the simple or more generalized specification is employed, electricity price measures and the measure of income are typically deflated by an index of all prices (such as the consumer price index), in keeping with the result from economic theory that real income and relative prices are the relevant variables.
33. Additional problems with the log-linear form are discussed in Andre Plourde and David Ryan [1985].
34. The classic underground paper on this subject is a 1967 University of Wisconsin Social Systems Research Institute discussion paper that was finally published in 1987. See Arthur S. Goldberger [1987].
35. For a fascinating discussion of experiences with the EDSAC (the electronic delay storage automatic calculator at the University Mathematical Laboratory, Cambridge University), see James A. C. Brown, Hendrik S. Houthakker, and S. J. Prais [1953].
36. See your econometric theory textbook for a demonstration of this important numerical equivalence.
37. This interpretation is based on Houthakker [1951b], pp. 18–19, in which he refers to his [1951a] paper and states that, "From pre-war information the long-term elasticity of demand with respect to the running charge in a two-part tariff has been estimated at about 0.9."
38. A summary of this extensive modeling effort is found in Andrew A. Goett and Daniel McFadden [1984].
39. Procedures for calculating robust standard errors were developed by Halbert L. White [1980].
40. On this, see Roger R. Betancourt and Harry Kelejian [1981].
41. Such computational algorithms are typically based on procedures developed by Charles M. Beach and James G. MacKinnon [1978]. Incidentally, one need not use ML to retain the first observation. Your econometric theory text might describe the Prais-Winsten estimator, which is similar to the one-step Cochrane-Orcutt procedure in transforming observations 2 through T, but retains and transforms the first observation by multiplying all variables by the square root of $(1 - \rho^2)$.
42. Not all econometric theory textbooks devote attention to these admittedly ad hoc forecasting procedures. If your text does not, you might consult Robert S. Pindyck and Daniel L. Rubinfeld [1990], especially Chapter 14; also see Spyros G. Makridakis and Steven C. Wheelwright [1983] and, for an overview of a wide variety of forecasting procedures, Wheelwright-Makridakis [1985] and Walter Vandaele [1983].
43. On the more general issue of conditions under which it is desirable to include in forecasts some other forecasts of macroeconomic variables, see Richard Ashley [1983].

CHAPTER REFERENCES

Aigner, Dennis J., ed. [1984], "Welfare Econometrics of Peak-Load Pricing for Electricity," *Annals of the Journal of Econometrics*, 26:1/2, September/October, 1–252.

Aigner, Dennis J. and Joseph G. Hirschberg [1983], "An Analysis of Commercial and

Industrial Customer Response to Time-of-Use Rates," *Energy Journal*, 4, Special Electricity Issue, 103–126.

Aigner, Dennis J. and Joseph G. Hirschberg [1985], "Commercial/Industrial Customer Response to Time-of-Use Electricity Prices: Some Experimental Results," *Rand Journal of Economics*, 16:3, Autumn, 341–355.

Ashley, Richard [1983], "On the Usefulness of Macroeconomic Forecasts as Inputs to Forecasting Models," *Journal of Forecasting*, 2:3, July/September, 211–223.

Beach, Charles M. and James G. MacKinnon [1978], "A Maximum Likelihood Procedure for Regression with Autocorrelated Errors," *Econometrica*, 46:1, January, 51–58.

Berndt, Ernst R. [1984], "Modeling the Aggregate Demand for Electricity: Simplicity vs. Virtuosity," in John R. Moroney, ed., *Advances in the Economics of Energy and Resources*, Vol. 5, Greenwich, Conn.: JAI Press, pp. 141–152.

Betancourt, Roger R. [1981], "An Econometric Analysis of Peak Demand in the Short-Run," *Energy Economics*, 3:1, January, 14–29.

Betancourt, Roger R. and Harry Kelejian [1981], "Lagged Endogenous Variables and the Cochrane-Orcutt Procedure," *Econometrica*, 49:4, July, 1073–1078.

Bohi, Douglas R. [1981], *Analyzing Demand Behavior: A Study of Energy Elasticities*, Baltimore, Md.: Johns Hopkins University Press for Resources for the Future.

Box, George E. P. and Gwilym M. Jenkins [1976], *Time Series Analysis: Forecasting and Control*, Revised Edition, San Francisco: Holden-Day.

Brown, James A. C., Hendrik S. Houthakker, and S. J. Prais [1953], "Electronic Computation in Economic Statistics," *Journal of the American Statistical Association*, 48:263, 414–428.

Burtless, Gary and Jerry A. Hausman [1978], "The Effect of Taxation on Labor Supply: Evaluating the Gary Negative Income Tax Experiment," *Journal of Political Economy*, 86:6, December, 1103–1130.

Caves, Douglas W., Laurits R. Christensen, and Joseph A. Herriges [1987], "The Neoclassical Model of Consumer Demand with Identically Priced Commodities: An Application to Time-of-Use Electricity Pricing," *The Rand Journal of Economics*, 18:4, Winter, 564–580.

Corio, Marie [1982], "Aggregate Residential Electricity Demand: Methods for Integrating Over Declining Block Rates," Final Report by National Economic Research Associates, Palo Alto, Calif.: Electric Power Research Institute, EA-2767, Research Project 1361, December.

Dhrymes, Phoebus J. [1969], "Efficient Estimation of Distributed Lags with Autocorrelated Error Terms," *International Economic Review*, 10:1, February, 47–67.

Durbin, James M. [1970], "Testing for Serial Correlation in Least Squares Regression When Some of the Regressors Are Lagged Dependent Variables," *Econometrica*, 38:3, May, 410–421.

Fisher, Franklin M., in association with Carl Kaysen [1962], *A Study in Econometrics: The Demand for Electricity in the United States*, Amsterdam: North-Holland.

Friedman, Milton [1957], *A Theory of the Consumption Function*, Princeton: Princeton University Press for the National Bureau of Economic Research.

Gabor, Andre [1955], "A Note on Block Tariffs," *Review of Economic Studies*, 23:1, 32–41.

Goett, Andrew A. and Daniel McFadden [1984], "The Residential End-Use Energy Planning System: Simulation Model Structure and Empirical Analysis," in John R. Moroney, ed., *Advances in the Economics of Energy and Resources*, Vol. 5, Greenwich, Conn.: JAI Press, pp. 153–210.

Goldberger, Arthur S. [1968], *Topics in Regression Analysis*, New York: The Macmillan Company.

Goldberger, Arthur S. [1987], *Functional Form and Utility: A Review of Consumer Demand Theory*, Boulder, Colo.: Westview Press.

Griliches, Zvi [1957], "Specification Bias in Estimates of Production Functions," *Journal of Farm Economics*, 39:1, March, 8–20.

Halvorsen, Robert [1978], *Econometric Models of U.S. Energy Demand*, Lexington, Mass,: D.C. Heath.

Hartman, Raymond S. [1978], "A Critical Review of Single Fuel and Interfuel Substitution Residential Energy Demand Models," Cambridge, Mass.: Massachusetts Institute of Technology, Energy Laboratory Report MIT-EL-78-003.

Hartman, Raymond S. [1979], "Frontiers in Energy Demand Modeling," *Annual Review of Energy*, 4, 433–466.

Hartman, Raymond S. [1982], "A Note on the Use of Aggregate Data in Individual Choice Models: Discrete Consumer Choice among Alternative Fuels for Residential Appliances," *Journal of Econometrics*, 18:3, April, 313–335.

Hartman, Raymond S. [1983], "The Estimation of Short-Run Household Electricity Demand Using Pooled Aggregate Data," *Journal of Business and Economic Statistics*, 1:2, April, 127–135.

Henderson, J. Stephen [1983], "The Economics of Electricity Demand Charges," *The Energy Journal*, 4, Special Electricity Issue, 127–140.

Houthakker, Hendrik S. [1951a], "Some Calculations of Electricity Consumption in Great Britain," *Journal of the Royal Statistical Society (A)*, No. 114, Part III, 351–371.

Houthakker, Hendrik S. [1951b], "Electricity Tariffs in Theory and Practice," *Economic Journal*, 61:241, March, 1–25.

Huss, William R. [1985], "What Makes a Good Load Forecast," *Public Utilities Fortnightly*, 116:11, 28 November, 27–35.

Koyck, Leendert M. [1954], *Distributed Lags and Investment Analysis*, Amsterdam: North-Holland.

Makridakis, Spyros G. and Steven C. Wheelwright [1983], *Forecasting Methods and Applications*, Second Edition, New York: John Wiley and Sons.

McFadden, Daniel, Carlos Puig, and Daniel Kirshner [1977], "Determinants of the Long-Run Demand for Electricity," in American Statistical Association, *1977 Proceedings of the Business and Economic Statistics Section*, Part 2, 109–117.

Mitchell, Bridger M., Rolla E. Park, and Francis Labrune [1986], "Projecting the Demand for Electricity: A Survey and Forecast," Santa Monica, Calif.: The Rand Corporation, Series 3312-PSSP, February.

Mount, Timothy D., L. Duane Chapman, and Timothy J. Tyrrell [1973], "Electricity Demand in the United States: An Econometric Analysis," Oak Ridge, Tenn.: Oak Ridge National Laboratory, Report ORNL-NSF-EP-49.

Murray, Michael P., Robert Spann, Lawrence Pulley, and Edward Beauvais [1978], "The Demand for Electricity in Virginia, *Review of Economics and Statistics*, 60:4, November, 585–600.

Muth, John F. [1960], "Optimal Properties of Exponentially Weighted Forecasts," *Journal of the American Statistical Association*, 55:290, June, 299–306.

National Research Council (Tjalling C. Koopmans, Chairman) [1978], "Report of the Modeling Resource Group, Synthesis Panel, Committee on Nuclear and Alternative Energy Systems," Washington, D.C.: National Academy of Sciences, Supporting Paper 2.

Nelson, Charles R. and Stephen C. Peck [1985], "The NERC Fan: A Retrospective Analysis of NERC Summary Forecasts," *Journal of Business and Economic Statistics*, 3:3, July, 179–187.

Nelson, Charles R., Stephen C. Peck, and Robert G. Uhler [1989], "The NERC Fan in Retrospect and Lessons for the Future," *Energy Journal*, 10:2, April, 91–107.

Pindyck, Robert S. and Daniel L. Rubinfeld [1990], *Econometric Models and Economic Forecasts*, Third Edition, New York: McGraw-Hill.

Plourde, Andre and David Ryan [1985], "On the Use of Double-Log Forms in Energy Demand Analysis," *The Energy Journal*, 6:4, October, 105–113.

Strauss, Lewis L. [1954], Remarks prepared for delivery at the Founder's Day Dinner, National Association of Science Writers, New York, September 16.

Taylor, Lester D. [1975], "The Demand for Electricity: A Survey," *Bell Journal of Economics and Management Science*, 6:1, Spring, 74–110.

Taylor, Lester D., Gail R. Blattenberger, and Robert K. Rennhack [1984a], "Residential Energy Demand in the United States: Introduction and Overview of Alternative Models," in John R. Moroney, ed., *Advances in the Economics of Energy and Resources*, Vol. 5, Greenwich, Conn.: JAI Press, pp. 85–102.

Taylor, Lester D., Gail R. Blattenberger, and Robert Rennhack [1984b], "Residential Energy Demand in the United States: Empirical Results for Electricity," in John R. Moroney, ed., *Advances in the Economics of Energy and Resources*, Vol. 5, Greenwich, Conn.: JAI Press, pp. 103–127.

Taylor, Lester D., Gail R. Blattenberger, and Philip K. Verleger, Jr. [1977], *The Residential Demand for Energy*, Palo Alto, Calif.: Electric Power Research Institute, Final Report EPRI EA-235, Vol. 1, January.

Theil, Henri S. [1957], "Specification Errors and the Estimation of Economic Relationships," *Review of the International Statistical Institute*, 25, 41–51.

Vandaele, Walter [1983], *Applied Time Series and Box-Jenkins Models*, New York: Academic Press.

Wales, Terence J. and Alan D. Woodland [1979], "Labour Supply and Progressive Taxes," *Review of Economic Studies*, 46:1, 83–96.

Wheelwright, Steven C. and Spyros G. Makridakis [1985], *Forecasting Methods for Management*, Fourth Edition, New York: John Wiley and Sons.

White, Halbert L. [1980], "A Heteroskedasticity-Consistent Covariance Matrix Estimator and a Direct Test for Heteroskedasticity," *Econometrica*, 48:4, May, 817–838.

Woo, Chi-Keung, Philip Hanser, and Nate Toyama [1986], "Estimating Hourly Electric Load with Generalized Least Squares Procedures, *The Energy Journal*, 7:2, April, 153–170.

Zellner, Arnold, and Martin S. Geisel [1970], "Analysis of Distributed Lag Models with Application to Consumption Function Estimation," *Econometrica*, 38:6, November, 865–888.

FURTHER READINGS

Granger, Clive W. J. [1989], *Forecasting in Business and Economics*, Second Edition, New York, Academic Press. An introductory-level textbook on forecasting using time series and regression techniques.

Harvey, Andrew C. [1981], *The Econometric Analysis of Time Series*, Oxford, England. Philip Allan Publishers, Ltd. (Second Edition published by MIT

Press, Cambridge, Mass. 1990.) A useful text on time series estimation and forecasting.

Journal of Forecasting [1987], Special Section on Electricity Load Forecasting, 6:2, April/June. Considers alternative forecasting approaches, classic and contemporary.

Nelson, Charles R. [1973], *Applied Time Series Analysis for Managerial Forecasting*, San Francisco: Holden-Day. A simple and elegant introductory treatment of time series analysis.

Peck, Stephen C. and John P. Weyant [1985], "Electricity Growth in the Future," *The Energy Journal*, 6:1, January, 23–43. An overview of problems and findings in forecasting electricity demand.

Chapter 8

Causality and Simultaneity Between Advertising and Sales

"If you think advertising doesn't pay—we understand there are twenty-five mountains in Colorado higher than Pike's Peak. Can you name one?"

THE AMERICAN SALESMAN[1]

"Advertisements contain the only truths to be relied on in a newspaper."

THOMAS JEFFERSON, Letter to Nathaniel Macon, 1819

"The conclusion that advertising's effect on sales lasts for months rather than years is strongly supported."

DARRAL G. CLARKE (1976, p. 355)

"Advertising may shift purchases between firms or even between industries, but consumer saving does not appear to be at all affected. Advertising cannot be praised for booms, damned for recessions, or blamed for keeping funds from the public treasury."

RICHARD SCHMALENSEE (1972, p. 58)

In this chapter we consider econometric issues involved in attempting to quantify the causes and consequences of advertising. Advertising has been with us for a long time, although its forms have changed along with technology. For example, in ancient Athens, Rome, and Carthage, street criers announced to all who would hear the imminent sales of slaves, cattle, and imports. Later, when most of the populace was still illiterate, merchants displayed signs with symbols calling attention to their shops, such as a loaf of bread for a baker or a horseshoe for a cobbler. With the advent of the printing press and the spread of literacy, sellers placed advertisements on handbills and in newspapers. In the United States in the 1700s, Benjamin Franklin pioneered the use of print advertising. Today, much advertising employs electronic media such as radio and television.

Although advertising is but one instrument in the marketing mix, even by itself it entails a massive expenditure of funds. As can be seen in Table 8.1, for example, from 1940 to 1970, advertising outlays increased from 2 billion to 20 billion dollars.[2] In 1988, expenditures for advertising are estimated to have been 118 billion dollars, or about $450 per person in the United States. Since 1975, advertising as a percentage of GNP has risen steadily, reaching almost 2.5% in 1988.[3] It is clear that advertising is a very important industry.

While advertising has been with us for centuries, so too have its critics. Early on, advertising generated much public skepticism, due in part to its involvement with occasional fraudulent promotions of herbal and other medicines. Writing in *The Idler* in 1758, for example, a disgruntled Doctor Samuel Johnson observed, "Advertisements are now so numerous that they are very negligently perused and it is therefore necessary to gain attention by magnificence of promise and by eloquence, sometimes sublime and sometimes pathetick."

More recently, in widely read books such as *The Hucksters* and *The*

Table 8.1 Annual U.S. Advertising Expenditures and GNP, Selected Years, in Billions of Current Dollars

Year	ADV	GNP	ADV/GNP	Year	ADV	GNP	ADV/GNP
1940	2.11	100.4	2.10%	1980	53.55	2732.0	1.96%
1950	5.70	288.3	1.98%	1981	60.43	3052.6	1.98%
1960	11.96	515.3	2.32%	1982	66.58	3166.0	2.10%
1970	19.55	1015.5	1.93%	1983	75.85	3405.7	2.23%
1975	27.90	1598.4	1.75%	1984	87.82	3765.0	2.33%
1976	33.30	1782.8	1.87%	1985	94.75	3998.1	2.37%
1977	37.44	1990.5	1.88%	1986	102.14	4235.0	2.41%
1978	43.33	2249.7	1.93%	1987	109.65	4526.7	2.42%
1979	48.78	2508.2	1.94%	1988	118.05	4864.3	2.43%

Notes: ADV is advertising, GNP is gross national product for the United States.
Sources: Advertising expenditure data from Robert J. Coen, McCann-Erickson, Inc., prepared for *Advertising Age;* GNP data through 1988, from the 1987 *Economic Report of the President* and from the April 1989 issue of the *Survey of Current Business.*

Hidden Persuaders,[4] critics have emphasized the less visible and perhaps even subliminal effects of advertising, arguing that because advertising influences the formation of consumers' tastes, it can affect consumers' spending decisions in major and perhaps socially undesirable ways. Economist John Kenneth Galbraith [1971, p. 286] has gone even further, charging that "The economy for its success requires organized public bamboozlement."[5]

Other economists, such as Neil Borden [1942], Alvin Hansen [1960], and Gardner Ackley [1961], have contended that variations in aggregate advertising have a procyclical impact on macroeconomic aggregate demand. In fact, Hansen and Ackley, both prominent Keynesian economists of their time, once proposed that advertising spending and other marketing promotions might be regulated or managed countercyclically to mitigate macroeconomic fluctations.[6]

Among mainstream economists today, few believe that advertising plays as large a role—negative or positive—as has been hypothesized by Borden et al. Most believe, for example, that advertising has little if any impact on the choice between aggregate consumption and aggregate saving. In reviewing the meager empirical research underlying Galbraith's wide-ranging claims in *The New Industrial State*, Robert M. Solow [1967, p. 101] concludes, "It is a book for the dinner table, not for the desk."

Advertising is a fascinating topic, especially for econometricians. In this chapter we examine a number of economic issues concerning the causes and effects of advertising. We begin in Section 8.1 with insights from economic theory. When advertising is viewed as another input, we show what factors affect the firm's optimal advertising budget. This implies that advertising is endogenous, depending in part on sales, the price elasticity of demand, the effectiveness of advertising, and rivals' advertising. An interesting feature of this theory is that it highlights the fact that causality may run from sales to advertising, not just from advertising to sales. Hence on theoretical grounds, advertising and sales may be simultaneously determined. This has important econometric implications. We also briefly relate the sales responsiveness of advertising to the theory of consumer demand and note in particular that it is not necessary to assume that advertising can affect consumers' demands only by changing the parameters of their utility functions.

With these considerations from economic theory as background, in Section 8.2 we introduce a number of econometric issues that arise when one attempts to infer empirically the causes and effects of advertising. Econometric issues that we address here include problems in the measurement of advertising quantity and price, issues of simultaneous equations specifications and identification, procedures for implementing the Hausman specification test and checking for Granger causality, the importance of noting potential pitfalls when constructing logically consistent market share specifications, accounting properly for autocorrelation when attempting to measure the cumulative or lingering effects of advertising with alternative distributed lag specifications, and dealing with problems of temporal aggregation.

Then we move on to consider a number of published empirical studies in advertising. In Section 8.3 we examine three studies that address the issue of whether aggregate advertising affects aggregate consumption, aggregate consumption affects aggregate advertising, or causation runs in both directions. The results might surprise you.

In Section 8.4 we begin by discussing empirical research on the effectiveness of advertising undertaken by voluntary trade associations. We then examine in detail a classic and somewhat amusing study that attempts to measure the cumulative impact of advertising on sales over time in a market in which no clear rivals exist. This study of the Lydia E. Pinkham Medicine Company has inspired a prodigious number of econometric analyses, recently enshrined as "Lydiametrics." It is worth noting that the extent to which advertising creates lingering effects on future product demand is important for policy purposes. Some critics have argued that for tax purposes, advertising outlays should be treated as long-lived investments and therefore amortized over time, rather than being entirely expensed in the year in which they occur. According to this view, since current U.S. tax provisions permit full expensing, the tax code is nonneutral and favors advertising over other investment outlays. This implies that the measurement of the duration of time over which advertising affects sales is a very important empirical policy issue. Is the duration interval less than or greater than one year? We review this literature, and again we conjecture that the results might surprise you.

Another empirical study that we assess in Section 8.4 is a 1947 classic involving two brands of a drug product advertised exclusively in magazines. The cross and own effects of advertising are analyzed by regression analysis based on detailed biweekly information on about 1500 families in 1943. Last, we review an article that distinguishes the effects on sales of the quantity of advertising from its quality, where the latter involves experts' subjective ratings of the creative copy quality of the advertising.

Much empirical research on the effectiveness of advertising has dealt with the cigarette and tobacco industry, a very large advertiser. In Section 8.5 we examine a provocative study that measures the effectiveness of various public policies on the demand for cigarettes, such as mandatory health warnings and a ban on all broadcast TV and radio cigarette advertising. This study concludes that the broadcast advertising ban has not been particularly effective in reducing cigarette consumption but that consumers have responded very significantly to the information supplied them by public health authorities, such as the U.S. Surgeon General's Advisory Committee [1964]. Fortunately, the data underlying this study have been made available, and so in the exercises you will be able to pursue further this important set of empirical issues.

Finally, in Section 8.6 we briefly outline a number of other important current empirical issues in advertising. Specifically, we overview literature on the effectiveness of alternative "pulsing" strategies for advertising, the extent to which advertising and the firm's "goodwill stock" constitute a barrier to entry, the degree of economies of scale and scope in advertising, and the role of traditional regression analysis in marketing research.

The exercises at the end of this chapter are particularly interesting and useful. Because we have reproduced on your data diskette the underlying data from a number of classic studies, you will have the opportunity to replicate, revise, and perhaps even reinterpret published empirical findings. In particular, in the exercises you will obtain hands-on experience concerning the effects of the Sunkist and Florida Citrus Commission trade association advertising outlays on the market price and demand for oranges; you will measure the carryover effects of current advertising on future sales of the pain reliever sold by the monopolist and legendary advertiser, the Lydia E. Pinkham Medicine Company; and you will engage in an exercise involving choice among alternative formulations of the cumulative effects of advertising.

In the exercises you will also learn how to avoid embarrassment from making a common mistake in specifying market share models, and you will have the opportunity to use a variety of time series, Granger causality, Hausman specification, and simultaneous equations procedures in determining causality and/or simultaneity between aggregate advertising and aggregate consumption. You will become immersed in assessing the validity and robustness of a provocative study on the ineffectiveness of the broadcast ban on cigarette advertising in the United States. Finally, you will distinguish between advertising quantity and advertising copy quality, obtaining distinct estimates of their effectiveness on sales. In brief, the exercises of this chapter provide exciting opportunities for you to engage in a variety of empirical encounters with models relating sales and advertising. Each exercise will provide you with an important and useful learning experience.

8.1 CONSIDERATIONS FROM ECONOMIC THEORY

The theoretical and empirical literature on the advertising-sales relationship is large, spanning disciplines such as psychology, psychophysics, management science, and economics. We begin this chapter with a brief overview of insights into advertising-sales relationships that are provided by economic theory. We initially consider determinants of advertising outlay, and then we examine determinants of sales.

8.1.A Determinants of Advertising Outlay

The basic economic framework for analyzing determinants of advertising outlay has been developed by Norman Buchanan [1942], Nicholas Kaldor [1950–1951], Arne Rasmussen [1952], Robert Dorfman and Peter O. Steiner [1954], Marc Nerlove and Kenneth J. Arrow [1962], Lester G. Telser [1966], and Richard Schmalensee [1972, Chapter 6; 1978]. In making their decisions on the optimal amount of advertising expenditures, profit-maximizing firms are envisaged as treating advertising as one of many inputs. Unlike other inputs, however, advertising not only affects costs, but also shifts the demand curve. According to the economic theory of the firm, each input should be purchased until its marginal revenue product (marginal physical product times marginal revenue) just equals its marginal cost. In the context of advertising, as we now show, this basic result still holds, except that the optimal amount of advertising will occur where the *net* marginal revenue product equals marginal cost.

In terms of notation, let M be the number of advertising messages, let T be the cost per message, and let the product demand function have the form $Q = Q(M, P)$, where Q is output quantity and P is output price. Define profits as being equal to total revenue minus production costs minus advertising costs:

$$\pi = P \cdot Q(M, P) - C[Q(M, P)] - M \cdot T \tag{8.1}$$

where $C[Q(M, P)]$ indicates that production costs depend on output Q, which in turn depends on price P and the number of advertising messages M. Further, T is assumed to be unaffected by the number of messages purchased; that is, the supply curve of messages is perfectly elastic.

If the firm is a monopolist maximizing current period profits, the first-order condition for maximizing Eq. (8.1) with respect to P is

$$\partial\pi/\partial P = P \cdot \partial Q/\partial P + Q - (\partial C/\partial Q\,) \cdot (\partial Q/\partial P = 0 \tag{8.2}$$

Now name marginal cost $MC = \partial C/\partial Q$, collect terms in Eq. (8.2), and rearrange:

$$(P - MC) \cdot \partial Q/\partial P = -Q \tag{8.3}$$

Finally, divide both sides of Eq. (8.3) by P and then by $\partial Q/\partial P$. This results in

$$(P - MC)/P = -1/E \tag{8.4}$$

where $E \equiv (\partial Q/\partial P) \cdot (P/Q\,) = \partial \ln Q/\partial \ln P$ is the price elasticity of demand. As usual, the monopolist is assumed to operate on the elastic portion of its demand curve, that is, $E < -1$, or $|E| > 1$.

The left-hand side of Eq. (8.4) is the percent markup, often called the Lerner index of monopoly power.[7] Note that the markup (Lerner index of monopoly power) increases as E becomes smaller in absolute value, that is, as demand becomes more price inelastic.

The first-order condition for maximizing profits with respect to the number of advertising messages M is

$$\partial\pi/\partial M = (P - MC) \cdot \partial Q/\partial M - T = 0 \tag{8.5}$$

which implies that

$$(P - MC) \cdot \partial Q/\partial M = \mathrm{T} \tag{8.6}$$

The left-hand side of Eq. (8.6) is the product of two terms, profits from sales times the impact of advertising messages on sales, while the right-hand side is the marginal cost of messages. At a profit-maximizing optimum the net marginal revenue of messages (the left-hand side of Eq. (8.6)) just equals the marginal cost of messages.[8]

To obtain a more interpretable result, define the elasticity of quantity demanded with respect to advertising messages as $m \equiv (\partial Q/\partial M) \cdot (M/Q)$. This implies that $\partial Q/\partial M = m \cdot Q/M$. If this is substituted into Eq. (8.6), one obtains

$$(P - MC) \cdot m \cdot Q/M = T \tag{8.7}$$

which implies that

$$(P - MC)/P = (1/m) \cdot (M \cdot T)/(P \cdot Q) \tag{8.8}$$

Since the left-hand sides of Eqs. (8.4) and (8.8) are identical, we can equate their right-hand sides. Doing this and then rearranging, we obtain the very useful result

$$(M \cdot T)/(P \cdot Q) = -m/E \tag{8.9}$$

that is, the optimal advertising/sales ratio depends only on the ratio of the advertising message elasticity to the price elasticity of demand.

Equation (8.9) has very important implications. First, the optimal advertising/sales ratio increases with a decrease in $|E|$. Hence profit-maximizing monopolistic firms will employ additional advertising rather than price cutting for their marketing strategy as demand becomes more price-inelastic.

Second, for mature products it may often be the case that m and E are relatively constant. When this occurs, even if prices of advertising media change sharply, the optimal advertising/sales ratio will be constant. Equation (8.9) therefore provides an interpretative rationale for the oft-observed stability of advertising/sales ratios for mature products, as well as the widespread industry practice of setting advertising budgets as a fixed proportion of expected sales.

Third, for new products it is often hypothesized that the sales-message elasticity m is initially high (a large portion of initial advertising is often purely informative) and then gradually falls, whereas the price elasticity E is initially small and then becomes larger in absolute value. This suggests that for new products the initial sales/advertising ratio will typically be much larger than the ratio when the product reaches the mature stage of its life cycle.

Finally, note that as sales grow, one would expect advertising outlay to change proportionately unless the m or E elasticities change. It is possible, however, that optimal advertising expenditures could increase even as demand falls. For example, the introduction of cable television and home videocassette recorders undoubtedly shifted downward the demand curve facing movie theatres. If this downward shift in demand left only the price-insensitive movie theatre aficionados as remaining possible customers, then in response it might have been optimal for movie theatres to increase their advertising/sales ratios and possibly even increase their advertising outlays.

The above framework is instructive, but it is based on a number of restrictive and potentially important assumptions. For example, one assumption that is implicit in the discussion is that the effect of advertising on sales is transitory in that it lasts only one time period. Suppose, however, that advertising as well as other marketing instruments have a lingering effect on demand; call this the "goodwill stock," and name it K.

Schmalensee [1972, pp. 26–32] has shown that (a) if a monopolistic firm chooses advertising and pricing decisions over time so as to maximize the present value of its profits (discounting future profits by the interest rate r), (b) if the goodwill stock K deteriorates exponentially, and (c) if actual demand Q_t moves toward long-run equilibrium demand Q_t^* only gradually as, for example, in $dQ/dt = \eta(Q_t^* - Q_t)$, then along the optimal present-value-maximizing time path it is always the case that the optimal advertising/sales ratio equals

$$(MT)/PQ) = -m^*/E^* \tag{8.10}$$

Here m^* and E^* are *long-run* elasticities of demand with respect to advertising and price, defined as follows:

$$m^* \equiv (\partial Q^*/\partial M) \cdot (M/Q^*) \qquad \text{and} \qquad E^* \equiv (\partial Q^*/\partial P) \cdot (P/Q^*)$$

This is a strong result; it states that if the long-run elasticities m^* and E^* are constant, then neither changes in interest rates nor variations in the price of advertising messages have any impact on the optimal advertising/sales ratio. Even though current advertising decisions affect the time path of the goodwill stock S, which in turn affects profits, pricing decisions also affect the present value of profits; according to Eq. (8.10), the pricing and advertising decisions are influenced in the same way by dynamic considerations.[9]

A second important assumption that is made in the above analysis is that the firm has monopoly power, and in its optimizing decisions it does not worry about the price or advertising behavior of competitors. As has been emphasized since at least the classic book of Edward H. Chamberlin [1933] on monopolistic competition, in one sense the very purpose of product marketing is to create a differentiated product over which the producer can exercise limited monopoly power. Yet in spite of attempts by firms to differentiate their products, in many industries the products of several firms are highly substitutable, resulting in limited price competition and often intense oligopolistic rivalry. This implies that analyses of advertising-sales relationships must take into account the pricing and marketing interactions of competitors and rivals.

Traditional models of pricing under oligopoly that yield unique determinate outcomes invariably have been based on rather simplified notions of industries producing undifferentiated products, for example, the Cournot or Bertrand models of oligopoly. Once one introduces product differentiation, the analytical framework rapidly becomes very messy. Schmalensee [1972, pp. 32–33], for example, notes that if an increase in a firm's advertising has any effect, it must permit the firm to increase its sales without lowering price or to raise price without lowering sales. If this latter possibility is acknowledged, it becomes possible for there simultaneously to be more than one price prevailing in an industry, thereby calling into question the very notion of what one means by an industry and by industry equilibrium.

The existing literature on the economic theory of joint pricing and advertising decisions in the oligopoly context is extremely sparse, and as of this date it does not yet include empirically implementable models.[10] Within the marketing literature, however, models have been constructed in which advertising decisions are made in an interdependent oligopoly setting but price is exogenous. Such models have been rationalized on the basis that in some oligopolistic industries (such as cigarettes and beer), price competition is rare. While it would of course be preferable to work with empirically implementable models in which both price and advertising expenditures are endogenous, these marketing models should be viewed as being in principle no more restrictive than the economic oligopoly models that focus on price competition but ignore advertising decisions.[11]

Schmalensee [1972, pp. 32–43] has presented a useful simple static model of advertising expenditures in an oligopoly framework, analogous to the static Cournot and Bertrand oligopoly output and pricing models. Consider an industry in which all firms charge the same price, P. Let the ith firm's sales, q^i, be a function of its own advertising messages, M^i, the advertising messages purchased by its competitors, $\tilde{M}^i$, and P. The typical firm's per period profit is written, using notation similar to that above, as

$$\pi^i = P \cdot q^i(M^i, \tilde{M}^i, P) - C^i[q^i(M^i, \tilde{M}^i, P)] - M^i \cdot T \qquad \textbf{(8.11)}$$

Setting the first derivative of Eq. (8.11) with respect to M^i equal to zero, we obtain the necessary conditions for profit maximization,

$$(P - MC^i) \cdot [\partial q^i/\partial M^i + (\partial q^i/\partial \tilde{M}^i) \cdot (d\tilde{M}^i/dM^i)] = T \qquad \textbf{(8.12)}$$

where $MC^i \equiv dC^i/dq^i$ and $d\tilde{M}^i/dM^i$ is the conjectured or expected reaction of competitors to an increase in firm i's advertising messages.

Now define the elasticities of firm i's sales with respect to its own messages, m^i, firm i's sales with respect to its competitors' messages, $\tilde{m}^i$, and the conjectured response elasticity of competitors' messages with respect to changes in firm i's messages, μ^i, as

$$m^i \equiv (\partial q^i/\partial M^i) \cdot M^i/q^i, \qquad \tilde{m}^i \equiv (\partial q^i/\partial \tilde{M}^i) \cdot \tilde{M}^i/q^i, \qquad \text{and}$$
$$\mu^i \equiv (\partial \tilde{M}^i/\partial M^i) \cdot M^i/\tilde{M}^i$$

Note that in order for the second order conditions for profit maximization to be satisfied, it is sufficient that diminishing returns to advertising messages occur, that is, that $0 \leqslant m^i < 1$. Now if these elasticities are substituted into Eq. (8.12), one obtains the simple result that the firm's optimal advertising/

sales ratio depends on its Lerner index of monopoly power (in turn a function of its price elasticity of demand), its advertising effectiveness elasticity, the conjectural advertising elasticity, and the effectiveness of competitors' advertising elasticity,

$$M^iT/Pq^i = L^i(m^i + \tilde{m}^i \cdot \mu^i) \quad \textbf{(8.13)}$$

where L^i is firm i's Lerner index of monopoly power, $L^i \equiv (P - MC^i)/P$.

Two special cases of Eq. (8.13) are of interest. First, if firm i's sales are unaffected by competitors' advertising, that is, if $\tilde{m}^i = 0$, then firm i is in effect a monopolist. By Eq. (8.4), such a firm will set $L^i = -1/E$; hence in this case, Eq. (8.13) reduces to Eq. (8.9).

A second special case occurs when firm i conjectures that competitors' advertising messages will not change in response to changes in firm i's advertising messages, that is, when $\mu^i = 0$. This no-retaliation case is analogous to the familiar Cournot model, in which it is assumed that other firms' output quantities will not be changed in response to a change in firm i's output. In this case, with $\mu^i = 0$, Eq. (8.13) collapses to Eq. (8.8).[12]

Interestingly, it has been argued that this second special case of $\mu^i = 0$ provides a reasonable approximation to reality. Julian L. Simon [1970] notes, for example, that firms tend to vary their advertising expenditures quite frequently over the calendar year, and so it becomes rather difficult for competitors to detect overall changes in firm i's advertising outlays, particularly since data on advertising outlays tend to be proprietary. Moreover, since it takes time to change promotion outlays and copy, any firm that increases its advertising can reasonably expect a nontrivial lag before its competitors retaliate. Incidentally, one significant implication of the existence of such a lag is that it creates incentives for firms to increase their advertising outlays.

The above static oligopolistic framework can be generalized to accommodate the accumulation of goodwill stocks of advertising in the context of dynamic optimization. In particular, Schmalensee [1972, pp. 39–43] has shown that if output price is taken as exogenously given (but is still permitted to vary over time), if the typical oligopolistic firm discounts profits using the interest rate r, and if the oligopoly's pricing responds to dynamic considerations as would a monopolist's, then a relationship very similar to Eq. (8.13) emerges, namely,

$$M^iT/Pq^i = L^{*i}(m^{*i} + \tilde{m}^{*i} \cdot \mu^i) \quad \textbf{(8.14)}$$

where the elasticities again refer to long-run, not short-run, values. Moreover, if the ordinary Lerner index of monopoly power L^i is fixed, then L^{*i} is a negative function of the discount rate r.[13]

This analysis therefore suggests very strongly that under both static and dynamic conditions, if certain elasticities are constant, then the optimal advertising/sales ratio will also be constant. When these elasticities vary, however, so too will the optimal advertising/sales ratios.

For this type of model to be useful a firm must have some knowledge concerning the effectiveness of its, and its competitors', advertising. This therefore raises the issue of how advertising affects sales. Note that this implies a causation in the exact opposite direction of what has been considered so far in this section, namely, instead of examining how advertising is affected by sales as in Eq. (8.13), we now assess how sales are affected by advertising. This brings us to the economic theory of consumer behavior.

8.1.B Determinants of Sales

The traditional economic theory of consumer demand is based on the assumption that consumers' preferences are unchanging or, in some cases, at least stable. Yet one alleged purpose of advertising is to "bend" consumers' tastes toward the product being marketed. Attempts have been made to integrate these two approaches, with some success. As we shall see, however, economic theory has not yet been able to provide clear guidance on functional specifications for sales demand equations.

In one line of literature, rather than defining a consumer's utility function over consumption of goods X_l through X_n as $U(X_1, \ldots, X_n)$, Robert L. Basmann [1956] and Franklin M. Fisher and Karl Shell [1968] specified a particular form of a utility function in which advertising is viewed as being "consumption augmenting":

$$U[V^1(a_n)X_1, \ldots, V^n(a_n)X_n] \tag{8.15}$$

where the V^i represent information knowledge and are monotonically increasing and stable functions of, say, advertising outlay or the goodwill stock of good X_n. This approach has not proved to be fruitful for a number of reasons.

First, as has been pointed out by Schmalensee [1972, pp. 101–104], this type of theoretical framework does not yield any new testable generalizations for consumer demand equations. Further, implementation necessitates taking into account the effects of advertising for good i on the demand for good j. Empirical execution would therefore require specification, data gathering, and estimation for entire systems of demand equations. While certainly possible, such a substantial effort does not appear to be useful, given that the underlying theory is not able to generate any new testable restrictions.

Second, and more basic, the textbook presentation of consumer demand theory based on utility functions typically stresses the requirement that all results should be invariant to monotonic transformations of the utility function; that is, the theory stresses ordinal rather than cardinal utility. Any results that lack invariance to such transformations are viewed as dubious, since they could easily be changed by merely scaling the cardinal utility function in an arbitrary manner. In this context, William F. Massy [1960] has noted that with specifications such as Eq. (8.15) the direction of change in substitution elasticities between goods i and j in response to changes in advertising for good k is not sign-invariant under monotonic transformations of the utility function. According to Schmalensee [1972, p. 104], this result "indicates that neoclassical consumer theory, derived on the basis of constant tastes, simply cannot be used as it stands in situations where tastes change."

Some analysts have looked to other disciplines for help in specifying demand equations. According to the Weber-Fechner "law" of psychophysics, for example, the perceived intensity of a stimulus, I, is related to the actual intensity of the stimulus, A, according to $I = a + \ln(bA)$ over some relevant range. Results from psychometric experimentation have not been kind to this law, however, and it no longer commands much following among psychologists.[14] Even if this law commanded a substantial following, it is not clear how one could generalize it in a tractable manner to include the effects of other stimuli such as changes in prices and income. Hence at this point the psychology of perception cannot yet tell us much about the sorts of models that ought to be specified in detecting relationships between advertising and sales.

The most successful attempt to date to integrate advertising into a consistent theoretical framework of consumer demand is by Vinod K. Verma [1980], who builds on the household theory of production. Here, households are viewed as combining the inputs of time, information, and market goods, subject to constraints provided by a household production function, to produce unobserved, latent commodities that ultimately create value or utility. Information is itself not freely provided but also requires the inputs of time and goods. Moreover, the productivity of goods and time in producing information is conditioned by the exogenous amount of advertising messages to which the household is exposed. This advertising is produced by firms, not households. As a result, according to Verma, advertising plays the role of an exogenous shift variable in the household's production functions for information and hence, ultimately, for goods and services. This implies that in empirical demand equations for market goods, advertising variables should be added, in addition to the usual price and income variables. Note that in the Verma framework, increases in advertising are viewed as increasing the endowments of productive inputs available to households and therefore have the effect of increasing the consumer's wealth or income, other things being equal. This advertising-as-information notion of Verma is therefore somewhat different from the more traditional view of advertising as changing preferences.

Although Verma's notion of advertising facilitating household production provides an innovative and constructive way of integrating advertising with consumer demand theory, unfortunately it does not provide much insight into empirical specifications. In particular, as has been noted by Sherwin Rosen [1980], it provides no new guidelines for econometric specification, other than suggesting that demand equations derived from an indirect utility function should have as arguments not only price and income variables, but also advertising levels.

In summary, the economic theory of consumer demand can be extended to incorporate advertising, without requiring that advertising actually change consumers' preferences. However, such theoretical developments still have not been able to provide much help to practicing econometricians in specifying a functional relationship between sales and advertising. While in one sense unfortunate, this lack of clear guidance from theory implies that the empirical researcher has been able to exercise considerable freedom in specifying such equations for empirical analyses. We now turn attention to a number of econometric issues that have emerged as researchers have implemented sales-advertising models empirically.

8.2 ISSUES IN ECONOMETRIC IMPLEMENTATION

In this section we overview six important issues emerging from econometric analyses of the sales-advertising relationship.[15] These issues include (a) the measurement of advertising messages and their prices; (b) simultaneity between advertising and sales and use of the Hausman specification test; (c) Granger causality between advertising and sales; (d) the logically consistent specification of market share models; (e) alternative distributed lag specifications for measuring the current and cumulative impact of advertising efforts; and (f) aggregation over time, including the "data interval bias."

8.2.A Measurement Issues

One task of marketing divisions in firms is to choose sets of marketing activities that transmit persuasive messages and product information to target markets. The marketing communications mix chosen by firms includes a variety of promotional activities such as product samples, gifts, price discounts, and other literature, as well as differing forms of electronic and print media advertising. Public goodwill is also built up through acts of corporate good citizenship, such as charitable donations. Not only is advertising but one part of a larger marketing effort, but even within advertising, numerous different types of messages are produced and transmitted to target audiences. For example, it is estimated that of the roughly $118 billion expended on advertising in the United States in 1988, about 26% involved the use of newspaper media, 22% utilized television, 18% direct mail, 7% radio, 5% magazines, and 2% other business publications, while the remaining portion employed a variety of other media.[16] These media differ in the number of messages delivered as well as in their effectiveness.

The theoretical framework considered in Section 8.1 conveniently abstracted from these various types of marketing and advertising instruments and simply employed the notion of "advertising messages," denoted as M. For empirical implementation it is of course necessary to measure M and perhaps its price. But how is one to construct such measures? This is a very important measurement issue that has confounded empirical research in marketing for quite some time.

Currently, a great deal of marketing research attempts to quantify the number of people exposed at least once to an advertising campaign during some time period (often called the *reach*), the number of times within the specified time period that an average person or household is exposed to the message (*frequency*), and the impact of the message, measured alternatively by memory recall, market awareness, or, if possible, actual purchase in the current or some future time period.[17] On the basis of this information, a variety of measures have been constructed that attempt to quantify the effectiveness or quality of various types of advertising media and copy per dollar expended. Although reach and frequency data are now widely accepted, not surprisingly, it is the measurement of consumer response, given exposure, that remains most controversial. Finally, in terms of price, note that once one has a value for M, a corresponding price index or implicit deflator can be computed simply by dividing total advertising outlay by the quantity measure M.

In the United States the usual sources of official price indexes are the Bureau of Labor Statistics (BLS) and the U.S. Department of Commerce. In large part because of the above-mentioned difficulties, neither agency computes or publishes official price indexes for advertising. Within the private sector, major advertising research firms such as McCann-Erickson regularly compute and often make publicly available their best estimates of price indexes for various types of advertising media, as well as for overall advertising. Such firms have not disclosed publicly precisely how such price indexes are computed, for a variety of proprietary reasons.

The practicing econometrician, however, must often proceed, even if the preferred data are not available. Two common procedures have been employed in the published econometric literature to deflate advertising outlay, neither of which is particularly attractive. First, on the basis of anecdotal evidence, their own judgment, or sheer frustration, some researchers have argued that the productivity of various advertising media such as television and newspaper has increased along with their costs and that it may therefore be reasonable to make no adjustment whatsoever to the current dollar outlay values.[18] This is tantamount to stating that the price deflator for advertising over the relevant time period has remained constant at, say, 1.00.[19]

A second procedure employed by some researchers is to assume that the advertising price deflator changes over time at the same percentage rate as some overall consumption price index, such as the official Consumer or Producer Price Index published by the BLS or the gross national product deflator published by the U.S. Department of Commerce. The empirical validity of this assumption is not clear, but there is some evidence suggesting that price increases for advertising messages have not been as high as those for overall consumption. Richard Ashley, Clive Granger, and Richard Schmalensee, for example, have computed an aggregate advertising deflator for the United States, quarterly from 1956 to 1975, based on data for six media provided to them by McCann-Erickson and *Printer's Ink*. They report that over this time period the advertising deflator grew at an average annual rate of 2.2% per year, while the GNP deflator increased at an average of 3.5%. Further, the simple correlation between the first differences of the two series was only 0.60.[20]

Future progress in understanding more fully the empirical relationships between advertising and sales will depend critically on the availability of better marketing data. Although a great deal of research effort on advertising quantity measures and their effectiveness is currently being undertaken by the marketing divisions of various firms, unfortunately in most cases the underlying data sets remain proprietary and are not available to outside researchers. Private sector, public policy, and academic researchers well recognize the potential mutual benefits of cooperation, and substantial efforts are underway to improve data availability.[21]

8.2.B Simultaneity, Identification, and the Hausman Specification Test

An important implication of the economic theory underlying advertising-sales relationships, summarized in Section 8.1, is that if relevant elasticities are constant, then advertising budgets should be set so as to preserve a constant ratio between advertising outlay and sales. This implies that advertising is endogenous. On the other hand, one principal reason that firms undertake advertising is because they believe that advertising has an impact on sales; this implies that sales are endogenous. Underlying theory and intuition therefore suggest that both sales and advertising should be viewed as being endogenous; that is, they are simultaneously determined.

Econometric implications of the joint endogeneity of advertising and sales have long been recognized.[22] Consider the following stylized simple two-equation structural model:

$$S_t = a + bM_t + cP_{s,t} + u_t \tag{8.16a}$$

$$M_t = d + eS_t + fP_{m,t} + w_t \tag{8.16b}$$

where S is the quantity sales of output, M is the number of advertising messages, P_s and P_m are real price indexes for output and advertising, respectively, and u and w are random disturbance terms, all for a firm at time t. Assume that u_t and w_t are independently and identically normally distributed, that u_t is distributed independently of $P_{s,t}$ and w_t is distributed independently of $P_{m,t}$, and that u_t and w_t could be contemporaneously correlated. We expect that b and e are positive, while c and f are negative. Although this structural equation system is extremely simple, it is useful for pedagogical purposes, and it will be generalized later on. Hereafter, we refer to an equation by its left-hand variable; for example, Eq. (8.16a) is called the sales equation.

Suppose that a realization of the random disturbance term u_t in the sales equation is positive, implying that, other things being equal, S_t increased; with an increased S_t in the advertising equation, provided that $e > 0$ and that u_t

and w_t were not sufficiently negatively correlated to offset one another, M_t would also increase. This implies that within the sales equation the regressor M_t and the disturbance term u_t are positively correlated; hence estimation by ordinary least squares (OLS) would yield biased and inconsistent estimates of the structural parameters. Using analogous reasoning, one can conclude that within the advertising equation, S_t and w_t are also positively correlated, so that OLS estimation of that equation would yield biased and inconsistent parameter estimates as well. In fact, under the above assumptions it has been shown that OLS estimates of b and e are upward biased; for a proof, see Schmalensee [1972, pp. 98–100].

In addition, it can easily be verified, using the conventional rank and order conditions, that each of the above two equations is just identified. However, if some other explanatory variable X_t were added to the sales equation but excluded from the advertising equation (say, a demand variable such as income per capita), and if its true coefficient were nonzero, then the advertising equation would be overidentified, while the sales equation would be just identified. Analogously, if some regressor R_t were added to the advertising equation but excluded from the sales equation (say, the proportion of households that are connected to cable television), and if its true coefficient were nonzero, then the sales equation would be overidentified while the advertising equation would be just identified. If X_t were included in Eq. (8.16a) and not in Eq. (8.16b), while R_t simultaneously appeared in Eq. (8.16b) but not in Eq. (8.16a), then both equations would be overidentified.

To examine the consequences of just identification and possibilities for underidentification, it is instructive to compute the reduced form corresponding to the structural equation system (8.16). Specifically, solve Eq. (8.16b) for S_t, equate this to Eq. (8.16a), and then solve for M_t. Similarly, solve Eq. (8.16a) for M_t, equate this to Eq. (8.16b), and then solve for S_t. This yields the following two reduced form equations:

$$M_t = \alpha_0 + \alpha_1 P_{s,t} + \alpha_2 P_{m,t} + \nu_t \tag{8.17a}$$

$$S_t = \beta_0 + \beta_1 P_{s,t} + \beta_2 P_{m,t} + \omega_t \tag{8.17b}$$

where

$$\alpha_0 \equiv \frac{ae + d}{1 - eb}, \quad \alpha_1 \equiv \frac{ce}{1 - eb}, \quad \alpha_2 \equiv \frac{f}{1 - eb}, \quad \nu_t \equiv \frac{w_t + eu_t}{1 - eb}$$

$$\beta_0 \equiv \frac{a + bd}{1 - eb}, \quad \beta_1 \equiv \frac{c}{1 - eb}, \quad \beta_2 \equiv \frac{bf}{1 - eb}, \quad \omega_t \equiv \frac{u_t + bw_t}{1 - eb} \tag{8.18}$$

Notice that with the reduced form system (8.17), given the above stochastic specification, the disturbances ν_t and ω_t are each distributed independently of the regressors $P_{s,t}$ and $P_{m,t}$. Hence estimation of the reduced form equations in Eqs. (8.17) by OLS yields best linear unbiased estimates of the reduced form parameters.

One potential problem with OLS estimation of Eq. (8.17) is that the reduced form parameters are not of much direct interest; rather, what is desired is consistent estimates of the structural parameters. This raises the identification issue: How can one employ unbiased estimates of the reduced form parameters in Eqs. (8.17) to obtain consistent estimates of the structural parameters in Eqs. (8.16), given the relationships among them in Eqs. (8.18)?

With this just identified two-equation structural model there are six reduced form and six structural parameters. In this case, unique estimates of the structural parameters can be obtained indirectly by employing the reduced form estimates and the relations in Eqs. (8.18); this procedure is called indirect least squares (ILS).

More specifically, if we denote parameter estimates with a circumflex, from Eqs. (8.18) it follows that

$$\hat{b} = \hat{\beta}_2/\hat{\alpha}_2 \quad \text{and} \quad \hat{e} = \hat{\alpha}_1/\hat{\beta}_1 \quad \text{implying that} \quad \hat{b} \cdot \hat{e} = \frac{\hat{\beta}_2\hat{\alpha}_1}{\hat{\alpha}_2\hat{\beta}_1} \tag{8.19}$$

Using Eqs. (8.19) and the relationship for β_1 in Eqs. (8.18), one can solve for c as

$$\hat{c} = \hat{\beta}_1 - (\hat{\beta}_2\hat{\alpha}_1/\hat{\alpha}_2) \tag{8.20}$$

Similarly, from α_2 in Eqs. (8.18) and using Eqs. (8.19), f can be estimated as

$$\hat{f} = \hat{\alpha}_2 - (\hat{\beta}_2\hat{\alpha}_1/\hat{\beta}_1) \tag{8.21}$$

This yields ILS estimates of the four slope coefficients in the structural equation system (8.16). Given these estimated structural slope coefficients as well as reduced form estimates of α_0 and β_0, estimates of the intercept terms a and d in the structural equations can be obtained by using Eqs. (8.18).

Our discussion so far has emphasized that this two-equation structural model (8.16) is just identified. Suppose, however, that a priori we excluded the $P_{m,t}$ variable from the structural advertising equation (8.16b) because of, say, difficulties in obtaining a measure of $P_{m,t}$; this is equivalent to specifying that $f = 0$. Notice that with $P_{m,t}$ excluded, the new reduced form equation system would also exclude $P_{m,t}$, and so there would be four reduced form parameters (α_0, α_1, β_0, and β_1) but five structural parameters (a, b, c, d, and e). With f set to zero we could not estimate the reduced form parameters α_2 and β_2, and thus we could not employ the first relation in Eqs. (8.19) to estimate the structural parameter b. Hence with $P_{m,t}$ excluded from the advertising equation we would be unable to identify b in the sales equation; that is, the sales equation would be underidentified, although the advertising equation would be just identified. With the structural sales equation being underidentified, there is no way to obtain consistent estimates of all its parameters.

Similarly, suppose that one believed that price competition was virtually nonexistent and that therefore the variable $P_{s,t}$ should be excluded from the sales structural equation (8.16a). This is equivalent to setting $c = 0$ and results in a reduced form equation system with $P_{s,t}$ excluded from both reduced form equations. Since the reduced form parameters α_1 and β_1 could not be estimated, there would be four reduced form parameters (α_0, α_2, β_0, and β_2), but five structural parameters (a, b, d, e, and f); the second relation in Eqs. (8.19) could not be used to estimate the structural parameter e. Therefore with $P_{s,t}$ excluded from the sales equation, it would be impossible to identify e in the advertising equation; while the sales equation would be just identified, the advertising equation would be underidentified.

Let us return to the full just identified model (8.16). Although we have shown it to be computationally feasible, use of ILS and the reduced form estimator is still somewhat unsatisfactory, since it is not clear how one could test hypotheses involving the structural parameters. In particular, the variances and covariances of the structural parameters are a very nonlinear function of the reduced form variances and covariances, and computing them appropriately could be very cumbersome.

One alternative possibility is to employ nonlinear least squares procedures and directly estimate the structural parameters in the two reduced form equations incorporating the appropriate cross-equation constraints; statistical inference could then be carried out by using direct estimates of the variances and covariances of the (nonlinear) structural parameters. Note that since all six structural parameters appear in each reduced form equation, in order to obtain identification it would be necessary to estimate the two equations as a system. In times past, the possible use of this nonlinear procedure was acknowledged, but it was usually discarded because of prohibitive computational costs. Even though computational costs have now fallen dramatically, in practice this nonlinear procedure is seldom employed today because a still simpler approach involving instrumental variables is available.

Specifically, notice that in the structural sales equation (8.16a), although M_t is endogenous and appears as a regressor, the exogenous variable $P_{m,t}$ is excluded. Since one would expect M_t and $P_{m,t}$ to have a nonzero (most likely negative) covariance, and since by assumption $P_{m,t}$ and the structural disturbance term u_t are independently distributed, it follows that $P_{m,t}$ is a legitimate instrument for M_t in the sales equation. Similarly, in the structural advertising equation (8.16b), while S_t is endogenous and appears as a regressor, the exogenous variable $P_{s,t}$ is not a regressor. Since one would expect S_t and $P_{s,t}$ to have a nonzero (most likely negative) covariance, and since by assumption $P_{s,t}$ and the structural disturbance term w_t are independently distributed, $P_{s,t}$ is a legitimate instrument for S_t in the advertising equation. Given that a legitimate instrument is available for each equation, consistent estimates of the structural parameters could be obtained by employing the instrumental variable (IV) estimator. Although, in general, small sample properties of the IV estimator are unknown, statistical inference can proceed on the basis of asymptotic theory.[23]

One remarkable aspect of this IV estimator in the context of the just identified model is that in this particular case it is numerically equivalent to the ILS estimator; if either of the structural equations were overidentified, however, this numerical equivalence of the IV and ILS estimator would no longer generally hold.[24]

Finally, it is widely known that the two-stage least squares (2SLS) estimator is a member of the class of IV estimators. In our context it is useful to note that with 2SLS the first-stage estimation would involve a regression of the endogenous regressor on all exogenous variables in the two-equation system. For example, in the first stage of 2SLS estimation of the sales equation (8.16a), M_t would be regressed on a constant and the exogenous variables $P_{m,t}$ and $P_{s,t}$; the fitted value from this first-stage regression would then be used as an instrument for M_t. Note, however, that this first-stage regression is precisely the same regression as that of the reduced form equation (8.17a). An analogous procedure would occur in the first stage of 2SLS estimation of the advertising equation (8.16b), where the fitted value from the reduced form equation (8.17b) would be used as an instrument for S_t.

This suggests that in the just identified model there might be a close relationship between the ILS, IV, and 2SLS estimators. In fact, it can be shown that they are numerically equivalent. When equations are overidentified, however, a variety of alternative IV estimators could be employed. In general, although their parameter estimates might each be consistent, these differing IV estimators will not be numerically equivalent to the asymptotically more efficient 2SLS estimator. As a result, 2SLS is commonly used in the context of an overidentified equation.

One other issue of considerable interest concerns how one might employ statistical criteria to choose between a sales-advertising model that permitted simultaneity and one that did not. One procedure for doing this is called the Hausman specification test.[25]

In our context, suppose, for example, that one wanted to test whether in the sales equation (8.16a) the regressor M_t was correlated with the disturbance term u_t. Under the null hypothesis that in large samples, M_t and u_t are uncorrelated, OLS estimation of Eq. (8.16a) results in consistent and efficient estimates of the parameters, whereas 2SLS estimation yields only consistent estimates. Under the alternative hypothesis that in large samples, M_t and u_t are correlated, however, 2SLS yields consistent estimates, but OLS does not. Hausman has shown that a large sample test of the null hypothesis that M_t and u_t are uncorrelated is very simple to implement and essentially amounts to nothing more than a test of whether the 2SLS estimates are significantly different from the OLS estimates.

To implement the Hausman specification test, first estimate the reduced form equation (8.17a) by OLS, retrieve the fitted values from this regression, and denote them $\hat{M}_t$. Next estimate by OLS the expanded regression equation

$$S_t = a + bM_t + cP_{s,t} + h\hat{M}_t + u_t \qquad \textbf{(8.22)}$$

where $\hat{M}$ is an added regressor. The null hypothesis that M_t and u_t are uncorrelated in large samples then reduces to a test of the simple hypothesis that $h = 0$, which can easily be tested by computing the ratio of the estimated h to its standard error and comparing it to a critical value drawn from the normal distribution.

A related Hausman specification test of the null hypothesis that S_t and w_t in the advertising equation (8.16b) are uncorrelated can be performed in an analogous manner. Specifically, add the fitted value for sales in the reduced form equation (8.17b) as a regressor in the advertising equation (8.16b), and then test whether its coefficient is significantly different from zero.

As a matter of historical note, a number of researchers have attempted to estimate parameters of a sales equation in which advertising is a regressor, without taking account of possible simultaneity; such studies include classic efforts by, among others, E. H. Schoenberg [1933], Neil H. Borden [1942], Lester G. Telser [1962] and Kristian Palda [1964]. Others, such as Kendrick B. Melrose [1969], have sought to examine determinants of advertising without examining possible simultaneity with sales.

It appears that the first simultaneous equations estimation is by Quandt [1964], who unfortunately does not report 2SLS estimates but instead simply states that results were "discouraging" and that standard error estimates were very large in relation to the estimated coefficients. In comparison to OLS results, Quandt [1964, p. 60] concludes that when a variety of $P_{m,t}$ measures were included to identify the sales equation, "no improvement . . . [was] . . . obtained by the relatively more sophisticated formulation."

Several years later, Bass and Parsons [1969] estimated a structural model that was somewhat similar to Eqs. (8.16) using the 2SLS method, where the model was just identified through use of lagged advertising variables. Using bimonthly data for 16 years, Bass and Parsons were unable to obtain sharp estimates of their structural parameters; in most cases, standard errors of their estimated structural parameters were larger than the estimated parameters.

Finally, in Schmalensee's [1972] quarterly study of the effects of advertising on aggregate consumption in the United States, 1956–1967, 2SLS estimation was undertaken with advertising considered endogenous, using as instruments population, the Federal Reserve Bank of New York discount rate, a time trend, net exports, and last quarter's investment in residential and nonresidential structures. Very few if any 2SLS coefficients were found to be statistically significantly different from zero. However, in the advertising equation, Schmalensee found that advertising responded very quickly to changes in sales, between 75% and 85% of the total response occurring within four quarters. As a result, Schmalensee conjectured that it would be quite difficult, using annual data, to measure the impact of advertising upon demand, since advertising simultaneously responds very quickly to changes in demand. We will return to this important point later.

8.2.C Granger Causality

In the previous paragraphs we examined econometric implications of simultaneity between advertising and sales. This raises a related methodological issue: How might one test hypotheses concerning one-way or mutual causation in a bivariate time series setting? In our context this problem is complicated by the fact that time series of both advertising and sales are highly positively autocorrelated, making it more difficult to detect causation between them. It is well known that failing to account for the own autocorrelation of a variable, say, that of sales, can give a misleading account of both the importance and pattern of the effect of a covariate, such as advertising.

The seemingly simple concept that X causes Y must be considered carefully, since it raises subtle and difficult issues that transcend econometrics.[26] Although a universally acceptable definition of causation certainly does not exist, one procedure for dealing with causality issues in data analysis has gained considerable usage over the last decade and is called the Granger causality test.[27] Essentially, Granger causality testing involves using F-tests to determine whether lagged information on a variable, say, X, has any statistically significant role in explaining Y_t in the presence of lagged Y. If, in the presence of lagged Y's, lagged X's make no statistically significant contribution to explaining Y_t, then it is said that "X does not Granger-cause Y." Similarly, if lagged Y's make no statistically significant contribution to the explanation of X_t in the presence of lagged X's, then it is said that "Y does not Granger-cause X." Although some might wish to attach deep philosophical meanings to use of the word "causal," it is best simply to interpret Granger causality as assessing whether another variable's lags either do or do not make a net significant incremental contribution to the movement of a dependent variable, once the own correlation of the dependent variable is taken into account.

More formally, let Ω_t be the information set that includes information up to and including time period t on $X_{t-\tau}$ and $Y_{t-\tau}$, $\tau = 0, 1, \ldots, T$. According to the Granger definition, given the information set Ω_t, X causes Y if Y_t can be predicted better by using past X than by not using it. A symmetric statement can be made for Y causing X. It is also possible for causation to proceed in both directions simultaneously (called "feedback").

Within the advertising-sales context, Granger causality might be investigated as follows. Let us now denote advertising quantity by A_t rather than M_t. Consider first an advertising equation of the form

$$A_t = \alpha + \sum_{i=1}^{I} \beta_i A_{t-i} + \sum_{j=1}^{J} \gamma_j S_{t-j} + \epsilon_t \tag{8.23}$$

where ϵ_t is assumed to be a "white noise" error term with mean zero and variance σ^2, and I and J are chosen by the investigator to be sufficiently large to permit a variety of autocorrelation patterns. The regression equation (8.23) is run with and without the S_{t-j} variables included, and then an F-test is performed to test the null hypothesis that $\gamma_j = 0, j = 1, \ldots, J$. If the calculated F-statistic is greater than the critical value, then it is said that sales Granger-cause advertising; otherwise, nothing is inferred concerning this Granger causality from sales to advertising.

Next consider a sales equation having the form

$$S_t = \delta + \sum_{k=1}^{K} \mu_k S_{t-k} + \sum_{\ell=1}^{L} \pi_\ell A_{t-\ell} + u_t \tag{8.24}$$

where u_t has properties analogous to ϵ_t, and K and L are determined similarly to I and J. The regression equation (8.24) is run with and without the $A_{t-\ell}$ variables included, and then an F-test is performed to test the null hypothesis that $\pi_\ell = 0$, $\ell = 1, \ldots, L$. If the calculated F-statistic is greater than the critical value, then it is said that advertising Granger-causes sales; otherwise, nothing is presumed concerning this Granger causality from advertising to sales.

If it is found both that sales Granger-causes advertising and that advertising Granger-causes sales, then feedback is said to exist. Other procedures can be employed to test for Granger causality, including cases in which contemporaneous significance (called "instantaneous causality") is assessed by including $j = 0$ in Eq. (8.23) and $\ell = 0$ in Eq. (8.24). Also, in some cases, both lead and lag values are included as regressors. For further discussion of these and other methodological issues concerning Granger causality, see the survey by David A. Pierce and Larry D. Haugh [1977].

One alternative, yet not totally satisfactory, procedure for assessing Granger causality involves a two-step process. In the first stage the two time series are fitted to univariate, integrated, autoregressive moving average error (ARIMA) specifications using Box-Jenkins techniques. The residuals from each of these estimated ARIMA models are then interpreted as representing movements in the variable other than those due to its own autocorrelations; they are typically called "prewhitened" data series for the two variables. Call such ARIMA residuals from the advertising equation e_{at} and those from the sales equation e_{st}.

In the second stage, a sample cross-correlogram between these two residual series is calculated:

$$r_k \equiv \text{corr}\,(e_{a,t}, e_{s,t-k}) \tag{8.25}$$

If any r_k for $k > 0$ is significantly different from zero, then there is an indication that sales is Granger-causing advertising, since the correlogram indicates that past sales may be useful in forecasting current advertising. Similarly, if any r_k is significantly nonzero for $k < 0$, advertising appears to be Granger-causing sales. If both these results occur, two-way causality or feedback between the series is indicated.

To undertake statistical inference based on measures of r_k, sampling distribution information must be utilized. Unfortunately, the sampling distribution of r_k depends on the exact, unknown relationship between the series. Under the null hypothesis that the two series are not causally related, the r_k are asymptotically independently and normally distributed with mean zero and variance $1/N$, where N is the number of observations employed in estimation. Further, if one wishes to test the null hypothesis that $q = 1, \ldots, m$ sample correlations are simultaneously equal to zero, one can employ the Box-Pierce statistic

$$N \sum_{q=1}^{m} r_q^2 \tag{8.26}$$

which, under the null hypothesis, is asymptotically distributed as a chi-square random variable with m degrees of freedom.

Practicing econometricians occasionally find the Granger causality results difficult to interpret. In our context, three potential pitfalls are of particular importance.[28] First, the analysis of Granger causality is based on an information set that includes observations on only two variables, advertising and sales. If some third variable were affecting both sales and advertising, the Granger causality results could be misleading.[29] Second, the process of deciding on I, J, K, and L or, alternatively, the use of Box-Jenkins "prewhitening" procedures can distort causal relationships among the original series. Third, the sampling distributions of various statistics used to determine statistical significance are often valid only in large samples. In the context of small samples their use might result in unreliable inference. There is some evidence that this is particularly true for the Box-Pierce statistic (8.26).[30]

As an historical matter, it is worth noting that Granger causality tests have been employed in several econometric studies on sales-advertising relationships. Using quarterly U.S. data from 1956 to 1975, Ashley, Granger, and Schmalensee [1980], for example, have found evidence supporting the notion that aggregate national consumption (sales) Granger-causes advertising, but they could not find empirical support for the symmetric hypothesis that advertising Granger-causes aggregate national consumption. Causality results will be discussed further in Section 8.3.

8.2.D Consistent Market Share Specifications

Our discussion of the economic theory underlying advertising outlay decisions indicated that advertising outlay was likely to be particularly substantial when price elasticities were small in absolute value. Moreover, in the context of oligopolies, nonprice competition was seen to be of considerable importance in that sales for firm i depended in part on the advertising messages transmitted by firm j.

This interdependence of firms' advertising decisions has led to the formulation of a number of models in which the market share of sales gained by firm i in time t, s_{it}, depends in part on the *relative* share of advertising undertaken by firm i, $w_{it} \equiv$ (firm i advertising/all other firms' advertising), and the carryover effects of brand loyalty, as captured by the lagged sales share $s_{i,t-1}$.

In his study of cigarette advertising, for example, Lester Telser [1962] estimated parameters of the equation

$$s_{it} = \alpha_i + \beta_i w_{it} + \gamma_i s_{i,t-1} + \epsilon_{it} \tag{8.27}$$

where ϵ_{it} was assumed to have the usual optimal properties. Equation (8.27) appears to be plausible and innocuous, but as we shall now see, it suffers from a logical inconsistency, and it should not be used.

To see this, consider the case of a two-firm industry in which the sum of sales market shares always equals 1 and the relative advertising shares are therefore reciprocals, that is, $s_{1t} + s_{2t} = s_{1,t-1} + s_{2,t-1} = 1$ and $w_{2t} = 1/w_{1t}$. In order for this market share model to make sense, it is necessary that the sum of the predicted shares also equal 1. In the case of a duopoly, write the estimate of the market share equation (8.27) for firm 1 as

$$\hat{s}_{1t} = \hat{\alpha}_1 + \hat{\beta}_1 w_{1t} + \hat{\gamma}_1 s_{1,t-1} \tag{8.28}$$

and that for firm 2 as

$$\hat{s}_{2t} = \hat{\alpha}_2 + \hat{\beta}_2 w_{2t} + \hat{\gamma}_2 s_{2,t-1} \tag{8.29}$$

where the circumflexes denote parameter estimates. But since shares sum to unity, one can substitute $\hat{s}_{2t} = 1 - \hat{s}_{1t}$, $s_{2,t-1} = 1 - s_{1,t-1}$, and $w_{2t} = 1/w_{1t}$ into Eq. (8.29), yielding

$$1 - \hat{s}_{1t} = \hat{\alpha}_2 + \hat{\beta}_2(1/w_{1t}) + \hat{\gamma}_2(1 - s_{1,t-1}) \tag{8.30}$$

The problem of logical consistency becomes apparent when one takes the two share equations (8.28) and (8.30) and constrains their sum to equal unity:

$$1 = \hat{\alpha}_1 + \hat{\alpha}_2 + \hat{\beta}_1 w_{1t} + \hat{\beta}_2/w_{1t} + s_{1,t-1}(\hat{\gamma}_1 - \hat{\gamma}_2) + \hat{\gamma}_2 \tag{8.31}$$

Notice that the only way in which the sum of the shares (8.31) will always equal 1, regardless of the values of w_{1t} and $s_{1,t-1}$, is if

$$\hat{\alpha}_1 + \hat{\alpha}_2 = 1 \qquad \text{and} \qquad \hat{\beta}_1 = \hat{\beta}_2 = \hat{\gamma}_1 = \hat{\gamma}_2 = 0$$

that is, the specification will be logically consistent if and only if all slope coefficients simultaneously equal zero, and Eqs. (8.28) and (8.29) reduce to share equations with only an intercept term. Hence no matter how the parameters β_i and γ_i are estimated, this type of share specification will not make sense unless all these slope parameters equal zero. Incidentally, these results generalize to cases in which more than two share equations are involved.

In fact, a substantial number of empirical researchers have estimated equations very similar to Eq. (8.27) that suffer from this flaw of logical inconsistency.[31] Moreover, the flaw is fatal in that there is no easy fix. If, for example, there are n firms, it would of course be possible to estimate only $n - 1$ share equations and then to construct the fitted value of the remaining share as 1 minus the sum of the directly estimated $n - 1$ fitted share equations. In this way, one could constrain the fitted shares to sum to unity. But with such a procedure, all results would depend on which share was originally deleted in estimation, a decision that is truly arbitrary yet could substantially affect results.

The essential problem with a share specification such as Eq. (8.27) is that it fails to come to terms with the fact that if any regressor is included in one share equation, the same variable must also be included in a similar way in an least one other share equation. Note that w_{1t} is in Eq. (8.28) but $w_{2t} = 1/w_{1t}$ is in Eq. (8.29). The sum of the effects of any regressor (other than a constant) over all share equations must always be zero, since if a regressor affects one share positively, it must affect at least one other share negatively.

Share equations are a special case of singular equation systems, whose specification requires particular care. In this chapter we limit our focus to single equation estimation methods. However, estimation and inference in systems of singular equations are discussed at much greater length in Chapter 9.

For the moment, therefore, simply remember always to take care when specifying share models so that their adding-up properties are logically consistent. For the practicing econometrician it would be embarrassing indeed to realize that after expending a great deal of effort in estimating a complex share model with data from a large number of firms, the predicted shares over all firms summed to 1.378, or 0.837! Defending that result would be difficult.

8.2.E Distributed Lags and the Measurement of the Cumulative Effects of Advertising

One issue of great importance in the marketing literature is the time response pattern of sales to advertising. Here the goal of empirical research is to measure how rapidly sales respond as advertising is increased, at what rate sales decay when advertising is decreased, and what the cumulative impact of advertising is on sales. The length of the time response of advertising on sales is also an important public policy issue. Recall from the introduction to this chapter that critics have argued that if the effects of advertising linger for more than one year, then for tax purposes, advertising should be treated as an investment and not be entirely expensed in the year in which it occurs.

Econometric specifications that incorporate the lagged effects of advertising on sales fall into a class of models called distributed lags. Since distributed lags have already been discussed in Chapters 6 and 7, here we present but a brief overview. Assume that a firm's sales at time t are a linear function of its own present and past outlays only, plus an independently and identically distributed random disturbance term:

$$S_t = \alpha + \beta_0 A_t + \beta_1 A_{t-1} + \cdots + \epsilon_t \qquad \textbf{(8.32)}$$

Given that econometricians typically have access to only a finite number of observations, estimation of Eq. (8.32) is not feasible, since the number of regressors is infinite. Even if the lag were arbitrarily truncated after some time period, it might still be difficult to obtain precise estimates of the distributed lag coefficients, since the advertising expenditure series is likely to be highly autocorrelated, implying potentially severe multicollinearity.

One simplifying step is to specify that after a certain lag length, say, k, the distributed lag coefficients begin to decline geometrically such that $\beta_{k+m} = \lambda^m \beta_k$, where λ is a decay factor for advertising effectiveness, $0 \leqslant \lambda < 1$:

$$S_t = \alpha + \beta_0 A_t + \beta_1 A_{t-1} + \cdots + \beta_k A_{t-k} + \beta_k \lambda A_{t-k-1} + \beta_k \lambda^2 A_{t-k-2} + \cdots + u_t \tag{8.33}$$

In this specification, the first k distributed lag coefficients are unconstrained (permitting, for example, first an increasing and then a decreasing impact of advertising on sales), but the remaining, more distant lag coefficients are constrained to decline geometrically.

A special case of Eq. (8.33) occurs when it is further assumed that geometric decay begins immediately, rather than only after k time periods. In this case, Eq. (8.33) reduces to

$$S_t = \alpha + \beta_0 A_t + \beta_0 \lambda A_{t-1} + \beta_0 \lambda^2 A_{t-2} + \cdots + u_t \tag{8.34}$$

Equation (8.34) is still not useful for empirical implementation, because although it contains only three estimable parameters, it requires use of an infinite number of lagged advertising terms. However, if one employs the Koyck transformation, an estimable form emerges.[32] In particular, lag Eq. (8.34) once, multiply the lagged equation by λ, subtract the result from Eq. (8.34), and rearrange. This yields

$$S_t = \alpha(1 - \lambda) + \beta_0 A_t + \lambda S_{t-1} + v_t, \qquad v_t \equiv u_t - \lambda u_{t-1} \tag{8.35}$$

an equation in which current sales depends on current advertising, lagged sales, and a moving average disturbance. Equation (8.35) has formed the basis of numerous empirical studies, including Palda's [1964] classic work on the cumulative effects of advertising. Hereafter, we call it the Koyck *lingering effects* model.

Several features of Eq. (8.35) merit attention. First, note that the disturbance v_t in Eq. (8.35) follows a first order moving average process and is therefore correlated with the S_{t-1} regressor. Hence estimation by OLS yields biased and inconsistent estimates of the parameters. Other techniques, such as instrumental variables or a maximum likelihood method, can be used instead to obtain consistent parameter estimates. Moreover, in this context, one cannot employ the Durbin-Watson test for autocorrelation, since it is biased toward 2. See your econometric theory textbook for further details.[33]

Second, an estimate of the immediate carryover effect of advertising, the parameter λ, is obtained directly from the coefficient on the lagged sales variable; hence $1 - \lambda$ represents the rate of advertising decay. The cumulative effect of advertising on sales after two periods, that is, the instantaneous plus the carryover effect, is $\beta_0(1 + \lambda)$, while the cumulative impact after m time periods equals

$$\beta_0[1 + \lambda + \lambda^2 + \cdots + \lambda^{m-1}] = \beta_0(1 - \lambda^m)/(1 - \lambda)$$

As m approaches infinity, the total cumulative impact of advertising on sales converges to $\beta_0/(1 - \lambda)$.

Third, the proportion of the total cumulative impact of advertising on sales realized after m time periods, denoted p, equals $1 - \lambda^m$. Hence if one wishes to compute the length of time required to attain proportion p of the total sales response, one can solve $p = 1 - \lambda^m$ for m, yielding

$$m = \ln(1 - p)/\ln \lambda \tag{8.36}$$

An alternative formulation of the advertising-sales model, based on the notion that advertising has only a current and not a lingering impact on sales, is known as the *current effects* model; it is due to Darral G. Clarke and John M. McCann [1973] and has the form

$$S_t = \alpha + \beta A_t + u_t \tag{8.37}$$

However, the disturbance term is specified to follow a traditional first-order autoregressive scheme,

$$u_t = \rho u_{t-1} + \epsilon_t \tag{8.38}$$

reflecting the possible carryover effects of other marketing efforts and not necessarily those of past advertising outlays. Lagging Eq. (8.37) one time period, multiplying this lagged equation by ρ, subtracting the result from Eq. (8.37) and employing Eq. (8.38) yield the expression

$$S_t = \alpha(1 - \rho) + \beta A_t - \beta\rho A_{t-1} + \rho S_{t-1} + \epsilon_t \tag{8.39}$$

Compared to the lingering effects specification (8.35), the current effects model (8.39) has an additional regressor, A_{t-1}; further, while disturbances in Eq. (8.35) follow a first-order moving average process, in Eq. (8.39) disturbances are "white noise." However, if the u_t in the lingering effects model (8.35) followed a first order autoregressive process such as Eq. (8.38) and if it coincidentally were the case that $\lambda = \rho$, then the apparent first order moving average error in Eq. (8.35) would actually simply be ϵ_t, a "white noise" error. In such a case, Eq. (8.35) would be a simple testable special case of Eq. (8.39), and lingering effects could be tested as a special case of the current effects specification.

In an important paper, Zvi Griliches [1967, especially Section 4] has demonstrated that if the current effects model with autocorrelation were true but one instead estimated the lingering effects model, one would often obtain statistically significant and sensible coefficient estimates and would observe little if any autocorrelation among the residuals, even though the lingering effects model is "wrong." One way of checking this is to estimate an equation such as Eq. (8.39) without imposing the nonlinear restrictions, that is, estimate

$$S_t = \gamma_0 + \gamma_1 A_t + \gamma_2 A_{t-1} + \gamma_3 S_{t-1} + \epsilon_t \tag{8.40}$$

Note that if $\gamma_2 = 0$ and $\rho = \lambda = \gamma_3$, then Eq. (8.40) reduces to Eq. (8.35), and there is support for the Koyck geometrically declining lingering effects specification. If $\gamma_2 > 0$, then the shape of the lag distribution is different from the Koyck model, perhaps initially increasing with the time lag but then eventually decreasing. If estimates of γ_2 are approximately equal to the negative of the product of the estimated γ_1 and γ_3, as they should be if Eq. (8.39) is true, then there is support for the current effects model with autocorrelation. Hence if one estimates Eq. (8.40) in addition to Eq. (8.35), and if one finds that estimates of γ_2 are significantly different from zero, then one could conclude that results from the Koyck specification are spurious and unreliable.

Another distributed lag specification of the sales-advertising model, called the *brand loyalty* model, has been introduced by Franklin S. Houston and Doyle L. Weiss [1975]. In this model the geometric decay hypothesis of advertising is not explicitly invoked to justify inclusion of the lagged sales term. Rather, S_{t-1} as a regressor is simply rationalized as being attributable to marketing carryover effects that are more general than just advertising. Specifically, Houston and Weiss propose that

$$S_t = \delta_0 + \delta_1 A_t + \delta_2 S_{t-1} + u_t \tag{8.41}$$

where u_t follows the first-order autoregressive process (8.38). Use of the Koyck transformation then yields the estimable equation

$$S_t = \delta_0(1 - \rho) + (\delta_2 + \rho)S_{t-1} - \delta_2 \rho S_{t-2} + \delta_1 A_t - \delta_1 \rho A_{t-1} + \epsilon_t \tag{8.42}$$

whose parameters can be estimated consistently by nonlinear least squares. Alternatively, parameters in Eq. (8.41) can be estimated by using any of the various generalized least squares (GLS) estimators such as the iterative Cochrane-Orcutt or Hildreth-Lu procedures. Notice, however, that since Eq. (8.41) contains a lagged dependent variable and u_t follows a first-order autoregressive process, use of the one-step Cochrane-Orcutt GLS procedure yields inconsistent estimates of the parameters.

One feature of this brand loyalty specification is that if $\rho = 0$, then Eq. (8.42) reduces to the lingering effects model (8.35), except for the disturbance term. Further, the current effects model (8.39) with autocorrelation is a special case of Eq. (8.42) when δ_2 in the latter equals zero. Hence the brand loyalty specification provides considerable generality.

Numerous other combinations of autoregressive and mathematically more complex distributed lag representations could be specified, and some have in fact been estimated.[34] However, as we shall now see, empirical results based on these rather simple specifications have been found to yield a striking pattern of results that has turned the attention of researchers to a heretofore neglected issue, namely, that of bias due to temporal aggregation. We now examine this important topic.

8.2.F Temporal Aggregation and the Data Interval Bias

One issue of great practical importance is how long the cumulative effect of advertising persists. Estimates of this time length, called the *duration level,* have differed widely.[35] In his survey of more than 70 studies that estimated duration levels, Clarke [1976] classified studies on the basis of whether they employed weekly, monthly, bimonthly, quarterly, or annual data. In the process he uncovered a striking systematic association between estimates of the duration level and the length of the data interval.

In particular, using a relationship similar to Eq. (8.36) and estimates of λ from numerous published studies using lingering effects specifications, Clarke computed how long a period of time it would take for 90% of the total response to occur; he called this the 90% duration interval and expressed it in months. Estimates of this 90% duration interval were found to differ widely, ranging from 1.3 to 1368 months. While Clarke expected considerable variation due to differences among products studied, he concluded that such volatility was excessive. Even within the cigarette industry, for example, estimates of the 90% duration interval varied from 17 to 677 months.

From Eq. (8.36) it is clear that variations in estimates of the 90% duration interval depend entirely on variations in the estimates of λ, the coefficient on the lagged dependent variable. Clarke noted that if estimates of λ are to be consistent across studies based on data with varying periodicity, then one would expect estimates of λ to decrease as the data interval increased, say, from weekly to annually. This, Clarke discovered, was not the case.

Clarke's findings are reproduced in the first two columns of Table 8.2. In the first column the periodicity of the data is indicated, while in the second column the arithmetic mean of the estimate of λ, the coefficient on the lagged sales variable, is presented; in computing this mean, Clarke eliminated "unreasonable" studies with 90% duration levels exceeding 120 months. Instead of decreasing as the data interval increased from weekly to annually, mean estimates of λ increased from 0.537 (weekly) and 0.440 (monthly) to 0.599 (quarterly) and 0.560 (annually). This is in sharp contrast to what would be expected. For example, if the estimate of λ based on monthly data is 0.440, then the consistent three-month (quarterly) estimate would approximately equal $(0.440)^3 = 0.085$, yet the reported mean quarterly estimate is 0.599. Conversely, an annual estimate of 0.560 corresponds to a monthly estimate of approximately $0.560^{1/12}$, or 0.953, yet the reported monthly estimate is only 0.440.

These estimates of λ imply vastly differing estimates of the 90% duration level. As is shown in the third column of Table 8.2, the mean implied 90% duration interval derived from annual data (56.5 months) is more than 17

Table 8.2 Effect of Data Interval on Implied Duration Interval, in Months, as Computed by Clarke (Standard Deviations in Parentheses)

Data Interval	Mean Estimate of λ	Mean Estimate of 90% Duration Interval	Number of Studies
Weekly	0.537	0.9	2
	(0.057)	(0.2)	
Monthly	0.440	3.0	10
	(0.027)	(0.2)	
Bimonthly	0.493	9.0	10
	(0.086)	(6.9)	
Quarterly	0.599	25.1	10
	(0.086)	(6.9)	
Annually	0.560	56.5	27
	(0.031)	(5.1)	

Source: Data from Darral G. Clarke [1976], Table 2, p. 351.

times as long as the average implied duration interval derived from monthly data (3.0 months). Clearly, a substantial portion of the variation among studies is simply due to the fact that the implied duration interval increased significantly as the length of the data interval increased.

To determine which data interval yielded "correct" estimates of the duration interval, Clarke used Griliches' criteria (see the discussion in Section 8.2.E near Eq. (8.40)) to choose between the lingering effects and the current effects with autocorrelation specifications. Recall that with the current effects model it is implicitly assumed that if there is a cumulative effect attributable to advertising, it is of a shorter duration than the data interval. Using the annual data provided by Palda [1964], Clarke estimated Eq. (8.40) by GLS and found that the negative of the product of estimated γ_1 and γ_3 was very close to the estimate of γ_2 (-0.465 versus -0.382, with a standard error on γ_2 equal to 0.102). Clarke took this to imply that with the annual data there was support for the current effects model with autocorrelation, that is, the duration interval was less than one year. However, since the estimate of γ_2 was significantly different from zero and since estimates of ρ and λ were quite different (0.186 versus 0.765), Clarke was also able to conclude that Palda's results from annual data suggesting duration levels of greater than one year based on the Koyck lingering effects model "are the result of data interval bias and should be rejected."[36]

Clarke performed the same type of calculations with monthly, quarterly, and annual data made available from other studies. When the data interval was quarterly or shorter, in no case could he find support for the current effects model with autocorrelation. On the other hand, for nine of the 12 annual studies, Clarke found that the current effects specification was preferable. From this Clarke [1976, p. 353] concluded that

> the long implied duration intervals obtained from the annual models are due to data interval bias and the shorter implied duration intervals

> obtained from the monthly, bimonthly, and quarterly data are more likely to be accurate descriptions of the duration of the cumulative advertising effect.

Furthermore, "The conclusion that advertising's effect on sales lasts for months rather than years is strongly supported."[37]

Clarke's provocative survey of empirical findings generated a number of studies that sought to provide theoretical underpinnings to the alleged data interval bias. For example, on the basis of earlier research by Henri Theil [1954], Yair Mundlak [1961], C. Moriguchi [1970], Arnold Zellner and Claude Montmarquette [1971], and Robert Rowe [1976] on temporal aggregation in other contexts, Frank Bass and Robert Leone [1983] analyzed the data interval bias in the sales-advertising context by adding up models with brief data intervals into a corresponding model for longer data intervals and then examining relationships among parameters in the temporally aggregated and disaggregated models.

Bass and Leone demonstrated both analytically and empirically that the lag coefficient decreases and the advertising coefficient increases with the length of data interval employed in the analysis. Moreover, given these relationships, they also showed how parameter estimates for models that apply to brief intervals can be recovered approximately (but inefficiently) when only aggregate data, for example, annual data, are available.

These results raised the important question of what the appropriate data interval should be to obtain reliable and efficient estimates of the parameters of the sales-advertising relationship. On the basis of other theoretical work relating the way in which advertising effects carry over from one interval to another, Bass and Leone [1983, p. 7] tentatively suggested,

> It is probably best to think of the appropriate micro data interval as having a length which coincides with the average interval between purchases of the product. In this way the implied duration for advertising would be related to the number of purchases occasions.

As long as purchases are made more than once annually, Bass and Leone provide theoretical support for Clarke's empirical proposition that the very long carryover effects of advertising that are obtained in the context of annual data are misleading and are the result of data interval bias.

The extent to which autocorrelation in combination with temporal aggregation yields spuriously large estimates of the lagged dependent variable coefficient continues to be the focus of much recent marketing research. In a precursor to the Bass-Leone study of the lingering effects model, Pierre Windal and Doyle Weiss [1980] devised an iterative GLS procedure for generating estimates of microperiod parameters from a temporally aggregated model, provided that the model is a current effects one with autocorrelation. Charles B. Weinberg and Doyle Weiss [1982] examined the data interval bias in the context of a Koyck lingering effects model, but they tentatively concluded that the upward biased duration intervals based on estimation with annual data are not simply due to the choice of data interval.

This tentative conclusion is reinforced in the Monte Carlo study of Weiss, Weinberg, and Windal [1983]. Here, computer-simulated monthly data are generated on the basis of alternative "true" variants of the Koyck lingering effects, current effects with autocorrelation, and brand loyalty with autocorrelation specifications, each with random realizations of equation disturbances. Parameter estimates are then calculated by using the simulated monthly data, as well as the semiannual and annual aggregations of these data. To reduce effects of sampling error, a large sample of 1200 monthly observations is generated. Weiss et al. find that temporal aggregation alone is not the major source of the reported overestimation of λ, but that there are subtle and important misspecifications that occur as one attempts to aggregate from micro to more temporally aggregated analytical relationships. In some cases, analytical relationships among the micro and macro specifications involve approximations that introduce considerable misspecification. According to this view, therefore, it is the analytical aggregation of the micro relationship, not the simple aggregation of data, that is the primary source of the so-called "data interval bias." This makes it difficult if not impossible to infer reliable microperiod parameters when only temporally aggregated (e.g., annual) data are available.

The principal lesson to be learned from this is that since it is now widely believed that the "true" 90% duration interval of advertising for most established products is a matter of months and certainly is less than a year, one simply should not use annual data to estimate parameters of the sales-advertising relationship. For most purposes, data from shorter time intervals are required. Further, use of annual data can yield spurious results.

Before leaving this section on econometric issues we note one other very interesting survey of sales-advertising econometric studies. Using a rather different framework called "meta-analysis," Gert Assmus, John U. Farley, and Donald R. Lehmann [1984] survey and summarize the short-run impacts of advertising on sales, the estimated lag coefficient, and the goodness of fit for 128 models reported in 22 studies published before 1981.[38] Although they report results that are in large part consistent with those of Clarke and of Bass and Leone, the Assmus et al. study is of interest because of the meta-analysis methodology employed.

In essence, meta-analysis takes an important quantifiable implication of a number of estimated models, say, the models' short-run elasticity of sales with respect to advertising, and treats this as a left-hand variable in a regression equation. The right-hand variables might include continuous variables such as the number of observations, as well as dummy variables for, say, estimation method (OLS, 2SLS, GLS), data interval employed (monthly, quarterly, annually), type of product (new, mature), functional form (logarithmic, linear), and numerous other characteristics.[39] On the basis of these estimated relationships, meta-analysis can then be employed to "predict" consequences of altering one's research procedures; for example, one could project the effect on the short-run advertising elasticity of estimating a quarterly model using

2SLS rather than OLS. Incidentally, with 24 regressors, Assmus et al. are able to "explain" 50.1% of the variation among studies in the estimated short-run advertising elasticity, 59.9% of the variation in the estimated lag coefficient, and 59.1% of the variation in R^2.

This concludes our discussion of issues in econometric implementation of sales-advertising relationships. We turn now to a brief review of selected empirical findings. We begin with a controversial issue that was noted in the introduction, namely, does aggregate advertising affect aggregate consumption?

8.3 DOES AGGREGATE ADVERTISING AFFECT AGGREGATE CONSUMPTION? EMPIRICAL RESULTS

Some of the earliest empirical research on whether aggregate advertising affects aggregate consumption focused on their relationships at cyclical turning points. A common finding from this research was that aggregate advertising generally lagged the rest of the economy at such points, thereby casting doubt on the hypothesis that aggregate advertising affected aggregate consumption.[40] While of some interest, turning point studies do not employ all of the available time series data, nor do they typically provide formal tests of statistical hypotheses.

One of the first statistical analyses of sales-advertising relationships was that by Walter A. Verdon, Campbell R. McConnell, and Theodore W. Roesler [1968]. It related a *Printer's Ink* monthly index of advertising spending (denoted PII), GNP, and the Federal Reserve index of industrial production. After detrending these three time series and then smoothing them by use of a weighted moving average, Verdon et al. examined correlations between the transformed PII series and the other two transformed series at various leads and lags and for various periods. The correlations that they obtained indicated no clear patterns.

The Verdon et al. study was critiqued by Robert B. Ekelund, Jr. and William P. Gramm [1969], who argued that only consumption spending, not entire GNP or an index of industrial production, should be used in analyzing aggregate sales-advertising relationships. The reason for excluding the investment and government spending GNP components is that they are not likely to be greatly affected by advertising (other marketing instruments might be more effective). Ekelund and Gramm regressed detrended quarterly advertising data from Blank [1962] and detrended consumption spending and found that all regressions yielded insignificant results.

A much more detailed econometric study was undertaken by Richard Schmalensee in his 1970 Ph.D. dissertation, eventually published as Schmalensee [1972]. Using quarterly data from Blank [1962] and updating it with figures provided by the Columbia Broadcasting System and other sources, Schmalensee constructed current and constant dollar measures of aggregate advertising outlay. The price index for advertising varied by media type and was constructed as current dollar expenditure by media type divided by the estimated number of people exposed to the media, that is, a "cost per million" index.[41]

Schmalensee began by looking at correlations at various leads and lags between per capita aggregate consumption (C) and per capita aggregate advertising (A), where both series were deflated to 1958 dollars. Over the 1956:2 to 1967:3 time period, simple correlations for C_t, A_{t-1}, for C_t, A_t, and for C_t, A_{t+1} were 0.968, 0.978, and 0.980, respectively, while corresponding ones for aggregate consumption defined as consumption for goods only were 0.972, 0.985, and 0.986. Schmalensee [1972, pp. 51–52] interpreted this as follows:

> The second set of correlations are all higher than the first set, but the pattern is the same in both. Real advertising in the next quarter is more closely correlated with consumption in the current quarter than is advertising last quarter. This suggests that causation runs from consumption to advertising. We cannot, however, rule out an impact of lagged advertising on consumption; a correlation of .968 is by no means tiny. When data are generated by a simultaneous system in which structural equations involve distributed lags, simple correlations are of little use in making judgments about the true structure.

Proceeding with a more structured approach, Schmalensee specified several standard consumption functions, augmented by advertising variables. One typical model is of the form

$$C_t = b_0 + b_1 Y_t + b_2 C_{t-1} + b_3 A_\tau + u_t \qquad \textbf{(8.43)}$$

where τ is alternatively set at $t-1$, t, and $t+1$; Y is per capita disposable income; and u_t is permitted to follow a first-order autoregressive scheme. C_t was measured alternatively as total consumption and consumption on goods only. Schmalensee observed that if aggregate advertising influenced aggregate consumption spending, then one would expect both the coefficient of advertising and its associated t-statistic to be largest with A_t, next largest with A_{t-1}, and quite small when A_{t+1} is introduced into Eq. (8.43).

Results based on OLS estimation did not bear this out, however. In particular, in no case did A_{t-1} have a positive coefficient, and while the coefficient on A_t was positive and often statistically significant, that on A_{t+1} was even larger and was almost always statistically significant.

A second set of regressions was then run using the 2SLS estimator, allowing A_t to be endogenous. In the first stage, A_t was specified to be a linear function of a constant term, population, the Federal Reserve Bank of New York discount rate, a time trend, net exports, and last quarter's investment in residential and nonresidential structures, where the last three quantities were expressed in current dollars per capita. The R^2 from this first stage regression was 0.9845. In the second stage of 2SLS the same pattern of results emerged as with OLS estimation; coefficients and t-statistics increased as one went from A_{t-1} to A_t and to A_{t+1} as a regressor.

RICHARD SCHMALENSEE

Assessing the Causes and Consequences of Advertising

Richard Schmalensee's interest in the interfaces between economics and management grew when he was an undergraduate economics major at MIT, having come from a family business environment. At MIT, interactions between economics and marketing became the focus of his Ph.D. dissertation, which was eventually published in 1972 by North-Holland and entitled *The Economics of Advertising*. As is discussed in detail in this chapter, Schmalensee's econometric analysis on causality between aggregate advertising and aggregate sales produced the now-classic finding that while aggregate sales appears to causally affect aggregate advertising, the reverse is apparently not true.

Schmalensee's interests have broadened considerably since 1972 (although he still maintains an active interest in the border between marketing and economics), and he is now widely regarded as a leading scholar of modern industrial economics, with major contributions both theoretical and empirical. He has written extensively on the economics of antitrust policy and on regulatory policy, is co-editor (with Robert Willig) of the *Handbook of Industrial Organization*, and is founding editor of the MIT Press *Regulation of Economic Activity* series.

After attending public schools in Belleville, Illinois, Schmalensee went to MIT in 1961 for undergraduate studies in economics, politics, and science. He continued graduate work at MIT, and in 1970 he received the Ph.D. degree in economics. Schmalensee's first academic appointment was at the University of California, San Diego. He returned to MIT as Associate Professor in the School of Management in 1977 and is now the Gordon Y. Billard Professor of Economics and Management. Schmalensee has served on the editorial board of several journals and has been elected a Fellow of the Econometric Society. In 1989 he was asked by President Bush to serve as a member of the President's Council of Economic Advisers, focusing on microeconomic policy issues.

Note that if u_t in Eq. (8.43) followed a first-order autocorrelation process, since C_{t-1} appears as a regressor, C_{t-1} and u_t would be correlated, and so neither OLS nor 2SLS would provide consistent parameter estimates. Schmalensee dealt with this possibility, following a suggestion of Nissan Liviatan [1963], by using as another instrument in Eq. (8.43) the fitted value from a first-stage regression where C_{t-1} was regressed on a constant and contemporaneous values of the Federal Reserve Bank of New York discount rate, a time trend, population, net exports, and federal nondefense spending (with the last two quantities in current dollars per capita). When total consumption was the dependent variable, the first-stage regression yielded an R^2 of 0.9928, while for consumption of goods and services it was 0.9865. With both A_t and C_{t-1} instrumented, Schmalensee again found that all coefficients of A_{t-1} were negative, that coefficients on A_t were mixed in sign but always insignificantly different from zero, and that coefficients on A_{t+1} were always positive and statistically significant.

Together, these results led Schmalensee [1972, p. 58] to conclude that "we find no real evidence that national advertising influences either aggregate total consumption or aggregate consumption of goods," and that

> Advertising may shift purchases between firms or even between industries, but consumer saving does not appear to be at all affected. Advertising cannot be praised for booms, damned for recessions, or blamed for keeping funds from the public treasury.

Schmalensee then moved on to examine determinants of aggregate advertising. Since aggregate consumption is not affected by aggregate advertising, consumption could be viewed as exogenous, and so use of OLS was justified. Schmalensee employed Griliches' [1967] reasoning to distinguish empirically between a consumption model with lingering effects on advertising and a current effects model. The preferred model ended up being a current effects one in which the long-run equilibrium level of the advertising/sales ratio depended on the percentage change in consumption goods spending from one quarter to the next. This equation had an intercept term that was constrained to zero and took the form

$$\begin{aligned} A_t = {} & \underset{(2.631)}{6.102\, C_t} + \underset{(1.996)}{0.09960\, (\%\Delta C_t)} + \underset{(6.243)}{0.7054\, A_{t-1}} \qquad R^2 = 0.9926 \qquad \textbf{(8.44)} \end{aligned}$$

where A_t is advertising outlay in current dollars, C_t and $\%\Delta C_t$ are the level and percent change in current dollar consumption of durable and nondurable goods, and t-statistics are in parentheses. With this model and using the Hildreth-Lu scanning method, the null hypothesis of no autocorrelation was not rejected at the 95% level of significance.

One important implication of Eq. (8.44) is that advertising adjusts very rapidly to changes in consumption. In particular, with Eq. (8.44), 29.65% of the adjustment of advertising to a maintained increase in C_t is realized in the quarter in which the increase occurs, and 75.25% is completed at the end of one year. Given this rapid adjustment of advertising to sales, Schmalensee concluded that any studies that attempt to measure the impact of advertising on demand using annual data will encounter a severe identification problem, since attempts to isolate the effect of advertising on sales will be confounded by reverse causality where advertising outlay is almost a fixed proportion of sales.

With this cautionary advice in mind we now look at another study that reached rather different conclusions concerning the aggregate effects of aggregate advertising. Using annual advertising data from the *Statistical Abstract of the United States*, Lester D. Taylor and Daniel Weiserbs [1972] concluded that "advertising does in fact tend to increase consumption at the expense of saving."[42]

The Taylor and Weiserbs study differs from that of Schmalensee in several respects. First, the data are annual, not quarterly, and therefore are potentially vulnerable to Schmalensee's identification critique. Second, although Taylor and Weiserbs use both deflated and undeflated advertising data, the deflator they employ is simply the implict GNP deflator. Hence no attempt is made to obtain a deflator specific to advertising outlays on various media. Third, while their theoretical model implies a specification with a lagged dependent variable and a first-order moving average disturbance, implying that a regressor and the disturbance are correlated, estimation is carried out using OLS or 2SLS, not GLS. However, Taylor and Weiserbs report that the Durbin test statistic for the null hypothesis of no autocorrelation against an alternative hypothesis of first-order autoregressive errors, in the presence of a lagged dependent variable, could not be rejected for their OLS-estimated models.

Taylor and Weiserbs estimated a number of formulations of the Houthakker-Taylor state-adjustment model, augmented to include advertising.[43] When real consumption per capita is the dependent variable, although the coefficient on advertising is positive and statistically significant, other features of the model are quite unsatisfactory. This leads Taylor and Weiserbs [1972, p. 648] to conclude that "the overall quality of results leaves much to be desired."

However, of their three alternative models with real savings per capita as the dependent variable, one is particularly striking. On the basis of annual 1929–1968 data excluding 1942–1945, Taylor and Weiserbs obtain the estimated equation

$$\begin{aligned} y_t = {} & \underset{(31.30)}{0.8889 y_{t-1}} + \underset{(10.85)}{0.5057 \Delta x_t} - \underset{(4.353)}{3.8863 \Delta a_t} \qquad \bar{R}^2 = 0.903 \qquad \textbf{(8.45)} \end{aligned}$$

where y_t is real savings per capita, Δx_t is the change from year $t-1$ in real per capita disposable income (excluding personal transfer payments), Δa_t is the corresponding change in real per capita advertising expenditure, and numbers in parentheses are absolute values of t-statistics. The parameters of Eq. (8.45) are a nonlinear combination of structural parameters; and when these implicit structural parameters are estimated, they imply that the short-run effect of a \$1.00 increase in advertising is to reduce saving (increase consumption) by a substantial amount, \$4.12 (with an estimated standard error of \$0.95). To compute a long-run effect, Taylor and Weiserbs calculate the difference in the saving rate between steady exponential growth of 2.5% per annum in advertising and no growth; this increase in advertising is found to decrease the saving rate from 0.093 to 0.070, a very large amount.

To account for possible simultaneity, Taylor and Weiserbs estimate by OLS a reduced-form advertising equation in which a_t is a linear function of lagged advertising, lagged consumption, lagged income, and a constant term; the coefficients on lagged income and lagged consumption are insignificantly different from zero at the usual significance levels, and the adjusted R^2 of 0.939 reflects primarily the effect of the lagged advertising variable, whose t-statistic is 5.87. The fitted value from this reduced form regression is then used as an instrument for a_t, yielding the 2SLS equation

$$y_t = \underset{(25.74)}{0.8983} y_{t-1} + \underset{(8.650)}{0.4256} \Delta x_t - \underset{(1.960)}{2.5738} \Delta a_t \qquad \bar{R}^2 = 0.726 \qquad \textbf{(8.46)}$$

Here the 2SLS coefficient on Δa_t is about a third smaller than the OLS estimate in Eq. (8.45), and its statistical significance is marginal, using common levels of confidence.[44] In terms of the implied long-run effect on saving rates, parameters in Eq. (8.46) indicate that a steady-state change of from 0% to 2.5% growth in advertising would reduce the saving rate from 0.085 to 0.068, which is still a very large effect.

In interpreting these striking results, note that the 2SLS advertising coefficient is of marginal statistical significance and that the only statistically significant coefficient in the reduced form regression is lagged advertising. Therefore identifiability is not clear. Moreover, Schmalensee's results, as well as those of Clarke [1976], suggest that identifiability of the effect of advertising on sales is extremely difficult when annual data are employed.[45] Finally, if disturbances in the structural equation are autocorrelated, then estimation by this 2SLS procedure yields inconsistent parameter estimates. Incidentally, Taylor and Weiserb do not report results of a Durbin test with the 2SLS equation (8.46).[46]

The final empirical study examined here is a time-series analysis of Granger causality between advertising and consumption by Ashley, Granger, and Schmalensee [1980]. One important methodological innovation of this study is that alternative models of causality are estimated by using quarterly data for 60 observations over the 1956:1–1970:4 time period, and then their ex post forecasting properties are compared on the basis of quarterly data for 20 observations from 1971:1 to 1975:4. The advertising data are updated series from Blank [1962] and Schmalensee [1972] and in particular incorporate media-specific cost per million messages deflation procedures. Unfortunately, both the quarterly advertising data and the published quarterly consumption data were seasonally adjusted by a U.S. Bureau of the Census procedure called X-11. Because it is known that use of seasonally adjusted data can introduce bias into investigations of causality,[47] Ashley et al. obtained the unpublished U.S. Department of Commerce raw data on quarterly consumption, not seasonally adjusted. However, their advertising data were still seasonally adjusted.

Using both nominal and real series, seasonally adjusted and not (for consumption), Ashley et al. employed univariate Box-Jenkins techniques to prewhiten the various advertising and consumption time series and then calculated cross-correlograms between residuals from these series. Results were quite similar among the various data series, although use of seasonally unadjusted data yielded preferable results. With the seasonally unadjusted nominal consumption goods expenditure data per capita, denoted UCGN, the following univariate model was identified, estimated, and checked (all data were logarithmically transformed):

$$\underset{}{(1 - B)(1 - B^4)\text{UCGN}_t} = \underset{(0.00043)}{0.00086} + (1 - \underset{(0.082)}{0.204}B^2 - \underset{(0.075)}{0.747}B^4)\epsilon_{\text{UCGN},t} \qquad \textbf{(8.47)}$$

where B is the lag or backward shift operator, $\epsilon_{\text{UCGN},t}$ is the residual, numbers in parentheses are standard errors, and $(1 - B^4)$ reflects the use of seasonal differencing.[48] The corresponding univariate model for nominal advertising expenditures per capita was

$$(1 - B)\text{ADN}_t = \underset{(0.0022)}{0.00911} + (1 - \underset{(0.13)}{0.256}B^5)\epsilon_{\text{ADN},t} \qquad \textbf{(8.48)}$$

The cross-correlogram between $\epsilon_{\text{ADN},t}$ and $\epsilon_{\text{UCGN},t-k}$ indicated sample correlations of 0.05, 0.06, −0.14, −0.13, −0.19, 0.09 and 0.04 for $k = -7$ to -1, respectively; 0.50 at $k = 0$; and 0.18, −0.02, 0.16, −0.13, 0.16 −0.13, and −0.13 for $k = 1$ to 7. Since the standard error for each correlation coefficient is about 0.14, the correlation at $k = 0$ is clearly significant, while that at $k = 1$ (0.18) is marginal. Ashley et al. took the $k = 0$ and $k = 1$ results together as being suggestive of a lag structure in which consumption causes advertising. Although correlations at $k = -3$ to -5 are not significant, they are nonnegligible. Since these correlations are negative and those at $k = -2$ and $k = -1$ are clearly insignificant, Ashley et al. concluded that no sensible lag structure could be put together for advertising causing sales.

With this preliminary information on cross-correlograms of residuals in mind, Ashley et al. proceeded nonetheless with estimation of a bivariate model relating the original (not residual) series. The final form for advertising as a function of consumption turned out to be

$$\begin{aligned}(1 + \underset{(0.13)}{0.327}B - \underset{(0.16)}{0.625}B^2)(1 - B)\text{ADN}_t &= \underset{(0.0025)}{0.00665} + \\ &+ (\underset{(0.21)}{0.636}B + \underset{(0.19)}{0.317}B^5)\text{UCGN}_t + (1 - \underset{(0.19)}{0.686}B^2)\eta_{\text{ADN},t}\end{aligned} \qquad \textbf{(8.49)}$$

while that for consumption as a function of advertising was

$$\begin{aligned}(1 - B)(1 - B^4)\text{UCGN}_t &= \underset{(0.00090)}{0.001885} - \underset{(0.076)}{0.121}(1 - B)\text{ADN}_t \\ &+ (1 - \underset{(0.15)}{0.162}B^2 - \underset{(0.11)}{0.684}B^4)\eta_{\text{UCGN},t}\end{aligned}$$

where the η's are residual series.

As their final step, Ashley et al. compared the mean squared errors of a set of one-period forecasts for the 20 postsample observations, based alternatively on the univariate models (8.47) and (8.48) and the bivariate models (8.49) and (8.50).[49] For advertising causing consumption the overall postsample mean-squared error of forecast was only 5.1% less with the bivariate model (8.50) relative to the univariate model (8.47), an improvement that was too small to be statistically significantly different from zero. Since past advertising does not seem to be helpful in forecasting consumption, Ashley et al. concluded that the null hypothesis that aggregate advertising does not cause aggregate consumption should be retained.

By contrast, the bivariate model (8.49) for advertising reduced the postsample mean-squared error or forecast relative to the univariate model (8.48) by some 26%, a statistically significant improvement at something less than the 9.2% level of significance. While the evidence was therefore not overwhelming, Ashley et al. concluded that aggregate consumption is useful in forecasting aggregate advertising and in this sense that aggregate consumption Granger-causes aggregate advertising.

In interpreting the divergent findings among the Schmalensee, Taylor and Weiserbs, and Ashley et al. studies, note that the Taylor and Weiserbs study suffers from the use of annual data and potential stochastic specification problems. On the other hand, although Schmalensee employs 2SLS with quarterly data, potentially useful and informative procedures such as the Hausman specification test are not employed. While the Granger causality results from Ashley et al. are significant, they are not overwhelming, and bivariate advertising-sales causality measures could be affected by a common omitted other variable, such as disposable income. Finally, by now all these studies are somewhat dated. Even the most recent 1980 article by Ashley et al. employs data only through 1975:4. Since that time in the United States the saving rate has fallen considerably, even as the ratio of advertising to GNP has risen dramatically (see Table 8.1). This suggests that the use of more recent data, as well as some of the various relatively new econometric procedures discussed earlier, could provide the basis of an empirical study that might finally lay to rest the aggregate advertising-consumption controversy. For the moment, however, it is safest to assume that causality occurs from aggregate consumption to aggregate advertising but does not occur in the reverse direction.

8.4 OVERVIEW OF SELECTED CLASSIC AND RECENT EMPIRICAL STUDIES ON SALES-ADVERTISING RELATIONSHIPS WITH AND WITHOUT RIVALS

We now turn our attention to a selected number of classic and recent empirical studies focusing on the effects of advertising in a more disaggregated context, such as at the level of an industry or a particular product, not the entire national economy. Although numerous studies could be included, here we limit our attention to several that identify important issues; further, for most of these studies, the underlying data are available, thus facilitating replication.

One of the earliest econometric studies on the cumulative effects of advertising was by Marc Nerlove and Frederick Waugh [1961], who considered the issue of how voluntary trade associations or other cooperatives should make advertising outlay decisions. An important aspect of the trade association is that it has no impact on the output decisions of its member companies, but instead simply provides informational and promotional advertising designed to benefit its members.

Nerlove and Waugh chose to implement their theoretical model empirically, using advertising, sales, and price data for oranges over a 50-year period beginning in 1907. To assess whether advertising was one of the reasons behind the substantial growth in demand for oranges, Nerlove and Waugh related q_t (per capita deliveries of oranges in boxes in year t) to p_t (price of oranges per box), y_t (per capita disposable income of consumers), and a_t (per capita advertising expenditures for oranges by Sunkist Growers and the Florida Citrus Commission), where all nominal values were deflated by the CPI.

Nerlove and Waugh experimented with a number of distributed lag formulations for a_t and discovered that the Koyck exponentially declining lag gave rather unreasonable results, indicating no decline over time in the effectiveness of advertising. When current and several lagged advertising terms were included with no constraints placed on the parameters, results indicated that the effect of current advertising was larger than that of lagged terms but that the effect of lagged terms was relatively constant over a finite number of past expenditures. This led them to a demand for oranges equation formulation:

$$q_t = kp_t^{\eta} y_t^{\beta} a_t^{\gamma} A_t^{\delta} \tag{8.51}$$

where k is a constant, η and β are the price and income elasticities of demand, and A_t is the arithmetic average of advertising expenditures over the ten years preceding t, that is, $A_t \equiv (1/10)(a_{t-1} + \cdots + a_{t-10})$. In this formulation, γ is the short-run elasticity of demand with respect to current advertising, and $\gamma + \delta$ represents the long-run or cumulative elasticity of demand with respect to a maintained change in advertising.

Nerlove and Waugh did not actually estimate Eq. (8.51), but instead solved it for p_t, multiplied through by q_t, and then took logarithms. This resulted in a demand equation with revenue $v_t \equiv p_t \cdot q_t$ as the dependent variable

$$\begin{aligned} \ln v_t = {} & c + (1 + 1/\eta) \ln q_t - (\beta/\eta) \ln y_t \\ & - (\gamma/\eta) \ln a_t - (\delta/\eta) \ln A_t \end{aligned} \tag{8.52}$$

Nerlove and Waugh added a random disturbance term and, using annual data from the period 1907–1958 but excluding the World War II years 1941–1945, obtained the OLS equation

$$\ln v_t = -2.939 - \underset{(0.198)}{0.390*\ln q_t} + \underset{(0.191)}{0.924*\ln y_t} + \underset{(0.125)}{0.233*\ln a_t} + \underset{(0.045)}{0.103*\ln A_t} \tag{8.53}$$

with an R^2 of 0.72, where numbers in parentheses are standard errors. Using Eqs. (8.53) and (8.52), this implied estimates of the elasticities η, β, γ, δ, and $\gamma + \delta$ equal to -0.72, 0.67, 0.17, 0.07 and 0.24, respectively. Hence long-run price and income elasticity estimates were -0.72 and 0.67, while current and lagged advertising elasticity estimates were 0.17 and 0.07, respectively.

It is worth remarking here that if advertising affects quantity demanded, then in an equation such as Eq. (8.52), q_t may be correlated with the disturbance term, implying that estimation by OLS yields inconsistent parameter estimates. Nerlove and Waugh do not state why they treat q_t as exogenous and revenue v_t (hence, price p_t) as endogenous, nor do they report results with a logarithmic version of Eq. (8.51) estimated directly. However, they do point out that OLS estimates of all the elasticities would be unaffected (although R^2 would change) if $\ln q_t$ were subtracted from both sides of Eq. (8.53) and if $\ln p_t$ rather than $\ln v_t$ were the dependent variable.

Although the Nerlove and Waugh econometric analysis of the long-run impact of advertising is well known and often cited, another study is much more famous and arguably has had more impact on econometric research in advertising than any other research. This legendary study is the 1963 University of Chicago Ph.D. dissertation by Kristian S. Palda, "The Measurement of Cumulative Advertising Effects," published as Palda [1964].

Palda focused on the Lydia E. Pinkham Medicine Company, which since 1873 had manufactured a patent medicine that was alleged not only to be a pain reliever, but also to cure a wide variety of other ills. The Pinkham data base was viewed as ideal for studying the effects of advertising on sales for several reasons. First, Pinkham's product was not subject to advertising by rivals, and advertising was essentially the only form of marketing that was employed. In particular, Pinkham's compound had no direct competitor, it did not employ salespeople or sales agents, and it had no distribution system worthy of mention except for advertising.

Second, Pinkham was one of the first large national advertisers in the United States and was controversial as well. Advertising/sales ratios were phenomenally large, up to 85% in 1934 and only occasionally dipping below 40%. Controversy emerged because the Lydia Pinkham vegetable compound consisted of an herbal extract in an alcoholic solution. In 1914 the 18% alcoholic content of the alleged pain reliever prompted the Internal Revenue Service to threaten to tax it as an alcoholic beverage and the Food and Drug Administration to cite the company for false and misleading advertising. In response, Pinkham sharply reduced the claims of its vast curative powers and reduced its alcoholic content slightly, to about 15%. Further actions by the Food and Drug Administration in 1925 required Pinkham to advertise its compound as only a vegetable tonic, upon which sales immediately declined. After becoming a director in 1926, Lydia Gove, a granddaughter of the founder, dominated company advertising decisions and refused to cut advertising when sales fell, thereby incurring the ire of other officers. A lawsuit, settled in July 1937, ended her reign, after which advertising expenditures were drastically reduced, and media changed from primarily newspapers and magazines to radio.[50]

Palda therefore argued that if advertising had a cumulative effect on sales, it should surely become manifest through an analysis of this relatively "clean" Pinkham data.

One problem that Palda faced with the Pinkham data, however, was that price variables could not be used as regressors or deflators. Although it was known that wholesale price changes occurred only very seldom, data on retail prices could not be obtained, and further, changes in retail and wholesale prices were often unrelated because the Pinkham product was frequently used as a "loss leader" in retail stores. Moreover, since the form of the product changed over time from liquid tonic eventually to tablets, a measure of sales in physical units was unavailable, and therefore Palda could not compute a per unit price as sales divided by the number of physical units. Palda therefore argued that it was best simply to ignore the effects on demand of product price. Similarly, difficulties in finding a deflator for advertising motivated Palda to relate sales to advertising outlay in a simple manner, in which both were measured in current dollars.

Computational constraints at the University of Chicago's Univac I computer facility forced Palda to submit most of his dissertation regressions in one batch, thereby preventing him from using past results to explore more promising model revisions, although he was able to do a few second-round estimations on the IBM 1620 computer at the École des Hautes Études Commerciales de l'Université de Montreal. Using a Koyck distributed lag specification, Palda reported that preferred results based on annual data, 1908–1960, for his initial batch of regressions, were

$$\begin{aligned} S_t = 212 + &\underset{(7.39)}{0.628 S_{t-1}} + \underset{(3.76)}{0.537 A_t} - \underset{(1.04)}{102 D1} + \underset{(2.66)}{181 D2} - \underset{(2.90)}{203 D3} \\ R^2 &= 0.922 \end{aligned} \qquad \textbf{(8.54)}$$

where $D1$, $D2$, and $D3$ are dummy variable series reflecting changes in advertising copy, taking on the values of 1 in 1908–1914, 1915–1925, and 1926–1940, respectively. Numbers in parentheses are t-statistics. The statistically significant coefficient on lagged sales was taken to suggest the importance of cumulative advertising. The magnitude of this carryover effect is large; if one substitutes this estimate of λ into Eq. (8.36), one obtains a 90% duration interval of 4.95 years, or 59.4 months.

From his second batch of computer runs in Montreal, Palda's preferred equation took the form

$$\begin{aligned} S_t = -3649 + &\underset{(10.56)}{0.665 S_{t-1}} + \underset{(4.86)}{1180 \log_{10} A_t} + \underset{(7.23)}{774 D} + \underset{(5.4)}{32 T} - \underset{(4.22)}{2.83 Y_t} \\ R^2 &= 0.941 \end{aligned} \qquad \textbf{(8.55)}$$

where $\log_{10}$ refers to a logarithmic transformation to base 10, D is a dummy variable having the value 1 in years 1908–1925, and 0 otherwise, T is a time counter equal to 1 in 1908 and 53 in 1960, and Y is disposable income in billions of current dollars. Note that since A_t is in logarithms, whereas the dependent variable S_t is not, Eq. (8.55) permits diminishing returns to advertising. Again, the coefficient on lagged sales is statistically significant, indicating a substantial carryover or lingering effect for advertising; the implied 90% duration level is 5.64 years or 67.7 months.

Although a lagged dependent variable appeared as a regressor in Eqs. (8.54) and (8.55), Palda used the Durbin-Watson test statistic to check for autocorrelation; in one case he even employed the OLS-based Durbin-Watson test statistic to estimate ρ, the first-order autocorrelation coefficient, and then using this estimate of ρ to transform the data, he reestimated by OLS an equation similar to Eq. (8.55).[51]

Palda compared cumulative effects models such as those above to more naive ones that permitted only current effects, using as a criterion the ability of models estimated on data through 1934 to forecast the sales consequences in 1935–1936 of sharp cutbacks in advertising; on the basis of the absolute value of their mean percentage errors, the cumulative effects models dominated. From these results, Palda concluded that the hypothesis that advertising has a lagged and cumulative effect received strong support.

Palda's seminal research on the Lydia E. Pinkham Medicine company has generated a whole subfield of empirical research in advertising, dubbed "Lydiametrics" by the advertising historian Richard W. Pollay [1979, 1984]. As was noted in Section 8.2, much has been written on pitfalls in estimating advertising duration levels using annual data, on alternative forms of the distributed lag relationship, and on stochastic specification. Owing in part to the diversity in results, not all scholars of advertising believe that the Lydiametrics experience has been a productive one. Pollay's view, for example, is that too much of Lydiametrics has emphasized methodological technique, that use of annual data is inappropriate, that the absence of deflated sales and advertising data is very important, and that not enough of Lydiametrics has dealt adequately with the historical context. As a result, the promise of using more sophisticated econometric methodology to clarify issues raised by Palda has not materialized. In the words of Pollay [1984, p. 21], "What at first appeared sophisticated now seems like sophistry. This unfortunately parallels the worst of advertising, where the promise far exceeds the product." Fellow econometricians, take note.

One aspect that makes the Lydia Pinkham data set particularly attractive for econometric research is the fact that the Pinkham compound was widely viewed as having no effective competitor. Given this monopolistic position, analyses of the effects of advertising on sales did not need to be concerned with competitors' advertising. In most markets, however, this monopolistic situation does not arise, and so one must incorporate interdependent effects of firm i's advertising on the sales of firm j, as well as the own effects.

Perhaps the most classic study of advertising in a market with rivals is that by Harry V. Roberts [1947], who considered the situation in which:

> Both manufacturers of a drug product have approximately the same distribution, they share the major part of the market between them, they are exclusively magazine advertisers, and the market is relatively free of "deals" and special price promotions."[52]

Roberts designated the two products "A" and "B," and analyzed cross and own effects of advertising using detailed biweekly information available on 1504 families for a six-month period in 1943. Advertising for A and B was recorded for each family in units of opportunity for exposure, where an exposure opportunity was measured each time a magazine entered a household. Two equations were estimated using OLS, the dependent variable being either total family purchases of brand A or brand B, in cents, over the six-month period. Right-hand variables included advertising exposure measures for brands A and B, a number of other variables, such as number of people in the family, and dummy variables for city size, age, economic class, education, occupation, and region. Calculations were carried out by hand (electronic computers were not yet available) using the normal equation solution algorithm outlined by Roberts's Chicago colleague, Henry Schultz [1938, Appendix C].

Notice that with this type of model based on family data, it is unlikely that advertising is endogenous, and so use of OLS is justified. Two aspects of the study worried Roberts, however. First, the correlation between the advertising of A and B was quite high, $r = 0.84$, implying that estimation of the separate effects of A and B advertising on purchases might be imprecise. Second, Roberts was unable to obtain data on the family's exposure to A and B advertising prior to the 1943 sample period. Hence if there were a carryover effect, it could not be incorporated. To Roberts [1947, p. 138], this constituted "the most important qualifications to the . . . conclusions."

Roberts found that in the regression equation explaining A's sales, the coefficient of A's advertising was positive and significant at the 1% level, and although the coefficient on B's advertising was negative as expected, it was not significant at the 10% level. On the other hand, in the equation explaining B's sales, both advertising coefficients were positive, though neither was significant. In large part these insignificant results could be attributed to collinearity between A and B's advertising. Not surprisingly, given this type of microdata, the R^2 figures were also quite low, 0.045 for the A equation and 0.035 for B. Roberts took the results of the A equation and found that they were consistent with diminishing returns to A's advertising, that is, the family's marginal revenue curve declined with increases in A's advertising. Roberts noted that a comparison of this marginal revenue with the marginal cost of advertising could provide the basis for determining an optimal amount of advertising.

Since Roberts's classic 1947 study, a large number of papers, both experimental and econometric, have been published attempting to measure sales

HARRY ROBERTS

Pioneer in Studying the Effectiveness of Advertising

Born in Peoria, Illinois in 1923, Harry Roberts came to the University of Chicago in 1940 and chose business because it was a major that he could complete in two and a half years, the time he had before being drafted into the Army. After graduating in 1943 with a Phi Beta Kappa key, Roberts was drafted and assigned to a U.S. Army tank crew and saw action in France and Belgium. He was captured in the Battle of the Bulge and spent the rest of the war in several German POW camps. He returned to Chicago to pursue an MBA degree in 1945 and became interested in studying the effectiveness of advertising. Roberts's Chicago M.B.A. thesis, which is discussed in this chapter, was a pioneering empirical study on the effects of advertising in a market with rivals. A principal finding was that advertising is often less effective than people had thought.

After completing his M.B.A. degree in 1947, Roberts joined one of Chicago's largest advertising firms, McCann-Erickson, where he soon became manager of marketing research. But the topic of Roberts' M.B.A. thesis kept nagging him, and he soon saw that the questions in which he was most interested were really statistical questions. This led Roberts to return to the University of Chicago to study statistics. Teaching statistics to business school students while he continued his own doctoral studies, Roberts completed the Ph.D. degree requirements in 1955 and was immediately appointed Associate Professor of Statistics at Chicago's Graduate School of Business. Roberts has been at Chicago ever since.

Roberts's distinguished contributions to applied statistics are numerous and wide ranging. His first textbook, *Basic Methods of Marketing Research* (written jointly with James Lorie), is widely recognized as having brought modern statistical sampling theory to marketing research. He has also written in fields as diverse as finance, microcomputing, quality control, productivity, hypothesis testing, Bayesian statistics, and the measurement of discrimination by race and gender (see Chapter 5 of this book). With Lorie and Roman Weil, Roberts has written a book of special significance to Chicago's Ph.D. student community; it is entitled *Dissertations with Fewer Tears.*

Among his colleagues at Chicago, however, Roberts has become legendary as the school's primary consultant for quantitative research. According to colleague James Lorie, "Harry has a great weakness. If you can interest him intellectually in your problem, he'll work extremely hard to help you."*

Roberts has served on the editorial boards of numerous statistical and marketing journals and has been on the Board of Directors of the National Opinion Research Center since 1980. He is an avid runner, having completed more than 40 marathons since 1973, and has recently begun competing in triathlons (biking, swimming, and running for a total of about three hours). He considers himself a compulsive computer addict, an amateur astronomer, and an amateur expert on sports medicine. (He once presented a colloquium at Chicago in which he used time series methods to trace his body weight, concluding that his weight was autoregressive with a systematic component of variation by day of the week.)

* Quoted from Larry Arbeiter, "Harry Roberts, Marathon Man," *GSB Chicago*, Autumn 1987, p. 4.

effects of advertising in markets with rivals.[53] In a provocative survey of some of this literature, David Aaker and James Carman [1982] have suggested that firms might be spending too much on purchasing media time and space and not enough on analyzing the quality of the advertising copy. In particular, Aaker and Carman cite evidence suggesting that at current levels of spending, there is more response to variations in advertising quality than there is to variations in purchasing media time and space. Moreover, from other sources, Aaker and Carman note that within typical advertising budgets of firms, media tend to get the largest share of resources and that only something under 5% of the advertising budget is allocated to creativity and testing. This suggests that advertising copy quality deserves further examination.

In a recent exploratory study of sales-advertising relationships in which experts' measures of advertising copy quality were available, Stephen J. Arnold, Tae H. Oum, Bohumir Pazderka, and Douglas W. Snetsinger [1987] integrated the hedonic price theory (see Chapter 4 of this book) with traditional sales-response specifications.[54] In particular, Arnold et al. defined quality-adjusted advertising outlay θ_t as the product

$$\theta_t \equiv \phi_t \cdot A_t = [q_{1t}^{\tau_1} \cdot q_{2t}^{\tau_2} \cdot \ldots \cdot q_{kt}^{\tau_k}] \cdot A_t \tag{8.56}$$

where A_t is traditional advertising outlay and the quality adjustment coefficient ϕ_t depends on k observed attributes of the advertising copy at time t, q_{1t} through q_{kt}, each affecting overall advertising quality ϕ_t by the unknown parameter τ_k.[55] Arnold et al. substitute θ_t into a traditional log-log sales-response model,

$$\begin{aligned} \ln y_t &= \alpha_0 + \beta \ln \theta_t + \Sigma_t \delta_i \ln X_{it} + \Sigma_j \alpha_j D_{it} + \epsilon_t \\ &= \alpha_0 + \beta[\Sigma_k \tau_k \ln q_{kt} + \ln A_t] + \Sigma_i \delta_i \ln X_{it} + \Sigma_j \alpha_j D_{it} + \epsilon_t \end{aligned} \tag{8.57}$$

where y_t is sales, X_{it} are other variables affecting sales (including competitors' prices and advertising outlays), D_{it} are dummy variables, ϵ_t is a traditional disturbance term, and α, β, τ, and δ are parameters to be estimated. Note that with this specification the parameter β is estimated simultaneously with the τ_k, thereby permitting separate identification of the effects of advertising quality and outlay on sales.

Arnold et al. specify a "partial adjustment" framework for Eq. (8.57) in which a proportion η of the cumulative effect of advertising occurs each time period. This yields the estimable equation

$$\ln y_t = \eta\alpha_0 + (1 + \eta) \ln y_{t-1} + \eta\beta[\Sigma_k\tau_k \ln q_{kt} + \ln A_t] + \eta\Sigma_i\delta_i \ln X_{it} + \eta\Sigma_j\alpha_j D_{it} + \epsilon_t^* \quad \textbf{(8.58)}$$

which is nonlinear in the parameters. They actually estimate a linear version of Eq. (8.58) directly and then obtain indirect estimates of the nonlinear parameters, that is, they estimate

$$\ln y_t = \alpha_0^* + \eta^* \ln y_{t-1} + \beta^* \ln A_t + \Sigma_k\tau_k^* \ln q_{kt} + \Sigma_i\delta_i^* \ln X_{it} + \Sigma_j\alpha_j^* D_{it} + \epsilon_{it}^* \quad \textbf{(8.59a)}$$

where

$$\alpha_0^* \equiv \eta\alpha_0, \qquad \eta^* \equiv 1 - \eta, \qquad \beta^* \equiv \eta\beta, \qquad \tau_k^* \equiv \eta\tau_k,$$

$$\delta_i^* \equiv \eta\delta_i, \qquad \text{and} \qquad \alpha_j^* \equiv \eta\alpha_j \quad \textbf{(8.59b)}$$

With this specification the long-run elasticity of sales with respect to quality-adjusted advertising θ_t is the same as the long-run elasticity with respect to advertising outlay, both equaling $\beta^*/1 - \eta^*$. However, the long-run elasticity of sales with respect to quality attribute k is $\tau_k^*/1 - \eta^*$.

The data set used to illustrate this procedure came from a company that sells a low-priced, frequently purchased packaged good sold in food, drug, tobacco, confectionery, and variety stores, eating and drinking places, and vending machines in Canada. A total of 54 bimonthly observations were used covering the 1973–1982 time period for each of five geographical regions. The data included observations on sales and the primary marketing variables for the brand of interest, as well as advertising expenditures, distribution levels, and prices for all competing brands in each of the regions.

As measures of the quality attributes of advertising copy, Arnold et al. prepared a questionnaire measuring the extent to which advertising strategies were met by the commercial (16 distinct variables were rated) and the performance of each commercial against the target audience (seven measures). This questionnaire was administered to five expert raters for each commercial that was aired during the 1973–1982 period. The ratings were averaged across the five judges and were then inserted into the data base according to the period when each commercial was aired. Since the 16 variables from the first set were highly correlated, only one was used in estimation, namely, the log copy rating of "creative device." Note, however, that these experts' ratings of copy quality were taken ex post, and they might therefore already reflect feedback from the market. For this reason their interpretation requires considerable caution.

Arnold et al. deflated prices to 1971 constant dollars using regional consumer price indexes, and advertising outlay was deflated by using "an industry-produced media price index," further details of which were not given. The strong seasonal pattern of sales data suggested the use of six dummy variables for each of the bimonthly periods in the year, and three product reformulations were also accommodated by including appropriate dummy variables.

Estimation of this model was somewhat complex. On the basis of F- and t-tests, it was concluded that the slope coefficients in Eq. (8.59a) were equal across regions but that intercept terms were not. Results from Hausman specification tests suggested that brand i's advertising outlay was not correlated with the disturbance term in that brand's sales equation, nor was the advertising outlay on brand j correlated.

The final estimates reported by Arnold et al. were based on an estimation procedure that accounted for heteroskedasticity across regions and first-order autocorrelation, described by Jan Kmenta.[56] Point estimates (and t-ratios) for parameters in Eq. (8.59a) were 0.01339 (2.29) for β^*, the own-advertising outlay short-run elasticity; 0.27132 (3.29) for τ_1^*, the short-run elasticity with respect to copy rating "creative device"; −0.53053 (−4.92) for δ_1^*, the short-run price elasticity; 0.15765 (2.52) for the carryover sales elasticity η^*; and a number of dummy variable terms. No cross-advertising terms appeared in the final specification.

Of particular interest, however, are the implied long-run elasticity estimates. Using Eq. (8.59), estimates of η, β, τ_1, and $\tau_1\beta$ are calculated as 0.84235, 0.01590, 20.258, and 0.32210, respectively. The long-run elasticity with respect to the advertising quality attribute "creative device" of 0.32210 is about 20 times the size of the elasticity of sales with respect to advertising outlay, 0.01590. This suggests that at least one dimension of advertising quality has a very important effect. Whether there is overspending or underspending on overall advertising relative to that on quality, however, depends in part on the marginal costs of improving the "creative device" attribute.[57]

This concludes our overview of several classic and recent empirical studies of the sales-advertising relationship in markets with and without rivals. We now turn to a related issue, one involving public policy toward regulation of broadcast advertising for cigarettes and tobacco.

8.5 ADVERTISING AND PUBLIC POLICY: BANNING BROADCAST ADS FOR CIGARETTES

Critics of advertising have alleged that its effect in part is to stimulate consumption of products that are harmful to consumers, such as liquor and tobacco. Others have argued, however, that advertising does not affect aggregate consumption of, say, tobacco, but only influences the composition of sales among brands. Hence advertising should not be blamed for stimulating aggregate cigarette consumption.

In 1953, both the American Cancer Society and the British Medical Research Council published reports claiming higher death rates for smokers, and in 1964 the U.S. Surgeon General's Report concluded that cigarette smoking was causally related to lung cancer. In response, many public officials argued that advertising should inform consumers about the health hazards that are associated with cigarette smoking and should even discourage cigarette consumption.

A number of policies were enacted in the United States. In 1965, health warnings were required on all cigarette packages. These warnings were strengthened in 1970 and were extended to print advertising in 1972. Since 1971, cigarette companies have been obligated to disclose the tar and nicotine content of cigarettes in their advertising. Under the Fairness Doctrine, in 1968 the Federal Communications Commission required television and radio stations to air anti-cigarette commercials in a ratio of approximately one to every four cigarette commercials broadcast. Finally, on January 1, 1971, federal law prohibited all broadcast cigarette advertising.

One important issue concerns the effect of these various public policy regulations on cigarette and tobacco consumption and, ultimately, on the number of lives saved. Did public information on the health aspects of cigarettes reduce consumption sufficiently that further regulation in the form of a broadcast ban was ineffective? Did the broadcast ban on advertising have any effect on aggregate cigarette consumption? Would price increases for cigarettes have been equally or more effective? Was cigarette advertising after 1971 less effective, since it could not employ broadcast media? Some of these issues are the focus of a study by Lynne Schneider, Benjamin Klein, and Kevin M. Murphy [1981], who compare effects of information and outright regulation on tobacco and cigarette consumption.

Basing their study in part on earlier cigarette demand studies by Schoenberg [1933], Telser [1962], Schmalensee [1972], and others, Schneider et al. begin by estimating a simple demand function using annual 1930–1970 data, a period before the advertising ban was instituted. This yields the OLS equation

$$\begin{aligned} \ln C_t = {} & \underset{(1.41)}{2.116} + \underset{(1.7.7)}{1.289} \ln y_t - \underset{(2.38)}{0.724} \ln p_t + \underset{(0.33)}{0.032} \ln A_t \\ & - \underset{(1.84)}{0.114}\, D_{F,t} + \underset{(0.50)}{0.038}\, D_{53,t} - \underset{(1.71)}{0.115} D_{64,t} \\ & R^2 = 0.960, \qquad DW = 0.67 \end{aligned} \tag{8.60}$$

where C is per capita consumption of cigarettes; y is real per capita income; p is the real retail price of cigarettes; A is the advertising goodwill stock, which is assumed to have an annual depreciation rate of 0.33; D_F is a dummy variable for the Fairness Doctrine period, 7/1/67–12/31/70, standardized annually for the estimated quantity of anticigarette advertising during the period; and D_{53} and D_{64} are two dummy variables representing health information events occurring in 1953 and 1964 that are generally thought to have permanently lowered consumption. Numbers in parentheses are t-ratios.

Some of the results in Eq. (8.60) appear plausible. For example, the negative and statistically significant price elasticity is in line with other studies, and negative coefficients on D_F and D_{64} appear reasonable. The finding that advertising has an effect on aggregate cigarette consumption that is insignificantly different from zero is consistent with the position that advertising affects only the composition and not the level of cigarette consumption. However, the large estimated income elasticity of 1.289 suggests that cigarettes are a luxury good, a result that is inconsistent with industry opinion and most previous studies. Further, when actual values of the exogenous variables from the postsample 1971–1978 time period are substituted into Eq. (8.60), the model fares very poorly, overpredicting actual consumption by about 78% in 1978.

To check for stability, Schneider et al. reestimate Eq. (8.60) using data through 1978, adding a D_{71} dummy variable for the postadvertising ban period, and find that coefficients are highly unstable, some even becoming meaningless. Clearly, they argue, something is wrong with this specification. Schneider et al. focus on three specification issues.

Previous studies, such as that of Telser [1962] and numerous others cited by Schneider et al., have noted that large income elasticity estimates could be reduced by adding a time trend variable, since income and time are positively correlated. Schneider et al. argue, however, that such a procedure is "*ad hoc* curve fitting" and unsatisfactory. Rather, after examining the history of cigarette consumption from "rolling your own" to prerolled cigarettes, Schneider et al. conclude that prerolled cigarettes were initially a luxury good, that poorer folks tended to roll their own, and that the time series of cigarette consumption data must accommodate the fact that self-rolled cigarettes did not enter the data.

If this hypothesis were true, overall tobacco consumption and the number of cigarettes consumed should have differing time trends. In fact, Schneider et al. find that per capita tobacco consumption behaves very differently than per capita cigarette consumption, the former peaking in 1953, ten years before the latter. Further, per capita tobacco consumption in 1978 was 42% below its 1953 peak, whereas per capita cigarette consumption was only 7% below its 1962 peak. Since per capita income had been steadily rising over this period, this suggested to Schneider et al. [1981, p. 586] that "the average income elasticity of demand for total tobacco consumption is significantly lower than the demand for the cigarette element of that consumption."

To incorporate the effects of self-rolled cigarettes that were not in the data series, Schneider et al. sought to specify and add a variable reflecting the effects of changes in the level and distribution of income on the amount of tobacco consumed in the form of self-rolled cigarettes. They assume that below a critical cutoff level of income y_c, all tobacco is consumed in forms other than prerolled cigarettes, whereas above this level, potential cigarette consumers consume all their tobacco in the form of cigarettes. Schneider et al. specify a particular form of the distribution of income function that relates the proportion of tobacco consumers who smoke cigarettes, T_c/T, to a function of the cutoff income, y_c, and the mean disposable personal income at time t, y_{mt}. This relationship is

$$\ln (T_c/T)_t = \alpha + \ln [1 + 2(y_c/y_{mt})] - 2y_c/y_{mt} \tag{8.61}$$

whose parameters are estimated by nonlinear least squares using annual data from 1925–1978. The estimated values of α and y_c are -0.0299 and 551 (constant 1929 dollars), with t-statistics of 1.64 and 32.6, respectively; the R^2 is 0.92. Fitted values from this regression are then employed as a regressor in a cigarette demand equation, thereby accounting for the income-induced "switch" over time from self-rolled to prerolled cigarettes. Schneider et al. expect the coefficient on this variable to have the value unity.

A second problem with Eq. (8.60) that is of concern to Schneider et al. is that if the broadcast advertising ban had been effective, it should have resulted in less productive advertising. Hence one would expect advertising expenditures after 1971 to have a smaller effect on sales than earlier advertising. Schneider et al. deal with this by allowing all advertising expenditures to have the same depreciation rate of 33% per year but replace the old advertising measure with a new variable $A_t \equiv A_{1t} + rA_{2t}$, where A_1 is the advertising stock created before the 1971 ban, A_2 is that from 1971 onward, and r is a relative productivity parameter to be estimated. If the postban advertising is less effective, then $r < 1$.

A third problem with Eq. (8.60), Schneider et al. argue, is that the 0–1 dummy variables D_{53} and D_{64} are not able to capture the gradual diffusion of knowledge concerning the adverse health effects of smoking, nor the sluggish response of consumers to this information. As alternative measures of the diffusion of the health information produced by the 1953 and 1964 disclosures, Schneider et al. propose using in place of D_{53} the market share of filter cigarettes and for D_{64} the market share of cigarettes yielding 15 mg or less of tar. Filter cigarettes were introduced in 1953, and their market share rose from 3% in 1953 to 90% in 1978. The low tar cigarettes were introduced in 1964, and their market share rose from 0.3% in 1964 to 27.5% in 1978. These two variables, called F for filter and L for low-tar, as well as the fitted value from Eq. (8.61) are then used as regressors in a modified estimation of Eq. (8.60).

Not surprisingly, Schneider et al. report that the fitted value from Eq. (8.61) and real income per capita variable are highly collinear, resulting in very imprecise estimates of the income elasticity. To cope with this, Schneider et al. estimate by OLS a tobacco (not cigarette) demand equation with $\ln y$, $\ln p$, $\ln (A_1 + rA_2)$, D_F, F, and L as regressors, obtaining an income elasticity estimate of 0.426, with a t-statistic of 12.17. This extraneous estimate of the income elasticity is then inserted into a cigarette demand equation, estimated by OLS, resulting in

$$\begin{aligned}
\ln C - 0.462 \ln y = {} & \underset{(0.57)}{2.243} - \underset{(5.47)}{1.218} \ln P + \underset{(10.45)}{0.971} \ln I \\
& + \underset{(0.70)}{0.046} \ln (A_1\, 0.264 A_2) - \underset{(0.11)}{0.075} D_F - \underset{(1.41)}{0.0021}\, F \quad (0.76) \\
& - \underset{(4.11)}{0.0235} L - \underset{(1.98)}{1.386} \ln \mathrm{TPC} \\
R^2 = 0.957, \qquad DW = {} & 0.98
\end{aligned} \tag{8.62}$$

where ln I is the fitted value from (8.61), TPC is the average annual amount of tobacco in each cigarette consumed, and t-ratios are in parentheses.

Several comments are in order. First, the coefficients on both advertising stocks are positive but have very low t-ratios. Therefore the null hypothesis that advertising has no impact on aggregate cigarette consumption cannot be rejected. This result casts doubt on the effectiveness of the broadcast ban in reducing overall cigarette consumption.

Second, the price elasticity estimate of -1.218 suggests that demand is price-responsive and that imposition of additional taxes on cigarettes could reduce cigarette consumption significantly.

Third, in terms of the impact of new information concerning adverse health effects of smoking, the estimated coefficients on F (for filter cigarettes, which were introduced after the American Cancer Association report in 1953), on L (low-tar cigarettes, which were introduced after the Surgeon General's Report in 1964) and on the 1968 Fairness Doctrine dummy variable D_F are all negative, although only the 1964-related low-tar coefficient is significant. The interpretation of the significant coefficient on L is somewhat ambiguous, however, since health warnings were also required on all cigarette packages beginning in 1965.[58] This suggests that widespread health information, more than advertising restrictions, may have affected aggregate cigarette consumption.

Fourth, the coefficient on ln I is 0.971, which is very close to the expected 1.00 value. Fifth, to check on the validity of the extraneous 0.426 income elasticity estimate imposed in Eq. (8.62), Schneider et al. estimated a model without this constraint. The null hypothesis that this elasticity equaled 0.426 could not be rejected. Finally, Schneider et al. report that an examination of residuals from Eq. (8.62) suggested they might follow a first-order moving average process, not a first-order autoregressive one as might be presumed by the low Durbin-Watson statistic. Nonetheless, they chose not to reestimate using GLS.

In summary, the Schneider et al. study suggests that the broadcast advertising ban was not particularly effective in reducing cigarette consumption but that consumers have reacted quite vigorously to the information supplied to them regarding the health dangers of smoking. In addition to such information, consumer demand has been responsive to changes in the real price of cigarettes, as well as to the level and distribution of income.

The issues raised in this study are obviously very important and remain controversial even today as governments look to cigarette taxes as possible sources of revenue.[59] Our brief discussion also makes clear that there are a number of ambiguities in interpreting the Schneider et al. econometric results. Fortunately, the data underlying the Schneider et al. study have been made available, and in the exercises at the end of this chapter you will have the opportunity to replicate, extend, revise, and reinterpret the findings of this provocative study.

8.6 OTHER CURRENT EMPIRICAL ISSUES

In the previous sections we identified a number of important econometric issues that occur when sales-advertising models are implemented empirically. We have also surveyed a selected set of classic and more recent econometric studies. In this section we briefly outline several other current empirical issues involving advertising.

In an important survey of the state of the art in aggregate advertising models to the late 1970s, John D. C. Little [1979] focuses particular attention on the shape of advertising response functions. Not only should advertising response models admit the possibility of positive sales with nonzero advertising (which can easily be accomplished by including an intercept term in the sales equation), but, according to Little, they should also be nonlinear and perhaps S-shaped, exhibiting increasing returns to advertising at low advertising rates and diminishing returns at high rates. Further, the sales response to an increase in advertising might not be symmetric to that of a decrease in advertising.

Whether advertising response functions are in fact S-shaped is still a controversial empirical issue; Ambar G. Rao and P. B. Miller [1975], for example, report evidence supporting the S shape, whereas Julian L. Simon and Johan Arndt [1980] find only diminishing returns. If advertising response functions are S-shaped, then over a given time period with fixed advertising budgets, firms might be able to generate additional sales per dollar of advertising by implementing a cyclic or pulsing advertising policy instead of an even policy that involves constant spending over time.

The theoretical conditions under which a pulsing policy might be optimal were originally examined by Maurice W. Sasieni [1971]. Recent research on advertising wearout and the optimality of pulsing policies, both theoretical and empirical, has been reported by Hermann Simon [1982], and by Vijay Mahajan and Eitan Muller [1986]. Mahajan and Muller show that a pulsing policy is optimal *only* under an S-shaped response function. Further, they conjecture that the reason that Simon and Arndt and others find diminishing returns in their empirical analyses is that even if firms faced S-shaped response functions, statisticians using temporally aggregated data on advertising levels and sales responses would be unable to recover an S-shaped function, since the effect of pulsing is always to linearize the convex (increasing returns) portion of the response function. In essence, Mahajan and Muller believe that for some small time interval the sales response function must be S-shaped. As Little [1986] notes, however, since all advertising is inherently discrete in a fine enough time frame, for practical progress to be made in this area it will be necessary to develop empirically based definitions of what is "even" and what is "pulsed."[60]

Another substantial body of empirical literature, not considered in this chapter, is concerned with the effects of advertising on erecting barriers to competition. There are a number of different strands of research here.[61] One body of literature deals with the proposition that advertising erects patterns of brand loyalty that work to the advantage of established firms.

Joseph Bain [1956, Chapter 4; 1968], for example, has argued that as a result, the minimum efficient size of a potential entrant firm is larger, thereby inhibiting entry. This hypothesis has attracted a great deal of attention from empirical analysts in industrial organization, who have attempted, with only limited success, to uncover stable relationships among advertising outlays, pricing behavior, profitability, and industry concentration.[62] A major problem with Bain's hypothesis, however, is that advertising has the hypothesized impact of erecting entry barriers only if its duration level is quite long; if today's advertising does not affect tomorrow's sales, an entrant tomorrow need only advertise at the same rate as incumbent firms to match their goodwill with customers. As was emphasized in Section 8.2.F and in the survey by Clarke [1976], 90% duration levels for most products are less than one year. Therefore the empirical evidence on duration levels provides little support for this aspect of Bain's hypothesis.

A related body of literature deals with the issue of whether scale economies exist for advertising.[63] If they do, and if the lower costs at larger volumes of advertising result in lower prices to the larger clients of advertising agencies, then the monopsony power of larger firms could result in an effective barrier to entry.[64] This scale economy issue also relates to a long-standing puzzle in marketing as to why most firms limit in-house advertising efforts and instead primarily farm out their advertising efforts to advertising agencies. The existence of scale economies could help provide a satisfactory explanation for this observed phenomenon.

Surprisingly little econometric research has focused on the issue of scale economies for advertising agencies. The most detailed study to date is that by Richard Schmalensee, Alvin J. Silk, and Robert Bojanek [1983], who estimate advertising agency cost functions and find that economies of scale are exhausted at relatively small output levels. Their estimates imply that in 1977, more than 200 advertising agencies in the United States had essentially exploited all scale-related efficiencies and that economies of scale could not help explain the low incidence of in-house advertising efforts. However, Schmalensee et al. also find that agencies' costs are sensitive to the mix of media in which their clients advertise and that larger agencies tend to derive larger shares of their billings from media with lower unit costs than do smaller agencies. They conclude by suggesting that size-related differences in agencies' media mixes are a reflection of size-related differences in the clientele being served rather than being due to any cost advantage arising from economies of scale.

Finally, although in this advertising-sales chapter we have summarized a very substantial literature involving numerous econometric studies, it should be emphasized that in much marketing research, traditional regression methods are simply not useful. For example, a great deal of empirical research in marketing is based on experimental designs involving individual consumers, in which their responses to various advertising stimuli are meticulously observed and, where possible, quantified. In cases in which the response of an individual consumer involves a discrete choice of whether or not to purchase a particular product in response to some stimulus, the dependent variable is discrete rather than continuous. It is well known that traditional regression analysis is ill suited for estimating parameters of such models in which the dependent variable can take on only a limited number of values. Other estimation procedures, such as the logit or probit methods, however, may be appropriate. Incidentally, under carefully designed experimental situations, potential problems involving advertising simultaneity can also be circumvented.

This chapter is already very long, and so we will not consider experimentally based applications of discrete choice models in advertising. However, logit and probit models in the context of family labor force supply decisions are discussed extensively in Chapter 11.[65]

8.7 HANDS-ON ESTIMATION OF SALES-ADVERTISING RELATIONSHIPS

By now you have probably spent enough time reading and are ready, willing, and able to gain hands-on experience in estimating and interpreting sales-advertising relationships. The exercises of this chapter have been designed to involve you directly in analyzing empirically various facets of the causes and effects of advertising. Econometric techniques that you implement in the exercises of this chapter include Hausman specification tests (Exercises 1 and 6), two-stage least squares estimation (Exercises 1 and 6), 2SLS with first-order autocorrelation (Exercise 6), nonlinear estimation (Exercises 1 and 7), dummy variables (Exercises 2, 3, 7, and 8), model comparisons with distributed lags (Exercise 3), adding-up relationships in market share specifications (Exercise 4), univariate and bivariate ARIMA estimation and forecasting (Exercise 5), Granger causality (Exercise 5), some open-ended specification issues (Exercise 7), and the pooling of cross-sectional and time series data (Exercise 8).

Seven data files have been placed in a subdirectory named CHAP8.DAT on your data diskette. The Nerlove-Waugh data on orange demand are in ORANGE, the Palda annual data on the Lydia E. Pinkham Medicine Company are in PALDA, and the Palda monthly data are in a file called PALDAM. Some classic data of Nicholls on pre–World War II major brand advertising and sales of cigarettes in the United States are in NICHOL. Data underlying the analysis of causality between aggregate advertising and aggregate U.S. consumption by Ashley et al. are found in a file called CAUSAL, while data from the provocative study by Schneider et al. on the effectiveness of the broadcast cigarette advertising ban are in CIGAD. Finally, the pooled cross-sectional, time series data on advertising quantity and quality analyzed by Arnold et al. are found in a data file called QUAL. Further details concerning the data in each of these files can be found in the README.DOC file of the subdirectory CHAP8.DAT.

EXERCISES

EXERCISE 1: Assessing Price and Quantity Endogeneity in a Sales-Advertising Model for Oranges

The purpose of this exercise is to help you gain experience in dealing with potential simultaneous equations biases. You will replicate the Nerlove-Waugh results, you will uncover a subtle exogeneity assumption that will lead you to estimate an alternative specification, and then you will test the Nerlove-Waugh formulation using the Hausman specification test. You will also estimate the Nerlove-Waugh equation using 2SLS rather than OLS, and you will discover that doing 2SLS estimation is different from doing OLS estimation with the endogenous regressor simply being replaced by its fitted value from a first-stage regression. This exercise should therefore make you more comfortable with simultaneous equations estimation and with using the Hausman specification test.

In the data diskette directory CHAP8.DAT three is a data file called ORANGE containing 1910–1959 annual data used by Nerlove and Waugh in their study of the effects of advertising by two voluntary trade associations, Sunkist Growers and the Flordia Citrus Commission, on the demand for oranges. Variables in this ORANGE data set include the year (YEAR), per capita real revenue from sales in dollars (REV), per capita real income in dollars (INC), per capita boxes of oranges sold (QTY), per capita current year real advertising expenditures in cents (CURADV), the average real advertising expenditures per capita in the ten preceding years in cents (AVEADV), the U.S. population in millions (POP), and the consumer price index (CPI), where 1947–1949 = 100. These data are taken from Nerlove and Waugh [1961, Table 1, p. 827], a study that we reviewed in Section 8.3. Recall in particular that Nerlove and Waugh constructed AVEADV after experimenting with alternative advertising lingering effects formulations.

Note: For each part of this exercise, follow Nerlove and Waugh and employ the 1910–1959 data, *excluding* the war years 1942–1946.

(a) Arguing that voluntary trade associations advertise without taking into account the output and pricing decisions of its members, Nerlove and Waugh treated advertising expenditures as exogenous and estimated by least squares the parameters in Eq. (8.52). Following Nerlove and Waugh, construct natural logarithms of REV, INC, QTY, CURADV, and AVEADV; denote these as LREV, LINC, LQTY, LCURADV, and LAVEADV, respectively; and then estimate by OLS parameters of Eq. (8.52). You should be able to replicate the Nerlove and Waugh results, reproduced in Eq. (8.53), except for the constant term, which should be about -6.766, not the -2.939 reported by Nerlove and Waugh (the difference in intercepts could be due to scaling variations, such as the use of base 10 logs). Using your parameter estimates and the relations in Eq. (8.52), solve for the implied estimates of η, β, γ, δ, and $\gamma + \delta$. Do your estimates match those of Nerlove and Waugh, reproduced underneath Eq. (8.53)? (*Optional:* If nonlinear estimation software is available, estimate Eq. (8.52) by nonlinear least squares, and obtain direct estimates of the various elasticity parameters. What is the statistical significance of each of these parameters?)

(b) A curious feature of the Nerlove-Waugh estimating equation, Eq. (8.52), is that the logarithm of revenue (price times quantity) is the dependent variable, while the logarithm of quantity is one of the regressors. Assuming that the LQTY variable is exogenous and uncorrelated with the disturbance term (which must be the case if OLS is to provide consistent parameter estimates), show that even though LREV is the dependent variable, in essence the Nerlove-Waugh specification is treating the logarithm of price as endogenous. What do you think would happen to parameter estimates if Eq. (8.52) were therefore revised so that the logarithm of price rather than that of revenue were the dependent variable? Why? To check on your conjecture, construct LPRI as LPRI $\equiv$ log (REV/QTY), and then run the regression similar to Eq. (8.52) with LPRI replacing LREV. Are your parameter and elasticity estimates related as expected? Why or why not?

(c) In part (b) you showed that the demand equation estimated by Nerlove and Waugh treats price as endogenous and quantity as exogenous. Suppose that advertising expenditures shifted the demand curve for oranges outward, other things being equal. Using the supply-demand framework of basic microeconomics with a downward-sloping demand curve, show that if the supply curve were perfectly inelastic, an increase in advertising expenditures would not change the quantity demanded (quantity would be exogenous), but that it would increase the price (price would be endogenous). In the opposite extreme case, show that if the supply curve were perfectly elastic, in response to an exogenous increase in advertising expenditures, quantity would be endogenous while price would be exogenous. If the Nerlove-Waugh implicit exogeneity specification in Eq. (8.52) is valid, what must be the corresponding assumption on the elasticity of the supply curve? Comment on the plausibility of this assumption. (*Hint:* In the short run of a year or so, can orange growers affect the quantity of oranges they bring to market? Why or why not? What about imports?)

(d) The issues raised in part (c) suggest that one might be able to argue that supply is somewhat price responsive, particularly if one believed (realistically?) that oranges from Central and South America could have been imported freely into the United States. Suppose one took the extreme view that price was exogenous and quantity was endogenous and that one could then justify estimating a logarithmic transformation of Eq. (8.51) by OLS. Estimate parameters of such an equation by OLS. What are the estimates of the various elasticities now? Do any of the price- or advertising-related elasticity estimates change significantly from that obtained in part (a) when price was endogenous and quantity was exogenous? For a priori reasons, which estimates do you prefer, if any, those in part (a) or here? Why?

(e) One way of handling the potential correlation of a regressor with the equation disturbance term is to perform a Hausman specification test, as discussed in Section 8.2.B. To implement the Hausman test here, one or more variables are needed that are excluded from the demand equation (8.51) yet that could plausibly be argued to be included in an orange supply equation. One obvious candidate would be a weather-related variable, but no such variable is available in the Nerlove-Waugh study. Two variables whose data series are printed in Nerlove and Waugh are population (POP) and the consumer price index (CPI). Recognizing that rationalizing the inclusion of the CPI in an orange supply equation requires substantial imagination and creativity, let us nonetheless use it now in a Hausman specification context. In particular, construct the natural logarithm of CPI, call it LCPI, and then run a reduced form OLS regression of LQTY on a constant, LINC, LCURADV, LAVEADV, and LCPI. Retrieve the fitted value from this regression, denote it LQTYFIT, and then run another OLS regression with LREV (or, if you prefer, LPRI) as the dependent variable and a constant, LQTY, LINC, LCURADV, LAVEADV, and LQTYFIT as regressors. Test the null hypothesis of no correlation between LQTY and the disturbance term by inspecting the *t*-statistic on the coefficient corresponding with the LQTYFIT variable (since the Hausman test relies on large-sample theory, use a critical value from the normal distribution table). Does the Hausman specification test support or call into question the Nerlove-Waugh formulation? Why? Intepret your finding.

(f) If one believes that both the price and quantity of oranges are affected by advertising, then one might want to estimate a demand equation accounting for simultaneity. Suppose, as in part (e), that the CPI variable affects the supply of, but not the demand for, oranges. In such a case, would the demand equation (8.52) be underidentified, just identified, or overidentified? Why? Using the 2SLS estimation procedure, estimate parameters in an equation similar to Eq. (8.52) but with LPR rather than LREV as the dependent variable, assuming that LINC, LCURADV, and LAVEADV are exogenous, that LPR and LQTY are endogenous, and that LCPI is a legitimate instrument. How are results affected when estimation is by 2SLS rather than OLS as in part (a)? How do you interpret this?

(g) Finally, an error that is commonly made by empirical researchers is to assume that 2SLS estimation is equivalent to OLS estimation of an equation in which the endogenous regressor is simply replaced with the fitted value from the first-stage regression. You will now see that this is only partly true. To see this, do an OLS regression of LQTY on a constant, LINC, LCURADV, LAVEADV, and LCPI. Retrieve the fitted value from this regression, and call it LQTYFIT. Now run a second-stage OLS regression of LPR on a constant, LQTYFIT, LINC, LCURADV, and LAVEADV. The parameter estimates should be identical to the 2SLS estimates in part (f), but the standard error estimates and t-statistics should be different. Is this what you find? Interpret your results.

EXERCISE 2: Estimating 90% Duration Levels for Advertising with Annual and Monthly Data for the Lydia E. Pinkham Medicine Company

The purpose of this exercise is to engage you in empirically estimating the cumulative impact of advertising by measuring the 90% duration level implicit in Palda's classic results. Further, to help you interpret the empirical significance of the data interval bias discussed in Section 8.2.F, you will compare estimates of the 90% duration level using annual, quarterly, and monthly data.

(a) Part of the reason that the Lydia E. Pinkham data set has been so widely used is because of its unique features. One striking aspect of this company is that its advertising/sales ratios were remarkably high. Using the data in the data file PALDA, construct and then print out advertising/sales ratios annually over the 1908–1960 time period. Then, using the monthly data in the data file PALDAM, construct and print out advertising/sales ratios monthly from 1907:01 through 1926:12 and from 1937:01 through 1960:06. What are minimum and maximum advertising/sales ratios? Is there more monthly than annual variation? What patterns from these data series are particularly eye-catching?

(b) Palda's preferred results, using annual data for 1908–1960, were reproduced in Eq. (8.54) of this chapter. Using OLS procedures and the data in the annual PALDA data file, replicate the results reported in Eq. (8.54). Your results will be close to, but not quite identical with, those of Palda.[66]

(c) Given your estimates in part (b), use the duration interval formula in Eq. (8.36) with $p = 0.9$ and your estimate of λ, the coefficient on the lagged dependent variable, to estimate m, the 90% duration interval for advertising. Since this value of m is based on annual data, convert it to months by multiplying it by 12. Interpret this 90% duration interval. Is it plausible? Why or why not? Does it compare well with Palda's estimate?

(d) Now proceed to estimate the 90% duration interval using data of varying periodicity but from roughly the same time period. Begin with annual data. Estimate the same equation as in part (b), using annual data for the 1908–1926 and 1938–1960 time spans. Following the procedures outlined in part (c), construct a 90% duration interval. Compare your estimates of λ, as well as estimates of the 90% duration interval, with those reported by Palda and those that you obtained in parts (b) and (c). Are the estimates reasonably stable?

(e) Now do comparable estimation using monthly data. First, using data series in the PALDAM data file, create monthly dummy variables that are analogous to the annual DUM1, DUM2, and DUM3 variables, defined as MDUM1 $\equiv$ 1.0 from 1907:1 through 1914:12, otherwise zero; MDUM2 $\equiv$ 1.0 from 1915:01 through 1925:12, otherwise zero; and MDUM3 $\equiv$ 1.0 from 1926:01 through 1926:12 and from 1937:01 through 1940:12, otherwise zero. (Recall that monthly data are not available from 1927:01 through 1936:12.) Next, using the monthly observations from 1907:2 through 1926:12 and from 1937:02 through 1960:06 in the PALDAM data file, estimate by OLS an equation with MSALES_t as the dependent variable and a constant, MSALES_{t-1}, MADV_t, MDUM1_t, MDUM2_t, and MDUM3_t as regressors. Compute the implied 90% duration interval using Eq. (8.36) with $p = 0.9$ and your monthly estimate of λ. Compare these estimates of the duration interval to those from parts (c) and (d). What do you conclude so far? Is there a systematic trend in the duration interval estimates that depends on the data periodicity?

(f) Finally, estimate a similar equation using quarterly data. First, convert your 522 monthly observations to 174 quarterly observations. Some computer software programs have specific commands to perform such conversions. If your computer software does not, convert the data as follows. For each year from 1907 through 1960, define quarter 1 as months 1, 2, and 3; quarter 2 as months 4, 5, and 6; and so on. Construct a variable for quarterly advertising, called QADV, as the sum of the three months' advertising outlays; similarly, construct quarterly sales, QSALES, as the sum of the three months' sales. Compute the variables QDUM1, QDUM2, and QDUM3 as the sample averages of the underlying monthly variables MDUM1, MDUM2, and MDUM3, respectively. Then, given this new quarterly data series and using the 1907:2–1926:4 and 1937:2–1960:2 quarterly observations, estimate by

OLS the parameters of an equation with $QSALES_t$ as the dependent variable and a constant, $QSALES_{t-1}$, $QADV_t$, $QDUM1_t$, $QDUM2_t$, and $QDUM3_t$ as regressors. Compute the implied 90% duration interval using Eq. (8.36) with $p = 0.9$ and your estimate of λ. Since this estimate is based on quarterly data, convert it to months by multiplying it by 3. Finally, compare your estimate of the 90% duration interval from quarterly data with those based on annual (parts (c) and (d)) and monthly (part (e)) data. Do your results correspond with the data interval bias hypothesis advanced by Darral Clarke, discussed in Section 8.2.F? Why or why not? How do you interpret this bias?

EXERCISE 3: Choosing Between Current and Lingering Effects Models

In this exercise you will learn how one can use econometric procedures to choose among alternative formulations measuring the carryover effect of current advertising on future sales. In particular, you will estimate and compare a Koyck lingering effects model, a current effects model with autocorrelation, and a brand loyalty model with autocorrelation, each discussed in Section 8.2.E and each using Palda's data from the legendary Lydia E. Pinkham Company.

In the data diskette subdirectory CHAP8.DAT you will find a data file called PALDA containing *annual* data, as well as a data file called PALDAM containing *monthly* data relating to the Lydia E. Pinkham Medicine Company. The first part of the PALDA file contains annual data from 1907 to 1960 on the year (YEAR), current year sales in thousands of current dollars (SALES), current year advertising outlay in thousands of current dollars (ADVER), and disposable personal income in billions of current year dollars (INC) and three dummy variables representing the various advertising policy eras, DUM1 for 1908–1914, DUM2 for 1915–1925, and DUM3 for 1926–1940. The data file PALDAM contains 522 observations on monthly data from 1907:01 through 1926:12 and from 1937:01 through 1960:6. Notice that monthly data do not exist for the time interval from 1927:01 through 1936:12. The monthly data from 1954:01 to 1960:06 were originally published by Palda [1964], while data for other months are unpublished and were graciously provided us by him. In the PALDAM data file are three variables: the time period—the year and month (YRMON), current monthly advertising outlay in current dollars (MADV), and current monthly sales in current dollars (MSALES).

The first task facing you is to choose which data set you will examine. Choose between the annual data set in PALDA and the monthly data set PALDAM. Use your chosen data for the remainder of this exercise. If you are using monthly data, construct three monthly dummy variables corresponding to the annual DUM1, DUM2, and DUM3 variables, defined as MDUM1 ≡

1.0 from 1907:1 through 1914:12, otherwise zero; MDUM2 = 1.0 from 1915:01 through 1925:12, otherwise zero; and MDUM3 = 1.0 from 1926:01 through 1926:12 and from 1937:01 through 1940:12, otherwise zero. (Recall that monthly data are not available from 1927:01 through 1936:12.)

(a) Given your data, estimate by OLS the Koyck lingering effects model (8.35). If you are using annual data, employ data for 1912–1960 and, following Palda as in Eq. (8.54) add as regressors to Eq. (8.35) the dummy variables DUM1, DUM2, and DUM3. If you are using monthly data, employ data for 1907:03 through 1926:12 and from 1937:03 to 1960:06, and add as regressors to Eq. (8.35) the dummy variables MDUM1, MDUM2, and MDUM3. Comment on your parameter estimates and their interpretation.

(b) In Section 8.2.E an alternative formulation was introduced, called the current effects model with autocorrelation. Using a generalized least squares estimator that allows for first-order autocorrelation in the disturbances, estimate parameters of this model. (For annual data, estimate over 1912–1960 and, as in part (a), and add the dummy variables DUM1, DUM2, and DUM3 to the current effects specification (8.37)–(8.39). For monthly data, add the dummy variables MDUM1, MDUM2, and MDUM3 to the current effects specification (8.37)–(8.39), and estimate using the observations from 1907:03 through 1926:12 and from 1937:03 through 1960:06). Is the autocorrelation coefficient statistically significant? Compare parameter estimates with those based on the Koyck lingering effects model in part (a). Which do you prefer? Why?

(c) Recall from Section 8.2.E that Griliches has suggested a procedure for choosing between the two specifications in parts (a) and (b). Following Griliches, estimate by OLS a model such as Eq. (8.40) with sales as the dependent variable and with a constant term, current advertising, lagged advertising, and lagged sales as regressors. (For the annual model, add DUM1, DUM2, and DUM3 to Eq. (8.40), and estimate using 1912–1960 data; for monthly data, add MDUM1, MDUM2, and MDUM3, and estimate over the 1907:03–1926:12 and from 1937:03–1960:06 time periods.) Given this more general estimated model, use Griliches' procedures to choose between the Koyck lingering effects and the current effects with autocorrelation specification. Which do you prefer? Why?

(d) An alternative procedure for choosing between parts (a) and (b) is to estimate the brand loyalty model (8.41) with first-order autocorrelation, which yields Eq. (8.42). As was discussed in Section 8.2.E, the brand loyalty model with autocorrelation takes on as testable special cases the Koyck lingering effects specification and the current effects model with autocorrelation. Using an appropriate generalized least squares algorithm (recall that a lagged dependent variable is a regressor) such as the

Hildreth-Lu procedure, estimate parameters of the brand loyalty model with autocorrelation. (If using annual data, add DUM1, DUM2, and DUM3 to Eq. (8.41), and estimate over 1912–1960; if using monthly series, add MDUM1, MDUM2, and MDUM3, and estimate over the 1907:03–1926:12 and 1937:03–1960:06 time periods.) Test for the lingering and current effects models as special cases. Which specification is preferred, and why? Are these results consistent with those obtained in part (c)? Why or why not?

EXERCISE 4: Avoiding Embarrassment with Consistent Market Share Specifications

The purpose of this exercise is to help you avoid the embarrassing situation in which you estimate a model with sales market shares as dependent variables but find (or, worse yet, do not realize) that the sum of the fitted shares does not equal unity. As was noted in Section 8.2.D, there is unfortunately ample precedent for finding oneself in this humbling predicament.

In the data diskette subdirectory CHAP8.DAT there is a data file called NICHOL containing 1931–1949 annual data on the sales (in billions of cigarettes) of three predominant cigarette brands of the time, Camels (CAMELS), Lucky Strike (LUCKY), and Chesterfield (CHEST), as well as the annual advertising outlays of the tobacco-producing companies Reynolds (REYADV, for CAMELS), American (AMEADV, for LUCKY), and Liggett-Myers (LIGADV, for CHEST), in thousands of current dollars. The variable YEAR is also included, beginning with 1931 and ending in 1949. The final variable in this data file is U.S. real disposable personal income, in billions of 1958 dollars, named RLINC. These data are taken from a well-known study of the cigarette industry pricing behavior by William H. Nicholls [1951], based in part on earlier data provided by Borden [1942].

(a) Problems with inconsistent market share specifications can be illustrated with a two-firm model. Consider the two leading brands, CAMELS and LUCKY. Construct annual sales market share variables over the 1931–1949 time period as SHCAM ≡ CAMELS/SALES and SHLUC = LUCKY/SALES where SALES ≡ CAMELS + LUCKY. Then construct relative advertising outlay variables as WCAM ≡ REYADV/AMEADV and WLUC ≡ AMEADV/REYADV. Note that WLUC = 1/WCAM. Print these variables, as well as AMEADV and REYADV, and examine their time trends. Did you find surprises? What happened to cigarette sales and advertising during the Depression? During and after World War II?

(b) Next estimate by OLS an equation similar to Eq. (8.28) where SHCAM_t is the dependent variable, and the regressors include a constant term, WCAM_t, RLINC_t, and the lagged dependent variable, SHCAM_{t-1}. (Since SHCAM_{t-1} is a regressor, estimate using data from 1932 to 1949.)

Retrieve the fitted or predicted values from this regression, and then construct an implicit fitted market share series for LUCKY as 1 minus the fitted market share for CAMELS. Call this implicit share IMPLUC. Print out the fitted value series for SHCAM and IMPLUC.

(c) Now estimate by OLS the LUCKY market share equation over the same 1932–1949 interval, where $SHLUC_t$ is the dependent variable and the regressors include a constant term, $WLUC_t$, $RLINC_t$, and the lagged dependent variable $SHLUC_{t-1}$. Retrieve the fitted or predicted values from this regression, and then construct an implicit fitted market share series for CAMELS as 1 minus the fitted market share for LUCKY. Call this implicit share IMPCAM. Print out the fitted value series for SHLUC and IMPCAM. To check on consistency, first compare the fitted share for SHCAM with the implicit CAMELS share IMPCAM. If the model is consistent, they should be identical. Are they? (Look especially at 1932.) Next compare the fitted value series for SHLUC with the implicit LUCKY share IMPLUC. Are they identical? Then sum the two directly estimated fitted market share series, SHCAM and SHLUC, and call their share sum SUMSH. If the model is consistent, SUMSH should always equal 1. Does this occur? What do you conclude? Why is this lack of consistency a significant practical problem?

(d) The following variation on the above model yields rather different results. Redo parts (b) and (c), but instead of using $WCAM_t$ and $WLUC_t$ as regressors, take their natural logarithms $LWCAM_t \equiv \log(WCAM_t)$ and $LWLUC_t \equiv \log(WLUC_t)$ and replace $WCAM_t$ with $LWCAM_t$, and $WLUC_t$ with $LWLUC_t$ as regressors. What happens to logical consistency now? Why does this occur? (*Hint:* What is the sum of the two regressors $LWCAM_t$ and $LWLUC_t$ at each observation?) One other alternative is to use in place of $WCAM_t$ and $WLUC_t$ the advertising share (not the relative share) variables $ASHCAM_t \equiv$ REYADV/TOTADV and $ASHLUC_t \equiv$ AMEADV/TOTADV, where the total advertising variable TOTADV $\equiv$ REYADV + AMEADV. Redo parts (b) and (c) using ASHCAM and ASHLUC in place of WCAM and WLUC. What happens to logical consistency now? Compare values of the parameters in the two equations. Why does this occur? (*Hint:* What is the sum of ASHCAM and ASHLUC at each observation?)

(e) We now want to convince you that the strange results obtained in part (d) are for the most part perverse and will generally occur only when but two firms or two brands are considered. In particular, we want you to demonstrate that the apparent consistency obtained in part (d) will no longer hold when three brands are considered. We begin by demonstrating that the inconsistency obtained in parts (b) and (c) still occurs in the three-brand case. To do this, first construct sales market share variables SHCAM, SHLUC *and* SHCHE over the entire 1931–1949 time span, where SALES $\equiv$ CAMELS + LUCKY + CHEST, SHCAM $\equiv$ CAMELS/SALES, SHLUC $\equiv$ LUCKY/SALES, and SHCHE $\equiv$ CHEST/

SALES. Then construct relative advertising outlay variables as (us/them), that is, WCAM ≡ REYADV/(AMEADV + LIGADV), WLUC ≡ AMEADV/(REYADV + LIGADV) and WCHE ≡ LIGADV/(REYADV + AMEADV). Next do three OLS equation estimations where $SH_{i,t}$ is the dependent variable and the regressors include a constant term, $W_{i,t}$, $RLINC_t$, and $SH_{i,t-1}$, separately for i = CAM, LUC, and SHE. Retrieve the fitted values from each of these three regressions, and then form a SUMSH variable as the sum of these predicted shares at each observation. Does SUMSH always equal unity, as it should if the market share specification is consistent? Another way of demonstrating inconsistency is to form, for example, the implicit fitted market share for CHEST as 1 minus the sum of the fitted shares SHCAM and SHLUC; call this implicit CHEST share IMPCHE, and compare it to the directly estimated fitted share SHCHE. Are they identical?

(f) Now we show that the consistencies obtained in part (d) with the two-brand model vanish as soon as one specifies a three-brand framework. Redo the three estimations in part (e) replacing WCAM, WLUC, and WCHE with their natural logarithms, denoted LWCAM, LWLUC, and LWCHE. Construct fitted shares, sums of fitted shares, and implicit shares as in part (e). Does the consistency that occurred when only two brands were considered in part (d) still occur when three brands are included? Why not? (*Hint:* In the three-brand case, is the sum LWCAM + LWLUC + LWCHE still a constant or zero as it was in the two-brand case?) Finally, construct instead of relative (us/them) advertising outlay variables the advertising share variables ASHCAM, ASHLUC, and ASHCHE defined as REYADV/TOTADV, AMEADV/TOTADV, and LIGADV/TOTADV, respectively, where TOTADV ≡ REYADV + AMEADV + LIGADV. Redo the three estimations in part (e), replacing WCAM, WLUC, and WCHE with ASHCAM, ASHLUC, and ASHCHE, respectively. Construct fitted shares, sums of fitted shares, and implicit shares as in part (e). Does the consistency still occur?

Remark: Note that consistency no longer holds in this last case, even though the sum of ASHCAM + ASHLUC + ASHCHE equals unity at each observation. This particular specification can be rescued so as to make it consistent, but consistency requires the use of systems of equations estimation methods with cross-equation constraints. These procedures are discussed in Chapter 9 and are the focus of Exercises 4 and 8 in that chapter.

EXERCISE 5: Using Granger's Method to Determine Causality Between Aggregate Advertising and Aggregate Sales

The purpose of this exercise is to engage you in a study of causality between aggregate advertising and aggregate consumption using the techniques of time series analysis. The data to be analyzed here are taken from the article by

Ashley, Granger, and Schmalensee [1980], an important study that we discussed in detail in Section 8.3.

In the subdirectory CHAP8.DAT of your data diskette there is a data file named CAUSAL, containing quarterly observations over the 1956:1–1975:4 time period on a number of variables for the U.S. economy. There are two sets of variables; in this exercise, only the first set is employed.

The first set of variables includes the following: Observation number, in year and quarter form YYQ, 561 to 754 (OBSNO); advertising expenditures per capita, current dollars, seasonally adjusted (ADN); real advertising expenditures per capita, 1972 dollars, seasonally adjusted (ADR); total personal consumption expenditures, thousands of current dollars per capita, seasonally adjusted (CTN); real total personal consumption expenditures, thousands of 1972 dollars per capita, seasonally adjusted (CTR); personal consumption expenditures on goods, thousands of current dollars per capita, seasonally adjusted (CGN); real personal consumption expenditures on goods, thousands of 1972 dollars per capita, seasonally adjusted (CGR); total personal consumption expenditures, thousands of current dollars per capita, not seasonally adjusted (UCTN); and personal consumption expenditures on goods, thousands of current dollars per capita, not seasonally adjusted (UCGN). Note that the two advertising series and all but the last two consumption series involve seasonally adjusted data.

For the remainder of this exercise, choose one advertising series (real or nominal advertising, ADR or ADN) and one corresponding real or nominal consumption series (one of CTR or CGR if you chose ADR or one of CTN, CGN, UCTN or UCGN if you chose ADN). If you wish to attempt to replicate Ashley et al. [1980], choose ADN and UCGN. In this exercise you will relate your two data series using time-series techniques. The first 60 observations are used for estimation, and the remaining 20 are reserved for forecasting.

Note 1: In preparing this exercise we noticed that when moving average specifications are estimated, various software programs often give different results based on identical data. In some cases these differences are substantial. We conjecture that such differences are due in large part to differences in backcasting procedures used in the various programs to initialize the out-of-sample lagged residuals. An implication of this is that you might find it difficult to replicate Ashley et al.'s findings. Check with your instructor regarding which software program currently best handles these time series computational nuances.

Note 2: When estimating various ARIMA models in this exercise, use as many as possible of the first 60 observations. This means dropping observations at the beginning of the sample in order to account for any differencing of the data and for the degree of the AR process. It is not necessary to drop observations for the MA process.

(a) Begin by taking natural logarithms of your advertising and your consumption variables for the entire 1956:1–1975:4 time period. (Hereafter any reference in this exercise to an advertising or consumption variable assumes that the variable has been logarithmically transformed.) Following Ashley et al., first estimate univariate ARIMA models and thereby obtain "prewhitened" data series as residuals from these ARIMA estimations. Specifically, using only the data for the first 60 observations, 1956:1–1970:4, check for stationarity of your two data series, and difference the data in each series until stationarity is achieved. (Note that if your data series is not seasonally adjusted, fourth differencing is often also recommended to capture the effects of seasonality.) Print out the autocorrelation and partial autocorrelation functions of your stationary data series; and on the basis of these printouts, choose several ARIMA specifications for further examination. Estimate these various ARIMA models for each data series, and choose a preferred specification. Check that the residuals from these regressions are close to "white noise." If you are replicating Ashley et al., the preferred specifications should be reasonably close to results reproduced in Eqs. (8.47) and (8.48).

(b) Now use these residuals to investigate causality. In particular, take the residuals from the preferred advertising specification and the preferred consumption specification, and construct a cross-correlogram between them, as in Eq. (8.25). On the basis of these cross correlations, does it appear that advertising causes consumption or that consumption causes advertising? Why? (If you are replicating Ashley et al., your correlations should be reasonably close to those reproduced underneath Eq. (8.49).) Then employ ARIMA techniques and the causality information found in the cross-correlogram and regress the residual of the Y equation on the residual of the X equation, where X is thought to Granger-cause Y. If you are replicating Ashley et al., this involves an ARIMA equation in which the residual from the advertising equation in part (a) is regressed on the once-lagged residual from the consumption equation in part (a), with no constant but allowing for an AR(1) disturbance process. Check the residuals from this double residual regression to ensure that they are close to "white noise."

(c) Next, return to the original data series and reassess causality. The information that you obtained in parts (a) and (b) should suggest forms for the relationship between the original (not the residual) advertising and consumption data series. In time series analysis this is often called the final form, and in cases in which X Granger-causes Y, it involves a bivariate transfer function in which Y is some function of X. Estimate an implied final form for the advertising equation, and then reestimate, deleting insignificant terms. (The procedure employed by Ashley et al. was to retain terms having t-values greater than one in absolute value.) If you are replicating Ashley et al., you might end up with something like Eq. (8.49) for the advertising equation. However, in preparing this exercise we found a more preferable specification involved a constant and a once-lagged, first-differenced transform of UCG as regressors, with an MA(5) error process. Then estimate an implied final form for the consumption equation, and reestimate, deleting insignificant terms. Since Ashley et al. found that causation was unidirectional from consumption to advertising, but not the reverse, their final form for the consumption equation was the univariate equation (8.47), whereas the transfer function for the advertising equation turned out to be the bivariate equation (8.49).

(d) Following Ashley et al. and assuming that you have found that X Granger-causes Y, but not the reverse, now estimate a bivariate transfer function equation for the X equation. If you are replicating Ashley et al., this involves estimating parameters of the bivariate equation (8.50).

(e) Finally, compare the forecasting properties of the univariate and bivariate specifications and determine whether forecasting properties conform to in-sample estimation results. In particular, using the preferred univariate specification for advertising obtained in part (a) and the preferred bivariate specification "explaining" advertising from part (c) or (d), follow Ashley et al. and construct two distinct series of advertising forecasts for the 1971:1–1975:4 time period (use actual values of the right-hand variables), one univariate and the other bivariate. Then compute mean squared errors of these two forecast series and compare them. Does adding lagged consumption help forecast advertising? Why or why not? Similarly, using the preferred univariate specification for consumption obtained in part (a) and the preferred bivariate specification "explaining" consumption from part (c) or (d), generate two distinct series of consumption forecasts for the 1971:1–1975:4 time span. Then compute mean squared errors of these two forecast series, and compare them. Does adding lagged advertising help forecast consumption? In terms of these four forecasts, does advertising cause consumption, does consumption cause advertising, or is causation bidirectional? Why? Do these forecasting results conform with your estimation results obtained in part (b)? Why or why not?

EXERCISE 6: Estimating A Simultaneous Equations Model of Aggregate Sales and Aggregate Advertising

The purpose of this exercise is to help you gain experience in uncovering and dealing with simultaneous equations biases when estimating sales-advertising models. More specifically, in this exercise you will employ OLS and 2SLS estimation techniques with and without first-order autocorrelation. You will also implement the Hausman specification test to examine the nature of interactions between aggregate sales and aggregate advertising in the U.S. economy, using an updated and somewhat revised data set that was initially examined by Schmalensee [1972].

In the subdirectory CHAP8.DAT of your data diskette there is a data file named CAUSAL, containing quarterly observations over the 1956:1–1975:4 time period on a number of variables for the U.S. economy. The variables are incorporated in two records. From the first record in CAUSAL, variables to be used in this exercise include observation number, year and quarter, 561 to 754 (OBSNO); real advertising expenditures per capita, 1972 dollars, seasonally adjusted (ADR); real total personal consumption expenditures, thousands of 1972 dollars per capita, seasonally adjusted (CTR); real personal consumption expenditures on goods, thousands of 1972 dollars per capita, seasonally adjusted (CGR); and, real disposable income, thousands of dollars per capita, seasonally adjusted (YPCR).

Variables in the second record of CAUSAL include several exogenous variables that you can use in doing instrumental variable estimation. These variables include real U.S. government defense spending on goods and services in 1972 dollars per capita, seasonally adjusted (GOVDEFR); real U.S. government nondefense spending on goods and services in 1972 dollars per capita, seasonally adjusted (GNONDEFR); real exports from the United States in 1972 dollars per capita, seasonally adjusted (EXPORTR); U.S. resident population, in thousands (POPN); and the Moody AAA bond yield, annual rate in percentage points (MOODY). The data file CAUSAL also contains other variables, which you will most likely not use in this exercise. Further details on all variables in CAUSAL are found in the README.DOC file in the subdirectory CHAP8.DAT.

Note: The quarterly data in CAUSAL cover the 1956:1–1975:4 time period, whereas the Schmalensee [1972] study used an earlier version of data for a shorter time period, covering 1956:1 to 1967:4.

(a) As in Schmalensee [1972, Chapter 3], begin by estimating with OLS a simple consumption function equation from 1956:2 to 1967:3 where real goods consumption per capita CGR_t is the dependent variable and the regressors include a constant, real per capita disposable income, YPCR_t; the lagged dependent variable, CGR_{t-1}; and lagged real advertising per capita, ADR_{t-1}. Then do the same regression, but replace the lagged ADR_{t-1} with current ADR_t. Finally, do this regression again but employ as the advertising regressor ADR_{t+1}. If advertising "caused" consumption, what pattern would you expect to observe in these three regressions on the coefficient of advertising ? Why? What if instead consumption "caused" advertising? What do you observe, and how do you interpret this pattern? Is this consistent with the findings reported by Schmalensee, discussed in Section 8.3?

(b) As Schmalensee noted, there are many problems with the OLS regression in part (a). One problem, that concerning the endogeneity of YPCR, can be checked by using the Hausman specification test. Recall that according to national income accounting conventions, consumption is a component of gross national product (GNP). In turn, disposable income is determined in large part by GNP and is very highly correlated with it. It is therefore reasonable to expect that the regressor YPCR is correlated with the disturbance term in the equation in part (a), implying that OLS yields inconsistent estimates of the parameters. To check on whether this correlation exists, do three Hausman specification tests as follows: (i) Using OLS and data from 1956:2–1967:4, regress $YPCR_t$ on a constant, CGR_{t-1}, ADR_{t-1}, and several other exogenous variables, such as real U.S. government defense ($GOVDEFR_t$) and nondefense ($GNONDEFR_t$) spending, real U.S. exports ($EXPORTR_t$), the Moody AAA bond yield ($MOODY_t$), and U.S. resident population (POPN). Retrieve the fitted value from this first-stage regression and call it $YPCRFIT1_t$. Now redo the first regression in part (a) but add $YPCRFIT1_t$ as a regressor. Test the null hypothesis that YPCR is uncorrelated with the disturbance term by examining the t-statistic on the estimated coefficient of the $YPCRFIT1_t$ regressor. (Use a critical value from the normal table, since the Hausman test is a large-sample test.) (ii) Next, form a fitted value variable when ADR_t rather than ADR_{t-1} is the regressor. In particular, run the same first-stage regression as you did in step (i), but replace ADR_{t-1} with ADR_t, and then retrieve the fitted value and call it $YPCRFIT2_t$. Adding $YPCRFIT2_t$ to the second equation estimated in part (a), run an expanded regression and perform the Hausman test procedure. (iii) Finally, form $YPCRFIT3_t$ as the fitted value from the OLS first-stage equation in which ADR_{t+1}, rather than ADR_{t-1} or ADR_t, is one of the regressors. Then do the second-stage regression as in steps (i) and (ii), but include $YPCRFIT3_t$ as a regressor. Test the null hypothesis that $YPCR_t$ and the disturbance term are uncorrelated by using the Hausman procedure, as in step (i). What do you conclude concerning the validity of this null hypothesis in the three regressions? Does estimation by OLS introduce a significant simultaneous equations bias? Why or why not?

(c) Now examine the robustness of the results obtained in part (a) when endogeneity of YPCR is accommodated. Since the Hausman test suggests a simultaneous equations problem, reestimate the three equations in part (a) over the 1956:2–1967:3 time period by two-stage least squares (2SLS) treating $YPCR_t$ as endogenous, where the first-stage regressions use as instruments a constant, CGR_{t-1}, ADR_{t-1} (or ADR_t or ADR_{t+1}, depending on which advertising variable is a regressor in the second stage), $GOVDEFR_t$, $GNONDEFR_t$, $EXPORTR_t$, $MOODY_t$, and $POPN_t$. Compare the values and t-statistics of the estimated coefficients on the advertising variable in the three 2SLS regressions. You should find that the pattern observed in part (a) emerges again, although the t-statistic on ADR_t is now even larger and more significant than with the OLS regression in part (a). Why could this result suggest that ADR_t might also be an endogenous variable, simultaneously determined with CGR_t?

(d) If both ADR and YPCR are endogenous variables correlated with the disturbance term in part (a), a different 2SLS procedure is required to ensure consistent parameter estimates. Therefore, as in part (c), reestimate the three equations in part (a) by 2SLS, but now treat *both* YPCR_t and ADR_{t-1} (or ADR_t or ADR_{t+1}, depending on which advertising variable is a regressor in the second stage) as endogenous. Employ the same instruments as in part (c). Compare the values and *t*-statistics of the estimated coefficients on the advertising variable in these three 2SLS regressions. You should now uncover a different pattern, in which the coefficients on ADR_{t-1} and ADR_t are insignificant, but that on ADR_{t+1} remains significant at the 5% level of confidence. Is this what you find? Interpret these results. Do you agree with Schmalensee, who concluded that the evidence suggested that consumption "causes" advertising but advertising does not "cause" consumption in the aggregate?

(e) Finally, check further on the validity of the stochastic specification that is implicit in the above computations. In particular, employing a generalized least squares procedure that allows for a first-order autoregressive process, use instrumental variables and reestimate the three equations in part (d).[67] How large is the value of the estimated autocorrelation coefficient in the three regressions? Is it statistically significant? What pattern do you find on the estimated coefficients of the advertising variable in the three equations? What do you conclude concerning simultaneity or "causality" between advertising and consumption?

(f) *Optional:* The data used in this exercise, 1956:2–1967:3, are only a portion of the data set, which continues through 1975:4. Choose a different sample, and redo parts (a) through (e) to determine the robustness of Schmalensee's classic findings.

EXERCISE 7: Evaluating the Effects of the Cigarette Broadcast Ban

The purpose of this exercise is to help you understand more completely the empirical findings reported by Schneider, Klein, and Murphy [1981] concerning the apparent ineffectiveness of the 1971 broadcast ban on cigarette advertising in the United States. As was noted in Section 8.5, Schneider et al.'s findings are controversial, and so it is particularly appropriate that we take advantage of the opportunity to examine them in detail. Incidentally, this exercise is a challenging and exciting one, and it could involve various teams within a class, particularly for part (f).

In your data diskette subdirectory CHAP8.DAT there is a data file called CIGAD containing 1930–1978 annual observations on two sets of variables used in the Schneider et al. study..The first set includes year (YEAR); cigarette consumption in millions of cigarettes (SALES); cigarette consumption per capita, population 14 and over (SALESPC); real per capita income, total population (INCPC); real cigarette price, defined as the CPI (consumer price index) for tobacco divided by the CPI for all commodities (RPRICE); the percentage of total tobacco consumed by cigarette consumption (CIGTOB); tobacco consumption per capita in pounds, population 14 and over (TOBPC); the real price of tobacco, defined as the CPI for tobacco divided by the CPI for all commodities (PRTOB); a standardized dummy variable for the effects of the Fairness Doctrine, where standardization accounts for the number of antismoking commercials aired (DF); and the stock of advertising (ASTOCK).

The second set of variables in CIGAD includes year minus 1900 (TIME); nominal advertising expenditures (ADV); tobacco advertising expenditures (TOBADV); real advertising expenditures (REALAD); tobacco per cigarette, in pounds (TPERCIG); the advertising stock before the broadcast ban (ASTOCK1); the advertising stock after the broadcast ban (ASTOCK2); the market share of filter cigarettes (F); the market share of low-tar cigarettes with 15 mg of tar or less (L); and the logarithm of the predicted value of the income instrument regression (8.61) (LNI). Further details on these variables are given in the README.DOC file of the CHAP8.DAT subdirectory and in the references cited therein.

(a) Schneider et al. argue that a simple estimated demand for cigarettes equation such as Eq. (8.60) is unacceptable, owing in part to the high income elasticity. Using 1930–1978 data in CIGAD, construct natural logarithms for SALESPC, INCPC, RPRICE, and ASTOCK; call these variables LSALESPC, LINCPC, LRPRICE, and LASTOCK, respectively. Then construct a dummy variable D53 that takes on the value of 1 for 1953–1978, otherwise zero; and D64, which is 1 from 1964 through 1978, otherwise zero. Using OLS regression and data only through 1970, estimate parameters of Eq. (8.60) and replicate Schneider et al.'s results. Interpret coefficients on the dummy variables, noting the health effect information that they represent. Comment on the statistical significance of other parameter estimates. Given these parameter estimates and values of the 1971–1978 exogenous variables, follow Schneider et al. and forecast LSALESPC for 1971–1978. Exponentiate your forecasts, and then compare the forecasts in 1978 with the actual sales. Is your forecast in 1978 about 78% higher than the actual, as Schneider et al. report?

(b) Schneider et al. then estimate an equation identical to Eq. (8.60) over the entire 1930–1978 time period but add a dummy variable D71 to capture the effects of the cigarette advertising broadcast ban; D71 is 1 in years 1971–1978, otherwise zero. Using OLS, follow Schneider et al. and estimate such an equation. Do your results match those of Schneider et al., who report that several parameter estimates become meaningless, that the income elasticity estimate is now much too large, and that the estimated model is unstable?

(c) The large income elasticity estimate is particularly troubling to Schneider et al., as are several other aspects of the equation estimated in parts (a) and (b). Refresh your memory by rereading the material in Section 8.5 following Eq. (8.60). To account for the impact of self-rolled cigarettes, Schneider et al. estimated Eq. (8.61) and then suggested using the fitted value from this regression as a regressor in a cigarette demand equation. Comment on the appropriateness of this procedure. Do you agree with Schneider et al. that the coefficient on this variable should be unity? Why or why not? With the log of CIGTOB (the proportion of total tobacco consumption accounted for by cigarette consumption) as dependent variable and with INCPC as the measure of y_{mt} in Eq. (8.61), use nonlinear least squares and replicate the Schneider et al. results reproduced underneath Eq. (8.61). (*Notes:* This is a highly nonlinear model, and estimation may be much affected by your choice of starting values for the parameters α and y_c. Also, though Schneider et al. report using data for 1925–1978 (not 1930–1978) and indicate y_{mt} is the mean real disposable personal income, in preparing this exercise we have found that we are able to replicate their y_c estimate of \$551 (and t-value of 32.66) using 1930–1978 data and INCPC as a measure of y_{mt}. However, our estimated intercept is 4.575 (t-value of 251.69), not the −0.0299 reported by Schneider et al.)

(d) The fitted value from the nonlinear regression in part (c) is denoted LNI and is found in your data file CIGAD. Schneider et al. initially hoped that use of this variable would yield more sensible income elasticity estimates. Given your 1930–1978 data, what is the correlation between LNI and LINCPC? What do you think this implies for use of both LNI and LINCPC in a regression equation? An alternative procedure that might possibly yield smaller income elasticity estimates, particularly in the later years of the sample, would involve adding $(\text{LINCPC})^2$ as a regressor in the equation estimated in part (b). Construct such a variable, call it LINCPC2, compute simple correlations between LINCPC, LINCPC2, and LNI, and then estimate by OLS an equation identical to that in part (b) but with LINCPC2 added as a regressor. Compute and print out the implied income elasticity estimates. (Note that this elasticity, or logarithmic derivative, now depends on the level of LINCPC.) Compare this equation to that estimated in part (b). Which do you prefer, and why?

(e) If the effect of the cigarette advertising broadcast ban in 1971 made advertising expenditures by the cigarette industry less "productive," then the advertising stock consisting of post-1971 expenditures should be distinguished from that of pre-1971 expenditures in a cigarette demand equation. To do this, Schneider et al. constructed pre- and post-1971 advertising stock estimates (assuming a common annual depreciation rate of 33%) called ASTOCK1 and ASTOCK2, respectively, and then they let log (ASTOCK1 + r*ASTOCK2) be a regressor, where they expected $0 < r < 1$. In addition, as seen in Eq. (8.62), they inserted other variables, such as the market shares of filter (F) and low-tar (L) cigarettes as regressors.

To interpret Schneider et al.'s findings, first estimate Eq. (8.62) without imposing the constraint that the income elasticity equals 0.462; that is, add LINCPC as a regressor on the right-hand side of Eq. (8.62), and have ln C be the dependent variable. (*Notes:* This is also a nonlinear regression, and starting values could be important. We suggest using as starting values the parameter estimates reported in Eq. (8.62) and 0.462 as the starting value for the income elasticity parameter. Although we experienced some problems in obtaining convergence, we were able to estimate this equation and obtained an income elasticity estimate of 1.1024, with a standard error of 0.372.) Does your estimate of the income elasticity agree with this? What is your estimate of r, and how precise an estimate is it? Interpret this result. Then estimate Eq. (8.62) with the 0.462 income elasticity constraint imposed. (An easy way to do this is to redefine the dependent variable, as in Eq. (8.62).) Can you replicate Schneider et al.'s results? (We have been able to come quite close but have not been able to replicate their results exactly.) Compare results from these two specifications, noting in particular the sensitivity of the parameter estimate on the LNI variable and on the health information variables. Comment on the estimated impact of advertising on cigarette consumption. Schneider et al. conclude that the broadcast ban was ineffective and that to the extent that it made advertising less productive, advertising expenditures were reduced, resulting in lower cigarette prices, which in turn stimulated cigarette demand because of the large price elasticity estimate. Do you agree with these conclusions? Why or why not?

(f) There are numerous potential problems with the Schneider et al. specification. Develop arguments for alternative specifications, and then experiment empirically with them, assessing whether Schneider et al.'s finding that the broadcast ban was ineffective is robust. Note that there are some additional variables in the CIGAD data file that were not used by Schneider et al. Here are several ideas to set you thinking: (i) Schneider et al. treat the market shares of filter (F) and low-tar (L) as exogenous, whereas they might well be endogenous. Why? How about estimating separate demand equations for nonfilter (1930–1978) and filter (say, 1955–1978) cigarettes? Or you might estimate a logistic function in which log $(F/1 - F)$ is the dependent variable, using 1955–1978 data. Are all low-tar cigarettes also filter cigarettes? (ii) Schneider et al. always use the advertising stock as an explanatory variable, assuming a 0.33 annual depreciation rate. Several advertising variables are available in your data file, and you might construct and then experiment with an alternative advertising stock series. Or you might simply assume that the 90% duration interval is less than a year and therefore have only current real advertising as a regressor. But if you do this, what would you do concerning the potential endogeneity of current advertising?

EXERCISE 8: Distinguishing the Sales Effects of Advertising Quality and Advertising Quantity

The purpose of this exercise is to give you experience in distinguishing empirically the effects on sales of advertising quality from those of advertising quantity. Econometric techniques that you will employ in this exercise include ordinary least squares, generalized least squares, and a pooled cross-sectional, time series estimation procedure. The data for this study are 54 bimonthly observations from September/October 1973 to July/August 1982 for five regions within Canada, used by Arnold, Oum, Pazderka and Snetsinger in their 1987 hedonic study of advertising quality and quantity. We discussed this article in detail near the end of Section 8.4.

In your data diskette subdirectory CHAP8.DAT there is a data file called QUAL, containing three records of data as follows. In the first record the first variable is the observation number, beginning with 1 and ending with 54 (OBSNO). This is followed by the log of the copy creative device, a measure of advertising quality (LQUAL), the log of sales in 1971 dollars for regions 1–5 (LY1–LY5), a dummy variable for a product change (DMR), and dummy variables for January/February (PJF) and November/December (PND). In the second record, variables include the observation number (OBSN) and the log of the real price—a nominal price divided by a regional consumer price index—for each of the five regions (LPR1–LPR5). In the third and final record, variables include the observation number (OBS) and the log of real advertising in each of the five regions (LADR1–LADR5).

(a) Begin by examining the data. Print out the data series for LY1–LY5, LPR1–LPR5, LADR1–LADR5, and LQUAL. Is there much variation within regions over time in LY? What about the between-region variance in LPR? Something curious seems to have happened to LADR in observations 30–32 (July/August 1978 to November/December 1978) in several of the regions. What might account for this? How might this affect results from estimation? Is there much variation in the sample in LQUAL, the advertising quality variable constructed from experts' judgments?

(b) Now proceed with region-specific estimation. Using observations 2 through 54, run five OLS regressions of LY_{it} on a constant, $LY_{i,t-1}$, LPR_{it}, $LADR_{it}$, $LQUAL_t$, DMR_t, PJF_t, and PND_t, for $i = 1, \ldots, 5$, as in Eq. (8.59a). Interpret the parameter estimates. Using Eq. (8.59), construct implied estimates of the long-run elasticities. Do results appear to differ significantly across regions? Does advertising quality have a distinguishable impact on sales? Why or why not?

(c) Next, allow for first-order autocorrelation. Specifically, using observations 3 through 54, do five regressions as in part (b), but now employ a generalized least squares procedure such as the Hildreth-Lu grid search algorithm. (*Note:* In preparing this exercise we found that in some regions, negative values of the estimated first order autocorrelation coefficient may emerge. To permit this, make sure your GLS software allows for negative values.) Is autocorrelation statistically significant? How are your results in part (b) affected by autocorrelation?

(d) Arnold et al.'s preferred results are based on a regression in which all coefficients except the intercept term are constrained to be equal across the five regions. The stochastic specification underlying their estimation allows for cross-sectional heteroskedasticity across regions and first-order autocorrelation within regions, as described by Kmenta [1986, pp. 622–625]. Using this cross-sectionally heteroskedastic and timewise autoregressive stochastic specification, estimate such a model for observations 3–54. How well do your results correspond to those reported by Arnold et al., which are reproduced at the end of Section 8.4? Is advertising quality distinguishable from advertising quantity? Why or why not?

(e) In part (a) of this exercise you found that in certain observations the advertising outlays equaled zero. To allow for the possibility that these might be outlier observations, reestimate part (d) with these observations omitted from all regions. Are your results substantially affected? Interpret your findings.

CHAPTER NOTES

1. Quotation taken from Philip Kotler [1988], p. 617.
2. Advertising outlays are defined here as all expenditures by U.S. advertisers—including those at the national, local, and individual levels.
3. There is some controversy in interpreting trends in the ratio of measured advertising outlays to GNP. For discussions of measurement issues concerning this historical relationship, see David M. Blank [1963] and Kenneth H. Myers [1959].
4. See Frederic Wakeman [1946] and Vance Packard [1957], respectively. For careful reviews and analyses of issues raised by Wakeman, Packard, and others concerning the social effects of advertising, see William Leiss, Stephen Kline, and Sut Jhally [1986] and Michael Schudson [1984].
5. Also see Galbraith [1958].
6. Hansen [1960, pp. 36–37] and Ackley [1961], p. 268.
7. See Abba P. Lerner [1934].
8. Notice that in Eq. (8.6) it is net marginal revenue, not marginal revenue, that is set equal to marginal cost. Setting marginal revenue equal to marginal cost would ignore the effect of M on costs.
9. An alternative derivation that employs dynamic optimization, yet yields similar results, is found in Alain V. Bultez and Philippe A. Naert [1979].
10. For a static oligopolistic model in which advertising is endogenous but output pricing or quantity is not, see Richard Schmalensee [1976]. Dynamic issues, including the existence of a unique equilibrium in a model with both output and advertising endogenous, are considered by James W. Friedman [1983].
11. See Marc Nerlove and Frederick V. Waugh [1961], who consider an interesting intermediate case in which firms jointly determine advertising outlays (e.g.,

through a trade association) but then act independently in choosing output levels for their homogenous product.

12. Implications for industry equilibrium in this oligopolistic model of firm behavior are outlined in Schmalensee [1972, pp. 34–39]. For a pioneering empirical study of reaction functions in an oligopoly context, see Jean-Jacques Lambin, Philippe A. Naert, and Alain Bultez [1975].
13. For an analysis of dynamic relationships in a duopoly, see the simulations reported by Julian L. Simon and Joseph Ben-Ur [1982].
14. See, for example, Joseph C. Stevens [1968].
15. Some of these issues have been discussed in an early paper describing both the satisfactions and frustrations of one econometrician in initially estimating advertising-sales models; see Richard E. Quandt [1964]. For a discussion of how econometric models have been employed in actual marketing situations, see Frank M. Bass [1980].
16. These figures are taken from *Advertising Age* [1989], p. 24, based on information supplied by McCann-Erickson.
17. For more detailed information on this and related marketing research, see a marketing textbook; several well-known ones are noted at the end of this chapter under the heading "Further Reading."
18. See, for example, Lester Telser [1962] and the classic study by Kristian S. Palda [1964], especially Chapter 4. It is worth noting that in Telser's study, a time trend variable was added, in part to reduce the grosser effects of not deflating.
19. There is precedent. As was discussed in Chapter 4 of this book, until 1986 the U.S. Department of Commerce implicitly assumed that the price index for computers had remained constant at 1.00 since World War II. That agency now uses hedonic price indexes to adjust for quality changes in computers over time. Later in this chapter (in Section 8.4), we discuss how hedonic methods might be employed in the advertising context.
20. Richard Ashley et al. [1980, fn. 6, p. 1150].
21. One major effort is that by the Marketing Science Institute (MSI), a nonprofit center for research in marketing with member companies coming from a wide variety of consumer and industrial product and service businesses. MSI is an organization that attempts to bring together the interests and resources of industry and academia to address important marketing issues. MSI is currently in the process of developing a series of data bases from commercial sources that could be used by full-time academics for scholarly research on the effects of advertising and other market mix variables. MSI is located at 1000 Massachusetts Avenue, Cambridge, MA 02138, phone 617-491-2060.
22. In addition to the previously cited studies by Quandt [1964] and Schmalensee [1972], see, for example, Frank M. Bass and Leonard J. Parsons [1969].
23. Note that large sample theory must also be employed in doing inference in models nonlinear in the parameters. For a discussion of inference with instrumental variable estimators, see Kimio Morimune [1989].
24. Note that to employ the ILS estimator in an overidentified context, some of the overidentifying restrictions must arbitrarily be ignored. For further discussion, see the simultaneous equations chapters in your econometric theory textbook. One of the earliest textbook discussions of relationships among ILS, IV, and 2SLS estimators is found in Arthur S. Goldberger [1964, Chapter 7].
25. Jerry A. Hausman [1978]. Hausman's test builds on earlier work by James Durbin [1954] and De-Min Wu [1973].
26. A useful discussion of causality is that by Arnold Zellner [1979]; also see the spe-

cial issue of the *Journal of Econometrics* on causality edited by Dennis J. Aigner and Arnold Zellner [1988].

27. See Clive W. J. Granger [1969].
28. These three problems, as well as several others, were first discussed in the money-interest rate context by David A. Pierce [1977].
29. Such a variable could represent technological developments, such as the revolution in information technology. For a more general discussion, see Christopher A. Sims [1977].
30. See Nicholas Davies, C. M. Triggs, and Paul Newbold [1977].
31. In private correspondence, Lester Telser has informed me that in his 1962 study on advertising and cigarettes, the quantitative effect of this consistency problem turns out to be rather minor. In particular, the sum of predicted market shares for Camels, Lucky Strikes, and Chesterfield varies from a low of 0.9846 in 1934 to a high of 1.0291 in 1930. It is worth noting, however, that there is no reason for one to expect the consistency problem always to be so small in empirical magnitude.
32. See Leendert M. Koyck [1954].
33. Specific references are also given in Chapters 6 (Section 6.7.C), 7 (Section 7.3), and 10 (Section 10.3) of this book.
34. See, for example, David B. Montgomery and Alvin J. Silk [1972], Doyle L. Weiss, Franklin S. Houston, and Pierre Windal [1978], and Russel S. Winer [1979].
35. This literature is vast; for surveys, see, among others, Darral G. Clarke [1976], Norman K. Dhalla [1978], and Robert P. Leone and Randall L. Schultz [1980].
36. Clarke [1976, p. 353].
37. Clarke [1976, p. 355].
38. The meta-analysis methodology is described in further detail in John U. Farley and Donald R. Lehmann [1986].
39. Actually, Assmus et al. employ analysis-of-variance techniques, which are equivalent to dummy variable procedures. The number of regressors employed is reduced by using principal components methods. See Farley and Lehmann [1986] for further details.
40. A classic study in this context is by David M. Blank [1962]. For surveys of this literature, see Julian Simon [1970, pp. 67–74] and Richard Schmalensee [1972, pp. 17–18].
41. For further discussion, see Schmalensee [1972, Appendix A, "Advertising Price Indices," pp. 245–264.].
42. Taylor and Weiserbs [1972, p. 642].
43. The state-adjustment model is developed in Hendrik S. Houthakker and Lester D. Taylor [1970], especially pp. 281–293.
44. Recall that with 2SLS, in some cases, standard errors do not even exist, and at best one should use large sample inference.
45. Interestingly, when Schmalensee [1972, pp. 52–58] estimated a Houthakker-Taylor consumption goods state-adjustment model analogous to Eq. (8.45) by OLS using quarterly data, the coefficients on a_{t-1}, a_t, and a_{t+1} were each statistically insignificant; with 2SLS and advertising endogenous, only the a_{t+1} coefficient was significant, again suggesting causality from consumption to advertising rather than from advertising to consumption.
46. It is worth noting, however, that a U.K. study by Keith Cowling, John Cable, Michael Kelly, and Tony McGuinness [1975, Chapter 9] based on quarterly aggregate U.K. data, 1956:1–1966:4, reports results that are somewhat similar to those of Taylor and Weiserbs in that advertising is found to have a significant effect on aggregate consumption, using both OLS and 2SLS estimation procedures. In a

Canadian study by Eben Otuteye and Kristian S. Palda [1987] based on annual data, 1952–1985, results that are slightly less favorable to Taylor and Weiserbs and more in line with Schmalensee are reported, although some evidence of simultaneous feedback is obtained.

47. On this, see Christopher A. Sims [1974] and Kenneth F. Wallis [1974].
48. The $(1 - B)$ term on the left-hand side of Eq. (8.47) indicates that $UCGN_t$ was first-differenced prior to estimation, while the B^2 and B^4 terms refer to parameters of the second- and fourth-order moving average process.
49. Actually, the univariate model used for consumption was slightly different from Eq. (8.47), since a bivariate software program was employed that used an alternative computational algorithm. The results were virtually identical, however. For further discussion, see Ashley et al. [1980, pp. 1161–1162.].
50. The history of the Lydia Pinkham company is a most fascinating one. For an overview, see Palda [1964, Chapter 3] and the references cited therein.
51. See Palda [1964, pp. 60–69]. It appears that Palda inappropriately omitted transforming the constant vector, as well as the dummy variable vectors, by his 0.37 estimate of ρ. For a correct transformation, see Montgomery and Silk [1972].
52. Roberts [1947], p. 133.
53. For a review and interpretation of some of this literature, see Darral G. Clarke [1973] and Dominique M. Hanssens, Leonard J. Parsons, and Randall L. Schultz [1990].
54. This paper also provides references to the large number of other studies that have examined quality issues.
55. Although the multiplicative specification is useful, it is not the only one that might be employed. For alternatives, see the experimental study by Joseph O. Eastlack and Amber G. Rao [1986].
56. This is the cross-sectionally heteroskedastic and timewise autoregressive model described by Kmenta [1986, pp. 622–625].
57. Issues in determining what amount of quality is optimal and how long an ad agency should search before choosing advertising copy have been considered by Simeon Chow and Alvin J. Silk [1988].
58. Schneider et al. find that in their tobacco demand equation, both F and L are negative and highly significant. Hence F and L might have had more of an impact on tobacco consumption than on cigarette consumption, by reducing tobacco consumption per cigarette.
59. For a relatively recent discussion, along with interesting historical examples, see *Consumer Reports* [1987].
60. A related literature on optimal advertising is based on specifications of diffusion processes. In this context, see, for example, studies by Dan Horsky [1977], Horsky and Leonard S. Simon [1983], Gerald L. Thompson and Jinn-Tsair Teng [1984], Shlomo Kalish [1985], and Ram C. Rao [1986].
61. For a brief overview, see Schmalensee [1987].
62. See, for example, Robert Ayanian [1983], William S. Comanor and Thomas A. Wilson [1967, 1979], James M. Ferguson [1974], George J. Stigler [1968], and Lester G. Telser [1964, 1969]. A review of the theoretical and empirical literature concerning interactions between pricing and advertising behavior is found in Paul W. Farris and Mark S. Albion [1980] and in the comment by James M. Ferguson [1982]; a recent empirical study is that by Lakshman Krishnamurthi and S. P. Raj

[1985]. Another strand of literature relates stock returns to advertising capital; see, for example, Harry Bloch [1974] and Mark Hirschey [1982]. Simultaneous equations problems abound in all this literature. For a useful discussion, see Stephen Martin [1979] and the references cited therein.

63. See studies by Julian L. Simon [1969] and Kenneth D. Boyer and Kent M. Lancaster [1986] and the references cited therein.
64. This and other size-related issues are considered by William S. Comanor and Thomas A. Wilson [1969].
65. Applications of discrete choice models to statistical marketing research are the focus of several articles in a special issue of *Marketing Science* [1986].
66. Parameter estimates and standard errors that you obtain (in the same order as in Eq. (8.54), with standard errors in parentheses) should be about 254.64 (96.308), 0.607 (0.081), 0.534 (0.136), −133.35 (88.96), 216.84 (67.22), and −202.50 (67.06); the R^2 is 0.929.
67. Care should be taken in choosing the list of instruments. For discussion, see Ray C. Fair [1970].

CHAPTER REFERENCES

Aaker, David A. and James M. Carman [1982], "Are You Overadvertising?" *Journal of Advertising Research*, 22:4, August/September, 57–70.

Ackley, Gardner M. [1961], *Macroeconomic Theory*, New York: Macmillan.

Advertising Age [1989], "US Advertising Volume," 60, May 15.

Aigner, Dennis J. and Arnold Zellner, ed. [1988], "Special Issue on Causality," *Journal of Econometrics*, 39:1/2, September/October.

Arnold, Stephen J., Tae H. Oum, Bohumir Pazderka, and Douglas W. Snetsinger [1987], "Advertising Quality in Sales Response Models," *Journal of Marketing Research*, 24:1, February, 106–113.

Ashley, Richard, Clive W. J. Granger, and Richard Schmalensee [1980], "Advertising and Aggregate Consumption: An Analysis of Causality," *Econometrica*, 48:5, July, 1149–1168.

Assmus, Gert, John U. Farley, and Donald R. Lehmann [1984], "How Advertising Affects Sales: Meta-Analysis of Econometric Results," *Journal of Marketing Research*, 21:1, February, 65–74.

Ayanian, Robert [1983], "The Advertising Capital Controversy," *Journal of Business*, 56:3, July, 349–364.

Bain, Joseph [1956], *Barriers to New Competition*, Cambridge, Mass.: Harvard University Press.

Bain, Joseph [1968], *Industrial Organization*, Second Edition, New York: John Wiley and Sons.

Basmann, Robert L. [1956], "A Theory of Demand with Variable Consumer Preferences," *Econometrica*, 24:1, January, 47–58.

Bass, Frank M. [1980], "Some Case Histories of Econometric Modeling in Marketing: What Really Happened," *Interfaces*, 10:1, February, 86–90.

Bass, Frank M. and Robert P. Leone [1983], "Temporal Aggregation, the Data Interval Bias, and Empirical Estimation of Bimonthly Relations from Annual Data," *Management Science*, 29:1, January, 1–11.

Bass, Frank M. and Leonard J. Parsons [1969], "Simultaneous Equation Regression Analysis of Sales and Advertising," *Applied Economics*, 1:2, May, 103–124.

Blank, David M. [1962], "Cyclical Behavior of National Advertising," *Journal of Business*, 35:1, January, 14–27.

Blank, David M. [1963], "A Note on the Golden Age of Advertising," *Journal of Business*, 36:1, January, 33–38.

Bloch, Harry [1974], "Advertising and Profitability: A Reappraisal," *Journal of Political Economy*, 82:2, Part I, March/April, 267–286.

Borden, Neil H. [1942], *The Economic Effects of Advertising*, Chicago: Richard D. Irwin.

Boyer, Kenneth D. and Kent M. Lancaster [1986], "Are There Scale Economies in Advertising?" *Journal of Business*, 59:3, July, 509–526.

Buchanan, Norman S. [1942], "Advertising Expenditures: A Suggested Treatment," *Journal of Political Economy*, 50:4, August, 537–557.

Bultez, Alain V. and Philippe A. Naert [1979], "Does Lag Structure Really Matter in Optimizing Advertising Expenditures?" *Management Science*, 25:5, May, 454–465.

Chamberlin, Edward H. [1933], *The Theory of Monopolistic Competition*, Cambridge, Mass.: Harvard University Press.

Chow, Simeon and Alvin J. Silk [1988], "Advertising Copy Development and Optimal Search," Cambridge, Mass.: Massachusetts Institute of Technology, A. P. Sloan School of Management, Working Paper, March.

Clarke, Darral G. [1973], "Sales-Advertising Cross-Elasticities and Advertising Competition," *Journal of Marketing Research*, 10:3, August, 250–262.

Clarke, Darral G. [1976], "Econometric Measurement of the Duration of Advertising Effects on Sales," *Journal of Marketing Research*, 13:4, November, 345–357.

Clarke, Darral G. and John M. McCann [1973], "Measuring the Cumulative Effects of Advertising: A Reappraisal," in Thomas V. Greer, ed., *1973 Combined Proceedings*, Chicago: American Marketing Association, pp. 135–139.

Comanor, William S. and Thomas A. Wilson [1967], "Advertising Market Structure and Performance," *Review of Economics and Statistics*, 49:4, November, 423–440.

Comanor, William S. and Thomas A. Wilson [1969], "Advertising and the Advantage of Size," *American Economic Review*, 59:2, May, 87–98.

Comanor, William S. and Thomas A. Wilson [1979], "The Effect of Advertising on Competition," *Journal of Economic Literature*, 17:2, June, 453–476.

Consumer Reports [1987], "Ban Cigarette Advertising?" 52:9, September, 565–569.

Cowling, Keith, John Cable, Michael Kelly, and Tony McGuinness [1975], *Advertising and Economic Behaviour*, London: The Macmillan Press, Ltd.

Davies, Nicholas, C. M. Triggs, and Paul Newbold [1977], "Significance Levels of the Box-Pierce Portmanteau Statistic in Finite Samples," *Biometrika*, 64:3, September, 517–522.

Dhalla, Norman K. [1978], "Assessing the Long-term Value of Advertising," *Harvard Business Review*, 56:1, January/February, 87–95.

Dorfman, Robert and Peter O. Steiner [1954], "Optimal Advertising and Optimal Quality," *American Economic Review*, 44:5, December, 826–836.

Durbin, James [1954], "Errors in Variables," *Review of the International Statistical Institute*, 22, 23–32.

Eastlack, Joseph O. and Amber G. Rao [1986], "Modeling Response to Advertising and Pricing Changes for V-8 Vegetable Cocktail Juice," *Marketing Science*, 5:3, Summer, 245–259.

Ekelund, Robert B., Jr., and William P. Gramm [1969], "A Reconsideration of Advertising Expenditures, Aggregate Demand, and Economic Stabilization," *Quarterly Review of Economics and Business*, 9:2, Summer, 71–77.

Fair, Ray C. [1970], "The Estimation of Simultaneous Equation Models with Lagged Endogenous Variables and First Order Serially Correlated Errors," *Econometrica*, 38:3, May, 507–516.

Farley, John U. and Donald R. Lehmann [1986], *Meta-Analysis in Marketing: Generalization of Response Models*, Lexington, Mass.: Lexington Books, D.C. Heath and Company, in cooperation with the Marketing Science Institute.

Farris, Paul W. and Mark S. Albion [1980], "The Impact of Advertising on the Price of Consumer Products," *Journal of Marketing*, 44:3, Summer, 17–35.

Ferguson, James M. [1974], *Advertising and Competition: Theory, Measurement, Facts*, Cambridge, Mass.: Ballinger Publishing Company.

Ferguson, James M. [1982], "Comments on 'The Impact of Advertising on the Price of Consumer Products,'" *Journal of Marketing*, 46:1, Winter, 102–105.

Fisher, Franklin M. and Karl Shell [1968], "Taste and Quality Change in the Pure Theory of the True Cost-of-Living Index," in J. N. Wolfe, ed., *Value, Capital and Growth: Essays in Honour of Sir John Hicks*, Edinburgh: University of Edinburgh Press. Reprinted in Chapter 2 of Zvi Griliches, ed., *Price Indexes and Quality Change*, Cambridge, Mass.: Harvard University Press, 1971, 16–54.

Friedman, James W. [1983], "Advertising and Oligopolistic Equilibrium," *The Bell Journal of Economics*, 14:2, Autumn, 464–473.

Galbraith, John Kenneth [1958], *The Affluent Society*, Boston: Houghton Mifflin.

Galbraith, John Kenneth [1971], *The New Industrial State*, Second Edition, New York: The New American Library, Inc., 1971.

Goldberger, Arthur S. [1964], *Econometric Theory*, New York: John Wiley and Sons.

Granger, Clive W. J. [1969], "Investigating Causal Relations by Econometric Methods and Cross-Spectral Methods," *Econometrica*, 34:4, July, 424–438.

Griliches, Zvi [1967], "Distributed Lags: A Survey," *Econometrica*, 35:1, January, 16–49.

Hansen, Alvin H. [1960], *Economic Issues of the 1960's*, New York: McGraw-Hill.

Hanssens, Dominique M., Leonard J. Parsons, and Randall L. Schultz [1990], *Market Response Models: Econometric and Time Series Analysis*, Norwell, Mass.: Kluwer Academic Publishers.

Hausman, Jerry A. [1978], "Specification Tests in Econometrics," *Econometrica*, 46:6, November, 1251–1272.

Hirschey, Mark [1982], "Intangible Capital Aspects of Advertising and R&D Expenditures," *Journal of Industrial Economics*, 30:4, June, 375–390.

Horsky, Dan [1977], "A Theoretical and Empirical Analysis of the Optimal Advertising Policy," *Management Science*, 23:6, June, 1037–1049.

Horsky, Dan and Leonard S. Simon [1983], "Advertising and the Diffusion of New Products," *Marketing Science*, 2:1, 1–18.

Houston, Franklin S. and Doyle L. Weiss [1975], "Cumulative Advertising Effects: The Role of Serial Correlation," *Decision Sciences*, 6:3, July, 471–481.

Houthakker, Hendrik S. and Lester D. Taylor [1970], *Consumer Demand in the United States*, Second Edition, Cambridge, Mass.: Harvard University Press.

Kaldor, Nicholas [1950–1951], "The Economic Aspects of Advertising," *Review of Economic Studies*, 18, 1–27.

Kalish, Shlomo [1985], "A New Product Adoption Model with Price, Advertising and Uncertainty," *Management Science*, 31:12, 1569–1585.

Kmenta, Jan [1986], *Elements of Econometrics*, Second Edition, New York: Macmillan.

Kotler, Philip [1980], *Marketing Management: Analysis, Planning and Control*, Fourth Edition, Englewood Cliffs, N.J.: Prentice Hall.

Koyck, Leendert M. [1954], *Distributed Lags and Investment Analysis*, Amsterdam: North-Holland.

Krishnamurthi, Lakshman and S. P. Raj [1985], "The Effect of Advertising on Consumer Price Sensitivity," *Journal of Marketing Research*, 22:2, May, 119–129.

Lambin, Jean-Jacques, Philippe A. Naert, and Alain Bultez [1975], "Optimal Marketing Behavior in Oligopoly," *European Economic Review*, 6:2, 105–128.

Leiss, William, Stephen Kline, and Sat Jhally [1986], *Social Communication in Advertising: Persons, Products, and Images of Well-Being*, New York: Methuen.

Leone, Robert P. and Randall L. Schultz [1980], "A Study of Marketing Generalization," *Journal of Marketing*, 44:1, Winter, 10–18.

Lerner, Abba P. [1934], "The Concept of Monopoly and the Measurement of Monopoly Power," *Review of Economic Studies*, 1, June, 157–175.

Little, John D. C. [1979], "Aggregate Advertising Models: The State of the Art," *Operations Research*, 27:4, July/August, 629–667.

Little, John D. C. [1986], "Comments on Mahajan-Muller," *Marketing Science*, 5:2, Spring, 107–108.

Liviatan, Nissan [1963], "Consistent Estimation of Distributed Lags," *International Economic Review*, 4:1, January, 44–52.

Mahajan, Vijay and Eitan Muller [1986], "Advertising Pulsing Policies for Generating Awareness for New Products," *Marketing Science*, 5:2, Spring, 89–106.

Marketing Science [1986], Special Issue on Consumer Choice Models, 5:4, Fall.

Martin, Stephen [1979], "Advertising, Concentration, and Profitability: The Simultaneity Problem," *The Bell Journal of Economics*, 10:2, Autumn, 639–647.

Massy, William F. [1960], "Innovation and Market Penetration," unpublished Ph. D. dissertation, Massachusetts Institute of Technology, Department of Economics.

Melrose, Kendrick B. [1969], "An Empirical Study on Optimizing Advertising Policy," *Journal of Business*, 42:3, July, 282–292.

Montgomery, David B. and Alvin J. Silk [1972], "Estimating Dynamic Effects of Market Communications Expenditures," *Management Science*, 18:10, June, B485–B501.

Moriguchi, C. [1970], "Aggregation over Time in Macroeconomic Relations," *International Economic Review*, 11:3, October, 427–440.

Morimune, Kimio [1989], "*t*-Test in a Structural Equation," *Econometrica*, 57:6, November, 1341–1360.

Mundlak, Yair [1961], "Aggregation over Time in Distributed Lag Models," *International Economic Review*, 2:2, May, 154–163.

Myers, Kenneth H. [1959], "Have We a Decline in Advertising Appropriations?" *Journal of Marketing*, 23:4, April, 370–375.

Nerlove, Marc and Kenneth J. Arrow [1962], "Optimal Advertising Policy Under Dynamic Conditions," *Economica*, 29:114, New Series, May, 129–142.

Nerlove, Marc and Frederick V. Waugh [1961], "Advertising without Supply Control:

Some Implications of a Study of the Advertising of Oranges," *Journal of Farm Economics*, 43:4, Part I, November, 813–837.

Nicholls, William H. [1951], *Price Policies in the Cigarette Industry*, Nashville, Tenn.: Vanderbilt University Press.

Otuteye, Eben and Kristian S. Palda [1987], "Testing for Causality between Aggregate Advertising and Consumption in Canada," paper presented at the 1987 Administrative Science Association of Canada, University of Toronto.

Packard, Vance [1957], *The Hidden Persuaders*, New York: David McKay.

Palda, Kristian S. [1964], *The Measurement of Cumulative Advertising Effects*, Englewood Cliffs, N.J.: Prentice Hall.

Pierce, David A. [1977], "Relationships—and the Lack Thereof—Between Economic Time Series, with Special Reference to Money and Interest Rates," *Journal of the American Statistical Association*, 72:357, March, 11–21.

Pierce, David A. and Larry D. Haugh [1977], "Causality in Temporal Systems: Characterizations and a Survey," *Journal of Econometrics*, 5:3, May, 265–293.

Pollay, Richard W. [1979], "Lydiametrics: Applications of Econometrics to the History of Advertising," *Journal of Advertising History*, 1:2, January, 3–18.

Pollay, Richard W. [1984], "The Languishing of 'Lydiametrics': The Ineffectiveness of Econometric Research on Advertising Effects," *Journal of Communications*, 34:2, Spring, 8–23.

Quandt, Richard E. [1964], "Estimating the Effectiveness of Advertising: Some Pitfalls in Econometric Methods," *Journal of Marketing Research*, 1:2, May, 51–60.

Rao, Ambar G. and P. B. Miller [1975], "Advertising/Sales Response Functions," *Journal of Advertising Research*, 15:2, April, 7–15.

Rao, Ram C. [1986], "Estimating Continuous Time Advertising-Sales Models," *Marketing Science*, 5:2, Spring, 125–142.

Rasmussen, Arne [1952], "The Determination of Advertising Expenditures," *Journal of Marketing*, 16:4, April, 439–446.

Roberts, Harry V. [1947], "The Measurement of Advertising Results," *Journal of Business*, 20:3, July, 131–145.

Rosen, Sherwin [1980], "Comments on 'A Price Theoretic Approach to the Specification and Estimation of the Sales-Advertising Function,'" *Journal of Business*, 53:3, Part 2, July, S139–S142.

Rowe, Robert D. [1976], "The Effects of Aggregation over Time on t-Ratios and R^2's," *International Economic Review*, 17:3, October, 751–757.

Sasieni, Maurice W. [1971], "Optimal Advertising Expenditure," *Management Science*, 18:4, Part II, December, P64–P72.

Schmalensee, Richard [1972], *The Economics of Advertising*, Amsterdam: North-Holland.

Schmalensee, Richard [1976], "A Model of Promotional Competition in Oligopoly," *Review of Economic Studies*, 43, 493–507.

Schmalensee, Richard [1978], "A Model of Advertising and Product Quality," *Journal of Political Economy*, 86:3, June, 485–503.

Schmalensee, Richard [1987], "Advertising," in John Eatwell, Murray Milgate, and Peter Newman, eds., *The New Palgrave: A Dictionary of Economics*, Vol. 1, London: The Macmillan Press, Ltd., pp. 34–36.

Schmalensee, Richard, Alvin J. Silk, and Robert Bojanek [1983], "The Impact of Scale and Media Mix on Advertising Agency Costs," *Journal of Business*, 56:4, October, 453–475.

Schneider, Lynne, Benjamin Klein, and Kevin M. Murphy [1981], "Governmental Regulation of Cigarette Health Information," *Journal of Law and Economics*, 24:3, December, 575–612.

Schoenberg, E. H. [1933], "The Demand Curve for Cigarettes," *Journal of Business*, 6:1, January, 15–35.

Schudson, Michael [1984], *Advertising—The Uneasy Persuasion: Its Dubious Impact on American Society*, New York: Basic Books.

Schultz, Henry [1938], *The Theory and Measurement of Demand*, Chicago: University of Chicago Press.

Simon, Hermann [1982], "ADPULS: An Advertising Model with Wearout and Pulsation," *Journal of Marketing Research*, 19:3, August, 352–363.

Simon, Julian L. [1969], "New Evidence for No Effect of Scale in Advertising," *Journal of Advertising Research*, 9:1, March, 38–42.

Simon, Julian L. [1970], *Issues in the Economics of Advertising*, Urbana, Ill.: University of Illinois Press.

Simon, Julian L. and Johan Arndt [1980], "The Shape of the Advertising Response Function," *Journal of Advertising Research*, 20:4, August, 11–28.

Simon, Julian L. and Joseph Ben-Ur [1982], "The Advertising Budget's Determinants in a Market with Two Competing Firms," *Management Science*, 28:5, May, 500–519.

Sims, Christopher A. [1974], "Seasonality in Regression," *Journal of the American Statistical Association*, 69:3, September, 618–626.

Sims, Christopher A. [1977], "Exogeneity and Causal Ordering in Macroeconomic Models," in Christopher A. Sims, ed., *New Methods in Business Cycle Research*, (Proceedings of a 1975 Conference Sponsored by the Federal Reserve Bank of Minneapolis), Minneapolis: Federal Reserve Bank, 23–43.

Solow, Robert M. [1967], "The New Industrial State, or Son of Affluence," *The Public Interest*, 9, Fall, 100–108.

Stevens, Joseph C. [1968], "Psychophysics," in *International Encyclopedia of the Social Sciences*, Vol. 13, New York: Macmillan, pp. 120–126.

Stigler, George J. [1968], "Price and Non-Price Competition," *Journal of Political Economy*, 76:1, January/February, 149–154.

Taylor, Lester D. and Daniel Weiserbs, [1972] "Advertising and the Aggregate Consumption Function," *American Economic Review*, 62:4, September, 642–655.

Telser, Lester G. [1962], "Advertising and Cigarettes," *Journal of Political Economy*, 70:5, October, 471–499.

Telser, Lester G. [1964], "Advertising and Competition," *Journal of Political Economy*, 72:6, December, 537–562.

Telser, Lester G. [1966], "Supply and Demand for Advertising Messages," *American Economic Review*, 56:2, May, 457–466.

Telser, Lester G. [1969], "Another Look at Advertising and Concentration," *Journal of Industrial Economics*, 18:1, November, 85–94.

Theil, Henri [1954], *Linear Aggregation of Economic Relations*, Amsterdam: North-Holland.

Thompson, Gerald L. and Jinn-Tsair Teng [1984], "Optimal Pricing and Advertising for New Product Oligopoly Models," *Marketing Science*, 3:2, Spring, 148–168.

U.S. Surgeon General's Advisory Committee [1964], *Smoking and Health*, Washington, D.C.: U.S. Government Printing Office.

Verdon, Walter A., Campbell R. McConnell, and Theodore W. Roesler [1968],

"Advertising Expenditures as an Economic Stabilizer: 1945–64," *Quarterly Review of Economics and Business*, 8:2, Summer, 7–18.

Verma, Vinod K. [1980], "A Price Theoretic Approach to the Specification and Estimation of the Sales-Advertising Function," *Journal of Business*, 53:3, Part 2, July, S115–S138.

Wakeman, Frederic [1946], *The Hucksters*, New York: Rinehart.

Wallis, Kenneth F. [1974], "Seasonal Adjustment and Relations between Variables," *Journal of the American Statistical Association*, 69:1, March, 18–31.

Weinberg, Charles B. and Doyle L. Weiss [1982], "On the Econometric Measurement of the Duration of Advertising Effect on Sales," *Journal of Marketing Research*, 19:4, November, 585–591.

Weiss, Doyle L., Franklin S. Houston, and Pierre Windal [1978], "The Periodic Pain of Lydia E. Pinkham," *Journal of Business*, 51:1, January, 91–101.

Weiss, Doyle L., Charles B. Weinberg, and Pierre M. Windal [1983], "The Effects of Serial Correlation and Data Aggregation on Advertising Measurement," *Journal of Marketing Research*, 20:3, August, 268–279.

Windal, Pierre M. and Doyle L. Weiss [1980], "An Iterative GLS Procedure for Estimating the Parameters of Models with Autocorrelated Errors Using Data Aggregated over Time," *Journal of Business*, 53:4, October, 415–424.

Winer, Russel S. [1979], "An Analysis of the Time-Varying Effects of Advertising: The Case of Lydia Pinkham," *Journal of Business*, 52:4, October, 563–576.

Wu, De-Min [1973], "Tests of Independence between Stochastic Regressors and Disturbances," *Econometrica*, 41:4, July, 733–750.

Zellner, Arnold [1979], "Causality and Econometrics," in Karl Brunner and Allan H. Meltzer, eds., *Three Aspects of Policy and Policymaking*, Amsterdam: North-Holland, pp. 9–54.

Zellner, Arnold and Claude Montmarquette [1971], "A Study of Some Aspects of Temporal Aggregation Problems in Econometric Analysis," *Review of Economics and Statistics*, 53:6, November, 335–342.

FURTHER READINGS

Aaker, David A. and John G. Myers [1982], *Advertising Management*, Second Edition, Englewood Cliffs, N.J.: Prentice Hall. A well-known textbook on advertising.

Aigner, Dennis J. and Arnold Zellner, ed. [1988], "Special Issue on Causality," *Journal of Econometrics*, 39:1/2, September/October. A broad overview on recent developments in modeling, assessing, and interpreting causality.

Journal of Business [1980], "Special Issue on Interfaces between Marketing and Economics," 53:3, Part 2, July. A useful statement of research issues.

Kotler, Philip [1980], *Marketing Management: Analysis, Planning and Control*, Fourth Edition, Englewood Cliffs, N.J.: Prentice Hall. A well-known textbook on marketing, including advertising.

Lambin, Jean-Jacques [1976], *Advertising, Competition and Market Conduct in Oligopoly over Time*, Amsterdam: North-Holland. A classic econometric study.

Lilien, Gary and Philip Kotler [1983], *Marketing Decision Making: A Model-Building Approach*, New York: Harper & Row, 1983, especially Chapter 14, "Advertising Decision Models." A well-known marketing textbook.

Marketing Science [1986], Special Issue on Consumer Choice Models, 5:4, Fall. Focuses on discrete choice models in the marketing context.

Parsons, Leonard J. and Randall L. Schultz [1976], *Marketing Models and Econometric Research*, New York: North-Holland. A useful summary of research to 1976.

Pollay, Richard W., ed. [1979], *Information Sources in Advertising History*, Westport, Conn.: Greenwood Press. A useful, comprehensive guide to the advertising literature.

Chapter 9

Modeling the Interrelated Demands for Factors of Production: Estimation and Inference in Equation Systems

"The relative desirability of estimation of the production function, its dual profit or cost function, factor demand or supply equations, or their inverse first-order conditions, depends primarily on the stochastic structure of the data. In the general case, these equations together constitute a simultaneous system, and the most efficient estimators are obtained by estimation of the complete system."

MELVYN FUSS, DANIEL McFADDEN, and YAIR MUNDLAK (1978), p. 266.

"A currently favored specification is the transcendental logarithmic (or translog) function. This is a very flexible form, capable of approximating a wide variety of functional forms."

JACK JOHNSTON (1984), p. 335.

"Although we are not bound to the view that in all industries over any time period, energy and capital are complements, there appears to be a substantial and growing body of econometric evidence supporting the notion of Hicks-Allen energy-capital complementarity."

ERNST R. BERNDT and DAVID O. WOOD (1979), p. 351.

The empirical analysis of input demands and input substitution patterns provides a striking example of the strong links between economic theory and econometric implementation. For example, while the underlying economic theory of cost and production emphasizes the joint nature of input demand decisions, econometric implementations of this interdependence typically involve simultaneous estimation of parameters in systems of factor demand equations having cross-equation constraints. In this chapter we therefore focus our attention on econometric techniques that are used to analyze the interrelated demands for energy, labor, and other inputs in firms' production processes.

The econometric techniques that we employ in this chapter deal with estimation of parameters in systems of equations. We also consider alternative procedures for obtaining statistical inference on the empirical validity of hypotheses involving cross-equation parameter restrictions, the measurement of goodness of fit in equation systems, special properties of singular equation systems, and the specification and estimation of vector autoregressive stochastic processes in multivariate equation systems.

We begin this chapter with an historical overview of the literature on the demand for factors of production, beginning with the famous Cobb-Douglas model, moving on to the constant elasticity of substitution (CES) specification, and concluding with "flexible" functional forms such as the generalized Leontief and transcendental logarithmic (translog) representations. We then proceed with a discussion of issues involved in empirical implementation and focus in particular on econometric issues involved in estimating parameters of the generalized Leontief and translog functional forms.

The exercises in this chapter highlight problems that are typically encountered by econometricians estimating factor demand models, particularly in the context of systems of equations. The data set underlying these exercises is from a well-known and controversial study by Ernst R. Berndt and David O. Wood [1975], based on annual U.S. manufacturing data from 1947 to 1971.

9.1 HISTORICAL OVERVIEW

The notion of a production function has been with us for a long time. In the theoretical literature, already in the first edition of his famous *Principles of Economics* text in 1890, Alfred Marshall devoted considerable attention to theoretical relationships among production functions and factor demands. As is frequently the case, however, empirical analysis lagged considerably behind theoretical developments.

The empirical analysis of production relationships arose from a number of motivations and diverse intellectual interests. For example, Paul Douglas, a distinguished labor economist, was very much interested in explaining movements of labor productivity and real wages over time. To Douglas, an important issue was whether labor was in fact paid the value of its marginal product. Douglas wanted to test the marginal productivity theory, but he realized that, to do this, he needed a mathematical representation for a production function. Teaming up with an applied mathematician colleague at Amherst College named Charles Cobb, Douglas published a classic article in 1928 that purported to test empirically the theory of marginal productivity.[1] Cobb and Douglas assumed that production was characterized by constant returns to scale and then empirically related value-added output Y to the inputs of capital (K) and labor (L) in U.S. manufacturing using the log-log form

$$\ln Y = \ln A + \alpha_K \ln K + \alpha_L \ln L \tag{9.1}$$

based on annual data over the 1899–1922 time period.[2] The assumption of constant returns to scale (homogeneity of degree 1 in input quantities) implied the parameter restriction $\alpha_K + \alpha_L = 1$.[3] Substituting this restriction into Eq. (9.1) and rearranging yield an equation relating average labor productivity (Y/L) to the capital/labor ratio (K/L):

$$\ln (Y/L) = \ln A + \alpha_K \ln (K/L) \tag{9.2}$$

Let us now consider empirical implementation of this log-log specification. Denote the prices of K, L, and Y as P_K, P_L, and P, respectively, and rewrite Eq. (9.1) in nonlogarithmic form with constant returns to scale imposed as

$$Y = A \cdot K^{\alpha} L^{1-\alpha} \tag{9.3}$$

Next take partial derivatives of Y in Eq. (9.3) with respect to K and to L, yielding an expression for marginal products. If firms are maximizing profits, these marginal products can be equated to the real input prices, $\partial Y/\partial K = P_K/P$ and $\partial Y/\partial L = P_L/P$. After rearranging, this yields the relationships

$$\alpha_K = \frac{P_K K}{P \cdot Y} \qquad \alpha_L = 1 - \alpha_K = \frac{P_L L}{P \cdot Y} \tag{9.4}$$

Therefore one important empirical implication of this log-log specification is that the α_K and α_L parameters must equal the value shares of inputs in the value of output. Cobb-Douglas argued that if markets were competitive, if firms chose inputs such that marginal products equaled real prices, and if the production technology in U.S. manufacturing over the 1899–1922 time period followed the constant returns to scale log-log specification (9.2), then least squares estimates of the parameters α_K and α_L should be approximately equal to the values shares of K and L in the value of output, as in Eq. (9.4).

Adding a random disturbance term to Eq. (9.2) and using their time series data, Cobb and Douglas obtained least squares estimates of α_K and α_L equal to 0.25 and 0.75, respectively, as well as a respectable R^2 of 0.97. Since these estimates were consistent with actual shares of total product received by the K and L inputs—which, according to contemporary National Bureau of Economic Research estimates, were 0.259 and 0.741, respectively—Cobb and Douglas argued that the theory of marginal productivity had been validated empirically.[4]

Although the production function (9.1) was useful for the particular labor value share application that was of interest to Cobb and Douglas, other economists who were more interested in measuring substitution elasticities among inputs found the form of Eq. (9.1) too restrictive. In particular, define the elasticity of substitution between capital and labor as

$$\sigma = \frac{\partial \ln (K/L)}{\partial \ln (F_L/F_K)} = \frac{\partial \ln (K/L)}{\partial \ln (P_L/P_K)} \tag{9.5}$$

where F_L and F_K are marginal products of L and K. If one solves for optimal K and L and substitutes these into Eq. (9.5), one can easily show that for the Cobb-Douglas case, this σ always equals unity.

Economists who were interested in estimating σ rather than assuming that $\sigma = 1$ extended the basic production function modeling approach in two different ways. Apparently the first published empirical paper attempting to measure substitution elasticities among inputs within the theory of cost and production was an article by the Nobel Laureate Ragnar Frisch [1935], who sought to measure input substitution possibilities in the chocolate-manufacturing industry. Frisch empirically illustrated the principle of substitution by estimating a substitution coefficient (the ratio of marginal productivities) between the inputs of cocoa paste and the labor time involved in shaping and remolding in the manufacture of chocolate. To accomplish this, Frisch made a number of mathematical approximations and then computed substitution coefficients directly, rather than using regression or other statistical methods.

A second generalization involved a more direct extension of the Cobb-Douglas function. In an important paper, Kenneth J. Arrow, Hollis B. Chenery, Bagicha Minhas, and Robert M. Solow [1961] asked, "For what functional form would σ be constant but not be constrained to equal unity?" The solution involved integrating Eq. (9.5), resulting in

$$\ln (K/L) = \text{constant} + \sigma \ln (F_K/F_L) \tag{9.6}$$

They then integrated the marginal rate of substitution (F_K/F_L) to obtain the implied production function. Such a mathematical exercise generated the now widely known constant elasticity of substitution (CES) production function, which, with constant returns to scale imposed, is written as

$$Y = A \cdot [\delta K^{-\rho} + (1 - \delta)L^{-\rho}]^{-1/\rho} \tag{9.7}$$

where $\sigma = 1/(1 + \rho)$. In the limiting case in which $\rho \rightarrow 0$, $\sigma \rightarrow 1$, and so the Cobb-Douglas function is a limiting form of the CES specification.

It is worth noting that, as with the Cobb-Douglas function, in fact this CES specification has older roots, having been derived independently a quarter century earlier in the literature on consumer demand analysis. Specifically, Eq. (9.7) is an example of the mean value function

$$Y^{-\rho} = A\left(\sum_{i=1}^{n} \delta_i X_i^{-\rho}\right) \tag{9.8}$$

considered in the economics literature earlier by Abraham Bergson [1936].

An entirely different motivation for empirical production function estimation arose within the agricultural economics literature. Beginning shortly after World War II, Earl Heady and his associates at Iowa State University designed crop, seed, and fertilizer experiments for a large number of crops at the Agriculture Experiment Station in Iowa and then used these data and least squares methods to estimate input-output relationships with alternative forms of production functions.

Heady et al. wanted to include in their experiments input combinations that resulted in negative marginal products, that is, regions of the production function that were noneconomic. With the Cobb-Douglas function, such economic regions cannot exist (marginal products are always positive), and so it was necessary for Heady et al. to generalize that form.

Heady and his associates experimented with Taylor's series expansions as polynomial approximations to unknown algebraic forms. In their 1961 book *Agricultural Production Functions*, Heady and John Dillon introduced the second-degree polynomial in logarithms that added quadratic and cross-terms to the Cobb-Douglas function (9.1). As we shall soon see, Heady's form was dubbed the translog function almost a decade later by Laurits R. Christensen, Dale W. Jorgenson, and Lawrence J. Lau [1970]. Heady and Dillon also reported least squares estimates of a square root transformation that included as a special case the generalized linear production function introduced by W. Erwin Diewert [1971].

In terms of econometric procedures, Heady et al. estimated the production function directly using least squares methods and called this procedure production function contour fitting. Moreover, because the underlying data were based on controlled experiments, the right-hand variables in the regression equations (usually input quantities) were by design uncorrelated with the random disturbance term. This contrasts with the nonexperimental case in which having input quantities as regressors often leaves one vulnerable to a simultaneous equations estimation problem.

The efforts of Frisch, Arrow et al., and Heady and Dillon all involved attempts to generalize the restrictive Cobb-Douglas function. Since the CES generalization by Arrow et al. has been used so widely in empirical research, it is worth exploring a number of its econometric issues further. We begin by examining the sensitivity of the estimated elasticity of substitution to the choice of equation to be estimated.

Suppose that production is characterized by constant returns to scale

(CRTS) and that there are zero economic profits and competitive markets (note that in this case, optimal output is indeterminate). Taking logarithms of the marginal productivity relations from Eq. (9.7), rearranging, and adding a random disturbance term u, one obtains factor demand equations for K and L as

$$\ln(Y/K) = a_1 + \sigma_1 \ln(P_K/P) + u_1 \tag{9.9}$$

$$\ln(Y/L) = a_1 + \sigma_2 \ln(P_L/P) + u_2 \tag{9.10}$$

where σ_1 and σ_2 are alternative estimates of the elasticity of substitution between capital and labor from the two differing estimable equations, the constant terms a_1 and a_2 are associated nonlinear combinations of δ and σ, and u_1 and u_2 are random disturbance terms.

The source of these random disturbance terms merits discussion. One possible source is the fact that firms undoubtedly choose optimal input demands with occasional error, and such optimization errors could manifest themselves as random disturbances. Managerial skills may also vary across firms. If these managerial abilities affected the efficiency parameter A in Eq. (9.7), and if these efficiency parameters were randomly distributed among firms, then disturbances at the more aggregate level could reflect the distribution of managerial talent across firms.

Another estimable equation can be obtained as follows. If Eq. (9.9) is subtracted from Eq. (9.10)—or if one assumes only cost minimization with output fixed rather than profit maximization—one obtains the *relative* factor demand equation

$$\ln(K/L) = a_3 - \sigma_3 \ln(P_K/P_L) + u_3 \tag{9.11}$$

Variants of Eqs. (9.9), (9.10), and (9.11) have been estimated by a number of researchers with differing results. Empirical findings to 1965 have been surveyed by Marc Nerlove [1967], while additional empirical results to 1973 have been summarized by Ernst R. Berndt [1976]. We now briefly review this empirical literature to see why estimates of σ might differ depending on the equation that is fitted.

One assumption that is typically made in cross-sectional empirical studies (say, for disaggregated two-digit SIC manufacturing industries by state or province) is that product (but not input) prices are equal across geographical regions.[5] In such cases, Eqs. (9.9) and (9.10) can be modified to

$$\ln(PY/K) = a_1' + \sigma_1' \ln(P_K/P) \tag{9.12}$$

and

$$\ln(PY/L) = a_2' + \sigma_2' \ln(P_L/P) \tag{9.13}$$

In almost all such studies, it is assumed that input prices are exogenous.

A typical empirical finding emerging from two-digit cross-sectional studies in the United States based on the labor productivity demand equation

(9.13) is that there is substantial support for the notion that $\sigma = 1$. In particular, in most cases the null hypothesis that σ equals 1 cannot be rejected. By contrast, cross-sectional two-digit estimates of σ based on the capital productivity demand equation (9.12) have usually been less than unity. One conjecture rationalizing this result is that investment in capital plant and equipment tends to be gradual and not as instantaneous as that for certain types of labor. Since less substitution is observed in the short run when the capital input is partially fixed, cross-sectional estimates of σ based on the capital equation (9.12) might be expected to be smaller than those based on the labor equation (9.13).

To examine this capital lagged adjustment hypothesis further, some researchers have employed either time series data or else pooled cross-sectional, time series data and then compared results with cross-sectional estimates. In most studies, least squares estimates of σ based on time series data have been statistically significantly less than unity, regardless of whether the labor or capital equation was estimated. Typical estimates of σ based on distributed lag variants of Eq. (9.9) or (9.10) range from 0.3 to 0.5.

These results provide an example of a familiar empirical finding in demand analysis that time series estimates of elasticities are smaller than cross-sectional ones. Numerous researchers have attempted to reconcile the seemingly disparate cross-sectional and time series estimates of σ. For example, Robert E. Lucas, Jr. [1969] attempted to attain a reconciliation by employing variants of the lagged adjustment process. His results were unsuccessful, however, and he was forced to conclude that the lagged adjustment hypotheses "make essentially no contribution to the reconciling of time series and cross-sectional evidence of substitution." Later in this chapter, in the context of distinguishing between short- and long-run cost functions, we will return to this partial adjustment hypothesis.

Several other curious empirical results have been reported in the literature, based on the CES production function. One set of results can be explained analytically. Suppose that one estimated equations such as Eq. (9.9) or (9.10) using highly aggregated economywide data. In such circumstances it might be more appropriate to assume that prices (rather than quantities) are endogenous and that quantities (rather than prices) are exogenous. In these cases (or if one simply persisted in ignoring possible simultaneous equations biases), one could estimate the reciprocals of equations Eqs. (9.9)–(9.11) by ordinary least squares,

$$\ln (P_K/P) = a_4 + (1/\sigma_4) \ln (Y/K) + u_4 \quad \textbf{(9.14)}$$

$$\ln (P_L/P) = a_5 + (1/\sigma_5) \ln (Y/L) + u_5 \quad \textbf{(9.15)}$$

$$\ln (P_K/P_L) = a_6 - (1/\sigma_6) \ln (K/L) + u_6 \quad \textbf{(9.16)}$$

and then calculate the implied estimate of σ by inverting the least squares estimated slope coefficient in each of these equations. A number of researchers have in fact estimated σ on the basis of such reciprocal relationships; their findings are surveyed by Berndt [1976].

A somewhat surprising and useful discovery is that one can show analytically that a systematic variation in σ estimates is due solely to the choice of the equation fitted. To see this, recall that in bivariate regression analysis it is well known that the R^2 based on a simple regression model $Y_i = \alpha + \beta X_i + u_i$ is numerically equal to the R^2 from the reciprocal regression $X_i = \phi + \gamma Y_i + v_i$ (or, denoting deviations of variables from their means with lowercase letters, the R^2 from $y_i = \beta x_i + u_i$ must equal that from $x_i = \gamma y_i + v_i$). This equality occurs because R^2 is merely the squared sample correlation coefficient between X_i and Y_i. Furthermore, denoting the parameter estimates and fitted values of y with a circumflex, we know that

$$R^2 = \frac{\sum_{i=1}^{n} \hat{y}_i^2}{\sum_{i=1}^{n} y_i^2} = \frac{\hat{\beta}^2 \sum_{i=1}^{n} x_i^2}{\sum_{i=1}^{n} y_i^2} = \frac{\hat{\beta} \sum_{i=1}^{n} x_i y_i}{\sum_{i=1}^{n} y_i^2} = \hat{\beta} \cdot \hat{\gamma} \tag{9.17}$$

where

$$\hat{\beta} = \frac{\sum_{i=1}^{n} x_i y_i}{\sum_{i=1}^{n} x_i^2} \quad \text{and} \quad \hat{\gamma} = \frac{\sum_{i=1}^{n} x_i y_i}{\sum_{i=1}^{n} y_i^2} \tag{9.18}$$

It follows that once one estimates a bivariate regression equation by least squares and obtains the R^2 value, all one need do to obtain an estimate of the regression coefficient from the other reciprocal regression is to employ Eq. (9.17). In particular, one need not actually run the reciprocal regression to infer the corresponding parameter estimate.

If, for example, one estimated by least squares the reciprocal regression equations (9.9) and (9.14), the estimates of β and γ would correspond with estimates of σ_1 and $1/\sigma_4$, and therefore one would obtain the relationship

$$\hat{\beta} \cdot \hat{\gamma} = \hat{\sigma}_1/\hat{\sigma}_4 = R_1^2 = R_4^2$$

where the i subscript on R^2 refers to the squared correlation coefficient of the σ_i equation being estimated. Since $R^2 \leqslant 1$, it follows that ordinary least squares estimates of σ will always be subject to the following inequality relationship:

$$\hat{\sigma}_1/\hat{\sigma}_4 = R_1^2 = R_4^2 \rightarrow \hat{\sigma}_1 \leqslant \hat{\sigma}_4 \tag{9.19}$$

Similarly,

$$\hat{\sigma}_2/\hat{\sigma}_5 = R_2^2 = R_5^2 \rightarrow \hat{\sigma}_2 \leqslant \hat{\sigma}_5$$

and

$$\hat{\sigma}_3/\hat{\sigma}_6 = R_3^2 = R_6^2 \rightarrow \hat{\sigma}_3 \leqslant \hat{\sigma}_6 \qquad 9.20)$$

Hence the choice of estimating equation based on the CES functional form systematically affects the estimated substitution elasticity.

This choice of estimating equation has an important economic interpretation in that the selection is tantamount to choosing whether input quantities or input prices are exogenous right-hand variables. In this context it is generally held that if industries are reasonably competitive, the more disaggregated the data are, the more likely prices rather than quantities are to be exogenous, and therefore that with disaggregated data the lower σ_1, σ_2, or σ_3 estimates are preferred to the larger σ_4, σ_5, or σ_6 estimates.

To this point we have discussed only estimation of the production function itself or of its first-order (marginal productivity) conditions. An alternative approach is based on the dual cost function. More specifically, assume that the optimization problem facing the firm is to choose inputs so that costs of production are minimized, given input prices, the level of output, and the form of the production function. The solution to such an optimization problem yields a cost function that is dual to the production function.

Econometric implementations of cost and production functions differ in their assumptions concerning exogeneity. In the production function regression equation, output is endogenous, and input quantities are exogenous. By contrast, in the dual cost function, production costs and input quantities are endogenous, while input prices and the level of output are exogenous. It follows that whenever output level and input prices can plausibly be assumed to be exogenous (the latter is more likely to be the case when disaggregated data are available), it is preferable to employ a cost function that has input prices as regressors, rather than a production function in which input quantities are the right-hand variables.[6]

In some cases, one can solve analytically for the form of the cost function that is dual to the underlying primal production function. Such a cost function is dual in the sense that it embodies all the parameters of the underlying production function. Moreover, the production function parameters can be uniquely recovered from estimation of the demand equations derived from the dual cost function. Notable examples of such analytically solvable dual cost relationships include the Cobb-Douglas and CES dual cost functions.

In Chapter 3 of this book, for example, we noted that in a pioneering study by Marc Nerlove [1963] the Cobb-Douglas dual cost function was derived and estimated by using data from the electric utility industry. Nerlove reasoned that in the electric utility industry, electricity rate schedules were set by regulators and so were exogenous. Given these rate schedules, the demand for kilowatt hours was also exogenous, and since electricity output cannot be stored, profit maximization and cost minimization were equivalent behavioral assumptions. Nerlove specified and estimated a three-input (capital, labor, and fuels) Cobb-Douglas cost function that permitted returns to scale to be other than constant. One significant empirical finding that he reported was that the estimated returns to scale were generally increasing, rather than constant.

While Nerlove was gratified with his empirical findings and use of the dual cost function, he was clearly unsatisfied with the assumptions on substitution elasticities implied by the Cobb-Douglas specification, which required that the σ elasticities between capital and labor, capital and fuel, and fuel and labor were all equal to unity. One possibility was to employ instead a cost function that was dual to the CES production function, but such a form was unattractive to Nerlove because, while it did not constrain these elasticities all to equal unity, it still restricted them to be constant and to be equal to each other. Such a priori restrictions would be unfortunate, since it was quite likely, Nerlove reasoned, that the substitution elasticity between fuels and capital was larger than that between fuels and labor.

Nerlove and his colleague, Hirofumi Uzawa, encouraged their research assistant at that time at Stanford University, Daniel McFadden, to examine further both the use of duality theory and the problem of generating more flexible functional forms with three or more inputs, forms that were less restrictive than the CES or Cobb-Douglas cost function specifications.

In the years that followed, McFadden focused a great deal of his attention on the theory and applications of duality in production,[7] but it was left to a student of his at the University of California–Berkeley, W. Erwin Diewert, to solve the problem of developing flexible functional forms with three or more inputs, on both the primal and dual sides. Diewert's Ph.D. dissertation at Berkeley and his subsequent classic 1971 article made widely available to empirical researchers functional forms that placed no a priori restrictions on substitution elasticities, yet were consistent with the constraints that are typically assumed in economic theory.[8]

Diewert's generalized Leontief functional form was the first in a series of developments in the theory of dual cost and production, most of them emanating from the economics department at the Berkeley campus, where, ironically, some of Earl Heady's students also taught contemporaneously in the Department of Agricultural Economics. (Recall that the specification of very general functional forms of the production function was also the focus of the much earlier research conducted by Heady and other agricultural economists, research that resulted in Taylor's series production function relationships.)

At the 1970 meetings of the Second World Congress of the Econometric Society, a combination of Berkeley economics faculty and graduate students, Laurits R. Christensen, Dale W. Jorgenson, and Lawrence J. Lau, presented a paper introducing the translog functional form for production, transformation, cost and profit functions, a form that also placed no prior restrictions on substitution elasticities.[9] The translog was a second-order Taylor's series in logarithms and was identical to the production function considered by Heady several decades earlier. Heady and his associates, however, focused only on the primal production function and did not consider the dual cost or profit function specifications.

In the sections of this chapter that follow, we will devote considerable

W. ERWIN DIEWERT

Duality and Flexible Functional Forms

Born in Vancouver, British Columbia in 1941, Erwin Diewert attended public elementary and secondary schools in Vancouver and then went on to earn both his B.A. and M.A. degrees in mathematics from the University of British Columbia. Already as a UBC student, Diewert became fascinated with interfaces among mathematics, statistics, and economics. His M.A. thesis, for example, investigated estimators for the seasonal adjustment of economic time series.

In 1964, Diewert decided to travel south for further graduate studies, enrolling as a Ph.D. student in economics at the University of California–Berkeley. There he interacted with fellow graduate students such as Lawrence J. Lau and Laurits R. Christensen and studied under distinguished young faculty members such as Dale W. Jorgenson and Daniel McFadden. Although graduate student life was not always easy (readers might be comforted to learn that Diewert failed to pass his first set of Ph.D. comprehensive exams and was rescued on his second attempt by Professors Jorgenson and McFadden), it was clear to many that Diewert was an extraordinarily talented student.

Along with McFadden and Jorgenson, Diewert became interested in the duality theory of cost and production developed by a Berkeley engineering professor named Ronald Shepard. Under the prodding of McFadden, Diewert also researched the possibility of deriving empirically implementable mathematical formulations of production or cost functions that were "flexible," that is, that placed no a priori restrictions on substitution elasticities. In his pioneering 1969 Ph.D. dissertation, Diewert integrated these two themes, introducing the generalized linear production function and the generalized Leontief cost function and then using duality theory to investigate their properties. This dissertation, which won him the University of California Best Thesis in Economics Award, formed the basis of his classic 1971 *Journal of Political Economy* article, "An Application of the Shephard Duality Theorem: A Generalized Linear Production Function."

Diewert's first academic appointment was at the University of Chicago. Soon after arriving there, he told his Chicago colleagues that he longed to return to Vancouver. (Rumor has it that Chicago Professor Arnold Harberger was astonished by this attitude and stated, "Diewert may have a great production function, but he sure has a strange utility function.") In 1970, Diewert did just that, accepting an offer from the University of British Columbia.

Duality theory has always been an important component of Diewert's research. He has used duality approaches not only to address functional form problems in producer and consumer theory, but also in the context of general equilibrium modeling, international trade theory, index number theory, and the measurement of waste and welfare and in a number of empirical studies. In 1975, Diewert was elected a Fellow of the Econometric Society, and in 1982 he was inducted as a Fellow of the Royal Society of Canada. Since 1983 he has served as Chairman of the Statistics Canada Prices Advisory Committee.

additional attention to the econometric issues that are involved in the estimation of these more general specifications. Note at this point, however, that issues of whether input prices or input quantities are exogenous, similar to those discussed in the context of the CES function, also pervade the more general functional form implementations. Because of the desire to account for possible heterogeneity of production technologies among industries, many econometricians today prefer to work with more disaggregated data in which prices rather than quantities are exogenous. As a result, most recent econometric studies of substitution relationships among inputs employ general cost or profit functions in which input prices are exogenous and quantities are endogenous, rather than production or transformation functions in which quantities are exogenous and prices are endogenous.

Let us now summarize this historical overview. Empirical research on estimating cost and production relationships has a long history in the economics profession, stemming in part from efforts to explain average labor productivity, to quantify relationships among inputs and outputs in agriculture, to estimate substitution elasticities among inputs, and to estimate returns to scale. Major theoretical and econometric developments facilitating empirical research have involved the introduction of more generalized yet empirically implementable functional forms—from the Cobb-Douglas of Wicksell to the CES of Bergson and finally to the Taylor's series formulations initiated by Heady and his associates.

In the following sections we will consider issues of empirical implementation for two flexible cost functions. We begin with Diewert's generalized Leontief cost function, digress to consider procedures for obtaining statistical inference in equation systems and measuring goodness of fit, and then turn to the translog function of Christensen, Jorgenson, and Lau.

9.2 THE GENERALIZED LEONTIEF COST FUNCTION

Let us now name prices of n inputs as P_i, $i = 1, \ldots, n$, the n input quantities X_i, total costs C, and output Y. Assume that the P_i and Y are exogenous but that the X_i and C are endogenous. With constant returns to scale imposed, the generalized Leontief (GL) cost function can be written as

$$C = Y \cdot \left[\sum_{i=1}^{n} \sum_{j=1}^{n} d_{ij}(P_iP_j)^{1/2} \right] \tag{9.21}$$

where $d_{ij} = d_{ji}$. To obtain equations that are amenable to estimation, it is convenient to employ Shephard's Lemma, which states that the optimal, cost-minimizing demand for input i can simply be derived by differentiating the cost function with respect to P_i. In the GL context, therefore, optimal factor demands are obtained by differentiating Eq. (9.21) with respect to the P_i, yielding

$$\frac{\partial C}{\partial P_i} = X_i = Y \cdot \left[\sum_{j=1}^{n} d_{ij}(P_j/P_i)^{1/2} \right], \qquad i = 1, \ldots, n \tag{9.22}$$

A more convenient equation for estimation purposes can be obtained by dividing through by Y, yielding optimal input-output demand equations, denoted by a_i:

$$a_i \equiv \frac{X_i}{Y} = \sum_{j=1}^{n} d_{ij}(P_j/P_i)^{1/2}, \qquad i = 1, \ldots, n \tag{9.23}$$

Notice that when $i = j$, $(P_j/P_i)^{1/2}$ equals 1, and so d_{ii} is a constant term in the ith input-output equation.

As an example, consider the case in which there are four inputs: capital (K), labor (L), energy (E), and nonenergy intermediate materials (M). With the E and M intermediate inputs included, the appropriate measure of output quantity Y is gross output (sales quantity plus net changes in output inventory quantities), not value-added. In this four-input case, by Eqs. (9.22) the GL cost-minimizing input-output equations are

$$a_K \equiv \frac{K}{Y} = d_{KK} + d_{KL}(P_L/P_K)^{1/2} + d_{KE}(P_E/P_K)^{1/2} + d_{KM}(P_M/P_K)^{1/2} \tag{9.24}$$

$$a_L \equiv \frac{L}{Y} = d_{LL} + d_{KL}(P_K/P_L)^{1/2} + d_{LE}(P_E/P_L)^{1/2} + d_{LM}/(P_M/P_L)^{1/2} \tag{9.25}$$

$$a_E \equiv \frac{E}{Y} = d_{EE} + d_{KE}(P_K/P_E)^{1/2} + d_{LE}(P_L/P_E)^{1/2} + d_{EM}(P_M/P_E)^{1/2} \tag{9.26}$$

$$a_M \equiv \frac{M}{Y} = d_{MM} + d_{KM}(P_K/P_M)^{1/2} + d_{LM}(P_L/P_M)^{1/2} + d_{EM}(P_E/P_M)^{1/2} \tag{9.27}$$

Note that while each of the four equations has four parameters, the six cross-equation symmetry constraints reduce the number of free parameters to be estimated from 16 to ten. Further, estimates of all the parameters in the GL cost function (9.21) can be obtained by estimating only the input-output demand equations (9.24)–(9.27); this occurs because there is no intercept term in the GL cost function, owing to the constant-returns-to-scale assump-

Table 9.1 Equation-by-Equation OLS and IZEF/ML Estimates of Parameters in the Generalized Leontief Input-Output Demand Equations (9.24)–(9.27), without Symmetry Imposed, U.S. Manufacturing, 1947–1971

	K/Y Equation		L/Y Equation		E/Y Equation		M/Y Equation	
d_{ij}	OLS	IZEF	OLS	IZEF	OLS	IZEF	OLS	IZEF
$j = K$	0.0232	0.0263	0.0485	0.0517	−0.0139	−0.0111	−0.0550	−0.0542
	(0.0157)	(0.0143)	(0.0269)	(0.0245)	(0.0097)	(0.0088)	(0.0459)	(0.0420)
$j = L$	0.0048	0.0036	−0.0692	−0.0719	−0.0041	−0.0048	−0.1372	−0.1374
	(0.0097)	(0.0088)	(0.0166)	(0.0151)	(0.0058)	(0.0053)	(0.0281)	(0.0258)
$j = E$	0.0605	0.0649	0.2183	0.2200	0.0373	0.0403	0.0385	0.0399
	(0.0331)	(0.0301)	(0.0523)	(0.0476)	(0.0201)	(0.0183)	(0.0933)	(0.0855)
$j = M$	−0.0381	−0.0443	0.0281	0.0264	0.0199	0.0150	0.7420	0.7401
	(0.0469)	(0.0426)	(0.0743)	(0.0676)	(0.0285)	(0.0259)	(0.1325)	(0.1214)

Source: Data from Berndt and Wood [1975]. Estimation by the author.

tion. Finally, if $d_{ij} = 0$ for all $i, j, i \neq j$, then input-output demand equations are independent of relative input prices, and all cross-price elasticities equal zero.

To implement this GL model empirically, a stochastic framework must be specified. An additive disturbance term is appended to each of the four input-output equations, and it is typically assumed that the resulting disturbance vector is independently and identically normally distributed with mean vector zero and constant, nonsingular covariance matrix Ω. These disturbances could simply reflect optimization errors on the part of firms. Alternatively, firms could be envisaged as differing from each other according to parameters that are known by the firms' managers but not by the econometrician examining the aggregate data. To the econometrician, such firm effects can manifest themselves as random parameters in the GL cost function (9.21) and as additive disturbances in the input demand functions (9.24)–(9.27).

Although equation-by-equation OLS estimation might appear attractive, since the input demand functions (9.24)–(9.27) are linear in the parameters, these demand equations have cross-equation symmetry constraints. Even if these constraints hold in the population, for any given sample equation-by-equation OLS estimates will not reveal such restrictions; for example, d_{KE} in the K/Y equation estimated by OLS will not necessarily equal d_{KE} estimated in the E/Y equation. This is demonstrated empirically in Table 9.1, where the columns indicate which of Eqs. (9.24)–(9.27) is being estimated and the rows denote the numerator of the relative price regressor. Note, for example, that while the OLS estimate of d_{KE} in the K/Y equation is positive (0.0605), in the E/Y equation the OLS estimate of d_{KE} is negative (−0.0139). To impose these cross-equation constraints, it is necessary instead to use a systems estimator.

One possibility is to use Zellner's seemingly unrelated estimator (often shortened to ZEF and also called the seemingly unrelated regression estimator (SUR) or the minimum chi-square estimator). Even if one ignored the cross-equation constraints, one would still expect the ZEF systems estimator to yield different parameter estimates than those from equation-by-equation OLS, for two reasons. First, one would expect disturbances across input-output equations to be contemporaneously correlated, implying that the disturbance covariance matrix would be nondiagonal. Second, as is seen in Eqs. (9.24)–(9.27), each input-output equation contains different regressors. For both these reasons, in large samples the ZEF estimator would provide more efficient estimates of parameters than OLS.

In effect, the ZEF estimator uses equation-by-equation OLS to obtain an estimate of the disturbance covariance matrix Ω and then does generalized least squares, given this initial estimate of Ω, on an appropriately "stacked" set of equations. Furthermore, one can update the estimates of Ω and iterate the Zellner procedure until changes from one iteration to the next in the estimated parameters *and* the estimated Ω become arbitrarily small. This iterative Zellner-efficient estimator is typically termed IZEF, and in this case it yields parameter estimates that are numerically equivalent to those of the maximum likelihood (ML) estimator.[10]

For purposes of comparison, in Table 9.1 we therefore also present IZEF estimates of the generalized Leontief parameters, without the symmetry constraints imposed. Notice that in this case the IZEF and equation-by-equation OLS estimates do not differ greatly, although the IZEF estimated standard errors are generally smaller than those from OLS. Of course, even more efficient estimates of the parameters could be obtained if one imposed the cross-equation symmetry constraints in the IZEF estimation.[11]

As an alternative specification, suppose one suspected that input prices were endogenous and that failure to account for this might lead to a simultaneous equations bias. Assuming that appropriate instruments were available, one could employ instrumental variable estimation techniques. Equation-by-equation two-stage least squares (2SLS) estimation would again be inappropriate, since it could not impose the requisite cross-equation parameter restrictions. Instead, one could employ the three-stage least squares (3SLS) estimation procedure. It is worth noting that even if one iterated the 3SLS estimator (I3SLS), the estimated parameters would not in general be numerically equivalent to those of the full information maximum likelihood technique, even though their asymptotic properties are identical.[12]

One attractive feature of flexible functional forms like the GL cost function (9.21) is that they place no a priori restrictions on the substitution elasticities. Indeed, as was pointed out in the previous section, flexible functional forms were developed because of the desire to estimate substitution elasticities without imposing prior constraints. The Hicks-Allen partial elasticities of substitution between inputs i and j for a general dual cost function C having n inputs are computed as

$$\sigma_{ij} = \frac{C \cdot C_{ij}}{C_i \cdot C_j} \tag{9.28}$$

where the i, j subscripts refer to first and second partial derivatives of the cost function C with respect to input prices P_i, P_j.[13] For the generalized Leontief cost function these elasticities turn out to be

$$\sigma_{ij} = \frac{1}{2} \cdot \frac{Cd_{ij}(P_iP_j)^{-1/2}}{Ya_ia_j}, \qquad i, j = 1, \ldots, n \qquad \text{but} \quad i \neq j \qquad \textbf{(9.29)}$$

while the own Hicks-Allen elasticity equals

$$\sigma_{ii} = \frac{-\frac{1}{2} C \sum_{\substack{j=1 \\ j \neq i}}^{n} d_{ij} P_j^{1/2} P_i^{-3/2}}{Ya_i^2}, \qquad i = 1, \ldots, n \qquad \textbf{(9.30)}$$

These Hicks-Allen elasticities can be computed, once estimates of the GL parameters are available. For example, based on the IZEF/ML parameter estimates presented in note 11 at the end of the chapter, estimates of the σ_{ij} for 1971 are σ_{KL}, 6.84; σ_{KE}, -1.98; σ_{KM}, -0.87; σ_{LM}, 1.04, σ_{EM}, 0.15; and σ_{LE}, 11.14; the own-elasticity estimates are σ_{KK}, -5.50; σ_{LL}, -1.27; σ_{EE}, -13.72; and σ_{MM}, -0.09. These estimates suggest that in U.S. manufacturing in 1971, capital was substitutable with labor but complementary with energy; further, labor and energy inputs were also substitutable.

If one instead wanted to compute the familiar price elasticities $\epsilon_{ij} \equiv (\partial \ln X_i / \partial \ln P_j = (\partial X_i / \partial P_j) \cdot (P_j / X_i)$, output quantity and all other input prices fixed), this could be done by calculating $\epsilon_{ij} = S_j \sigma_{ij}$, where S_j is the cost share of the jth input in total production costs. For the generalized Leontief function the cross-price elasticities are computed as

$$\epsilon_{ij} = \frac{1}{2} \cdot \frac{d_{ij}(P_i/P_j)^{-1/2}}{a_i}, \qquad i, j = 1, \ldots, n \qquad \text{but} \quad i \neq j \qquad \textbf{(9.31)}$$

while the own-price elasticities equal

$$\epsilon_{ii} = \frac{-\frac{1}{2} \sum_{\substack{j=1 \\ j \neq 1}}^{n} d_{ij}(P_i/P_j)^{-1/2}}{a_i}, \qquad i = 1, \ldots, n \qquad \textbf{(9.32)}$$

For example, the 1971 IZEF/ML estimates of price elasticities based on parameters of the generalized Leontief cost function given in note 11 turn out to be ϵ_{KL}, 0.62; ϵ_{KE}, -0.05; ϵ_{KM}, -0.28; ϵ_{KK}, -0.29; ϵ_{LK}, 0.11; ϵ_{LE}, 0.13; ϵ_{LM}, 0.14, ϵ_{LL}, -0.38; ϵ_{EK}, -0.05; ϵ_{EL}, 0.74; ϵ_{EM}, 0.03; ϵ_{EE}, -0.72; ϵ_{MK}, -0.02; ϵ_{ML}, 0.07; ϵ_{ME}, 0.003; and ϵ_{MM}, -0.05.

Several comments should be made regarding these elasticities. First, note that since the input prices and a_i vary over observations, in general the σ_{ij} and ϵ_{ij} estimates also differ over observations. The values given above are for 1971; for other years they differ. Second, although by construction $\sigma_{ij} = \sigma_{ji}$, in general, $\epsilon_{ij} \neq \epsilon_{ji}$; unlike the Allen elasticities, the price elasticities are not symmetric. Third, inspection of Eqs. (9.29) and (9.31) reveals that inputs

i and j are substitutes, independent inputs, or complements, depending on whether the estimated d_{ij} is positive, zero, or negative. Moreover, in order that the own-price elasticity be negative, it is necessary that the summation portion in the numerator of Eq. (9.32) be positive.

Fourth, since C and the a_i, a_j appear in the above elasticity expressions, computations of these estimated elasticities are based on the estimated parameters and the predicted or fitted values of C and the a_i, a_j, not on their observed values. It is quite easy, incidentally, to make computational errors when using the above equations. One useful check on elasticity calculations involves the following summation of elasticities, which must always hold:

$$\sum_{j=1}^{n} \epsilon_{ij} = 0, \qquad i = 1, \ldots, n \tag{9.33}$$

(You might want to verify that the estimates given underneath Eq. (9.32) satisfy this condition.)

Fifth, to ensure that the estimated cost function is monotonically increasing and strictly quasi-concave in input prices, as is required by theory, one must verify that the fitted values for all of the input-output equations are positive and that the $n \times n$ matrix of the σ_{ij} substitution elasticities is negative semidefinite at each observation. This latter condition is often checked within computer software programs by using matrix algebra commands that calculate the appropriate eigenvalues or determinants.

Finally, since the computed elasticities depend on the estimated parameters and hence are stochastic, the estimated elasticities also have variances and covariances. The substantial nonlinearities that are inherent in elasticity calculations have forced empirical researchers typically to employ approximation techniques in calculating these variances. Moreover, since distribution properties of such elasticity estimates have not yet been derived, the basis for employing statistical inference on them does not yet exist.[14]

Estimation of the equation system (9.24)–(9.27) enables one to perform hypothesis tests on the empirical validity of parameter restrictions. We now digress briefly and consider alternative procedures for testing hypotheses in the multivariate equation systems context.

9.3 STATISTICAL INFERENCE AND THE MEASUREMENT OF FIT IN EQUATION SYSTEMS

Statistical inference on the validity of parameter restrictions in systems of equations can be undertaken in a number of alternative ways. We now briefly outline three common test statistics: the Wald, likelihood ratio (LR), and Lagrange multiplier (LM) test procedures. We begin by naming the $T \times 1$ vector of residuals for the ith input-output equation e_i and the $T \times n$ matrix of residuals as E, where T is the number of observations in each equation.[15] The n columns of E thus consist of the e_i vectors, $i = 1, \ldots, n$, one for each estimated equation. Maximum likelihood (ML) estimation of a multiequation system such as Eqs. (9.24)–(9.27) chooses the set of parameter estimates minimizing the determinant of the residual cross-products matrix, that is, ML minimizes $|E'E|$.[16]

Suppose that in the four-equation system (9.24)–(9.27), one wanted to test the null hypothesis of symmetry (the d_{KL} in Eqs. (9.24) and (9.25) are equal, d_{KE} in Eq. (9.24) equals d_{KE} in Eq. (9.26), the d_{KM} in Eqs. (9.24) and (9.27) are equal, d_{LE} in Eq. (9.25) equals d_{LE} in Eq. (9.26), the d_{LM} in Eqs. (9.25) and (9.27) are equal, and d_{EM} in Eq. (9.26) equals d_{EM} in Eq. (9.27)) against an alternative hypothesis in which these symmetry restrictions are not imposed. To use the Wald test statistic, first estimate the unconstrained model (without symmetry imposed) by ML, and denote the resulting residual cross-products matrix by S. Then do one-step Zellner-efficient estimation of the constrained model (with the cross-equation symmetry restrictions imposed), conditional on this estimate of S. Denote the resulting residual cross-products matrix from this constrained model by W_1. Finally, construct the Wald test statistic as

$$\textbf{Wald test statistic:} \qquad T \operatorname{tr} S^{-1}(W_1 - S) = T \operatorname{tr} S^{-1}H_1 \qquad \textbf{(9.34)}$$

where tr refers to the trace of the matrix and $H_1 \equiv W_1 - S$ is the "loss-of-fit matrix" due to the imposition of the null hypotheses.

This Wald test statistic is distributed asymptotically as a chi-square random variable, with degrees of freedom equal to the difference between the number of free parameters estimated in the unconstrained and constrained models. In our particular GL example there are 16 parameters in the unconstrained model and ten in the constrained model, implying that the degrees of freedom for this Wald test statistic is 6. The resulting test statistic should then be compared with a chi-square critical value at a predetermined level of significance. Incidentally, since $S^{-1}S$ in Eq. (9.34) is an identity matrix with trace equal to n (in this case, 4), to obtain the Wald statistic, one need only calculate $T \operatorname{tr} (S^{-1}W_1 - 4)$. Moreover, some computer software programs provide as standard or optional output the product $S^{-1}W_1$, and so it is relatively straightforward to implement the Wald test procedure. It might also be noted that the asymptotic t-statistics for each coefficient accompanying most computer outputs of equation system estimation are actually square roots of the Wald test statistic corresponding to the null hypothesis that a particular coefficient equals zero.

An alternative test procedure is based on the likelihood ratio principle. To implement the LR test, first estimate the unconstrained model by ML, and then estimate the constrained model, also using the ML procedure. Denote the values of the sample maximized log-likelihood functions under the constrained and unconstrained models as $\ln L_0$ and $\ln L_1$, respectively. The LR test statistic is then simply computed as

$$\textbf{LR test statistic:} \qquad -2\,(\ln L_0 - \ln L_1) \qquad \textbf{(9.35)}$$

This LR test statistic is distributed asymptotically as a chi-square random variable, with degrees of freedom computed in the same manner as in the Wald test. The LR test procedure is easy to implement, since virtually all computer software programs that estimate parameters in systems of equations by the ML method provide as standard output the value of the sample maximized log-likelihood function.

The LR test statistic can be implemented in a different but numerically equivalent manner. Denote the residual cross-products matrices from the ML unconstrained and ML constrained models by S and W_0. Then form the LR test statistic as follows:[17]

$$\textbf{LR test statistic:} \qquad -T(\ln|S| - \ln|W_0|) \tag{9.36}$$

The final test statistic procedure that we consider in testing the symmetry hypothesis is the Lagrange multiplier (LM) test. To implement this LM test, first estimate the constrained model by ML, and again denote the resulting residual cross-products matrix by W_0. Then do one-step Zellner-efficient estimation of the unconstrained model, conditional on W_0, and denote the resulting cross-products matrix of residuals by S_1. Using these matrices, compute the LM statistic as follows:

$$\textbf{LM test statistic:} \qquad T \operatorname{tr} W_0^{-1}(W_0 - S_1) = T \operatorname{tr} W_0^{-1} H_0 \tag{9.37}$$

where $H_0 \equiv W_0 - S_1$, again a "loss-of-fit matrix." This LM test statistic is distributed asymptotically as a chi-square random variable, similar to the Wald and LR test procedures and with identical degrees of freedom.

Although in principle these three alternative test procedures can be used interchangeably because they have identical limiting distributions, whenever the null hypothesis does not hold exactly in the sample (and this happens with a probability of virtually 1), the calculated Wald, LR, and LM test statistics are subject to the following inequality relationship:[18]

$$\textbf{Inequality:} \qquad \text{Wald} > \text{LR} > \text{LM} \tag{9.38}$$

This implies that in practice there will always be a level of significance for which these three test procedures will yield conflicting statistical inference. However, when the null hypothesis is true, the dispersion among the test statistics will tend to decrease as the sample size increases.

Empirical econometricians therefore have some choice of whether to use the Wald, LR, or LM procedure when testing hypotheses in equation systems. Thomas J. Rothenberg [1984] has shown that when the number of restrictions being tested is greater than one, the power functions of the three test procedures cross and that no one of the tests is uniformly more powerful than the others. Although Rothenberg develops some adjustments to correct critical values for power, conflicting inference can still emerge. Hence choice among them is unclear. In practice the LR test procedure appears to be used most frequently, but as was noted above, the asymptotic t-statistics for each coefficient of typical computer outputs are actually square roots of Wald tests.[19]

This completes our discussion of test procedures in the system of equations context when estimation is by ML. LR and Wald test procedures in the context of instrumental variable estimation are considered further in the final portion of Section 9.4.

One other issue that merits brief discussion in the context of estimation and inference in systems of regression equations concerns the measurement of goodness of fit. In the single equation context in which $Y = X\beta + u$, most computer regression programs compute R^2 as

$$R^2 = 1 - \frac{e'e}{(Y - \overline{Y})'(Y - \overline{Y})} \tag{9.39}$$

where e is the vector of T residuals and $\overline{Y}$ is the sample mean of Y. Note that in the single-equation context, $e'e = (e - \overline{e})'(e - \overline{e})$, since least squares estimation ensures that the sum of residuals is zero and therefore that their mean also equals zero.

There are two major reasons why single-equation R^2 measures are not appropriate in an equation system context. First, it is possible that the R^2 from a particular equation computed by using Eq. (9.39) could be negative, since with system estimation in general it is not the case that within each equation the sum of residuals is zero. Hence it is possible that the numerator in Eq. (9.39) could be larger than the denominator, resulting in a negative R^2 value. Second, and more important, while single-equation least squares minimizes $e'e$ and therefore maximizes R^2, in general, system estimation methods do not minimize $e'e$. For example, as was noted earlier in this section, the maximum likelihood estimator minimizes the determinant of the residual cross-products matrix; that is ML minimizes $|E'E|$. Hence in general, ML does not maximize the individual equation R^2 values.

Since single-equation R^2 measures are flawed in the equation systems context, a different goodness-of-fit measure should be employed. Define the generalized variance of the matrix Y as the determinant of $y'y$, where $y \equiv (Y - \overline{Y})$ and Y, like E, is now a $T \times n$ matrix of observations on the Y_i, $i = 1, \ldots, n$. The generalized R^2 measure, $\tilde{R}^2$, indicates the proportion of the generalized variance in Y "explained" by variation in the right-hand variables in the system of equations, and is computed as follows:

$$\tilde{R}^2 = 1 - \frac{|E'E|}{|y'y|} \tag{9.40}$$

Notice that since the ML estimator minimizes $|E'E|$, ML also maximizes $\tilde{R}^2$.

Recall that in the single equation context the equation F-statistic corresponding to the null hypothesis that all k slope coefficients simultaneously equal zero is related to the traditional R^2 measure by

$$[R^2/(1 - R^2)] \cdot (T - k)/k \sim F_{k,T-k}$$

For systems of equations the LR test statistic of the null hypothesis that all slope coefficients in all equations are simultaneously equal to zero can be shown to be equal to

$$\text{LR test statistic} = -T \cdot \ln(1 - \tilde{R}^2) \sim \chi^2 \tag{9.41}$$

and is distributed as a chi-square random variable with degrees of freedom equal to the number of independent slope coefficients in the equation system.

As an example, consider goodness of fit in the context of the system of input-output equations (9.24)–(9.27) derived from the GL cost function. In this case, by Eq. (9.31) it follows that the LR test statistic (9.41) corresponding to the null hypothesis that all the $d_{ij} = 0$, $i \neq j$, has a useful economic interpretation. In particular, this test statistic corresponds to the null hypothesis that all cross-price elasticities are zero, that is, that input-output coefficients are not price-responsive.

This concludes our digression on alternative procedures that are available for obtaining statistical inference in equation systems and for measuring goodness of fit. We now turn to a discussion of econometric issues that are involved in implementing a different flexible functional form, namely, the translog cost function specification.

9.4 THE TRANSLOG SPECIFICATION

The nonhomothetic translog cost function can be envisaged as a second-order Taylor's series approximation in logarithms to an arbitrary cost function. Nonhomothetic functions are very general, since their ratios of cost-minimizing inputs demands are allowed to depend on the level of output; by contrast, with homothetic functions, relative input demands are independent of the level of output.[20] The nonhomothetic translog is written as

$$\begin{aligned} \ln C = \ln \alpha_0 &+ \sum_{i=1}^{n} \alpha_i \ln P_i + \frac{1}{2} \cdot \sum_{i=1}^{n} \sum_{j=1}^{n} \gamma_{ij} \ln P_i \ln P_j \\ &+ \alpha_Y \ln Y + \frac{1}{2} \gamma_{YY} (\ln Y)^2 + \sum_{i=1}^{n} \gamma_{iY} \ln P_i \ln Y \end{aligned} \tag{9.42}$$

where $\gamma_{ij} = \gamma_{ji}$. For a cost function to be well behaved, among other things it must be homogeneous of degree 1 in prices, given Y. This implies the following restrictions on Eq. (9.42):

$$\sum_{i=1}^{n} \alpha_i = 1, \qquad \sum_{i=1}^{n} \gamma_{ij} = \sum_{j=1}^{n} \gamma_{ji} = \sum_{i=1}^{n} \gamma_{iY} = 0 \tag{9.43}$$

A number of additional parameter restrictions can be imposed on the translog cost function, corresponding with further restrictions on the underlying technology. For the translog cost function to be homothetic it is necessary and sufficient that $\gamma_{iy} = 0 \; \forall \; i = 1, \ldots, n$. Homogeneity of a constant degree in output occurs if, in addition to these homotheticity restrictions,

$\gamma_{YY} = 0$; in this case the degree of homogeneity equals $1/\alpha_Y$. Constant returns to scale of the dual production function occurs when, in addition to the above homotheticity and homogeneity restrictions, $\alpha_Y = 1$. Finally, the translog function reduces to the constant-returns-to-scale Cobb-Douglas function when, in addition to all the above restrictions, each of the $\gamma_{ij} = 0$, $i, j = 1, \ldots, n$.

One could of course estimate the translog cost function (9.42) directly, but gains in efficiency can be realized by estimating the optimal, cost-minimizing input demand equations, transformed here into cost share equations. If one logarithmically differentiates Eq. (9.42) with respect to input prices and then employs Shephard's Lemma (see the discussion at the beginning of Section 9.2), one obtains cost share (not input-output) equations of the form

$$\frac{\partial \ln C}{\partial \ln P_i} = \frac{P_i}{C} \cdot \frac{\partial C}{\partial P_i} = \frac{P_i X_i}{C} = \alpha_i + \sum_{j=1}^{n} \gamma_{ij} \ln P_j + \gamma_{iY} \ln Y \qquad \textbf{(9.44)}$$

where $\Sigma_{i=1}^{n} P_i X_i = C$. Defining the cost shares $S_i \equiv P_i X_i / C$, it follows that

$$\sum_{i=1}^{n} S_i = 1$$

This "adding-up condition" of the share equation system (9.44) has important implications for econometric estimation.

To illustrate these issues, let us again consider a four-input (K, L, E and M) cost function, now having the translog form (9.42). In this case the cost share equations (9.44) for the four inputs become

$$\begin{aligned}
S_K &= \alpha_K + \gamma_{KK} \ln P_K + \gamma_{KL} \ln P_L + \gamma_{KE} \ln P_E + \gamma_{KM} \ln P_M + \gamma_{KY} \ln Y \\
S_L &= \alpha_L + \gamma_{LK} \ln P_K + \gamma_{LL} \ln P_L + \gamma_{LE} \ln P_E + \gamma_{LM} \ln P_M + \gamma_{LY} \ln Y \\
S_E &= \alpha_E + \gamma_{EK} \ln P_K + \gamma_{EL} \ln P_L + \gamma_{EE} \ln P_E + \gamma_{EM} \ln P_M + \gamma_{EY} \ln Y \\
S_M &= \alpha_M + \gamma_{MK} \ln P_K + \gamma_{ML} \ln P_L + \gamma_{ME} \ln P_E + \gamma_{MM} \ln P_M + \gamma_{MY} \ln Y
\end{aligned} \qquad \textbf{(9.45)}$$

Notice that in the absence of symmetry restrictions there are 24 parameters to estimate, six in each of the four share equations. When the six cross-equation symmetry conditions are imposed ($\gamma_{KL} = \gamma_{LK}$, $\gamma_{KE} = \gamma_{EK}$, $\gamma_{KM} = \gamma_{MK}$, $\gamma_{LE} = \gamma_{EL}$, $\gamma_{LM} = \gamma_{ML}$, and $\gamma_{EM} = \gamma_{ME}$), the number of parameters drops to 18.

As we noted above, the underlying economic theory also requires that this translog function be homogeneous of degree 1 in input prices. In the above *KLEM* framework the restrictions corresponding to Eq. (9.43) turn out to be

$$\begin{aligned}
\alpha_K + \alpha_L + \alpha_E + \alpha_M &= 1 \\
\gamma_{KK} + \gamma_{KL} + \gamma_{KE} + \gamma_{KM} &= 0 \\
\gamma_{KL} + \gamma_{LL} + \gamma_{LE} + \gamma_{LM} &= 0 \\
\gamma_{KE} + \gamma_{LE} + \gamma_{EE} + \gamma_{EM} &= 0 \\
\gamma_{KM} + \gamma_{LM} + \gamma_{EM} + \gamma_{MM} &= 0 \\
\gamma_{KY} + \gamma_{LY} + \gamma_{EY} + \gamma_{MY} &= 0
\end{aligned} \qquad \textbf{(9.46)}$$

These six restrictions reduce the number of free parameters to be estimated from 18 to 12. If other restrictions such as constant returns to scale were also imposed, the number of free parameters would be reduced further, in this case to nine.

To implement this share equation system empirically, it is necessary to specify a stochastic framework. Empirical researchers have typically added a random disturbance term u_i to each share equation, $i = K, L, E, M$, and have then assumed that the resulting disturbance vector $u \equiv \{u_K, u_L, u_E, u_M\}$ is multivariate normally distributed with mean vector zero and constant covariance matrix Ω^*. More general stochastic specifications, such as those involving first-order vector autocorrelation, will be considered further in Section 9.5.

The rationale for the stochastic specification can simply consist of the argument that firms make random errors in choosing their cost-minimizing input bundles. Alternatively, following Marjorie McElroy [1987], one might argue that errors are in the eyes of the beholding econometrician and are not due to firms. Specifically, McElroy suggests embedding the entire optimization problem within a stochastic framework and assumes that firms differ from one another according to parameters that are known by the firms' managers but are not observed by the econometrician. Depending on how one specifies these parameters, the firm effects can manifest themselves as additive or multiplicative error terms in the cost function, demand equations, or share equations. Note that if one wants to estimate the cost function jointly with the demand or share equations, then an internally consistent stochastic specification cannot in general involve additive and homoskedastic disturbances in both the cost function and demand or share equations. Also, in some cases, information from the cost function is totally redundant in that it is already entirely captured by disturbances in the demand or share equations.[21]

Suppose, then, that one were interested only in estimating parameters of the cost share equations (9.45) and that one specified additive disturbances that are multivariate normally distributed with mean vector zero and constant covariance matrix Ω^*.

The share equation system (9.44) or (9.45) possesses a special property, in that for each observation the sum of the dependent variables (the cost shares) over all equations always equals 1. Hence if there are n factor share equations, only $n-1$ of them are linearly independent. This adding-up feature of the share equation system (9.44) or (9.45) has several important econometric implications, to which we now turn our attention.

First, since the shares always sum to unity and only $n-1$ of the share equations are linearly independent, for each observation the sum of the disturbances across equations must always equal zero. This implies that the disturbance covariance matrix Ω^* is singular and nondiagonal.

Second, because the shares sum to unity at each observation, when the six symmetry restrictions are not imposed, the simple arithmetic of equation-by-equation ordinary least squares yields parameter estimates that always obey the following column sum adding-up conditions:

$$\begin{aligned} a_K + a_L + a_E + a_M = 1, \qquad g_{KK} + g_{LK} + g_{EK} + g_{MK} = \\ g_{KL} + g_{LL} + g_{EL} + g_{ML} = g_{KE} + g_{LE} + g_{EE} + g_{ME} = \\ g_{KM} + g_{LM} + g_{EM} + g_{MM} = g_{KY} + g_{LY} + g_{EY} + g_{MY} = 0 \end{aligned} \tag{9.47}$$

where the a_i and g_{ij} are estimates of the α_i and γ_{ij} parameters. These relationships in Eqs. (9.47) also imply that the OLS residuals e_i across equations will sum to zero at each observation, that is,

$$e_K + e_L + e_E + e_M = 0$$

Thus the residual cross-products matrix resulting from OLS equation-by-equation estimation will be nondiagonal and singular. These parameter adding-up relationships are demonstrated empirically in Table 9.2, in which equation-by-equation OLS parameter estimates are presented in columns with the heading "OLS"; it can easily be verified that with these estimates, the adding-up restrictions in Eq. (9.47) are satisfied.[22]

Third, because the disturbance covariance and residual cross-products matrices will both be singular, ML estimation, which minimizes the determinant of $E'E$, will not be feasible, since this determinant will be zero for any set of parameters satisfying Eq. (9.47). The most common procedure for handling this singularity problem is to drop an arbitrary equation and then estimate the remaining $n-1$ share equations by ML.

For example, in our four-equation symmetry-constrained translog example, one could impose the homogeneity restrictions (9.46), delete the M share equation, and directly estimate the 12 free parameters in the K, L, and E equations as follows:

$$\begin{aligned} S_K &= \alpha_K + \gamma_{KK} \ln (P_K/P_M) + \gamma_{KL} \ln (P_L/P_M) + \gamma_{KE} \ln (P_E/P_M) + \gamma_{KY} \ln Y \\ S_L &= \alpha_L + \gamma_{KL} \ln (P_K/P_M) + \gamma_{LL} \ln (P_L/P_M) + \gamma_{LE} \ln (P_E/P_M) + \gamma_{LY} \ln Y \\ S_E &= \alpha_E + \gamma_{KE} \ln (P_K/P_M) + \gamma_{LE} \ln (P_L/P_M) + \gamma_{EE} \ln (P_E/P_M) + \gamma_{EY} \ln Y \end{aligned} \tag{9.48}$$

Indirect parameter estimates of the six other parameters in the omitted M share equation could then be obtained by rearranging the homogeneity

Table 9.2 Equation-by-Equation OLS Estimates and IZEF/ML Parameter Estimates of Translog Share Equations (9.45), U.S. Manufacturing, 1947–1971, Standard Errors in Parentheses

Parameter	OLS	IZEF	Parameter	OLS	IZEF	Parameter	OLS	IZEF
a_K	0.279	0.057	g_{LL}	0.101	0.075	g_{EM}	−0.013	−0.004
	(0.035)	(0.001)		(0.035)	(0.007)		(0.008)	(0.009)
g_{KK}	0.045	0.030	g_{LE}	0.041	−0.004	g_{EY}	−0.031	0.000
	(0.004)	(0.006)		(0.034)	(0.002)		(0.003)	
g_{KL}	0.031	−0.000	g_{LM}	−0.123	−0.071	a_M	0.119	0.645
	(0.011)	(0.004)		(0.048)	(0.011)		(0.127)	(0.003)
g_{KE}	0.000	−0.010	g_{LY}	−0.028	0.000	g_{MK}	−0.062	−0.019
	(0.010)	(0.003)		(0.021)			(0.013)	(0.010)
g_{KM}	−0.015	−0.019	a_E	0.205	0.044	g_{ML}	−0.161	−0.071
	(0.015)	(0.010)		(0.018)	(0.001)		(0.039)	(0.011)
g_{KY}	−0.043	0.000	g_{EK}	−0.004	−0.010	g_{ME}	−0.053	−0.004
	(0.007)			(0.002)	(0.003)		(0.038)	(0.009)
a_L	0.398	0.253	g_{EL}	0.029	−0.004	g_{MM}	0.150	0.094
	(0.114)	(0.002)		(0.005)	(0.002)		(0.054)	(0.023)
g_{LK}	0.021	−0.000	g_{EE}	0.011	0.019	g_{MY}	0.102	0.000
	(0.012)	(0.004)		(0.005)	(0.005)		(0.024)	

Notes: Data are from Berndt and Wood [1975, 1979]. Estimation by the author. Equation-by-equation OLS and IZEF/ML estimates coincide when no restrictions are imposed. The IZEF/ML estimates presented are with symmetry, linear homogeneity in prices, and constant returns to scale imposed.

restrictions (9.46) in terms of the directly estimated parameters as follows:

$$a_M = 1 - a_K - a_L - a_E \; g_{KM} = -(g_{KK} + g_{KL} + g_{KE})$$
$$g_{LM} = -(g_{KL} + g_{LL} + g_{LE}) \; g_{EM} = -(g_{KE} + g_{LE} + g_{EE})$$
$$g_{MY} = -(g_{KY} + g_{LY} + g_{EY}), \quad \text{and} \quad g_{MM} = -(g_{KM} + g_{LM} + g_{EM})$$
$$\Rightarrow g_{MM} = g_{KK} + g_{LL} + g_{EE} + 2(g_{KL} + g_{KE} + g_{LE}) \tag{9.49}$$

Note that since these indirectly estimated parameters are linear combinations of the directly estimated coefficients, variances of the indirectly estimated parameters can be calculated as a linear combination of the directly estimated variances and covariances. Statistical software programs currently differ in the user commands that are required to make such indirect computations.

Fourth, although arbitrarily dropping one share equation in the direct estimation of parameters appears to be a reasonable procedure, it does raise the issue of whether the parameter estimates are invariant to the choice of which equation is deleted. If such invariance were lacking, it would be a troubling feature of the estimation process, since it would permit users to report only those estimation results that are most agreeable with prior beliefs or judgments. Fortunately, as long as ML estimation procedures are employed on the $n-1$ share equations, all parameter estimates, log-likelihood values, and estimated standard errors will be invariant to the choice of which $n-1$ equations are directly estimated. This invariance also holds for the one-step Zellner-efficient estimator, *provided* that the first-round estimate of Ω_n (the disturbance covariance matrix Ω^* with the nth row and column deleted) is based on equation-by-equation least squares estimation without the symmetry restrictions imposed. However, if one-step ZEF estimation is undertaken in which the estimate of Ω_n is based on, for example, ordinary least squares estimation of a stacked $n-1$ equation system with symmetry restrictions imposed (frequently called a trace minimization estimator), then the direct and indirect ZEF parameter estimates will vary depending on which $n-1$ share equations are directly estimated.

Fifth and finally, if one were estimating the translog share equation system (9.48) using highly aggregated data and therefore believed that input prices were endogenous, to avoid simultaneous equations problems, one could employ an instrumental variable estimator, provided that appropriate instruments were available. Equation-by-equation two-stage least squares (2SLS) would be inappropriate, since the requisite cross-equation symmetry conditions could not be properly imposed. As with the ZEF estimator discussed above, if one employed the three-stage least squares estimator (3SLS), and if the estimate of Ω_n were based on equation-by-equation 2SLS estimation of $n-1$ equations without the symmetry restrictions imposed, then the 3SLS estimates would also be invariant to the choice of which $n-1$ equations were directly estimated. By contrast, if 3SLS estimation were performed where the estimate of Ω_n were based on 2SLS trace minimization of an $n-1$ equation system with symmetry restrictions imposed, then the choice of which $n-1$ share equations were directly estimated would affect the parameter estimates. This lack of invariance could be eliminated, however, if one iterated the 3SLS procedure until changes from one iteration to the next in the directly estimated parameters and Ω_n became arbitrarily small.

For the translog function estimated by ML, hypothesis testing can be undertaken using any of the three test procedures discussed in Section 9.3, that is, the Wald, LR, or LM test statistic. For the singular share equation system these test procedures must be based on direct estimation of $n-1$ share equations. If instrumental variable estimation such as 3SLS is employed, then the LR test statistic would not be appropriate (the likelihood function is not the maximand). However, the Wald or LM test statistic can be used in the context of instrumental variable estimation.

A common Wald test procedure is first to estimate the unconstrained model by 3SLS or I3SLS such that parameter estimates are invariant to the choice of deleted equation. Let the corresponding residual cross-products matrix be S. Conditional on this S, estimate the constrained model by 3SLS, and denote the resulting residual cross-products matrix by W_1. Finally, to obtain the Wald test statistic, use Eq. (9.34), and compare the value of this chi-square random variable to the critical value at a predetermined level of significance.[23]

The LM test statistic can also be employed, first by estimating the W_0 matrix by 3SLS or I3SLS, then by estimating by 3SLS the unconstrained model conditional on W_0, and finally, by substituting into Eq. (9.37).[24] Note that the inequality in Eq. (9.38) involving Wald and LM statistics under ML estimation will no longer necessarily hold with instrumental variable estimation.

We now move on to a discussion of estimation of substitution elasticities based on the translog functional form. Using Eq. (9.28), the Allen partial elasticities of substitution for the translog cost function turn out to be equal to

$$\sigma_{ij} = \frac{\gamma_{ij} + S_i S_j}{S_i S_j}, \qquad i, j = 1, \ldots, n, \qquad \text{but} \quad i \neq j$$
$$\sigma_{ii} = \frac{\gamma_{ii} + S_i^2 - S_i}{S_i^2}, \qquad i = 1, \ldots, n \tag{9.50}$$

For example, based on the IZEF/ML translog parameter estimates presented in Table 9.2, 1971 estimates of the σ_{ij} are σ_{KL}, 0.97; σ_{KE}, -3.60; σ_{KM}, 0.35; σ_{LM}, 0.61; σ_{EM}, 0.83; and σ_{LE}, 0.68; while σ_{ii} estimates are σ_{KK}, -6.99; σ_{LL}, -1.51; σ_{EE}, -11.74; and σ_{MM}, -0.39. Notice that with these translog estimates, capital and energy are complements, capital and labor are substitutes, and energy and labor are substitutable inputs.

Further, since the price elasticities $\epsilon_{ij} = S_j \sigma_{ij}$, it follows that for the translog cost function, price elasticites are calculated as

$$\epsilon_{ij} = \frac{\gamma_{ij} + S_i S_j}{S_i}, \qquad i, j = 1, \ldots, n, \qquad \text{but} \quad i \neq j$$
$$\epsilon_{ii} = \frac{\gamma_{ii} + S_i^2 - S_i}{S_i}, \qquad i = 1, \ldots, n \tag{9.51}$$

Based on the IZEF/ML translog parameter estimates presented in Table 9.2, the implied 1971 price elasticity estimates are as follows: ϵ_{KK}, -0.34; ϵ_{KL}, 0.29; ϵ_{KE}, -0.16; ϵ_{KM}, 0.21, ϵ_{LK}, 0.05; ϵ_{LL}, -0.45; ϵ_{LE}, 0.03; ϵ_{LM}, 0.37; ϵ_{EK}, -0.17; ϵ_{EL}, 0.20; ϵ_{EE}, -0.53; ϵ_{EM}, 0.51; ϵ_{MK}, 0.02; ϵ_{ML}, 0.18; ϵ_{ME}, 0.04; and ϵ_{MM}, -0.24.

Several comments should be made concerning these substitution elasticity estimates. First, parameter estimates and fitted shares should replace the γ's and S's when computing estimates of the σ_{ij} and ϵ_{ij}. This implies that in general the estimated elasticities will vary across observations. Second, since the parameter estimates and fitted shares have variances and covariances, the estimated substitution elasticities also have stochastic distributions. The fact that these elasticities are highly nonlinear functions of the estimated γ's and S's has made it difficult to obtain estimates of the variances of the estimated elasticities. Progress on this and related issues, using first-order approximations, has been reported by Nalin Kulatilaka [1985] and, based on Monte Carlo techniques, by Richard G. Anderson and Jerry G. Thursby [1986].[25] Third, if the translog form is restricted to the Cobb-Douglas function so that

γ_{ij}, $i, j = 1, \ldots, n$, simultaneously equal zero, by Eq. (9.50) all the σ_{ij} will equal unity, $i, j = 1, \ldots, n$ but $i \neq j$.

Fourth, as with the generalized Leontief function, the estimated translog cost function should be checked to ensure that it is monotonically increasing and strictly quasi-concave in input prices, as is required by theory. For monotonicity it is required that the fitted shares all be positive, and for strict quasi-concavity the $n \times n$ matrix of substitution elasticities must be negative semidefinite at each observation. Finally, a useful check on the validity of the elasticity calculations is to ensure that at each observation the additive relationship (9.33) holds.

The translog cost function as specified in Eq. (9.42) was a highly general, nonhomothetic form, which implies that returns to scale are not constrained a priori. As has been shown by Giora Hanoch [1975], returns to scale (here, called μ) are computed as the inverse of the elasticity of costs with respect to output. More specifically,

$$\mu = 1/\epsilon_{CY} \qquad \text{where} \qquad \epsilon_{CY} \equiv \frac{\partial \ln C}{\partial \ln Y} \tag{9.52}$$

and where for the translog function

$$\begin{aligned}\epsilon_{CY} = \alpha_Y &+ \gamma_{KY} \ln P_K + \gamma_{LY} \ln P_L + \gamma_{EY} \ln P_E \\ &+ \gamma_{MY} \ln P_M + \gamma_{YY} \ln Y\end{aligned} \tag{9.53}$$

Hypothesis tests regarding the empirical validity of the homotheticity, homogeneity, and constant-returns-to-scale restrictions can be implemented by using the statistical inference procedures outlined above.

One potential problem with estimation of scale economies, however, is that the α_Y and γ_{YY} parameters do not appear in the share equations, and so these parameters cannot be estimated by using only the share equation system (9.44) or (9.45). To estimate returns to scale, it is usually necessary to add the translog cost function to the share equation system to be estimated.[26] If, for example, one were estimating the *KLEM* model, estimates of all the substitution and scale economy elasticities could be obtained by estimating the translog cost function (9.42) plus the three share equations in Eq. (9.48). In this case it would also be necessary to impose the symmetry restrictions, as well as the homogeneity constraints in Eq. (9.46), on the cost function equation.

9.5 AUTOREGRESSIVE STOCHASTIC PROCESSES IN MULTIVARIATE EQUATION SYSTEMS

The discussion of stochastic specification to this point has been limited to specifying that the vector U of additive disturbance terms to the n input-output equations (for the GL cost function) or to the $n-1$ share equations (for the translog function) is independently and identically multivariate normally distributed with mean vector zero and constant nonsingular covariance matrix Ω. An obvious generalization involves the use of a first-order stationary vector autoregressive process specification.

Let U_t be an $n \times 1$ vector of disturbances following a first-order vector autoregressive process, let ϵ_t be an $n \times 1$ vector of independently and identically normally distributed random error terms, and let R be an $n \times n$ autocovariance matrix consisting of n^2 parameters, where R is in general nondiagonal and asymmetric. By using matrix notation the first-order vector or multivariate autoregressive stochastic process can be written as

$$U_t = RU_{t-1} + \epsilon_t \tag{9.54}$$

This is analogous to the single-equation context, in which u_t in the regression model

$$y_t = \alpha + \beta X_t + u_t, \qquad t = 1, \ldots, T \tag{9.55}$$

follows a first-order stationary univariate autoregressive scheme,

$$u_t = \rho u_{t-1} + \epsilon_t, \qquad t = 2, \ldots, T \tag{9.56}$$

$|\rho| < 1$, and ϵ_t is a "white noise" independent and identically normally distributed disturbance term. Although OLS estimates of α and β in Eq. (9.55) are unbiased and consistent, they are not efficient; further, the estimates of the variances of the OLS estimated parameters are biased and inconsistent.

A common way of circumventing these problems and accounting properly for autocorrelation in the single equation context is to transform Eq. (9.55) into an equation having "clean" disturbances. For example, lag Eq. (9.55) once, multiply by ρ, and then subtract the lagged version from the original Eq. (9.55). After rearranging and substituting in Eq. (9.56), this yields

$$y_t = \alpha(1 - \rho) + \rho y_{t-1} + \beta(X_t - \rho X_{t-1}) + \epsilon_t, \qquad t = 2, \ldots, T \tag{9.57}$$

Note that estimation of Eq. (9.57) by single-equation nonlinear least squares methods yields consistent and efficient estimates of the parameters, since ϵ_t is "white noise." Also, the null hypothesis of no autocorrelation corresponds to a test that $\rho = 0$.

Vector autocorrelation in systems of equations is analogous. Consider, for example, the n-equation system

$$Y_t = X_t\beta + U_t, \qquad t = 1, \ldots, T \tag{9.58}$$

where Y is an $n \times 1$ vector, X_t is an $n \times K$ matrix, and β is a $K \times 1$ vector of parameters. Note that since β includes parameters from all the equations, K can be very large; for example, if there were k right-hand variables in each equation and no cross-equation restrictions, $K = nk$. Further, let U_t in Eq. (9.58) follow the vector autoregressive process specified in Eq. (9.54), namely, $U_t = RU_{t-1} + \epsilon_t$.

To accommodate autocorrelation, lag Eq. (9.58) once, premultiply by R, and then subtract the product from Eq. (9.58). After rearrangement and substitution, this yields the multivariate equation system

$$Y_t = RY_{t-1} + (X_t - RX_{t-1})\beta + \epsilon_t, \qquad t = 2, \ldots, T \tag{9.59}$$

which is analogous to Eq. (9.57). This equation system (9.59) can be estimated by using system estimation methods that incorporate nonlinear parameter restrictions.

As an example, consider the n input-output demand equations (9.23) derived from the generalized Leontief cost function. If additive disturbance terms are appended to each equation in Eq.(9.23), and if the resulting vector of disturbances is assumed to follow the first-order vector autoregressive process (9.54), then following the procedure outlined above, one can obtain an equation system analogous to Eq. (9.59), whose ith equation is written as

$$a_{it} = \sum_{m=1}^{n} \rho_{im} a_{m,t-1} + \sum_{j=1}^{n} d_{ij}(w_{jt}/w_{it})^{1/2} - \sum_{m=1}^{n}\sum_{j=1}^{n} \rho_{mj} d_{ij}(w_{j,t-1}/w_{i,t-1})^{1/2} + \epsilon_{it},$$
$$i = 1, \ldots, n; \qquad t = 2, \ldots, T \tag{9.60}$$

Special cases of Eq.(9.60) include the diagonal autocovariance matrix R (when all $\rho_{ij} = 0$, $i, j = 1, \ldots, n$ but $i \neq j$), and the case of no autocorrelation when all $\rho_{ij} = 0$, $i, j = 1, \ldots, n$. Each of these special cases can be tested by using the statistical inference methods outlined in Section 9.3.

For the translog function, vector autocorrelation can be accommodated in a completely analogous manner, except for one major exception. Recall that with the translog form, the cost shares are dependent variables, and at each observation these shares must sum to unity, implying that only $n - 1$ share equations are independent, that the n disturbances must sum to zero at each observation, and that the $n \times n$ disturbance covariance and residual cross-products matrices are singular. This singularity imposes severe identifiability and diagonality constraints on the autocovariance matrix R.

To see this, note that if an additive disturbance term u_{it} is appended to each of the n share equations (9.44) derived from the translog cost function, and if the resulting $n \times 1$ disturbance vector U_t follows the first-order vector autoregressive process $U_t = RU_{t-1} + \epsilon_t$ as in Eq. (9.54), then the restriction that the disturbances sum to zero at each observation implies that

$$i'U_t = i'RU_{t-1} + i'\epsilon_t = 0, \qquad t = 2, \ldots, T \tag{9.61}$$

where i' is a $1 \times n$ vector of 1's. For Eq. (9.61) to hold for all possible statistically independent ϵ_t, U_{t-1} pairs, it is necessary and sufficient that each of the right-hand side terms of Eq. (9.61) equal zero, that is,

$$i'RU_{t-1} = i'\epsilon_t = 0 \tag{9.62}$$

While the second equality in Eq. (9.62) presents no unusual problems, the first relation will hold if and only if each column of the R matrix sums to the same unknown constant, say, λ.[27] This is a very strong restriction. For example, if R is specified to be diagonal, then Eq. (9.62) requires that all diagonal elements equal λ. This implies that empirical implementation of vector autoregressive processes in singular equation systems such as the share system derived from the translog cost function requires considerable care.

A further problem arises in that when $n-1$ cost share equations are directly estimated, it is not possible to identify all the $n(n-1)$ independent elements of R unless n–1 independent additional zero or other equality restrictions on the elements of R are imposed a priori. While further discussion of this can be found in Berndt and Savin [1975], it is worth remarking here that this identification problem for R is generally not very damaging, since empirical researchers seldom have an economic interest in identifying the elements of R. Note also that even though the elements of R may be underidentified, the α_i, γ_{ij}, and γ_{iY} translog parameters are still all identified.

Finally, with respect to hypothesis testing in the vector autocorrelation context, a test of $R = 0$ can be accomplished by estimating a translog share version of Eq. (9.60) with and without $R = 0$ being imposed and then using any of the test statistic procedures discussed above. Tests concerning R in the GL function are analogous, except that the absence of singularity implies that R can assume any form. In particular, with the GL function, a diagonal R can have unequal elements.

9.6 THE TRANSLOG FUNCTION IN AN INTERINDUSTRY GENERAL EQUILIBRIUM MODEL

Up to this point we have considered only econometric issues that are involved in estimating the production structure of a single firm, industry, or sector. In a series of articles with various coauthors, Dale W. Jorgenson has introduced procedures for implementing empirically multisectoral models of a macroeconomy in which interindustry flows (the outputs of one sector being inputs into another sector) are explicitly incorporated.[28] We now briefly consider economic theory and econometric issues that are involved in performing such general equilibrium econometrics.

Jorgenson begins by assuming that in all production sectors, production is characterized by constant returns to scale. This is a useful assumption because it means that average (and marginal) costs for each sector are invariant to the scale of output and therefore to any changes in the composition of final demand among sectors. A second important assumption that Jorgenson makes is that in each sector, inputs adjust instantaneously (more on this in Section 9.7) to full equilibrium levels and that economic profits are zero. Under these conditions, output price equals unit cost, and since cost depends on input prices, output prices for each sector can be directly related to input prices, that is, each sector has a well-defined price-possibility frontier.

Although Jorgenson's earliest general equilibrium models included nine production sectors and one final demand consumption sector, his more recent models for the United States have incorporated more than 30 sectors.[29] In such cases it is of course infeasible to estimate all equations for all sectors as a full simultaneous equations system. Instead, the system of translog share

DALE JORGENSON

Integrating Theory and Practice

In 1970, at the World Congress of the Econometric Society in Cambridge, England, Dale W. Jorgenson presented a now classic paper entitled "Conjugate Duality and the Transcendental Logarithmic Production Function," that was jointly written with his Berkeley students Laurits R. Christensen and Lawrence J. Lau. The translog function introduced in that paper and discussed in this chapter is widely used today in econometric studies of producer and consumer behavior.

Born in Bozeman, Montana in 1933, Dale Jorgenson attended public schools in Helena, Montana. After receiving his B.A. degree in economics from Reed College in Portland, Oregon in 1955, he enrolled at Harvard for graduate studies. He wrote a Ph.D. dissertation on dynamic input-ouput analysis under the supervision of Wassily Leontief. Jorgenson then joined the economics faculty at the University of California–Berkeley. There his early research focused on the modeling of investment behavior. Jorgenson made pioneering theoretical and econometric contributions, developing neoclassical models of investment, formulae for the user cost of capital, and rational distributed lag functions (see Chapter 6 for further discussion).

In a subsequent line of research, Jorgenson and a number of co-authors utilized the neoclassical model of production to develop now standard procedures for measuring multifactor productivity growth. One important outcome of this productivity research was that it focused attention on the critical need to employ national income and product accounting procedures that are consistent with the economic theory of producer and consumer behavior.

Because of these contributions, in 1971 the American Economic Association awarded Jorgenson the prestigious John Bates Clark Medal, citing him as "preeminently a master of the territory between economics and statistics" and his investment research as "one of the finest examples in the marriage of theory and practice in economics."

Jorgenson's integration of economic theory, statistics, accounting, and econometrics has continued at an even more rapid pace in the last two decades. Together with a number of coauthors, Jorgenson has pioneered in empirically implementing general equilibrium models of production and consumption. These general equilibrium models, based on the translog functional form, have been applied to important policy issues such as the economywide effects of energy price shocks, alternative environmental policies, and changes in tax policy in the United States, Japan, Germany, and elsewhere.

Dale Jorgenson returned to Harvard in 1969. He is currently the Frederic Eaton Abbe Professor of Economics at Harvard as well as Director of the Program on Technology and Economic Policy at Harvard's Kennedy School of Government. Jorgenson is an elected Member of the National Academy of Sciences and the American Academy of Arts and Sciences and is a Fellow of the Econometric Society, the American Statistical Association, and the American Association for the Advancement of Science. In 1987 he served as President of the Econometric Society.

An important feature of Jorgenson's research process has been the collaboration with students at Berkeley and Harvard, primarily through his supervision of doctoral research. Collaboration is often an outgrowth of the student's Ph.D. dissertation, leading to subsequent joint publications. At last count, Jorgenson had collaborated on publications with more than 35 individual economists.

equations is estimated by using I3SLS separately for each sector, the same set of instruments being employed in each sector. It is worth noting that the reason that I3SLS is employed rather than IZEF is to take account of the interindustry flow nature of a general equilibrium model, since in such a model the input and output prices are simultaneously determined; hence it is inappropriate to assume that input prices are exogenous in each sector.

Jorgenson's general equilibrium econometric approach has attracted a great deal of attention, in large part because it has proved to be a very useful and instructive way to analyze economywide impacts of energy price shocks in the 1970s and of alternative tax policies in the 1980s.

9.7 ISSUES ADDRESSED BY RECENT RESEARCH ON FACTOR DEMAND MODELS

We now outline several extensions of the basic or classic models of production that were considered in previous sections of this chapter. We also briefly survey a number of related research issues.[30]

A common feature of the GL and translog functions that were discussed in Sections 9.2 and 9.4 is that each specification includes a single output measure. This type of specification can be extended in at least two ways. First, Richard H. Spady and Ann F. Friedlaender [1978] have integrated the hedonic approach that emphasizes attributes of outputs (see Chapter 4 of this book) with the flexible functional form literature. Specifically, noting that in many industries, physical output varies with respect to attributes or qualities, Spady and Friedlaender construct an hedonic measure of output as a function of output characteristics. They call this hedonic measure an "effective" or "quality-adjusted" output. They then argue that failure to take these output characteristics into account can create serious specification errors. For example, inferences concerning economies of scale and factor demand elasticities differ substantially between the hedonic and nonhedonic formulations of the cost function.

Spady and Friedlaender illustrate this point empirically by examining the regulated trucking industry in the United States, where ton-miles is the conventional measure of output. They distinguish the ton-miles of the short-haul, small-load, less-than-truckload (LTL) traffic from those of the long-haul, large-load, truckload traffic, not by treating them as separate outputs, but rather by specifying an effective output that depends on a generic measure of physical output (ton-miles) and on the attributes of this output (e.g., average shipment size, average length of haul, and proportion of tons shipped in LTL lots).[31]

An alternative generalization is to specify multiple outputs. With multiproduct firms, economies of scope become of interest, and procedures for measuring scale economies become more ambiguous.[32] Although multiproduct cost function specifications generally entail estimation of a larger number of parameters than the hedonic cost functions with a comparable number of attributes, the multiproduct formulation permits a richer analysis of effects on costs and factor demands of various changes in the composition and levels of output. Recent examples of empirical implementations of multiproduct cost functions, as well as associated econometric issues, are found in, among others, Douglas W. Caves, Laurits R. Christensen, and Michael W. Tretheway [1981]; Thomas G. Cowing and Alphonse Holtmann [1983]; and Judy S. Wang Chiang and Ann F. Friedlaender [1985].

Another body of literature has dealt with alternative flexible functional forms, representations that in some cases are even more general than the GL and translog. Such functional forms include the symmetric generalized McFadden,[33] the generalized Box-Cox,[34] the Fourier,[35] and the minflex Laurent.[36] While very general, these functional forms are more cumbersome to implement empirically because the associated likelihood functions are exceedingly nonlinear and therefore more complex. In a related literature, researchers have compared a number of the existing flexible functional forms empirically, examining in particular their approximation properties; see, for example, David Guilkey, C. A. Knox Lovell, and Robin C. Sickles [1983].

A different but increasingly important extension deals with the fixity of certain inputs. Specifically, an important assumption that has been implicit in the discussion of the GL and translog forms to now is that all inputs adjust instantaneously to their long-run, equilibrium values. Recall that in our overview of empirical results based on the CES production function, it was hypothesized that the reason that estimates of σ based on the capital demand equation were lower than those based on the labor demand equation was that, within one time period, capital adjusted only partially to its full equilibrium level.

Rather than assuming that all inputs adjust instantaneously to their full equilibrium levels, researchers in the last decade have increasingly adopted a framework that distinguishes variable from quasi-fixed inputs, where the latter adjust only partially to their full equilibrium levels within one time period. Following the Marshallian tradition, empirical researchers have therefore distinguished short-run cost functions (in which some inputs are fixed at levels other than their full equilibrium values) from long-run cost functions (in which all inputs are at their full equilibrium values).[37]

One line of research specifies that variable costs (expenditures on variable inputs) are a function of the variable input prices, the level of output, and quantities of the fixed factors. For example, a *KLEM* translog variable cost function with K fixed and L, E, and M as variable inputs can be written as

$$\begin{aligned}\ln VC = {} & \ln \beta_0 + \beta_L \ln P_L + \beta_E \ln P_E + \beta_M \ln P_M + \beta_K \ln K + \beta_Y \ln Y \\ & + \tfrac{1}{2}[\beta_{LL} (\ln P_L)^2 + \beta_{EE} (\ln P_E)^2 + \beta_{MM} (\ln P_M)^2 + \beta_{KK} (\ln K)^2 \\ & + \beta_{YY} (\ln Y)^2] + \beta_{LE} \ln P_L \ln P_E + \beta_{LM} \ln P_L \ln P_M \\ & + \beta_{EM} \ln P_E \ln P_M + \beta_{KL} \ln K \ln P_L + \beta_{KE} \ln K \ln P_E \\ & + \beta_{KM} \ln K \ln P_M + \beta_{KY} \ln K \ln Y + \beta_{LY} \ln P_L \ln Y \\ & + \beta_{EY} \ln P_E \ln Y + \beta_{MY} \ln P_M \ln Y \end{aligned} \tag{9.63}$$

where variable costs $VC \equiv P_L L + P_E E + P_M M$. In contrast to the full equilibrium translog cost function (9.42), the translog variable or restricted cost function has variable (rather than total) costs as a left-hand variable and various linear and quadratic forms of the (beginning of time period) *quantity* of the fixed capital input, not its price, as right-hand variables. To be consistent with economic theory, parameter restrictions that are analogous to Eq. (9.46) must be adapted to this framework so that this variable cost function is homogeneous of degree 1 in variable input prices, given K and Y.

Estimating equations for the variable inputs based on the translog variable cost function can be obtained by using Shephard's Lemma, as with a long-run cost function. For example, the share equations for the variable inputs turn out to be

$$\begin{aligned}\frac{\partial \ln VC}{\partial \ln P_L} = \frac{P_L L}{VC} &= \beta_L + \beta_{LL} \ln P_L + \beta_{LE} \ln P_E + \beta_{LM} \ln P_M \\ & \quad + \beta_{KL} \ln K + \beta_{LY} \ln Y \\ \frac{\partial \ln VC}{\partial \ln P_E} = \frac{P_E E}{VC} &= \beta_E + \beta_{LE} \ln P_L + \beta_{EE} \ln P_E + \beta_{EM} \ln P_M \\ & \quad + \beta_{KE} \ln K + \beta_{EY} \ln Y \\ \frac{\partial \ln VC}{\partial \ln P_M} = \frac{P_M M}{VC} &= \beta_M + \beta_{LM} \ln P_L + \beta_{EM} \ln P_E + \beta_{MM} \ln P_M \\ & \quad + \beta_{KM} \ln K + \beta_{MY} \ln Y \end{aligned} \tag{9.64}$$

These share equations differ from those based on the full equilibrium cost function in that the left-hand variables are cost shares in variable (not total) costs and $\ln K$ replaces $\ln P_K$ as a right-hand variable. For empirical implementation, researchers typically append an additive disturbance term to each share equation. Since the shares again sum to unity at each observation, the disturbance covariance matrix is still singular, and so one variable input share equation is typically arbitrarily deleted.

A distinguishing feature of the variable cost function is that it permits one to calculate the shadow value of the fixed inputs. For example, in the *KLEM* framework, one can define the shadow value of the fixed capital input as $-\partial VC/\partial K$ and denote it as R_K; $\partial VC/\partial K$ represents the one-period reduction in variable costs attainable if, holding output quantity and variable input prices constant, the quantity of capital services were increased by one unit.

Further, since it is reasonable to expect that in the short run the shadow or ex post value of capital services R_K would not always equal the ex ante or market price of capital P_K (for example, because of unexpected cyclical changes in demand), one might want to define the full equilibrium level of K given Y as that level of K^* at which R_K equals P_K. One implication of this is that one can distinguish short-run substitution elasticities (when $R_K \neq P_K$) from those in the long run (when $R_K = P_K$).

Empirical implementations of flexible variable cost or restricted profit functions that treat some inputs as fixed and others as variable in the short run include, for example, a study by Scott E. Atkinson and Robert Halvorsen [1976] of steam electric power generation, an examination of substitution possibilities in the U.S. agriculture sector by Randall S. Brown and Laurits R. Christensen [1981], and an assessment of economic capacity utilization in the manufacturing sectors of nine OECD countries by Berndt and Dieter M. Hesse [1986]. While each of these studies employs a translog form, a short-run variant of the GL function can also be used. Indeed, Catherine J. Morrison [1988a] finds that the GL form might be preferred to the translog in the variable or restricted cost function context.

Another line of recent research not only distinguishes between fixed and variable inputs, but also derives analytically the optimal transition path from short to long run. This endogenous partial adjustment of fixed inputs is the outcome of a dynamic optimization process by which firms choose investment paths and variable input demands to maximize the present value of net benefits. Early research in this area assumed either a flexible functional form and static expectations[38] or a restrictive functional form with complex nonstatic expectations.[39] Recent research efforts have been based on flexible functional forms and have permitted a variety of nonstatic expectations representations, including the rational expectations hypothesis (REH).

A study by Robert S. Pindyck and Julio R. Rotemberg [1983], for example, uses lagged values of the exogenous variables as instruments and then estimates a translog variable cost function along with an equation representing optimal investment using the iterative three-stage least squares (I3SLS) estimator. An attractive feature of this estimation technique is that the residuals are orthogonal to the fitted right-hand variables, and so the I3SLS estimator is consistent with the REH. Research by Morrison [1986] and by Ingmar R. Prucha and M. Ishaq Nadiri [1986] suggests, however, that the REH specification might not be the most preferable empirically and that the I3SLS estimator in this context tends to suffer from efficiency problems.

Another strand in the recent literature extends the cost function approach to endogenize pricing in the output market under the assumption of imperfect competition in the output market. In such models, a demand equation is specified for the output of the firm or industry, and from this demand equation an expression for marginal revenue (MR) is obtained. Assuming profit maximization, this MR is then set equal to marginal cost (MC), and the $MR = MC$ condition is then used to solve for endogenous output; the corresponding profit-maximizing price is obtained by inverting the demand curve.

Within such a framework it is therefore possible to examine the effects of various changes (such as supply or demand shocks) on the optimal markups of profit maximizing firms. Note that to implement such a model econometrically, it is necessary to incorporate into the estimation in addition to the input demand (or cost share) equations, an inverted demand equation and the output quantity equation based on the $MR = MC$ condition. Obviously, a simultaneous equation estimation procedure such as 3SLS, I3SLS, or FIML needs to be employed in the estimation.[40]

Finally, any survey of interrelated factor demand modeling would be seriously incomplete if it did not devote some attention to efforts to model the effects of technical progress on factor demands and costs. Under constant returns to scale the effects of technical progress are manifested either in increased output or in reduced factor demands and costs and are typically called multifactor productivity (MFP) growth. Virtually all of the MFP research has assumed that technical progress is disembodied, which means that its effects are assumed not to depend on the vintage structure of the inputs. In particular, variations over time in the composition and characteristics of the surviving vintages of capital plant and equipment do not affect the measure of capital input, as would be the case if technical progress were embodied. Typically, researchers have proceeded by assuming that disembodied technical progress proceeds lockstep with the passage of time and, like "manna from heaven," is free. This type of technical progress is implemented empirically by simply inserting the variable t, or $\ln t$, for time into the cost function specification.

For example, linear (t) and quadratic forms of t ($t \cdot \ln P_i$, $t \cdot \ln Y$, t^2) are added to the translog cost function (9.42), and by Shephard's Lemma, t also appears as a regressor in the cost-minimizing share equations (9.42). The partial derivative $-\partial C/\partial t$ is then interpreted as the "shadow value" of time, and under constant returns to scale, $-\partial \ln C/\partial t$ is the rate of MFP growth; it represents the one-period reduction in costs, with prices and output fixed, due to disembodied technical progress. Note that this MFP derivative is a function of the prices of the various inputs. A well-known empirical implementation of such a disembodied technical progress model is that by Dale W. Jorgenson and Barbara Fraumeni [1981].

Relatively little research has been reported to date using flexible functional form models incorporating embodied technical progress. Measurable attributes of capital plant and equipment could be included by integrating the hedonic approach of Chapter 4 with the flexible functional form framework from this chapter, similar to procedures used for output by Spady and Friedlaender.[41]

This concludes our brief overview of extensions to the classic GL and translog models and of other issues that have been addressed by recent research on factor demand models. With this background we are now ready to engage you in hands-on empirical implementations.

9.8 HANDS-ON ESTIMATION OF INTERRELATED DEMANDS FOR FACTORS OF PRODUCTION

The purpose of the following exercises is to help you gain experience with, and an empirical understanding of, econometric issues that are frequently encountered in estimating demand equations for factors of production. The data underlying these exercises are those from a study by Berndt and Wood [1975], who reported the controversial finding that energy and capital inputs in U.S. manufacturing were complements, rather than substitutes.

In Exercise 1 you become familiar with the Berndt-Wood data, generate several variables, and examine their time trends and intercorrelations. In Exercise 2 you become involved in single-equation estimation of parameters in Cobb-Douglas and CES production functions, while in Exercise 3 you compare equation-by-equation with system estimation. In Exercise 4 you encounter issues of singularity, adding up, and invariance to the choice of which equations are directly estimated, while in Exercise 5 you compute substitution elasticities based on the translog and generalized Leontief functional forms.

In Exercise 6 you implement alternative procedures for obtaining statistical inference in systems of equations, and in Exercise 7 you relate this statistical inference to a system generalization of the single-equation R^2 measure. In Exercise 8 you generalize the stochastic specification to permit first-order vector autocorrelation, and you then implement it empirically. Finally, in Exercise 9 you extend the translog model to permit estimation and measurement of multifactor productivity growth.

In the data diskette provided, you will find a subdirectory called CHAP9.DAT with a data file called KLEM. This data file contains annual time series on U.S. manufacturing for the following variables: quantities of capital, labor, energy and nonenergy intermediate material inputs, denoted

QK, QL, QE, and QM, respectively, along with their nominal (current dollar) prices, named PK, PL, PE, and PM, respectively. The quantity of gross output is called QY, while the value-added quantity is QV; the corresponding nominal output prices are PY and PV, respectively. The variable YEAR indexes time. Finally, there are ten other variables, assumed to be exogenous, that can serve as potential instrumental variables. These variables are U.S. population (Z1), U.S. population of working age (Z2), the effective rate of sales and excise taxation (Z3), the effective rate of property taxation (Z4), government purchases of durable goods (Z5), government purchases of nondurable goods and services (Z6), government purchases of labor services (Z7), real exports of durable goods (Z8), real exports of nondurable goods and services (Z9), and U.S. tangible capital stock at the end of the previous year (Z10). These data are described in greater detail in Berndt and Wood [1975].

EXERCISE 1: Inspecting the Berndt-Wood KLEM Data for U.S. Manufacturing

The purpose of this exercise is to help you become familiar with features of the Berndt-Wood KLEM data set for U.S. manufacturing over the 1947–1971 time period. You will examine time trends of variables, generate several new variables, and interpret intercorrelations among them.

(a) In your data diskette subdirectory CHAP9.DAT there is a data file called KLEM. Using the data in this data file, print out the time series of input prices PK, PL, PE, and PM, as well as the gross output deflator PY, over the entire 1947–1971 time period. Also print out time series for input quantities QK, QL, QE, and QM, as well as gross output quantity, QY, over the 1947–1971 time span. Do prices and quantities all increase with time?

(b) The prices that you printed out in part (a) are nominal, not real prices and are indexed to 1.00 in 1947. Generate new relative price variables for the inputs, defined as PKP = PK/PY, PLP = PL/PY, PEP = PE/PY, and PMP = PM/PY, and print them out for the 1947–1971 time span. Notice the time trends of these relative prices. Which relative input prices are increasing, which are relatively constant, and which are decreasing? How might such prices have been affected by governmental policies?

(c) The quantities that you printed out in part (a) reflect the overall growth of the manufacturing sector's output during the 1947–1971 time period. To assess input or factor intensity, generate input-output coefficients defined as KY = QK/QY, LY = QL/QY, EY = QE/QY, and MY = QM/QY for the 1947–1971 time span, and print them out. What are the time trends of factor intensities? Was production in U.S. manufacturing becoming more or less labor intensive during this time period? What about energy and capital intensities?

(d) Compute the means and standard deviations of the relative price variables generated in part (b) and of the input-output coefficients generated in part (c). Which input prices are most volatile? Why might this be the case? Then compute simple correlations between these eight variables. Comment on these intercorrelations. Might any of them give you some hints on which inputs are substitutes and which are complements? Why or why not?

(e) Next, compute nominal total costs of production as NTCOST ≡ PK∗QK + PL∗QL + PE∗QE + PM∗QM, nominal average or unit costs as NUCOST ≡ NTCOST/QY, and real average or unit costs as RUCOST ≡ NUCOST/PY. Print out these three series, and comment on the time trend of RUCOST. How do you interpret this? Compute and print out the simple correlation between RUCOST and the time variable called YEAR. Does the sign of this correlation suggest anything to you concerning possible multifactor productivity growth over the 1947–1971 time period in U.S. manufacturing? Why or why not?

(f) Finally, verify the accounting relationship between gross output and value added. Specifically, verify that value-added output quantity QV is in fact equal to gross output quantity QY minus the intermediate input quantities QE and QM, all expressed in 1947 dollars, that is, QV ≡ QY − QE − QM. Also verify that value added in current dollars, QV∗PV, is equal to gross output in current dollars minus current dollar expenditures on all the intermediate inputs, that is, QV∗PV ≡ QY∗PY − QE∗PE − QM∗PM. These measures of output are clearly different. Which measure of output do you prefer—gross output or value added? Why?

EXERCISE 2: Single-Equation Estimation of Cobb-Douglas and CES Forms

The purpose of this exercise is to engage you in estimating and interpreting parameters of the Cobb-Douglas and CES production functions. You also examine relationships among the R^2 values and alternative estimates of σ.

In your data diskette subdirectory CHAP9.DAT, data file KLEM, there are data series on the quantities of value-added output (QV), capital input services (QK), and labor input (QL), as well as the corresponding nominal prices PV, PK and PL.

(a) Generate the variables corresponding to average labor productivity QV/QL (value-added output over labor input) and the capital/labor ratio QK/QL; then take natural logarithms of these ratios and denote them LNQVQL and LNQKQL. Estimate the Cobb-Douglas equation (9.2), which in this case involves a regression of LNQVQL on a constant term and LNQKQL. Why does the least squares estimate of α_K not make sense here empirically? (Recall the discussion surrounding Eq. (9.4) in the text.) Comment on the possible presence of autocorrelation. Why might simultaneous equations be a potential problem? What do you conclude concerning this specification?

(b) Generate the additional variables QV/QK, PK/PV, PL/PV, and PK/PL; take their natural logarithms and call the resulting variables LNQVQK, LNPKPV, LNPLPV, and LNPKPL, respectively. Using single-equation least squares methods, obtain three alternative estimates of the elasticity of substitution between capital and labor, based on Eqs. (9.9), LNQVQK on a constant and LNPKPV; (9.10), LNQVQL on a constant and LNPLPV; and (9.11), LNQKQL on a constant and LNPKPL; the estimates that you obtain should be 0.713, 0.932, and 0.656, respectively. Denote these estimates of σ with subscripts 1, 2, and 3, respectively. Compare the relative sizes of these three estimates of σ. Are the results based on this data set consistent with those typically found in the empirical literature? (See Section 9.1 for further discussion.) Using either an F- or a t-test statistic, test the null hypothesis that $\sigma = 0$ against the alternative hypothesis that $\sigma \neq 0$ for each of the three equations estimated; then test the null hypothesis that $\sigma = 1$ (the Cobb-Douglas case) against the alternative hypothesis that $\sigma \neq 1$ for each of the three equations estimated. Is there much empirical support for the fixed coefficient, zero-price elasticity specification? For the Cobb-Douglas case?

(c) Using the estimated elasticities and R^2 values obtained in part (b), calculate what the R^2 values and substitution elasticity estimates would be were you to estimate the reciprocal regression equations (9.14)–(9.16). (These calculations should be based on the relationships (9.19) and (9.20).) Choose one of these three reciprocal regression equations in Eq. (9.14)–(9.16) and, using the same variables generated in part (b), verify empirically that the relationships in Eqs. (9.19) and (9.20) do in fact hold by running the appropriate reciprocal regression. Did you get any surprising results?

EXERCISE 3: Comparing Equation-by-Equation and IZEF Estimates

The purpose of this exercise is to have you compare equation-by-equation estimates of parameters with those generated by using the iterative Zellner-efficient estimator (IZEF, here numerically equivalent to maximum likelihood). This exercise involves estimation of demand equations derived from the generalized Leontief (GL) and translog cost functions.

(a) Using the data file KLEM in the subdirectory CHAP9.DAT, form the input-output coefficients and square root transformations of variables required to estimate equations (9.24)–(9.27) based on the GL cost function. (Note that in the KLEM file, factor quantities are denoted QK, QL, QE, and QM rather than K, L, E, and M as in the text. Further, unlike the value-added output measure used in Exercise 2, note that in this exercise the appropriate output measure is gross output QY, since intermediate inputs such as QE and QM are included.) Once these variables are formed, estimate parameters in each of the four equations (9.24)–(9.27) using equation-by-equation ordinary least squares methods. Your results should be identical to those given in Table 9.1 in columns with the heading "OLS." Verify empirically that this estimation procedure results in parameter estimates that are not consistent with the appropriate cross-equation symmetry constraints found in Eqs. (9.24)–(9.27), for example, $\gamma_{KL} = \gamma_{LK}$, $\gamma_{KE} = \gamma_{EK}$, and so on.

Next, without imposing these cross-equation symmetry constraints, estimate the 16 parameters in equation system (9.24)–(9.27) using the IZEF estimator, which is numerically equivalent to the ML estimator. Your results should be the same as those in Table 9.1 in columns with the heading "IZEF." Verify empirically that the equation-by-equation and IZEF estimates of parameters differ numerically. If your computer software permits, compute the 4×4 residual cross-products matrix, which, when divided by sample size T is an estimate of Ω. Given this estimate of Ω and the specification of the equation system (9.24)–(9.27), comment on why one might expect IZEF and equation-by-equation estimates to differ. Does the IZEF estimator have smaller estimated standard errors of parameters than do the equation-by-equation estimators? Why or why not?

(b) Using the data file KLEM in the subdirectory CHAP9.DAT on your data diskette, form the cost shares S_K, S_L, S_E, and S_M; the logarithmic transformations of input prices P_K, P_L, P_E, and P_M; and the logarithm of gross output quantity QY, as specified in equation system (9.45). Once these variables are formed, estimate parameters in the first three of the four share equations (where the dependent variables are S_K, S_L, and S_E) in Eq. (9.45) using equation-by-equation ordinary least squares methods. Your results should be identical to those in Table 9.2 in columns with the heading "OLS." Verify empirically that this estimation procedure results in parameter estimates that are inconsistent with the cross-equation symmetry constraints (e.g., $\gamma_{KL} = \gamma_{LK}$, $\gamma_{KE} = \gamma_{EK}$, and so on).

Next, without imposing these cross-equation symmetry constraints, delete the S_M share equation and estimate the S_K, S_L, and S_E equation system in Eq. (9.45) first using the one-step Zellner (ZEF) and then using the IZEF/ML estimator. Compare the 15 parameter estimates based on equation-by-equation methods with those based on the ZEF and the IZEF/ML estimators. Why does this relationship hold? Does it also hold for estimates of the standard errors of the parameters? Why or why not?

EXERCISE 4: Special Issues in Estimating Singular Equation Systems

The purpose of this exercise is to help you understand better the adding-up and invariance issues that arise in the estimation of parameters in singular equation systems.

(a) As in Exercise 3, part (b), using the data file KLEM in the subdirectory CHAP9.DAT on your data diskette, form the cost shares S_K, S_L, S_E, and S_M; the logarithmic transformations of input prices P_K, P_L, P_E, and P_M; and the logarithm of gross output quantity QY, as specified in equation system (9.45). Once these variables are formed, estimate parameters in each of the four share equations using equation-by-equation ordinary least squares (OLS) methods. Your results should match those presented in Table 9.2 in columns with the heading "OLS." Verify empirically that the parameter estimates obtained satisfy the adding-up conditions (9.47). Comment on why the OLS estimates satisfy these adding-up restrictions. Using the variance of a sum rule, and noting that by Eqs. (9.47), $g_{MK} = -(g_{KK} + g_{LK} + g_{EK})$, verify that the estimated standard error of the g_{MK} parameter estimate equals the estimated standard error of $(g_{KK} + g_{LK} + g_{EK})$.

(b) Now consider the case in which the cross-equation symmetry restrictions, the linear homogeneity in prices conditions, and constant returns to scale are simultaneously imposed on the translog cost function. This yields the estimable equation system

$$S_K = \alpha_K + \gamma_{KK} \ln (P_K/P_M) + \gamma_{KL} \ln (P_L/P_M) + \gamma_{KE} \ln (P_E/P_M) \tag{9.65a}$$

$$S_L = \alpha_L + \gamma_{KL} \ln (P_K/P_M) + \gamma_{LL} \ln (P_L/P_M) + \gamma_{LE} \ln (P_E/P_M) \tag{9.65b}$$

$$S_E = \alpha_E + \gamma_{KE} \ln (P_K/P_M) + \gamma_{LE} \ln (P_L/P_M) + \gamma_{EE} \ln (P_E/P_M) \tag{9.65c}$$

$$S_M = \alpha_M + \gamma_{KM} \ln (P_K/P_M) + \gamma_{LM} \ln (P_L/P_M) + \gamma_{EM} \ln (P_E/P_M) \tag{9.65d}$$

Using the IZEF/ML estimator, directly estimate parameters in the S_K, S_L, and S_E equations of (9.65), and then compute the implied estimates of α_M, γ_{KM}, γ_{LM}, γ_{EM}, and γ_{MM} using the relationships in Eqs. (9.49). Your results should be identical to those given in Table 9.2 in columns with the heading "IZEF."

Now consider deleting a different share equation and modifying the share equations appropriately. In particular, directly estimate by IZEF/ML parameters in the share system consisting of the S_L, S_E, and S_M equations, with the S_K share deleted, as follows:

$$S_L = \alpha_L + \gamma_{LL} \ln (P_L/P_K) + \gamma_{LE} \ln (P_E/P_K) + \gamma_{LM} \ln (P_M/P_K) \tag{9.66a}$$

$$S_E = \alpha_E + \gamma_{LE} \ln (P_L/P_K) + \gamma_{EE} \ln (P_E/P_K) + \gamma_{EM} \ln (P_M/P_K) \tag{9.66b}$$

$$S_M = \alpha_M + \gamma_{LM} \ln (P_L/P_K) + \gamma_{EM} \ln (P_E/P_K) + \gamma_{MM} \ln (P_M/P_K) \tag{9.66c}$$

Obtain indirect estimates of α_K, γ_{KK}, γ_{KL}, γ_{KE}, and γ_{KM} by appropriately rearranging Eqs. (9.49), for example, $a_K = 1.0 - a_L - a_E - a_M$. Verify that the directly and indirectly estimated parameters are numerically invariant to the choice of which three share equations are directly estimated and which single equation is deleted. (Incidentally, you might want to attempt estimating the full four-equation system (9.65) by IZEF/ML. Most computer programs will "blow up" and give you an error message indicating problems in inverting a singular matrix. What happens with your software?)

(c) As was noted in the text, depending in particular on the level of aggregation, input prices might be endogenous variables, and so estimation of equation system (9.65) by IZEF could leave one vulnerable to a simultaneous equations estimation problem. Using the ten instrumental variables described at the beginning of this section and the three-stage least squares (3SLS) estimator, directly estimate parameters in the S_K, S_L, and S_E equations of Eqs. (9.65), and compute the implied estimates of α_M, γ_{KM}, γ_{LM}, γ_{EM}, and γ_{MM} using the relationships in Eqs. (9.49). Then, again with the 3SLS estimator, directly estimate parameters in the S_L, S_E, and S_M equations of Eqs. (9.66), and obtain indirect estimates of α_K, γ_{KK}, γ_{KL}, γ_{KE}, and γ_{KM} using appropriate variants of Eqs. (9.49). Are the directly and indirectly estimated parameters numerically invariant to the choice of which three share equations are directly estimated? (*Note:* The answer to this last question will depend on the software package that you are using and in particular on how the initial estimate of Ω_n is obtained, as was discussed in Section 9.4 underneath Eqs. (9.49). If you find that your 3SLS parameter estimates lack invariance, redo the above estimation, employing instead the iterative 3SLS estimator, for which invariance should always be the case.)

(d) Suppose that a researcher wanted to delete the $\ln(P_E/P_M)$ variable from the S_K, S_L, and S_E share equations in Eqs. (9.65), that is, to constrain $\gamma_{KE} = \gamma_{LE} = \gamma_{EE} = 0$. However, suppose also that this researcher did not want to delete this variable from the S_M share equation, that is, he or she wanted $\gamma_{EM} \neq 0$. Why would such a specification not be consistent with the adding-up conditions in Eqs. (9.49)? Can a particular regressor ever appear in only one share equation? Why not?

EXERCISE 5: Substitution Elasticities and Curvature Checks

The purpose of this exercise is to help you gain experience in computing substitution elasticities based on the generalized Leontief and translog functional forms and in checking for monotonicity and strict quasi-concavity.

(a) Using the data file KLEM in the subdirectory CHAP9.DAT, form the input-output coefficients and square root transformations of variables required to estimate Eqs. (9.24)–(9.27) based on the GL cost function. Once these variables are formed, estimate parameters in each of the four equations (9.24)–(9.27) imposing the cross-equation symmetry constraints and using the IZEF/ML system estimation method. Your estimates should agree with those given in note 11 at the end of this chapter. On the basis of these parameter estimates and Eqs. (9.24)–(9.27), compute the fitted a_i (predicted input-output coefficients). Verify that these fitted a_i are all positive, a condition that is required to satisfy the monotonicity conditions. Then, using Eqs. (9.31) and (9.32), compute the 16 possible price elasticity estimates for each year in the sample. For 1971 your estimates should agree with those given underneath Eq. (9.32) in the text. Check your calculations by verifying that the price elasticities satisfy condition (9.33). On the basis of these price elasticity estimates, which inputs appear to be substitutes and which appear to be complements? Do you obtain energy-capital complementarity, as Berndt and Wood reported when they employed these data and estimated the translog form? Are all own-price elasticities negative? Are own-price responses elastic or inelastic for each of the inputs?

(b) On the basis of the GL parameter estimates obtained in part (a), employ Eqs. (9.29) and (9.30) and compute the Allen partial elasticities of substitution σ_{ij} for each year in the sample. To do this, it will be necessary to calculate the predicted C/Y (unit cost), which you can do by multiplying each of your fitted input-output demand equations by P_i and then summing, that is

$$(C/Y)_{\text{fit}} = P_K{*}(K/Y)_{\text{fit}} + P_L{*}(L/Y)_{\text{fit}} + P_E{*}(E/Y)_{\text{fit}} + P_M{*}(M/Y)_{\text{fit}}$$

Note that unlike the ϵ_{ij} price elasticities, the σ_{ij} are symmetric, and so it is necessary to compute only ten σ_{ij}. For 1971 your results should match those given underneath Eq. (9.30) in the text. To check for strict quasi-concavity of the cost function in input prices, verify that the σ_{ij} matrix is negative semidefinite by showing that (i) all own four σ_{ii} are negative at each observation, (ii) the six possible 2×2 matrices whose elements consist of

$$\begin{bmatrix} \sigma_{ii} & \sigma_{ij} \\ \sigma_{ij} & \sigma_{jj} \end{bmatrix} \quad \text{for} \quad i, j = K, L, E, M \qquad \text{but} \quad i \neq j \qquad \textbf{(9.67)}$$

each has a positive determinant at every observation, (iii) the four possible 3×3 matrices whose elements consist of

$$\begin{bmatrix} \sigma_{ii} & \sigma_{ij} & \sigma_{ik} \\ \sigma_{ij} & \sigma_{jj} & \sigma_{jk} \\ \sigma_{ik} & \sigma_{jk} & \sigma_{kk} \end{bmatrix} \qquad \begin{matrix} \text{for} \quad i, j, k = K, L, E, M \\ \text{but} \quad i \neq j, \quad i \neq k, \quad j \neq k \end{matrix} \qquad \textbf{(9.68)}$$

each has a negative determinant at every observation, and (iv) the 4×4 matrix consisting of all the σ_{ij}, $i, j = K, L, E$, and M, has a determinant whose value is zero (or extremely close to it, reflecting computational rounding error) at each annual observation. *Note:* Do not be surprised if you find some violations of curvature for this estimated model.

(c) Using the data file KLEM in the subdirectory CHAP9.DAT on your data diskette, form the cost shares S_K, S_L, S_E, and S_M and the logarithmic transformations of the relative input prices P_K/P_M, P_L/P_M, and P_E/P_M as specified in equation system (9.65). Once these variables are formed, with symmetry restrictions imposed and employing the IZEF/ML estimator, directly estimate parameters in the S_K, S_L, and S_E share equations, and obtain indirect estimates of α_M, γ_{KM}, γ_{LM}, γ_{EM}, and γ_{MM} based on Eqs. (9.49). Your estimates should match those in Table 9.2 in columns with the heading "IZEF." Compute the fitted cost shares for the directly estimated equations, calculate the implied fitted cost share for M, and verify that for each share at each annual observation the fitted value is positive, as is required for monotonicity of the cost function in input prices. Then calculate the 16 possible own- and cross-price elasticity estimates involving the K, L, E, and M inputs, using Eqs. (9.51). For 1971 your estimates should be identical to those given underneath Eqs. (9.51). Verify that the adding-up condition (9.33) holds. On the basis of these price elasticity estimates, which input pairs are substitutes and which are complements? Are own-price demands elastic or inelastic?

(d) Using the translog parameter estimates obtained in part (c), employ Eqs. (9.50) and compute the Allen partial elasticities of substitution σ_{ij} for each year in the sample. Note that as with the GL form in part (b), because the σ_{ij} are symmetric, it is necessary to compute only ten σ_{ij}. For 1971 your estimates should match those given underneath Eqs. (9.50). To check for strict quasi-concavity of the cost function in input prices, verify that (i) all own four σ_{ii} are negative at each observation, (ii) the six possible 2×2 matrices whose elements are defined in Eq. (9.67) each has a positive determinant at every observation, (iii) the four possible 3×3 matrices whose elements are defined at Eq. (9.68) each has a negative determinant at every observation, and (iv) the 4×4 matrix consisting of all the σ_{ij}, $i, j = K, L, E$, and M, has a determinant whose value is zero (or extremely close to it, reflecting computational rounding error) at each annual observation.

(e) Compare the ϵ_{ij} and σ_{ij} elasticity estimates based on the GL and translog functional forms. Are there any sign reversals? Any substantial differences between the GL and translog estimates? Which form is easier to work with? Do you prefer one form over the other? Why?

EXERCISE 6: Obtaining Statistical Inference in Equation Systems

The purpose of this exercise is to involve you in implementing three alternative test procedures, the Wald, likelihood ratio (LR), and Lagrange multiplier (LM) test statistics, for testing a particular null hypothesis and to verify empirically the inequality relationship among them, Wald > LR > LM.

(a) Choose either the generalized Leontief (GL) or the translog functional form. Noting the form of the estimating equations (Eqs. (9.24)–(9.27) for the GL or (9.65a)–(9.65c) for the translog), generate the appropriate variables from the KLEM data file in the subdirectory CHAP9.DAT so that estimation can proceed. With symmetry constraints imposed, estimate parameters in either the GL or the translog equation system using the IZEF/ML estimation technique; your IZEF/ML estimates for the GL should match those given in note 11, while IZEF/ML estimates for the translog should be identical with those given in Table 9.2 in columns with the heading "IZEF." For either form, call this the unconstrained model. Note the value of the sample maximized log-likelihood function (calling it $\ln L_1$), and retrieve the residual cross-products matrix, which is now denoted as S. Recall that S/T is an estimate of Ω, where T is the number of observations in each equation.

(b) Now, using the same GL or translog function as in part (a), specify a constrained model in which all the slope parameters are restricted to equal zero (the d_{ij}, $i \neq j$, for the GL or the γ_{ij} for the translog). For the GL this is equivalent to specifying a model in which all price and Allen elasticities are zero, while for the translog this set of restrictions corresponds to the Cobb-Douglas case in which all $\sigma_{ij} = 1$, $i \neq j$. Next do one-step Zellner estimation of this restricted model, *conditional* on the implied S estimate of Ω from part (a). Retrieve the residual cross-products matrix from this restricted model, and denote it as W_1. Noting that the sample size in this case is $T = 25$, compute the Wald test statistic using Eq. (9.34), and compare it to the χ^2 critical value at the 0.01 and 0.05 levels of significance. (Recall that the degrees of freedom for this test are computed as the number of free parameters estimated in the unconstrained model minus the number of free parameters estimated in the constrained model.)

(c) Next, instead of estimating the constrained model conditional on S (as in part (b)), estimate Ω and the other parameters of the constrained model using the IZEF/ML estimator. Call the value of the sample maximized log-likelihood function $\ln L_0$, and retrieve the residual cross-products matrix from this constrained model, calling it W_0. Using the sample maximized log-likelihood function values from the unconstrained ($\ln L_1$) and constrained ($\ln L_0$) estimated models, calculate the LR test statistic based on Eq. (9.35). Also calculate the LR test statistic using the alternative computational formula (9.36), and verify that its numerical value is identical. Compare the LR test statistic to the χ^2 critical value at the 0.01 and 0.05 levels of significance.

(d) Do one-step Zellner estimation of the unrestricted model in part (a), *conditional* on W_0, where W_0/T is the estimate of Ω based on the restricted estimates obtained in part (c). Retrieve the residual cross-products matrix from this estimation, and call it S_1. Compute the LM test statistic using Eq. (9.37), and compare it to the χ^2 critical value at the 0.01 and 0.05 levels of significance.

(e) Verify that the Wald, LR, and LM test statistics that you obtained in parts (b), (c), and (d) follow the inequality noted in Eq. (9.38), namely, that Wald > LR > LM. At the 0.01 or 0.05 level of significance, is there any conflict in inference regarding the empirical validity of the null hypothesis?

EXERCISE 7: Goodness of Fit in GL or Translog Equation Systems

The purpose of this exercise is to have you construct a measure of goodness of fit in equation systems that is related to the null hypothesis that all slope coefficients are simultaneously equal to zero.

(a) Choose either the generalized Leontief (GL) or the translog functional form. Noting the form of the estimating equations (Eqs. (9.24)–(9.27) for the GL and Eqs. (9.65a)–(9.65c) for the translog), generate the appropriate variables from the KLEM data file in the subdirectory CHAP9.DAT. Estimate parameters either in the GL input-output equations (9.24)–(9.27) or in the first three translog share equations (9.65a)–(9.65c) using the IZEF/ML estimator, with symmetry constraints imposed; your IZEF/ML estimates for the GL should match those given in footnote 11, while IZEF/ML estimates for the translog should be identical with those given in Table 9.2 in columns with the heading "IZEF." Retrieve the value of the determinant of the residual cross-products matrix, and call this determinant $|E'E|$. Also denote the value of the sample maximized log-likelihood function as $\ln L_1$.

To obtain the generalized total sum of squares, using the same GL or translog function, specify and estimate by ML a model in which all the slope parameters are simultaneously restricted to equal zero (the $d_{ij} = 0$, $i \neq j$, for the GL or the $\gamma_{ij} = 0$ for the translog). In this restricted model, the only regressor is a vector of 1's, and so the estimated constant terms in each equation equal the sample means of the dependent variables. Retrieve the value of the determinant of the residual cross-products matrix from this restricted model, and call this determinant $|y'y|$. Also note the value of the sample maximized log-likelihood function, and call it $\ln L_0$. Finally, using Eq. (9.40), compute the generalized or system $\tilde{R}^2$.

(b) Relate the measure of $\tilde{R}^2$ obtained in part (a) to the null hypothesis that all slope coefficients are simultaneously equal to zero by calculating the LR test statistic using Eq. (9.41). Compare the value of this LR test statistic to a χ^2 critical value at the 0.01 and 0.05 levels of significance. Verify your computation by checking whether this value of the LR test statistic is the same as that obtained by using relationship (9.35) and the values of $\ln L_1$ and $\ln L_0$ generated in part (a).

EXERCISE 8: Estimating Interrelated Factor Demand Models with Vector Autocorrelation

The purpose of this exercise is to involve you in estimating an interrelated factor demand model allowing for first-order vector autocorrelation of the disturbances. To reduce computational requirements, you will assume that the autocovariance matrix is diagonal. You then test the null hypothesis of no autocorrelation using the LR test procedure.

(a) Choose either the generalized Leontief (GL) or the translog functional form. Depending on the form of the chosen estimating equations (Eqs. (9.24)–(9.27) for the GL and Eqs. (9.65a)–(9.65c) for the translog), generate the required variables from the KLEM data file in the subdirectory CHAP9.DAT. Assuming that the autocovariance matrix R is diagonal, specify and estimate by ML the equation system (9.60) (for the GL) or the translog share system that is analogous to Eq. (9.59). Note that (i) since the first observation is lost owing to the presence of lagged variables, estimation is done over the 1948–1971 time span, not 1947–1971 and (ii) with the translog model the elements of the diagonal autocovariance matrix must be equal, as discussed in Section 9.5. Denote the value of the sample maximized log-likelihood function from this model $\ln L_1$.

(b) Estimate the same model as in part (a) over the 1948–1971 time period, where the autocovariance matrix R is now restricted to equal zero. This is done to test the null hypothesis that there is no autocorrelation ($R = 0$) against the alternative hypothesis that $R \neq 0$. Denote the value of the sample maximized log-likelihood function from this restricted model $\ln L_0$. Using Eq. (9.35), compute the LR test statistic and compare it to the χ^2 critical values at the 0.01 and 0.05 levels of significance, taking particular care in computing degrees of freedom. Is the null hypothesis rejected or not rejected? Which parameters appear to be most affected by the presence of autocorrelation? Do the estimates of R correspond with the implied estimates based on the equation-by-equation Durbin-Watson test statistics? Interpret these statistics.

EXERCISE 9: Obtaining Estimates of Multifactor Productivity Growth

The purpose of this exercise is to engage you in extending the empirical implementation of the translog cost function to accommodate the effects of biased technical change and multifactor productivity (MFP) growth.[42] You will assume that all technical progress is disembodied and that disembodied technical progress proceeds in lockstep with the passage of time. You incorporate this by adding a time counter as an argument to the translog function (t can be formed as $t \equiv \text{YEAR} - 1947$). Denote the time variable by t, and let $t = 0$ in 1947, 1 in 1948, . . . , and 24 in 1971.

(a) Take the translog cost function specification (9.42) and add to it a linear term in t, cross-products terms in t and the ln P_i, and a t^2 term. Call the parameters on these additional variables α_t, γ_{it}, and γ_{tt}, respectively. Consider a model with constant returns to scale imposed, that is, in which $\alpha_Y = 1$, $\gamma_{iY} = 0$, $i = K, L, E, M$, and $\gamma_{YY} = 0$. Solve out analytically the translog cost function with symmetry and the linear homogeneity in prices restrictions (9.43) imposed, as well as the above constant-returns-to-scale constraints. *Note:* This will result in a new dependent variable involving the logarithm of average, not total costs.

The addition of the time-related variables entails a further linear homogeneity in prices restriction, namely, $\gamma_{Kt} + \gamma_{Lt} + \gamma_{Et} + \gamma_{Mt} = 0$. Differentiate this translog average cost function with respect to the ln P_i, and obtain estimating equations identical to Eqs. (9.65a)–(9.65d) with, however, $\gamma_{it} \cdot t$ terms added to each of the share equations, $i = K, L, E$, and M. Estimate by IZEF/ML the equation system consisting of the translog average cost function (with time terms included) and any three of the four share equations in Eqs. (9.65a)–(9.65d), each with the corresponding $\gamma_{it} \cdot t$ term included.

(b) Although technical progress typically involves savings on all inputs, such progress may save on some inputs more than on others. Therefore technical progress is said to be relative input i-saving, i-neutral, or i-using when the estimated γ_{it} parameter is negative, zero, or positive, respectively.[43] In the model estimated in part (a), what is the pattern of the estimated bias of technical change? Using either the Wald, LR, or LM test procedure, test the null hypothesis that technical progress is Hicks-neutral, that is, test that the parameter restrictions $\gamma_{KT} = \gamma_{LT} = \gamma_{ET} = \gamma_{MT} = 0$ are simultaneously valid in this sample.

(c) Write out the partial derivative $\partial \ln C/\partial t$ for the translog cost function with disembodied technical progress specified in part (a). This derivative is interpreted as the change in costs due to disembodied technical progress (here, the passage of time), given output quantity, input prices, and time, and is typically called the measure of multifactor productivity (MFP) growth. Using the parameter estimates obtained in part (a), where technical change was permitted to be biased, substitute in these parameters and values of variables, and then obtain an annual time series of predicted MFP. Does this data series appear reasonable? Why or why not?

CHAPTER NOTES

1. Charles Cobb and Paul H. Douglas [1928].
2. Although the functional form in Eq. (9.1) has traditionally been called the Cobb-Douglas production function, this log-log specification had already been employed in 1896 by Knut Wicksell. On this and other historical issues, see Paul A. Samuelson [1979].

3. In nonlogarithmic form, Eq. (9.1) is $Y = A \cdot K^{\alpha}L^{\beta}$. Multiply Y, K, and L by $\lambda > 1$: $\lambda^{\mu}Y = A \cdot (\lambda K)^{\alpha}(\lambda L)^{\beta} = A \cdot K^{\alpha}L^{\beta}\lambda^{\alpha+\beta}$. This function is homogeneous of degree $\mu = \alpha + \beta$. When $\mu = 1$, $\alpha + \beta = 1$.
4. It is interesting to note that Cobb-Douglas also estimated parameters of an alternative functional form, $Y = aL + bK$. Although this form is inconsistent with the usual theory of production (it does not permit diminishing returns), it generated the same 0.97 R^2 as the log-log equation (9.2). *Moral:* A high R^2 does not necessarily imply that a model is reasonable. Also, Cobb and Douglas's interpretations of these results have been critiqued by a number of researchers; see, for example, Alan A. Walters [1963]. The Walters article includes an extensive survey of empirical work on factor demands prior to 1960, based on the Cobb-Douglas functional form.
5. In most industrialized countries, the SIC (*S*tandard *I*ndustrial *C*lassification) code specifies major sectors by one-digit numbers (e.g., agriculture, manufacturing, mining, and services are all one-digit industries) and components of the one-digit industries by two-digits. In the United States, for example, there are approximately 20 two-digit industries in the one-digit manufacturing sector.
6. On this, see, however, Arnold Zellner, Jan Kmenta, and Jacques Dréze [1966].
7. See, for example, Daniel McFadden [1978a, b].
8. W. Erwin Diewert [1971]. Other researchers dedicated attention to flexible functional forms with only two inputs and focused only on the primal production function. See, for example, Shih-Fan Chu, Dennis J. Aigner,and Marvin Frankel [1970]; Jan Kmenta [1967]; and J. Denis Sargan [1971].
9. This paper was abstracted in Christensen, Jorgenson, and Lau [1971] and appeared in more complete form as Christensen, Jorgenson, and Lau [1972]. While the 1970 and 1972 papers were theoretical, they were soon followed by an empirical implementation with two outputs (consumption goods and investment goods) and two inputs (K and L) based on a translog transformation function and annual U.S. data; see Christensen, Jorgenson, and Lau [1973].
10. For a proof of this result, see Walter Oberhofer and Jan Kmenta [1974].
11. When the equation system (9.24)–(9.27) is estimated by IZEF/ML with symmetry restrictions imposed, the resulting parameter estimates (and standard errors) are: d_{KK}, 0.0281 (0.0117); d_{KL}, 0.0549 (0.0058); d_{KE}, −0.0060 (0.0066); d_{KM}, −0.0327 (0.0175); d_{LL}, 0.0393 (0.0097); d_{LE}, 0.0552 (0.0036); d_{LM}, 0.0640 (0.0147); d_{EE}, −0.0212 (0.0110); d_{EM}, 0.0035 (0.0167); and d_{MM}, 0.5244 (0.0382).
12. For discussion, see Jerry A. Hausman [1975].
13. This result is originally due to Hirofumi Uzawa [1964] and is discussed in many microeconomic theory textbooks. Also see W. Erwin Diewert [1974].
14. See, however, the related discussion in Section 9.4 on estimating variances of the translog substitution elasticity estimates.
15. This matrix of residuals E is not to be confused with the quantity of energy demanded, which was also denoted as E earlier in this section.
16. See your econometric theory textbook for further details. A classic discussion on fitting criteria in the multivariate equation system model is given by Arthur S. Goldberger [1970].
17. One potential problem with standard computer programs is that they often print out the sample maximized value of the likelihood function or the determinant of the appropriate residual cross-products matrix, rather than the natural logarithms of these variables. This can result in a common computational error, since the LR

test statistic formulae (9.35) and (9.36) involve logarithmically transformed variables.

18. This has been shown by Ernst R. Berndt and N. Eugene Savin [1977].
19. One drawback with the Wald test is that when the restrictions involve nonlinearities in the parameters, the calculated value of the Wald test will vary depending on how one algebraically solves out the nonlinearities. By contrast, the LM and LR tests do not suffer from this drawback. See Allan W. Gregory and Michael R. Veall [1985], Francine Lafontaine and Kenneth J. White [1986], and Peter C. B. Phillips and Joon Y. Park [1988].
20. See a microeconomic theory textbook for further details. A useful discussion is given by Giora Hanoch [1975], while a more extensive presentation is found in Robert G. Chambers [1988].
21. Unless constant returns to scale is imposed, use of the McElroy procedure results in problems of identification of the parameters; see J. R. Norsworthy [1990]. Another problem with the traditional multivariate normal stochastic specification for disturbances is that cost shares must always be nonnegative, which implies restrictions on the distribution-generating disturbances. For a discussion of this issue and an examination of the Dirichlet distribution, see Alan D. Woodland [1979].
22. Because of rounding, the sums might not be precisely as in Eqs. (9.47).
23. Further information on the Wald test statistic in the instrumental variable context, including a discussion of nonlinear hypothesis tests, is found in A. Ronald Gallant and Dale W. Jorgenson [1979]. It is worth noting that in some computer programs, such as TSP and PC-TSP, the value of $T \text{ tr } S^{-1}H_1$ in Eq. (9.34) can also be computed simply as the difference between values of $E'HH'E$ in the unconstrained and constrained (conditional on S) estimations.
24. See A. Ronald Gallant [1987], especially pp. 460–463.
25. Additional discussions on this issue are given in Alden L. Toevs [1980, 1982] and Itzhak Krinsky and A. Leslie Robb [1986].
26. Obviously, one also needs to estimate the cost function if one needs an estimate of its intercept term α_0; this would be necessary whenever a calculation required the predicted cost.
27. For further discussion, see Ernst R. Berndt and N. Eugene Savin [1975]; also see Lawrence J. Lau [1978].
28. See, for example, Ernst R. Berndt and Dale W. Jorgenson [1973], Edward A. Hudson and Jorgenson [1974, 1978], and, for an overview, Jorgenson [1984].
29. See, for example, the 35 sector production model by Jorgenson and Barbara Fraumeni [1981].
30. An extensive survey on factor demand modeling, with emphasis placed on the static translog specification, is found in Dale W. Jorgenson [1986].
31. For a further discussion of the integration of hedonic specifications with modern demand analysis, see Ernst R. Berndt [1983].
32. Conceptual issues in measuring economies of scope and scale for multiproduct firms, as well as a survey of empirical studies of multiproduct cost functions, are addressed by Elizabeth E. Bailey and Ann F. Friedlaender [1982].
33. This form was developed in Daniel McFadden [1978b] and discussed further by W. Erwin Diewert and Terence J. Wales [1987].
34. See Ernst R. Berndt and Mohammed S. Khaled [1979].
35. See A. Ronald Gallant [1981].

36. See William A. Barnett [1985].
37. The literature on dynamic factor demand modeling to 1980 is surveyed in Ernst R. Berndt, Catherine J. Morrison, and G. Campbell Watkins [1981].
38. See Ernst R. Berndt, Melvyn A. Fuss, and Leonard Waverman [1980] and Catherine J. Morrison and Ernst R. Berndt [1981].
39. Lars P. Hansen and Thomas J. Sargent [1980].
40. For examples of this approach, see Catherine J. Morrison [1988b, 1989].
41. A rather simple but useful formulation is the average age of firms' generating equipment, a vintage measure that was developed and implemented for the electric utility industry by Randy A. Nelson [1986].
42. For a discussion of issues involved in specifying and estimating translog models with various types of technical progress, see Ernst R. Berndt and David O. Wood [1982].
43. See Berndt and Wood [1982] for further interpretation of biased technical change in the translog context.

CHAPTER REFERENCES

Anderson, Richard G. and Jerry G. Thursby [1986], "Confidence Intervals for Elasticity Estimators in Translog Models," *Review of Economics and Statistics*, 68:4, November, 647–656.

Arrow, Kenneth J., Hollis B. Chenery, Bagicha Minhas, and Robert M. Solow [1961], "Capital-Labor Substitution and Economic Efficiency," *Review of Economics and Statistics*, 43:5, August, 225–254.

Atkinson, Scott E. and Robert Halvorsen [1976], "Interfuel Substitution in Steam Electric Power Generation," *Journal of Political Economy*, 84:5, October, 959–978.

Bailey, Elizabeth E. and Ann F. Friedlaender [1982], "Market Structure and Multiproduct Industries," *Journal of Economic Literature*, 20:3, September, 1024–1048.

Barnett, William A. [1985], "The Minflex-Laurent Translog Flexible Functional Form," *Journal of Econometrics*, 30:1/2, October/November, 33–44.

Bergson (Burk), Abraham [1936], "Real Income, Expenditure Proportionality, and Frisch's 'New Method of Measuring Marginal Utility,'" *Review of Economic Studies*, 4:1, October, 33–52.

Berndt, Ernst R. [1976], "Reconciling Alternative Estimates of the Elasticity of Substitution," *Review of Economics and Statistics*, 58:1, February, 59–68.

Berndt, Ernst R. [1983], "Quality Adjustment, Hedonics, and Modern Empirical Demand Analysis," in W. Erwin Diewert and Claude Montmarquette, eds., *Price Level Measurement* (Proceedings from a Conference Sponsored by Statistics Canada), Ottawa: Minister of Supply and Services Canada, October, pp. 817–863.

Berndt, Ernst R. and Dieter M. Hesse [1986], "Measuring and Assessing Capacity Utilization in the Manufacturing Sectors of Nine OECD Countries," *European Economic Review*, 30:5, October, 961–989.

Berndt, Ernst R. and Dale W. Jorgenson [1973], "Production Structure," in Dale W. Jorgenson and Hendrik S. Houthakker, eds., *US Energy Resources and Economic Growth*, Washington, D.C.: Ford Foundation Energy Policy Project.

Berndt, Ernst R. and Mohammed S. Khaled [1979], "Parametric Productivity Measurement and Choice among Flexible Functional Forms," *Journal of Political Economy*, 87:6, December, 1220–1245.

Berndt, Ernst R. and N. Eugene Savin [1975], "Estimation and Hypothesis Testing in Singular Equation Systems with Autoregressive Disturbances," *Econometrica*, 43:5–6, September/November, 937–957.

Berndt, Ernst R. and N. Eugene Savin [1977], "Conflict among Criteria for Testing Hypotheses in the Multivariate Linear Regression Model," *Econometrica*, 45:5, July, 1263–1277.

Berndt, Ernst R. and David O. Wood [1975], "Technology, Prices and the Derived Demand for Energy," *Review of Economics and Statistics*, 57:3, August, 259–268.

Berndt, Ernst R. and David O. Wood [1979], "Engineering and Econometric Interpretations of Energy-Capital Complementarity," *American Economic Review*, 69:3, June, 342–354.

Berndt, Ernst R. and David O. Wood [1982], "The Specification and Measurement of Technical Change in U.S. Manufacturing," Chapter 7 in John R. Moroney, ed., *Advances in the Economics of Energy and Natural Resources*, Vol. 4, Greenwich, Conn.: JAI Press, pp. 199–221.

Berndt, Ernst R., Melvyn A. Fuss, and Leonard Waverman [1980], "Dynamic Adjustment Models of Industrial Energy Demand: Empirical Analysis for U.S. Manufacturing, 1947–74," EPRI Reserach Project 683-1, Report EA-1613, Palo Alto, Calif.: Electric Power Research Institute.

Berndt, Ernst R., Catherine J. Morrison, and G. Campbell Watkins [1981], "Dynamic Models of Energy Demand: An Assessment and Comparison," in Ernst R. Berndt and Barry C. Field, eds., *Modeling and Measuring Natural Resource Substitution*, Cambridge, Mass.: MIT Press, pp. 259–289.

Brown, Randall S. and Laurits R. Christensen [1981], "Estimates of Elasticities of Substitution in a Model of Partial Static Equilibrium: An Application to U.S. Agriculture, 1947–1974," in Ernst R. Berndt and Barry C. Field, eds., *Modeling and Measuring Natural Resource Substitution*, Cambridge, Mass.: MIT Press, pp. 209–229.

Caves, Douglas W., Laurits R. Christensen, and Michael W. Tretheway [1981], "Flexible Cost Functions for Multiproduct Firms," *Review of Economics and Statistics*, 62:3, August, 477–481.

Chambers, Robert G. [1988], *Applied Production Analysis*, New York: Cambridge University Press.

Chiang, Judy S. Wang and Ann F. Friedlaender [1985], "Truck Technology and Efficient Market Structure," *Review of Economics and Statistics*, 67:3, August, 250–258.

Christensen, Laurits R., Dale W. Jorgenson, and Lawrence J. Lau [1970], "Conjugate Duality and the Transcendental Logarithmic Production Function," unpublished paper presented at the Second World Congress of the Econometric Society, Cambridge, England, September.

Christensen, Laurits R., Dale W. Jorgenson, and Lawrence J. Lau [1971], "Conjugate Duality and the Transcendental Logarithmic Production Function," *Econometrica*, 39:4, July, 255–256.

Christensen, Laurits R., Dale W. Jorgenson, and Lawrence J. Lau [1972], "Conjugate Duality and the Transcendental Logarithmic Production Frontiers," Discussion Paper 238, Cambridge, Mass.: Harvard Institute of Economic Research, April.

Christensen, Laurits R., Dale W. Jorgenson, and Lawrence J. Lau [1973], "Transcendental Logarithmic Production Frontiers," *Review of Economics and Statistics*, 55:1, February, 28–45.

Chu, Shih-Fan, Dennis J. Aigner, and Marvin Frankel [1970], "On the Log-Quadratic Law of Production," *Southern Economic Journal*, 37:1, July, 32–39.

Cobb, Charles and Paul H. Douglas [1928], "A Theory of Production," *American Economic Review*, Supplement to Vol. 18, 1928, 139–165.

Cowing, Thomas G. and Alphonse Holtmann [1983], "Multiproduct Short-Run Hospital Cost Functions: Empirical Evidence and Policy Implications from Cross-Sectional Data," *Southern Economic Journal*, 49:1, January, 637–653.

Diewert, W. Erwin [1971], "An Application of the Shepard Duality Theorem: A Generalized Linear Production Function," *Journal of Political Economy*, 79:3, May/June, 482–507.

Diewert, W. Erwin [1974], "Applications of Duality Theory," in Michael D. Intriligator and David A. Kendrick, eds., *Frontiers of Quantitative Economics*, Vol. II, Amsterdam: North-Holland, pp.106–171.

Diewert, W. Erwin and Terence J. Wales [1987], "Flexible Functional Forms and Global Curvature Conditions," *Econometrica*, 55:1, January, 43–68.

Frisch, Ragnar [1935], "The Principle of Substitution: An Example of Its Application in the Chocolate Industry," *Nordisk Tidsskrift for Teknisk Okonomi*, 1:1, 12–27.

Fuss, Melvyn, Daniel McFadden and Yair Mundlak [1978], "A Survey of Functional Forms in the Economic Analysis of Production," Chapter II.1 in Melvyn A. Fuss and Daniel McFadden, eds., *Production Economics: A Dual Approach to Theory and Applications*, Amsterdam: North-Holland, pp. 219–268.

Gallant, A. Ronald [1981], "On the Bias in Flexible Functional Forms and an Essentially Unbiased Form: The Fourier Flexible Form," *Journal of Econometrics*, 15:2, February, 211–245.

Gallant, A. Ronald [1987], *Nonlinear Statistical Models*, New York: John Wiley and Sons.

Gallant, A. Ronald and Dale W. Jorgenson [1979], "Statistical Inference for a System of Simultaneous, Nonlinear, Implicit Equations in the Context of Instrumental Variable Estimation," *Journal of Econometrics*, 11:2/3, October/November, 275–302.

Goldberger, Arthur S. [1970], "Criteria and Constraints in Multivariate Regression," Madison, Wisc.: Social Science Research Institute, Working Paper EME 7026, July.

Gregory, Allan W. and Michael R. Veall [1985], "Formulating Wald Tests of Nonlinear Restrictions," *Econometrica*, 53:6, November, 1465–1468.

Guilkey, David, C. A. Knox Lovell, and Robin C. Sickles [1983], "A Comparison of the Performance of Three Flexible Functional Forms," *International Economic Review*, 24:3, October, 591–616.

Hanoch, Giora [1975], "The Elasticity of Scale and the Shape of Average Costs," *American Economic Review*, 65:3, June, 492–497.

Hansen, Lars P. and Thomas J. Sargent [1980], "Formulating and Estimating Dynamic Linear Rational Expectations Models," *Journal of Economic Dynamics and Control*, 2:1, February, 7–46.

Hausman, Jerry A. [1975], "An Instrumental Variable Approach to Full Information Estimates for Linear and Certain Nonlinear Econometric Models," *Econometrica*, 43:4, July, 727–738.

Heady, Earl O. and John L. Dillon [1961], *Agricultural Production Functions*, Ames,

Iowa: Iowa State University Press.

Hudson, Edward A. and Dale W. Jorgenson [1974], "U.S. Energy Policy and Economic Growth, 1975–2000," *Bell Journal of Economics and Management Science*, 5:2, Autumn, 461–514.

Hudson, Edward A. and Dale W. Jorgenson [1978], "The Economic Impact of Policies to Reduce US Energy Growth," *Resources and Energy*, 1:3, November, 205–230.

Johnston, Jack [1984], *Econometric Methods*, Third Edition, New York: McGraw-Hill.

Jorgenson, Dale W. [1984], "Econometric Methods for Applied General Equilibrium Analysis," in Herbert E. Scarf and John B. Shoven, eds., *Applied General Equilibrium Analysis*, Cambridge; England.: Cambridge University Press, pp. 139–203.

Jorgenson, Dale W. [1986], "Econometric Methods for Modeling Producer Behavior," Chapter 31 in Zvi Griliches and Michael D. Intriligator, eds., *Handbook of Econometrics*, Vol. 3, Amsterdam: North-Holland, pp. 1841–1915.

Jorgenson, Dale W. and Barbara Fraumeni [1981], "Relative Prices and Technical Change," in Ernst R. Berndt and Barry C. Field, eds., *Modeling and Measuring Natural Resource Substitution*, Cambridge, Mass.: MIT Press, pp. 17–47.

Kmenta, Jan [1967], "On Estimation of the CES Production Function," *International Economic Review*, 8:2, June, 180–189.

Krinsky, Itzhak and A. Leslie Robb [1986], "On Approximating the Statistical Properties of Elasticities," *Review of Economics and Statistics*, 68:4, November, 715–719.

Kulatilaka, Nalin [1985], "Tests on the Validity of Static Equilibrium Models," *Journal of Econometrics*, 28:2, May, 253–268.

Lafontaine, Francine and Kenneth J. White [1986], "Obtaining Any Wald Statistic You Want," *Economics Letters*, 21:1, 35–40.

Lau, Lawrence J. [1978], "A Note on the Compatibility of a System of Difference Equations and a Time-Independent Linear Equation," *Economics Letters*, 1:3, 243–247.

Lucas, Robert E., Jr. [1969], "Labor-Capital Substitution in U.S. Manufacturing," in Arnold C. Harberger and Martin J. Bailey, eds., *The Taxation of Income from Capital*, Washington, D.C.: The Brookings Institution, pp. 223–274.

McElroy, Marjorie B. [1987], "Additive General Error Models for Production, Cost, and Derived Demand or Share Equations," *Journal of Political Economy*, 95:4, August, 737–757.

McFadden, Daniel [1978a], "Cost, Revenue and Profit Functions," Chapter I.1 in Melvyn Fuss and Daniel McFadden, eds., *Production Economics: A Dual Approach to Theory and Applications*, Vol. 1, Amsterdam: North-Holland, pp. 1–109.

McFadden, Daniel [1978b], "The General Linear Profit Function," Chapter II.2 in Melvyn Fuss and Daniel McFadden, eds., *Production Economics: A Dual Approach to Theory and Applications*, Vol. 1, Amsterdam: North-Holland, 1, pp. 269–286.

Morrison, Catherine J. [1986], "Structural Models of Dynamic Factor Demands with Nonstatic Expectations: An Empirical Assessment of Alternative Expectations Specifications," *International Economic Review*, 27:2, June, 365–386.

Morrison, Catherine J. [1988a], "Quasi-Fixed Inputs in US and Japanese Manufacturing: A Generalized Leontief Restricted Cost Function Approach," *Review of Economics and Statistics*, 70:2, May, 275–287.

Morrison, Catherine J. [1988b], "Markups in US and Japanese Manufacturing: A Short Run Econometric Analysis," Cambridge, Mass.: NBER Working Paper No. 2799, December.

Morrison, Catherine J. [1989], "Markup Behavior in Durable and Nondurable Manufacturing: A Production Theory Approach," Cambridge, Mass: NBER Working Paper No. 2941, April.

Morrison, Catherine J. and Ernst R. Berndt [1981], "Short Run Labor Productivity in a Dynamic Model," *Journal of Econometrics*, 16:3, December, 339–365.

Nelson, Randy A. [1986], "Capital Vintage, Time Trends, and Technical Change in the Electric Power Industry," *Southern Economic Journal*, 53:2, June, 315–332.

Nerlove, Marc [1963], "Returns to Scale in Electricity Supply," in Carl Christ, ed., *Measurement in Economics: Studies in Mathematical Economics and Econometrics in Memory of Yehuda Grunfeld*, Stanford, Calif.: Stanford University Press, 167–198.

Nerlove, Marc [1967], "Recent Empirical Studies of the CES and Related Production Functions," in Murray Brown, ed., *The Theory and Empirical Analysis of Production*, Studies in Income and Wealth, Vol. 32, New York: Columbia University Press for the National Bureau of Economic Research, pp. 55–122.

Norsworthy, J. Randolph [1990], "Cost Function Estimation and the Additive General Error Model," Troy, N.Y.: Renssalaer Polytechnic Institute, Dept. of Economics, Unpublished Working Paper, April.

Oberhofer, Walter and Jan Kmenta [1974], "A General Procedure for Obtaining Maximum Likelihood Estimates in Generalized Regression Models," *Econometrica*, 42:3, May, 579–590.

Phillips, Peter C. B. and Joon Y. Park [1988], "On the Formulation of Wald Tests of Nonlinear Restrictions," *Econometrica*, 56:5, September, 1065–1083.

Pindyck, Robert S. and Julio R. Rotemberg [1983], "Dynamic Factor Demands and the Effects of Energy Price Shocks," *American Economic Review*, 73:5, December, 1066–1079.

Prucha, Ingmar R. and M. Ishaq Nadiri [1986], "A Comparison of Alternative Methods for the Estimation of Dynamic Factor Demand Models under Nonstatic Expectations," *Journal of Econometrics*, 33:1/2, October/November, 187–211.

Rothenberg, Thomas J. [1984], "Hypothesis Testing in Linear Models when the Error Covariance Matrix Is Nonscalar," *Econometrica*, 52:4, July, 827–842.

Samuelson, Paul A. [1979], "Paul Douglas' Measurement of Production Functions and Marginal Productivities," *Journal of Political Economy*, 87:5, Part 1, October, 923–939.

Sargan, J. Denis [1971], "Production Functions," Part V of Richard G. Layard, J. Denis Sargan, Margaret E. Ager, and Deborah J. Jones, eds., *Qualified Manpower and Economic Performance*, London: The Penguin Press, pp. 145–204.

Spady, Richard H. and Ann F. Friedlaender [1978], "Hedonic Cost Functions for the Regulated Trucking Industry," *Bell Journal of Economics*, 9:1, Spring, 159–179.

Toevs, Alden L. [1980], "Approximate Variance Formulas for the Elasticities of Substitution Obtained from Translog Production Functions," *Economics Letters*, 5:2, 155–160.

Uzawa, Hirofumi [1964], "Duality Principles in the Theory of Cost and Production," *International Economic Review*, 5:2, 216–220.

Walters, Alan A. [1963], "Production and Cost Functions: An Econometric Survey," *Econometrica*, 31:1, January/April 1963, 1–66.

Woodland, Alan D., [1979], "Stochastic Specification and the Estimation of Share Equations," *Journal of Econometrics*, 10:3, August, 361–383.

Zellner, Arnold, Jan Kmenta and Jacques Drèze [1966], "Specification and Estimation of Cobb-Douglas Production Function Models," *Econometrica*, 34:3, October, 784–795.

FURTHER READINGS

Berndt, Ernst R. and Melvyn A. Fuss, eds. [1986], "The Econometrics of Temporary Equilibrium," Special Issue of the *Journal of Econometrics*, Vol. 33, No. 1/2, October/November. A set of papers dealing with production-cost models in which some inputs are fixed in the short run, while others are variable.

Chambers, Robert G. [1988], *Applied Production Analysis*, New York: Cambridge University Press. An extensive discussion of modern production theory, with literature surveys.

Fuss, Melvyn A. and Daniel McFadden, eds., [1978] *Production Economics: A Dual Approach to Theory and Applications*, Amsterdam: North-Holland, 2 volumes. A classic set of studies using modern duality theory.

Jorgenson, Dale W., Frank M. Gollop, and Barbara M. Fraumeni [1987], *Productivity and U.S. Economic Growth*, Cambridge, Mass.: Harvard University Press. An extensive study of productivity growth, using the translog cost function framework. The underlying data are also provided.

Morrison, Catherine J. [1991], *A Microeconomic Approach to the Measurement of Economic Performance: Productivity Growth, Capacity Utilization, and Related Performance Indicators*, New York: Springer-Verlag, forthcoming. An overview of productivity modeling and measurement based on the theory of cost and production.

Chapter 10

Parameter Estimation in Structural and Reduced Form Equations of Small Macroeconometric Models

". . . there is always a temporary trade-off between inflation and unemployment; there is no permanent trade-off."

MILTON FRIEDMAN (1968, p. 11)

"Since 1970 the Phillips curve has become an unidentified flying object and has eluded all econometric efforts to nail it down."

ARTHUR M. OKUN (1980, p. 166)

"Why is our money ever less valuable? Perhaps it is simply that we have inflation because we expect inflation, and we expect inflation because we've had it."

ROBERT M. SOLOW (1979, p. 31)

". . . existing Keynesian macroeconometric models are incapable of providing reliable guidance in formulating monetary, fiscal, or other types of policy. This conclusion is based in part on the spectacular recent failures of these models, and in part on their lack of a sound theoretical or econometric basis."

ROBERT E. LUCAS, JR. and THOMAS J. SARGENT (1978, p. 316)

"It is hard to avoid the conclusion that for short-run analysis the Lucas supply function and with it applications of rational expectations to economic policy should be relegated to the same scrap heap of discarded ideas where lie the earlier classical models of perfect market clearing laid to rest by Keynes forty years ago."

ROBERT J. GORDON (1977, p. 132)

In macroeconomic theory, attention is focused on factors that affect fluctuations in national aggregate economic performance. The specific measures of aggregate performance include, for example, a country's output, employment, price level, balance of trade, and exchange rates. In turn, movements in these aggregate measures reflect changes in the behavior of firms, households, and governments; such underlying behavioral factors include, among others, the consumption, savings, and investment behavior of firms and households; the determinants of changes in wages and prices; monetary and fiscal policies; the stock of money and other liquid assets; the federal budget; and the national debt.

One goal of macroeconomic theory is to relate these underlying behavioral factors to the specific measures of aggregate economic performance. Much of the fascination and challenge of macroeconomic theory derive from the fact that it deals with such important interrelationships. As a result, developments in macroeconomic theory are frequently closely related to current and controversial economic problems of the day.

Empirical implementations of theoretical macroeconomics are often called *macroeconometric models*. Macroeconometric models are very diverse, ranging from small two- or three-equation models to huge edifices containing hundreds, occasionally even thousands, of equations. Although their diversity is striking, macroeconometric models typically share a focus on economic aggregates. Thus a common feature of macroeconometric models is that they deal with a small number of aggregated markets, and by necessity they abstract from the microeconomic details surrounding individual industries, firms, and households. Nonetheless, most macroeconomists are mindful of the microeconomic foundations underlying aggregate models. There is, of course, much art and disagreement among macroeconomists in choosing which factors ought to be emphasized in macroeconometric models, how heterogeneity and aggregation problems affect the reliability of microeconomic optimization theory, and what details can safely be ignored or circumvented through the use of judicious assumptions.[1]

In this chapter we concern ourselves with estimation and inference issues in structural and reduced form equations of small macroeconometric models. We restrict our attention to small models, since most of the important issues of identification, estimation, and inference in simultaneous equation models can be illustrated by using models having only several, say, three or so equations.[2] Moreover, since many of the most recent developments in macroeconometrics involve highly sophisticated and rather advanced estimation techniques, in this chapter we focus primarily on classic issues and econometric models. We will also, of course, devote some attention to the more recent literature.

The macroeconomic literature has long reflected a tension between theory and observation. We begin our survey of small macroeconometric models in Section 10.2 by overviewing the history of the interplay between theory and observation for one of the best-known classic empirical discoveries in macroeconomics, the *Phillips curve.*[3] In its original form the Phillips curve summarized an inverse empirical relationship between wage inflation (the dependent variable) and the unemployment rate (an explanatory variable); it was rationalized as reflecting the price movements of a commodity (labor) facing excess demand (low unemployment). As we shall see in Section 10.2, econometric estimation of the original Phillips curve estimation was quite unusual.

Phillips's 1958 article had a considerable impact on macroeconomists and among macro policymakers. In response to Phillips's empirical findings, both cautious and downright skeptical macroeconomic theorists attempted to provide a more detailed theoretical underpinning for the Phillips curve. One very important paper by Robert E. Lucas, Jr. and Leonard A. Rapping [1970] reversed the causation and emphasized market-clearing rather than excess demand factors; in particular, Lucas and Rapping related an endogenous unemployment rate to expected wage inflation. A clear implication of their "backward" Phillips curve was that any observed relationship between inflation and unemployment must reflect the price expectations of firms and households; one should therefore not expect a Phillips curve to be stable unless these expectations are also stable. In fact, during the 1970s the Phillips curve became so volatile that the well-known macroeconomic policy analyst Arthur M. Okun called it an "unidentified flying object" (see the quote from Okun at the beginning of this chapter). In Section 10.3 of this chapter we therefore consider the stability of the Phillips curve and the Lucas-Rapping critique in detail. Later in the chapter we employ the data underlying the original Lucas-Rapping three-equation simultaneous equations model in doing a number of hands-on applications and exercises.

An important contribution of the Lucas-Rapping paper was that it highlighted the role of expectations in interpreting the Phillips curve. But how is one to model the process by which firms and households form expectations? In recent years this issue has been at the center of many controversies among macroeconometricians. Naive econometric modelers have often assumed that firms and households are myopic and that they form essentially static expectations (either in levels or in growth rates); more sophisticated macroeconometricians have specified that expectations are formed in an adaptive manner, conditioned in a stable way by recent historical experiences. According to the *rational expectations hypothesis* (REH), however, economic agents form expectations using all available economically relevant information. When combined with the assumption that markets are in instantaneous full equilibrium, the REH provides explicit guidance on how econometricians should model the expectations formation process; these procedures often differ dramatically from those involved in implementing empirically the myopic or adaptive expectation formation processes.

The REH has had an enormous impact in macroeconometrics, and therefore in Section 10.4 we consider the specification, estimation, and interpretation of a relatively simple two-equation model of output and inflation in the United States that incorporates the REH; this model, developed by John

B. Taylor [1979], is especially attractive in that the cross-equation restrictions implied by the REH are testable by using traditional procedures for statistical inference. The data underlying Taylor's study are provided on the floppy diskette accompanying this text, and in the hands-on applications of this chapter we will investigate empirically the consequences of estimating this simultaneous equations model using alternative estimation procedures.

In Section 10.5 we consider a rather different but traditionally equally important body of literature. Specifically, much has been written in macroeconometrics on the sensitivity of parameter estimates and inference to alternative simultaneous equations estimators, including instrumental variables, two- and three-stage least squares, reduced form versus structural estimation, and limited and full information maximum likelihood estimation. It is somewhat remarkable that when econometricians have developed a new simultaneous equations estimator, one data set that they have often used for purposes of comparison is the data set developed for one of the very first macroeconometric models of the U.S. economy, namely, the three-equation Model I, published in 1950 by Lawrence R. Klein.[4] Accordingly, in Section 10.5 we summarize results reported by investigators employing different simultaneous equations estimators on the same Klein Model I annual data for the U.S. economy, 1921–1941. In the hands-on applications of this chapter we will attempt to replicate several of the more important empirical findings from this literature.

Before initiating our survey of the econometric issues that are involved in estimating small macroeconomic models, we must first overview some very important measurement issues. Specifically, we begin by focusing our attention on one variable whose measurement and interpretation is particularly important in recent macroeconometric controversies, namely, the unemployment rate.

10.1 MEASUREMENT ISSUES: THE UNEMPLOYMENT RATE

Numerous measurement issues are of great concern to macroeconometric modelers. Among them are appropriate measurements for money supply, real output and price deflators, net investment, the government budget deficit, and the balance of trade. Space constraints prevent us from discussing each of these; however, in Chapter 4 we consider issues in constructing hedonic (quality adjusted) price deflators, in Chapter 5 we devoted attention to the measurement of wage rates, and in Chapter 6 we overview measurement issues for net investment. In this chapter we briefly discuss issues in measuring unemployment, a variable whose interpretation is surrounded with considerable controversy. Additional discussion on employment and unemployment measurement is provided in Chapter 11 in the context of modeling the labor supply decision.

Official data on monthly labor force, employment, and unemployment statistics in the United States are typically announced by the Bureau of Labor

Statistics on the first Friday of each month and are drawn from the Current Population Survey.[5] This survey is based on interviews conducted by an employee of the U.S. Bureau of the Census during the week following the twelfth day of the previous month—called the reference week. The sample consists of people in about 60,000 households in over 700 separate geographic areas of the United States. Households are chosen to reflect the principal characteristics of the population (e.g., age, gender, race, ethnicity, and marital status), as taken from the most recent decennial census. The same household is included in the survey for four consecutive months, is removed from the survey for eight months, and is then included again for a final four consecutive months.

The *employed* are defined as those individuals who worked one hour or more for wages or salary during the reference week or did 15 hours or more of unpaid work in a family business or farm. Individuals who were absent from work because of vacation, illness, inclement weather, or strikes and lockouts are also counted as employed but are included in the separate subcategory "with a job but not at work." The *unemployed* are those who are on layoff from a job, who have no job but have looked for work during the preceding four weeks and were available for work during the reference week, or who are waiting to report to a new job within the next 30 days.

On the basis of questions asked by the interviewer the labor force status of each civilian aged 16 or over is determined in an all-or-nothing manner. A person is either in or out of the labor force; by definition, one cannot be partly in the labor force and partly out.

As currently defined in the United States, the *labor force* is limited to those individuals 16 years of age and older who are not institutionalized in prisons, mental institutions, and the like. Any labor supplied by individuals under age 16 is ignored, presumably because such an amount is small. Note that students aged 16 or over are counted as being in the labor force, and many in fact participate on a part-time or part-year basis. Separate data are compiled on the civilian and total labor forces; the latter adds resident military personnel to the civilian labor force. In most macroeconometric studies, the measures of employment and unemployment that are used for analysis refer only to the civilian labor force.

Census Bureau interviewers therefore decompose the entire civilian noninstitutionalized population P into the employed, E, the unemployed, U, and those who are out of the labor force, O, such that $P \equiv E + U + O$. The labor force L is limited to the employed and unemployed, $L \equiv E + U$, while the labor force participation rate, in percentage points, is measured as LFPR $\equiv 100*(L/P)$. The civilian unemployment rate, also measured in percentage points, is defined as $UR \equiv 100*(U/L)$. Data on the civilian UR for selected years in the United States are presented in Table 10.1. There it is seen that the UR has varied from a high of 24.9% in 1933 to a low of 1.9% in 1945. Even in the 1980s the UR has varied substantially, from 5.5% in 1988 to 9.7% in 1982.[6]

Table 10.1 The Civilian Unemployment Rate in the United States, Selected Years

Year	UR	Year	UR	Year	UR	Year	UR
1929	3.2	1947	3.9	1961	6.7	1983	9.6
1933	24.9	1949	5.9	1967	3.8	1984	7.5
1939	17.2	1952	3.0	1975	8.5	1985	7.2
1942	4.7	1955	4.4	1979	5.8	1986	7.0
1945	1.9	1958	6.8	1982	9.7	1988	5.5

Source: U.S. Economic Report of the President, Selected Years.

Considerable disagreement exists, however, concerning the interpretation of the measured unemployment rate and, in particular, the extent to which it accurately quantifies the rate of underutilization of labor supply. In the Keynesian literature it has been traditional to distinguish people who are voluntarily unemployed (those who have quit jobs to search for new employment) from those who for a variety of reasons are involuntarily unemployed. As we shall see in Section 10.3.D, modern classical economists deny the existence of involuntary unemployment in market economies such as the United States. Much of the controversy between modern Keynesians and modern classicists derives from the fact that the unemployment rate is a quantity measure that is constructed independently of price (the wage rate); therefore there is disagreement concerning whether unemployment quantity measures fully reflect the optimizing behavior of individuals and firms (including possible optimal labor hoarding by firms).[7] Some of these issues will be discussed in further detail in Section 10.3. Other issues, particularly those concerning "added" and "discouraged" workers and their impacts on measured unemployment rates, are discussed in Chapter 11. For our purposes in this chapter, however, we now focus our attention on a classic debate in the macroeconometrics literature involving measured unemployment and inflation, namely, the Phillips curve.

10.2 EXTRAORDINARY ECONOMETRICS: THE ORIGINAL PHILLIPS CURVE

The history surrounding the Phillips curve is a most fascinating one. In his widely cited 1958 article analyzing the relationship between unemployment and the rate of change of money wage rates in the United Kingdom for the almost 100-year time period between 1861 and 1957, A. William Phillips summarized his simple and modest theoretical framework in three opening sentences:

> When the demand for a commodity or service is high relatively to the supply of it we expect the price to rise, the rate of rise being greater the greater the excess demand. Conversely when the demand is low relatively

> to the supply we expect the price to fall, the rate of fall being greater the greater the deficiency of demand. It seems plausible that this principle should operate as one of the factors determining the rate of change of money wage rates.[8]

Using this reasoning, Phillips postulated that the relationship between the unemployment rate u and the rate of change of money wage rates $\dot{w}/w$ would be nonlinear. With $\dot{w}/w$ on the vertical axis and u on the horizontal axis, Phillips conjectured that at higher rates of unemployment the relationship would become quite flat, since "workers are reluctant to offer their services at less than the prevailing rates when the demand for labour is low and unemployment is high."[9]

Further, Phillips argued that the rate of change in the unemployment rate, $\dot{u}/u$, would also affect $\dot{w}/w$. During a year when $\dot{u}/u$ was falling, employers would bid for workers' services more vigorously than they would in a year when $\dot{u}/u$ was zero but u was at the same average rate; similarly, when $\dot{u}/u$ was rising, workers would be less able to demand wage increases, and employers would be less willing to grant them than they would in a year when $\dot{u}/u$ was zero but u was at the same average rate.

Finally, owing to provisions of cost-of-living adjustments in negotiated wage contracts, Phillips argued that $\dot{w}/w$ might also depend on the rate of change in retail prices, particularly when rates of price increase for imported goods greatly exceeded those for domestically produced goods. Together, these considerations suggested to Phillips a model of the form

$$\dot{w}/w = f(u, \dot{u}/u, \dot{p}_i/p_i) \tag{10.1}$$

where $\dot{p}_i/p_i$ is the difference between rates of price increase for imported and for domestically produced goods.

With this as theoretical background, Phillips then initiated an empirical investigation, whose goal was to examine

> whether statistical evidence supports the hypothesis that the rate of change of money wage rates in the United Kingdom can be explained by the level of unemployment and the rate of change in unemployment, except in or immediately after those years in which there was a very rapid rise in import prices, and if so to form some quantitative estimate of the relation between unemployment and the rate of change of money wage rates.[10]

As we shall now see, while Phillips's goals were straightforward, the econometric tools that he employed were, let us say, rather unconventional.

Phillips disaggregated his 1861–1957 near-century of annual data into three time periods: 1861–1913, 1913–1948, and 1948–1957.[11] Using the 1861–1913 annual data, he began by constructing a scatter diagram with $\dot{w}/w$ on the vertical axis and u on the horizontal axis; apparently, he did not consider the price variable $\dot{p}_i/p_i$ further, since it was substantial only in 1862. The resulting scatter diagram suggested a nonlinear relationship between $\dot{w}/w$ and u, although a number of outlier observations were rationalized as possibly being due to the effects of $\dot{u}/u$ on $\dot{w}/w$.

To isolate the effects on $\dot{w}/w$ of u from those of $\dot{u}/u$, Phillips constructed from the original 53 annual time periods six "average" observations consisting of average values for $\dot{w}/w$ and u when u lay between 0 and 2, 2 and 3, 3 and 4, 4 and 5, 5 and 7, and 7 and 11 percent, respectively. This averaging, he argued, canceled out the effects of $\dot{u}/u$, since "each interval includes years in which unemployment was increasing and years in which it was decreasing."[12] With this averaged data in hand, Phillips then proceeded to examine the relationship between $\dot{w}/w$ and u, disregarding $\dot{u}/u$.

Phillips considered using multiple regression analysis but rejected this procedure, since he believed that the linear regression framework would not approximate the hypothesized nonlinear relationship adequately. Instead, Phillips employed the six average observations and specified an equation having the form

$$\dot{w}/w + \alpha = \beta u^{\gamma}$$

which, when logarithmically transformed, became

$$\log(\dot{w}/w + \alpha) = \log\beta + \gamma\log u \tag{10.2}$$

The parameter α deserves comment. In the two average observations when u was greater than 5%, $\dot{w}/w$ was negative; to rule out negative values and thereby to ensure that a logarithmic transformation was possible, Phillips appended a parameter α, which was assumed to be sufficiently positive that at these two observations, $(\dot{w}/w + \alpha) > 0$.

Using the four observations for which $\dot{w}/w$ was positive, Phillips initially ignored the parameter α in Eq. (10.2) and ran a linear regression of $\log(\dot{w}/w)$ on a constant term and $\log u$, thereby obtaining estimates of $\log\beta$ and γ. He then used these estimates of $\log\beta$ and γ and a "trial-and-error" graphical inspection to find that value of the parameter α that made the curve pass "as close as possible" to the two remaining observations where u was greater than 5% and $\dot{w}/w$ was negative.[13] This resulted in the fitted curve

$$\log(\dot{w}/w + 0.900) = 0.984 - 1.394\log u \tag{10.3}$$

Phillips plotted this fitted curve and compared it to the 1861–1913 historical data; except for 1862 (when $\dot{p}_i/p_i$ was large) and to a lesser extent 1863, the visual "fit" was quite good (Phillips did not report an R^2 measure, nor did he provide standard error estimates for the parameters).

On the basis of this equation fitted from six averages of the first 53 annual observations (1861–1913), and using historical data on $\log u$, Phillips then generated annual predicted values of $\dot{w}/w$ for 1913 to 1948 and for 1948 to 1957. Although some residuals were large (Phillips commented on them at length), the overall fit was phenomenal, particularly for the 1948–1957 time period. To Phillips these results drawn from a near-century data set provided preliminary support for the existence of a stable empirical relationship between $\dot{w}/w$ and u.

The extent of this stability is demonstrated in Fig. 10.1, which reproduces Phillips's original Figure 11; here Phillips used parameters in Eq. (10.3) estimated from the six average observations over the 1861–1913 time period to predict annual values of $\dot{w}/w$ for many years later, from 1948 to 1957. As can be seen, Phillips's equation appears to predict $\dot{w}/w$ with remarkable accuracy.

By today's standards, Phillips's econometric technique—least squares combined with graphical inspection using six averaged observations—is somewhat lacking in finesse. Phillips applied it in part because at that time, nonlinear estimation methods were not widely available. Evidence reported by Nancy J. Walwick [1989] suggests that Phillips, an electrical engineer turned economist who made major contributions in statistics, wanted to finish this research project quickly so that he could depart from London for a sabbatical year in New Zealand. According to Walwick, Phillips thought that the tools he used were appropriate for a "quick and dirty" initial study. Interestingly, Christopher L. Gilbert [1976] has employed Phillips's original data, appended a stochastic specification to Eq. (10.2), and then estimated it and other specifications using nonlinear maximum likelihood procedures, utilizing each of the annual observations from 1861 to 1913, not just the six averaged ones. Gilbert reports that when these high-tech estimation methods are employed, the point estimates of α, β, and γ become 0.8826, 0.9513, and -1.3837, respectively, surprisingly close to Phillips's original estimates—see Eq. (10.3).[14]

In terms of policy implications, Phillips noted that his estimated equation provided support for the notion that policymakers might be able to choose between different combinations of unemployment and wage inflation;

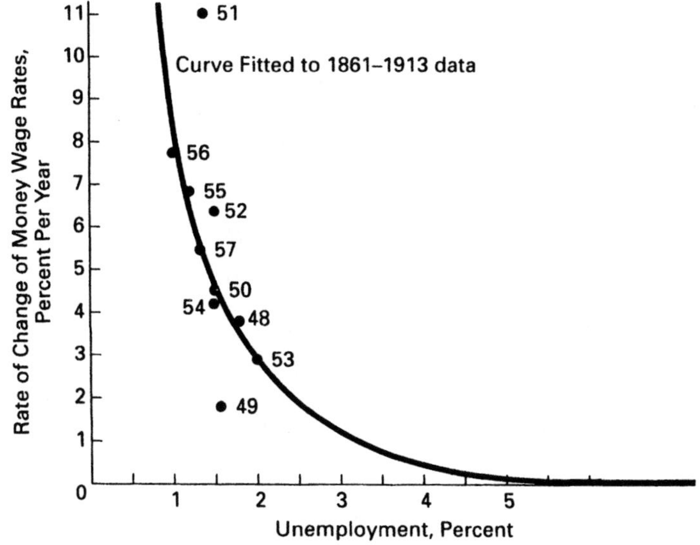

Figure 10.1 The Phillips Curve for the United Kingdom, 1948–1957
(Source: Phillips [1958]. Reprinted with permission.)

in his conclusion, for example, Phillips wrote that his estimated equation implied that wage rates would stabilize if there were about 5% unemployment and that wage rate increases of about 2–3% (corresponding with labor productivity growth) would be consistent with a 2.5% unemployment rate.[15] Notably, however, Phillips did not distinguish short-run from possible long-run tradeoffs, nor in his policy discussion did he clearly differentiate money wage inflation from real wage changes. As we shall see, these distinctions became critical in the subsequent policy debate.

Three other matters concerning Phillips's analysis merit brief comment. First, while Phillips is usually credited with having discovered the empirical relationship between $\dot{w}/w$ and u, more than 30 years earlier, in 1926, Irving Fisher reported results of a study in which he related the overall rate of price inflation, $\dot{p}/p$, to u (actually, to $1 - u$, the employment rate).[16] Using monthly data for the United States from September 1915 through December 1924, Fisher began by constructing a variable representing the effects of a moving sum or distributed lag of rates of price changes:

> for any particular spurt P' in prices, about three percent of the effect will be felt in a month; six per cent in the second month; seven per cent in the third, fourth and fifth months respectively, after which the effects will gradually taper off.[17]

He then correlated this rate of change of prices series reflecting previous "dances of the dollar" with an employment rate series, obtaining a correlation of 0.90, which he called "remarkably high." In interpreting these findings, however, Fisher argued that the causation ran primarily from $\dot{p}/p$ to u and that u was therefore endogenous;[18] by contrast, Phillips treated $\dot{w}/w$ as endogenous and u as exogenous.

Second, although Fisher's study was disseminated in 1926, macroeconomists were apparently unaware of it until well after Phillips's 1958 article was published. Independently, Arthur Donner and James F. McCollum [1972] cited Fisher in an historical note on the Phillips curve, while in 1973 the editors of the *Journal of Political Economy* reprinted it in the "Lost and Found" section of the March/April issue under Fisher's authorship, but retitled "I Discovered the Phillips Curve."

Third, while Phillips's original relation was one between wage rate changes and u, numerous studies that followed (as well as the earlier Fisher research) instead postulated a relation between overall price changes and u. The two approaches can be related, under strong assumptions, as follows. Let y be the constant dollar level of output, e be the level of labor employment, and let μ be the markup of the value of output over the wage bill. Then $p \cdot y = \mu \cdot w \cdot e$. Rewriting this in terms of proportional growth rates and rearranging, we obtain

$$\dot{p}/p = \dot{\mu}/\mu + \dot{w}/w - (\dot{y}/y - \dot{e}/e) \tag{10.4}$$

where $(\dot{y}/y - \dot{e}/e)$ is the growth rate of average labor productivity. If one assumes a constant markup over labor costs, $\dot{\mu}/\mu = 0$, and if the growth in average labor productivity occurs at a constant rate of ϕ percent per time period, then Eq. (10.4) reduces to

$$\dot{p}/p = \dot{w}/w - \phi \tag{10.5}$$

Note that since $\dot{p}/p$ depends on $\dot{w}/w$ which in turn is a function of u, one can modify the Phillips curve and relate $\dot{p}/p$ to u. Although the empirical validity of these required assumptions has often been called into question,[19] Phillips's equation (10.2) is frequently reformulated in a way that relates $\dot{p}/p$, rather than $\dot{w}/w$, to u.

10.3 THEORY AND OBSERVATION: SHOULD THE PHILLIPS CURVE BE STABLE? IS IT?

Phillips's discovery of an inverse relationship between $\dot{w}/w$ and u generated a great deal of empirical and theoretical research, much of which is beyond the scope of this chapter.[20] In the paragraphs that follow, we will highlight interactions between theory and observation and will focus on significant econometric aspects, including OLS and two-stage least squares (2SLS) estimation issues, identifiability, and structural versus reduced form estimation. Although we will focus primarily on econometric aspects of this literature, readers should understand that much of this research took place in the context of vigorous policy debates. Passions, polemics, and analyses were frequently intertwined.

10.3.A Early Extensions of Phillips's Findings

One of the first discussions on the possible shape of a Phillips curve for the United States (rather than for the United Kingdom) was given by Paul A. Samuelson and Robert M. Solow at the December 1959 annual meetings of the American Economic Association.[21] Following Phillips, Samuelson and Solow constructed a scatter diagram relating $\dot{w}/w$ and u. They noted that although the diagram indicated some outlier observations (around World War I and the years from 1933 to 1941), the "bulk of the observations . . . all show a rather consistent pattern. Wage rates do tend to rise when the labor market is tight, and the tighter the faster."[22] Further, Samuelson and Solow found an apparent upward shift in the inverse relationship in the 1940s and 1950s, one that was consistent from 1946 to 1958. On the basis of this more recent data, and "using no more than a couple of rules of thumb and educated guessing," Samuelson and Solow "converted these postwar observations into a hypothetical relation between the rate of price inflation and the unemployment rate."[23] The U.S. Phillips curve that they drew was more like Fisher's than Phillips's, however, in that it related the rate of overall inflation $\dot{p}/p$ to u, rather than $\dot{w}/w$ to u.

The Samuelson-Solow U.S. modified Phillips curve is reproduced in Fig. 10.2; note that its shape is roughly similar to the original Phillips curve reproduced in Fig. 10.1.

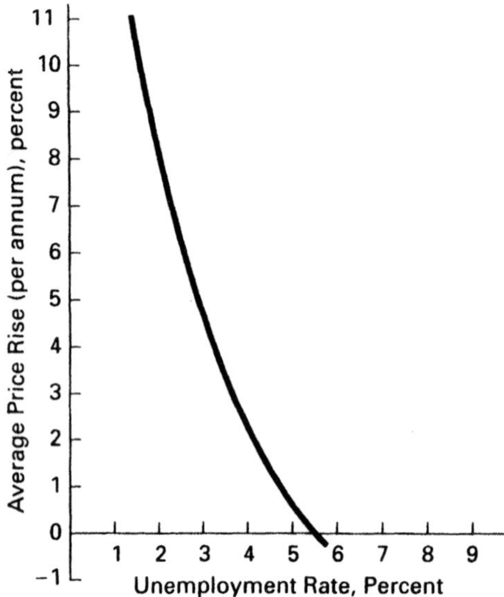

Figure 10.2 The Samuelson-Solow Modified Phillips Curve for the United States (Source: Samuelson and Solow [1965]. Reprinted with permission.)

Unlike Phillips, however, Samuelson and Solow explicitly argued that the tradeoff implied by their Phillips curve was only a short-run one. In particular, they acknowledged that government policies might change the shape of, or shift, the Phillips curve:

> It would be wrong, though, to think that our . . . menu that relates obtainable price and unemployment behavior will maintain its same shape in the longer run. What we do in a policy way during the next few years might cause it to shift in a definite way.[24]

Another study, that by Richard G. Lipsey [1960], was also stimulated by the important policy issues raised by Phillips's article. Lipsey's goal was to provide more credible theoretical and empirical foundations. His plan was first to subject the data to estimation procedures that were more traditional than those of Phillips to uncover what phenomena would require explanation and then to attempt to provide the requisite theoretical foundations that would help "explain" these phenomena.

Lipsey began by modifying Phillips's functional form to another whose plot of fitted values was virtually indistinguishable from Phillips's nonlinear form. Specifically, using 1862–1913 annual U.K. data, Lipsey obtained results from OLS estimation as follows:

$$\dot{w}/w = -1.42 + 7.06u^{-1} + 2.31u^{-2} \qquad \textbf{(10.6)}$$

where $u^{-1} \equiv 1/u$ and $u^{-2} \equiv 1/u^2$; Lipsey reported an R^2 of 0.64, but did not disclose t-statistics or standard errors. An expanded version of Eq. (10.6) with $\dot{u}$ added as a regressor yielded an estimated equation of the form

$$\dot{w}/w = -1.52 + 7.60u^{-1} + 1.61u^{-2} - 0.023\dot{u} \quad \textbf{(10.7)}$$

and an R^2 of 0.82. Although Lipsey did not report it, one can conclude (simply by examining the change in R^2 from these two regressions) that the estimated coefficient on $\dot{u}$ was statistically significantly different from zero at the usual significance levels.[25]

Next, Lipsey added a regressor measuring the change in the cost of living, which we denoted earlier as the overall rate of inflation $\dot{p}/p$. This resulted in a least squares estimated equation

$$\begin{aligned}\dot{w}/w = -1.21 + &6.45u^{-1} + 2.26u^{-2} - 0.019\dot{u} + 0.21\dot{p}/p \\ &(2.12) \qquad (2.13) \qquad (0.004) \quad (0.07)\end{aligned} \quad \textbf{(10.8)}$$

having an R^2 of 0.85, where standard errors are in parentheses. Note that the implied coefficient t-statistics are larger than 2.5 for all variables except u^{-2}. It is also worth noting that the coefficient on $\dot{p}/p$ is small, certainly less than unity. One might expect this coefficient to equal unity if one interpreted Eq. (10.8) as a short-run labor supply equation in which labor supply depended on real (rather than nominal) wages—but more on this later. Lipsey acknowledged that there might be some simultaneity problems with having $\dot{p}/p$ as a regressor, but he argued that the small value of its coefficient was credible, since the ordinary least squares bias on the $\dot{p}/p$ coefficient was upward, the extent of the bias depending in part on the relationship between $\dot{w}/w$ and $\dot{p}/p$. To his surprise, Lipsey found that for the 1862–1913 time period the R^2 from a simple regression of $\dot{w}/w$ on $\dot{p}/p$ was only 0.27; it had the form $\dot{w}/w = 1.14 + 0.55\dot{p}/p$. He interpreted this result as implying that in his data set the likely bias from using OLS was small.

On the basis of this preliminary empirical research, Lipsey concluded that in fact both u and $\dot{u}$ significantly affected $\dot{w}/w$ and that it was now time to do some theorizing as to what causal factors might help to explain these observed phenomena.

To analyze the relationship between $\dot{w}/w$ and u incorporating dynamic effects, Lipsey introduced the hypothesis that the rate at which w changes is proportional to the gap between the demand (d) and supply (s) for labor:

$$\dot{w}/w = \alpha[(\mathrm{d} - \mathrm{s})/\mathrm{s}] \quad \textbf{(10.9)}$$

where α is now the speed of adjustment parameter. One possible measure of the numerator in $[\cdot]$ was the difference between unfilled vacancies and the number of unemployed workers. Since the vacancy data were generally unavailable, however, Lipsey instead specified the unemployment rate u as a measure of excess demand.[26] Further, since for a number of reasons, workers take time to change jobs, Lipsey argued that even when excess demand was zero, there would be some positive frictional unemployment. Hence Lipsey interpreted the Phillips curve of Fig. 10.1 as representing the speed at which wage rates adjust to a disequilibrium; he called this relationship an adjustment function. Lipsey cautioned, however, that even if one had knowledge of the shape of the adjustment function, such information would not be sufficient to identify and distinguish between causes of any disequilibrium, since that would require additional details on the factors affecting the underlying supply and demand curves for labor.

The interpretation that Lipsey gave Eq. (10.9) was that it applied to a single market. This raised the issue of what happens when one aggregates over markets and attempts to fit an equation analogous to Eq. (10.9) using national data. Lipsey demonstrated that whenever individual markets had differing but stable adjustment parameters α_j (as they might be expected to have, for example, in the different geographic regions of the United Kingdom), compositional changes in unemployment among markets would cause the aggregate α for the country as a whole to be unstable. Moreover, even when the α_j were equal across markets, because the common relationship between $\dot{w}/w$ and u is nonlinear (convex), the macro observations will always lie above the individual market curves, the difference being greater the larger the degree of inequality in u among markets.

To see this, assume a two-market economy in which each market is of equal size and each market has identical Phillips curves. In one market, however, the wage inflation is high and u is low (say, point 1 on a Phillips curve), while in the other market, wage inflation is low and u is high (point 2). For the economy as a whole, the national values for $\dot{w}/w$ and u are simply the arithmetic means of values in the two markets. Therefore the macro Phillips curve observation corresponding with these two markets will be the midpoint on a straight line drawn between points 1 and 2, a point that will always be farther out from the origin than those on the market-specific Phillips curves, owing to their convexity.

On the basis of such reasoning, Lipsey concluded that he would not necessarily expect a macro Phillips curve to be stable—the α_j might differ, and even if they were identical, compositional changes in u among markets would cause the macro curve to shift.[27] This also suggested to Lipsey an important short-run, long-run distinction:

> Finally, great caution must be exercised in trying to infer from a statistically fitted relation between $\dot{w}$ and u what would happen to wage rates if unemployment were held constant at any level for a long time. If unemployment were held constant, we would expect the degree of inequality in its distribution between markets to change substantially. We would thus expect the macro-adjustment function to shift.[28]

With this additional theory as background, Lipsey then returned to empirical analysis, seeking to examine the stability of the parameters in the estimated macro equations. In brief, what Lipsey found was that when macro

U.K. data from 1923–39 and 1948–57 were used to estimate equations analogous to Eq. (10.8), the R^2 values remained very high, but the individual parameter estimates varied considerably, often corresponding with known changes in the intermarket distribution of u. Furthermore, the coefficient on the overall inflation term $\dot{p}/p$ appeared to rise dramatically after World War I, from its 0.21 value in Eq. (10.8) based on 1862–1913 data to 0.69 for 1923–1939 and 1948–1957; while such a value was still less than unity, Lipsey acknowledged that this estimate was not inconsistent with the "cost-push" or labor supply view of wage inflation, which argues that a great deal of the rise in wages is due to wages chasing prices.[29] Together, these results led Lipsey to conclude on a most cautious note:

> Thus, although it might be held with a high degree of confidence that a significant and very interesting relation had been discovered, a very low degree of confidence might be attached at this stage to a particular estimate of the parameters.[30]

10.3.B Phelps, Friedman and the Expectations-Augmented Phillips Curve

Lipsey's analysis damaged the hypothesis that a stable short-run relationship might be expected between $\dot{w}/w$ and u, one that might be of great use to policymakers. But another theoretical assault, this one having to do with the $\dot{p}/p$ term and the price expectations of workers and employers, was even more destructive. We now briefly summarize this other attack, argued with particular vigor initially by Edmund S. Phelps [1968] and Milton Friedman [1966, 1968].

According to the neoclassical theory of consumer demand, individuals choose goods and leisure consumption so as to maximize their utility, given exogenous prices of goods p, a money wage rate w, and money wealth holdings A. The first-order conditions from such utility maximization imply that the supply of labor is homogeneous of degree zero in w, p and A, that is, that labor supply depends on real wages w/p, not money wages w. Furthermore, from the vantage of employers the first-order conditions derived from profit maximization behavior generate labor demand equations that depend on real wages w/p, not money wages w.

Phelps extended this simple supply-demand framework by incorporating heterogeneity. Individuals are heterogeneous in their preferences regarding work, and employers' job requirements also differ. In pursuing their optimizing objectives, both workers and employers search over possible jobs and people to generate the best possible employment matches. But since it is costly to process all the information in the labor market, this job-matching process takes time. At any point in time, even though real wages are equating market supply and demand, one would expect at least two types of unemployed: those who are actively searching for a new job at a wage rate that they believe they should be able to earn steadily (the frictionally unemployed) and those who might be called "passively" or "wait" unemployed, who choose to have a reservation price for their services such that they expect only intermittent employment.[31]

It is worth noting, incidentally, that disagreements still exist over whether in practice the search activities and mobility of workers in the labor market are substantial. For example, John Abowd and Arnold Zellner [1985] have estimated that in each month in the United States, close to 7 million workers move either into or out of employment.[32] On the other hand, Kim B. Clark and Lawrence H. Summers [1979] report that only 7% of the unemployed had ever turned down a job offer. Considerable controversy also remains over whether workers must in fact quit their jobs before searching for employment elsewhere.[33]

Some analysts of labor markets go the additional step to argue that the search and the wait unemployed are the *only* types of unemployed that are possible in a market economy. In particular, to the new classical economists, within a market-clearing supply-demand framework the existence of Keynes's involuntary unemployment is not possible, since in an instantaneous full equilibrium the equality of labor supply and labor demand at a market-determined real wage rate implies that the only types of unemployment that can occur are the frictional and the wait unemployment. We will return to this point later.

But what features of such a market-clearing economy could generate a short-run tradeoff between inflation and measured unemployment? Suppose that in a macroeconomy having a fixed population the labor market is in full equilibrium in the sense that the rate of actual price inflation just equaled that rate expected by all optimizing firms and individuals and that this happy coincidence had occurred for quite some time, so that real wages had fully adapted. As a result, the total amount of labor supplied and demanded by all individuals in the economy is determinate and is stable. In such a no-surprise economy, the amount of unemployment would still be nonzero, but it would simply reflect the two types of unemployment described above (search and wait); this rate of unemployment is called the *natural rate*. Given the country's capital stock, its production function, and the level of technology, the amount of output produced in such a macroeconomy at the natural rate of unemployment is also determinate; this is called a country's *potential output*, or its natural rate of output.

To understand why a Phillips curve relation might occur, for simplicity and without loss of generality, assume that the expected and actual inflation rates initially are zero, that is, that wages and prices are stable and that unemployment equals the natural rate. Now suppose that the government wishes to reduce the unemployment rate below the natural rate by stimulating aggregate demand and that this results in unexpected inflation. Employers offering the preexisting stable money wage rate to searchers might in fact "trick" some individuals into accepting job offers at that money wage (but at a lower real wage than expected), since some searchers would be unaware of the "surprise" inflation. Employers might even raise their money wage rate offers slightly, perhaps in response to finding fewer unemployed individuals sampling their job offers, and searchers might mistake the larger money wage offer as corresponding to a more attractive real wage offer than expected. In either case, as a result of the surprise inflation, unemployed individuals will prematurely abandon their job search, the mean duration of spells of unemployment might decrease, reducing u even as $\dot{p}/p$ becomes positive, and increasing output beyond its natural rate. Such an inverse relationship between $\dot{p}/p$ and u corresponds with a movement along a short-run Phillips curve.

However, workers will soon notice that inflation has in fact occurred and that their real wages have fallen. As a result, they will demand higher money wage rates to regain their real wage position. How much higher the money wage rates demanded will be will depend of course on how much inflation workers expect to occur in the future. If workers simply expect a new rate of inflation equal to that just experienced, and if this inflation rate is realized, then the tricking will cease, searchers will no longer be surprised, and the premature abandonment of job search will cease; as a result, real wages will rise, u will begin to increase, and output growth will decline, both returning toward their natural rates. This will shift the Phillips curve outward.

But seeing their attempts to decrease u being frustrated, government authorities will conclude that they can attain their target unemployment rate only by surprising workers further, that is, only by bringing about an inflation rate that is even greater than expected. This will shift the Phillips curve outward even farther. This wage-price process will spiral at an ever-accelerating rate (which is why the natural rate notion is often associated with the accelerationist view of inflation) until the government backtracks and pursues instead a deflationary policy in which the rate of inflation is less than expected. Such a deflationary policy will initially involve accepting an increased u, but once workers' expectations adjust to the lower rate of inflation and real wages rise to the expected level, u will gradually return to its natural rate.[34]

On the basis of such arguments, Phelps, Friedman, and others stated that the standard Phillips curve ought to be augmented by price expectations; movements along a Phillips curve should reflect only the effects of "surprise" inflation, not expected inflation. In terms of a Phillips curve equation such as Eq. (10.8) this reasoning implies that the $\dot{p}/p$ variable should be replaced by an expected price inflation term and that its coefficient should equal unity.[35] Hence for each rate of expected price inflation a different short-run Phillips curve relation exists; movements along any such Phillips curves correspond only with surprise inflation. Apparent shifts in the Phillips curve between two time periods could therefore reflect nothing more than the differing price expectations that occurred in each of them. Moreover, according to Phelps and Friedman, since the same natural rate could coexist with any fully anticipated rate of inflation, the long-run Phillips curve must be vertical.

10.3.C Parameter Stability When Government Policies Change

An interesting implication of the Phelps-Friedman paradigm is that to the extent that government wage and price, or incomes, policies affect the expectations of workers and employers, they would presumably shift the Phillips curves in a corresponding manner. Extending such reasoning, Richard G. Lipsey and J. Michael Parkin [1970] specified a two-equation model of wage and price determination and then estimated it, using quarterly U.K. data. Two aspects of their study are of special interest. First, Lipsey and Parkin outlined the transmission mechanisms by which incomes policies might affect wages and prices and noted that such effects would frequently involve changes in the values of one or more slope coefficients; in such cases it would of course be inappropriate to use only dummy variable intercept terms to capture the effects of incomes policies. This has obvious implications for the specification of wage and price equations.

Second, to account for such parameter changes, Lipsey and Parkin estimated parameters of their two-equation model separately for data from time periods during which government incomes policies were in effect ("policy-on" quarters) and from periods in which no government incomes policies were in effect ("policy-off"). These useful insights of Lipsey and Parkin were, unfortunately, offset by several serious problems in econometric implementation.[36]

The two-equation simultaneous equations model specified and estimated by Lipsey-Parkin is relatively straightforward:

$$\dot{p}/p = a_1 + a_2\dot{w}/w + a_3\dot{p}_i/p_i + a_4\dot{q}/q + \epsilon \tag{10.10}$$

$$\dot{w}/w = a_5 + a_6 u + a_7\dot{p}/p + a_8\dot{n} + \delta \tag{10.11}$$

where $\dot{p}_i/p_i$ is the percent growth rate of import prices, $\dot{q}/q$ is the percent change in average labor productivity (defined earlier as $\dot{y}/y - \dot{e}/e$), $\dot{n}$ is the change in the percent of the labor force unionized (reflecting union aggressiveness), other variables are as defined earlier, the a_i are unknown parameters to be estimated, and ϵ and δ are random disturbance terms that are assumed to be independently and identically normally distributed. Some of the regressors include distributed lag terms, but the two-equation model is simultaneous in $\dot{p}/p$ and $\dot{w}/w$.

Assuming that $\dot{p}/p$ and $\dot{w}/w$ are the only two jointly determined endogenous variables (a very strong assumption) and that no autocorrelation is present, one can assess whether necessary conditions for identification are satisfied. Specifically, since $\dot{p}_i/p_i$ and $\dot{q}/q$ are included in the price equation but are excluded from the wage equation, the necessary conditions for the wage equation to be identified are satisfied (in this case, overidentification is implied, since there are two excluded exogenous variables and one included endogenous variable on the right-hand side of the wage equation). Further, since u and $\dot{n}$ are included in the wage equation but are excluded from the price equation, necessary conditions for the price equation to be identified are also satisfied. As in the wage equation, overidentification is implied in the price equation.

Lipsey and Parkin estimated this two-equation model by OLS, stating that while estimation by 2SLS would be preferable, it would not be feasible.[37] According to Kenneth F. Wallis [1971], however, the paragraph in which Lipsey and Parkin defend their OLS approach is "remarkable for the frequency of mistakes."[38] Specifically, Lipsey and Parkin first argue that to do 2SLS estimation, it is necessary to "treat all the variables in the two equation subsystem, except $\dot{p}/p$ and $\dot{w}/w$, as exogenous and as the only exogenous variables in the entire economy."[39] That is clearly not correct, since one could specify that some of the other regressors are correlated with disturbance terms due to simultaneity; and provided that other legitimate instrumental variables were available, one could still estimate each of these two structural equations by 2SLS.

Second, Lipsey and Parkin state that, in their judgment, not only should $\dot{p}/p$ and $\dot{w}/w$ be viewed as jointly determined endogenous variables, but so too should u, $\dot{q}/q$ and $\dot{n}$ (but not $\dot{p}_i/p_i$). To obtain 2SLS estimates with all these jointly determined variables, Lipsey and Parkin asserted that it is necessary to "specify the complete macro model."[40] Again, that is not correct, since 2SLS estimation of the wage and price equations could be accomplished simply by employing as instruments other excluded exogenous variables, without needing to specify the precise form of other equations in a larger macro model. As Wallis notes, the single-equation 2SLS estimator is a limited information estimator and does not require specification of a full model. In fact, that is one of the more attractive features of 2SLS.

In any case, Lipsey and Parkin argued that the most likely set of legitimate instrumental variables would include government expenditures, taxes, exports, and bank rates, but that unfortunately, quarterly data series for such variables were simply not available before 1955, whereas the remainder of their data set began in 1948. Therefore they proceeded with OLS estimation of Eqs. (10.10) and (10.11).

The Lipsey and Parkin OLS estimates for the entire 1948:3–1968:2 time period and separate estimates for the policy-on and the policy-off time periods are presented in Table 10.2. As can be seen, point estimates of the $\dot{w}/w$ coefficient in the price equation and the $\dot{p}/p$ coefficient in the wage equation are much smaller in the policy-on time periods, suggesting that incomes policies might affect parameter estimates, but it is also clear that the precision with which parameters are estimated declines dramatically in the policy-on equations.

Lipsey and Parkin therefore conducted Chow tests for parameter equality. In the wage equation the null hypothesis that all parameters are equal in the policy-off and policy-on periods was rejected at the 95% confidence level, but the low Durbin-Watson test statistic suggested the presence of autocorrelation. The corresponding null hypothesis of parameter equality in the price equation was rejected at the 95% (and 99%) confidence level. Lipsey and Par-

Table 10.2 Lipsey-Parkin Parameter Estimates Using Quarterly U.K. Data, Two-Equation Wage and Price Change Model (t-Statistics Are in Parentheses)

	Price Equation				Wage Equation		
Variable	Entire Sample	Policy Off	Policy On	Variable	Entire Sample	Policy Off	Policy On
Constant	1.374	−0.140	3.874	Constant	4.147	6.672	3.919
	(2.51)	(0.16)	(5.65)		(4.26)	(5.79)	(2.27)
$\dot{w}/w$	0.562	0.851	0.014	u	−0.891	−2.372	−0.404
	(5.53)	(5.52)	(0.10)		(1.77)	(3.64)	(0.56)
$\dot{p}_i/p_i$	0.085	0.073	0.001	$\dot{p}/p$	0.482	0.457	0.227
	(4.60)	(2.93)	(0.04)		(5.76)	(6.25)	(0.93)
$\dot{q}/q$	−0.145	−0.092	−0.198	$\dot{n}$	3.315	0.136	3.764
	(3.48)	(1.90)	(2.68)		(2.09)	(0.07)	(1.61)
R^2	0.697	0.843	0.241	R^2	0.616	0.856	0.138
DW	0.946	1.274	1.088	DW	0.742	1.231	0.724

Source: Data from Lipsey and Parkin [1970]. Reprinted with permission.

kin then performed a modified Chow test, in which the null hypothesis is that only the slope coefficients are identical in the two time periods (the intercepts are allowed to differ). For the wage equation the results were mixed; the null hypothesis of slope coefficient parameter equality was not rejected at the 95% confidence level but was at the 90% level of confidence. However, for the price equation this null hypothesis was rejected decisively, even at a level of confidence as high as 99.9%. Lipsey and Parkin therefore concluded that the estimated Phillips curve did not appear to be stable. Parameters are policy-dependent.

To examine the impact of incomes policies on wages and prices, Lipsey and Parkin used equations estimated in policy-off time periods to predict $\dot{w}/w$ and $\dot{p}/p$ during policy-on periods. Specifically, Lipsey and Parkin employed the structural equations (10.10) and (10.11) originally estimated with policy-off data, and using actual values of the right-hand variables, they compared the predicted values of $\dot{w}/w$ and $\dot{p}/p$ with those that were actually observed; they concluded that

> the data are not inconsistent with the view that wage and price restraints have usually been ineffective in restraining inflation, and also that the restraints have sometimes actually had the effect of raising the rate of inflation above what it would otherwise have been.[41]

In commenting on the Lipsey-Parkin paper, Wallis has noted that if one is to do this type of model simulation, one should not predict wage and price inflation employing the structural equations (10.10) and (10.11) using actual values of $\dot{w}/w$ in the $\dot{p}/p$ equation and actual values of $\dot{p}/p$ in the $\dot{w}/w$ equation. Such simulation ignores the feedback effects that simultaneous equation systems are designed to capture. Rather, one should use the reduced form equations for $\dot{p}/p$ and $\dot{w}/w$, since each reduced form equation is a function of all the other exogenous variables in the system, and each thereby incorporates feedback, such as "a rise in wages raises prices and thus will cause a further rise in wages."

Given the policy-off structural estimates reported by Lipsey and Parkin and the structural model in Eqs. (10.10) and (10.11), Wallis derived the reduced form equation system for this model. This turned out to be

$$\dot{p}/p = 9.289 - 3.387u + 0.122\dot{p}_i/p_i - 0.154\dot{q}/q + 0.194\dot{n} \qquad \textbf{(10.12)}$$

$$\dot{w}/w = 11.080 - 3.980u + 0.058\dot{p}_i/p_i - 0.073\dot{q}/q + 0.228\dot{n} \qquad \textbf{(10.13)}$$

Wallis substituted actual values of the exogenous variables in the policy-on period into these reduced form equations and then compared predicted values with actual values. His conclusions were quite different: "once allowance is made for the feedback between wages and prices, incomes policies appear to have been rather more effective than claimed by Lipsey-Parkin."[42]

This chapter is not the appropriate forum in which to discuss the very important policy issue concerning the effectiveness of wage and price controls. For our purposes, however, it is worth noting that Wallis's results, as well as those reported by Lipsey and Parkin, are consistent with the view that the Phillips curve is not stable and that it can be affected by changes in government policies, operating in part through their effects on expectations. Moreover, relationships between wage and price changes include feedback and therefore require a simultaneous equations specification.

10.3.D Inverting the Phillips Curve: The Lucas-Rapping Equilibrium Model

The final study that we examine in detail in this review of the Phillips curve literature also highlights the role of expectations, yet it is very different in spirit from the original Phillips orientation, since it emphasizes an equilibrium labor supply relation rather than an excess labor demand interpretation of the Phillips curve. It is the now-classic paper by Robert E. Lucas, Jr. and Leonard A. Rapping [1970].[43]

Lucas and Rapping begin by assuming that when individuals make their consumption and leisure decisions, they do so in an intertemporal context. Specifically, assume that there are four arguments in the utility function of a representative household: current goods consumption C, current labor supply N, future goods consumption C^*, and future labor supply N^*. The household maximizes the utility function

$$U(C, C^*, N, N^*), \qquad U_1, U_2 > 0, \qquad U_3, U_4 < 0 \qquad \textbf{(10.14)}$$

where the U_i indicate partial derivatives with respect to the sequence of arguments in $U(\cdot)$. This utility function is maximized subject to the constraint that the present value of consumption cannot exceed the present value of income. The initial nonhuman assets are valued in money terms at A, the nominal interest rate is r, and present and future goods prices and money wage rates are P, P^*, W, and W^*, respectively. Hence the budget constraint is written as

$$PC + [(P^*/(1 + r))C^*] \leqslant A + WN + [(W^*/(1 + r))N^* \quad \textbf{(10.15)}$$

Assuming the existence of a unique solution to this constrained maximization problem with positive prices, Lucas and Rapping write in implicit form the current labor supply function, homogeneous of degree zero in its four arguments:

$$N = f\left[\frac{W}{P}, \frac{W^*}{P(1 + r)}, \frac{P^*}{P(1 + r)}, \frac{A}{P}\right] \quad \textbf{(10.16)}$$

Provided that future goods and leisure are substitutes for current leisure, that leisure is not an inferior good, and that the asset effect is small, this model implies that $f_1 > 0$, but that f_2, f_3, and $f_4 < 0$, where the subscript number refers to the partial derivative of f in Eq. (10.16) with respect to the sequence number of the arguments.

This simple theory of a single household suggests an aggregate empirical labor supply function relating total hours supplied annually N_t, divided by an index of the number of households M_t, to current and future money wages W_t and W_t^*, current and future prices (GNP deflators) P_t, and P_t^*, a nominal interest rate r_t, and the market value of assets held by the household sector A_t. Lucas and Rapping postulated an aggregate log-linear relationship

$$\begin{aligned}\ln (N_t/M_t) &= \beta_0 + \beta_1 \ln (W_t/P_t) + \beta_2 \ln [W_t^*/(P_t(1 + r_t))] \\ &\quad + \beta_3' \ln [P_t^*/(P_t(1 + r_t))] + \beta_4 \ln [A_t/(P_tM_t)] \quad \textbf{(10.17)}\end{aligned}$$

where they expected β_1 to be positive but β_2, β_3', and β_4 to be negative; the sign of β_0 was indeterminate a priori. Defining real values with lowercase letters, $w_t \equiv W_t/P_t$, $w_t^* \equiv W_t^*/P_t^*$, $a_t \equiv A_t/P_t$, letting $\beta_3 \equiv -(\beta_2 + \beta_3') > 0$, and noting that $\ln (1 + r_t) \approx r_t$, they rewrote Eq. (10.17) in the more familar form

$$\begin{aligned}\ln (N_t/M_t) &= \beta_0 + \beta_1 \ln w_t + \beta_2 \ln w_t^* + \beta_3[r_t - \ln (P_t^*/P_t)] \\ &\quad + \beta_4 \ln (a_t/M_t) \quad \textbf{(10.18)}\end{aligned}$$

According to Eq. (10.18), current labor supply depends on current and expected real wages, on the expected real interest rate $[r_t - \ln (P_t^*/P_t)]$, and on real asset holdings.

Equation (10.18) was modified for empirical purposes in several ways. First, since Lucas and Rapping expected the effects of real asset holdings on labor supply to be small, and since it was difficult to obtain reliable measures of a_t/M_t, they set $a_4 = 0$ and excluded this regressor; also, although they reported some results with r_t included, Lucas and Rapping noted that "our most satisfactory models exclude this variable, and it will be dropped from the discussion that follows."[44] Finally, to account for the special effects of

World War II on labor supply to both the military and nonmilitary sectors, in some of their estimated equations, Lucas and Rapping added a dummy variable D_t, equal to 1 in 1941–1945 and otherwise equal to zero.

This left Lucas and Rapping with the problem of modeling the mechanism by which expectations of the real wage w_t^* and prices P_t^* were formed. They postulated the *adaptive expectations* scheme,

$$\frac{w_t^*}{w_{t-1}^*} = \left[\frac{w_t}{w_{t-1}^*}\right]^{\lambda} e^{\lambda'} \tag{10.19}$$

where λ is the adaptive expectations parameter, $0 < \lambda < 1$, and where $e^{\lambda'}$ is added to permit an anticipated trend in real wages. In this adaptive specification the greater the reliance of current expectations on the more recent past, the larger is λ; small values of λ imply a long memory, larger values a shorter recall. In logarithmic form, Eq. (10.19) becomes

$$\ln w_t^* - \ln w_{t-1}^* = \lambda(\ln w_t - \ln w_{t-1}^*) + \lambda' \tag{10.20a}$$

or

$$\ln w_t^* = \lambda \ln w_t + (1 - \lambda) \ln w_{t-1}^* + \lambda' \tag{10.20b}$$

Note that in Eq. (10.20a), the change or "correction" in the expected rate of wage inflation is a constant proportion λ of the forecast error ($\ln w_t - \ln w_{t-1}^*$); hence the adaptive expectations scheme can be viewed as an error correction process. Alternatively, if one employs repeated substitution procedures in Eq. (10.20b), it becomes clear that with the adaptive expectations specification the unobservable expected wage rates are in fact a function of an infinite set of observable past rates of wage inflation.

Lucas and Rapping went on to assume that price anticipations are also formed adaptively, and that they had the same error correction parameter λ:

$$\ln P_t^* = \lambda \ln P_t + (1 - \lambda) \ln P_{t-1}^* + \lambda'' \tag{10.21}$$

where the trend parameter λ'' was envisaged as depending "on major political and military events as well as the past development of prices."[45]

Deleting r_t and a_t/M_t as noted above, inserting repeated substitution versions of Eqs. (10.20) and (10.21) into Eq. (10.18), and then doing a Koyck transformation (lagging the expanded Eq. (10.21) one time period, multiplying through by $(1-\lambda)$, subtracting the product from the expanded Eq. (10.21), and setting to zero the terms in which λ and $(1-\lambda)$ are raised to large powers), Lucas and Rapping obtained the labor supply equation

$$\begin{aligned}\ln (N_t/M_t) = {} & [\beta_0\lambda + \beta_2\lambda' - \beta_3\lambda''] + (\beta_1 + \lambda\beta_2) \ln w_t \\ & - (1 - \lambda)\beta_1 \ln w_{t-1} + (1 - \lambda)\beta_3 \ln (P_t/P_{t-1}) \\ & + (1 - \lambda) \ln (N_{t-1}/M_{t-1})\end{aligned} \tag{10.22}$$

which they then reparameterized as

$$\begin{aligned}\ln (N_t/M_t) = {} & \beta_{10} + \beta_{11} \ln w_t - \beta_{12} \ln w_{t-1} + \beta_{13} \ln (P_t/P_{t-1}) \\ & + \beta_{14} \ln (N_{t-1}/M_{t-1})\end{aligned} \tag{10.23}$$

The economic theory underlying the derivation of this equation implied four inequality restrictions on the parameters in Eq. (10.23), namely,

$$0 < \beta_{11} < \beta_{12}/\beta_{14}, \ \beta_{12} > 0, \ \beta_{13} > 0, \text{ and } 0 < \beta_{14} < 1 \qquad \textbf{(10.24)}$$

To facilitate estimation, Lucas and Rapping added a stochastic disturbance term to Eq. (10.22) and assumed that it was serially independently distributed.[46]

An interesting feature of the labor supply equation (10.22) is that as long as $0 < \lambda < 1$, labor supply is responsive to nominal (not just real) wage rate changes, since the adaptive expectations specification (10.21) implies that suppliers of labor ultimately expect a return to normal price levels, *regardless* of current prices; the elasticity of expectations to actual nominal wage rate changes, λ, is positive but less than unity. In such cases and with these expectations it is perfectly rational for an individual to act as though there were money illusion, that is, to increase his or her current supply of labor when prices rise. Lucas and Rapping emphasized, however, that if there were a marked and sustained change in the trend rate of inflation (from one λ" to another), this would lead households using Eq. (10.21) "to consistently over- or under-forecast prices, in which case some other forecasting scheme would presumably be adopted." They then went on to say that for the 1929–1965 data period in the United States that they used in their estimation, they believed that the assumption of a constant λ was "plausible."[47] Nonetheless, they underscored the fact that if the expectation coefficient λ ever changes, as it well might, then there is no reason to assume that the coefficient on $\ln (P_t/P_{t-1})$ in Eq. (10.22) is constant and that in such cases it is illegitimate to use it to obtain estimates of the long-run effects of inflation on labor supply.

For their labor demand equation, Lucas and Rapping employed a constant elasticity of substitution (CES) production function; owing to space constraints, we will not discuss this production relation in detail.[48] Suffice it to say that Lucas and Rapping assumed that the CES production function was characterized by constant returns to scale, that firms chose inputs so as to maximize profits, and that input and output markets were competitive. Rearranging a logarithmic version of the marginal product of labor equals wage rate equation derived from the CES production function and permitting partial adjustment of firms' labor demands to their long-run equilibrium levels, Lucas and Rapping derived a labor demand equation having the form

$$\begin{aligned}\ln (Q_t N_t/Y_t) = \beta_{20} + \beta_{21} \ln (w_t/Q_t) + \beta_{22} \ln (Q_{t-1} N_{t-1}/Y_{t-1}) \\ + \beta_{23} \ln (Y_t/Y_{t-1}) \qquad \textbf{(10.25)}\end{aligned}$$

where N_t and w_t are the quantities and real wage rate for labor, Y_t is the level of output in constant dollars, and Q_t is an index of labor quality, which in practice is a years-of-schooling-completed index. In terms of parameters, β_{21} represents the negative of the short-run elasticity of substitution between capital and labor inputs, and β_{22} and β_{23} reflect the effects of the gradual adjustment of employment and output to long-run equilibrium. On the basis of the underlying theory, Lucas-Rapping predicted that

$$\beta_{21} < 0 \qquad \text{and} \qquad 0 < \beta_{22} < 1 \tag{10.26}$$

For empirical implementation, Lucas and Rapping appended an additive disturbance term to Eq. (10.26) and assumed that it was distributed in a serially independent manner. Moreover, in their empirical work they assumed that Y_t is exogenous, even though the profit maximization theory underlying the derivation of the labor demand equation implies that Y_t is also a choice variable.

The third and final equation of the Lucas-Rapping model is of special importance because it relates changes in the measured unemployment rate to inflation. Lucas and Rapping explicitly assumed that the current wage rate equates labor supply with labor demand. But from where does unemployment emerge in such an equilibrium model? To allow for the existence of measured unemployment consistent with their equilibrium view of the labor market, Lucas and Rapping offered an alternative hypothesis about what people mean when they classify themselves as unemployed.

Specifically, Lucas and Rapping built on the Phelps-Friedman view of the labor market, discussed in Section 10.3.B. In this paradigm, workers and employers are heterogeneous, information on employment possibilities and wage rates is costly to process, and job mobility is gradual, since acting on the basis of information acquired from job search sometimes requires large resource investments in moving and retraining. It follows that even in long-run equilibrium there will be a nonzero amount of unemployment, since job search and job mobility are ever-present activities. These considerations led Lucas and Rapping to state:

> The labor force as measured by the employment survey consists of those who are employed *plus* those who are unemployed but would accept work at what they regard as their normal wage rates (or, equivalently, in their normal occupation).[49]

Lucas and Rapping related this notion of the labor market to their model of labor supply as follows. They postulated that workers regard the current real wage rate as normal provided that there are no current surprises, that is, $w_t = w^*_{t-1}$; they specified a normal price level analogously, $P_t = P^*_{t-1}$. They then expressed *normal labor supply* N^*_t as the labor supply function (10.18) evaluated at these normal wages and prices:

$$\begin{aligned}\ln (N^*_t/M_t) = \beta_0 + \beta_1 \ln w^*_{t-1} + \beta_2 \ln w^*_t \\ + \beta_3[r_t - \ln (P^*_t/P^*_{t-1})] + \beta_4 \ln (a_t/M_t)\end{aligned} \tag{10.27}$$

Next they subtracted Eq. (10.18) from Eq. (10.27), and obtained

$$\ln (N^*_t/N_t) = \beta_1 \ln (w^*_{t-1}/w_t) + \beta_3 \ln (P^*_{t-1}/P_t) \tag{10.28}$$

Since $\ln (N^*_t/N_t) \approx (N^*_t - N_t)/N^*_t$, the left-hand side of Eq. (10.28) might be interpreted as some type of unemployment rate. Lucas and Rapping hypothesized, however, that this unemployment rate differed from the traditionally measured unemployment rate because of the discouraged worker effect,[50] and because of frictional unemployment. This led them to assume that the measured unemployment rate u_t is linearly related to ln (N_t^*/N_t) according to

$$u_t = \gamma_0 + \gamma_1 \ln (N_t^*/N_t) \qquad \text{with} \qquad \gamma_0, \gamma_1 > 0 \tag{10.29}$$

Substituting Eq. (10.28) into Eq. (10.29) then yielded

$$u_t = \gamma_0 + \gamma_1\beta_1 \ln (w_{t-1}^*/w_t) + \gamma_1\beta_3 \ln (P_{t-1}^*/P_t) \tag{10.30}$$

To eliminate w_{t-1}^* and P_{t-1}^*, Lucas and Rapping substituted into Eq. (10.30) repeated substitution versions of Eqs. (10.20) and (10.21), lagged this expanded (10.30) equation one time period, multiplied it by $(1 - \lambda)$, and then subtracted the product from the expanded Eq. (10.30). Setting to zero any terms that were raised to very large powers of λ and $(1 - \lambda)$, Lucas and Rapping finally obtained their inverted Phillips curve, in which measured unemployment is a function of price and wage inflation:

$$\begin{aligned} u_t = {} & [\gamma_0\lambda + \gamma_1\beta_1\lambda' + \gamma_1\beta_3\lambda''] - \gamma_1\beta_1 \ln (w_t/w_{t-1}) \\ & - \gamma_1\beta_3 \ln (P_t/P_{t-1}) + (1 - \lambda)u_{t-1} \end{aligned} \tag{10.31}$$

which they reparameterized as

$$u_t = \beta_{30} - \beta_{31} \ln (w_t/w_{t-1}) - \beta_{32} \ln (P_t/P_{t-1}) + \beta_{33}u_{t-1} \tag{10.32}$$

Several features of Eq. (10.31) merit comment. First, since both components of the product $\gamma_1\beta_3$ in Eq. (10.31) are expected to be positive, it is clear that there is an expected short-run negative relationship between inflation and unemployment; it is noteworthy that Lucas and Rapping were able to derive this Phillips curve relation from a framework emphasizing labor market equilibrium. Equation (10.30) does not necessarily imply a long-term tradeoff, however; that depends on how the wage and price expectations terms adjust to experience.

Second, Lucas and Rapping argued that since the trend rates of real wages λ' and prices λ'' appear in the constant term of Eq. (10.31), one should not expect the Phillips curve to be stable whenever economies experience sharp changes in wages and prices; given sufficient cause, firms and households will eventually revise their expectations accordingly.

Third, although Lucas and Rapping reported results from estimation of the full three-equation system consisting of the labor supply curve (10.23), the labor demand curve (10.25), and the market unemployment relation (10.32), they clearly stated that in their view, Eq. (10.32) added nothing to the theory of labor market behavior already contained in Eqs. (10.23) and (10.25); they estimated Eq. (10.32) since it had independent interest because of its resemblance to the Phillips curve.

In terms of econometric implementation, Lucas and Rapping appended additive disturbance terms to each of their three structural equations (10.23), (10.25), and (10.32) and assumed that the resulting disturbance vector was independently and identically normally distributed with a mean vector of zero and a finite covariance matrix. The variables Q_t, Y_t, M_t, and P_t (and their lags) were taken to be exogenous, while the three endogenous variables were N_t, w_t, and u_t. Using the necessary order conditions for identification, they concluded that all three equations were overidentified.

The right-hand sides of the reduced form equations for $\ln w_t$ and $\ln (N_t/M_t)$ corresponding to Eqs. (10.23) and (10.25) turn out to have the form

$$\pi_{i0} + \pi_{i1} \ln w_{t-1} + \pi_{i2} \ln (P_t/P_{t-1}) + \pi_{i3} \ln (Y_t/M_t) + \pi_{i4} \ln Q_t + \pi_{i5} \ln (Q_{t-1}N_{t-1}/Y_{t-1}) + \pi_{i6} \ln (Y_t/Y_{t-1}) + \pi_{i7} \ln (N_{t-1}/M_{t-1}) + \epsilon_{it} \quad \mathbf{(10.33)}$$

where ϵ_{it} is a random disturbance term, $i = 1$ for the reduced form wage equation, and $i = 2$ for the reduced form employment equation. Since the ϵ_{it} are functions of the parameters and the identically and independently distributed structural disturbance terms, the ϵ_{it} are also identically and independently distributed with mean zero and finite constant covariance matrix. Further, given the restrictions implied by the underlying economic theory and the relations among structural parameters embodied in the reduced form equations (10.33), Lucas and Rapping noted that of the eight parameters in the reduced form wage equation, five were restricted as follows:

$$\pi_{11} > 0, \quad \pi_{12} < 0, \quad \pi_{13} > 0, \quad \pi_{15} > 0, \quad \text{and} \quad \pi_{17} < 0 \quad \mathbf{(10.34)}$$

Similarly, five of the eight parameters in the reduced form employment equation had predictable signs. These are

$$\pi_{21} < 0, \quad \pi_{22} > 0, \quad \pi_{23} > 0, \quad \pi_{25} > 0, \quad \text{and} \quad \pi_{27} > 0 \quad \mathbf{(10.35)}$$

Lucas and Rapping then reported results based on OLS estimation of the reduced form equations (10.33) and from 2SLS estimation of the labor supply equation (10.23), the labor demand equation (10.25), and the measured unemployment equation (10.32), all using aggregate annual U.S. time series data from 1930 to 1965. Their results for the three structural equations were as follows (standard errors are in parentheses, $\overline{R}^2$ is the degrees of freedom adjusted R^2, and DW is the Durbin-Watson test statistic):

Labor supply:

$$\begin{aligned} \ln (N_t/M_t) = \; & \underset{(0.93)}{3.81} + \underset{(0.51)}{1.40} \ln \hat{w}_t - \underset{(0.51)}{1.39} \ln w_{t-1} + \underset{(0.17)}{0.74} \ln (P_t/P_{t-1}) \\ & + \underset{(0.09)}{0.64} \ln (N_{t-1}/M_{t-1}) \qquad \overline{R}^2 = 0.798 \qquad DW = 1.56 \end{aligned} \quad \mathbf{(10.36)}$$

Labor demand:

$$\begin{aligned} \ln (NQ/Y)_t = \; & \underset{(0.70)}{-2.21} - \underset{(0.12)}{0.46} \ln (\hat{w}_t/Q_t) + \underset{(0.11)}{0.58} \ln (NQ/Y)_{t-1} \\ & \underset{(0.04)}{-0.21} \ln (Y_t/Y_{t-1}) \qquad \overline{R}^2 = 0.993 \qquad DW = 1.84 \end{aligned} \quad \mathbf{(10.37)}$$

Unemployment:

$$u_t = \underset{(0.01)}{0.042} - \underset{(0.08)}{0.59} \ln (P_t/P_{t-1}) - \underset{(0.24)}{0.41} \ln (\hat{w}_t/w_{t-1}) + \underset{(0.05)}{0.80} u_{t-1}$$

$$\bar{R}^2 = 0.925 \qquad DW = 1.50 \tag{10.38}$$

where ln $\hat{w}_t$ is the first-stage fitted value from the wage rate reduced form equation (10.33). (See Exercise 2 at the end of this chapter for further details.)

Lucas and Rapping were particularly interested in examining whether signs and inequalities among the estimated structural coefficients were consistent with those predicted by the underlying theory. For the estimated labor supply equation (10.36), point estimates of the parameters were consistent with all four of the predictions from theory, summarized in Eqs. (10.24). Similarly, for the estimated labor demand equation (10.37), point estimates of the structural parameters matched both inequality relationships noted in Eq. (10.26). In most cases the parameters were estimated with sufficient precision that the inequality relations were statistically significant at the usual confidence levels.

For the unemployment equation (10.32), the focal point of analysis, the parameter inequality relations predicted by the underlying theory are

$$\beta_{31} > 0, \qquad \beta_{32} > 0, \qquad \text{and} \qquad 0 < \beta_{33} < 1 \tag{10.39}$$

As is seen in Eq. (10.38), point estimates of the parameters satisfied these three inequality relationships (and were statistically significant). Lucas and Rapping also noted that since the unemployment equation is in fact derived from the labor demand and labor supply equations, testable cross-equation parameter restrictions occur. These parameter restrictions turn out to be

$$\beta_{31}/\beta_{32} = \beta_{11}/\beta_{13} \qquad \text{and} \qquad \beta_{33} = \beta_{14} \tag{10.40}$$

If one substitutes point estimates from Eq. (10.38) into the first equality in Eqs. (10.40), one obtains ratios of 0.70 and 1.89. Using a linear approximation rather than nonlinear statistical inference, Lucas and Rapping concluded that these ratios were insignificantly different from each other. Similarly, using standard error estimates and ignoring possible covariances, they concluded that point estimates of their estimated parameters were consistent with the other cross-equation constraint in Eqs. (10.40), that $\beta_{33} = \beta_{14}$. Buoyed by these results, Lucas and Rapping concluded that their estimated unemployment equation (10.38) "is a satisfactory Phillips curve, and further, the predicted link between [it] and the rest of the model appears to be consistent with the data."[51]

Lucas and Rapping reported Durbin-Watson test statistics ("as a rough measure of serial correlation, although nothing is known about its distribution in models such as ours").[52] We now know that the Durbin-Watson test statistic is inappropriate whenever one of the regressors is a lagged dependent variable, as is the case in each of the Lucas-Rapping three structural equations and both reduced form equations; while Durbin's *m*- and *h*-statistic procedures are now often used in such a context, those procedures were not available when the Lucas-Rapping article was written.[53] Note that if autocorrelation were present, since one of the regressors is a lagged dependent variable, then the Lucas-Rapping structural and reduced form estimates would be biased and inconsistent. Further, to obtain consistent estimates of the structural parameters using the 2SLS procedure in the context of first-order autocorrelation, it would be necessary to employ in addition lagged values of the instruments; this has been shown by Ray C. Fair [1970]. Together, these comments imply that whether the disturbances are serially correlated is an important econometric issue, one that, understandably, was not addressed by Lucas and Rapping. (In the hands-on exercises at the end of this chapter you will find that the evidence on this issue is mixed.)

Lucas and Rapping also estimated the two reduced form equations by OLS. Since the labor demand and labor supply structural equations are overidentified, one could derive and impose the implied cross-equation constraints on the reduced form equations; this would yield consistent and efficient estimates of the structural coefficients. As is often the case, however, Lucas and Rapping did not impose these cross-equation constraints; instead, they simply estimated Eq. (10.33) using unrestricted equation-by-equation OLS. Their results were as follows:

Wage rate:

$$\begin{aligned}\ln w_t = & -15.65 + 0.44 \ln w_{t-1} - 0.22 \ln (P_t/P_{t-1}) \\ & \quad (3.50) \quad (0.17) \qquad\qquad (0.07) \\ & + 1.25 \ln (Y_t/M_t) + 0.27 \ln Q_t + 1.24 \ln (Q_{t-1}N_{t-1}/Y_{t-1}) \\ & \quad (0.44) \qquad\qquad (0.55) \qquad\quad (0.44) \\ & - 1.22 \ln (Y_t/Y_{t-1}) - 1.15 \ln (N_{t-1}/M_{t-1}) \\ & \quad (0.45) \qquad\qquad (0.45) \\ & \bar{R}^2 = 0.997 \qquad DW = 2.26\end{aligned} \tag{10.41}$$

Employment:

$$\begin{aligned}\ln (N_t/M_t) = & \; 11.60 + 0.08 \ln w_{t-1} + 0.06 \ln (P_t/P_{t-1}) \\ & \quad (3.50) \quad (0.17) \qquad\qquad (0.07) \\ & + 0.02 \ln (Y_t/M_t) - 1.02 \ln Q_t - 0.39 \ln (Q_{t-1}N_{t-1}/Y_{t-1}) \\ & \quad (0.44) \qquad\qquad (0.55) \qquad\quad (0.44) \\ & + 0.80 \ln (Y_t/Y_{t-1}) + 0.91 \ln (N_{t-1}/M_{t-1}) \\ & \quad (0.45) \qquad\qquad (0.45) \\ & \bar{R}^2 = 0.970 \qquad DW = 1.73\end{aligned} \tag{10.42}$$

On the basis of one-tail tests of significance, for the estimated wage equation (10.41), not only were the point estimates of the reduced form parameters consistent with the restrictions in Eqs. (10.34), but the inequalities were also statistically significant. Results were not quite as satisfying, however, for the estimated employment equation. Of the five constraints in Eqs. (10.35), only the estimate of π_{27} was positive and statistically different from zero; point estimates satisfied two of the remaining four inequality restrictions, but since each of the four estimated coefficients was insignificantly different from zero, these four restrictions were neither confirmed nor contradicted. One interpretation of these results is that, unlike the structural estimates, the OLS reduced form estimates do not incorporate appropriate cross-equation constraints, and as a result, parameter estimates are less precise.

As we have seen, the Lucas-Rapping model represented an important intellectual accomplishment. Perhaps its most significant contribution was the demonstration that it is possible to have a short-run tradeoff between inflation and unemployment, even though such a tradeoff need not exist in the long run. Moreover, if workers, searchers, and firms form expectations of wages and prices in an adaptive manner, this short-run tradeoff is consistent with individual rational behavior. Finally, it is worth emphasizing that the Lucas-Rapping interpretation of the Phillips curve rests critically on the notion that the labor market is in equilibrium and that there is no involuntary unemployment.

10.3.E A Brief Overview of Related Research

The Lucas-Rapping study created grave doubts concerning the possibility of a stable short-run tradeoff between inflation and unemployment. Since the early 1970s a substantial literature has emerged that has moved away from the original Phillips curve interpretation and now for the most part rejects the plausibility of any long-run tradeoff. In the final paragraphs of this section we highlight some of the more prominent strands of this and related research.

One significant theme emerging from the work of Phelps, Friedman, Lucas and Rapping, and others is that attempts by government authorities to move along a Phillips curve may be frustrated by changes in people's expectations, changes that could shift the curve and offset policy effectiveness. In his well-known econometric policy evaluation critique, Robert E. Lucas [1976] argued that because government policies are likely to change people's expectations, one cannot naively simulate the effects of policy changes and implicitly assume that parameters reflecting expectations will remain unchanged once policy changes are put into place. (Recall that in the Lipsey-Parkin paper that we discusssed earlier, the same point was made.) Lucas therefore argued that, in undertaking simulations on the effects of policy changes, econometricians must take into account how the policy changes will alter people's expectations, and consequently, how policies might change parameter values. Therefore, to be reliable for policy evaluation, econometric models must incorporate a credible theory of expectations formation.

But how might one formulate and implement such a credible theory of expectations formation? This issue was examined by Robert E. Lucas [1972], building on the earlier work of John F. Muth [1961]. Lucas began by arguing that in the long run, any expectations formation process must rule out the possibility of money illusion, since money illusion is inconsistent with the

ROBERT E. LUCAS, Jr.

On Modeling Expectations

No individual has had a greater impact on the practice of macroeconometric modeling in the last two decades than Robert E. Lucas, Jr. In a series of papers beginning in 1969, Lucas dramatically changed the profession's view of the Phillips curve, emphasizing an equilibrium rather than an excess demand interpretation. Moreover, unsatisfied with his own early research which employed adaptive expectations (see this chapter for further discussion), Lucas soon realized that any specification of expectations that was simply backward- rather than forward-looking was unlikely to be credible and useful. To Lucas, the frequent econometric finding of unstable parameter estimates often reflected an inappropriate modeling of expectations because in such models, parameters typically lacked policy invariance.

Building on earlier work by John Muth, Lucas went on to argue that the specification of expectations formation in econometric models should account for the fact that economic agents are rational, using all the information available to them, including information on how the economy functions. Today, almost all macroeconometric models incorporate the rational expectations hypothesis, although substantial differences still remain concerning the specification of the market clearing process and the nature of price flexibility.

Robert E. Lucas, Jr. was born in Yakima, Washington in 1937. Recipient of a Procter & Gamble Scholarship, Lucas pursued undergraduate studies at the University of Chicago, majoring in history and graduating with a Phi Beta Kappa key in 1959. Lucas remained at Chicago for doctoral studies but changed fields from history to economics and earned his Ph.D. degree in 1964, studying under Arnold Harberger. His first academic appointment was at Carnegie-Mellon University, but in 1974, Lucas returned to Chicago, where, except for occasional visits, he has been ever since. He is currently the John Dewey Distinguished Service Professor of Economics at Chicago.

Lucas has served on the editorial boards of several journals and is currently editor of the *Journal of Political Economy*. He has been elected a Fellow of the Econometric Society and of the American Academy of Arts and Sciences and is a Member of the National Academy of Sciences.

individual optimization theory of consumers and employers that underlies long-run equilibrium; for example, long-run labor supply must depend on real wages, not money wages, and in the long run, unemployment and real output must equal their natural rates. Lucas then examined the adaptive expectations hypothesis as formalized in Eqs. (10.19) and (10.20), where λ (the elasticity of expectations with respect to realized price inflation) is the adaptive expectations parameter, $0 < \lambda < 1$. Although the adaptive expectations process predicts that a once-and-for-all change in the price *level* will have no long-run effect on labor supply and on real output and in this sense rules out money illusion, as long as the *rate* of inflation increases over time and $\lambda < 1$, price expectations will always fall short of realized prices, that is, $E[P_t^* - P_t] < 0$. (Recall that according to the accelerationists, this will occur when the government persists in pursuing target levels of u below the natural rate.) In such cases there would be a long-run tradeoff between inflation and real output. That, Lucas argued, is simply not consistent with basic economic theory.

Another critical shortcoming of the adaptive expectations specification is that if an economic agent has information in addition to a data series of past observation values of the variable to be forecasted (such as observations on other economic variables and knowledge of how an economy in fact functions), then the use of adaptive expectations would lead the agent to waste that information. Lucas argued that if the economic agent were rational, he or she would instead use economic theory to process that information and to use it accordingly in forming expectations. Since adaptive expectations do not rule out this possibility of systematically biased expectations and the resulting long-run tradeoff between inflation and real output, and since the concept of adaptive expectations implies that economic agents willingly waste useful and scarce information, Lucas concluded that the adaptive expectations hypothesis was unacceptable.[54]

As an alternative, therefore, Lucas suggested that since the natural rate hypothesis requires that in the long run, expectations and experience must converge to equality, and since economic agents are fully aware of the implications of this when forming their expectations, one might simply impose the constraint that

$$E[P_t^* - P_t] = 0 \tag{10.43}$$

a restriction that Muth [1961] called the *rational expectations hypothesis* (REH). In the Muth and Lucas formulation the restriction (10.43) is imposed at *each* time period. Further, at each time period, prices are assumed to be sufficiently flexible that instantaneous equality between supply and demand is attained. It is worth noting that since the notion of such rapid price adjustment is similar to that espoused by classical economists, macroeconomists who espouse both rational expectations and rapid price adjustment are frequently called members of the *new classical school.*[55]

Lucas's instantaneous market-clearing assumption is a decisive and controversial one. Critics of Lucas note that such instantaneous market clearing and perfect wage and price flexibility are implausible in real-world markets. For example, some point to the widespread existence of long-term labor contracts with horizons of two or more years; in practice, such contracts promote wage rigidity and reduce potential wage and price flexibility.[56] Among these critics of Lucas, the "new Keynesians" accept the notion of rational expectations (defined as, roughly, the idea that economic agents use all of the information available to them, not just knowledge of prior data trends), but they maintain that wages and prices adjust slowly and that this gradual adjustment is the key to explaining short-run macroeconomic fluctuations.

This split between new classicists and new Keynesians is not just a recent one; it was evident immediately when Lucas presented his paper in 1970. The discussant of that paper, Franklin M. Fisher, made the following distinction

> Lucas appears to believe that the notion that one cannot fool all of the people all of the time implies one cannot fool all the people even some of the time. I fully accept the view that if a policy goes on long enough people will have correct expectations on the average. But this certainly does not imply that, when policies change, average expectations will be right in the short run. A proper view of rational expectations seems to me to be that the limit of the expected value of the expected prices is the same as the limit of the expected value of actual prices given that there are no policy shifts; I see no reason, however, why the two expected values should be equal at every moment in time.[57]

Other critics of Lucas have expressed their objections in less statistical language. For example, in assessing the Lucas-Sargent view of the labor market as being in continuous equilibrium, Franco Modigliani [1977] has pointed to the historical experiences of unemployment in the United States during the Depression of the 1930s. According to Modigliani, viewing such high unemployment rates as the outcome of instantaneous market clearing is possible only if "what happened to the United States in the 1930's was a severe attack of contagious laziness!"[58]

The price flexibility–market-clearing assumption is therefore a most controversial and important one. In the next section we will examine a model with rational expectations, but one in which prices are sticky. Before doing that, however, we briefly comment on several other related recent research themes.[59]

An important feature of the Lucas-Rapping labor supply function (10.14) is that intertemporal substitution can substantially affect current labor supply. In one line of research the extent of intertemporal substitution has been estimated, extending the Lucas-Rapping framework to incorporate expectations formations that are more general than adaptive. Such studies include those by Joseph G. Altonji [1982]; Orley Ashenfelter and David Card [1982]; N. Gregory Mankiw, Julio J. Rotemberg, and Lawrence H. Summers [1985]; John C. Ham [1986]; and Stephen P. Zeldes [1989]. Although the evidence is somewhat mixed, the majority of work appears to suggest that intertemporal substitution in labor supply is modest.

Another strand of research has defined potential output in a way that differs somewhat from the natural rate notion described earlier. This alternative notion of potential output is generally attributed to Arthur M. Okun [1962], who derived a well-known empirical relationship, often called Okun's Law:

$$Y_{pot} = Y[1 + 0.032(U - U^*)] \tag{10.44}$$

where Y_{pot} is potential real output in percentage points, Y is measured real output, U is the measured rate of unemployment, and U^* is the nonaccelerating inflation rate of unemployment.[60] According to Okun's Law, if current unemployment were, say, 1% greater than U^*, then Y_{pot} would be 1.032 times actual current real output. This relationship is often envisaged as implying that the forgone output cost of "excessive" unemployment is substantial.

Until the late 1960s it was thought that the value of U^* in the United States underlying the Y_{pot} series was relatively stable at 4%. In the 1970s, both U^* and the 0.032 value appeared to become less stable, but it was also found that some of the apparent instability could be eliminated if one adjusted Y_{pot} for compositional changes in the labor force.[61] The economic argument for such demographic compositional adjustments was based on the following reasoning. Since the amount of output forgone by unemployment depends on workers' marginal products if the unemployed were at work, and since these marginal products vary demographically, compositional changes among the unemployed correspond with differing incremental outputs if they were employed. This has led a number of researchers to define and compute a demographically adjusted measure of Y_{pot}, and, implicitly, of U^*.

In related research, Jeffrey M. Perloff and Michael L. Wachter [1979] used an aggregate production function framework and defined the nonaccelerating inflation rate of unemployment as that level of U corresponding to the amount of labor input that resulted in increasing (rather than constant) marginal costs of output. Based on this and other procedures, estimates of demographically adjusted U^* for the late 1970s in the United States typically tended to be about 6%,[62] and according to Robert J. Gordon [1988a], U^* has remained remarkably constant at about 6% throughout most of the 1980s. Estimates of U^* for countries other than the United States, however, are not necessarily similar, and some may differ over time.[63] Incidentally, in the United States, the Council of Economic Advisors has on occasion published an official series of its estimates of potential output, based on updated variants of Eq. (10.44).

In the previous paragraphs we attempted to highlight the interaction between theory and observation in interpreting the Phillips curve. As we have seen, a great deal has been learned—both by theorists and by econometricians. This debate among economists has not, however, been limited to the pages of detached academic journals. Rather, much of the research has occurred amidst vigorous policy debates concerning the role and effectiveness of government policies. By the beginning of the 1980s this lively interaction among economic theorists, econometricians, and government policymakers in the United States had led to a remarkable new consensus. For example, Arthur M. Okun, a distinguished policy advisor to various Democratic presidents and a widely acknowledged "liberal," analyzed the 1970s by summarizing what policy mistakes were made and what was learned as follows:

> The big errors in assessing the split [of nominal GNP growth into its real and inflation components] stemmed initially from continued econometric reliance on the short-run Phillips curve. It was hard to cast aside a tool that had traced the United States record so well from 1954 through the late sixties. And it was easy to ignore the Friedman and Phelps attack on the stability of the short-run Phillips curve, and their prophetic warning (issued at a time when the Phillips curve was performing admirably) that the curve would come unstuck in a prolonged period of excess demand. Unfortunately, most of the profession (including me) took too long to recognize that. Since 1970, the Phillips curve has become an unidentified flying object and has eluded all econometric efforts to nail it down.[64]

Only seldom do such major and widespread changes in thinking occur so rapidly within our profession. The history of the Phillips curve is truly exceptional.

10.4 A TWO-EQUATION MACROECONOMETRIC MODEL WITH RATIONAL EXPECTATIONS

In the previous section we showed that two critical aspects of the Lucas-Rapping attack on the Phillips curve involved their assumption that labor markets are always in equilibrium and their argument that expectations should not be adaptive, particularly in times of substantial and/or sustained price instability. We now consider an extension of this reasoning, a simple two-equation macroeconometric model constructed by John B. Taylor [1979] in which expectations are formed in a rational manner but prices are sticky and are not necessarily in instantaneous equilibrium. In current parlance this type of framework is often called a neo-Keynesian model. Moreover, while aggregate output price and quantity are exogenous in the Lucas-Rapping model, in the Taylor framework these are the only two endogenous variables. Taylor's two-equation model is a highly aggregated one, but it has the advantage of helping us to focus on technical problems of estimation. Moreover, it highlights the important role of cross-equation restrictions, a common feature of REH models.

Taylor's aggregate demand equation can be envisaged as being derived from conventional macroeconomic IS-LM relationships. Define y_t as the log of real expenditures measured as a deviation from the log of potential output (the latter being the estimated series prepared by the U.S. Council of Economic Advisers), $m_t - p_t$ as the log of real money balances (where m_t is the log of money balances and p_t is the log of the GNP deflator), and π_t as the rate of inflation defined as $p_{t+1} - p_t$. Taylor specifies the aggregate demand equation

$$y_t = \beta_0 + \beta_1 y_{t-1} + \beta_2 y_{t-2} + \beta_3(m - p)_t + \beta_4(m - p)_{t-1} + \beta_5\hat{\pi}_t + \beta_6 t + u_t \qquad \textbf{(10.45)}$$

where $\hat{\pi}_t$ is the conditional expectation of π_t given information available through period $t-1$ and u_t is a random disturbance term.

The two lagged output values in Eq. (10.45) can be viewed as capturing multiplier-accelerator effects, but they can also be interpreted as representing other sources of persistence. Both current and once-lagged real money balances affect real output, the lagged value reflecting the partial adjustment of real money balances to changes in interest rates and income. Taylor hypothesizes that because of partial adjustment, β_4 should be opposite in sign to β_3 and less in absolute value. Taylor assumes that both m_t and p_t are predetermined at time $t-1$. The expected inflation rate variable can be viewed as representing the effects of intertemporal substitution, in which case β_5 should be positive, since a higher price of future goods relative to current goods should stimulate current expenditures. The time trend variable allows for long run secular trends in the money demand function and in the components of aggregate demand. Taylor argues that it is plausible that the β parameters in Eq. (10.45) are invariant to changes in government policy and therefore assumes such policy invariance.

For the aggregate price determination equation, Taylor specifies that

$$\pi_t = \gamma_0 + \pi_{t-1} + \gamma_1\hat{y}_t + \nu_t \qquad \textbf{(10.46)}$$

where $\hat{y}_t$ is the conditional expectation of y_t given information through period $t-1$, and ν_t is a random disturbance term. The rationale underlying Eq. (10.46) is that prices and wages are set in advance of the periods during which they apply (recall that $\pi_t \equiv p_{t+1} - p_t$ and that $\pi_{t-1} \equiv p_t - p_{t-1}$), that prices and wages are not set by all firms simultaneously, and moreover, that on the basis of long-term profit considerations these prices are maintained for more than one time period. Hence the aggregate price determination equation (10.46) allows for staggered and multiperiod overlapping contracts. Taylor expects that firms' pricing behavior will be reflected by the most recent price and wage decisions of other firms and therefore specifies that π_{t-1} affects π_t with an implicit coefficient of unity. Moreover, when markets are expected to be tighter than average ($\hat{y}_t > 0$), Taylor expects that prices will increase more rapidly than π_{t-1}, that is, $\gamma_1 > 0$.

Although the aggregate price determination equation (10.46) looks something like a Phillips curve, Taylor emphasizes that in his model π_{t-1} does not represent an expectations-augmented Phillips curve; rather, π_{t-1} captures the fact that price and wage decisions of some firms are predetermined at the same time that other firms are setting prices and wages, and hence current decisions must be made in relation to those predetermined values. It is also worth noting that according to Eq. (10.46), provided that $\gamma_1 > 0$, there is no way that output can be raised *permanently* above its natural or potential rate without accelerating the rate of inflation. While the long-run Phillips curve is therefore vertical, in the short-run with π_{t-1} predetermined, it is not. Further, the intercept term γ_0 allows for the possibility that at the zero change inflation point (where $\pi_t = \pi_{t-1}$, that is, $\Delta\pi_t = 0$), in the short run, y_t need not also be zero (actual and potential output might still differ).

For this aggregate inflation equation (10.46), Taylor specifies that the stochastic disturbance term ν_t has a first-order moving average form

$$\nu_t = \epsilon_t - \theta_2 \epsilon_{t-1} \tag{10.47}$$

where the fraction θ_2 of a given shock to the inflation rate is transitory, with the remaining $(1 - \theta_2)$ proportion persisting into the next time period. The rationale that Taylor employs to justify this is again based on the notion of overlapping and staggered contracts. Specifically, firms realize that there are some nonrecurrent errors or mistakes in the pricing behavior of other firms and that these should not be fully incorporated into their own price-setting behavior.[65]

Since the aggregate demand equation (10.45) already includes two lagged dependent variables, it would appear that there is little additional role for serial correlation in the stochastic disturbance term u_t. However, aggregate demand is affected by lagged *real* money balances, and this suggests that the lagged shock from the price equation, ϵ_{t-1}, should be included in the error structure of u_t. This reasoning leads Taylor to specify a stochastic disturbance structure for u_t as

$$u_t = \eta_t - \theta_1 \epsilon_{t-1} \tag{10.48}$$

Note that as a result, while both ϵ_t and ϵ_{t-1} affect p_t and therefore real money balances $(m_t - p_t)$ equally, one might expect ϵ_{t-1} to have a smaller effect on aggregate demand; by adding the lagged price shock ϵ_{t-1} to the aggregate demand equation (10.45), Taylor allows for this differential effect.

In terms of stochastic specification, Taylor assumes that the vector of disturbances e_t, $e_t \equiv (\epsilon_t, \eta_t)'$, is independently and identically distributed with mean vector zero and constant nonsingular covariance matrix Ω. Although he does not assume multivariate normality, it turns out to be a convenient additional assumption.

Since m_t and p_t are assumed to be predetermined, both these variables can be treated as part of the information set available to all economic agents at time $t-1$, and so Taylor notes that the conditional expectation of m_t and of p_t, given information through period $t-1$, is simply equal to m_t and p_t. When Eqs. (10.47) and (10.48) are substituted into Eqs. (10.45) and (10.46), the conditional expectations of Eqs. (10.45) and (10.46), given information through period $t - 1$, equal

$$\hat{y}_t = \beta_0 + \beta_1 y_{t-1} + \beta_2 y_{t-2} + \beta_3(m - p)_t + \beta_4(m - p)_{t-1} + \beta_5\hat{\pi}_t + \beta_6 t - \theta_1\epsilon_{t-1} \quad \textbf{(10.49)}$$

and

$$\hat{\pi}_t = \gamma_0 + \pi_{t-1} + \gamma_1\hat{y}_t - \theta_2\epsilon_{t-1} \quad \textbf{(10.50)}$$

Next, Taylor solves the two equations (10.49) and (10.50) for the two unknowns $\hat{y}_t$ and $\hat{\pi}_t$ and substitutes the solution values into Eq. (10.45) and (10.46). Finally, he invokes the model-consistent rational expectations hypothesis (REH),

$$\hat{y}_t = y_t \qquad \text{and} \qquad \hat{\pi}_t = \pi_t \quad \textbf{(10.51)}$$

which gives him the two reduced form equations

$$y_t = a[\beta_0 + \beta_1 y_{t-1} + \beta_2 y_{t-2} + \beta_3(m - p)_t + \beta_4(m - p)_{t-1} + \beta_5\pi_{t-1} + \beta_6 t + \beta_5\gamma_0 - (\beta_5\theta_2 + \theta_1)\epsilon_{t-1}] + \eta_t \quad \textbf{(10.52)}$$

and

$$\pi_t = a[\gamma_1(\beta_1 y_{t-1} + \beta_2 y_{t-2} + \beta_3(m - p)_t + \beta_4(m - p)_{t-1}) + \pi_{t-1} + \gamma_1\beta_6 t + \gamma_1\beta_0 + \gamma_0 - (\gamma_1\theta_1 + \theta_2)\epsilon_{t-1}] + \epsilon_t \quad \textbf{(10.53)}$$

where $a \equiv 1/(1 - \beta_5\gamma_1)$.

Several comments should be made concerning these two reduced form equations. First, note that the REH in Eq. (10.51) reflects the assumption that economic agents understand the workings of this two-equation economy, that expectations are model consistent and that, as a result, the REH places restrictions on the coefficients of these two reduced form equations; in particular, the 16 coefficients on the predetermined variables (including ϵ_{t-1}) depend on only 11 unknown structural parameters. Therefore the REH imposes testable cross-equation parameter restrictions on the two-equation reduced form model; such testable cross-equation restrictions are a common feature of REH models. Second, since the parameters of the structural model are policy invariant (m_t and p_t are assumed to be predetermined at time $t-1$), the coefficients of the reduced form are also policy invariant. Third, Taylor emphasizes that this policy invariance would not hold if $\hat{\pi}_t$ and $\hat{y}_t$ were instead generated by adaptive expectations schemes analogous to Eq. (10.21), since then the λ and λ'' expectations coefficients would change when policy rules were altered; in turn, this would imply changes in the coefficients of the two reduced form equations for π_t and y_t. Fourth, the reduced form equations (10.52) and (10.53) form a first-order vector autoregressive moving average model with cross-equation restrictions, a specification whose estimation presents some special problems. We now turn to a discussion of these estimation issues.

If the moving average parameters θ_1 and θ_2 were both equal to zero, then one could estimate the two-equation system of reduced form equations (10.52) and (10.53) using the minimum distance estimator (MDE), which minimizes

$$\sum_{t=1}^{T} \hat{e}_t' \hat{\Omega}^{-1} \hat{e}_t \tag{10.54}$$

where the residual vector $\hat{e}_t$ corresponds to the disturbance vector e_t, $\hat{e}_t \equiv (\hat{\epsilon}_t, \hat{\eta}_t)'$. Edmond Malinvaud [1970] has proposed iterating the MDE, using as an estimate of Ω the residuals from the previous iteration, that is, minimizing Eq. (10.54) with respect to the unknown parameters, where

$$\hat{\Omega} = \sum_{t=1}^{T} \hat{e}_t \hat{e}_t'/T \tag{10.55}$$

If the iterative MDE converges to a global minimum, and if the disturbance vector e_t is normally distributed, then as has been shown by Peter C. B. Phillips [1976], the iterative MDE is numerically equivalent to the maximum likelihood estimator; it is also numerically identical to the iterative Zellner-efficient estimator.[66]

It is also worth noting that as long as $\theta_1 = \theta_2 = 0$, consistent estimates of the parameters could be obtained by estimating the structural (rather than reduced form) equations using instrumental variable procedures. For example, one could directly estimate the aggregate demand structural equation (10.45) by two-stage least squares, using π_{t-1} as an instrument for $\hat{\pi}_t$; similarly, one could estimate the aggregate price equation (10.46) by 2SLS. If disturbances were autoregressive, then 2SLS estimation would need to be modified along the lines suggested by Fair [1970] and McCallum [1979b]. (You will have an opportunity to consider such estimation issues in further detail in Exercise 3 at the end of this chapter.) Other structural equation estimation methods such as three-stage least squares (3SLS) and full information maximum likelihood could be employed as well, modified to allow for any autoregressive or moving average error structures.[67]

The problem with each of these estimation methods, however, is that in general θ_1 and θ_2 are not equal to zero. Taylor notes that as long as θ_1 and θ_2 were known and nonzero, one could modify the iterated MDE to deal with the serial correlation as follows. Let the vector of composite disturbances in the two reduced form equations be w_t,

$$w_t \equiv e_t - \theta e_{t-1} \tag{10.56}$$

where $e_t \equiv (\eta_t, \epsilon_t)'$, and

$$\theta \equiv a \begin{bmatrix} 0 & \beta_5\theta_2 + \theta_1 \\ 0 & \gamma_1\theta_1 + \theta_2 \end{bmatrix}, \qquad a \equiv 1/(1 - \beta_5\gamma_1)$$

RAY C. FAIR

Computation in Macroeconometric Models

As a graduate student at MIT working with Edwin Kuh and Robert Solow, Ray Fair became interested in a host of computational issues that are encountered in estimating and simulating macroeconometric models. In one of his first published articles, Fair showed that considerable care must be taken in estimating simultaneous equations models with lagged endogenous variables and first-order serially correlated errors, particularly in specifying the set of instrumental variables (see this chapter for further discussion).

Fair has written extensively on econometric issues in simultaneous equations models, developing maximum likelihood estimators for linear equation systems with autoregressive residuals, deriving computational algorithms for implementation of models with rational expectations, comparing alternative estimators, constructing measures to evaluate the predictive accuracy of alternative models, and implementing these procedures empirically. Much of Fair's research is summarized in his 1984 Harvard University Press book, *The Specification, Estimation, and Analysis of Macroeconometric Models.* In addition to his research in econometrics and macroeconomics, Fair has made important contributions in international economics, in using optimal control theory to measure economic performance, and in analyzing the effects of economic events on voting behavior in the U.S. Presidential elections.

Born in Fresno, California in 1942, Fair received his B.A. degree in economics from Fresno State College in 1964 and then went on to MIT for doctoral studies, earning his Ph.D. degree in 1968. Fair's first academic appointment was at Princeton University. In 1974 he left for the Cowles Foundation and the Department of Economics at Yale University, where he now teaches macroeconomics and econometrics. Fair has been elected a Fellow of the Econometric Society, and since 1977 he has served as Associate Editor of the *Review of Economics and Statistics.*

By repeated substitution, e_t can be rewritten as

$$e_t = \sum_{i=1}^{t} \theta^{t-i} w_i + \theta^t e_0 \qquad \textbf{(10.57)}$$

Given e_0 and known values of θ, one could use Eq. (10.57) to calculate e_t and then employ the iterated MDE, minimizing Eq. (10.54). Under normality this iterative MDE is numerically equivalent to the maximum likelihood estimator.

When θ is not known, estimation could become more complicated. However, it turns out that in Taylor's model, no restrictions are placed on the elements of θ; as is seen in Eq. (10.56), there are only two unknown elements in θ, and there are two free parameters, θ_1 and θ_2, which do not appear elsewhere in the model. For this reason, Taylor suggests using the following two-dimensional grid search: Given any two-dimensional grid value of θ, use Eq. (10.57) to compute the corresponding e_t, minimize Eq. (10.54) with respect to the remaining nine unknown structural parameters, and then choose as the preferred iterative MDE that set of θ and the corresponding structural parameter estimates that yields the smallest value for the minimum of Eq. (10.54). Note that since the set of parameters that minimizes Eq. (10.54) is equivalent to the parameter set that minimizes the determinant $|\hat{e}'\hat{e}|$ one could perform the same grid search procedure and instead employ as the fitting criterion the minimum value of the determinant of $\hat{e}'\hat{e}$.[68]

To facilitate this computation, Taylor shows that a simple recursive relationship can be used to calculate e_t as a function of the elements of θ and that if one transforms the data in a corresponding way using this relationship, one can use the algorithms of the traditional iterated MDE and the transformed data to obtain conditional maximum likelihood parameter estimates. Specifically, Taylor sets e_0 in Eq. (10.57) to zero and obtains the $\hat{e}_t$ from $\hat{\theta}$ as follows: For each variable x_{1t} in the aggregate demand reduced form equation (10.52)—the dependent variable, constant term, and each of the right-hand variables—he transforms the T observations recursively, using

$$\begin{aligned} x^*_{11} &= x_{11} \\ x^*_{12} &= x_{12} + \phi_1 x^*_{11} \\ &\vdots \\ x^*_{1T} &= x_{1T} + \phi_1 x^*_{1,T-1} \end{aligned} \tag{10.58}$$

Similarly, for each variable x_{2t} in the inflation equation (10.53)—the dependent variable, constant term, and each of the right-hand variables—he transforms the T observations recursively, using

$$\begin{aligned} x^*_{21} &= x_{21} \\ x^*_{22} &= x_{22} + \phi_2 x^*_{21} \\ &\vdots \\ x^*_{2T} &= x_{2T} + \phi_2 x^*_{2,T-1} \end{aligned} \tag{10.59}$$

where ϕ_1 and ϕ_2 represent the two unknown elements in θ from Eq. (10.56), that is, $\phi_1 = a(\beta_5\theta_2 + \theta_1)$, and $\phi_2 = a(\gamma_1\theta_1 + \theta_2)$. Once these data series were transformed for alternative grid values of θ_1 and θ_2 (or equivalently, ϕ_1 and ϕ_2),[69] Taylor employed the traditional iterated MDE on the sequentially transformed data and chose as his final set of parameters that set of estimates yielding the smallest value of Eq. (10.54).

Using quarterly U.S. data from 1953:3–1975:3 (the first two quarter observations for 1953 were lost owing to the inclusion of a twice-lagged dependent variable, and the final 1975:4 observation was lost in forming π for 1975:3), Taylor employed this modified iterative MDE technique and obtained as estimates

$$\begin{aligned} y_t = {} & \underset{(2.1)}{0.0720} + \underset{(13.3)}{1.167 y_{t-2}} - \underset{(3.6)}{0.324 y_{t-2}} + \underset{(3.3)}{0.578(m - p_t)} - \\ & \underset{(2.5)}{0.484(m - p)_{t-1}} - \underset{(1.4)}{0.447\hat{\pi}_t} + \underset{(1.1)}{0.0000843t} + u_t \\ & u_t = \eta_t + 0.38\epsilon_{t-1}, \qquad \hat{\omega}_\eta = 0.007916 \end{aligned} \tag{10.60}$$

and

$$\begin{aligned} \pi_t &= \underset{(3.0)}{0.000515} + \pi_{t-1} + \underset{(3.1)}{0.0180\hat{y}_t} + \nu_t, \\ \nu_t &= \epsilon_t - 0.67\epsilon_{t-1}, \qquad \hat{\omega}_\epsilon = 0.003661 \end{aligned} \tag{10.61}$$

where absolute values of asymptotic t-ratios are in parentheses and $\hat{\omega}_\eta$ and $\hat{\omega}_\epsilon$ are the standard errors of the estimated disturbances. Note that since the standard errors of the coefficients are conditional on values of $\hat{\theta}_1$ and $\hat{\theta}_2$, these estimates likely understate the true standard errors.

In the estimated aggregate demand equation (10.60), parameter estimates on the lagged dependent variables suggest the presence of a substantial but stable acceleration component; to see this, rewrite the expression $1.17y_{t-1} - 0.32y_{t-2}$ as $0.85y_{t-1} + 0.32(y_{t-1} - y_{t-2})$. The estimated coefficient on each of the real money balance terms is significantly different from zero, and Taylor reports that so too is their sum; moreover, the coefficient on lagged real balances is negative with an absolute value less than that on current real balances, consistent with the partial adjustment hypothesis on the money demand equation. Contrary to Taylor's expectation, the coefficient on the expected inflation term is negative, but it is insignificantly different from zero. Finally, note that in the error process of the aggregate demand equation, the implied estimated negative value of θ_1 ($= -0.38$) suggests that nominal money balances do not adjust fully to every shock in the price level.

For the inflation equation (10.61) the coefficient on the excess aggregate demand variable is positive, indicating that excess demand accelerates inflation (recall that $\hat{y}_t$ is the expected deviation from potential output). The intercept term in this equation is positive and significantly different from zero, implying that inflation will be accelerating when $\hat{y}_t$ is zero (since then $\pi_t - \pi_{t-1} > 0$, where $\pi_t \equiv p_{t+1} - p_t$). The nonaccelerating inflation point occurs at a GNP gap of about 2.9%, that is, $\Delta\pi_t \equiv \pi_t - \pi_{t-1} = 0$ when $y_t = -0.029$. Further, the estimated coefficient of 0.0180 on excess demand in the inflation equation suggests that inflation will be reduced by 0.29 percentage points (at annual rates) for each year (not quarter) that GNP is 1% below the nonaccelerating point (that is, 0.018*4*4 = 0.288). With regard to the error structure in the inflation equation, the 0.67 estimate of the moving average parameter θ_2 implies that on average, 67% of any shock to the inflation equation is temporary and disappears in the following quarter.

Finally, as a test for model specification and for the constraints imposed by the REH (10.51), Taylor estimates the reduced form equations (10.52)–(10.53) over the same sample time period with and without imposing the five cross-equation constraints. Using a likelihood ratio test statistic, Taylor obtains a chi-square test statistic of 12.8, which, when compared with the 0.05, 0.025, and 0.01 critical values of 11.1, 12.8, and 15.1, respectively, leads him to conclude that "the constraints imposed by the rational expectations hypothesis are not strongly rejected by the data."[70] It is worth noting, incidentally, that the result that the constraints implied by the REH are rejected by the data is not an uncommon one in the empirical literature to date, although it is often not clear whether the REH or some other coincident hypothesis (such as the perfect markets assumption) is the cause of the rejection; see, for example, the empirical studies in Robert E. Lucas, Jr. and Thomas J. Sargent [1981] as well as those surveyed by David K. H. Begg [1982], G. S. Maddala [1988, Chapter 10], and especially Frederic Mishkin [1983].

This completes our discussion of the classic econometric issues that are involved in empirically implementing REH macroeconometric models. Our goal in this section has been to acquaint readers with the most important econometric implications of the REH. We have accomplished this by focusing on a simple two-equation macroeconometric model, in which it is possible to obtain (conditional) maximum likelihood parameter estimates by using a modified iterative MDE.

It is worth emphasizing, however, that in the last decade, numerous other macroeconometric models have been constructed and estimated, each incorporating the REH. Some REH models still include the instantaneous market-clearing assumption; in other models, some markets are envisaged as clearing instantaneously while others are more sluggish.[71] Although Bennett McCallum [1979b] discusses single equation estimation procedures that are consistent with the REH, in many of these macroeconometric models, explicit imposition of the REH requires the use of far more complex estimation methods and computational algorithms. For a discussion and review of some of these studies and econometric procedures, see, among others, David K. H. Begg [1982], Gregory C. Chow [1980], Ray C. Fair [1981, 1984], Fair and John Taylor [1983], Robert P. Flood and Peter M. Garber [1980], Frederic Mishkin [1983], Steven M. Sheffrin [1983], and Kenneth F. Wallis [1980].

While much of this recent research incorporating REH into estimation is exciting and technically challenging, for pedagogical purposes it is also useful to step back in time and examine more closely the first macroeconometric model of the United States that was estimated using simultaneous equations methods, namely, Klein's Model I.

10.5 PARAMETER ESTIMATES OF KLEIN'S MODEL I USING ALTERNATIVE SIMULTANEOUS EQUATIONS ESTIMATORS

The literature on macroeconometric models in the last two decades has been largely dominated by implementation issues and implications of the REH. A survey chapter on simultaneous equations estimation such as this would be seriously deficient, however, if it failed to discuss and reference, at least briefly, the very substantial literature on structural and reduced form estimation of macroeconometric models that existed before the REH debate.[72] This literature is particularly important because it deals with relationships among alternative estimators, issues that are still important today. Incidentally, the historical development of simultaneous equations estimation is discussed by, among others, Klein [1953, Chapter 3; 1972, Chapters 4–7], Jerry A. Hausman [1983], Roy J. Epstein [1987], and Neil de Marchi and Christopher L. Gilbert [1989].

The three-equation macroeconometric Model I was the first of three models presented in Klein's now-classic 1950 book, published as Monograph No. 11 by the Cowles Commission for Research in Economics.[73] Although Jan Tinbergen had constructed and estimated several macroeconometric models more than a decade earlier,[74] it appears that Klein's Model I was the first to exploit simultaneous equation estimation methods such as maximum likelihood.

Klein's Model I is a highly aggregative one, a fact that he well recognized, but it is very simple and useful for pedagogical purposes; in its time it also had the advantage of being estimable using relatively simple computational algorithms. It is a model that highlights Keynesian demand features (although supply is implicit), and it focuses only on real, not nominal magnitudes; the quantity of money is ignored entirely.[75] Interestingly, Klein noted that the three equations of his model could be viewed as being consistent with two rather diverse traditions in economic thought, the Marxian and the individual maximization paradigms:

> It is possible to develop this model, as we have shown, from the un-Marxian principles of utility and profit maximization, but it is also possible to develop this model from purely Marxian principles. The same model can be consistent with a multiplicity of hypotheses.[76]

We begin this section by briefly outlining Klein's three-equation model, as formulated by Arthur S. Goldberger [1964, pp. 303–304].

The first equation in Klein's Model I is a consumption function, and it relates consumption CN to the total wage bill earned by workers W and to current and lagged nonwage income (profits) P. In turn, the total wage bill W is the sum of wages earned by workers in the private sector, W_1, and wages earned by government workers, W_2, where all values are in constant 1934 dollars. Klein's consumption function takes the form

$$CN_t = \alpha_0 + \alpha_1(W_{1t} + W_{2t}) + \alpha_2 P_t + \alpha_3 P_{t-1} + \epsilon_{1t} \tag{10.62}$$

where ϵ_{1t} is a random disturbance term, assumed to be serially uncorrelated. Note that although the marginal propensity to consume from wage income is permitted to differ from that for profit income, the effect on consumption is the same from private sector and public sector wage income.

For the investment equation, Klein specified a cash flow–type equation relating net investment I (including net change in inventories, whether desired or not) to current and lagged profits and to the beginning-of-year capital stock,

$$I_t = \beta_0 + \beta_1 P_t + \beta_2 P_{t-1} + \beta_3 K_{t-1} + \epsilon_{2t} \tag{10.63}$$

where ϵ_{2t} is a random disturbance term, assumed to be serially uncorrelated.

As his third and final stochastic equation, Klein specified a demand for labor equation that related the private wage bill W_1 to current and lagged values of a private product measure E, defined as national income Y plus indirect business taxes TX minus government wage bill W_2, and to time T, where T is measured as YEAR minus 1931:

$$W_{1t} = \gamma_0 + \gamma_1 E_t + \gamma_2 E_{t-1} + \gamma_3(\text{YEAR} - 1931) + \epsilon_{3t} \tag{10.64}$$

Again, the random disturbance term ϵ_{3t} was assumed to be serially uncorrelated. Although inclusion of the time variable (YEAR − 1931) in Eq. (10.64) might have been rationalized on the basis of improvements over time in average labor productivity, Klein envisaged a different justification, "to reflect an institutional phenomenon, namely, the growing bargaining strength of labor."[77]

In addition to these three stochastic equations, Klein specified five identities, several of which have already been noted:

$$\begin{aligned}
&\text{Total product:} && Y_t + TX_t \equiv CN_t + I_t + G_t \\
&\text{Income:} && Y_t \equiv P_t + W_t \\
&\text{Capital:} && K_t \equiv I_t + K_{t-1} \\
&\text{Wage bill:} && W_t \equiv W_{1t} + W_{2t} \\
&\text{Private product:} && E_t \equiv Y_t + TX_t - W_{2t}
\end{aligned} \tag{10.65}$$

The first identity states that total national product is the sum of goods and services demanded by consumers plus investors plus net government demands.[78] The second identity states that total income is the sum of profits and wages, while the third (not used in estimation but employed in dynamic simulations) defines the end-of-year capital stock as last year's end-of-year capital stock plus this year's net investment. The last two identities define total wage bill as the sum of private and government sector wage bills and private product as total product minus the government wage bill.

Within this equation system, Klein specified that CN_t, I_t, W_{1t}, Y_t, P_t, K_t, W_t, and E_t were endogenous; that the exogenous variables were the constant vector, G_t, W_{2t}, TX_t, and (YEAR − 1931); and that the predetermined variables were K_{t-1}, P_{t-1}, and E_{t-1}. Note that there happen to be as many dependent as exogenous plus predetermined variables, namely, eight. The data for this model were annual U.S. data from 1920 to 1941; owing to the presence of lagged regressors, estimation covered the 1921–1941 time period. All variables except the constant and (YEAR − 1931) were measured in billions of 1934 dollars.

In terms of identification, in each stochastic equation the number of excluded exogenous (and predetermined) variables is greater than the number of included endogenous variables appearing as regressors, and so in each equation the necessary conditions for identification are satisfied. Specifically, for the consumption equation the number of excluded exogenous (and predetermined) variables and the number of endogenous regressors are six and two, respectively, while for the investment equation they are five and one, and in the private wage bill equation they are five and one, respectively. The necessary order condition therefore suggests that each of the three equations is overidentified.

Klein estimated parameters of Model I using a variety of estimation methods, and since publication of his model, numerous other researchers have estimated its parameters using different estimators. In Table 10.3 we present parameter estimates based on a number of alternative estimation procedures, as reported in well-known econometrics textbooks and articles. The OLS column reports equation-by-equation ordinary least squares estimates; 2SLS refers to the equation-by-equation two-stage least squares estimates;[79] 3SLS the three-stage least squares system method estimates;[80] FIML refers to the estimates yielded by the full information maximum likelihood estimator;[81] I3SLS refers to the iterative three-stage least squares system estimates;[82] OLS-AR(1) refers to the equation-by-equation generalized least squares estimates, assuming that disturbances in each equation follow a first-order autoregressive process; and 2SLS-AR(1) refers to the equation-by-equation 2SLS estimates with first-order autocorrelation, using the appropriately lagged instruments as outlined by Ray C. Fair [1970].[83] Note that with the OLS, 2SLS, 3SLS, I3SLS, OLS-AR(1), and 2SLS-AR(1) estimation procedures, parameter estimates lack invariance to the choice of which endogenous variable is the dependent variable; this is not the case, however, with FIML or with the limited information maximum likelihood (LIML) estimation procedure.

Several comments are in order concerning the various parameter estimates in Table 10.3. First, for the consumption function the alternative estimates of α_1, the marginal propensity to consume out of wage income, are very similar, all near 0.8, provided that autocorrelation is not taken into account.

Table 10.3 Structural Parameter Estimates of Klein's Model I Using Alternative Estimators (Asymptotic Standard Errors Are in Parentheses)

Structural Parameter	Estimation Procedure						
	OLS	2SLS	3SLS	FIML	I3SLS	OLS-AR(1)	2SLS-AR(1)
α_0	16.237	16.555	16.441	17.165	16.559	26.438	21.584
	(1.303)	(1.468)	(1.304)	(7.363)	(1.224)	(4.069)	(2.380)
α_1	0.796	0.810	0.790	0.791	0.766	0.478	0.644
	(0.040)	(0.045)	(0.038)	(0.066)	(0.035)	(0.116)	(0.079)
α_2	0.193	0.017	0.125	−0.062	0.164	0.419	0.301
	(0.091)	(0.131)	(0.108)	(1.09)	(0.096)	(0.118)	(0.123)
α_3	0.090	0.216	0.163	0.310	0.176	0.165	0.066
	(0.091)	(0.119)	(0.100)	(0.629)	(0.090)	(0.103)	(0.096)
ρ						0.868	0.599
						(0.111)	(0.184)
R^2	0.981	0.977	0.980		0.980	0.916	0.950
DW	1.368	1.485	1.425	1.483	1.335	2.023	2.059
β_0	10.126	20.278	28.178	29.837	42.716	10.196	12.981
	(5.466)	(8.383)	(6.79)	(23.77)	(10.56)	(7.399)	(8.618)
β_1	0.480	0.150	−0.013	−0.625	−0.353	0.490	0.425
	(0.097)	(0.193)	(0.162)	(1.48)	(0.259)	(0.111)	(0.134)
β_2	0.333	0.616	0.756	1.020	1.009	0.324	0.375
	(0.101)	(0.181)	(0.153)	(0.999)	(0.248)	(0.108)	(0.126)
β_3	−0.112	−0.158	−0.195	−0.173	−0.259	−0.112	−0.125
	(0.027)	(0.040)	(0.033)	(0.106)	(0.051)	(0.035)	(0.041)
ρ						0.094	0.043
						(0.223)	(0.229)
R^2	0.931	0.885	0.826		0.644	0.921	0.925
DW	1.810	2.085	1.996	1.427	1.786	1.960	1.887
γ_0	1.497	1.500	1.797	4.790	2.614	2.097	2.210
	(1.270)	(1.276)	(1.12)	(4.82)	(1.19)	(1.06)	(1.10)
γ_1	0.439	0.439	0.400	0.278	0.375	0.430	0.433
	(0.032)	(0.040)	(0.032)	(0.084)	(0.031)	(0.028)	(0.030)
γ_2	0.146	0.147	0.181	0.257	0.194	0.147	0.142
	(0.037)	(0.043)	(0.034)	(0.052)	(0.032)	(0.032)	(0.035)
γ_3	0.130	0.130	0.150	0.213	0.168	0.118	0.114
	(0.032)	(0.032)	(0.028)	(0.078)	(0.029)	(0.026)	(0.028)
ρ						−0.141	−0.181
						(0.221)	(0.226)
R^2	0.987	0.987	0.986		0.985	0.991	0.990
DW	1.958	1.963	2.155	1.669	2.109	2.083	1.825

Notes: In cases with AR(1) processes, the R^2 and DW statistics refer to the ρ-transformed data. OLS estimates are taken from G. S. Maddala [1977, p. 242]; 2SLS from Arthur S. Goldberger [1964, p. 364]; 3SLS from Henri Theil [1971, p. 517], with corrections; and FIML from the present author, using the TSP software program. When R^2 and DW values were not reported in these texts and articles, they were supplied by the present author, based on replication attempts.

Estimates of the autoregressive parameter are significantly different from zero for both the OLS-AR(1) and 2SLS-AR(1) procedures. Estimates of α_2, the marginal propensity to consume out of current profits, vary considerably, from a high OLS-AR(1) estimate of 0.419 to a low FIML estimate of -0.062; for all but the OLS, OLS-AR(1), and 2SLS-AR(1) estimators, estimates of α_3 (the marginal propensity to consume out of lagged profits) are larger than those of α_2, but each of the standard error estimates is large in relation to point estimates of α_2.

In the investment equation, while estimates of β_2 vary substantially, they all indicate that lagged profits have a significant effect on current investment; estimates of β_1 vary a great deal, even in sign, suggesting that the effect of current profits on current investment either is insignificant or else is simply estimated very imprecisely. First-order autocorrelation does not appear to be significant in the investment equation.[84]

Finally, in the private wage bill equation, both current (γ_1) and lagged (γ_2) values of private product affect current payments to labor positively, but estimates of γ_1 are uniformly larger than those of γ_2. The FIML estimates appear to be quite different from those of other estimators. First-order autoregression does not appear to be statistically significant.

An alternative estimation procedure involves estimating parameters of the reduced form of Klein's Model I. In the first three columns of Table 10.4 the OLS equation-by-equation parameter estimates are presented for the unrestricted reduced form equations; when the overidentifying restrictions from the structure of Klein's Model I are imposed on the reduced form parameters, one obtains restricted estimates. In the final three columns of Table 10.4 we reproduce Arthur S. Goldberger's restricted reduced form estimates of Klein's Model I. (See your econometric or macroeconomic theory text for a discussion of the interpretation of the reduced form parameters, which in this case turn out to be closely related to the notion of impact multipliers.) A cursory examination of the two sets of estimates appears to suggest that there are substantial differences in parameter estimates based on the unrestricted and restricted reduced form estimation; see, for example, estimates on the T, TX, G, and W_2 variables. A likelihood ratio test statistic for the 12 overidentifying restrictions is equal to $2*[-63.7675 - (-83.4665)] = 2*19.699 = 39.398$, which is larger than the 0.01 (0.05) chi-square critical value of 26.22 (21.03), a result suggesting that the overidentifying restrictions are not consistent with the data. This result is not that surprising, since Klein's Model I is obviously a highly aggregated and simplified model, useful for pedagogical purposes but not necessarily an accurate model of the U.S. economy. In the exercises that follow, you will have an opportunity to replicate and then interpret these estimates of the Klein Model I in greater detail.

This concludes our discussion of estimation and inference issues on small macroeconometric models. Our purpose in this chapter has been to introduce problems and issues that one encounters when specifying and estimating small macroeconometric models, particularly models with simulta-

Table 10.4 Reduced Form Estimates of Klein's Model I of the U.S. Economy (Asymptotic Standard Errors Are in Parentheses)

	Dependent Variable					
	OLS Unrestricted Reduced Form			ML Restricted Reduced Form		
Regressor	CN	I	W_1	CN	I	W_1
Constant	58.3022	35.5181	43.4358	42.826	25.841	31.635
	(30.631)	(24.976)	(25.419)	(8.619)	(7.567)	(7.240)
P_{-1}	0.7480	0.9264	0.8719	0.768	0.743	0.664
	(0.5025)	(0.4097)	(0.4170)	(0.197)	(0.173)	(0.165)
K_{-1}	−0.1465	−0.1925	−0.1230	−0.105	−0.182	−0.126
	(0.1154)	(0.0941)	(0.0957)	(0.037)	(0.033)	(0.031)
E_{-1}	0.2301	−0.1127	0.0953	0.179	−0.008	0.222
	(0.2732)	(0.2228)	(0.2268)	(0.024)	(0.010)	(0.016)
T	0.7011	0.3319	0.7136	0.159	−0.007	0.197
	(0.7536)	(0.6144)	(0.6253)	(0.021)	(0.009)	(0.014)
TX	−0.3657	−0.1615	−0.6042	−0.128	−0.176	−0.134
	(0.4201)	(0.3425)	(0.3486)	(0.276)	(0.238)	(0.214)
G	0.2050	0.1002	0.8662	0.664	0.153	0.797
	(0.3788)	(0.3089)	(0.3143)	(0.237)	(0.208)	(0.198)
W_2	0.1933	−0.7166	−0.4437	0.684	−0.029	−0.151
	(2.454)	(2.001)	(2.036)	(0.062)	(0.040)	(0.054)
R^2	0.9383	0.8469	0.9497	0.9155	0.8112	0.9152
DW	2.0244	2.1459	2.3449	1.6813	1.8156	1.8613
ln L (for the equation system)			−63.7675			−83.4665

Notes: The OLS unrestricted reduced form estimates are taken from Goldberger [1964, p. 325], with standard errors estimated by the present author, taking account of the redefined W_2 variable. The reduced form estimates are drawn from Goldberger [1964, p. 368]. The values of R^2, DW, and ln L were estimated by the present author, using the TSP software program.

neity and/or nonstatic expectations. With this material as background you are now ready for hands-on involvement.

10.6 HANDS ON WITH PARAMETER ESTIMATION IN STRUCTURAL AND REDUCED FORM EQUATIONS OF SMALL MACROECONOMETRIC MODELS

We have now come to the hands-on portion of this chapter. The goal of these exercises is to increase your familiarity with and understanding of estimation and inference issues in simultaneous equations models by engaging you in hands-on estimation. The exercises that follow are designed to involve you in some of the more common problems of estimation and inference in simultaneous equations models. Since the literature on simultaneous equations estimation is very large, it is simply not possible to introduce you to all of the important issues. Your instructor might therefore wish to supplement the exercises below, focusing on other significant issues in estimation, inference, and interpretation.

Exercises 1 and 2 are particularly important and useful; in these exercises, among other tasks, you construct variables that are used in subsequent exercises. Further, in Exercise 1 you replicate the estimation of Klein's Model I using single-equation estimation procedures such as OLS and 2SLS, with and without allowance for first-order autoregressive disturbances. In Exercise 2 you gain further understanding of the two steps in 2SLS estimation by replicating the Lucas and Rapping estimates; you discover that their estimation procedure was apparently not quite correct, although their results are not substantially affected.

Exercise 3 is also a most useful and important one; in it you employ the concept of an information set and use 2SLS estimation procedures to obtain estimates that are consistent with the orthogonality condition of the rational expectations hypothesis. In particular, using data underlying Taylor's two-equation model of the U.S. economy, you implement a variety of instrumental variable estimation procedures.

Then in Exercise 4 you will learn how to test for the exogeneity of a regressor based on the Hausman specification test, which you implement using the Klein Model I data. In Exercise 5 you will test for serial correlation in the reduced form and structural equations of the Lucas-Rapping model, equations whose regressors include lagged dependent variables and therefore complicate the testing procedure.

The next four exercises focus on numerical relationships among parameter estimates with alternative estimators. Specifically, in Exercise 6 you will estimate a modified version of Klein's Model I in which each equation is just identified, and you will demonstrate that in such just identified models, a variety of estimators yield numerically equivalent parameter estimates. In Exercise 7 you will find that this equivalence among parameter estimators breaks down in general when one has a model with overidentified equations; you will discover such differences among the 2SLS, 3SLS, FIML, and I3SLS estimators, using your choice of the Klein Model I or the Lucas-Rapping model. In Exercise 8 you show, however, that if one estimates the structure of Klein's overidentified Model I by FIML, or if one estimates the implied restricted reduced form by ML, one obtains numerically identical parameter estimates. Moreover, using the reduced form, you will be able to test for the empirical validity of the overidentifying restrictions in Klein's Model I. Then in Exercise 9 you compare the successive least squares procedure with FIML estimation of a structurally recursive variant of Klein's Model I, and you also note a somewhat surprising equivalence of parameter estimates based on FIML and the iterative-Zellner efficient estimator in this special type of simultaneous equations model.

In the final exercise you will estimate a model incorporating rational expectations using the method of maximum likelihood, with cross-equation parameter restrictions. Specifically, in Exercise 10 you will replicate Taylor's maximum likelihood estimation procedure for his two reduced form equations and test for the empirical validity of the overidentifying restrictions.

EXERCISE 1: OLS, 2SLS, and GLS Estimation of Klein's Model I

The purpose of this exercise is to have you replicate other researchers' attempts at estimating the three-equation Klein Model I of the U.S. economy, using a variety of single-equation structural estimation methods: equation-by-equation OLS, 2SLS, and variants of OLS and 2SLS that allow for AR(1) autoregressive disturbances.

The subdirectory CHAP10.DAT in your data diskette contains a data file called KLEIN. This data file includes annual time series from 1920 to 1941 for ten variables: YEAR, CN, P, W1, I, KLAG, E, W2, G, and TX. The variable YEAR is the year of observation, and KLAG is the beginning-of-year capital stock, earlier denoted as K_{-1}; all other variables are defined in Section 10.5 of the text.

(a) Following Klein, begin by generating a variable "time," denoted T, and defined as $T \equiv$ YEAR $-$ 1931. Also, define and generate the total wage bill variable W as $W = W_1 + W_2$. Finally, generate an aggregate demand variable defined as $Y \equiv CN + I + G - TX$. Print out the entire 1920–1941 annual data series for T, W, Y, and the nine other variables—CN, P, W1, I, KLAG, E, W2, G, and TX. Make sure the data series in your software is identical to that in the KLEIN data file.

(b) Next, replicate Klein's OLS regressions (which he called classical least squares). Specifically, estimate by OLS parameters in the consumption equation (10.62), the investment equation (10.63), and the private wage bill equation (10.64). Since lagged values of regressors appear as regressors in each of these equations, you will need to drop the first observation from your sample and estimate using data covering the 1921–1941 time period. Compare your results with the OLS estimates reported in Table 10.3. Do you believe that these OLS estimates are plausible? Why or why not? Are they consistent estimates of the true parameters? Why or why not?

(c) Now replicate the 2SLS equation-by-equation estimates. You should take care in specifying the instrument list. For the consumption equation (10.62) the instrument list should consist of a constant term, P_{-1}, KLAG, E_{-1}, T, TX, G, and W_2. Why? The same list of variables should comprise the list of instruments in the investment equation (10.63) and in the private wage bill equation (10.64). Why? (*Hint:* Look at the list of regressors in the reduced form equations of Table 10.4.) Using the 2SLS estimator in your computer software program, estimate parameters in the consumption, investment, and private wage bill structural equations. How well do you replicate results reported in Table 10.3? What are the properties of these 2SLS estimates? Do any of the 2SLS estimates differ considerably from their OLS counterparts? Which do you prefer? Why?[85]

(d) For purposes of comparison, estimate the three structural equations (10.62)–(10.64) by least squares, but allow for a first-order autoregressive scheme, that is, use one of the single equation generalized least squares estimators in your computer software program, such as iterative Cochrane-Orcutt or Hildreth-Lu. Is your estimate of the first-order autoregressive parameter statistically different from zero? Why? Compare your OLS-AR(1) estimates with those reported in Table 10.3 and with the OLS estimates. What are the properties of this OLS-AR(1) estimator? Can you choose between the OLS and OLS-AR(1) estimates? Why?

(e) Finally, reestimate the three structural equations using single-equation 2SLS procedures, but allow for a first-order autoregressive error process in each equation. As was pointed out by Ray C. Fair [1970], in this case the list of instruments must be expanded to include not only the constant and the seven variables noted in part (c), but also the lagged values $W_{2,t-1}$, TX_{t-1}, G_{-1}, P_{-2}, KLAG$_{-1}$ and E_{-2}.[86] Briefly outline the intuition explaining why this list of instruments must be expanded in this way. Using this 2SLS-AR(1) estimation procedure, estimate parameters of the three structural equations (10.62)–(10.64), and compare your results to those reported in the last column of Table 10.3. Are they identical? What are the properties of this 2SLS-AR(1) estimator? Compare your 2SLS-AR(1) results with the traditional 2SLS estimates. Which do you prefer? Why?

EXERCISE 2: The Two OLS Steps of 2SLS: A Lucas-Rapping Faux Pas?

The purpose of this exercise is to help you better understand and interpret the procedures involved in 2SLS estimation of simultaneous equation systems. Your econometric theory text discusses the theory of this estimator; in this exercise you have the opportunity to verify the textbook algebra. You will also encounter a nuance concerning the estimation of residuals in the second stage and will discover implications for the appropriate estimation of the variance-covariance matrix of the parameters. As you will see, in the classic Lucas-Rapping model there appears to be a computational error in the 2SLS estimation, although the basic qualitative results are not substantially affected.

In your data diskette subdirectory CHAP10.DAT there is a data file called LUCAS containing 1929–1965 annual time series data on nine variables: The year of observation (YR), an index of real hourly wage compensation (HW), the implicit GNP deflator (PGNP), an index of employment—persons engaged times annual hours worked by full-time employees (N), a population index with fixed age-sex distribution (POP), a measure of labor quality based in large part on educational attainment (QL), real GNP (RGNP), the percent of the labor force unemployed (U), and Moody's AAA bond yield rate (R). The variables HW, PGNP, N, POP, QL, and RGNP are in index form, with 1929 = 100. It is worth noting that in Lucas and Rapping [1970, p. 257] the authors state that "all regression results reported in this paper are based on data series to more significant digits than those reported in this table. The data were rounded to make the table more readable." It turns out that although you will not be able to replicate the Lucas-Rapping results exactly, you should be able to come very close.

To attempt replication of the Lucas-Rapping study, it is first necessary to perform some logarithmic data transformations. Specifically, define and generate the following nine variables:

For 1929–1965:	*For 1930–1965:*
$y_1 \equiv \ln (\text{N/POP})$	$x_1 \equiv \ln (\text{PGNP/PGNP}_{-1})$
$y_2 \equiv \ln (\text{QL*N/RGNP})$	$x_4 \equiv \ln (\text{RGNP/RGNP}_{-1})$
$y_3 \equiv \ln (\text{HW})$	$y_5 \equiv \ln (\text{HW/HW}_{-1})$
$y_4 \equiv \ln (\text{HW/QL})$	
$x_2 \equiv \ln (\text{RGNP/POP})$	
$x_3 \equiv \ln (\text{QL})$	

(a) First, try to replicate the Lucas-Rapping 2SLS estimates of the three structural equations reproduced in Eqs. (10.36)–(10.38). Using the 1930–1965 annual data (you lose one observation because of the presence of lagged variables), estimate by 2SLS each of their three structural equations, where in each equation the following variables are treated as exogenous or predetermined: a constant vector, x_1, x_2, x_3, x_4, and once-lagged values of y_1, y_2, and y_3. Run the following 2SLS regressions:
  (i) y_1 on a constant, y_3, y_3 lagged, x_1, and y_1 lagged: Eq. (10.36)
  (ii) y_2 on a constant, y_4, y_2 lagged, and x_4: Eq. (10.37)
  (iii) U on a constant, x_1, y_5, and U lagged: Eq. (10.38).
  Your parameter estimates (except the intercept term) should match the estimates reported in Eqs. (10.36)–(10.38) reasonably well, but estimates are not quite as close for the inverted Phillips curve equation (10.38). Verify these results.

(b) Upon closer inspection, you might notice that the standard error estimates, $\bar{R}^2$, and the Durbin-Watson test statistics that you obtained in part (a) are in most cases quite different from those reported by Lucas and Rapping. Let us now do some detective work to see whether we can determine why this difference arises and what this implies for the interpretation of the Lucas-Rapping 2SLS estimation procedure. Notice first that in Eq. (10.36) the variable $\ln \hat{w}_t$ appears as a regressor and that

$\ln(\hat{w}_t/Q_t)$ is a right-hand variable in Eq. (10.37), as is $\ln(\hat{w}_t/w_{t-1})$ in Eq. (10.38). These variables are fitted value expressions derived from the first-stage portion of 2SLS. Proceed by running the following reduced form regression: Using OLS, regress y_3 (which is $\ln w_t$) on a constant, x_1, x_2, x_3, x_4, and once-lagged values of y_1, y_2 and y_3; retrieve the fitted value from this OLS reduced form regression, and call it $y_{3,\text{fit}}$. Next perform the second stage of 2SLS. Specifically, for the labor supply equation (10.36), run an OLS regression in which the y_3 regressor is replaced by $y_{3,\text{fit}}$, that is, regress y_1 on a constant, $y_{3,\text{fit}}$, y_3 lagged, x_1, and y_1 lagged. Your parameter estimates should be numerically identical to those you obtained in part (a), but your standard error estimates should now be virtually identical to those reported by Lucas and Răpping. Your $\bar{R}^2$ and Durbin-Watson test statistics should now also be very close to those given in Eq. (10.36). Check to make sure this is the case.

(c) To assess whether you are replicating what in fact Lucas and Rapping did, let us now examine whether similar results obtain if one reestimates the labor demand (10.37) and unemployment (Phillips curve) equations using this two-step OLS procedure. Specifically, since a fitted value version of y_4—$\ln(\hat{w}_t/Q_t)$—is a regressor in Eq. (10.37), generate this fitted variable as a new variable $y_{4,\text{fit}}$, defined as $y_{4,\text{fit}} \equiv y_{3,\text{fit}} - x_3$, where $y_{3,\text{fit}}$ is from part (b). Then run an OLS regression of y_2 on a constant, $y_{4,\text{fit}}$, y_2 lagged, and x_4; your parameter estimates should be numerically equivalent to those you obtained in the 2SLS estimation of part (a), but the standard error estimates, $\bar{R}^2$ and Durbin-Watson test statistics that you now obtain should differ from your 2SLS estimates and instead should be very close to the Lucas-Rapping values in Eq. (10.37). Check to make sure this is the case. Finally, since a fitted value version of y_5—$\ln(\hat{w}_t/w_{t-1})$—is a regressor in the inverted Phillips curve equation, generate $y_{5,\text{fit}}$ as $y_{5,\text{fit}} \equiv y_{3,\text{fit}} - y_{3,t-1}$. Then run an OLS regression of U on a constant, x_1, $y_{5,\text{fit}}$, and U lagged once. Compare your parameter estimates, standard errors, $\bar{R}^2$ and Durbin-Watson test statistic values to those you obtained in part (a) and to those reported by Lucas and Rapping in Eq. (10.38).

(d) On the basis of this detective activity you now have a reasonably good idea of what Lucas and Rapping did, and you now know that the 2SLS parameter estimates in a linear regression model are numerically equivalent to a two-step OLS procedure. To see why the standard errors, $\bar{R}^2$, and Durbin-Watson test statistic values differ, however, note that in forming the residuals that are used to calculate the estimated variance-covariance matrix of the coefficients and other residual-based equation statistics, what 2SLS does is to form the fitted value using the *actual* value of the right-hand side endogenous variable (e.g., in the labor supply equation (10.36), it uses $\ln w_t$ rather than $\ln \hat{w}_t$) and *not* the fitted value from the first-stage OLS regression. In the brute-force two-step OLS procedure that you (and apparently, Lucas and Rapping) have done, ln $\hat{w}_t$ rather than ln w_t is employed in computing the residuals. Why is the two-step OLS procedure for computing the residuals inappropriate? Why is the 2SLS calculation correct? (If you have problems understanding this, check your econometric theory textbook for further details.)

(e) You have demonstrated that Lucas and Rapping apparently made a computational error in their 2SLS estimation. Given the correct standard error calculations that you have now made, assess whether any of the Lucas-Rapping findings are affected substantially, particularly those involving inequalities predicted by the underlying economic theory. Are the correct 2SLS standard errors always larger than the inappropriate two-step OLS values? Explain your findings.

EXERCISE 3: REH-Consistent Estimation Using 2SLS

The purpose of this exercise is to engage you in several alternative procedures for obtaining consistent (but not necessarily efficient) estimates of parameters in models with rational expectations, using Taylor's two-equation model of the U.S. economy. You will first implement procedures outlined by Bennett T. McCallum [1979b] for relatively simple yet consistent estimation of models with the REH. This will involve the use of a concept called the *information set*. You will also consider estimation of a model in which adapative and rational expectations coincide.

It should be noted at the outset that there are numerous alternative possibilities for obtaining consistent estimates of parameters in models with rational expectations or with adaptive expectations. In this exercise you are introduced to just several of these possibilities. Your instructor or econometrics theory textbook can provide you with further options and details.[87]

In your data diskette you will find a file called TAYLOR in the subdirectory named CHAP10.DAT. This data file contains quarterly data from 1953:1 to 1975:4 (92 observations) on six variables: the observation date—a three-digit variable named DATE whose first two digits are the year 19xx and whose last digit is the quarter (e.g., the first quarter in 1953 is 531); a potential GNP series named POTGNP, in billions of 1972 dollars, as estimated and revised by the U.S. Council of Economic Advisers; the narrow definition of the U.S. money supply in billions of current dollars, called M1; GNPDEF, the GNP deflator in index form with 1972 = 100; GNP, real GNP in billions of 1972 dollars; and a time counter named TIME, equal to 1 in 1953:1 and 92 in 1975:4. Note that the POTGNP, M1, GNPDEF and GNP variables are all seasonally adjusted.

(a) First you must construct the variables used by Taylor. For the entire 1953:1–1975:4 sample, construct Taylor's output deviation from trend variable as YDEV ≡ log (GNP/POTGNP). Then generate a real money supply variable RM1 as RM1 $\equiv$ log (M1/GNPDEF). Finally, construct Taylor's inflation rate variable as INF $\equiv$ log (GNPDEF(+1)/GNPDEF). Since by construction this variable involves a lead, you will lose the last observation and will be able to construct INF for only 91 observations from 1953:1 to 1975:3. Using these 91 observations, print out values for YDEV, RM1, and INF, and compute their sample means and sample correlations. Are there any clear trends in the data? For further reference, note that in terms of the notation of Section 10.4, $\text{YDEV}_t \equiv y_t$, $\text{RM1}_t \equiv (m - p)_t$, and $\text{INF}_t \equiv \pi_t = p_{t+1} - p_t$.

(b) An important concept in the estimation of models with rational expectations is the notion of an *information set*—the set of information that is available to economic agents at a given point in time. To avoid confusion with an investment variable that we denoted earlier as I_t, we now define the information set at time t, called IS_t, as those variables and economic relationships that are known to economic agents at the beginning of time t. Given the assumptions that Taylor made concerning the timing of variables and which variables were predetermined, review the discussion in Section 10.4 and verify that Taylor's information set at time $t-1$, IS_{t-1}, includes the following variables: IS_{t-1}: M1_t, GNPDEF_t, RM1_t, RM1_{t-1}, YDEV_{t-1}, YDEV_{t-2}, INF_{t-1}, TIME, and further lagged values of these variables. Variables in IS_{t-1} are often used as instrumental variables in the estimation of REH models, provided that disturbances are not serially correlated. However, if disturbances follow a first-order scheme such as an AR(1) or an MA(1), consistent estimation based on IV procedures often requires using as instruments instead of IS_{t-1} the information set that was available one period earlier, that is, IS_{t-2}. This has been shown by, among others, Bennett T. McCallum [1979b]. Verify that in Taylor's model, IS_{t-2} includes the following variables: IS_{t-2}: M1_{t-1}, GNPDEF_{t-1}, RM1_{t-1}, RM1_{t-2}, YDEV_{t-2}, YDEV_{t-3}, INF_{t-2}, TIME, and further lagged values of these variables. In the remaining portion of this exercise, to obtain consistent estimates of the parameters you will use either IS_{t-1} or IS_{t-2}.

(c) Now estimate Taylor's two-equation model under the assumption that there is no serial dependence in the disturbances, using single-equation estimation procedures. Specifically, assume that in Taylor's two structural equations, (10.45) and (10.46), the composite disturbance terms consist of two parts—an equation disturbance reflecting a variety of optimization errors and an expectations "surprise"; let both of these components be serially independent with constant variances. To obtain consistent estimates of parameters in the output equation, using data from 1953:3 to 1975:3, run a 2SLS regression of YDEV_t on a constant, YDEV_{t-1}, YDEV_{t-2}, RM1_t, RM1_{t-1}, INF_t, and TIME, where the instrument list consists of variables in the period t information set IS_{t-1}, namely, a constant term, M1_t, GNPDEF_t, RM1_t, RM1_{t-1}, YDEV_{t-1}, YDEV_{t-2}, INF_{t-1}, and TIME. Note that this 2SLS procedure represents an attempt to deal with a nonzero correlation between the INF_t regressor and the disturbance term. To understand why this 2SLS procedure is consistent with, yet does not fully incorporate the REH, consider the following questions:

(i) In what sense is the fitted value from the first-stage regression a conditional expectation of INF_t, conditional on IS_{t-1}? How might you interpret the residual from this first stage?

(ii) The algebra of least squares ensures that the fitted values are orthogonal to the residuals from the first-stage regression and that each regressor in this first stage is also orthogonal to the residual. What does this imply in terms of expectational errors being correlated with elements of the information set IS_{t-1}? In the second stage of 2SLS the residual is also orthogonal to each regressor, including in particular orthogonality with the conditional forecast of INF_t. Why does this occur?

(iii) Why is this orthogonality important in the context of the REH?

(iv) Can this 2SLS procedure impose the model-consistency and cross-equation restrictions that typically accompany the REH? In what sense, therefore, does this 2SLS procedure yield results that are consistent with, yet do not fully incorporate, the REH?

Now compare your 2SLS parameter estimates of the output equation to the ML reduced form estimates reported by Taylor, reproduced in Eq. (10.60). Are there any major differences? Then estimate this equation by OLS, rather than 2SLS. What are properties of the OLS estimator? Do results differ substantially? Which results make the most sense in terms of macroeconomic theory? Why?

Next, run 2SLS and OLS regressions for Taylor's inflation equation (10.46), using data from 1953:3 to 1975:3 and the same instrument set as you did earlier. In particular, regress INF_t on a constant, INF_{t-1}, and $YDEV_t$. Compare your OLS and 2SLS results with those of Taylor, reproduced in Eq. (10.61). In what sense is the 2SLS estimator here consistent with the REH? Note that in running this regression you have not imposed the restriction that the coefficient on the INF_{t-1} regressor equals unity, as Taylor did in Eq. (10.61). To impose this restriction, bring INF_{t-1} over to the left-hand side, that is, define and generate a new variable called ACCEL, where $ACCEL_t \equiv INF_t - INF_{t-1}$. Why does ACCEL measure the acceleration in the rate of inflation? Then run both OLS and 2SLS regressions of $ACCEL_t$ on a constant and $YDEV_t$. Compare your results here to those of Taylor.

(d) Among others, Bennett T. McCallum [1979b] has shown that when expectational processes are serially correlated, then to ensure consistency of the 2SLS estimation procedure, one must take care in choosing the information set that is used to form instruments. Specifically, consider an ARMA expectational process in which the process is AR(p) and MA(q), and define d as $d \equiv p + q$. To ensure consistent estimation by

2SLS, McCallum shows that in general, one needs to employ as the instrument set the list of variables in IS_{t-1-d}. For example, if the expectational process followed a first-order serial correlation scheme, say, an AR(1) or an MA(1) so that $d = 1$, then the appropriate information set is IS_{t-2}.

Using IS_{t-2} (namely, a constant term, $\mathrm{M1}_{t-1}$, GNPDEF_{t-1}, $\mathrm{RM1}_{t-1}$, $\mathrm{RM1}_{t-2}$, YDEV_{t-2}, YDEV_{t-3}, INF_{t-2}, and TIME) and data from the 1953:4–1975:3 time period, estimate Taylor's output equation (10.45) by 2SLS. Compare your results to those obtained in part (c). Next estimate the inflation equation (10.46) by 2SLS using IS_{t-2}, without imposing the restriction that the coefficient on INF_{t-1} equals unity. Finally, impose this restriction and estimate by 2SLS parameters in the equation of ACCEL_t on a constant term and YDEV_t. Compare these results to each other and to those reported by Taylor. Which do you prefer, and why?

(e) One drawback of the single-equation 2SLS estimation procedures that you employed in parts (c) and (d) is that they ignore possible efficiency gains that are made available by accounting for the contemporaneous covariances of the equation disturbances. Assuming that the contemporaneous disturbance covariance matrix is conditionally homoskedastic and that disturbances are serially independent, Lars P. Hansen and Kenneth Singleton [1982] have shown that gains in efficiency can be obtained in large samples by using the 3SLS estimator. What are the orthogonality properties of residuals from the 3SLS estimator, and why are they consistent with the REH? In this context, how does 3SLS differ from the 2SLS estimator?

To implement the Hansen-Singleton procedure under the assumption of serial independence and conditional homoskedasticity, employ the information set IS_{t-1} as in part (c) and estimate by 3SLS parameters in the output equation (10.45) and the inflation equation (10.46) without imposing the restriction that the coefficient on INF_{t-1} in the inflation equation equals unity. Compare your results to the analogous 2SLS estimates obtained in part (c). Finally, impose the unity restriction on the INF_{t-1} regressor in the inflation equation by employing ACCEL_t rather than INF_t as the dependent variable and deleting INF_{t-1} as a regressor, as in part (c); estimate the two-equation system by 3SLS, and compare your results to those of Taylor and to the results that you obtained in part (c). Which do you prefer, and why?

(f) (Optional) Finally, it has been shown that if the expectations processes for INF_t and YDEV_t follow MA(1) processes (as would be the case, for example, if expectations were adaptive), then estimation of an adaptive expectations model fully incorporates the REH. Why does this occur? In this case, several estimation procedures are available. One possibility is the following. Using Box-Jenkins estimation procedures and data from 1953:1 to 1975:3, estimate parameters of an MA(1) process for

INF_t and $YDEV_t$. Retrieve the fitted values from these time series estimations, and denote them as $INFFIT_t$ and $YDEVFIT_t$, respectively. Then, using data from the 1953:4–1975:3 time period, estimate first by OLS and then by 2SLS (using IS_{t-2}) the output equation (10.45) and the inflation equation (10.46). Compare your parameter estimates to those obtained by using alternative estimation procedures from this exercise. Which estimates do you prefer, and why?

EXERCISE 4: Testing for Exogeneity Using Hausman's Specification Test

The purpose of this exercise is to enable you to test the null hypothesis that the disturbance term in a stochastic equation is uncorrelated with a regressor, a condition that is required if the OLS estimator is to be consistent. In the context of simultaneous equation systems, if endogenous variables appear as regressors, they will generally be correlated with disturbance terms. Hence in the case of simultaneous equations this test corresponds to a test of the null hypothesis that a regressor is exogenous, when the alternative hypothesis is that the regressor is endogenous. The test that we implement in this exercise is called the Hausman specification test and is due to Jerry A. Hausman [1978].[88]

The subdirectory CHAP10.DAT in your data diskette contains a data file called KLEIN. This data file includes annual time series from 1920 to 1941 for ten variables: YEAR, CN, P, W1, I, KLAG, E, W2, G, and TX. The variable YEAR is the year of observation, and KLAG is the beginning-of-year capital stock, earlier denoted as K_{-1}; all other variables are defined in Section 10.5 of the text.

Note: For this exercise you will also need to use the variables T and W, which were defined and generated in part (a) of Exercise 1.

(a) Suppose that you had become familiar with Klein's Model I and that you knew that in the consumption equation (10.62) the regressors W_t and P_t were specified to be endogenous. Also, you knew that in the investment equation (10.63) the regressor P_t was endogenous and that in the private wage bill equation (10.64) the regressor E_t was endogenous. You understood that because of this endogeneity, these regressors were likely to be correlated with the equation disturbance terms and that as a result, estimation by OLS would result in biased and inconsistent estimates of the structural parameters. Nevertheless, you decided to be lazy and simply use OLS procedures. Run these three OLS regressions, using Klein's annual 1921–1941 data; your results should be identical to those reported in the first column of Table 10.3. Verify this equivalence. Note the residual sum of squares from the consumption equation, and call it SSE_{con}.

(b) Having performed this shameful act, your econometric conscience begins to bother you, and to eliminate the excessive burden of this guilt, you decide to test for the validity of your OLS procedure. You read about Hausman's specification test, and you realize that it amounts to testing whether OLS and 2SLS coefficient estimates on the "suspicious" regressors in each equation are identical. You implement Hausman's test as follows. You begin by running three additional regressions, one for each of the "suspicious" regressors, using the 1921–1941 annual data. First you regress W_t on the set of exogenous and predetermined variables (in this case this is the same as an unrestricted reduced form OLS estimation) consisting of a constant, W_2, TX, G, T, P_{-1}, KLAG, and E_{-1}, you retrieve the fitted values from this regression, and you call them W_{fit}. Next, you run an OLS regression of P_t on this same set of exogenous and predetermined variables, you retrieve the fitted values from this regression, and you call them P_{fit}. Finally, you run another OLS regression, this time regressing E_t on the identical set of exogenous and predetermined variables, you retrieve the fitted values from this regression, and you call them E_{fit}. The three series of fitted value variables, W_{fit}, P_{fit}, and E_{fit}, are now used in expanded regression equations.

(c) Next you run three expanded OLS regressions. For the consumption structural equation you add to Eq. (10.62) the regressors W_{fit} and E_{fit}, and you estimate the expanded equation by OLS, denoting the residual sum of squares SSE_{unc}. Next you estimate by OLS an expanded investment structural equation, in which you add to Eq. (10.63) the regressor P_{fit}. Third, run an OLS regression of an expanded private wage bill structural equation, in which you add to Eq. (10.64) the regressor E_{fit}.

(d) To test the null hypothesis that W and P are exogenous in the consumption equation, test the joint null hypothesis that the coefficients on the W_{fit} and P_{fit} variables are simultaneously equal to zero. You can do this by computing the statistic $[(\text{SSE}_{\text{con}} - \text{SSE}_{\text{unc}})/\text{SSE}_{\text{unc}}]*[(21 - 6)/2]$, where SSE_{con} and SSE_{unc} were computed in parts (b) and (c) and the term in the second set of square brackets reflects degrees of freedom in the unconstrained regression (21 − 6) divided by the number of independent parameter restrictions being tested, namely, 2. Multiply this F-statistic by the number of restrictions (here, two), and you obtain a test statistic whose large sample distribution approximates a χ^2 distribution with two degrees of freedom. Then compare this test statistic to the χ^2 critical value for two degrees of freedom, using a reasonable level of significance. Do you reject or do you not reject the null hypothesis that W and P are exogenous in the consumption equation? Why? What are the implications for obtaining consistent estimates of the structural parameters?

(e) To test the null hypothesis that P is exogenous in the investment equation, simply test whether the coefficient on P_{fit} in the second regression of part (c) is equal to zero, using an asymptotic t-test procedure at a predetermined reasonable confidence level. Similarly, to test the null hypothesis that E is exogenous in the private wage bill equation, simply test whether the coefficient on E_{fit} from the last regression in part (c) is significantly different from zero, using an asymptotic t-test procedure and a reasonable level of significance. Comment on your test results. Was your guilt from estimating by OLS well deserved, or were you lucky? Why?

(f) Finally, provide some intuition on why the Hausman specification test procedure that you undertook in parts (a) through (e) is in fact a test for exogeneity. If you have problems with the interpretation of your test procedure, consult your econometric theory textbook or the Hausman [1978] article for further details.

EXERCISE 5: Testing for Serial Correlation in the Lucas-Rapping Model

The purpose of this exercise is to engage you in testing for various types of serial correlation in the Lucas-Rapping simultaneous equations model, a model whose equations have lagged dependent variables as regressors. The tests that you employ include Durbin's m-test, as well as the Breusch-Godfrey test for serial correlation. Both test statistic procedures are valid when the list of regressors includes lagged dependent variables, unlike the traditional Durbin-Watson test statistic. See your econometrics theory text for further details.[89]

In your data diskette subdirectory CHAP10.DAT there is a data file called LUCAS containing 1929–1965 annual time series data on nine variables. This data set was described at the beginning of Exercise 2.

Note: To do this exercise, it will be necessary for you to perform the data transformations on the Lucas data set that are described at the beginning of Exercise 2. Make sure the appropriate x and y variables have been generated.

(a) The two unrestricted reduced form equations underlying the Lucas-Rapping model are given in Eq. (10.33), and estimated versions of them are in Eqs. (10.41) and (10.42). First, using OLS and data from 1930 to 1965 (you lose one observation because of the presence of lagged dependent variables), run a regression of y_3 on a constant, y_3 lagged, x_1, x_2, x_3, y_2 lagged, x_4 and y_1 lagged. Your results should be quite close to the Lucas-Rapping findings reported in Eq. (10.41), except for the intercept term. Retrieve the residuals from this regression and call them RESY3. Next run an OLS regression of y_1 on the same set of regressors; except for the constant term, your results should be very close to those of Lucas and Rapping, reproduced in Eq. (10.42). Retrieve the residuals from this regression and call them RESY1. (A question for the curious: Note that the standard error estimates reported by Lucas and Rapping, reproduced in Eqs. (10.41)–(10.42), are the same for each regressor in both equations. Should this be the case, is it coincidental, or is it a computational error? Why?)

(b) Notice that the lagged dependent variable appears in each of these reduced form equations and that if there were first-order autocorrelation, estimation by OLS would be biased and inconsistent. Furthermore, in this circumstance the traditional Durbin-Watson test statistic is inappropriate. Why is this the case? One possibility in testing for first-order autoregressive disturbances is to use Durbin's m-statistic (see Durbin [1970]). To do this, run two more regressions, one based on each reduced form equation, this time from 1931 to 1965. First, run an OLS regression of RESY3 on the same set of regressors as in part (a) plus the lagged residual RESY3. To test the null hypothesis that $\rho = 0$ in an AR(1) process, compute the ratio of the estimated coefficient on the RESY3 regressor to its standard error; in large samples this ratio is distributed as a standard normal variable. Using a 5% level of significance, test whether this coefficient equals zero. Second, run another OLS regression, this one having RESY1 as the dependent variable, the same set of regressors as in part (a) but with RESY1 lagged as an additional regressor. Using the 95% significance level, test whether $\rho = 0$ in the employment reduced form equation by computing the ratio of the estimated coefficient on the lagged RESY1 regressor to its estimated standard error, and compare this test statistic to the critical value from a normal distribution table. For either of these equations, what do you conclude concerning the presence of an AR(1) disturbance process?

(c) Trevor S. Breusch [1978] and Leslie G. Godfrey [1978] have generalized the Durbin m-test to testing for autoregressive processes of order q—AR(q)—where $q \geqslant 1$. All that one need do is run an OLS regression as in part (a), retrieve the residuals, and then run another OLS regression of the residuals on the same set of regressors as in the original OLS regression (deleting q additional observations at the beginning of the sample) plus q lagged residuals. The test of the null hypothesis that $\rho_1 = \rho_2 \cdots = p_q = 0$ is accomplished by testing whether the coefficients on the q lagged residual terms simultaneously equal zero, using the traditional analysis-of-variance F-test procedure; in large samples, the test statistic computed as $q*F$ is distributed as a χ^2 random variable. Using the Breusch-Godfrey procedure in each of the two reduced form equations, set $q = 2$ and test for the absence of autocorrelation. (*Note:* To do the analysis-of-variance F-test, it will be necessary to do two regressions over the same sample of observations, one a constrained one with the lagged residuals omitted as regressors and the other an unconstrained one in which the lagged residuals are included as regressors.) Do disturbances in either reduced form equation appear to follow an AR(2) process? Why or why not? It is worth noting that the Breusch-Godfrey test procedure is the same for an AR(q) process as for a moving average process of order q—MA(q). Recall also that with the adaptive expectations framework, one frequently obtains an MA(1) error structure. With these comments in mind, interpret the results that you have just obtained on testing for second-order serial correlation in the reduced form equations of the Lucas-Rapping model.

(d) The Breusch-Godfrey test can also be implemented in the context of structural simultaneous equations, provided that an instrumental variable procedure is used at each of the steps. Begin by assuming the absence of serial correlation, and using 1930–1965 annual data, estimate the following three equations by 2SLS:

(i) y_1 on a constant, y_3, y_3 lagged, x_1, and y_1 lagged;
(ii) y_2 on a constant, y_4, y_2 lagged, and x_4;
(iii) U on a constant, x_1, y_5, and U lagged.

In each equation, treat the following variables as exogenous or predetermined: a constant vector, current values of x_1, x_2, x_3, and x_4, and once-lagged values of y_1, y_2, and y_3. Your 2SLS parameter estimates should be very close to those of Lucas-Rapping, reproduced in Eqs. (10.36)–(10.38). (*Note:* Reasons why your 2SLS standard error and residual statistics do not replicate those of Lucas and Rapping are investigated in Exercise 2.) Retrieve the vector of residuals from these three 2SLS regressions, and call them RES1, RES2, and RES3, respectively.

Using data from 1931 to 1965, for the labor supply structural equation run a 2SLS regression of RES1 on a constant and the same regressors as in (i) and with RES1 once-lagged added as a regressor; however, to ensure consistency of parameter estimates under the alternative hypothesis, add to the list of instruments once-lagged values of x_1, x_2, x_3, and x_4, and twice-lagged values of y_1, y_2, and y_3. Test for the absence of a first-order autoregresive process by testing whether the coefficient on the lagged RES1 variable is equal to zero (use a large sample, normal distribution critical value).

For the labor demand equation, again use data from 1931 to 1965 and run a 2SLS regression of RES2 on the same regressors as in (ii) with the lagged RES2 variable added as a right-hand variable; add to the list of instruments the additional lagged variables, as in the previous paragraph. Test for the absence of an AR(1) process in this equation by testing whether the estimated coefficient on the lagged RES2 variable equals zero.

Finally, for the inverted Phillips curve equation, use 1931–1965 annual data and run a 2SLS regression (using the larger list of instrumental variables, as in the previous two paragraphs) of RES3 on the same regressors as in (iii) with the once-lagged RES3 variable added as a regressor. Test whether autocorrelation is absent in the inverted Phillips curve equation by testing whether the coefficient on the lagged RES3 variable is equal to zero.

Were Lucas and Rapping justified in assuming that disturbances in their three structural equations were serially uncorrelated? Why or why not?

EXERCISE 6: The Equivalence of Alternative Estimators in a Just Identified Model

The purpose of this exercise is to have you demonstrate the numerical equivalence of a number of alternative estimators when each of the equations in a model is just identified. To accomplish this, consider a simplified adaptation of Klein's Model I, a model specification that is designed to illustrate numerical relationships rather than to represent "true" structural relationships. Let the economy consist of only a private sector and no government. Consider a three-equation model consisting of a consumption function

$$CN_t = a_0^* + a_1^* Y_t + a_2^* T + u_{1t}^* \quad \textbf{(10.66)}$$

an investment equation

$$I_t = b_0^* + b_1^* Y_t + b_2^* K_{t-1} + u_{2t}^* \quad \textbf{(10.67)}$$

and the identity

$$Y_t = CN_t + I_t \quad \textbf{(10.68)}$$

where variables are defined at the beginning of Exercise 1, $K_{t-1} \equiv$ KLAG, and the u^*'s are serially uncorrelated random disturbances. To obtain estimable structural equations, substitute Eq. (10.68) into Eqs. (10.66) and (10.67), rearrange, and then reparameterize. This process yields the equations

$$CN = a_0 + a_1 I + a_2 T + u_1 \quad \textbf{(10.69)}$$

$$I = b_0 + b_1 C + b_2 \text{KLAG} + u_2 \quad \textbf{(10.70)}$$

where the a's, b's, and u's are functions of the a^*'s, b^*'s and u^*'s and for simplicity the time subscripts have been deleted. Assume that u_1 and u_2 are independently and identically normally distributed disturbance vectors with mean vector zero and nonsingular contemporaneous covariance matrix Σ.

(a) Using the necessary order conditions for identification, verify that each of the equations (10.69) and (10.70) is just identified. Then, using 1920–1941 annual data from the data file KLEIN, estimate the a and b parameters in Eqs. (10.69) and (10.70) by 2SLS, where the list of exogenous variables in each equation consists of a constant vector, T, and KLAG.[90]

(b) Now estimate parameters in Eqs. (10.69) and (10.70) using the 3SLS estimator. Your parameter and standard error estimates should be numerically equivalent to the 2SLS estimates from part (a). Verify that this occurs.[91]

(c) Another possible estimation method is to use equation-by-equation OLS on the reduced form equations, and then work backward to estimate the structural equations. This procedure is feasible whenever each of the structural equations is just identified and is called the method of indirect least squares (ILS). To implement ILS, first solve out analytically for the reduced form equations. In particular, substitute Eq. (10.70) into Eq. (10.69) and rearrange, obtaining

$$CN = \frac{a_0 + a_1 b_0}{1 - a_1 b_1} + \frac{a_1 b_2}{1 - a_1 b_1} \cdot \text{KLAG} + \frac{a_2}{1 - a_1 b_1} \cdot T + \frac{a_1 u_2 + u_1}{1 - a_1 b_1} \tag{10.71}$$

Reparameterize this consumption function reduced form equation as

$$CN = \pi_{10} + \pi_{11} \cdot \text{KLAG} + \pi_{12} \cdot T + v_1 \tag{10.72}$$

where the π's and v_1 are functions of the a's, b's, and u's. In an analogous manner, substitute Eq. (10.69) into Eq. (10.70), collect terms, and rearrange, resulting in the investment reduced form equation

$$I = \frac{b_0 + b_1 a_0}{1 - a_1 b_1} + \frac{b_2}{1 - a_1 b_1} \cdot \text{KLAG} + \frac{b_1 a_2}{1 - a_1 b_1} \cdot T + \frac{b_1 u_1 + u_2}{1 - a_1 b_1} \tag{10.73}$$

and then reparameterize this as

$$I = \pi_{20} + \pi_{21} \cdot \text{KLAG} + \pi_{22} \cdot T + v_2 \tag{10.74}$$

where the π's and v_2 are functions of the a's, b's, and u's. Given the stochastic assumptions on the u's, what is the implied stochastic specification for the v's? How many reduced form parameters can be estimated in the reduced form equations (10.72) and (10.74)? How many structural parameters are there in the structural equations (10.69) and (10.70)? Estimate the reduced form equations (10.72) and (10.74) using equation-by-equation OLS and the 1920–1941 data from the data file KLEIN. Then, using the reduced form parameter estimates and the relations between reduced form and structural parameters in Eqs. (10.71)–(10.74), for example, $b_1 = \pi_{22}/\pi_{12}$, $a_1 = \pi_{11}/\pi_{21}$, obtain ILS estimates of the structural parameters. Compare these ILS estimates to the 2SLS and 3SLS estimates you obtained in parts (a) and (b). They should be numerically equivalent. Are they? What computational problems emerge when you attempt to obtain standard errors of the parameters using the ILS procedure?

(d) It is also possible to estimate parameters in the reduced form equations (10.72) by using the Zellner "seemingly unrelated" equation systems estimation procedure. In this just identified model, what would the relationship be between the Zellner estimator and the equation-by-equation OLS parameter estimates? Why?

(e) What do you conclude concerning parameter equivalence of alternative estimators in models in which each equation is just identified?

EXERCISE 7: Comparing 2SLS, 3SLS, and I3SLS Estimates in an Overidentified Model

The purpose of this exercise is to involve you in estimating and comparing three simultaneous equations estimators—2SLS, 3SLS, and I3SLS. Under traditional stochastic specifications, each of these three estimators generates consistent estimates of the structural parameters, although in large samples, 3SLS and I3SLS are more efficient than 2SLS. The large sample efficiency properties of 3SLS and I3SLS are identical. In small samples, however, the numerical values of the 2SLS, 3SLS, and I3SLS parameter estimates can vary considerably, provided that the model is overidentified. See your econometrics theory text for further discussion and references.

For this exercise, choose either the Klein Model I or the Lucas-Rapping model. As was noted in the text, both models are overidentified. Data for Klein's model are discussed at the beginning of Exercise 1; the data underlying the Lucas-Rapping model are discussed at the beginning of Exercise 2. Given your choice of model, generate the required transformed variables, as discussed at the beginning of Exercise 1 or 2. Note that in both the Klein and Lucas-Rapping models, the presence of once-lagged variables implies that one observation is lost in the estimation. Hence if you choose the Klein model, estimate using data from 1921–1941, and if you choose the Lucas-Rapping model, estimate over the 1930–1965 time period.

For Klein's Model I the relevant structural equations are Eqs. (10.62)–(10.64). For the Lucas-Rapping model, confine your attention to the labor supply equation (10.23) and the labor demand equation (10.25); omit the measured unemployment equation (10.32), since as Lucas and Rapping note, it is essentially implicit from the labor demand and labor supply equations. Finally, in Klein's Model I, treat the regressors W_t, P_t, and E_t as endogenous right-hand variables; in the Lucas-Rapping model, treat $\ln w_t$ as an endogenous right-hand variable. All other right-hand variables in both models should be treated either as exogenous or as predetermined. The list of exogenous and predetermined variables in Klein's Model I is given in Table 10.4; the corresponding list for the Lucas-Rapping model appears in Eqs. (10.41) and (10.42).

(a) Choose either Klein's Model I or the Lucas-Rapping model. Estimate its structural equations (see the above discussion) using the 2SLS estimation method. Compare your results to those reported in the text (in Table 10.3 for Klein's Model I and in Eqs. (10.36) and (10.37) for the Lucas-Rapping model). Retrieve the residuals from your estimated 2SLS equations, and compute the simple contemporaneous correlations among residuals in the equations estimated. Do these contemporaneous correlation coefficients have signs as you expected? Why or why not? Do you think that undertaking system estimation such as 3SLS or I3SLS will change your 2SLS parameter estimates substantially? Why or why not?

(b) Using the same model as was estimated in part (a), estimate the equation system using the 3SLS estimator. Which, if any, of the 2SLS parameter estimates change substantially when you employ the 3SLS estimator? Does this affect your interpretation of the estimated model? Why? Which estimates do you prefer? Why? (You might want to consult your econometric theory textbook on results from Monte Carlo studies that compare the 2SLS and 3SLS estimators in small samples.)

(c) The I3SLS estimator keeps the same set of instruments from one iteration to the next, but it continues iterating until changes in the estimated parameters and the estimated residual covariance matrix from one iteration to the next become arbitrarily small (until their changes become less than some predetermined convergence tolerance level). Using the I3SLS estimation method and the same model as was estimated in parts (a) and (b), estimate parameters of your equation system. Compare the 2SLS, 3SLS, and I3SLS parameter estimates. Which do you prefer, and why? Are the results uniformly consistent with the theoretical inequalities predicted by Klein or by Lucas and Rapping? Discuss.

EXERCISE 8: Maximum Likelihood Structural and Reduced Form Estimation of Klein's Model I

The purpose of this exercise is to engage you in full information maximum likelihood (FIML) estimation of parameters in the three structural equations of Klein's Model I and in maximum likelihood (ML) estimation of parameters in the three implied restricted reduced form equations of this model. On the basis of your hands-on experience you should be able to conclude that you obtain the same estimates of the structural parameters when you estimate either the structure by FIML or the restricted reduced form by ML. You will also perform a test for the validity of the overidentifying restrictions.

The subdirectory CHAP10.DAT in your data diskette contains a data file called KLEIN. This data file includes annual time series from 1920 to 1941 for ten variables: YEAR, CN, P, W1, I, KLAG, E, W2, G, and TX. The variable YEAR is the year of observation, and KLAG is the beginning-of-year capital stock, earlier denoted as K_{-1}; all other variables are defined in Section 10.5 of the text.

Note: For this exercise you will also need to use the variables T, Y, and W, defined and generated in part (a) of Exercise 1.

(a) Assuming that the ϵ are identically and independently joint normally distributed with mean vector zero and constant nonsingular covariance matrix, employ the FIML method to estimate parameters in the three structural equations (10.62)–(10.64) over the 1921–1941 time period, incorporating all the relevant identities in Eq. (10.65). Your parameter and standard error estimates should agree with those reported in the FIML column of Table 10.3. Note the sample maximized log-likelihood value.

(b) Using the identities in Eq. (10.65) and the three structural equations (10.62)–(10.64), solve out analytically the three reduced form equations in which the three endogenous variables CN, I, and W1 are related to the eight exogenous and predetermined variables (see Table 10.4) and the 12 structural parameters. This is tedious but well worth your time. (*Hint:* It is convenient to proceed in three steps. First, use the identities and rewrite Eqs. (10.62)–(10.64) in terms of the parameters, the exogenous variables, the disturbances, and Y. Second, using the identity $Y \equiv CN + I + G - TX$ and the expressions obtained in the first step, express Y as a function of the parameters, exogenous variables, and disturbances. Third, using this expression for Y, substitute back into the three equations from step 1, and collect terms. Incidentally, from step 2 it is possible to compute the government spending impact multiplier as $\partial Y/\partial G = 1/[1 - (\alpha_2 + \beta_1) - \gamma_1(\alpha_1 - \alpha_2 - \beta_1)]$. Verify that this is the case.) Finally, show that since the structural disturbances are identically and independently joint normally distributed with mean zero and constant nonsingular covariance matrix, so too are the reduced form disturbances.

(c) Next, interpret this three-equation restricted reduced form system of equations as a set of nonlinearly restricted equations, in which each of the regressors is either exogenous or predetermined. Estimate structural parameters in this set of restricted "seemingly unrelated" equations using the method of maximum likelihood. Compare your estimates based on this restricted reduced form estimation to the FIML structural estimates of part (a). The estimates should be identical. Why? Also compare the values of the two sample maximized log-likelihoods. Did you find any surprises? Compute the implied restricted reduced form parameters. These estimates should agree with those computed by Arthur S. Goldberger [1964], reproduced in the last three columns of Table 10.4. Finally, what is the estimated value of the government-spending impact multiplier (written out in part (b))? Is this plausible? Why?

(d) To test for the validity of the overidentifying restrictions, next estimate by maximum likelihood the unrestricted reduced form equation system, as in the first three columns of Table 10.4. There are two different yet equivalent ways of estimating this unrestricted reduced form. First, estimate the three unrestricted reduced form equations using equation-by-equation OLS; these estimates should be identical to those reported in the first three columns of Table 10.4. Next, treating the three unrestricted reduced form equations as a set of "seemingly unrelated" equations, estimate parameters in the three equations using the method of maximum likelihood. Verify that these ML estimates are numerically identical to the equation-by-equation unrestricted reduced form estimates. Why is this case? (In some cases the ML procedures provide asymptotic standard error estimates, which tend to be smaller than the equation-by-equation OLS unbiased estimates. Is this the case with your ML software?) Note the value of the sample maximized log-likelihood function from this unrestricted reduced form estimation.

(e) Finally, compute the difference between the sample maximized log-likelihood value from the unrestricted reduced form of part (d) and that from the restricted reduced form of part (c); multiply this difference by 2. This is a likelihood ratio test statistic, and it should be compared to the chi-square critical value given a predetermined level of significance. To compute the appropriate degrees of freedom for the critical value, note that in the unrestricted reduced form estimation there are 24 free parameters (eight in each of the three equations), while in the restricted reduced form estimation there are only 12 free structural parameters; hence the degrees of freedom are 24 − 12, or 12. Do you reject or not reject the overidentifying restrictions in Klein's Model I? Interpret your results.

(f) (Optional) Suppose you estimated by maximum likelihood, instead of the three reduced form equations having CN, I, and W1 as dependent variables, three other reduced form equations with different endogenous variables from Klein's Model I as dependent variables, but having the same set of regressors as in part (c). Under what conditions would the test for overidentifying restrictions from part (e) yield the same likelihood ratio test statistic? Why?

EXERCISE 9: Estimation of a Structurally Recursive Model

The purpose of this exercise is to help you understand relations among alternative estimators in the special case of structurally recursive models. A model is said to be structurally recursive if its Jacobian can be triangularized. In this exercise you will first verify that Klein's Model I is not recursive, then you will consider an alternative model put forward by Klein [1953, Chapter III, Part 2] and demonstrate that it is recursive, and finally, you will implement and compare alternative estimation procedures.

The subdirectory CHAP10.DAT in your data diskette contains a data file called KLEIN. This data file includes annual time series from 1920 to 1941 for ten variables: YEAR, CN, P, W1, I, KLAG, E, W2, G, and TX. The variable YEAR is the year of observation, and KLAG is the beginning-of-year capital stock, denoted earlier as K_{-1}; all other variables are defined in Section 10.5 of the text.

Note: For this exercise you will also need to use the variables W and Y, which were defined and generated in part (a) of Exercise 1.

(a) Begin by reconsidering Klein's Model I of the U.S. economy, summarized in Eqs. (10.62)–(10.64). Rewrite each of the three equations so that the disturbance term ϵ_i is the left-hand variable, $i = 1, 2, 3$, take partial derivatives of the ϵ_i with respect to each of the endogenous variables CN, I, and W1, and using these derivatives, form the Jacobian transformation matrix. Note first that since this model is linear in the endogenous variables, the Jacobian is constant and does not vary by observation. Note also that the diagonal elements of this Jacobian are unity, reflecting the implicit normalization concerning which endogenous variable in each equation is chosen as the dependent variable. If a matrix such as this were triangular or could be triangularized, its determinant would be unity. Demonstrate that this Jacobian cannot be triangularized by calculating its determinant.

(b) Next consider a variant of Model I introduced and estimated by Klein [1953, Chapter III]. Klein modified his consumption equation (10.62) by replacing W_1 with Y, excluding current and lagged π, and including lagged Y,

$$CN_t = \alpha_0 + \alpha_1 Y_t + \alpha_2 Y_{t-1} + \epsilon_{1t} \tag{10.62'}$$

He then altered his investment equation (10.63) by including only lagged (and not current) profits,

$$I_t = \beta_0 + \beta_1 P_{t-1} + \beta_2 K_{t-1} + \epsilon_{2t} \tag{10.63'}$$

and deleted the $T \equiv$ YEAR $-$ 1931 variable from his private wage bill equation (10.64):

$$W_{1t} = \gamma_0 + \gamma_1(Y + TX - W_2)_t + \gamma_2(Y + TX - W_2)_{t-1} + \epsilon_{3t} \tag{10.64'}$$

Note that in Eq. (10.64′) the variable $(Y + TX - W_2)$ was defined earlier as being equal to E. Klein then added three identities to this model:

$$\begin{aligned} &\text{Total product:} && CN_t + I_t + G_t \equiv Y_t + TX_t \\ &\text{National income:} && W_{1t} + W_{2t} + P_t \equiv Y_t \\ &\text{Capital stock:} && K_t \equiv I_t + K_{t-1} \end{aligned} \tag{10.65'}$$

where all variables are defined as in the text. The six endogenous variables in this equation system are therefore C, Y, I, P, W_1, and K; the exogenous variables are W_2, TX, and G; and the predetermined variables include the exogenous and endogenous lagged variables plus the exogenous current variables.

Begin by demonstrating that this model is structurally recursive. First rewrite Eqs. (10.62′)–(10.64′) so that in each equation the disturbance term ϵ_{it} is the left-hand variable, $i = 1, 2, 3$, and then take partial derivatives of the ϵ_{it} with respect to the endogenous variables CN_t, I_t, and W_{1t}. Then form the 3×3 Jacobian transformation matrix whose top row consists of the partial derivatives of ϵ_2 with respect to I, CN and W_1, respectively, whose second row contains the partial derivatives of ϵ_1 with respect to I, CN and W_1, respectively, and whose bottom row is comprised of the partial derivatives ϵ_3 with respect to I, CN, and W_1, respectively. Verify that this Jacobian matrix is triangular and that its determinant is unity at all observations.[92]

(c) Surprisingly, Klein was able to estimate the parameters of this model consistently using successive least squares procedures, even when Σ, the contemporaneous disturbance covariance matrix, was nondiagonal. To do this, first notice that in Eq. (10.62′), each of the regressors is exogenous or predetermined. Therefore estimate Eq. (10.62′) by OLS using Klein's 1921–1941 annual data, and retrieve the fitted values, calling them I_{fit}. What are the properties of these OLS estimates? Next substitute the first identity in Eq. (10.65′) into Eq. (10.62′), collect terms, and rearrange. This yields

$$Y_t = [1/(1 - \alpha_1)] \cdot [\alpha_0 + \alpha_2 Y_{t-1} + J_t + \epsilon_{1t}]$$

$$\text{where} \qquad J_t \equiv (I - TX + G)_t \tag{10.75}$$

Generate a new variable called $J_{\text{fit},t}$ defined as $J_{\text{fit},t} \equiv (I_{\text{fit}} - TX + G)_t$, where I_{fit} is the fitted value series that you retrieved earlier. Replace J_t with $J_{\text{fit},t}$ in Eq. (10.75), and noting that this equation is linear in the variables and that each of its regressors is predetermined, exogenous, or a linear function of predetermined and exogenous variables, estimate its parameters by OLS, using 1921–1941 data. Retrieve the fitted values from this OLS regression, and call them Y_{fit}. What are the properties of OLS estimates in this equation? Finally, recalling that E_t was earlier defined as $E_t \equiv Y_t + TX_t - W_{2t}$, generate a new variable $E_{\text{fit},t}$ defined as $E_{\text{fit},t} \equiv Y_{\text{fit},t} + TX_t - W_{2t}$, and then estimate by OLS parameters in the modified equation (10.64′), that is, regress W_1 on a constant, $E_{\text{fit},t}$ and E_{t-1}. What are the properties of this OLS estimator? Why?

(d) Klein argued that if Σ, the contemporaneous disturbance covariance matrix of the ϵ's, were diagonal, this method of successive least squares would provide maximum likelihood estimates of the structural parameters in this structurally recursive model. Do you agree? Why or why not? (*Hint:* Write out the likelihood function, and note what happens to the Jacobian and contemporaneous disturbance covariance matrix terms.) In what way is this method of successive least squares an instrumental variable method? Is it the same as equation-by-equation 2SLS? Why or why not? Incidentally, this method of successive least squares can easily be generalized to equation systems that are block recursive. For further discussion of recursive systems, see the early paper by Ragnar Bentzel and Herman Wold [1946] and the extension to block recursive systems by Franklin M. Fisher [1965].

(e) In the more general case in which the Σ matrix is not diagonal, does the method of successive least squares provide consistent estimates of the parameters? Why? Now, assuming that Σ is nondiagonal, employ the FIML estimation method and estimate parameters in Eqs. (10.62′)–(10.64′), taking account of the identities in Eq. (10.65′). What are properties of these FIML estimates? Do they differ substantially from the successive least squares estimates? Interpret your findings.

(f) (Optional) Because the model of this exercise is structurally recursive, the determinant of the Jacobian matrix is unity, and its logarithm is zero, implying that the Jacobian term drops out of the log-likelihood function. This implies also that parameter estimates numerically identical to FIML can be obtained by using the iterative Zellner-efficient (IZEF) estimator. Why is this the case? Verify this numerically by estimating the equation system (10.62′)–(10.64′) using the IZEF estimator. According to Ingmar Prucha [1987], however, the standard error estimates from the IZEF estimator are not correct and are never larger than (and usually are less than) the correct FIML standard error estimates in a structurally recursive model. Are Prucha's arguments upheld by your data? Why or why not? Interpret the difference between the IZEF and FIML asymptotic standard error estimates.

EXERCISE 10: Replicating the Estimation of Taylor's REH Model

The purpose of this exercise is to implement the maximum likelihood estimation procedure that Taylor used in estimating parameters of his two-equation reduced form model. Although the conceptual basis of this ML estimation procedure is relatively straightforward (see the discussion in Section 10.4 of this chapter), the computational procedure is a bit messy. We will do our best to help you replicate Taylor's ML procedure on the appropriately transformed data in his two reduced form equations.

Note: To do this exercise, it will first be necessary to construct the variables used by Taylor. Procedures for doing this are given in Exercise 3, part (a). Make sure the required variables are generated and available to you.

(a) First, estimate Taylor's two-equation reduced form model (10.52) and (10.53) by ML, assuming that disturbances are serially independent, that is, assume that $\theta_1 = \theta_2 = 0$. To do this, using data from 1953:3 to 1975:3, employ the iterative Zellner-efficient (ML) estimator and estimate parameters in Eqs. (10.52) and (10.53), incorporating the cross-equation restrictions. There are nine free parameters in this model. If this model is empirically valid, the cross-equation restrictions should be consistent with the data. To test these cross-equation overidentifying restrictions, estimate parameters in the same two equations, but allow the parameters on each regressor (including the constant term) to differ in the two equations; this involves estimation of 14 parameters, seven in each equation. Using the likelihood ratio test procedure and a reasonable level of significance, test the validity of these five parameter restrictions. Interpret your results.

(b) Next, write up a computer code that appropriately transforms each of the variables in the output equations (as in Eq. (10.58)) as a function of ϕ_1 and each of the variables in the inflation equation (see Eq. (10.59)) as a function of ϕ_2. Place this data transformation subroutine into a "DO" loop, where the ϕ_1 and ϕ_2 are explicit functions of θ_1 and θ_2, as noted underneath Eq. (10.59). Begin with a coarse 2×2 grid search, where each of θ_1 and θ_2 takes on values of -0.99, -0.66, -0.33, 0, 0.33, 0.66, and 0.99, and for each element of this two-dimensional grid, estimate parameters of the two equations (10.52) and (10.53), using the iterative-Zellner estimator and Eq. (10.57) to compute Eq. (10.54). This is the iterative MDE procedure used by Taylor. Compare values of the minimum value of Eq. (10.54) given alternative values of the two-dimensional grid, and then refine your grid search procedure by redoing the grid search in the apparent minimum value region of Eq. (10.54). How closely do your results match those of Taylor, reproduced in Eqs. (10.60) and (10.61)? Do you agree with Taylor's interpretation of his (conditional) standard error estimates? Why or why not?

(c) Finally, to test the overidentifying, cross-equation restrictions implied by Taylor's REH model, follow the same procedures as in part (b), but do not impose any cross-equation parameter restrictions. Using a likelihood ratio test procedure, test the empirical validity of these five restrictions. Do your findings agree with those of Taylor, discussed near the end of Section 10.4? Interpret your findings and Taylor's discussion of them. Do you believe in the REH for this model? Why or why not?

CHAPTER NOTES

1. For an early discussion of aggregation issues and the microeconomic foundations of macroeconometric models, see Lawrence R. Klein [1946]. The issues raised by Klein continue to be controversial. For more recent developments, see Thomas M. Stoker [1986a, b] and the references cited therein.
2. Although larger models may be more realistic and preferable as descriptions of reality, our instructional goals can be fulfilled more easily by using the smaller macroeconometric models.
3. Named from the classic article by A. William Phillips [1958].
4. See Klein [1950]. The first macroeconometric model of the U.S. economy is that by Jan Tinbergen [1939].
5. Detailed data on U.S. government household surveys are found in two U.S. Bureau of Labor Statistics publications, an occasional one called the *Handbook of Labor Statistics*, Technical Notes, and the monthly publication called *Employment and Earnings*. The discussion that follows is based in large part on Daniel Hamermesh and Albert Rees [1988], Chapter 1.

6. These data are annual. A number of important measurement issues are involved in constructing data on month-to-month changes in the seasonally adjusted unemployment rate. These issues are discussed by, among others, Lawrence H. Summers [1981], Jerry A. Hausman and Mark W. Watson [1985], and Peter Burridge and Kenneth F. Wallis [1985].
7. There is a substantial literature on both hidden unemployment and labor hoarding and their implications for the interpretation of measured unemployment rates. For a brief survey and references, see Jim Taylor [1970].
8. Phillips [1958, p. 283.]
9. Ibid.
10. Ibid.
11. Apparently, these data breaks were chosen on the basis of changes in data sources and data construction procedures, although the first break corresponds roughly with the beginning of World War I.
12. Phillips [1958, p. 290.]
13. This sequence is consistent with Phillips's own description of his procedure [1958, p. 290]. However, Meghnad Desai [1975] has reported that when he employed this procedure, he was unable to replicate Phillips's original findings. But Christopher L. Gilbert [1976] has pointed out that if one reverses the procedure—first choosing the parameter α by graphical inspection and next estimating log β and γ using linear least squares—then Phillips's results can be replicated exactly.
14. Gilbert's estimated asymptotic standard error of γ—the coefficient of the unemployment rate variable—is 0.3178, implying an asymptotic t-statistic of 4.35. The equation R^2 is 0.6828, but there is some evidence of autocorrelation, since the Durbin-Watson test statistic is only 0.7775. For another discussion of Phillips's original estimation, see Meghnad Desai [1975].
15. Phillips [1958, p. 299].
16. Irving Fisher [1926]. Other very closely related analyses relating wage rate changes to unemployment rates include Lawrence R. Klein and Arthur S. Goldberger [1955, pp. 18–19], and Bent Hansen and Gösta Rehn [1956]. Also see Klein [1950].
17. Ibid., p. 790.
18. Although Fisher acknowledged the possibility of simultaneity, he explicitly argued that the dominant causality ran from price inflation to employment. For example, Fisher [1926, p. 792] concluded that "what the charts show is largely, if not mostly, a genuine and straightforward causal relationship; that the ups and downs of employment are the effects, in large measure, of the rises and falls of prices, due in turn to the inflation and deflation of money and credit."
19. See, for example, Frank R. Brechling [1968], who argues that markups and average labor productivity tend to vary over the business cycle and generally are not constant.
20. Many of the earliest Phillips curve studies are referenced in Edmund S. Phelps [1968, 1970]. An extensive survey of research to 1975 is presented in David E. W. Laidler and J. Michael Parkin [1975].
21. Samuelson and Solow [1960]. Portions of this are reprinted in Samuelson and Solow [1965].
22. Ibid., p. 189.
23. Solow [1979, p. 39.]
24. Ibid., p. 193.

25. The t-statistic on the $\hat{u}$ variable can be computed indirectly as the square root of the traditional analysis-of-variance F-statistic based on the two R^2 measures. Specifically, in this case the relative change in R^2 times the degrees of freedom adjustment gives us an F-statistic with 1 and 48 degrees of freedom, $F = [(0.82 - 0.64)/0.82]*48 = 10.536$. The square root of this, 3.246, is a t-statistic with 48 degrees of freedom.
26. A related framework was presented much earlier by Lord Beveridge, in which the number of new hires is related to the number of vacancies and the number of people unemployed. For a discussion of Beveridge and Phillips curves, see Peter A. Diamond and Olivier Jean Blanchard [1989a, b].
27. Aggregation issues have been considered in further detail, both theoretically and empirically, by G. Christopher Archibald [1969]; a more detailed analysis is given in Archibald, Robyn Kemmis, and J. W. Perkins [1974].
28. Lipsey [1960, p. 19.].
29. Similar results based on U.S. data were reported several years later by George L. Perry [1964].
30. Lipsey [1960, p. 30].
31. For a more detailed discussion of this search process, see Charles C. Holt [1971].
32. Information on gross flows of workers in the United States is based on the monthly *Current Population Survey* of the Census Bureau. It is widely believed that measurement errors lead to an upward bias in the raw data on gross flows. Various adjustments have been suggested to eliminate the bias. The 7 million number cited in the text refers to gross flows as adjusted by Abowd and Zellner. Using a different method of adjustment, James Poterba and Lawrence Summers [1986] have reported an estimate of gross flows equal to only 60% of the Abowd-Zellner estimates.
33. On this, see, for example, Roger E. Brinner [1977] and Robert E. Hall [1980].
34. Some critics of the natural rate hypothesis argue that the time path response of unemployment to inflation surprises is asymmetric and that unemployment increases more slowly in response to negative inflation surprises than it decreases in response to positive inflation shocks; on this, see, for example, Robert J. Gordon [1985].
35. Two early prominent attempts to estimate this coefficient were by Robert M. Solow [1969] and Robert J. Gordon [1970]. They each assumed that expectations were formed adaptively and resulted in estimates of about 0.5. However, when Thomas J. Sargent [1973] and Bennett T. McCallum [1976] allowed expectations to be rational, estimates of this coefficient became very close to 1.0.
36. We do not consider here the possible sample selectivity problem resulting from the fact that "policy-on" might in fact be endogenous. Although the context is different, sample selectivity issues are discussed in detail in Chapter 11.
37. Recall that 2SLS is not always preferable to OLS, particularly in small samples, when 2SLS and other consistent estimators often have large finite sample bias. See your econometrics theory textbook for further details.
38. Wallis [1971, p. 308].
39. Lipsey and Parkin [1970, p. 127].
40. Ibid., p. 127.
41. Ibid., p. 115.
42. Wallis [1971, p. 306]. Wallis also raises other issues concerning model specifica-

tion and the treatment of autocorrelation. Identification issues in the context of a more general autoregressive specification are dealt with in detail by Desai [1976, Chapter 7].

43. As the Lucas and Rapping [1970] reference indicates, except for material in Appendix 2, the 1970 chapter is the same as that which appeared in the September/October 1969 issue of the *Journal of Political Economy,* Vol. 77, No. 5, pp. 721–754. Another closely related paper is Lucas and Rapping [1969].
44. Lucas and Rapping [1970, p. 267].
45. Ibid., p. 268.
46. In their footnote 15, Lucas and Rapping [1970, p. 268] note that for this serial independence to occur, the disturbance terms originally appended to Eqs. (10.20) and (10.21) would have been serially correlated and that the subsequent Koyck transformation would have broken this dependence.
47. Ibid., p. 270.
48. Further details on the CES production function and its estimation are given in Chapter 9.
49. Lucas and Rapping [1970, pp. 273–274].
50. Further discussion of the discouraged worker effect is found in Chapter 11, Section 11.2.C.
51. Lucas and Rapping [1970, p. 282].
52. Ibid., p. 278.
53. In particular, the important article by James M. Durbin did not appear until 1970, and early versions of the Lucas-Rapping paper were already circulating in 1969.
54. On related grounds, Lucas also rejected a generalization of the adaptive scheme developed by Dale W. Jorgenson [1966]. Incidentally, although Jorgenson's generalization is called a rational distributed lag, the word "rational" refers to a mathematical property, not to rational decision making on the part of economic agents; therefore Jorgenson's specification should not be identified with the rational expectations hypothesis.
55. See, for example, Robert E. Hall and John B. Taylor [1988, pp. 16–17].
56. See, for example, Stanley Fischer [1977] and John B. Taylor [1980]. In response, Lucas and Sargent [1978] suggest that the length of wage contracts might be endogenous.
57. Franklin M. Fisher [1970, p. 113].
58. Modigliani [1977, p. 6].
59. An interesting line of research that we will not have time to discuss is one that attempts to quantify the flexibility of wages, prices, and interest rates and economic agents' expectations of these variables; this literature also tests for the neutrality of money. See studies by, among others, Robert J. Barro [1977, 1978], Robert E. Lucas, Jr. [1980], Bennett T. McCallum [1979a], Salih Neftci and Thomas J. Sargent [1978], Sargent [1976], Christopher A. Sims [1980], and Steven J. Turnovsky and Michael L. Wachter [1972].
60. The closely related term "noninflationary rate of unemployment" was coined by Franco Modigliani and Lucas Papademos [1975] and was defined (p. 142) "as a rate such that, as long as unemployment is above it, inflation can be expected to decline."
61. See, for example, George L. Perry [1970] and Franco Modigliani and Lucas Papademos [1975].
62. See, for example, Robert J. Gordon [1980, 1982a] and James Tobin [1980].

63. See, for example, Robert M. Coen and Bert G. Hickman [1987], Robert J. Gordon [1982b, 1985, 1988b], and George L. Perry [1975].
64. Okun [1980, p. 166]. The words in brackets have been added for clarification.
65. A further discussion of staggered contracts is found in Taylor [1980].
66. On this, see Walter Oberhofer and Jan Kmenta [1974].
67. In this context, the 3SLS estimator can have a special interpretation if one assumes that the disturbance terms reflect only the random errors in expectations, that is, the differences between expectations and realizations. Use of the 3SLS estimator in this context ensures that the residuals are orthogonal to any regressor, including in particular the expectation variables. Therefore it is consistent with the REH in that it employs all the available information and any expectational "mistakes" are uncorrelated with the available information set. For a further theoretical discussion, see Lars P. Hansen and Kenneth Singleton [1982], and for an empirical implementation, see Robert S. Pindyck and Julio J. Rotemberg [1983]. For a discussion of FIML estimation in the context of vector autoregressive error structures, see David F. Hendry [1971].
68. For a discussion relating these and other alternative fitting criteria, see Arthur S. Goldberger [1970].
69. Notice that ϕ_1 and ϕ_2 depend not only on θ_1 and θ_2, but also on γ_1 and β_5. As was stated earlier, however, θ_1 and θ_2 are the only two free parameters in θ, and since they appear nowhere else in the model, they are totally unrestricted. In practice, therefore, Taylor's method involves use of a two-dimensional grid search for ϕ_1 and ϕ_2, and then computes the implicit corresponding grid values for θ_1 and θ_2 as $\theta_1 = \phi_1 - \beta_5\phi_2$ and $\theta_2 = \phi_2 - \gamma_1\phi_1$. Further details on Taylor's estimation procedure are discussed in Exercise 10 of this chapter.
70. Taylor [1979, p. 1275, fn. 9].
71. Examples of partly rational models include Rudiger Dornbusch [1976], Ray C. Fair [1979], and Olivier J. Blanchard [1981].
72. For a summary survey of the specification and estimation of macroeconometric models to the mid-1960s, see Marc Nerlove [1966].
73. Klein's Model II was a small just identified model, designed to illustrate indirect least squares procedures, while Model III was a larger 12-equation model.
74. Tinbergen's first macroeconometric model was a 24-equation model of the Dutch economy, published in Dutch in 1936, and was translated into English in Tinbergen [1959]. Tinbergen also constructed and estimated a similarly sized model of the U.S. economy in 1939. In both models, each of the stochastic equations was estimated by ordinary least squares. For a discussion of Tinbergen's contributions, see, among others, Roy J. Epstein [1987] and A. J. Hughes Hallett [1989].
75. In personal correspondence, Klein has noted that Model I should have been specified in nominal, not real terms. "That would, however, make the system nonlinear, which we were not prepared to do, given the hardware of the 1940's."
76. Klein [1950, p. 63]. The Marxian derivation is discussed in Klein [1947].
77. Klein [1950, p. 62].
78. The G_t variable includes net foreign demand, defined as exports minus imports. To satisfy accounting identities in Eqs. (10.65), it also includes the government wage bill W_{2t}, and in this way the G series differs slightly from that given by Henri Theil [1971, p. 456].
79. The 2SLS estimator was developed independently by Henri Theil [1958, pp. 336–338] and by Robert L. Basmann [1957].

80. Development of the 3SLS estimator is due to Arnold Zellner and Henri Theil [1962].
81. The FIML estimator is originally due to Trygve Haavelmo [1943] and Henry B. Mann and Abraham Wald [1943], but its practical development is generally attributed to the Cowles Commission research team; see in particular Tjalling C. Koopmans and William C. Hood [1953], who developed computational algorithms.
82. I3SLS is a natural generalization of 3SLS, but its asymptotic properties are generally identical to 3SLS; for a discussion, see Albert Madansky [1964]. In the case of singular equation systems, however, I3SLS estimates can be invariant to a number of alternative specifications, unlike 3SLS; see Chapter 9 of this book for further discussion.
83. Other estimators have also been proposed but, for reasons of parsimony, are not discussed here. See, for example, Arnold Zellner and Soo-Bin Park [1979] for minimum expected loss estimation of Klein's Model I.
84. The absence of serial correlation in an investment equation is a relatively rare occurrence; see Chapter 6 for further discussion.
85. You should be aware of the fact that in finite samples, the 2SLS estimator is not always preferred. Moreover, in some cases the moments of the 2SLS estimator are not even well defined. For a discussion and references, see Takamitsu Sawa [1972].
86. Note that to avoid perfect multicollinearity among regressors in this expanded list of instruments, the lagged constant term and T_{-1} are not included. All other instruments are, however, lagged once and then included in the expanded instrument list for first-stage estimation.
87. For a compact, introductory discussion of the econometric issues that are involved in estimating models with rational and adaptive expectations, see G. S. Maddala [1988, Chapter 10].
88. For earlier, related discussions, see James M. Durbin [1954] and De-Min Wu [1973].
89. The classic articles in this context include James M. Durbin [1970], Trevor S. Breusch [1978], and Leslie G. Godfrey [1978].
90. Note that to do this, you will first need to generate the T variable, which you do at the beginning of Exercise 1.
91. In some computer software programs the 3SLS estimated standard errors are not adjusted by a degrees of freedom term, and in such cases the 2SLS and 3SLS estimated standard errors may differ. Check your results to determine whether this is the case with your software program.
92. See Klein [1953, p. 112] for further discussion.

CHAPTER REFERENCES

Abowd, John and Arnold Zellner [1985], "Estimating Gross Labor Force Flows," *Journal of Economic and Business Statistics*, 3:3, July, 254–293.

Altonji, Joseph G. [1982], "The Intertemporal Substitution Model of Labour Market Fluctuations: An Empirical Analysis," *Review of Economic Studies*, Special Issue on Unemployment, 49, 783–824.

Archibald, G. Christopher [1969], "The Phillips Curve and the Distribution of Unemployment," *American Economic Review*, 59:2, May, 124–134.

Archibald, G. Christopher, Robyn Kemmis, and J. W. Perkins [1974], "Excess Demand for Labour, Unemployment and the Phillips Curve: A Theoretical and Empirical Study," Chapter 5 in David E. Laider and David L. Purdy, eds., *Inflation and Labour Markets*, Manchester, England: Manchester University Press, pp. 109–163.

Ashenfelter, Orley and David Card [1982], "Time Series Representations of Economic Variables and Alternative Models of the Labour Market," *Review of Economic Studies*, Special Issue on Unemployment, 49, 761–782.

Barro, Robert J. [1977], "Unanticipated Money Growth and Unemployment in the United States," *American Economic Review*, 67:1, March, 101–115.

Barro, Robert J. [1978], "Unanticipated Money, Output, and the Price Level in the United States," *Journal of Political Economy*, 86:4, August, 549–580.

Basmann, Robert L. [1957], "A Generalized Classical Method of Linear Estimation of Coefficients in a Structural Equation," *Econometrica*, 25:1, January, 77–83.

Begg, David K. H. [1982], *The Rational Expectations Revolution in Macroeconomics: Theories and Evidence*, Baltimore: Johns Hopkins University Press.

Bentzel, Ragnar and Herman Wold [1946], "On Statistical Demand Analysis from the Viewpoint of Simultaneous Equations," *Skandinavisk Aktuarietidskrift*, 29, 95–114.

Blanchard, Olivier J. [1981], "Output, the Stock Market, and Interest Rates," *American Economic Review*, 71:1, March, 132–143.

Brechling, Frank R. [1968], "The Trade-off between Inflation and Unemployment," *Journal of Political Economy*, 76:4, July/August, 712–737.

Breusch, Trevor S. [1978], "Testing for Autocorrelation in Dynamic Linear Models," *Australian Economic Papers*, 17:31, December, 334–355.

Brinner, Roger E. [1977], "The Death of the Phillips Curve Reconsidered," *Quarterly Journal of Economics*, 91:3, August, 389–418.

Burridge, Peter and Kenneth F. Wallis [1985], "Calculating the Variance of Seasonally Adjusted Series," *Journal of the American Statistical Association*, 80:391, September, 541–552.

Clark, Kim B. and Lawrence H. Summers [1979], "Labor Market Dynamics and Unemployment: A Reconsideration," *Brookings Papers on Economic Activity*, 1:1979, 13–60.

Chow, Gregory C. [1980], "Estimation of Rational Expectations Models," *Journal of Economic Dynamics and Control*, 2:3, August, 241–255.

Coen, Robert M. and Bert G. Hickman [1987], "Keynesian and Classical Unemployment in Four Countries," *Brookings Papers on Economic Activity*, 1:1987, 123–193.

de Marchi, Neil and Christopher L. Gilbert, eds. [1989], "History and Methodology of Econometrics," Special Issue of the *Oxford Economic Papers*, 41:1, January.

Desai, Meghnad [1975], "The Phillips Curve: A Revisionist Interpretation," *Economica*, New Series, 42:165, February, 1–20.

Desai, Meghnad [1976], *Applied Econometrics*, New York: McGraw-Hill.

Diamond, Peter A. and Olivier Jean Blanchard [1989a], "The Beveridge Curve," *Brookings Papers on Economic Activity*, 1:1989, 1–60.

Diamond, Peter A. and Olivier Jean Blanchard [1989b], "Beveridge and Phillips

Curves," paper presented at the 65th birthday celebration of Robert M. Solow, Cambridge, Mass., April.

Donner, Arthur and James F. McCollum [1972], "The Phillips Curve: An Historical Note," *Economica*, 39:155, August, 322–323.

Dornbusch, Rudiger [1976], "Expectations and Exchange Rate Dynamics," *Journal of Political Economy*, 84:6, November/December, 1161–1176.

Durbin, James M. [1954], "Errors in Variables," *Review of the International Statistical Institute*, 22, 23–32.

Durbin, James M. [1970], "Testing for Serial Correlation in Least Squares Regression When Some of the Regressors Are Lagged Dependent Variables," *Econometrica*, 38:3, May, 410–421.

Epstein, Roy J. [1987], *A History of Econometrics*, Amsterdam: North-Holland.

Fair, Ray C. [1970], "The Estimation of Simultaneous Equation Models with Lagged Endogenous Variables and First Order Serially Correlated Errors," *Econometrica*, 38:3, May, 507–516.

Fair, Ray C. [1979], "An Analysis of a Macro-Economic Model with Rational Expectations in the Bond and Stock Markets," *American Economic Review*, 69:4, September, 539–552.

Fair, Ray C. [1984], *Specification, Estimation, and Analysis of Macroeconometric Models*, Cambridge, Mass.: Harvard University Press.

Fair, Ray C. and John B. Taylor [1983], "Solution and Maximum Likelihood Estimation of Dynamic Rational Expectations Models," *Econometrica*, 51:4, July, 1169–1185.

Fischer, Stanley [1977], "Long-Term Contracts, Rational Expectations, and the Optimal Money Supply Rule," *Journal of Political Economy*, 85:1, February, 191–205.

Fisher, Franklin M. [1965], "Dynamic Structure and Estimation in Economy-Wide Econometric Models," in James Duesenberry et al., eds., *The Brookings Quarterly Econometric Model of the United States*, Chicago: Rand McNally, pp. 588–635.

Fisher, Franklin M. [1970], "Discussion of Papers," in Otto Eckstein, ed., *The Econometrics of Price Determination*, Washington, D.C.: Board of Governors of the Federal Reserve System, pp. 113–115.

Fisher, Irving [1926], "A Statistical Relation between Unemployment and Price Changes," *International Labor Review*, 13:6, June, 785–792.

Fisher, Irving [1973], "I Discovered the Phillips Curve," *Journal of Political Economy*, 81:2, Part I, March/April, 496–502.

Flood, Robert P. and Peter M. Garber [1980], "A Pitfall in Estimation of Models with Rational Expectations," *Journal of Monetary Economics*, 6:3, July, 433–435.

Friedman, Milton [1966], "Comments," in George P. Schultz and Robert Z. Aliber, eds., *Guidelines, Informal Controls, and the Market Place*, Chicago: University of Chicago Press, pp. 55–61.

Friedman, Milton [1968], "The Role of Monetary Policy," *American Economic Review*, 58:1, March, 1–17.

Gilbert, Christopher L. [1976], "The Original Phillips Curve Estimates," *Economica*, New Series, 43:169, February, 51–57.

Godfrey, Leslie G. [1978], "Testing against General Autoregressive and Moving Average Models When the Regressors Include Lagged Dependent Variables," *Econometrica*, 46:6, November, 1293–1301.

Goldberger, Arthur S. [1964], *Econometric Theory*, New York: John Wiley and Sons.

Goldberger, Arthur S. [1970], "Criteria and Constraints in Multivariate Regression," Madison: University of Wisconsin, Social Science Research Institute, EME 7026, July.

Gordon, Robert J. [1970], "The Recent Acceleration of Inflation and Its Lessons for the Future," *Brookings Papers on Economic Activity*, 1:1970, 8–41.

Gordon, Robert J. [1977], "The Theory of Domestic Inflation," *American Economic Review*, 67:1, March, 128–134.

Gordon, Robert J. [1980], "A Consistent Characterization of a Near-Century of Price Behavior," *American Economic Review*, 70:2, May, 243–249.

Gordon, Robert J. [1982a], "Inflation, Flexible Exchange Rates, and the Natural Rate of Unemployment," in Martin N. Baily, ed., *Workers, Jobs and Inflation*, Washington, D.C.: The Brookings Institution, pp. 89–158.

Gordon, Robert J. [1982b], "Why U.S. Wage and Employment Behavior Differs from That in Britain and Japan," *Economic Journal*, 92:1, March, 13–44.

Gordon, Robert J. [1985], "Understanding Inflation in the 1980s," *Brookings Papers on Economic Activity*, 1985:1, 263–299.

Gordon, Robert J. [1988a], "U.S. Inflation, Labor's Share, and the Natural Rate of Unemployment," Cambridge, Mass.: National Bureau of Economic Research, Working Paper No. 2585, May.

Gordon, Robert J. [1988b], "Back to the Future: European Unemployment Today Viewed from America in 1939," *Brookings Papers on Economic Activity*, 1:1988, 271–304.

Haavelmo, Trygve [1943], "The Statistical Implications of a System of Simultaneous Equations," *Econometrica*, 11:1, January, 1–12.

Hall, Robert E. [1980], "Employment Fluctuations and Wage Rigidity," *Brookings Papers on Economic Activity*, 1980:1, 91–123.

Hall, Robert E. and John B. Taylor [1988], *Macroeconomics: Theory, Performance, and Policy*, Second Edition, New York: W.W. Norton.

Hallett, A. J. Hughes [1989], "Econometrics and the Theory of Economic Policy: The Tinbergen-Theil Contributions 40 Years On," *Oxford Economic Papers*, 41:1, January, 189–214.

Ham, John C. [1986], "Testing Whether Unemployment Represents Intertemporal Labour Supply Behaviour," *Review of Economic Studies*, 53, August, 559–578.

Hamermesh, Daniel S. and Albert Rees [1988], *The Economics of Work and Pay*, Fourth Edition, New York: Harper & Row.

Hansen, Bent and Gösta Rehn [1956], "On Wage-Drift: A Problem of Money-Wage Dynamics," in *Twenty-Five Essays (In English, German and Scandinavian Languages) in Honour of Erik Lindahl)*, Stockholm: Ekonomisk Tidskrift, 21 November.

Hansen, Lars P. and Kenneth Singleton [1982], "Generalized Instrumental Variables Estimation of Nonlinear Rational Expectations Models," *Econometrica*, 50:5, September, 1269–1286.

Hausman, Jerry A. [1978], "Specification Tests in Econometrics," *Econometrica*, 46:6, November, 1251–1271.

Hausman, Jerry A. [1983], "Specification and Estimation of Simultaneous Equations Models," Chapter 7 in Zvi Griliches and Michael D. Intriligator, eds., *Handbook of Econometrics*, Vol. 1, Amsterdam: North-Holland, pp. 391–448.

Hausman, Jerry A. and Mark W. Watson [1985], "Errors in Variables and Seasonal Adjustment Procedures," *Journal of the American Statistical Association*, 80:391, September, 531–540.

Hendry, David F. [1971], "Maximum Likelihood Estimation of Systems of Simultaneous Regression Equations with Errors Generated by a Vector Autoregressive Process," *International Economic Review*, 12:2, June, 257–272.

Holt, Charles C. [1971], "Job Search, Phillips' Wage Relation, and Union Influence: Theory and Evidence," in Edmund S. Phelps, ed., *Microeconomic Foundations of Employment and Inflation Theory*, New York: Macmillan, pp. 53–123.

Jorgenson, Dale W. [1966], "Rational Distributed Lag Functions," *Econometrica*, 29:1, January, 135–149.

Klein, Lawrence R. [1946], "Macroeconomics and the Theory of Rational Behavior," *Econometrica*, 14:2, April, 93–108.

Klein, Lawrence R. [1947], "Theories of Effective Demand and Employment," *Journal of Political Economy*, 55:2, April, 108–131.

Klein, Lawrence R. [1950], *Economic Fluctuations in the United States, 1921–1941*, Cowles Commission for Research in Economics, Monograph No. 11, New York: John Wiley and Sons.

Klein, Lawrence R. [1953], *A Textbook of Econometrics*, Evanston, Ill.: Row, Peterson.

Klein, Lawrence R. [1972], *A Textbook of Econometrics*, Second Edition, Englewood Cliffs, N.J.: Prentice Hall.

Klein, Lawrence R. and Arthur S. Goldberger [1955], *An Econometric Model of the United States 1929–1952*, Amsterdam: North-Holland.

Koopmans, Tjalling C. and William C. Hood [1953], "The Estimation of Simultaneous Linear Economic Relationships," in William C. Hood and Tjalling C. Koopmans, eds., *Statistical Inference in Dynamic Economic Models*, Cowles Commission for Research in Economics, Monograph No. 14, New York: John Wiley and Sons, pp. 53–237.

Laidler, David E. W. and J. Michael Parkin [1975], "Inflation: A Survey," *Economic Journal*, 85:4, December, 741–809.

Lipsey, Richard G. [1960], "The Relationship between Unemployment and the Rate of Change of Money Wage Rates in the U.K., 1862–1957," *Economica*, New Series, 27:105, February, 1–31.

Lipsey, Richard G. and J. Michael Parkin [1970], "Incomes Policy: A Reappraisal," *Economica*, New Series, 37:146, July, 115–138.

Lucas, Robert E., Jr. [1970], "Econometric Testing of the Natural Rate Hypothesis," in Otto Eckstein, ed., *The Econometrics of Price Determination*, Washington, D.C.: Board of Governors of the Federal Reserve System, pp. 50–59.

Lucas, Robert E., Jr. [1976], "Econometric Policy Evaluation: A Critique, in Karl Brunner and Allan H. Meltzer, eds., *The Phillips Curve and Labor Economics*, Carnegie-Rochester Series on Public Policy, Supplementary Series to the *Journal of Monetary Economics*, 1:1, January, 19–46.

Lucas, Robert E., Jr. [1980], "Two Illustrations of the Quantity Theory of Money," *American Economic Review*, 70:5, December, 1005–1014.

Lucas, Robert E., Jr. and Leonard A. Rapping [1969], "Price Expectations and the Phillips Curve," *American Economic Review*, 59:3, June, 342–351.

Lucas, Robert E., Jr. and Leonard A. Rapping [1970], "Real Wages, Employment, and Inflation," in Edmund S. Phelps, ed., *Microeconomic Foundations of Employment and Inflation Theory*, New York: W.W. Norton, pp. 257–305. With the exception of material in Appendix 2 this is reprinted from the *Journal of Political Economy*, 77:5, September/October 1969, 721–754.

Lucas, Robert E., Jr. and Thomas J. Sargent [1978], "After Keynesian Macroeconomics," in *After the Phillips Curve: Persistence of High Inflation and High Unemployment*, Boston: Federal Reserve Bank of Boston, Conference Series 19, pp. 49–72. Reprinted in Robert E. Lucas, Jr. and Thomas J. Sargent, eds., *Rational Expectations and Econometric Practice*, Vol. 1, Minneapolis: University of Minnesota Press, 1981, pp. 295–319.

Madansky, Albert [1964], "On the Efficiency of Three-Stage Least Squares Estimation," *Econometrica*, 32:1, January/April, 51–56.

Maddala, G. S. [1977], *Econometrics*, New York: McGraw-Hill.

Maddala, G. S. [1988], *Introduction to Econometrics*, New York: Macmillan.

Malinvaud, Edmond [1970], *Statistical Methods of Econometrics*, Amsterdam: North-Holland.

Mankiw, N. Gregory, Julio J. Rotemberg, and Lawrence H. Summers [1985], "Intertemporal Substitution in Macroeconomics," *Quarterly Journal of Economics*, 100, February, 225–251.

Mann, Henry B. and Abraham Wald [1943], "On the Statistical Treatment of Linear Stochastic Difference Equations," *Econometrica*, 11:2, July/October, 173–220.

McCallum, Bennett T. [1976], "Rational Expectations and the Natural Rate Hypothesis: Some Consistent Estimates," *Econometrica*, 44:1, January, 43–52.

McCallum, Bennett T. [1979a], "On the Observational Inequivalence of Classical and Keynesian Models," *Journal of Political Economy*, 87:2, April, 395–402.

McCallum, Bennett T. [1979b], "Topics Concerning the Formulation, Estimation, and Use of Macroeconometric Models with Rational Expectations," *1979 Proceedings of the Business and Economics Statistics Section of the American Statistical Association*, Washington, D.C., pp. 65–72.

Mishkin, Frederic [1983], *A Rational Expectations Approach to Macroeconomics: Testing Policy Ineffectiveness and Efficient-Markets Models*, Chicago: University of Chicago Press.

Modigliani, Franco [1977], "The Monetarist Controversy or, Should We Forsake Stabilization Policies?" *American Economic Review*, 67:2, March, 1–19.

Modigliani, Franco and Lucas Papademos [1975], "Targets for Monetary Policy in the Coming Year," *Brookings Papers on Economic Activity*, 1:1975, 141–163.

Muth, John F. [1961], "Rational Expectations and the Theory of Price Movements," *Econometrica*, 29:3, July, 315–335.

Neftci, Salih and Thomas J. Sargent [1978], "A Little Bit of Evidence on the Natural Rate Hypothesis from the U.S.," *Journal of Monetary Economics*, 4:2, April, 315–319.

Nerlove, Marc [1966], "A Tabular Survey of Macroeconometric Models," *International Economic Review*, 7:2, May, 127–175.

Oberhofer, Walter and Jan Kmenta [1974], "A General Procedure for Obtaining Maximum Likelihood Estimates in Generalized Regression Models," *Econometrica*, 42:3, May, 579–590.

Okun, Arthur M. [1962], "Potential GNP: Its Measurement and Significance," *Pro-*

ceedings of the Business and Economics Section of the American Statistical Association, Washington, D.C.: American Statistical Association, pp. 98–104.

Okun, Arthur M. [1980], "Postwar Macroeconomic Performance," in Martin S. Feldstein, ed., *The American Economy in Transition*, Chicago: University of Chicago Press, pp. 162–169.

Perloff, Jeffrey M. and Michael L. Wachter [1979], "A Production Function–Nonaccelerating Inflation Approach to Potential Output: Is Measured Potential Output Too High?" in Karl Brunner and Allan H. Meltzer, eds., *Three Aspects of Policy and Policymaking: Knowledge, Data and Institutions*, Supplementary Series to the *Journal of Monetary Economics*, Vol. 10, 113–164.

Perry, George L. [1964], "The Determinants of Wage Rate Changes and the Inflation-Unemployment Trade-off in the United States," *Review of Economic Studies*, 31, 287–308.

Perry, George L. [1970], "Changing Labor Markets and Inflation," *Brookings Papers on Economic Activity*, 1970:3, 411–441.

Perry, George L. [1975], "Determinants of Wage Inflation around the World," *Brookings Papers on Economic Activity*, 1975:2, 403–435.

Phelps, Edmund S. [1968], "Money Wage Dynamics and Labor Market Equilibrium," *Journal of Political Economy*, 76:4, July/August, 678–711.

Phelps, Edmund S. [1970], "Money Wage Dynamics and Labor Market Equilibrium," in Edmund S. Phelps, ed., *Microeconomic Foundations of Employment and Inflation Theory*, New York: Norton, pp. 124–166.

Phillips, A. William [1958], "The Relation between Unemployment and the Rate of Change of Money Wage Rates in the United Kingdom, 1861–1957," *Economica*, New Series, 25:100, November, 283–299.

Phillips, Peter C. B. [1976], "The Iterated Minimum Distance Estimator and the Quasi-Maximum Likelihood Estimator," *Econometrica*, 44:3, May, 449–460.

Pindyck, Robert S. and Julio J. Rotemberg [1983], "Dynamic Factor Demands, Energy Use, and the Effects of Energy Price Shocks," *American Economic Review*, 73:5, December, 1066–1079.

Poterba, James and Lawrence Summers [1986], "Reporting Errors and Labor Force Dynamics," *Econometrica*, 54:6, November, 1319–1339.

Prucha, Ingmar [1987], "The Variance-Covariance Matrix of the Maximum Likelihood Estimator in Triangular Structural Systems: Consistent Estimation," *Econometrica*, 55:4, July, 977–978.

Samuelson, Paul A. and Robert M. Solow [1960], "Analytical Aspects of Anti-Inflation Policy," *American Economic Review*, 40:2, May, 177–194.

Samuelson, Paul A. and Robert M. Solow [1965], "Our Menu of Policy Choices," in Arthur M. Okun, ed., *The Battle against Unemployment*, New York: W.W. Norton, pp. 71–76.

Sargan, J. Denis [1964], "Wages and Prices in the United Kingdom: A Study in Econometric Methodology," in Peter Hart, Gordon Mills, and John K. Whitaker, eds., *Econometric Analysis for National Planning*, London: Butterworths, pp. 25–54.

Sargent, Thomas J. [1973], "A Note on the Accelerationist Controversy," *Journal of Money, Credit and Banking*, 3:1, August, 50–60.

Sargent, Thomas J. [1976], "The Observational Equivalence of Natural and Unnatural Rate Theories of Macroeconomics," *Journal of Political Economy*, 84:3, June, 631–640.

Sawa, Takamitsu [1972], "Finite Sample Properties of the k-Class Estimators," *Econometrica*, 40:4, July, 653–680.

Sheffrin, Steven M. [1983], *Rational Expectations*, Cambridge, England: Cambridge University Press.

Sims, Christopher A. [1980], "Macroeconomics and Reality," *Econometrica*, 48:1, January, 1–48.

Solow, Robert M. [1969], *Price Expectations and the Behavior of the Price Level*, Manchester, England: Manchester University Press.

Solow, Robert M. [1979], "What We Know and Don't Know about Inflation," *Technology Review*, 81:3, December 1978/January 1979, 30–44.

Stoker, Thomas M. [1986a], "Aggregation, Efficiency and Cross-Section Regression," *Econometrica*, 54:1, January, 171–188.

Stoker, Thomas M. [1986b], "Simple Tests of Distributional Effects on Macroeconomic Equations," *Journal of Political Economy*, 94:4, August, 763–796.

Summers, Lawrence H. [1981], "Measuring Unemployment," *Brookings Papers on Economic Activity*, 2:1981, 609–620.

Taylor, John B. [1979], "Estimation and Control of a Macroeconomic Model with Rational Expectations," *Econometrica*, 47:5, September, 1267–1286.

Taylor, John B. [1980], "Aggregate Dynamics and Staggered Contracts," *Journal of Political Economy*, 88:1, February, 1–23.

Taylor, Jim [1970], "Hidden Unemployment, Hoarded Labor, and the Phillips Curve," *Southern Economic Journal*, 37:1, July, 1–16.

Theil, Henri [1958], *Economic Forecasts and Policy*, Amsterdam: North-Holland.

Theil, Henri [1971], *Principles of Econometrics*, New York: John Wiley and Sons.

Tinbergen, Jan [1939], *Statistical Testing of Business-Cycle Theories*, Vol. 1: *A Method and Its Application to Investment Activity*, and Vol. II: *Business Cycles in the United States of America, 1919–1932*, Geneva: League of Nations Economic Intelligence Service.

Tinbergen, Jan [1959], "Types of Equilibrium and Business-Cycle Movements: An Economic Policy for 1936," in Leo H. Klaassen, Leendert M. Koyck, and Hendrik J. Witteveen, eds., *Jan Tinbergen: Selected Papers*, Amsterdam: North-Holland, pp. 15–84.

Tobin, James [1980], "Stabilization Policy Ten Years After," *Brookings Papers on Economic Activity*, 1980:1, 19–85.

Turnovsky, Stephen J. and Michael L. Wachter [1972], "A Test of the Expectations Hypothesis Using Directly Observed Wage and Price Expectations," *Review of Economics and Statistics*, 54:1, February, 47–54.

Wallis, Kenneth F. [1971], "Wages, Prices and Incomes Policies: Some Comments," *Economica*, New Series, 38:151, August, 304–310.

Wallis, Kenneth F. [1980], "Econometric Implications of the Rational Expectations Hypothesis," *Econometrica*, 48:1, January, 49–73.

Walwick, Nancy J. [1989], "Phillips' Approximate Regression," *Oxford Economic Papers*, 41:1, January, 170–188.

Wu, De-Min [1973], "Tests of Independence between Stochastic Regressors and Disturbances," *Econometrica*, 41:4, July, 733–750.

Zeldes, Stephen P. [1989], "Consumption and Liquidity Constraints: An Empirical Investigation," *Journal of Political Economy*, 97:2, April, 305–346.

Zellner, Arnold and Soo-Bin Park [1979], "Minimum Expected Loss (MELO) Estimators for Functions of Parameters and Structural Coefficients of Econometric Models," *Journal of the American Statistical Association*, 74:365, March, 185–193.

Zellner, Arnold and Henri Theil [1962], "Three-Stage Least Squares: Simultaneous Estimation of Simultaneous Equations," *Econometrica*, 30:1, January, 54–78.

FURTHER READINGS

Addison, John T. and W. Stanley Siebert [1979], *The Market for Labor: An Analytical Treatment*, Santa Monica, Calif.: Goodyear. See especially Chapter 12, "Wage Inflation," pp. 414–464.

Barro, Robert J. [1987], *Macroeconomics*, Second Edition, New York: John Wiley and Sons. See especially Chapter 16, "The Interplay between Nominal and Real Variables—What Is the Evidence?," pp. 455–461.

de Marchi, Neil and Christopher L. Gilbert, eds. [1989], "History and Methodology of Econometrics," Special Issue of the *Oxford Economic Papers*, 41:1, January. A lively discussion on the historical development of econometrics with special emphasis on simultaneous equations procedures.

Desai, Meghnad [1976], *Applied Econometrics*, New York: McGraw-Hill. See especially Chapter 7, "Dynamic Simultaneous Equation Models: Wages and Prices," pp. 205–232, and Chapter 8, "Macroeconomic Models: Simulation and Policy Applications," pp. 233–268.

Ehrenberg, Ronald G. and Robert S. Smith [1985], *Modern Labor Economics*, Second Edition, Glenview, Ill.: Scott, Foresman. See especially Chapter 16, "Inflation and Unemployment," pp. 524–564.

Fleisher, Belton and Thomas Kniesner [1984], *Labor Economics: Theory, Evidence and Policy*, Third Edition, Englewood Cliffs, N.J.: Prentice-Hall. See especially Chapter 12, "Unemployment and Wage Inflation," pp. 462–527.

Lucas, Robert E., Jr. and Thomas J. Sargent [1981], eds., *Rational Expectations and Econometric Practice*, Minneapolis: University of Minnesota Press. A collection of oft-cited papers dealing with rational expectations.

McCallum, Bennett T. [1989], *Monetary Economics: Theory and Policy*, New York: Macmillan. See especially Chapter 9, "Inflation and Unemployment: Alternative Theories," pp. 174–200.

Sargent, Thomas J. [1987], *Macroeconomic Theory*, Second Edition, Boston: Academic Press. See especially Chapter 16, "The Phillips Curve," pp. 438–446.

Tauchen, George, ed. [1990], Special Issue on "Solving Nonlinear Rational Expectations Models," *Journal of Business and Economic Statistics*, 8:1, January, 1–52. A collection of eleven articles introducing and comparing alternative computational algorithms for solving nonlinear rational expectations models.

Wallis, Kenneth F. [1973], *Topics in Applied Econometrics*, London: Gray-Mills Publishing, Ltd. See especially Chapter 4, "Simultaneous Equation Systems," pp. 98–127.

Chapter 11

Whether and How Much Women Work for Pay: Applications of Limited Dependent Variable Procedures

". . . most of the available evidence suggests that female labor supply, measured either as labor force participation or as hours of work, is considerably more wage and property income elastic than male labor supply."

MARK R. KILLINGSWORTH (1983, p. 432)

"One unexpected finding is that working wives in Canada tend to work fewer hours per year when paid more per hour. . . . Our resulting uncompensated wage elasticities of hours of work are shown to be very similar to those reported by other researchers for men."

ALICE NAKAMURA, MASAO NAKAMURA, and DALLAS CULLEN (1979, p. 787)

"High taxes, sometimes by diminishing the consumption of the taxed commodities, and sometimes by encouraging smuggling, frequently afford a smaller revenue to government than what might be drawn from more moderate taxes."

ADAM SMITH (1776, Book V, p. 835)

". . . reasonable estimates of an aggregate labor supply elasticity and of an overall marginal labor tax rate are both low enough to suggest that broad-based cuts in labor tax rates would not increase [government] revenues."

DON FULLERTON (1982, p. 20)

Many contemporary public policy debates involve issues concerning the supply of labor. For example, controversies surrounding welfare payments, social security, and the income tax system often focus on incentives for work. Even macroeconomic analyses of unemployment and wage rigidity often raise microeconomic issues concerning choices between leisure and labor supply.

The notion of labor supply, however, encompasses several dimensions: the size and demographic composition of the population, the proportion of the working-age population that is working for pay or seeking such work (called the labor force participation rate, LFPR), the number of hours worked per week or per year, and the quality of labor. In this chapter we focus on factors that affect the decisions of household members, particularly women, on whether to work for pay and, if so, for how many hours. The econometric tools that we employ include various limited and censored dependent variable procedures.

In the United States since World War II the agggregate LFPR was fairly stable to 1968 and then trended upward. In 1948, for example, the aggregate LFPR was 58.8%, in 1968 it was 59.6%, but in 1988 it stood at 65.9%. This trending pattern in the aggregate LFPR, however, masks two dramatic and almost offsetting drifts, those of males and those of females. For example, in 1948, 1968, and 1988 the LFPR rate for females increased from 32.7% to 41.6% to 56.1%, while that for males decreased from 86.6% to 80.1% to 76.2%.[1]

Labor market analysts have offered numerous explanations for growth in the female LFPR.[2] Although increases in male real wages and male real incomes since World War II have provided opportunities for married women to reduce their commitment to the labor force (an income effect), this negative effect has apparently been more than offset by improvements in the real wages offered women (both income and substitution effects) and by increased availability of daycare services for children, as well as by the enhanced employment possibilities that are available to women. Moreover, the greater educational attainment of females not only has resulted in improved real wages (see Chapter 5), but may also have changed women's preferences toward obtaining meaningful work outside the home. These factors, plus widespread growth in the availability of birth control, have undoubtedly contributed to the substantial decline in birth rates since World War II, a phenomenon that has greatly facilitated increased female labor force participation. Finally, rising productivity in the household due to labor-saving technological progress (such as freezers, microwave ovens, self-defrosting refrigerators, and automatic dishwashers) has also contributed to encouraging women to engage in part- and full-time employment in the labor market.

The explanations underlying the gradual decline in the LFPR of males are somewhat different from those explaining the increased female LFPR and are highlighted when one disaggregates the male population by age. For male teenagers there has been little if any change in the LFPR from World War II to the present, and for prime-aged males (those in the 25–54 age group) the aggregate LFPR has been relatively stable, declining slightly from around 96% or 97% in 1949 to about 94% in 1984.

The decline in the overall LFPR of males since World War II is due primarily to decreases in the LFPR of those in the 55–64 and 65 and over age groups. While the sharp drop in the LFPR of males who are 65 years of age and over from 47% in 1949 to 16.1% in 1984 might not be surprising, given growth in earned benefits available from private pension and U.S. social security programs, there has also been a substantial decrease in the LFPR of males in the traditional preretirement years of ages 55–64; in 1949, for example, this LFPR was 87.5%, while by 1984 it had fallen 18.9 percentage points to 68.6%.[3]

Econometric research on labor supply has a long history. Much of this research has been policy oriented, attempting to measure the effects on labor supply of changes in transfer programs or the effects on tax revenues and labor supply of changes in income tax rates. Although the ordinary least squares estimator was used in much early econometric research, several factors caused econometricians to worry about biases resulting from the use of OLS. For example, the domain of the dependent variable in many regressions—hours worked—is censored; observed hours worked are never negative, and in many samples the number of hours worked is zero for a large number of individuals. Further, labor supply data are often truncated in that data on wages are typically unobserved for individuals who are not working.[4] Finally, for those working individuals for whom the wage is observed, issues emerge concerning the simultaneity of wages and hours worked.

To deal with limited dependent variable, sample selectivity, censored and truncated data, and other statistical issues that arise in the empirical analysis of labor supply, within the last two decades, econometricians have developed and implemented a host of sophisticated econometric techniques. In this chapter we examine several of the more common limited dependent variable estimators, focusing on the analysis of labor supply, particularly the labor force decisions of women.

We begin in Section 11.1 with definitions of variables and a brief discussion of common data sources. Then in Section 11.2 we review the economic theory of labor force participation and labor supply. Here we examine individual and household labor supply decision making, summarize the effects on labor supply of changes in aggregate demand, briefly discuss the allocation of time over the life cycle, and note implications for labor supply of the fixed costs of employment.

In Section 11.3 we consider econometric issues and representative empirical findings, using the paradigm of Mark R. Killingsworth [1983] that distinguishes first- and second-generation studies of labor supply. We then assess the sensitivity of empirical results to alternative econometric procedures that rely on differing statistical and economic assumptions; this discussion is drawn in large part from Thomas A. Mroz [1987]. We conclude this section with an overview of issues in dynamic labor supply.

Finally, in the hands on portion of this chapter we enable you to obtain first-hand experience with implementing empirically a variety of estimation techniques, including the OLS, instrumental variable, logit, probit, Tobit, and generalized Tobit (Heckit) procedures. This is accomplished by engaging you in a number of exercises, each of which uses a portion of Mroz's original 1976 Panel Study of Income Dynamics data set.

11.1 DEFINITIONS AND COMMON DATA SOURCES

The supply of labor is typically defined as the amount of effort offered by a population of a given size. In turn, this amount is conveniently decomposed into four factors: (1) the percentage of the population engaged in or seeking gainful employment, usually called the *labor force participation rate;* (2) the number of hours people are willing to work per day, per week, or per year while they are in the labor force; (3) the amount of effort that people put forth per hour or day while at work; and (4) the level of training and skills that workers bring to their jobs. In this chapter we focus attention primarily on components 1 and 2 of labor supply and emphasize the labor supply of women.[5] Not much is known yet concerning component 3;[6] some aspects of component 4 are discussed in Chapter 5 of this book.

In practice, researchers have used a wide variety of measures of labor supply; a survey by Glen Cain and Harold Watts [1973a, Table 9.3], for example, identified 18 distinct measures of labor supply. It is therefore imperative that we devote some attention to measurement issues.[7]

Statistics on labor force participation rates (LFPR) and number of hours supplied are gathered by a number of private and governmental organizations. In terms of LFPR in the United States, official data on monthly labor force, employment, and unemployment statistics are typically announced by the Bureau of Labor Statistics on the first Friday of each month and are drawn from the Current Population Survey.[8] This survey is based on interviews conducted by an employee of the U.S. Bureau of the Census during the week following the twelfth day of the previous month—called the reference week. The sample consists of people in about 60,000 households in over 700 separate geographic areas. Households are chosen to reflect the principal characteristics of the population (e.g., age, gender, race, ethnicity, and marital status), as taken from the most recent decennial census. The same household is included in the survey for four consecutive months, is removed from the survey for eight months, and then is included again for a final four consecutive months.

As currently defined in the United States, the *labor force* is limited to those individuals 16 years of age and older who are not institutionalized in prisons, mental institutions, and the like and who either are employed, are searching for gainful employment, or are unemployed. Any labor supplied by individuals under age 16 is ignored, presumably because such an amount is small. Note that students aged 16 or over are counted as being in the labor force, and many in fact participate on a part-time or part-year basis. Separate data are kept on the civilian and total labor forces; the latter adds resident military personnel to the civilian labor force. For our purposes in this chapter the focus of the economic theory and econometric analyses of labor supply will be confined to the civilian portion of the labor force.[9]

The *employed* are defined as those individuals who worked one hour or more for wages or salary during the reference week or did 15 hours or more of unpaid work in a family business or farm. Individuals who were absent from work because of vacation, illness, inclement weather, or strikes and lockouts are also counted as employed but are included in the separate subcategory "with a job but not at work." The *unemployed* are those who are on layoff from a job, who have no job but have looked for work during the preceding four weeks and were available for work during the reference week, or who are waiting to report to a new job within the next 30 days.

On the basis of questions asked by the interviewer the labor force status of each civilian aged 16 or over is determined in an all-or-nothing manner. A person is either in or out of the labor force; by definition, one cannot be partly in the labor force and partly out. Thus the entire civilian noninstitutionalized population P is decomposed into employed, E, unemployed, UN, and out of the labor force, O, where

$$P \equiv E + UN + O \tag{11.1}$$

The labor force LF is limited to those who are employed or unemployed,

$$LF \equiv E + UN \tag{11.2}$$

while the labor force participation rate, in percentages, is measured as

$$\text{LFPR} \equiv 100\,(LF/P) \tag{11.3}$$

The unemployment rate UR, also measured in percentages, is

$$UR \equiv 100\,(UN/LF) \tag{11.4}$$

An important focus of this chapter is the LFPR of women. As is seen in Table 11.1, this LFPR varies considerably by age and has increased dramatically over time for all age groups. In 1988, for example, the LFPR for women aged 25–34 was 72.7%, more than twice the 34.9% of 33 years earlier. Sharp increases in the LFPR of women aged 20–24 and 35–44 also occurred after 1955 (especially after 1965), while the LFPR of women aged 45–54 increased more than 50% from 43.8% in 1955 to 69.0% in 1988.

In terms of hours of labor supplied, in practice most empirical labor economists use hours of employment as a measure of hours supplied. However, this employment measure might not reflect the number of hours an individual is willing to supply at a given wage rate. This raises several issues. Many employers specify standard weekly hours of work equal to, say, 35, 37.5, or 40 hours per week, but to some extent, employees can choose among employ-

Table 11.1 U.S. Female Labor Force Participation, 1955–1985, Women Aged 20–54

Year	20–24	25–34	35–44	45–54
1955	45.9	34.9	41.6	43.8
1960	46.1	36.0	43.4	49.8
1965	49.9	38.5	46.1	50.9
1970	57.7	45.0	51.1	54.4
1975	64.1	54.6	55.8	54.6
1980	69.0	65.4	65.5	59.9
1985	71.8	70.9	71.8	64.4
1988	72.7	72.7	75.2	69.0

Sources: Reproduced from Daniel S. Hamermesh and Albert Rees, *The Economics of Work and Pay*, Fourth Edition, New York: Harper & Row, 1988, Table 1.2. 1988 data are from the January 1989 issue of U.S. Bureau of Labor Statistics, *Employment and Earnings*.

ers with differing standard workweeks. Employers also vary in terms of possibilities for part-time and overtime work. Furthermore, firms with the same 40-hour standard workweek often offer different yearly hours of work because of varying layoff, vacation, and holiday policies. Finally, occupational choice has a working-hours dimension. The weekly or yearly hours of work may differ if one chooses to become an elementary school teacher rather than a realtor, an assembly line worker rather than a funeral director, or a New York City lawyer rather than a small-town one. Hence, although there are constraints, employees can still exercise a substantial choice over hours at work.

It is also useful to distinguish hours at work from hours paid. Since World War II in the United States, the wedge between hours at work and hours paid has increased, owing to the growing importance of paid holidays, paid vacations, and other paid leaves. The U.S. Chamber of Commerce has estimated, for example, that paid time not at work as a percent of total wage and salary costs increased from 5.9% in 1955 to 7.3%, 9.4% and 10.3% in 1965, 1975, and 1985, respectively.[10] In this chapter, unless otherwise specified, the measure of labor supply used refers to hours at work, not hours paid.

One important measurement issue concerns the source of the hours at work data. The monthly *Current Population Survey* asks the respondent to list not only his or her hours at work during the reference week, but also the hours of work for all other adult household members. Inability to recall one's own hours the previous week or those of other household members can result in serious measurement error. Moreover, the self-employed and many salaried workers might not accurately recollect when they were working and when they were not. Measures of hours at work are therefore likely to include errors.

An alternative governmental source of data on hours at work is based on surveys of firms and establishments rather than of households. Data provided by business firms and establishments for all manufacturing firms are collected by the U.S. Census Bureau once every five or six years *(Census of Manufactures)*, while a smaller sample of manufacturing firms is surveyed each year *(Annual Survey of Manufactures)*.[11] Data from a sample of all firms and establishments, including those in nonmanufacturing sectors, are gathered on a monthly basis and are published in summary form by the Bureau of Labor Statistics (the *Employment and Earnings Surveys*). Although labor economists have long advocated that the government match data from its household surveys with those from establishments, such data have not yet been developed, in part because of issues of confidentiality and budgetary considerations.[12]

A number of nongovernmental institutions produce data on individual and household labor supply. Two that are of particular importance to empirical labor economists are the Center for Human Resource Research at Ohio State University, which conducts National Longitudinal Surveys (NLS), often called the Parnes data, and the Survey Research Center at the University of Michigan, which provides data from its Survey of Working Conditions. Quality of Employment Survey, and the Panel Study of Income Dynamics (PSID).[13] The NLS and the PSID have become increasingly useful to empirical researchers, owing in part to the fact that both generate panel data, that is, they interview the same households year after year. Moreover, in the PSID, attempts are made to distinguish desired hours of labor supply from hours at work.

Although labor force participation and hours of labor supply are the principal focus of this chapter, other variables are also typically used in empirical studies explaining labor supply. Such variables include the wage rate, measures of experience, the educational attainment of the individual, and nonlabor (often called property) income. Measurement of these variables introduces additional problems of accuracy and interpretation. For a discussion of measurement issues for the wage and education variables, see Section 5.2.A of Chapter 5 in this book; the measurement of property income and other variables in the context of labor supply is discussed by, among others, Mark Killingsworth [1983, pp. 87–100].

It is important that difficulties in the measurement of labor supply and its determinants be borne in mind when working through the economic theory and econometric analyses surveyed in this chapter. As we shall see, measurement issues turn out to be very important.

11.2 THE ECONOMIC THEORY OF LABOR FORCE PARTICIPATION AND LABOR SUPPLY

We now briefly review the economic theory underlying labor supply. We begin by examining the individual's participation decision and the hours supplied by the individual, given that participation. This framework is then extended to encompass the household rather than the individual as a decision unit. Hypotheses concerning the effects of demand shifts, known as the added and discouraged worker hypotheses, are addressed. A more general treatment of the allocation of time, both static and over the life cycle, is presented, followed by a discussion of implications of fixed costs of employment. By necessity this review of the economic theory underlying labor supply is brief; more thorough and detailed analyses are found in the labor economics textbooks listed under the heading Further Readings at the end of this chapter, and especially in Mark Killingsworth [1983, Chapters 2, 5 and 6].

11.2.A Individual Labor Supply

The neoclassical model of the supply of labor is in essence an application of the theory of consumer behavior. The individual is assumed to allocate time to market work and to nonmarketable activities; the latter are typically called, erroneously, "leisure." Utility is maximized by choosing combinations of goods and leisure hours subject to time, price, and income constraints.[14]

More specifically, let the individual's preferences be represented by a twice differentiable utility function $U = U(G, L)$, indicating the utility (U) obtained from consuming alternative quantities of goods (G) and leisure (L). (*Note:* Hereafter, U refers to utility, not to the unemployed; further, L is leisure, not labor.) The marginal utilities of G and of L ($MU_G \equiv \partial U/\partial G$ and $MU_L \equiv \partial U/\partial L$) are both assumed to be positive, and the utility function is concave in G and L, implying that $\partial^2 U/\partial G^2, \partial^2 U/\partial L^2 < 0$, and $\partial^2 U/\partial G \partial L > 0$.

Along an individual's indifference curve, alternative combinations of L and G generate the same level of satisfaction. In Fig. 11.1, four indifference curves are drawn, I_0, I_1, I_2, and I_3, each corresponding with successively greater levels of U.

Two important properties of the indifference curve are its slope and its shape. The slope is derived as follows. The total differential of the utility function $U(G, L)$ is

$$(\partial U/\partial G)dG + (\partial U/\partial L)dL = dU \tag{11.5}$$

Along a given indifference curve, $dU = 0$. Substituting $dU = 0$ into Eq. (11.5) and rearranging yield the slope of indifference curves in Fig. 11.1, dG/dL, also known as the negative of the marginal rate of substitution of leisure for consumer goods and denoted here as $-MRS_{LG}$,

$$\frac{dG}{dL} = -\frac{\partial U}{\partial L} \div \frac{\partial U}{\partial G} = -\frac{MU_L}{MU_G} \equiv -MRS_{LG} \tag{11.6}$$

Since by assumption, MU_L and MU_G are both positive, indifference curves slope downward. Further, concavity implies that indifference curves are convex to the origin. Hence, although it is possible to substitute L for G and hold utility fixed, the greater the ratio of L to G, the greater the marginal amount of L required to compensate for giving up a marginal amount of G.

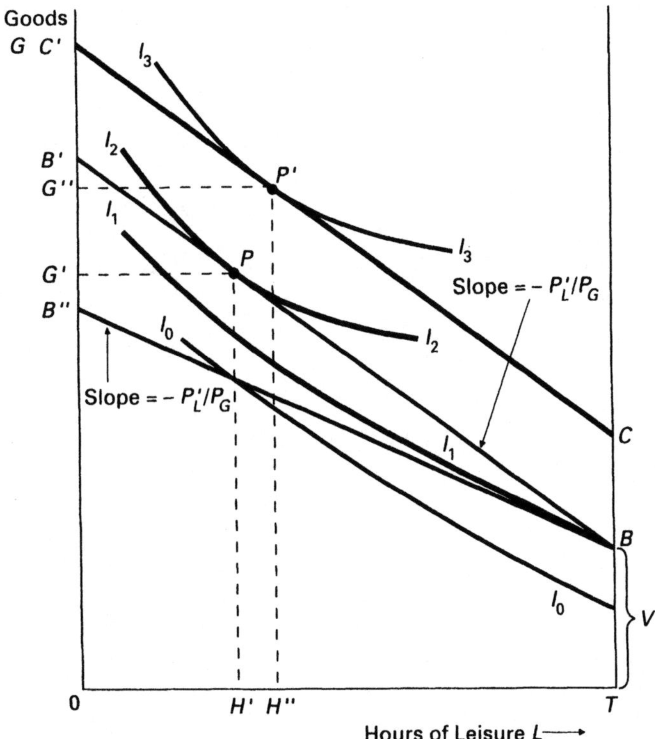

Figure 11.1 Indifference Curves and the Budget Constraint

Since indifference curves that are farther away from the origin represent successively higher levels of utility, the utility-maximizing individual will choose the highest possible indifference curve, given his or her budget constraint.

Three factors affect the budget constraint—prices, nonlabor income, and time. First, let the unit price of goods be P_G, and let the exogenous and constant wage rate be P_L; thus the individual's real wage is P_L/P_G. Second, let the individual's nonlabor or property income be denoted as V; in terms of consumption goods the real amount of nonlabor income is V/P_G. Third, because only a finite number of hours T are available in any time period, leisure (nonmarket) hours L plus hours devoted to market work H must exhaust T, that is, $L + H = T$. Further, labor income equals the product P_LH, and the real labor income forgone by choosing one more unit of leisure instead of working equals P_L/P_G.

If it is further assumed that the individual spends all of his or her available income, the above three factors imply the budget constraint

$$Y \equiv P_LH + V = P_L(T - L) + V = P_GG \tag{11.7}$$

where Y, total money income, is the sum of labor and nonlabor income.

Equation (11.7) is often rewritten in two ways. To emphasize the notion that an individual's "full income" F is spent on goods and leisure, Gary Becker [1965] has added $P_L L$ to both sides of Eq. (11.7), obtaining

$$F \equiv Y + P_L L = P_G G + P_L L \equiv P_L T + V \tag{11.8}$$

In this formulation the full income budget constraint consists of the total amount of time available, T, evaluated at the constant wage rate P_L, plus nonlabor income V. This full income F is then totally expended on leisure ($P_L L$) and on goods ($P_G G$).

Alternatively, to facilitate graphical analysis, one can rewrite Eq. (11.7) in terms of real income,

$$G = \left[\frac{P_L}{P_G} \cdot T + \frac{V}{P_G}\right] - \frac{P_L}{P_G} \cdot L \tag{11.9}$$

When Eq. (11.9) is graphed as in Fig. 11.1, the budget line embodying the income constraint is line $B'B$, with intercept equal to $[(P_L/P_G) \cdot T + V/P_G]$ and slope equal to $-(P_L/P_G)$. Note that even if $L = T$ (when all time is devoted to leisure and none to market work), the budget line $B'B$ does not cross the horizontal axis unless nonlabor income V is zero.

Maximization of utility subject to the budget constraint Eq. (11.9) involves choosing the set of G and L that is feasible (on the budget line) and is on the highest indifference curve that touches the budget line $B'B$. In Fig. 11.1, such a point is at P, where the slope of the indifference curve I_2 $(-MRS_{LG})$ equals the slope of the budget line $-P_L/P_G$. At this point the individual purchases goods OG', chooses leisure OH', and supplies hours of labor $H'T$ to the market.

More formally, the individual solves his or her maximization problem by maximizing $U = U(G, L)$ subject to the budget constraint $P_G G = P_L (T - L) + V$. This is done by setting up the Lagrangian function,

$$\Psi = U(G, L) - \lambda[P_G G - P_L(T - L) - V] \tag{11.10}$$

taking first partial derivatives of Ψ with respect to G and L, setting them equal to zero, and then solving. This yields

$$\frac{\partial U/\partial L}{\partial U/\partial G} = \frac{MU_L}{MU_G} = MRS_{LG} = \frac{P_L}{P_G} \tag{11.11}$$

Notice that according to Eq. (11.11), at the point at which utility is maximized, the MRS_{LG} (the negative of which, by Eq. (11.6), equals the slope of the indifference curve) is equal to the real wage rate P_L/P_G (the negative of which, by Eq. (11.9), equals the slope of the budget line $B'B$).

The way in which Fig. 11.1 has been drawn allows the individual to maximize his or her utility at an interior solution point P where $L < T$ and $H > 0$, that is, where the individual participates in the labor force with nonzero H. This need not be the case and in fact is critical to understanding the labor force participation decision. To see this, assume that the wage rate the individual would earn were he or she to work in the market was P'_L, which is lower than P_L. Further, let the individual have the same nonlabor income V and preferences as before. In such a case the budget constraint facing the individual would be $P_G G = P'_L(T - L) + V$, which is drawn in Fig. 11.1 as the flatter budget line $B''B$. Now the highest indifference curve the individual could attain, given his or her preferences and the budget constraint $B''B$, is I_1. At point B the indifference curve I_1 touches the budget line $B''B$, where $L = T$ and $H = 0$, that is, at the point at which the individual is a nonparticipant in the labor force, spending all of his or her time in leisure (nonmarket activities). Any higher indifference curve is simply unattainable to individuals with such preferences and budget constraints.

Points such as B represent a corner solution to the individual's utility maximization problem, rather than an interior solution. Note in particular that at the corner solution B, instead of Eq. (11.11) holding, where $MRS_{LG} = P_L/P_G$, the slope of the indifference curve is steeper than that of the budget line, implying that $MRS_{LG} > P_L/P_G$. This suggests that the labor force participation decision can be simply envisaged as corresponding to whether the individual's utility maximization problem, given budget constraints, yields a corner solution or an interior solution. Specifically, if at the solution point, $MRS_{LG} = P_L/P_G$, then $H > 0$ and $L < T$—an interior solution occurs; but if instead at the solution point, $MRS_{LG} > P_L/P_G$, then $H = 0$ and $L = T$—a corner solution obtains.

An important concept underlying the labor force participation decision is the notion of the *reservation wage.* At point B the slope of the indifference curve I_1, $-MRS_{LG}$, indicates how much extra earnings the individual would require to be induced to give up one unit of leisure, when he or she is not working at all. This amount of extra earnings is called the reservation wage, which we denote as w^*.[15] Note that as drawn in Fig. 11.1 with budget line $B''B$, the reservation wage w^* is greater than the market wage P_L, that is, the extra satisfaction from an hour of leisure is greater than the wage rate. However, if the wage rate rose so that the budget line rotated upward from $B''B$ to $B'B$, then at some point the wage rate would exceed the reservation wage, resulting in a positive labor force supply. Hence the condition for positive labor force participation is simply that $P_L > w^*$.

Several important implications of this economic theory of labor force participation are worth noting. First, for individuals with identical reservation wages those with higher (potential) wage rates are more likely to be in the labor force. Second, for individuals with identical potential wage rates those with lower reservation wages are more likely to be in the labor force. Since "workaholics" have lower reservation wages than, say, avid hobbyists, given identical potential wage rates, workaholics are more likely to be in the labor force. Similarly, women with very young children at home and with only very expensive daycare possibilities are likely to have higher reservation wages than single, career-oriented women with no children; other things being equal, we would expect the latter to have higher labor force participation rates. Note that such differences in preferences among individuals are reflected in the shape and slope of their indifference curves. Moreover, for a given individual the shape of the indifference curve may change at various points during his or her life cycle.

The theoretical framework presented above can be generalized to cases in which only several options for hours at work are available to employees, for example, one could only work zero, 20, or 40 hours per week. In such situations the optimal corner solution is the largest amount of hours of work for which the market wage is greater than or equal to the reservation wage.

We now consider the effects on labor supply of changes in nonlabor income and in the wage rate. Suppose that the nonlabor income of the individual increased from TB to TC in Fig. 11.1 but that the wage rate remained constant at P_L. This results in a new budget line $C'C$ parallel to the old budget line $B'B$. Relative to the initial equilibrium at P, the increase in nonlabor income now permits the utility-maximizing individual to move to a higher indifference curve, I_3, tangent to the new budget line $C'C$ at point P', where the hours of leisure consumed increases to OH'', the amount of labor supplied decreases to $H''T$, and the amount of goods consumed increases to OG''. This outward movement from P to P' reflects a pure income effect in which L and G both increase in response to the increase in nonlabor income. Note, however, that the pure income effect on hours of labor supplied is negative, reflecting the implicit assumption here that leisure is a normal good.

Matters are not quite as simple when the individual experiences a change in the wage rate, since the response reflects both income and substitution effects. To see this, consider Fig. 11.2. Let the initial equilibrium be at point P, where the I_0 indifference curve is tangent to the original budget line $B'B$, resulting in OG units of goods and OH hours of leisure consumed and HT hours of labor supplied. Now let the wage rate increase while goods prices, preferences, and nonlabor income remain unchanged. The increase in the wage rate results in an upwardly rotated new budget line $B''B$, tangent to the higher indifference curve I_1 at point P'. At this new equilibrium the utility-maximizing individual increases goods consumed from OG to OG', decreases the amount of leisure chosen from OH to OH', and increases hours of labor supplied to the market from HT to $H'T$.

It is useful to decompose the movement from P to P' into pure income and compensated substitution effects. The compensated substitution effect is defined as the response of the individual to a change in the wage rate *holding utility fixed.* Hence the compensated substitution effect involves a movement along the original indifference curve I_0. To show this graphically, let us notionally decrease the individual's nonlabor income by imposing a tax on it such that the new notional budget line $D'D$ has the same slope as the new budget line $B''B$ (reflecting the higher wage rate) but is just tangent to the original indifference curve I_0 at point P''. Note that in terms of utility this notional budget line $D'D$ just offsets or compensates for the improvement in earning power that results from the increased wage rate.

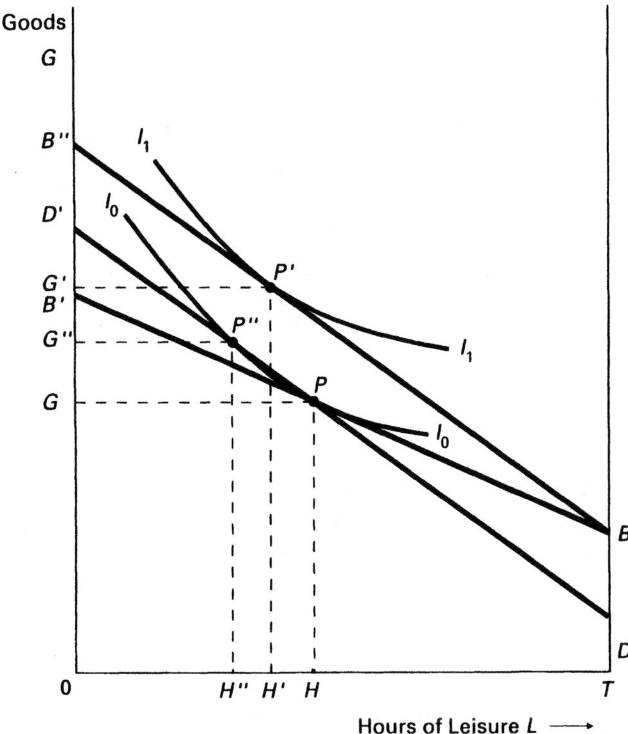

Figure 11.2 Income and Substitution Effects in Response to a Change in the Wage Rate

As is shown in Fig. 11.2, the movement from P to P'' is the compensated substitution effect; it results in reduced leisure OH'' and increased labor supply $H''T$, reflecting the fact that leisure has become more expensive as the wage rate has increased. Once this compensated substitution effect has been isolated, the pure income effect (with no prices changing) is the residual movement from P'' to P', with leisure increasing from OH'' to OH' and labor supplied to the market falling from $H''T$ to $H'T$. Incidentally, although the nomenclature can be confusing, it is worth noting that in much of the literature the total movement from P to P' in response to an increase in the wage rate is called the *uncompensated* or gross substitution effect. Hence the uncompensated or gross substitution effect is the sum of the compensated substitution effect and the pure income effect.

An important implication of the above graphical analysis is that in response to an increase in the wage rate, the utility-maximizing individual responds in two different ways: The uncompensated substitution effect results in more labor supply and less leisure, while the pure income effect results in less labor supply and more leisure. Figure 11.2 has been drawn in such a way that the positive compensated substitution effect on labor supply dominates the negative pure income effect, but this need not be the case. Had we drawn the indifference curves with different shapes (but still downward sloping and convex to the origin), we could have obtained a new equilibrium in which the pure income effect dominated the compensated substitution effect. It is therefore important to note that even when leisure is a normal good, on the basis of economic theory, one cannot determine a priori whether an increase in the wage rate, *ceteris paribus*, results in increased or reduced hours of labor supplied; this depends on the relative magnitudes of the compensated substitution and pure income effects, which in turn are empirical, not theoretical issues. In terms of traditional labor supply curves, therefore, one needs empirical evidence to determine whether the labor supply curve is upward sloping or backward bending.

Two further remarks are worth noting. First, the above analysis of income and substitution effects has assumed that interior solutions occur both before and after the wage rate increase, that is, it is conditional on positive labor force participation. Although it is not demonstrated here, it can be shown that if the original solution was a corner one with no participation, then a sufficiently large wage increase, *ceteris paribus*, could result in positive labor force participation, as could a reduction in nonlabor income, *ceteris paribus*. Hence participation decisions can also be assessed in terms of income and substitution effects.

Second, following the traditional theory of consumer demand as, for example, in R. G. D. Allen [1938] and Angus Deaton and John M. Muellbauer [1980], one can write the gross, compensated substitution and pure income effects of a wage rate change in terms of the calculus and in elasticity form. In particular, this results in the well-known Slutsky equation,

$$\left.\frac{\partial H}{\partial P_L}\right|_{\text{gross}} = \left.\frac{\partial H}{\partial P_L}\right|_{U=\bar{U}} + H \cdot \frac{\partial H}{\partial Y} \tag{11.12}$$

where Y is money income. The first term on the right-hand side of Eq. (11.12) is the compensated substitution effect with utility held constant, and the second term is the pure income effect. If one multiplies the entire expression in Eq. (11.1) by P_L/H and then multiplies and divides the income effect by Y, one obtains a Slutsky relation in elasticity form,

$$\left.\frac{\partial H}{\partial P_L} \cdot \frac{P_L}{H}\right|_{\text{gross}} = \left.\frac{\partial H}{\partial P_L} \cdot \frac{P_L}{H}\right|_{U=\bar{U}} + \frac{P_L H}{Y} \cdot \frac{\partial H}{\partial Y} \cdot \frac{Y}{H} \tag{11.13}$$

which in turn can be rewritten as

$$\epsilon^{g}_{H,P_L} = \epsilon^{c}_{H,P_L} + S_L \cdot \epsilon_{H,Y} \tag{11.14}$$

where S_L is the share of labor in total money income and where the g and c superscripts on the substitution elasticities refer to gross and compensated changes, respectively.[16]

11.2.B Household Labor Supply

The theoretical framework just presented envisages an individual as making labor supply decisions in isolation. In fact, however, the labor supply decision is typically made in the context of decisions taken by other members of the household or family within which the individual resides. Killingsworth [1983, Chapter 2] distinguishes three approaches that link family membership to labor supply.

In the "male chauvinist" model it is assumed that, when making her labor supply decisions, the wife views her husband's earnings as a form of property or nonlabor income, whereas the husband decides on his labor supply solely on the basis of his own wage and the family's actual nonlabor income, without reference to his wife's labor supply decisions.[17] The only difference in this model compared to that considered in Section 11.2.A is that in the male chauvinist framework the property income V relevant to the wife's labor supply decision is assumed to include the husband's labor income as well as all nonlabor income.[18]

A second approach assumes the existence of a family or household aggregate utility function $U = U(G, L_1, L_2, \ldots, L_n)$, where L_i is the leisure consumed by the ith individual in the family. This family utility function is maximized subject to a family budget constraint.[19]

The family utility approach has become a familiar one in labor supply analyses, owing in part to the fact that many of the well-known comparative statics results of the individual utility maximization framework carry over with little adaptation. An important generalization that is afforded by the family utility function approach is that there now are four substitution effects. In particular, not only do both family members have own-substitution effects (the response of the ith family member's labor supply to a change in his or her own wage rate), but two cross-substitution effects also occur, involving the ith family member's labor supply response to a change in the wage rate of the jth family member and vice versa.

Because of the assumed existence of an aggregate family utility function, the compensated cross-substitution effect of a change in the ith individual's wage rate on the jth member's labor supply must equal the effect of the jth member's wage rate on the ith member's labor supply. Further, although these compensated cross-substitution effects must be equal in magnitude, their signs can be either positive (indicating substitutability) or negative (complementarity). However, because the pure income effects on the two family members need not be identical, the gross (uncompensated) cross-substitution effects are not necessarily equal. Hence the gross effect of a change in the wife's wage rate on the husband's labor supply need not equal the gross effect of a change in the husband's wage rate on the wife's labor supply.

A special case of the family utility function framework, considered in detail by Malcolm S. Cohen, Samuel A. Rea, and Robert I. Lerman [1970] and by Orley Ashenfelter and James J. Heckman [1974], occurs when the compensated cross-substitution effects equal zero for all family members. In this instance a change in the *i*th member's wage rate imparts only a pure income effect on the labor supply of the *j*th individual. This implies that the labor supply function of the *j*th family member depends only on his or her wage rate and on the sum of all other family members' labor incomes plus family nonlabor income.

Because of its analytical simplicity, the family utility function approach is common in empirical labor supply studies. It is worth noting, however, that this framework has a number of drawbacks. Because the aggregate utility function implies that the family derives utility from consumption as a whole, the distribution of goods consumption does not matter; while this might make sense for family "public goods" such as heat and light, it is obviously questionable for "private goods" such as food, clothing, and entertainment. Moreover, the family utility function approach is silent concerning the process that actually generates an aggregate utility function that is mutually agreeable to all family members.

Owing in part to such considerations, a variety of alternative frameworks have been developed that treat labor supply within a household setting, yet emphasize the individual behavior of family members. Jane Leuthold [1968], for example, has presented a model in which individuals' reactions to other family members' labor supplies and wage rates are analogous to the Cournot or Stackelberg reaction curves of duopolists or oligopolists. As in modern game theory, such a framework requires stringent assumptions to ensure the existence and stability of a unique equilibrium.[20]

Bargaining models of family members' behavior are another example of recent developments in "family economics" emphasizing the individual utilities approach. As formulated by, among others, Marilyn E. Manser and Murray Brown [1979, 1980] and Marjorie B. McElroy and Mary Jean Horney [1981], family members arrive at decisions about labor supply and consumption spending through a complex process of bargaining. Without stringent assumptions, such models seldom generate closed form solutions that are amenable to empirical implementation. As with the aggregate utility function approach, in these bargaining models, the total effects of changes in, say, the husband's wage on the wife's labor supply need not equal the total effects of changes in the wife's wage on the husband's labor supply.[21] However, unlike the family utility function framework, in the bargaining models, both the level and distribution of consumption among household members can affect the labor supply of each member. Unfortunately, these bargaining models have not, as yet, generated any discriminating testable restrictions.

Marital status is clearly important in the modeling of household labor supply. In this context, recent work by Gary Becker [1974, 1981, 1988] seeks to endogenize jointly the marital status, consumption, and labor supply decisions of individuals, but at this point, no fully empirically implementable model has been developed.

11.2.C Effects on Labor Supply of Changes in Aggregate Demand

The relative importance of income and substitution effects has also played an important role in assessing the effects on labor supply of cyclical changes in aggregate demand. Here the important issue concerns the net impact on LFPR of changes in aggregate demand, for example, of recessions or booms. In the 1930s an hypothesis emerged that when the usual breadwinner became unemployed, additional members of the household enter the labor force in order to maintain the family's income, the implication being that labor force participation rates would rise along with unemployment. This was called the *added-worker hypothesis*.[22] A counter view, known as the *discouraged-worker hypothesis*, holds that when unemployment increases, searching for employment becomes so disheartening that some of the unemployed give up and withdraw from the labor force, while others who would ordinarily enter the labor force choose not to do so.

These two hypotheses have very different implications for the measurement and interpretation of the aggregate unemployment rate. According to the added-worker hypothesis, the labor force is above the long-term trend during recessions, implying that the unemployment rate is overestimated in the sense that creating one new job might reduce the number of unemployed by two people. On the other hand, according to the discouraged-worker hypothesis, the size of the aggregate labor force varies in the same direction as aggregate demand rather than in the opposite direction. Since unemployment is measured as the number of people who report themselves as seeking work, the discouraged-worker hypothesis suggests that unemployment is underestimated, since one should add to those enumerated as unemployed another group, the hidden unemployed, who would be searching for employment were the search not as likely to be fruitless. Which of these two hypotheses is most valid has been viewed as having important policy implications, since the theories can differ sharply in implying whether increases in the measured unemployment rate might warrant expansionary or contractionary macroeconomic policy responses.

In terms of economic theory the added-worker hypothesis essentially involves a household income effect, since it implies that the reduction in aggregate demand lowers the income of those family members who are in the labor force (those who lose their jobs or are put on shorter workweeks), thereby reducing the nonlabor income available to family members who are not currently in the labor force. Given this reduction in nonlabor income, reservation wages drop, the demand for leisure (a normal good) falls, and labor supply increases.

In contrast, the discouraged-worker hypothesis involves a substitution effect for two reasons. First, when aggregate demand for labor falls, real wage rates will often also tend to fall, making leisure hours less expensive. Second, the probability of successfully finding a job with a given wage falls during a recession. If one defines the expected wage from job search as the product of the wage rate of people who have the job and the probability of finding the job, then both components of the expected wage from job search may fall during recessionary periods, thereby lowering the attractiveness of job search and reducing the opportunity cost of leisure hours.

It is of course possible that both the added-worker (income) effect and the discouraged-worker (substitution) effect coexist; the added and discouraged workers might well be different groups of people. Which group tends to dominate is again an empirical issue. Although researchers such as Jacob Mincer [1962], Shelly Lundberg, [1985] and Olivia S. Mitchell [1980] have obtained results suggesting a significant number of added workers, many of them married women, the added-worker impact emerges only from families whose normal breadwinner loses a job, and this income effect tends to occur for only a relatively small portion of the labor force (unemployment rates in the United States seldom go above 10%). By contrast, the fall in expected real wages that occurs in recessions affects nearly every household, and so it is not surprising that empirical researchers have generally concluded that the discouraged-worker (substitution) effect is considerably larger than the added-worker effect.[23] Hence, other things being equal, the labor force tends to shrink during recessions and grow during periods of economic recovery.[24]

11.2.D The Allocation of Time: A More General Treatment

The theoretical framework that we have discussed so far assumes that all time is allocated either to market work or to leisure. This is clearly unrealistic, since much nonmarket time is spent in "producing" consumable services at home, using both time and goods. For example, the preparation of meals at home consumes both time and food; this time is neither leisure nor market work. In an important paper, Gary Becker [1965] called such activities *nonmarket work*. We now briefly examine factors that affect market labor supply when the choice set of alternative activities is expanded to also include nonmarket work.

Becker's essential insight was that neither time nor consumer goods are consumed by themselves, since time is usually not enjoyed without goods, and virtually all goods require time in order to be consumed. This implies that consumption decisions of individuals and households are made from a menu of alternative activities with varying amounts of both goods and time inputs. The total price of any consumption activity is the sum of its market goods price plus the value of time required to produce or consume it. Other things being equal, an increase in the wage rate raises the relative price of time-intensive activities, induces substitution against them, and thereby might result in an increase in hours worked. Note that in this broader framework the individual's supply of labor hours is determined jointly with consumption; it no longer involves just a labor-leisure tradeoff.

More formally, a model with such time consumption costs begins with a utility function $U = U(Z_1, Z_2, \ldots, Z_m)$, where the Z_i are household activities depending on both goods and time inputs.[25] Households are assumed to combine time and market goods to produce the "basic commodities" Z_i, subject to household production functions $Z_i = Z_i(G_i, t_i)$, $i = 1, \ldots, m$, where the G_i and t_i are goods and time inputs. Becker specifies that the household production function is of the fixed coefficient type,

$$Z_i = G_i/a_i \qquad \text{and} \qquad Z_i = t_i/b_i \tag{11.15}$$

where the a_i and b_i are units of goods and units of time per unit of activity, respectively. Since the time and money income constraints imply that

$$T = \sum_{i=1}^{m} t_i + H \qquad \text{and} \qquad \sum_{i=1}^{m} P_{G_i} G_i = P_L H + V \tag{11.16}$$

one can rewrite the full income constraint (11.8)—the income that would be realized if $T = H$—as

$$\sum_{i=1}^{m} P_{G_i} G_i + P_L \cdot \sum_{i=1}^{m} t_i = P_L T + V = F \tag{11.17}$$

When Eq. (11.15) is substituted in Eq. (11.17), one obtains the expression

$$\sum_{i=1}^{m} P_{G_i} Z_i a_i + P_L \cdot \sum_{i=1}^{m} Z_i b_i = \sum_{i=1}^{m} \pi_i Z_i = F \tag{11.18}$$

where

$$\pi_i \equiv P_{G_i} a_i + P_L b_i \qquad i = 1, \ldots, m \tag{11.19}$$

Note that π_i is the full cost of consuming or producing activity Z_i, including both the goods cost and forgone-earnings components.

If one maximizes the utility function subject to the budget constraint (11.19), one obtains from the first-order conditions the equilibrium relation

$$\frac{\partial U/\partial Z_i}{\partial U/\partial Z_j} = \frac{MU_i}{MU_j} = \frac{\pi_i}{\pi_j} \qquad i, j = 1, \ldots, m \qquad i \neq j \tag{11.20}$$

According to Eq. (11.20), the utility-maximizing individual consumes/produces activities i and j such that the marginal rate of substitution between any two activities just equals the ratio of their full costs, including time costs.

To see the usefulness of this more general framework, consider the effect of a wage increase on an individual's market labor supply. The income effect will bring about an increase in the consumption of all normal commodities;

if the time-intensive nonmarket commodities are normal, the income effect will cause less time to be devoted to market work and more to be allocated to nonmarket activities. In terms of substitution effects, however, note that the wage increase will raise the cost of all commodities (assuming that each requires a nonzero amount of time) but will raise the relative cost of the more time-intensive ones. This results in a shift away from more time-intensive toward less time-intensive nonmarket activities and toward market labor supply.

Within the household, for example, the increased wage might result in purchases of time-saving devices such as a microwave oven and a computer-activated water-sprinkling system. Note that although the income and substitution effects on an individual's labor supply are therefore essentially similar in sign to those derived in the earlier, simpler case, in this more general framework, insights can be gained into factors affecting the division of nonmarket time into more and less time-intensive activities. Further, to the extent that technological advances result in increasing the labor productivity of home activities, such advances could be viewed as facilitating increased market labor supply. Hence, although this more general treatment of time probably has principal implications for "home economics," it also has a nontrivial impact on market labor supply because of interactions among market and nonmarket activities.

The most important contribution of the more general treatment of time to understanding family labor supply behavior, however, concerns household decisions regarding family size and child-rearing. Since child-rearing is clearly a time-intensive process, the full costs of having children depend in part on the opportunity costs of the parents' time. Although beyond the scope of this chapter, it is worth noting that a substantial literature exists relating fertility rates to, among other things, wage rates of married women and incomes of married men; not surprisingly, empirical evidence suggests that other things being equal, married women with higher earnings potentials appear to have fewer children and participate to a greater extent in the labor force.[26] A number of studies have also been made of how one might valuate the contribution of the nonmarket working time of married women, including that portion allocated to child-rearing; on this, see, for example, Reuben Gronau [1973a, b, c, 1977, 1986].

Much recent research in the labor supply literature has involved an even more general treatment of time, analyzing the allocation of time over the life cycle.[27] Significantly, once one considers the longer life cycle horizon, decisions involving education, training, hours of labor supplied at different ages, and retirement all become interdependent and to a certain extent endogenous. What may have been exogenous or predetermined in a static context now becomes in part endogenous. Some of these issues are discussed briefly in Chapter 5, particularly in Section 5.1. For our present purposes, however, it is worth noting that not only do married women currently appear to be having smaller families than in previous decades, but the time duration between children has also declined, implying that the time devoted to child-rearing has been compressed, while that allocated to market labor supply has expanded.

11.2.E Implications of Costs of Employment

In general, it is costly to hold a job. *Money* costs must be incurred by workers to pay for transportation to work, purchase appropriate work clothing, buy meals away from home, and, in many cases, pay for babysitting, daycare, or other child care services. *Time* costs are also typically incurred by workers, since most people take time in traveling from home to job; further, children must often be transported to child care locations before the parent can travel to work. There are also *nonpecuniary* costs to job holding, such as dealing with traffic hassles or traveling through areas where personal safety may be at risk. A substantial portion of these job costs are fixed in the sense that they are incurred regardless of whether one works ten minutes or eight hours per day; a portion of child care costs, however, is variable, depending on the amount of time for which child care is required. We now briefly consider the effects on labor force participation and labor supply of changes in fixed and variable costs of employment.

John F. Cogan [1977, 1980b, 1981] has modeled the effects of job costs on labor force participation and labor supply.[28] When job-holding costs are only time costs and are fixed, the budget constraint line of Fig. 11.1 becomes kinked, with a flat, horizontal segment emanating from $H = 0$ to, say, $H = h'$, indicating that the fixed time cost of h' contributes nothing to earnings. As a result, either individuals tend to perform no market work at all (a corner solution) or they enter the labor force at a significant number of hours per week (a "very interior" solution); hence fixed job time costs imply that interior solutions are less likely to occur near the corner point where $H = 0$. One implication is that because of the fixed time costs of holding a job, much of the upward-sloping portion of labor supply curves will not be observed in data on hours of work.

Cogan also shows that if an exogenous increase in fixed time costs occurs (say, an increase in traffic congestion, implying a longer commuting time), the individual's reservation wage w^* is raised, and owing to the reduced full income that is available as a result of the increased fixed time cost (a downward parallel shift in the budget constraint, total hours available still fixed at T), hours of labor supplied H will decrease; provided that L is a normal good, hours in L will also decrease, compensating in part for the increased fixed time costs of employment.

Costs of employment are in practice very significant and are of prime importance in determining the labor supply behavior of married women. For working women, Cogan [1981] estimates that in the United States in 1967, average annual fixed costs as a percentage of the average annual earnings of working women were 28.3%; furthermore, this figure increases considerably with the number of children in the household under age six and with additional years of education for the mother. Cogan also reports that for an average woman the discontinuity in the labor supply function from $H = 0$ to $H > 0$ occurs at about 1300 hours annually (more than half-time work), indicating that when the equilibrium solution changes from a corner to an interior one, the result is a very substantial increase in the number of hours worked.

This concludes our brief overview of the theoretical issues underlying the labor force participation and labor supply decisions of individuals and households. We now move on to a more detailed discussion of econometric issues and empirical results, focusing particular attention on factors that affect female labor supply.

11.3 ECONOMETRIC ISSUES AND REPRESENTATIVE EMPIRICAL FINDINGS

The vast proportion of empirical studies of labor supply, beginning with the pioneering effort of Erika Schoenberg and Paul H. Douglas [1937], has been based on the neoclassical analysis of choice, as outlined in the previous section. This empirical literature has been surveyed by, among others, Mark R. Killingsworth [1983] and Killingsworth and James J. Heckman [1986]. For our purposes it is useful to employ the paradigm developed by Killingsworth, in which studies are classified as first or second generation depending on the attention paid to econometric issues and the underlying economic theory.[29]

11.3.A First Generation Studies

First-generation studies of labor supply are characterized by Killingsworth as relying on ordinary least squares estimation of parameters in equations whose functional form is chosen either arbitrarily or on the basis of specific ad hoc considerations; in particular, the functional forms are not derived explicitly from utility or indirect utility functions. Although dates are not precise, first-generation research began in the 1930s and continued into the early 1970s; a well-known first-generation study using aggregate data is by Glen Cain [1966], while representative studies using microdata are found in the volume edited by Glen Cain and Harold Watts [1973b].

Some examples of linear specifications that are commonly used in first-generation research include

$$H = a + bW + cV + \epsilon \tag{11.21a}$$

$$H_i = a_i + \sum_{j=1}^{J} b_{ij} W_j + c_i V + \epsilon_i \tag{11.21b}$$

$$H_i = a_i + b_i W_i + c_i \left(V + \sum_{j=1, j \neq i}^{J} W_j H_j\right) + \epsilon_i \tag{11.21c}$$

where H is hours work time, W is the real wage rate, V is per period real property income, ϵ is a stochastic term, and the i, j subscripts refer to differing household members. Equation (11.21a) refers to the labor supply of a given individual, Eq. (11.21b) to the labor supply of a given household member allowing for nonzero intrahousehold (cross-substitution) effects on i's labor supply, and Eq. (11.21c) constrains these intrahousehold substitution effects to zero. Intercept terms in these equations are often made a function of various variables such as age, gender, and race, reflecting tastes for work. Further, in many studies, transformations of the variables in Eqs. (11.21) are used, including logarithms and polynomials. Finally, as Killingsworth notes, questions concerning the sources underlying the error term ϵ are typically ignored in first-generation studies. Most of this research proceeds on the assumption that the error term is randomly distributed and makes no distinction between the measurement error or omitted regressors that might have generated ϵ. As we shall see, this last issue receives much more explicit treatment in second-generation research.

In terms of empirical findings, most first-generation studies conclude that female labor supply is considerably more sensitive to changes in wage rates and property income than is male labor supply. Most also find that leisure is a normal good for both men and women. Another common finding is that an income-compensated increase in one's own wage increases one's labor supply.

Although these qualitative conclusions are roughly consistent across studies, the quantitative estimates of the labor supply elasticities obtained from first-generation studies of labor supply differ very dramatically. As Heckman, Killingsworth, and MaCurdy [1981, Table 1.1, p. 80] note, estimates of the compensated own-wage rate labor supply elasticities range widely from -0.05 to $+0.96$ for males and from -0.05 to $+2.00$ for females; gross own-wage rate labor supply elasticities vary from -0.45 to $+0.55$ for males and from -0.10 to $+1.60$ for females, while labor supply elasticities with respect to property income extend from 0 to -0.16 for males and from -0.1 to -0.75 for females. Moreover, in almost all cases the symmetry of compensated wage effects among household members is rejected by first-generation empirical results, and at times the estimated compensated own-wage effect on labor supply has been positive, contrary to theory. These disappointing results (and some well-timed financial support from research funding agencies) have led labor researchers to examine more closely the theory underlying labor supply models, as well as the econometric and statistical procedures that have been used to obtain parameter estimates.

Three issues have received particularly close attention because of the unsatisfactory first-generation results. First, although first-generation empirical studies appear to have used interchangably alternative measures of labor supply H such as labor force participation, hours worked per week, weeks worked per year, lifetime participation, and the fraction of a lifetime spent working, in second-generation research, distinct theoretical models have been constructed to consider separately the participation, hours of work per week, lifetime participation, and lifetime hours of work decisions. These distinct theoretical models have helped in part to reconcile persistent differences in estimates of labor supply responses obtained by fitting the same function to data on temporally different perspectives of labor supply.

Second, empirical labor economists began focusing more attention on functional form and econometric technique. In turn, this entailed a more explicit treatment of unobservable variables and introduced the issue of sample selection bias. Equations such as (11.21) were now viewed more formally as representing the outcome of utility maximization and in that context were found to be woefully inadequate. Specifically, with even the simplest type of utility maximization model, the labor supply function for a single individual can be stated as

$$H = a + bW + cV + \epsilon \qquad \text{if and only if } W > W_r \qquad \textbf{(11.22a)}$$

$$H = 0 \qquad \text{otherwise} \qquad \textbf{(11.22b)}$$

where W_r is the individual's reservation wage, derived by setting H in Eq. (11.22a) equal to zero and solving for W.

First-generation studies ignored this distinction, typically either by fitting equations such as Eq. (11.21a) to a random sample taken from the population with the labor supply of nonworking individuals set at zero[30]—hereafter called Procedure I—or by fitting the equation by OLS using population subsamples that consist only of working individuals—called Procedure II.[31] Procedure I (setting H for all nonworkers equal to zero) implicitly assumes that Eqs. (11.21) or Eq. (11.22a) holds for all values of W, not just for values in excess of the reservation wage, and therefore involves a model misspecification, yielding inconsistent estimates of the parameters. Use of Procedure II (limiting the sample to workers) results in a nonrandom selection of ϵ, since by Eq. (11.22a) an individual will be included in the estimation subsample if and only if $H > 0$, that is, if and only if $\epsilon > -(a + bW + cV) \equiv -J$. Hence the data on H is censored, and ϵ must necessarily be correlated with W and V (unless $b = c = 0$, or if everyone in the population works, as was virtually the case in certain studies of the labor supply of prime-aged males).

Since observations under Procedure II are systematically selected into the estimation subsample according to the criterion $\epsilon > -J$, OLS parameter estimates based on such subsamples do not provide consistent estimates of the total labor supply response parameters. This $\epsilon > -J$ condition therefore draws attention to corner solutions in which labor force participation (a binary variable) is determined and interior solutions in which hours of work are then determined, given positive *LFP*. As Heckman et al. [1981] emphasize, while generated from the same preference function, the hours of work equation and the participation equation are fundamentally very different.

The third issue that drew the attention of researchers who were unsatisfied with first-generation empirical studies was that of nonlinear budget constraints. Once one introduces into the model common income tax structures, various types of income transfer programs, fixed costs of work, or employers' preferences for minimum hours of work, the simple straight-line budget constraints drawn in Figs. 11.1 and 11.2 disappear and give way to complex forms with kinks, discontinuities, gaps, and nonconvexities. Moreover, when tax rates depend on the level of income, the after-tax wage rate becomes endogenous, and simultaneous equations problems can emerge. Most first-generation work ignored these phenomena altogether, in spite of the fact that in the late 1960s and early 1970s a great deal of policy-oriented econometric research focused on the labor supply effects of alternative social benefit programs (such as the negative income tax), programs that clearly implied complex budget constraints.

These shortcomings of first-generation studies suggested numerous opportunities for improvement. As Heckman, Killingsworth, and MaCurdy noted,

> analysis and technique go together, and first-generation work, which glossed over some of the structural aspects of labor supply decisions and used empirical techniques that did not adequately address some of the complexities of that structure, suffered from a number of serious problems. The results of second-generation work . . . suggest that solving these problems makes a considerable difference for estimates of labor supply parameters, with correspondingly considerable implications for analysis and policy.[32]

11.3.B Second-Generation Studies

We now turn to a dicussion of second-generation studies. We first consider issues of specification and estimation, then we introduce taxes into the labor supply model, and finally, we briefly summarize empirical findings from second generation research.

11.3.B.1 SPECIFICATION AND ESTIMATION ISSUES A distinguishing feature of second-generation models of labor supply is the explicit treatment of utility functions and unobservable variables. As an example, consider the utility function

$$U = [W(H + e) + V]^{\alpha}[1 - (H + e)]^{\beta} \qquad \textbf{(11.23)}$$

where W and V are real wage and real property income, total time T is normalized to 1 so that H is the *proportion* of time spent at market work, $1 - H \equiv L$ is the proportion of time in leisure (nonmarket activities), e is an unobservable error term varying from one person to another, and the term in the first set of square brackets is real goods consumption G. The error term e is interpreted as representing interpersonal differences in tastes for leisure and for goods consumption.[33] Note that Eq. (11.23) implies that even though two people have identical W and V, they are permitted to derive differing utility U from the same amount of observable H.

The marginal rate of substitution M implied by the utility function (11.23), $M \equiv (\partial U/\partial L)/(\partial U/\partial G)$, can be shown to equal

$$M = [b/(1 - b)] \cdot [W(H + e) + V]/[1 - (H + e)] \qquad \textbf{(11.24)}$$

where $b \equiv \beta/(\alpha + \beta)$. To compute the reservation wage W_r, evaluate M in Eq. (11.24) at the point where $H = 0$ and $L = 1$. At such a point,

$$W_r = [b/(1 - b)] \cdot [We + V]/[1 - e] \qquad \textbf{(11.25)}$$

An individual with a given value of e will provide positive labor supply if and only if (hereafter abbreviated as iff) $W > W_r$. Setting $W > W_r$ and rearranging implies that $H > 0$ iff $\epsilon_h > -J$, where

$$\epsilon_h \equiv -e \qquad \text{and} \qquad J \equiv [(1 - b) - bV/W] \qquad \textbf{(11.26)}$$

This implies that

$$H > 0 \qquad \text{iff } \epsilon_h > -J \qquad \textbf{(11.27)}$$

$$H = 0 \qquad \text{iff } \epsilon_h \leqslant -J \qquad \textbf{(11.28)}$$

Further, if $H > 0$, then H is determined by the condition that the $M = W$ in Eq. (11.24).[34] Therefore if one sets $M = W$ in Eq. (11.24) and solves for H, one obtains the empirical labor supply function (given $H > 0$) as

$$H = (1 - b) - bV/W + \epsilon_h \qquad H > 0 \qquad \textbf{(11.29)}$$

More generally, one can specify a utility function $U = U(G, L, e)$, in which case the marginal rate of substitution function M is $M(G, L, e) = M(WH + V, 1 - H, e)$ and the reservation wage function at $H = 0$ is $W_r = M(V, 1, e)$. The individual will work iff $W > W_r$, and for these individuals, W equals M, implying that the labor supply function can be derived by solving $W = M(WH + V, 1 - H, e)$ for $H > 0$.

Although the labor supply function (11.29) looks quite similar to first-generation equations such as Eq. (11.21a), in fact the equation system (11.27), (11.28), and (11.29) provides much more information and does so in an integrated and coherent manner. To see this, first note that Eqs. (11.27) and (11.28) emphasize a crucial threshold condition summarizing the labor force participation (LFP) decision (for given V and W, an individual will work iff $\epsilon_h > -J$). Second, the equation system (11.27)–(11.29) highlights the fact that the labor supply function is in fact two functions—Eq. (11.29), which holds iff $W > W_r$, and Eq. (11.28), which holds iff $W \leqslant W_r$. Third, notice that the same observable variables, unobservable variables, and parameters—namely, W, V, e, and b—affect both the LFP decision and the amount of labor force supply conditional on positive LFP. While first-generation models overlooked these aspects of labor supply, second-generation models emphasize them. Let us now briefly examine some of the principles of estimation implied by second-generation models of labor supply.

Initially, assume that measures of the real wage rate W are available for all individuals in the population, including nonworkers. For the ith individual, from Eq. (11.26), denote values concerning tastes for work as $\epsilon_{Hi} \equiv -e_i$ and the value of J given b, W_i, V_i, and e_i as J_i. A common assumption is that ϵ_{Hi} has a mean of zero, has a standard deviation of σ_H, and is normally distributed in the population as a whole, implying that the standardized normal variable ϵ_{Hi}/σ_H has a mean of zero and a variance of 1.

Given this assumption concerning the population distribution of ϵ_{Hi}, the probability that a given individual i will work is given by

$$P[i \text{ works}] = P[(\epsilon_{Hi}/\sigma_H) > (-J_i/\sigma_H)$$
$$= \int_{-J_i/\sigma_H}^{\infty} f(t)dt = 1 - F(-J_i/\sigma_H) \qquad \textbf{(11.30)}$$

where f and F are the standard normal and cumulative normal density functions, respectively. Using Eqs. (11.27) and (11.28), write the likelihood function for a sample of individuals who are either working or not working as

$$\ell = \prod_{i\in\Omega} \{1 - F[-(1-b)^* + b^*(V_i/W_i)]\} \cdot$$
$$\prod_{i\in\Omega'} F[-(1-b)^* + b^*(V_i/W_i)] \qquad \textbf{(11.31)}$$

where Ω is the set of people who are working, Ω' is the set of people who are not working, $b^* \equiv b/\sigma_H$, and $(1-b)^* \equiv (1-b)/\sigma_H$.

Equation (11.31) is the standard *probit* equation, and its parameters b^* and $(1-b)^*$ can be estimated by maximizing the sample likelihood function ℓ (or its logarithm) with respect to b^* and $(1-b)^*$.[35] Given these estimates, one can then uniquely compute the maximum likelihood estimates of σ_H as $1/[b^* + (1-b)^*]$ and of b as $b^*/[b^* + (1-b)^*]$. Hypothesis tests can be implemented using the likelihood ratio test procedure.

An interesting feature of this probit model is that although it provides estimates of b and σ_H and therefore provides information on parameters governing labor supply, its computation in Eq. (11.31) uses information only on V_i, W_i, and whether the individual works, but does not utilize any information on hours worked, H_i. Further, the conditional expectation of $F[-J_i/\sigma_H]$ in Eq. (11.26) simply equals the probability that individual i is not working, that is, the probability that $H_i = 0$. A number of alternative procedures can be used to incorporate the additional information provided by nonzero data on H_i.

For the moment, assume again that data on wages are available for both workers and nonworkers. The probability that individual i works H_i hours *and* that this amount H_i is positive can be written as

$$P[i \text{ works } H_i \text{ hours and } H_i > 0] =$$
$$P[i \text{ works } H_i] \cdot P[H_i > 0 \,|\, i \text{ works } H_i] = P[i \text{ works } H_i] \cdot 1 = f(\cdot)$$

where the probability density of observing individual i working *exactly* H_i hours is $f(\epsilon_{Hi}/\sigma_H)/\sigma_H$. Hence the likelihood function for the entire sample of Ω workers and Ω' nonworkers is

$$\ell = \prod_{i\in\Omega} [f(\epsilon_{Hi}/\sigma_H)/\sigma_H] \cdot \prod_{i\in\Omega'} F[-J_i/\sigma_H] \tag{11.32}$$

where $\epsilon_{Hi} \equiv H_i - J_i$ and $J_i \equiv [(1 - b) - b(V_i/W_i)]$. Equation (11.32) is called a *Tobit* likelihood function.[36] Nonlinear methods can be employed to find estimates of b and σ_H that maximize the sample likelihood function (11.32), and hypotheses can be tested by using the likelihood ratio test procedure.[37]

The first part of the right-hand side of Eq. (11.32) refers to workers, while the second refers to nonworkers. Moreover, the first part is identical to the likelihood function that is implicit in a traditional OLS regression, whereas the second part resembles the nonworking probability portion of the probit likelihood function (11.31). In a sense, therefore, Tobit combines regression and probit frameworks. Note also that if everyone worked, then the last part of Eq. (11.32) would disappear, and estimation of Eq. (11.29) by OLS would yield unbiased estimates of b and σ_H. However, if some individuals do not work, Tobit is more appropriate than OLS, since Tobit not only predicts the number of hours worked for each worker (see Eq. (11.29)), but also produces the estimated probability that an individual will not work and thereby helps explain why a number of observations are clustered at the point $H = 0$ (see Eq. (11.28)).

The probit and Tobit models that we have discussed so far are based on a simple form of J derived from the specific utility function (11.23), namely, $J_i \equiv [(1 - b) - b(V_i/W_i)]$.[38] In a more general case, one might write a labor supply model

$$\begin{aligned} H_i &= X_i\beta + u_{Hi} && \text{if } X_i\beta + u_{Hi} > 0 \\ H_i &= 0 && \text{if } X_i\beta + u_{Hi} \leq 0, \quad i = 1, \ldots, N \end{aligned} \tag{11.33}$$

where X_i is a vector of regressors, β is the corresponding unknown coefficient vector, N is the total number of individuals, and u_{Hi} is an independently normally distributed "tastes for work" random variable with mean zero and variance σ^2. The stochastic index $X_i\beta + u_{Hi}$ is observed only when it is positive and thus results in censored samples. This index can be substituted into the probit likelihood function (11.31) or the Tobit likelihood function (11.32) in place of J_i, and maximum likelihood estimates of β and σ can then be obtained by using nonlinear optimization procedures.

It is tempting but incorrect to interpret the Tobit β coefficients as measuring the effect on $E(H_i)$ given a change in X for individuals who are working, that is, $\partial E(H_i)/\partial X_i = \beta$ for those $H_i > 0$, where $E(\cdot)$ refers to the expected value operator. In the above model (11.33), and ignoring individual subscripts i, the $E(H) = X\beta F(z) + \sigma f(z)$, where $z \equiv X\beta/\sigma$, $f(z)$ is the unit normal density, and $F(z)$ is the cumulative normal distribution function. As has been emphasized by Amemiya [1973], the expected value of H for observations that are above the threshold (with positive labor supply), now called H^*, is simply $X\beta$ plus the expected value of the truncated normal error term,

$$E(H^*) = E(H \mid H > 0) = E(H \mid u_H > -X\beta) = X\beta + \sigma f(z)/F(z) \quad \textbf{(11.34)}$$

This implies that the relationship among expected values of all observations, $E(H)$, the expected value conditional upon being above the limit, $E(H^*)$, and the probability of being above the limit, $F(z)$, is $E(H) = F(z)E(H^*)$.

John F. McDonald and Robert A. Moffitt [1980] have noted that if one differentiates this last expression with respect to X_k, where X_k is the kth regressor, one obtains

$$\frac{\partial E(H)}{\partial X_k} = F(z) \cdot \frac{\partial E(H^*)}{\partial X_k} + E(H^*) \cdot \frac{\partial F(z)}{\partial X_k} \quad \textbf{(11.35)}$$

In the labor supply context the total effect of a change in X_k on $E(H)$ can therefore be decomposed into two intuitively appealing components: (1) the change in hours worked for individuals who are already working, weighted by the probability of working, plus (2) the change in the probability of working, weighted by the expected value of hours for those who work.

McDonald and Moffitt go on to show that it is relatively simple to compute these two components of the total effect, as well as their relative importance. Specifically, one can use as an estimate of $F(z)$ the fraction of the sample above the limit (that is, the sample labor force participation rate), and one can estimate $E(H^*)$ using Eq. (11.34), along with entries from standard normal tables evaluating $F(z)$, parameter estimates, and data evaluated at sample means. Also, the derivative $\partial E(H^*)/\partial X_k$ equals $\beta_k \cdot A$, where $A \equiv \{1 - [zf(z)/F(z)] - [f(z)^2/F(z)^2]\}$, a fraction between zero and 1.[39] Finally, since $\partial F(z)/\partial X_k = f(z)\beta_k/\sigma$, one can estimate the *proportion* of the total effect of a change in X_k on labor supply due to the effect from those already working simply as A.[40]

The fraction A therefore not only provides the appropriate adjustment on β_k to obtain consistent estimates of the effects of changes in X_k on H for those already above the threshold index, but also indicates the proportion of the total effect due to induced changes in the behavior of those above the threshold. This distinction can be important; for example, not only is it often useful for policy purposes to know the effect of a policy variable such as as a specific income tax rate change on total labor supply, but it is also pertinent to be able to distinguish what portion of the total effect represents a change in LFPR (and hence a change in unemployment rates) from that portion of the effect on people who are already working.

Although the Tobit procedure utilizes information on both LFP and hours supplied given positive participation, it is but one of several procedures that are available for estimating labor supply models. Two variants on one prominent alternative, called the *selection bias–corrected regression* method, use both regression analysis and probit techniques, but as we now see, they do so in a manner that is very different from Tobit.

To understand selection bias more clearly, consider a labor supply function generated from a utility-optimizing framework and having the form $H_i = X_i\beta + u_{Hi}$, where the normally distributed u_{Hi} have a population mean of zero and standard deviation of σ, as in Eq. (11.33). (Often, H_i or some of the X_i are logarithmic transformations.) Suppose that one estimated this equation by OLS using data only from working individuals. As was noted in the previous section, such a procedure results in inconsistent estimates of the parameters in Eq. (11.33), since with such samples, the conditional expectation of u_{Hi} is nonzero and u_{Hi} is correlated with X.

The nature of the OLS bias has been considered by, among others, Arthur S. Goldberger [1981] and William H. Greene [1981]. Under the assumption that all independent variables and the dependent variable are multivariate normally distributed in the population (this therefore excludes dummy variables as regressors), Goldberger obtains the strong result that the OLS regression coefficients are biased downward in the sense that the OLS coefficient vector is a scalar multiple of the "true" labor supply coefficient vector, where the scalar lies within the 0–1 interval. Moreover, Greene shows that to obtain consistent estimates of the true labor supply parameters in Eq. (11.33), all one need do is divide each element of the OLS coefficient vector by the proportion of observations for which, in our context, $H > 0$.

Although Goldberger shows analytically that this remarkable result does not hold when the multivariate normality assumption is relaxed, Greene finds that with a variety of nonnormal situations (including dummy variable regressors), this simple adjustment of OLS estimates provides a surprisingly robust approximation to maximum likelihood estimates of the labor supply parameters in Eq. (11.33). The OLS-based estimates of standard errors, however, are inconsistent, and as Greene shows, they cannot be easily adjusted. Hence one possible way of dealing with sample selectivity is to do probit estimation of the LFP decision based on all observations, then do OLS estimation of the hours worked equation, limiting the sample to workers, and finally, obtain consistent estimates of the hours worked parameters by multiplying the OLS coefficient vector by the sample proportion of observations for which $H > 0$. Note that tests of significance cannot be done with this procedure, since OLS-based estimated standard errors are unreliable.

A second variant on the sample selectivity bias procedure involves OLS estimation of an expanded regression equation. Recall that, using Eq. (11.34), one can write the conditional expectation of hours worked for workers as

$$E(H^*) \equiv E(H \mid H > 0) = X_i\beta + K_i \qquad \textbf{(11.36)}$$

where K_i, the conditional mean of u_i given $H > 0$, is

$$K_i = \sigma \cdot [f(z_i)]/[F(Z_i)] = \sigma \cdot \lambda_i \qquad \textbf{(11.37)}$$

λ_i is often called the inverse of Mill's ratio, and in reliability theory it is known as the hazard rate. Since K_i is essentially an omitted variable in the linear regression equation $H_i = X_i\beta + u_{Hi}$, James Heckman [1976, 1979, 1980] has suggested adding an estimate of λ_i as a regressor to such an equation and then estimating the expanded regression equation by OLS while limiting the sample to individuals for which $H > 0$.

Heckman suggests estimating λ_i initially on the basis of a probit regression using data from all workers and nonworkers and shows that when this estimate of λ_i is appended as a regressor to the equation $H_i = X_i\beta + u_{Hi}$, OLS estimates of the labor supply parameters are consistent. However, since the disturbance term from this expanded regression equation turns out to be heteroskedastic, OLS estimates of β are inefficient, and estimates of standard errors are biased and inconsistent.

Yet another alternative procedure for handling this sample selectivity issue has been suggested by Randall J. Olsen [1980]. Olsen proposes estimating by OLS a linear probability model in which the dependent variable is a 0–1 dummy variable (equaling 1 if $H > 0$, otherwise zero) and the regressors are the same as in Eq. (11.33), then retrieving the fitted values from this OLS regression (calling them $\hat{P}$), and finally, adding $(\hat{P} - 1)$ as a regressor in the hours worked equation confined to the sample for which $H > 0$. Olsen shows that under the uniform distribution this procedure provides consistent estimates of the labor supply parameters in (11.33).[41]

The Goldberger-Greene, Heckman, and Olsen two-step procedures are in a sense generalizations of the Tobit technique, since the underlying utility function and labor supply parameters in the first-stage probit estimation are not constrained to equal numerically the values that are obtained from the OLS or adjusted OLS estimates in the second stage, even if the underlying economic theory suggests that they should be identical. By contrast, the Tobit procedure constrains these parameters to be equal in both the labor force participation and labor supply equations. Note, however, that if one initially specifies a more general model with discontinuities in the labor supply schedule due to, say, fixed costs of work, then the two-stage estimator might well be preferable.

Unfortunately, the Goldberger-Greene, Heckman, and Olsen two-step structural procedures require wage data for workers and nonworkers, as does Tobit. A major problem confronting second-generation researchers, however, is the fact that typically wage data are available only for workers. This data problem creates other econometric issues, to which we now turn our attention.

A number of alternative procedures have been employed by second-generation researchers to obtain estimates of labor supply parameters when wages are unobserved for nonworkers. Many of these approaches use an additional population wage equation of the form

$$W_i = Z_i\Gamma + \epsilon_{Wi} \tag{11.38}$$

where Z_i is a vector of variables observed for all workers, including, for example, age, education, gender, region, and experience, and ϵ_{Wi} is a mean zero normally distributed random error term representing the effects of unobserved factors such as motivation and abilities.[42] Killingsworth [1983] has distinguished eight estimation procedures that attempt in alternative ways to deal with missing wage data for nonworkers.[43] We now summarize his detailed discussion.

In *Procedure I*, two steps are taken. First, the wage equation (11.38) is estimated by OLS using data on workers only, and then the resulting OLS parameters and data on Z_i are used to create predicted wages $\hat{W}_i$ for both workers and nonworkers. Second, the predicted wages are used as a regressor in the hours worked equation $H_i = X_i\beta + u_{Hi}$, which is estimated by OLS using data on all individuals and setting hours worked of nonworkers equal to zero. As was noted earlier, this procedure produces inconsistent parameter estimates, since it assumes that the hours worked equation applies to all people, rather than only to those for whom $H > 0$.

Procedure II is simply a one-step procedure in which the hours worked equation

$$H_i = X_i\beta + u_{Hi} \qquad \textbf{(11.39)}$$

is estimated by OLS using data only on workers. A variant of Procedure II uses predicted rather than actual wages as a regressor but still limits the sample for which Eq. (11.39) is estimated to individuals who work. Recall that since people for whom $H = 0$ are excluded from estimation, Procedure II suffers from sample selectivity and yields biased parameter estimates.

Procedure III is the Tobit estimator discussed above but uses as a measure of the unobserved wage for nonworkers the predicted wage from Procedure I. Unfortunately, this procedure results in inconsistent parameter estimates, since it is highly likely that sample selectivity problems also bedevil estimation of the wage equation (11.38), which by necessity is estimated by using data only on workers.[44] Specifically, the disturbance term ϵ_{Wi} in Eq. (11.38) reflecting unobserved factors that affect wage rates (such as productivity, abilities, and motivation) is very likely correlated with the disturbance term u_{Hi} representing unobserved factors that influence labor supply (such as tastes for work). This implies that σ_{WH}, the covariance between ϵ_{Wi} and u_{Hi}, is nonzero; alternatively, it implies that the wage variable in the hours worked equation (11.39) is endogenous, correlated with the u_{Hi} disturbance term. As a result, neither use of imputed wage data derived from OLS estimates nor use of actual wage data (if they were somehow available for all workers) would yield consistent estimates of the labor supply model under any of Procedures I, II, or III. To be valid, each of these procedures would require that W_i be exogenous or, equivalently, that σ_{WH} be zero.

Procedure IV is one of several different procedures discussed by Heckman [1974b, 1976a]. It attempts to deal with this endogeneity issue by using a reduced form procedure. Let the marginal rate of substitution function derived from a utility function have the linear form

$$M_i = X_i^*\Phi + \epsilon_{Mi} \qquad \textbf{(11.40)}$$

where the X^* matrix is the X matrix of Eq. (11.39) plus an additional column vector, hours worked H_i, and where the mean zero normally distributed ϵ_{Mi} random error term represents unobservable taste factors. When expression (11.40) is solved for that wage rate at which $H = 0$, one obtains the reservation wage equation

$$W_{ri} = X_i^{**}\theta + \epsilon_{Ri} \tag{11.41}$$

where the X^{**} matrix is the X^* matrix of Eq. (11.40) with the W_i and H_i vectors deleted.

Heckman begins by adopting an analytically convenient proportionality hypothesis (consistent with linear labor supply) where hours of work H_i are proportional to the difference between W_i and W_{ri} whenever $W_i > W_{ri}$ and otherwise are zero:[45]

$$H_i = b(W_i - W_{ri}) = bW_i - bX_i^{**}\theta - b\epsilon_{Ri} \quad \text{iff } W_i > W_{ri} \tag{11.42a}$$

$$H_i = 0 \quad \text{iff } W_i \leq W_{ri} \tag{11.42b}$$

The participation equation implied by this equation system is

$$\begin{aligned} P[i \text{ works}] &= P[W_i > W_{ri}] = P[Z_i\Gamma + \epsilon_{Wi} > X_i^{**}\theta + \epsilon_{Ri}] \\ &= P[\epsilon_{Di} > -J_i] \end{aligned} \tag{11.43}$$

where $\epsilon_{Di} \equiv \epsilon_{Wi} - \epsilon_{Ri}$ and $J_i \equiv Z_i\Gamma - X_i^{**}\theta$. Since ϵ_{Wi} and ϵ_{Ri} are zero mean normally distributed random variables, so too is ϵ_{Di}; the variance of ϵ_{Di} is $\sigma_D^2 = \sigma_W^2 + \sigma_R^2 + 2\sigma_{WR}$. The likelihood function for LFP observations from a sample consisting of workers Ω and nonworkers Ω' can then be written as

$$\ell = \prod_{i\in\Omega} [1 - F(-J_i/\sigma_D)] \cdot \prod_{i\in\Omega'} [F(-J_i/\sigma_D)] \tag{11.44}$$

whose estimation involves standard probit procedures.

The hours of work equation that is consistent with this framework is most interesting. Heckman first estimates the wage determination equation (11.38) by OLS or GLS, using data for workers only, and then directly substitutes this into Eqs. (11.42a) and (11.42b), resulting in

$$H_i = b[Z_i]\,\hat{\Gamma} - X_i^{**}\theta + \epsilon_{Di} \quad \text{iff } [\cdot] > 0 \tag{11.45a}$$

$$H_i = 0 \quad \text{iff } [\cdot] \leq 0 \tag{11.45b}$$

Hence by substituting out the endogenous wage in Eqs. (11.42) using Eq. (11.38), Heckman obtains a reduced form equation (11.45), whose right-hand variables are all exogenous. Three issues merit brief discussion.

First, note that certain variables in the Z matrix from the wage determination equation (11.38) might be identical to those in the X^{**} matrix from the reservation wage equation (11.41), for example, age, education, gender, race, and years of work experience. This raises issues of identification, a problem that arises whenever wages are endogenous. Heckman [1974b, 1979] notes that a condition sufficient for identification is that at least one variable included in Z must be excluded from X^{**}.[46] Second, the data in the Z and X^{**} matrices of the reduced form equations (11.45) are typically observed for both workers and nonworkers, in contrast with traditional labor supply equations such as Eq. (11.29), for which data on W are available only for workers. Hence it appears possible to utilize data on the entire population, not just workers. Third, note that one could estimate Eq. (11.45a) by nonlinear least squares (or by OLS with the parameter estimates from Eq. (11.38) directly substituted in), using data on the entire population and setting $H = 0$ for nonworkers. Killingsworth [1983] calls such a reduced form estimation method Procedure IV.

A major problem with Procedure IV, unfortunately, is that if it is based on data for all individuals with nonworkers H set to zero, it involves a misspecification similar to Procedure I, since in fact Eq. (11.45a) refers only to workers. If one instead estimates Eq. (11.45a) only for workers, sample selectivity problems emerge, similar to those in Procedure II. Hence while it is apparently promising, Procedure IV does not solve the hours worked–wage rate endogeneity problem.

There is, however, a related two-stage estimation procedure that effectively deals with this problem. In *Procedure V*, one takes advantage of the fact that ϵ_{Di} in Eqs. (11.45a) and (11.45b) is normally distributed and that H_i can never be negative. One then specifies the Tobit likelihood function (11.32) adjusted to account for the fact that the disturbance term $b\epsilon_{Di}$ is the product of an unknown parameter to be estimated and the mean zero normally distributed random variable ϵ_{Di}. This yields

$$\ell = \prod_{i \in \Omega} [f(b\epsilon_{Di}/b\sigma_D)/b\sigma_D] \cdot \prod_{i \in \Omega'} F[-J_i/\sigma_D] \qquad \textbf{(11.46)}$$

where $b\epsilon_{Di} \equiv H_i - bJ_i$ and J_i is defined underneath Eq. (11.43).

In the second stage the parameter estimates that are obtained by maximizing the Tobit sample likelihood function (11.46) with respect to b, Γ, θ, and σ_D, along with data on X_i^{**} and Z_i, are used to calculate the inverse Mills ratio $\lambda_i = f(-J_i/\sigma_D)/[1 - F(-J_i/\sigma_D)]$, that is, one uses parameters and data to estimate the probability that an individual with given X_i^{**} and Z_i will work. This estimate of λ_i is then inserted as an additional variable in the wage equation (11.38), whose parameters are estimated by OLS using data on workers only. Note that with Procedure V, estimation of the participation–hours worked equations is based on a reduced form Tobit specification, while estimation of the wage structural equation for workers allows for sample selectivity. However, since the underlying parameters in the reduced form equation are not constrained to equality with structural parameters of the wage equation, parameter estimates are not efficient.

In *Procedure VI*, also discussed in Heckman [1974b], parameters of the entire equation system consisting of Eqs. (11.38) and (11.41) and the Tobit equations (11.42a) and (11.42b) are estimated by using full information maximum likelihood (FIML) simultaneous equation techniques, with cross-equation parameter constraints fully imposed. This FIML specification builds on the assumption of joint normally distributed random disturbance terms ϵ_{Wi} in the wage equation (11.38) and ϵ_{Ri} in the reservation equation (11.41), having covariance σ_{WR} and implying that the random variable $\epsilon_{Di} \equiv \epsilon_{Wi} - \epsilon_{Ri}$ in the hours equation (11.42) is also joint normally distributed with ϵ_{Wi}, having covariance $\sigma_{DW} = \sigma_W^2 - \sigma_{WR}$. As a result, the likelihood function for the wage rate, hours of work, and participation decisions of working individuals in set Ω and nonworking individuals in set Ω' is

$$\ell = \prod_{i \in \Omega} [\, j(b\epsilon_{Di}/b\sigma_D, \epsilon_{Wi}/\sigma_W)] \cdot \prod_{i \in \Omega'} F[-J_i/\sigma_D] \qquad \textbf{(11.47)}$$

where j is the joint probability density function for ϵ_{Di} and ϵ_{Wi} and other terms are as defined above.

The important distinction between the FIML (11.47) and Tobit (11.32) likelihood functions is therefore that while FIML treats W and H as simultaneously determined because of the possible correlation between ϵ_W and ϵ_R, Tobit treats W as strictly exogenous. Further, unlike the Tobit specification (11.45), the FIML estimation of Eq. (11.47) utilizes all available information on W and H for workers.

A common feature of all the above estimation procedures is that they assume that labor supply falls continuously to zero as wage rates or property income declines; see, for example, Eqs. (11.33) and (11.42a). If there are fixed costs of employment, however, one might want to develop a procedure that allows for discontinuous labor supply schedules, that is, one that permits the lowest nonzero number of hours supplied by a worker to be substantially in excess of zero. Two estimation procedures, both known as *generalized Tobit estimators* and often called *Heckit procedures*, allow for such discontinuities.

In *Procedure VII* a three-stage method is implemented. Stage 1 is the same as in Procedure V, except that one now estimates parameters of a probit (not a Tobit) likelihood function for participation, such as Eq. (11.44). By using a probit rather than a Tobit specification, continuity of the labor supply schedule is not imposed. In the second stage of Procedure VII, one uses the probit parameter estimates to compute probit estimates of the inverse Mills ratio $\lambda_i = f(-J_i/\sigma_D)/[1 - F(-J_i/\sigma_D)]$ and then appends λ_i as an additional regressor to the wage equation (11.38) to obtain OLS selection bias–corrected parameter estimates using data on workers only; Killingsworth [1983, p. 159] notes that the parameter estimate on λ_i in this second stage should be interpreted as an estimate of σ_{WD}, the covariance between ϵ_{Wi} and ϵ_{Di}.

In the third and final stage of Procedure VII, one estimates by OLS the reduced form hours equation (11.45a) with the probit inverse Mills ratio variable added, based on data for workers only, which, along with the structural wage parameter estimates from Stage 2, yields consistent estimates of the labor supply structural parameters. In this case the parameter estimate on λ_i is interpreted as an estimate of $[(\sigma_{HD}/\sigma_D) + b(\sigma_{WD}/\sigma_D)]$, where σ_{HD} is the covariance between u_{Hi} and ϵ_{Di}. Formulae for the asymptotic variance-covari-

JAMES HECKMAN

Labor Econometrician

More than any other economist in the last two decades, James Heckman has affected the econometric modeling of the labor force participation and labor supply decisions. Heckman's contributions began with his 1971 Ph.D. thesis at Princeton, "Three Essays on Household Labor Supply and the Demand for Market Goods." Since then, as detailed in this chapter, Heckman's research has essentially built the core of what are now called the "second-generation models" of labor supply. Two distinguishing features of this research are that the various estimating equations are derived explicitly from neoclassical utility theory and that the stochastic disturbance terms are an integral part of the model, rather than being "tacked on" at the end of the derivation. Heckman's analysis of self-selection in labor supply has produced a new methodology for solving self-selection and sample selection problems, often called the "Heckit" procedure; it is now widely used in a variety of contexts. Although they are not discussed in this chapter, Heckman has also developed and implemented empirically a number of dynamic discrete choice models, as well as models for the analysis of duration data. Some of this research has involved new uses of semiparametric and nonparametric methods.

Born in Chicago in 1944, Heckman pursued undergraduate studies at Colorado College, majoring in mathematics, earning a Phi Beta Kappa key, and graduating summa cum laude. He then went on to study economics at Princeton, and after spending a summer as Junior Economist at the Council of Economic Advisors in Washington, D.C., Heckman was awarded the Ph.D. degree in 1971, studying under Stanley Black, E. Phillip Howrey, Harry Kelejian, Richard Quandt, and Albert Rees.

Heckman's first academic appointment was at Columbia University. In 1973 he accepted a position at the University of Chicago, and in 1985 he was named its Henry Schultz Professor of Economics. In 1988 he moved to Yale University, where he now is the A. Whitney Griswold Professor of Economics. Heckman has been elected a Fellow of the Econometric Society and of the American Academy of Arts and Sciences. In 1983 he was awarded the distinguished John Bates Clark Medal by the American Economics Association.

ance matrix of estimates obtained from this three-stage procedure have been derived by Lung-Fei Lee [1982], but consistent estimates of standard errors for the third-stage parameters can be obtained in a computationally less burdensome manner by using the Halbert White [1980] robust estimator.

Finally, in *Procedure VIII* the first two stages are identical to those in Procedure VII, but in the third stage, instead of using the reduced form specification (11.45a), one employs instrumental variable and selectivity bias-corrected techniques to estimate parameters of the structural hours equation (11.33) for workers. More specifically, λ_i is added as a regressor to the first equation in (11.33), and instrumental variable estimation is undertaken with the actual wage rates of workers replaced by fitted values derived from the second-stage selectivity bias–corrected wage equation estimates; hence the probit λ_i appears as a regressor in both the wage and hours equations.

It is worth noting that if in fact the labor supply schedule is continuous, parameter estimates from the Heckit multistage Procedures VII and VIII should be identical to those from the FIML Procedure VI. On the other hand, if the labor supply schedule is discontinuous owing to, say, fixed costs of employment, then the Heckit multistage generalized Tobit estimators of Procedures VII and VIII should differ from FIML. However, unless one specifies explicitly the nature of the optimization problem facing individuals—including, for example, the budget constraint implications of fixed costs of employment, the Heckit parameter estimates are "black box" in the sense that they are unable to provide insights on what factors have generated the discontinuities. For further discussion of such important specification issues, see Killingsworth [1983, pp. 161–168], who considers theoretical and econometric aspects of several explicit models of discontinuous labor supply.

11.3.B.2 INCORPORATING TAXES INTO LABOR SUPPLY To this point, our discussion of labor supply has ignored the presence of taxes. Since consumption expenditures derive from after-tax income, the relevant budget constraint set for the analysis of individual labor supply is the after-tax constraint, not the before-tax one. Taxes on wage and property income can significantly affect labor supply, in part because taxes often introduce a wedge between average and marginal after-tax wage rates. Moreover, since much public policy discussion has focused on the labor supply effects of changing statutory provisions of the income tax code, it is important that we focus attention on the effects of taxes on labor supply. Second-generation research on this topic has been substantial, with noteworthy contributions made by Harvey S. Rosen [1976], Gary Burtless and Jerry A. Hausman [1978], Hausman [1979; 1980; 1981a, b; 1985], Terence J. Wales and Alan D. Woodland [1979], James J. Heckman and Thomas E. MaCurdy [1981], and Alice Nakamura and Masao Nakamura [1981a].

To see the impact of taxes, let us assume that the individual receives real property income V and earns a gross (before-tax) real wage of W per hour worked. As is shown in Fig. 11.3, in the absence of taxes the budget constraint

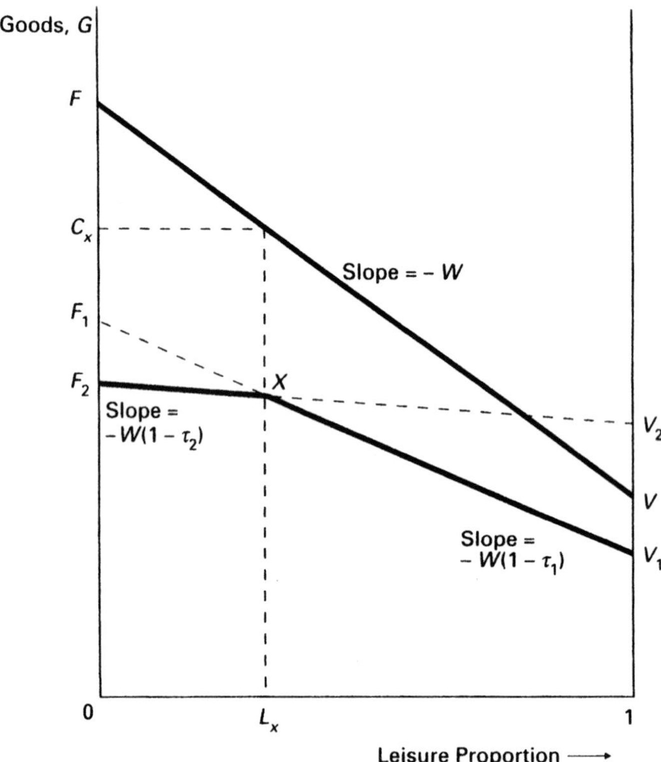

Figure 11.3 The Effects of Varying Marginal Tax Rates on the Budget Constraint

is $1VF$, with the nonvertical portion having a slope of $-W$. Suppose, however, that the individual is taxed on the sum of property and wage income. If this total income is C_x or less, let the tax rate be $100 \cdot \tau_1$ percent; if total income is greater than C_x, let the marginal tax rate on total income above C_x be $100 \cdot \tau_2$ percent, where $\tau_2 > \tau_1$. In Fig. 11.3 this implies that if the individual works hours between zero and $1 - L_x$ and chooses a leisure amount between L_x and 1, the marginal after-tax wage rate is $W(1 - \tau_1)$, while if the individual works more than $1 - L_x$ hours (chooses less L than L_x), the marginal after-tax wage rate is $W(1 - \tau_2)$; thus the kinked after-tax budget constraint is $1V_1XF_2$. Note also that in Fig. 11.3 the vertical distance between the two budget constraints represents the total amount of taxes paid at various proportions of L.

The budget constraint set in Fig. 11.3 is rather simple. It is relatively straightforward to extend the analysis to a progressive tax structure with m distinct and successively flatter linear segments, corresponding to increasing marginal tax rates $\tau_m > \tau_{m-1} > \cdots > \tau_1$; in such a case the budget constraint set would be quasi-concave to the origin. Note that with such a quasi-concave budget constraint set, given strictly convex indifference curves, the equilibrium point of tangency between the indifference curve and the budget set is unique and occurs either at one of the kinks or at an interior location between kinks.

However, if one introduces other real-world statutory tax provisions into the analysis such as exemptions, deductibles, and transfer payments tied to hours worked, then the budget constraint set may include nonconcave regions, and as a result, multiple tangencies of indifference curves to the budget set might occur. As Wales and Woodland [1979] and Hausman [1981a] emphasize, in such cases, to determine the utility-maximizing hours of work, one must know the form of the utility function and compare utility at the various tangency points. This introduces complications into the estimation of the effects of taxes on labor supply.

One way of simplifying the potentially complex budget constraint set involves linearization; this has been implemented empirically by, among others, Hall [1973] and Wales [1973]. Specifically, for an individual who works somewhere along segment V_1X, when confronted with the budget set $1V_1XF_2$, that individual could be assumed to act *as if* he or she faced a simple straight-line budget constraint $1V_1XF_1$ with real property income equal to V_1 and a real marginal wage rate of $W(1 - \tau_1)$. The effects of small changes in property income or before-tax wage rates could then be analyzed by assuming that the individual does not shift onto a different segment of the budget constraint set. Incidentally, in this case the after-tax property income V_1 is the amount of disposable income that is available to the individual assuming that $H = 0$ and $L = 1$. Following W. Erwin Diewert [1971], Burtless and Hausman [1978] call this the individual's *virtual income;* hence virtual income corresponds with the before-tax property income V and the tax rate τ_1.

Similarly, for an individual who is working somewhere along segment XF_2, when confronted with the same kinked budget constraint set, that individual might be envisaged as acting *as if* he or she faced the simple straight-line budget constraint $1V_2XF_2$ with a virtual income of V_2 and a real marginal wage rate of $W(1 - \tau_2)$. Hence complex budget constraints can be made considerably less complicated simply by linearizing them at the individual's equilibrium point. Note that in econometric implementation, at each observation the measures of after-tax W and virtual income V used must be changed to reflect the after-tax wage and property income corresponding with the individual's marginal tax rate at the equilibrium point.

Although this linearized budget constraint approach is attractive, it also introduces new econometric problems. Several issues are of particular importance in empirical implementation. First, because the after-tax W and V measures depend on H (the marginal tax rate τ varies with $H = 1 - L$), the disturbance term in the hours worked equation is by construction correlated with the after-tax measures of W and V; hence estimation by OLS provides inconsistent estimates of the parameters, and instrumental variable (IV) estimation may be preferable. IV estimates have been reported by, among others, Jerry A. Hausman and David A. Wise [1976] and Harvey S. Rosen [1976]. Rosen's study is of special interest, since in it he examines tax perception.

Rosen finds that he cannot reject the null hypothesis that individuals perceive the effects of taxes and react to the net after-tax wage rather than to the before-tax gross wage.

Second, and closely related to the previous point, it might be that in response to a change in before-tax V or W, the individual would shift to an entirely different segment on the budget constraint set. Estimation and model predictions based on predetermined marginal tax rates would therefore be unreliable. As might be expected, such estimation problems increase when the concave budget set is kinked rather than continuous, that is, when marginal tax rate changes are discrete rather than continuous. Problems of estimation become even more severe if the budget set has nonconcave and kinked portions.

Such problems with the linearization or local approximation approach have given rise to a variety of alternative procedures in which the complete budget set is evaluated.[47] In one procedure the previous no-tax estimation framework in which the probability of $H > 0$ is estimated along with an hours worked equation conditional on $H > 0$—a single-threshold framework—is generalized to include multiple marginal tax rates by permitting multiple thresholds, each corresponding with a different segment of the budget set in which the hours worked decision entails a different marginal tax rate. This type of model can be estimated by using the ordered probit function; see Takeshi Amemiya [1975, 1981] for a discussion of this estimator and Antoni Zabalza [1983] and John C. Ham and Cheng Hsiao [1984] for empirical implementations.

Yet another procedure assumes that random disturbances arise either from individuals' errors in optimization or from measurement error of H and involves evaluating utility at each point of the individual's budget constraint set (including the kink points), given values of the relevant structural parameters of an assumed direct or indirect utility function. This procedure, which is often called the complete budget constraint approach (CBC), literally solves the individual's utility maximization problem for each set of parameter values and is obviously very computationally intensive. Notice in particular that for each set of parameter values, the individual's entire maximization problem is solved; estimation proceeds, as has been noted by Wales and Woodland [1980], by maximizing the likelihood of observed hours with respect to the entire set of structural parameters of the utility or indirect utility function.

The Wales-Woodland approach has been generalized by Burtless and Hausman [1978] and by Hausman [1980] to allow the disturbance term in the hours worked equation to originate not only from errors in optimization or errors in the measurement of H, but also from omitted variables that are known by the individual but are not observable by the econometrician. Remarkably, this more general conceptual framework can be implemented without resort to the laborious Woodland-Wales maximizing procedure, provided that one makes very strong assumptions about the functional form of the hours worked equation.

The above discussion therefore suggests that while the presence of taxes considerably complicates the analysis of labor supply, empirical analysis can proceed, provided that one is willing to make tradeoffs concerning computational complexity and flexibility of the functional form. This type of tradeoff is, of course, a familiar quandary to the practicing econometrician.

11.3.B.3 EMPIRICAL FINDINGS We now conclude our discussion of second-generation research in labor supply by providing a brief summary of empirical findings. More detailed surveys can be found in, among others, Heckman, Killingsworth, and MaCurdy [1981, pp. 106–112], Killingsworth [1983, pp. 179–206]; and Killingsworth and Heckman [1986, pp. 185–197].

Most of the second-generation studies avoid the pitfalls associated with first-generation research. In particular, second-generation analyses explicitly distinguish the LFP function from the hours supplied function, yet they also note that both derive from a common utility-maximizing framework. Within this framework a substantial proportion of second-generation studies treat hours worked and the wage rate as endogenous. Finally, most of the second-generation studies take account of the selectivity bias in estimating labor supply functions, using one or more of the Procedures V through VIII summarized above.

A vast majority of second-generation work has been concerned either with fixed costs and discontinuities in the labor supply function (Cogan [1980b, 1981], Giora Hanoch [1976, 1980], Heckman [1980], and T. Paul Schultz [1980]) or with taxes and nonlinear budget constraints (Burtless and Hausman [1978], Rosen [1976], and Wales and Woodland [1979]). With the notable exception of Hausman [1980; 1981a, b; 1983] and Alice Nakamura and Masao Nakamura [1981a], most studies have focused on either fixed costs or taxes but have not considered them jointly. As might be expected, the numerous second-generation studies differ not only in estimation procedures employed, but also in terms of the underlying data samples. This heterogeneity makes it somewhat difficult to provide a concise comparison and summary of research results.

Two criteria might be used in assessing this research. First, do second-generation results suggest important stylized facts of labor supply that are not apparent from first-generation studies? Second, do estimates of labor supply responses based on second-generation research differ appreciably from those based on OLS estimation of first-generation equations? The answer to the first question appears to be "perhaps," while the answer to the second is an emphatic "yes."

In terms of the first criterion, like the first-generation studies, most (but not all, as we shall soon see) second-generation results generally conclude that female labor supply is considerably more responsive to changes in property income and wage rates than is male labor supply. Killingsworth [1983, p. 206] goes even further, concluding that "female labor supply responses are somewhat larger than was apparent in first-generation research" (see also his quote at the beginning of this chapter). He notes as well that second-generation studies that are based on continuous labor supply schedules (using Procedures III, V, and VI) tend to produce greater estimates of female labor supply elasticities than do second-generation studies that allow for a discontinuous labor supply schedule (Procedures VII and VIII). Moreover, most second-generation research explicitly considering discontinuities in the labor supply schedule finds that such discontinuities are substantial. Estimates of the "point of discontinuity"—the minimum amount of annual hours at which wages are sufficiently high to overcome fixed costs—are reasonably consistent over diverse studies. For example, Heckman [1980] and Cogan [1980b, 1981] report estimates that range between only 1126 and 1383 hours, while Hanoch's lowest estimate is 820 hours.

Unfortunately, however, like their first-generation counterparts, in terms of wage and income elasticity estimates, the second-generation estimates of labor supply responses are very diverse. In fact, noting that estimates of the female uncompensated wage elasticity of annual hours vary from −0.30 to +14.00, Killingsworth and Heckman [1986, p. 185] reach the saddening conclusion that

> It is not uncommon for authors of empirical papers on labor supply to point to results in other studies similar to the ones they have obtained, but . . . such comparisons may not always be informative; it is all too easy to find at least one other set of results similar to almost any set of estimates one may have obtained.[48]

In spite of this diversity, and in terms of the second criterion for evaluating second-generation studies, on the basis of research to 1980, Heckman, Killingsworth, and MaCurdy [1981] have argued that elasticity estimates obtained from second-generation studies tend to be greater—sometimes considerably greater—in absolute value than those based on first-generation techniques. They cite two types of evidence to support their tentative conclusion. First, an important Monte Carlo study by Wales and Woodland [1980] indicated that, given joint normality, OLS estimates are badly biased toward zero (though perhaps not as much in the wage equation as in the hours equation), whereas techniques that correct for sample selection bias are much closer to the "true" parameter values. Second, studies of female labor supply by, among others, Cogan [1980a], Heckman [1976a], and Schultz [1980], found that labor supply elasticity estimates that were based on second-generation estimation procedures were consistently larger than those based on first-generation OLS methods.

Not all labor econometricians agree with Heckman, Killingsworth, and MaCurdy's assessment. In particular, already in the late 1970s, Alice Nakamura and Masao Nakamura [1979] reported results of a second-generation study that found female labor supply to be basically unresponsive to changes in wage rates, similar to the findings reported by others for males (see their quote at the beginning of this chapter); additional supporting findings were presented later in Nakamura and Nakamura [1981a; 1985a, b]. This controversy about whether males and females respond differentially to wage rate changes is of considerable interest, and therefore in Section 11.3.C we will discuss it further when we consider the Mroz [1987] article.

Finally, in terms of analyzing the effects of taxes on labor supply, not much is known yet concerning the consequences and relative merits of using linearized (LBC) or complete budget constraint (CBC) estimation procedures. Killingsworth [1983, pp. 204–205] notes that the LBC and CBC estimates differ considerably, but since most CBC studies employed restrictive utility function specifications or limited samples,[49] it is not clear how much of the difference is due to LBC versus CBC, versus the choice of a restrictive functional form.

The empirical results on the effects of taxes on labor supply reported by Hausman [1981a] are of particular interest, however. Hausman incorporates effects of a progressive income tax schedule, as well as provisions of numerous U.S. transfer programs resulting in budget constraint sets with both concave and nonconcave regions. Following the previous tradition, Hausman treats the husband as the primary worker in the family and specifies that in making her labor supply decisions, the wife treats the husband's income as predetermined.[50] Significantly, the functional form and stochastic specification employed by Hausman constrain leisure to be a normal good. Fixed costs of working are incorporated into the model. Hausman computes virtual incomes corresponding to each individual's equilibrium marginal tax rate and employs a specification in which increases in income never raise desired hours of work. However, heterogeneity in preferences among individuals can result in income effects that vary across the population. A CBC estimation procedure is employed, and estimation results are compared on the basis of a combined concave, nonconcave budget constraint set with results from a globally concave approximation to a complex budget constraint set.

For husbands, Hausman finds that the uncompensated wage elasticity is essentially zero but that the income effect is negative and substantial. Results from the concave and nonconcave estimation procedures are similar. Given these estimated income effects, Hausman concludes that for husbands with average tastes and in the $8000–$12,000 federal tax bracket in 1980, the progressive income tax structure reduces labor supply by 8% compared to a no-tax situation and by 7% compared to a proportional tax system generating equal tax revenue.

For wives, Hausman uses results from his earlier research that suggested that the wives' wage rates before taxes are not a function of hours worked; moreover, he also concludes that sample selectivity is not a significant problem in the female wage rate equation. Hausman estimates the uncompensated wage elasticity for the average woman working full time as being equal to a rather substantial 0.995 and, if fixed costs are taken into account, at 0.906. The income elasticity is negative and substantial, reflecting in part the leisure normality assumption. These results imply that progressive income taxes

JERRY A. HAUSMAN

Modeling the Effects of Taxes on Labor Supply

Jerry Hausman's contributions to the theory and practice of econometrics have been numerous and wide ranging. While students might recognize him best for the oft-used specification test procedure that he developed, Hausman has written extensively in econometric theory on simultaneous equations estimation, the interpretation of instrumental variable estimators, estimation of models with errors in variables, computational algorithms for nonlinear structural models, and panel data estimators.

Although Hausman has made major contributions in econometric theory, he considers himself essentially an applied econometrician. He has long been interested in public finance (he currently serves as a Member of the Massachusetts Governor's Advisory Council for Revenue and Taxation), and this interest led him to research the effects of taxes on labor supply. One of Hausman's important econometric findings, discussed in this chapter, is that the U.S. income tax system leads to greater deadweight loss than had previously been believed and that an equal revenue-generating tax structure with personal exemptions and then a proportional tax would involve much smaller efficiency losses.

In addition to his work on the effects of taxes on labor supply, Hausman has published empirical studies on the effects of alternative rate structures on the demand for electricity, on factors affecting the purchase and utilization of energy-using durable goods, on the relationship between patents and research and development, and most recently, on the effects of competition and technical progress in telecommunications.

Born in West Virginia in 1946, Jerry Hausman obtained his A.B. degree (summa cum laude) from Brown University in 1968. After spending two years with the U.S. Army Corps of Engineers in Anchorage, Alaska, Hausman resumed studies at Oxford University, where he was a Marshall Scholar. At Oxford, Hausman earned a B.Phil. degree in 1972, and a D.Phil. in 1973; his dissertation was entitled "A Theoretical and Empirical Study of Vintage Investment and Production in Great Britain."

Hausman's first academic appointment was at MIT in 1972, and aside from occasional visiting appointments, he has been there ever since, teaching courses in econometric theory, microeconomics, public finance and a course in the industrial organization of telecommunications. Hausman has been elected a Fellow of the Econometric Society, and in 1985 he was awarded the John Bates Clark Medal by the American Economic Association.

reduce wives' labor supply in large part by decreasing the net after-tax wage. Specifically, to the extent that the wife is a "secondary" worker, Hausman notes that she faces a "marriage tax," since the first dollar of her earnings is taxed at the rate that is applicable to the last dollar of her husband's earnings.[51] Hausman also examines the effects of taxes on labor supply of female heads of families and reports significant sensitivity to taxes.

Overall, Hausman estimates that the progressive federal U.S. income tax structure existing in 1980 results in an 8.6% decline in labor supply compared to a no-tax situation and estimates that the deadweight loss as a percent of income tax revenues raised is 28.7%. Owing to progressivity, deadweight loss increases sharply with market wage rates and associated marginal taxes. By contrast, a proportional income tax system that generated identical tax revenues would reduce labor supply by only slightly more than 1%, and the average deadweight loss as a proportion of tax revenues raised would be only 7.1%. Arguing that a proportional tax system with an initial exemption provides an alternative way of implementing progressivity without entailing as large a deadweight loss, Hausman concludes that "the progressive income tax system may be a costly way to seek income redistribution. Other, more cost-effective means of income redistribution may well exist."[52]

Hausman's findings are not universally accepted, however. For example, in commenting on Hausman [1983], Heckman [1983] conjectures that Hausman's rather large wage responsiveness estimates reflect at least in part the effects of his assumption, imposed on the data, that leisure is a normal good.

11.3.C On the Sensitivity of Results to Alternative Statistical and Economic Assumptions: The Mroz Study

In reviewing second generation empirical results in the previous section we emphasized that the substantial heterogeneity that is observed in the estimates of wage and income elasticities could be due in part to the fact that the various studies differ in terms of estimation method, functional form, and data base. This suggests that an informative research project would involve undertaking detailed sensitivity analyses of existing alternative second-generation estimation methods but using a common data base and functional form. That is precisely the approach taken by Thomas Mroz [1987], who employs data from the 1976 Panel Study of Income Dynamics (PSID) sample consisting of 753 white married women aged 30–60, of whom 428 worked at some time during 1975. Using these data, Mroz compares elasticity estimates based on a variety of alternative statistical and economic assumptions that were made by authors of previous studies.

Mroz's study is of considerable interest because, although it does not focus on new methodological developments, it yields important results concerning sensitivity, and it follows up on Nakamura and Nakamura [1979;

1981a; 1985a, b] in challenging the conventional wisdom of labor economists that the responsiveness of female labor supply to changes in wage rates and income is larger than that of men.[53] We now examine the Mroz study and the associated second-generation empirical literature in more detail.

Mroz begins by noting the very large diversity of reported estimates of female labor supply responses to variations in wage rates and income.[54] To make the results of various studies comparable, Mroz evaluates the implied effects of these studies on annual hours worked in 1975, assuming that the wife's wage is $4.50 and her hours worked are 1500, the husband's wage is $7.00 and his hours are 2000, the household nonlabor income is $1000, and the labor and nonlabor marginal tax rates are 0.339 and 0.280, respectively. Mroz's evidence on the wide range of labor supply response estimates is presented in Table 11.2, which reproduces Table 1 of Mroz [1987, p. 766]. There it is seen that while the vast majority of uncompensated wage effect estimates

Table 11.2 MROZ's Survey of Estimates of Married Women's Labor Supply Responses

Study	Estimation Method	Wage Effect	Income Effect
Boskin [1973]	Instrumental variables	29	−16.9
Cogan [1980a]	Tobit	865	−32.3
Cogan [1980a]	Instrumental variables	349	−11.7
Cogan [1980b]	Tobit	632	−22.8
Cogan [1980b]	Fixed costs	196	−8.5
Cogan [1981]	Fixed costs	269	−22.4
Greenhalgh [1980]	Instrumental variables	213	−65.6
Hausman [1981a]	Convex budget sets	328	−125.0
Hausman [1981a]	Nonconvex budget sets	335	−118.0
Hausman [1981a]	Fixed costs	305	−113.0
Heckman [1976a]	Tobit	1462	−73.4
Heckman [1976a]	Generalized Tobit	−499	51.0
Heckman [1980]	Generalized Tobit	1401	−18.7
Layard et al. [1980]	Tobit	128	−118.2
Layard et al. [1980]	Instrumental variables	22	−11.8
Leuthold [1978]	1967 estimates	14	−3.0
Leuthold [1978]	1969 estimates	45	−7.1
Leuthold [1978]	1971 estimates	33	5.8
Nakamura and Nakamura [1981a]	Generalized Tobit	−16	−15.0
Schultz [1980]	Tobit	123	−67.0
Schultz [1980]	Instrumental variables	−26	−1.9

Notes: These effects are evaluated at a wife's wage of $4.50, wife's hours at 1500, husband's wage of $7.00, husband's hours at 2000, household nonlabor income of $1000, and labor and nonlabor marginal tax rates of 0.339 and 0.280, respectively. The income effect is per $1000 in 1975 dollars.
Source: Data from Thomas A. Mroz "The Sensitivity of an Empirical Model of Married Women's Hours of Work to Economic and Statistical Assumptions," *Econometrica*, Vol. 55, No. 4, 1987, Table 1, p. 766.

are positive, the range is substantial, varying from -499 to $+1462$ for a \$1 change in the wage rate; estimated income effects per \$1000 in 1975 dollars are primarily negative but range from -125 to $+51$. Further, there does not appear to be any obvious relationship between the estimation method that is employed and the magnitude or sign of the estimated labor supply response.

Mroz proceeds by choosing a simple functional form for the labor supply equation, one that Nicholas Stern [1986] derived explicitly from an indirect utility function. This labor supply equation is

$$H_i = a_0 + a_1 \ln (W_i) + a_2 V_i + a_3' Z_i + \epsilon_i \tag{11.48}$$

where H_i is the ith woman's hours of work in 1975, W_i is a measure of her wage rate, V_i is a measure of other income received by the household in thousands of 1975 dollars, Z_i is a vector of additional control variables (including the wife's age, her years of schooling, the number of children less than six years old in the household, and the number of children between the ages of six and 18), and ϵ_i is a stochastic disturbance term. At a given wage rate, Mroz computes the uncompensated wage effect on hours worked for a \$1 wage rate change as simply $\partial H_i/\partial W_i = a_1/W_i$ and the income effect as $\partial H_i/\partial V_i = a_2$. The corresponding uncompensated wage and income elasticities are then computed as $\partial \ln H_i/\partial \ln W_i = a_1/H_i$ and $\partial \ln H_i/\partial \ln V_i = a_2 V_i/H_i$, respectively.

The 1976 PSID data sample (for year 1975) is employed by Mroz in this study because only in 1976 did the PSID survey directly interview wives in households. During all other years the household head supplied information about the wife's labor market experiences during the previous year. As Mroz notes, "one suspects that the own reporting is more accurate, and it is for this reason that many recent studies of married women's labor supply have used these data."[55] Annual hours worked H_i is measured as the product of the number of weeks the wife worked for pay in 1975 and the average number of hours of work per week during the weeks she worked. The wage rate W_i is measured as average hourly earnings, calculated as total labor income of the wife in 1975 divided by H_i. Note that if there is a random measurement error in annual hours worked, a spurious negative correlation will emerge between hours worked and this wage rate measure. Finally, the property income measure V_i is defined as the household's total money income minus the wife's labor income, in thousands of 1975 dollars.

For a "base case estimation," Mroz reports results when parameters in Eq. (11.48) are estimated by OLS and the sample is restricted to those who work (recall from Section 11.3.B.1 that this is Procedure II)

$$\begin{aligned} H_i = a_0 - &\underset{(81)}{17} \ln (W_i) - \underset{(3.1)}{4.2}\, V_i - \underset{(131)}{342}\, \text{KL6}_i - \underset{(29)}{115}\, \text{K618}_i + \text{others} \end{aligned} \tag{11.49}$$

Here KL6_i is the number of children under age six in the household, K618_i is the number of children between ages six and 18, numbers in parentheses are estimated standard errors (adjusted for arbitrary forms of heteroskedasticity, using the Halbert White [1980] procedure), and "others" refers to the additional variables (wife's age and wife's education), whose parameter estimates, along with the intercept, are not reported by Mroz. Note that these OLS estimates imply that both the uncompensated wage effect and income effect are negative (the elasticities are $-17/1500 = -0.0113$ and $-4.2/1500 = -0.0028$, respectively) and that the presence of children in the household (particularly those under age six) reduces labor supply substantially, other things being equal. The negative OLS estimated wage effect is not surprising, since as was noted above, if there is a random measurement error in H_i, then a spurious negative relationship occurs between H_i and W_i.

With Eq. (11.49) as a basis of comparison, Mroz then examines the effects of three variations: (1) alternative exogeneity assumptions on the regressors, issues that are raised in particular by Nakamura and Nakamura [1981a]; (2) statistical control for self-selection into the labor force—a classic issue; and (3) the impacts of controlling for taxes. We begin by summarizing results that occur once Mroz controls for possible correlation between regressors and the disturbance term in Eq. (11.48) through the use of an instrumental variable procedure such as two-stage least squares (2SLS).

Treating ln (W_i) as an endogenous variable that might be correlated with the disturbance term ϵ_i in Eq. (11.48), Mroz uses as instruments the wife's reported labor market experience (the number of years the woman has worked for pay since her eighteenth birthday), this variable squared, and several different polynomials in the wife's and husband's age and education. This variant on Procedure II (see Section 11.3.B.1) results in an estimated 2SLS equation whose wage and income parameters are much different from the OLS estimates of Eq. (11.49):

$$H_i = a_0 + \underset{(217)}{672} \ln(W_i) - \underset{(3.6)}{6.4}\, V_i - \underset{(147)}{283}\, \text{KL6}_i - \underset{(36)}{85}\, \text{K618}_i + \cdots \tag{11.50}$$

Note that unlike the OLS estimates, here the 2SLS estimate of the uncompensated wage response is positive and highly significant; in fact, this large 2SLS estimate on the wage coefficient is similar to some of the largest wage effects reported in Table 11.2. The 2SLS income effect, however, is more negative than the OLS estimate, and the 2SLS estimates of the effects of children on labor supply, while also negative, are smaller than OLS estimates. Further, using the elasticity formulae underneath Eq. (11.48) and evaluating derivatives at $H_i = 1500$ and $V_i = 1$ (recall V_i is measured in thousands of 1975 dollars), we see that the implied 2SLS uncompensated wage elasticity estimate is $672/1500 = 0.448$, while the income elasticity estimate is very small, $-6.4*1/1500 = -0.0043$.

Following a conjecture by Nakamura and Nakamura [1981a, p. 480], Mroz then examines whether the disturbance term in Eq. (11.48) reflects in part the unobservable preferences of the individual, including her attitude toward work. If this were true, it is likely that a variable such as the wife's labor market experience would also be correlated with the disturbance term and that as a result this variable and its square would not be legitimate instruments. Mroz therefore reestimates Eq. (11.48) by 2SLS but excludes the experience variable and its square as instruments. This yields an equation with a much smaller and statistically insignificant estimated wage effect:

$$\underset{}{H_i} = a_0 + \underset{(220)}{46} \ln(W_i) - \underset{(3.3)}{4.4}\, V_i - \underset{(131)}{337}\, \text{KL6}_i - \underset{(30)}{112}\, \text{K618}_i + \cdots \tag{11.51}$$

With the experience variables excluded as instruments the uncompensated wage elasticity falls to $46/1500 = 0.031$, and the income elasticity to $-4.4*1/1500 = -0.0029$. Such low estimates match some of the smallest estimates reported in Table 11.2. The estimated effects of children on labor supply, however, are not affected as much and in fact are quite similar in the various OLS and 2SLS specifications. These results therefore demonstrate that estimates of the wage and income responses are very sensitive to assumptions concerning the endogeneity of regressors and the choice of instruments.

To make the choice of instruments less arbitrary, Mroz proceeds with a variant of the Durbin-Wu-Hausman-White specification test.[56] In this context the null hypothesis is that the experience instruments are uncorrelated with ϵ_i, and the alternative hypothesis is that they are correlated. Mroz shows that a test of this hypothesis amounts to testing whether the estimated wage coefficient in the 2SLS equation (11.50) with the experience variables included as instruments is equal to the estimated wage coefficient in the 2SLS equation (11.51) with experience variables excluded as instruments. He derives the formulae for the asymptotic variances and covariances and obtains an asymptotic normal test statistic of 3.0, implying that the null hypothesis is rejected at any reasonable level of significance. Mroz therefore concludes that the wife's previous labor market experience is not exogenous in the labor supply equation and that as a result the experience variables are invalid instruments, consistent with the Nakamura and Nakamura [1981a] conjecture. Interestingly, Mroz undertakes similar exogeneity tests for the KL6_i, K618_i, and V_i variables and finds that the exogeneity of these children and nonwife income variables cannot be rejected at reasonable levels of significance.[57]

Second, as was discussed in Section 11.3.B.1, a major problem with each of the above Procedure II estimates is that they are based on a subsample of working women only and therefore do not control for self-selection into the labor force. To examine the impact of ignoring self-selection bias, Mroz estimates the labor supply equation using the Heckit multistage Procedure VIII. In particular, using the full sample of 753 married women, Mroz first estimates a probit model of labor force participation in which the explanatory variables include KL6, K618, V, polynomials in the wife's age and education, the education of the wife's mother and father, the county's unemployment rate, a dummy variable for large city, and the wife's previous labor market experience and its square (note that the wife's wage is not included). Of the 18 regressors, only the coefficients on KL6, V, experience, and its square are more than twice their estimated standard error. Mroz then uses this probit model to estimate the inverse Mills ratio λ (see the discussion in Section 11.3.B.1, especially that on Procedures VII and VIII) and appends this variable as a regressor in a wage rate determination equation in which the other right-hand variables are the same as in the estimated probit equation but where the sample is limited to workers (428 of the 753 observations). In the third and final stage, Mroz uses the fitted value from the wage determination equation as an instrument in a 2SLS estimation of the hours worked equation (11.48) but with the inverse Mills ratio λ_i added as a regressor. It is worth noting that since the wife's previous labor market experience and its square are regressors in the first two stages of this Heckit procedure, this particular estimation assumes that these experience variables are exogenous.

The resulting estimated labor supply equation has a small positive uncompensated wage effect and a small positive income effect, neither of which is statistically different from zero:

$$\begin{aligned} H_i = a_0 &+ \underset{(225)}{122} \ln(W_i) + \underset{(4.5)}{3.9}\, V_i + \underset{(173)}{53}\, \mathrm{KL6}_i \\ &- \underset{(34)}{87}\, \mathrm{K618}_i - \underset{(171)}{758}\, \lambda_i + \cdots \end{aligned} \tag{11.52}$$

In this case, when evaluated at the same wage and income as earlier, the estimated uncompensated wage elasticity is but 0.081 (122/1500), and the income elasticity is 0.0026 (3.9/1500). Surprisingly. the estimated coefficient on young children KL6 is now positive (but insignificantly different from zero), while that on K618 is still negative but considerably smaller in absolute value than in Eq. (11.50). Since the ratio of the estimated coefficient on λ_i to its standard error is 753/171 = 4.43, a number that is greater than the critical value for the normal distribution at reasonable levels of significance, Mroz rejects the null hypothesis that there is no self-selection bias.

However, when the same multistage Heckit estimation Procedure VIII is employed but the wife's labor market experience and its square are omitted as regressors in the probit and wage determination equations, a rather different labor supply equation is obtained:

$$\begin{aligned} H_i = a_0 &+ \underset{(227)}{64} \ln(W_i) - \underset{(9.2)}{1.0}\, V_i - \underset{(408)}{183}\, \mathrm{KL6}_i \\ &- \underset{(34)}{106}\, \mathrm{K618}_i - \underset{(467)}{294}\, \lambda_i + \cdots \end{aligned} \tag{11.53}$$

Not only is the uncompensated wage effect coefficient small and insignificantly different from zero, but the income effect is negative, small, and also insignificant. Further, the estimated coefficient on λ_i is insignificantly different from zero, implying that one cannot reject the null hypothesis that there is no self-selection bias.[58]

These results suggest that whether the experience variables are assumed to be exogenous has a decisive impact on whether the self-selection bias is statistically significant in the labor supply equation. To test for exogeneity of the experience variables, Mroz uses the same specification test procedure as was described earlier, but with the asymptotic variance formulae adjusted to include sample selectivity. The null hypothesis of exogeneity reduces again to a very simple test—whether the estimated wage coefficient in Eq. (11.53) is equal to that in Eq. (11.52); since the difference in estimated coefficients is 58 (122 − 64) and the estimated asymptotic standard error is 163, the null hypothesis of exogeneity is not rejected.

On the basis of results from these four estimated equations, Mroz draws a number of conclusions. First, the estimated uncompensated wage effect is positive but typically very small, provided that one treats the wife's experience variables as "endogenous" and/or one allows for sample selectivity bias in the wage determination and labor supply equations. Further, under the same estimation procedures the income effect is usually negative but also rather small.

Mroz [1987, p. 794] therefore concurs with Nakamura and Nakamura [1979; 1981a; 1985a, b] and rejects the conventional wisdom based on second-generation studies, concluding that

> the small income and wage effects found in this study provide a much more accurate picture of the behavioral responses of working women to variations in nonlabor income and wages than those found in most previous studies.

Such findings suggest as well that the modest responsiveness of married women's labor supply to changes in wage rates and income is not much different from that found in studies of the labor supply of prime-aged married males. Second, the sample selectivity bias is significant only if the wife's experience variables are treated as exogenous. Third, the wife's labor market experience variables are exogenous provided that one allows for sample selectivity bias. Fourth, the results are consistent with the view that a woman's tastes for work are unobserved omitted variables that affect both her previous and current labor market participation and hours of work, over and above their influence on her wage rate.[59]

In addition to estimating the labor supply equation using the Heckit multistage Procedure VIII, Mroz employs the full Tobit simultaneous equation estimation Procedure VI. Recall that unlike Procedures VII and VIII, which allow for discontinuities in the labor supply schedule due to, say, fixed costs of employment, the Tobit Procedure VI assumes continuity. In fact, the Procedure VI estimates will be equal to those from Procedures VII and VIII whenever the labor supply schedule is continuous in wages. Mroz reports that his Procedure VI Tobit estimates of the labor supply equation are

$$\underset{}{H_i} = a_0 + \underset{(357)}{261 \ln(W_i)} - \underset{(5.1)}{22.9\, V_i} - \underset{(140)}{1035\, \mathrm{KL6}_i} - \underset{(48)}{97\, \mathrm{K618}_i} + \cdots \tag{11.54}$$

Hence the Tobit uncompensated wage elasticity estimate is also quite small (261/1500 = 0.174) and insignificantly different from zero, while the income effect is significant and larger than those estimated above (−22.9/1500 = −0.015) but is still rather small. Further, with the Tobit specification the null hypothesis of exogeneity of the experience variables is rejected. Mroz then tests for this Tobit specification (11.54) as a special case of the multistage Heckit Procedure VIII and in all cases rejects the null hypothesis. This leads Mroz to conclude that the restrictions implied by the Tobit Procedure VI must be rejected, a conclusion that is consistent with the view that fixed costs of employment are substantial.

In the third phase of his study, Mroz assesses the effects of including a measure of the marginal tax rate into the labor supply equation. Following Hall [1973], Mroz uses a linearization of the budget set in which the marginal after-tax wage rate replaces the previous wage measure and virtual income is measured as the intercept of the linearized budget set at zero hours of work; unlike Hall, however, Mroz treats both the after-tax wage rate and virtual income as endogenous variables. Using similar estimation procedures as before,[60] Mroz finds that the estimated wage coefficient falls and in fact becomes negative but that the magnitude of the change is at most 33 hours and is always within 20% of one standard deviation of the estimates obtained without taxes. This leads Mroz [1987, p. 786] to conclude, "In the light of the other possible sources of bias examined in the previous sections, the influences of taxes on the estimates of the labor supply parameters appears to be at most a second order effect."

Finally, following Rosen [1976], Mroz rewrites Eq. (11.48) in after-tax form as the expanded equation

$$\begin{aligned} H_i = a_0 + a_1 \ln [W_i(1 - \tau_i)] + b_1 \ln (1 - \tau_i) \\ + a_2 V_i + b_2 YV_i + a_3' Z_i + \epsilon_i \end{aligned} \qquad \textbf{(11.55)}$$

where τ_i is the marginal tax rate and YV_i is virtual income. The null hypothesis that married women optimally take taxes into consideration is that $b_1 = a_2 = 0$, while the alternative hypothesis is that $b_1 \neq 0$, $a_2 \neq 0$. One might also consider testing the hypothesis that married women completely ignore taxes when making labor supply decisions. This corresponds to the null hypothesis that $b_1 = -a_1$ and $b_2 = 0$, while the alternative hypothesis is $b_1 \neq -a_1$, $b_2 \neq 0$. Unlike Rosen, Mroz finds that neither of these two distinct null hypotheses can be rejected, perhaps reflecting the relatively large standard errors on the estimated wage coefficients and income terms.

As can be seen, therefore, the significance of Mroz's study is that it highlights the empirical consequences of employing alternative assumptions concerning exogeneity, sample selectivity, and taxes on estimates of the labor supply responsiveness of married women. These assumptions do matter.

11.3.D Issues in Dynamic Labor Supply

One interpretation of Mroz's results on the importance of the labor force experience variables is that labor supply might better be viewed in a dynamic life cycle context. Before concluding this chapter, therefore, we briefly overview the rapidly growing theoretical literature on dynamic labor supply.

Within the last decade, considerable theoretical research has focused on dynamic labor supply models. In dynamic models of labor supply, economic agents act knowing that today's decisions will have consequences in the future. Further, in dynamic models, the accumulation of nonhuman and/or human capital is modeled explicitly. Our overview of this literature is by necessity brief; more detailed discussions can be found in Killingsworth [1983, Chapter 5], Killingsworth and Heckman [1986, pp. 144–179], and, in particular, Pencavel [1986]. We begin by discussing models in which wages at each point in time are exogenous and then examine models in which wages are determined endogenously through human capital accumulation.

Although discussions of the timing of labor supply and human capital accumulation during the life cycle of women have a long history in labor economics, one of the most influential early contributions on dynamic issues is that by Jacob Mincer [1962]. Mincer suggested that one way of thinking through dynamic issues is simply to reinterpret the static analyses of labor supply in lifetime terms, where variables such as consumption, leisure, work at home, wages, budget constraints, and time are envisaged as lifetime variables. Note that in this view, the woman's real asset holdings should be reinterpreted as those occurring at the beginning of the (lifetime) time period and not as her actual lifetime or current exogenous income.

Following Killingsworth and Heckman [1986], let us assume that the life cycle consists of T periods, and let us then sort single-period real wage rates in descending order so that $w(1)$ denotes the highest real wage and $w(T)$ denotes the lowest. For the moment, assume that consumption and leisure at different points in time are perfect substitutes. Under these conditions an individual will work sometime during her life if $w(1)$ exceeds her lifetime reservation or shadow wage rate $MRS(0)$, where the latter is the marginal rate of substitution evaluated at zero lifetime hours of work. To determine the total number of periods worked, compare discounted real wage rates to the MRS; the individual will work exactly k time periods if

$$w(k) \geqslant MRS(k) \geqslant w(k+1) \qquad \textbf{(11.56)}$$

where at least one of the inequalities is strict.[61] Thus the total number of periods worked k is a function of an unobserved taste or household production variable e that affects lifetime utility, real initial wealth A, and the "marginal wage" $w(k)$, that is,

$$k = k[w(k), A, T, e] \qquad \textbf{(11.57)}$$

In this case the proportion of all periods in the woman's lifetime that is devoted to work, h, is simply $h = k/T$, which together with Eq. (11.57) implies that

$$h = h[w(k), A, T, e] \tag{11.58}$$

One practical problem with implementing empirically equations such as Eq. (11.57) or Eq. (11.58) is that it would appear that each requires k or h data on labor supply over the entire life cycle—a truly formidable obstacle. As Mincer [1962] and Heckman [1978] have noted, however, if one abstracts from "transitory" factors, one might assume that the timing of work over the life cycle is random. If this were true, and if all individuals worked at some point in their lives, then one could estimate parameters of Eq. (11.58) by replacing h (which refers to lifetime participation) with, say, Q, where Q now refers to participation as of a given date; the resulting parameter estimates could then be used to obtain estimates of elasticities of labor supply with respect to (permanent) wage changes and with respect to income (here, initial wealth).

While apparently promising, however, this approach suffers from the practical ambiguity of determining the appropriate measure of the "marginal wage" $w(k)$ that could clearly differ from the wage prevailing as of the date referenced by the Q variable; specifically, while data on lifetime labor supply might not be necessary, one still needs to be able to determine which particular wage rate—of all the wages the individual will earn during her lifetime—happens to be the appropriate marginal wage rate in Eq. (11.56).

Another problem with this approach, emphasized by Killingsworth and Heckman [1986, pp. 148–149], is that using estimates of Eq. (11.58) with Q replacing h to obtain measures of substitution and income effects is appropriate only when h is strictly positive, that is, only when individuals have an interior solution to their lifetime labor supply optimization problem. As Heckman [1978] notes, although appropriate data are rather scarce, there is reason to believe that a nonnegligible portion of the female population never undertakes market work for pay. Therefore this approach might not provide useful estimates of income and substitution effects.

Much recent work has focused on modeling more explicitly the factors that affect an individual's equilibrium sequence of lifetime labor supply, leisure, and consumption; the solution to the lifetime optimization problem is often called the individual's equilibrium dynamics. A common approach is to assume perfect certainty and specify lifetime utility as an additively separable utility function

$$U = \sum_{t=0}^{T} (1 + s)^{-t} u[C(t), L(t)] \tag{11.59}$$

where T is fixed, $L(t) + H(t)$ exhausts all available time during period t, s is the individual's subjective rate of time preference, and $u[\cdot]$ is the utility function for period t, depending on consumption $C(t)$ and leisure $L(t)$. Incidentally, in this additively separable specification, $C(t)$ and $C(t')$, as well as $L(t)$ and $L(t')$, are not assumed to be perfect substitutes for $t \neq t'$.[62]

Lifetime utility is maximized subject to a lifetime budget constraint

$$A(0) + \sum_{t=0}^{T} (1 + r)^{-t} \cdot [W(t)H(t) - P(t)C(t)] \geqslant 0 \qquad \textbf{(11.60)}$$

where $A(0)$ is the individual's initial asset holdings, r is the market rate of interest, and $W(t)$, $H(t)$, and $P(t)$ are the wage rate, hours of work, and price levels in period t, respectively.

More formally, using Lagrangian procedures, maximize Eq. (11.59) over $C(t)$ and $H(t)$ subject to the lifetime budget constraint (11.60), and interpret the Lagrangian multiplier in front of Eq. (11.60), say, λ, as the marginal lifetime utility of initial asset holdings. The first-order conditions yield an intertemporal equilibrium plan, given a set of wage rates and price levels $W(t)$ and $P(t)$, $t = 0, \ldots, T$, for $C(t)$, $L(t)$, and λ. One can of course assess how the equilibrium paths of differing individuals would vary as a result of their holding different $A(0)$ or facing diverse wage rates $W(t)$; such mental experiments are called *comparative dynamics* and should be distinguished from the individual's initial intertemporal equilibrium sequence, called her *equilibrium dynamics.*

In carrying through comparative dynamics, one must of course be careful in specifying what is being held fixed. One common approach, called the Frisch λ-fixed or Frisch demand notion, examines the equilibrium time path effects of a change in, say, $W(t)$, treating the marginal lifetime utility of assets λ as fixed; an alternative procedure, dubbed λ-variable, allows this marginal utility of assets to vary in response to a change in $W(t)$.[63] In either case it can be shown that variation in a wage at any given date may have consequences not only at that point in time, but also at other dates.

It is worth noting here that within the labor economics literature, much ink has been spilt concerning the effects of changes in "permanent" or "transitory" income on labor supply over the life cycle. Controversy has occurred, for example, concerning whether one should include only measures of permanent income in labor supply equations or whether one should also include a measure of transitory income. Although much of this literature is informal rather than rigorous, it can be assessed within a comparative dynamics framework.

Specifically, define permanent income W_p as the present value of the stream of an individual's future rates from $t = 0$ to $t = T$, discounted at rate r, and transitory income w_t as the difference between the actual wage $W(t)$ and the permanent wage W_p, that is, $w_t \equiv W(t) - W_p$. As Killingsworth and Heckman [1986] emphasize, empirical measures of W_p have been constructed in practice by using essentially ad hoc procedures, depending in large part on the nature of the available data.

One body of literature adopts what Killingsworth and Heckman [1986] call the PO position, according to which hours of work and labor force participation in any period t depend on the permanent wage *only*, analogous to Milton Friedman's [1957] permanent income theory of consumption. Under the PO hypothesis, one need never include the transitory wage measure w_t in an equation such as Eq. (11.50), since its coefficient should be zero.

An alternative to the PO position, called PT, hypothesizes that both W_p and $w(t)$ should appear in labor supply equations; moreover, according to this literature, the coefficient on w_t should be positive and algebraically greater than the coefficient on W_p, since the latter represents the sum of a positive substitution effect and a negative income effect, whereas the former reflects only a positive substitution effect.[64]

Using comparative dynamic procedures with both λ-constant and λ-variable, Killingsworth and Heckman [1986, pp. 156–158] show that contrary to PO, leisure and labor supply are responsive to transitory wage differences, owing to the fact that life cycle asset accumulation is affected. Further, contrary to PT, it is not necessarily the case that labor supply at time t is positively correlated with w_t. However, if one examines instead the comparative dynamics of changes in exogenous income (such as the income of other family members) on an individual's equilibrium dynamics (rather than changes in her W_p or w_t), it turns out that labor supply depends only on permanent exogenous income and not on transitory exogenous income.[65]

Not surprisingly, Killingsworth and Heckman conclude that much of the ambiguity in the transitory-permanent income controversy arises because of a lack of proper theoretical foundations. As an alternative, they suggest employing the Frisch demand framework, in which the marginal utility of assets λ constitutes a type of "permanent wage" and variations in the observed wage $W(t)$ with λ constant correspond to a type of "transitory" wage variation, since with λ constant it can be shown that differences in $W(t)$ must always be negatively correlated with $L(t)$.

Our discussion on dynamic labor supply to this point has assumed that wages are exogenous. By contrast, and as discussed more fully in Chapter 5 of this book (see especially Section 5.1), there is a great deal of literature suggesting that wage rates for women are endogenous, affected in large part by intermittent labor supply and expectations concerning child-rearing. More specifically, since current wage rates depend in part on human capital endowments, and since human capital formation is affected by educational attainment and on-the-job training, the choices that women make concerning marriage, child-rearing, and work affect their time paths of wage rates. As a result, in the more complete and necessarily more complex dynamic models of female labor supply, educational attainment, marriage, the desired number and spacing of children, the time path of market labor supply, and the time paths of wages and consumption are all endogenous.

In large part because of their mathematical complexity, formal theoretical models of joint labor supply and wage determination have not yet yielded much empirical insight into the dynamics of women's work and wages. However, this topic is currently attracting a great deal of attention both from theorists and from econometricians.[66]

11.4 ADDITIONAL REMARKS ON ECONOMETRIC ANALYSES OF LABOR SUPPLY

As we have seen, the literature on factors that affect female labor supply provides a useful example of how economic theory, measurement issues, and econometric technique can interact to enhance our understanding of important public policy issues. But this literature has also amply illustrated that in spite of enormous progress in theory, technique, and, to some extent, measurement, it is still frustratingly difficult to "nail down" precise estimates of important elasticities. While critics of recent econometric practice might interpret this difficulty as further evidence that the payoffs of state-of-the art econometric research are often meager, many econometricians who work on labor supply remain strongly optimistic. Killingsworth [1983, p. 432], for example, concludes his summary of what we do and don't know about labor supply by stating, "At least temporarily, then, uncertainty about, and variation in, actual magnitudes of labor supply estimates seems larger than it used to be." Whether Killingsworth's 1983 assessment that this large range of elasticity estimates is but a temporary condition in the history of the analysis of labor supply remains to be seen.

Finally, it is worth noting that some students of labor supply argue that one reason for the large variability in labor supply elasticity estimates, which is evident in Table 11.2, is that existing theoretical models of labor supply are simply too crude. Although we have attempted in this chapter to discuss the current labor supply literature in a relatively thorough manner and have demonstrated some of its complexity, in fact the labor supply literature is extremely large, much of it still needs to be synthesized, and by necessity we have ignored potentially important strands of research. For example, we have only skimmed the literature on family or household decision-making processes, as well as the significance of hours worked quantity restrictions on labor supply.[67] Further, we have entirely overlooked labor supply issues concerning the quality of work, the amount of leisure time spent at work, and the risk and uncertainty of job search. In terms of econometric matters we have considered only the relatively simple limited dependent variable models,[68] and among other omissions we have not dealt with issues concerning the possibility of obtaining better econometric estimates of labor supply elasticities by employing data from well-designed experiments,[69] nor have we examined issues of specification, estimation, and inference when the labor supply observations are taken from a panel data set.[70] Fortunately, readers who are interested in pursuing these related issues can begin by working through the references given here and those provided in leading labor economics textbooks, such as those referenced at the end of this chapter.

11.5 HANDS ON WITH LIMITED DEPENDENT VARIABLE TECHNIQUES TO ASSESS THE LABOR SUPPLY OF MARRIED WOMEN

We have now come to the hands-on portion of this chapter. The goal of the following exercises is to engage you in obtaining firsthand experience in implementing and interpreting alternative procedures that attempt to measure factors affecting female labor force participation and hours worked; in particular, you will have the opportunity to carry out on your own a number of estimation methods, including most of the second generation procedures discussed in Section 11.3.B.1.

Note: Although the exercises of this chapter have been carefully designed to introduce you to some of the most important computational and interpretive issues in the econometric analysis of labor supply, they are but an introduction, and your instructor may use the data set in this chapter for other useful and more elaborate exercises. For example, although data on the husband's hours of work and wages are provided in the MROZ data file on your diskette, we make no use of those data in the exercises. Such data could be useful in a model of family labor supply. Alternatively, your instructor might want to provide you with a different set of data. Hence we urge you to envisage these exercises as a beginning step to understanding better the applicability of limited dependent variable procedures to the analysis of labor supply.

The exercises of this chapter can be summarized as follows. Because it is extremely important to examine data sets before becoming involved in econometric estimation, we highly recommend that all readers work through Exercise 1, "Inspecting Mroz's 1975 Panel Study of Income Dynamics Data." Moreover, this exercise is essential because in it you generate two data series that are necessary for completion of subsequent exercises. In Exercise 2 we introduce you to a common but inappropriate estimation procedure in which an hours worked equation is estimated by OLS with hours of nonworkers set to zero (Procedure I). Then in Exercise 3 we invite you to explore the female labor force participation decision using OLS, probit, and logit estimation procedures and to examine numerical relationships among them. In Exercise 4 we ask you to compare the conditional OLS and Tobit estimators of the hours worked equation (Procedures II and III) and to implement the Goldberger-Greene procedure for assessing the OLS bias. Next, in Exercise 5 we have you consider identification issues when both the wage rate and labor supply equations are estimated by using Procedure IV. In Exercise 6 we lead you through estimation of the hours worked equation based on the increasingly common Heckit multistage procedure (generalized Tobit), which Killingsworth called Procedure VIII. In Exercise 7 we have you estimate a Heckit model in which taxes are taken into account, and finally, in Exercise 8 we work with you in specifying and estimating an extended Tobit model (Procedure VI).

••••••••••

Many of the data sets that are used to estimate models of labor supply are large, often involving over 10,000 observations, and it is simply infeasible to provide such a large data base on your 360K data diskette. However, the 1976 PSID data set employed by Mroz [1987] in his sensitivity study is useful and convenient, since it is rather small (it contains 753 observations on 19 variables and occupies only about 60K of space on your data diskette), and it permits replication of some of Mroz's most important findings.[71]

In the subdirectory called CHAP11.DAT of your data diskette you will find a data file called MROZ. This data file contains 753 observations on married white women aged 30–60 in 1975 for 19 variables. The first 428 observations are those for women whose hours of work in 1975 were positive, while the final 325 observations are those for women who did not work for pay in 1975. Each 80-column row of this data set corresponds to one observation.

The first variable, LFP, is a labor force participation dummy variable that equals 1 if the woman's hours of work in 1975 were positive; otherwise, it equals zero. WHRS is the wife's hours of work in 1975, while KL6 and K618 indicate the number of children in the household under age six and between ages six and 18, respectively. WA is the wife's age in years, WE is the wife's educational attainment in years of schooling, WW is the wife's 1975 average hourly earnings in 1975 dollars, and RPWG is the wife's wage reported at the time of the 1976 interview, in dollars. The HHRS variable is the husband's hours worked in 1975, HA is his age, HE is his educational attainment in years of schooling, and HW is his 1975 wage in 1975 dollars. FAMINC is the family income in 1975 dollars; hence to calculate the wife's property income, one must subtract the product of WW and WHRS from FAMINC. MTR is the wife's marginal tax rate evaluated if her hours of work were zero. MTR is taken from published federal tax tables (it excludes state and local income taxes but includes any applicable social security benefits). WMED is the wife's mother's years of schooling, and WFED is the wife's father's years of schooling. UN is the unemployment rate in the county of residence, in percentage points, while CIT is a dummy variable that equals 1 if the family lives in a large city (a Standard Metropolitan Statistical Area, SMSA); otherwise, it equals zero. Finally, AX is the wife's previous labor market experience, in years. Further details on these variables are given in the README.DOC file in the subdirectory CHAP11.DAT and in Mroz [1987].

EXERCISE 1: Inspecting Mroz's 1975 Panel Study of Income Dynamics Data

The purpose of this exercise is to help you become familiar with salient features of the data series in the MROZ data file. While exploring this data set, you will compute arithmetic means, standard deviations, and minimum and maximum values for variables in the entire sample and for the data sorted into various subgroups. You will also construct and save two variables that will be used in the subsequent exercises of this chapter.

(a) To check whether the data are the same as those employed by Mroz [1987, Table III, p. 769], compute and print out the arithmetic means and standard deviations of each of the 19 variables in the MROZ data file, using the entire sample of 753 observations. The results that you obtain from such a calculation should equal (for each variable named, followed with parentheses enclosing first the mean and then the standard deviation): LFP (0.56839, 0.49563), WHRS (740.57636, 871.31422), KL6 (0.23772, 0.52396), K618 (1.35325, 1.31987), WA (42.53785, 8.07257), WE (12.28685, 2.28025), WW (2.37457, 3.24183), RPWG (1.84973, 2.41989), HHRS (2267.27092, 595.56665), HA (45.12085, 8.05879), HE (12.49137, 3.02080), HW (7.48218, 4.23056), FAMINC (23080.59495, 12190.20203), MTR (0.67886, 0.08350), WMED (9.25100, 3.36747), WFED (8.80876, 3.57229), UN (8.62351, 3.11493), CIT (0.64276, 0.47950), and AX (10.63081, 8.06913). Do your results match those of Mroz? (Because of differing rounding conventions, your computer software program might generate slightly different values. But the means and standard deviations should be very close to those reported here.) Also compute minimum and maximum values for each of these variables; this is a particularly useful practice, since by doing this, one can often spot data coding errors. Are any of your min-max values "suspicious"? Why or why not?

(b) Now compare the sample of working women (the first 428 observations in the MROZ data file) with those not working for pay in 1975 (the final 325 observations). Compute arithmetic means and standard deviations for each of the 19 variables in these two subsamples, then print and compare them. Mroz notes that arithmetic means in the working and nonworking samples are quite similar for variables such as WA, WE, K618, HA, HE, and HHRS. Do you also find this to be the case? However, means in the working and nonworking samples tend to differ more for variables such as KL6 and HW. How do they differ, and what might this imply concerning the reservation wages of women in these two samples? Why? To the extent that the previous labor market experience of women (AX) reflects their preferences or tastes for market work, one might expect means of AX to differ between the working and nonworking samples. Is this the case? Interpret this difference. Are there any other differences in means of variables in the two subsamples that might affect labor force participation or hours worked? If so, comment on them.

(c) In the model of labor supply estimated by Mroz, it is assumed that in making her labor supply decisions the wife takes as given the household's entire nonlabor income plus her husband's labor income. Mroz calls this sum the wife's property income and computes it as total family income minus the labor income earned by the wife. For the entire sample of 753 observations, compute this property income variable (named, say, PRIN) as PRIN ≡ FAMINC − (WHRS · WW). Also calculate and print its mean and standard deviation; these should equal 20129 and 11635, respectively. Save PRIN for use in subsequent exercises of this chapter.

(d) One of the variables that is often employed in empirical analyses of labor force participation is the wage rate. As was emphasized earlier in this chapter, however, the wage rate is typically not observed for women who are not working. Some analysts have attempted to deal with this problem (albeit in an unsatisfactory manner—see Section 11.3.B.1) by estimating a wage determination equation using data on workers only and then using the resulting parameter estimates and characteristics of the nonworking sample to construct fitted or predicted wages for each of the nonworkers.

Restricting your sample to workers (the first 428 observations), take the natural logarithm of the wife's wage rate variable WW and call this log-transformed variable LWW. Compute and print out the mean and standard deviation of LWW for this sample. Then, for the entire sample of 753 observations, construct the square of the wife's experience variable and call it AX2, that is, generate AX2 ≡ AX*AX (and, for later use, the square of the wife's age, WA2 ≡ WA*WA). Next, following the human capital literature on wage determination summarized in Chapter 5 of this book and using only the 428 observations from the working sample, estimate by OLS a typical wage determination equation in which LWW is regressed on a constant term, WA, WE, CIT, AX, and AX2. Does this equation make sense? Why or why not? Then use the parameter estimates from this equation and values of the WA, WE, CIT, AX, and AX2 variables for the 325 women in the nonworking sample to generate the predicted or fitted log-wage for the nonworkers. Call this fitted log-wage variable for the nonworkers FLWW. Compute the arithmetic mean and standard deviation of FLWW for the nonworkers, and compare them to those for LWW from the working sample. Is the difference in means substantial? How do you interpret this result? Finally, for the entire sample of 753 observations and for use in subsequent exercises of this chapter, generate a variable called LWW1 for which the first 428 observations (the working sample) LWW1 = LWW and for which the last 325 observations (the nonworking sample) LWW1 = FLWW from above. Note that your constructed LWW1 variable should include either the actual or a predicted wage for each individual in the sample. To ensure that you have computed the data series LWW1 correctly, compute and print out its mean and standard deviation; they should equal 1.10432 and 0.58268, respectively. Save the LWW1 data series for use in subsequent exercises of this chapter.

EXERCISE 2: Estimating the Hours Worked Equation Using Procedure I

The purpose of this exercise is to introduce you to a common, but unfortunately inappropriate, procedure for estimating the hours worked equation. Specifically, in this exercise you implement Procedure I, in which you estimate by OLS an hours worked equation using the entire sample of 753 observations and predicted wages for nonworkers and you set hours worked for nonworkers equal to zero. Such an equation is often called a *truncated normal regression equation*. You also compute the implied responses to changes in the wage rate and in property income, both in level and in elasticity form.

(a) Inspect the WHRS variable (wife's hours worked) and verify that whenever the LFP (labor force participation) variable equals zero, the value of WHRS is also zero. Then, using the OLS estimation procedure and the entire set of 753 observations in the MROZ data file, regress WHRS on a constant term and on the variables KL6, K618, WA, WE, LWW1 (constructed in part (d) of Exercise 1), and PRIN (constructed in part (c) of Exercise 1). Do the signs of the estimated parameters agree with your intuition? Why or why not? What is the value of R^2? Why might this value be so low when Procedure I is employed?

(b) Using the above OLS parameter estimates and the elasticity formulae underneath Eq. (11.48) evaluated at the same points as noted at the bottom of Table 11.2, compute the elasticity of hours worked with respect to wages and with respect to property income. Is the wage elasticity a compensated or an uncompensated one? Why? Then, following Mroz's procedures, which are also discussed underneath Eq. (11.48), compute the implied response of hours worked to a \$1 change in the wage rate, evaluated at the same point. How does this estimate compare with those presented in Table 11.2? Finally, compute the implied response of hours worked to a \$1000 increase in property income. Comment on how this estimate compares with those presented in Table 11.2.

(c) Although this Procedure I is simple and easy to implement, it has a number of serious flaws. What are the principal shortcomings?

EXERCISE 3: Comparing OLS, Probit, and Logit Estimates of the Labor Force Participation Decision

The goal of this exercise is to help you gain experience with simple limited dependent variable estimation techniques by computing and then comparing OLS, probit, and logit estimates of a typical labor force participation equation. The numerical comparison of these various estimators is based in large part on the work of Takeshi Amemiya [1981], who has derived relationships among them.[72]

(a) Econometrics textbooks typically point out that if the dependent variable in an equation is a dichotomous dummy variable, and if an equation is estimated by OLS in which this dependent variable is related linearly to an intercept term, a number of regressors, and a stochastic error term, then the resulting equation (often called a *linear probability model*) suffers from at least two defects: (1) the fitted values are not confined to the 0–1 interval, and so their interpretation as probabilities is inappropriate; and (2) the residuals from such an equation are heteroskedastic. Note that in our context, LFP is such a dichotomous dependent variable.

Using OLS estimation procedures and the MROZ data file for all 753 observations, estimate parameters of a linear probability model in which LFP is related linearly to an intercept term, the LWW1 variable constructed in part (d) of Exercise 1, KL6, K618, WA, WE, UN, CIT, the wife's property income PRIN (constructed in part (c) of Exercise 1), and a stochastic error term. Do signs of these OLS estimated parameters make sense? Why or why not? Comment on the appropriateness of using the OLS estimated standard errors to conduct tests of statistical significance. Next retrieve and print out the fitted values from this estimated linear probability model. For how many observations are the fitted values negative? For how many are they greater than 1? Why does this complicate the interpretation of this model? What is R^2 in this model? Does it have any useful interpretation? Why or why not?

(b) One possible estimation procedure that is more appropriate when the dependent variable is dichotomous is based on the assumption that the cumulative distribution of the stochastic disturbances is the logistic; the resulting maximum likelihood estimator is usually called logit.[73]

With LFP as the dependent variable and with a constant term, LWW1 (from part (d) of Exercise 1), KL6, K618, WA, WE, UN, CIT, and PRIN (from part (c) of Exercise 1) as explanatory variables, use the entire sample of 753 observations in the MROZ data file and estimate parameters based on a logit maximum likelihood procedure. Do the signs of these estimated logit parameters make sense? Why or why not? Which of the estimated logit parameters is significantly different from zero? Interpret. Does the nonlinear logit computational algorithm in your computer software program reach convergence quickly, after only a few iterations (say, fewer than five)? Some computer programs provide "goodness-of-fit" output for the estimated logit model, such as a pseudo-R^2 measure or a measure indicating what percent of the predictions are "correct." Check your computer output and manual for the interpretation of any such goodness-of-fit measures.[74] Finally, compare your logit estimates to the OLS or linear probability model estimates from part (a). In particular, following Takeshi Amemiya [1981], each of the OLS *slope* parameter estimates should approximately equal 0.25 times the corresponding logit slope parameter estimate. How well does Amemiya's approximation work in this sample? Further, Amemiya shows that each of the OLS *intercept* and OLS *dummy variable* intercept terms should approximately equal 0.25 times the corresponding logit parameter estimate, plus 0.5. Do your OLS and logit intercept and dummy variable intercept terms correspond well with Amemiya's approximation?

(c) Another common estimation procedure that is used in the estimation of dichotomous dependent variable models is based on the assumption that the cumulative distribution of the disturbances is normal; this is usually called the probit model. Likelihood functions based on the probit model have been discussed in Section 11.3.B.1 of this chapter.

With LFP as the dependent variable and with a constant term, LWW1 (from part (d) of Exercise 1), KL6, K618, WA, WE, UN, CIT, and PRIN (from part (c) of Exercise 1) as explanatory variables, use the entire sample of 753 observations in the MROZ data file and estimate parameters based on a probit maximum likelihood procedure. Do the signs of these estimated probit parameters make sense? Why? Which of the estimated probit parameters is significantly different from zero? Why? Does the probit computational algorithm in your computer software program reach convergence quickly, after only a few iterations? Is convergence more or less rapid than with the logit model? As in part (b), interpret any goodness-of-fit measures that are provided as output by your computer software program.

(d) Because the cumulative normal distribution and the logistic distribution are very close to each other, in most cases the logit and probit estimated models will be quite similar.[75] Are the sample maximized log-likelihoods in your estimated logit and probit models similar? Which is larger? What about the signs and statistical significance of the estimated parameters—are they similar? The estimated effect of a change in a regressor on the probability of participating in the labor force, $\partial P/\partial X_i$, is equal to $P*(1 - P)*\hat{\beta}_{Li}$ in the logit model and $f(P)*\hat{\beta}_{Pi}$ in the probit model, where P is the probability of LFP, $\hat{\beta}_{Li}$ and $\hat{\beta}_{Pi}$ are the estimated logit and probit coefficients, respectively, on the ith explanatory variable, and $f(P)$ is the cumulative normal function corresponding to P.[76] Evaluate these estimated derivatives for the logit and probit models, using the sample LFPR of 425/753 = 0.568 as an estimate of P and noting that $f(P) = f(0.568) = 0.393$. At this sample mean, are the estimated effects similar for the logit and probit models? What happens if you evaluate these effects at the tail of the distribution, such as at $P = 0.9$ where $f(P) = 0.175$?

(e) Since the logistic distribution has a variation of $\pi^2/3$, whereas the variation from the probit model is usually normalized to unity, one way to compare the logit and probit estimates is to multiply each of the logit estimates by $\sqrt{3}/\pi \cong 1.73205/3.14159 \cong 0.5513$, and then compare these transformed logit parameters to the actual probit estimates. Amemiya [1981] argues, however, that a better approximation emerges if one multiplies the logit parameter estimates by 0.625 and then compares these transformed logit parameters to the probit estimates. Which of these two approximations best transforms your logit estimates to comparable probit estimates? Why?

(f) In this exercise we have compared OLS linear probability model, logit, and probit estimates of a labor force participation equation and have focused on numerical relationships among the estimated parameters. As was pointed out in Section 11.3.B.1, however, there are serious statistical problems with each of the particular OLS, logit, and probit procedures that were employed in this exercise. What are these problems?

EXERCISE 4: Relating the Tobit and Conditional OLS Estimates

The purpose of this exercise is to engage you in the estimation and interpretation of a labor supply model based on the Tobit Procedure III and to enrich your understanding of how this Tobit model relates to the conditional OLS framework of Procedure II. You will also have the opportunity to implement empirically the analytical results of Goldberger [1981], Greene [1981], and McDonald and Moffitt [1980], which were discussed in Section 11.3.B.1.

(a) First, estimate a conditional OLS model of labor supply (Procedure II). In particular, restricting your sample to the women who worked for pay in 1975 (the first 428 observations in the MROZ data file), run a regression of WHRS on a constant term, KL6, K618, WA, WE, PRIN, and LWW (see part (d) of Exercise 1 for a discussion of LWW and PRIN). Compare your results to those obtained by Mroz, reproduced in Eq. (11.49). Your standard error estimates might differ from those reported by Mroz, since his estimates are adjusted for heteroskedasticity using the Halbert White [1980] robust estimation procedure. If your computer software program permits, also compute the White robust standard errors; your results should be very close to those reported by Mroz.

(b) In Section 11.3.B.1 it was pointed out that these conditional OLS estimates are biased estimates of the parameters in Eq. (11.33). Why are they biased? Following Goldberger and Greene, compute consistent estimates of each of the labor supply parameters using the LFP adjustment. In particular, calculate the sample proportion of observations for which WHRS is positive—in the MROZ data file this is 428/753 = 0.568. Then divide each of the conditional OLS parameter estimates from part (a) by this proportion. According to Goldberger and Greene, these transformed conditional OLS estimates are consistent estimates of the labor supply parameters in Eq. (11.33). Are these transformed, consistent estimates plausible? What can you say regarding the statistical significance of these transformed parameters? Why?

(c) Now obtain consistent estimates using the Tobit estimation method

(Procedure III). In particular, using the Tobit maximum likelihood procedure (the sample likelihood function corresponding to Eq. (11.33) is Eq. (11.32) with J_i now equal to $X_i\beta + u_{Hi}$) and the same functional form as in part (a), compute the Tobit parameter estimates and asymptotic standard errors. How do these estimates compare to the Goldberger and Greene approximations from part (b)? What can you say regarding the statistical significance of these Tobit parameters?

(d) As was discussed in Section 11.3.B.1, McDonald and Moffitt have shown (see Eq. (11.35)) that the total effect of the change in a regressor on expected hours worked in the Tobit model can be decomposed into two parts: the change in hours worked for those already working weighted by the probability of working plus the change in the probability of working weighted by the expected value of hours worked for those who work. Using the sample proportion of those who work (428/753 = 0.568) as an estimate of $F(z)$, the Tobit parameter estimates from part (c), and data evaluated at sample means, calculate A as outlined underneath Eq. (11.35). *Note:* For $F(z) = 0.568$, $z = 0.175$ and $f(z) = 0.393$. Of the total change in hours worked due to a $1 change in the wage rate, what amount results from changes in hours worked from those who are already working? What amount comes from new entrants into the labor force? What is the proportion of the total effect on hours worked of a change in any of the variables that derives from those women who are already working?

(e) The likelihood function (11.32) for the Tobit model indicates that the Tobit can be envisaged as combining a probit model of labor force participation with a standard regression model of hours worked for those who work (see Section 11.3.B.1). One might therefore conclude that if the sample were limited to those who work, Tobit estimates would be numerically equivalent to OLS estimates. Would such a conclusion be correct? Why or why not? Verify your intuition numerically, using data in the MROZ data file, by estimating a Tobit model, restricting the sample to the first 428 observations (the workers) and comparing these Tobit estimates with the OLS estimates of part (a).

(f) In this exercise we have numerically related the Tobit and conditional OLS estimates in a model of labor supply. As was pointed out in Section 11.3.B.1, however, there are serious statistical problems with the Tobit and conditional OLS procedures that were employed in this exercise. What are these problems?

EXERCISE 5: Identifying Parameters in a Reduced Form Estimation

The purpose of this exercise is to explore issues of identification of the structural parameters when the reduced form Procedure IV method is implemented empirically. In essence, this procedure involves first estimating a wage equation using a sample of workers only, then using the entire sample of observations with hours of nonworkers set to zero to estimate a reduced form hours worked equation derived from a reservation wage relationship, and finally, identifying the structural parameters of the reservation wage equation by using the reduced form and the wage equation parameter estimates. As we shall see, the reservation wage equation is underidentified, just identified, or overidentified depending on whether zero, one, or more than one regressor in the wage equation is excluded from the reservation wage equation.

(a) Retrieve from Exercise 1, part (d), the parameter estimates from the OLS wage determination equation in which LWW was regressed on a constant, WA, WE, AX, WA2, and CIT and the sample was confined to those who worked (the first 428 observations). This corresponds to the equation, with i subscripts deleted for simplicity,

$$\begin{aligned} \text{LWW} = {} & g_0 + g_1 \text{ WA} + g_2 \text{ WA2} + g_3 \text{ WE} \\ & + g_4 \text{ CIT} + g_5 \text{ AX} + e_W \end{aligned} \quad \textbf{(11.61)}$$

where the g's are OLS parameter estimates and e_W is the OLS residual.

(b) Next specify three alternative structural reservation wage equations, and then using a transform of Heckman's proportionality relation (11.42), write out their corresponding reduced form representations. Specifically, three possible structural representations for the log of the reservation wage (LWR) equation, analogous to Eq. (11.41), are

Just identified:

$$\begin{aligned} \text{LWR} = {} & a_0 + a_1 \text{ WA} + a_2 \text{ WA2} + a_3 \text{ WE} + a_4 \text{ CIT} \\ & + a_5 \text{ KL6} + a_6 \text{ K618} + a_7 \text{ PRIN} + a_8 \text{ UN} + \epsilon \end{aligned} \quad \textbf{(11.62)}$$

Overidentified:

$$\begin{aligned} \text{LWR} = {} & b_0 + b_1 \text{ WA} + b_2 \text{ WA2} + b_3 \text{ WE} + b_4 \text{ KL6} \\ & + b_5 \text{ K618} + b_6 \text{ PRIN} + b_7 \text{ UN} + \epsilon \end{aligned} \quad \textbf{(11.63)}$$

Underidentified:

$$\begin{aligned} \text{LWR} = {} & c_0 + c_1 \text{ WA} + c_2 \text{ WA2} + c_3 \text{ WE} + c_4 \text{ CIT} + c_5 \text{ AX} \\ & + c_6 \text{ KL6} + c_7 \text{ K618} + c_8 \text{ PRIN} + c_9 \text{ UN} + \epsilon \end{aligned} \quad \textbf{(11.64)}$$

where PRIN is the property income variable constructed in part (c) of Exercise 1 and ϵ is a random disturbance. Note that in Eqs. (11.62), (11.63), and (11.64) there are one (AX), two (AX and CIT), and zero variables, respectively, included in the LWW equation (11.61) but excluded from the LWR equation. For each of these three reservation wage equations, first employ a log-transformation of Heckman's proportionality relation (11.42),

$$H_i = d*(\text{LWW}_i - \text{LWR}_i) \qquad \text{iff LWW}_i > \text{LWR}_i \quad \textbf{(11.65a)}$$

$$H_i = 0 \qquad \text{iff LWW}_i \leq \text{LWR}_i \quad \textbf{(11.65b)}$$

then substitute into Eqs. (11.65) for LWW the OLS estimated wage determination equation (11.61) and for LWR one of the LWR specifications in Eqs. (11.62)–(11.64). Having done this, you should have obtained three alternative reduced form equations for hours worked, each in terms of the underlying structural parameters, exogenous variables, and disturbances.

(c) Using the entire sample of 753 observations in the MROZ data file and setting hours of nonworkers to zero, estimate by OLS the reduced form equation corresponding to the just identified equation (11.62) derived in part (b), using the g estimates from Eq. (11.61) to solve for the a parameters in Eq. (11.62). This procedure is often called indirect least squares. Do these structural estimates of the a parameters make sense? Why or why not? What about your estimate of d? Next, employ a more direct estimation procedure. Specifically, using your reduced form equation corresponding to Eq. (11.62), construct transformed regressors variables as the product of the original regressors in Eq. (11.61) and their estimated g coefficients, and then estimate by OLS the resulting equation with these transformed variables as regressors. Verify that you obtain the same structural estimates of the a and d parameters as you did with the indirect least squares procedure. Are the standard error estimates from this direct procedure appropriate for doing inference? Why or why not?

(d) To understand complications that arise when the reservation wage equation is over-identified, first show that in the reduced form equation corresponding to Eq. (11.63) derived in part (b) a parameter restriction must be imposed so that a unique estimate of d is obtained. Using the entire sample of 753 observations in the MROZ data file and setting hours of nonworkers to zero, impose this parameter restriction, estimate by OLS the constrained, overidentified reduced form equation, and solve for the b parameters in Eq. (11.63) and for d. Do these structural estimates of the b and d parameters make sense? Why or why not? Derive, interpret, and then implement empirically a test for the over-identified model (11.63) as a special case of the just identified model (11.62).

(e) Show that if you were to estimate by OLS the reduced form equation corresponding to the underidentified reservation wage equation (11.64) derived in part (b), there is no way that you can obtain unique estimates of the c and d structural parameters. If you nonetheless estimated this reduced form equation by OLS, what would the R^2 be relative to that from the just identified reduced form estimation of part (c)? Why does this occur?

(f) There is a serious drawback with the Procedure IV estimation you have done in this exercise. What is this problem?

EXERCISE 6: Implementing the Heckit Generalized Tobit Estimator

The purpose of Exercise 6 is to have you implement and interpret the Heckit multistage Procedure VIII. This is accomplished by having you replicate results reported by Mroz [1987]. You also will compare the Heckit sample selectivity procedure to an OLS-based method due to Olsen [1980].

(a) In the first stage of the Heckit procedure, one estimates a probit LFP equation and retrieves from this estimated equation the inverse Mills ratio λ. Mroz first generates a number of polynomial transformations of the wife's age, education and experience variables to be used as explanatory variables in the LFP equation. For the entire sample of 753 observations in the MROZ data file, following Mroz, generate AX2 ≡ AX*AX, WA2 ≡ WA*WA, WE2 ≡ WE*WE, WA3 ≡ WA2*WA, WE3 ≡ WE2*WE, WAWE ≡ WA*WE, WA2WE ≡ WA2*WE, and WAWE2 ≡ WA*WE2. With this sample, estimate by maximum likelihood a probit model in which LFP is the dependent variable and the explanatory variables include a constant term, KL6, K618, WA, WE, WA2, WE2, WAWE, WA3, WE3, WA2WE, WAWE2, WFED, WMED, UN, CIT, and PRIN (this last variable was calculated in part (c) of Exercise 1). From this estimated probit model, calculate the inverse Mills ratio for each observation, save this variable, and call it INVR1. (Some computer software programs offer this calculation as an optional command; for others, it must be computed by brute force, using Eq. (11.37) and values from the normal distribution.) Now redo the probit estimation, this time adding the experience variables AX and AX2 and calling the corresponding inverse Mills ratio values INVR2. Comment on the statistical significance of parameters estimated in these two probit equations. Note that the LWW1 wage variable is excluded as an explanatory variable in this probit model. Since economic theory suggests that LFP is affected by the wage rate, why is this LWW1 variable excluded? In what sense, however, might it be included indirectly?

(b) Next, restricting your sample to those who work for pay (the first 428 observations in MROZ), estimate by OLS a wage determination equation allowing for sample selectivity and compare results to an equation that does not take into account the sample selectivity. In particular, following Mroz, let LWW be a linear function of a constant term, KL6, K618, WA, WE, WA2, WE2, WAWE, WA3, WE3, WA2WE, WAWE2, WMED, WFED, UN, CIT, and PRIN. Call this set of explanatory variables "Set A." Estimate this equation by OLS (if your software permits, employ the White [1980] robust standard error procedure), and comment on the signs and statistical significance of the estimated parameters. Redo this OLS estimation, adding to Set A the experience variables AX and AX2. Interpret any changes in results. Then, with the same 428 observations, estimate by OLS two wage determination equations that allow for sample selectivity: first, an LWW wage determination equation with the Set A variables and the INVR1 inverse Mills ratio variable (from part (a)) included as regressors and second, an LWW wage determination equation with the Set A variables included, but with the AX, AX2 experience measures and the corresponding INVR2 variable also included. Comment on the sensitivity of the estimated parameters to inclusion of the experience variables and to the sample selectivity adjustment. Is sample selectivity significant? (You may use large sample distribution theory and the White [1980] robust standard error method to conduct statistical inference.)

(c) Finally, restricting your sample to those who work for pay (the first 428 observations in MROZ), use the fitted values from the wage determination equation in part (b) as instruments in a sample selectivity–adjusted two-stage least squares estimation of the hours worked equation. Specifically, following Mroz, for a base case comparison, first employ instrumental variable (IV) estimation (with the White robust standard error procedure if it is available in your software) of an hours worked equation in which WHRS is the dependent variable and the explanatory variables include a constant term, KL6, K618, WA, WE, LWW, and PRIN; call this set of explanatory variables "Set B." In this IV or 2SLS estimation, treat LWW as an endogenous variable, and use the Set A variables defined in part (b) to form instruments. How do your results compare with those reported by Mroz, reproduced in Eq. (11.51)? (*Note:* Mroz's standard error estimates employ the White robust standard error procedure. If your software does not permit this, your OLS standard error estimates will differ slightly from those in Eq. (11.51)). Next allow for sample selectivity, but exclude the experience variables. Specifically, using the same Set A variables plus the INVR1 inverse Mills ratio variable to form the instrument for LWW, estimate by IV or 2SLS an hours worked equation with the Set B variables as regressors (using robust standard error methods if possible), but with INVR1 added as a regressor. How do your results compare with those reported by Mroz, given in Eq. (11.53)? Is sample selectivity significant? Why or why not? (*Note:* Mroz's standard error estimates are based on a formula derived in his Appendix—his estimates will differ slightly from those of the White robust standard error procedure.) Then estimate a model by 2SLS in which the experience variables AX and AX2 are included along with the Set A variables in the first-stage wage determination equation, but in which sample selectivity is not taken into account and only the Set B variables are regressors. Compare your results with those of Mroz, reproduced in Eq. (11.50). Finally, include the experience variables AX and AX2, the Set A variables, and the INVR2 inverse Mills ratio as variables in forming the instrument for LWW, and then estimate by 2SLS the hours worked equation including as regressors the Set B variables and INVR2. Your results should conform closely with those reported by Mroz, reproduced in Eq. (11.52). Is sample selectivity important when the experience variables are treated as exogenous? Why or why not?

(d) Interpret your findings in part (c), commenting in particular on the importance of allowing for sample selectivity and how this sensitivity is affected by the assumption of exogeneity of the experience variables. Mroz concludes that with his preferred specifications the uncompensated wage effect for his sample is small, as is the estimated income effect. Do you agree? Why or why not? (You might want to compare results here with those from other studies, reported in Table 11.2.)

(e) Now compare the Heckit inverse Mills ratio procedure to the OLS-based linear probability model method proposed by Olsen [1980]. In particular, using a model either with or without the AX and AX2 experience variables, follow the Olsen procedure outlined in Section 11.3.B.1 underneath Eq. (11.37) and use as a regressor in the wage rate determination and hours worked equations, instead of the inverse Mills ratio, the fitted probability minus 1 from an OLS-estimated linear probability model. Compare these results with those obtained from the Heckit procedure. Do they differ substantially?

(f) In what sense is the estimation procedure of this exercise a generalized Tobit estimator?

EXERCISE 7: Incorporating Income Taxes into a Model of Labor Supply

The purpose of this exercise is to enable you to assess the impacts of incorporating income taxes on your estimates of the wage and income responsiveness of labor supply. This will involve creating virtual income and after-tax wage rate variables that are consistent with a linearized budget constraint (LBC) budget constraint specification, estimating by using the Heckit generalized Tobit procedure, and comparing results with those reported by Mroz [1987].

(a) Our first task is to create several tax-related variables. For the entire sample of 753 observations in the MROZ data file, first create and save a virtual property income variable defined as VPRIN ≡ (1 − MTR)*PRIN, where PRIN was created in part (c) of Exercise 1 and MTR is the marginal tax rate variable provided in the MROZ data file. Next, generate and save LTAX ≡ LOG(1−MTR) and the logarithm of an after-tax wage variable as LTWW ≡ LTAX + LWW1, where LWW1 is the wage variable created in Exercise 1.

(b) To implement the Heckit multistage procedure that allows for sample selectivity, we must initially estimate a probit LFP equation for the entire sample of 753 observations and compute from this estimation the Heckman inverse Mills ratio. Following Mroz, first generate polynomial transformations of the wife's age, education, and experience variables, to be used as explanatory variables in the LFP equation. In particular, for the entire sample of 753 observations in the MROZ data file, generate and save WA2 = WA*WA, WE2 = WE*WE, WA3 = WA2*WA, WE3 = WE2*WE, WAWE = WA*WE, WA2WE = WA2*WE, and WAWE2 = WA*WE2. With this sample, estimate by maximum likelihood a probit model in which LFP is the dependent variable and the explanatory variables include a constant term, KL6, K618, WA, WE, WA2, WE2, WAWE, WA3, WE3, WA2WE, WAWE2, WFED, WMED, UN, CIT, and PRIN (this last variable was calculated in part (c) of Exercise 1). From this estimated probit model, calculate the inverse Mills ratio for each observation, save this variable, and call it INVR. (Some computer software programs offer this calculation as an optional command; for others it must be computed by brute force using Eq. (11.37) and values from the normal distribution.)

(c) Now estimate a model with taxes included, similar to that presented in Eq. (11.55), by 2SLS. Specifically, using as exogenous variables a constant term, KL6, K618, WA, WE, WA2, WE2, WAWE, WA3, WE3, WA2WE, WAWE2, WMED, WFED, UN, CIT, PRIN and the inverse Mills ratio variable INVR from part (b), form an instrument for the log of the after-tax wage rate variable LTWW (created in part (a)). With these instruments for LTWW, estimate by 2SLS a model in which WHRS is a linear function of a constant term, LTWW, LTAX, KL6, K618, WA, WE, PRIN, VPRIN, INVR, and a random disturbance term. If your software permits, obtain the White robust standard error estimates. Comment on the sign and magnitude of the estimated wage, property income, and tax coefficients. Using the information given underneath Eq. (11.55) and your estimated variance-covariance matrix of the estimated coefficients, formulate and test the hypothesis that women optimally take income taxes into account when making labor supply decisions. Then formulate and test the hypothesis that women entirely ignore income taxes when making labor supply decisions. Interpret your test results. Do your conclusions agree with those reported by Mroz and by Rosen [1976]? Why or why not?

(d) Experiment with any two other plausible specifications for the probit, wage determination, and/or hours worked equations with taxes included, and comment on the sensitivity of your results to changes in specification. Do Mroz's results on the unimportance of income taxes appear to be robust?

EXERCISE 8: Specifying and Estimating an Extended Tobit Model

In this exercise you will specify and estimate an extended Tobit simultaneous equations model in which parameters of the wage rate, reservation wage (and implicitly, hours of work), and labor force participation equations are estimated simultaneously by using the method of full information maximum likelihood (FIML), with cross-equation parameter constraints imposed. As was noted in Section 11.3.B.1, Killingsworth [1983] has called this Procedure VI.

(a) We begin by specifying the wage equation for workers only, where LWW is specified to be a linear function of a constant term, WA, WA2, WE, CIT, AX, and a random disturbance term ϵ_{Wi}, as in Eqs. (11.38) and (11.61). Next we specify the functional form of the reservation wage equation derived from the marginal rate of substitution function. In particular, let the logarithm of the reservation wage equation be LWR and let it have the functional form as in the overidentified equation (11.63) but denote the disturbance term in Eq. (11.63) by ϵ_{Ri}, as in Eq. (11.41). Finally, following Heckman [1974b], specify that hours worked, WHRS, is a proportion d of the difference between LWW and LWR iff $\text{LWW}_i > \text{LWR}_i$ and is zero iff $\text{LWW}_i \leq \text{LWR}_i$, analogous to Eqs. (11.65a) and (11.65b). Finally, analytically substitute into the hours worked equations (11.65a) and (11.65b) your specifications for the LWW and LWR equations, and note that in Eq. (11.65a) the disturbance term, now denoted $d\epsilon_{Di}$, is equal to $d\epsilon_{Di} \equiv d(\epsilon_{Wi} - \epsilon_{Ri})$, which is similar to Eq. (11.45a) but with d replacing b.

(b) Now assume that ϵ_{Wi} and ϵ_{Ri} are joint normally distributed with variances σ_W^2 and σ_R^2 and covariance σ_{WR}. This implies that in the hours worked equation that you constructed in part (a) the disturbance term ϵ_{Di} is normally distributed with variance $\sigma_D^2 = \sigma_W^2 + \sigma_R^2 - 2\sigma_{WR}$ and is joint normally distributed with ϵ_{Wi}, having covariance $\sigma_{DW} = \sigma_W^2 - \sigma_{WR}$. Given these distributional assumptions, write out the likelihood function for the entire sample of 753 observations, analogous to Eq. (11.47), where d now replaces b and other terms are as defined by Eq. (11.47).

(c) Using the appropriate computer software and the 753 observations from the MROZ data file as well as the likelihood function constructed in part (b), estimate by maximum likelihood the parameters appearing in the extended Tobit model consisting of the wage and hours worked equations. Mroz reports that when he estimated a model similar to this, he obtained a large positive and statistically significant coefficient on LWW but a negative and marginally significant coefficient on PRIN. Are your results qualitatively similar to those of Mroz?

(d) Finally, following Mroz, specify an alternative model in which the experience variable AX is excluded from the wage rate determination equation. As in parts (a) and (b), write out the corresponding likelihood function, and then estimate parameters using the FIML method. Compare your results to those obtained in part (c). Mroz found that when the AX experience variable was omitted from the wage determination equation, the estimated FIML coefficient on LWW in the hours worked equation was positive but much smaller than when AX was included (and statistically insignificantly different from zero). However, the estimated coefficient on PRIN was negative and statistically significant, but smaller in absolute value than when the AX variable was included in Eq. (11.61). Do your results conform with those of Mroz? Why or why not?

(e) The model specified and estimated in this exercise is based implicitly on an important assumption concerning the continuity of the hours worked relationship. What is this assumption, and under what practical considerations might it be violated? What estimation procedures are available that do not require this strong assumption?

CHAPTER NOTES

1. These data are taken from the *1989 Economic Report of the President*, Washington, D.C.: U.S. Government Printing Office, Table B-36, p. 349.
2. For a detailed discussion of factors affecting the time series growth of the female labor force supply, see James P. Smith and Michael Ward [1985] and the references cited therein.
3. Reasons for this decline are discussed and surveyed by, among others, John Pencavel [1986].
4. To a first approximation the effect of truncation occurs when sample data are drawn from a subset of a larger population of interest (e.g., those in the labor force are selected from those in the population as a whole), whereas censoring occurs when values over a range of a variable are reported simply as being less than (or greater than) some given value (e.g., the unobserved reservation wage is less than the market wage facing an individual). Unlike truncation, censoring is essentially a defect in the sample data.
5. For a survey of issues concerning the labor supply of males, see John Pencavel [1986].
6. However, see the classic study by P. Sargant Florence [1924].
7. For a more detailed discussion of measurement issues, see, for example, Harold Watts et al. [1977] and Shirley J. Smith [1983].
8. Detailed data on U.S. government household surveys are found in two U.S. Bureau of Labor Statistics publications, an occasional one called *Handbook of Labor Statistics*, Technical Notes, and the monthly publication called *Employment and Earnings*. International comparisons of labor force participation and international data sources are discussed in, among others, Constance Sorrentino [1983]. The discussion that follows is based in large part on Daniel Hamermesh and Albert Rees [1988], Chapter 1.
9. Issues involved in assessing factors that affect the supply of labor to the U.S. military are discussed in, among others, Colin Ash, Bernard Udis, and Robert F. McNown [1983].
10. These figures are taken from Hamermesh and Rees [1988, Table 2.5].
11. Another, less commonly used data set is one that focuses particular attention on the variety of sources of income. It is the U.S. Bureau of Census *Survey of Income and Program Participation*, undertaken as a joint project with the U.S. Department of Health and Human Services. For a discussion of this data set, see U.S. Department of Commerce, Bureau of the Census [1987].
12. For additional discussion, see Daniel S. Hamermesh [1990].

13. Descriptions of the data gathered at Ohio State are found in Parnes et al. [1970], while those of data collected at the University of Michigan are presented in Morgan et al. [1966, 1974].
14. For a classic presentation of the individual labor supply model, see H. Gregg Lewis [1957].
15. This reservation wage notion is apparently due to Jacob Mincer [1963]. Important extensions and applications include those of Reuben Gronau [1973b] and James Heckman [1974b]; also see Gronau [1986].
16. The expressions in Eqs. (11.12)–(11.14) implicitly assume that interior solutions occur both before and after the small change in P_L.
17. This choice of nomenclature is somewhat unfortunate, since while chauvinism is clearly undesirable, this particular model might or might not be a reasonable description of household decision making.
18. For examples of the use of the male chauvinist model, see, among others, Bowen and Finegan [1965, 1969] and Hausman [1981a].
19. Applications of this model include Marvin Kosters [1966]; Malcolm Cohen, Sam Rea, and Robert Lerman [1970]; Robert Hall [1973]; Orley Ashenfelter and James Heckman [1974]; and Jerry Hausman and Paul Ruud [1984].
20. This duopoly type of model of labor supply has been implemented by J. S. Ashworth and David T. Ulph [1981].
21. For a discussion of such indirect income effects, see Killingsworth [1983, pp. 36–38].
22. The added worker hypothesis appears to have been first pointed out by Wladimir S. Woytinsky [1940].
23. On this, see, for example, Mincer [1962, 1966] and Belton M. Fleisher and George F. Rhodes, Jr. [1976].
24. Ronald G. Ehrenberg and Robert S. Smith [1985, p. 204] note that if one incorporated estimates of discouraged workers into official unemployment rate statistics, then the U.S. unemployment rate in 1973, for example, would have increased from 4.9 to 5.6%. There is some evidence, however, that for a substantial number of discouraged workers the attachment to the labor force is loose, and so it is not clear how one should interpret the welfare consequences of the discouraged-worker effect; see, for example, Paul Flaim [1984]. For this and other reasons, considerable controversy exists concerning whether published unemployment rates should include estimates of discouraged workers. A useful discussion of this set of issues is found in the final report of the National Commission on Employment and Unemployment Statistics [1979, pp. 44–49].
25. The discussion that follows is based in large part on Addison and Siebert [1979, pp. 79–85].
26. For a discussion of such family economics issues and additional references, see Gary S. Becker [1981, 1988].
27. A partial list of studies includes the theoretical and econometric analyses by Martin Browning et al. [1985], Kim B. Clark and Lawrence H. Summers [1982], Gilbert R. Ghez and Gary S. Becker [1975], James J. Heckman [1978], James J. Heckman and Thomas E. MaCurdy [1980, 1986], Richard Layard and Jacob Mincer [1985], Thomas E. MaCurdy [1981], Robert A. Moffitt [1984], Alice Nakamura and Masao Nakamura [1985a, b], and T. Paul Schultz [1980].
28. Other early studies estimating the effects of fixed costs on labor supply include those by Giora Hanoch [1976, 1980] and Jerry A. Hausman [1980].

29. This classification scheme was actually developed earlier by James J. Heckman, Mark R. Killingsworth, and Thomas E. MaCurdy [1981].
30. See, for example, Robert E. Hall [1973].
31. This procedure is followed by each of the authors in Cain and Watts [1973b], except for Hall [1973].
32. Heckman, Killingsworth, and MaCurdy [1981, pp. 83–84].
33. When this type of model is implemented using panel data, it is often assumed that although e varies across people at any given point in time, for any one person it is fixed over time. A discussion of econometric techniques that exploit panel data is beyond the scope of this chapter; see, however, Zvi Griliches, Bronwyn H. Hall, and Jerry A. Hausman [1978]; Griliches and Hausman [1986]; and Cheng Hsiao [1986].
34. Recall that the first-order conditions for utility maximization at an interior solution imply that the marginal rate of substitution M equals the real wage rate W, that is, that the slope of the indifference curve equals the slope of the budget line.
35. Probit analysis has a long history in biometrics; see, for example, David J. Finney [1947] and Jerome Cornfield and Nathan Mantel [1950]. For early discussions in the context of econometrics, see James Tobin [1955] and Arthur S. Goldberger [1964, pp. 248–251].
36. For further discussion, see, *inter alia*, Tobin [1958], Amemiya [1973], and Maddala [1983, Chapter 6]. The etymology of Tobit is unclear, although Goldberger [1964, p. 253] refers to it as Tobin's probit. Maddala [1983, p. 151] suggests that there is presumably no connection with the prophet Tobit or the book of Tobit in the Apocrypha. It is known that James Tobin achieved a distinguished record in the U.S. Navy during World War II, including anti-submarine duty. Further, Killingsworth [1983, fn. 7, p. 142] notes that the novelist Herman Wouk was a classmate of Tobin's in naval officer training school and that in his best-seller *The Caine Mutiny*, Wouk created a midshipman character named "Tobit."
37. Computational issues concerning estimation of the Tobit model have been considered by, among others, Richard N. Rosett and Forrest D. Nelson [1975] and Ray Fair [1977].
38. For a discussion of more general utility functions and their implied consumer demand and labor supply equations, see Arthur S. Goldberger [1987].
39. McDonald and Moffitt emphasize that A will equal 1 only if X is infinity, in which case $F(z) = 1$ and $f(z) = 0$.
40. In practice, this is typically done by evaluating the expressions at sample means of the variables and using estimated parameters.
41. For further discussion, see Olsen [1980], and for a generalization to accommodate other distributions, see Lung-Fei Lee [1982].
42. For further discussion of issues concerning the functional form of the wage determination equation (11.38), see Chapter 5 of this book.
43. See Killingsworth [1983, Table 4.1, p. 151] and Killingsworth and Heckman [1986, Table 2.26, p. 192] for a very brief tabular summary of these eight methods.
44. One of the first statements of this sample selectivity problem in the context of labor supply is found in Reuben Gronau [1973a].
45. In practice, this factor of proportionality often applies to the difference in the natural logarithms of W_i and W_{ri}.
46. For further discussion of identification issues, see Killingsworth [1983, pp. 154–156, especially footnotes 14 and 17] and Olsen [1980].

47. There are other important problems in analyzing the labor supply effects of taxes. To determine the appropriate marginal after-tax wage rate, researchers typically must employ published statutory tax rate information. However, actual marginal after-tax wage rates may differ substantially from statutory rates, owing to complex exemptions and deductible expense provisions, underreporting or concealment of income by individuals, and/or to discretionary administrative behavior by tax-collecting agencies. With the exception of William Gould [1979], hardly any empirical work has been done to date on the labor supply implications of tax avoidance and tax evasion; however, for theoretical discussions of this topic, see Jonathan C. Baldry [1979], Arne J. Isachsen and Steiner Strøm [1980], Agnar Sandmo [1981], and James J. Heckman [1983]. Further, it is widely believed that the available data on hours worked measure actual hours worked with error, which implies that the budget constraint segment facing the individual might be misspecified. This issue has been addressed by, among others, Burtless and Hausman [1978], Hausman [1980], and Wales and Woodland [1980].
48. This is slightly better than the cynical summary offered by George Johnson [1976, p. 107, fn. 9] concerning estimates of input substitutability in production: "In recent years, economists have narrowed its value down to a range between zero and infinity."
49. Wales and Woodland [1979] and Zabalza [1983] employ the CES direct utility function, while Burtless and Hausman [1978] and Hausman [1980, 1981a, 1983] adopt a form that places a priori inequality (negative) restrictions on the total income elasticity. Ashworth and Ulph [1981] restrict their sample to people who work at least eight hours per week but do not correct for the potential sample selectivity bias.
50. Orley Ashenfelter and James J. Heckman [1974] consider a joint labor supply model but do not incorporate the effects of taxation. For another attempt at including taxes in the family labor supply context, see Jerry A. Hausman and Paul Ruud [1984].
51. Note that in countries such as Canada where spouses file separate income tax returns, this marriage tax is less of an issue. For further discussion, see Alice Nakamura and Masao Nakamura [1981a].
52. Hausman [1981a, p. 63]. Also see Hausman [1986].
53. This conventional wisdom has also been persistently attacked by Alice Nakamura and Masao Nakamura [1981b; 1985a, b].
54. A more complete survey of female labor supply is presented in Table 2.26 of Killingsworth and Heckman [1986, pp. 189–192].
55. Mroz [1987, p. 769].
56. See James Durbin [1954], De-Min Wu [1973], Jerry Hausman [1978], and Halbert White [1982].
57. That $KL6_i$, the number of children under age six, and perhaps $K618_i$ are exogenous is a somewhat surprising finding. One possibility is that the power of the Durbin-Wu-Hausman-White specification test may be low, particularly when the fit from the first-stage regressions is low. For a discussion of such power issues for this test, see Nakamura and Nakamura [1985c].
58. It is worth noting that when the two experience variables are excluded from the first-stage probit equation, the sample likelihood function falls from -398 to -450, and of the 16 regressors, only $KL6_i$ and V_i have estimated coefficients that are more than twice their estimated standard errors.

59. Mroz also reports that these findings are essentially unchanged when the first-stage probit equation is altered to reflect alternative distributions such as the logit or log normal. Furthermore, tests for the exogeneity of KL6, K618, and V uniformly indicate nonrejection of the null hypothesis of exogeneity.
60. It is worth noting, however, that use of the simple conditional mean or inverse Mills ratio adjustment to account for sample selectivity is at best a "first-order approximation" when taxes are incorporated into the model; unless strong assumptions are made similar to those specified by Hausman [1981a], the appropriate procedure is very complex and computationally cumbersome. Mroz's results concerning the effects of taxes should therefore be viewed as tentative.
61. Note the similarity of this framework to that of progressive taxation in static labor supply discussed in Section 11.3.B.2; in both cases the budget constraint set consists of numerous segments having differing slopes.
62. An implication of this additive separability is that $C(t)$ or $L(t)$ does not affect the marginal utility of $C(t')$ or $L(t')$ for $t \neq t'$. Further, if leisure is a normal good in each time period, then additive separability implies that leisure times at different points over the life cycle must be net substitutes (holding lifetime utility constant). For further discussion, see Angus Deaton [1974].
63. For further discussion, see Martin Browning, Angus Deaton, and Margaret Irish [1985] and the references cited therein.
64. See Harold Watts, Dale Poirier, and Chris Mallar [1977], among others, for a study implementing PO and Edward Kalachek, Wesley Mellow, and Fredric Raines [1978] for PT.
65. For details, see Killingsworth and Heckman [1986, pp. 159–161].
66. For a general theoretical discussion on models of endogenous dynamic wage determination, see Yoram Weiss [1986]. Recent econometric studies on various aspects of dynamic labor supply include Joseph Altonji [1986], Richard Blundell and Ian Walker [1982], James Heckman and Thomas MaCurdy [1980], Richard Layard and Jacob Mincer [1985], Thomas MaCurdy [1981], Robert Moffitt [1984], Alice Nakamura and Masao Nakamura [1985a, b], and James P. Smith [1977, 1980].
67. The labor supply effects of such quantity restrictions have been considered by, among others, Angus Deaton and John M. Muellbauer [1981], Robert A. Moffitt [1982], and John C. Ham [1982, 1986].
68. For a survey of econometric problems with more general qualitative dependent variable specifications, see, for example, Takeshi Amemiya [1981, 1984], Richard Blundell [1987], James Heckman [1976b], G. S. Maddala [1983], and Daniel McFadden [1984]. In the context of family labor force participation studies, see Jules Theeuwes [1981] for an application of the multinomial logit specification.
69. For discussions on inference from experimental data, see, for example, Dennis J. Aigner [1979]; Michael C. Keeley [1981]; Michael C. Keeley, Philip K. Robins, Robert G. Spiegelman, and Richard W. West [1978]; and Charles E. Metcalf [1973].
70. Panel data issues are discussed by, among others, Zvi Griliches, Bronwyn H. Hall, and Jerry A. Hausman [1978]; Griliches and Hausman [1986]; and Cheng Hsiao [1986].
71. Thanks are due to Thomas Mroz, who made this data set available for our use.
72. For an empirical comparison of the OLS, logit, and probit estimators in the context of the labor force participation decision, see Morley K. Gunderson [1980]. Gunderson [1980, p. 217] finds that, "When the probability of labor force partic-

ipation is .50, . . . , the results of all three statistical techniques are similar. However, when the actual probability of participation is nearer to zero or one, then the probit or logit results differ substantially from the linear probability function."

73. Historical aspects of the logit specification in bioassay studies are discussed briefly in Joseph Berkson [1951].
74. A discussion of goodness-of-fit measures in the context of limited dependent variable models is given in, for example, G. S. Maddala [1983, pp. 37–41, 76–77].
75. However, among others, Joseph Berkson [1951] has argued that the logit is preferable to the probit.
76. For a discussion and derivation, see G. S. Maddala [1983, pp. 23–24].

CHAPTER REFERENCES

Addison, John T. and W. Stanley Siebert [1979], *The Market for Labor: An Analytical Treatment,* Santa Monica, Calif.: Goodyear.

Aigner, Dennis J. [1979], "A Brief Introduction to the Methodology of Optimal Experimental Design," *Journal of Econometrics,* 11:1, September, 7–26.

Allen, R. G. D. [1938], *Mathematical Analysis for Economists,* London: Macmillan.

Altonji, Joseph G. [1986], "Intertemporal Substitution in Labor Supply: Evidence from Micro Data," *Journal of Political Economy,* 94:3, Part 2, June, S176-S215.

Amemiya, Takeshi [1973], "Regression Analysis When the Dependent Variable Is Truncated Normal," *Econometrica,* 41:6, November, 997–1017.

Amemiya, Takeshi [1975], "Qualitative Response Models," *Annals of Economic and Social Measurement,* 4:2, Summer, 363–372.

Amemiya, Takeshi [1981], "Qualitative Response Models: A Survey," *Journal of Economic Literature,* 19:4, December, 1483–1536.

Amemiya, Takeshi, ed. [1984], "Censored or Truncated Regression Models," *Journal of Econometrics,* 24:1/2, January/February, 1–222.

Ash, Colin, Bernard Udis, and Robert F. McNown [1983], "Enlistments in the All-Volunteer Force: A Military Personnel Supply Model and Its Forecasts," *American Economic Review,* 73:1, March, 145–155.

Ashenfelter, Orley and James J. Heckman [1974], "The Estimation of Income and Substitution Effects in a Model of Family Labor Supply," *Econometrica,* 42:1, January, 73–86.

Ashworth, J. S. and David T. Ulph [1981], "Endogeneity I: Estimating Labor Supply with Piecewise Linear Budget Constraints," in Charles V. Brown, ed., *Taxation and Labor Supply,* London: Allen & Unwin, pp. 53–68.

Baldry, Jonathan C. [1979], "Tax Evasion and Labor Supply," *Economics Letters,* 3:1, January, 53–56.

Becker, Gary S. [1965], "A Theory of the Allocation of Time," *Economic Journal,* 75:299, September, 493–517.

Becker, Gary S. [1974], "A Theory of Marriage," in Theodore W. Schultz, ed., *Economics of the Family,* Chicago: University of Chicago Press, pp. 293–344.

Becker, Gary S. [1981], *A Treatise on the Family,* Cambridge, Mass.: Harvard University Press.

Becker, Gary S. [1988], "Family Economics and Macro Behavior," *American Economic Review,* 78:1, March, 1–13.

Berkson, Joseph [1951], "Why I Prefer Logits to Probits," *Biometrics*, 7:4, December, 327–339.

Blundell, Richard, ed. [1987], "Specification Testing in Limited and Discrete Dependent Variable Models," *Journal of Econometrics*, 34:1/2, January/February, 1–274.

Blundell, Richard and Ian Walker [1982], "Modelling the Joint Determination of Household Labor Supplies and Commodity Demands," *Economic Journal*, 92, June, 351–364.

Boskin, Michael J. [1973], "The Economics of Labor Supply," in Glen C. Cain and Harold W. Watts, eds., *Income Maintenance and Labor Supply*, Chicago: Rand McNally, pp. 163–181.

Bowen, William G. and T. Aldrich Finegan [1965], "Labor Force Participation and Unemployment," in Arthur M. Ross, ed., *Employment Policy and the Labor Market*, Berkeley, Calif.: University of California Press, pp. 115–161.

Bowen, William G. and T. Aldrich Finegan [1969], *The Economics of Labor Force Participation*, Princeton, N.J.: Princeton University Press.

Browning, Martin, Angus Deaton, and Margaret Irish [1985], "A Profitable Approach to Labor Supply and Commodity Demands over the Life-Cycle," *Econometrica*, 53:3, May, 503–543.

Burtless, Gary and Jerry A. Hausman [1978], "The Effect of Taxation on Labor Supply: Evaluating the Gary Negative Income Tax Experiment," *Journal of Political Economy*, 86:6, December, 1103–1130.

Cain, Glen G. [1966], *The Labor Force Participation of Married Women*, Chicago: University of Chicago Press.

Cain, Glen C. and Harold W. Watts [1973a], "Toward a Summary and Synthesis of the Evidence," in Cain and Watts, eds., *Income Maintenance and Labor Supply*, Chicago: Rand McNally, pp. 328–367.

Cain, Glen C. and Harold W. Watts, eds. [1973b], *Income Maintenance and Labor Supply*, Chicago: Rand McNally.

Clark, Kim B. and Lawrence H. Summers [1982], "Labour Force Participation: Timing and Persistence," *Review of Economic Studies*, 49, Supplement, 825–844.

Cogan, John F. [1977], *Labor Supply with Time and Money Costs of Participation:* Report No. R-2044 to the U.S. Department of Health, Education and Welfare, Santa Monica, Calif.: The Rand Corporation.

Cogan, John F. [1980a], "Married Women's Labor Supply: A Comparison of Alternative Estimation Procedures," in James P. Smith, ed., *Female Labor Supply: Theory and Estimation*, Princeton, N.J.: Princeton University Press, pp. 90–118.

Cogan, John F. [1980b], "Labor Supply with Fixed Costs of Labor Market Entry," in James P. Smith, ed., *Female Labor Supply: Theory and Estimation*, Princeton, N.J.: Princeton University Press, pp. 327–364.

Cogan, John F. [1981], "Fixed Costs and Labor Supply," *Econometrica*, 49:4, July, 945–963.

Cohen, Malcolm S., Samuel A. Rea, and Robert I. Lerman [1970], "A Micro Model of Labor Supply," Washington, D.C.: U.S. Bureau of Labor Statistics, BLS Staff Paper No. 4.

Cornfield, Jerome and Nathan Mantel [1950], "Some New Aspects of the Application of Maximum Likelihood to the Calculation of the Dosage Response Curve," *Journal of the American Statistical Association*, 45:250, June, 181–210.

Deaton, Angus [1974], "A Reconsideration of the Empirical Implications of Additive Preferences," *Economic Journal*, 84:334, June, 338–348.

Deaton, Angus and John M. Muellbauer [1980], *Economics and Consumer Behavior*, New York: Cambridge University Press.

Deaton, Angus and John M. Muellbauer [1981], "Functional Forms for Labor Supply and Commodity Demands with and without Quantity Restrictions," *Econometrica*, 49:6, November, 1521–1532.

Diewert, W. Erwin [1971], "Choice on Labour Markets and the Theory of the Allocation of Time," Ottawa, Ontario: Government of Canada, Department of Manpower and Immigration, Research Branch, mimeo.

Durbin, James [1954], "Errors in Variables," *Review of the International Statistical Institute*, 22:1, 23–32.

Ehrenberg, Ronald G. and Robert S. Smith [1985], Modern Labor Economics: Theory and Public Policy, Second Edition, Glenview, Ill.: Scott, Foresman.

Fair, Ray C. [1977], "A Note on the Computation of the Tobit Estimator," *Econometrica*, 41:7, October, 1723–1727.

Finney, David J. [1947], *Probit Analysis*, Cambridge, England: Cambridge University Press.

Flaim, Paul O. [1984], "Discouraged Workers: How Strong Are Their Links to the Job Market," *Monthly Labor Review*, 107:8, August, 8–11.

Fleisher, Belton M. and George F. Rhodes, Jr. [1976], "Labor Force Participation of Married Men and Women: A Simultaneous Model," *Review of Economics and Statistics*, 58:6, November, 398–406.

Florence, P. Sargant [1924], *The Economics of Fatigue and Unrest*, New York: Holt.

Friedman, Milton [1957], *A Theory of the Consumption Function*, Princeton N.J.: Princeton University Press.

Fullerton, Don [1982], "On the Possibility of an Inverse Relationship between Tax Rates and Government Revenues," *Journal of Public Economics*, 19:1, October, 3–22.

Ghez, Gilbert R. and Gary S. Becker [1975], *The Allocation of Time and Goods over the Life Cycle*, New York: Columbia University Press.

Goldberger, Arthur S. [1964], *Econometric Theory*, New York: John Wiley and Sons.

Goldberger, Arthur S. [1981], "Linear Regression after Selection," *Journal of Econometrics*, 15:3, April, 357–366.

Goldberger, Arthur S. [1987], *Functional Form and Utility: A Review of Consumer Demand Theory*, Boulder, Colo.: Westview Press.

Gould, William [1979], "Taxes and Female Labor Supply," unpublished Ph.D. dissertation, University of California at Los Angeles.

Greene, William H. [1981], "On the Asymptotic Bias of the Ordinary Least Squares Estimator," *Econometrica*, 49:2, March, 505–513.

Greenhalgh, Christine [1980], "Participation and Hours of Work for Married Women in Great Britain," *Oxford Economic Papers*, 32:2, July, 296–318.

Griliches, Zvi and Jerry A. Hausman [1986], "Errors in Variables in Panel Data," *Journal of Econometrics*, 31:1, February, 93–118.

Griliches, Zvi, Bronwyn H. Hall, and Jerry A. Hausman [1978], "Missing Data and Self-Selection in Large Panels," *Annales de l'INSEE*, No. 30/31, April/September, 137–176.

Gronau, Reuben [1973a], "The Effect of Children on the Housewife's Value of Time," *Journal of Political Economy*, 81:2, Part II, March/April, S168–S199.

Gronau, Reuben [1973b], "Home Production: A Forgotten Industry," *Review of Economics and Statistics*, 62:5, August, 408–415.

Gronau, Reuben [1973c], "The Intrafamily Allocation of Time: The Value of the Housewives' Time," *American Economic Review*, 63:4, September, 634–651.

Gronau, Reuben [1977], "Leisure, Home Production, and Work—The Theory of the Allocation of Time Revisited," *Journal of Political Economy*, 85:6, December, 1099–1124.

Gronau, Reuben [1986], "Home Production: A Survey," Chapter 4 in Orley Ashenfelter and Richard Layard, eds., *Handbook of Labor Economics*, Vol. 1, New York: Elsevier Sciences BV, pp. 273–304.

Gunderson, Morley K. [1980], "Probit and Logit Estimates of Labor Force Participation," *Industrial Relations*, 19:2, Spring, 216–220.

Hall, Robert E. [1973], "Wages, Income and Hours of Work in the U.S. Labor Force," in Glen C. Cain and Harold W. Watts, eds., *Income Maintenance and Labor Supply*, Chicago: Rand McNally, pp. 102–162.

Ham, John C. [1982], "Estimation of a Labour Supply Model with Censoring Due to Unemployment and Underemployment," *Review of Economic Studies*, 49:3, July, 335–354.

Ham, John C. [1986], "Testing Whether Unemployment Represents Intertemporal Labour Supply Behavior," *Review of Economic Studies*, 53:4, August, 559–578.

Ham, John C. and Cheng Hsiao [1984], "Two Stage Estimation of Structural Labor Supply Parameters Using Interval Data from the 1971 Canadian Census," *Journal of Econometrics*, 24:1/2, January/February, 133–158.

Hamermesh, Daniel S. [1990], "Data Difficulties in Labor Economics," in Ernst R. Berndt and Jack E. Triplett, eds., *Fifty Years of Economic Measurement*, Chicago: University of Chicago Press.

Hamermesh, Daniel S. and Albert Rees [1988], *The Economics of Work and Pay*, Fourth Edition, New York: Harper & Row.

Hanoch, Giora [1980], "A Multivariate Model of Labor Supply: Methodology and Estimation," in James P. Smith, ed., *Female Labor Supply*, Princeton, N.J.: Princeton University Press, pp. 249–326.

Hausman, Jerry A. [1978], "Specification Tests in Econometrics," *Econometrica*, 46:6, November, 1251–1272.

Hausman, Jerry A. [1979], "The Econometrics of Labor Supply on Convex Budget Sets," *Economics Letters*, 3:2, 171–174.

Hausman, Jerry A. [1980], "The Effects of Wages, Taxes and Fixed Costs on Women's Labor Force Participation," *Journal of Public Economics*, 14:2, October, 161–194.

Hausman, Jerry A. [1981a], "Labor Supply," in Henry J. Aaron and Joseph A. Pechman, eds., *How Taxes Affect Economic Behavior*, Washington, D.C.: The Brookings Instiution, pp. 27–72.

Hausman, Jerry A. [1981b], "Income and Payroll Tax Policy and Labor Supply," in Lawrence H. Meyer, ed., *The Supply-Side Effects of Economic Policy*, St. Louis, Mo.: Center for the Study of American Business, Washington University, 173–202.

Hausman, Jerry A. [1983], "Stochastic Problems in the Simulation of Labor Supply," in Martin S. Feldstein, ed., *Behavioral Simulation Methods in Tax Policy Analysis*, Chicago: University of Chicago Press for the National Bureau of Economic Research, pp. 47–69.

Hausman, Jerry A. [1985], "Taxes and Labor Supply," in Alan Auerbach and Martin Feldstein, eds., *Handbook of Public Economics*, New York: Elsevier Science Publishers BV, pp. 213–263.

Hausman, Jerry A. and Paul Ruud [1984], "Family Labor Supply with Taxes," *American Economic Review*, 74:2, May, 242–248.

Hausman, Jerry A. and David A. Wise [1976], "The Evaluation of Results from Truncated Samples: The New Jersey Income Maintenance Experiment," *Annals of Economic and Social Measurement*, 5:4, Fall, 391–420.

Heckman, James J. [1971], "Three Essays on the Supply of Labor and the Demand for Market Goods," Ph.D. dissertation, Princeton University, Department of Economics.

Heckman, James J. [1974a], "Life Cycle Consumption and Labor Supply: An Explanation of the Relationship between Income and Consumption over the Life Cycle," *American Economic Review*, 64:1, March, 188–194.

Heckman, James J. [1974b], "Shadow Prices, Market Wages and Labor Supply," *Econometrica*, 42:4, July, 679–694.

Heckman, James J. [1976a], "The Common Structure of Statistical Models of Truncation, Sample Selection and Limited Dependent Variables, and a Simple Estimator for Such Models," *Annals of Economic and Social Measurement*, 5:4, Fall, 475–492.

Heckman, James J., ed. [1976b], "Special Issue on Discrete, Qualitative and Limited Dependent Variables," *Annals of Economic and Social Measurement*, 5:4, Fall.

Heckman, James J. [1978], "A Partial Survey of Recent Research on the Labor Supply of Women," *American Economic Review*, 68:2, May, 200–207.

Heckman, James J. [1979], "Sample Selection Bias as a Specification Error," *Econometrica*, 47:1, January, 153–162.

Heckman, James J. [1980], "Sample Selection Bias as a Specification Error," in James P. Smith, ed., *Female Labor Supply*, Princeton, N.J.: Princeton University Press, pp. 206–248.

Heckman, James J. [1983], "Comment on Hausman," in Martin S. Feldstein, ed., *Behavioral Simulation Methods in Tax Policy Analysis*, Chicago: University of Chicago Press for the National Bureau of Economic Research, pp. 70–82.

Heckman, James J. and Thomas E. MaCurdy [1980], "A Life-Cycle Model of Female Labor Supply," *Review of Economic Studies*, 47:1, January, 47–74.

Heckman, James J. and Thomas E. MaCurdy [1981], "New Methods for Estimating Labor Supply Functions: A Survey," in Ronald G. Ehrenberg, ed., *Research in Labor Economics*, Vol. 4, Greenwich, Conn.: JAI Press, pp. 65–102.

Heckman, James J. and Thomas E. MaCurdy [1986], "Labor Econometrics," Chapter 32 in Zvi Griliches and Michael D. Intriligator, eds., *Handbook of Econometrics*, Vol. 3, New York: Elsevier Science Publishers, pp. 1917–1977.

Heckman, James J., Mark R. Killingsworth, and Thomas E. MaCurdy [1981], "Empirical Evidence on Static Labour Supply Models: A Survey of Recent Developments," in Zmira Hornstein, Joseph Grice, and Alfred Webb, eds., *The Economics of the Labour Market*, London: Her Majesty's Stationery Office, pp. 73–122.

Hsiao, Cheng [1986], *Analysis of Panel Data*, Cambridge, England: Cambridge University Press.

Isachsen, Arne J. and Steiner Strøm [1980], "The Hidden Economy: The Labor Market and Tax Evasion," *Scandinavian Journal of Economics*, 82:2, 304–311.

Johnson, George E. [1976], "Evaluating the Macroeconomic Effects of Public Employment Programs," in Orley Ashenfelter and James Blum, eds., *Evaluating the Labor Market Effects of Social Programs*, Princeton, N.J.: Industrial Relations Section, Princeton University, pp. 90–123.

Kalachek, Edward D., Wesley Mellow, and Fredric Raines [1978], "The Male Labor Supply Function Reconsidered," *Industrial and Labor Relations Review*, 31:3, April, 356–367.

Keeley, Michael C. [1981], *Labor Supply and Public Policy*, New York: Academic Press.

Keeley, Michael C., Philip K. Robins, Robert G. Spiegelman, and Richard W. West [1978], "The Estimation of Labor Supply Models Using Experimental Data," *American Economic Review*, 68:5, December, 873–887.

Killingsworth, Mark R. [1983], *Labor Supply*, New York: Cambridge University Press.

Killingsworth, Mark R. and James J. Heckman [1986], "Female Labor Supply: A Survey," Chapter 2 in Orley Ashenfelter and Richard Layard, eds., *Handbook of Labor Economics*, Vol. 1, New York: Elsevier Science Publishers BV, pp. 103–204.

Kosters, Marvin [1966], "Income and Substitution Effects in a Family Labor Supply Model," Santa Monica, Calif.: The Rand Corporation, Report No. P3339.

Layard, Richard, Margaret Barton, and Antoni Zabalza [1980], "Married Women's Participation and Hours," *Economica*, 47:185, February, 51–72.

Layard, Richard and Jacob Mincer, eds. [1985], "Trends in Women's Work, Education and Family Building," *Journal of Labor Economics*, 3:1, Supplement, January, S1–S396.

Lee, Lung-Fei [1982], "Some Approaches to the Correction of Selectivity Bias," *Review of Economic Studies*, 49:3, July, 355–372.

Leuthold, Jane H. [1968], "An Empirical Study of Formula Income Transfers and the Work Decision of the Poor," *Journal of Human Resources*, 3:3, Summer, 312–323.

Leuthold, Jane H. [1978], "The Effect of Taxation on the Hours Worked by Married Women," *Industrial and Labor Relations Review*, 31:4, July, 520–526.

Lewis, H. Gregg [1957], "Hours of Work and Hours of Leisure," *Proceedings of the Industrial Relations Research Association*, pp. 196–206.

Lundberg, Shelley [1985], "The Added Worker Effect," *Journal of Labor Economics*, 3:1, Supplement, January, S11–S37.

MaCurdy, Thomas E. [1981], "An Empirical Model of Labor Supply in a Life-Cycle Setting," *Journal of Political Economy*, 89:6, December, 1059–1085.

Maddala, G. S. [1983], *Limited Dependent and Qualitative Variables in Econometrics*, Cambridge, England: Cambridge University Press, Econometric Society Monographs No. 3.

Manser, Marilyn E. and Murray Brown [1979], "Bargaining Analyses of Household Decisions," in Cynthia B. Lloyd, Emily S. Andrews, and Curtis L. Gilroy, eds., *Women in the Labor Market*, New York: Columbia University Press, pp. 3–26.

Manser, Marilyn E. and Murray Brown [1980], "Marriage and Household Decision-Making: A Bargaining Analysis," *International Economic Review*, 21:1, February, 31–44.

McDonald, John F. and Robert A. Moffitt [1980], "The Uses of Tobit Analysis," *Review of Economics and Statistics*, 67:2, May, 318–321.

McElroy, Marjorie B. and Mary Jean Horney [1981], "Nash-Bargained Household Decisions: Toward a Generalization of the Theory of Demand," *International Economic Review*, 22:2, June, 333–349.

McFadden, Daniel [1984], "Econometric Analysis of Qualitative Response Models," Chapter 24 in Zvi Griliches and Michael D. Intriligator, eds., *Handbook of Econometrics*, Vol. 2, New York: Elsevier Science Publishers BV, pp. 1395–1457.

Metcalf, Charles E. [1973], "Making Inferences from Controlled Income Maintenance Experiments," *American Economic Review*, 63:3, June, 478–483.

Mincer, Jacob [1962], "Labor Force Participation of Married Women: A Study of Labor Supply," in H. Gregg Lewis, ed., *Aspects of Labor Economics*, Princeton, N.J.: Princeton University Press, pp. 63–97.

Mincer, Jacob [1963], "Market Prices, Opportunity Costs, and Income Effects," in Carl Christ, ed., *Measurement in Economics: Essays in Honor of Yehuda Grunfeld*, Stanford, Calif.: Stanford University Press, pp. 67–82.

Mincer, Jacob [1966], "Labor Force Participation and Unemployment: A Review of Recent Evidence," in Robert A. Gordon and Margaret S. Gordon, eds., *Prosperity and Unemployment*, New York: John Wiley and Sons, pp. 73–112.

Mitchell, Olivia S. [1980], "Labor Force Activity of Married Women as a Response to Changing Jobless Rates," *Monthly Labor Review*, 103:6, June, 32–33.

Moffitt, Robert A. [1982], "The Tobit Model, Hours of Work and Institutional Constraints," *Review of Economics and Statistics*, 64:3, August, 510–515.

Moffitt, Robert A. [1984], "Profiles of Fertility, Labour Supply and Wages of Married Women: A Complete Life-Cycle Model," *Review of Economic Studies*, 51:2, April, 263–278.

Moffitt, Robert A. and Ken Kehrer [1981], "The Effect of Tax and Transfer Programs on Labor Supply: The Evidence from the Income Maintenance Experiments," in Ronald G. Ehrenberg, ed., *Research in Labor Economics*, Vol. 4, Greenwich, Conn.: JAI Press, pp. 103–150.

Morgan, James N., et al. [1966], *Productive Americans: A Study of How Individuals Contribute to Economic Progress*, Ann Arbor, Mich.: Survey Research Center, University of Michigan.

Morgan, James N. et al. [1974], *Five Thousand American Families—Patterns of Economic Progress*, Ann Arbor, Mich.: Survey Research Center, University of Michigan.

Mroz, Thomas A. [1987], "The Sensitivity of an Empirical Model of Married Women's Hours of Work to Economic and Statistical Assumptions," *Econometrica*, 55:4, July, 765–799.

Nakamura, Alice and Masao Nakamura [1981a], "A Comparison of the Labor Force Behavior of Married Women in the United States and Canada, with Special Attention to the Impact of Income Taxes," *Econometrica*, 49:2, March, 451–489.

Nakamura, Alice and Masao Nakamura [1981b], "On the Relationships among Several Specification Error Tests Presented by Durbin, Wu and Hausman," *Econometrica*, 49:6, November, 1583–1588.

Nakamura, Alice and Masao Nakamura [1985a], "Dynamic Models of the Labor Force Behavior of Married Women Which Can Be Estimated Using Limited Amounts of Past Information," *Journal of Econometrics*, 27:3, March, 273–298.

Nakamura, Alice and Masao Nakamura [1985b], *The Second Paycheck: A Socioeconomic Analysis of Earnings*, Orlando, Fla.: Academic Press.

Nakamura, Alice and Masao Nakamura [1985c], "On the Performance of Tests by

Wu and by Hausman for Detecting the Ordinary Least Squares Bias Problem," *Journal of Econometrics*, 29:3, September, 213–227.

Nakamura, Alice, Masao Nakamura, and Dallas Cullen [1979], "Job Opportunities, the Offered Wage, and the Labor Supply of Married Women," *American Economic Review*, 69:5, December, 787–805.

National Commission on Employment and Unemployment Statistics [1979], *Counting the Labor Force*, Washington, D.C.: U.S. Government Printing Office.

Olsen, Randall J. [1980], "A Least Squares Correction for Selectivity Bias," *Econometrica*, 48:7, November, 1815–1820.

Parnes, Herbert S. et al. [1970], *The Pre-Retirement Years: A Longitudinal Study of the Labor Market Experience of Men*, Vol. 1, Washington, D.C.: U.S. Department of Labor, Manpower Administration.

Pencavel, John [1986], "Labor Supply of Men: A Survey," Chapter 1 in Orley Ashenfelter and Richard Layard, eds., *Handbook of Labor Economics*, Vol. 1, New York: Elsevier Science Publishers BV, pp. 3–101.

Rosen, Harvey S. [1976], "Taxes in a Labor Supply Model with Joint Wage-Hours Determination," *Econometrica*, 44:3, May, 485–507.

Rosett, Richard N. and Forrest D. Nelson [1975], "Estimation of the Two-Limit Probit Regression Model," *Econometrica*, 43:1, January, 141–146.

Sandmo, Agnar [1981], "Income Tax Evasion, Labour Supply and the Equity-Efficiency Tradeoff," *Journal of Public Economics*, 6:1, February, 37–54.

Schoenberg, Erika and Paul H. Douglas [1937], "Studies in the Supply Curve of Labor: The Relation between Average Earnings in American Cities and the Proportion Seeking Employment," *Journal of Political Economy*, 45:1, February, 45–62.

Schultz, T. Paul [1980], "Estimating Labor Supply Functions for Married Women," in James P. Smith, ed., *Female Labor Supply*, Princeton N.J.: Princeton University Press, pp. 25–89.

Smith, Adam [1776], *The Wealth of Nations*, London: J. M. Dent & Sons. Reprinted in 1937 as the Cannan edition by The Modern Library, Random House, New York.

Smith, James P. [1977], "Assets, Savings and Labor Supply," *Economic Inquiry*, 15:4, October, 551–573.

Smith, James P. [1980], "Assets and Labor Supply," in James P. Smith, ed., *Female Labor Supply*, Princeton N.J.: Princeton University Press, pp. 166–205.

Smith, James P. and Michael Ward [1985], "Time-Series Growth in the Female Labor Force," *Journal of Labor Economics*, 3:1, January, Supplement, S59–S90.

Smith, Shirley J. [1983], "Estimating Annual Hours of Labor Force Activity," *Monthly Labor Review*, 106:2, 13–22.

Sorrentino, Constance [1983], "International Comparisons of Labor Force Participation, 1960–1981," *Monthly Labor Review*, 106:2, 23–36.

Stern, Nicholas [1986], "On the Specification of Labor Supply Functions," in Richard Blundell and Ian Walker, eds., *Unemployment, Search and Labour Supply*, Cambridge, England: Cambridge University Press, pp. 143–189.

Theeuwes, Jules [1981], "Family Labour Force Participation: Multinomial Logit Estimates," *Applied Economics*, 13:4, December, 481–498.

Tobin, James [1955], "The Application of Multivariate Probit Analysis to Economic Survey Data," Cowles Foundation Discussion Paper 1.

Tobin, James [1958], "Estimation of Relationships for Limited Dependent Variables," *Econometrica*, 26:1, January, 24–36.

U.S. Department of Commerce, Bureau of the Census [1987], *Survey of Income and*

Program Participation: Users' Guide, Washington, D.C.: Customer Services, Data User Services Division.

Wales, Terence J. [1973], "Estimation of a Labor Supply Curve for Self-Employed Business Proprietors," *International Economic Review*, 14:1, February, 69–80.

Wales, Terence J. and Alan D. Woodland [1977], "Estimation of the Allocation of Time for Work, Leisure and Housework," *Econometrica*, 45:1, January, 115–132.

Wales, Terence J. and Alan D. Woodland [1979], "Labour Supply and Progressive Taxes," *Review of Economic Studies*, 46:1, January, 83–95.

Wales, Terence J. and Alan D. Woodland [1980], "Sample Selectivity and the Estimation of Labor Supply Functions," *International Economic Review*, 21:2, June, 437–468.

Watts, Harold, Dale Poirier, and Charles Mallar [1977], "Sample, Variables and Concepts Used in the Analysis," in Harold Watts and Albert Rees, eds., *The New Jersey Income Maintenance Experiment: Labor Supply Response*, Vol. 2, New York: Academic Press, pp. 33–56.

Weiss, Yoram [1986], "The Determinants of Life Cycle Earnings: A Survey," Chapter 11 in Orley Ashenfelter and Richard Layard, eds., *Handbook of Labor Economics*, Vol. 1, New York: Elsevier Science Publishers BV, pp. 603–640.

White, Halbert J., [1980], "A Heteroskedasticity-Consistent Covariance Matrix Estimator and a Direct Test for Heteroskedasticity," *Econometrica*, 48:4, May, 817–838.

White, Halbert J. [1982], "Maximum Likelihood Estimation of Misspecified Models," *Econometrica*, 50:2, March, 483–499.

Woytinsky, Wladimir S. [1940], *Additional Workers and the Volume of Unemployment in the Depression*, Washington, D.C.: Social Science Research Council.

Wu, De-Min [1973], "Tests of Independence between Stochastic Regressors and Disturbances," *Econometrica*, 41:4, July, 733–750.

Zabalza, Antoni [1983], "The CES Utility Function, Nonlinear Budget Constraints and Labour Supply: Results on Female Participation and Hours," *Economic Journal*, 93:370, June, 312–320.

FURTHER READINGS (All are textbooks in labor economics)

Addison, John T. and W. Stanley Siebert [1979], *The Market for Labor: An Analytical Treatment*, Santa Monica, Calif: Goodyear.

Ehrenberg, Ronald G. and Robert S. Smith [1985], *Modern Labor Economics: Theory and Public Policy*, Second Edition, Glenview, Ill.: Scott, Foresman.

Fleisher, Belton and Thomas Kniesner [1984], *Labor Economics: Theory, Evidence and Policy*, Third Edition, Englewood Cliffs, N.J.: Prentice Hall.

Gunderson, Morley and W. Craig Riddell [1988], *Labor Market Economics: Theory, Evidence and Policy in Canada*, Second Edition, Toronto: McGraw-Hill Ryerson, Ltd.

Hamermesh, Daniel S. and Albert Rees [1988], *The Economics of Work and Pay*, Fourth Edition, New York: Harper & Row.

McConnell, Campbell R. and Stanley L. Brue [1986], *Contemporary Labor Economics*, New York: McGraw-Hill.

Reynolds, Lloyd G., Stanley H. Masters, and Colletta H. Moser [1987], *Economics of Labor*, Englewood Cliffs, N.J.: Prentice Hall.

(credits continued from copyright page)

General Series No. 73, NY: Columbia University Press for the National Bureau of Economic Research, 1961, p. 35. Reprinted with permission. Griliches: *Technology, Education and Productivity,* NY: Basil Blackwell, Inc., 1988, p. 120. Reprinted with permission. Forester, ed., *The Information Technology Review,* Cambridge, MA. The MIT Press, 1985, p.i. Reprinted with permission. Machlup, *Journal of Political Economy,* 82:4, July/August, 1974, p. 892. Reprinted with permission. Hall and Taylor, *Macroeconomics: Theory, Performance, and Policy,* 2/e, NY: W.W. Norton and Co., Inc., 1988, p. 237. Reprinted with permission. Griliches, "Comments on Sims," in Intriligator/Kendrick, eds., *Frontiers of Quantitative Economics,* Vol. II, Amsterdam: North-Holland, 1974, p. 335. Reprinted with permission. Koopmans: Reprinted from "Report of the Modeling Resource Group, 1978, with permission from the National Academy of Sciences, Washington, DC. Reprinted by permission of AMERICAN SALESMAN, © The National Research Bureau, Inc., 424 North Third St., Burlington, Iowa 52601-5224. Clarke, "Econometric Measurement of the Duration of Advertising Effects on Sales," *Journal of Marketing Research,* 13:4, November, 1976, p. 355. Reprinted with permission. Schmalensee, *The Economics of Advertising,* Amsterdam: North-Holland, 1972, p. 58. Reprinted with permission. Fuss, McFadden and Mundlak, "A Survey of Functional Forms in the Economics Analysis of Production," in Fuss/McFadden, eds., *Production Economics: A Dual Approach to Theory and Applications,* Amsterdam: North-Holland, 1978, p. 266. Reprinted with permission. Berndt and Wood, "Engineering and Econometric Interpretations of Energy-Capital Complementarity," *American Economic Review,* 69:3, June 1979, p. 351. Reprinted with permission. Friedman, "The Role of Monetary Policy," *American Economic Review,* 58:1, March 1968, p. 11. Reprinted with permission. Okun, "Postwar Macroeconomic Performance," in Martin S. Feldstein, ed., *The American Economy in Transition,* Chicago: The University of Chicago Press, 1980, p. 166. Reprinted with permission. Solow, "What We Know and Don't Know About Inflation," *Technology Review,* 81:3, December 1978/January 1979, p. 31. Reprinted with permission from Technology Review, copyright 1978. Lucas, Jr. and Sargent, "After Kenyesian Macroeconomics," in After the Phillips Curve: Persistence of High Inflation and High Unemployment, BOSTON: Federal Reserve Bank of Boston, Conference Series, No. 19, p. 69. Gordon, "The Theory of Domestic Inflation," *American Economic Review,* 67:1, March 1977, p. 132. Reprinted with permission. Killingsworth, *Labor Supply,* NY: Cambridge University Press, 1983, p. 432. Reprinted with permission. Nakamura, Nakamura, and Cullen, "Job Opportunities, the Offered Wage, and the Labor Supply of Married Women," *American Economics Review,* 69:5, December 1979, p. 787. Reprinted with permission. Fullerton, "On the Possibility of an Inverse Relationship between Tax Rates and Government Revenues," *Journal of Public Economics,* 19:1, October 1982, p. 20. Reprinted with permission. Jack Johnston, *Econometric Methods,* 3/e, © 1984, p. 335. Reprinted with permission of McGraw-Hill, Inc. Rudiger Dornbusch and Stanley Fischer, *Macroeconomics,* 4/e, © 1987, p. 315. Reprinted with permission of McGraw-Hill, Inc.

PHOTO CREDITS

Page 4: courtesy of Guy Orcutt. Page 5: Maurice V. Wilkes, David J. Wheeler, and Stanley Gill. *Preparation of Programs for an Electronic Digital Computer.* © 1951, renewed 1985; Addison-Wesley Publishing Company. Reprinted with permission of the publisher. Page 24: courtesy of Harry M. Markowitz. Page 38: courtesy of Steven A. Ross. Page 82: courtesy of Marc Nerlove. Page 115: courtesy of Zvi Griliches. Page 119: courtesy of Gregory C. Chow. Page 168: courtesy of Jacob Mincer. Page 185: courtesy of Alan Blinder. Page 246: courtesy of Robert Hall. Page 258: courtesy of James Tobin. Page 329: courtesy of Hendrik Houthakker. Page 334: photo of Daniel McFadden: courtesy of Tito Simboli. Page 395: courtesy of Richard Schmalensee. Page 406: courtesy of Harry V. Roberts. Page 459: courtesy of W. Erwin Diewert. Page 480: courtesy of Dale Jongenson. Page 537: courtesy of Robert E. Lucas, Jr. Page 546: courtesy of Ray C. Fair. Page 628: courtesy of James Heekman. Page 636: courtesy of Jerry A. Hausman.

Author Index

Subject Index